1st edition, February 1998

ISBN 0 7495 1721 2

Published by AA Publishing (a trading name of The Automobile Association Developments Limited, whose registered office is Norfolk House, Priestly Road, Basingstoke, Hampshire, RG24 9NY. Registered number 1878835).

Printed by G Canale & C. S.P.A., Torino, Italy

A CIP catalogue record for this book is available from the British Library.

contents

Route-planning map	**inside front cover**
Map symbols	**II**
Map pages	**III**
Road atlas	**1 - 230**
Principal city street plans	**231 - 245**
Bordeaux	235
Bruxelles/Brussel	245
Lille	237
Lyon	243
Marseille	244
Montpellier	238
Nantes	240
Nice	239
Paris - centre	233 - 234
Paris - environ	231 - 232
Rennes	236
Strasbourg	242
Toulouse	241
Index	**246-301**
Department map	**inside back cover**

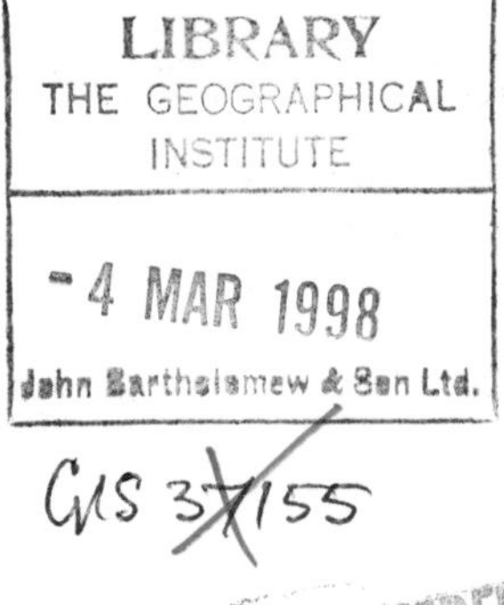

LEGENDE • KEY • VERKLARING • ZEICHENERKLÄRUNG • LEGGENDA

AUTOROUTES		MOTORWAYS AUTOBAHNEN	AUTOWEG AUTOSTRADA
Autoroute, point de jonction, n° et nom de la sortie	3 ST-PAUL A 4	Motorway, junctions Nr and name of the exit Autobahn, Anschlussstelle, Nr und Ausfahrtsname	Autoweg, aansluiting, Nr.en naam van de afrit Autostrada, punto di guizone, n° e nome dell'uscita
Aire de service, péage	St-Jean	Service area, toll Service - Center, Gebühr	Service center, betaling Aera di servizio, pedaggio
Aire de repos, poste d'essence		Resting area, service station Raststätte, Tankstelle	Rutsplaats, Benzinepomp Aera di riposo,stazione di benzina
Restaurant, hôtel		Restaurant, Hotel Restaurant, Hotel	Spijshuis, hotel Ristorante, albergo
Kilométrage ① global ② partiel	① 15 ② 5 10②	Kilometre-distance ① in total ② partial Entfernungsangaben ① Fern- ② Nahkilometer	Afstand in kilometers ① totale ② gedeeltelijke Kilometraggio ① totale ② parziale
Autoroute ① en construction ② en projet	① ②	Motorway ① under construction ② projected Autobahn ① im Bau ② in Planung	Autoweg ① in aanbouw ② project Autostrada ① in construzione ② in progetto

ROUTES		ROADS STRASSEN	WEGEN STRADA
Route à chaussées indépendantes		Dual carriageways Zweibahnige Schnellstrasse	Weg met gescheiden rijbanen Strada a doppia carreggiata
Route à quatre voies		Four-lane roads Vierspurige Schnellstrasse	Vierbaansnelweg Strada a quatro corsie
Grand itinéraire	N.7	Primary route Fernverkehrsstrasse	Grote hoofdweg Grande Itinerario
Route à grande circulation	N 151 D 940	Trunk road Hauptverkehrsstrasse	Doorgaande route Strada a grande circolazione
Route recommandée ou liaison principale	D 97	Recommended route or principal connection Wichtige Verbindungsstrasse	Aanbevolen weg of voornaamste verbinding Strada consigliata oppure collegamento principale
Autres routes	D.18	Other roads Sonstige Strassen	Overige wegen Altre strada
Route étroite ou de viabilité incertaine	D.42	Narrow road or of incertain viability Schmale Strasse oder von zweifelhafter Befahrbarkeit	Smalle weg of weg met onzekere begaanbaarheid Strada stretta oppure di incerta viabilità
Route forestière, sentier	R.F.	Forest road, path Forstrasse, Fussweg	Bosweg, pad Strada forestale, sentiero
Route en construction, en projet		Road under construction,projected Strasse im Bau, in Planung	Weg in aanleg, in ontwerp Strada in construzione, in progetto
Hauteur limitée Limite de charge en tonnes	3m9 6 4	Low headroom Load limit in T. Zulässige Gesamthöhe Höchstbelastung in T.	Vrije hoogte max. draagvermogen in T. Limite di altezza Limite di carico in T.
Col, altitude	2099	Pass, height Pass, Höhenangabe	Bergpas, hoogte Valico, altitudine
Montée 10% et plus		Steep hill 10 % and more Steigung 10 % und mehr	Helling van 10 % of meer Salita 10 % e più
Col fermé en période d'enneigement	1509	Pass closed at periods of snowfall Pass, während der Schneeperiode geschlossen	Bergpas gesloten tijdens Sneeuwperiode Passo chiuso in periodo di neve
Route interdite		Prohibited road Gesperrte Strasse	Verboden weg Transito vietato
Kilométrage ①global ②partiel	13 ① 4 9 ②	Kilometre-distance ①in total ②partial Entfernungsangaben ①Fern- ②Nahkilometer	Afstand in kilometers ①Totaal ②gedetailleerd Kilometraggio ①totale ②parziale

HYDROGRAPHIE		WATERWAYS GEWÄSSER	HYDROGRAFIE IDROGRAFIA
Canal navigable, écluse		Navigable canal, lock Schiffbarer Kanal, Schleuse	Bevaarbaar Kanaal, sluis Canale navigabile, chiusa
Marais, aqueduc		Swamp, Aqueduct Moor, Aquädukt	Moeras, Aquaduct Palude, Acquedotto
Bacs (piétons, autos)		Ferries (pedestrians, cars) Fähren (Personen, Auto)	Ponten (voetgangers, autos) Traghetti (pedoni, auto)
Barrage, cascade		Dam, cascade Staudamm, Wasserfall	Stuwdam, waterval Diga, cascata
Plage, dunes		Beach, dunes Strand, dünen	Strand, Duinen Spiaggia, Dune
Rochers, falaises		Rocks, cliffs Felsen, Klippen	Rotsen, Kliffen Scogli, Scogliere
Phare, sémaphore		Lighthouse, semaphore Leuchtturm, Signalmast	Vuurtorens, seinpost Faro, semaforo
Route maritime		Sea route Seeweg	Zeeweg Vià marittima

LOCALITES		LOCALITIES ORTE	BEBOUWDE KOM. LOCALITA
Préfecture(France) Chef lieu de province(Belgique)	ARRAS NIMES NIORT	Prefecture(France) Provincial capital(Belgium) Präfektur(Frankreich) Hauptort der Provinz(Belgien)	Prefectuur(Frankrijk) Provinciehoofdplaats(België) Prefettura(Francia) Capoluogo di provincia(Belgio)
Sous-préfecture(France) Chef-lieu d'arrondissement (Belgique)	SENLIS ALÈS CHOLET	Sub-prefecture(France) Principal town of arrondissement (Belgium) Unterpräfektur(Frankreich) Hauptort der Bezirks(Belgien)	Onderprefectuur(Frankrijk) Arrondissementshoofdplaats (België) Sottoprefettura(Francia) Capoluogo di distretto(Belgio)
Chef-lieu de canton(France) Commune(Belgique)	DUREN Uzès AYTRE	Canton market town(France) Commune(Belgium) Kantonssitz (Frankreich) Gemeinde(Belgien)	Kantonhoofdplaats(Frankrijk) Gemeente(België) Capoluogo distrettuale(Francia) Comune(Belgio)
Commune(France) Ancienne commune(Belgique)	Tralonca Caseneuve Marcillac	Commune(France) Former commune(Belgium) Gemeinde(Frankreich) Ehemalige Gemeinde(Belgien)	Gemeente(Frankrijk) Gemeente voor de fusie(België) Comune(Francia) Vecchio comune(Belgio)
Hameau	Beauregard St-Pancrace Pont-Bernard le Corbier	Hamlet Weiler	Gehucht Frazione
Localité à grand intérêt touristique	*	Picturesque locality Ort von touristischem Interesse	Toeristisch centrum Località di notevole interesse turistico

LIMITES		BOUNDARIES GRENZEN	GRENZEN LIMITI
d'Etat, douane		National boundary, customs Staatsgrenze, Zollamt	Staatsgrenzen, douane di Stato, dogana
de département , de province		County , province boundary Departements - Provinzgrenze	Departements , Provinciegrenzen di Provincia, di provincia
Parc naturel		Natural park Naturpark	Natuurpark Parco Naturale

TOURISME		TOURISM TOURISMUS	TOERISME TURISMO
*Particulièrement remarquable		*Particulary interesting *Bezonders bemerkenswert	*Bijzondere bezienswaardigheid *Particolarmente notevoli
Château , manoir		Castle, manor-house Schloss, Landchloss	Kasteel, Slot Castello, maniero
Tour, monument		Tower, monument Turm, Denkmal	Toren, monument Torre, monumento
Fort, citadelle		Fortress, citadel Festung	Fort, citadel Fortezza, cittadella
Eglise		Church Kirche	Kerk Chiesa
Chapelle		Chapel Kapelle	Kapel Cappella
Abbaye, monastère		Abbey, monastery Abtei, Kloster	Abdij, klooster Abbazia, monastero
Croix, calvaire		Cross, calvary Kreuz, Bildstock	Kruis, Kruisheuvel Croce, calvario
Pèlerinage		Pilgrimage Wallfahrtsort	Bedevaartsplaats Pellegrinaggio
Ruines, ruines romaines		Ruines, roman ruins Ruinen,römische Ruinen	Ruines, romeinse ruines Rovine, ruderi romani
Menhir, dolmen		Standing stone, dolmen Steinsäule, Steintisch	Menhir, hunnebed Menhir, dolmen
Grotte,gouffre, tumulus		Cave, chasm, tumulus Höhle, Abgrund, Grabhügel	Grot, Afgrond, grafheuvel Grotta, abisso, tumulo
Musée, halle	M	Museum, market Museum, Halle	Museum, hal Museo, mercato coperto
Vieilles maisons		Old houses Alte Bauten	Oude huizen Vecchie case
Curiosité, site		Curiosity, site Sehenswürdigkeit, Landschaft	Bezienswaardigheid, oord Curiosità, paesaggio
Point de vue, panorama		View-point, panorama Aussichtspunkt, Panoramablick	Uitkijkpunt, panorama Punto di vista,Veduta panoramica
Table d'orientation		Orientation table Orientierungstisch	Uitkijktoren Tavola di orientamento
Camping, auberge de jeunesse		Camping, youth hostel Campingplatz, Jugendherberge	Kampeerterrein, Jeugdherberg Campeggio,Albergo della gioventù
Station verte		Country pleasure center Ferienorte	Rekreatiecentrum Stazione verde
Route pittoresque		Picturesque road Landschaftlich schöne St.	Schilderachtige weg Strada panoramica
Train touristique		Touristical railway Touristischer Eisenbahn	Touristischer spoorwegen Treno turistico

SPORT		SPORT	SPORT
Station de sports d'hiver		Winter sports resort Wintersportplatz	Wintersportstation Stazione di sports invernali
Téléphérique, télésiège		Telepheric, teleseat Seilbahn, Sesselbahn	Kabelspoorweg, Stoeljeslft Funivia, seggiovia
Refuge en montagne		Moutain refuge Bergschutzhütte	Schuilhut in de bergen Rifugio in montagna
Yachting		Yachting Segelsport	Jachthaven Navigazione da diporto
Plage en eau douce, piscine		Beach, pool Strand, Schwimmbad	Strand, Zwembad Spiaggia, piscina
Golf		Golf	Golf
Hippodrome		Race-course Pferderennbahn	Renbaan Ippodromo
Sentier de grande randonnée	GR 2	Rambling tour path Markierter Wanderweg	Zwerfpad Sentiero per lunghe gite
Piste cyclable		Cycle track Radweg	Rijwielpad Pista ciclabile

VOIES FERREES		RAILWAYS EISENBAHNEN	SPOORWEGEN FERROVIE
Voyageurs et marchandises		Passengers and goods Reisende und Güter	Passagiers en goederen Viaggiatori e merci
Marchandises seulement		Goods only Nur-Güter	Alleen goederen Merci soltanto
Chemin de fer à crémaillère		Rack railway Zahnradbahn	Tandradbaan Ferrovia a cremagliera

AVIATION		AVIATION FLUGVEKEHR	LUCHTVAART AVIAZONE
Aéroport		Civil airport Flughafen	Vlieghaven Aeroporto
Aérodrome:		Airport: Flugplatz :	Vliegterrein: Aerodromo:
- ouvert à la C.A.P. (Circulation A. Publique)		- open civil aviation - öffentlicher Luftverkehr	- open voor het publiek Luchtverkeer - Aperto all'aviazione civile
- à usage restreint		- limited use - Eingeschränkt	- met beperkt gebruik - usaggio limitato
- Administrations de l'Etat		-Government controlled - Staatlich verwaltet	- Staatsadministraties - Amministraz. del Strato
Hydroaérodrome, altiport		Sea-plane base, altiport Wasserflugplatz, Gebirgflugplatz	Watervliegtuig, altiport Idroaerodromo, altiport

DIVERS		DIVERS SONSTIGE ZEICHEN	DIVERSE AANDUIDINGEN VARIE
Maison forestière	MF	Forest ranger station Forsthaus	Boswachterswoning Casa forestale
Usine, mine		Factory, mine Fabrik, Bergwerk	Fabriek, mijn Stabilimento, miniera
Pont mobile	PM	Swing bridge Bewegliche Brücke	Beweegbare brug Ponte mobile
Réserve de chasse		Game reserve Gehege	Jachtreservaat Riserva di caccia
Station thermale		Spa Heilbad	Kuurinrichting Stazione termale
Hôpital isolé, sanatorium		Isolated hospital, sanatorium Einzelstehendes Krankenhaus, Sanatorium	Geisoleerd ziekenhuis,sanatorium Ospedale isolato, sanatorio
Moulin à vent		Windmill Windmühle	Windmolen Mulino a vento
Cimetière (militaire)		Cemetery (military) Friedhof (Soldaten)	Kerkhof Cimitero (militare)
Sommet	1059 ▲	Summit Bergspitze	Bergtop Vetta
Transport aérien industriel		Industrial air transport Industrielle Drahtseilbahn	Industrieel Luchtvervoerde Trasportatore elevato indutriale

Tableau d'assemblage - How to assemble. Bauanleitung - Montageschema. Indice delle carte.

■ Nantes
Plans de villes
Maps of towns
Stadtpläne
Stadsplattegronden
Piante di città

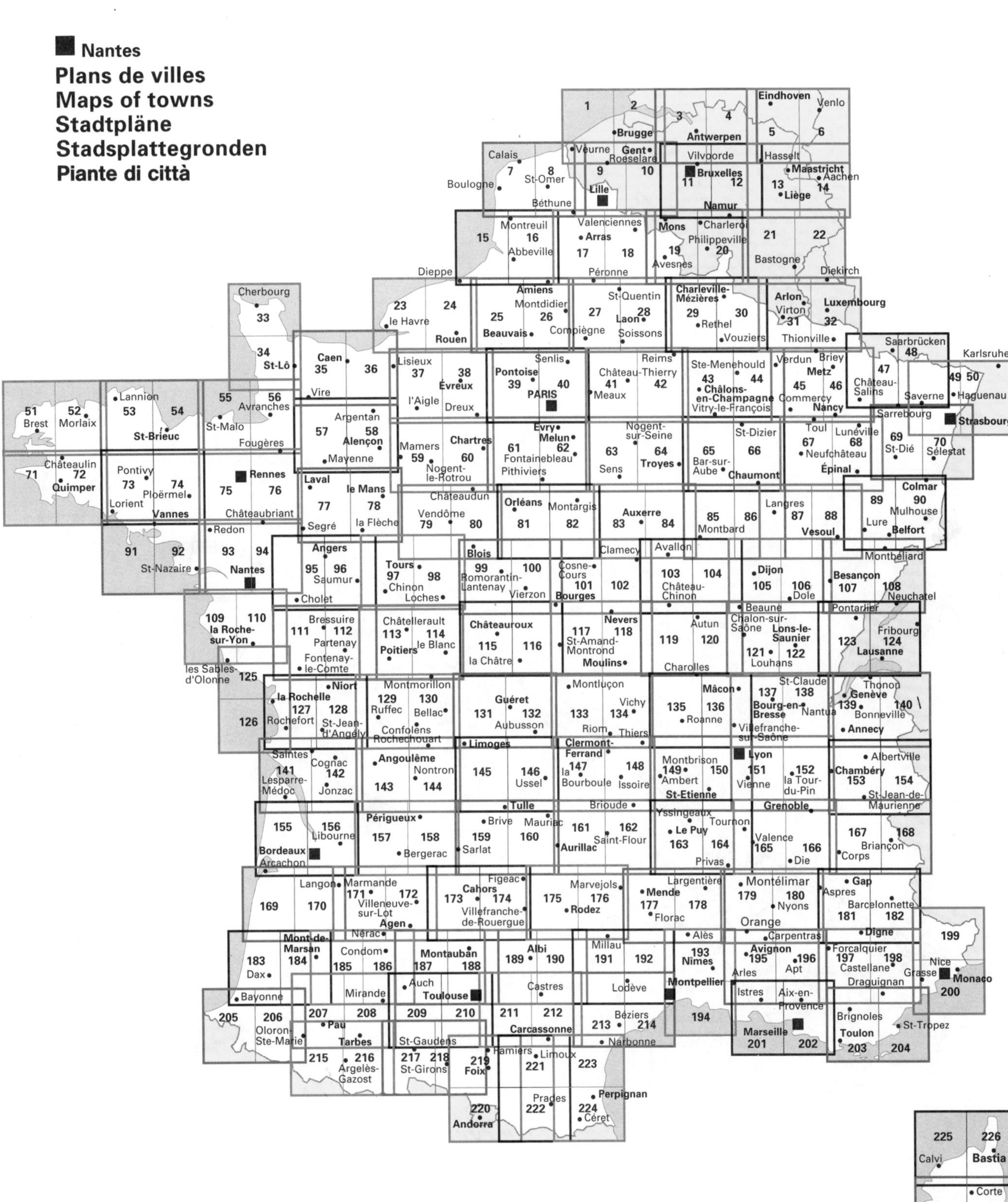

189913653

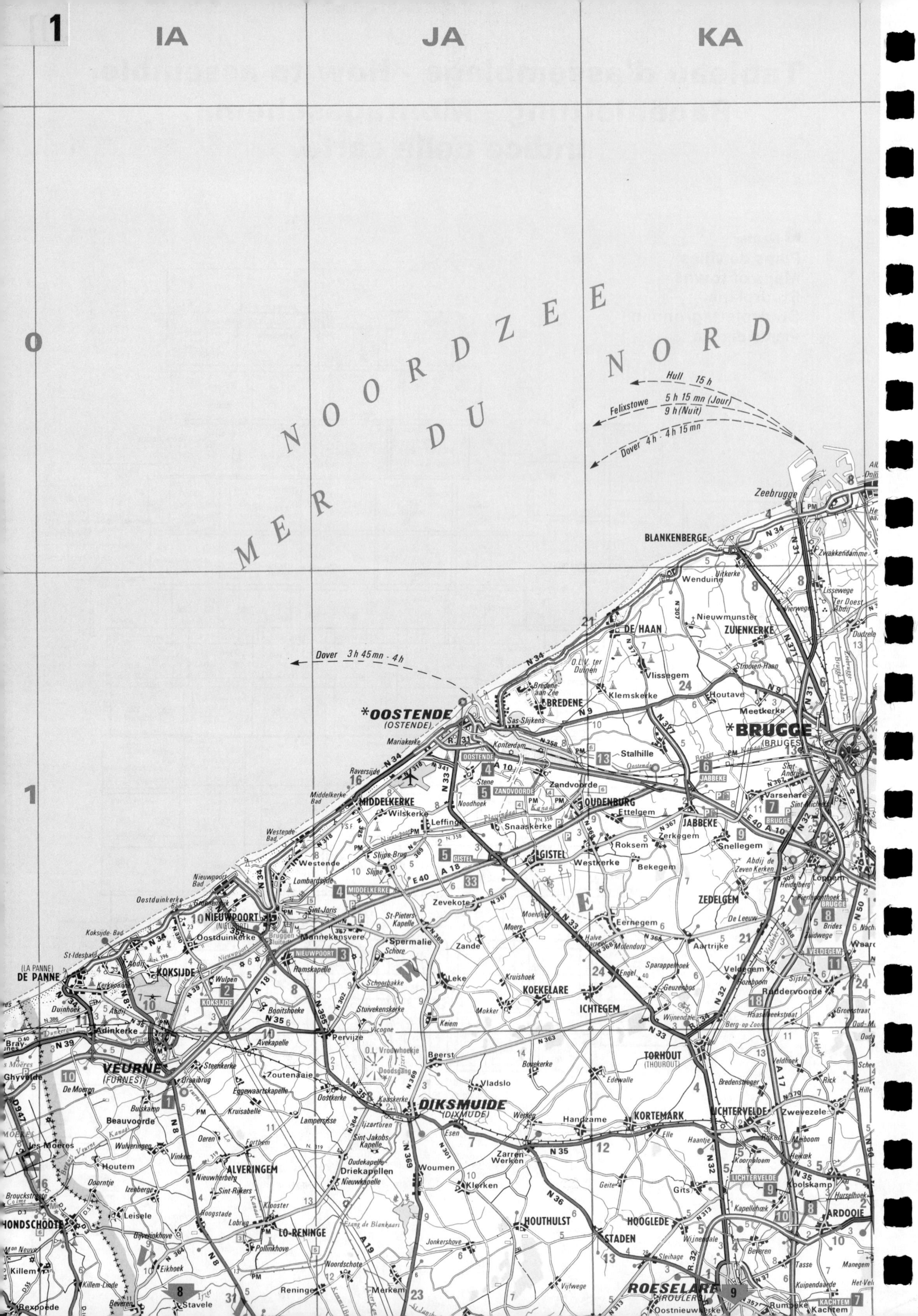
IA
JA
KA
0
1
NOORDZEE
MER DU NORD
Hull 15 h
Felixstowe 5 h 15 mn (Jour) 9 h (Nuit)
Dover 4 h - 4 h 15 mn
Dover 3 h 45 mn - 4 h
Zeebrugge
BLANKENBERGE
Wenduine
Uitkerke
Zwakkendamme
Lissewege
Ter Doest Abdij
Dudzele
Nieuwmunster
ZUIENKERKE
DE HAAN
Vlissegem
Klemskerke
BREDENE
Bredene-aan-Zee
Sas-Slijkens
Houtave
Meetkerke
Stroobrugge
*BRUGGE
(BRUGES)
*OOSTENDE
(OSTENDE)
Mariakerke
Konterdam
Stalhille
Raversijde
Stene
Zandvoorde
OUDENBURG
Ettelgem
JABBEKE
Varsenare
Sint-Andries
Sint-Michiels
Middelkerke Bad
MIDDELKERKE
Wilskerke
Leffinge
Snaaskerke
Roksem
Zerkegem
Snellegem
Westende Bad
Westende
Slijpe
GISTEL
Westkerke
Bekegem
Abdij de Zeven Kerken
Loppem
Lombardsijde
Nieuwpoort Bad
Oostduinkerke Bad
NIEUWPOORT
Sint-Joris
St-Pieters Kapelle
Zevekote
Moerdijk
Eernegem
ZEDELGEM
De Leeuw
Koksijde-Bad
Oostduinkerke
Mannekensvere
Spermalie
Zande
Moere
Halve Barreel
Molendorp
Aartrijke
Brides
St-Idesbald
(LA PANNE)
DE PANNE
KOKSIJDE
Wulpen
Ramskapelle
Schoorbakke
Leke
Kruishoek
KOEKELARE
ICHTEGEM
Sparappelhoek
Engel
Geuzenbos
Veldegem
Ruddervoorde
Duinhoek
Adinkerke
Booitshoeke
Stuivekenskerke
Mokker
Keiem
Wijnendale
Haasebeekstraat
Berg-op-Zoom
Pervijze
Avekapelle
Beerst
TORHOUT
(THOUROUT)
Ghyvelde
VEURNE
(FURNES)
Steenkerke
Zoutenaaie
O.L. Vrouwhoekje
Doodsgang
Bovekerke
Vladslo
Edewalle
Bredensweger
Veldhoek
Rick
De Moeren
Bulskamp
Eggewaartskapelle
Oostkerke
Kaaskerke
DIKSMUIDE
(DIXMUDE)
Handzame
KORTEMARK
LICHTERVELDE
Zwevezele
Beauvoorde
Kruisabelle
Lampernisse
IJzertoren
Sint-Jakobs Kapelle
Werken
Esen
Elle
Haantje
Rijken
Meiboom
Les Moëres
Wulveringem
Oeren
Forthem
Vinkem
Oudekapelle
Driekapellen
Nieuwkapelle
Zarren
Werken
N 35
Koornbloem
Heikoek
Houtem
ALVERINGEM
Woumen
Klerken
Geite
Gits
Koolskamp
Hurselhoek
Brouckstraete
Doorntje
Izenberge
Nieuwkerke
Sint-Rikers
Klooster
Hoogstade
Lobrug
LO-RENINGE
Pollinkhove
Étang de Blankaart
HOUTHULST
HOOGLEDE
STADEN
Kapellehoek
ARDOOIE
HONDSCHOOTE
Leisele
Gijverinkhove
Jonkershove
Wijnendale
Beveren
Tasse
Manegem
Killem
Eikhoek
Noordschote
Sleihage
Kuipendaarde
Het-Veld
Killem-Linde
Bevern
Reninge
Merkem
Vijfwege
ROESELARE
(ROULERS)
Oostnieuwkerke
Rumbeke
Kachtem
Rexpoede
Stavele
OOSTENDE
ZANDVOORDE
GISTEL
MIDDELKERKE
NIEUWPOORT
KOKSIJDE
JABBEKE
BRUGGE
VELDEGEM
LICHTERVELDE
KACHTEM
A 10
A 18
E 40
A 19
A 17
N 34
N 33
N 32
N 31
N 9
N 35
N 36
N 8
N 39
N 369
N 355
N 50

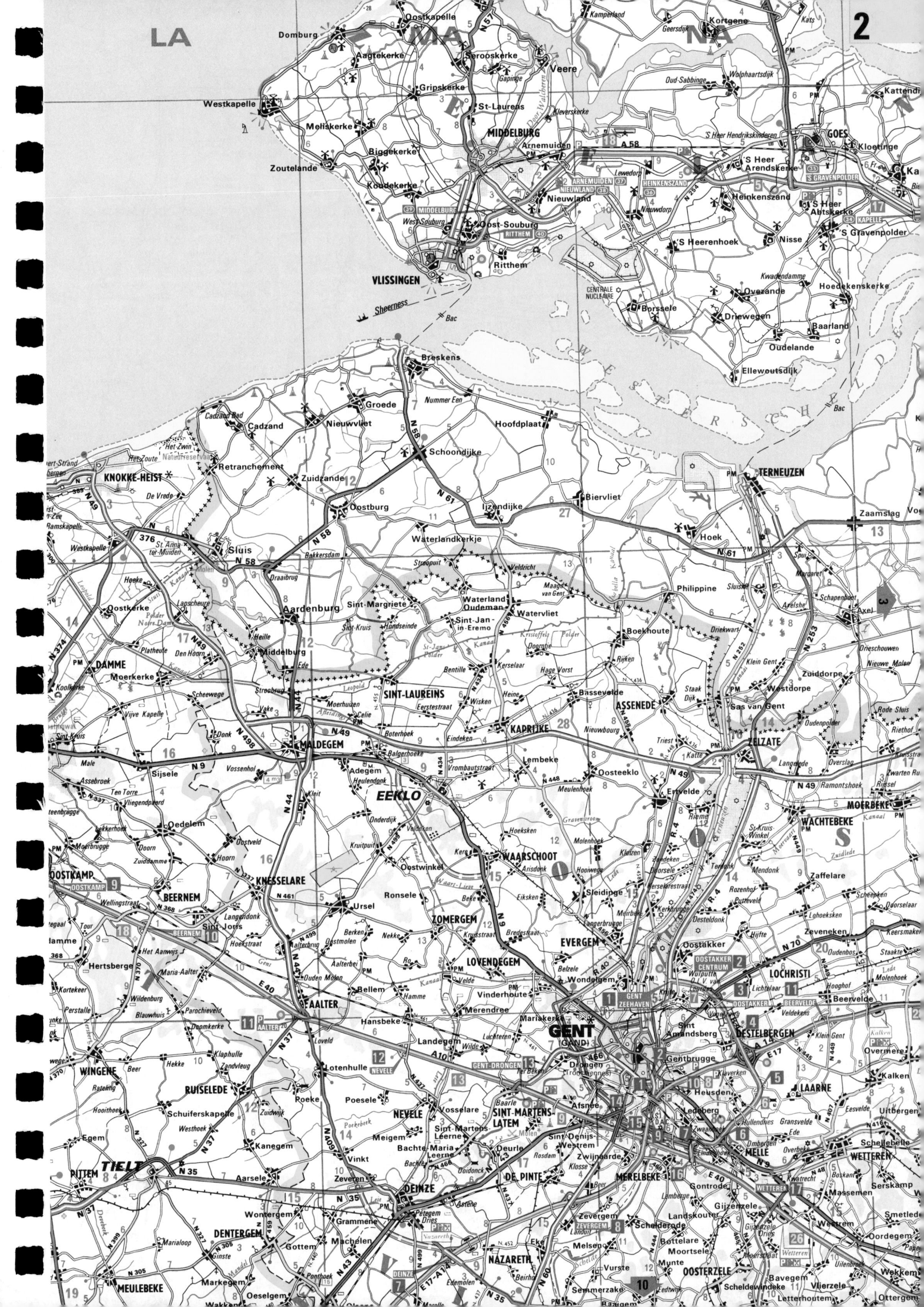
LA MANCHE
Domburg
Oostkapelle
Aagtekerke
Serooskerke
Veere
Kamperland
Geersdijk
Kortgene
Kats
Westkapelle
Gripskerke
St-Laurens
Meliskerke
MIDDELBURG
Arnemuiden
Biggekerke
Zoutelande
Koudekerke
Nieuwland
West Souburg
Oost-Souburg
Ritthem
VLISSINGEN
Sheerness
Bac
Oud-Sabbinge
Wolphaartsdijk
'S Heer Hendrikskinderen
GOES
Kloetinge
'S Heer Arendskerke
Lewedorp
Heinkenszand
Nieuwdorp
'S Heer Abtskerke
'S Gravenpolder
Nisse
'S Heerenhoek
Borssele
Ovezande
Driewegen
Hoedekenskerke
Baarland
Oudelande
Ellewoutsdijk
WESTERSCHELDE
Breskens
Groede
Nummer Een
Cadzand Bad
Cadzand
Nieuwvliet
Hoofdplaat
Schoondijke
Retranchement
KNOKKE-HEIST
Het Zoute
Het Zwin Natuurreservaat
Zuidzande
De Vrede
Oostburg
Ijzendijke
Biervliet
TERNEUZEN
Zaamslag
Waterlandkerkje
Westkapelle
Sluis
Ramskapelle
Bakkersdam
Draaibrug
Hoek
Philippine
Sluiskil
Axel
Aardenburg
Sint-Margriete
Waterland Oudeman
Watervliet
Sint-Jan-in-Eremo
Boekhoute
Oostkerke
Heille
Middelburg
Den Hoorn
Damme
Moerkerke
Kerselaar
Bentille
Hage Vorst
Rijken
Sint-Laureins
Bassevelde
Assenede
Sas van Gent
Westdorpe
Zuiddorpe
Nieuwe Molen
Vijve Kapelle
Strobrug
Moerhuizen
Celie
Eerstestraat
Wisken
Kaprijke
Nieuwbourg
Maldegem
Balgerhoeke
Eindeken
Zelzate
Sijsele
Vossenhol
Adegem
Lembeke
Oosteeklo
Ertvelde
Ramontshoek
Moerbeke
Assebroek
Ten Torre
Vliegendpaard
Eeklo
Wachtebeke
Oedelem
Oostveld
Moerbrugge
Doorn
Hoorn
Waarschoot
Kluizen
Zaffelare
Oostkamp
Knesselare
Ursel
Ronsele
Sleidinge
Beernem
Sint-Joris
Zomergem
Evergem
Oostakker
Zeveneken
Lochristi
Hertsberge
Maria-Aalter
Lovendegem
Wondelgem
Aalter
Bellem
Hamme
Vinderhoute
Merendree
Mariakerke
GENT
Sint-Amandsberg
Destelbergen
Beervelde
Wingene
Hansbeke
Landegem
Drongen
Gentbrugge
Kalken
Ruiselede
Lotenhulle
Poesele
Nevele
Vosselare
Sint-Martens-Latem
Afsnee
Heusden
Laarne
Schuiferskapelle
Kanegem
Meigem
Sint-Denijs-Westrem
Zwijnaarde
Ledeberg
Melle
Wetteren
Egem
Pittem
Tielt
Aarsele
Vinkt
Zeveren
Deinze
De Pinte
Merelbeke
Gontrode
Massemen
Serskamp
Wontergem
Grammene
Petegem
Zevergem
Landskouter
Gijzenzele
Dentergem
Gottem
Machelen
Nazareth
Melsen
Bottelare
Moortsele
Munte
Oosterzele
Meulebeke
Markegem
Oeselgem
Semmerzake
Vurste
Scheldewindeke
Letterhoutem
Vlierzele
Bavegem
Ottergem
Wichelen
N 61
N 58
N 49
N 9
N 44
E 40
E 17
A 10
A 58
R 4

Oud-Vossemeer
Scherpenisse
Poortvliet
St-Maartensdijk
Tholen
Halsteren
Wouw
Kruisland
Rucphen
ROOSENDAAL
Kattendijke
Wemeldinge
GOES
Kloetinge
Yerseke
Kapelle
Biezelinge
BERGEN OP ZOOM
Wouwse Plantage
Nispen
ESSEN
Horendonk
'S Heer Abtskerke
'S Gravenpolder
Nisse
Kruiningen
Hansweert
Krabbendijke
Woensdrecht
Hoogerheide
Huijbergen
Wildert
Nieuwmoer
Hoedekenskerke
Waarde
Rilland
Bath
Baarland
Oudelande
Ossendrecht
Achterbroek
KALMTHOUT
Kruisstraat
Putte
Heide
Zandvliet
Stabroek
Berendrecht
Kloosterzande
Walsoorden
Hengstdijk
Kuitaart
Lamswaarde
TERNEUZEN
Graauw
Prosper-Polder
Galgestraat
KAPELLEN
Maria-ter-Heide
Zaamslag
Vogelwaarde
Ter Hole
Doel
Lillo
Hoevenen
Hoge-Kaart
BRASSCHAAT
Nieuw Namen
Kieldrecht
Hulst
Axel
Schapenbout
EKEREN
MERKSEM
Clinge
Kapellebrug
Meerdonk
Sint-Jansteen
De Klinge
Verrebroek
Kallo
ANTWERPEN
(ANVERS)
Merksem
SCHOTEN
Zuiddorpe
Westdorpe
Koewacht
Zwijndrecht
Melsele
Deurne
Borgerhout
WIJNEGEM
Sint-Gillis-Waas
Vrasene
BEVEREN
STEKENE
Kemzeke
Sint-Pauwels
Nieuwkerken-Waas
Haasdonk
Burcht
Berchem
BORSBEEK
Moerbeke
Wachtebeke
SINT-NIKLAAS
(ST-NICOLAS)
KRUIBEKE
HOBOKEN
WILRIJK
EDEGEM
MORTSEL
BOECHOUT
Sinaai
Belsele
Bazel
HEMIKSEM
HOVE
Zaffelare
Eksaarde
Daknam
Elversele
TEMSE
Tielrode
Steendorp
Rupelmonde
SCHELLE
AARTSELAAR
KONTICH
LINT
Zeveneken
LOCHRISTI
LOKEREN
WAASMUNSTER
HAMME
Weert
Hingene
NIEL
BOOM
Terhagen
Waarloos
DUFFEL
Beervelde
ZELE
Moerzeke
BORNEM
PUURS
RUMST
Walem
Heindonk
Oppuurs
Mariekerke
SINT-AMANDS
Liezele
WILLEBROEK
Blaasveld
Heffen
Overmere
Grembergen
Kalken
LAARNE
DENDERMONDE
(TERMONDE)
Baasrode
Lippelo
Breendonk
Leest
MECHELEN
(MALINES)
BERLARE
Uitbergen
Appels
Malderen
Ramsdonk
KAPELLE-OP-DEN-BOS
Hombeek
WICHELEN
Schellebelle
WETTEREN
Schoonaarde
Oudegem
LEBBEKE
BUGGENHOUT
LONDERZEEL
Steenhuffel
Hofstade
ZEMST
Serskamp
Wanzele
Gijzegem
Wieze
Massemen
Smetlede
LEDE
OPWIJK
Nieuwenrode
Weerde
Eppegem
Elewijt
Wetteren
Oordegem
Impe
Herdersem
Hofstade
AALST
(ALOST)
MERCHTEM
Humbeek
Bavegem
Erondegem
Moorsel
Mazenzele
Mollem
Wolvertem
MEISE
VILVOORDE
(VILVORDE)
KAMP
Perk

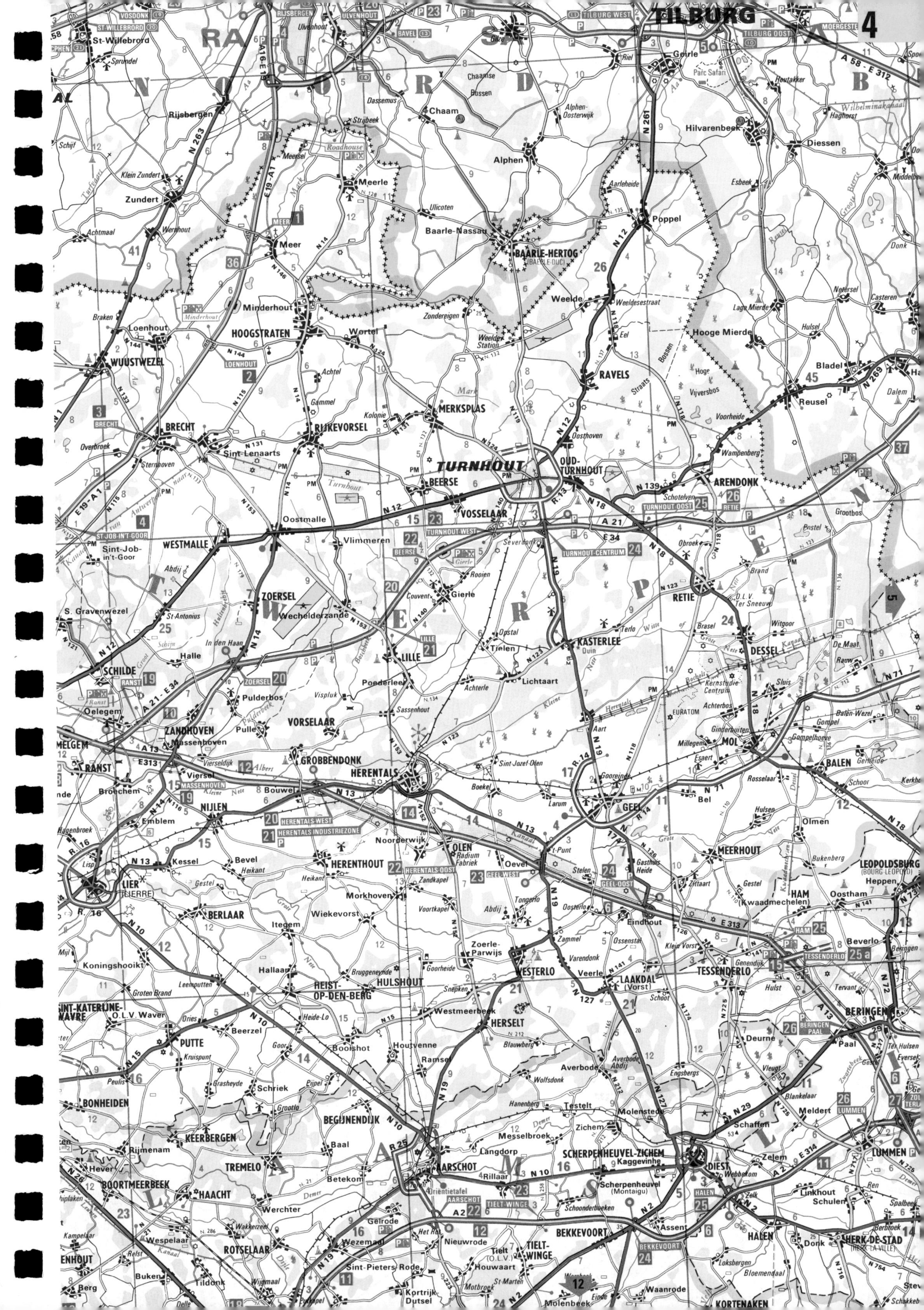
TILBURG
St-Willebrord
Sprundel
Rijsbergen
Ulvenhout
Gilze
Riel
Goirle
Chaamse Bossen
Dassemus
Chaam
Alphen-Oosterwijk
Hilvarenbeek
Diessen
Strijbeek
Meersel
Roadhouse
Klein Zundert
Zundert
Meerle
Alphen
Esbeek
Middelbeers
Achtmaal
Wernhout
Meer
Ulicoten
Baarle-Nassau
BAARLE-HERTOG
(BAERLE-DUC)
Poppel
Aarleheide
Donk
Braken
Minderhout
Weelde
Weeldesestraat
Lage Mierde
Netersel
Casteren
Loenhout
HOOGSTRATEN
Wortel
Zondereigen
Weelde Station
Eel
Hooge Mierde
Hulsel
WUUSTWEZEL
Achtel
Gammel
RAVELS
Hoge Vijversbos
Bladel
Reusel
Dalem
Kolonie
MERKSPLAS
Voorheide
BRECHT
RIJKEVORSEL
Oosthoven
Overbroek
Sint-Lenaarts
Sternhoven
TURNHOUT
OUD-TURNHOUT
Wampenberg
ARENDONK
BEERSE
Schotelven
Oostmalle
VOSSELAAR
TURNHOUT-WEST
TURNHOUT-OOST
Grootbos
WESTMALLE
Vlimmeren
Severdonk
TURNHOUT-CENTRUM
Obroek
Sint-Job-in't-Goor
Postel
Rooien
Brand
Gierle
S. Gravenwezel
St-Antonius
ZOERSEL
Wechelderzande
Couvent
RETIE
O.L.V. Ter Sneeuw
Witgoor
Opstal
Tielen
KASTERLEE
Terlo
Brasel
Duin
DESSEL
De Maat
Rauw
Halle
In den Haan
LILLE
SCHILDE
Poederlee
Lichtaart
Achterle
Kernstudie Centrum
Sluis
Pulderbos
Vispluk
Oelegem
ZANDHOVEN
Massenhoven
VORSELAAR
Sassenhout
Aart
EURATOM
Achterbos
Balen-Wezel
Gompel
Gompelhoeve
MELGEM
RANST
Vierseldijk
Viersel
GROBBENDONK
HERENTALS
Sint-Jozef-Olen
Millegem
MOL
Esaert
BALEN
Gerheide
Broechem
Bouwel
Boekel
Gooreinde
Larum
GEEL
Bel
Rosselaar
Schoor
Kerkhoven
NIJLEN
Emblem
HERENTALS-WEST
HERENTALS INDUSTRIEZONE
Noorderwijk
OLEN
Radium Fabriek
Oevel
't-Punt
Hulsen
Olmen
Kessel
Bevel
Heikant
HERENTHOUT
HERENTALS-OOST
Zandkapel
GEEL-WEST
Stelen
GEEL-OOST
Gasthuis Heide
Zittaart
MEERHOUT
Bukenberg
LEOPOLDSBURG
(BOURG-LEOPOLD)
Heppen
LIER
(LIERRE)
Gestel
Morkhoven
Voortkapel
Abdij
Tongerlo
Oosterlo
Eindhout
Kwaadmechelen
HAM
Oostham
BERLAAR
Itegem
Wiekevorst
Zoerle-Parwijs
WESTERLO
Zammel
Ossenstal
Varendonk
Klein Vorst
Genendijk
Beverlo
Mijl
Koningshooikt
Hallaar
Bruggenende
Goorheide
Veerle
LAAKDAL
(Vorst)
TESSENDERLO
Groten Brand
Leemputten
HEIST-OP-DEN-BERG
HULSHOUT
Snepken
Schoot
Hulst
Tervant
SINT-KATELIJNE-WAVRE
O.L.V. Waver
Ories
Heide-Lo
Westmeerbeek
HERSELT
BERINGEN
Beerzel
PUTTE
Kruispunt
Goor
Boorshot
Houtvenne
Ramsel
Blauwberg
Deurne
BERINGEN PAAL
Paal
Averbode
Abdij
Engsbergs
Vleugt
Peulis
Grasheyde
Schriek
Pijpel
Wolfsdonk
BONHEIDEN
Grootlo
BEGIJNENDIJK
Hanenberg
Testelt
Molenstede
Blankelaar
Meldert
LUMMEN
KEERBERGEN
Rijmenam
Baal
Messelbroek
Zichem
Schaffen
Langdorp
SCHERPENHEUVEL-ZICHEM
Kaggevinne
DIEST
Zelem
Hever
BOORTMEERBEEK
TREMELO
AARSCHOT
Rillaar
Scherpenheuvel
(Montaigu)
Webbekom
Linkhout
Schulen
HAACHT
Betekom
Oriëntietafel
TIELT-WINGE
Schoonderbuken
HALEN
Zelk
Spalbeek
Werchter
Gelrode
Het Hof
Nieuwrode
BEKKEVOORT
Assent
Berbroek
Kampelaar
Wespelaar
Wakkerzeel
ROTSELAAR
Wezemaal
Tielt
(O.L.V.)
TIELT-WINGE
Houwaart
HALEN
Donk
HERK-DE-STAD
(HERK-LA-VILLE)
Relst
Sint-Pieters-Rode
Loksbergen
Bloemendaal
Buken
Tildonk
Wijgmaal
St-Marten
Kortrijk-Dutsel
Motbroek
Molenbeek
Waanrode
KORTENAKEN
Schakkebroek
Berg
Pakapel

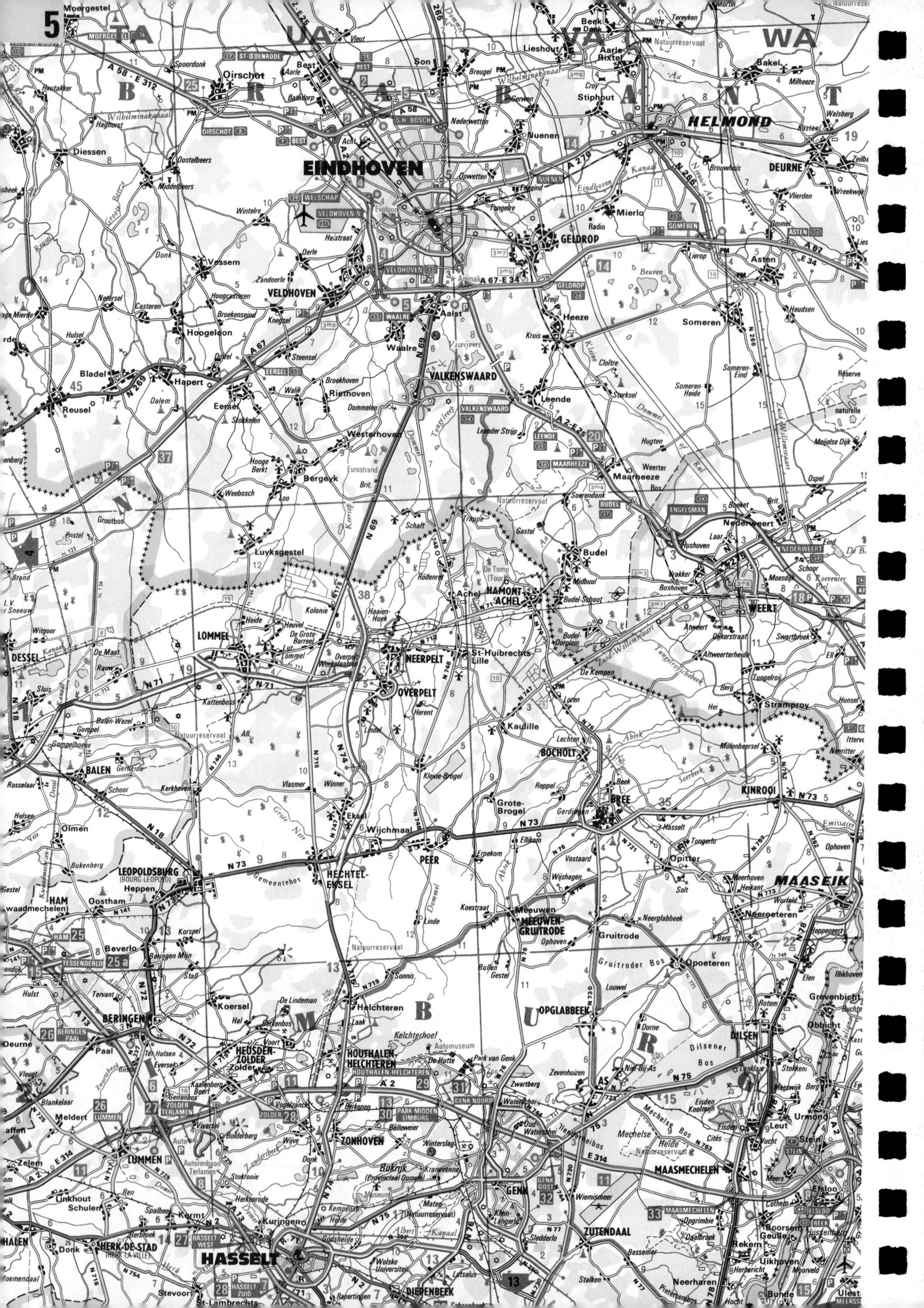
Moergestel
Oirschot
Best
Son
Lieshout
Beek en Donk
Aarle Rixtel
Bakel
Milheeze
Stiphout
HELMOND
Nuenen
Gerwen
Nederwetten
Diessen
Oostelbeers
Middelbeers
EINDHOVEN
DEURNE
Vlierden
Mierlo
GELDROP
Asten
Wintelre
Vessem
Veldhoven
VELDHOVEN
Aalst
Heeze
Someren
Hoogeloon
Bladel
Hapert
Reusel
Eersel
Waalre
VALKENSWAARD
Riethoven
Westerhoven
Leende
Bergeyk
Maarheeze
Luyksgestel
Budel
Nederweert
WEERT
HAMONT-ACHEL
Achel
LOMMEL
DESSEL
NEERPELT
OVERPELT
St-Huibrechts-Lille
Kaulille
BOCHOLT
BREE
KINROOI
BALEN
Olmen
LEOPOLDSBURG
(BOURG-LEOPOLD)
Heppen
HAM
Oostham
HECHTEL-EKSEL
PEER
Wijchmaal
Grote-Brogel
Kleine-Brogel
MAASEIK
Opitter
Tongerlo
MEEUWEN-GRUITRODE
Gruitrode
Opoeteren
Beverlo
BERINGEN
Koersel
Helchteren
OPGLABBEEK
DILSEN
HEUSDEN-ZOLDER
HOUTHALEN-HELCHTEREN
LUMMEN
ZONHOVEN
GENK
As
MAASMECHELEN
HASSELT
HERK-DE-STAD
ZUTENDAAL
DIEPENBEEK
Stevoort
Kuringen
Urmond
Stein
Elsloo
Geulle
Rekem
Uikhoven
Ulestraten

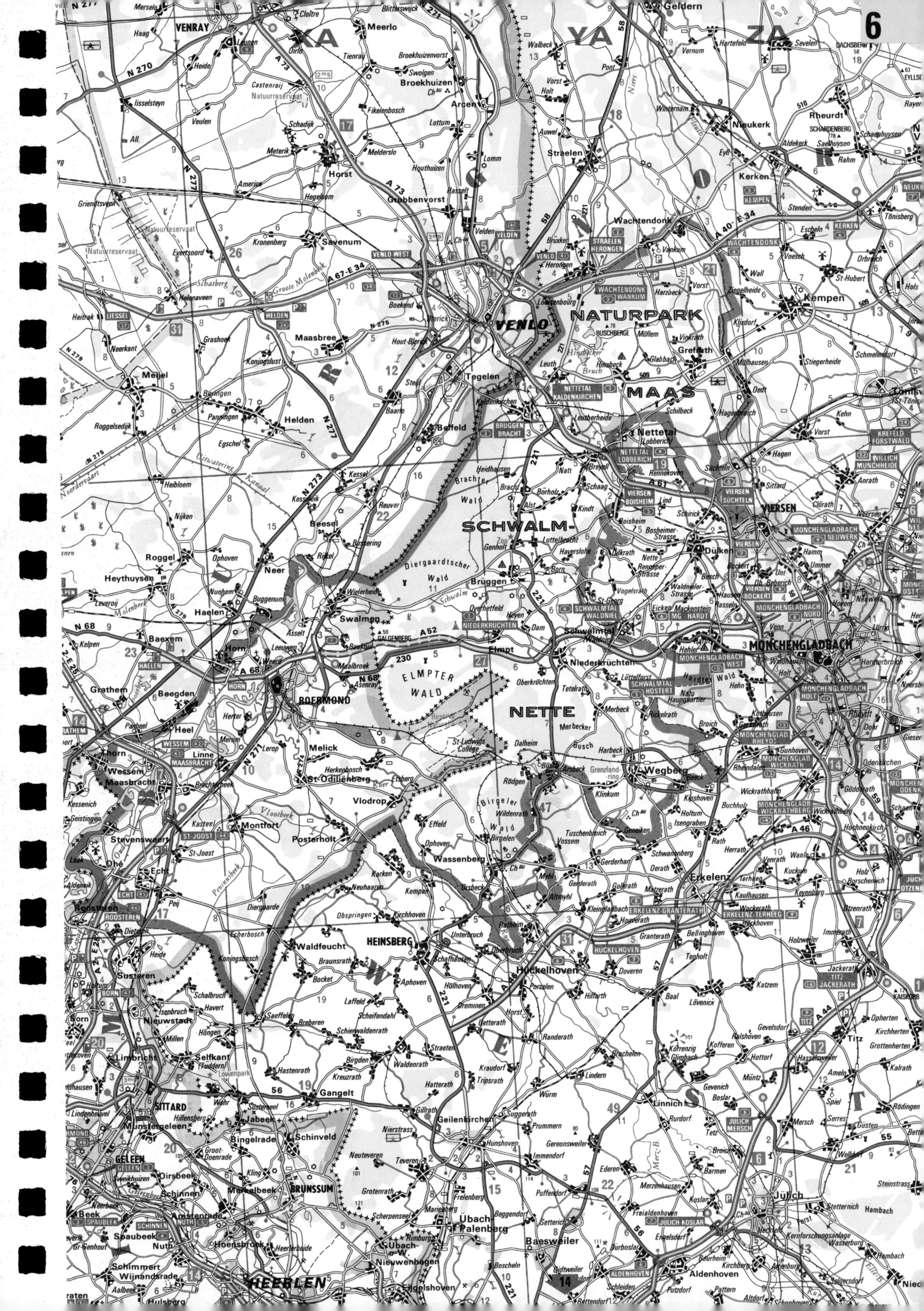

VENRAY
Merselo
Cloître
Blitterswijck
Geldern
Meerlo
Haag
Oirlo
Tienray
Broekhuizenvorst
Swolgen
Broekhuizen
Walbeck
Vernum
Hartefeld
Sevelen
N 270
Castenraij
Natuurreservaat
Arcen
Fikelenbosch
Vorst
Holt
Pont
Ysselsteyn
Veulen
Schadijk
Lottum
Wintemam
Nieukerk
Rheurdt
Schaephuysen
Rahm
Aldekerk
Meterik
Horst
Melderslo
Lomm
Auwel
Straelen
Houthuizen
Kerken
America
Hegelsom
Hasselt
Grubbenvorst
Griendtsveen
Wachtendonk
Stenden
Tönisberg
Sevenum
Kronenberg
Evertsoord
Velden
VENLO WEST
VELDEN
Brüxken
Herongen
STRAELEN HERONGEN
Vankum
WACHTENDONK
Voesch
Orbroich
Eschein
KERKEN
A 40 - E 34
A 67 - E 34
A 73
Schatberg
Groote Molenbeek
Helenaveen
Heitrak
LIESSEL
HELDEN
Boekend
Blerick
VENLO
Louisenbourg
WACHTENDONK WANKUM
Harzbeck
Vorst
Ziegelheide
St-Hubert
Kempen
Klixdorf
NATURPARK
BUSCHBERGE
Müllem
Vinkrath
Grefrath
Neerkant
Grashoek
Maasbree
N 275
Hout-Blerick
Koningslust
Leuth
Hinsbeck
Glabbach
Mülhausen
Stiegerheide
Schmelendorf
Meijel
Steyl
Tegelen
NETTETAL KALDENKIRCHEN
MAAS
Oedt
Beringen
Panningen
Helden
Baarlo
Kaldenkirchen
Leutherheide
Schilbeck
Hagenbroich
Vorst
Kehn
Roggelsedijk
Egschel
Belfeld
BRUGGEN BRACHT
Nettetal (Lobberich)
NETTETAL LOBBERICH
Hagen
KREFELD FORSTWALD
WILLICH MÜNCHHEIDE
Anrath
Uitwatering Kanaal
Noordervaart
Heibloem
Kessel
Heidhausen
Brachter Wald
Bracht
Breyell
Natt
Rennekoven
Schaag
Bõrholz
Alst
Kindt
VIERSEN BOISHEIM
Lind
VIERSEN SÜCHTELN
Slicheln
Sittard
Clörath
VIERSEN
N 273
Kesseleik
Reuver
Nijken
Beesel
SCHWALM-
Boisheim
Schirick
Bosheimer-Strasse
MÖNCHENGLADBACH NEUWERK
Roggel
Ophoven
Bussering
Rijkel
Zoo
Genholt
Luttelbracht
Haverslohe
Dülkrath
Dülken
Nette
Rennpeper-Strasse
Hamm
Ummer
Heythuysen
Neer
Diergaardtscher Wald
Bruggen
Born
Waldnieler-Strasse
Vogelsrath
Bösch
Wielerheide
Nunhem
Buggenum
Overhetfeld
St-Georg
SCHWALMTAL WALDNIEL
Eicken
Mackenstein
MG HARDT
Hausen
Rasseln
MÖNCHENGLADBACH NORD
VIERSEN BÖCKERT
Leveroij
Molenbeek
Haelen
Swalmen
Heyen
NIEDERKRÜCHTEN
Dam
Schwalmtal (Waldniel)
N 68
Baexem
Kelpen
Asselt
GALGENBERG
A 52
Elmpt
Hehler
MÖNCHENGLADBACH WEST
MÖNCHENGLADBACH
Horn
Leeuwen
Boukoul
Maalbroek
230
Niederkrüchten
Venn
HAELEN
A 68
Weerd
ELMPTER WALD
Oberkrüchten
Lüttelforst
SCHWALMTAL HOSTERT
Hardter Wald
Hehn
Waldhausen
Holt
Grathem
Beegden
HORN
ROERMOND
Asenray
Tetelrath
Nato Hauptquartier
MÖNCHENGLADBACH HOLT
NETTE
Merbeck
Rickelrath
Herten
Heel
Panheel
Réserve Naturelle
Merbecker
Broich
Kothausen
Rheydt
Geneicken
MÖNCHENGLADBACH RHEYDT
THORN
Wessem
WESSEM
Merum
Linne
MAASBRACHT
Lerop
Melick
St-Ludwigs College
Dalheim
Busch
Harbeck
Gunhoven
MÖNCHENGLADBACH WICKRATH
Odenkirchen
Maasbracht
Brachterbeek
N 271
Herkenbosch
St-Odiliënberg
Roer
Etsberg
Rödgen
Arsbeck
Grenzlandring
Wegberg
Beeck
Rheindalen
Kessenich
Geistingen
Vlodrop
Birgeler Wald
Wildenrath
Klinkum
Kipshoven
Wickrathhahn
MÖNCHENGLADBACH WICKRATHBERG
Wickrathberg
Güdderath
Vlootbeek
Kasteel
ST JOOST
Montfort
Stevensweert
St-Joost
Posterholt
Effeld
Ophoven
Birgelen
Tuschenbroich
Vossem
Geneiken
Holtum
Isengraben
Buchholz
A 46
Hochneukirch
Ohé
Laak
Echt
Peij
Peminsbeek
Wassenberg
Karken
Kempen
Neuhaaren
Orsbeck
Myhl
Gerderhan
Schwanenberg
Oerath
Rath
Herrath
Venrath
Kuckum
Wanlo
Holz
Borschemich
Erkelenz
Terheeg
Kaulhausen
Keyenberg
ECHT
ROOSTEREN
Roosteren
Diergaarde
Obspringen
Kirchhoven
Gerderath
Golkrath
Matzerath
Altmyhl
Kleingladbach
ERKELENZ GRANTERATH
ERKELENZ TERHEEG
Hückhoven
Wockerath
Otzenrath
Dieteren
Echterbosch
Waldfeucht
HEINSBERG
Unterbruch
Ratheim
Houverath
Granterath
Bellinghoven
Immerath
Holzweiler
Heide
Koningsbosch
Braunsrath
Schafhausen
Oberbruch
HÜCKELHOVEN
Tenholt
Jackerath
JACKERATH
Susteren
Bocket
Aphoven
Hückelhoven
Porselen
Doveren
Baal
Lövenich
Katzem
Holtum
BORN
Schalbruch
Havert
Isenbruch
Nieuwstadt
Laffeld
Scheifendahl
Hülhoven
Bremmen
Hilfarth
Horst
Titz
Opherten
Kirchherten
Grottenherten
Born
Millen
Höngen
Saeffelen
Breberen
Schierwaldenrath
Hetterath
Randerath
Gevelsdorf
Ralshoven
Körrenzig
Glimbach
Kofferen
Hottorf
Hasselsweiler
Kalrath
Limbricht
Selfkant (Tüddern)
Lowenpark
Birgden
Waldenrath
Straeten
Kraudorf
Tripsrath
Brachelen
Lindern
Müntz
Ameln
Hastenrath
Kreuzrath
Hatterath
Würm
Gevenich
Boslar
Spiel
Rödingen
SITTARD
Wehr
Süsterseel
Jabeek
Hillensberg
Gangelt
Gillrath
Geilenkirchen
Suggerath
Linnich
Rurdorf
JÜLICH MERSCH
Mersch
Serrest
Güsten
Lindenheuvel
Munstergeleen
Schinveld
Nierstrass
Prummern
Tetz
Bingelrade
Groot-Doenrade
Gereonsweiler
Immendorf
Broich
Welldorf
GELEEN
Geleen
Oirsbeek
Kling
Neuteveren
Teveren
Hunshoven
Ederen
Barmen
Steinstrass
Schinnen
Merkelbeek
BRUNSSUM
Grotenrath
Frelenberg
Puffendorf
Merzenhausen
Koslar
Jülich
Hambach
Stetternich
Beek
SPAUBEEK
SCHINNEN
NUTH
Amstenrade
Scherpenseel
Marienberg
Übach-Palenberg
Beggendorf
Setterich
Freialdenhoven
JÜLICH KOSLAR
Heckfeld
Kernforschungsanlage
Spaubeek
Gr-Genhout
Nuth
Hoensbroek
Heerlerheide
Rimburg
Übach-o-W.
Baesweiler
Dürboslar
Engelsdorf
Wasserburg
Schimmert
Wijnandsrade
Nieuwenhagen
Boscheln
Bourheim
Kirchberg
Altenburg
Hambach
Aalbeek
Hulsberg
HEERLEN
Eygelshoven
Bettendorf
ALDENHOVEN
Aldenhoven
Schleiden
Putzdorf
Pattern
Altdorf
Schophoven
Selgersdorf
Niederzier

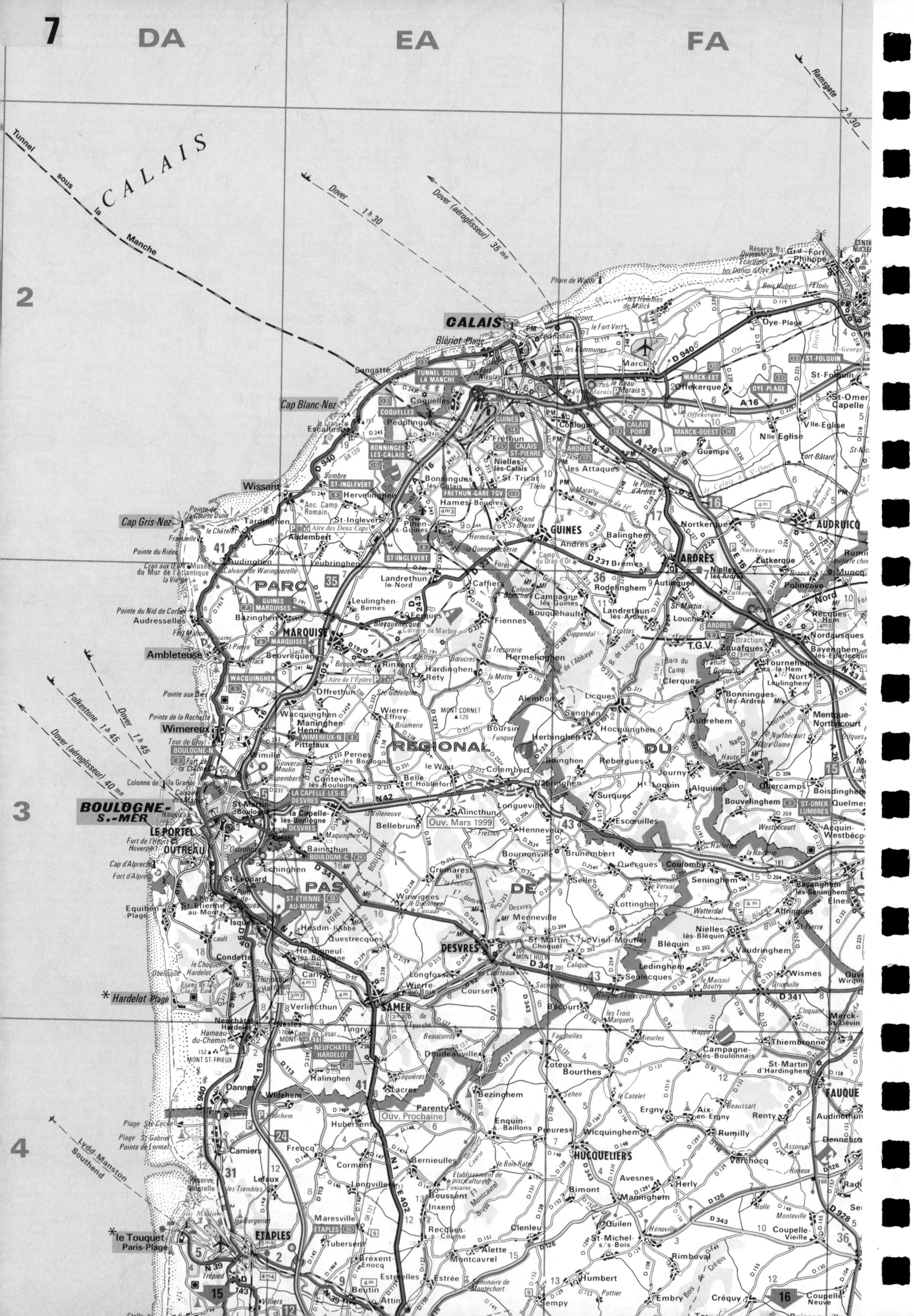

DA
EA
FA
2
3
4
Tunnel sous la Manche
CALAIS
Dover 1 h 30
Dover (aéroglisseur) 35 mn
Ramsgate 2 h 30
Folkestone 1 h 45
Dover 1 h 45
Dover (aéroglisseur) 40 mn
Lydd-Manston Southend
CALAIS
Blériot-Plage
Sangatte
TUNNEL SOUS LA MANCHE
Cap Blanc-Nez
COQUELLES
Coquelles
Peuplingues
Escalles
BONNINGES LES-CALAIS
GUINES
CALAIS ST-PIERRE
CALAIS PORT
Fréthun
Nielles-lès-Calais
St-Tricat
Marck
Oye-Plage
MARCK-EST
Offekerque
OYE-PLAGE
ST-FOLQUIN
St-Folquin
St-Omer Capelle
MARCK-OUEST
Vlle-Eglise
Nlle Eglise
Guemps
Coulogne
les Attaques
Wissant
ST-INGLEVERT
Hervelinghen
Bonningues lès-Calais
FRETHUN-GARE TGV
Hames-Boucres
Cap Gris-Nez
Tardinghen
Audembert
St-Inglevert
Pihen lès-Guînes
Aire des Deux Caps
GUINES
Andres
Balinghem
Nortkerque
AUDRUICQ
ARDRES
Zutkerque
Polincove
Audinghen
Leubringhen
Landrethun le-Nord
Caffiers
Rodelinghem
Autingues
PARC
GUINES MARQUISES
Audresselles
Bazinghen
MARQUISE
Leulinghen-Bernes
Ferques
Fiennes
Campagne lès-Guines
Bouquehault
Landrethun lès-Ardres
Louches
ARDRES
Recques s-Hem
Nordausques
Ambleteuse
Beuvrequen
Rinxent
Hardinghen
Rety
Hermelinghen
T.G.V.
Zouafques
Bayenghem lès-Eperlecques
Tournehem s-la-Hem
Nort Leulinghen
WACQUINGHEN
Offrethun
Clerques
Licques
Alembon
Bonningues lès-Ardres
Wimereux
Wacquinghen
Maninghen Henne
WIMEREUX-N.
Pittefaux
Wierre-Effroy
MONT CORNET
Boursin
Sanghen
Hocquinghen
Audrehem
Mentque Nortbécourt
BOULOGNE-N.
Wimille
Pernes lès-Boulogne
REGIONAL
Herbinghen
DU
Conteville lès-Boulogne
le Wast
Colembert
Bainghen
Rebergues
Journy
Alquines
Quercamps
Boisdinghem
BOULOGNE-S.-MER
LA CAPELLE-LES-B DESVRES
Belle-et-Houllefort
Nabringhen
Ht-Loquin
Bouvelinghem
ST-OMER LUMBRES
St-Martin-Boulogne
la Capelle-lès-Boulogne
Alincthun
Longueville
Surques
Escœuilles
Acquin-Westbécourt
LE PORTEL
OUTREAU
Bellebrune
Ouv. Mars 1999
Henneveux
Bainethun
BOULOGNE-C.
Echinghen
Bournonville
Brunembert
Quesques
Coulomby
St-Léonard
PAS
Cremarest
Selles
Seninghem
Bayenghem lès-Seninghem
Equihen-Plage
ST-ETIENNE AU-MONT
Wirwignes
DE
Lottinghen
Affringues
Isques
Hesdin-l'Abbé
Questrecques
Menneville
Nielles-lès-Bléquin
Condette
Hesdigneul-lès-Boulogne
DESVRES
St-Martin-Choquel
Vieil-Moutier
Bléquin
Vaudringhem
Hardelot-Plage
Carly
Longfossé
Courset
Ledinghem
Seulecques
Wismes
Verlincthun
SAMER
Bécourt
D 341
Neufchâtel-Hardelot
Nesles
Tingry
Campagne-lès-Boulonnais
Thiembronne
MONT ST-FRIEUX
NEUFCHATEL-HARDELOT
Doudeauville
Zoteux
Bourthes
St-Martin d'Hardinghen
Dannes
Widehem
Halinghen
Lacres
Bezinghem
FAUQUE
Parenty
Ouv. Prochaine
Hubersent
Enquin-s.-Baillons
Preures
Wicquinghem
Ergny
Aix-en-Ergny
Renty
Camiers
Frencq
Bernieulles
HUCQUELIERS
Rumilly
Verchocq
Cormont
Lefaux
Longvilliers
Beussent
Inxent
Bimont
Avesnes
Maninghem
Herly
Maresville
ETAPLES
le Touquet Paris-Plage
Recques-s.-Course
Clenleu
Quilen
St-Michel-s/s-Bois
Coupelle-Vieille
Tubersent
Alette
Montcavrel
Rimboval
Bréxent-Enocq
Estréelles
Estrée
Humbert
Beutin
Attin
Embry
Créquy
Coupelle-Neuve

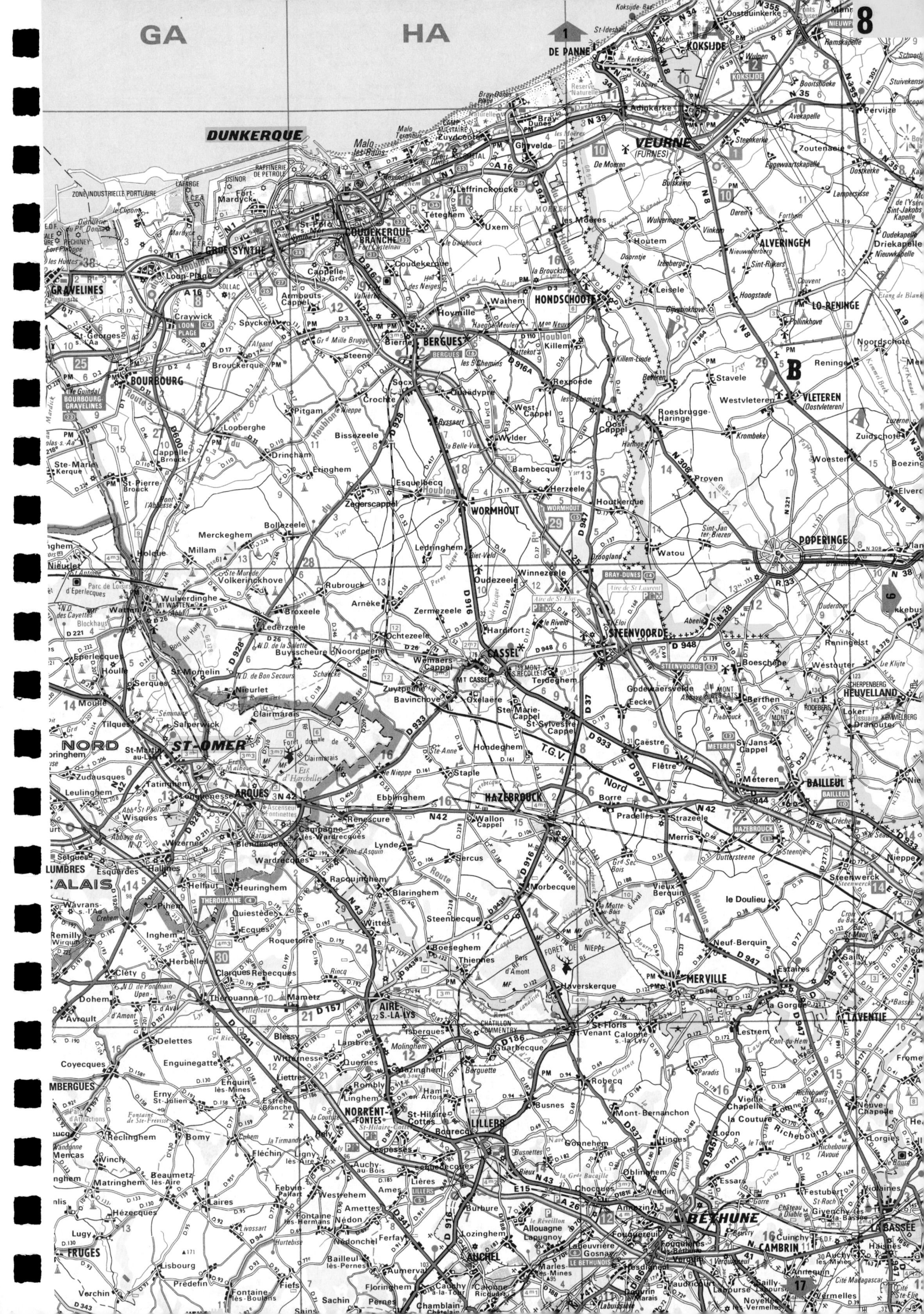
GA
HA
1
DE PANNE
KOKSIJDE
Oostduinkerke
St-Idesbald
Koksijde-Bad
Nieuwpoort
Ramskapelle
DUNKERQUE
Malo-les-Bains
Bray-Dunes
Zuydcoote
Ghyvelde
VEURNE
(FURNES)
De Moeren
Adinkerke
Bulskamp
Steenkerke
Avekapelle
Pervijze
Zoutenaaie
Eggewaartskapelle
Oostkerke
Lampernisse
Oeren
ALVERINGEM
Oudekapelle
Driekapelle
Nieuwkapelle
Wulveringem
Vinkem
Houtem
Izenberge
Sint-Rijkers
Leisele
Hoogstade
LO-RENINGE
Pollinkhove
Gijverinkhove
Stavele
Reninge
Noordschote
B
VLETEREN
(Oostvleteren)
Westvleteren
Roesbrugge-Haringe
Krombeke
Zuidschote
Woesten
Boezinge
Proven
Elverdinge
POPERINGE
Watou
Abeele
Reningelst
Westouter
Boeschepe
HEUVELLAND
Loker
Dranouter
Berthen
Mont des Cats
Godewaersvelde
Méteren
BAILLEUL
Nieppe
Steenwerck
Le Doulieu
Neuf-Berquin
Estaires
Merville
La Gorgue
LAVENTIE
Lestrem
Vieille-Chapelle
La Couture
Richebourg
Locon
Festubert
Essars
BÉTHUNE
Beuvry
Cuinchy
LA BASSÉE
CAMBRIN
Vermelles
Auchy-lès-Mines
Annequin
Noyelles
Sailly-Labourse
Verquin
Fouquereuil
Fouquières
Hinges
Chocques
Oblinghem
Vendin
Annezin
Gonnehem
Mont-Bernanchon
Robecq
Busnes
LILLERS
Burbure
Allouagne
Lozinghem
AUCHEL
Calonne-Ricouart
Marles-les-Mines
Gosnay
Labeuvrière
Lapugnoy
Ferfay
Ames
Lières
Amettes
Auchy-au-Bois
Ecquedecques
Lespesses
Ham-en-Artois
St-Hilaire-Cottes
NORRENT-FONTES
Linghem
Rombly
Mazinghem
Guarbecque
Isbergues
Molinghem
Berguette
St-Venant
St-Floris
Calonne-s.-la-Lys
Haverskerque
Forêt de Nieppe
Thiennes
Boëseghem
Steenbecque
Morbecque
Blaringhem
Racquinghem
Wardrecques
Campagne-lès-Wardrecques
Renescure
Ebblinghem
Lynde
Sercus
Wallon-Cappel
HAZEBROUCK
Borre
Pradelles
Strazeele
Merris
Vieux-Berquin
Caëstre
Flêtre
St-Jans-Cappel
Hondeghem
Staple
Le Nieppe
St-Sylvestre-Cappel
Ste-Marie-Cappel
Oxelaëre
Bavinchove
Zuytpeene
CASSEL
Wemaers-Cappel
Terdeghem
STEENVOORDE
Winnezeele
Oudezeele
Hardifort
Zermezeele
Ochtezeele
Noordpeene
Buysscheure
Arnèke
Rubrouck
Broxeele
Lederzeele
Volkerinckhove
Wulverdinghe
Watten
Millam
Merckeghem
Bollezeele
Holque
Zegerscappel
Esquelbecq
Ledringhem
WORMHOUT
Herzeele
Houtkerque
Bambecque
Wylder
West-Cappel
Oost-Cappel
Rexpoëde
Killem
HONDSCHOOTE
Warhem
Hoymille
BERGUES
Bierne
Socx
Quaëdypre
Crochte
Pitgam
Bissezeele
Drincham
Eringhem
Looberghe
Cappelle-Brouck
Ste-Marie-Kerque
St-Pierre-Brouck
BOURBOURG
Brouckerque
Steene
Spycker
Craywick
Armbouts-Cappel
Cappelle-la-Grande
Coudekerque
COUDEKERQUE-BRANCHE
Téteghem
Uxem
Leffrinckoucke
Les Moëres
GRANDE-SYNTHE
St-Pol-s-Mer
Fort-Mardyck
Loon-Plage
GRAVELINES
St-Georges-s.-Aa
Mardyck
Eperlecques
Houlle
Serques
St-Momelin
Nieurlet
Clairmarais
Moulle
Tilques
Salperwick
ST-OMER
St-Martin-au-Laërt
Tatinghem
Longuenesse
ARQUES
Blendecques
Wizernes
Hallines
Esquerdes
Setques
LUMBRES
Helfaut
Heuringhem
Pihem
Inghem
Quiestède
Ecques
Roquetoire
Wittes
Herbelles
Cléty
Clarques
Rebecques
Thérouanne
Mametz
AIRE-S.-LA-LYS
Blessy
Lambres
Witternesse
Quernes
Liettres
Estrée-Blanche
Enquin-lès-Mines
Enguinegatte
Erny-St-Julien
Delettes
Coyecques
Dohem
Avroult
Bomy
Reclinghem
Vincly
Fléchin
Ligny-lès-Aire
Beaumetz-lès-Aire
Matringhem
Laires
Febvin-Palfart
Westrehem
Fontaine-lès-Hermans
Nédon
Nédonchel
Hézecques
Lugy
FRUGES
Lisbourg
Prédefin
Fontaine-lès-Boulans
Fiefs
Sachin
Pernes
Floringhem
Camblain-Châtelain
Cauchy-à-la-Tour
Aumerval
Bailleul-lès-Pernes
Verchin
NORD
PAS-DE-CALAIS
T.G.V. Nord
N 1
N 39
N 35
N 8
N 38
N 42
N 43
A 16
A 25
A 26
D 916
D 933
D 947
D 928
E 15
9
17

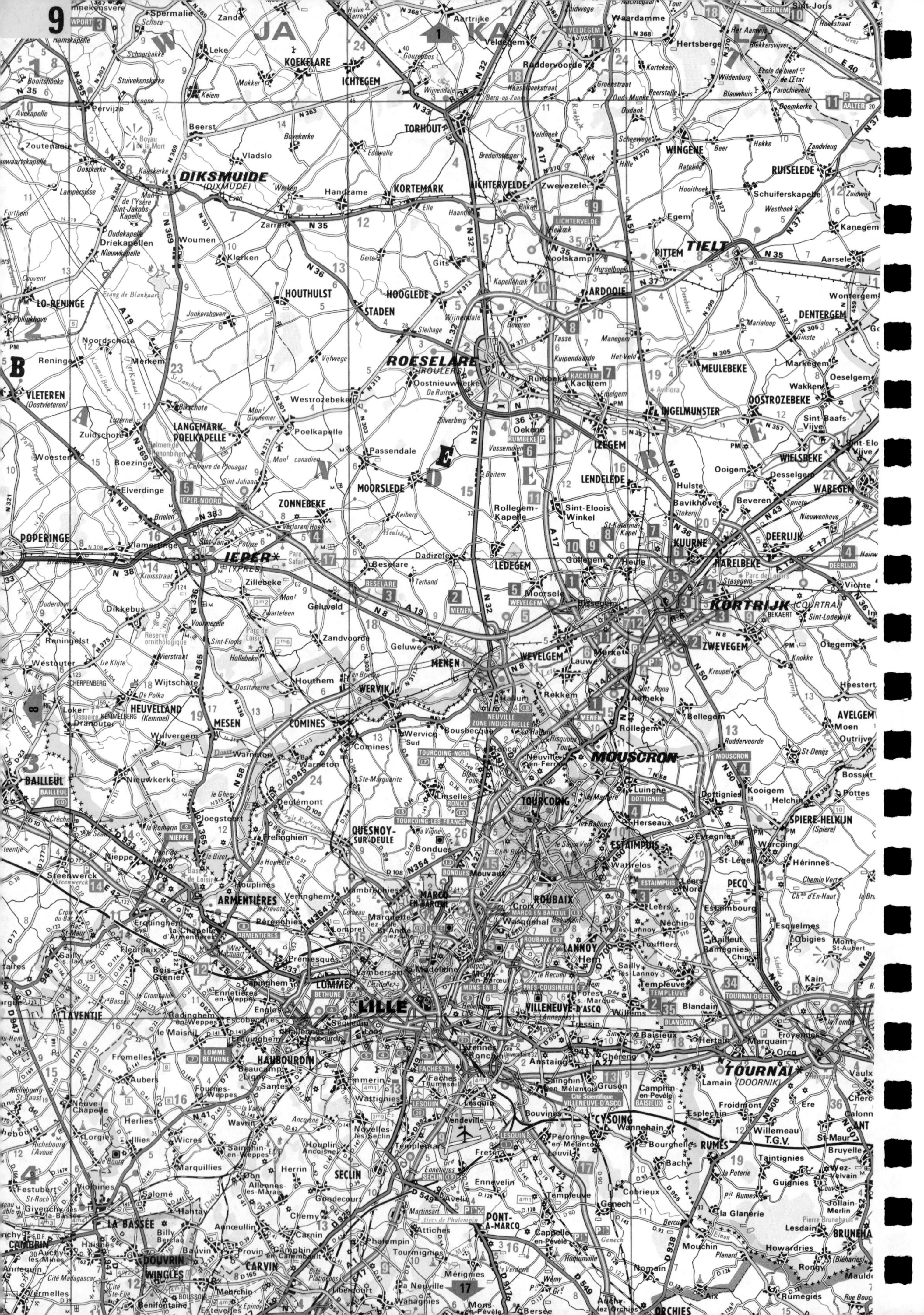
DIKSMUIDE
(DIXMUDE)
KOEKELARE
ICHTEGEM
TORHOUT
KORTEMARK
LICHTERVELDE
WINGENE
RUISELEDE
TIELT
PITTEM
ARDOOIE
HOUTHULST
HOOGLEDE
STADEN
LO-RENINGE
ROESELARE
(ROULERS)
MEULEBEKE
DENTERGEM
VLETEREN
(Oostvleteren)
LANGEMARK-
POELKAPELLE
INGELMUNSTER
OOSTROZEBEKE
IZEGEM
LENDELEDE
WIELSBEKE
WAREGEM
MOORSLEDE
ZONNEBEKE
POPERINGE
IEPER
(YPRES)
LEDEGEM
KUURNE
HARELBEKE
DEERLIJK
KORTRIJK
(COURTRAI)
ZWEVEGEM
WEVELGEM
MENEN
WERVIK
HEUVELLAND
(Kemmel)
MESEN
COMINES
AVELGEM
MOUSCRON
BAILLEUL
TOURCOING
SPIERE-HELKIJN
(Spiere)
ESTAIMPUIS
QUESNOY-
SUR-DEULE
ARMENTIÈRES
ROUBAIX
PECQ
LANNOY
LILLE
VILLENEUVE-D'ASCQ
LAVENTIE
HAUBOURDIN
TOURNAI
(DOORNIK)
CYSOING
RUMES
SECLIN
LA BASSÉE
PONT-
À-MARCQ
BRUNEHAUT
CAMBRIN
DOUVRIN
WINGLES
CARVIN
ORCHIES

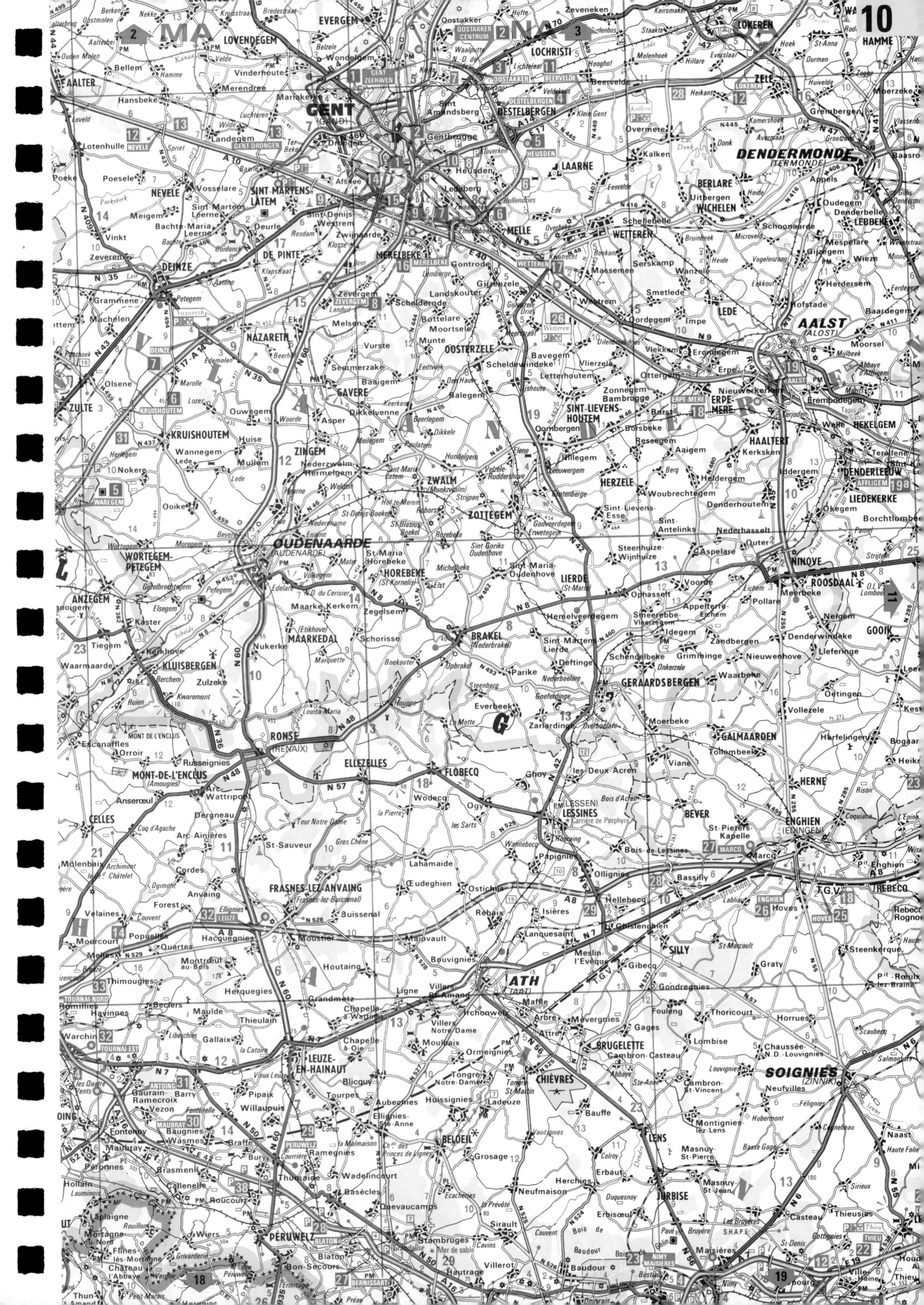
EVERGEM
LOVENDEGEM
LOCHRISTI
LOKEREN
HAMME
AALTER
GENT
(GAND)
DESTELBERGEN
ZELE
DENDERMONDE
(TERMONDE)
LAARNE
BERLARE
WICHELEN
NEVELE
SINT-MARTENS-LATEM
MELLE
WETTEREN
DEINZE
DE PINTE
MERELBEKE
LEBBEKE
NAZARETH
OOSTERZELE
LEDE
AALST
(ALOST)
ZULTE
GAVERE
ERPE-MERE
SINT-LIEVENS-HOUTEM
KRUISHOUTEM
ZINGEM
HAALTERT
ZWALM
ZOTTEGEM
HERZELE
DENDERLEEUW
LIEDEKERKE
OUDENAARDE
(AUDENARDE)
WORTEGEM-PETEGEM
HOREBEKE
LIERDE
NINOVE
ROOSDAAL
ANZEGEM
MAARKEDAL
BRAKEL
GOOIK
KLUISBERGEN
GERAARDSBERGEN
RONSE
(RENAIX)
GALMAARDEN
ELLEZELLES
FLOBECQ
MONT-DE-L'ENCLUS
HERNE
LESSINES
BEVER
ENGHIEN
(EDINGEN)
CELLES
FRASNES-LEZ-ANVAING
SILLY
ATH
LEUZE-EN-HAINAUT
BRUGELETTE
CHIÈVRES
SOIGNIES
(ZINNIK)
BELOEIL
LENS
JURBISE
PÉRUWELZ

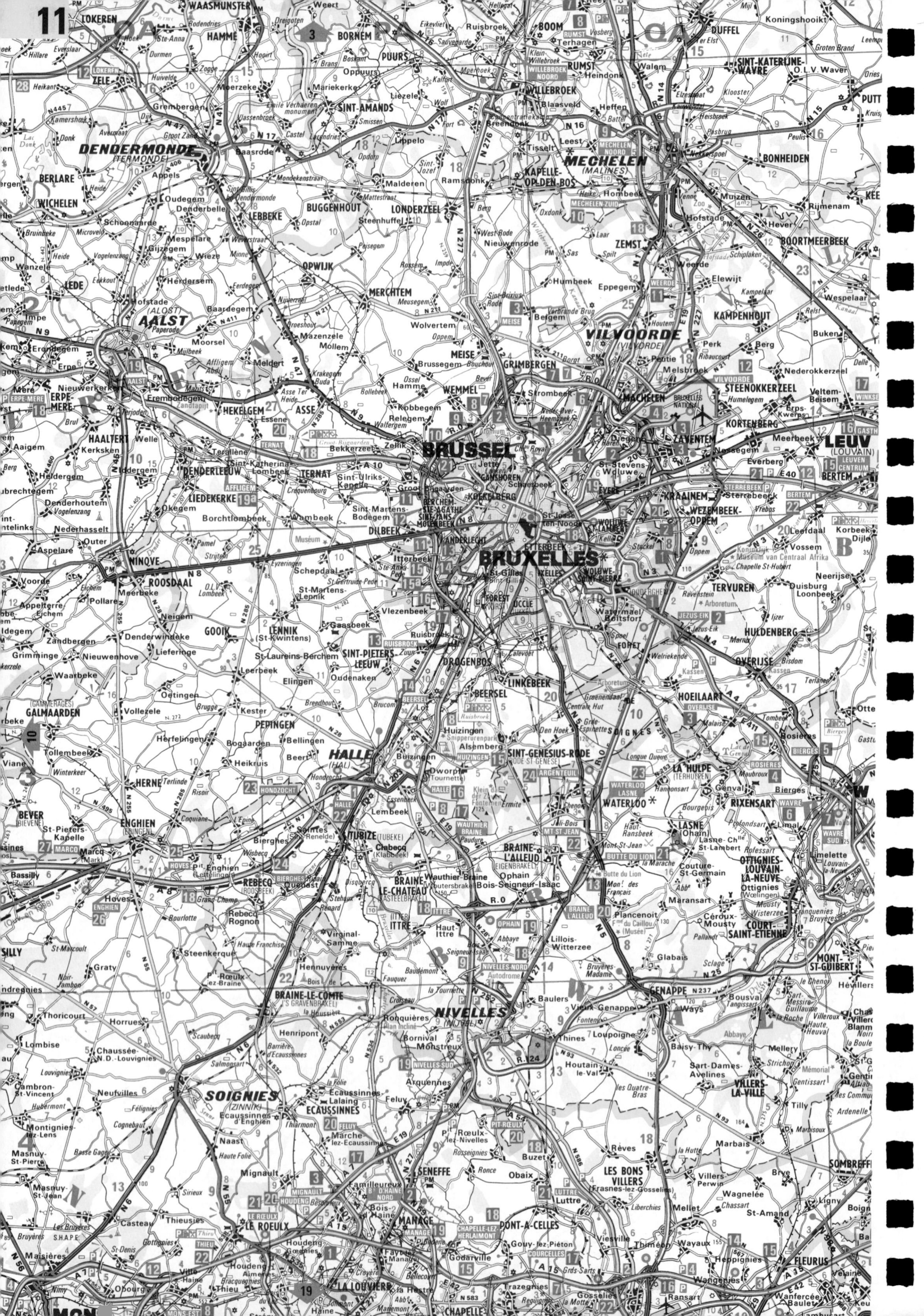

LOKEREN
WAASMUNSTER
HAMME
BORNEM
PUURS
BOOM
RUMST
DUFFEL
Koningshooikt
SINT-KATERIJNE-WAVRE
O.L.V. Waver
ZELE
Mariekerke
Liezele
SINT-AMANDS
WILLEBROEK
Breendonk
Heffen
PUTT
Grembergen
Lippelo
Tisselt
Leest
MECHELEN
(MALINES)
BONHEIDEN
DENDERMONDE
(TERMONDE)
Baasrode
Malderen
Ramsdonk
KAPELLE-OP-DEN-BOS
BERLARE
Appels
WICHELEN
Oudegem
BUGGENHOUT
LONDERZEEL
Hombeek
Muizen
Rijmenam
LEBBEKE
Hofstade
BOORTMEERBEEK
Wieze
Nieuwenrode
ZEMST
OPWIJK
LEDE
Herdersem
MERCHTEM
Humbeek
Eppegem
Elewijt
Wespelaar
Hofstade
AALST
(ALOST)
Baardegem
Wolvertem
Grimbergen
VILVOORDE
KAMPENHOUT
Moorsel
Mazenzele
Meise
Perk
Berg
Buken
Erpe
Meldert
Brussegem
Melsbroek
STEENOKKERZEEL
Nederokkerzeel
ERPE-MERE
Wemmel
MACHELEN
Veltem-Beisem
HAALTERT
HEKELGEM
ASSE
Strombeek
KORTENBERG
Kerksken
Aaigem
Welle
Relegem
ZAVENTEM
BRUSSEL
LEUV
(LOUVAIN)
Heldergem
Ternat
Zellik
Jette
St-Stevens-Woluwe
Everberg
BERTEM
DENDERLEEUW
Sint-Ulriks-Kapelle
Ganshoren
Evere
Kraainem
Sterrebeek
LIEDEKERKE
Koekelberg
Wezembeek-Oppem
Denderhoutem
Okegem
Berchem-Ste-Agathe
Sint-Martens-Bodegem
Nederhasselt
Borchtlombeek
Dilbeek
Wambeek
Anderlecht
Etterbeek
BRUXELLES
Outer
Leefdaal
Korbeek-Dijle
Aspelare
NINOVE
Vossem
ROOSDAAL
Schepdaal
Itterbeek
St-Gilles
Ixelles
Woluwe-Saint-Pierre
Voorde
Meerbeke
Pollare
St-Martens-Lennik
Forest
Uccle
TERVUREN
Neerijse
Duisburg
Loonbeek
Appelterre-Eichem
Vlezenbeek
Watermael-Boitsfort
Neigem
GOOIK
LENNIK
(St-Kwintens)
Gaasbeek
Denderwindeke
Ruisbroek
HULDENBERG
Zandbergen
Lieferinge
Grimminge
Nieuwenhove
St-Laureins-Berchem
SINT-PIETERS-LEEUW
Drogenbos
Linkebeek
OVERIJSE
Waarbeke
Leerbeek
Oudenaken
Elingen
Beersel
Oetingen
Vollezele
Kester
HOEILAART
GALMAARDEN
Pepingen
Bellingen
Herfelingen
Huizingen
Alsemberg
SINT-GENESIUS-RODE
(RHODE-ST-GENESE)
Tollembeek
Bogaarden
HALLE
(HAL)
Beert
Buizingen
Heikruis
Dworp
LA HULPE
(TERHULPEN)
Genval
Bierges
HERNE
WATERLOO
RIXENSART
BEVER
ENGHIEN
(EDINGEN)
Lembeek
St-Pieters-Kapelle
Saintes
TUBIZE
(TUBEKE)
Clabecq
BRAINE-L'ALLEUD
(EIGENBRAKEL)
Ophain
LASNE
(Ohain)
Limal
Marcq
Bierghes
Rebecq
OTTIGNIES-LOUVAIN-LA-NEUVE
Bassilly
BRAINE-LE-CHATEAU
Wauthier-Braine
Bois-Seigneur-Isaac
Couture-St-Germain
Hoves
Ittre
Plancenoit
Maransart
Rognon
Virginal-Samme
Lillois-Witterzee
Céroux-Mousty
COURT-SAINT-ETIENNE
SILLY
Steenkerque
Glabais
MONT-ST-GUIBERT
Graty
Hennuyères
Bruyères-Madame
GENAPPE
Hévillers
BRAINE-LE-COMTE
Baulers
Vieux-Genappe
Ways
Thoricourt
Horrues
Ronquières
NIVELLES
Henripont
Thines
Loupoigne
Lombise
Chaussée-N.D.-Louvignies
Monstreux
Baisy-Thy
Mellery
Houtain-le-Val
Sart-Dames-Avelines
Cambron-St-Vincent
Neufvilles
SOIGNIES
(ZINNIK)
Arquennes
VILLERS-LA-VILLE
Ecaussinnes-Lalaing
ECAUSSINNES
Feluy
Tilly
Montignies-lez-Lens
Naast
Marche-lez-Ecaussinnes
Rèves
Marbais
Masnuy-St-Pierre
SENEFFE
Obaix
Buzet
LES BONS VILLERS
Mignault
Villers-Perwin
Wagnelée
SOMBREFFE
Masnuy-St-Jean
Familleureux
Ligny
Luttre
Mellet
Casteau
Thieusies
LE ROEULX
MANAGE
PONT-A-CELLES
St-Amand
Houdeng-Goegnies
Gouy-lez-Piéton
Viesville
Thiméon
Wayaux
Heppignies
FLEURUS
Godarville
Obourg
Thieu
LA LOUVIERE
Trazegnies
Gosselies
Ransart
Wanfercée-Baulet
CHAPELLE

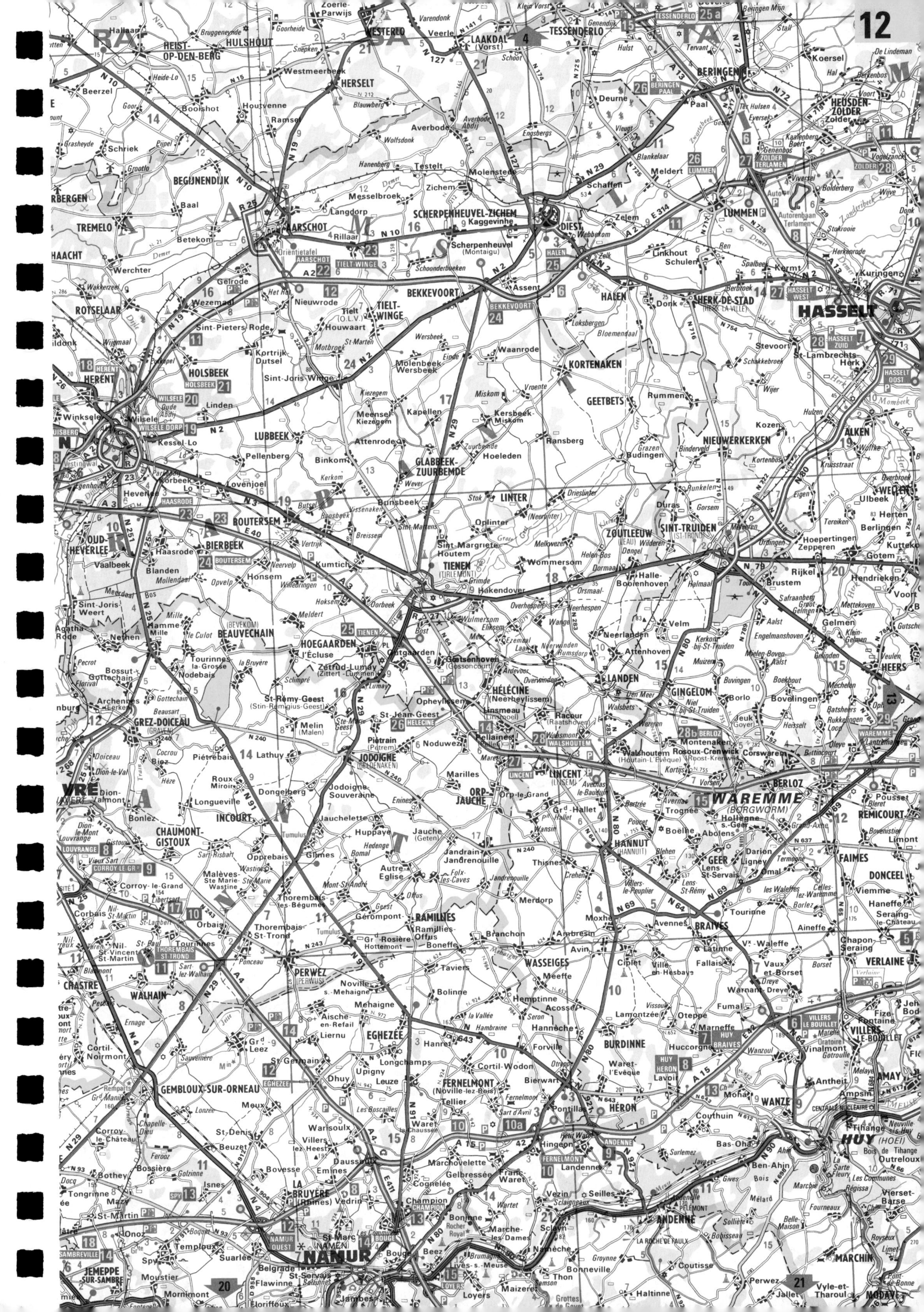

12
Hallaar
Heist-op-den-Berg
Hulshout
Westerlo
Zoerle-Parwijs
Veerle
Laakdal (Vorst)
Tessenderlo
Beringen
Koersel
Heusden-Zolder
Herselt
Westmeerbeek
Beerzel
Booischot
Houtvenne
Ramsel
Averbode
Testelt
Molenstede
Deurne
Paal
Schriek
Begijnendijk
Tremelo
Baal
Aarschot
Langdorp
Messelbroek
Zichem
Scherpenheuvel-Zichem
Kaggevinne
Diest
Schaffen
Meldert
Zelem
Lummen
Haacht
Werchter
Betekom
Rillaar
Scherpenheuvel (Montaigu)
Schoonderbuken
Halen
Linkhout
Schulen
Herk-de-Stad
Kermt
Kuringen
Hasselt
Rotselaar
Gelrode
Wezemaal
Nieuwrode
Bekkevoort
Assent
Tielt-Winge
Tielt (O.L.V.)
Houwaart
Donk
Sint-Pieters-Rode
Kortrijk-Dutsel
Holsbeek
Herent
Sint-Joris-Winge
Molenbeek-Wersbeek
Waanrode
Kortenaken
Stevoort
St-Lambrechts-Herk
Winksele
Wilsele
Linden
Kessel-Lo
Lubbeek
Pellenberg
Binkom
Kapellen
Meensel-Kiezegem
Kersbeek-Miskom
Geetbets
Rummen
Attenrode
Glabbeek-Zuurbemde
Hoeleden
Ransberg
Nieuwerkerken
Kozen
Alken
Budingen
Heverlee
Lovenjoel
Korbeek-Lo
Bunsbeek
Linter
Wellen
Ulbeek
Herten
Berlingen
Boutersem
Bierbeek
Oud-Heverlee
Haasrode
Vaalbeek
Blanden
Honsem
Kumtich
Sint-Margriete-Houtem
Tienen (Tirlemont)
Oplinter
Zoutleeuw (Léau)
Sint-Truiden (St-Trond)
Duras
Gorsem
Wommersom
Halle-Booienhoven
Brustem
Rijkel
Gotem
Hoepertingen
Zepperen
Hakendover
Orsmaal
Sint-Joris-Weert
Hamme-Mille
Beauvechain (Bevekom)
Nethen
Hoegaarden
l'Écluse
Meldert
Oorbeek
Outgaarden
Goetsenhoven (Gossoncourt)
Neerlanden
Attenhoven
Velm
Aalst
Gelmen
Heers
Tourinnes-la-Grosse
Nodebais
Zétrud-Lumay (Zittert-Lummen)
Hélécine (Neerheylissem)
Landen
Gingelom
Borlo
Bovelingen
Grez-Doiceau (Graven)
Archennes (Eerken)
Bossut-Gottechain
St-Rémy-Geest (Stin-Remigius-Geest)
Melin (Malen)
Opheylissem
St-Jean-Geest
Linsmeau (Linsmoel)
Racour (Raatshoven)
Walsbets
Montenaken
Pietrain (Petrem)
Noduwez
Jodoigne (Geldenaken)
Pellaines
Walshoutem (Houtain-L'Évêque)
Rosoux-Crenwick
Corswarem
Lathuy
Piétrebais
Bonlez
Dongelberg
Jodoigne-Souveraine
Marilles
Orp-Jauche
Orp-le-Grand
Lincent (Lijsem)
Berloz
Waremme (Borgworm)
Remicourt
Pousset
Longueville
Incourt
Jauchelette
Huppaye
Jauche (Geten)
Grand-Hallet
Hannut (Hanuit)
Trognée
Hollogne-s.-Geer
Chaumont-Gistoux
Opprebais
Glimes
Jandrain-Jandrenouille
Thisnes
Geer
Faimes
Donceel
Corroy-le-Grand
Autre Eglise
Merdorp
Crehen
Lens-St-Servais
Omal
Viemme
Thorembais-les-Béguines
Gérompont
Ramillies
Ramillies-Offus
Moxhe
Avennes
Braives
Tourinne
Thorembais-St-Trond
Orbais
Perwez (Perwijs)
Branchon
Ambresin
Wasseiges
Latinne
Fallais
Chapon-Seraing
Verlaine
Chastre
Walhain
Noville-s.-Mehaigne
Taviers
Bolinne
Meeffe
Ciplet
Vaux-et-Borset
Mehaigne
Hemptinne
Acosse
Lamontzée
Fumal
Villers-le-Bouillet
Aische-en-Refail
Liernu
Eghezée
Hanret
Hanneche
Burdinne
Marneffe
Huccorgne
Grand-Leez
Cortil-Noirmont
St-Germain
Longchamps
Cortil-Wodon
Forville
Waret-l'Évêque
Lavoir
Gembloux-sur-Orneau
Upigny
Leuze
Dhuy
Fernelmont (Noville-les-Bois)
Tellier
Bierwart
Héron
Moha
Wanze
Amay
Huy (Hoei)
Warisoulx
Waret-la-Chaussée
Pontillas
Couthuin
Villers-lez-Heest
Dausse
Hingeon
Bas-Oha
Bovesse
Emines
Marchovelette
Franc-Waret
Landenne
Ben-Ahin
Isnes
La Bruyère (Rhines)
Vedrin
Gelbressée
Cognelée
Champion
Bonninne
Vezin
Seilles
Andenne
Marche-les-Dames
Sclayn
Namêche
Namur (Namen)
Beez
Bouge
Lives-s.-Meuse
Bonneville
Coutisse
Thon
Maizeret
Loyers
Jambes
Flawinne
Belgrade
St-Servais
Suarlée
Temploux
Spy
Moustier
Mornimont
Jemeppe-sur-Sambre
Perwez
Haltinne
Jallet
Vyle-et-Tharoul
Marchin
Modave
20
21

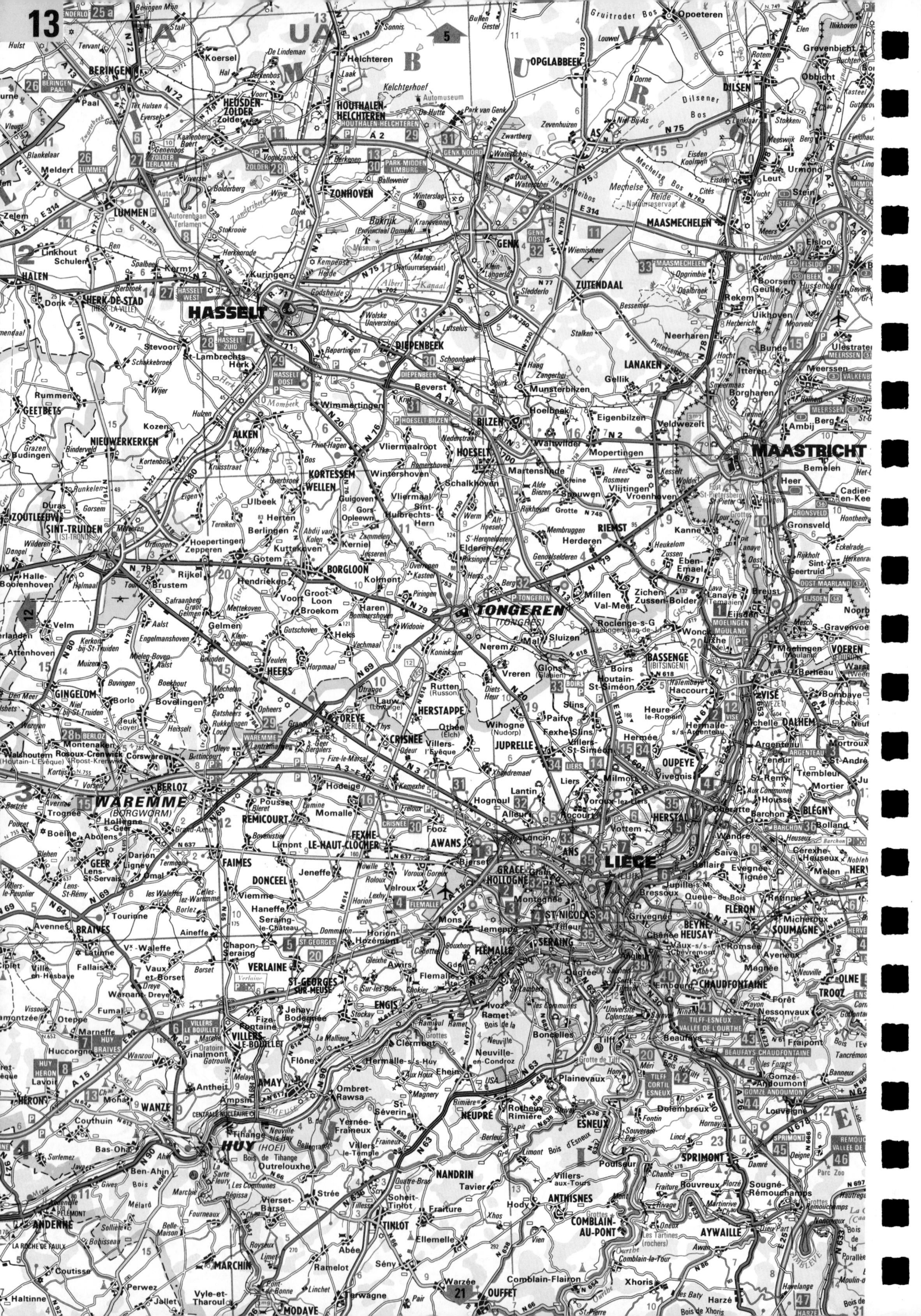
BERINGEN
HEUSDEN-ZOLDER
HOUTHALEN-HELCHTEREN
OPGLABBEEK
DILSEN
LUMMEN
ZONHOVEN
GENK
MAASMECHELEN
HALEN
HERK-DE-STAD
HASSELT
DIEPENBEEK
ZUTENDAAL
LANAKEN
ALKEN
BILZEN
HOESELT
MAASTRICHT
NIEUWERKERKEN
KORTESSEM
WELLEN
RIEMST
GEETBETS
ZOUTLEEUW
SINT-TRUIDEN
BORGLOON
TONGEREN
(TONGRES)
HEERS
BASSENGE
GINGELOM
HERSTAPPE
OREYE
CRISNEE
JUPRELLE
OUPEYE
VISÉ
VOEREN
DALHEM
BERLOZ
WAREMME
(BORGWORM)
REMICOURT
FEXHE-LE-HAUT-CLOCHER
AWANS
ANS
HERSTAL
BLÉGNY
GEER
FAIMES
DONCEEL
GRACE-HOLLOGNE
LIEGE
FLERON
SOUMAGNE
BRAIVES
ST-NICOLAS
SERAING
BEYNE-HEUSAY
FLEMALLE
VERLAINE
ST-GEORGES-SUR-MEUSE
CHAUDFONTAINE
OLNE
TROOZ
ENGIS
VILLERS-LE-BOUILLET
AMAY
WANZE
HERON
NEUPRÉ
ESNEUX
SPRIMONT
HUY
(HOEI)
NANDRIN
ANTHISNES
COMBLAIN-AU-PONT
AYWAILLE
ANDENNE
TINLOT
MARCHIN
OUFFET
MODAVE

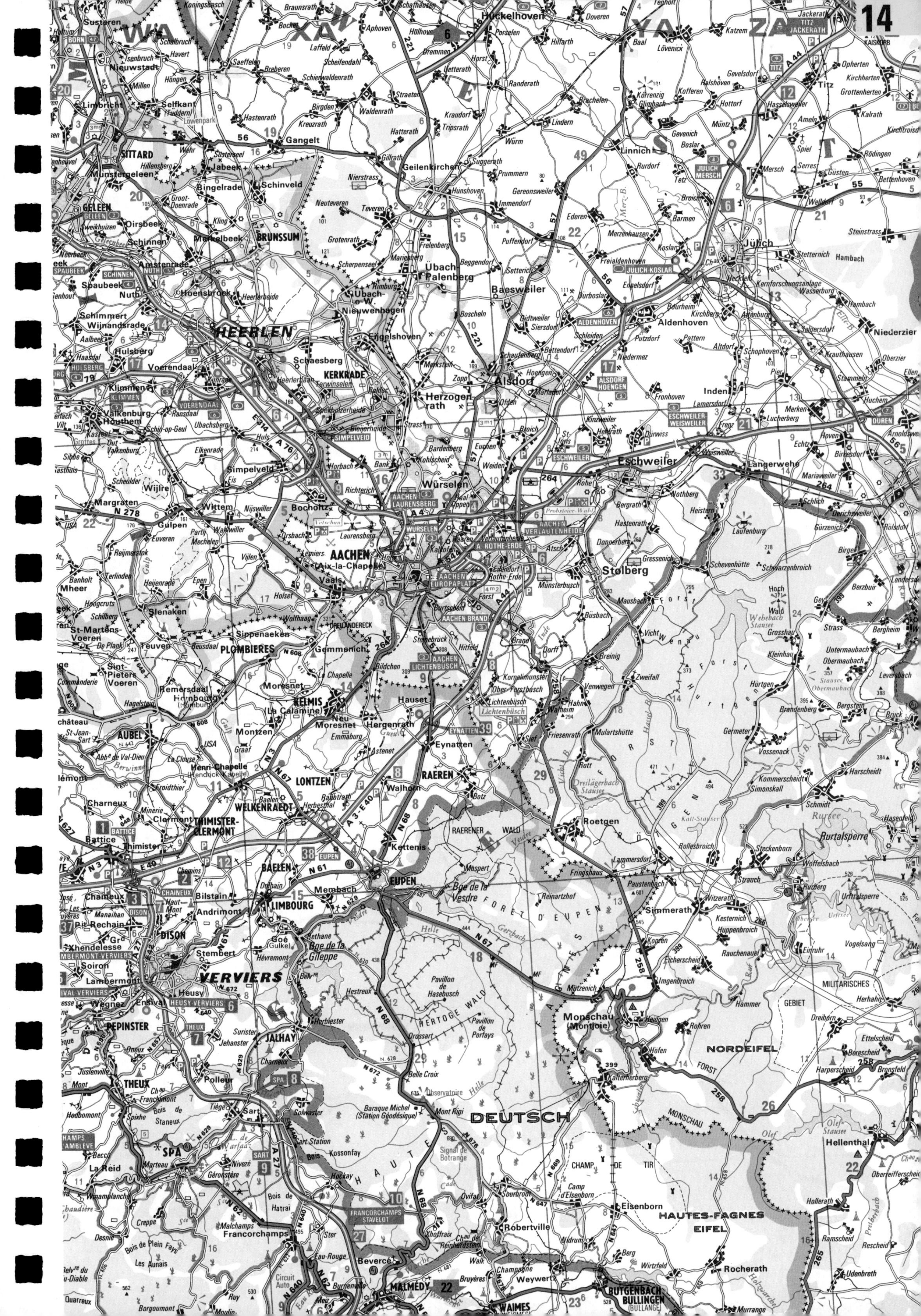
Susteren
Braunsrath
Schafhausen
Hückelhoven
Doveren
Baal
Lövenick
Katzem
Jackerath
Havert
Nieuwstadt
Saeffelen
Breberen
Schierwaldenrath
Hilfarth
Ratheim
Randerath
Brachelen
Kofferen
Ralshoven
Hottorf
Titz
Opherten
Kirchherten
Grottenherten
Limbricht
Selfkant (Tüddern)
Millen
Höngen
Waldenrath
Straeten
Kraudorf
Tripsrath
Hastenrath
Birgden
Kreuzrath
Hatterath
Lindern
Würm
Gangelt
Linnich
Gevenich
Boslar
Müntz
Hasselsweiler
Ameln
Kalrath
SITTARD
Wehr
Süsterseel
Jabeek
Gillrath
Geilenkirchen
Suggerath
Prummern
Rurdorf
Tetz
Mersch
Spiel
Rödingen
Munstergeleen
Hillensberg
Bingelrade
Schinveld
Nierstrass
Hünshoven
Gereonsweiler
JÜLICH MERSCH
Serrest
Gusten
Bettenhoven
GELEEN
Oirsbeek
Neuteveren
Teveren
Immendorf
Ederen
Broich
Barmen
Welldorf
Schinnen
Merkelbeek
BRUNSSUM
Grotenrath
Frelenberg
Puffendorf
Merzenhausen
Koslar
Jülich
Steinstrass
Amstenrade
Scherpenseel
Marienberg
Übach-Palenberg
Beggendorf
Setterich
Freialdenhoven
JULICH KOSLAR
Stetternich
Hambach
Spaubeek
Nuth
Hoensbroek
Heerlerheide
Rimburg
Übach-o-W.
Nieuwenhagen
Baesweiler
Engelsdorf
Dürboslar
Kernforschungsanlage
Wasserburg
Schimmert
Wijnandsrade
HEERLEN
Boscheln
Oidtweiler
Siersdorf
ALDENHOVEN
Aldenhoven
Bourheim
Kirchberg
Niederzier
Aalbeek
Hulsberg
Eygelshoven
Schleiden
Putzdorf
Pattern
Altdorf
Schophoven
Krauthausen
Oberzier
Voerendaal
Schaesberg
Merkstein
Schaufenberg
Bettendorf
Niedermerz
KERKRADE
Zopp
Alsdorf
Hoengen
ALSDORF HOENGEN
Pier
Stammeln
Klimmen
Herzogenrath
Mariadorf
Fronhoven
Inden
Lamersdorf
Merken
Huchem
Valkenburg-Houthem
Ransdaal
Ofden
Kinzweiler
Hehlrath
ESCHWEILER-WEISWEILER
Frenz
Lucherberg
DÜREN
Ubachsberg
Spekholzerheide
Bleijerheide
SIMPELVELD
Strass
Bardenberg
Broich
St. Jöris
Dürwiss
Hoven
Arnoldsweiler
Elkenrade
Huls
Kohlscheid
Euchen
ESCHWEILER
Eschweiler
Weisweiler
Langerwehe
Echtz
Birgelsdorf
Simpelveld
Horbach
Bank
Weiden
Mariaweiler
Schaesberg
Wijlre
Richterich
Würselen
AACHEN LAURENSBERG
Rohe
Nothberg
Heistern
Schlich
Derichsweiler
Margraten
Wittem
Nijswiller
Bocholtz
Bergrath
Hastenrath
Laufenburg
Gürzenich
Gulpen
Euveren
Wahlwiller
Mechelen
Laurensberg
Orsbach
WÜRSELEN
Verlautenheide
AACHEN VERLAUTENHEIDE
Donnerberg
Schevenhütte
Rölsdorf
Reijmerstok
Vijlen
Lemiers
AACHEN (Aix-la-Chapelle)
A. ROTHE-ERDE
Atsch
Gressenich
Stolberg
Schwarzenbroich
Birgel
Banholt
Mheer
Terlinden
Heijenrade
Epen
Vaals
AACHEN EUROPAPLATZ
Eilendorf
Rothe-Erde
Münsterbusch
Forst
Holset
Mausbach
Hoch Wald
Gey
Berzbuir
Burtscheid
Büsbach
Wehebach Stausee
Grosshau
Strass
Bergheim
Slenaken
Wolfhaag
DREILÄNDERECK
AACHEN BRAND
Brand
Vicht
Wenau
Kleinhau
St-Martens-Voeren
Sippenaeken
Teuven
PLOMBIERES
Gemmenich
Stenebrück
Hitfeld
Dorff
Breinig
Untermaubach
Obermaubach
AACHEN LICHTENBUSCH
Kornelimünster
Ober-Forstbach
Zweifall
Hurtgen
Sint-Pieters-Voeren
Moresnet
La Chapelle
Bildchen
Verwegen
Leversbach
Remersdaal
Homburg
KELMIS (La Calamine)
Neu-Moresnet
Hergenrath
Hauset
Lichtenbusch
Walheim
Hahn
Hürtgen
Bergstein
Brandenberg
Bruck
AUBEL
Montzen
Emmaburg
EYNATTEN
Eynatten
Friesenrath
Mulartshütte
Germeter
Vossenack
Abbe de Val-Dieu
La Clouse
Henri-Chapelle
Astenet
Graaf
Rott
Harscheidt
Froidthier
LONTZEN
Walhorn
RAEREN
Raeren
Dreilägerbach Stausee
Kommerscheidt
Simonskall
Charneux
Minerie
Clermont
THIMISTER-CLERMONT
WELKENRAEDT
Baelen
Herbesthal
Botz
Kalt-Stausee
Schmidt
Rursee
Hasenfeld
BATTICE
Battice
Thimister
RAERENER WALD
Roetgen
Rollesbroich
Rurtalsperre
Steckenborn
Woffelsbach
Kettenis
BAELEN
EUPEN
Mospert
Fringshaus
Lammersdorf
Chaineux
CHAINEUX
Haut-Mont
Bilstain
Dolhain
Membach
Eupen
Bge de la Vesdre
Reinartzhof
Paustenbach
Strauch
Rurberg
Urftalsperre
Manaihan
Andrimont
LIMBOURG
FORET D'EUPEN
Simmerath
Witzerath
Kesternich
Huppenbroich
Pt-Rechain
DISON
Bethane
Goé
Konzen
Xhendelesse
Stembert
Hévremont
Bge de la Gileppe
Eicherscheid
Rauchenauel
Einruhr
Vogelsang
Soiron
VERVIERS
Lambermont
Heusy
Pavillon de Hasebusch
Mützenich
Imgenbroich
MILITARISCHES GEBIET
Wegnez
Ensival
HEUSY-VERVIERS
Hestreux
Hammer
Herhahn
PEPINSTER
Herbiester
HERTOGE WALD
Monschau (Montjoie)
Heidgen
Rohren
Dreiborn
Suriste
Jehanster
JALHAY
Drossart
Pavillon de Porfays
Ettelscheid
Oneux
Charneux
NORDEIFEL
Berescheid
Juslenville
THEUX
Polleur
Belle Croix
Höfen
Kalterherberg
FORST
Harperscheid
Bronsfeld
Mont
Franchimont
Bois de Staneux
Observatoire
Hodbomont
Spixhe
Tiège
Sart
Solwaster
Baraque Michel (Station Géodésique)
Mont Rigi
DEUTSCH
MONSCHAU
Olef Stausee
Hellenthal
SPA
La Reid
Marteau
Nivezé
Géronstère
Sart-Station
Bois
Kossonfay
Signal de Botrange
HAUTE
CHAMP DE TIR
Hockay
Wimmplanche
Bois de Hatrai
FRANCORCHAMPS STAVELOT
Ovifat
Sourbrodt
Camp d'Elsenborn
Elsenborn
HAUTES-FAGNES EIFEL
Hollerath
Creppe
Desnie
Malchamps
Francorchamps
Ster
Xhoffraix
Robertville
Nidrum
Bois de Plein Fays
Les Aunais
Eau-Rouge
Beverce
Reinhardstein
Walk
Champagne
Weywertz
Berg
Wirtzfeld
Rocherath
Ramscheid
Rescheid
Circuit Auto
MALMEDY
Bruyères
WAIMES
BUTGENBACH BULLINGEN (BULLANGE)
Udenbreth
Ruy
Burnenville
Quarreux
Borgoumont
Murrange

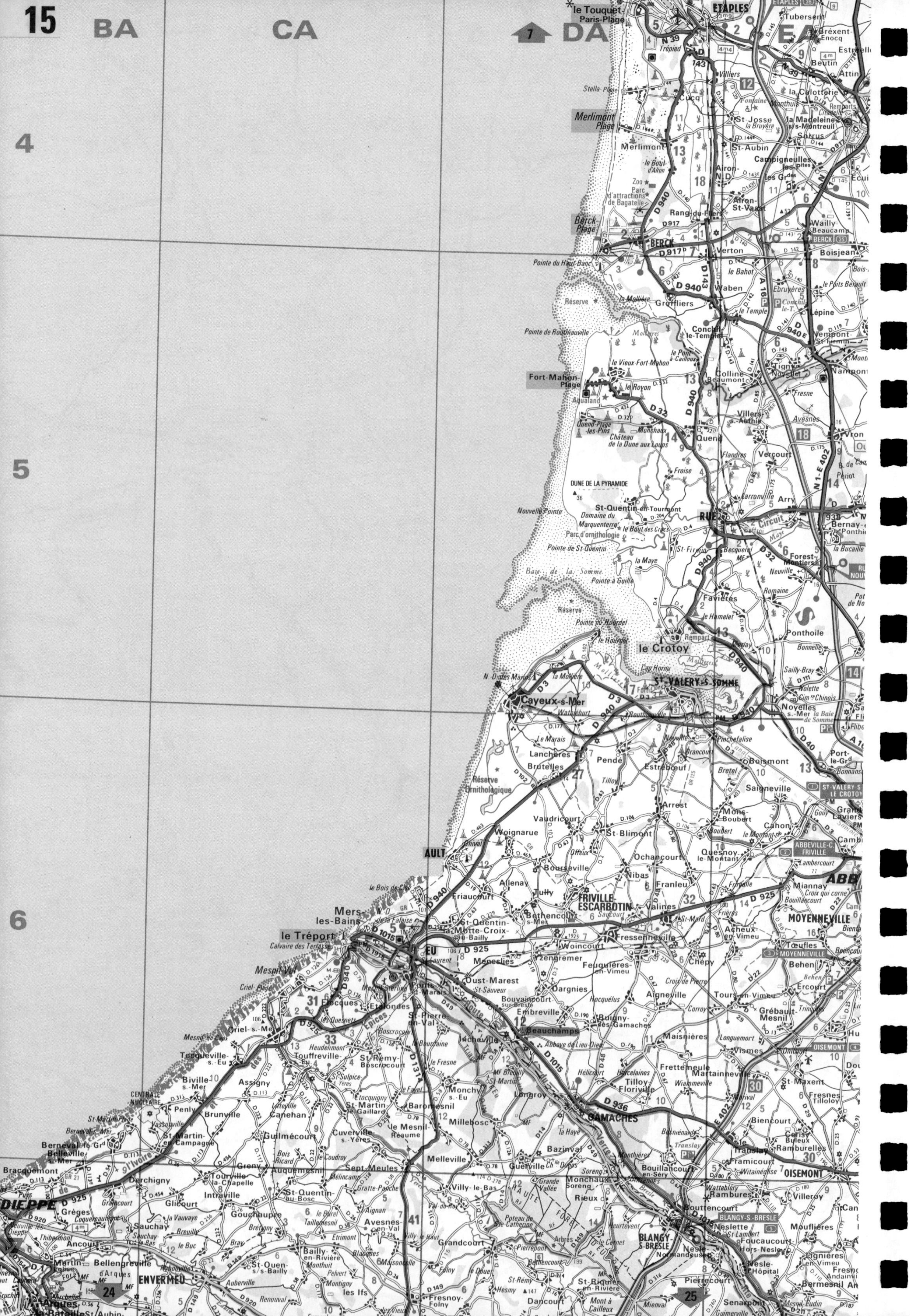
BA
CA
DA
EA
4
5
6
7
24
25
ETAPLES
le Touquet-Paris-Plage
BERCK
Berck-Plage
Merlimont Plage
Fort-Mahon-Plage
RUE
le Crotoy
St-VALERY-S-SOMME
Cayeux-s-Mer
AULT
Mers-les-Bains
le Tréport
EU
FRIVILLE-ESCARBOTIN
MOYENNEVILLE
GAMACHES
OISEMONT
BLANGY-S-BRESLE
DIEPPE
ENVERMEU

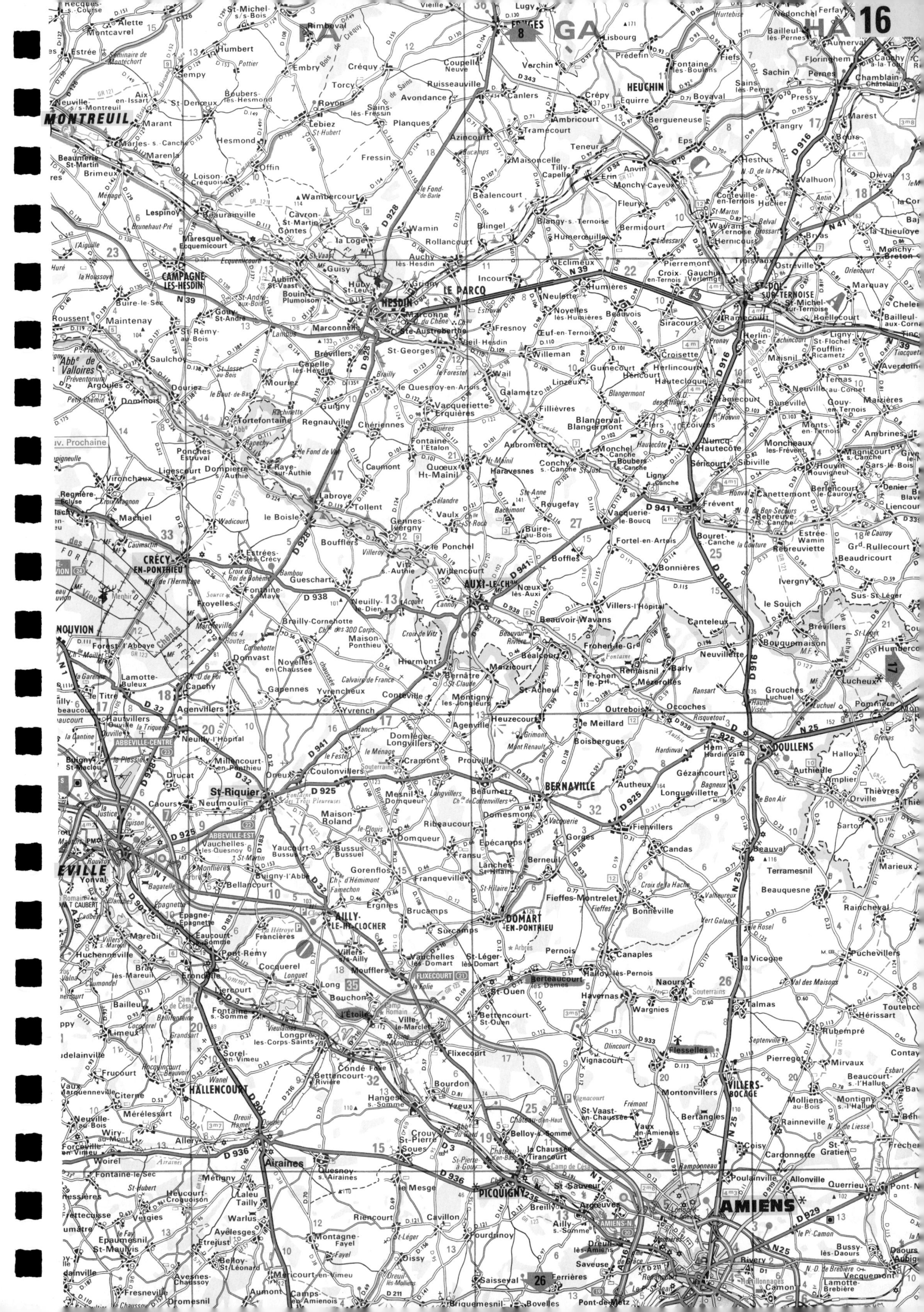
MONTREUIL
HESDIN
LE PARCQ
HEUCHIN
ST-POL-SUR-TERNOISE
FRUGES
CAMPAGNE-LES-HESDIN
CRÉCY-EN-PONTHIEU
NOUVION
AUXI-LE-CHau
St-Riquier
BERNAVILLE
DOULLENS
AILLY-LE-HT-CLOCHER
DOMART-EN-PONTHIEU
HALLENCOURT
VILLERS-BOCAGE
PICQUIGNY
AMIENS
Airaines
ABBEVILLE-CENTRE
ABBEVILLE-EST
FLIXECOURT
AMIENS-N.
Abbe de Valloires
Alette
Montcavrel
Estrée
Sempy
Aix-en-Issart
Neuville-s/s-Montreuil
Marant
Marles-s.-Canche
Hesmond
Offin
Loison
Lespinoy
Beaurainville
Maresquel-Ecquemicourt
Humbert
Embry
Créquy
Torcy
Royon
Lebiez
Sains-lès-Fressin
Planques
Fressin
Avondance
Ruisseauville
Coupelle-Neuve
Azincourt
Tramecourt
Maisoncelle
Canlers
Verchin
Lisbourg
Prédefin
Fontaine-lès-Boulans
Crépy
Equirre
Ambricourt
Bergueneuse
Teneur
Eps
Anvin
Erin
Tilly-Capelle
Monchy-Cayeux
Fleury
Bealencourt
Blingel
Blangy-s.-Ternoise
Bermicourt
Wamin
Rollancourt
Auchy-lès-Hesdin
Grigny
Incourt
Éclimeux
Humières
Humerœuille
Croix-en-Ternois
Gauchin-Verloingt
Pierremont
Ostreville
Siracourt
Beauvois
Noyelles-lès-Humières
Neulette
Wail
Fresnoy
Vieil-Hesdin
St-Georges
Willeman
Œuf-en-Ternois
Croisette
Gueschart
Brévillers
Capelle-lès-Hesdin
Marconne
Marconnelle
Ste-Austreberthe
Huby-St-Leu
Aubin-St-Vaast
Bouin-Plumoison
Guisy
Tortefontaine
Regnauville
Guigny
Chériennes
Vacqueriette-Erquières
Galametz
Fillièvres
Linzeux
Gennes-Ivergny
Boufflers
Le Ponchel
Vitz-s.-Authie
Willencourt
Tollent
Labroye
Caumont
Quœux-Ht-Mainil
Haravesnes
Conchy-s.-Canche
Rougefay
Vacquerie-le-Boucq
Frévent
Fortel-en-Artois
Boffles
Bonnières
Villers-l'Hôpital
Nœux-lès-Auxi
Beauvoir-Wavans
Frohen-le-Grd
Remaisnil
Barly
Mézerolles
Occoches
Outrebois
Heuzecourt
Le Meillard
Boisbergues
Hem-Hardinval
Gézaincourt
Longuevillette
Autheux
Fienvillers
Candas
Beauval
Terramesnil
Beauquesne
Bonneville
Fieffes-Montrelet
Canaples
Naours
Talmas
Havernas
Wargnies
Flesselles
Vignacourt
Montonvillers
Bertangles
Poulainville
Allonville
Querrieu
Rainneville
Cardonnette
Coisy
Molliens-au-Bois
Lucheux
Neuvillette
Bouquemaison
Canteleux
Le Souich
Ivergny
Grouches-Luchuel
Hiermont
Bernâtre
Montigny-les-Jongleurs
Agenville
Prouville
Cramont
Domléger-Longvillers
Coulonvillers
Oneux
Drucat
Caours
Neufmoulin
Vauchelles-lès-Quesnoy
Mesnil-Domqueur
Maison-Roland
Domqueur
Ribeaucourt
Domesmont
Beaumetz
Épécamps
Gorges
Berneuil
Lanches-St-Hilaire
Franqueville
Fransu
Gorenflos
Bussus-Bussuel
Yaucourt-Bussus
Ergnies
Brucamps
Surcamps
Vauchelles-lès-Domart
St-Léger-lès-Domart
Berteaucourt-les-Dames
St-Ouen
Bettencourt-St-Ouen
Ville-le-Marclet
Bouchon
L'Étoile
Long
Longpré-les-Corps-Saints
Condé-Folie
Bettencourt-Rivière
Hangest-s.-Somme
Bourdon
Yzeux
Belloy-s.-Somme
La Chaussée-Tirancourt
St-Sauveur
Ailly-s.-Somme
Breilly
Argœuves
Dreuil-lès-Amiens
Saveuse
Crouy
St-Pierre-à-Gouy
Soues
Le Mesge
Cavillon
Riencourt
Fourdrinoy
Oissy
Montagne-Fayel
Saisseval
Ferrières
Bovelles
Pont-de-Metz
Briquemesnil
Camps-en-Amiénois
Métigny
Laleu
Tailly
Warlus
Avelesges
Belloy-St-Léonard
Aumont
Quesnoy-s.-Airaines
Allery
Wiry-au-Mont
Mérélessart
Citerne
Frucourt
Sorel-en-Vimeu
Limeux
Fontaine-s.-Somme
Pont-Remy
Érondelle
Liercourt
Bailleul
Huchenneville
Eaucourt-s.-Somme
Épagne-Épagnette
Mareuil
Bray-lès-Mareuil
Yonval
Bellancourt
Buigny-l'Abbé
Francières
Cocquerel
Villers-s.-Ailly
Moufflers
Millencourt-en-Ponthieu
Neuilly-l'Hôpital
Agenvillers
Canchy
Lamotte-Buleux
Forest-l'Abbaye
Domvast
Noyelles-en-Chaussée
Gapennes
Yvrencheux
Yvrench
Conteville
Brailly-Cornehotte
Maison-Ponthieu
Neuilly-le-Dien
Fontaine-s.-Maye
Froyelles
Marcheville
Estrées-lès-Crécy
Machiel
Le Boisle
Vironchaux
Ligescourt
Dompierre-s.-Authie
Raye-s.-Authie
Ponches-Estruval
Dominois
Argoules
Saulchoy
Douriez
Mouriez
Maintenay
Roussent
Buire-le-Sec
St-Rémy-au-Bois
Gouy-St-André
Nempont-St-Firmin
Bréxent
Auxi
Fontaine-l'Étalon
Aubrometz
Blangerval-Blangermont
Monchel
Boubers-s.-Canche
Ligny-s.-Canche
Nuncq-Hautecôte
Séricourt
Sibiville
Flers
Écoivres
Hautecloque
Herlincourt
Gumecourt
Héricourt
Framecourt
Ramecourt
Herlin-le-Sec
Maisnil
Ligny-St-Flochel
Foufflin-Ricametz
Ternas
Neuville-au-Cornet
Buneville
Gouy-en-Ternois
Monts-en-Ternois
Moncheaux-lès-Frévent
Houvin-Houvigneul
Canettemont
Berlencourt-le-Cauroy
Rebreuve-s.-Canche
Bouret-s.-Canche
Estrée-Wamin
Rebreuviette
Grd-Rullecourt
Beaudricourt
Sus-St-Léger
Brévillers
Humbercourt
Pommera
Halloy
Authieule
Amplier
Orville
Thièvres
Sarton
Marieux
Raincheval
Puchevillers
Toutencourt
Hérissart
Rubempré
Pierregot
Mirvaux
Contay
Beaucourt-s.-l'Hallue
Montigny-s.-l'Hallue
St-Gratien
Fréchencourt
Pont-Noyelles
Bussy-lès-Daours
Daours
Vecquemont
Lamotte-Brebière
Camon
Rivery
Longpré
Pernes
Floringhem
Cauchy-à-la-Tour
Chamblain-Châtelain
Sachin
Pressy
Tangry
Marest
Bours
Valhuon
Diéval
Hestrus
Conteville-en-Ternois
Huclier
Wavrans-s.-Ternoise
Brias
Hernicourt
La Thieuloye
Monchy-Breton
Marquay
Orlencourt
St-Michel-s.-Ternoise
Roëllecourt
Bailleul-aux-Cornailles
Averdoingt
Maizières
Ambrines
Magnicourt-s.-Canche
Denier
Liencourt
Ferfay
Nédonchel
Bailleul-lès-Pernes
Auchy-au-Bois
Fiefs
Boyaval
Sains-lès-Pernes
Heuringhem
Rimboval
St-Michel-s/s-Bois
Lugy
Vieille
Recques-s.-Course
Wambercourt
Cavron-St-Martin
Contes
la Loge
Beaumerie-St-Martin
Brimeux
Bois-Jean
Buigny-St-Maclou
Hautvillers-Ouville
Le Titre
Caumartin
St-Acheul
Maizicourt
Lannoy
Bealcourt
Frohen-le-Pt
N 39
N 41
N 1
N 25
D 928
D 916
D 941
D 938
D 925
D 933
D 936
D 901
D 929
D 343
D 340
Forêt de Crécy
Canche
Authie
Somme

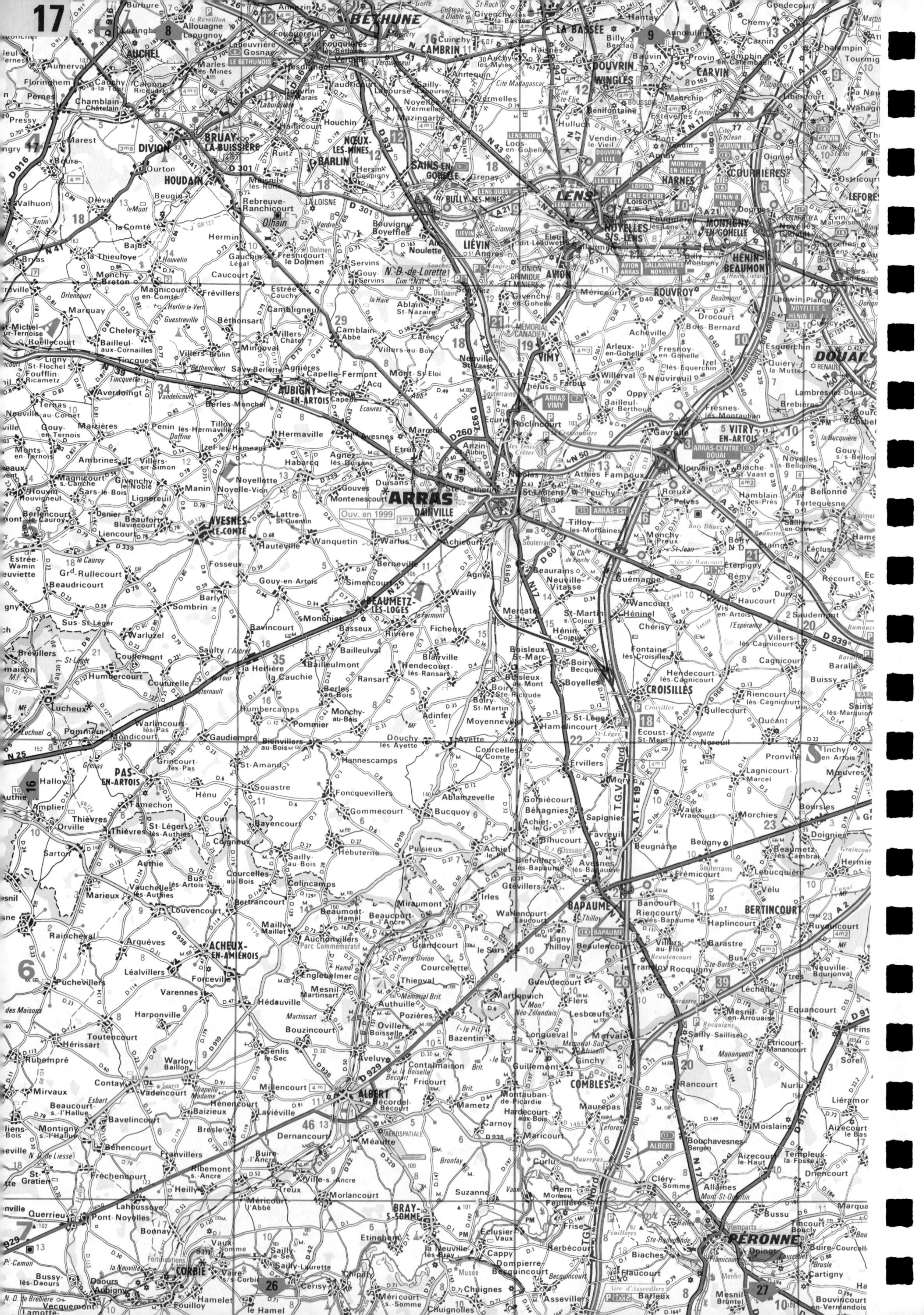
BÉTHUNE
LA BASSÉE
AUCHEL
CAMBRIN
DOUVRIN
WINGLES
CARVIN
BRUAY-LA-BUISSIÈRE
DIVION
NŒUX-LES-MINES
BARLIN
HOUDAIN
SAINS-EN-GOHELLE
BULLY-LES-MINES
LENS
HARNES
COURRIÈRES
NOYELLES S/S-LENS
LIÉVIN
AVION
MONTIGNY EN-GOHELLE
HÉNIN-BEAUMONT
ROUVROY
N.-D.-de-Lorette
VIMY
DOUAI
AUBIGNY-EN-ARTOIS
VITRY-EN-ARTOIS
ARRAS
DAINVILLE
Ouv. en 1999
AVESNES-LE-COMTE
BEAUMETZ-LES-LOGES
CROISILLES
PAS-EN-ARTOIS
BAPAUME
BERTINCOURT
ACHEUX-EN-AMIÉNOIS
COMBLES
ALBERT
BRAY-S-SOMME
CORBIE
PÉRONNE

PARC RÉGIONAL DU NORD

PAS DE CALAIS

Genech, la Glanerie, Lesdain, BRUNEHAUT, Laplaigne, Roucourt, Quevaucamps, PÉRUWELZ, PONT-à-MARCQ, Cappelle-en-Pévèle, Mouchin, Howardries, Mortagne-du-Nord, Wiers, Stambruges, Mérignies, Nomain, Rongy, Maulde, Flines-lès-Mortagne, Bon-Secours, Hautrage, ORCHIES, Aix, Rumegies, Thun-St-Amand, Château l'Abbaye, Hergnies, BERNISSART, Mons-en-Pévèle, Bersée, Landas, Saméon, Lecelles, Bruille-St-Amand, Nivelle, Pommerœul, Beuvry-la-Forêt, Rosult, ST-AMAND-LES-EAUX, Vieux-Condé, St-Aybert, Faumont, Coutiches, Odomez, CONDÉ-SUR-L'ESCAUT, Moncheaux, Sars-et-Rosières, Thivencelle, Montrœul-s.-Haine, Raimbeaucourt, Bouvignies, Brillon, Millonfosse, Fresnes-s.-Escaut, HENSIES, Thulin, Flines-lès-Raches, Bousignies, Tilloy-lès-Marchiennes, Hasnon, Escautpont, Roost-Warendin, Crespin, Vicq, Raches, Anhiers, MARCHIENNES, Warlaing, Wandignies-Hamage, Elouges, QUIÉVRAIN, Lallaing, Rieulay, Raismes, Beuvrages, Bruay-s.-l'Escaut, Onnaing, Baisieux, Pecquencourt, Wallers, ANZIN, Quarouble, Quiévrechain, Marchipont, Audregnies, Waziers, Fenain, Aubry-du-Hainaut, Rombies-et-Marchipont, Montignies-s.-Roc, Montigny-en-Ostrevent, Bruille-lez-Marchiennes, Hornaing, Erre, Hélesmes, Haveluy, Bellaing, Oisy, Hérin, VALENCIENNES, Marly, Estreux, Onnezies, HONNELLES, Sin-le-Noble, Dechy, Loffre, Masny, Ecaillon, Somain, Escaudain, DENAIN, Wavrechain-s/-Denain, Sentinelle, Saultain, Sebourg, Guesnain, Lewarde, Roucourt, Auberchicourt, Aniche, Abscon, Lourches, Trith-St-Léger, Aulnoy-lez-Valenciennes, Curgies, Roisin, Erchin, Rœulx, Mastaing, Haulchin, Prouvy, Famars, Préseau, Jenlain, Eth, Bry, Wargnies-le-Gd, Villers-au-Tertre, Emerchicourt, Monchecourt, Marcq-en-Ostrevent, Marquette-en-Ostrevant, BOUCHAIN, Neuville-s.-Escaut, Noyelles-s-Selle, Douchy-les-Mines, Thiant, Maing, Artres, Quérénaing, Maresches, Villers-Pol, Wargnies-le-Pt, Preux-au-Sart, Estrées, Bugnicourt, Fressain, Monchaux-s.-Ecaillon, Sepmeries, Frasnoy, Gommegnies, Brunémont, Wavrechain-s.-Faulx, Lieu-St-Amand, Orsinval, ARLEUX, Aubigny-au-Bac, Féchain, Wasnes-au-Bac, Hordain, Haspres, Verchain-Maugré, Sommaing, Vendegies-s.-Ecaillon, Ruesnes, Villereau, Palluel, Hem-Lenglet, Avesnes-le-Sec, Bermerain, LE QUESNOY, Potelle, Oisy-le-Verger, Aubencheul-au-Bac, Fressies, Estrun, Saulzoir, St-Martin-s.-Ecaillon, Capelle, Jolimetz, Rumaucourt, Abancourt, Paillencourt, Beaudignies, Sauchy-Cauchy, Epinoy, Sauchy-Lestrée, Bantigny, Thun-l'Évêque, Iwuy, Villers-en-Cauchies, Montrécourt, Escarmain, Ghissignies, Louvignies-Quesnoy, Cuvillers, Thun-St-Martin, Eswars, Haussy, Vertain, MARQUION, Blécourt, Sancourt, Ramillies, Naves, St-Aubert, Romeries, Salesches, Raucourt-au-Bois, Locquignol, Haynecourt, Tilloy, Sailly-lez-Cambrai, Neuville-St-Rémy, Escaudœuvres, Rieux-en-Cambrésis, Avesnes-lès-Aubert, Neuville-en-Avesnois, Poix-du-Nord, Englefontaine, Raillencourt-Ste-Olle, CAMBRAI, Cagnoncles, St-Hilaire-lez-Cambrai, St-Vaast-en-Cambrésis, St-Python, SOLESMES, Beaurain, Vendegies-au-Bois, Hecq, Bourlon, Cauroir, Boussières-en-Cambrésis, Fontaine-N.-D., Proville, CARNIÈRES, Quiévy, Briastre, Robersart, Preux-au-Bois, Anneux, Awoingt, Boistrancourt, Bévillers, Viesly, Croix-Caluyau, Bousies, Cantaing-s.-Escaut, Niergnies, Estourmel, Cattenières, Beauvois-en-Cambrésis, Bethencourt, Neuvilly, Forest-en-Cambrésis, Fontaine-au-Bois, LANDRECIES, Noyelles-s.-Escaut, Flesquières, Rumilly-en-Cambrésis, Fontaine-au-Pire, Caudry, Beaumont-en-Cambrésis, Inchy, Montay, Pommereuil, MARCOING, Masnières, Séranvillers-Forenville, Wambaix, Audencourt, Ribecourt-la-Tour, Havrincourt, Crèvecœur-s.-l'Escaut, Esnes, Haucourt, Ligny-Haucourt, Montigny-en-Cambrésis, Troisvilles, LE CATEAU-CAMBRESIS, Ors, le Favril, les Rues-des-Vignes, Lesdain, Caullery, Bertry, Reumont, Bazuel, Trescault, Villers-Plouich, Walincourt-Selvigny, CLARY, Maurois, Honnechy, Catillon-s.-Sambre, la Groise, Metz-en-Couture, Bantouzelle, Banteux, Dehéries, Maretz, St-Benin, St-Souplet, Mazinghien, Gouzeaucourt, Gonnelieu, Malincourt, Elincourt, Busigny, St-Martin-Rivière, Ribeauville, Rejet-de-Beaulieu, Fesmy-le-Sart, Barzy-en-Thiérache, Bergues-s.-Sambre, Villers-Guislain, Honnecourt-s.-Escaut, Aubencheul-aux-Bois, Villers-Outréaux, Serain, Molain, Vaux-Andigny, la Vallée-Mulâtre, WASSIGNY, Oisy, Boué, Heudicourt, Epehy, Vendhuile, LE CATELET, Prémont, Becquigny, Guyencourt-Saulcourt, Gouy, Beaurevoir, BOHAIN-EN-VERMANDOIS, Étreux, la Neuville-lès-Dorengt, Vénérolles, Villers-Faucon, Lempire, Ronssoy, Bony, Brancourt-le-Gd, Mennevret, Hannapes, Dorengt, Estrées, Montbrehain, Petit-Verly, Longavesnes, Bellicourt, Joncourt, Nauroy, Ramicourt, Fresnoy-le-Gd, Seboncourt, Tupigny, Iron, Lavaquerie, ROISEL, Templeux-le-Guérard, Hargicourt, Villeret, Hesbécourt, Magny-la-Fosse, Levergies, Étaves-et-Bocquiaux, Grougis, Grand-Verly, Vadencourt, Lesquielles-St-Germain, Hervilly, Jeancourt, Sequehart, Aisonville-et-Bernoville, Villers-lès-Guise, le Verguier, Bellenglise, le Haucourt, Croix-Fonsommes, Malzy, Bernes, Fontaine-Uterte, Monceau-s.-Oise, Vendelles, Pontru, Essigny-le-Petit, Fonsommes, Montigny-en-Arrouaise, Noyales, Proix, GUISE, Lesdins, Fieulaine, Remaucourt, Flavigny-le-Gd-et-Beaurain

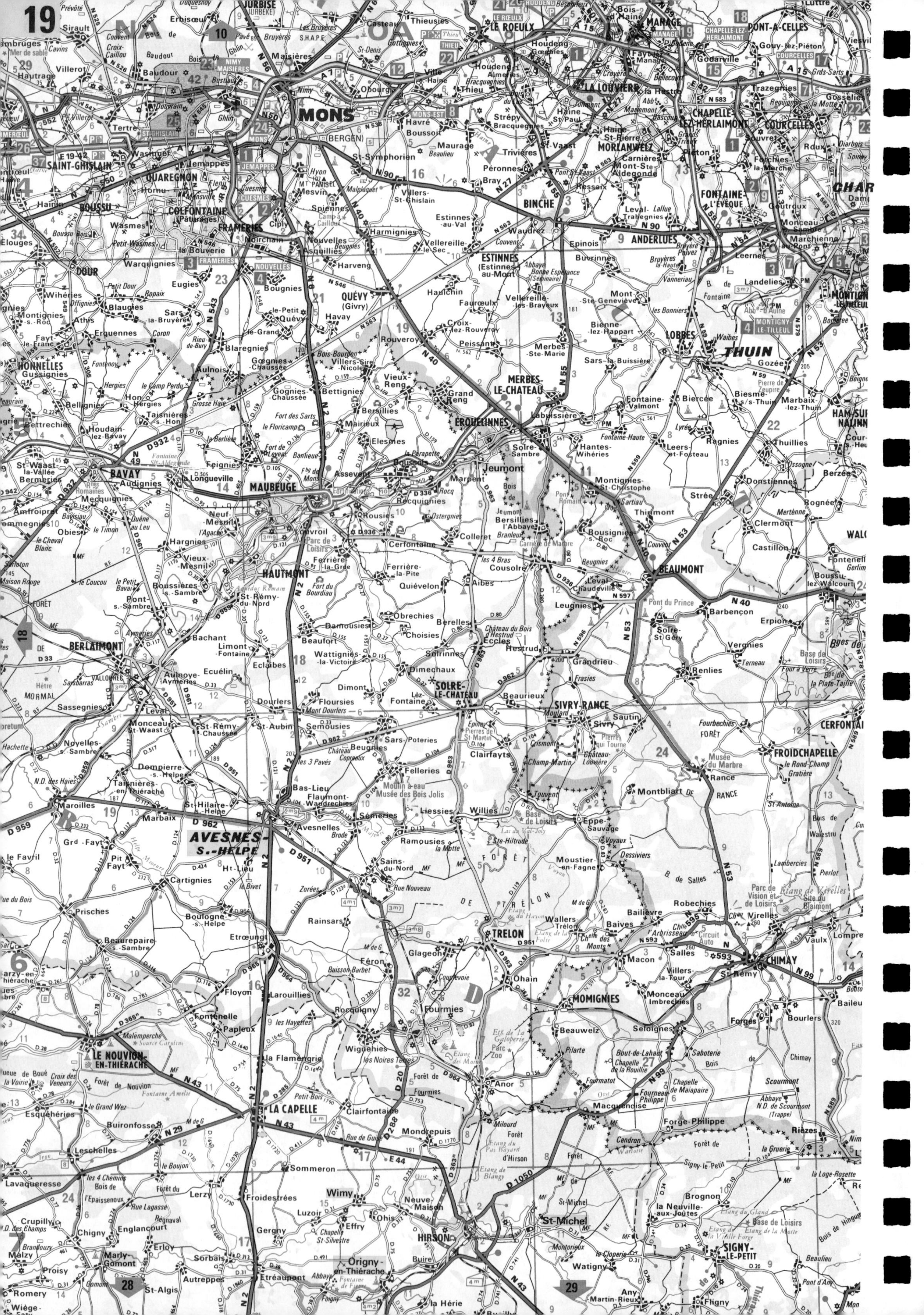
MONS
(BERGEN)
LE ROEULX
MANAGE
PONT-A-CELLES
LA LOUVIERE
CHAPELLE-LEZ-HERLAIMONT
COURCELLES
MORLANWELZ
BINCHE
SAINT-GHISLAIN
QUAREGNON
BOUSSU
COLFONTAINE
FRAMERIES
DOUR
ESTINNES
ANDERLUES
FONTAINE-L'EVEQUE
CHAR
LOBBES
THUIN
MONTIGNY-LE-TILLEUL
QUÉVY
(Givry)
HONNELLES
MERBES-LE-CHATEAU
ERQUELINNES
BAVAY
MAUBEUGE
Jeumont
HAUTMONT
BEAUMONT
HAM-SUR-HEURE-NALINNES
BERLAIMONT
SOLRE-LE-CHATEAU
SIVRY-RANCE
FROIDCHAPELLE
CERFONTAINE
AVESNES-S.-HELPE
TRELON
CHIMAY
MOMIGNIES
Fourmies
LE NOUVION-EN-THIÉRACHE
LA CAPELLE
HIRSON
St-Michel
SIGNY-LE-PETIT
Wimy
Origny-en-Thiérache
Marly-Gomont
Forêt de Nouvion
Forêt de Trélon
Forêt de Rance
Lac du Val Joly
Etang de Virelles
N 40
N 53
N 90
N 2
N 43
N 29
D 962
D 951
D 1050
E 44
10
23
24
28
29
18

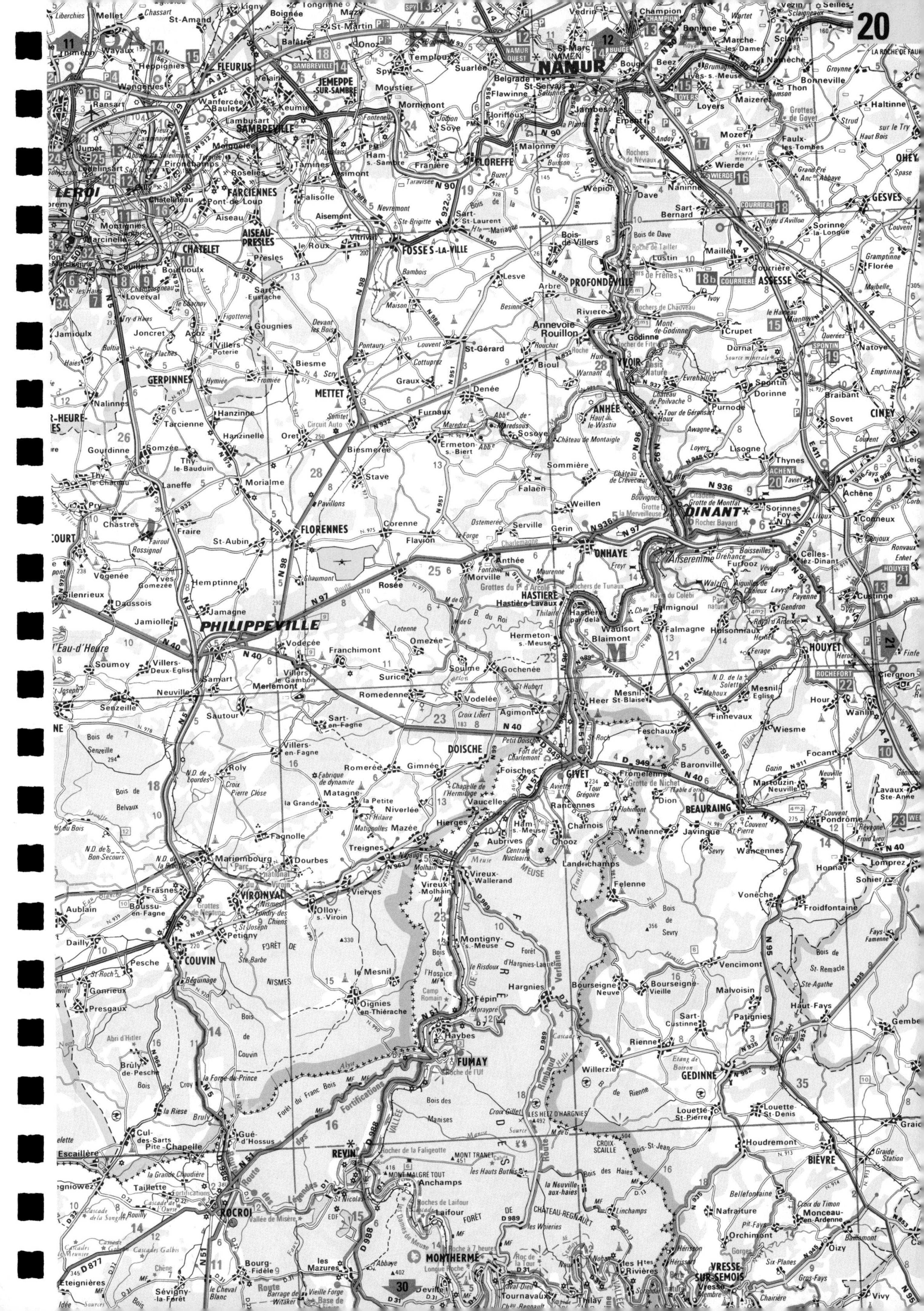

NAMUR
FLEURUS
SAMBREVILLE
JEMEPPE SUR-SAMBRE
FLOREFFE
FARCIENNES
CHATELET
AISEAU-PRESLES
FOSSES-LA-VILLE
PROFONDEVILLE
ASSESSE
GESVES
OHEY
GERPINNES
METTET
YVOIR
ANHÉE
CINEY
DINANT
FLORENNES
ONHAYE
PHILIPPEVILLE
HASTIÈRE
HOUYET
DOISCHE
GIVET
BEAURAING
VIROINVAL
COUVIN
FUMAY
GEDINNE
BIÈVRE
REVIN
ROCROI
MONTHERMÉ
VRESSE-SUR-SEMOIS
Jambes
Malonne
Wépion
Lustin
Godinne
Crupet
Spontin
Purnode
Sovet
Achêne
Thynes
Lisogne
Anseremme
Celles-lez-Dinant
Falmignoul
Falmagne
Blaimont
Hermeton-s.-Meuse
Heer
Agimont
Vodelée
Gochenée
Soulme
Surice
Romedenne
Franchimont
Villers-le-Gambon
Merlemont
Samart
Neuville
Senzeille
Sautour
Roly
Matagne
Niverlée
Mazée
Treignes
Vierves
Olloy-s.-Viroin
Nismes
Mariembourg
Frasnes
Aublain
Dailly
Pesche
Petigny
Vaucelles
Hierges
Aubrives
Chooz
Rancennes
Landrichamps
Felenne
Winenne
Javingue
Wancennes
Pondrôme
Focant
Wiesme
Finnevaux
Vencimont
Malvoisin
Patignies
Bourseigne-Neuve
Bourseigne-Vieille
Rienne
Willerzie
Louette-St-Pierre
Louette-St-Denis
Houdremont
Nafraiture
Orchimont
Oizy
Haybes
Fépin
Hargnies
Montigny-s.-Meuse
Vireux-Molhain
Vireux-Wallerand
Anchamps
Laifour
Deville
Les Hautes Rivières
Thilay
Tournavaux
les Mazures
Bourg-Fidèle
Sévigny-la-Forêt
Éteignières
Taillette
Gué-d'Hossus
Cul-des-Sarts
Brûly-de-Pesche
Gonrieux
Presgaux
Stave
Biesmerée
Oret
Morialme
Laneffe
Fraire
Chastrès
Vogenée
Yves-Gomezée
Hemptinne
Jamagne
Jamiolle
Daussois
Silenrieux
Soumoy
Villers-Deux-Eglises
Somzée
Thy-le-Château
Pry
Tarcienne
Hanzinne
Hanzinelle
Nalinnes
Gourdinne
Joncret
Acoz
Gougnies
Biesme
Graux
St-Gérard
Denée
Furnaux
Ermeton-s.-Biert
Sosoye
Maredsous
Falaën
Sommière
Weillen
Serville
Gerin
Anthée
Flavion
Corenne
Rosée
Morville
Omezée
Bioul
Annevoie Rouillon
Rivière
Lesve
Arbre
Bois-de-Villers
Dave
Naninne
Wierde
Sart-Bernard
Courrière
Florée
Sorinne-la-Longue
Maillen
Mozet
Faulx-les-Tombes
Haltinne
Loyers
Maizeret
Thon
Bonneville
Namêche
Sclayn
Marche-les-Dames
Beez
Bouge
Champion
Vedrin
Erpent
Belgrade
Flawinne
Suarlée
Temploux
Spy
Onoz
Balâtre
Ligny
Boignée
Velaine
Moustier
Mornimont
Franière
Soye
Tamines
Aisemont
Falisolle
Vitrival
Sart-St-Laurent
Presles
Roselies
Pont-de-Loup
Aiseau
Bouffioulx
Loverval
Châtelineau
Montignies
Marcinelle
Couillet
Jumet
Ransart
Heppignies
Wangenies
Wanfercée-Baulet
Lambusart
Moignelée
Keumiée
Pironchamps
Gilly
Mellet
Chassart
St-Amand
Wayaux
Villers-Poterie
Jamioulx
Mesnil-St-Blaise
Mesnil-Eglise
Hour
Wanlin
Custinne
Furfooz
Dréhance
Sorinnes
Foy-N.D.
Conneux
Haut-Fays
Vonêche
Froidfontaine
Honnay
Sohier
Lomprez
Martouzin-Neuville
Baronville
Feschaux
Fromelennes
Dion
Charnois
Ham-s.-Meuse
Foisches
Gimnée
Romerée
Villers-en-Fagne
Sart-en-Fagne
Fagnolle
Dourbes
Boussu-en-Fagne
Oignies-en-Thiérache
le Mesnil
Regniowez
Croix-Scaille
Bois-St-Jean
Linchamps
Château-Regnault
Les Hêtes d'Hargnies
Monceau-en-Ardenne
Bellefontaine
Croix du Timon
Graide Station
Vivy
Chairière
Gros-Fays
Six-Planes
Bohan
Membre
Vresse

MARCHIN
MODAVE
CLAVIER
OUFFET
ANTHISMES
COMBLAIN-AU-PONT
AYWAILLE
HAMOIR
OHEY
GESVES
HAVELANGE
FERRIÈRES
DURBUY
SOMME-LEUZE
HAMOIS
CINEY
EREZÉE
MANHAY
HOTTON
MARCHE EN-FAMENNE
RENDEUX
LA ROCHE EN-ARDENNE
ROCHEFORT
NASSOGNE
PARC NATIONAL DE LESSE ET LOMME
WELLIN
TELLIN
TENNEVILLE
BERTOGNE
SAINT-HUBERT
SAINTE-ODE
BASTOGNE (BASTENAKEN)
DAVERDISSE
LIBIN
LIBRAMONT CHEVIGNY
VAUX-SUR-SURE
PALISEUL
BERTRIX
FERRIÈRES VALLÉE DE L'OURTHE
VIELSALM BARAQUE DE FRAITURE
LAVAUX STE-ANNE
LONGLIER NEUFCHÂTEAU
LIBRAMONT CHEVIGNY
VERLAINE NEUFCHÂTEAU
NIVES-VAUX-S-SURE
VILLEROUX BASTOGNE
HOUYET
WELLIN
TELLIN
TRANSINNE
HARRE
MANHAY VALLÉE DE LA LIENNE

W
X
Y
Z
CÔTE
7
8
9
Veulettes-s.-Mer
CENTRALE NUCLÉAIRE
St-Sylvain
Malleville-les-Grès
St-Martin-aux-Buneaux
Auberville-la-Manuel
Butot-Venesville
Paluel
St-Riquier-ès-Plains
Vittefleur
St-Pierre-en-Port
Vinnemerville
Canouville
Ocqueville
Sassetot-le-Mauconduit
Criquetot-le-Mauconduit
Clasville
CANY-BARVILLE
Ecrettevile-s.-Mer
Elétot
Ste-Hélène-Bondeville
Ancretteville-s.-Mer
Ourville
Sasseville
Senneville-s.-Fécamp
Angerville-la-Martel
Theuville-aux-Maillots
Bertreville
Barville
N.D. du Salut
FÉCAMP
Thérouldeville
Bertheauville
Grainville-la-Teinturière
Bosville
Colleville
Criquebeuf-en-Caux
Gerponville
St-Léonard
Toussaint
VALMONT
Vattetot-s.-Mer
Yport
Ganzeville
Riville
OURVILLE-EN-CAUX
le Hanouard
Aiguille de Belval
Froberville
Contremoulins
Thiergeville
Beuzeville-la-Guérard
Oherville
Falaise d'Amont
Bénouville
Tourville-les-Ifs
Étretat
Aiguille d'Étretat
Falaise d'Aval
Bordeaux-St-Clair
les Loges
Epreville
Bec-de-Mortagne
Thiétreville
Sorquainville
Cleuville
Ancourteville-s.-Héricourt
Cap d'Antifer
Gerville
Maniquerville
Mentheville
Daubeuf-Serville
Normanville
la Place
le Tilleul
Auberville-la-Renault
Annouville-Vilmesnil
Limpiville
Ypreville-Biville
Thiouville
Fongueusemare
la Poterie-Cap-d'Antifer
Pierrefiques
Bretteville-du-Grand-Caux
Angerville-Bailleul
Bénarville
Bennetot
Ste-Marguerite-s.-Fauville
Beaurepaire
Tremanville
Clipponville
Ste-Marie-au-Bosc
Sausseuzemare-en-Caux
Cuverville
Grainville-Ymauville
Tocqueville-les-Murs
Villainville
St-Pierre-Lavis
Port du Havre-Antifer
St-Jouin-Bruneval
Gonneville-la-Mallet
Ecrainville
St-Maclou-la-Brière
Hattenville
FAUVILLE-EN-CAUX
YVETOT OUEST
Hautot-le-Vatois
GODERVILLE
Gonfreville-Caillot
Bermonville
CRIQUETOT-L'ESNEVAL
Aire de Bolleville
Anglesqueville-l'Esneval
Bréauté
Vattetot-s.-Beaumont
Yébleron
Auzouville-Auberbosc
Ricarville
Heuqueville
Bornambusc
Bernières
Cleville
Ecretteville-les-Baons
Vergetot
St-Sauveur-d'Emalleville
Manneville-la-Goupil
Mirville
Rouville
Foucart
Turretot
Houquetot
Cauville
St-Martin-du-Bec
Raffetot
Alvimare
Mannevillette
Hermeville
Virville
Beuzeville-la-Grenier
Nointot
Bolleville
N.-D.-du-Bec
Rolleville
Angerville-l'Orcher
Parc-d'Anxtot
St-Gilles-de-la-Neuville
Lanquetot
Bois-Himont
Gainneville
Ecqueville
St-Barthélémy
Graimbouville
St-Jean-de-la-Neuville
St-Aubin-de-Crétot
Octeville-s.-Mer
Epouville
Maneglise
Etainhus
BOLBEC
Beuzevillette
Trouville
Fontenay
Sainneville
Gommerville
Gruchet-le-Valasse
Lintot
Grand-Camp
St-Gilles-de-Crétot
St-Andrieux
MONTIVILLIERS
ST-ROMAIN-DE-COLBOSC
les Trois-Pierres
St-Eustache-la-Forêt
St-Nicolas-de-la-Haie
Fontaine-la-Mallet
Epretot
la Trinité-du-Mont
le Grand Hameau
Cap de la Hève
St-Laurent-de-Brèvedent
Auberville-la-Campagne
Anquetierville
St-Martin-du-Manoir
St-Antoine-la-Forêt
Mélamare
St-Arnoult
Montgeon
Gainneville
la Remuée
St-Jean-de-Folleville
Touffreville-la-Cable
Bléville
Sanvic
Graville
GONFREVILLE-L'ORCHER
Rogerville
Oudalle
St-Aubin-Routot
St-Vincent-Cramesnil
Beaufils
St-Nicolas-de-la-Taille
LILLEBONNE
Ste-Adresse
Sandouville
Cerlangue
Triquerville
Villequier
St-Vigor-d'Ymonville
Tancarville
N.-D.-de-Gravenchon
RAFFINERIE DE PÉTROLE
St-Georges-de-Gravenchon
LE HAVRE
COMPLEXE PÉTROCHIMIQUE
QUILLEBEUF-S.-SEINE
Norville
St-Aubin-s.-Quillebeuf
Petiville
St-Maurice-d'Etelan
Pont de Normandie (péage)
PARC REGIONAL DE
CÔTE DE GRACE
HONFLEUR
Berville-s.-Mer
St-Samson-de-la-Roque
Marais-Vernier
Aizier
Vieux-Port
Ste-Croix-s.-Aizier
Pte de Villerville
Conteville
Ste-Opportune-la-Mare
Trouville-la-Haule
Cricquebœuf
Pennedepie
Fatouville-Grestain
St-Thurien
Villerville
Equemauville
St-Pierre-du-Val
Foulbec
Bouquelon
TANCARVILLE
Bourneville
Hennequeville
Gonneville-s.-Honfleur
la Rivière-St-Sauveur
Fiquefleur-Equainville
Barneville-la-Bertran
Ablon
TROUVILLE-S.-MER
Deauville
Montessard
St-Sulpice-de-Grimbouville
St-Ouen-des-Champs
St-Mards-de-Blacarville
Fourmetot
PONT AUDEMER
Manneville-la-Raoult
Vallotot
Etreville
les Sablons
Genneville
St-Maclou
Toutainville
Fourneville
Boulleville
Eturqueraye
Manneville-s.-Risle
Touques
Bonneville-s.-Touques
St-Gatien-des-Bois
le Theil-en-Auge
BEUZEVILLE
Cauverville-en-Roumois
St-Germain-Village
PONT-AUDEMER
Colletot
St-Arnoult
Englesqueville-en-Auge
Quetteville
AUTOROUTE DE NORMANDIE
Triqueville
Tourville-s.-Pont-Audemer
Corneville-s.-Risle
Gatien
Tourville-en-Auge
le Torpt
Fort-Moville
Rondemare
Blonville
Tourgéville
Vauville
Canapville
St-Martin-aux-Chartrains
St-Benoît-d'Hébertot
St-André-d'Hébertot
les Préaux
Appeville-Annebault
Vieux-Bourg
Surville
Martainville
Vannecrocq
St-Symphorien
Campigny
Condé-s.-Risle
Glatigny
Coudray-Rabut
les Authieux-s.-Calonne
St-Léger-s.-Bonneville
Toutainville
Selles
St-Etienne-la-Thillaye
St-Julien-s.-Calonne
St-Philbert-s.-Risle
MONTFORT-S.-RISLE
St-Christophe
36
37
A 29
A 131
N 15
N 175
N 178
D 925
D 940
D 982

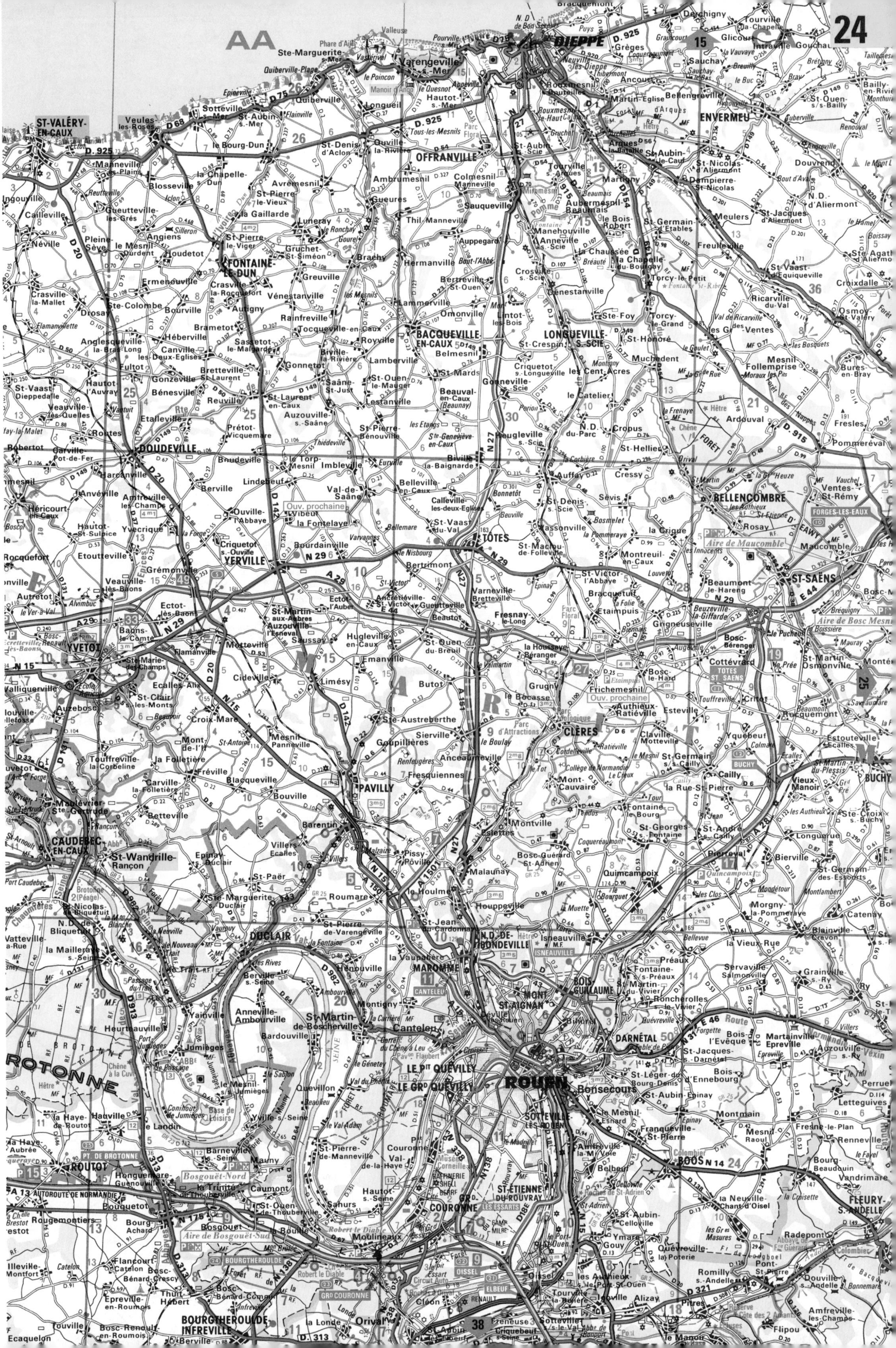

AA

Dieppe
St-Valéry-en-Caux
Veules-les-Roses
Sotteville-s.-Mer
Quiberville
Ste-Marguerite-s.-Mer
Varengeville-s.-Mer
Hautot-s.-Mer
Offranville
Arques-la-Bataille
Envermeu
Derchigny
Tourville-la-Chapelle
Glicourt
Grèges
Neuville-lès-Dieppe
Rouxmesnil-Bouteilles
Martin-Église
Bellengreville
Ancourt
Sauchay
St-Nicolas-d'Aliermont
Douvrend
St-Aubin-le-Cauf
Martigny
Dampierre-St-Nicolas
N.D.-d'Aliermont
St-Jacques-d'Aliermont
Meulers
St-Vaast-d'Équiqueville
Croixdalle
Osmoy-St-Valery
Ricarville-du-Val
Les Grandes-Ventes
Torcy-le-Grand
Torcy-le-Petit
Sauqueville
Tourville-s.-Arques
Aubermesnil-Beaumais
Manéhouville
Anneville-s.-Scie
Le Bois-Robert
St-Germain-d'Étables
Freulleville
La Chaussée
La Chapelle-du-Bourgay
Crosville-s.-Scie
Dénestanville
Lintot-les-Bois
Longueville-s.-Scie
Ste-Foy
St-Honoré
St-Crespin
Muchedent
Criquetot-s.-Longueville
Les Cent-Acres
Gonneville-s.-Scie
Le Catelier
Mesnil-Follemprise
Bures-en-Bray
Fresles
Ardouval
Pommeréval
Cropus
N.D.-du-Parc
St-Hellier
Heugleville-s.-Scie
Auffay
Cressy
Sévis
Bellencombre
Ventes-St-Rémy
Rosay
Maucomble
St-Saëns
Aire de Maucomble
La Crique
Bosc-Mesnil
Beaumont-le-Hareng
Bracquetuit
Étaimpuis
Grigneuseville
Beuzeville-la-Giffarde
Montreuil-en-Caux
St-Victor-l'Abbaye
Tôtes
St-Vaast-du-Val
Calleville-les-deux-Églises
Belleville-en-Caux
Biville-la-Baignarde
Bacqueville-en-Caux
Belmesnil
Ste-Geneviève-en-Caux
Beauval-en-Caux
Lamberville
St-Ouen-le-Mauger
Lestanville
St-Pierre-Bénouville
Royville
Tocqueville-en-Caux
Omonville
Hermanville
Bertreville-St-Ouen
Lammerville
Auppegard
Thil-Manneville
Colmesnil-Manneville
Ambrumesnil
Gueures
Luneray
Avremesnil
Ouville-la-Rivière
St-Denis-d'Aclon
Longueil
Brachy
Gruchet-St-Siméon
Greuville
Vénestanville
Rainfreville
Gonnetot
Saâne-St-Just
St-Laurent-en-Caux
Auzouville-s.-Saâne
Prétot-Vicquemare
Le Bourg-Dun
La Chapelle-s.-Dun
St-Pierre-le-Vieux
St-Pierre-le-Viger
Fontaine-le-Dun
Crasville-la-Rocquefort
Autigny
Bourville
Brametot
Sassetot-le-Malgardé
Héberville
Canville-les-Deux-Églises
Bretteville-St-Laurent
Gonzeville
Bénesville
Reuville
Étalleville
Routes
Doudeville
Anglesqueville-la-Bras-Long
Fultot
Hautot-l'Auvray
Drosay
Ste-Colombe
Ermenouville
Houdetot
Angiens
Pleine-Sève
Le Mesnil-Durdent
Gueutteville-les-Grès
Blosseville
Manneville-ès-Plains
Ingouville
Cailleville
Néville
Crasville-la-Mallet
St-Vaast-Dieppedalle
Veauville-lès-Quelles
Garville-Pot-de-Fer
Harcanville
Anvéville
Héricourt-en-Caux
Hautot-St-Sulpice
Rocquefort
Étoutteville
Yvecrique
Amfreville-les-Champs
Berville
Boudeville
Le Torp-Mesnil
Imbleville
Lindebeuf
Val-de-Saâne
Ouville-l'Abbaye
Criquetot-s.-Ouville
Yerville
Motteville
Grémonville
Veauville-lès-Baons
Autretot
Ectot-lès-Baons
Baons-le-Comte
Yvetot
Ste-Marie-des-Champs
Valliquerville
Écalles-Alix
St-Clair-s.-les-Monts
Auzebosc
Croix-Mare
Mont-de-l'If
La Folletière
Fréville
Touffreville-la-Corbeline
Carville-la-Folletière
Betteville
Maulévrier-Ste-Gertrude
Caudebec-en-Caux
St-Wandrille-Rançon
Épinay-Duclair
Villers-Écalles
Barentin
Pavilly
Bouville
Blacqueville
Mesnil-Panneville
Goupillières
Ste-Austreberthe
Limésy
Cideville
Emanville
Hugleville-en-Caux
Saussay
Auzouville-l'Esneval
St-Martin-aux-Arbres
Ectot-l'Auber
Bourdainville
La Fontelaye
Vibeuf
Bertrimont
Anctréville-St-Victor
Gueutteville
Varneville-Bretteville
Fresnay-le-Long
Beautot
St-Ouen-du-Breuil
Butot
Sierville
Anceaumeville
Fresquiennes
La Houssaye-Béranger
Grugny
Frichemesnil
Bosc-le-Hard
Clères
Authieux-Ratiéville
Esteville
Claville-Motteville
Cottévrard
Bosc-Bérenger
St-Martin-Osmonville
Yquebeuf
Rocquemont
Estouteville-Écalles
St-Germain-s.-Cailly
Cailly
La Rue-St-Pierre
Mont-Cauvaire
Fontaine-le-Bourg
St-Georges-s.-Fontaine
St-André-s.-Cailly
Vieux-Manoir
Buchy
Ste-Croix-s.-Buchy
Longuerue
Bierville
Pierreval
Quincampoix
Bosc-Guérard-St-Adrien
Montville
Eslettes
Malaunay
Le Houlme
Houppeville
N.D.-de-Bondeville
Isneauville
Bois-Guillaume
Mont-St-Aignan
Maromme
Déville
Canteleu
St-Jean-du-Cardonnay
Pissy-Pôville
Roumare
Ste-Marguerite-s.-Duclair
St-Paër
St-Pierre-de-Varengeville
Duclair
Le Trait
La Mailleraye-s.-Seine
N.D.-de-Bliquetuit
St-Nicolas-de-Bliquetuit
Vatteville-la-Rue
Yainville
Heurteauville
Jumièges
Le Mesnil-s.-Jumièges
Yville-s.-Seine
Berville-s.-Seine
Anneville-Ambourville
Hénouville
Bardouville
St-Martin-de-Boscherville
Quevillon
Le Petit-Quevilly
Le Grand-Quevilly
Rouen
Bonsecours
Darnétal
Sotteville-lès-Rouen
St-Étienne-du-Rouvray
Amfreville-la-Mi-Voie
Belbeuf
Franqueville-St-Pierre
Le Mesnil-Esnard
St-Léger-du-Bourg-Denis
St-Aubin-Épinay
Bois-d'Ennebourg
Montmain
Boos
Roncherolles
St-Martin-du-Vivier
Fontaine-s.-Préaux
Préaux
Servaville-Salmonville
Grainville-s.-Ry
Martainville-Épreville
Bois-l'Évêque
St-Jacques-s.-Darnétal
Auzouville-s.-Ry
Blainville-Crevon
La Vieux-Rue
Morgny-la-Pommeraye
Catenay
St-Germain-des-Essourts
Mesnil-Raoul
Fresne-le-Plan
Bourg-Beaudouin
Vandrimare
Fleury-s.-Andelle
Letteguives
Perruel
La Neuville-Chant-d'Oisel
Ymare
Gouy
St-Aubin-Celloville
Quévreville-la-Poterie
Radepont
Romilly-s.-Andelle
Pont-St-Pierre
Douville-s.-Andelle
Amfreville-les-Champs
Flipou
Pîtres
Alizay
Le Manoir
Les Authieux-Port-St-Ouen
Tourville-la-Rivière
Oissel
Sotteville-s.-le-Val
Freneuse
St-Aubin-lès-Elbeuf
Cléon
Orival
Grand-Couronne
Couronne
Moulineaux
La Bouille
Sahurs
Hautot-s.-Seine
Val-de-la-Haye
St-Pierre-de-Manneville
Caumont
La Trinité-de-Thouberville
St-Ouen-de-Thouberville
Bosgouet
Bourg-Achard
Honguemare-Guenouville
Routot
Hauville
La Haye-de-Routot
La Haye-Aubrée
Le Landin
Rougemontiers
Flancourt-Catelon
Bosc-Bénard-Crescy
Épreville-en-Roumois
Thuit-Hébert
Bosc-Bénard-Commin
Bourgtheroulde-Infreville
Bosc-Renoult-en-Roumois
La Londe
Écaquelon
Berville
Étréville
Illeville-Montfort

Forêt de Brotonne
Autoroute de Normandie
Aire de Bosgouët-Nord
Aire de Bosgouët-Sud
Aire de Bosc Mesnil
Ouv. prochaine
Forges-les-Eaux
Totes St Saëns
Bourgtheroulde
Dissel
Elbeuf
Isneauville
Canteleu
Les Essarts
Pt. de Brotonne

A 29 · A 13 · A 15 · A 150 · A 28 · N 27 · N 29 · N 15 · N 14 · N 31 · N 138 · N 175 · D. 925 · D. 915 · D 20 · D 142 · D 982 · D 313

15
25
38

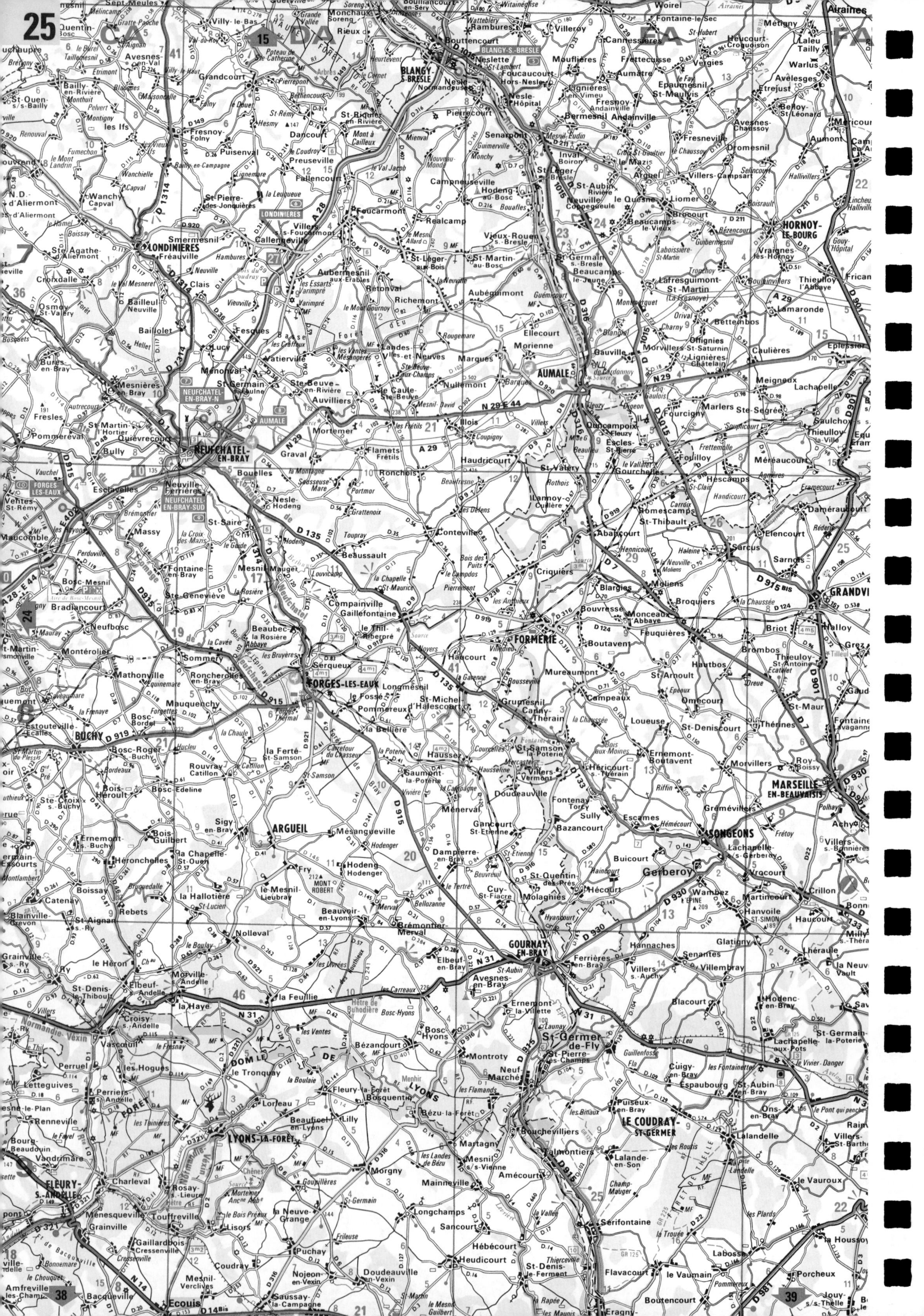
BLANGY-S-BRESLE
LONDINIERES
NEUFCHATEL-EN-BRAY
AUMALE
HORNOY-LE-BOURG
FORMERIE
FORGES-LES-EAUX
GRANDVILLIERS
MARSEILLE-EN-BEAUVAISIS
SONGEONS
Gerberoy
GOURNAY-EN-BRAY
ARGUEIL
BUCHY
LYONS-LA-FORÊT
LE COUDRAY-ST-GERMER
FLEURY-S.-ANDELLE
St-Germer-de-Fly
Ecouis
Airaines
Senarpont
Foucarmont
Gaillefontaine
Sommery
Saint-Saëns
Croixdalle
Bosc-Mesnil
Mesnières-en-Bray
Forêt d'Eu
Forêt de Lyons
A 28
A 29
N 29
N 31
N 14
D 915
D 919
D 930
D 1314
D 316
D 135
D 1015
15
24
38
39

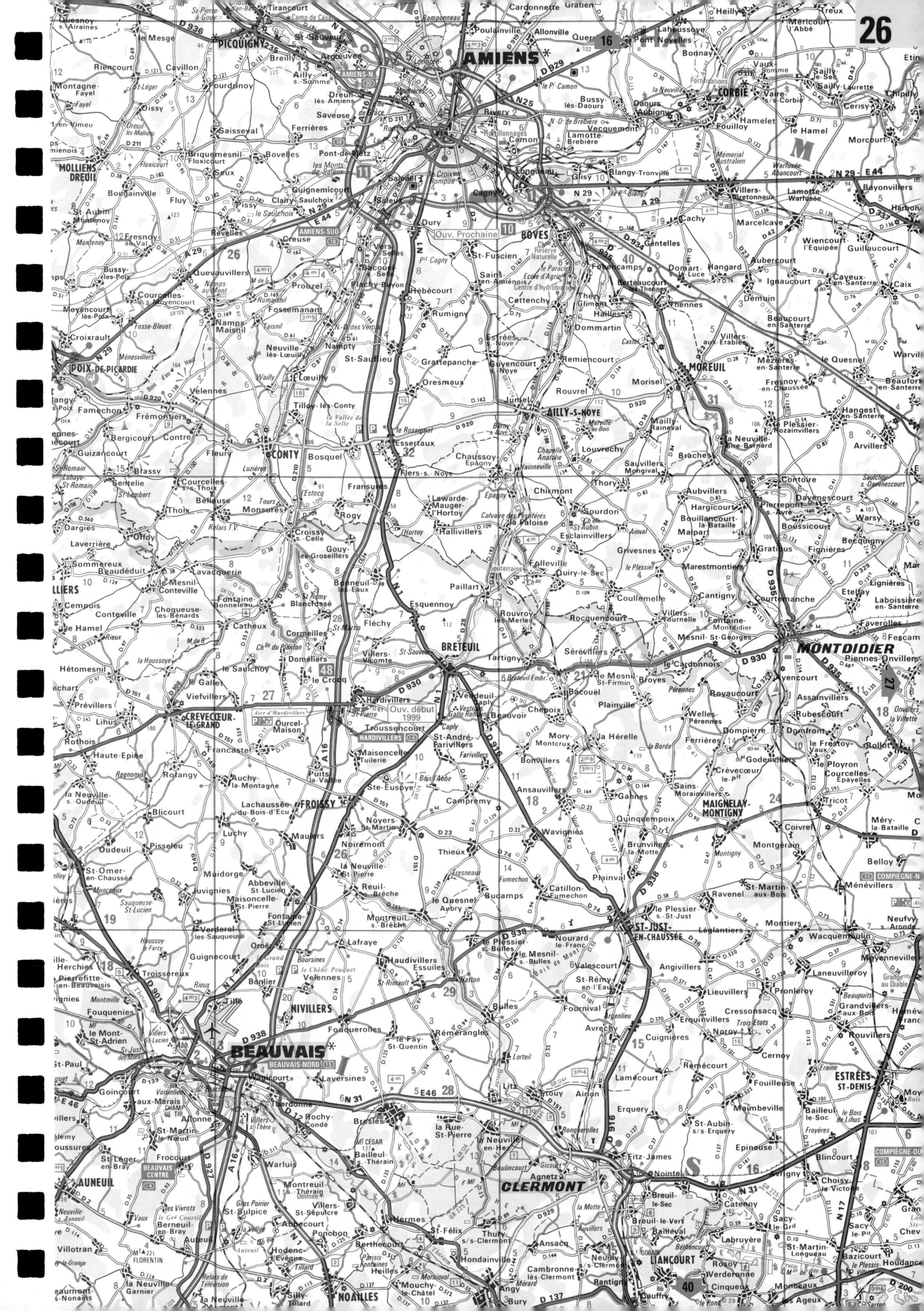
AMIENS
PICQUIGNY
Tirancourt
Cardonnette
Poulainville
Allonville
Querrieu
Pont-Noyelles
Lahoussoye
Heilly
Méricourt-l'Abbé
Bonnay
CORBIE
Vaux-sur-Somme
Sailly-le-Sec
Sailly-Laurette
Chipilly
Cerisy
Hamelet
Fouilloy
Vaire-s/s-Corbie
le Hamel
Morcourt
Daours
Aubigny
Bussy-lès-Daours
Vecquemont
Lamotte-Brebière
Camon
Rivery
Longueau
Glisy
Blangy-Tronville
Villers-Bretonneux
Marcelcave
Lamotte-Warfusée
Bayonvilles
Harbonnières
Wiencourt-l'Equipée
Guillaucourt
Cachy
Gentelles
BOVES
Dury
Ouv. Prochaine
St-Fuscien
Sains-en-Amiénois
Cottenchy
Fouencamps
Berteaucourt-lès-Thennes
Thennes
Domart-sur-la-Luce
Hangard
Aubercourt
Ignaucourt
Demuin
Caix
Cayeux-en-Santerre
Beaucourt-en-Santerre
Villers-aux-Erables
Mézières-en-Santerre
le Quesnel
Fresnoy-en-Chaussée
Beaufort-en-Santerre
MOREUIL
Morisel
Remiencourt
Dommartin
Hailles
Thézy-Glimont
Estrées-sur-Noye
Guyencourt-s-Noye
Grattepanche
Rumigny
Hébécourt
Plachy-Buyon
Bacouel-sur-Selle
Vers-sur-Selle
Saleux
Salouel
Pont-de-Metz
Saveuse
Ferrières
Dreuil-lès-Amiens
Ailly-s-Somme
Breilly
Argœuves
St-Sauveur
le Mesge
Riencourt
Cavillon
Fourdrinoy
Saisseval
Bovelles
Briquemesnil-Floxicourt
Seux
Guignemicourt
Clairy-Saulchoix
Pissy
Fluy
Bougainville
Revelles
Creuse
Prouzel
Quevauvillers
Fossemanant
Namps-Maisnil
Courcelles-s-Moyencourt
Moyencourt-lès-Poix
Croixrault
POIX-DE-PICARDIE
Bussy-les-Poix
Fresnoy-au-Val
St-Aubin-Montenoy
MOLLIENS-DREUIL
Oissy
St-Léger
Montagne-Fayel
Neuville-lès-Lœuilly
Lœuilly
Nampty
St-Sauflieu
Oresmaux
Tilloy-lès-Conty
Velennes
Frémontiers
Famechon
CONTY
Bosquel
Essertaux
Fleury
Contre
Bergicourt
Guizancourt
Brassy
Courcelles-s/s-Thoix
Thoix
Belleuse
Monsures
Rogy
Fransures
Flers-s.-Noye
Lawarde-Mauger-l'Hortoy
Hallivillers
Chaussoy-Epagny
Jumel
AILLY-S-NOYE
Rouvrel
Mailly-Raineval
Louvrechy
Sauvillers-Mongival
Thory
Braches
la Neuville-Sire-Bernard
Plessier-Rozainvillers
Hangest-en-Santerre
Arvillers
Contoire
Aubvillers
Hargicourt
Pierrepont-s.-Avre
Davenescourt
Bouillancourt-la-Bataille
Malpart
Boussicourt
Becquigny
Warsy
Grivesnes
Gratibus
Fignières
Marestmontiers
Cantigny
Coullemelle
Courtemanche
Lignières
Etelfay
Faverolles
MONTDIDIER
Fontaine-s.-Montdidier
Mesnil-St-Georges
Villers-Tournelle
Rocquencourt
Sérévillers
Tartigny
BRETEUIL
Esquennoy
Paillart
Folleville
Quiry-le-Sec
Chirmont
Sourdon
Esclainvillers
la Faloise
Epagny
Rouvroy-les-Merles
Bonneuil-les-Eaux
Fléchy
Villers-Vicomte
Croissy-s.-Celle
Gouy-les-Groseillers
Offoy
Dargies
Laverrière
Sommereux
Lavacquerie
le Mesnil-Conteville
Fontaine-Bonneleau
Choqueuse-les-Bénards
Conteville
Catheux
Cormeilles
Blancfossé
Doméliers
le Crocq
Hardivillers
Ouv. début 1999
HARDIVILLERS
Troussencourt
Vendeuil-Caply
Beauvoir
Chepoix
Bacouël
le Mesnil-St-Firmin
Broyes
Plainville
le Cardonnois
Ayencourt
Royaucourt
Welles-Pérennes
Dompierre
Rubescourt
Assainvillers
Domfront
Mory-Montcrux
la Hérelle
Ferrières
le Frestoy-Vaux
Godenvillers
Crèvecœur-le-Pt
le Ployron
Courcelles-Epayelles
Tricot
Sains-Morainvillers
MAIGNELAY-MONTIGNY
Méry-la-Bataille
Coivrel
Montgérain
Belloy
Ménévillers
COMPIEGNE-N
Gannes
Quinquempoix
Ansauvillers
Bonvillers
Wavignies
Brunvillers-la-Motte
Plainval
Catillon-Fumechon
Bucamps
le Quesnel-Aubry
Thieux
Noirémont
Noyers-St-Martin
Campremy
Ste-Eusoye
St-André-Farivillers
Maisoncelle-Tuilerie
Puits-la-Vallée
FROISSY
Auchy-la-Montagne
Lachaussée-du-Bois-d'Ecu
Rotangy
Francastel
Ourcel-Maison
CREVECŒUR-LE-GRAND
Viefvillers
le Gallet
le Saulchoy
Hétomesnil
Prévillers
Lihus
Rothois
Haute-Epine
la Neuville-s.-Oudeuil
Blicourt
Luchy
Pisseleu
Oudeuil
Muidorge
Juvignies
Abbeville-St-Lucien
Maisoncelle-St-Pierre
St-Omer-en-Chaussée
Verderel-les-Sauqueuse
Fontaine-St-Lucien
Maulers
la Neuville-St-Pierre
Reuil-s.-Brêche
Montreuil-s.-Brêche
Lafraye
Oroër
Guignecourt
Troissereux
Bonlier
Velennes
Haudivillers
Essuiles
St-Rimault
Hatton
le Plessier-s.-Bulles
le Mesnil-s.-Bulles
Nourard-le-Franc
ST-JUST-EN-CHAUSSÉE
le Plessier-s.-St-Just
Valescourt
St-Rémy-en-l'Eau
Angivillers
Léglantiers
Montiers
Ravenel
St-Martin-aux-Bois
Wacquemoulin
Moyenneville
Neufvy-s.-Aronde
Laneuvilleroy
Pronleroy
Lieuvillers
Cressonsacq
Erquinvillers
Noroy
Grandvillers-aux-Bois
Rouvillers
Cernoy
Cuignières
Avrechy
Fournival
Bulles
Nivillers
Tillé
Fouquerolles
le Fay-St-Quentin
Rémérangles
Lorteil
BEAUVAIS
BEAUVAIS-NORD
Laversines
Litz
Etouy
Airion
Lamécourt
Rémécourt
Fouilleuse
ESTRÉES-ST-DENIS
Maimbeville
Bailleul-le-Soc
Erquery
St-Aubin-s/s-Erquery
Epineuse
Blincourt
Avrigny
Choisy-la-Victoire
Sacy-le-Grd
Sacy-le-Pt
St-Martin-Longueau
Bazicourt
Fitz-James
Nointel
CLERMONT
Agnetz
Gicourt
Breuil-le-Sec
Breuil-le-Vert
Catenoy
Labruyère
LIANCOURT
Rosoy
Verderonne
Cinqueux
Monceaux
les Ageux
Cauffry
Rantigny
Neuilly-s/s-Clermont
Cambronne-lès-Clermont
Ansacq
Thury-s/s-Clermont
Hondainville
Angy
Bury
Mouchy-le-Châtel
NOAILLES
Heilles
Berthecourt
St-Félix
Hermes
Ponchon
Abbecourt
Villers-St-Sépulcre
Montreuil-s.-Thérain
Bailleul-s.-Thérain
Warluis
la Rue-St-Pierre
la Neuville-en-Hez
Bresles
Rochy-Condé
Therdonne
Allonne
St-Martin-le-Nœud
Frocourt
St-Léger-en-Bray
AUNEUIL
BEAUVAIS CENTRE
Goincourt
Aux-Marais
St-Paul
le Mont-St-Adrien
Fouquenies
Pierrefitte-en-Beauvaisis
Herchies
St-Sulpice
Berneuil-en-Bray
Auteuil
Villotran
FLORENTIN
la Neuville-Garnier
Hodenc-l'Evêque
Silly-Tillard
la Neuville-d'Aumont
Beaumont-les-Nonains
Ménévillers
Piennes-Onvillers
Fescamps
Onvillers
la Villette

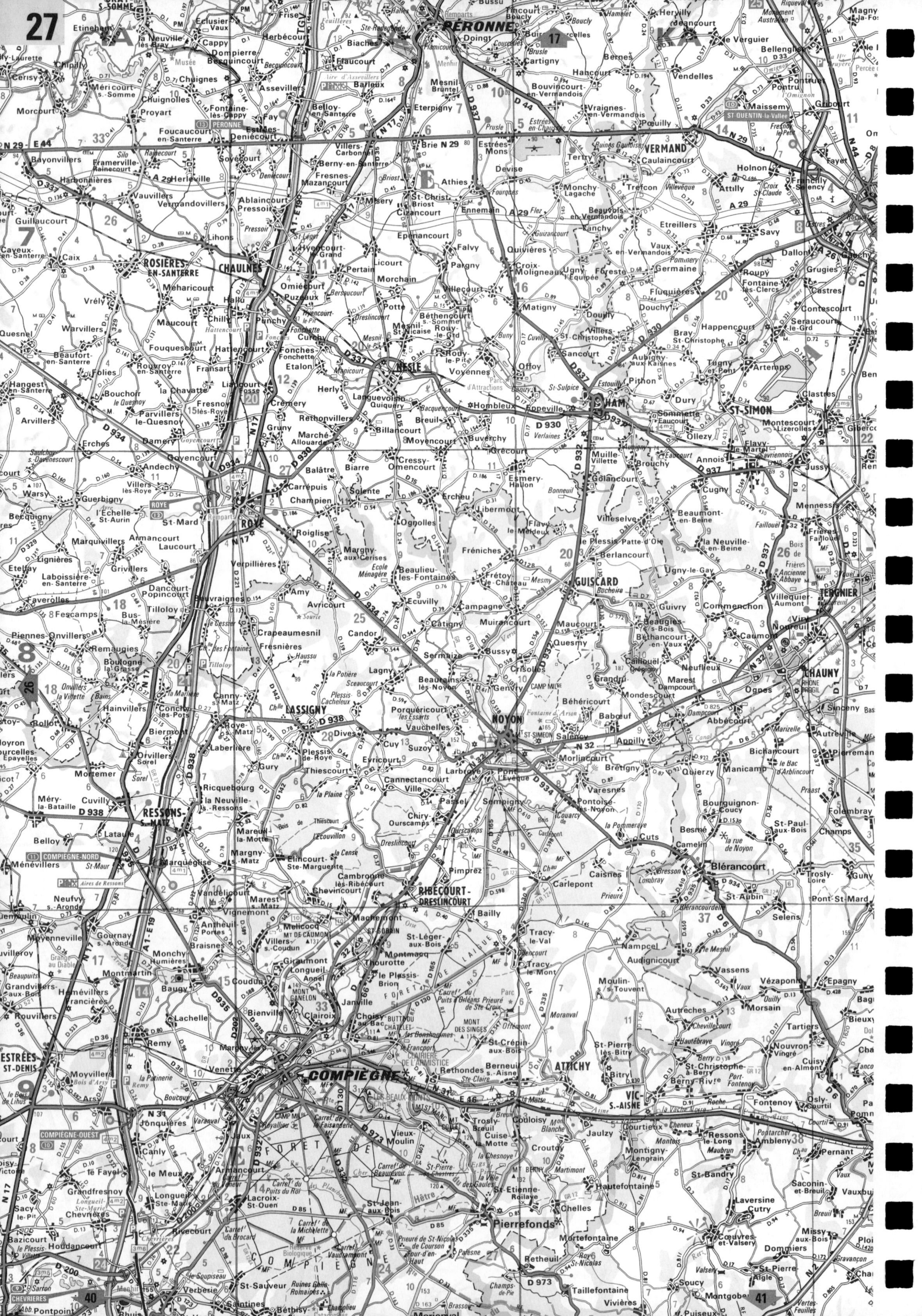
PÉRONNE
Doingt
Biaches
Flaucourt
Barleux
Assevillers
Herbécourt
Cappy
Éclusier-Vaux
Frise
Dompierre-Becquincourt
Chuignes
Chuignolles
Proyart
Foucaucourt-en-Santerre
Estrées-Deniécourt
Belloy-en-Santerre
Villers-Carbonnel
Berny-en-Santerre
Fresnes-Mazancourt
Misery
Eterpigny
Mesnil-Bruntel
Brie
Athies
Estrées-Mons
Devise
Ennemain
Cartigny
Hancourt
Bernes
Vendelles
Le Verguier
Bellenglise
Hervilly
Jeancourt
Bouvincourt-en-Vermandois
Vraignes-en-Vermandois
Pœuilly
VERMAND
Caulaincourt
Trefcon
Monchy-Lagache
Tertry
Maissemy
Holnon
Attilly
Francilly-Selency
Savy
Dallon
Fayet
ST-QUENTIN-la-Vallée
Bayonvillers
Harbonnières
Framerville-Rainecourt
Herleville
Soyécourt
Vauvillers
Vermandovillers
Ablaincourt-Pressoir
Guillaucourt
Lihons
Caix
ROSIÈRES-EN-SANTERRE
CHAULNES
Méharicourt
Hallu
Chilly
Maucourt
Puzeaux
Omiécourt
Punchy
Curchy
Fonches-Fonchette
Etalon
Hattencourt
Fouquescourt
Rouvroy-en-Santerre
Fransart
Liancourt
Fresnoy-lès-Roye
Parvillers-le-Quesnoy
Damery
Goyencourt
Andechy
Arvillers
Erches
Warvillers
Vrély
Beaufort-en-Santerre
Folies
Bouchoir
Hangest-en-Santerre
Quesnel
Cayeux-en-Santerre
NESLE
Languevoisin-Quiquery
Rethonvillers
Marché-Allouarde
Billancourt
Breuil
Moyencourt
Buverchy
Hombleux
Eppeville
HAM
Muille-Villette
Brouchy
Golancourt
Esmery-Hallon
Ercheu
Libermont
Flavy-le-Meldeux
Fréniches
Cressy-Omencourt
Balâtre
Biarre
Solente
Carrépuis
Champien
ROYE
St-Mard
Roiglise
Ognolles
Margny-aux-Cerises
Beaulieu-les-Fontaines
Fretoy-le-Château
GUISCARD
Berlancourt
Le Plessis-Patte-d'Oie
Villeselve
Beaumont-en-Beine
Cugny
Flavy-le-Martel
Annois
Jussy
Ollezy
Sommette-Eaucourt
Dury
ST-SIMON
Clastres
Montescourt-Lizerolles
Pithon
Aubigny-aux-Kaisnes
Tugny-et-Pont
Artemps
Happencourt
Bray-St-Christophe
Seraucourt-le-Grd
Contescourt
Castres
Grugies
Fontaine-lès-Clercs
Roupy
Fluquières
Douchy
Germaine
Vaux-en-Vermandois
Etreillers
Beauvois-en-Vermandois
Vaux-en-Vermandois
Foreste
Ugny-l'Équipée
Croix-Moligneaux
Matigny
Quivières
Douilly
Villers-St-Christophe
Sancourt
Offoy
Voyennes
Rouy-le-Pt
Rouy-le-Grd
Béthencourt-s-Somme
Mesnil-St-Nicaise
Potte
Morchain
Licourt
Pertain
Hyencourt-le-Grand
Falvy
Pargny
Villecourt
Épénancourt
Cizancourt
St-Christ-Briost
Herly
Cremery
Gruny
Verpillières
Tilloloy
Dancourt-Popincourt
Grivillers
Laboissière-en-Santerre
Armancourt
Laucourt
Marquivillers
Guerbigny
L'Échelle-St-Aurin
Becquigny
Warsy
Villers-lès-Roye
Lignières
Etelfay
Faverolles
Fescamps
Bus-la-Mésière
Piennes-Onvillers
Remaugies
Boulogne-la-Grasse
Hainvillers
Conchy-les-Pots
Canny-s-Matz
Beuvraignes
Crapeaumesnil
Fresnières
Amy
Avricourt
Candor
Lagny
Ecuvilly
Catigny
Campagne
Muirancourt
Sermaize
Beaurains-lès-Noyon
Bussy
Crisolles
Genvry
Maucourt
Quesmy
Grandrú
Béhéricourt
Babœuf
Salency
NOYON
Mondescourt
Marest-Dampcourt
Abbécourt
Appilly
Morlincourt
Bretigny
Quierzy
Manicamp
Varesnes
Pontoise-lès-Noyon
Ugny-le-Gay
Guivry
Commenchon
Beaugies-s-Bois
Béthancourt-en-Vaux
Caillouël-Crépigny
Neuflieux
Caumont
CHAUNY
Ognes
Sinceny
Autreville
Villequier-Aumont
Viry-Noureuil
TERGNIER
Frières-Faillouël
Menessis
LASSIGNY
Dives
Cuy
Suzoy
Porquéricourt
Vauchelles
Larbroye
Pont-l'Évêque
Sempigny
Passel
Chiry-Ourscamps
Ville
Cannectancourt
Evricourt
Thiescourt
Plessis-de-Roye
Lassigny
Roye-s-Matz
Laberlière
Gury
Ricquebourg
La Neuville-s-Ressons
RESSONS-S-MATZ
Mareuil-la-Motte
Margny-s-Matz
Marquéglise
Élincourt-Ste-Marguerite
Cambronne-lès-Ribécourt
Chevincourt
Pimprez
RIBÉCOURT-DRESLINCOURT
Bailly
Machemont
Mélicocq
Marest-s-Matz
Vandélicourt
Antheuil-Portes
Vignemont
Villers-s-Coudun
Giraumont
Thourotte
Montmacq
St-Léger-aux-Bois
Longueil-Annel
Le Plessis-Brion
Janville
Choisy-au-Bac
Clairoix
Coudun
Baugy
Monchy-Humières
Braisnes
Bienville
Margny
Venette
COMPIÈGNE
Lachelle
Remy
Montmartin
Moyvillers
Jonquières
Canly
Jaux
Le Meux
Armancourt
Le Fayel
Grandfresnoy
Chevrières
Longueil-Ste-Marie
Lacroix-St-Ouen
Rivecourt
Houdancourt
Bazicourt
Sacy-le-Pt
Verberie
St-Sauveur
Saintines
Béthisy-St-Pierre
Rhuis
Pontpoint
CHEVRIÈRES
COMPIÈGNE-OUEST
COMPIÈGNE-NORD
ESTRÉES-ST-DENIS
Ménévillers
Neufvy-s-Aronde
Gournay-s-Aronde
Moyenneville
Hémévillers
Grandvillers-aux-Bois
Rouvillers
Belloy
Lataule
Cuvilly
Méry-la-Bataille
Mortemer
Orvillers-Sorel
Biermont
Rollot
Boulogne
Vieux-Moulin
Rethondes
Berneuil-s-Aisne
St-Crépin-aux-Bois
Trosly-Breuil
Cuise-la-Motte
Couloisy
Jaulzy
Croutoy
Attichy
Bitry
St-Pierre-lès-Bitry
Moulin-s-Touvent
Autrêches
Nampcel
Audignicourt
Tracy-le-Val
Tracy-le-Mont
Carlepont
Caisnes
Cuts
Camelin
Besmé
Blérancourt
St-Aubin
Selens
Vassens
Vézaponin
Épagny
Morsain
Nouvron-Vingré
Tartiers
Cuisy-en-Almont
Bieuxy
St-Christophe-à-Berry
Berny-Rivière
VIC-S-AISNE
Fontenoy
Osly-Courtil
Ressons-le-Long
Montigny-Lengrain
Ambleny
Pernant
St-Bandry
Saconin-et-Breuil
Laversine
Cutry
Cœuvres-et-Valsery
Missy-aux-Bois
Dommiers
St-Pierre-Aigle
Montgobert
Soucy
Puiseux
Vivières
Taillefontaine
Retheuil
Mortefontaine
Chelles
Hautefontaine
St-Étienne-Roilaye
Pierrefonds
St-Jean-aux-Bois
Morienval
Folembray
Champs
St-Paul-aux-Bois
Bourguignon-s-Coucy
Trosly-Loire
Guny
Pont-St-Mard
FORÊT DE COMPIÈGNE
N 29 - E 44
A 29
A 26
A1-E19
N 17
D 930
D 934
D 938
D 932
N 32
N 31
D 973
D 935
17
22
26
35
40
41

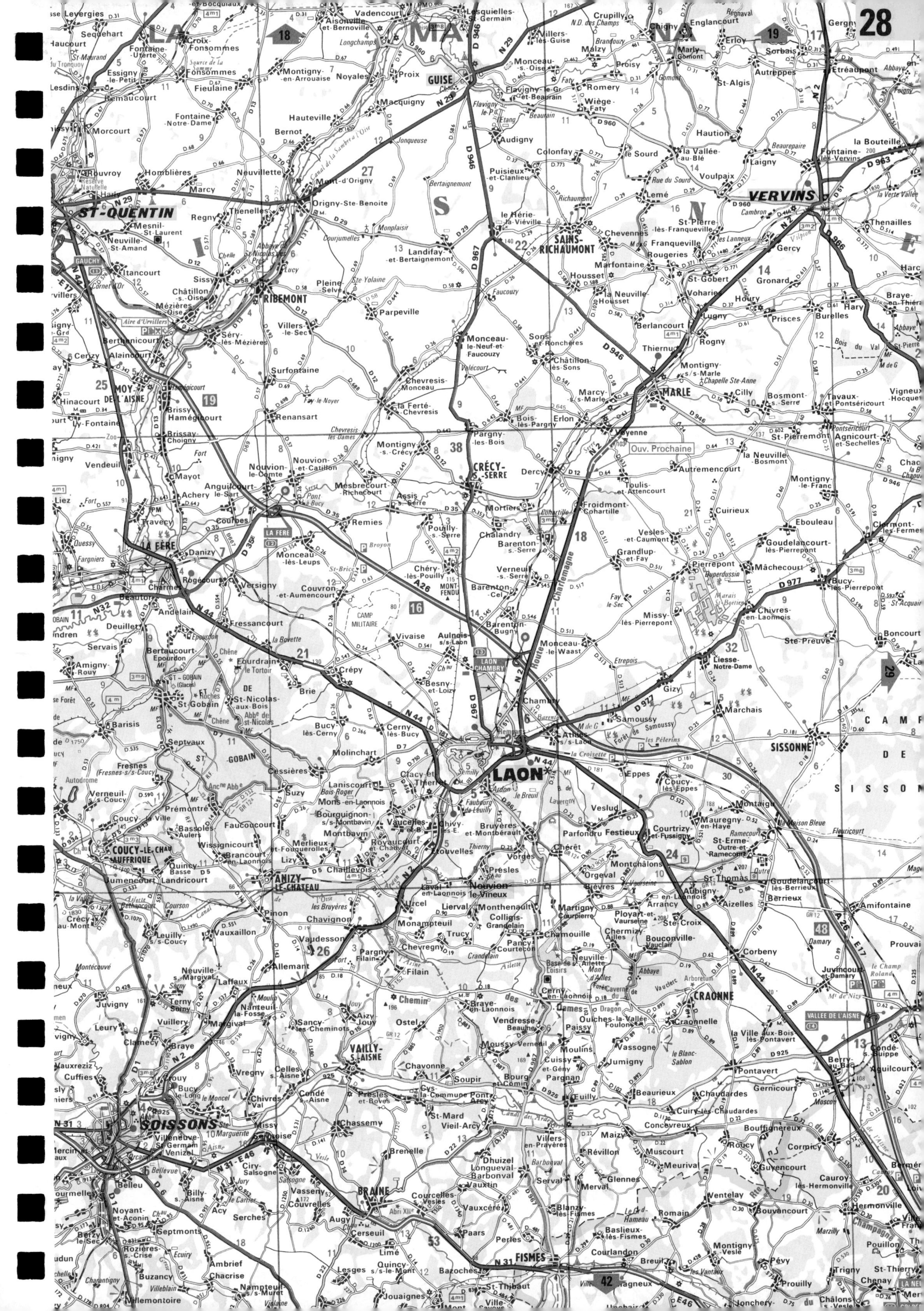

18
19
GUISE
VERVINS
ST-QUENTIN
RIBEMONT
SAINS-RICHAUMONT
MARLE
CRÉCY-SERRE
LA FÈRE
MOY-DE-L'AISNE
LAON
SISSONNE
COUCY-LE-CHÂTEAU AUFFRIQUE
ANIZY-LE-CHÂTEAU
CRAONNE
VAILLY-S-AISNE
SOISSONS
BRAINE
FISMES
Lesquielles-St-Germain
Vadencourt
Aisonville-et-Bernoville
Crupilly
Englancourt
Erloy
Sorbais
Étréaupont
Sequehart
Croix-Fonsommes
Fonsommes
Fieulaine
Montigny-en-Arrouaise
Noyales
Proix
Monceau-s.-Oise
Flavigny-le-Gr et-Beaurain
Romery
Wiège-Faty
Proisy
Malzy
Marly-Gomont
St-Algis
Autreppes
Hauteville
Macquigny
Bernot
Audigny
Colonfay
le Sourd
la Vallée-au-Blé
Haution
Voulpaix
Laigny
Fontaine-lès-Vervins
la Bouteille
Morcourt
Homblières
Neuvillette
Mont-d'Origny
Origny-Ste-Benoite
Puisieux-et-Clanlieu
le Hérie-la-Viéville
Lemé
Chevennes
St-Pierre-lès-Franqueville
Franqueville
Rougeries
Thenailles
Gercy
Harly
Marcy
Regny
Thenelles
Mesnil-St-Laurent
Neuville-St-Amand
Itancourt
Sissy
Châtillon-s.-Oise
Mézières-s.-Oise
Landifay-et-Bertaignemont
Pleine-Selve
Parpeville
Marfontaine
Housset
St-Gobert
Voharies
Houry
Gronard
Prisces
Burelles
Hary
Braye-en-Thiérache
la Neuville-Housset
Berlancourt
Lugny
Rogny
Thiernu
Séry-lès-Mézières
Berthenicourt
Alaincourt
Cerizy
Villers-le-Sec
Surfontaine
Monceau-le-Neuf-et-Faucouzy
Sons-et-Ronchères
Châtillon-lès-Sons
Montigny-s/s-Marle
Chevresis-Monceau
Marcy-s/s-Marle
Cilly
Bosmont-s.-Serre
Tavaux-et-Pontséricourt
Vigneux-Hocquet
Hinacourt
Ly-Fontaine
Brissy-Hamégicourt
Renansart
la Ferté-Chevresis
Bois-lès-Pargny
Erlon
Pargny-les-Bois
Montigny-s.-Crécy
Voyenne
St-Pierremont
Agnicourt-et-Séchelles
la Neuville-Bosmont
Autremencourt
Montigny-le-Franc
Brissay-Choigny
Vendeuil
Mayot
Nouvion-le-Comte
Nouvion-et-Catillon
Mesbrecourt-Richecourt
Dercy
Toulis-et-Attencourt
Anguilcourt-le-Sart
Achery
Travecy
Courbes
Remies
Assis-s.-Serre
Mortiers
Froidmont-Cohartille
Cuirieux
Eboulaeu
Clermont-les-Fermes
Quessy
Danizy
Monceau-lès-Leups
Pouilly-s.-Serre
Chalandry
Barenton-s.-Serre
Vesles-et-Caumont
Grandlup-et-Fay
Pierrepont
Goudelancourt-lès-Pierrepont
Mâchecourt
Bucy-lès-Pierrepont
Rogécourt
Versigny
Couvron-et-Aumencourt
Chéry-lès-Pouilly
Verneuil-s.-Serre
Barenton-Cel
Missy-lès-Pierrepont
Chivres-en-Laonnois
Charmes
Beautor
Andelain
Deuillet
Fressancourt
Servais
Amigny-Rouy
Bertaucourt-Epourdon
Fourdrain
Crépy
Vivaise
Aulnois-s/s-Laon
Barenton-Bugny
Monceau-le-Waast
Liesse-Notre-Dame
Ste-Preuve
Boncourt
St-Gobain
Barisis
St-Nicolas-aux-Bois
Brie
Besny-et-Loizy
Chambry
Gizy
Marchais
Septvaux
Bucy-lès-Cerny
Cerny-lès-Bucy
Samoussy
Athies-s/s-Laon
Fresnes
Verneuil-s.-Coucy
Cessières
Molinchart
Clacy-et-Thierret
Eppes
Coucy-lès-Eppes
Suzy
Laniscourt
Mons-en-Laonnois
Prémontré
Bourguignon-s/s-Montbavin
Vaucelles-et-B.
Chivy-lès-E.
Bruyères-et-Montbérault
Veslud
Parfondru
Festieux
Mauregny-en-Haye
Montaigu
Courtrizy-et-Fussigny
St-Erme-Outre-et-Ramecourt
Coucy
Bassoles-Aulers
Faucoucourt
Wissignicourt
Merlieux-et-Fouquerolles
Montbavin
Royaucourt
Etouvelles
Presles
Vorges
Chéret
Montchâlons
Orgeval
Bièvres
St-Thomas
Goudelancourt-lès-Berrieux
Berrieux
Aubigny
Aizelles
Amifontaine
Quincy-Basse
Landricourt
Brancourt-en-Laonnois
Lizy
Chaillevois
Jumencourt
Nouvion-le-Vineux
Laval-en-Laonnois
Urcel
Lierval
Monthenault
Colligis-Crandelain
Martigny-Courpierre
Ployart-et-Vaurseine
Arrancy
Ste-Croix
Pinon
Chavignon
Monampteuil
Trucy
Pancy-Courtecon
Chamouille
Chermizy-Ailles
Bouconville-Vauclair
Corbeny
Prouvais
Juvincourt-et-Damary
Leuilly-s/s-Coucy
Vauxaillon
Vaudesson
Chevregny
Filain
Pargny-Filain
Allemant
Neuville-s.-Ailette
Neuville-s.-Margival
Laffaux
Juvigny
Terny-Sorny
Nanteuil-la-Fosse
Aizy-Jouy
Chemin des Dames
Braye-en-Laonnois
Cerny-en-Laonnois
Vendresse-Beaulne
Oulches-la-Vallée-Foulon
Craonnelle
la Ville-aux-Bois-lès-Pontavert
Leury
Vuillery
Margival
Sancy-les-Cheminots
Ostel
Moussy-Verneuil
Paissy
Moulins
Vassogne
Jumigny
Condé-s.-Suippe
Aguilcourt
Berry-au-Bac
Clamecy
Braye
Vregny
Chavonne
Soupir
Bourg-et-Comin
Cuissy-et-Gény
Pargnan
Pontavert
Cuffies
Crouy
Bucy-le-Long
Chivres-Val
Celles-s.-Aisne
Condé-s.-Aisne
Presles-et-Boves
Gys-la-Commune
Pont-Arcy
Œuilly
Beaurieux
Chaudardes
Gernicourt
Villeneuve-St-Germain
Venizel
Missy
Sermoise
Chassemy
St-Mard
Vieil-Arcy
Villers-en-Prayères
Maizy
Cuiry-lès-Chaudardes
Concevreux
Bouffignereux
Roucy
Cormicy
Belleu
Ciry-Salsogne
Brenelle
Dhuizel
Longueval-Barbonval
Révillon
Muscourt
Meurival
Guyencourt
Cauroy-lès-Hermonville
Billy-s.-Aisne
Vasseny
Couvrelles
Courcelles-s-Vesles
Vauxtin
Serval
Merval
Glennes
Ventelay
Bouvancourt
Hermonville
Noyant-et-Aconin
Acy
Serches
Vauxcéré
Blanzy-lès-Fismes
Romain
Septmonts
Cerseuil
Paars
Perles
Basileux-lès-Fismes
Montigny-s/s-Vesle
Pouillon
St-Thierry
Limé
Ambrief
Chacrise
Buzancy
Quincy-s/s-le-Mont
Lesges
Bazoches
Courlandon
Breuil
Pévy
Trigny
Chenay
Prouilly
Nampteuil-s/s-Muret
Villemontoire
Jouaignes
St-Thibaut
Magneux
Jonchery
42
Ouv. Prochaine
CAMP MILITAIRE
CAMP DE SISSONNE
VALLEE DE L'AISNE
LAON CHAMBRY
LA FERE

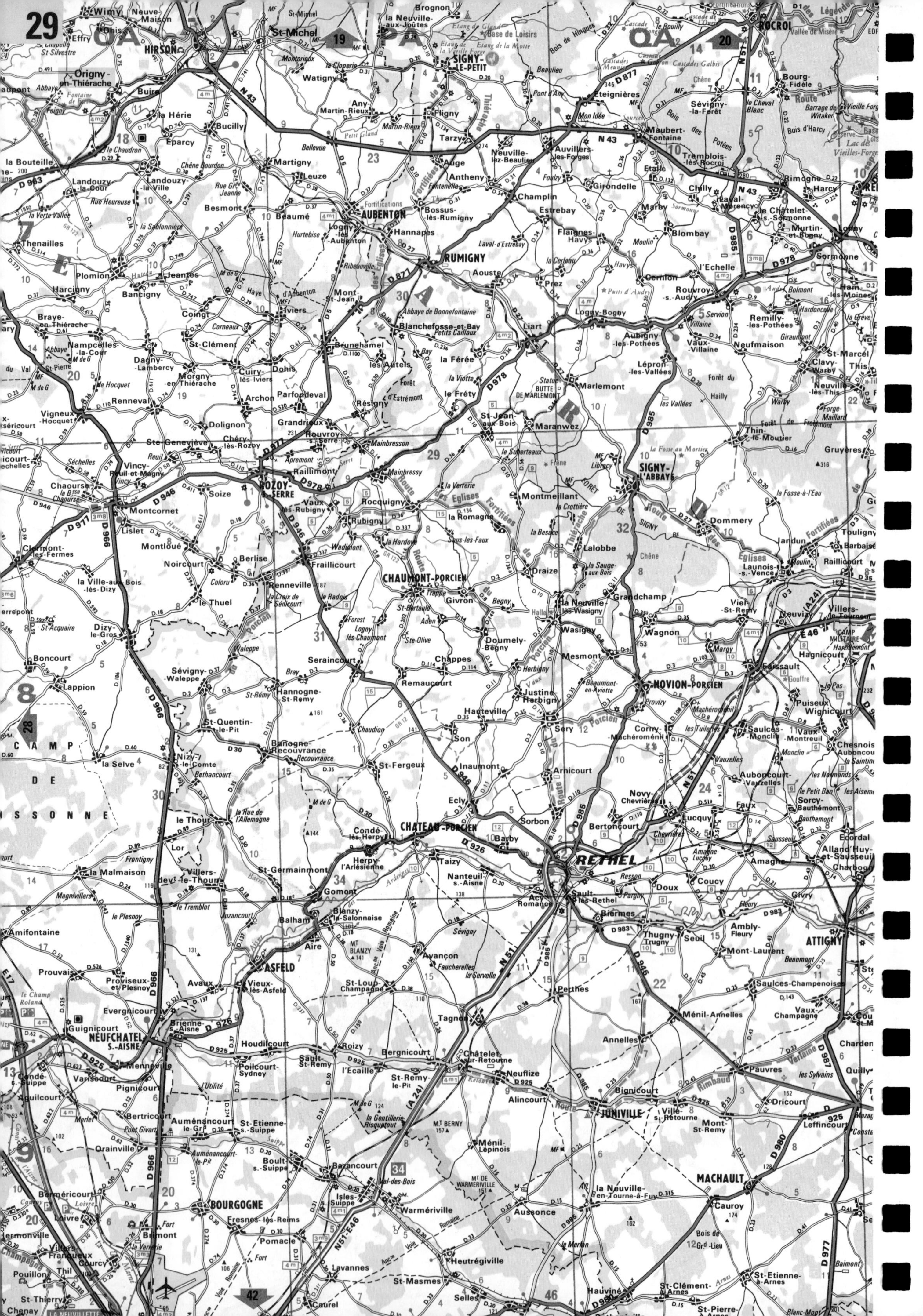

Wimy
Neuve-Maison
Brognon
St-Michel
la Neuville-aux-Joûtes
Etang de Gland
Base de Loisirs
ROCROI
Effry
Ohis
OA
PA
OA
19
20
HIRSON
St-Michel
SIGNY-LE-PETIT
Montorieux
Watigny
la Cloperie
Beaulieu
Origny-en-Thiérache
Buire
Any-Martin-Rieux
Fligny
Tarzy
Pont d'Any
Eteignières
Mon Idée
Maubert-Fontaine
Sévigny-la-Forêt
Bourg-Fidèle
Le Cheval Blanc
Bois d'Harcy
Bois des Potées
Tremblois-lès-Rocroi
la Hérie
Bucilly
Eparcy
Martigny
Petit Gland
Martin-Rieux
Auge
Neuville-lez-Beaulieu
Auvillers-les-Forges
N 43
D 877
la Bouteille
Landouzy-la-Cour
Landouzy-la-Ville
Leuze
Anthény
Champlin
Fontenelle
Etalle
Girondelle
Chilly
Laval-Morency
Le Châtelet-s.-Sormonne
Rimogne
Harcy
Rue Heureuse
Besmont
Beaumé
AUBENTON
Bossus-lès-Rumigny
Estrebay
Marby
Blombay
Murtin-et-Bogny
Lonny
Sormonne
la Verte Vallée
la Sablonnière
Logny-lès-Aubenton
Hannapes
RUMIGNY
Flaignes-Havys
Thenailles
Plomion
Jeantes
Ribeauville
Aouste
Prez
Cernion
Rouvroy-s.-Audry
l'Echelle
Harcigny
Bancigny
Haye d'Aubenton
Mont-St-Jean
Abbaye de Bonnefontaine
Blanchefosse-et-Bay
Liart
Logny-Bogny
Aubigny-les-Pothées
Remilly-les-Pothées
Servion
Braye-en-Thiérache
Coingt
Iviers
Nampcelles-la-Cour
St-Clément
Brunehamel
les Autels
la Férée
Vaux-Villaine
Neufmaison
St-Marcel
Clavy-Warby
Dagny-Lambercy
Cuiry-lès-Iviers
Dohis
Morgny-en-Thiérache
Lépron-les-Vallées
Marlemont
Statue BUTTE DE MARLEMONT
Neuville-lès-This
Renneval
Archon
Parfondeval
Résigny
le Fréty
Vigneux-Hocquet
Dolignon
Grandrieux
Rouvroy-s.-Serre
St-Jean-aux-Bois
Maranwez
les Vallées
Thin-le-Moutier
Ste-Geneviève
Chéry-lès-Rozoy
Mainbresson
Gruyères
Séchelles
Vincy-Reuil-et-Magny
Raillimont
Apremont
Mainbressy
le Suberteaux
SIGNY-L'ABBAYE
Chaourse
Soize
ROZOY-S.-SERRE
la Verrerie
Montmeillant
la Fosse-à-l'Eau
Montcornet
Vaux-lès-Rubigny
Rocquigny
la Crottière
Lislet
Rubigny
la Romagne
Dommery
Clermont-les-Fermes
Montloué
Wadimont
la Hardoye
la Besace
Lalobbe
Jandun
Touligny
Barbaise
Noircourt
Berlise
Fraillicourt
CHAUMONT-PORCIEN
Draize
la Sauge-aux-Bois
Chêne
Raillicourt
Launois-s.-Vence
la Ville-aux-Bois-lès-Dizy
Renneville
Grandchamp
le Thuel
la Croix de Sénicourt
le Radois
Givron
Bégny
la Neuville-lès-Wasigny
Viel-St-Remy
Neuvizy
Villers-le-Tourneur
St-Acquaire
St-Bertauld
Wasigny
Wagnon
Dizy-le-Gros
Forest
Logny-lès-Chaumont
Aden
Ste-Olive
Doumely-Bégny
CAMP MILITAIRE
Hagnicourt
Waleppe
Boncourt
Seraincourt
Chappes
Mesmont
Margy
Faissault
Herbigny
Lappion
Sévigny-Waleppe
Bray
Remaucourt
NOVION-PORCIEN
Puiseux
Wignicourt
St-Rémy
Hannogne-St-Remy
Justine-Herbigny
Beaumont-en-Aviotte
Provizy
Machéroménil
Hauteville
St-Quentin-le-Pit
Chaudion
Son
Sery
Corny-Machéroménil
les Tuileries
Saulces-Monclin
Chesnois-Auboncourt
CAMP DE SISSONNE
la Selve
Nizy-le-Comte
Banogne-Recouvrance
St-Fergeux
Inaumont
Arnicourt
Vauzelles
Auboncourt-Vauzelles
Bethancourt
les Normands
Novy-Chevrières
Faux
le Petit Ban
Sorcy-Bauthémont
le Thour
la Rue de l'Allemagne
Ecly
Sorbon
Lucquy
Bertoncourt
Ecordal
CHATEAU-PORCIEN
Condé-lès-Herpy
Barby
Lor
Frontigny
Herpy-l'Arlésienne
Taizy
RETHEL
Amagne
Alland'Huy-et-Sausseuil
la Malmaison
Villers-devant-le-Thour
St-Germainmont
Nanteuil-s.-Aisne
Doux
Coucy
Resson
Magnivillers
Gomont
Acy-Romance
Sault-lès-Rethel
Givry
le Plesnoy
le Tremblot
Juzancourt
Balham
Blanzy-la-Salonnaise
Biermes
Ambly-Fleury
Amifontaine
Sévigny
Aire
Thugny-Trugny
Seuil
Mont-Laurent
ATTIGNY
MT BLANZY
Avançon
Faucherelles
la Servelle
Prouvais
ASFELD
Proviseux-et-Plesnoy
Avaux
Vieux-lès-Asfeld
St-Loup-Champagne
Perthes
Saulces-Champenoises
Evergnicourt
Brienne-s.-Aisne
Tagnon
Ménil-Annelles
Vaux-Champagne
Guignicourt
NEUFCHATEL S.-AISNE
Houdilcourt
Roizy
Annelles
Menneville
Sault-St-Remy
Bergnicourt
Châtelet-sur-Retourne
Charden
Condé-s.-Suippe
Variscourt
Poilcourt-Sydney
l'Ecaille
St-Remy-le-Pit
Neuflize
Pauvres
Quilly
les Sylvains
Aguilcourt
Pignicourt
l'Utilité
Alincourt
Bignicourt
Dricourt
Merlet
Bertricourt
Auménancourt-le-Gd
St-Etienne-s.-Suippe
la Gentillerie
JUNIVILLE
Ville-s.-Retourne
Mont-St-Remy
Leffincourt
Pont Givart
MT BERNY
Ménil-Lépinois
Orainville
Auménancourt-le-Pit
Boult-s.-Suippe
Bazancourt
MACHAULT
Bermericourt
Val-des-Bois
MT DE WARMERIVILLE
la Neuville-en-Tourne-à-Fuy
Loivre
BOURGOGNE
Isles-s.-Suippe
Warmériville
Cauroy
Hermonville
Fresnes-lès-Reims
Aussonce
Brimont
Pomacle
Bois de Grd-Lieu
Villers-Franqueux
Courcy
Fort
Heutrégiville
Pouillon
Thil
Lavannes
Baimont
St-Thierry
St-Masmes
Hauviné
St-Clément-à-Arnes
St-Etienne-à-Arnes
Chenay
Caurel
Selles
St-Pierre-à-Arnes
Blanc-Mont
42
46
34
28

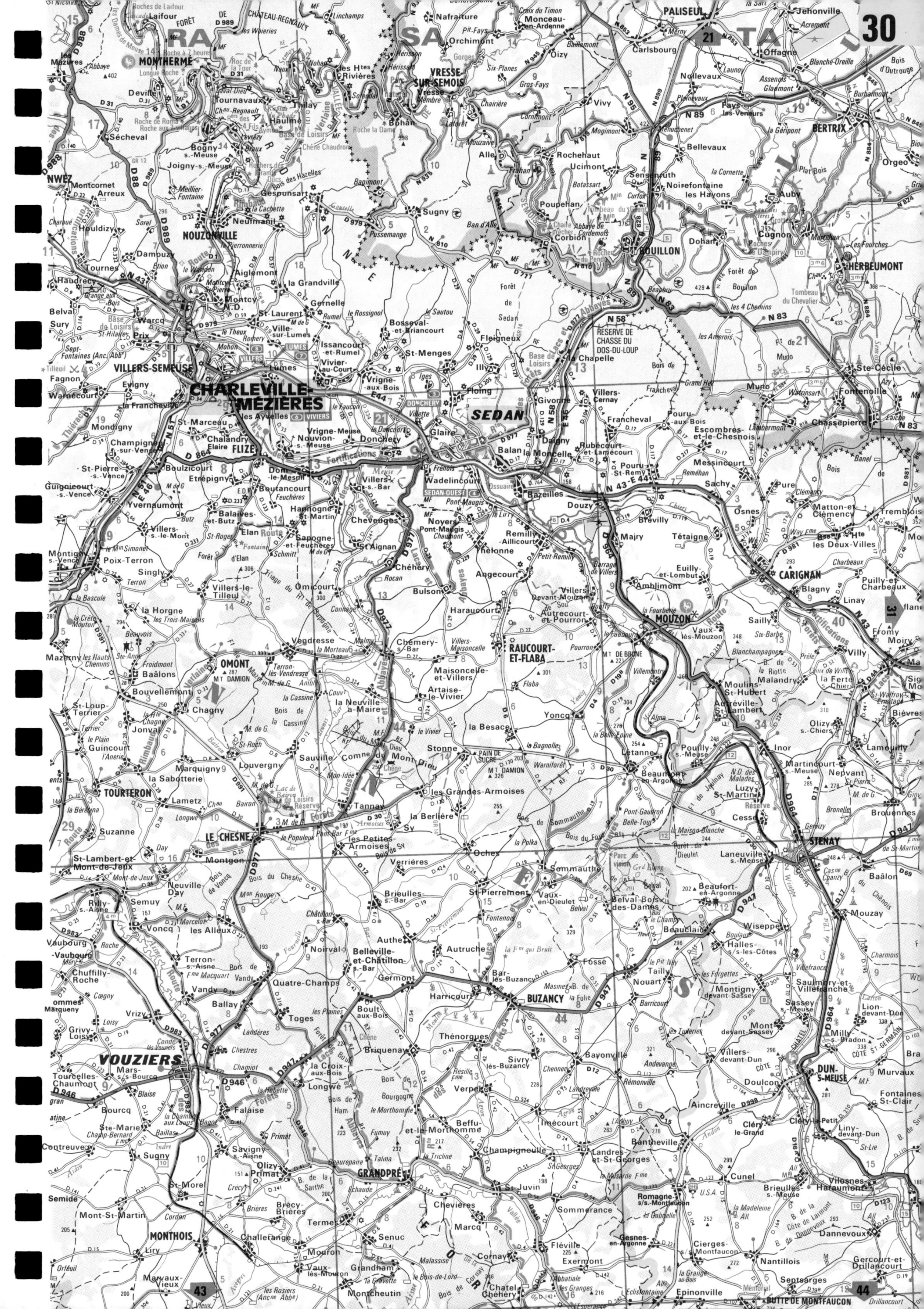

Laifour
Monthermé
Les Mazures
Deville
Tournavaux
Thilay
Haulmé
Les Hautes Rivières
Vresse-sur-Semois
Nafraiture
Orchimont
Monceau-en-Ardenne
Paliseul
Jehonville
Carlsbourg
Offagne
Bertrix
Orgeo
Sécheval
Bogny-s.-Meuse
Joigny-s.-Meuse
Bohan
Alle
Rochehaut
Vivy
Mogimont
Bellevaux
Noirefontaine
Auby
Montcornet
Arreux
Nouzonville
Neufmanil
Gespunsart
Sugny
Pussemange
Corbion
Bouillon
Dohan
Cugnon
Herbeumont
Houldizy
Tournes
Aiglemont
la Grandville
Gernelle
Montcy-N.-D.
St-Laurent
Ville-sur-Lumes
Bosseval-et-Briancourt
Fleigneux
Illy
Givonne
la Chapelle
Réserve de chasse du Dos-du-Loup
Warcq
Prix
Villers-Semeuse
Lumes
Issancourt-et-Rumel
Vivier-au-Court
St-Menges
Vrigne-aux-Bois
Iges
Floing
Charleville-Mézières
Sedan
Donchery
Villers-Cernay
Francheval
Pouru-aux-Bois
Escombres-et-le-Chesnois
Muno
Ste-Cécile
Fontenoille
Chassepierre
Fagnon
Warnécourt
Évigny
la Francheville
Mondigny
Champigneul-sur-Vence
St-Marceau
Chalandry-Elaire
Flize
Vrigne-Meuse
Nouvion-s.-Meuse
Glaire
Balan
Daigny
la Moncelle
Rubécourt-et-Lamécourt
Pouru-St-Remy
Messincourt
Sachy
Bazeilles
Douzy
Wadelincourt
Frénois
Boulzicourt
Étrépigny
Dom-le-Mesnil
Villers-s.-Bar
Boutancourt
Yvernaumont
Hannogne-St-Martin
Cheveuges
Noyers-Pont-Maugis
Remilly-Aillicourt
Brévilly
Tétaigne
Osnes
Matton-et-Clémency
Villers-s.-le-Mont
Balaives-et-Butz
Élan
Sapogne-et-Feuchères
St-Aignan
Thelonne
Majry
Carignan
les Deux-Villes
Poix-Terron
Singly
Chéhéry
Angecourt
Eully-et-Lombut
Amblimont
Blagny
Pouilly-s.-Charbeaux
Linay
Villers-le-Tilleul
Omicourt
Bulson
Haraucourt
Villers-devant-Mouzon
Autrecourt-et-Pourron
Mouzon
Vaux-lès-Mouzon
Sailly
Fromy
Moiry
Villy
la Horgne
Vendresse
Chémery-s.-Bar
Raucourt-et-Flaba
Omont
Baâlons
Maisoncelle-et-Villers
Artaise-le-Vivier
Bouvellemont
Chagny
la Neuville-à-Maire
Yoncq
Moulins-St-Hubert
Autréville-St-Lambert
Malandry
la Ferté-s.-Chiers
Olizy-s.-Chiers
St-Loup-Terrier
Jonval
Guincourt
la Besace
Stonne
Inor
Lamouilly
Sauville
Mont-Dieu
Létanne
Beaumont-en-Argonne
Pouilly-s.-Meuse
Martincourt-s.-Meuse
Nepvant
Marquigny
Louvergny
la Sabotterie
Tourteron
Lametz
les Grandes-Armoises
Tannay
la Berlière
Luzy-St-Martin
Cesse
Brouennes
Suzanne
Le Chesne
Sy
les Petites-Armoises
Oches
Stenay
Laneuville-s.-Meuse
St-Lambert-et-Mont-de-Jeux
Montgon
Verrières
Sommauthe
Beaufort-en-Argonne
Baâlon
Neuville-Day
Brieulles-s.-Bar
St-Pierremont
Vaux-en-Dieulet
Belval-Bois-des-Dames
Mouzay
Rilly-s.-Aisne
Semuy
Voncq
les Alleux
Châtillon-s.-Bar
Autruche
Wiseppe
Beauclair
Halles-s/s-les-Côtes
Vaubourg
Terron-s.-Aisne
Noirval
Authe
Belleville-et-Châtillon-s.-Bar
Fossé
Tailly
Nouart
Saulmory-et-Villefranche
Chuffilly-Roche
Vandy
Quatre-Champs
Germont
Bar-lès-Buzancy
Harricourt
Buzancy
Montigny-devant-Sassey
Sassey-s.-Meuse
Lion-devant-Dun
Ballay
Toges
Boult-aux-Bois
Vrizy
Grivy-Loisy
Thénorgues
Bayonville
Mont-devant-Sassey
Milly-s.-Bradon
Briquenay
Vouziers
Sivry-lès-Buzancy
Villers-devant-Dun
Dun-s.-Meuse
Murvaux
Tourcelles-Chaumont
Mars-s/s-Bourcq
la Croix-aux-Bois
Longwé
Verpel
Rémonville
Doulcon
Fontaines-St-Clair
Bourcq
Falaise
Beffu-et-le-Morthomme
Imécourt
Aincreville
Liny-devant-Dun
Ste-Marie
Contreuve
Savigny-s.-Aisne
Sugny
Champigneulle
Landres-et-St-Georges
Bantheville
Cléry-le-Grand
Cléry-le-Petit
Olizy-Primat
Grandpré
St-Juvin
Cunel
Vilosnes-Haraumont
St-Morel
Semide
Brieulles-s.-Meuse
Romagne-s/s-Montfaucon
Mont-St-Martin
Brécy-Brières
Chevières
Sommerance
Marcq
Monthois
Termes
Senuc
Dannevoux
Challerange
Fléville
Exermont
Cierges-s/s-Montfaucon
Liry
Mouron
Cornay
Gesnes-en-Argonne
Nantillois
Gercourt-et-Drillancourt
Marvaux-Vieux
Vaux-lès-Mouron
Grandham
Chatel-Chéhéry
Montcheutin
Épinonville
Septsarges
Butte de Montfaucon
43
44
31

NEUFCHATEAU
BERTRIX
HERBEUMONT
CHINY
FLORENVILLE
LÉGLISE
FAUVILLERS
MARTELANGE
ATTERT
HABAY
ARLON
ETALLE
TINTIGNY
SAINT-LÉGER
MESSANCY
AUBANGE
MUSSON
VIRTON
MEIX-DEVANT-VIRTON
ROUVROY
MONT-ST-MARTIN
HERSERANGE
LONGWY
MONTMEDY
STENAY
LONGUYON
DUN-S-MEUSE
DAMVILLERS
SPINCOURT
Mouzay
Avioth
Orval
Bouillon
Margut
Virton
Arlon
Longwy
Eton
Consenvoye
Pétange
Differdange
Mercy-le-Haut
Piennes
Landres
Fillières
Joudreville
Muzeray
Pillon
Azannes-et-Soumazannes
Brabant-s-Meuse
FORÊT DE CHINY
FORÊT DE WOEVRE
Forêt de Neufchâteau
Tellancourt
Cosnes-et-Romain
Villers-la-Chèvre
Torgny
Lamorteau
Harnoncourt
Ruette
Ethe
Latour
Bleid
Gerouville
Jamoigne
Izel
Les Bulles
Rossignol
Mellier
Suxy
Anlier
Vance
Chantemelle
Buzenol
Sainte-Marie
Bellefontaine
Habay-la-Neuve
Thiaumont
Nobressart
Hachy
Heinsch
Stockem
Udange
Toernich
Wolkrange
Hondelange
Selange
Châtillon
Meix-le-Tige
Rachecourt
Halanzy
Athus
Villécloye
Velosnes
Othe
Flassigny
Marville
Iré-le-Sec
Jametz
Louppy-s-Loison
Remoiville
Delut
Dombras
Vittarville
Brandeville
Murvaux
Fontaines-St-Clair
Liny-devant-Dun
Milly-s-Bradon
Lion-devant-Dun
Bréhéville
Lissey
Peuvillers
Ecurey-en-Verdunois
Réville-aux-Bois
Wavrille
Sivry-s-Meuse
Dannevoux
Vilosnes-Haraumont
Gercourt-et-Drillancourt
Moirey-Flabas-Crépion
Romagne-s/s-les-Côtes
Mangiennes
Billy-s/s-Mangiennes
Villers-lès-Mangiennes
Merles-s-Loison
Sorbey
St-Laurent-s-Othain
Rouvrois-s-Othain
Duzey
Nouillonpont
Vaudoncourt
Loison
Senon
Amel-s-l'Étang
Gouraincourt
Domremy-la-Canne
Bouligny
Dommary-Baroncourt
Avillers
Xivry-Circourt
Mercy-le-Bas
Joppécourt
Bazailles
Boismont
Pierrepont
Arrancy-s-Crusne
Beuveille
Doncourt-lès-Longuyon
Ugny
Cons-la-Grandville
Cutry
Rehon
Lexy
Mexy
Hussigny-Godbrange
Villers-la-Montagne
Morfontaine
Laix
Baslieux
Chenières
Fresnois-la-Montagne
Montigny-s-Chiers
Viviers-s-Chiers
Charency-Vezin
Villette
Colmey
Villers-le-Rond
St-Jean-lès-Longuyon
Fermont
Baâlon
Quincy-Landzécourt
Han-lès-Juvigny
Juvigny-s-Loison
Vigneul-s/s-Montmédy
Brouennes
Chauvency-le-Château
Chauvency-St-Hubert
Thonne-les-Prés
Thonnelle
Thonne-la-Long
Verneuil-Petit
Verneuil-Grand
Thonne-le-Thil
Breux
Sommethonne
Signy-Montlibert
Bièvres
Lamouilly
Nepvant
Olizy-s-Chiers
Villy
La Ferté-s-Chiers
Fromy
Moiry
Sapogne-s-Marche
Herbeuval
Margny
Villers-devant-Orval
Pure
Auflance
Linay
Pouilly-et-Charbeaux
Tremblois-lès-Carignan
Matton-et-Clémency
Mogues
Williers
Fontenoille
Sainte-Cécile
Chassepierre
Lacuisine
Orgeo
Grandvoir
Tournay
Longlier
Ebly
Juseret
Witry
Bodange
Wisembach
Tintange
Boulaide
Bigonville
Perlé
Rambrouch
Nothomb
Bonnert
Beckerich
Fontelange
Ell
Reda
Nagem
Guirsch
Autelbas
Bascharage
Sanem
Grevels
Eischen
Weyler
Beho
Strainchamps
Menufontaine
Volaiville
Chêne
Mon Idée
Hamipré
Nevraumont
Grapfontaine
St-Médart
Straimont
Assenois
Les Fosses
Thibésart
Behême
Louftemont
Vlessart
Heinstert
Schockville
Post
Lottert
Frassem
Waltzing
Turpange
Bébange
Differt
Guelff
Longeau
Habergy
Buvange
Musson
Mussy-la-Ville
Baranzy
Signeulx
Gomery
Dampicourt
St-Mard
Robelmont
Villers-la-Loue
Belmont
Croix-Rouge
Lahage
Lasoye
Mortinsart
Houdemont
Rulles
Termes
Moyen
Valansart
Prouvy
St-Vincent
Poncelle
Fratin
Sivry
Gévimont
Lacliareau
Hamawé
Cussigny
Gorcy
Ville-Houdlémont
St-Pancré
Saulnes
Hussigny
Herserange
Mont-St-Martin

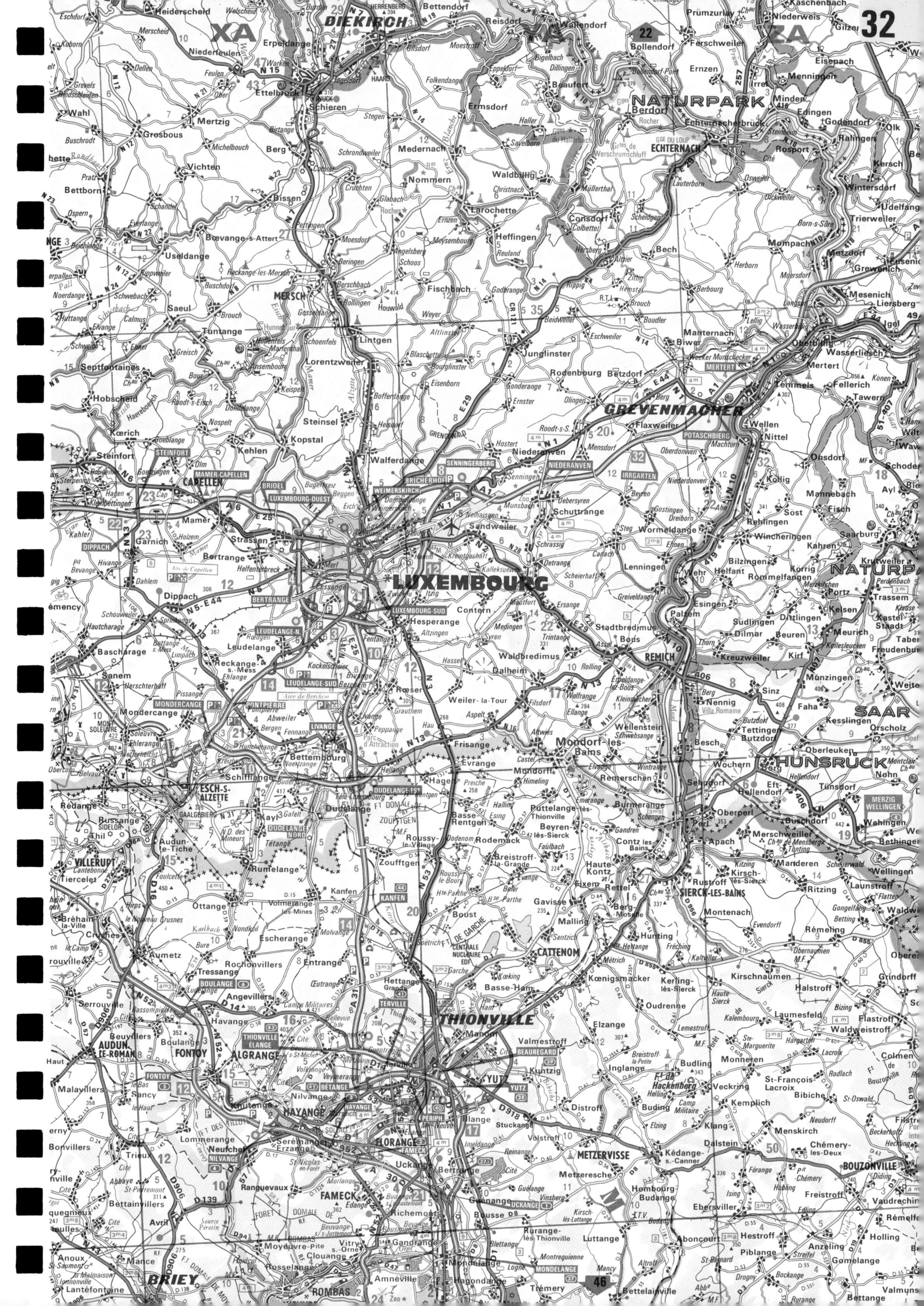
32
XA
ZA
DIEKIRCH
Heiderscheid
Bettendorf
Reisdorf
Wallendorf
Prümzurlay
Niederweis
Kaschenbach
Erpeldange
Niederfeulen
Ettelbruck
Schieren
Bollendorf
Ferschweiler
Ernzen
Menningen
Eisenach
NATURPARK
Berdorf
Beaufort
Ermsdorf
Mertzig
Grosbous
Wahl
Berg
Medernach
ECHTERNACH
Rosport
Ralingen
Echternacherbrück
Vichten
Bettborn
Nommern
Waldbillig
Bissen
Larochette
Heffingen
Consdorf
Boevange-s-Attert
Useldange
Bech
Mompach
Fischbach
MERSCH
Saeul
Tuntange
Lintgen
Junglinster
Manternach
Biwer
Igel
Septfontaines
Lorentzweiler
Rodenbourg
Betzdorf
Mertert
Wasserliesch
Hobscheid
Steinsel
GREVENMACHER
Flaxweiler
Wellen
Nittel
Koerich
Kopstal
Kehlen
Walferdange
Niederanven
Steinfort
CAPELLEN
Mamer
Strassen
Bertrange
Sandweiler
Schuttrange
Wormeldange
Saarburg
Garnich
Dippach
LUXEMBOURG
Hesperange
Contern
Lenningen
Wehr
NATURP
Bascharage
Leudelange
Reckange-s-Mess
Dalheim
Waldbredimus
Bous
REMICH
Stadtbredimus
Sanem
Mondercange
Bettembourg
Weiler-la-Tour
Frisange
Mondorf-les-Bains
Nennig
Sinz
SAAR
HUNSRÜCK
ESCH-S-ALZETTE
Schifflange
Dudelange
Kayl
Rumelange
Hagen
Evrange
Remerschen
Schengen
Perl
VILLERUPT
Audun-le-Tiche
Ottange
Kanfen
Zoufftgen
Rodemack
Breistroff-la-Grande
Haute Kontz
Contz les Bains
SIERCK-LES-BAINS
Apach
Aumetz
Tressange
Escherange
Entrange
CATTENOM
Koenigsmacker
Kerling-lès-Sierck
Halstroff
Angevillers
Havange
Basse-Ham
THIONVILLE
Elzange
Oudrenne
Laumesfeld
AUDUN-LE-ROMAN
FONTOY
ALGRANGE
Yutz
Kuntzig
Inglange
Budling
Monneren
Bibiche
Sancy
HAYANGE
Nilvange
Florange
Distroff
Stuckange
METZERVISSE
Kédange-s.-Canner
Dalstein
Menskirch
Chémery-les-Deux
BOUZONVILLE
Bonvillers
Trieux
Uckange
Metzeresche
Hombourg-Budange
Freistroff
Bettainvillers
Ranguevaux
FAMECK
Richemont
Bousse
Ebersviller
Avril
Vitry-s.-Orne
Gandrange
Rurange-lès-Thionville
Luttange
Hestroff
Anzeling
Gomelange
Moyeuvre
Clouange
Rosselange
Amnéville
Hagondange
Trémery
Bettelainville
Mancy
BRIEY
ROMBAS
Lantéfontaine
46
22

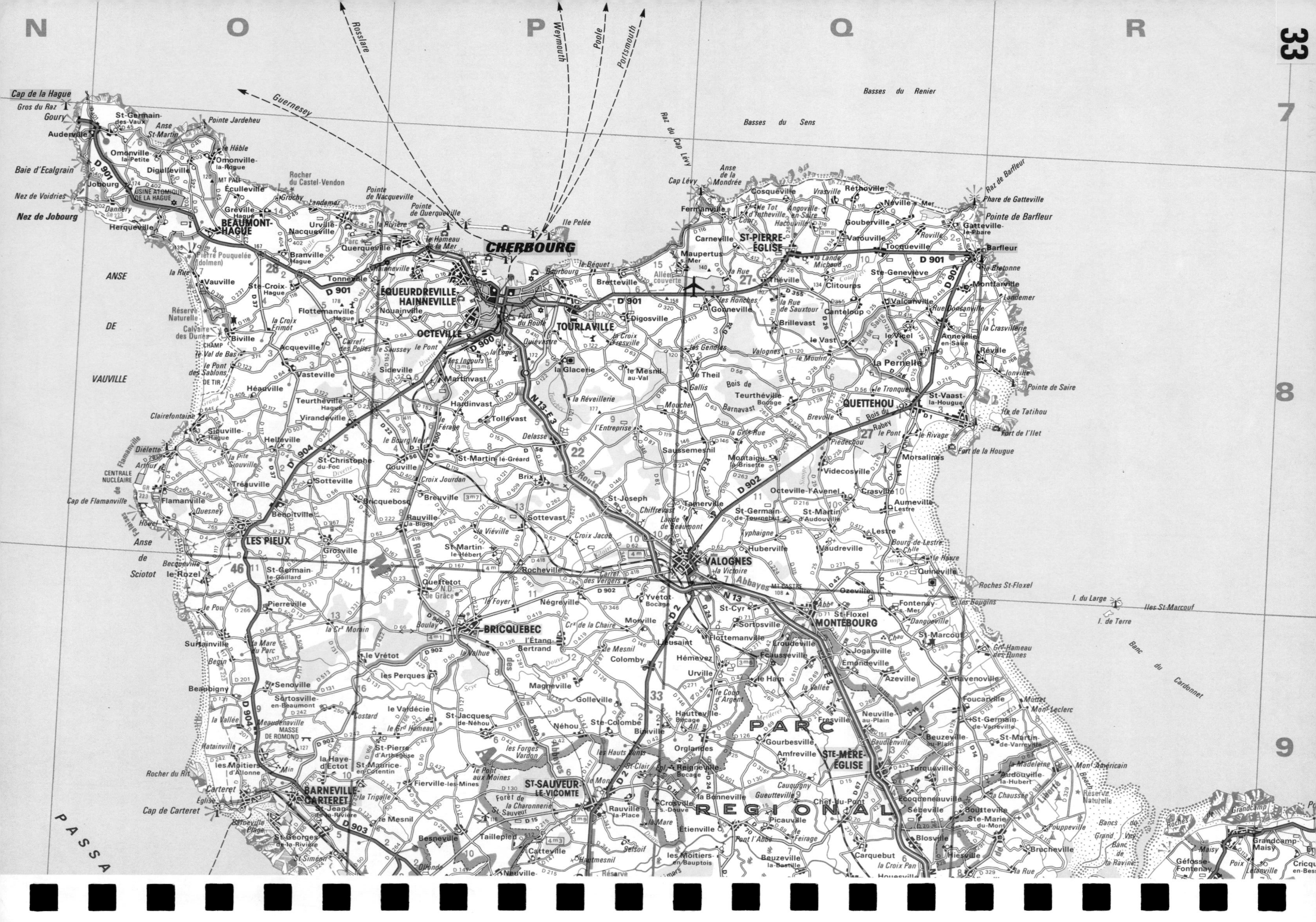

N
O
P
Q
R
7
8
9
CHERBOURG
VALOGNES
BRICQUEBEC
LES PIEUX
BARNEVILLE-CARTERET
ST-SAUVEUR-LE-VICOMTE
STE-MÈRE-ÉGLISE
MONTEBOURG
QUETTEHOU
ST-PIERRE-ÉGLISE
BEAUMONT-HAGUE
TOURLAVILLE
OCTEVILLE
ÉQUEURDREVILLE-HAINNEVILLE
Barfleur
St-Vaast-la-Hougue
Cap de la Hague
Nez de Jobourg
Cap de Carteret
Cap de Flamanville
Pointe de Barfleur
Pointe de Saire
Raz du Cap Lévy
Basses du Renier
Basses du Sens
Banc du Cardonnet
Iles St-Marcouf
ANSE DE VAUVILLE
PARC REGIONAL
Rosslare
Weymouth
Poole
Portsmouth
Guernesey
PASSA

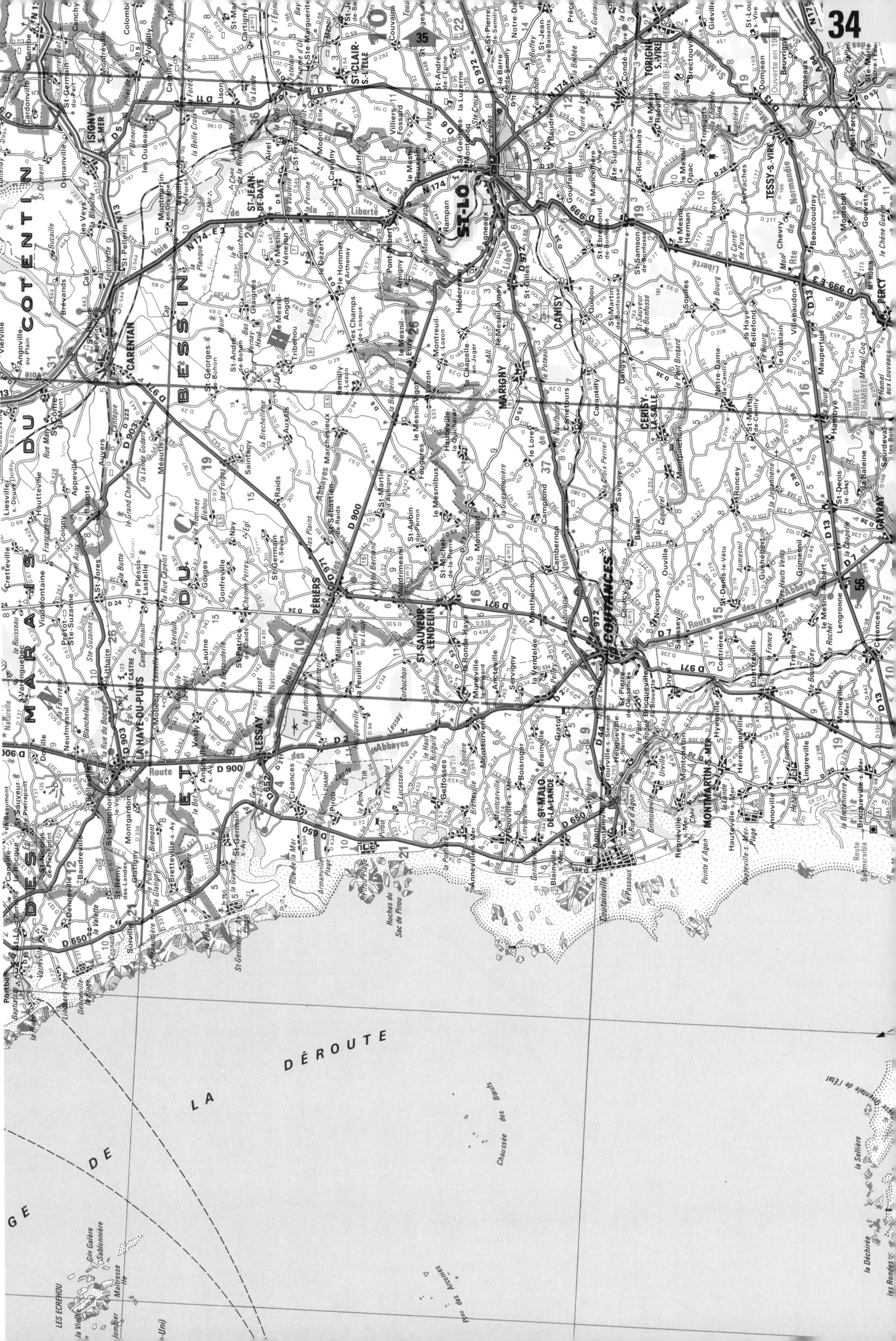

MARAIS DU COTENTIN ET DU BESSIN

ISIGNY-S-MER
CARENTAN
ST-JEAN-DE-DAYE
ST-CLAIR-S-L'ELLE
ST-LÔ
TORIGNI-S-VIRE
TESSY-S-VIRE
PERCY
CANISY
MARIGNY
CERISY-LA-SALLE
GAVRAY
COUTANCES
PÉRIERS
ST-SAUVEUR-LENDELIN
LA HAYE-DU-PUITS
LESSAY
ST-MALO-DE-LA-LANDE
MONTMARTIN-S-MER

Roches du Sac de Pirou

Pointe d'Agon

DÉROUTE

Chaussée des Bœufs

LES ECREHOU

35
56

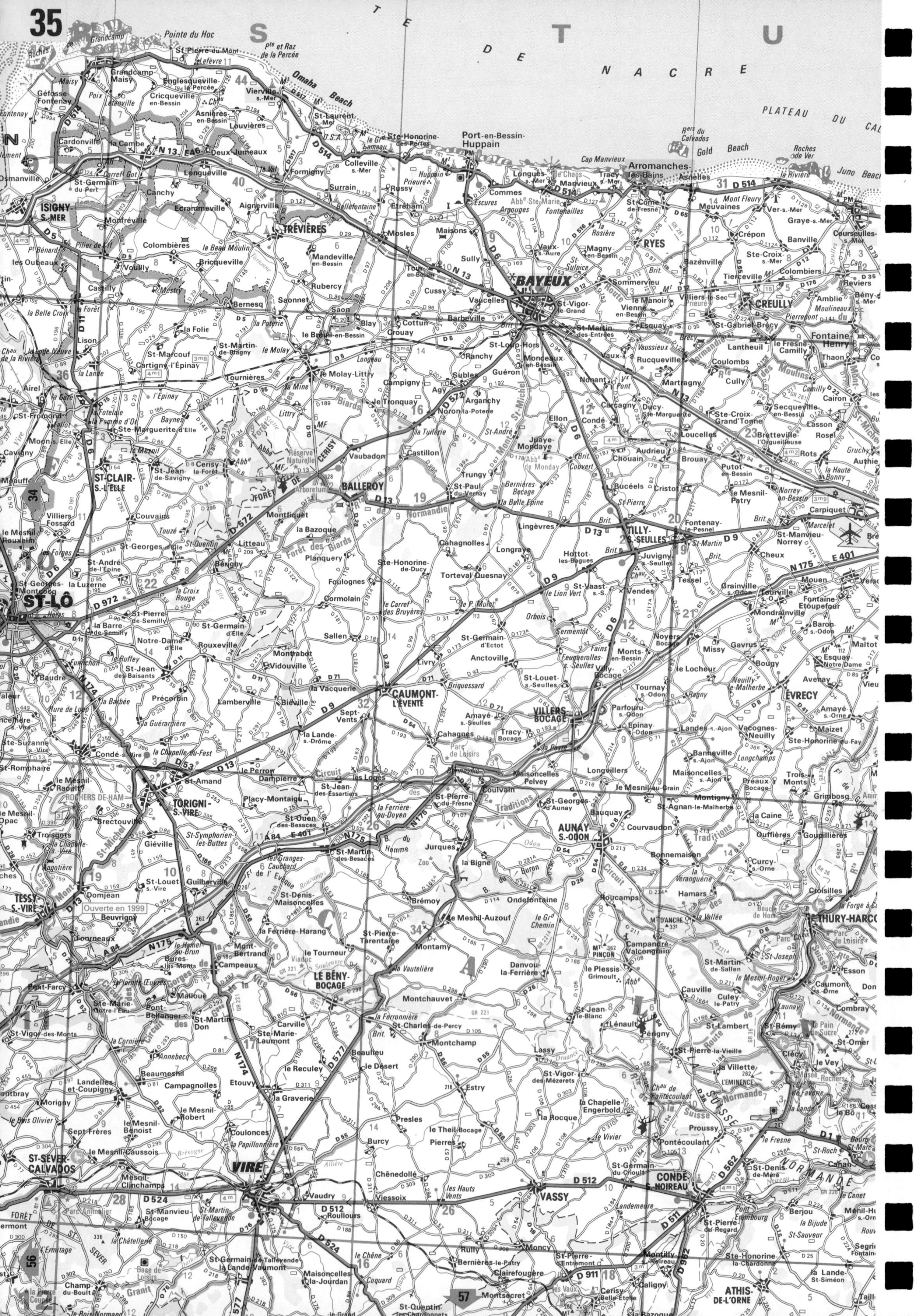
S
T
U
CÔTE DE NACRE
PLATEAU DU CALVADOS
Pointe du Hoc
Pte et Raz de la Percée
Omaha Beach
Gold Beach
Juno Beach
Cap Manvieux
Roches de Ver
Grandcamp-Maisy
St-Pierre-du-Mont
Englesqueville-la-Percée
Vierville-s.-Mer
Gefosse-Fontenay
Cricqueville-en-Bessin
Asnières-en-Bessin
Louvières
St-Laurent-s.-Mer
Ste-Honorine-des-Pertes
Port-en-Bessin-Huppain
Cardonville
la Cambe
Deux-Jumeaux
Colleville-s.-Mer
Formigny
Longueville
Osmanville
St-Germain-du-Pert
ISIGNY-S.-MER
Canchy
Ecrammeville
Aignerville
Surrain
Russy
Étréham
Commes
Escures
Longues-s.-Mer
Manvieux
Tracy-s.-Mer
Arromanches-les-Bains
Asnelles
St-Côme-de-Fresné
Meuvaines
Mont Fleury
Ver-s.-Mer
Graye-s.-Mer
Courseulles-s.-Mer
Monfréville
TRÉVIÈRES
Mosles
Maisons
Argouges
Fontenailles
la Rosière
RYES
Crépon
Banville
Colombières
le Beau Moulin
Mandeville-en-Bessin
Sully
Vaux-s.-Aure
Magny-en-Bessin
Ste-Croix-s.-Mer
les Oubeaux
Vouilly
Bricqueville
Tour-en-Bessin
BAYEUX
St-Sulpice
Sommervieu
Bazenville
Tierceville
Reviers
Castilly
Mestry
Rubercy
Cussy
Vaucelles
St-Vigor-le-Grand
le Manoir
Vienne-en-Bessin
Villiers-le-Sec
CREULLY
Amblie
Bény-s.-Mer
la Belle Croix
Bernesq
Saonnet
Saon
Barbeville
St-Martin-des-Entrées
Esquay-s.-S.
St-Gabriel-Brécy
Pierrepont
la Folie
le Breuil-en-Bessin
Blay
Cottun
Crouay
St-Loup-Hors
Fontaine-Henry
Lison
St-Marcouf
St-Martin-de-Blagny
le Molay
Ranchy
Vaussieux
Vaux-s.-S.
Rucqueville
Lantheuil
le Fresne-Camilly
Thaon
Cartigny-l'Épinay
le Molay-Littry
Monceaux-en-Bessin
Coulombs
Cully
Tournières
Campigny
Subles
Guéron
Nonant
Martragny
Airel
l'Épinay
la Mine
Agy
Argouges
Arganchy
Carcagny
Ducy-Ste-Marguerite
Ste-Croix-Grand'Tonne
Secqueville-en-Bessin
Cairon
St-Fromond
la Fotelaie
Baynes
le Tronquay
Noron-la-Poterie
Ellon
Condé-s.-S.
Loucelles
Bretteville-l'Orgueilleuse
Lasson
Rosel
Moon-s.-Elle
Ste-Marguerite-d'Elle
la Tuilerie
St-André
Juaye-Mondaye
Audrieu
Brouay
Cavigny
le Mesnil
Cerisy-la-Forêt
St-Jean-de-Savigny
Réserve Naturelle
FORÊT DE CERISY
Vaubadon
Castillon
Chouain
Rots
Authie
Putot-en-Bessin
la Haute Bonny
ST-CLAIR-S.-L'ELLE
Trungy
Bernières-Bocage
Bucéels
Cristot
BALLEROY
St-Paul-du-Vernay
la Belle Épine
St-Pierre
le Mesnil-Patry
Norrey-en-Bessin
Carpiquet
Villiers-Fossard
Couvains
Montfiquet
Lingèvres
TILLY-S.-SEULLES
Fontenay-le-Pesnel
St-Manvieu-Norrey
le Mesnil-Rouxelin
la Bazoque
Cahagnolles
Hottot-les-Bagues
St-Martin
les Forges
St-Georges-d'Elle
St-Quentin
Litteau
Planquery
Longraye
Juvigny-s.-Seulles
Cheux
St-André-de-l'Épine
Bérigny
Forêt des Biards
Ste-Honorine-de-Ducy
Torteval-Quesnay
Tessel
Grainville-s.-Odon
Tourville-s.-O.
Mouen
St-Georges-Montcocq
la Luzerne
Foulognes
St-Vaast-s.-S.
Vendes
Fontaine-Étoupefour
ST-LÔ
la Croix Rouge
Cormolain
le Carref des Bruyères
le P. Mulot
le Lion Vert
Mondrainville
St-Pierre-de-Semilly
la Barre-de-Semilly
St-Germain-d'Elle
Orbois
Sermentot
Baron-s.-Odon
Notre-Dame-d'Elle
Sallen
St-Germain-d'Ectot
Noyers-Bocage
Missy
Gavrus
Maltot
le Ruffey
Rouxeville
Montrabot
Vidouville
Anctoville
Feuguerolles-s.-Seulles
Fains
Monts-en-Bessin
Esquay-Notre-Dame
St-Jean-des-Baisants
Livry
Villy-Bocage
le Locheur
Bougy
Baudre
Précorbin
la Vacquerie
Briquessard
St-Louet-s.-Seulles
Tournay-s.-Odon
Neuilly-le-Malherbe
Avenay
ÉVRECY
la Barbée
Lamberville
Biéville
CAUMONT-L'ÉVENTÉ
la Guérardière
Sept-Vents
Amayé-s.-Seulles
VILLERS-BOCAGE
Parfouru-s.-Odon
Amayé-s.-Orne
Ste-Suzanne-s.-Vire
Condé-s.-Vire
la Lande-s.-Drôme
Cahagnes
Tracy-Bocage
Épinay-s.-Odon
Landes-s.-Ajon
Vacognes-Neuilly
Maizet
Ste-Honorine-du-Fay
la Chapelle-du-Fest
Parc de Loisirs
Banneville-s.-Ajon
Longchamps
St-Romphaire
le Perron
Dampierre
St-Amand
St-Jean-des-Essartiers
les Loges
Maisoncelles-Pelvey
Longvillers
Maisoncelles-s.-Ajon
Trois-Monts
le Mesnil-Raoult
ROCHERS DE HAM
TORIGNI-S.-VIRE
Placy-Montaigu
Coulvain
St-Pierre-du-Fresne
St-Georges-d'Aunay
le Mesnil-au-Grain
Montigny
Préaux-Bocage
Grimbosq
Brectouville
St-Ouen-des-Besaces
la Ferrière-au-Doyen
Bauquay
St-Agnan-le-Malherbe
la Caine
Troisgots
St-Symphorien-les-Buttes
AUNAY-S.-ODON
Courvaudon
Ouffières
Goupillières
Giéville
St-Martin-des-Besaces
Jurques
Bonnemaison
les Granges-Cauchard
la Bigne
Curcy-s.-Orne
St-Louet-s.-Vire
Guilberville
Roucamps
la Vérangueire
Hamars
TESSY-S.-VIRE
Domjean
Ouverte en 1999
St-Denis-Maisoncelles
Brémoy
Ondefontaine
Hucamps
Croisilles
Beuvrigny
le Mesnil-Auzouf
le Grd Chemin
la Vallée
THURY-HARCOURT
Fourneaux
la Ferrière-Harang
St-Pierre-Tarentaine
Campandré-Valcongrain
le Hamel-au-Brun
Bures-les-Monts
Mont-Bertrand
Campeaux
le Tourneur
Montamy
la Vautelière
Mt Pinçon
Danvou-la-Ferrière
le Plessis-Grimoult
St-Martin-de-Sallen
le Mesnil-Roger
St-Joseph
Esson
Pont-Farcy
LE BÉNY-BOCAGE
Cauville
Culey-le-Patry
Caumont-s.-Orne
Ste-Marie-Outre-l'Eau
Malloué
Montchauvet
Pont-Bellanger
St-Martin-Don
Carville
Ste-Marie-Laumont
la Ferronnière
St-Charles-de-Percy
Montchamp
St-Jean-le-Blanc
Lénault
St-Lambert
St-Rémy
Combray
le Pain de Sucre
St-Omer
St-Vigor-des-Monts
la Cornière
Pégny
Lassy
St-Pierre-la-Vieille
Clécy
le Vey
Annebecq
Beaulieu
le Désert
le Reculey
la Villette
L'ÉMINENCE
Beaumesnil
Landelles-et-Coupigny
Campagnolles
Etouvy
la Graverie
Estry
St-Vigor-des-Mézerets
Chau de Pontécoulant
SUISSE NORMANDE
Morigny
le Mesnil-Robert
la Chapelle-Engerbold
la Rocque
le Bois Olivier
Sept-Frères
le Mesnil-Benoist
Coulonces
la Papillonnière
Presles
le Theil-Bocage
Pierres
le Vivier
Proussy
Pontécoulant
Burcy
le Fresne
St-Roch
St-Marc
le Mesnil-Caussois
Brévogne
ST-SEVER-CALVADOS
VIRE
Chênedollé
St-Germain-du-Crioult
CONDÉ-S.-NOIREAU
St-Denis-de-Méré
Cahan
Mesnil-Clinchamps
Vaudry
Viessoix
les Hauts Vents
VASSY
St-Manvieu-Bocage
St-Martin-de-Tallevende
Roullours
Landemeure
Pont Erambourg
Berjou
la Bijude
St-Sauveur
FORÊT DE ST-SEVER
Parc Animalier
la Châtellerie
l'Ermitage
St-Pierre-du-Regard
Rully
Moncy
le Chêne
Bernières-le-Patry
St-Pierre-d'Entremont
Montilly-s.-Noireau
Ste-Honorine-la-Chardonne
St-Germain-de-Tallevende-la-Lande-Vaumont
Base de Loisirs
Maisoncelles-la-Jourdan
Clairefougère
Cerisy-Belle-Étoile
Caligny
la Lande-St-Siméon
Champ-du-Boult
Coquard
Montsecret
ATHIS-DE-L'ORNE
la Pierre Coupée
le Bois Normand
St-Quentin-les-Chardonnets
la Bazoque
57
56
34
36

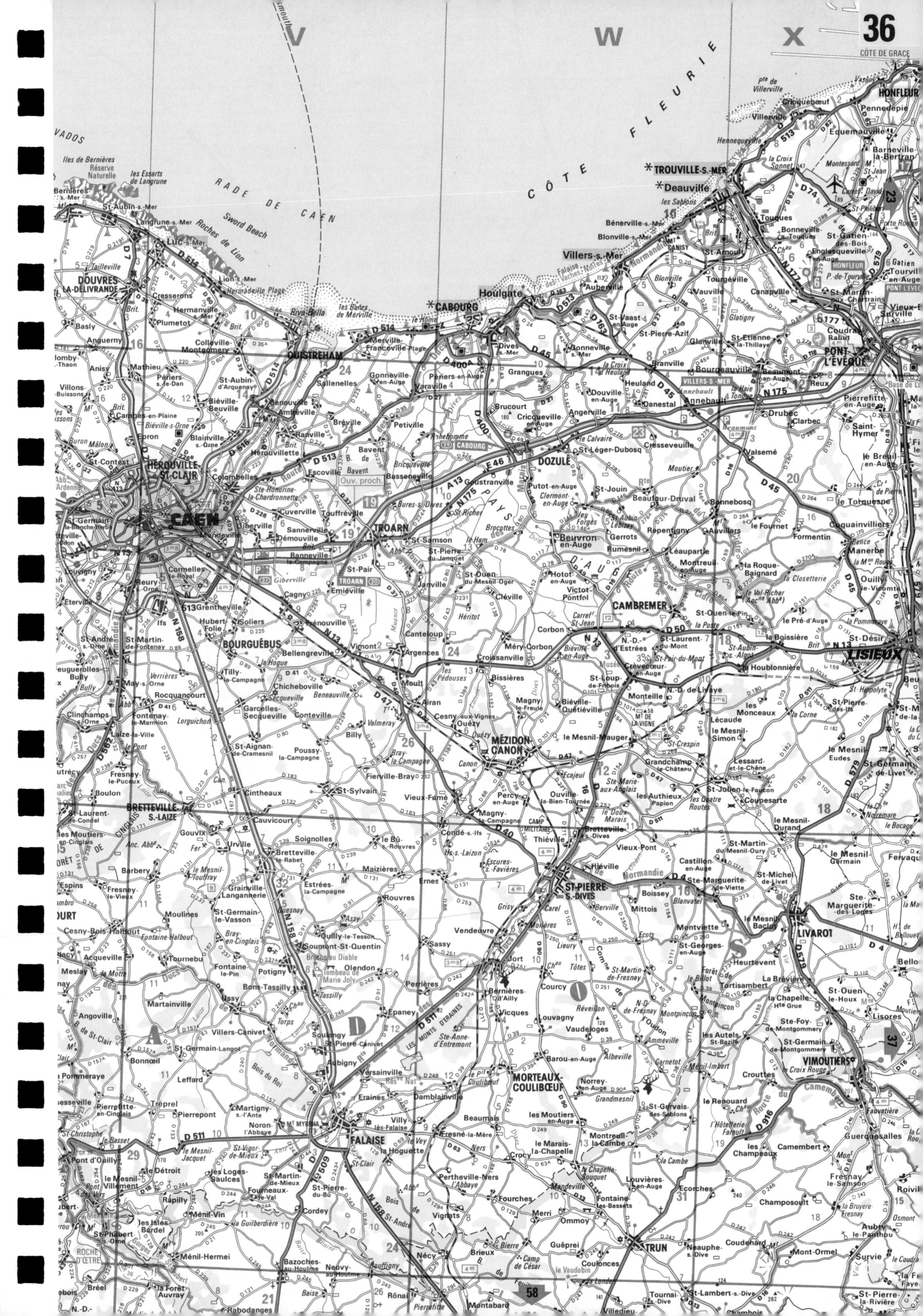
V
W
X
CÔTE DE GRACE
CÔTE FLEURIE
RADE DE CAEN
Sword Beach
Iles de Bernières
Réserve Naturelle
les Essarts de Langrune
Roches de Lion
HONFLEUR
Pennedepie
Equemauville
Cricquebœuf
Villerville
Hennequeville
TROUVILLE-S.-MER
Deauville
les Sablons
Bénerville-s.-Mer
Blonville-s.-Mer
Villers-s.-Mer
Houlgate
CABOURG
Dives s.-Mer
Touques
St-Arnoult
Tourgéville
Canapville
Bonneville-s.-Touques
St-Gatien-des-Bois
St-Vaast-en-Auge
St-Pierre-Azif
Auberville
Gonneville-s.-Mer
Branville
Glanville
St-Étienne-la-Thillaye
PONT-L'ÉVÊQUE
Beaumont-en-Auge
Bourgeauville
Annebault
Danestal
Heuland
Douville-en-Auge
Grangues
Périers-en-Auge
Varaville
Merville-Franceville-Plage
OUISTREHAM
Riva-Bella
Colleville-Montgomery
Hermanville-s.-Mer
Lion-s.-Mer
Luc-s.-Mer
Langrune-s.-Mer
St-Aubin-s.-Mer
Bernières-s.-Mer
DOUVRES-LA-DÉLIVRANDE
Tailleville
Basly
Anguerny
Anisy
Mathieu
Cresserons
Plumetot
Périers-s.-le-Dan
St-Aubin-d'Arquenay
Biéville-Beuville
Bénouville
Amfreville
Ranville
Sallenelles
Gonneville-en-Auge
Bréville
Petiville
Bavent
Brucourt
Cricqueville-en-Auge
Angerville
DOZULÉ
St-Léger-Dubosq
Cresseveuille
Valsemé
Drubec
Clarbec
Pierrefitte-en-Auge
Saint-Hymer
le Breuil-en-Auge
le Torquesne
Coquainvilliers
Formentin
Manerbe
Ouilly-le-Vicomte
Putot-en-Auge
Clermont-en-Auge
St-Jouin
Beaufour-Druval
Bonnebosq
Repentigny
Auvillars
Léaupartie
Beuvron-en-Auge
Gerrots
Rumesnil
Montreuil-en-Auge
la Roque-Baignard
HÉROUVILLE-ST-CLAIR
CAEN
Colombelles
Hérouvillette
Escoville
Basseneville
Goustranville
Cuverville
Touffréville
Sannerville
Démouville
Giberville
Mondeville
TROARN
St-Samson
St-Pierre-du-Jonquet
Banneville-la-Campagne
St-Pair
Émiéville
Janville
St-Ouen-du-Mesnil-Oger
Hotot-en-Auge
Victot-Pontfol
Cléville
CAMBREMER
St-Ouen-le-Pin
Cormelles-le-Royal
Fleury-s.-Orne
Louvigny
Ifs
Grentheville
Soliers
Hubert-Folie
Cagny
Frénouville
St-André-s.-Orne
St-Martin-de-Fontenay
BOURGUÉBUS
Bellengreville
Vimont
Argences
Canteloup
Moult
Croissanville
Méry-Corbon
Corbon
Bissières
St-Loup-de-Fribois
Crèvecœur-en-Auge
St-Laurent-du-Mont
St-Aubin-s.-Algot
la Houblonnière
LISIEUX
la Boissière
St-Désir
Tilly-la-Campagne
Chicheboville
Conteville
Airan
Cesny-aux-Vignes-Ouézy
Magny-le-Freule
Biéville-Quétiéville
le Mesnil-Mauger
Monteille
N.-D.-de-Livaye
Lécaude
les Monceaux
la Corne
St-Pierre-des-Ifs
May-s.-Orne
Rocquancourt
Garcelles-Secqueville
Fontenay-le-Marmion
Billy
Valmeray
MÉZIDON-CANON
le Mesnil-Simon
St-Crespin
Grandchamp-le-Château
Lessard-et-le-Chêne
le Mesnil-Eudes
St-Germain-de-Livet
Laize-la-Ville
St-Aignan-de-Cramesnil
Poussy-la-Campagne
Bray-la-Campagne
Fierville-Bray
Vieux-Fumé
Percy-en-Auge
Ouville-la-Bien-Tournée
Ste-Marie-aux-Anglais
les Authieux-Papion
St-Julien-le-Faucon
Coupesarte
Fresney-le-Puceux
Boulon
Cintheaux
St-Sylvain
BRETTEVILLE-S.-LAIZE
St-Laurent-de-Condel
Gouvix
Cauvicourt
Magny-la-Campagne
Condé-s.-Ifs
Bretteville-s.-Dives
Thiéville
Vieux-Pont
le Mesnil-Durand
Urville
Soignolles
le Bû-s.-Rouvres
Bretteville-le-Rabet
Maizières
Escures-s.-Favières
Hiéville
ST-PIERRE-S.-DIVES
Castillon-en-Auge
St-Martin-du-Mesnil-Oury
Ste-Marguerite-de-Viette
St-Michel-de-Livet
le Mesnil-Germain
Fervaques
Barbery
Fresney-le-Vieux
Grainville-Langannerie
Estrées-la-Campagne
Ernes
Rouvres
Boissey
Mittois
le Mesnil-Bacley
LIVAROT
Ste-Marguerite-des-Loges
Moulines
St-Germain-le-Vasson
Cesny-Bois-Halbout
Ouilly-le-Tesson
Soumont-St-Quentin
Sassy
Vendeuvre
Montviette
St-Georges-en-Auge
Acqueville
Tournebu
Fontaine-le-Pin
Potigny
Olendon
Perrières
Jort
Courcy
St-Martin-de-Fresnay
Heurtevent
Tortisambert
la Brévière
St-Ouen-le-Houx
Bons-Tassilly
Martainville
Ussy
Bernières-d'Ailly
Vicques
Louvagny
Vaudeloges
la Chapelle-Hte Grue
Ste-Foy-de-Montgommery
Lisores
Angoville
Villers-Canivet
St-Germain-Langot
Soulangy
St-Pierre-Canivet
Epaney
Ste-Anne-d'Entremont
Barou-en-Auge
Albeville
les Autels-St-Bazile
St-Germain-de-Montgommery
VIMOUTIERS
Bonnœil
Aubigny
Versainville
MORTEAUX-COULIBŒUF
Norrey-en-Auge
Grandmesnil
Crouttes
Leffard
Martigny-s.-l'Ante
Eraines
Damblainville
Villy-lez-Falaise
Beaumais
les Moutiers-en-Auge
St-Gervais-des-Sablons
le Renouard
Tréprel
Pierrepont
Noron-l'Abbaye
FALAISE
la Hoguette
Fresné-la-Mère
Montreuil-la-Cambe
Guerquesalles
Camembert
les Champeaux
Pierrefitte-en-Cinglais
le Mesnil-Jacquet
St-Vigor-de-Mieux
le Détroit
les Loges-Saulces
St-Martin-de-Mieux
Fourneaux-le-Val
St-Pierre-du-Bû
Pertheville-Ners
Crocy
le Marais-la-Chapelle
la Chapelle-Souquet
Louvières-en-Auge
Ecorches
Fresnay-le-Samson
Champosoult
Rapilly
Ménil-Vin
Cordey
Fourches
Vignats
Merri
Ommoy
Fontaine-les-Bassets
les Isles-Bardel
St-Philbert-s.-Orne
Ménil-Hermei
Bazoches-au-Houlme
Neuvy-au-Houlme
Nécy
Brieux
Guêprei
TRUN
Neauphe-s.-Dive
Coudehard
Mont-Ormel
Survie
Aubry-le-Panthou
Bréel
la Forêt-Auvray
Rabodanges
Rônai
Montabard
Tournai-s.-Dive
St-Lambert-s.-Dive
St-Pierre-la-Rivière
Vieux-Fumé
37
58
A
D
O
S

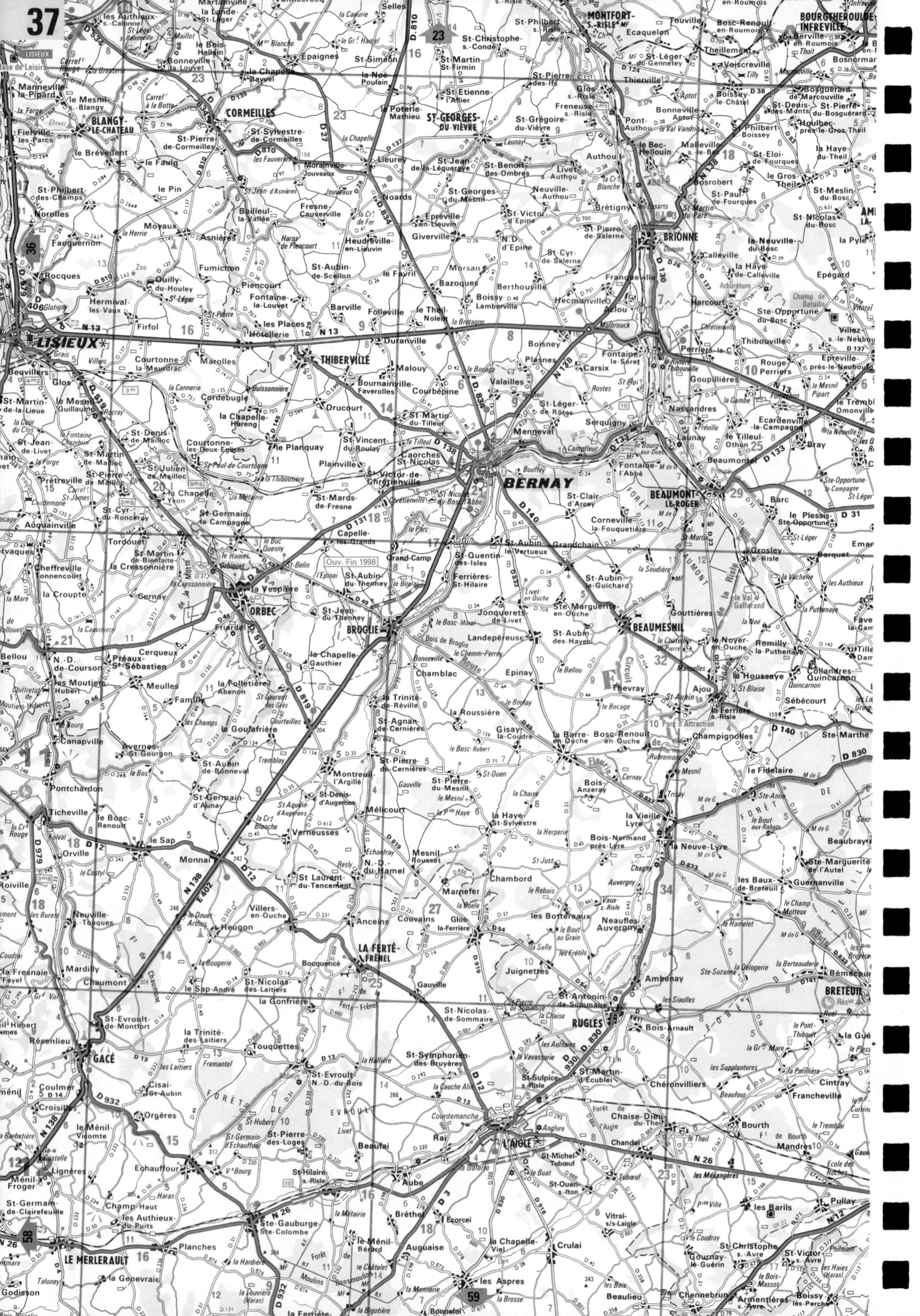

LISIEUX
Manneville-la-Pipard
le Mesnil-s.-Blangy
BLANGY-LE-CHATEAU
Fierville-les-Parcs
le Brévedent
le Faulq
St-Philbert-des-Champs
Norolles
Moyaux
Fauguernon
Rocques
Hermival-les-Vaux
Firfol
CORMEILLES
St-Sylvestre-de-Cormeilles
St-Pierre-de-Cormeilles
le Bois-Hellain
Bonneville-la-Louvet
la Chapelle-Bayvel
Epaignes
St-Siméon
la Noë-Poulain
la Poterie-Mathieu
Morainville-Jouveaux
Lieurey
Noards
Fresne-Cauverville
le Pin
Bailleul-la-Vallée
Asnières
Fumichon
Piencourt
Fontaine-la-Louvet
les Places
Hôtellerie
Barville
Folleville
le Theil-Nolent
Duranville
THIBERVILLE
Marolles
Courtonne-la-Meurdrac
Cordebugle
la Chapelle-Hareng
le Planquay
Courtonne-les-Deux-Eglises
St-Martin-de-Mailloc
St-Pierre-de-Mailloc
St-Julien-de-Mailloc
St-Denis-de-Mailloc
St-Jean-de-Livet
Prêtreville
St-Cyr-du-Ronceray
Auquainville
Tordouet
Cheffreville-Tonnencourt
la Croupte
la Cressonnière
St-Martin-de-Bienfaite
la Vespière
ORBEC
Cernay
Friardel
Cerqueux
Préaux-St-Sébastien
N.-D.-de-Courson
les Moutiers-Hubert
Meulles
la Folletière-Abenon
Familly
la Goulafrière
Avernes-St-Gourgon
St-Aubin-de-Bonneval
St-Germain-d'Aunay
Canapville
Pontchardon
Ticheville
le Bosc-Renoult
le Sap
Orville
Monnai
Villers-en-Ouche
Heugon
Neuville-sur-Touques
Mardilly
Chaumont
le Sap-André
St-Nicolas-des-Laitiers
la Gonfrière
St-Evroult-de-Montfort
Résenlieu
GACÉ
la Trinité-des-Laitiers
Touquettes
Cisai-St-Aubin
Coulmer
Croisilles
le Ménil-Vicomte
Orgères
St-Evroult-N.-D.-du-Bois
St-Pierre-des-Loges
Echauffour
Lignères
Ménil-Froger
St-Germain-de-Clairefeuille
Champ-Haut
les Authieux-du-Puits
Ste-Gauburge-Ste-Colombe
Planches
LE MERLERAULT
la Genevraie
Godisson
Ménil-Bérard
Bréthel
Auguaise
St-Hilaire-s.-Risle
Aube
Beaufai
Rai
L'AIGLE
St-Michel-Tubœuf
St-Ouen-s.-Iton
la Chapelle-Viel
Crulai
les Aspres
Vitrai-s/s-Laigle
Beaulieu
Chennebrun
Gournay-le-Guérin
St-Christophe-s.-Avre
St-Victor-s.-Avre
Armentières-s.-Avre
Boissy-lès-Perche
les Barils
Pullay
Bourth
Mandres
Chandai
Chaise-Dieu-du-Theil
Francheville
Cintray
Chéronvilliers
St-Sulpice-s.-Risle
St-Martin-d'Ecublei
St-Symphorien-des-Bruyères
RUGLES
Bois-Arnault
St-Antonin-de-Sommaire
St-Nicolas-de-Sommaire
Juignettes
Ambenay
Gauville
LA FERTÉ-FRÊNEL
Bocquencé
Anceins
Couvains
Glos-la-Ferrière
St Laurent-du-Tencement
Marnefer
Chambord
les Bottereaux
Neaufles-Auvergny
Mélicourt
Verneusses
Montreuil-l'Argillé
St-Denis-d'Augerons
St-Pierre-de-Cernières
St-Agnan-de-Cernières
la Trinité-de-Réville
la Chapelle-Gauthier
Chamblac
BROGLIE
St-Jean-du-Thenney
St-Aubin-du-Thenney
Capelle-les-Grands
Grand-Camp
St-Mards-de-Fresne
St-Victor-de-Chrétienville
Plainville
St-Vincent-du-Boulay
Drucourt
Bournainville-Faverolles
Malouy
Courbépine
St-Martin-du-Tilleul
BERNAY
Menneval
Valailles
St-Léger-de-Rôtes
Serquigny
Plasnes
Carsix
Fontaine-la-Soret
Boisney
St-Clair-d'Arcey
Corneville-la-Fouquetière
Grandchain
St-Aubin-le-Vertueux
St-Quentin-des-Isles
Ferrières-St-Hilaire
Jonquerets-de-Livet
Ste-Marguerite-en-Ouche
St-Aubin-le-Guichard
St-Aubin-des-Hayes
Landepéreuse
Epinay
la Roussière
Gisay-la-Coudre
la Barre-en-Ouche
Bosc-Renoult-en-Ouche
Thevray
BEAUMESNIL
Gouttières
Ajou
la Ferrière-s.-Risle
Champignolles
St-Pierre-du-Mesnil
Bois-Anzeray
la Haye-St-Sylvestre
la Vieille-Lyre
Bois-Normand-près-Lyre
la Neuve-Lyre
les Baux-de-Breteuil
Guernanville
Ste-Marguerite-de-l'Autel
Beaubray
le Fidelaire
Ste-Marthe
BRETEUIL
Bémécourt
Sébécourt
Collandres-Quincarnon
la Houssaye
Romilly-la-Puthenaye
le Noyer-en-Ouche
Grosley-s.-Risle
Barquet
le Plessis-Ste-Opportune
Barc
BEAUMONT-LE-ROGER
Fontaine-l'Abbé
Beaumontel
le Tilleul-Othon
Launay
Nassandres
Ecardenville-la-Campagne
Bray
Goupillières
Perriers-la-C.
Thibouville
Rouge-Perriers
Epreville-près-le-Neubourg
Ste-Opportune-du-Bosc
Villez-s.-le-Neubourg
Harcourt
Calleville
la Haye-de-Calleville
la Neuville-du-Bosc
Epégard
BRIONNE
Aclou
Hecmanville
Franqueville
Berthouville
Boissy-Lambeville
Bazoques
Morsan
le Favril
St-Aubin-de-Scellon
Heudreville-en-Lieuvin
Giverville
Epreville-en-Lieuvin
N.-D.-d'Epine
St-Victor-d'Epine
St-Cyr-de-Salerne
St-Pierre-de-Salerne
Neuville-s.-Authou
Livet-s.-Authou
Brétigny
St-Georges-du-Mesnil
St-Benoît-des-Ombres
St-Jean-de-la-Léquerave
ST-GEORGES-DU-VIÈVRE
St-Grégoire-du-Vièvre
St-Etienne-l'Allier
St-Martin-St-Firmin
St-Christophe-s.-Condé
St-Philbert-s.-Risle
MONTFORT-S.-RISLE
Ecaquelon
St-Pierre-des-Ifs
Glos-s.-Risle
Freneuse-s.-Risle
Pont-Authou
Authou
le Bec-Hellouin
Malleville-s.-le-Bec
St-Paul-de-Fourques
St-Martin-du-Parc
Bosrobert
St-Eloi-de-Fourques
le Gros-Theil
St-Meslin-du-Bosc
St-Nicolas-du-Bosc
St-Philbert-s.-Boissey
Boissey-le-Châtel
Bonneville-Aptot
Thierville
Voiscreville
St-Léger-du-Gennetey
Touville
Bosc-Renoult-en-Roumois
Thuillement
BOURGTHEROULDE-INFREVILLE
Berville-en-Roumois
Bosnormand
Bosguérard-de-Marcouville
St-Denis-des-Monts
St-Pierre-du-Bosguérard
Houlbec-près-le-Gros-Theil
la Haye-du-Theil
Selles
Martainville
Vannecrocq
les Authieux-s.-Calonne
Ouv. Fin 1998

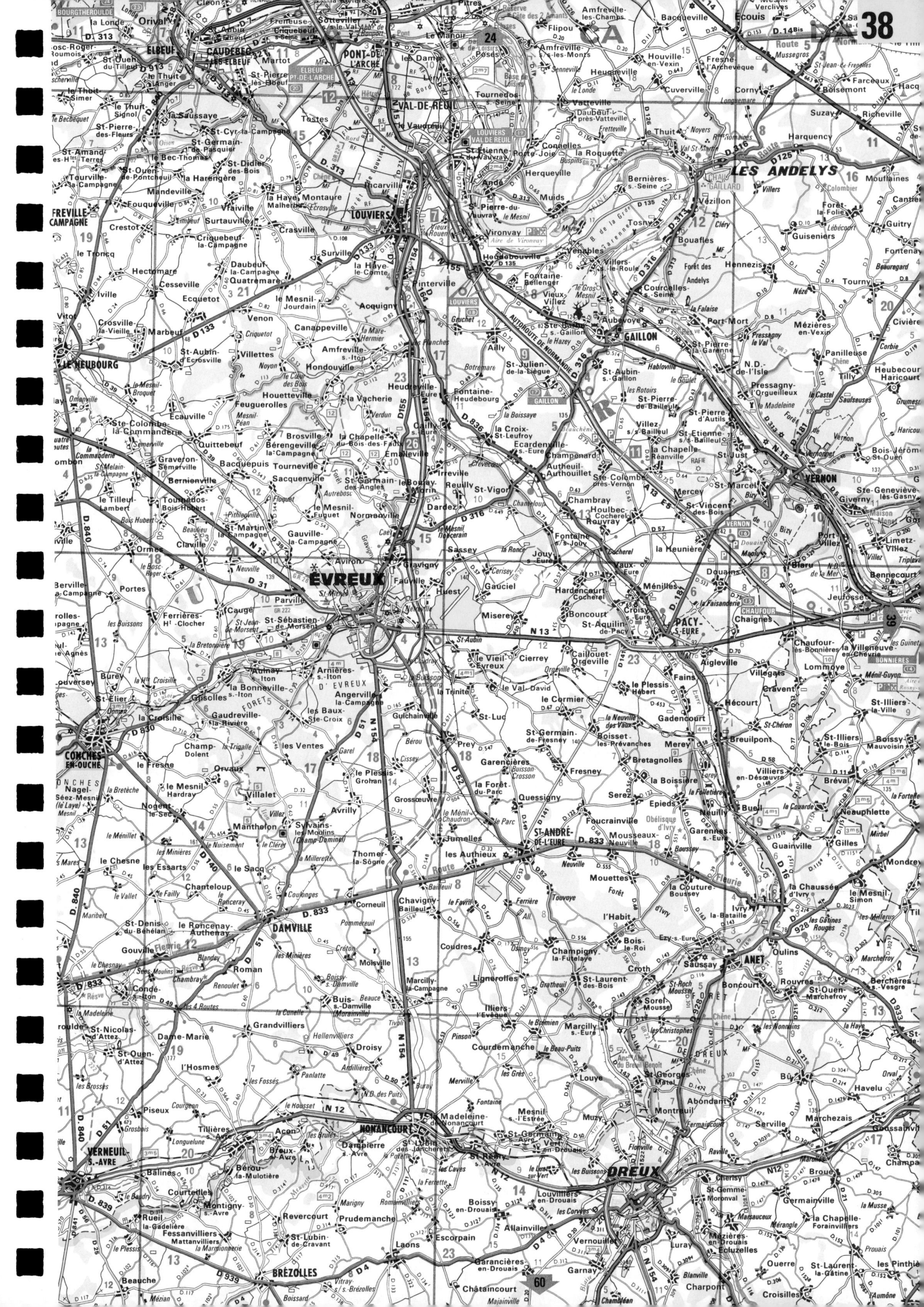
ELBEUF
CAUDEBEC-LES-ELBEUF
PONT-DE-L'ARCHE
VAL-DE-REUIL
LOUVIERS
LES ANDELYS
GAILLON
VERNON
LE NEUBOURG
ÉVREUX
PACY-S-EURE
CONCHES-EN-OUCHE
DAMVILLE
ST-ANDRÉ-DE-L'EURE
ANET
NONANCOURT
VERNEUIL-S.-AVRE
BRÉZOLLES
DREUX
AUTOROUTE DE NORMANDIE
Orival
Martot
Tostes
le Vaudreuil
Incarville
Acquigny
Pinterville
Heudebouville
Vironnay
Aire de Vironvay
Venables
Muids
Andé
Herqueville
Connelles
Porte-Joie
Tournedos-s.-Seine
Poses
Amfreville-sous-les-Monts
Flipou
Pîtres
Le Manoir
les Damps
Écouis
Bacqueville
Houville-en-Vexin
Fresne-l'Archevêque
Heuqueville
Cuverville
Corny
Boisemont
Farceaux
Suzay
Richeville
Harquency
Vatteville
Daubeuf-près-Vatteville
la Roquette
le Thuit
Bernières-s.-Seine
Tosny
Vézillon
Bouafles
Courcelles-s.-Seine
Hennezis
Tourny
Guiseniers
Forêt-la-Folie
Mouflaines
Guitry
Aubevoye
Port-Mort
Pressagny-l'Orgueilleux
Mézières-en-Vexin
Panilleuse
N.D.-de-l'Isle
Tilly
Heubecourt-Haricourt
St-Pierre-la-Garenne
St-Aubin-s.-Gaillon
St-Pierre-de-Bailleul
Villez-s/s-Bailleul
la Chapelle-Réanville
St-Just
St-Marcel
Ste-Geneviève-lès-Gasny
Giverny
Bois-Jérôme-St-Ouen
St-Vincent-des-Bois
Mercey
Chambray
Houlbec-Cocherel
Rouvray
Ste-Colombe-près-Vernon
Champenard
Autheuil-Authouillet
Ecardenville-s.-Eure
la Croix-St-Leufroy
St-Julien-de-la-Liègue
Aïlly
Fontaine-Heudebourg
Heudreville-s.-Eure
Cailly-s.-Eure
Émalleville
Irreville
Reuilly
St-Vigor
Dardez
Normanville
Gravigny
Fauville
Huest
Gauciel
Sassey
Jouy-s.-Eure
Fontaine-s/s-Jouy
Hardencourt-Cocherel
Ménilles
Douains
Boncourt
St-Aquilin-de-Pacy
Chaignes
Chaufour-lès-Bonnières
Miserey
Cierrey
le Vieil-Évreux
Caillouet-Orgeville
Aigleville
Fains
le Plessis-Hébert
Villegats
Lommoye
Hécourt
Gadencourt
le Cormier
la Trinité
St-Luc
Prey
St-Germain-de-Fresney
Fresney
Boisset-les-Prévanches
Merey
Breuilpont
Bretagnolles
la Boissière
Garencières
la Forêt-du-Parc
Quessigny
Serez
Epieds
Neuilly
Bueil
Villiers-en-Désœuvre
Bréval
Neauphlette
Foucrainville
Mousseaux-Neuville
Garennes-s.-Eure
Guainville
Gilles
Mouettes
la Couture-Boussey
Ivry-la-Bataille
la Chaussée-d'Ivry
l'Habit
Bois-le-Roi
Ezy-s.-Eure
Saussay
Oulins
Champigny-la-Futelaye
Croth
St-Laurent-des-Bois
Sorel-Moussel
Boncourt
Rouvres
St-Ouen-Marchefroy
Marcilly-s.-Eure
Louye
St-Georges-Motel
Abondant
Montreuil
Bû
Havelu
Marchezais
Serville
Broué
Germainville
la Chapelle-Forainvilliers
Cherisy
Ste-Gemme-Moronval
Mézières-en-Drouais
Écluzelles
Luray
Ouerre
St-Laurent-la-Gâtine
Charpont
Croisilles
Vernouillet
Garnay
Garancières-en-Drouais
Châtaincourt
Allainville
Louvilliers-en-Drouais
Boissy-en-Drouais
Escorpain
Laons
Prudemanche
Revercourt
St-Lubin-de-Cravant
Fessanvilliers-Mattanvilliers
Beauche
Rueil-la-Gadelière
Montigny-s.-Avre
Courteilles
Balines
Bérou-la-Mulotière
Breux-s.-Avre
Acon
Tillières
Piseux
Dampierre-s.-Avre
St-Lubin-des-Joncherets
St-Rémy-s.-Avre
Vert-en-Drouais
St-Germain-s.-Avre
Muzy
Mesnil-s.-l'Estrée
la Madeleine-de-Nonancourt
Droisy
Grandvilliers
Dame-Marie
St-Nicolas-d'Attez
St-Ouen-d'Attez
l'Hosmes
Courdemanche
Illiers-l'Évêque
Lignerolles
Coudres
Marcilly-la-Campagne
Buis-s.-Damville
Moisville
Roman
Condé-s.-Iton
Gouville
St-Denis-du-Béhélan
le Roncenay-Authenay
Corneuil
Chavigny-Bailleul
les Authieux
Jumelles
Thomer-la-Sôgne
Sylvains-les-Moulins
Grossœuvre
Avrilly
le Plessis-Grohan
Mantheion
Villalet
Orvaux
Nogent-le-Sec
le Mesnil-Hardray
Champ-Dolent
le Fresne
Chanteloup
le Sacq
les Essarts
le Chesne
Nagel-Séez-Mesnil
les Ventes
Angerville-la-Campagne
Arnières-s.-Iton
les Baux-Ste-Croix
Guichainville
la Bonneville-s.-Iton
Gaudreville-la-Rivière
Aulnay-s.-Iton
Glisolles
la Croisille
St-Élier
Burey
Louversey
Ferrières-Ht-Clocher
St-Sébastien-de-Morsent
Cauge
Parville
Portes
Berville-la-Campagne
Ormes
Claville
St-Martin-la-Campagne
Gauville-la-Campagne
Aviron
le Mesnil-Fuguet
Tourneville
Sacquenville
St-Germain-des-Angles
le Boulay-Morin
Tournedos-Bois-Hubert
le Tilleul-Lambert
Bernienville
Graveron-Sémerville
Bacquepuis
Brosville
Bérengeville-la-Campagne
la Chapelle-du-Bois-des-Faulx
Quittebeuf
Ste-Colombe-la-Commanderie
Ecauville
Feuguerolles
Houetteville
la Vacherie
Hondouville
Amfreville-s.-Iton
Canappeville
Villettes
St-Aubin-d'Ecrosville
Crosville-la-Vieille
Marbeuf
Venon
le Mesnil-Jourdain
Ecquetot
Iville
Cesseville
Quatremare
Daubeuf-la-Campagne
Hectomare
le Troncq
Crestot
Criquebeuf-la-Campagne
Surtauville
Crasville
Surville
la Haye-le-Comte
la Haye-Malherbe
Montaure
Vraiville
Fouqueville
Mandeville
la Harengère
Tourville-la-Campagne
St-Ouen-de-Pontcheuil
St-Didier-des-Bois
le Bec-Thomas
St-Amand-des-Hautes-Terres
St-Germain-de-Pasquier
St-Cyr-la-Campagne
la Saussaye
St-Pierre-des-Fleurs
le Thuit-Signol
le Thuit-Simer
le Thuit-Anger
St-Pierre-lès-Elbeuf
St-Ouen-du-Tilleul
la Londe
Criquebeuf-s.-Seine
Freneuse
Sotteville-s/s-le-Val
Cléon
Amfreville-les-Champs
Fréville-Campagne

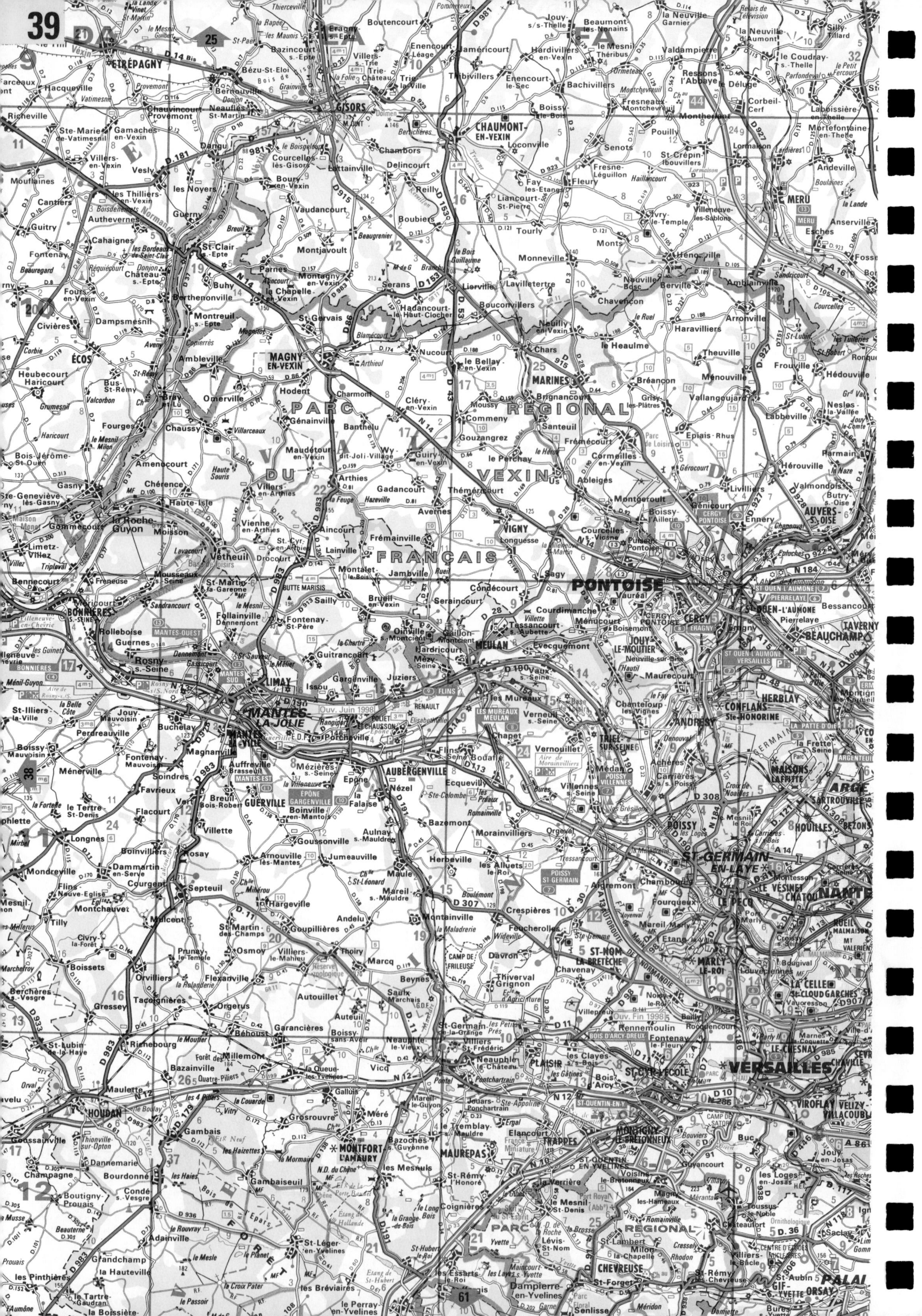

ÉTRÉPAGNY
GISORS
CHAUMONT-EN-VEXIN
MERU
MAGNY-EN-VEXIN
MARINES
PARC
RÉGIONAL
DU
VEXIN
FRANÇAIS
AUVERS-S.-OISE
PONTOISE
CERGY
TAVERNY
BEAUCHAMP
MEULAN
MANTES-LA-JOLIE
LIMAY
BONNIÈRES
HERBLAY
CONFLANS-Ste-HONORINE
ANDRESY
TRIEL-SUR-SEINE
POISSY
MAISONS-LAFFITTE
SARTROUVILLE
HOUILLES
ST-GERMAIN-EN-LAYE
LE VÉSINET
CHATOU
LE PECQ
GUERVILLE
AUBERGENVILLE
ST-NOM-LA-BRETÈCHE
MARLY-LE-ROI
LA CELLE-ST-CLOUD
GARCHES
LE CHESNAY
VERSAILLES
PLAISIR
ST-CYR-L'ÉCOLE
TRAPPES
MONTIGNY-LE-BRETONNEUX
VIROFLAY
VÉLIZY-VILLACOUBLAY
HOUDAN
MONTFORT-L'AMAURY
MAUREPAS
CHEVREUSE
GIF-S.-YVETTE
ORSAY
FORÊT
PARC
RÉGIONAL

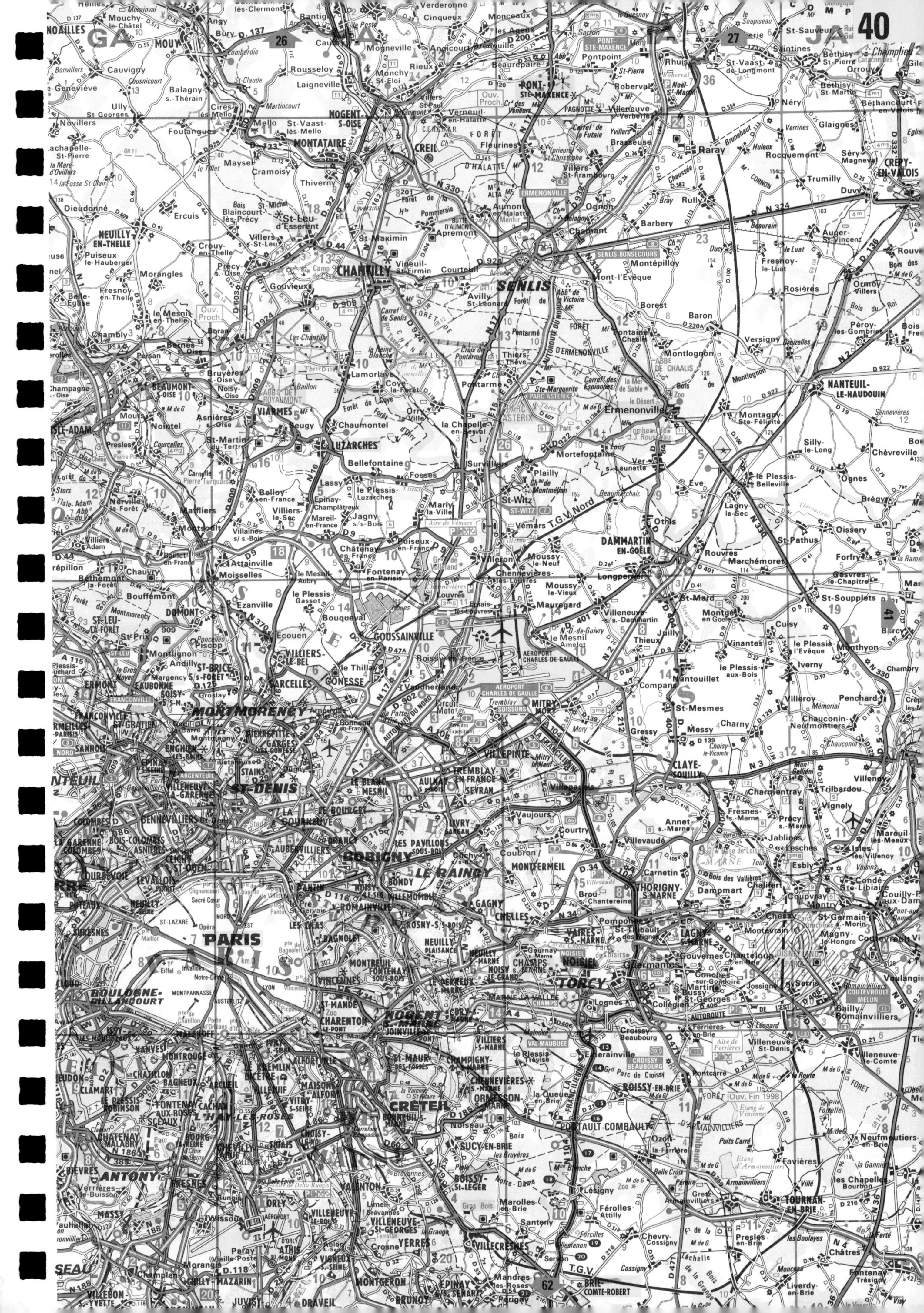
26
27
41
62
NOAILLES
MOUY
PONT-STE-MAXENCE
NOGENT-S-OISE
MONTATAIRE
CREIL
CHANTILLY
SENLIS
St-Leu-d'Esserent
Crépy-en-Valois
NEUILLY-EN-THELLE
BEAUMONT-S-OISE
VIARMES
LUZARCHES
Ermenonville
NANTEUIL-LE-HAUDOUIN
DAMMARTIN-EN-GOËLE
AÉROPORT CHARLES-DE-GAULLE
GOUSSAINVILLE
SARCELLES
GONESSE
VILLIERS-LE-BEL
DOMONT
MONTMORENCY
ST-DENIS
VILLEPINTE
TREMBLAY-EN-FRANCE
AULNAY-S-BOIS
SEVRAN
MITRY-MORY
CLAYE-SOUILLY
BOBIGNY
LE RAINCY
MONTFERMEIL
CHELLES
PARIS
BOULOGNE-BILLANCOURT
VINCENNES
NOGENT-S-MARNE
TORCY
LAGNY-S-MARNE
CRÉTEIL
SUCY-EN-BRIE
BOISSY-ST-LÉGER
ANTONY
MASSY
ORLY
VILLENEUVE-ST-GEORGES
YERRES
MONTGERON
PONTAULT-COMBAULT
TOURNAN-EN-BRIE
BRIE-COMTE-ROBERT
JUVISY
ST-DENIS
T.G.V. Nord
PARC ASTERIX
FORÊT D'ERMENONVILLE

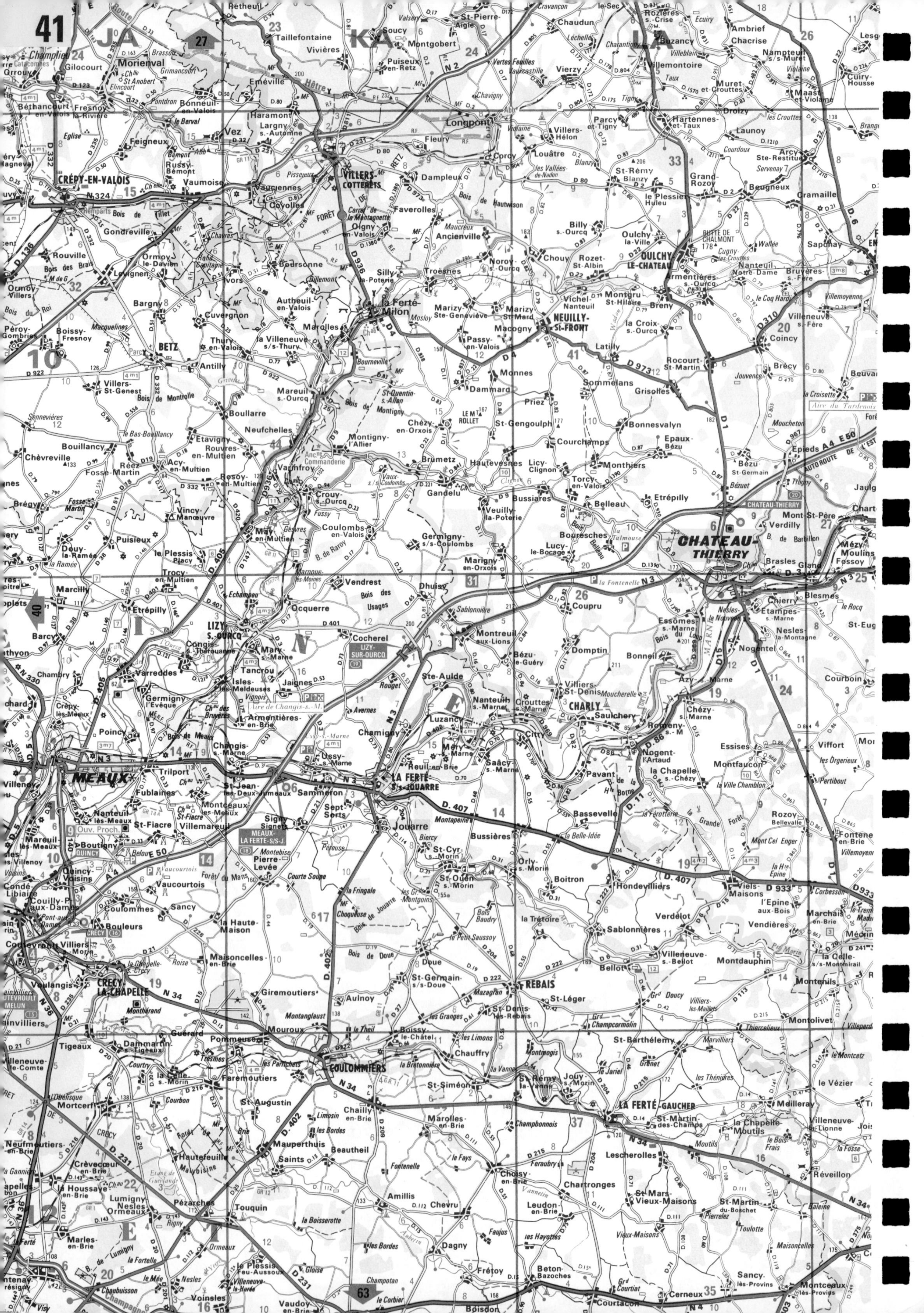
JA
KA
LA
27
Retheuil
Taillefontaine
Vivières
Soucy
Montgobert
Puiseux-en-Retz
St-Pierre-Aigle
Cravançon
Chaudun
Rozières-s.-Crise
Buzancy
Ecuiry
Ambrief
Chacrise
Nampteuil-s/s-Muret
Cuiry-Housse
Champlieu
Gilocourt
Morienval
Orrouy
Eméville
Vierzy
Villemontoire
Muret-et-Crouttes
Maast-et-Violaine
Béthancourt-en-Valois
Fresnoy-la-Rivière
Bonneuil-en-Valois
Haramont
Largny-s.-Automne
Longpont
Parcy-et-Tigny
Hartennes-et-Taux
Droizy
Feigneux
Vez
Fleury
Villers-Hélon
Launoy
Corcy
Louâtre
Arcy-Ste-Restitue
Russy-Bémont
St-Rémy-Blanzy
Grand-Rozoy
CRÉPY-EN-VALOIS
Vaumoise
Vauciennes
VILLERS-COTTERÊTS
Dampleux
Beugneux
Coyolles
le Plessier-Huleu
Cramaille
Faverolles
Gondreville
Ancienville
Billy-s.-Ourcq
Oulchy-la-Ville
OULCHY-LE-CHÂTEAU
Rouville
Ormoy-le-Davien
Oigny-en-Valois
Noroy-s.-Ourcq
Chouy
Rozet-St-Albin
Saponay
Levignen
Boursonne
Troësnes
Silly-la-Poterie
Armentières-s.-Ourcq
Nanteuil-Notre-Dame
Bruyères-s.-Fère
Ivors
Autheuil-en-Valois
LA FERTÉ-MILON
Marizy-Ste-Geneviève
Marizy-St-Mard
Vichel-Nanteuil
Montgru-St-Hilaire
Breny
Bargny
Cuvergnon
Marolles
NEUILLY-ST-FRONT
Macogny
La Croix-s.-Ourcq
Villeneuve-s.-Fère
Péroy-les-Gombries
Boissy-Fresnoy
BETZ
Thury-en-Valois
la Villeneuve-s/s-Thury
Passy-en-Valois
Latilly
Coincy
Rocourt-St-Martin
Brécy
Antilly
Villers-St-Genest
Mareuil-s.-Ourcq
Monnes
Dammard
Sommelans
Grisolles
Beuvardes
Boullarre
Neufchelles
Chézy-en-Orxois
Priez
St-Gengoulph
Bonnesvalyn
Sennevières
Etavigny
Montigny-l'Allier
Courchamps
Epaux-Bézu
Bouillancy
Chèvreville
Acy-en-Multien
Rouvres-en-Multien
Brumetz
Hautevesnes
Licy-Clignon
Monthiers
Bézu-St-Germain
Epieds
Rosoy-en-Multien
Varinfroy
Gandelu
Torcy-en-Valois
Fosse-Martin
Crouy-s.-Ourcq
Bussiares
Belleau
Etrépilly
Bréguy
Vincy-Manœuvre
Coulombs-en-Valois
Veuilly-la-Poterie
Verdilly
Mont-St-Père
May-en-Multien
Germigny-s/s-Coulombs
Bouresches
CHÂTEAU-THIERRY
Douy-la-Ramée
Puisieux
le Plessis-Placy
Lucy-le-Bocage
Marigny-en-Orxois
Brasles
Mézy-Moulins
Trocy-en-Multien
Vendrest
Dhuisy
Coupru
Fossoy
Marcilly
Etrépilly
LIZY-S.-OURCQ
Ocquerre
Chierry
Etampes-s.-Marne
Blesmes
Barcy
Cocherel
Montreuil-aux-Lions
Essômes-s.-Marne
Nesles-la-Montagne
Congis-s.-Thérouanne
Mary-s.-Marne
Domptin
Bonneil
Nogentel
Chambry
Varreddes
Tancrou
Jaignes
Bézu-le-Guéry
Courboin
Isles-lès-Meldeuses
Ste-Aulde
Villiers-St-Denis
Azy-s.-Marne
Germigny-l'Evêque
Armentières-en-Brie
Nanteuil-s.-Marne
Crouttes-s.-Marne
CHARLY
Saulchery
Chézy-s.-Marne
Crépy-lès-Meaux
Luzancy
Romeny-s.-M
Poincy
Chamigny
Citry
Essises
Viffort
Changis-s.-Marne
Ussy-s.-Marne
Méry-s.-Marne
Saâcy-s.-Marne
Nogent-l'Artaud
Montfaucon
MEAUX
Trilport
LA FERTÉ-S.-JOUARRE
Reuil-en-Brie
Pavant
la Chapelle-s.-Chézy
St-Jean-les-Deux-Jumeaux
Sammeron
Fublaines
Montceaux-lès-Meaux
Sept-Sorts
Bassevelle
Nanteuil-lès-Meaux
St-Fiacre
Villemareuil
Signy-Signets
Jouarre
Bussières
Rozoy-Bellevalle
Mareuil-lès-Meaux
Boutigny
Pierre-Levée
St-Cyr-s.-Morin
Orly-s.-Morin
Fontenelle-en-Brie
Quincy-Voisins
Vaucourtois
St-Ouen-s.-Morin
Boitron
Hondevilliers
Viels-Maisons
Condé-Sainte-Libiaire
Couilly-Pont-aux-Dames
Coulommes
Sancy
l'Epine-aux-Bois
Marchais-en-Brie
Bouleurs
la Haute-Maison
la Trétoire
Sablonnières
Verdelot
Vendières
Coupvray
Villiers-s.-Morin
Maisoncelles-en-Brie
Doue
Villeneuve-s.-Bellot
Montdauphin
la Celle-s/s-Montmirail
Voulangis
CRÉCY-LA-CHAPELLE
St-Germain-s/s-Doue
REBAIS
Bellot
Montenils
Giremoutiers
Aulnoy
St-Denis-lès-Rebais
St-Léger
Montolivet
Guérard
Pommeuse
Mouroux
Boissy-le-Châtel
Tigeaux
Dammartin-s.-Tigeaux
St-Barthélemy
COULOMMIERS
Chauffry
Faremoutiers
la Celle-s.-Morin
St-Siméon
St-Rémy-la-Vanne
Jouy-s.-Morin
le Vézier
Mortcerf
St-Augustin
LA FERTÉ-GAUCHER
Meilleray
Chailly-en-Brie
Marolles-en-Brie
St-Martin-des-Champs
la Chapelle-Moutils
Villeneuve-la-Lionne
Neufmoutiers-en-Brie
Hautefeuille
Mauperthuis
Beautheil
Lescherolles
Crèvecœur-en-Brie
Saints
Choisy-en-Brie
Réveillon
la Houssaye-en-Brie
Chartronges
Lumigny-Nesles-Ormeaux
Pézarches
Amillis
St-Mars-Vieux-Maisons
St-Martin-du-Boschet
Touquin
Chevru
Leudon-en-Brie
Marles-en-Brie
Dagny
le Plessis-Feu-Aussoux
Frétoy
Beton-Bazoches
Sancy-lès-Provins
Montceaux-lès-Provins
Voinsles
Vaudoy-en-Brie
Courtacon
Cerneux
Boisdon
63

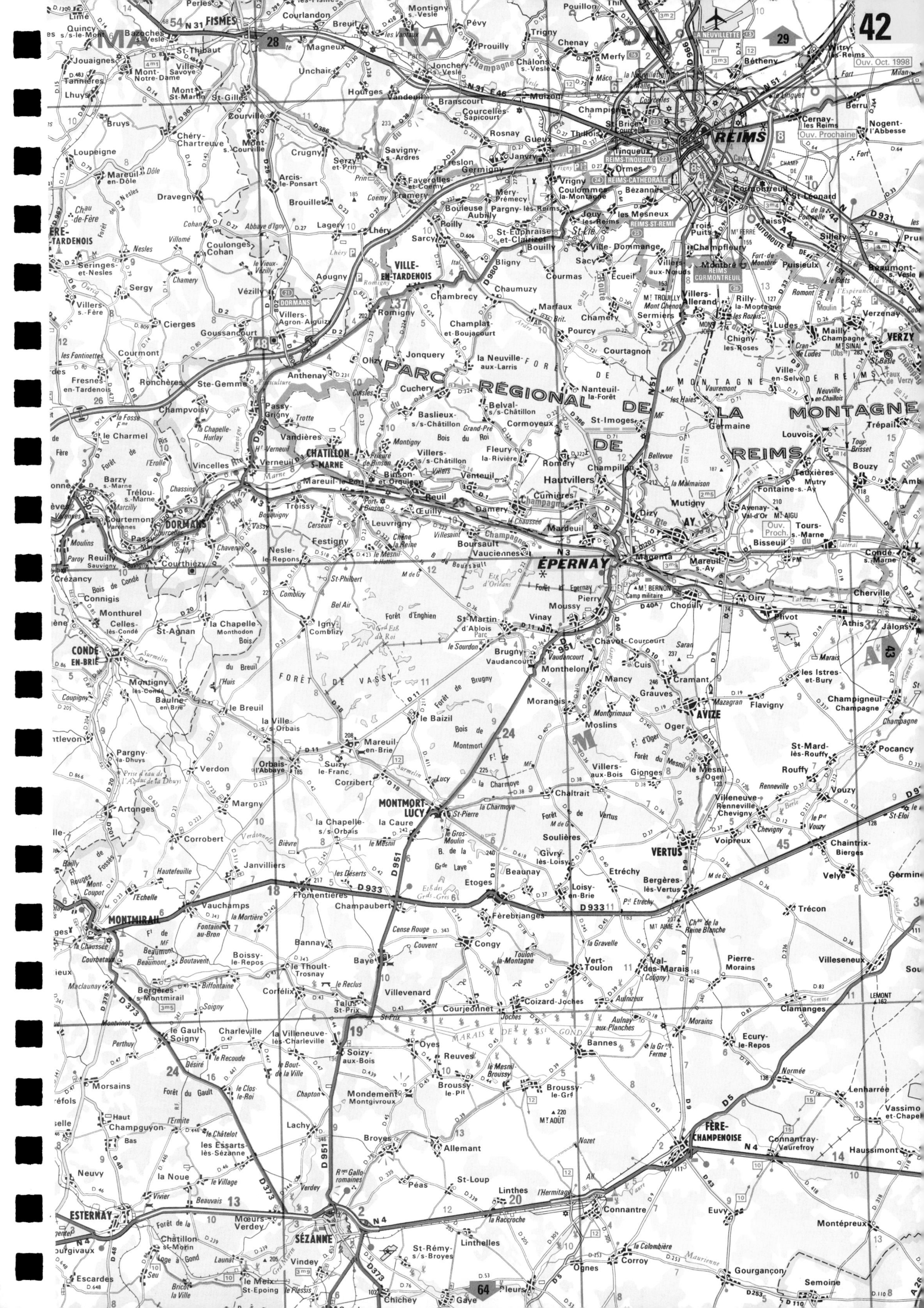
FISMES
Courlandon
Montigny-s.-Vesle
Pévy
Pouillon
Bazoches-s.-Vesle
St-Thibaut
Magneux
Prouilly
Trigny
Chenay
Merfy
Jouaignes
Mont-Notre-Dame
Unchair
Jonchery-s.-Vesle
Châlons-s.-Vesle
Bétheny
Hourges
Vandeuil
Branscourt
Muizon
Champigny
Mont-St-Martin
St-Gilles
Courcelles-Sapicourt
Bruys
Courville
Rosnay
Gueux
Thillois
REIMS
Cernay-lès-Reims
Nogent-l'Abbesse
Chéry-Chartreuve
Mont-s.-Courville
Crugny
Savigny-s.-Ardres
Serzy-et-Prin
Janvry
Tinqueux
Loupeigne
Mareuil-en-Dôle
Arcis-le-Ponsart
Faverolles-et-Coëmy
Treslon
Germigny
Ormes
Vrigny
Coulommes-la-Montagne
Bezannes
Cormontreuil
St-Léonard
Dravegny
Brouillet
Tramery
Méry-Prémecy
Bouleuse
Aubilly
Pargny-lès-Reims
Jouy-lès-Reims
les Mesneux
Taissy
Lagery
Lhéry
Sarcy
Poilly
St-Euphraise-et-Clairizet
Bouilly
Ville-Dommange
Trois-Puits
Champfleury
Sillery
FÈRE-EN-TARDENOIS
Coulonges-Cohan
Seringes-et-Nesles
VILLE-EN-TARDENOIS
Bligny
Sacy
Villers-aux-Noeuds
Montbré
Puisieulx
Beaumont-s.-Vesle
Sergy
Vézilly
Aougny
Courmas
Écueil
Chaumuzy
Chambrecy
Villers-Allerand
Rilly-la-Montagne
Villers-s.-Fère
Villers-Agron-Aiguizy
Romigny
Marfaux
Chamery
Sermiers
Verzenay
Cierges
Goussancourt
Champlat-et-Boujacourt
Pourcy
Chigny-les-Roses
Ludes
Mailly-Champagne
VERZY
Courmont
Jonquery
Olizy
La Neuville-aux-Larris
Courtagnon
Fresnes-en-Tardenois
Ronchères
Ste-Gemme
Anthenay
Ville-en-Selve
Cuchery
PARC RÉGIONAL DE LA MONTAGNE DE REIMS
Nanteuil-la-Forêt
Germaine
Champvoisy
Passy-Grigny
Baslieux-s/s-Châtillon
Belval-s/s-Châtillon
Cormoyeux
St-Imoges
Trépail
Louvois
le Charmel
Vandières
CHATILLON-S-MARNE
Villers-s/s-Châtillon
Fleury-la-Rivière
Romery
Champillon
Hautvillers
Bouzy
Tauxières-Mutry
Verneuil
Vincelles
Barzy-s.-Marne
Trélou-s.-Marne
Mareuil-le-Port
Binson-et-Orquigny
Venteuil
Cumières
Fontaine-s.-Ay
DORMANS
Courtemont-Varennes
Troissy
Reuil
Œuilly
Damery
Mutigny
Avenay-Val-d'Or
Dizy
AY
Passy
Leuvrigny
Mardeuil
Tours-s.-Marne
Bisseuil
Reuilly-Sauvigny
Festigny
Boursault
Vauciennes
Magenta
Mareuil-s.-Ay
Condé-s.-Marne
Courthiézy
Nesle-le-Repons
ÉPERNAY
Crézancy
St-Philibert
Connigis
Oiry
Chouilly
Cherville
Monthurel
Celles-lès-Condé
Comblizy
Forêt d'Enghien
Moussy
Pierry
Plivot
Athis
Jalons
St-Agnan
la Chapelle-Monthodon
Igny-Comblizy
St-Martin-d'Ablois
Vinay
Chavot-Courcourt
CONDÉ-EN-BRIE
Brugny-Vaudancourt
Cuis
Monthelon
Cramant
les Istres-et-Bury
Montigny-lès-Condé
FORÊT DE VASSY
Mancy
Grauves
Flavigny
Champigneul-Champagne
Baulne-en-Brie
Morangis
AVIZE
le Breuil
la Ville-s/s-Orbais
le Baizil
Moslins
Oger
Pargny-la-Dhuys
Mareuil-en-Brie
St-Mard-lès-Rouffy
Pocancy
Verdon
Orbais-l'Abbaye
Suizy-le-Franc
Corribert
Villers-aux-Bois
Gionges
le Mesnil-s.-Oger
Rouffy
Artonges
Margny
MONTMORT-LUCY
Chaltrait
Villeneuve-Renneville-Chevigny
Vouzy
Corrobert
la Chapelle-s/s-Orbais
la Caure
Soulières
Voipreux
VERTUS
Chaintrix-Bierges
Janvilliers
Givry-lès-Loisy
Étréchy
Bergères-lès-Vertus
Velye
Fromentières
Beaunay
Etoges
Loisy-en-Brie
MONTMIRAIL
Vauchamps
Champaubert
Fèrebrianges
Trécon
Boissy-le-Repos
Bannay
Congy
Vert-Toulon
Val-des-Marais
Pierre-Morains
Villeseneux
le Thoult-Trosnay
Baye
Bergères-s.-Montmirail
Corfélix
Villevenard
Coizard-Joches
Courjeonnet
Talus-St-Prix
Clamanges
le Gault-Soigny
Charleville
la Villeneuve-lès-Charleville
Soizy-aux-Bois
Oyes
Reuves
Bannes
Morains
Ecury-le-Repos
Morsains
Mondement-Montgivroux
Broussy-le-Pt
Broussy-le-Gd
Lenharrée
Champguyon
les Essarts-lès-Sézanne
Lachy
Broyes
Allemant
FÈRE-CHAMPENOISE
Connantray-Vaurefroy
Haussimont
Neuvy
la Noue
Péas
St-Loup
Linthes
Connantre
Euvy
Montépreux
ESTERNAY
Mœurs-Verdey
SÉZANNE
Linthelles
Châtillon-s-Morin
St-Rémy-s/s-Broyes
Corroy
Vindey
Ognes
Gourgançon
Escardes
le Meix-St-Epoing
Chichey
Gaye
Pleurs
Semoine
29
43
64

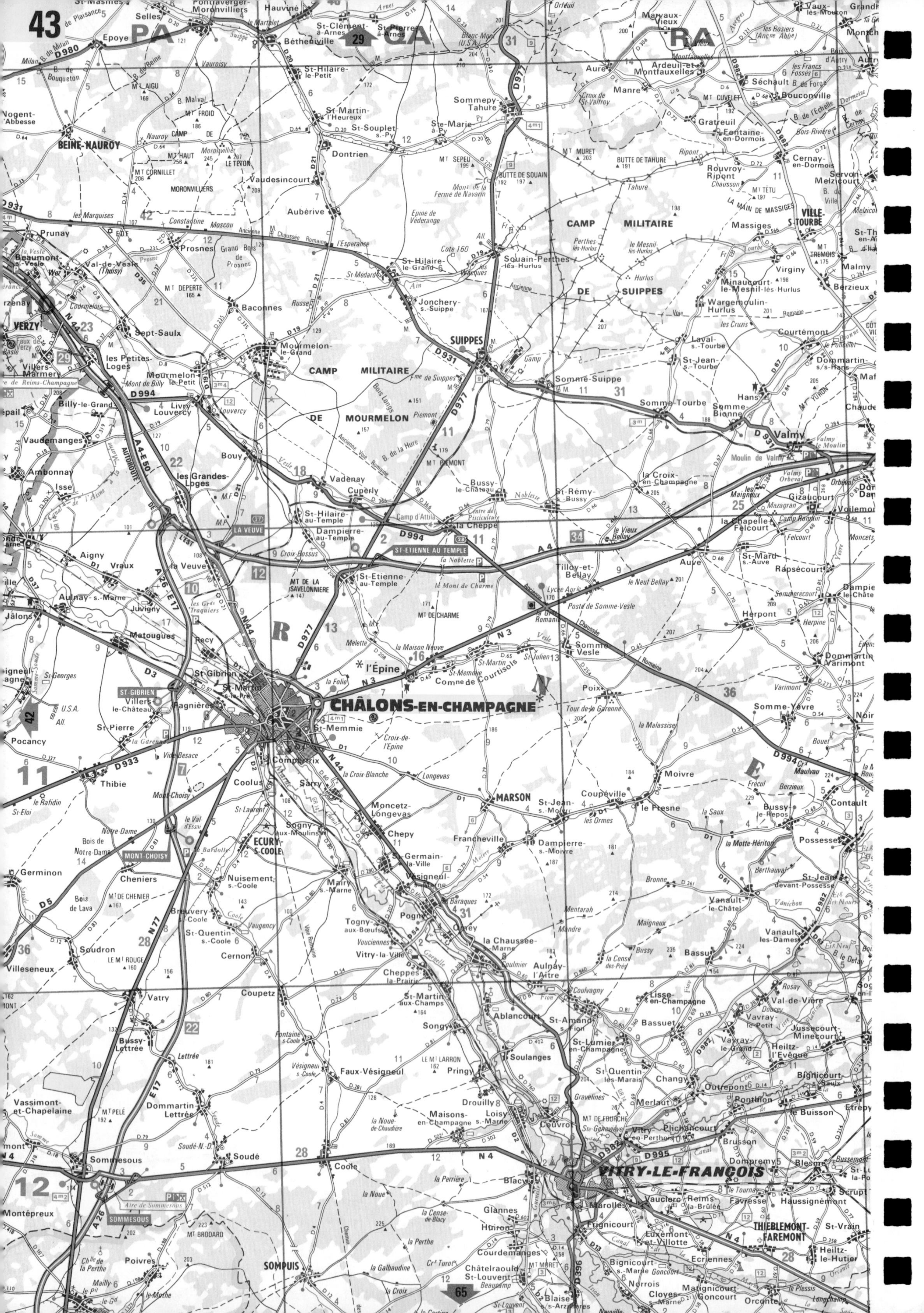
PA
QA
RA
29
Epoye
Selles
Pontfaverger-Moronvilliers
Hauviné
St-Clément-à-Arnes
St-Pierre-à-Arnes
Bétheniville
St-Hilaire-le-Petit
Sommepy-Tahure
Marvaux-Vieux
Aure
Ardeuil-et-Montfauxelles
Manre
Séchault
Bouconville
Gratreuil
Fontaine-en-Dormois
Cernay-en-Dormois
Nogent-l'Abbesse
BEINE-NAUROY
St-Martin-l'Heureux
St-Souplet-s.-Py
Ste-Marie-à-Py
Dontrien
Vaudesincourt
MORONVILLIERS
LE TÉTON
MT CORNILLET
MT SEPEU
BUTTE DE SOUAIN
BUTTE DE TAHURE
MT MURET
Rouvroy-Ripont
Servon-Melzicourt
Aubérive
Prunay
Prosnes
Beaumont-s.-Vesle
Val-de-Vesle
CAMP MILITAIRE DE SUIPPES
VILLE-S.-TOURBE
Massiges
Virginy
Minaucourt-le-Mesnil-lès-Hurlus
Wargemoulin-Hurlus
Malmy
Berzieux
St-Hilaire-le-Grand
Souain-Perthes-lès-Hurlus
Jonchery-s.-Suippe
Baconnes
Sept-Saulx
VERZY
Villers-Marmery
les Petites-Loges
Mourmelon-le-Grand
Mourmelon-le-Petit
CAMP MILITAIRE DE MOURMELON
SUIPPES
Laval-s.-Tourbe
St-Jean-s.-Tourbe
Courtémont
Dommartin-s/s-Hans
Hans
Somme-Suippe
Somme-Tourbe
Somme-Bionne
Valmy
Billy-le-Grand
Livry-Louvercy
Vaudemanges
Ambonnay
Isse
Bouy
les Grandes-Loges
Vadenay
Cuperly
Bussy-le-Château
St-Rémy-s.-Bussy
la Croix-en-Champagne
Gizaucourt
St-Hilaire-au-Temple
Dampierre-au-Temple
la Cheppe
LA VEUVE
ST-ETIENNE AU TEMPLE
St-Etienne-au-Temple
Aigny
Vraux
la Veuve
Tilloy-et-Bellay
Auve
St-Mard-s.-Auve
Rapsécourt
la Chapelle-Felcourt
Aulnay-s.-Marne
Juvigny
Jâlons
Matougues
Recy
St-Gibrien
l'Épine
CHÂLONS-EN-CHAMPAGNE
St-Memmie
Courtisols
Somme-Vesle
Poix
Herpont
Dommartin-Varimont
Somme-Yèvre
ST-GIBRIEN
Villers-le-Château
Fagnières
St-Pierre
Pocancy
Compertrix
Thibie
Coolus
Sarry
Moncetz-Longevas
MARSON
St-Jean-s.-Moivre
Coupéville
le Fresne
Moivre
Bussy-le-Repos
Contault
Possesse
Sogny-aux-Moulins
ECURY-S-COOLE
Chepy
Francheville
Dampierre-s.-Moivre
MONT-CHOISY
Germinon
Cheniers
Nuisement-s.-Coole
St-Germain-la-Ville
Vésigneul-s.-Marne
Mairy-s.-Marne
Pogny
Omey
Vanault-le-Châtel
St-Jean-devant-Possesse
Vanault-les-Dames
Breuvery-s.-Coole
St-Quentin-s.-Coole
Togny-aux-Bœufs
Vitry-la-Ville
la Chaussée-s.-Marne
Aulnay-l'Aître
Bassu
Soudron
Villeseneux
Cernon
Cheppes-la-Prairie
Coupetz
Vatry
St-Martin-aux-Champs
Songy
Ablancourt
St-Amand-s.-Fion
Lisse-en-Champagne
Bassuet
Val-de-Vière
Vavray-le-Grand
Heiltz-l'Évêque
Jussecourt-Minecourt
Bussy-Lettrée
Faux-Vésigneul
Pringy
Soulanges
St-Lumier-en-Champagne
St-Quentin-les-Marais
Changy
Outrepont
Bignicourt-s.-Saulx
Vassimont-et-Chapelaine
Dommartin-Lettrée
Drouilly
Loisy-s.-Marne
Maisons-en-Champagne
Couvrot
Vitry-en-Perthois
Merlaut
Plichancourt
Pontillon
le Buisson
Brusson
Sommesous
Soudé
Coole
Blacy
VITRY-LE-FRANÇOIS
Blesme
Montépreux
SOMMESOUS
Glannes
Huiron
Marolles
Frignicourt
Vauclerc
Reims-la-Brûlée
Favresse
Haussignémont
THIEBLEMONT-FAREMONT
St-Vrain
Poivres
SOMPUIS
Courdemanges
Châtelraould-St-Louvent
Luxémont-et-Villotte
Ecriennes
Heiltz-le-Hutier
Blaise-s/s-Arzillières
Bignicourt-s.-Marne
Norrois
Cloyes-s.-Marne
Matignicourt-Goncourt
Orconte
65

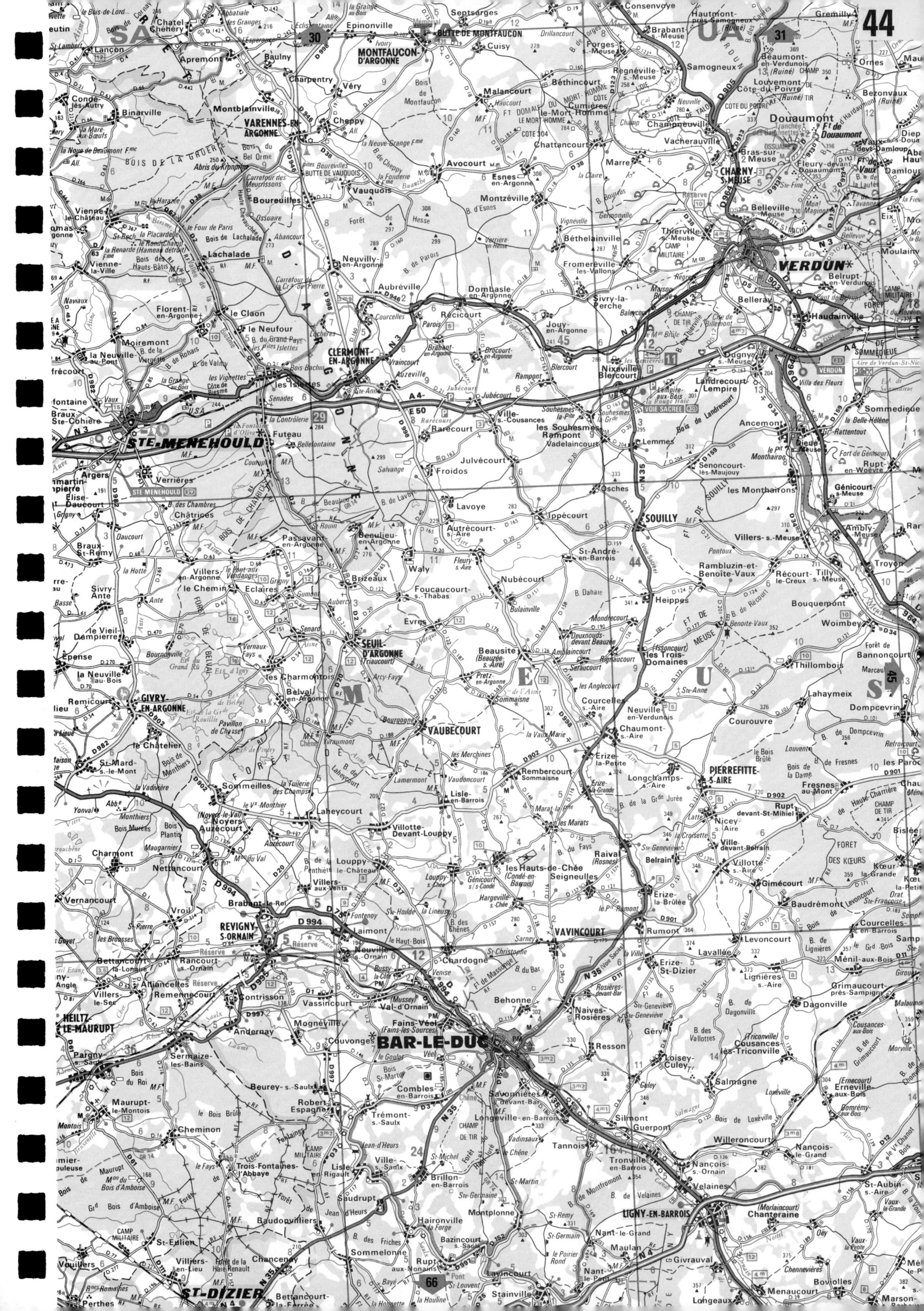
30
31
Epinonville
BUTTE DE MONTFAUCON
MONTFAUCON-D'ARGONNE
Septsarges
Cuisy
Consenvoye
Brabant-s.-Meuse
Forges-s.-Meuse
Samogneux
Apremont
Baulny
Charpentry
Véry
Malancourt
Béthincourt
Regnéville-s.-Meuse
Cumières-le-Mort-Homme
Champneuville
Binarville
Montblainville
VARENNES-EN-ARGONNE
Cheppy
Avocourt
Esnes-en-Argonne
Chattancourt
Marre
Vacherauville
Douaumont
Bras-sur-Meuse
CHARNY-S-MEUSE
Vauquois
Boureuilles
Montzéville
Belleville
Vienne-le-Château
Lachalade
Neuvilly-en-Argonne
Béthelainville
Thierville-s.-Meuse
VERDUN
Vienne-la-Ville
Aubréville
Fromeréville-les-Vallons
Belrupt-en-Verdunois
Florent-en-Argonne
le Claon
le Neufour
Récicourt
Dombasle-en-Argonne
Sivry-la-Perche
Belleray
Haudainville
Moiremont
la Neuville-au-Pont
CLERMONT-EN-ARGONNE
Brabant-en-Argonne
Brocourt-en-Argonne
Jouy-en-Argonne
Nixéville-Blercourt
Dugny-s.-Meuse
les Islettes
Auzéville
Jubécourt
Landrecourt-Lempire
Ste-MENEHOULD
Futeau
Rarécourt
Ville-s.-Cousances
les Souhesmes-Rampont
Ancemont
Dieue-s-Meuse
Argers
Verrières
Froidos
Julvécourt
Lemmes
Senoncourt-lès-Maujouy
Rupt-en-Woëvre
Osches
les Monthairons
Génicourt-s.-Meuse
Lavoye
Ippécourt
SOUILLY
Châtrices
Passavant-en-Argonne
Beaulieu-en-Argonne
Autrécourt-s.-Aire
Villers-s.-Meuse
Ambly-s.-Meuse
Braux-St-Remy
St-André-en-Barrois
Waly
Fleury-s.-Aire
Rambluzin-et-Benoite-Vaux
Récourt-le-Creux
Tilly-s.-Meuse
Troyon
Villers-en-Argonne
le Chemin
Eclaires
Brizeaux
Foucaucourt-s.-Thabas
Nubécourt
Heippes
Bouquemont
Sivry-Ante
Bulainville
Woimbey
Evres
le Vieil-Dampierre
SEUIL-D'ARGONNE
Beausite
Amblaincourt
les Trois-Domaines
Thillombois
Epense
la Neuville-aux-Bois
les Charmontois
Pretz-en-Argonne
Remicourt
Belval-en-Argonne
Courcelles-s.-Aire
Neuville-en-Verdunois
Lahaymeix
Dompcevrin
GIVRY-EN-ARGONNE
VAUBECOURT
Chaumont-s.-Aire
Courouvre
le Châtelier
St-Mard-s.-le-Mont
Erize-la-Petite
PIERREFITTE-S-AIRE
Rembercourt-Sommaisne
Longchamps-s.-Aire
Fresnes-au-Mont
Sommeilles
Lisle-en-Barrois
Rupt-devant-St-Mihiel
Noyers-Auzécourt
Laheycourt
Villotte-Devant-Louppy
Nicey-s.-Aire
Charmont
Louppy-le-Château
les Hauts-de-Chée
Raival
Belrain
Ville-devant-Belrain
Villotte-s.-Aire
Nettancourt
Seigneulles
Gimécourt
Vernancourt
Villers-aux-Vents
Erize-la-Brûlée
Baudrémont
Vroil
Brabant-le-Roi
REVIGNY-S-ORNAIN
Laimont
VAVINCOURT
Rumont
Levoncourt
Courcelles-en-Barrois
Bettancourt-la-Longue
Rancourt-s.-Ornain
Neuville-s.-Ornain
Chardogne
Erize-St-Dizier
Lavallée
Ménil-aux-Bois
Lignières-s.-Aire
Villers-le-Sec
Remennecourt
Contrisson
Vassincourt
Val-d'Ornain
Behonne
Naives-Rosières
Dagonville
Grimaucourt-près-Sampigny
HEILTZ-LE-MAURUPT
Andernay
Mognéville
Fains-Véel
BAR-LE-DUC
Resson
Géry
Cousances-lès-Triconville
Pargny
Sermaize-les-Bains
Couvonges
Savonnières-devant-Bar
Loisey-Culey
Salmagne
Erneville-aux-Bois
Beurey-s.-Saulx
Robert-Espagne
Combles-en-Barrois
Longeville-en-Barrois
Maurupt-le-Montois
Trémont-s.-Saulx
Silmont
Guerpont
Cheminon
Tannois
Willeroncourt
Trois-Fontaines-l'Abbaye
Lisle-en-Rigault
Ville-s.-Saulx
Brillon-en-Barrois
Tronville-en-Barrois
Nançois-s.-Ornain
Nançois-le-Grand
Velaines
St-Aubin-s.-Aire
Saudrupt
Montplonne
LIGNY-EN-BARROIS
Chanteraine
Baudonvilliers
Haironville
Nant-le-Grand
St-Eulien
Chancenay
Sommelonne
Bazincourt-s.-Saulx
Maulan
Givrauval
Villiers-en-Lieu
Rupt-aux-Nonains
Lavincourt
Nant-le-Petit
Boviolles
ST-DIZIER
Perthes
Bettancourt-la-Ferrée
66
Stainville
Longeaux
Menaucourt
MEUSE
ARGONNE

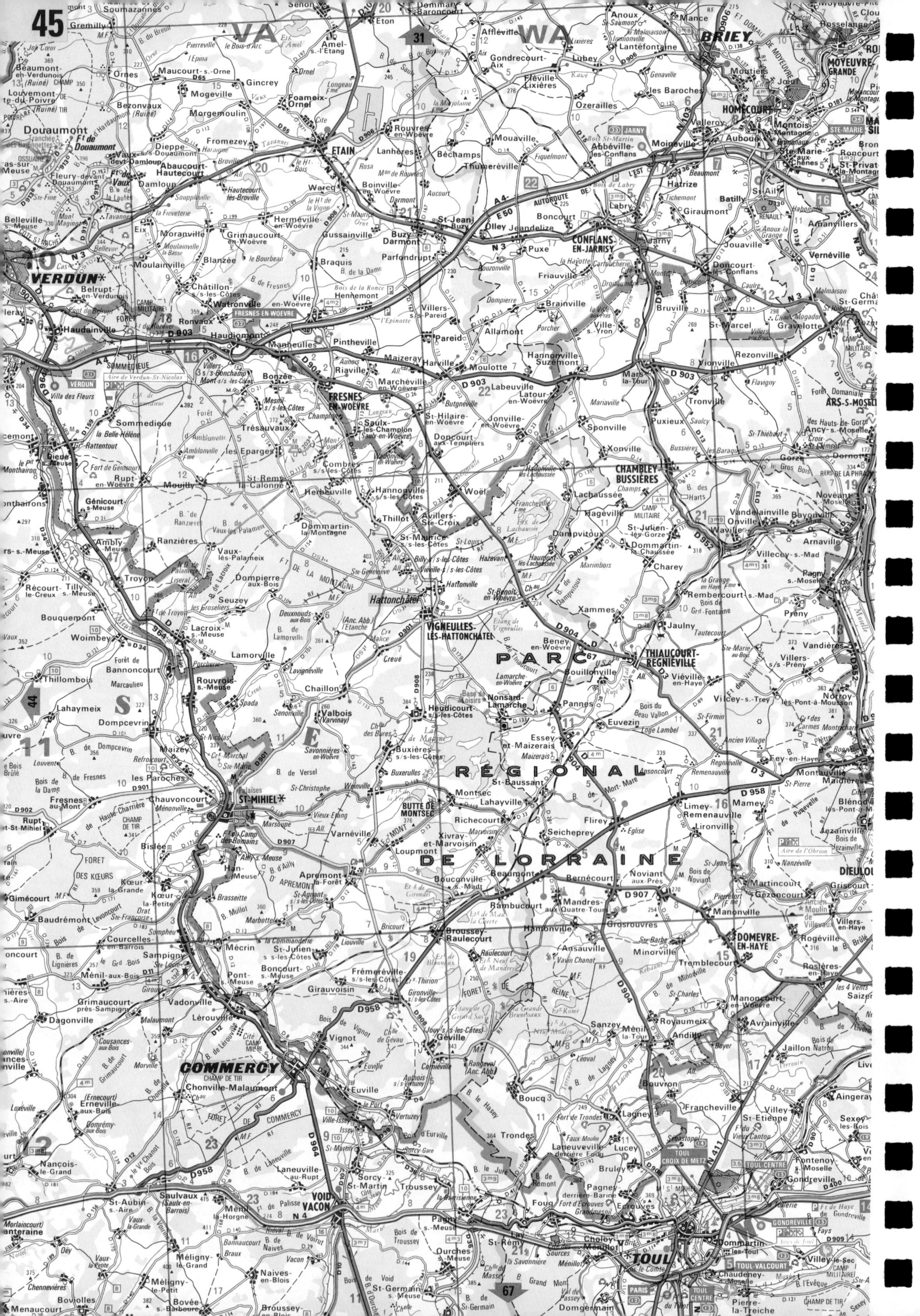
31
VERDUN
Douaumont
Ornes
Gincrey
Mogeville
Morgemoulin
Bezonvaux
Fromezey
Foameix-Ornel
Etain
Rouvres-en-Woëvre
Amel-s.-l'Etang
Affléville
Gondrecourt-Aix
Lantéfontaine
BRIEY
Mance
Anoux
Lubey
Fléville-Lixières
Ozerailles
Les Baroches
HOMÉCOURT
MOYEUVRE GRANDE
Joeuf
Auboué
Moineville
Valleroy
Mouaville
Béchamps
Thumeréville
Abbéville-lès-Conflans
JARNY
Hatrize
Batilly
St-Ail
Ste-Marie-aux-Chênes
St-Privat-la-Montagne
Roncourt
Amanvillers
Vernéville
Jouaville
Doncourt-lès-Conflans
Bruville
St-Marcel
Gravelotte
Rezonville
Vionville
Mars-la-Tour
Tronville
Puxieux
Sponville
Xonville
Labry
Giraumont
CONFLANS-EN-JARNISY
Boncourt
Jeandelize
Olley
St-Jean-lès-Buzy
Buzy-Darmont
Parfondrupt
Puxe
Friauville
Brainville
Allamont
Ville-s.-Yron
Hannonville-Suzémont
Labeuville
Latour-en-Woëvre
Jonville-en-Woëvre
Moulotte
Harville
Pareid
Villers-s/s-Pareid
Pintheville
Maizeray
Riaville
Marchéville-en-Woëvre
Manheulles
Haudiomont
Hennemont
Ville-en-Woëvre
Braquis
Gussainville
Herméville-en-Woëvre
Warcq
Boinville-en-Woëvre
Lanhères
Grimaucourt-en-Woëvre
Moranville
Moulainville
Eix
Blanzée
Châtillon-s/s-les-Côtes
Watronville
Ronvaux
Haudainville
Belrupt-en-Verdunois
Dieppe-s/s-Douaumont
Abaucourt-Hautecourt
Damloup
Vaux-devant-Damloup
Fleury-devant-Douaumont
Belleville-s.-Meuse
FRESNES-EN-WOËVRE
Bonzée
Mesnil-s/s-les-Côtes
Villers-s/s-Bonchamp
Sommedieue
Trésauvaux
Saulx-les-Champlon
Les Eparges
Combres-s/s-les-Côtes
Rupt-en-Woëvre
Mouilly
St-Remy-la-Calonne
Herbeuville
Hannonville-s/s-les-Côtes
Woël
Doncourt-aux-Templiers
St-Hilaire-en-Woëvre
Dieue-s.-Meuse
Génicourt-s.-Meuse
Ranzières
Dommartin-la-Montagne
Thillot
Avillers-Ste-Croix
St-Maurice-s/s-les-Côtes
Billy-s/s-les-Côtes
Viéville-s/s-les-Côtes
Hattonville
Hattonchâtel
VIGNEULLES-LÈS-HATTONCHÂTEL
St-Benoît-en-Woëvre
Lachaussée
Hagéville
CHAMBLEY-BUSSIÈRES
Dampvitoux
St-Julien-lès-Gorze
Dommartin-la-Chaussée
Charey
Xammes
Jaulny
Rembercourt-s.-Mad
THIAUCOURT-REGNIÉVILLE
Beney-en-Woëvre
Bouillonville
Vieville-en-Haye
Gorze
Vandelainville
Onville
Waville
Arnaville
Villecey-s.-Mad
Pagny-s.-Moselle
Prény
Vandières
Villers-s/s-Prény
Norroy-lès-Pont-à-Mousson
Vilcey-s.-Trey
Ars-s-Moselle
Ancy-s.-Moselle
Novéant-s.-Moselle
Ambly-s.-Meuse
Vaux-lès-Palameix
Dompierre-aux-Bois
Troyon
Seuzey
Lacroix-s.-Meuse
Lamorville
Rouvrois-s.-Meuse
Spada
Chaillon
Lavignéville
Creuë
Valbois
Heudicourt-s/s-les-Côtes
Nonsard-Lamarche
Pannes
Euvezin
Essey-et-Maizerais
Récourt
Tilly-s.-Meuse
Bouquemont
Woimbey
Thillombois
Lahaymeix
Dompcevrin
Maizey
Les Paroches
Chauvoncourt
ST-MIHIEL
Fresnes-au-Mont
Buxières-s/s-les-Côtes
Buxerulles
Woinville
Montsec
BUTTE DE MONTSEC
Lahayville
St-Baussant
Richecourt
Xivray-et-Marvoisin
Seicheprey
Flirey
Limey-Remenauville
Lironville
Mamey
Montauville
Varnéville
Loupmont
Apremont-la-Forêt
Bislée
Han-s.-Meuse
Kœur-la-Grande
Kœur-la-Petite
Brasseite
Baudrémont
Gimécourt
Courcelles-en-Barrois
Sampigny
Mécrin
St-Julien-s/s-les-Côtes
Boncourt-s.-Meuse
Pont-s.-Meuse
Ménil-aux-Bois
Grimaucourt-près-Sampigny
Dagonville
Vadonville
Lérouville
Girauvoisin
Fréméréville-s/s-les-Côtes
Gironville-s/s-les-Côtes
Broussey-Raulecourt
Bouconville-s.-Madt
Rambucourt
Beaumont
Bernécourt
Noviant-aux-Prés
Mandres-aux-Quatre-Tours
Hamonville
Ansauville
Grosrouvres
Minorville
Tremblecourt
DOMÈVRE-EN-HAYE
Manonville
Martincourt
Gézoncourt
Griscourt
DIEULOUARD
Manoncourt-en-Woëvre
Royaumeix
Andilly
Avrainville
Jaillon
Ménil-la-Tour
Sanzey
Vignot
Géville
COMMERCY
Chonville-Malaumont
Euville
Boucq
Bouvron
Francheville
Lagney
Trondes
Lucey
Laneuveville-derrière-Foug
Bruley
Erneville-aux-Bois
Nançois-le-Grand
Laneuville-au-Rupt
Sorcy-St-Martin
Troussey
VOID-VACON
Foug
Pagney-derrière-Barine
Écrouves
TOUL
Pagny-s.-Meuse
Ourches-s.-Meuse
St-Aubin-s.-Aire
Saulvaux
Méligny-le-Grand
Méligny-le-Petit
Naives-en-Blois
St-Germain-s.-Meuse
Bovée-s.-Barboure
Boviolles
Menaucourt
Broussey-en-Blois
Domgermain
Chaudeney-s.-Moselle
Dommartin-lès-Toul
Villey-le-Sec
Gondreville
Fontenoy-s.-Moselle
Villey-St-Etienne
Aingeray
Sexey-les-Bois
PARC RÉGIONAL DE LORRAINE
67

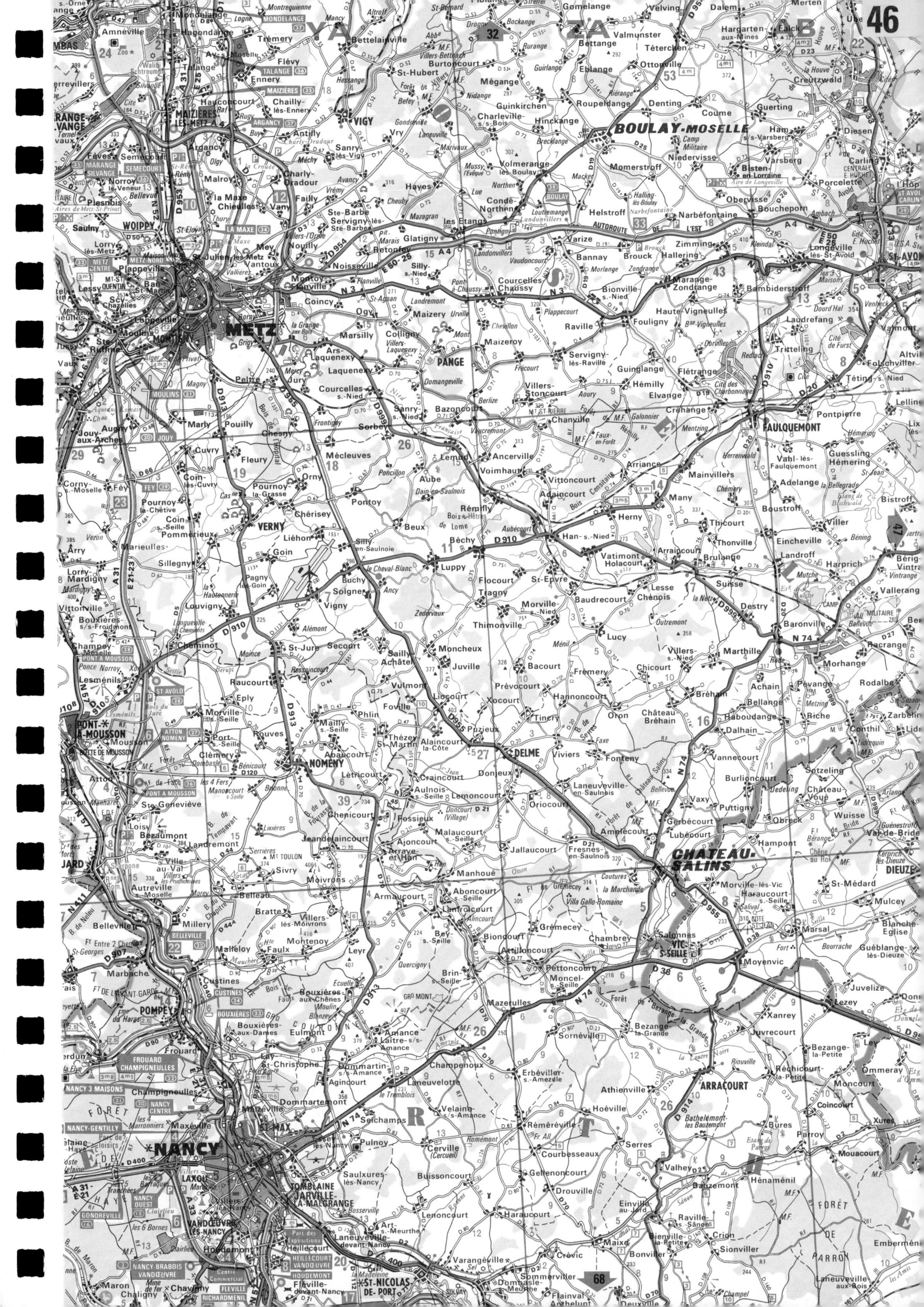
METZ
NANCY
BOULAY-MOSELLE
FAULQUEMONT
CHATEAU-SALINS
VIC-S-SEILLE
DELME
NOMENY
VERNY
PANGE
VIGY
ARRACOURT
PONT-A-MOUSSON
POMPEY
DIEUZE
MAIZIÈRES-LÈS-METZ
WOIPPY
TOMBLAINE
JARVILLE-LA-MALGRANGE
LAXOU
VANDŒUVRE-LÈS-NANCY
ST-NICOLAS-DE-PORT
ST-MAX
Hagondange
Talange
Trémery
Bettelainville
Creutzwald
Longeville-lès-St-Avold
Marange-Zondrange
Courcelles-Chaussy
Rémilly
Béchy
Luppy
Solgne
Han-s.-Nied
Morhange
Baronville
Château-Bréhain
Moyenvic
Marsal
Lezey
Juvelize
Bezange-la-Grande
Champenoux
Seichamps
Pulnoy
Essey-lès-Nancy
Maxéville
Champigneulles
Frouard
Custines
Marbache
Belleville
Dieulouard
Villers-lès-Nancy
Heillecourt
Houdemont
Laneuveville-devant-Nancy
Varangéville
Dombasle-s-Meurthe
Einville-au-Jard
Bauzemont
Hénaménil
Mouacourt
Parroy
Xures
Moncourt
Coincourt
Bures
Réméréville
Courbesseaux
Drouville
Haraucourt
Buissoncourt
Cerville
Velaine-s/s-Amance
Laneuvelotte
Dommartin-s/s-Amance
Agincourt
Amance
Laître-s/s-Amance
Eulmont
Lay-St-Christophe
Dommartemont
Bouxières-aux-Dames
Bouxières-aux-Chênes
Leyr
Faulx
Malleloy
Montenoy
Millery
Autreville-s-Moselle
Ville-au-Val
Bezaumont
Landremont
Loisy
Ste-Geneviève
Atton
Clémery
Port-s.-Seille
Morville-s.-Seille
Rouves
Phlin
Mailly-s.-Seille
Thézey-St-Martin
Abaucourt
Létricourt
Craincourt
Aulnois-s.-Seille
Lemoncourt
Fossieux
Malaucourt-s.-Seille
Ajoncourt
Arraye-et-Han
Jeandelaincourt
Chenicourt
Moivrons
Sivry
Armaucourt
Aboncourt-s.-Seille
Lanfroicourt
Bey-s.-Seille
Bioncourt
Attilloncourt
Pettoncourt
Moncel-s.-Seille
Mazerulles
Sornéville
Erbéviller-s.-Amezule
Athienville
Hoéville
Serres
Valhey
Raville-s.-Sânon
Crion
Sionviller
Bonviller
Maixe
Crévic
Sommerviller
Flainval
Deuxville
Laneuveville-aux-Bois
Embermenil
Xanrey
Juvrecourt
Bezange-la-Petite
Réchicourt-la-Petite
Ommeray
Salonnes
Chambrey
Grémecey
Manhoué
Jallaucourt
Fresnes-en-Saulnois
Amelécourt
Oriocourt
Laneuveville-en-Saulnois
Fonteny
Viviers
Faxe
Oron
Tincry
Hannoncourt
Frémery
Chicourt
Villers-s.-Nied
Marthille
Bréhain
Dalhain
Haboudange
Vannecourt
Burlioncourt
Vaxy
Puttigny
Gerbécourt
Lubécourt
Hampont
Obreck
Château-Voué
Sotzeling
Wuisse
Morville-lès-Vic
Haraucourt-s.-Seille
St-Médard
Mulcey
Blanche-Eglise
Guéblange-lès-Dieuze
Bourrache
Achain
Bellange
Pévange
Riche
Rodalbe
Conthil
Zarbeling
Racrange
Destry
Suisse
Harprich
Vallerange
Landroff
Eincheville
Viller
Bistroff
Boustroff
Adelange
Guessling-Hémering
Vahl-lès-Faulquemont
Mainvillers
Many
Thicourt
Thonville
Brulange
Arraincourt
Vatimont
Holacourt
Lesse
Chenois
Lucy
Baudrecourt
Morville-s.-Nied
Thimonville
Tragny
Flocourt
St-Epvre
Herny
Adaincourt
Vittoncourt
Arriance
Voimhaut
Ancerville
Lemud
Aube
Beux
Pontoy
Chérisey
Liéhon
Goin
Pagny-lès-Goin
Buchy
Vigny
Secourt
St-Jure
Sailly-Achâtel
Moncheux
Juville
Bacourt
Prévocourt
Xocourt
Liocourt
Vulmont
Foville
Alaincourt-la-Côte
Puzieux
Donjeux
Louvigny
Raucourt
Eply
Cheminot
Sillegny
Marieulles
Pommérieux
Coin-s.-Seille
Pournoy-la-Chétive
Pournoy-la-Grasse
Orny
Fleury
Cuvry
Coin-lès-Cuvry
Féy
Corny-s.-Moselle
Jouy-aux-Arches
Augny
Marly
Pouilly
Chesny
Mécleuves
Sorbey
Frontigny
Sanry-s.-Nied
Bazoncourt
Courcelles-s.-Nied
Laquenexy
Ars-Laquenexy
Mercy
Jury
Peltre
Marsilly
Colligny
Maizery
Ogy
Coincy
Montoy-Flanville
Noisseville
Silly-s.-Nied
Retonfey
Glatigny
Les Etangs
Servigny-lès-Ste-Barbe
Ste-Barbe
Failly
Vany
Chieulles
La Maxe
Malroy
Charly-Oradour
Argancy
Antilly
Chailly-lès-Ennery
Ennery
Flévy
Hauconcourt
Semécourt
Fèves
Norroy-le-Veneur
Plesnois
Saulny
Lorry-lès-Metz
Plappeville
Lessy
Scy-Chazelles
Longeville
Moulins
Ste-Ruffine
Montigny
St-Julien-lès-Metz
Mey
Vantoux
Vallières
Borny
Grigy
Amnéville
Mondelange
Ay-s.-Moselle
St-Hubert
Vry
Sanry-lès-Vigy
Hayes
Burtoncourt
Mégange
Charleville-s/s-Bois
Guinkirchen
Hinckange
Volmerange-lès-Boulay
Condé-Northen
Helstroff
Varize
Bannay
Brouck
Hallering
Zimming
Narbéfontaine
Bionville-s.-Nied
Raville
Servigny-lès-Raville
Maizeroy
Villers-Stoncourt
Chanville
Hémilly
Guinglange
Fouligny
Haute-Vigneulles
Bambiderstroff
Crehange
Elvange
Flétrange
Tritteling
Laudrefang
Téting-s.-Nied
Pontpierre
Folschviller
Valmont
Boucheporn
Obervisse
Porcelette
Bisten-en-Lorraine
Varsberg
Ham-s/s-Varsberg
Guerting
Coume
Denting
Momerstroff
Niedervisse
Roupeldange
Ottonville
Téterchen
Valmunster
Bettange
Eblange
Gomelange
Dalem
Hargarten-aux-Mines
Falck
Diesen
Carling
L'Hôpital
Gondreville
Chaligny
Chavigny
Fléville-devant-Nancy
Art-s.-Meurthe
Lenoncourt
Saulxures-lès-Nancy
Gellenoncourt
Maron
Ludres

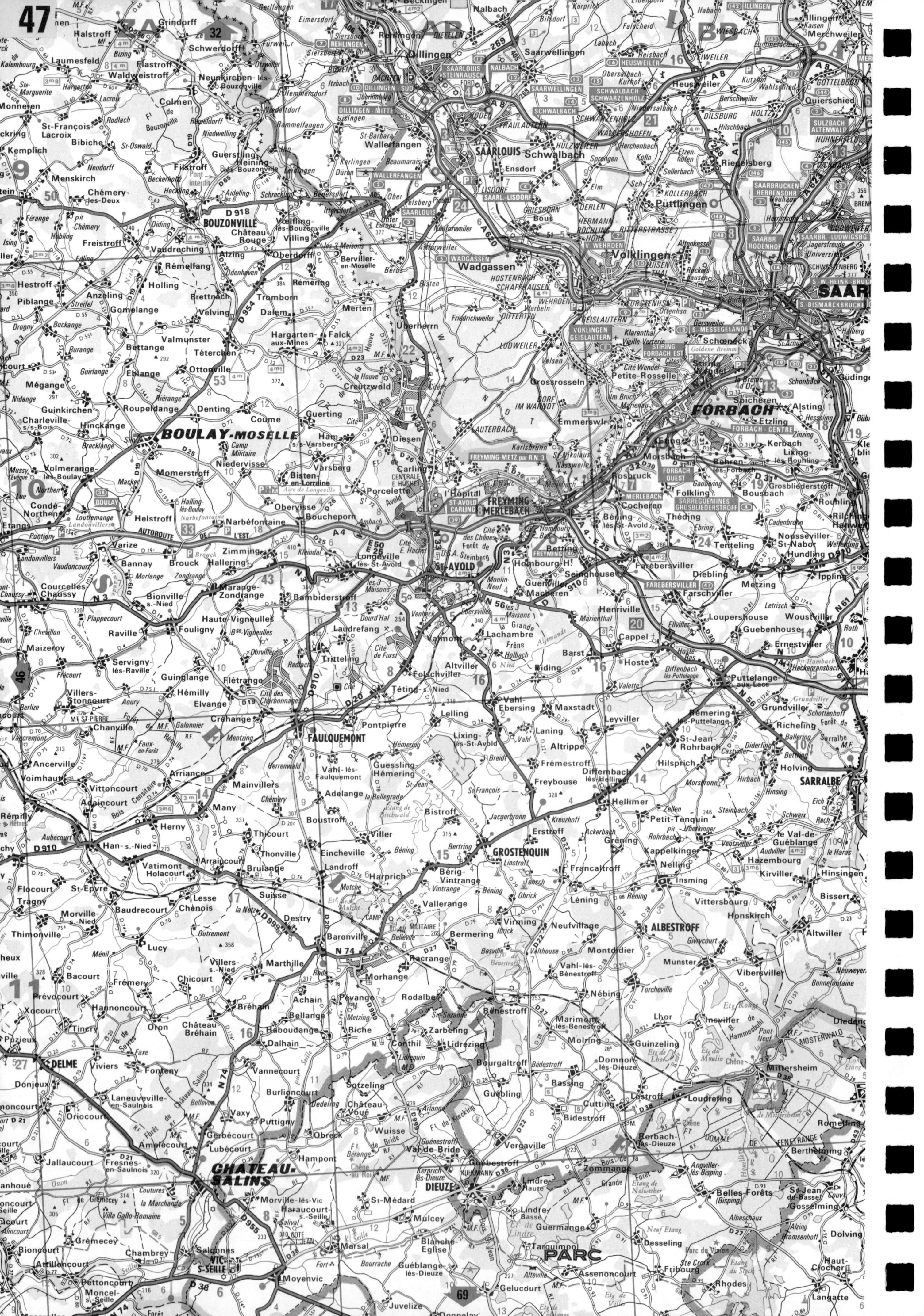
Halstroff
Grindorff
Schwerdorff
Laumesfeld
Flastroff
Waldweistroff
Neunkirchen-lès-Bouzonville
Colmen
St-François-Lacroix
Bibiche
Kemplich
Guerstling
Heining-lès-Bouzonville
Filstroff
Menskirch
Chémery-les-Deux
BOUZONVILLE
Château-Rouge
Vœlfling-lès-Bouzonville
Villing
Freistroff
Vaudreching
Alzing
Oberdorff
Rémelfang
Hestroff
Holling
Piblange
Anzeling
Brettnach
Tromborn
Gomelange
Velving
Dalem
Bettange
Valmunster
Téterchen
Ottonville
Mégange
Guinkirchen
Rouperdange
Denting
Coume
Charleville-s/s-Bois
Hinckange
BOULAY-MOSELLE
Volmerange-lès-Boulay
Momerstroff
Niedervisse
Condé-Northen
Helstroff
Narbéfontaine
Obervisse
Boucheporn
Varize
Bannay
Brouck
Hallering
Zimming
Courcelles-Chaussy
Bionville-s.-Nied
Marange-Zondrange
Raville
Fouligny
Haute-Vigneulles
Maizeroy
Servigny-lès-Raville
Guinglange
Flétrange
Villers-Stoncourt
Hémilly
Elvange
Créhange
Chanville
FAULQUEMONT
Ancerville
Arriance
Mainvillers
Vittoncourt
Many
Herny
Han-s.-Nied
Thicourt
Thonville
Vatimont
Holacourt
Brulange
Flocourt
St-Epvre
Tragny
Suisse
Morville-s.-Nied
Baudrecourt
Chenois
Lesse
Destry
Thimonville
Lucy
Baronville
Villers-s.-Nied
Marthille
Bacourt
Frémery
Chicourt
Prévocourt
Xocourt
Hannoncourt
Oron
Bréhain
Château-Bréhain
DELME
Viviers
Fonteny
Donjeux
Laneuveville-en-Saulnois
Oriocourt
Vaxy
Puttigny
Gerbécourt
Lubécourt
Amelécourt
Jallaucourt
Fresnes-en-Saulnois
CHATEAU-SALINS
Morville-lès-Vic
Haraucourt-s.-Seille
Grémecey
Chambrey
Salonnes
VIC-S-SEILLE
Moyenvic
Pettoncourt
Moncel-s.-Seille
Mazerulles
Dillingen
Saarlouis
Wallerfangen
Schwalbach
Ensdorf
Bous
Wadgassen
Völklingen
Püttlingen
Riegelsberg
Saarwellingen
Nalbach
Heusweiler
Quierschied
Illingen
Merchweiler
SAAR
Überherrn
Merten
Berviller-en-Moselle
Rémering
Hargarten-aux-Mines
Falck
Creutzwald
Guerting
Ham-s/s-Varsberg
Diesen
Varsberg
Bisten-en-Lorraine
Porcelette
Carling
l'Hôpital
FREYMING-MERLEBACH
Longeville-lès-St-Avold
ST-AVOLD
Bambiderstroff
Laudrefang
Tritteling
Folschviller
Téting-s.-Nied
Valmont
Altviller
Lachambre
Macheren
Seingbouse
Betting
Hombourg-H.
Grossrosseln
Petite-Rosselle
Stiring-Wendel
FORBACH
Schœneck
Spicheren
Alsting
Etzling
Kerbach
Morsbach
Behren-lès-Forbach
Rosbruck
Cocheren
Folkling
Bousbach
Théding
Tenteling
Farébersviller
Farschviller
Diebling
Metzing
Nousseviller-St-Nabor
Hundling
Henriville
Cappel
Barst
Hoste
Biding
Loupershouse
Guebenhouse
Ernestviller
Woustviller
Puttelange-aux-Lacs
Vahl-Ebersing
Maxstadt
Lelling
Leyviller
Pontpierre
Lixing-lès-St-Avold
Laning
Altrippe
Rémering-lès-Puttelange
St-Jean-Rohrbach
Grundviller
Richeling
Holving
SARRALBE
Hilsprich
Diffembach-lès-Hellimer
Frémestroff
Freybouse
Hellimer
Guessling-Hémering
Vahl-lès-Faulquemont
Adelange
Boustroff
Bistroff
Viller
Eincheville
Landroff
Harprich
Bérig-Vintrange
GROSTENQUIN
Erstroff
Francaltroff
Petit-Tenquin
Kappelkinger
Nelling
Insming
le Val-de-Guéblange
Hazembourg
Kirviller
Hinsingen
Vallerange
Virming
Bermering
Neufvillage
ALBESTROFF
Vittersbourg
Honskirch
Bissert
Altwiller
Racrange
Morhange
Montdidier
Vahl-lès-Bénestroff
Munster
Vibersviller
Achain
Pévange
Rodalbe
Bénestroff
Nébing
Torcheville
Bellange
Haboudange
Riche
Zarbeling
Lidrezing
Marimont-lès-Bénestroff
Molring
Lhor
Guinzeling
Insviller
Dalhain
Conthil
Bourgaltroff
Domnom-lès-Dieuze
Mittersheim
Vannecourt
Burlioncourt
Sotzeling
Château-Voué
Bassing
Guébling
Lostroff
Loudrefing
Wuisse
Obreck
Bidestroff
Cutting
Vergaville
Val-de-Bride
Rorbach-lès-Dieuze
Romelfing
Berthelming
Hampont
Guébestroff
DIEUZE
Lindre-Haute
Zommange
Angviller-lès-Bisping
Belles-Forêts
St-Jean-de-Bassel
Gosselming
St-Médard
Mulcey
Lindre-Basse
Guermange
Marsal
Blanche-Eglise
Desseling
Dolving
Tarquimpol
PARC
Guéblange-lès-Dieuze
Assenoncourt
Fribourg
Haut-Clocher
Alteville
Gelucourt
Rhodes
Langatte
Juvelize
Donnelay
AUTOROUTE DE L'EST
A4
N3
N74
D910
69

Neunkirchen
Bexbach
Homburg
Lambsborn
Bechhofen
Rosenkopf
Martinshohe
Kirchenarnbach
Schmaler
Wiesbach
Knopp-Labach
Hettenhsn.
Saalstadt
Horbach
Geiselberg
Heltersberg
Steinalben
Kashofen
Krahenbg.
Biedershsn
Wallhalben-Oberhausen
Hermersberg
Schauerberg
Herschberg
Waldfischbach-Burgalben
Gross-Klein-Budenbach
Schmitshsn
Winterbach
Reifenberg
Hoheinod
Thaleischweiler-Fröschen
Clausen
Donsieders
Merzalben
Sulzbach
St-Ingbert
Kirkel
Battweiler
Massweiler
Rieschweiler-Muhlbach
Contwig
Rodalben
Höhfröschen
Petersberg
Münchweiler
Zweibrucken
Blieskastel
Dellfeld
Hoheischweiler
Nunschweiler
Saarbrucken
Walshausen
Pirmasens
Althornbach
Klein-steinhausen
Ruppertsweiler
Dietrichingen
Gross-steinhausen
Bottenbach
Hornbach
Mauschbach
Riedelberg
Obersimten
Lemberg
Rolbing
Vinningen
Schweyen
Walschbronn
Kröppen
Mandelbachtal
Gersheim
Waldhouse
Trulben
Loutzviller
Breidenbach
Schweix
Ormersviller
Bousseviller
Liederschiedt
Hilst
Eppenbrunn
Epping
Volmunster
Lengelsheim
Fischbach
Obergailbach
Erching
Hanviller
Roppeviller
Frauenberg
Bliesbruck
Nousseviller-lès-Bitche
Haspelschiedt
Ludwigswinkel
Sarreguemines
Rimling
Sarreinsming
Bettviller
Hottviller
Schorbach
Camp de Bitche
Sturzelbronn
Rémelfing
Neufgrange
Woelfling-lès-Sarreguemines
Bitche
Zetting
Wiesviller
Gros-Réderching
Petit-Réderching
Reyersviller
Obersteinbach
Siltzheim
Wittring
Rohrbach-lès-Bitche
Siersthal
Achen
Bining
Lambach
Eguelshardt
Dambach
Etting
Enchenberg
Lemberg
Willerwald
Kalhausen
Herbitzheim
Schmittviller
St-Louis-lès-Bitche
Philippsbourg
Windstein
Oermingen
Rahling
Montbronn
Goetzenbruck
Mouterhouse
Baerenthal
Niederbronn-les-Bains
Dehlingen
Butten
Meisenthal
Keskastel
Ratzwiller
Volksberg
Soucht
Reipertswiller
Oberbronn
Voellerdingen
Lorentzen
Schopperten
Domfessel
Diemeringen
Rosteig
Wingen-s.-Moder
Zinswiller
Sarre-Union
Waldhambach
Lichtenberg
Gundershoffen
Frohmuhl
Weislingen
Puberg
Wimmenau
Offwiller
Rothbach
Gumbrechtshoffen
Rimsdorf
Mackwiller
Thal-Drulingen
Hinsbourg
Zittersheim
Bischholtz
Uttenhoffen
Sarrewerden
Rexingen
Adamswiller
Tieffenbach
Sparsbach
Ingwiller
Mulhausen
Engwiller
Dürstel
Struth
Schillersdorf
Uhrwiller
Mietesheim
Burbach
Berg
Bettwiller
Asswiller
Erckartswiller
Kindwiller
Mertzwiller
Wolfskirchen
Gungwiller
Petersbach
Weinbourg
Bitschhoffen
Eywiller
Drulingen
La Petite-Pierre
Obersoultzbach
Menchhoffen
Uberach
La Walck
Niederstinzel
Eschwiller
Ottwiller
Weiterswiller
Pfaffenhoffen
Niedermodern
Weyer
Lohr
Niedersoultzbach
Uttwiller
Obermodern-Zutzendorf
Dauendorf
Postroff
Siewiller
Neuwiller-lès-Saverne
Bouxwiller
Ringeldorf
Fénétrange
Veckersviller
Bust
Schoenbourg
Schalkendorf
Morschwiller
Baerendorf
Hirschland
Schalbach
Kirrwiller-Bosselshausen
Ettendorf
Grassendorf
Hellering-lès-Fénétrange
Kirrberg
Metting
Hangviller
Eschbourg
Dossenheim-s.-Zinsel
Ringendorf
Issenhausen
Lixhausen
Huttendorf
Zoebersdorf
Minversheim
Bettborn
Oberstinzel
Rauwiller
Bickenholtz
Berling
Pfalzweyer
Veschheim
Ernolsheim-lès-Saverne
Hattmatt
Printzheim
Geiswiller
Wickersheim-Wilshausen
Bossendorf
Alteckendorf
Hochfelden
Wintersbourg
Vilsberg
St-Jean-Saverne
Gottesheim
Schwindratzheim
Goerlingen
Vieux Lixheim
Fleisheim
Héange
Zilling
Steinbourg
Schwenheim
Dettwiller
Melsheim
Wilwisheim
Mommenheim
Lixheim
Mittelbronn
Phalsbourg
Danne-et-Quatre-Vents
Otterswiller
Monswiller
Mutzenhouse
Sarraltroff
Hilbesheim
Brouviller
Bourscheid
St-Jean-Kourtzerode
Waldolwisheim
Lupstein
Littenheim
Schaffhouse
Krautwiller
Réding
Waltembourg
Dannelbourg
Saverne
Ingenheim
Wingersheim
Hommarting
Lutzelbourg
Altenheim
Duntzenheim
Gingsheim
Hohatzenheim
Donnenheim
Bilwisheim
Henridorff
Sarrebourg
Parc Régional des Vosges du Nord
A4
A6
A8
D919
N61
N62
D421
49
70

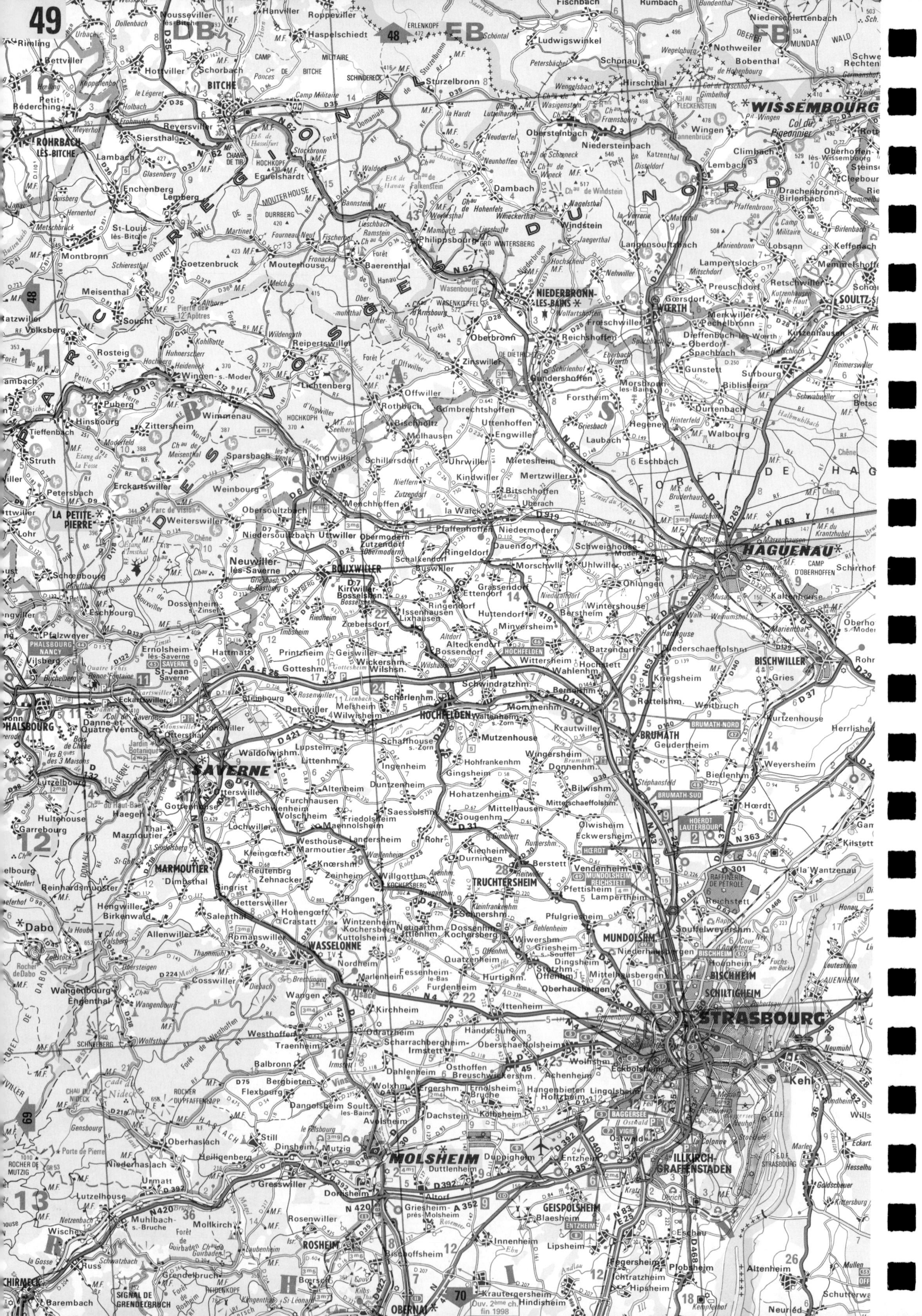

BITCHE
WISSEMBOURG
NIEDERBRONN-LES-BAINS
WŒRTH
HAGUENAU
SOULTZ-S
LA PETITE-PIERRE
BOUXWILLER
SAVERNE
PHALSBOURG
HOCHFELDEN
BRUMATH
BISCHWILLER
MARMOUTIER
WASSELONNE
TRUCHTERSHEIM
MUNDOLSHEIM
BISCHHEIM
SCHILTIGHEIM
STRASBOURG
Kehl
MOLSHEIM
ILLKIRCH-GRAFFENSTADEN
GEISPOLSHEIM
ROSHEIM
OBERNAI
SCHIRMECK
Dabo
ROHRBACH-LÈS-BITCHE
Lembach
Reichshoffen
Ingwiller
Zinswiller
Wingen-s.-Moder
Lichtenberg
Dettwiller
Mutzig
Dachstein
Eckbolsheim
Lingolsheim
Ostwald
Entzheim
Blaesheim
Plobsheim
Eschau
Fegersheim
Reichstett
Hoerdt
Weyersheim
La Wantzenau
Oberhausbergen
Achenheim
Wolfisheim
Ittenheim
Furdenheim
Kirchheim
Westhoffen
Wangen
Soultz-les-Bains
Avolsheim
Dinsheim
Still
Oberhaslach
Niederhaslach
Urmatt
Lutzelhouse
Muhlbach-s.-Bruche
Mollkirch
Grendelbruch
Barembach
Russ
Wisches
Rosenwiller
Griesheim-près-Molsheim
Bischoffsheim
Innenheim
Krautergersheim
Hindisheim
Lipsheim
Ichtratzheim
Hipsheim
Altenheim
Neuried
Schutterwald
Marlen
Goldscheuer
Kittersburg
Eckart.
Hesselhu
Wills
Sundheim
Neumühl
Auenheim
Leutesheim
Honau
Fuchs-am-Buckel
Gambsheim
Kilstett
Herrlisheim
Bietlenheim
Geudertheim
Kurtzenhouse
Gries
Weitbruch
Kriegsheim
Rottelsheim
Bernolsheim
Mommenheim
Schwindratzheim
Wittersheim
Wahlenheim
Hochstett
Batzendorf
Niederschaeffolsheim
Kaltenhouse
Oberhoffen-s.-Moder
Schirrhoffen
Marienthal
Ohlungen
Uhlwiller
Schweighouse-s.-Moder
Dauendorf
Ringeldorf
Niedermodern
Pfaffenhoffen
Uberach
La Walck
Bitschhoffen
Mertzwiller
Mietesheim
Engwiller
Uttenhoffen
Gumbrechtshoffen
Gundershoffen
Forstheim
Morsbronn-les-Bains
Durrenbach
Walbourg
Biblisheim
Surbourg
Gunstett
Eschbach
Laubach
Hegeney
Frœschwiller
Oberbronn
Offwiller
Rothbach
Bischholtz
Mulhausen
Uhrwiller
Kindwiller
Schillersdorf
Menchhoffen
Obersoultzbach
Weiterswiller
Weinbourg
Sparsbach
Erckartswiller
Zittersheim
Wimmenau
Puberg
Hinsbourg
Tieffenbach
Struth
Petersbach
Lohr
Schœnbourg
Eschbourg
Pfalzweyer
Vilsberg
Danne-et-Quatre-Vents
Lutzelbourg
Hultehouse
Garrebourg
Haegen
Gottenhouse
Otterswiller
Thal-Marmoutier
Reinhardsmunster
Dimbsthal
Hengwiller
Birkenwald
Allenwiller
Wangenbourg
Engenthal
Cosswiller
Romanswiller
Salenthal
Jetterswiller
Crastatt
Hohengœft
Zehnacker
Reutenbourg
Kleingœft
Westhouse-Marmoutier
Lochwiller
Schwenheim
Wolschheim
Furchhausen
Maennolsheim
Friedolsheim
Saessolsheim
Altenheim
Duntzenheim
Ingenheim
Littenheim
Lupstein
Waldolwisheim
Monswiller
Steinbourg
Eckartswiller
St-Jean-Saverne
Ernolsheim-lès-Saverne
Hattmatt
Dossenheim-s.-Zinsel
Neuwiller-lès-Saverne
Niedersoultzbach
Uttwiller
Obermodern-Zutzendorf
Kirrwiller-Bosselshausen
Issenhausen
Lixhausen
Ringendorf
Ettendorf
Grassendorf
Huttendorf
Minversheim
Berstheim
Wintershouse
Morschwiller
Alteckendorf
Bossendorf
Zœbersdorf
Riedheim
Imbsheim
Printzheim
Geiswiller
Wickersheim-Wilshausen
Gottesheim
Scherlenheim
Melsheim
Wilwisheim
Waltenheim-s.-Zorn
Mutzenhouse
Schaffhouse-s.-Zorn
Hohfrankenheim
Gingsheim
Hohatzenheim
Mittelhausen
Wingersheim
Donnenheim
Bilwisheim
Mittelschaeffolsheim
Olwisheim
Eckwersheim
Vendenheim
Berstett
Kienheim
Durningen
Gougenheim
Rohr
Landersheim
Knœrsheim
Zeinheim
Willgottheim
Rangen
Wintzenheim-Kochersberg
Kuttolsheim
Neugartheim-Ittlenheim
Dossenheim-Kochersberg
Schnersheim
Pfulgriesheim
Pfettisheim
Lampertheim
Souffelweyersheim
Niederhausbergen
Mittelhausbergen
Hœnheim
Griesheim-s.-Souffel
Dingsheim
Stutzheim-Offenheim
Wiwersheim
Quatzenheim
Hurtigheim
Fessenheim-le-Bas
Marlenheim
Nordheim
Odratzheim
Scharrachbergheim-Irmstett
Traenheim
Balbronn
Bergbieten
Flexbourg
Dangolsheim
Dahlenheim
Osthoffen
Breuschwickersheim
Handschuheim
Oberschaeffolsheim
Wolxheim
Ergersheim
Ernolsheim-Bruche
Kolbsheim
Hangenbieten
Holtzheim
Duppigheim
Duttlenheim
Dorlisheim
Altorf
Gresswiller
Heiligenberg
Boersch
Saverne
Hochfelden
Haguenau
Fischbach
Rumbach
Bundenthal
Niederschlettenbach
Nothweiler
Bobenthal
Schönau
Hirschthal
Ludwigswinkel
Roppeviller
Haspelschiedt
Hanviller
Nousseviller-lès-Bitche
Rimling
Bettviller
Hottviller
Schorbach
Petit-Réderching
Siersthal
Reyersviller
Lambach
Enchenberg
Lemberg
Eguelshardt
Sturzelbronn
Obersteinbach
Niedersteinbach
Wingen
Climbach
Oberhoffen-lès-Wissembourg
Cleebourg
Drachenbronn-Birlenbach
Keffenach
Lobsann
Lampertsloch
Preuschdorf
Mitschdorf
Retschwiller
Memmelshoffen
Gœrsdorf
Merkwiller-Pechelbronn
Kutzenhausen
Dieffenbach-lès-Wœrth
Oberdorf-Spachbach
Langensoultzbach
Windstein
Jaegerthal
Dambach
Neunhoffen
Philippsbourg
Baerenthal
Mouterhouse
Goetzenbruck
Montbronn
St-Louis-lès-Bitche
Meisenthal
Soucht
Volksberg
Rosteig
Reipertswiller
Wildenguth
PARC RÉGIONAL DES VOSGES DU NORD
FORÊT DE HAGUENAU
CAMP DE BITCHE
CAMP D'OBERHOFFEN
RAFFINERIE DE PÉTROLE
Duv. 2ème ch. fin 1998

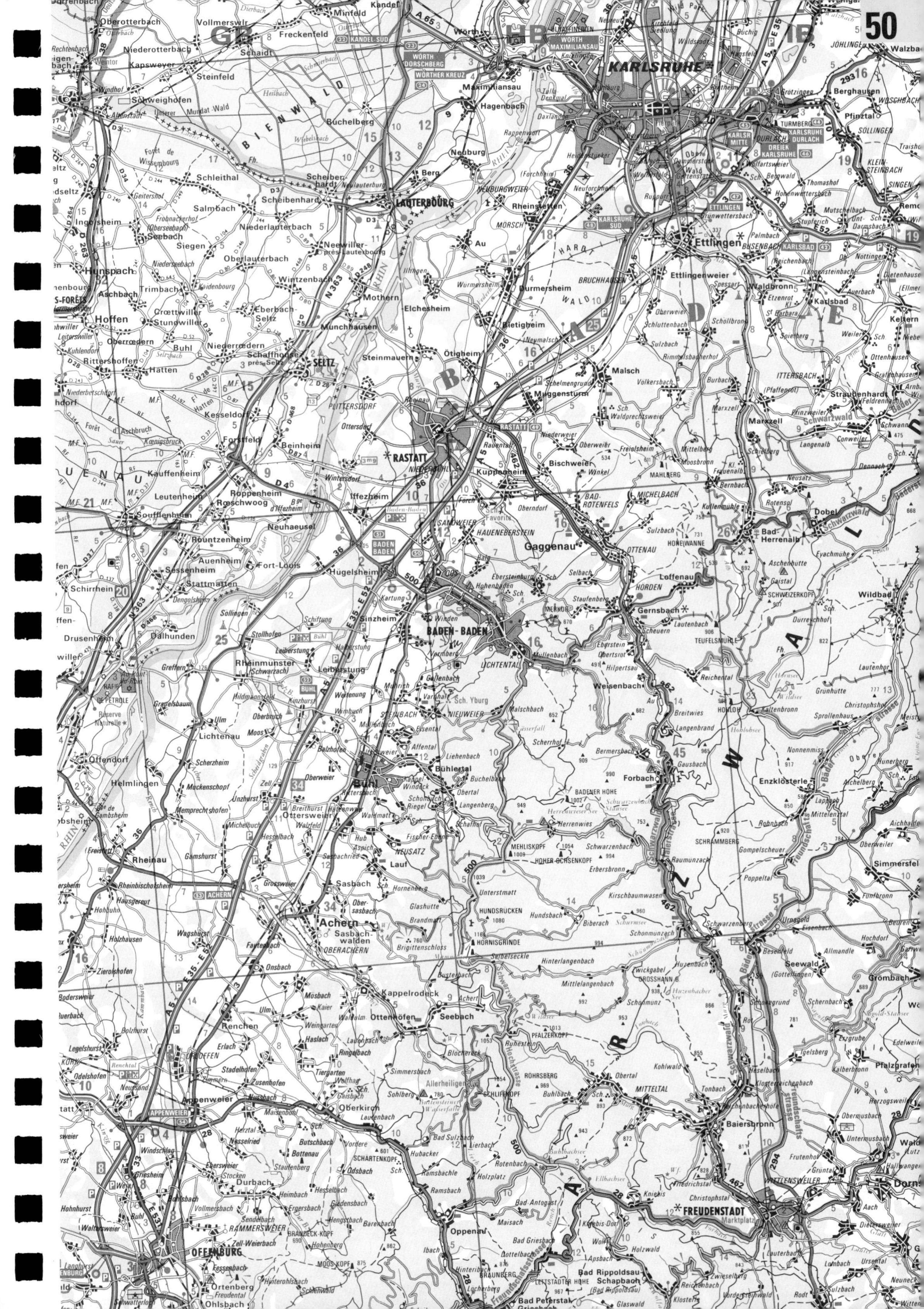
KARLSRUHE
Ettlingen
Malsch
Muggensturm
RASTATT
Kuppenheim
Gaggenau
BAD-ROTENFELS
Gernsbach
Loffenau
Bad-Herrenalb
Dobel
Wildbad
Enzklösterle
Forbach
BADEN-BADEN
LICHTENTAL
Sinzheim
Bühl
Bühlertal
Achern
Kappelrodeck
Ottenhöfen
Seebach
Renchen
Oberkirch
Appenweier
OFFENBURG
Durbach
Ortenberg
Ohlsbach
Baiersbronn
FREUDENSTADT
Bad Rippoldsau
Schapbach
Bad Peterstal
Oppenau
Rheinau
Lichtenau
Rheinmünster
Hügelsheim
Iffezheim
Durmersheim
Bietigheim
Ötigheim
Steinmauern
Elchesheim
Au
Rheinstetten
Neuburg
Hagenbach
Maximiliansau
Wörth
Kandel
Minfeld
Freckenfeld
LAUTERBOURG
SELTZ
Hatten
Hoffen
Hunspach
Soufflenheim
Drusenheim
Offendorf
Herrlisheim
Gambsheim
Mothern
Munchhausen
Beinheim
Roeschwoog
Fort-Louis
Marxzell
Waldbronn
Karlsbad
Straubenhardt
Pfinztal
HORNISGRINDE
MEHLISKOPF
BADENER HÖHE
SCHWARZWALD
BADEN
BIENWALD
Schwarzwaldhochstrasse
Badische Weinstrasse
Freudenstädter Strasse
Schwarzwald-Bäderstrasse

ILE D'OUESSANT
I. de Keller
Pnte Bac'haol
Stiff
Frugullou
Niou
Ecomusée
Lampaul
Creac'h
Penn Arlan
N.-D. de Bonne Espérance
OUESSANT
N.-D. de Bon Voyage
Feunteun Velen
Pnte de Porz Doun
la Jument
PASSAGE DU FROMVEUR
Kéréon
I. de Bannec
I. de Balanec
le Faix
les Trois Pierres
Lédénès de Molène
ILE MOLÈNE
Ile Molène
Ile de Trielen
Lédénès Quéménès
I. de Litiri
Ile de Quéménès
Morgol
12
C
A
B
13
14
Ile Vierge
GRAND CHENAL DE L'ABER VRAC'H
I. Stagadon
St-Michel
Kelerdut
Lilia
Grève du Vougo
Guissény
Kerlouan
Pnte de Beg-Pol
Pnte de Pontusval
Chapelle-Pol
Brignogan
St-Egarec
le Croazou
Lanhir
la Gare
Plouné
Kerbrézant
Lavengat
Goulven
Kerdivès
Plouider
Brendaouez
Plouguerneau
Leuré
I. Vrac'h
I. d'Erch
I. Guémioc
I. Tariec
Poulloc
l'Aber Vrac'h
I. Garo
I. de Rosservo
I. du Bec
I. Carn
Portsall
ROCHES DE PORTSALL
I. Verte
ROCHES D'ARGENTON
Trémazan
Pnte de Landunvez
Tréompan
Kergleuz
Lampaul-Ploudalmézeau
St-Pabu
Brouennou
Landéda
LANNILIS
Kerouartz
le Grouanec
St-Frégant
Penmarc'h
Kernouës
Kernilis
LESNEVEN
Kersaint
Landunvez
Ile d'Yoc'h
le Four
Argenton
Presqu'île St-Laurent
Porspoder
PLOUDALMÉZEAU
Loc Majan
Treglonou
Tariec
Loc-Brévalaire
le Folgoët
Lanarvily
Notre-Dame
Plouvien
St-Jaoua
St-Jean-Balanant
Locmaria
le Drennec
Ploudaniel
Plouguin
Kervignen
Plourin
Larret
Coat-Méal
Bourg-Blanc
PLABENNEC
Keranguéven
Kervezennec
Melon
I. de Melon
Lanildut
Brélès
Kergroadès
Tréouergat
Guipronvel
CHENAL DE L'ABER ILDUT
Aber Ildut
Lanrivoaré
Milizac
les 3 Curés
Lesquélen
St-Thonan
Trémaou
Porscav
Lampaul-Plouarzel
Porspaul
I. Ségal
le Faix
Kersaint-Plabennec
St-Eloi
Gouesnou
ST-RENAN
Plouarzel
Menhir de Kerloas
Trézien
Pnte de Corsen
Kerhornou
Lamber
Guilers
Bohars
Tromeur
St-Divy
la Forest-Landerneau
GUIPAVAS
Lavallot
Lambézellec
Ploumoguer
Kerzévéon
Penfeld
Chau de Keroual
le Relecq-Kerhuon
Kerbasquiou
Elorn
St-Marc
CHENAL DE LA HELLE
CHENAL DU FOUR
Ile Molène
I. de Litiri
I. de Morgol
Ile de Quéménès
la Grande Vinotière
Anse des Blancs Sablons
Lanfeust
Trébabu
Locmaria-Plouzané
Plouzané
Castel-Névez
St-Pierre-Quilbignon
Arsenal
Océanopolis
Pont A. Louppe
St-Jean
Dirinon
le Passage
Kérahou
Pnte de Kermorvan
le Conquet
Pnte des Renards
Kérambosquer
la Trinité
Cosquer
PM
Recouvrance
BREST
CALVAIRE
Plougastel-Daoulas
Loperhet
Ile de Béniguet
Lochrist
Porsmilin
Anse de Trez-Hir de Bertheaume
OCEANOGRAPHIQUE
Ste-Anne-du-Portzic
Pnte du Diable
Pnte de Portzic
RADE DE BREST
Kernisi
Plougonvelin
St-Mathieu
Pnte de St-Mathieu
Ste-Christine
St-Adrien
St-Guénolé
Pnte du Corbeau
Anse du Caro
le Caro
Porsguen
Pnte de Rostiviec
Rostiviec
DAOULAS
les Pierres Noires
Pnte du Pt Minou
GOULET DE BREST
Pnte des Espagnols
Kervinin
Roscanvel
Pnte de l'Armorique
Kerdéniel
Pnte de Kerdéniel
Kéramenez
BAIE DE DAOULAS
St-Jean
Prat-an-Dour
Logonna-Daoulas
Rungléo
Ste-Marguerite
PARC
CHAUSSÉE DES PIERRES NOIRES
I. Ronde
Pnte Doubidy
BAIE DE ROSCANVEL
I. Trébéron
I. des Morts
Ile Longue
Quélern
Rostellec
ANSE DU FRET
le Fret
Gr de Ile du Bindy
Min à Mer
Pnte du Grand Gouin
Pnte du Toulinguet
N.-D. de Roc'h Amadour
Alignements de Lagatjar
St-Fiacre
Camaret-s-Mer
Lanvéoc
ANSE DE POULMIC
Base Aéronautique
Lomergat
la Forêt
Landévennec
Abb.
la Parquette
Pointe de Pen Hir
Réserve Ornithologique
Kerloc'h
PRESQU'ÎLE DE CROZON
Mon Blanche
Térénez
I. de Térénez
Moulin à Mer
Pont Suspendu de Térénez
les Tas de Pois
Anse de Dinan
Gaoulac'h
CROZON
Tal ar Groas
Chau de Dinan
Pnte de Dinan
Tréboron
Argol
Morgat
ANSE DE MORGAT
Grotte de l'Autel
Lespiguet
Telgruc-s-Mer
Pnte de Morgat
I. de l'Aber
Croaz Sémenou
Trega
N 12-E 50
N 165
E 60
71

D
E
F
ILE DE BATZ
Ile de Batz
Plymouth
Cork
PLATEAU DE LA MÉLOINE
Pnte de Bloscon
Roscoff
Pnte de Primel
BAIE
BAIE DE MORLAIX
DE
LANNION
Réserve Ornithologique
Santec
Plouescat
Cléder
Sibiril
Plougoulm
ST-POL-DE-LÉON
Carantec
Plougasnou
St-Jean-du-Doigt
Locquirec
RADE DE MORLAIX
Plouézoch
Guimaëc
LANMEUR
PLESTIN-LES-GRÈVES
Tréflez
Plounevez-Lochrist
Tréflaouénan
Plouénan
Henvic
Locquénolé
Mespaul
Trézilidé
St-Vougay
PLOUZÉVÉDÉ
TAULÉ
Plouégat-Guérand
Lanhouarneau
St-Méen
Plouvorn
St-Martin-des-Champs
Garlan
Plougar
Plougourvest
Ste-Sève
MORLAIX
PLOUIGNEAU
Plouégat-Moysan
Guiclan
Base Aéronavale
Bodilis
Plounéventer
LANDIVISIAU
N 12 - E 50
Plourin-lès-Morlaix
St-Servais
ST-THÉGONNEC
Plougonven
Lanneuffret
Pleyber-Christ
Botsorhel
Guerlesquin
Lampaul-Guimiliau
Guimiliau
Loc-Eguiner
la Roche-Maurice
Lannéanou
la Martyre
PLOUDIRY
le Cloître-St-Thégonnec
Locmélar
Loc-Eguiner-St-Thégonnec
Pencran
St-Sauveur
Plounéour-Ménez
Tréflévénez
ROCHE ST-BARNABÉ
Bolazé
St-Urbain
SIZUN
Commana
Scrignac
le Tréhou
ROC'H TREDUDON
Trédudon-le-Moine
la Croix Rouge
Irvillac
ROC'H TREVEZEL
la Feuillée
Berrien
Quénéquen
Botmeur
St-Eloy
SIGNAL DE TOUSSAINES
MONTAGNES
M O N T A G N E S D' A R R É E
Hôpital-Camfrout
PEN-AR-HOAT
St-Rivoal
MONTAGNE ST-MICHEL
HUELGOAT
Brennilis
Locmaria-Berrien
Hanvec
FORÊT DU CRANOU
Poullaouen
le Moënnec
Loqueffret
St-Herbot
ROC'H BEGHEOR
Brasparts
Plouyé
LE FAOU
Lannédern
Quimerc'h
Lopérec
Rosnoën
Pont-de-Buis-lès-Quimerc'h
Collorec
Plounévézel
le Cloître-Pleyben
Plonévez-du-Faou
St-Ségal
Kergloff
CARHAIX
St-Laurent
72
53

53
G
H
11
12
13
14
CÔTE
GRANIT
LES SEPT ILES
I. Rouzic
Réserve Ornithologique
I. de Malban
I. Bono
Ile aux Moines
Guen Braz
les Héaux
Ile Grande
Ploumanac'h
Trégastel
PERROS-GUIREC
Trélévern
Trévou-Tréguignec
Penvénan
Plougrescant
Pleubian
Lanmodez
Kerbors
TRÉGUIER
Plouguiel
LÉZARDRIEUX
PAIMPOL
Ploubazlanec
Pleumeur-Bodou
Trébeurden
Louannec
Kermaria-Sulard
Coatréven
Trézény
Camlez
Minihy-Tréguier
Pouldouran
Pleudaniel
Pleumeur-Gautier
Trédarzec
LANNION
Ploulec'h
Rospez
Lanmérin
Langoat
LA ROCHE-DERRIEN
Quemperven
Troguéry
Hengoat
Pommerit-Jaudy
Ploëzal
Plourivo
Plouézec
Kerfot
Locquirec
Trédrez
St-Michel-en-Grève
Ploubezre
Caouënnec-Lanvézéac
Mantallot
Berhet
PONTRIEUX
Runan
Quemper-Guézennec
Yvias
PLESTIN-LES-GRÈVES
Ploumilliau
Tonquédec
Cavan
Prat
Coatascorn
Plouëc-du-Trieux
Le Faouët
Lanleff
Pléhédel
Tréduder
Plouzélambre
Pluzunet
Brélidy
St-Clet
St-Gilles-les-Bois
Tréméven
Lannebert
Lanvellec
PLOUARET
Plufur
Tréméi
BÉGARD
Landebaëron
Kermoroc'h
Squiffiec
Trévérec
Gommenec'h
LANVOLLON
Le Vieux-Marché
Tregrom
Pédernec
St-Laurent
Trégonneau
Pommerit-le-Vicomte
Plouégat-Moysan
Plounérin
MENEZ BRÉ
Louargat
Plouisy
GUINGAMP
Pabu
Goudelin
Plounévez-Moëdec
BELLE-ISLE-EN-TERRE
Tréglamus
Grâces
St-Agathon
Le Merzer
Bringolo
St-Jean-Kerdaniel
Guerlesquin
Loguivy-Plougras
Plougras
Loc-Envel
Gurunhuel
Moustéru
Ploumagoar
PLOUAGAT
Coadout
Lanrodec
Plougonver
Quilliac
St-Adrien
Bourbriac
St-Péver
Lohuec
Bolazec
la Chapelle-Neuve
Pont-Melvez
Plésidy
St-Fiacre
Senven-Léhart
Calanhel
Plourac'h
Bulat-Pestivien
CALLAC
Maël-Pestivien
Magoar
St-Connan
St-Gildas
Plusquellec
Carnoët
St-Servais
Kerien
Kerpert
St-Gilles-Pligeaux
le Vieux-Bourg
Duault
Peumerit-Quintin
Lanrivain
St-Nicodème
Trémargat
Canihuel
Locarn
Treffrin
Trébrivan
ST-NICOLAS-DU-PÉLEM
Kergrist-Moëlou
CORLAY
le Haut-Corlay
la Harmoye
MAËL-CARHAIX
CARHAIX-PLOUGUER
Plounévez-Quintin
St-Martin-des-Prés
N 12
N 12 - E 50
D 786
D 787
D 767
73
52

J
K
L
la Horaine
PLAU DES ECHAUDÉS
Phare du Paon
Ile de Bréhat
PLAU DE MEN - MARC'H
I. Lavrec
le Bourg
I. Logodec
Pointe de l'Arcouest
les Roho
I. St-Riom
Mez de Goëlo
Pointe de Bilfot
Port Lazo
Pointe de Minard
St-Riom
le Questel
Pnte Berjule
Bréhec
Pnte de la Tour
la Mauve
Port Moguer
Pnte Gwin-Zégal
Pnte de Plouha
la Trinité
Kermaria
Kérouziel
le Palus
Pnte du Bec de Vir
PLOUHA
St-Laurent
Kérégal
Pludual
St-Yves
Tréveneuc
Roches de St-Quay
Plateau des Hors
I. Harbour
Pnte de St-Quay
Kertugal
St-Quay-Portrieux
Pléguien
le Carrefour
Portrieux
N.D. de l'Espérance
Plourhan
ÉTABLES-SUR-MER
Lantic
Pnte de la Rognouze
Binic
Tréguidel
N.D.-de-la-Cour
le Vaudic
la Ville Rouault
Pnte de Pordic
Grève des Rosaires
la Cordenie
Trégomeur
Pordic
Plélo
Tréméloir
les Rosaires
St-Eloi
Pnte du Roselier
le Roselier
St-Mathurin
CHÂTELAUDREN
la Ville Agan
St-Laurent
N 12 - E 50
le Sépulcre
PLÉRIN
le Légué
Tour
Pnte de Cesson
Anse d'Yffiniac
Pnte des Guettes
Plouvara
Plerneuf
Trémuson
Cesson
ST-BRIEUC
St-Ilan
LANGUEUX
les Grèves
Hillion
St-Hervé
la Croix-Fichet
la Méaugon
Boqueho
PLOUFRAGAN
Trégueux
Yffiniac
St-René
St-Donan
le Créac'h
B. de Plédran
Camp Antique de Péran
St-Volon
Plaine-Haute
St-Julien
St-Nicolas
Plédran
le Foeil
l'Hôpital
Crézouard
la Croix-de Piruit
la Houssaye
Quessoy
Crénan
QUINTIN
Pays Gallo
St-Brandan
Plaintel
St-Guihen
St-Carreuc
le Colombier
Robien
St-Eutrope
Lanvia
Carestiemble
Hénon
Beau Soleil
Port-Martin
le Coudray
le Pas
Lanfains
FORÊT DE LORGE
PLŒUC-S.-LIÉ
St-Laurent
MONCONTOUR
l'Hermitage-Lorge
Belorient
Plémy
le Bodéo
le Bourgneuf
Rourhon
la Tantouille
N.D. de-la-Croix
Allineuc
les Forges
Bosméléac
la Porte-aux-Moines
Grand Léjon
BAIE DE ST-BRIEUC
Rohein
les Comtesses
le Four
le Grd Pourier
Rohinet
CÔTE
Chenal d'Erquy
Chlle St-Michel
Cap d'Erquy
Cap Fréhel
Pléhérel-Plage (Vieux Bourg)
Sables-d'Or-les-Pins
les Hôpitaux
Erquy
Plurien
Fréhel
Trécelin
la Carquois
le Verdelet
Réserve
Caroual
St-Pabu
St-Mathurin
Pnte de Pléneuf
le Val-André
la Couture
St-Laurent
Montbran
Tour
MATIGNON
Pléboulle
St-Aide
Dahouët
la Guette
Bien-Assis
St-Jean
PLÉNEUF-VAL-ANDRÉ
le Port-Morvan
St-Alban
la Ville-Clochard
la Bouillie
St-Samson
Ruca
la Cotentin
le Poirier
St-Jacques-le-Majeur
Hénanbihen
B. de Coron
la Ribourdais
Hénansal
le Grand-Chemin
St-Marc
les Rigaudais
Planguenoual
Morieux
Lermot
la Granville
les Ponts Neufs
le Tertre des-Noës
St-Aaron
St-Gueltas
St-Denoual
le Boulay
le Haut-des-Bois
Quintenic
Landébia
la Doberie
Andel
Coëtmieux
FT. DE ST-AUBIN
St-Aubin
St-Symphorien
LA HUNAUDAYE
Pléven
Tumulus
Chau de la Hunaudaye
la Berthière
la Poterie
Pommeret
Haras
LAMBALLE
Carnonen
Trégomar
le St-Esprit-des-Bois
Meslin
St-Julien
Trégenestre
Maroué
Noyal
Pledéliac
Maupry
Landéhen
St-Rieul
le Temple
Meudon
Plestan
Trémeudan
St-Blaise
le Vau-Jaune
Bréhand
Stulgneuc
Lescouët
Tramain
JUGON-LES-LACS
St-Trimoël
la Malhoure
Carbéhault
le Boissy
Dolo
Mont
Penguily
le Lorrain
Langouhèdre
Trédaniel
St-Glen
Plénée-Jugon
la Touche Trébry
Trébry
N.D. du Haut
la Touche-Joubin
ARMOR
Carsul
le Gouray
la Moussaye
Sévignac
Bel-Air
la Ville-Doualan
Abbe de Boquen
74
55

M
N
O
11
12
13
ILES CHAUSEY
la Déchirée
la Sellière
Passe Orientale de l'État
les Rondes de l'Ouest
la Houllée
Romond
la Meule
Grd Colombier
I. d'Ancre
la Conchée
Grande Ile
Longue
les Huguenans
Jersey
Guernesey
Sark
Portsmouth
(été)
St-Malo
D É M E R A U D E
la Pierre de Herpin
Pointe du Grouin
Ile des Landes
Réserve Naturelle
les Tintiaux
Pointe du Meinga
Pointe du Nez
Pointe du Nid
Port-Briac
Ile des Rimains
Pointe de la Chaine
CANCALE
St-Coulomb
Rothéneuf
Paramé
Terrelabouet
BAIE DU MONT
Cap Fréhel
Réserve
Anse des Sévignés
FORT LA LATTE
la Motte
St-Cast-le-Guildo
BAIE DE LA FRESNAYE
les Mielles
les Haies de la Conchée
I. de Cézembre
le Grd Jardin
Pte du Décollé
DINARD
ST-MALO
St-Enogat
St-Servan-s.-Mer
St-Lunaire
St-Briac-s.-Mer
Lancieux
la Buzardière
St-Méloir-des-Ondes
St-Benoît-des-Ondes
Vildé-la-Marine
Hirel
le Vivier-s.-Mer
Cherrueix
Ste-Anne
MATIGNON
la Richardais
USINE MAREMOTRICE
le Limonay
la Gouesnière
Bonaban
la Fresnais
la Guéhaine
St-Père
St-Jouan-des-Guérets
Tréméreuc
PLOUBALAY
Pleurtuit
Trégon
Créhen
St-Pôtan
St-Lormel
Pluduno
PLANCOËT
St-Guinoux
Lillemer
MONT-DOL
Mont-Dol
St-Broladre
l'Epinay
CHÂTEAUNEUF-D'ILLE-ET-VILAINE
St-Suliac
le Minihic-s.-Rance
Langrolay-s.-Rance
la Ville-ès-Nonais
Pleslin-Trigavou
Plouër-s.-Rance
Roz-Landrieux
DOL-DE-BRETAGNE
Baguer-Pican
Plerguer
Miniac-Morvan
Baguer-Morvan
Pleudihen-s.-Rance
la Vicomté-s.-Rance
Epiniac
St-Samson-s.-Rance
Corseul
Bourseul
Pléven
Plorec-s.-Arguenon
St-Michel-de-Plélan
St-Méloir
Aucaleuc
Quévert
DINAN
Lanvallay
Taden
St-Hélen
Tressé
le Tronchet
Bonnemain
Lanhélin
Lourmais
Cuguen
St-Maudez
Vildé-Guingalan
la Landec
PLELAN-LE-PETIT
Léhon
St-Pierre-de-Plesguen
Trélivan
JUGON-LES-LACS
St-Carné
les Champs-Géraux
Calorguen
Plesder
Meillac
Trémeheuc
COMBOURG
Trébédan
Bobital
Brusvily
le Hinglé
Languédias
Pleugueneuc
la Chapelle-aux-Filtzméens
Lanrigan
Mégrit
Trévron
EVRAN
St-André-des-Eaux
Trédias
Yvignac
Plumaudan
Trévérien
St-Domineuc
St-Judoce
Tréfumel
St-Juvat
le Quiou
St-Maden
St-Thual
Trimer
Québriac
Dingé
54
75
N 176
D 794
D 795
D 766
D 168
D 137

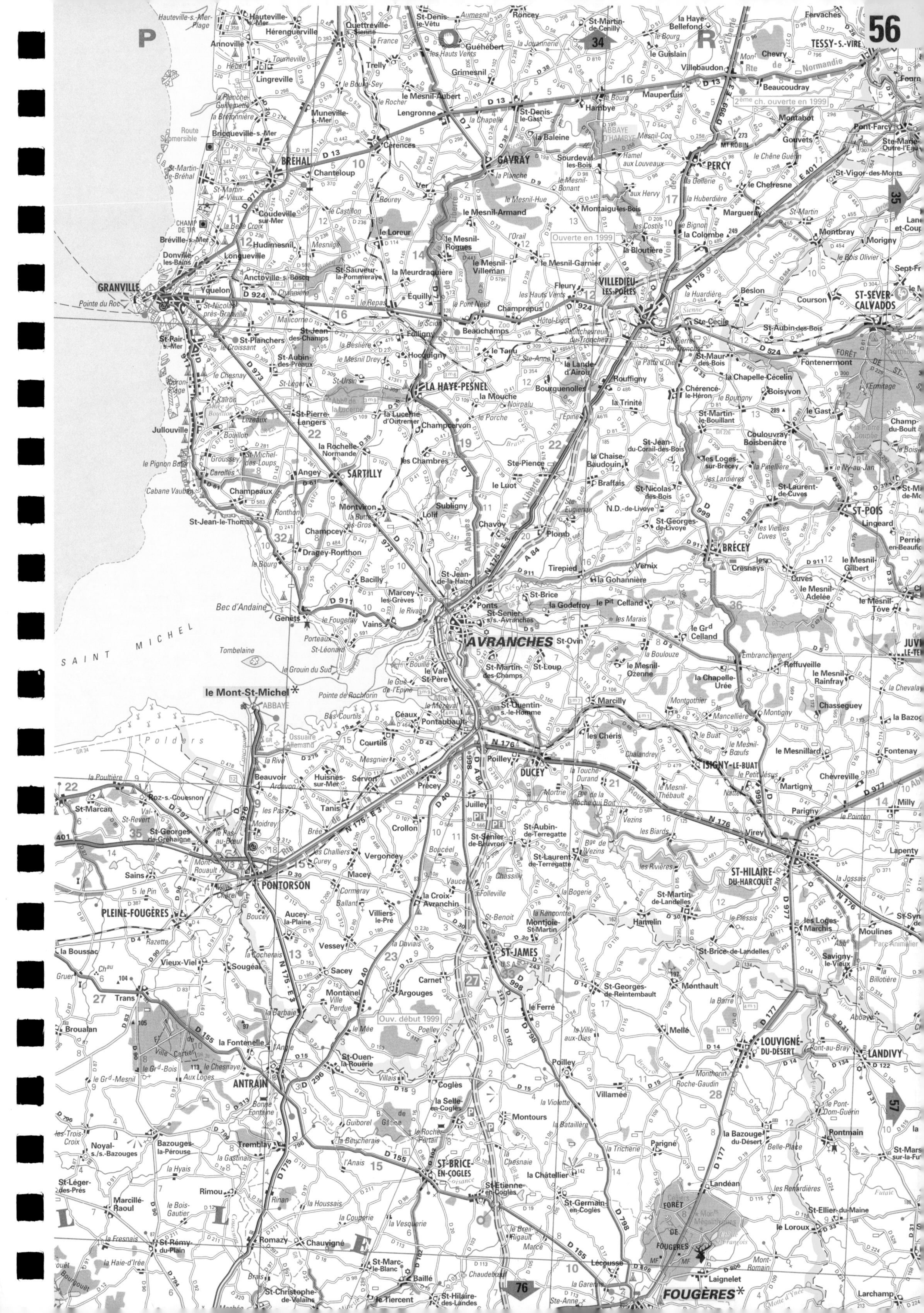
P
Q
R
Hauteville-s.-Mer-Plage
Hauteville-s.-Mer
Hérenguerville
Quettreville-s.-Sienne
St-Denis-le-Vêtu
Roncey
St-Martin-de-Cenilly
la Haye-Bellefond
Fervaches
Annoville
Guéhébert
TESSY-S.-VIRE
Tourneville
Trelly
le Guislain
Chevry
Lingreville
Grimesnil
Villebaudon
Rte de Normandie
le Mesnil-Aubert
Maupertuis
Beaucoudray
2ème ch. ouverte en 1999
la Planche-Guillemette
Hambye
la Bretonnière
Muneville-s.-Mer
Lengronne
St-Denis-le-Gast
ABBAYE D'HAMBYE
Montabot
Route Submersible
Bricqueville-s.-Mer
la Baleine
Mesnil-Coq
Pont-Farcy
Cérences
Gouvets
St-Martin-de-Bréhal
BRÉHAL
GAVRAY
Sourdeval-les-Bois
MT ROBIN
Ste-Marie-Outre-l'Eau
Chanteloup
PERCY
St-Vigor-des-Monts
St-Martin-le-Vieux
Ver
le Chefresne
CHAMP DE TIR
Coudeville-sur-Mer
le Castillon
le Mesnil-Armand
Montaigu-les-Bois
Margueray
Bréville-s.-Mer
le Loreur
le Mesnil-Rogues
Ouverte en 1999
la Colombe
Montbray
Morigny
Donville-les-Bains
Hudimesnil
la Bloutière
Longueville
le Mesnil-Villeman
le Mesnil-Garnier
Anctoville-s.-Bosq
la Meurdraquière
St-Sauveur-la-Pommeraye
GRANVILLE
Yquelon
Fleury
VILLEDIEU-LES-POÊLES
Beslon
Courson
ST-SEVER-CALVADOS
Pointe du Roc
St-Nicolas-près-Granville
la Chaussée
Équilly
Champrepus
Ste-Cécile
St-Aubin-des-Bois
St-Pair-s.-Mer
St-Planchers
St-Jean-des-Champs
Folligny
Beauchamps
le Tanu
la Lande-d'Airou
St-Maur-des-Bois
Fontenermont
St-Aubin-des-Préaux
Hocquigny
Rouffigny
la Chapelle-Cécelin
LA HAYE-PESNEL
la Mouche
Bourguenolles
Chérencé-le-Héron
Boisyvon
Kairon-Plage
la Lucerne-d'Outremer
la Trinité
St-Pierre-Langers
Champcervon
St-Martin-le-Bouillant
le Gast
Jullouville
la Rochelle-Normande
Coulouvray-Boisbenâtre
St-Jean-du-Corail-des-Bois
St-Michel-des-Loups
les Chambres
Ste-Pience
la Chaise-Baudouin
les Loges-sur-Brécey
Carolles
Angey
SARTILLY
Cabane Vauban
Champeaux
le Luot
Braffais
St-Nicolas-des-Bois
St-Laurent-de-Cuves
Montviron
Subligny
N.D.-de-Livoye
ST-POIS
St-Jean-le-Thomas
Lolif
Chavoy
St-Georges-de-Livoye
Lingeard
Champcey
Plomb
BRÉCEY
Dragey-Ronthon
Tirepied
Vernix
les Cresnays
le Mesnil-Gilbert
St-Jean-de-la-Haize
la Gohannière
Bacilly
Marcey-les-Grèves
St-Brice
Cuves
le Mesnil-Adelée
Bec d'Andaine
Genêts
Vains
Ponts
la Godefroy
le Pᵗ Celland
St-Senier-s/s.-Avranches
le Mesnil-Tôve
SAINT MICHEL
Tombelaine
St-Léonard
AVRANCHES
St-Ovin
le Grᵈ Celland
le Grouin du Sud
le Val-St-Père
St-Martin-des-Champs
St-Loup
le Mesnil-Ozenne
Embranchement
Reffuveille
le Mesnil-Rainfray
le Mont-St-Michel
ABBAYE
Pointe de Rochtorin
la Chapelle-Urée
Chasseguey
Céaux
Pontaubault
St-Quentin-s.-le-Homme
Marcilly
la Mancellière
Polders
Courtils
les Chéris
le Mesnillard
Fontenay
Beauvoir
Huisnes-sur-Mer
Servon
Poilley
DUCEY
ISIGNY-LE-BUAT
Chèvreville
Roz-s.-Couesnon
Précey
Martigny
St-Marcan
Tanis
Juilley
Milly
Parigny
St-Georges-de-Gréhaigne
Crollon
St-Aubin-de-Terregatte
Virey
Lapenty
St-Senier-de-Beuvron
St-Laurent-de-Terregatte
Sains
Vergoncey
Mont-Rouault
Macey
PONTORSON
ST-HILAIRE-DU-HARCOUËT
PLEINE-FOUGÈRES
la Croix-Avranchin
St-Martin-de-Landelles
Aucey-la-Plaine
Villiers-le-Pré
Montjoie-St-Martin
Hamelin
les Loges-Marchis
Moulines
Vessey
ST-JAMES
St-Brice-de-Landelles
la Boussac
Vieux-Viel
Sougéal
Savigny-le-Vieux
Sacey
Carnet
Trans
Montanel
Argouges
St-Georges-de-Reintembault
Monthault
Broualan
Ouv. début 1999
le Ferré
la Fontenelle
Mellé
LOUVIGNÉ-DU-DÉSERT
LANDIVY
St-Ouen-la-Rouërie
ANTRAIN
Poilley
Coglès
Villamée
la Selle-en-Coglès
Montours
Noyal-s./s.-Bazouges
Bazouges-la-Pérouse
Tremblay
Parigné
la Bazouge-du-Désert
Pontmain
St-Léger-des-Prés
ST-BRICE-EN-COGLES
la Châtellier
Rimou
St-Étienne-en-Coglès
Landéan
Marcillé-Raoul
St-Germain-en-Coglès
St-Ellier-du-Maine
FORÊT DE FOUGÈRES
le Loroux
Romazy
Chauvigné
St-Rémy-du-Plain
St-Marc-le-Blanc
Lécousse
Baillé
Laignelet
St-Christophe-de-Valains
le Tiercent
St-Hilaire-des-Landes
FOUGÈRES
Larchamp
34
35
57
76
D 13
D 924
D 973
D 911
D 976
D 155
D 175
D 798
D 177
N 175
N 176
A 84
E 3
E 401

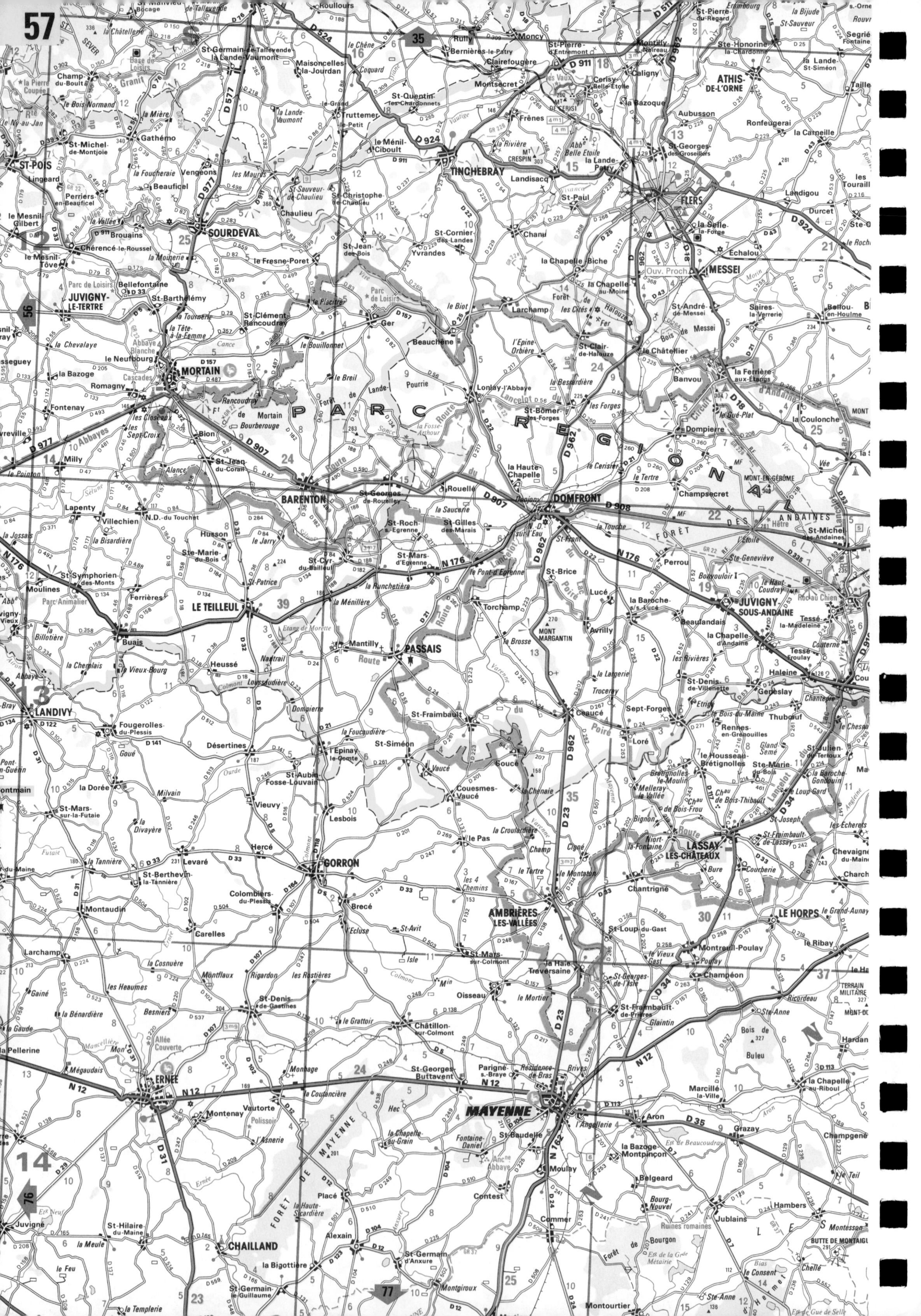
35
56
76
77
St-Pois
Lingeard
Perriers-en-Beauficel
le Mesnil-Gilbert
le Mesnil-Tôve
Chérencé-le-Roussel
Juvigny-le-Tertre
Bellefontaine
St-Barthélémy
Champ-du-Boult
le Bois Normand
St-Michel-de-Montjoie
Gathémo
la Mière
Vengeons
Beauficel
la Foucheraie
Brouains
Sourdeval
la Moinerie
le Fresne-Poret
St-Germain-de-Tallevende
la Lande-Vaumont
Maisoncelles-la-Jourdan
Coquard
Truttemer-le-Grand
Truttemer-le-Petit
St-Quentin-les-Chardonnets
le Ménil-Ciboult
St-Sauveur-de-Chaulieu
St-Christophe-de-Chaulieu
Chaulieu
St-Jean-des-Bois
Yvrandes
St-Cornier-des-Landes
Tinchebray
Rully
Bernières-le-Patry
Moncy
Clairefougère
Montsecret
Frênes
la Rivière
Mt Crespin
Landisacq
St-Paul
Chanu
St-Pierre-d'Entremont
Cerisy-Belle-Etoile
Caligny
Montilly-s.-Noireau
la Bazoque
Abb. Belle Etoile
la Lande-Patry
Flers
la Selle-la-Forge
Messei
Echalou
St-Pierre-du-Regard
Ste-Honorine-la-Chardonne
Athis-de-l'Orne
Aubusson
St-Georges-des-Groseillers
Ronfeugerai
la Carneille
Landigou
Durcet
la Lande-St-Siméon
Ouv. Proch.
la Chapelle-Biche
la Chapelle-au-Moine
Forêt de les Cités
Larchamp
le Biot
Ger
Parc de Loisirs
le Placître
St-Clément-Rancoudray
la Tournerie
la Tête-à-la-Femme
Abbaye Blanche
le Neufbourg
Mortain
Cascades
Romagny
la Chevalaye
la Bazoge
Fontenay
le Bouillonnet
le Breil
Forêt de Lande-Pourrie
Beauchêne
Lonlay-l'Abbaye
l'Epine-Orbière
St-Clair-de-Halouze
la Bessardière
St-Bômer-les-Forges
les Forges
le Châtellier
Banvou
la Ferrière-aux-Etangs
Bois de Messei
St-André-de-Messei
Saires-la-Verrerie
Bellou-en-Houlme
Dompierre
le Gué-Plat
la Coulonche
PARC RÉGIONAL
Rancoudray
Ft de Mortain
Bourberouge
les Closeaux
les Sept Croix
Bion
Milly
St-Jean-du-Corail
la Fosse-Arthour
la Haute-Chapelle
le Cerisier
le Tertre
Champsecret
Mont-en-Gérôme
Vée
Barenton
St-Georges-de-Rouelley
Rouellé
Domfront
Donjon
N.-D.-sur-l'Eau
St-Front
la Touche
Forêt des Andaines
l'Etoile
St-Michel-des-Andaines
Ste-Geneviève
Perrou
Bonvouloir
le Haut-Coudray
Roc au Chien
Lapenty
Villechien
N.D.-du-Touchet
Husson
le Jarry
Ste-Marie-du-Bois
St-Roch-s.-Egrenne
St-Gilles-des-Marais
la Saucerie
St-Cyr-du-Bailleul
St-Mars-d'Egrenne
le Pont-d'Egrenne
St-Brice
Luce
la Baroche-s/s-Lucé
Juvigny-sous-Andaine
Tessé-la-Madeleine
la Bisardière
St-Symphorien-des-Monts
Moulines
Parc Animalier
Ferrières
St-Patrice
Le Teilleul
la Ménillère
la Runchetière
Torchamp
Mont Margantin
Avrilly
Beaulandais
la Chapelle-d'Andaine
Tessé-Froulay
Couterne
la Billotière
Buais
Etang de Morette
Mantilly
Passais
la Brosse
les Rivières
Haleine
la Chemlais
Vieux-Bourg
Heussé
Nantrail
Loussaudière
la Largerie
Trocerny
St-Denis-de-Villenette
Geneslay
Chantepie
Landivy
Fougerolles-du-Plessis
Goué
Désertines
Dompierre
la Foucaudière
l'Epinay-le-Comte
St-Siméon
St-Fraimbault
Ceaucé
Sept-Forges
Etrigé
le Bois-du-Maine
Thubœuf
Rennes-en-Grenouilles
Loré
Glend Semé
St-Julien-du-Terroux
St-Aubin-Fosse-Louvain
Vaucé
Soucé
la Chenaie
le Housseau-Brétignolles
Brétignolles-le-Moulin
Ste-Marie-du-Bois
la Baroche-Gondouin
la Dorée
Milvain
Couesmes-Vaucé
Melleray-la-Vallée
Chau de Bois-Thibault
Chau de Bois-Frou
le Loup-Gard
St-Mars-sur-la-Futaie
la Divayère
Vieuvy
Lesbois
Bignon
St-Joseph
la Croulardière
Champ
le Pas
Niort-la-Fontaine
Lassay-les-Châteaux
St-Fraimbault-de-Lassay
Chevaigné-du-Maine
la Tannière
St-Berthevin-la-Tannière
Levaré
Hercé
Gorron
Cigné
le Montaton
le Tertre
Bure
Courberie
Chantrigné
les 4 Chemins
Montaudin
Colombiers-du-Plessis
Carelles
Brecé
l'Ecluse
St-Avit
Ambrières-les-Vallées
St-Loup-du-Gast
Montreuil-Poulay
le Horps
le Grand-Aunay
le Ribay
Larchamp
la Cosnuère
Montflaux
Rigardon
les Rostières
Isle
St-Mars-sur-Colmont
la Haie-Traversaine
le Vieux Gast
Poulay
Champéon
Terrain Militaire
Gainé
les Heaumes
la Bénardière
Besniers
St-Denis-de-Gastines
Oisseau
le Mortier
St-Georges-de-l'Isle
St-Fraimbault-de-Prières
Glaintin
Ricordeau
Ste-Anne
la Gaude
la Pellerine
Allée Couverte
le Grattoir
Châtillon-sur-Colmont
Bois de Buleu
Hardan
Mégaudais
Ernée
Montenay
Vautorte
Polissoir
l'Asnerie
la Coutancière
Monbage
St-Georges-Buttavent
Parigné-s.-Braye
Résidence de Bras
Brives
Mayenne
l'Angellerie
Aron
Grazay
Marcillé-la-Ville
la Chapelle-au-Riboul
Champgenéteux
Hec
la Chapelle-au-Grain
Fontaine-Daniel
Ancne Abbaye
St-Baudelle
Moulay
la Bazoge-Montpinçon
Et de Beaucoudray
Belgeard
Forêt de Mayenne
Placé
la Haute-Scardière
Contest
Bourg-Nouvel
Jublains
Hambers
Montesson
Butte de Montaigu
le Teil
Juvigné
St-Hilaire-du-Maine
la Meule
le Feu
Chailland
Alexain
la Bigottière
St-Germain-d'Anxure
Commer
Ruines romaines
Forêt de Bourgon
Et de la Gde Métairie
Bias
le Consent
Chellé
Montgiroux
St-Germain-le-Guillaume
la Templerie
Montourtier
Ste-Anne
la Barre
N 12
N 176
N 162
D 907
D 908
D 962
D 924
D 977
D 23
D 31
D 34
D 35

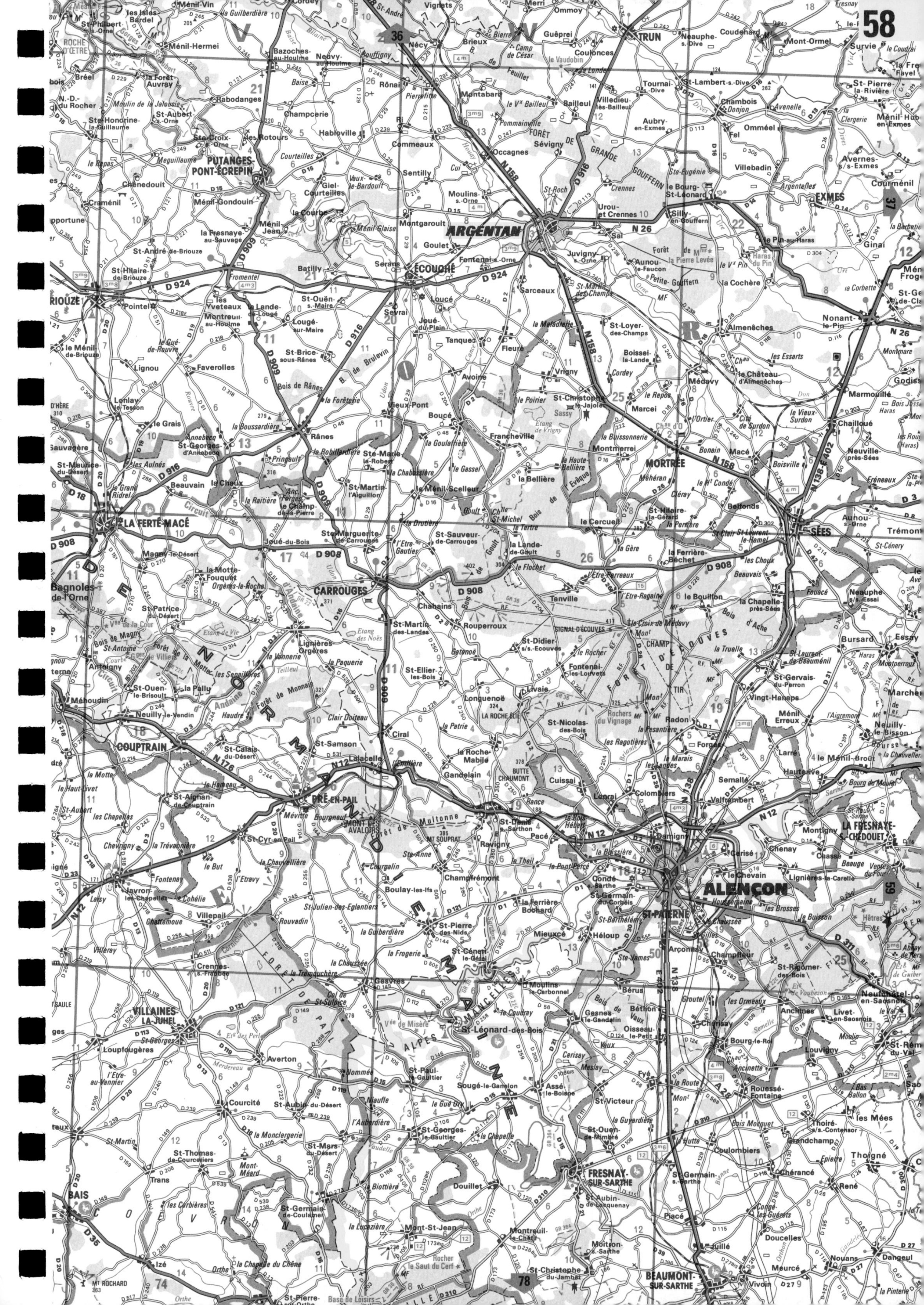

ARGENTAN
ÉCOUCHÉ
PUTANGES-PONT-ÉCREPIN
TRUN
Chambois
Exmes
Nonant-le-Pin
Almenêches
Mortrée
SÉES
LA FERTÉ-MACÉ
Bagnoles-de-l'Orne
Rânes
CARROUGES
Écouves
FORÊT D'ÉCOUVES
Signal d'Écouves
La Roche Elie
COUPTRAIN
PRÉ-EN-PAIL
Mont des Avaloirs
Mt Souprat
ALENÇON
St-Paterne
LA FRESNAYE-SUR-CHÉDOUET
VILLAINES-LA-JUHEL
St-Léonard-des-Bois
Alpes Mancelles
FRESNAY-SUR-SARTHE
BEAUMONT-SUR-SARTHE
BAIS
Mt Rochard
Courcité
Averton
Gesvres
Sougé-le-Ganelon
Assé-le-Boisne
Mamers
Forêt de Perseigne
Neufchâtel-en-Saosnois
Forêt de Multonne
Forêt de Monnaie
Forêt de Gouffern
Forêt Grande
Vimoutiers
St-Pierre-sur-Orthe
D 908
D 924
D 909
D 916
N 158
N 12
N 26
N 138
N 176
A 28
36
37
59
74
78

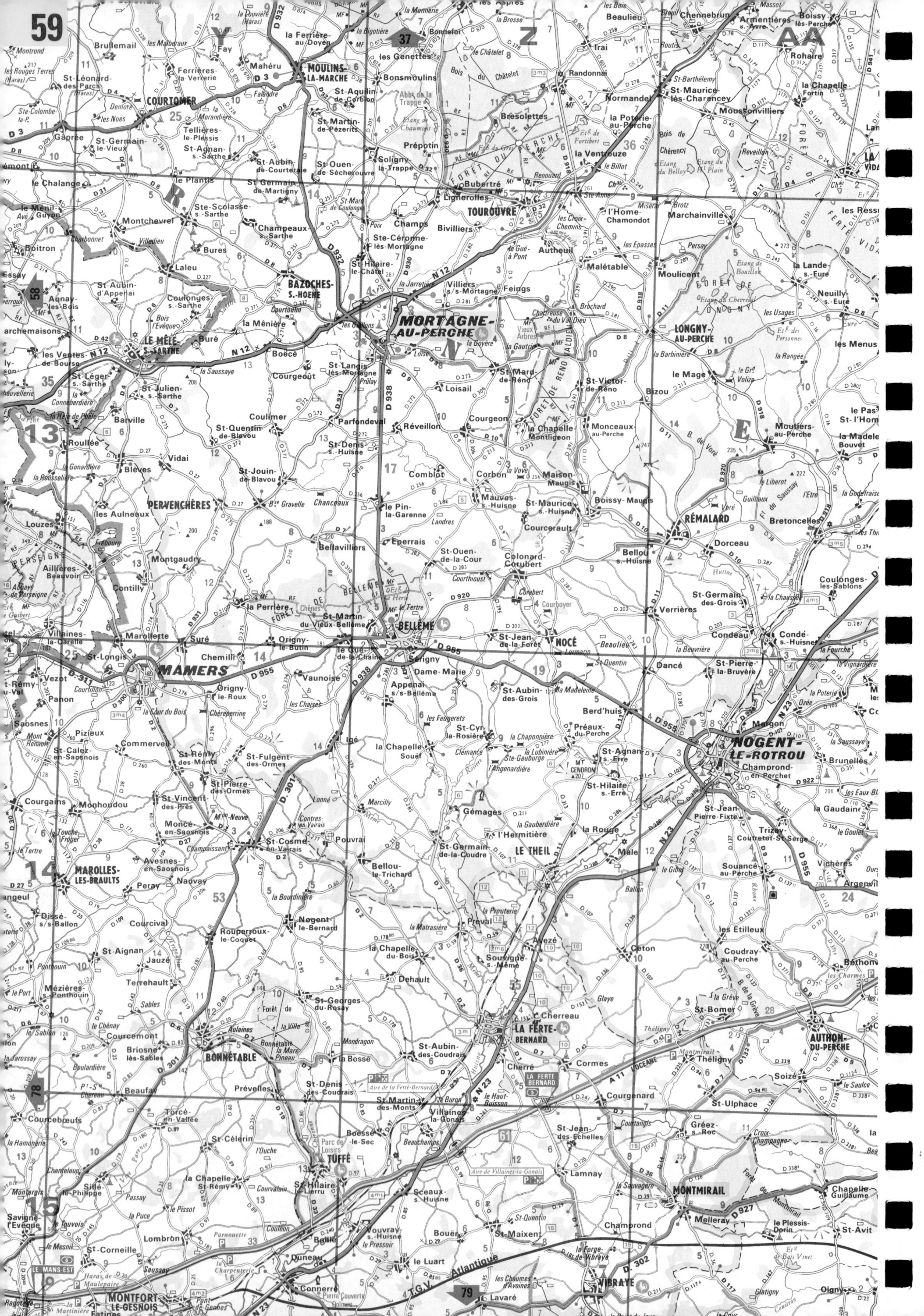

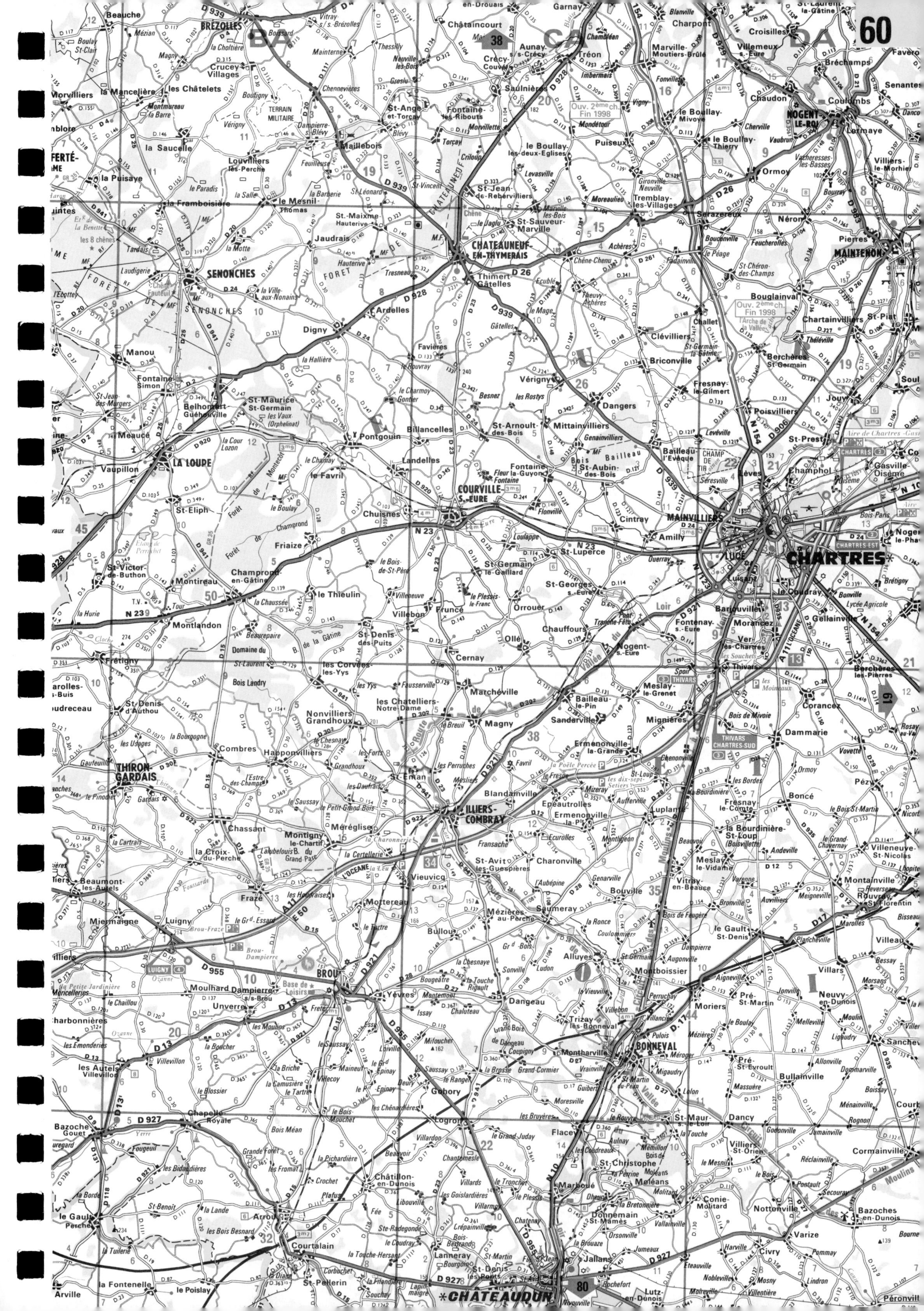
Beauche
Brezolles
Châtaincourt
Garnay
Blanville
Charpont
Croisilles
Senantes
Crucey Villages
Aunay-s/s-Crécy
Crécy-Couvé
Tréon
Marville-Moutiers-Brûlé
Villemeux-s-Eure
Bréchamps
Morvilliers
la Mancelière
les Châtelets
Saulnières
Fonvilliers
Chaudon
Coulombs
Nogent-le-Roi
Lormaye
Terrain Militaire
Chennevières
St-Ange-et-Torçay
Fontaine-les-Ribouts
Vigny
le Boullay-Mivoye
Maillebois
Louvilliers-lès-Perche
la Saucelle
le Boullay-les-deux-Eglises
Puiseux
le Boullay-Thierry
Villiers-le-Morhier
la Puisaye
Ormoy
la Framboisière
le Mesnil-Thomas
St-Jean-de-Rebervilliers
Tremblay-les-Villages
Serazereux
Néron
St-Maixme-Hauterive
St-Sauveur-Marville
Jaudrais
Châteauneuf-en-Thymerais
Maintenon
Pierres
Senonches
Thimert-Gâtelles
Chêne-Chenu
St-Chéron-des-Champs
Bouglainval
Ardelles
Chartainvilliers
St-Piat
Digny
Clévilliers
Briconville
Manou
Favières
Berchères-St-Germain
Fontaine-Simon
Vérigny
Fresnay-le-Gilmert
Jouy
St-Maurice-St-Germain
Dangers
Poisvilliers
Belhomert-Guéhouville
Billancelles
St-Arnoult-des-Bois
Mittainvilliers
Meaucé
Pontgouin
St-Prest
La Loupe
Landelles
Bailleau-l'Evêque
Vaupillon
Fontaine-la-Guyon
St-Aubin-des-Bois
Lèves
Champhol
Gasville-Oisème
Courville-s-Eure
St-Eliph
Chuisnes
Mainvilliers
Cintray
Amilly
Fraize
Lucé
Chartres
St-Victor-de-Buthon
St-Luperce
St-Germain-le-Gaillard
Champrond-en-Gâtine
Montireau
St-Georges-s-Eure
le Thieulin
Le Coudray
Fruncé
Orrouer
Barjouville
Montlandon
Villebon
Morancez
Gellainville
Fontenay-s-Eure
Chauffours
Ollé
St-Denis-des-Puits
Cernay
Nogent-s-Eure
Frétigny
Thivars
Berchères-les-Pierres
les Corvées-les-Yys
Marchéville
Meslay-le-Grenet
Bailleau-le-Pin
St-Denis-d'Authou
les Châtelliers-Notre-Dame
Corancez
Sandarville
Nonvilliers-Grandhoux
Magny
Mignières
Dammarie
Combres
Happonvilliers
Ermenonville-la-Grande
Thiron-Gardais
St-Eman
Blandainville
Pézy
Bonce
Illiers-Combray
Epeautrolles
Ermenonville-la-Petite
Luplanté
Fresnay-le-Comte
Chassant
Méréglise
Montigny-le-Chartif
la Bourdinière-St-Loup
Villeneuve-St-Nicolas
La Croix-du-Perche
St-Avit-les-Guespières
Charonville
Meslay-le-Vidame
Beaumont-les-Autels
Vieuvicq
Vitray-en-Beauce
Montainville
Frazé
Bouville
Mottereau
Mézières-au-Perche
Saumeray
Rouvray-St-Florentin
Miermaigne
Luigny
Bullou
le Gault-St-Denis
Alluyes
Brou
Montboissier
Villars
Moulhard
Dampierre-s/s-Brou
Unverre
Yèvres
Dangeau
Moriers
Pré-St-Martin
Neuvy-en-Dunois
Trizay-lès-Bonneval
Bonneval
Montharville
Pré-St-Evroult
Bullainville
Les Autels-Villevillon
Gohory
Chapelle-Royale
Bazoche-Gouet
Logron
Flacey
St-Maur-s-le-Loir
Dancy
Villiers-St-Orien
Cormainville
St-Christophe
Châtillon-en-Dunois
Marboué
Moléans
Conie-Molitard
Nottonville
Bazoches-en-Dunois
le Gault-Perche
Arrou
Donnemain-St-Mamès
Varize
Courtalain
Lanneray
Jallans
Civry
la Fontenelle
le Poislay
St-Pellerin
Châteaudun
Lutz-en-Dunois
Péronville
Arville

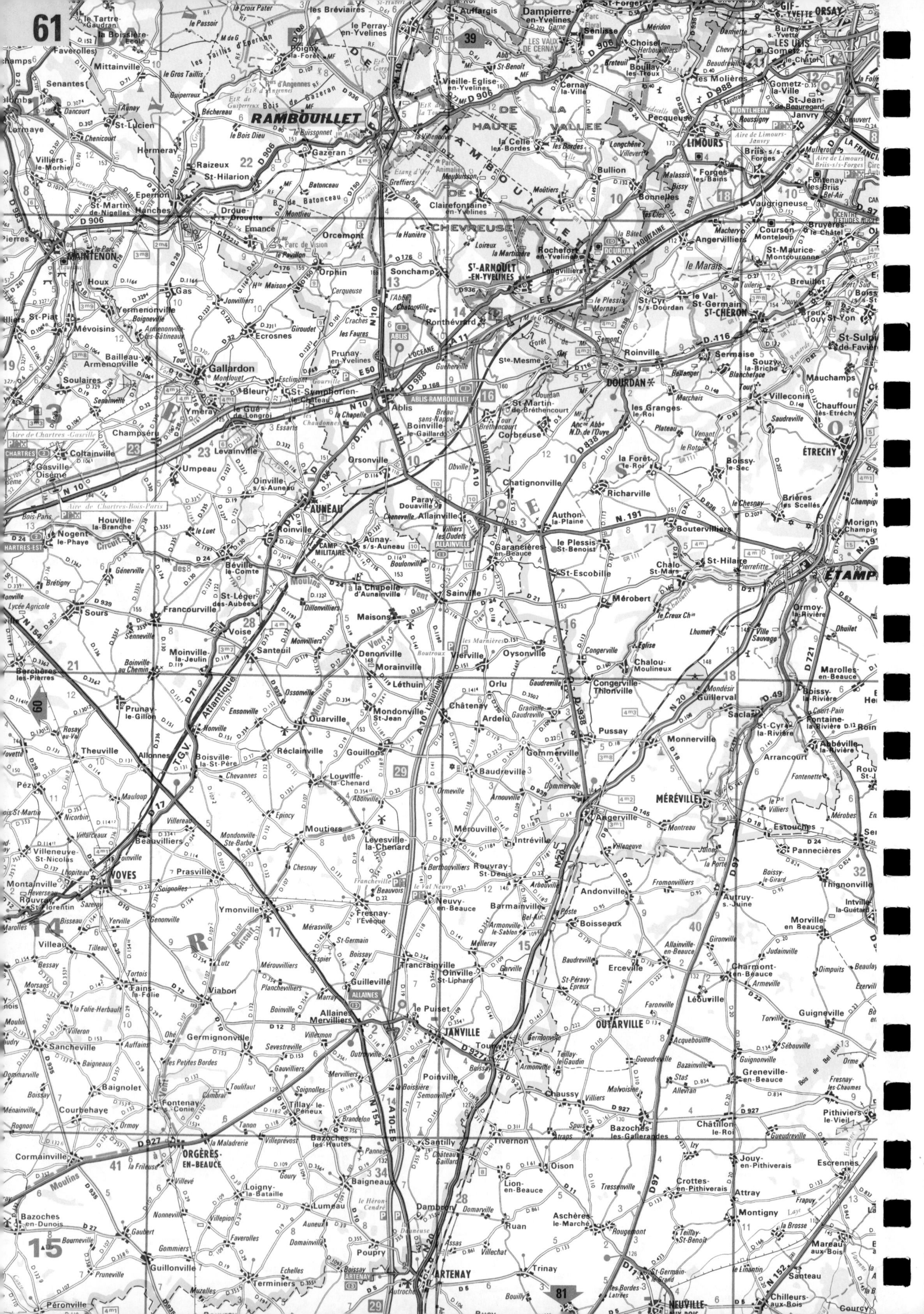
RAMBOUILLET
le Perray-en-Yvelines
Auffargis
Dampierre-en-Yvelines
Senlisse
Choisel
GIF-YVETTE
ORSAY
Bures-s.-Yvette
LES ULIS
Gometz-le-Châtel
Cernay-la-Ville
Vieille-Eglise-en-Yvelines
Poigny-la-Forêt
Mittainville
Faverolles
Senantes
St-Lucien
Hermeray
Raizeux
St-Hilarion
Gazeran
Epernon
Hanches
St-Martin-de-Nigelles
MAINTENON
Droue-s-Drouette
Emancé
Orcemont
Orphin
Sonchamp
Clairefontaine-en-Yvelines
CHEVREUSE
St-ARNOULT-EN-YVELINES
Rochefort-en-Yvelines
Bullion
Pecqueuse
LIMOURS
Briis-s/s-Forges
Forges-les-Bains
Bonnelles
Vaugrigneuse
Angervilliers
Courson-Monteloup
St-Maurice-Montcouronne
le Val-St-Germain
ST-CHÉRON
St-Cyr-s/s-Dourdan
Breuillet
St-Yon
Sermaise
Roinville
DOURDAN
Ste-Mesme
Ponthévrard
Prunay-en-Yvelines
ABLIS
Ablis
Gallardon
Ecrosnes
Gas
Houx
Vermenonville
Bailleau-Armenonville
Soulaires
Mévoisins
St-Piat
Bleury
St-Symphorien-le-Château
Ymeray
Champséru
Coltainville
Gasville-Oisème
Levainville
Umpeau
Oinville-s/s-Auneau
AUNEAU
Roinville
Aunay-s/s-Auneau
Boinville-le-Gaillard
Orsonville
Paray-Douaville
Allainville
Corbreuse
St-Martin-de-Bréthencourt
les Granges-le-Roi
Chatignonville
la Forêt-le-Roi
Richarville
Authon-la-Plaine
le Plessis-St-Benoist
Boutervilliers
Boissy-le-Sec
Villeconin
Chauffour-lès-Étréchy
ÉTRECHY
Souzy-la-Briche
Mauchamps
St-Sulpice-de-Favières
St-Hilaire
Chalo-St-Mars
ÉTAMPES
St-Escobille
Mérobert
Garancières-en-Beauce
Sainville
la Chapelle-d'Aunainville
Maisons
Béville-le-Comte
Houville-la-Branche
Nogent-le-Phaye
St-Léger-des-Aubées
Francourville
Sours
Voise
Santeuil
Moinville-la-Jeulin
Denonville
Morainville
Léthuin
Vierville
Oysonville
Orlu
Châtenay
Ardelu
Congerville-Thionville
Chalou-Moulineux
Guillerval
Saclas
Pussay
Gommerville
Monnerville
Mondonville-St-Jean
Ouarville
Réclainville
Gouillons
Louville-la-Chenard
Baudreville
Ormoy-la-Rivière
Marolles-en-Beauce
Boissy-la-Rivière
Abbéville-la-Rivière
Arrancourt
MÉRÉVILLE
Angerville
Estouches
Pannecières
Thignonville
Berchères-les-Pierres
Prunay-le-Gillon
Theuville
Allonnes
Boisville-la-St-Père
Moutiers
Levesville-la-Chenard
Mérouville
Intréville
Rouvray-St-Denis
Andonville
Autruy-s.-Juine
Beauvilliers
Villeneuve-St-Nicolas
VOVES
Prasville
Ymonville
Fresnay-l'Évêque
Neuvy-en-Beauce
Barmainville
Boisseaux
Erceville
Charmont-en-Beauce
Morville-en-Beauce
Léouville
Guigneville
Guilleville
Allaines-Mervilliers
Francrainville
Oinville-St-Liphard
OUTARVILLE
JANVILLE
Toury
Germignonville
Sancheville
Baignolet
Courbehaye
Fontenay-sur-Conie
Poinville
Tillay-le-Péneux
Chaussy
Bazoches-les-Gallerandes
Châtillon-le-Roi
Greneville-en-Beauce
Pithiviers-le-Vieil
ORGÈRES-EN-BEAUCE
Cormainville
Bazoches-les-Hautes
Santilly
Tivernon
Oison
Jouy-en-Pithiverais
Escrennes
Loigny-la-Bataille
Baigneaux
Lion-en-Beauce
Crottes-en-Pithiverais
Attray
Lumeau
Dambron
Aschères-le-Marché
Montigny
Ruan
Bazoches-en-Dunois
Poupry
Trinay
Guillonville
Terminiers
ARTENAY
Santeau
Mareau-aux-Bois
Chilleurs-aux-Bois
NEUVILLE
Péronville
81
39
60

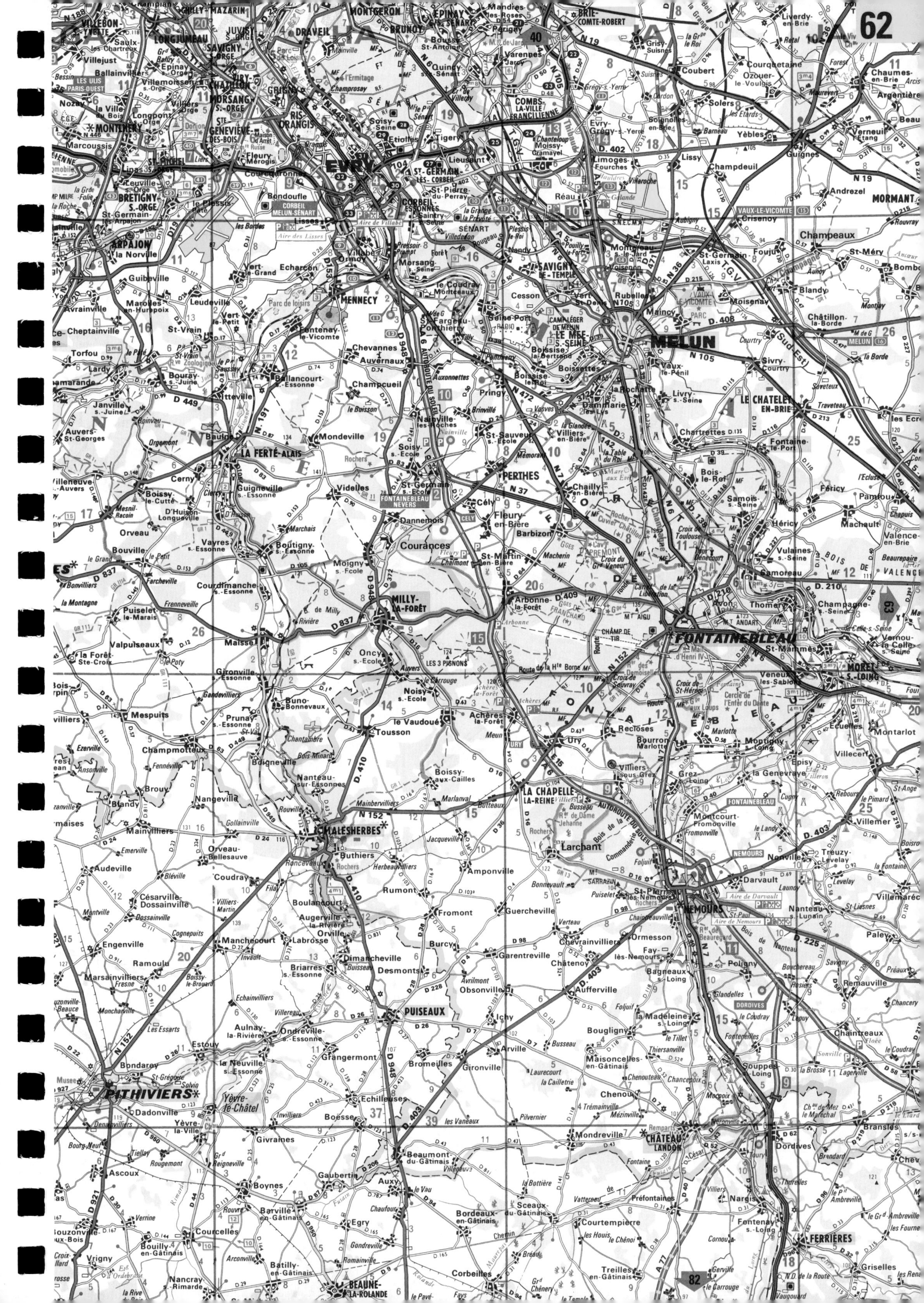
Longjumeau
Draveil
Montgeron
Brunoy
Brie-Comte-Robert
Villejust
Ballainvilliers
Montlhéry
Marcoussis
Morsang-s.-Orge
Ste-Geneviève-des-Bois
Ris-Orangis
Evry
Tigery
Lieusaint
Combs-la-Ville
Grisy-Suisnes
Coubert
Solers
Yèbles
Guignes
Courquetaine
Ozouer-le-Voulgis
Chaumes-en-Brie
Argentière
Brétigny-s.-Orge
Bondoufle
Corbeil-Essonnes
St-Germain-lès-Corbeil
Lissy
Champdeuil
Limoges-Fourches
Réau
Crisenoy
Andrezel
Mormant
Arpajon
La Norville
Lisses
Villabé
Ormoy
Morsang-s.-Seine
Nandy
Savigny-le-Temple
Cesson
Vert-St-Denis
Montereau-s.-le-Jard
St-Germain-Laxis
Fouju
Champeaux
St-Méry
Bombon
Guibeville
Vert-le-Grand
Echarcon
Mennecy
Le Coudray-Montceaux
Rubelles
Maincy
Moisenay
Blandy
Marolles-en-Hurepoix
Leudeville
Vert-le-Petit
Fontenay-le-Vicomte
Chevannes
Auvernaux
Seine-Port
Le Mée-s.-Seine
Boissise-la-Bertrand
Melun
Châtillon-la-Borde
Cheptainville
St-Vrain
Torfou
Lardy
Bouray-s.-Juine
Itteville
Ballancourt-s.-Essonne
Champcueil
Auxonnettes
Pringy
Boissettes
Vaux-le-Pénil
Livry-s.-Seine
Sivry-Courtry
Le Châtelet-en-Brie
Janville-s.-Juine
Auvers-St-Georges
Mondeville
Nainville-les-Roches
St-Sauveur-s.-Ecole
Dammarie-les-Lys
Villiers-en-Bière
Chartrettes
Fontaine-le-Port
La Ferté-Alais
Baulne
Soisy-s.-Ecole
Perthes
Chailly-en-Bière
Bois-le-Roi
Samois-s.-Seine
Féricy
Cerny
Guigneville-s.-Essonne
Videlles
St-Germain-s.-Ecole
Cély
Fleury-en-Bière
Barbizon
Héricy
Machault
Valence-en-Brie
Boissy-le-Cutté
D'Huison-Longueville
Orveau
Dannemois
Courances
St-Martin-en-Bière
Vulaines-s.-Seine
Samoreau
Vayres-s.-Essonne
Boutigny-s.-Essonne
Moigny-s.-Ecole
Bouville
Courdimanche-s.-Essonne
Milly-la-Forêt
Arbonne-la-Forêt
Avon
Thomery
Champagne-s.-Seine
Puiselet-le-Marais
Maisse
Fontainebleau
Valpuiseaux
La Forêt-Ste-Croix
Oncy-s.-Ecole
St-Mammès
Moret-s.-Loing
Vernou-la-Celle-s.-Seine
Gironville-s.-Essonne
Buno-Bonnevaux
Noisy-s.-Ecole
Veneux-les-Sablons
Mespuits
Prunay-s.-Essonne
Le Vaudoué
Tousson
Achères-la-Forêt
Recloses
Ury
Bourron-Marlotte
Montigny-s.-Loing
Ecuelles
Montarlot
Champmotteux
Boigneville
Boissy-aux-Cailles
La Chapelle-la-Reine
Villiers-sous-Grez
Grez-s.-Loing
Villecerf
Episy
La Genevraye
Nanteau-sur-Essonne
Brouy
Blandy
Nangeville
Mainvilliers
Malesherbes
Buthiers
Larchant
Montcourt-Fromonville
Villemer
Orveau-Bellesauve
Coudray
Amponville
Nemours
Treuzy-Levelay
Darvault
Audeville
Rumont
Fromont
Guercheville
St-Pierre-lès-Nemours
Nanteau-s.-Lunain
Césarville-Dossainville
Boulancourt
Augerville-la-Rivière
Orveau
Burcy
Chevrainvilliers
Ormesson
Paley
Engenville
Manchecourt
Labrosse
Dimancheville
Garentreville
Fay-lès-Nemours
Poligny
Ramoulu
Briarres-s.-Essonne
Desmonts
Châtenoy
Bagneaux-s.-Loing
Marsainvilliers
Obsonville
Aufferville
Remauville
Puiseaux
Ichy
La Madeleine-s.-Loing
Aulnay-la-Rivière
Ondreville-s.-Essonne
Bougligny
Chaintreaux
Estouy
Grangermont
Bromeilles
Arville
Gironville
Maisoncelles-en-Gâtinais
Bondaroy
La Neuville-s.-Essonne
Souppes-s.-Loing
Pithiviers
Yèvre-le-Châtel
Echilleuses
Boësse
Chenou
Dadonville
Yèvre-la-Ville
Givraines
Mondreville
Château-Landon
Bransles
Dordives
Beaumont-du-Gâtinais
Ascoux
Gaubertin
Auxy
Boynes
Barville-en-Gâtinais
Egry
Bordeaux-en-Gâtinais
Sceaux-du-Gâtinais
Préfontaines
Nargis
Courtempierre
Fontenay-s.-Loing
Courcelles
Bouilly-en-Gâtinais
Ferrières
Vrigny
Batilly-en-Gâtinais
Nancray-s.-Rimarde
Corbeilles
Treilles-en-Gâtinais
Griselles
Beaune-la-Rolande
AUTOROUTE DU SOLEIL
FONTAINEBLEAU

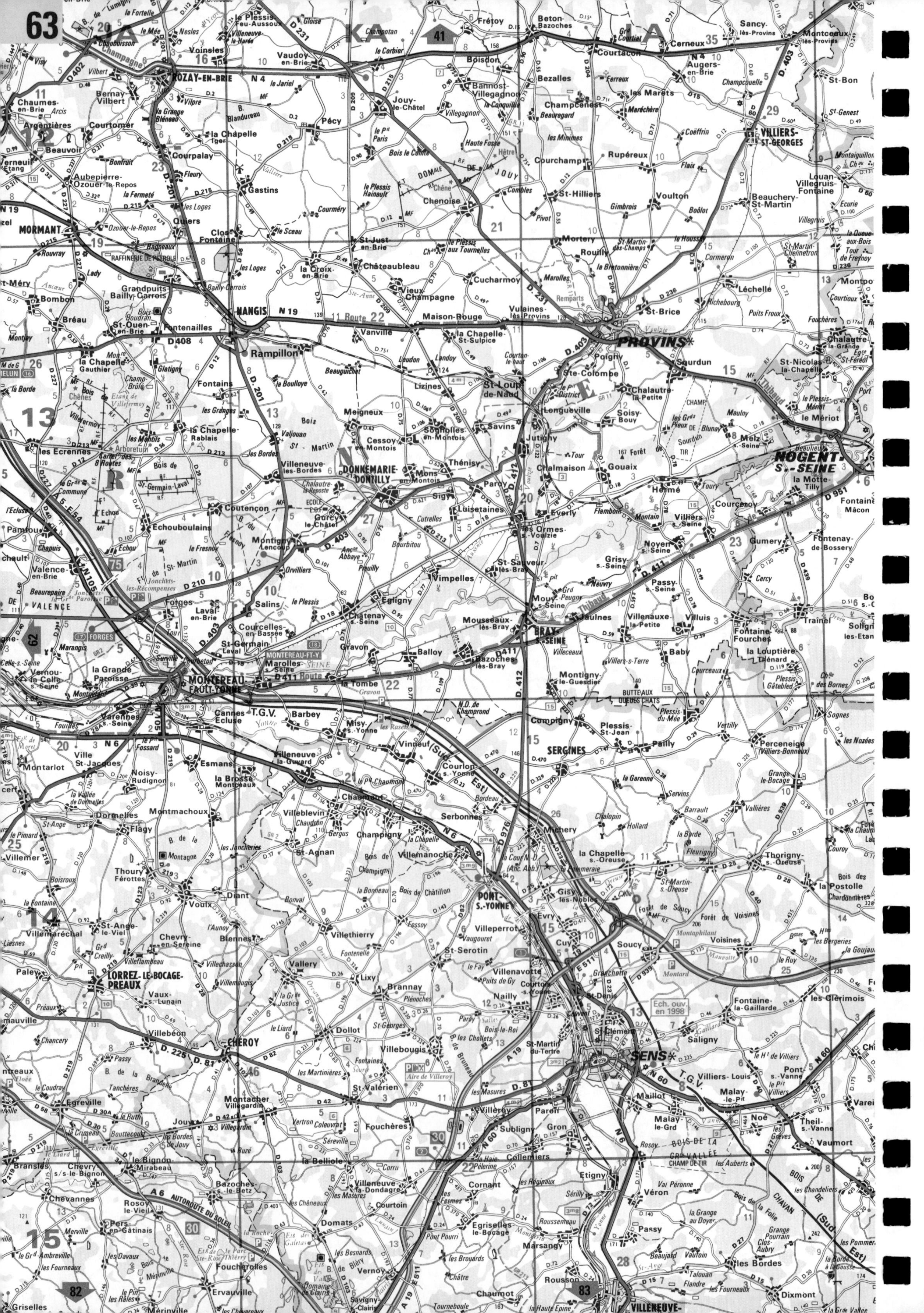

ROZAY-EN-BRIE
Voinsles
Vaudoy-en-Brie
Champotan
Frétoy
Beton-Bazoches
Sancy-lès-Provins
Cerneux
Montceaux-lès-Provins
Courtacon
Augers-en-Brie
Chaumes-en-Brie
Bernay-Vilbert
Jouy-le-Châtel
Pécy
Banno-Villegagnon
Bezalles
Champcenest
Les Marêts
St-Bon
Argentières
Courtomer
la Chapelle Iger
Villiers-St-Georges
Beauvoir
Courpalay
Rupéreux
Courchamp
Aubepierre-Ozouer-le-Repos
Gastins
Chenoise
St-Hilliers
Voulton
Beauchery-St-Martin
Louan-Villegruis-Fontaine
MORMANT
Quiers
Clos-Fontaine
St-Just-en-Brie
Mortery
Rouilly
Châteaubleau
la Croix-en-Brie
Cucharmoy
Léchelle
Grandpuits-Bailly-Carrois
Bombon
NANGIS
Vieux-Champagne
Maison-Rouge
Vulaines-lès-Provins
St-Brice
Bréau
St-Ouen-en-Brie
Fontenailles
Vanvillé
la Chapelle-St-Sulpice
PROVINS
Rampillon
Poigny
Sourdun
la Chapelle Gauthier
Fontains
Lizines
St-Loup-de-Naud
Ste-Colombe
Chalautre-la-Petite
St-Nicolas-la-Chapelle
Meigneux
Longueville
Soisy-Bouy
le Mériot
la Chapelle-Rablais
Cessoy-en-Montois
Sognolles-en-Montois
Savins
Jutigny
Melz-s.-Seine
NOGENT-S.-SEINE
les Ecrennes
Villeneuve-les-Bordes
DONNEMARIE-DONTILLY
Mons-en-Montois
Thénisy
Chalmaison
Gouaix
Hermé
la Motte-Tilly
Sigy
Paroy
Luisetaines
Everly
Villiers-s.-Seine
Courceroy
Coutençon
Echouboulains
Gurcy-le-Châtel
Les Ormes-s.-Voulzie
Noyen-s.-Seine
Gumery
Fontenay-de-Bossery
Montigny-Lencoup
St-Sauveur-lès-Bray
Grisy-s.-Seine
Valence-en-Brie
Vimpelles
Passy-s.-Seine
VALENCE
Forges
Laval-en-Brie
Salins
Egligny
Châtenay-s.-Seine
Mouy-s.-Seine
Mousseaux-lès-Bray
Jaulnes
Villenauxe-la-Petite
Villuis
Traînel
Courcelles-en-Bassée
St-Germain-Laval
Gravon
Balloy
BRAY-S.-SEINE
Bazoches-lès-Bray
Fontaine-Fourches
Baby
la Louptière-Thénard
Vernou-la-Celle-s.-Seine
la Grande Paroisse
Marolles-s.-Seine
MONTEREAU-FAULT-YONNE
la Tombe
Montigny-le-Guesdier
Varennes-s.-Seine
Cannes-Ecluse
Barbey
Misy-s.-Yonne
Compigny
Plessis-St-Jean
Plessis-du-Mée
Ville St-Jacques
Montarlot
Noisy-Rudignon
Esmans
Villeneuve-la-Guyard
Vinneuf
Courlon-s.-Yonne
SERGINES
Pailly
Perceneige
la Brosse-Montceaux
Chaumont
Dormelles
Montmachoux
Villeblevin
Champigny
Serbonnes
Michery
Flagy
St-Agnan
Villemanoche
la Chapelle-s.-Oreuse
Thorigny-s.-Oreuse
Villemer
Thoury-Férottes
PONT-S.-YONNE
Gisy-les-Nobles
la Postolle
Voulx
Diant
Villethierry
Villeperrot
Evry
Villemaréchal
St-Ange-le-Viel
Chevry-en-Sereine
Blennes
Cuy
Soucy
Voisines
St-Serotin
Paley
LORREZ-LE-BOCAGE-PREAUX
Vallery
Lixy
Brannay
Villenavotte
Naillly
St-Denis
Vaux-s.-Lunain
Fontaine-la-Gaillarde
les Clérimois
Villebéon
CHEROY
Dollot
Villebougis
St-Martin-du-Tertre
SENS
Saligny
St-Valérien
Villiers-Louis
Malay-le-Pt
Egreville
Montacher-Villegardin
Villeroy
Paron
Maillot
Jouy
Fouchères
Subligny
Gron
Malay-le-Grd
Noé
Theil-s.-Vanne
Vaumort
la Belliole
Collemiers
Etigny
Chevry s/s-le-Bignon
le Bignon-Mirabeau
Villeneuve-la-Dondagre
Cornant
Véron
Chevannes
Bazoches-s.-le-Betz
Rosoy-le-Vieil
Courtoin
Egriselles-le-Bocage
Domats
Passy
Marsangy
Fouchérolles
Vernoy
Les Bordes
Rousson
Ervauville
Chaumot
Dixmont
VILLENEUVE-
A 6 AUTOROUTE DU SOLEIL
T.G.V.
41
62
82
83

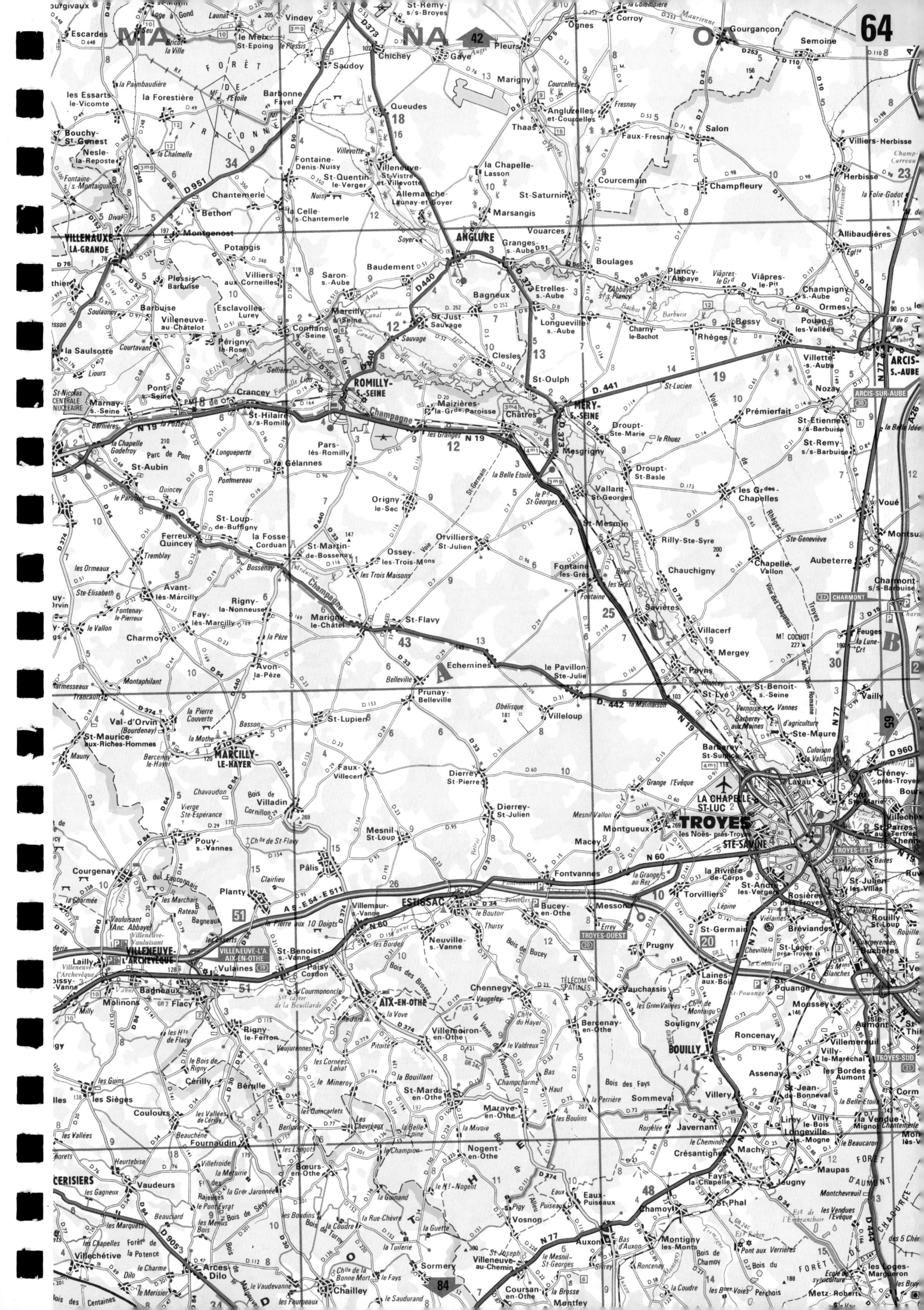

42
Escardes
Loge à Gond
le Meix St-Epoing
Vindey
Chichey
St-Remy-s/s-Broyes
Gaye
Pleurs
Ognes
Corroy
Gourgançon
Semoine
Saudoy
Marigny
Courcelles
Fresnay
Queudes
Anglure
Barbonne-Fayel
les Essarts-le-Vicomte
la Forestière
Forêt de la Traconne
Bouchy-St-Genest
Nesle-la-Reposte
Fontaine-Denis-Nuisy
Villeneuve-St-Vistre-et-Villevotte
St-Quentin-le-Verger
Allemanche-Launay-et-Soyer
la Chapelle-Lasson
Thaas
Angluzelles-et-Courcelles
Faux-Fresnay
Salon
Villiers-Herbisse
Herbisse
Courcemain
Champfleury
St-Saturnin
Marsangis
Chantemerle
la Celle-s/s-Chantemerle
Bethon
Villenauxe-la-Grande
Montgenost
Potangis
Vouarces
Granges-s.-Aube
Allibaudières
Boulages
Baudement
Saron-s.-Aube
Villiers-aux-Corneilles
Plessis-Barbuise
Plancy-l'Abbaye
Viâpres-le-Pt
Champigny-s.-Aube
Bagneux
Etrelles-s.-Aube
Esclavolles-Lurey
Barbuise
Villeneuve-au-Châtelot
Marcilly-s.-Seine
Conflans-s.-Seine
St-Just-Sauvage
Longueville-s.-Aube
Charny-le-Bachot
Rhèges
Bessy
Ormes
Pouan-les-Vallées
la Saulsotte
Périgny-la-Rose
Courtavant
Clesles
Villette-s.-Aube
Arcis-s.-Aube
Liours
Pont-s.-Seine
Romilly-s.-Seine
St-Oulph
St-Lucien
Nozay
Marnay-s.-Seine
Crancey
Maizières-la-Grde-Paroisse
Chatres
Méry-s.-Seine
Premierfait
St-Etienne-s/s-Barbuise
St-Hilaire-s/s-Romilly
Pars-lès-Romilly
Droupt-Ste-Marie
St-Remy-s/s-Barbuise
Mesgrigny
la Chapelle Godefroy
St-Aubin
Gélannes
Droupt-St-Basle
Vallant-St-Georges
les Grdes Chapelles
Origny-le-Sec
St-Loup-de-Buffigny
St-Mesmin
Voué
Ferreux-Quincey
la Fosse-Corduan
St-Martin-de-Bossenay
Orvilliers-St-Julien
Ossey-les-Trois-Mons
Rilly-Ste-Syre
Aubeterre
Fontaine-les-Grès
Chauchigny
Chapelle-Vallon
Charmont s/s-Barbuise
Avant-lès-Marcilly
Rigny-la-Nonneuse
Savières
Fay-lès-Marcilly
Marigny-le-Châtel
St-Flavy
Villacerf
Feuges
Charmoy
Mergey
Avon-la-Pèze
Echemines
le Pavillon-Ste-Julie
Payns
Prunay-Belleville
Villeloup
St-Benoit-s.-Seine
Vailly
St-Lyé
Val-d'Orvin
St-Maurice-aux-Riches-Hommes
St-Lupien
Marcilly-le-Hayer
Ste-Maure
Barberey-St-Sulpice
Faux-Villecerf
Dierrey-St-Pierre
Lavau
Créney-près-Troyes
La Chapelle-St-Luc
Troyes
Dierrey-St-Julien
Montgueux
Ste-Savine
Pouy-s.-Vannes
Mesnil-St-Loup
Macey
Courgenay
Pâlis
Fontvannes
la Rivière-de-Corps
St-André-les-Vergers
Planty
Estissac
Torvilliers
Rosières-près-Troyes
Villemaur-s.-Vanne
Bucey-en-Othe
Messon
St-Germain
Bréviandes
Villeneuve-l'Archevêque
Neuville-s.-Vanne
Prugny
St-Benoist-s.-Vanne
Paisy-Cosdon
Vulaines
Laines-aux-Bois
Bagneaux
Flacy
Aix-en-Othe
Chennegy
Vauchassis
St-Pouange
Molinons
Rigny-le-Ferron
Villemoiron-en-Othe
Bercenay-en-Othe
Souligny
Moussey
Roncenay
Bouilly
Villy-le-Maréchal
Cérilly
Bérulle
St-Mards-en-Othe
Assenay
Les Sièges
Coulours
Maraye-en-Othe
Sommeval
Villery
St-Jean-de-Bonneval
Fournaudin
Javernant
Lirey
Longeville-s.-Mogne
Nogent-en-Othe
Crésantignes
Machy
Bœurs-en-Othe
Maupas
Cerisiers
Vaudeurs
Eaux-Puiseaux
La Chapelle
Jeugny
St-Phal
Chamoy
Vosnon
Villechétive
Auxon
Montigny-les-Monts
Arces-Dilo
Sormery
Villeneuve-au-Chemin
Chailley
Coursan-en-Othe
Montfey
Metz-Robert
Les Loges-Margueron
Forêt d'Aumont
84
65
Troyes-Ouest
Troyes-Est
Troyes-Sud
Arcis-sur-Aube
Charmont
Villeneuve-l'A Aix-en-Othe

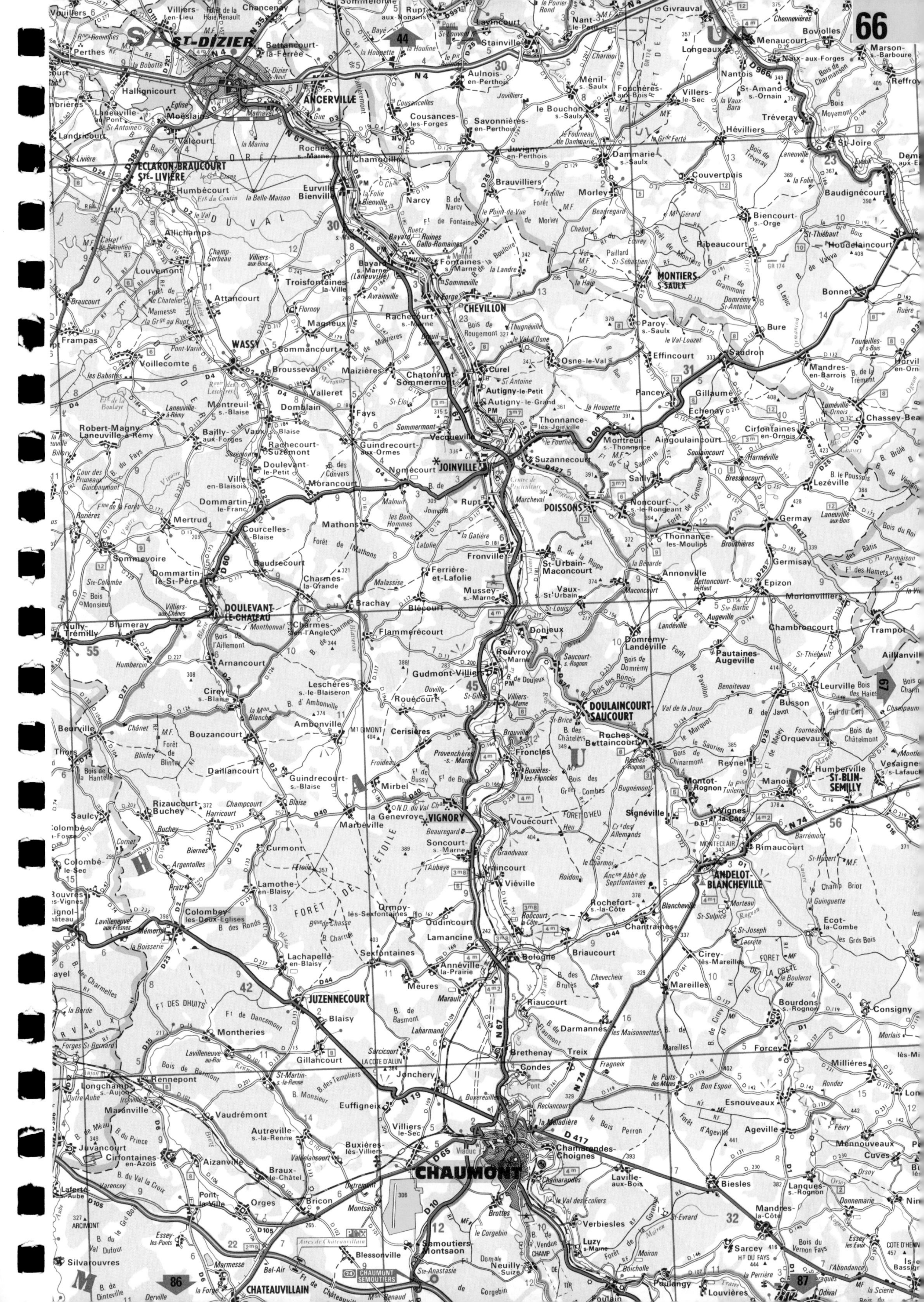
ST-DIZIER
ANCERVILLE
ECLARON-BRAUCOURT-STE-LIVIÈRE
Humbécourt
Eurville-Bienville
Chamouilley
Narcy
Bayard-s.-Marne
Fontaines-s.-Marne
CHEVILLON
Troisfontaines-la-Ville
Attancourt
WASSY
Sommancourt
Brousseval
Maizières
Curel
Chatonrupt-Sommermont
Autigny-le-Petit
Autigny-le-Grand
Thonnance-lès-Joinville
Vecqueville
JOINVILLE
Suzannecourt
POISSONS
Noncourt-s.-le-Rongeant
Montiers-s.-Saulx
Bure
Saudron
Effincourt
Gillaumé
Echenay
Aingoulaincourt
Cirfontaines-en-Ornois
Doulevant-le-Petit
Ville-en-Blaisois
Dommartin-le-Franc
Mertrud
Courcelles-s.-Blaise
Sommevoire
Dommartin-le-St-Père
DOULEVANT-LE-CHÂTEAU
Charmes-la-Grande
Brachay
Mathons
Rupt
Fronville
St-Urbain-Maconcourt
Mussey-s.-Marne
Donjeux
Rouvroy-s.-Marne
Gudmont-Villiers
DOULAINCOURT-SAUCOURT
Roches-Bettaincourt
Cirey-s.-Blaise
Arnancourt
Leschères-s.-le-Blaiseron
Cerisières
Froncles
Vouécourt
VIGNORY
Mirbel
Marbéville
Soncourt-s.-Marne
Viéville
Rochefort-s.-la-Côte
ANDELOT-BLANCHEVILLE
Rimaucourt
ST-BLIN-SEMILLY
Colombey-les-Deux-Eglises
Lamothe-en-Blaisy
Ormoy-lès-Sexfontaines
Oudincourt
Lamancine
Bologne
Annéville-la-Prairie
Sexfontaines
Lachapelle-en-Blaisy
JUZENNECOURT
Blaisy
Montheries
Riaucourt
Darmannes
Brethenay
Condes
Jonchery
Euffigneix
Gillancourt
Villiers-le-Sec
Buxières-lès-Villiers
CHAUMONT
Chamarandes-Choignes
Laville-aux-Bois
Biesles
Verbiesles
Luzy-s.-Marne
Brottes
Semoutiers-Montsaon
Bricon
Orges
CHATEAUVILLAIN
44
86
87
67

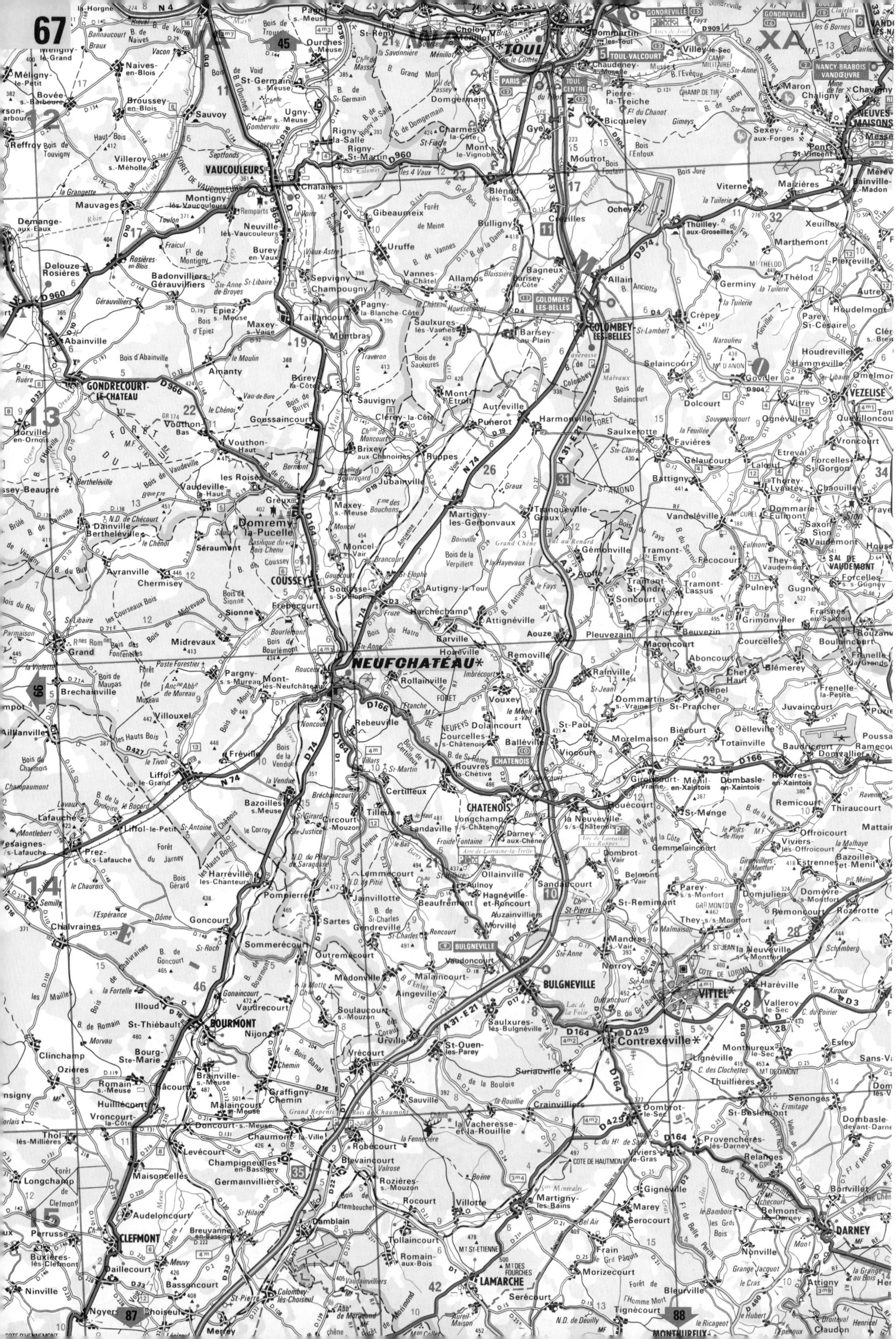

45

Toul
Dommartin-lès-Toul
Gondreville
Villey-le-Sec
Choloy-Ménillot
Ourches-s.-Meuse
Pagny-s.-Meuse
St-Germain-s.-Meuse
Void
Broussey-en-Blois
Naives-en-Blois
Méligny-le-Petit
Bovée-s.-Barboure
Sauvoy
Ugny-s.-Meuse
Domgermain
Chaudeney-s.-Moselle
Pierre-la-Treiche
Bicqueley
Maron
Chaligny
Chavigny
Neuves-Maisons
Sexey-aux-Forges
Pont-St-Vincent
Charmes-la-Côte
Mont-le-Vignoble
Gye
Rigny-la-Salle
Rigny-St-Martin
Villeroy-s.-Méholle
Reffroy
Vaucouleurs
Chalaines
Blénod-lès-Toul
Moutrot
Viterne
Mazières
Bainville-s.-Madon
Montigny-lès-Vaucouleurs
Mauvages
Demange-aux-Eaux
Neuville-lès-Vaucouleurs
Burey-en-Vaux
Gibeaumeix
Uruffe
Bulligny
Crézilles
Ochey
Thuilley-aux-Groseilles
Xeuilley
Marthemont
Pierreville
Delouze-Rosières
Badonvilliers-Gérauvilliers
Sepvigny
Champougny
Vannes-le-Châtel
Allamps
Bagneux
Barisey-la-Côte
Allain
Germiny
Thélod
Autrey
Épiez-s.-Meuse
Maxey-s.-Vaise
Taillancourt
Montbras
Pagny-la-Blanche-Côte
Saulxures-lès-Vannes
Barisey-au-Plain
Colombey-les-Belles
Crépey
Houdelmont
Parey-St-Césaire
Abainville
Amanty
Burey-la-Côte
Mont-l'Étroit
Selaincourt
Goviller
Houdreville
Hammeville
Omelmont
Gondrecourt-le-Château
Sauvigny
Autreville
Dolcourt
Vitrey
Vézelise
Horville-en-Ornois
Vouthon-Bas
Goussaincourt
Clérey-la-Côte
Punerot
Harmonville
Ognéville
Quevilloncourt
Vouthon-Haut
Brixey-aux-Chanoines
Ruppes
Saulxerotte
Favières
Vroncourt
Forcelles-St-Gorgon
Bertheléville
les Roises
Vaudeville-le-Haut
Greux
Jubainville
Gélaucourt
Battigny
Thorey-Lyautey
Chaouilley
Domremy-la-Pucelle
Maxey-s.-Meuse
Martigny-les-Gerbonvaux
Tranqueville-Graux
Vandeléville
Dommarie-Eulmont
Saxon-Sion
Praye
Dainville-Bertheléville
Séraumont
Moncel-Vair
Gémonville
Tramont-Emy
Fécocourt
Vaudémont
Avranville
Chermisey
Coussey
Soulosse-s.-St-Élophe
Autigny-la-Tour
Tramont-St-André
Tramont-Lassus
They-s.-Vaudémont
Gugney
Forcelles-s.-Gugney
Sionne
Frebécourt
Harchéchamp
Attignéville
Soncourt
Vicherey
Pulney
Grimonviller
Fraisnes-en-Saintois
Grand
Midrevaux
Barville
Aouze
Pleuvezain
Maconcourt
Beuvezin
Courcelles
Boulaincourt
Neufchâteau
Removille
Rainville
Aboncourt
Chef-Haut
Blémerey
Pargny-s.-Mureau
Mont-lès-Neufchâteau
Brechainville
Rollainville
Vouxey
Dommartin-s.-Vraine
Repel
Frenelle-la-Petite
Villouxel
Rebeuville
Dolaincourt
Balléville
St-Paul
St-Prancher
Juvaincourt
Aillianville
Fréville
Courcelles-s.-Châtenois
Rouvres-la-Chétive
Viocourt
Morelmaison
Biécourt
Oëlleville
Totainville
Liffol-le-Grand
St-Martin
Certilleux
Châtenois
Gironcourt-s.-Vraine
Ménil-en-Xaintois
Dombasle-en-Xaintois
Rouvres-en-Xaintois
Baudricourt
Domvallier
Bazoilles-s.-Meuse
Circourt-s.-Mouzon
Tilleux
Landaville
Longchamp-s.-Châtenois
Darney-aux-Chênes
La Neuveville-s.-Châtenois
Houécourt
St-Menge
Remicourt
Thiraucourt
Lafauche
Liffol-le-Petit
Prez-s.-Lafauche
Harréville-les-Chanteurs
Lemmecourt
Aulnoy
Ollainville
Sandaucourt
Dombrot-s.-Vair
Offroicourt
Viviers-lès-Offroicourt
Estrennes
Bazoilles-et-Ménil
Semilly
Pompierre
Jainvillotte
Beaufremont
Hagnéville-et-Roncourt
Belmont-s.-Vair
Parey-s.-Montfort
Domjulien
Domèvre-s.-Montfort
Chalvraines
Goncourt
Sartes
Gendreville
Auzainvilliers
St-Remimont
They-s.-Montfort
Remoncourt
Rozerotte
Sommerécourt
Outremécourt
Morville
Mandres-s.-Vair
La Neuveville-s.-Montfort
Vaudoncourt
Norroy
Médonville
Malaincourt
Aingeville
Bulgnéville
Vittel
Haréville
Valleroy-le-Sec
Gonaincourt
Illoud
Vaudrecourt
Soulaucourt-s.-Mouzon
Urville
Saulxures-lès-Bulgnéville
Contrexéville
Esley
St-Thiébault
Bourmont
Nijon
Bourg-Ste-Marie
St-Ouen-lès-Parey
Monthureux-le-Sec
Clinchamp
Ozières
Vrécourt
Lignéville
Thuillières
Sans-Vallois
Romain-s.-Meuse
Brainville-s.-Meuse
Hacourt
Graffigny-Chemin
Suriauville
Huilliécourt
Vroncourt-la-Côte
Malaincourt-s.-Meuse
Sauville
Crainvilliers
Dombrot-le-Sec
Senonges
St-Baslemont
Dombasle-devant-Darney
Thol-lès-Millières
Doncourt-s.-Meuse
Chaumont-la-Ville
La Vacheresse-et-la-Rouillie
Robécourt
Provenchères-lès-Darney
Levécourt
Champigneulles-en-Bassigny
Blevaincourt
Viviers-le-Gras
Relanges
Longchamp
Maisoncelles
Germainvilliers
Rozières-s.-Mouzon
Gignéville
Bonvillet
Audeloncourt
Rocourt
Villotte
Martigny-les-Bains
Marey
Serocourt
Belmont-lès-Darney
Darney
Perrusse
Clefmont
Breuvannes-en-Bassigny
Damblain
Tollaincourt
Frain
Nonville
Buxières-lès-Clefmont
Meuvy
Romain-aux-Bois
Lamarche
Morizecourt
Attigny
Daillecourt
Bassoncourt
Ninville
Serécourt
Bleurville
Noyers
Choiseul
Colombey-lès-Choiseul
Tignécourt
Claudon
Merrey
Monthureux-s.-Saône

66

87

88

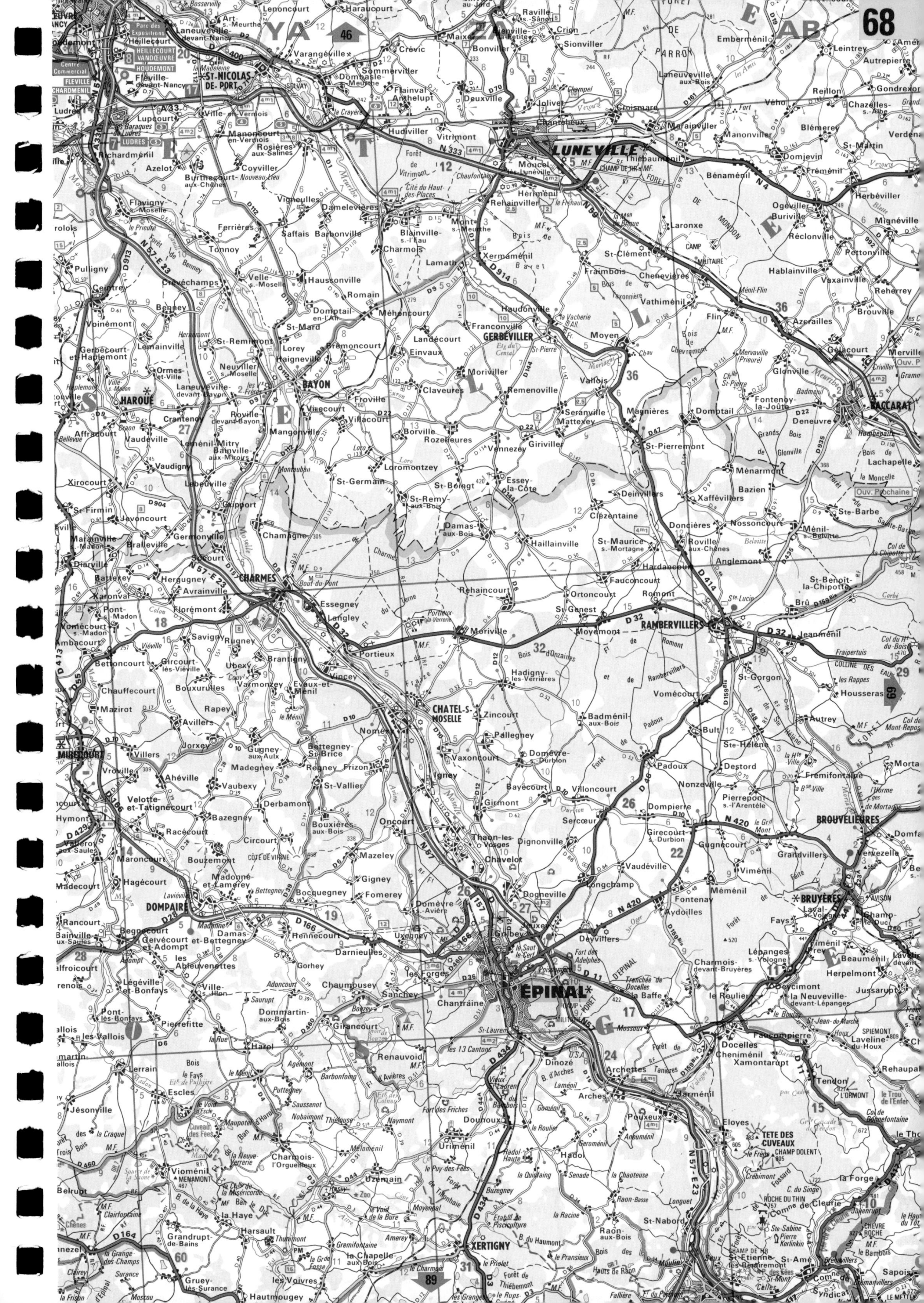
46
LUNEVILLE
ST-NICOLAS-DE-PORT
Laneuveville-devant-Nancy
Varangéville
Dombasle-Meurthe
Sommerviller
Crévic
Maixe
Bonviller
Einville-au-Jard
Raville-s.-Sânon
Sionviller
Crion
Emberménil
Leintrey
Autrepierre
Gondrexon
Reillon
Vého
Chazelles-s.-Albe
Blémerey
Domjevin
St-Martin
Fréménil
Verdenal
Herbéviller
Manonviller
Marainviller
Croismare
Laneuveville-aux-Bois
Jolivet
Chanteheux
Thiébauménil
Deuxville
Vitrimont
Hudiviller
Flainval
Anthelupt
Ville-en-Vermois
Lupcourt
Manoncourt-en-Vermois
Rosières-aux-Salines
Coyviller
Azelot
Burthecourt-aux-Chênes
Richardménil
Ludres
Fléville-devant-Nancy
Heillecourt
Houdemont
Forêt de Vitrimont
Moncel-lès-Lunéville
Hériménil
Rehainviller
Bénaménil
Ogéviller
Buriville
Reclonville
Mignéville
Pettonville
Hablainville
Vaxainville
Reherrey
Brouville
Azerailles
Gélacourt
Merviller
BACCARAT
Deneuvre
Glonville
Fontenoy-la-Joûte
Domptail
Flin
Vathiménil
Chenevières
St-Clément
Laronxe
Fraimbois
Moyen
Vallois
Magnières
Seranville
Mattexey
Giriviller
St-Pierremont
Ménarmont
Bazien
Xaffévillers
Nossoncourt
Ste-Barbe
Ménil-Belvitte
Anglemont
Doncières
Roville-aux-Chênes
St-Maurice-s.-Mortagne
Hardancourt
Clézentaine
Deinvillers
Haillainville
Damas-aux-Bois
Essey-la-Côte
Vennezey
Remenoville
Moriviller
Gerbéviller
Franconville
Haudonville
Xermaménil
Lamath
Mont-s.-Meurthe
Blainville-s.-l'Eau
Charmois
Damelevières
Barbonville
Saffais
Vigneulles
Haussonville
Romain
Méhoncourt
Domptail-en-l'Air
St-Mard
Lorey
Haigneville
Brémoncourt
Landécourt
Einvaux
BAYON
Froville
Virecourt
Villacourt
Claveures
Borville
Rozelieures
Loromontzey
St-Germain
St-Boingt
St-Remy-aux-Bois
Mangonville
Chamagne
CHARMES
Essegney
Langley
Portieux
Moriville
Rehaincourt
Ortoncourt
Fauconcourt
Romont
St-Genest
Moyemont
RAMBERVILLERS
Jeanménil
St-Gorgon
Housseras
Vomécourt
Autrey
Badménil-aux-Bois
Bult
Ste-Hélène
Padoux
Destord
Nonzeville
Fremifontaine
Pierrepont-s.-l'Arentèle
Dompierre
BROUVELIEURES
Grandvillers
Vimenil
Méménil
BRUYÈRES
Aydoilles
Fontenay
Gugnécourt
Girecourt-s.-Durbion
Sercœur
Villoncourt
Bayecourt
Domèvre-s.-Durbion
Pallegney
Zincourt
CHATEL-S-MOSELLE
Vaxoncourt
Igney
Girmont
Thaon-les-Vosges
Chavelot
Dignonville
Longchamp
Vaudéville
Dogneville
Jeuxey
Golbey
Deyvillers
ÉPINAL
Chantraine
Les Forges
Darnieulles
Uxegney
Domèvre-s.-Avière
Fomerey
Gigney
Mazeley
Oncourt
Bouxières-aux-Bois
Derbamont
St-Vallier
Regney
Frizon
Bettegney-St-Brice
Nomexy
Vincey
Evaux-et-Ménil
Varmonzey
Ubexy
Brantigny
Rugney
Savigny
Gircourt-lès-Viéville
Bouxurulles
Rapey
Avillers
Jorxey
Gugney-aux-Aulx
Madegney
Vaubexy
Ahéville
Villers
MIRECOURT
Vroville
Velotte-et-Tatignécourt
Bazegney
Racécourt
Circourt
Bouzemont
Madonne-et-Lamerey
Maroncourt
Hagécourt
DOMPAIRE
Bocquegney
Hennecourt
Damas-et-Bettegney
Gelvécourt-et-Adompt
Begnécourt
les Ableuvenettes
Ville-s.-Illon
Légéville-et-Bonfays
Pierrefitte
Dommartin-aux-Bois
Gorhey
Chaumousey
Sanchey
Girancourt
Renauvoid
Harol
Lerrain
Escles
Jésonville
Viomenil
Charmois-l'Orgueilleux
Uzemain
Urimenil
Dounoux
Hadol
Xertigny
Harsault
Grandrupt-de-Bains
Gruey-lès-Surance
Hautmougey
les Voivres
La Chapelle-aux-Bois
Raon-aux-Bois
St-Nabord
Pouxeux
Eloyes
Jarménil
Archettes
Arches
Dinozé
Docelles
Cheniménil
Xamontarupt
Tendon
Faucompierre
la Baffe
Charmois-devant-Bruyères
Le Roulier
Deycimont
Lépanges-s.-Vologne
Herpelmont
Beaumenil
Jussarupt
Laval-s.-Vologne
Champ-le-Duc
Fays
TETE DES CUVEAUX
St-Etienne-lès-Remiremont
St-Amé
89
69
Chaumont
Lemainville
Ormes-et-Ville
Laneuveville-devant-Bayon
Roville-devant-Bayon
Crantenoy
Affracourt
Vaudeville
Vaudigny
Xirocourt
St-Firmin
Jevoncourt
Germonville
Bralleville
Marainville-s.-Madon
Diarville
Battexey
Xaronval
Pont-s.-Madon
Florémont
Avrainville
Socourt
Chipport
Lebeuville
Lemainil-Mitry
Bainville-aux-Miroirs
Neuviller-s.-Moselle
St-Remimont
Velle-s.-Moselle
Crévéchamps
Benney
Voinémont
Ceintrey
Pulligny
Flavigny-s.-Moselle
Tonnoy
Ferrières
HAROUÉ
Gerbécourt-et-Haplemont
Vomécourt-s.-Madon
Ambacourt
Bettoncourt
Chauffecourt
Mazirot
Viéville

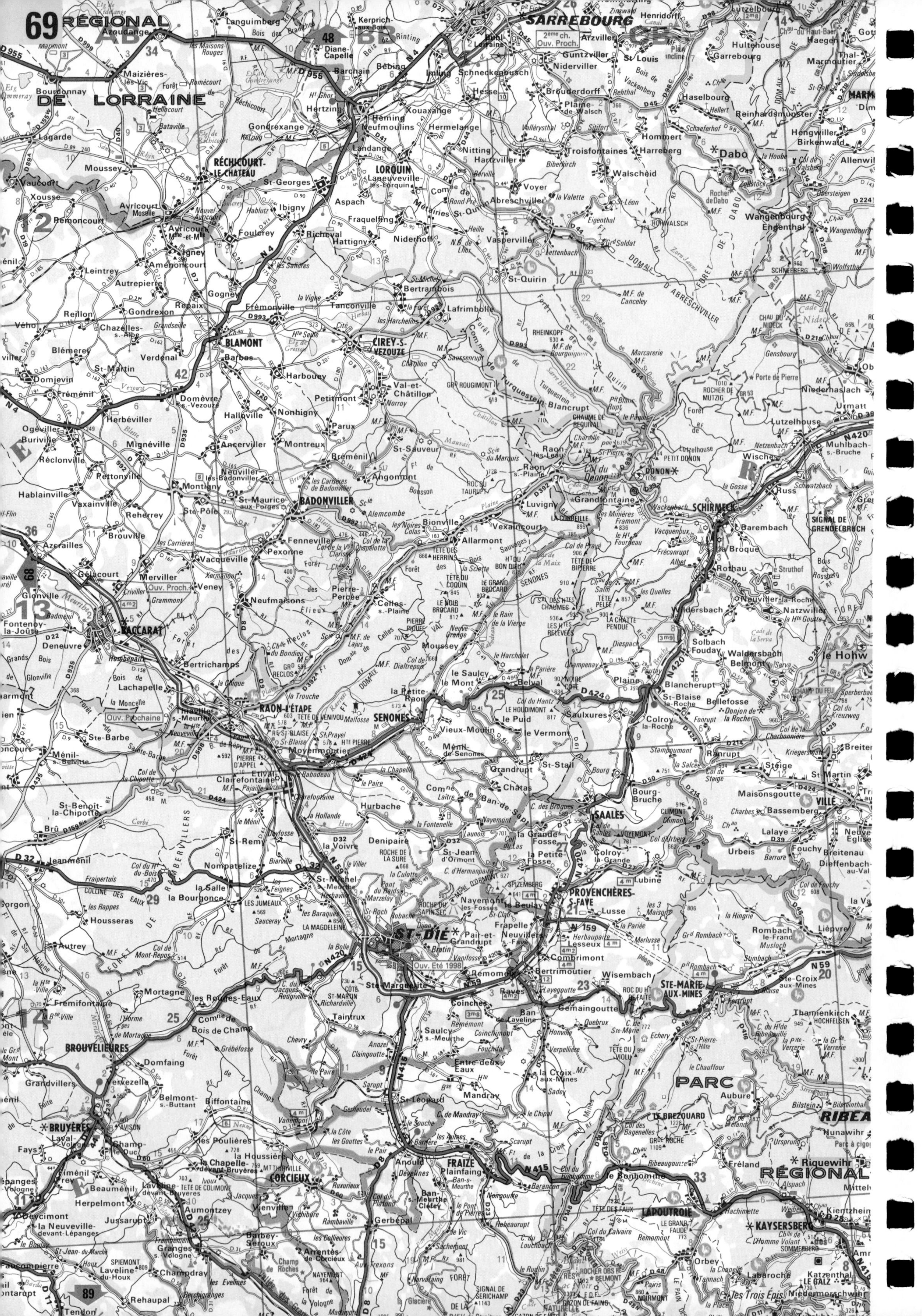
RÉGIONAL
DE LORRAINE
SARREBOURG
Réchicourt-le-Château
Lorquin
Blamont
Cirey-s-Vezouze
Badonviller
Baccarat
Raon-l'Étape
Senones
Schirmeck
Saales
St-Dié
Provenchères-s-Fave
Ste-Marie-aux-Mines
Fraize
Corcieux
Bruyères
Brouvelieures
Lapoutroie
Kaysersberg
Riquewihr
Villé
Dabo
Donon
Col du Donon
Moyenmoutier
Étival
Rambervillers
Gerbépal
Plainfaing
PARC
RÉGIONAL
Ouv. Prochaine
Ouv. Été 1998
2ème ch. Ouv. Proch.
N4
N59
N415
N420
D955
D993
D424
D392
48
68
89

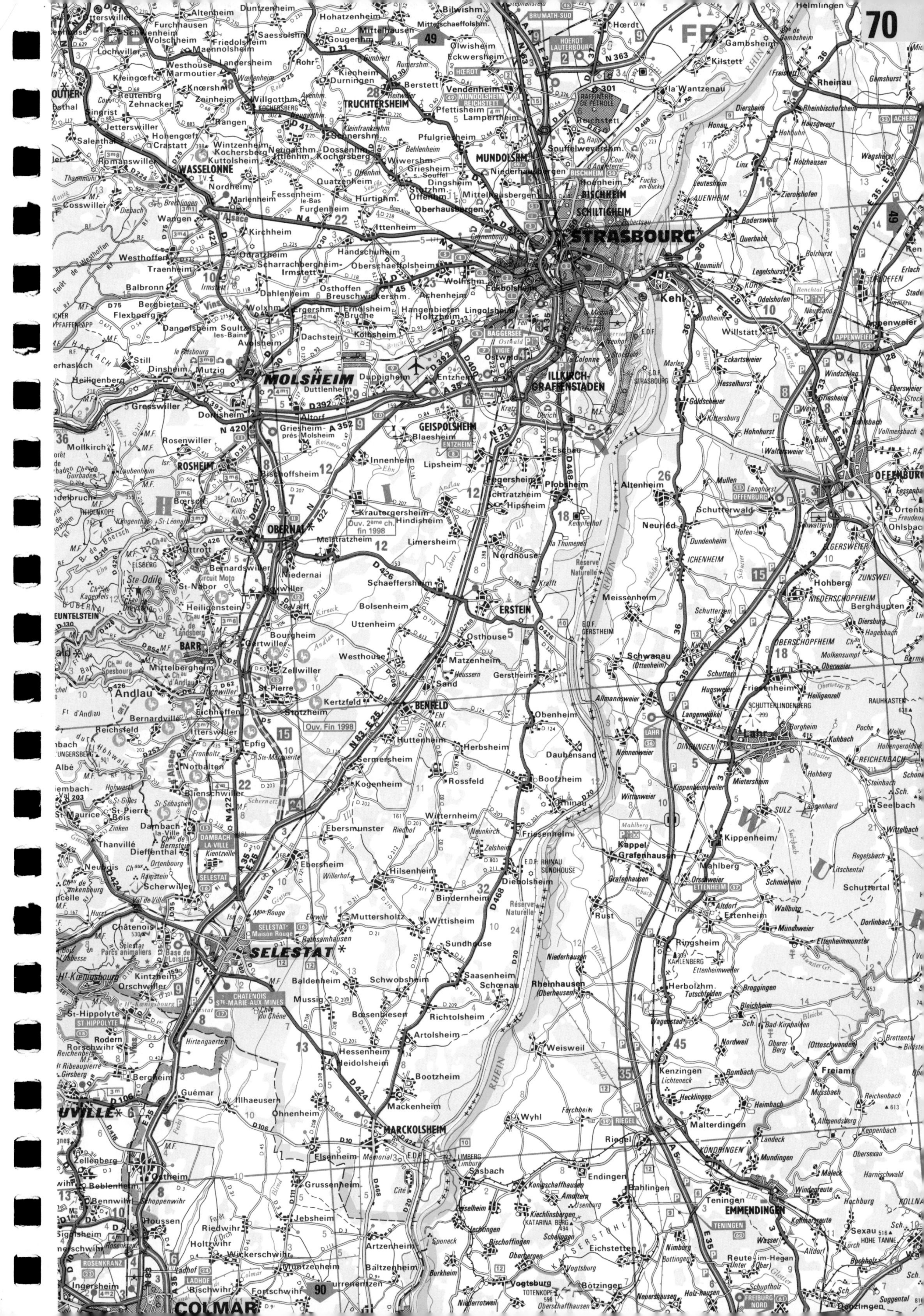
STRASBOURG
Kehl
MOLSHEIM
OBERNAI
BARR
SELESTAT
COLMAR
ERSTEIN
BENFELD
MARCKOLSHEIM
ILLKIRCH-GRAFFENSTADEN
SCHILTIGHEIM
BISCHHEIM
MUNDOLSHEIM
TRUCHTERSHEIM
WASSELONNE
ROSHEIM
Lahr
OFFENBURG
EMMENDINGEN
Teningen
Kenzingen
Endingen
Riegel
Rust
Ettenheim
Kippenheim
Mahlberg
Schwanau
Meissenheim
Neuried
Schutterwald
Altenheim
Willstätt
Appenweier
Rheinau
Gambsheim
Kilstett
Hœrdt
Brumath-Sud
Andlau
Dambach-la-Ville
Châtenois
Ste-Odile
Sasbach
Weisweil
Rheinhausen
Wyhl
Vogtsburg
Bötzingen
Eichstetten
Bahlingen
Freiamt
Sexau
Guémar
Ostheim
Ribeauvillé
Bergheim
St-Hippolyte
Kintzheim
Orschwiller
Marckolsheim
Sundhouse
Hilsenheim
Ebersheim
Boofzheim
Rhinau
Daubensand
Gerstheim
Plobsheim
Fegersheim
Geispolsheim
Entzheim
Duttlenheim
Dachstein
Wolfisheim
Eckbolsheim
Lingolsheim
Ostwald
Vendenheim
Reichstett
Souffelweyersheim
Hœnheim
Marlenheim
Westhoffen
Dinsheim
Mutzig
Still
Wangen
Kirchheim
Heiligenstein
Mittelbergheim
Epfig
Kertzfeld
Huttenheim
Herbsheim
Kogenheim
Sermersheim
Matzenheim
Osthouse
Hindisheim
Krautergersheim
Innenheim
Blaesheim
Lipsheim
RHIN
RHEIN
KAISERSTUHL

B
14
15
16
17
51
RÉGIONAL
ANSE DE MORGAT
Pnte de Morgat
I. de l'Aber
Grottes
la Palue
St-Hernot
Kerdreux
Rostudel
Cap de la Chèvre
Telgruc-s-Mer
Croaz Sémenou
Rostégoff
Pnte du Bellec
Elleguët
MENEZ-HOM
Ste-Marie du Menez-Hom
St-Nic
Pentrez
St-Côme
Plomodiern
Pnte de Talagrip
Kerviguen
Ploéven
Ty-an-Quer
Ste-Barbe
Ste-Anne-la-Palud
Pnte de Tréfeuntec
Tréfeuntec
Plonévez-Por
Kervel
BAIE DE DOUARNENEZ
Pnte de Leydé
Pnte de la Jument
Pnte du Milier
Ile Tristan
DOUARNENEZ
Locronan
Kerlaz
Tréboul
Pnte de Beuzec
Pnte de Luguénez
Réserve du Cap Sizun
Pnte de Brezellec
Tevennec
Pnte du Van
Pnte de Castelmeur
St-They
Kermeur
Baie des Trépassés
la Vieille
RAZ DE SEIN
Pointe du Raz
Lescoff
Kerrogel
Cléden-Cap-Sizun
Goulien
Beuzec-Cap-Sizun
Lescogan
Pors-Péron
Coat-Pin
Lesconil
Poullan-s-Mer
Ploaré
le Ris
Pouldavid
N.D. de Kérinec
Ft de Névet
le Juch
Plogon
Quatre-Vents
Lochrist
PONT-CROIX
Confort
Meilars
Mahalon
Plogoff
Pnte de Feunteunod
Pennéac'h
Primelin
St-Tugen
Esquibien
Audierne
Goyen
Ste-Evette
Poulgoazec
Pnte de Lervily
Tréboul
Tréheuzec
Plouhinec
Lambabu
Ty-Pic
Ty-Guen
Pouldergat
le Fort
Guengat
le Croëzou
Gourlizon
Ploneis
Guiler-s-Goyen
Landudec
Poul-ar-Marquis
la Trinité
Plozévet
Pors-Poulhan
Kerandoaré
Ste-Anne
QUIMP
PLOGASTEL-ST-GERMAIN
Pluguf
BAIE D'AUDIERNE
St-Demet
Mon
Lababan
Pouldreuzic
Kerveyen
St-Germain
Penhors
St-Joseph
Zoo
Peumerit
Chlle St-Honoré
Stang ar Bacol
Plovan
Chlle de Languidou
Tréogat
St-Sébastien
Etg de Kergalan
Etg de Trunvel
Languivoa
Tréméoc
Pérennou
le Croissant
Tréguennec
Plonéour-Lanvern
Combrit
St-Vio
PONT-L'ABBÉ
St-Jean-Trolimon
N.-D. de Tréminou
Kermaria
Anse du Pouldon
Eglise
CALVAIRE N.D.-DE TRONOËN
Beuzec
Pnte de la Torche
Rochers
la Madeleine
Musée Préhistorique
Plomeur
Kernuz
Kérézan
Ile Tudy
St-Guénolé
Pendreff
Plobannalec
Loctudy
Kerhervant
Kergall
N.-D. de la Joie
Phare d'Eckmühl
Penmarc'h
Treffiagat
Pnte de Penmarc'h
St-Pierre
Kérity
GUILVINEC
Léchiagat
Lesconil
Palud du Cosquer
Roches de Penmarc'h
CHAUSSÉE DE SEIN
Ar Men
ILE DE SEIN
Ile de Sein
Kelaourou
D 7
D 784
D 765
D 63
D 47
D 107
D 785
D 57
D 2
D 40
D 44
D 53
D 56
D 143
D 43
D 39
1H 30

CHÂTEAULIN
PLEYBEN
CHÂTEAUNEUF-DU-FAOU
Plonévez-du-Faou
Landeleau
Cléden-Poher
Port de Carhaix
St-Ségal
Dinéault
Lanvian
Port-Launay
St-Coulitz
Lothey
Lennon
Gouézec
St-Thois
Spézet
St-Hernin
Motreff
St-Goazec
ROC DE TOULLAËRON 326
Cast
Laz
Roudouallec
GOURIN
BRIEC
Edern
Trégourez
Leuhan
Landrévarzec
Quéménéven
Langolen
Landudal
Coray
Tourc'h
Elliant
Ergué-Gabéric
ROSPORDEN
SCAËR
Guiscriff
LE FAOUËT
St-Yvy
Lanvénégen
Pleuven
St-Evarzec
la Forêt-Fouesnant
FOUESNANT
Bénodet
Clohars-Fouesnant
Gouesnac'h
Plomelin
CONCARNEAU
Beg Meil
Melgven
BANNALEC
St-Thurien
Querrien
Mellac
Tréméven
QUIMPERLÉ
Baye
Le Trévoux
Trégunc
Nizon
PONT-AVEN
Riec-s.-Belon
Névez
Trévignon
Moëlan-s.-Mer
Clohars-Carnoët
Guidel
Guidel-Plages
le Pouldu
Port-Manec'h
Raguénez-Plage
Ile aux Moutons
Ecueils des Pourceaux
I. de St-Nicolas
I. de Penfret
Centre Nautique de Glénan
Réserve Ornithologique
ILES DE GLENAN
ANSE DE BENODET
Roches de Mousterlin
BAIE DE LA FORET
Anse du Pouldu
Basse des Bretons
ILE DE GROIX
N 164
N 165 - E 60
N 365
D 15
D 36
D 765
D 783
Ouv. 2ème sem. 1998
52
73

H
I
J
14
15
16
17
ROSTRENEN
GOUAREC
MÛR-DE-BRETAGNE
PONTIVY
LE FAOUËT
GUÉMENÉ-S.-SCORFF
CLÉGUÉREC
PLOUAY
ARZANO
PONT-SCORFF
HENNEBONT
LANESTER
LORIENT
PLOEMEUR
PORT-LOUIS
BAUD
PLUVIGNER
AURAY
GRAND-CHAMP
BELZ
Quintin
Plussulien
Ste-Tréphine
St-Igeaux
Laniscat
St-Gelven
Caurel
St-Mayeux
St-Gilles-Vieux-Marché
St-Guen
Merléac
Glomel
Plévin
Paule
Motreff
Tréogan
Plouguernével
Plélauff
Perret
Silfiac
Ste-Brigitte
St-Aignan
St-Connec
Kergrist
Neulliac
Plouray
Langonnet
Langoëlan
Séglien
Ploërdut
Locmalo
Malguénac
Noyal-Pontivy
Priziac
le Croisty
Lignol
Persquen
Guern
St-Tugdual
Kernascléden
Berné
Meslan
Inguiniel
Melrand
Bieuzy
Bubry
Pluméliau
Remungol
Moustoir-Remungol
Guilligomarc'h
Locunolé
Lanvaudan
Quistinic
Calan
Cléguer
Guénin
Inzinzac-Lochrist
Languidic
Caudan
Quéven
Gestel
Kervignac
Brandérion
Landévant
Nostang
Merlevenez
Ste-Hélène
Locmiquélic
Riantec
Gâvres
Plouhinec
Locoal-Mendon
Landaul
Brech
Plumergat
Camors
Plumelin
Brandivy
Ste-Anne-d'Auray
Etel
Erdeven
Larmor-Plage
Pluneret
N 164
N 24
N 165
E 60
D 769
D 768
D 767
D 782
D 764
D 790
53
72
91
FORÊT DE LANVAUX
Passe de l'Ouest
Passe du Sud
Port Tudy

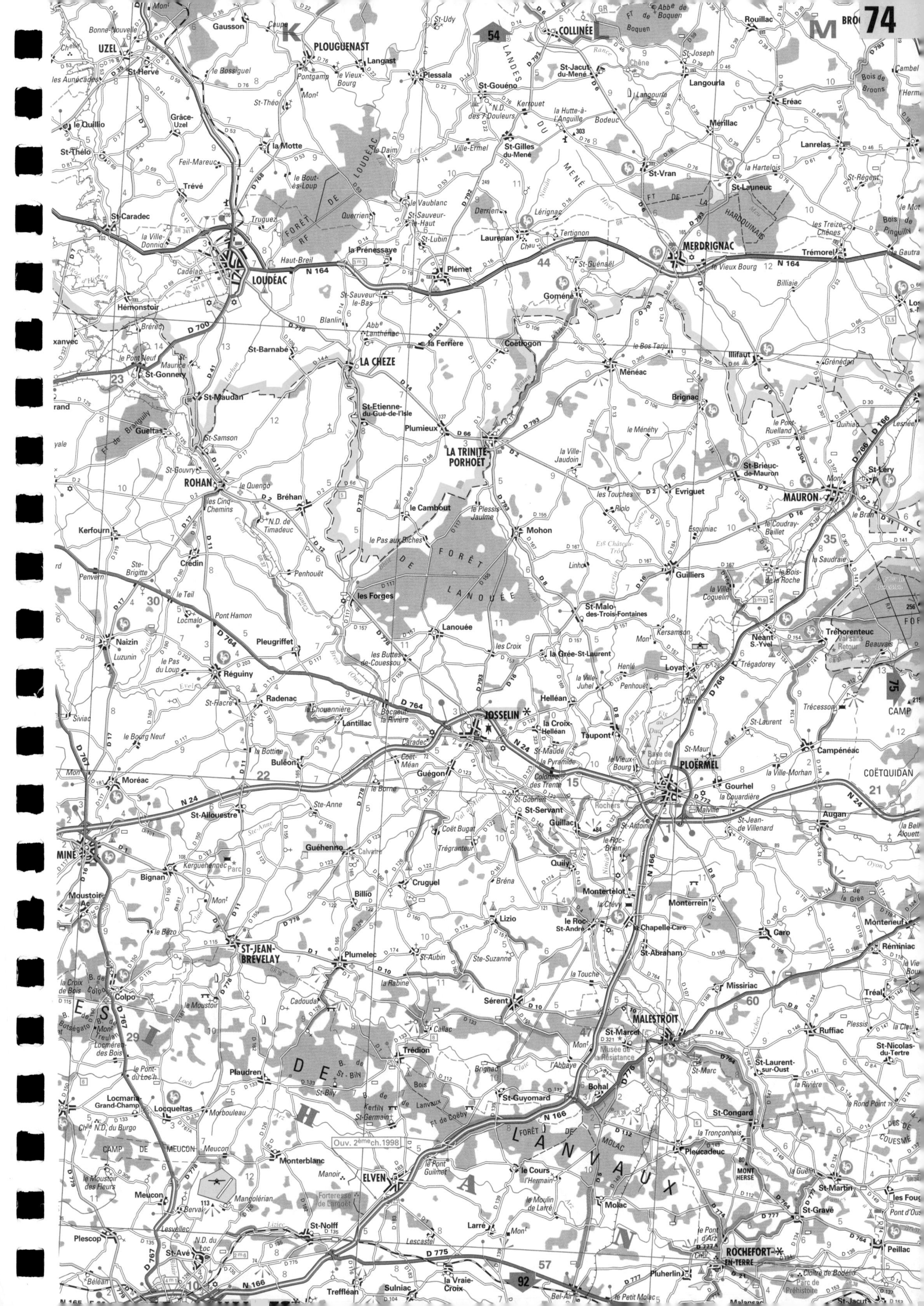
UZEL
PLOUGUENAST
COLLINÉE
Gausson
Langast
Plessala
St-Gouéno
St-Jacut-du-Mené
Langourla
Rouillac
Eréac
St-Hervé
le Quillio
St-Thélo
Grâce-Uzel
la Motte
Trévé
St-Caradec
LOUDÉAC
Hémonstoir
Mérillac
Lanrelas
St-Vran
St-Launeuc
St-Gilles-du-Mené
Laurenan
MERDRIGNAC
Trémorel
Plémet
la Prénessaye
Le Vaublanc
St-Sauveur-le-Haut
Goméné
FORÊT DE LOUDÉAC
LANDES DU MENÉ
FT DE LA HARDOUINAIS
N 164
la Ferrière
Coëtlogon
LA CHEZE
St-Barnabé
Ménéac
Illifaut
St-Gonnery
St-Maudan
Brignac
St-Etienne-du-Gué-de-l'Isle
Plumieux
LA TRINITÉ-PORHOËT
Gueltas
ROHAN
Bréhan
le Cambout
Evriguet
St-Brieuc-de-Mauron
MAURON
St-Léry
Kerfourn
Crédin
Mohon
Guilliers
FORÊT DE LANOUÉE
les Forges
Lanouée
St-Malo-des-Trois-Fontaines
Néant-S.-Yvel
Tréhorenteuc
Naizin
Pleugriffet
Réguiny
la Grée-St-Laurent
Loyat
Radenac
JOSSELIN
Helléan
Taupont
Lantillac
Campénéac
Moréac
Buléon
Guégon
PLOËRMEL
Gourhel
COËTQUIDAN
N 24
St-Allouestre
St-Servant
Guillac
Augan
Guéhenno
Bignan
Cruguel
Quily
Billio
Montertelot
Monterrein
Lizio
Caro
Moustoir-Ac
ST-JEAN-BREVELAY
Plumelec
St-Abraham
Réminiac
Colpo
Sérent
Missiriac
MALESTROIT
Tréal
Ruffiac
Tredion
St-Marcel
St-Nicolas-du-Tertre
Plaudren
St-Laurent-sur-Oust
Locmaria-Grand-Champ
Locqueltas
St-Guyomard
Bohal
St-Congard
FORÊT DE LANVAUX
Pleucadeuc
CAMP DE MEUCON
Monterblanc
ELVEN
le Cours
St-Martin
Meucon
Molac
St-Gravé
Plescop
St-Nolff
Larré
Peillac
St-Avé
ROCHEFORT-EN-TERRE
Pluherlin
Trefflean
Sulniac
la Vraie-Croix
D 775
N 166
D 766
D 767
Ouv. 2ème ch.1998

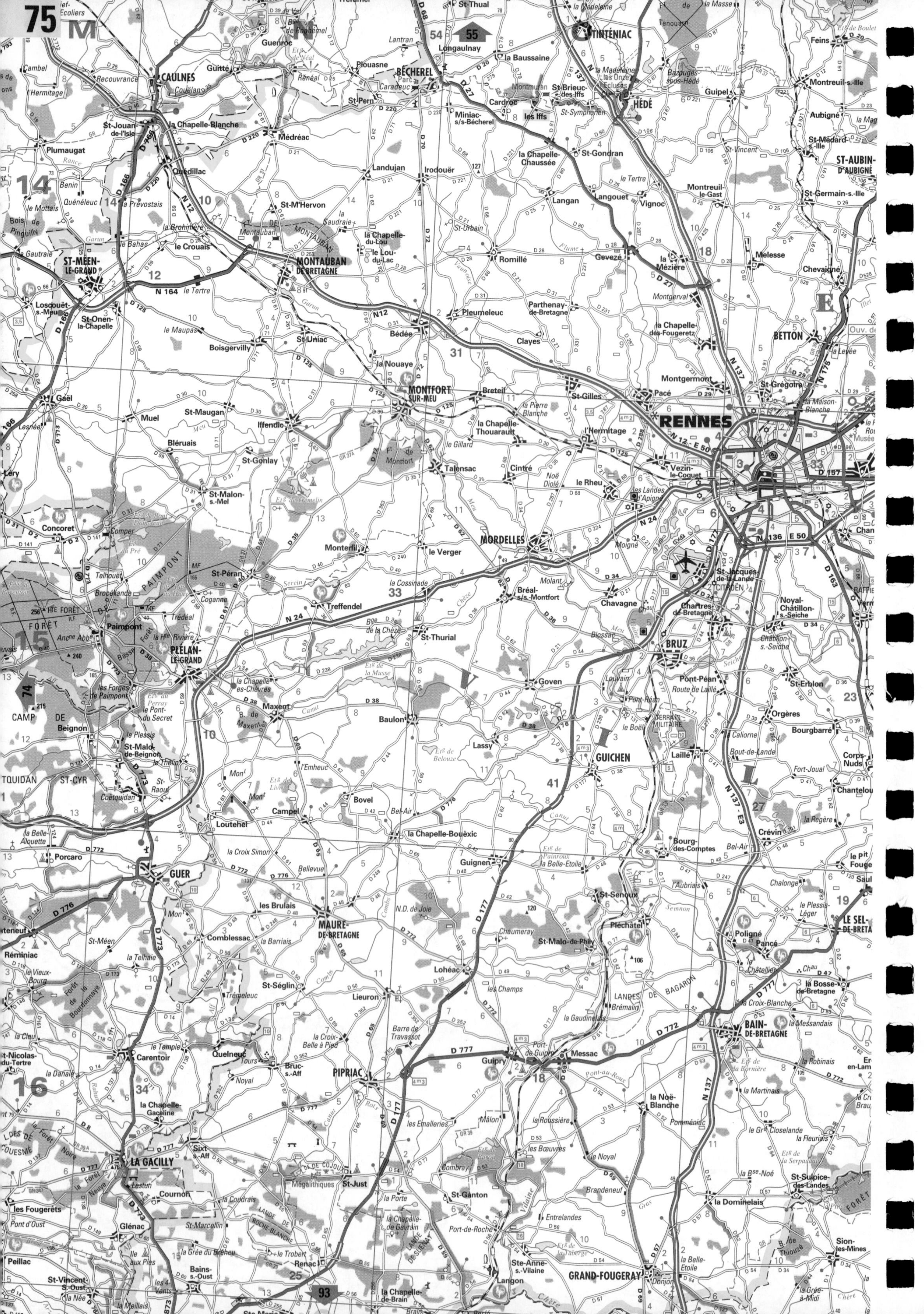
M
55
54
St-Thual
la Madeleine
TINTÉNIAC
Tanouarn
la Masse
Feins
Guenroc
Longaulnay
la Baussaine
CAULNES
Recouvrance
Guitté
Plouasne
BÉCHEREL
Caradeuc
Montmuran
St-Brieuc-des-Iffs
HÉDÉ
Bazouges-sous-Hédé
Guipel
Montreuil-s.-Ille
St-Pern
Miniac-s/s-Bécherel
Cardroc
les Iffs
St-Symphorien
Aubigné
St-Jouan-de-l'Isle
la Chapelle-Blanche
Médréac
la Chapelle-Chaussée
St-Gondran
St-Médard-s.-Ille
Plumaugat
Landujan
Irodouër
ST-AUBIN-D'AUBIGNÉ
Quédillac
Langouet
Vignoc
Montreuil-le-Gast
St-Germain-s.-Ille
Benin
Quénéleuc
la Prévostais
St-M'Hervon
Langan
le Mottais
Bois de Pinguilly
la Brohinière
Montauban
la Saudraie
la Chapelle-du-Lou
le Lou-du-Lac
St-Urbain
le Bahac
le Crouais
la Gautraie
ST-MÉEN-LE-GRAND
MONTAUBAN DE-BRETAGNE
Romillé
Gevezé
la Mézière
Melesse
Chevaigné
N 164
le Tertre
Montgerval
Loscouët-s.-Meu
St-Onen-la-Chapelle
Pleumeleuc
Parthenay-de-Bretagne
la Chapelle-des-Fougeretz
BETTON
le Maupas
Boisgervilly
St-Uniac
Bédée
Clayes
la Levée
la Nouaye
Montgermont
Gaël
MONTFORT-SUR-MEU
Breteil
St-Gilles
Pacé
St-Grégoire
la Maison-Blanche
Muel
St-Maugan
Iffendic
la Pierre Blanche
Lesnée
la Chapelle-Thouarault
l'Hermitage
RENNES
Bléruais
St-Gonlay
le Gillard
Talensac
Cintré
Vezin-le-Coquet
Léry
St-Malon-s.-Mel
Noë Diolé
le Rheu
les Landes d'Apigné
Concoret
Comper
Monterfil
le Verger
MORDELLES
Moigné
Telhouët
St-Péran
PAIMPONT
Brocéliande
Coganne
Treffendel
la Cossinade
Bréal-s/s.-Montfort
Molant
Chavagne
St-Jacques-de-la-Lande
CITROËN
Noyal-Châtillon-s.-Seiche
HTE FORÊT
FORÊT
Paimpont
Trédéal
St-Thurial
Blossac
Chartres-de-Bretagne
Châtillon-s.-Seiche
PLÉLAN-LE-GRAND
la Chapelle-es-Chèvres
BRUZ
Pont-Péan
St-Erblon
CAMP DE Beignon
les Forges de Paimpont
le Pont-du Secret
Maxent
Goven
Baulon
Pont-Réan
le Boël
Orgères
Bourgbarré
le Plessis
St-Malo-de-Beignon
Lassy
GUICHEN
Laillé
la Caliorne
Bout-de-Lande
Corps-Nuds
TQUIDAN
ST-CYR
Coëtquidan
St-Raoul
l'Emheuc
Bovel
Fort-Joual
Chanteloup
Campel
Loutehel
Bel-Air
la Chapelle-Bouëxic
Bourg-des-Comptes
Crévin
la Regère
la Belle-Alouette
Porcaro
la Croix Simon
Bellevue
Guignen
la Belle-Etoile
GUER
l'Aubriais
Chalonge
St-Senoux
les Brulais
N.D. de Joie
Pléchâtel
le Plessis-Léger
LE SEL-DE-BRETAGNE
MAURE-DE-BRETAGNE
Comblessac
la Barriais
Chaumeray
St-Malo-de-Phily
Poligné
Pancé
St-Méen
Réminiac
la Telhaie
le Vieux-Bourg
Forêt de la Bourdonnaye
Lohéac
le Châtellier
la Bosse-de-Bretagne
Trémeleuc
St-Séglin
Lieuron
les Champs
LANDES DE BAGARON
Brémalin
la Croix-Blanche
la Gaudinelais
BAIN-DE-BRETAGNE
la Messandais
St-Nicolas-du-Tertre
le Temple
Carentoir
Quelneuc
la Croix-Belle à Pied
Barre de Travassot
Port-de-Guipry
Messac
la Robinais
Guipry
Bruc-s.-Aff
PIPRIAC
Pont-au-Roux
la Danaïs
Noyal
la Martinais
la Noë-Blanche
la Chapelle-Gaceline
les Emalleries
Mâlon
la Roussière
Pommeniac
le Gd Closelande
la Fleuriais
Sixt-s.-Aff
les Bœuvres
le Noyal
LA GACILLY
St-Just
Combray
la Bse-Noé
St-Sulpice-des-Landes
Mégalithiques
Lestun
Cournon
Brandeneuf
la Dominelais
les Fougerêts
St-Ganton
la Porte
Pont d'Oust
la Coudrais
Glénac
St-Marcellin
LANDE DE ROCHE-BLANCHE
la Chapelle-de Gavrain
Port-de-Roche
Entrelandes
Sion-les-Mines
la Grée du Bréneu
le Trobert
Ille aux Pies
Thiouzé
Peillac
Renac
Bains-s.-Oust
Ste-Anne-s.-Vilaine
la Belle-Etoile
St-Vincent-S.-Oust
les 4 Vents
la Chapelle-de-Brain
Langon
GRAND-FOUGERAY
Donjon
la Grée-à-Midi
la Née
le Meillais
93
74
Ste-Marie
N 12
N 24
N 137
N 136
E 50
D 177
D 772
D 777
D 776
D 773
N 137 - E3
E 3
14
15
16

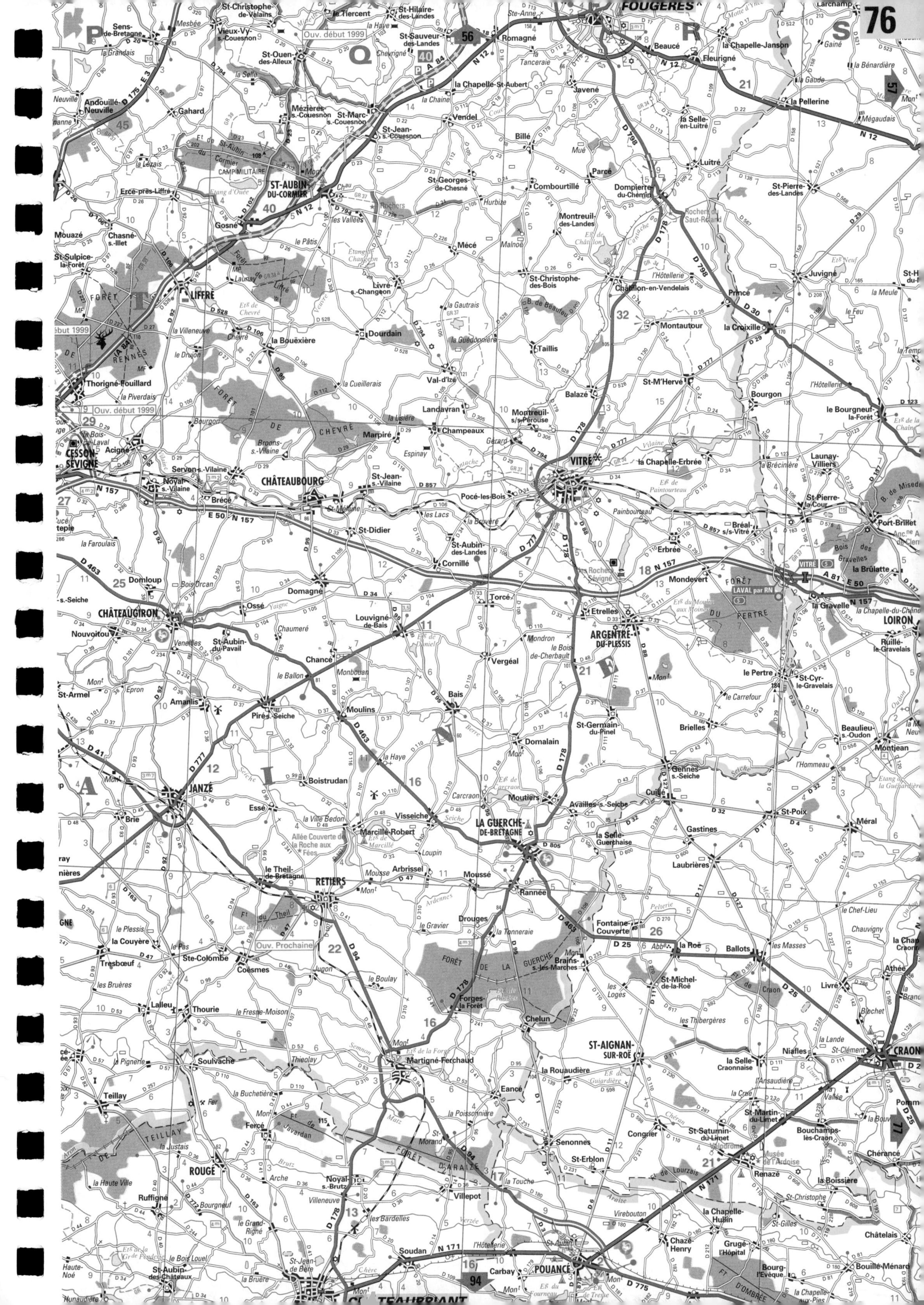
FOUGÈRES
St-Christophe-de-Valains
le Tiercent
St-Hilaire-des-Landes
Sens-de-Bretagne
Mesbée
Vieux-Vy-s.-Couesnon
Ouv. début 1999
St-Sauveur-des-Landes
Romagné
Beaucé
la Chapelle-Janson
St-Ouen-des-Alleux
Fleurigné
la Chapelle-St-Aubert
Javené
Andouillé-Neuville
Gahard
Mézières-s.-Couesnon
St-Marc-s.-Couesnon
Vendel
la Pellerine
St-Jean-s.-Couesnon
Billé
la Selle-en-Luitré
Luitré
Parcé
Dompierre-du-Chemin
Comboutillé
St-Georges-de-Chesné
St-Pierre-des-Landes
Ercé-près-Liffré
ST-AUBIN-DU-CORMIER
CAMP MILITAIRE
Gosné
Hurbize
Montreuil-des-Landes
Mouazé
Chasné-s.-Illet
Mecé
St-Sulpice-la-Forêt
Livré-s.-Changeon
St-Christophe-des-Bois
Châtillon-en-Vendelais
Juvigné
LIFFRÉ
FORÊT DE RENNES
Princé
Dourdain
la Bouëxière
Montautour
la Croixille
Taillis
Thorigné-Fouillard
Val-d'Izé
St-M'Hervé
la Cueillerais
Balazé
Bourgon
Landavran
Montreuil-s/s-Pérouse
le Bourgneuf-la-Forêt
Champeaux
Marpiré
FORÊT DE CHEVRÉ
CESSON-SÉVIGNÉ
Acigné
Servon-s.-Vilaine
Noyal-s.-Vilaine
CHÂTEAUBOURG
St-Jean-s.-Vilaine
VITRÉ
la Chapelle-Erbrée
Launay-Villiers
Brécé
Pocé-les-Bois
St-Pierre-la-Cour
Port-Brillet
St-Didier
Bréal-s/s-Vitré
Erbrée
St-Aubin-des-Landes
Cornillé
Mondevert
la Brûlatte
Domloup
Domagné
FORÊT DU PERTRE
la Gravelle
CHÂTEAUGIRON
Ossé
Torcé
Etrelles
LOIRON
Nouvoitou
Louvigné-de-Bais
ARGENTRÉ-DU-PLESSIS
Ruillé-le-Gravelais
St-Aubin-du-Pavail
Chancé
Vergéal
le Pertre
St-Cyr-le-Gravelais
St-Armel
Amanlis
Piré-s.-Seiche
Moulins
Bais
St-Germain-du-Pinel
Brielles
Beaulieu-s.-Oudon
Domalain
Montjean
JANZÉ
Boistrudan
Gennes-s.-Seiche
Carcraon
Moutiers
Availles-s.-Seiche
Cuillé
Brie
Essé
Visseiche
LA GUERCHE-DE-BRETAGNE
St-Poix
Méral
Marcillé-Robert
Allée Couverte de la Roche aux Fées
la Selle-Guerchaise
Gastines
Arbrissel
Laubrières
le Theil-de-Bretagne
RETIERS
Mousse
Moussé
Rannée
Drouges
Fontaine-Couverte
la Roë
Ballots
la Couyère
Tresbœuf
Ste-Colombe
Coësmes
Ouv. Prochaine
FORÊT DE LA GUERCHE
Brains-s.-les-Marches
St-Michel-de-la-Roë
Livré
Athée
Lalleu
Thourie
Forges-la-Forêt
Chelun
ST-AIGNAN-SUR-ROË
Niafles
CRAON
Soulvache
Martigné-Ferchaud
la Rouaudière
la Selle-Craonnaise
Teillay
Eancé
Ercé
FORÊT DE TEILLAY
Congrier
St-Saturnin-du-Limet
St-Martin-du-Limet
Bouchamps-lès-Craon
Senonnes
St-Erblon
Musée de l'Ardoise
Renazé
Chérancé
ROUGÉ
Noyal-s.-Brutz
la Boissière
Ruffigné
Villepot
la Chapelle-Hullin
Châtelais
Soudan
POUANCÉ
Chazé-Henry
Grugé-l'Hôpital
Bourg-l'Évêque
Bouillé-Ménard
St-Aubin-des-Châteaux
Carbay
Haute-Noé
St-Jean-de-Béré
CHÂTEAUBRIANT
la Chapelle-aux-Pies

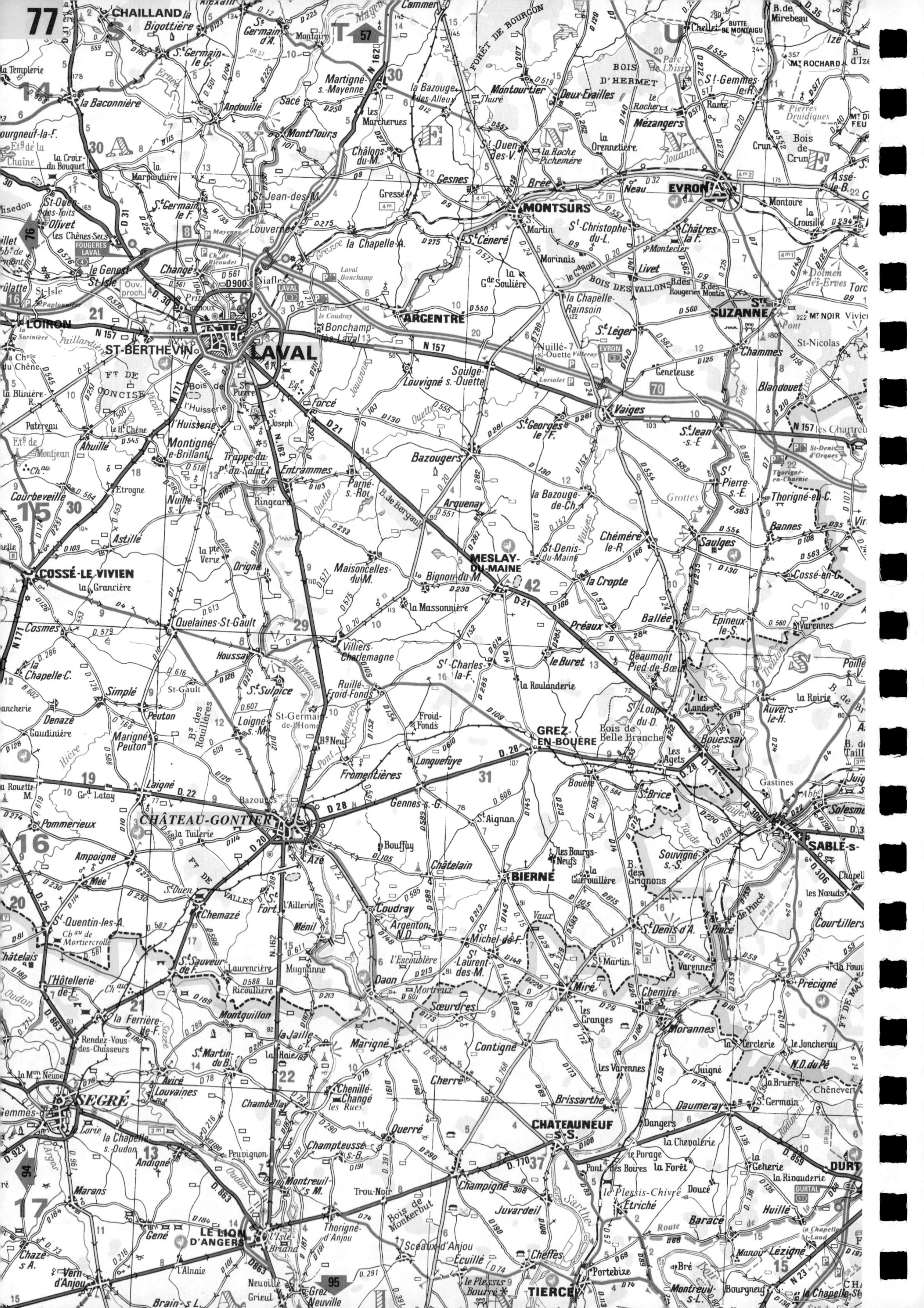
CHAILLAND
la Bigottière
St Germain d'A.
Montigny
Commer
FORÊT DE BOURGON
B. de Mirebeau
Izé
BUTTE DE MONTAIGU
Chellé
Mt ROCHARD
la Templerie
St Germain le G.
Martigné s.-Mayenne
la Baconnière
Andouillé
Sacé
la Bazouge des-Alleux
Montourtier
Deux-Evailles
BOIS D'HERMET
St-Gemmes-le-R.
Thuré
Mézangers
Pierres Druidiques
Bourgneuf-la-F.
Montflours
les Marcherues
Châlons du-M.
St-Ouen des-V.
la Roche Pichemère
la Orennetière
Crun
Bois de Crun
la Croix du Bouquet
la Marpandière
Gesnes
Brée
Neau
EVRON
Assé-le-B.
St-Ouen des-Toits
St Germain le F.
St-Jean-des-M.
Gressé
MONTSURS
Montoire
la Crousille
Olivet
les Chênes-Secs
FOUGERES LAVAL
Louverné
la Chapelle-A.
St Céneré
St Martin
St-Christophe du-L.
Châtres-la-F.
le Genest St-Isle
Changé
Ch. de Ricoudet
Laval Bonchamp
Morinais
Montecler
Livet
Dolmen des-Erves
Ouv. proch.
Niafles
la Gde Soulière
BOIS DES VALLONS
B. des Rougeries
B. des Montis
la Chapelle-Rainsoin
St SUZANNE
LOIRON
la Sorinière
St-Isle
Grenoux
ARGENTRÉ
Laval le Coudray
Bonchamp-lès-Laval
St Léger
Mt NOIR
Vivier
Pont
St-Nicolas
ST-BERTHEVIN
LAVAL
N 157
Nuillé-s.-Ouette
Villeray
Chammes
la Ch. du Chêne
Ft DE CONCISE
Bois de l'Huisserie
St Pierre
Louvigné
Soulgé s.-Ouette
Loriolet
Geneteuse
Blandouet
la Blinière-R.
l'Huisserie
Forcé
Vaiges
Patereau
le Ht Chêne
St Joseph
St Georges le F.
St Jean s.-E.
Etg de Montjean
Ahuillé
Montigné le-Brillant
Trappe-du-Pt du Salut
Bazougers
St-Denis d'Orques
St Pierre s.-E.
Thorigné en-Charnie
Thorigné-en-C.
Ch.au
Etrogne
Entrammes
Parné s.-Roc
Arquenay
la Bazouge de-Ch.
Grottes
Courbeveille
Nuillé s.-V.
Pt Ringeard
B. de Bergault
Chémeré le-R.
Bannes
Astillé
la Pte Verie
Origné
MESLAY DU-MAINE
St-Denis du-Maine
Saulges
COSSÉ-LE-VIVIEN
la Grancière
Maisoncelles du-M.
Bignon du M.
la Cropte
Cossé-en-C.
la Massonnière
Quelaines-St-Gault
Ballée
Préaux
Epineux le-S.
Varennes
Cosmes
Villiers Charlemagne
Houssay
la Chapelle-C.
St-Charles la-F.
le Buret
Beaumont Pied-de-Bœuf
Simplé
St-Gault
St Sulpice
Ruillé Froid-Fonds
la Roulanderie
la Roirie
Auvers le-H.
Denazé
Gaudinière
Peuton
Bs des Rouillères
Loigné s.-M.
St-Germain de-l'Home
Froid-Fonds
St Loup du-D.
les Landes
Marigné Peuton
Bg Neuf
GREZ-EN-BOUÈRE
Bois de Belle Branche
Bouessay
Fromentières
Longuefuye
Les Agets
Gastines
la Rouette-M.
Gr. Latay
Laigné
Bouère
St Brice
Bazouges
CHÂTEAU-GONTIER
Gennes-s.-G.
St Aignan
Pommerieux
la Tuilerie
SABLÉ-s-
Solesmes
Ampoigné
Azé
Bouffay
Les Bourgs-Neufs
Souvigné s.-S.
Mée
Ft DE VALLES
Châtelain
BIERNE
la Guerouillère
B. des Grignons
Chapelle
les Nœuds
St Ouen
St Fort
l'Aillerie
Coudray
Chemazé
Pincé
de Pincé
St-Quentin-les-A.
Chau de Mortiercrolle
Ménil
Argenton N.D.
St Michel-de-F.
St Denis-d'A.
Courtillers
St Sauveur de-F.
Laurencière
L'Escoublère
St Laurent des-M.
St Martin
Varennes
l'Hôtellerie de-F.
Ricoullière
Mugnanne
Daon
Mortreux
Miré
Chemiré
Précigné
la Ferrière de-F.
Montguillon
Sœurdres
les Granges
Morannes
Rendez-Vous des-Chasseurs
la Jaille-Y.
Marigné
Contigné
Tercleric
le Joncheray
St Martin du-B.
la Haie
N.D. du Pé
la Mon Neuve
Avire
Louvaines
Cherré
Les Varennes
Juigné
la Bruere
Chênevert
SEGRÉ
Chambellay
Chenillé-Changé
les Rues
Brissarthe
Daumeray
St Germain
Gemmes-d'A.
la Lorie
la Chapelle s.-Oudon
Peuvignon
Querré
CHATEAUNEUF s.S.
Dangers
la Chevalerie
Andigné
Champteussé s.-B.
le Porage
Pont des Boires
la Forêt
la Geherie
la Rivauderie
DURTAL
Marans
Montreuil s. M.
Trou-Noir
Champigné
le Plessis-Chivré
Douce
Etriché
Huillé
Bois de Monkerbut
Juvardeil
Baracé
Route
LE LION D'ANGERS
Gené
Thorigné d'Anjou
l'Isle-Briand
Sceaux-d'Anjou
la Chapelle St-Laud
Manoir
Lézigné
Chazé s.-A.
Vern d'Anjou
l'Alnaie
Ecuillé
Cheffes
Portebize
Bré
Neuville
Grieul
Grez Neuville
le Plessis Bourré
TIERCÉ
Montreuil s.-L.
Bourgneuf
la Chapelle-St
Brain-s-L.
Sarthe
Oudon
Mayenne
Vaiges
Erve
Jouanne
Ouette

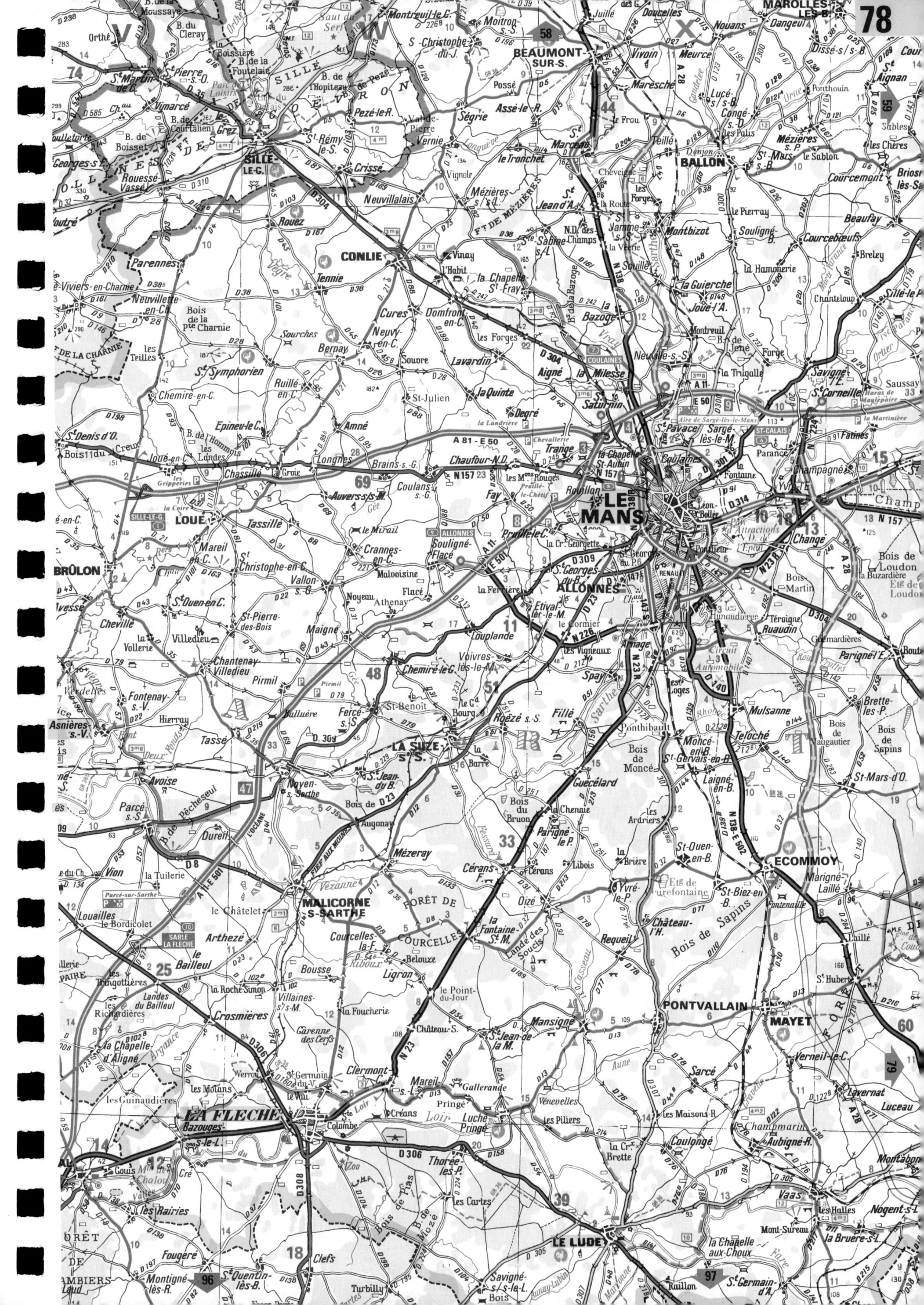

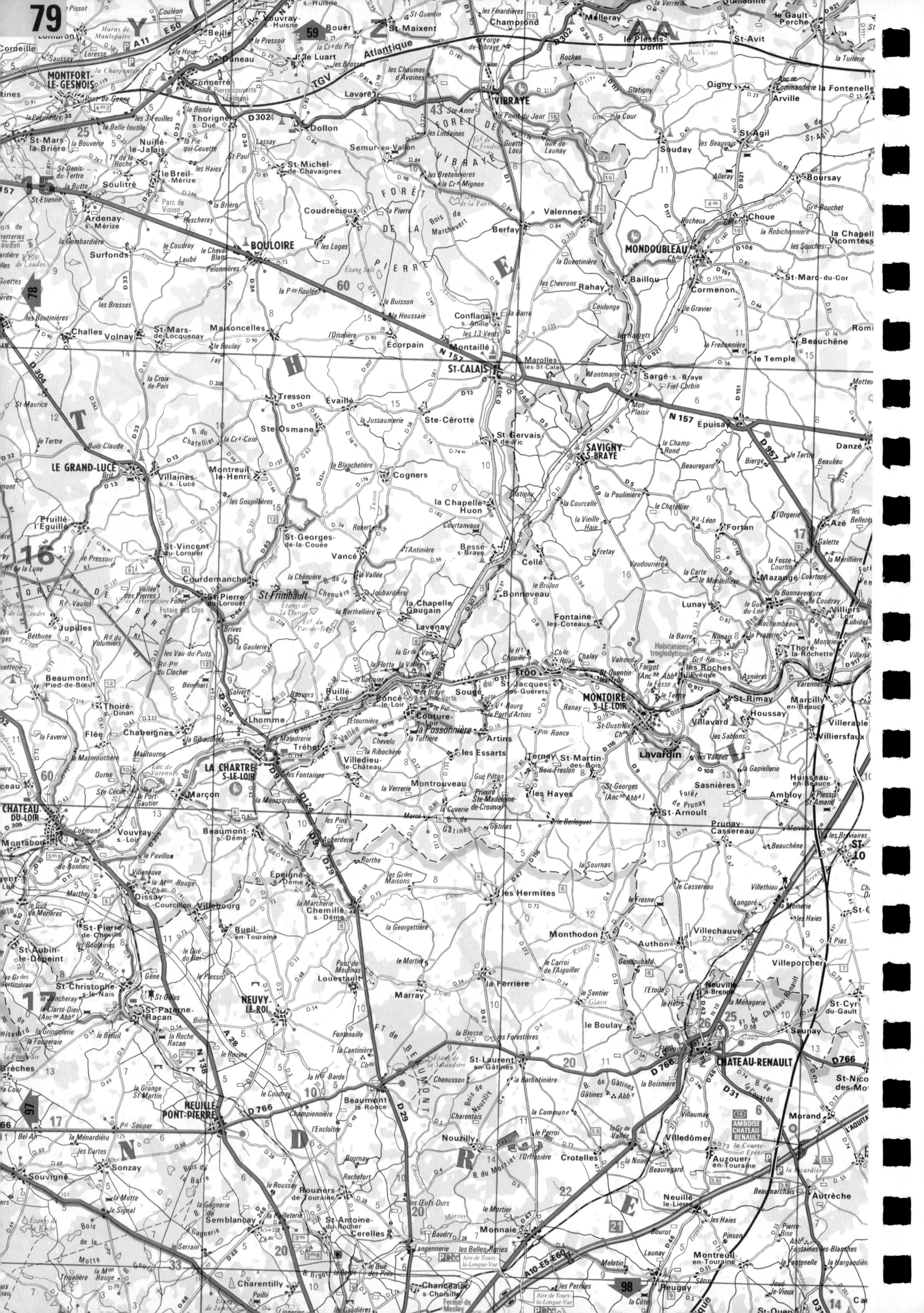

Y
Z
AA
59
Vouvray-s.-Huisne
Bouër
St-Maixent
Champrond
Melleray
le Plessis-Dorin
St-Avit
le Gault-Perche
MONTFORT-LE-GESNOIS
Connerré
Duneau
le Luart
TGV Atlantique
Lavaré
VIBRAYE
Oigny
Arville
la Fontenelle
Thorigné-s.-Dué
Dollon
St-Mars-la-Brière
Nuillé-le-Jalais
Semur-en-Vallon
FORÊT DE VIBRAYE
Souday
St-Agil
Soulitré
le Breil-s.-Mérize
St-Michel-de-Chavaignes
Boursay
Ardenay-s.-Mérize
Coudrecieux
FORÊT DE LA PIERRE
Valennes
Berfay
Choue
MONDOUBLEAU
BOULOIRE
Surfonds
Rahay
Baillou
Cormenon
St-Marc-du-Cor
78
Challes
Volnay
St-Mars-de-Locquenay
Maisoncelles
Écorpain
Conflans-s.-Anille
Montaillé
ST-CALAIS
Marolles-lès-St-Calais
Sargé-s.-Braye
Beauchêne
le Temple
Tresson
Évaillé
Ste-Cérotte
Ste-Osmane
St-Gervais-de-Vic
SAVIGNY-S.-BRAYE
Épuisay
Danzé
LE GRAND-LUCÉ
Villaines-s.-s.-Lucé
Montreuil-le-Henri
Cogners
la Chapelle-Huon
Fortan
Azé
Pruillé-l'Éguillé
St-Vincent-du-Lorouër
St-Georges-de-la-Couée
Vancé
Bessé-s.-Braye
Cellé
Mazangé
16
Courdemanche
St-Pierre-du-Lorouër
St-Frimbault
Bonneveau
Lunay
Villiers-s.-Loir
Jupilles
la Chapelle-Gaugain
Lavenay
Fontaine-les-Coteaux
Thoré-la-Rochette
Beaumont-Pied-de-Bœuf
Troo
Chalay
les Roches-l'Évêque
Ruillé-s.-Loir
Poncé-s.-le-Loir
Sougé
St-Jacques-des-Guérets
MONTOIRE-S.-LE-LOIR
St-Rimay
Houssay
Marcilly-en-Beauce
Thoiré-s.-Dinan
Flée
Chahaignes
Lhomme
Couture-s.-Loir
Artins
Villavard
Villerable
Villiersfaux
LA CHARTRE-S.-LE-LOIR
Tréhet
Villedieu-le-Château
les Essarts
Ternay
St-Martin-des-Bois
Lavardin
Huisseau-en-Beauce
CHÂTEAU-DU-LOIR
Marçon
Montrouveau
les Hayes
Sasnières
Ambloy
St-Arnoult
Montabon
Vouvray-s.-Loir
Beaumont-s.-Dême
Prunay-Cassereau
Épeigné-s.-Dême
les Hermites
Dissay-s.-Courcillon
Villebourg
Chemillé-s.-Dême
Bueil-en-Touraine
Monthodon
Authon
Villechauve
St-Pierre-de-Chevillé
St-Aubin-le-Dépeint
Louestault
Marray
la Ferrière
Villeporcher
St-Christophe-s.-le-Nais
NEUVY-LE-ROI
St-Paterne-Racan
le Boulay
Neuville-s.-Brenne
St-Cyr-du-Gault
Saunay
17
St-Laurent-en-Gâtines
CHÂTEAU-RENAULT
Beaumont-la-Ronce
Nouzilly
Villedômer
Morand
NEUILLÉ-PONT-PIERRE
Crotelles
Auzouer-en-Touraine
97
Sonzay
Souvigné
Rouziers-de-Touraine
Neuillé-le-Lierre
Autrèche
Semblançay
St-Antoine-du-Rocher
Cerelles
Monnaie
Charentilly
Chanceaux-s.-Choisille
Reugny
98
Montreuil-en-Touraine
A 28
N 138
N 157
D 766
A10-E5-E60

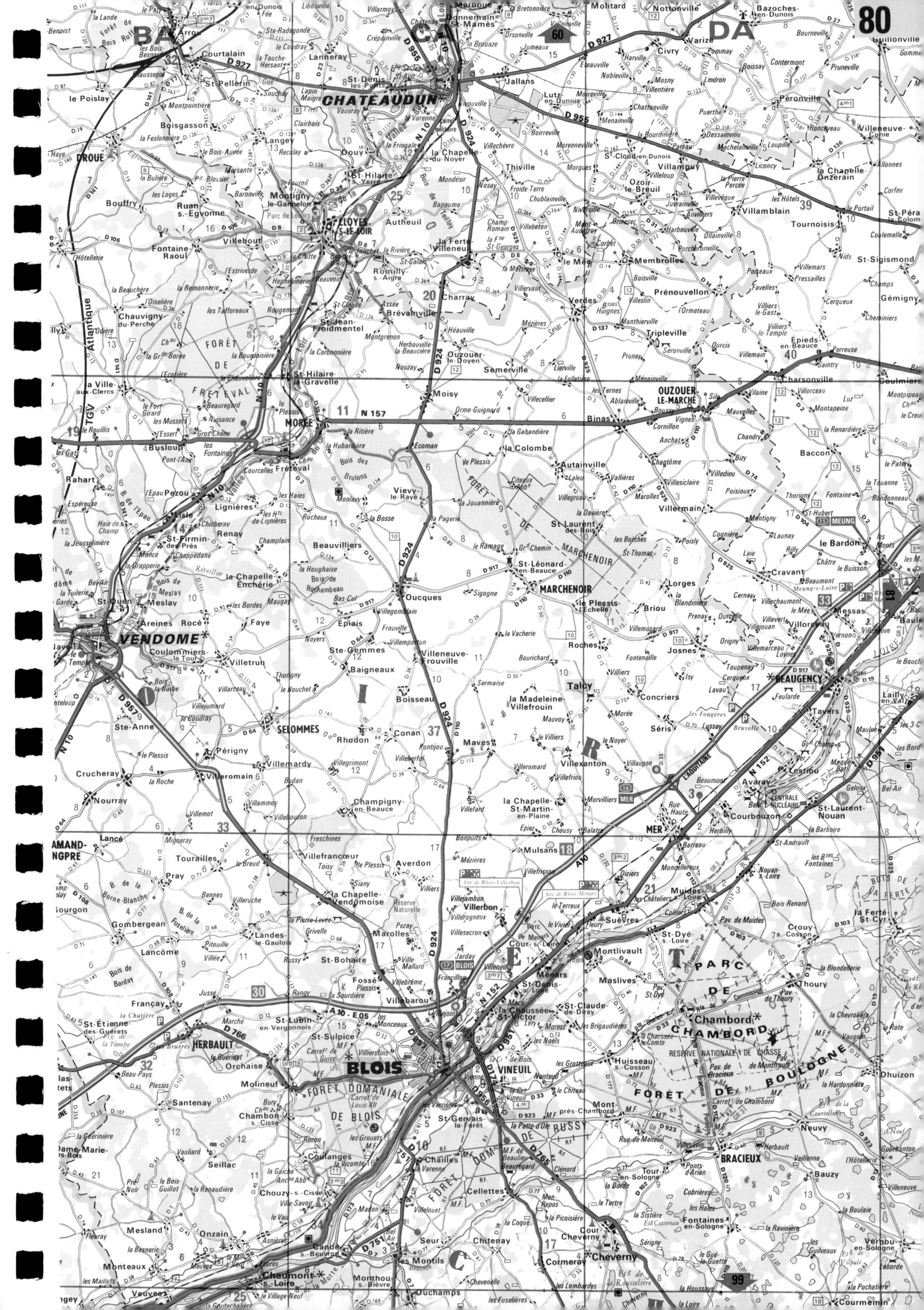
CHATEAUDUN
Cloyes-s-le-Loir
Morée
Fréteval
Vendome
Selommes
Oucques
Marchenoir
Ouzouer-le-Marché
Beaugency
Mer
Blois
Vineuil
Chambord
Parc de Chambord
Forêt de Boulogne
Bracieux
Cheverny
Cour-Cheverny
Herbault
Onzain
Chaumont-s-Loire
Droue
Courtalain
Jallans
Varize
Civry
Villamblain
Tournoisis
Verdes
Tripleville
Binas
Josnes
Talcy
Lorges
Villexanton
Suèvres
Muides-s-Loire
Montlivault
Saint-Dyé-s-Loire
Avaray
Lestiou
St-Laurent-Nouan
Villerbon
La Chapelle-Vendômoise
Villefrancœur
Averdon
Conan
Rhodon
Villemardy
Périgny
Villetrun
Coulommiers-la Tour
Ste-Anne
Crucheray
Nourray
Lancé
Pray
Gombergean
Lancôme
Françay
Molineuf
Orchaise
Santenay
Chambon-s-Cisse
Seillac
Mesland
Monteaux
Veuves
Chouzy-s-Cisse
Coulanges
Chailles
Cellettes
Seur
Chitenay
Les Montils
Ouchamps
Cormeray
Huisseau-s-Cosson
Mont-près-Chambord
Neuvy
Thoury
Crouy-s-Cosson
La Ferté-St-Cyr
Dhuizon
Forêt Domaniale de Blois
Forêt de Fréteval
Forêt de Marchenoir
N 10
N 157
N 152
D 924
D 927
D 955
A 10
TGV Atlantique
Loire

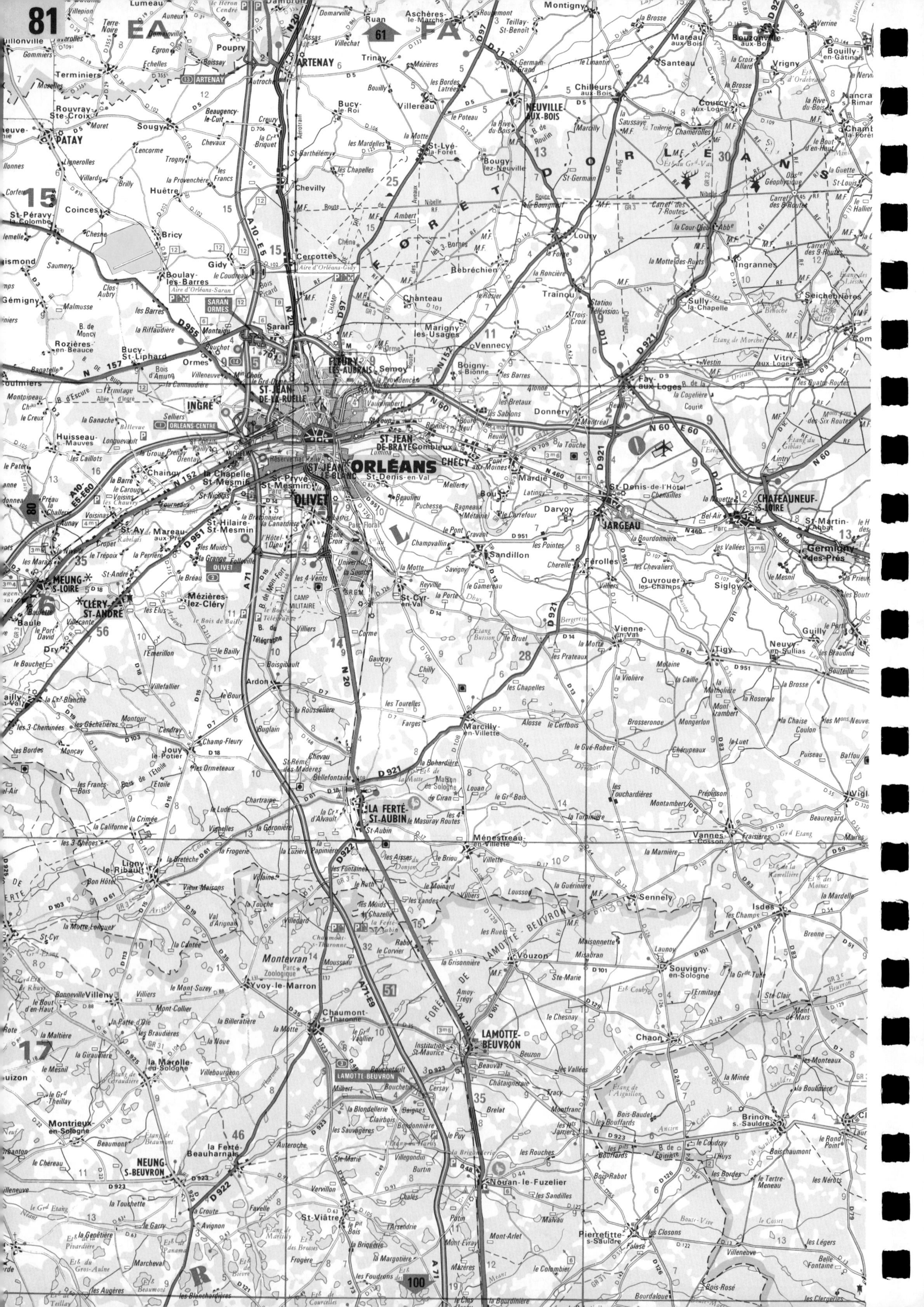
61
ARTENAY
PATAY
NEUVILLE-AUX-BOIS
FORÊT D'ORLÉANS
ORLÉANS
FLEURY-LES-AUBRAIS
ST-JEAN-DE-LA-RUELLE
ST-JEAN-DE-BRAYE
ST-JEAN-LE-BLANC
INGRÉ
OLIVET
CHÉCY
JARGEAU
CHATEAUNEUF-S-LOIRE
MEUNG-S-LOIRE
CLÉRY-ST-ANDRÉ
LA FERTÉ-ST-AUBIN
LAMOTTE-BEUVRON
NEUNG-S-BEUVRON
FORÊT DE LAMOTTE-BEUVRON
Montevran Parc Zoologique
80
100
LOIRE
A10-E5
A71
N 20
N 60
N 152
N 157
D 921
D 951
ORLEANS-CENTRE
SARAN ORMES
ARTENAY
OLIVET
LAMOTTE-BEUVRON

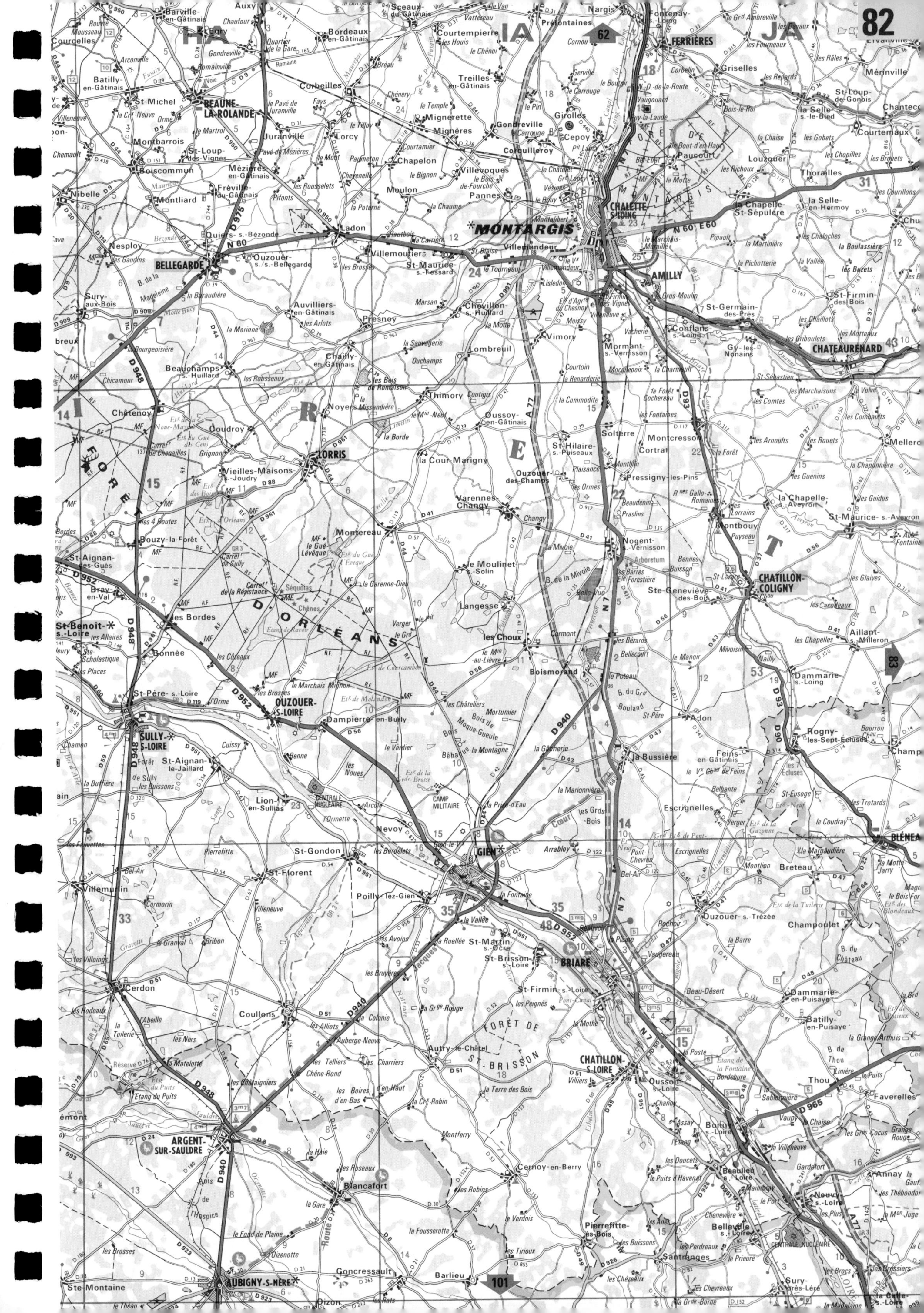
MONTARGIS
BELLEGARDE
BEAUNE-LA-ROLANDE
LORRIS
FERRIÈRES
CHALETTE-S-LOING
AMILLY
CHATEAURENARD
CHATILLON-COLIGNY
OUZOUER-S-LOIRE
SULLY-S-LOIRE
GIEN
BRIARE
CHATILLON-S-LOIRE
ARGENT-SUR-SAULDRE
AUBIGNY-S-NÈRE
BLÉNEAU
FORÊT D'ORLÉANS
FORÊT DE MONTARGIS
FORÊT DE ST-BRISSON
Nogent-s.-Vernisson
Ouzouer-des-Champs
Varennes-Changy
Bellegarde
Ladon
Boismorand
Dammarie-s.-Loing
Rogny-les-Sept-Ecluses
Ouzouer-s.-Trézée
Cerdon
Coullons
Blancafort
Cernoy-en-Berry
Pierrefitte-ès-Bois
Beaulieu-s.-Loire
Bonny-s.-Loire
Ousson-s.-Loire
Neuvy-s.-Loire
St-Florent
Poilly-lez-Gien
Autry-le-Châtel
St-Martin-s.-Ocre
St-Brisson-s.-Loire
Dampierre-en-Burly
Montereau
Châtenoy
Vieilles-Maisons-s.-Joudry
Bouzy-la-Forêt
St-Aignan-des-Gués
St-Benoît-s.-Loire
St-Père-s.-Loire
Lion-en-Sullias
CENTRALE NUCLÉAIRE
CAMP MILITAIRE
A77
N7
N60
E60
D940
D948
D952
D961
62
83
101

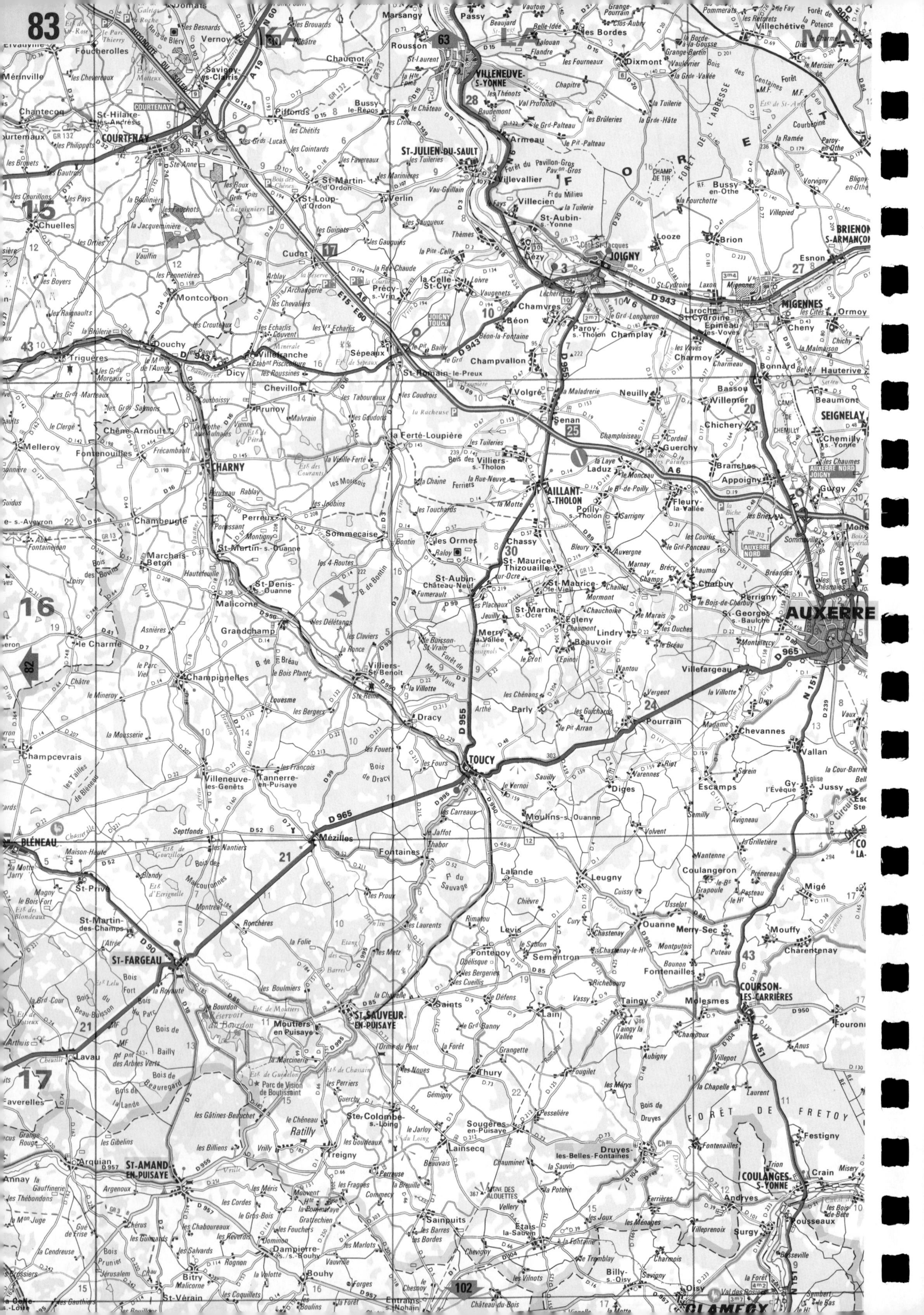

Courtenay
Foucherolles
Vernoy
Marsangy
Rousson
Passy
Villeneuve-s-Yonne
Chaumot
Dixmont
Savigny-s-Clairis
Chantecoq
St-Hilaire-les-Andrésis
Piffonds
Bussy-le-Repos
St-Julien-du-Sault
Villevallier
Villecien
St-Aubin-s-Yonne
St-Martin-d'Ordon
St-Loup-d'Ordon
Verlin
Chuelles
Cudot
Joigny
Brion
Looze
Bussy-en-Othe
Brienon-s-Armançon
Esnon
Migennes
Ormoy
Cheny
Laroche-St-Cydroine
Épineau-les-Voves
Charmoy
Bonnard
Hauterive
Montcorbon
Précy-s-Vrin
La Celle-St-Cyr
Chamvres
Béon
Paroy-s-Tholon
Champlay
Champvallon
Douchy
Triguères
Villefranche
Dicy
Sépeaux
St-Romain-le-Preux
Chevillon
Prunoy
Volgré
Neuilly
Bassou
Villemer
Beaumont
Seignelay
Chemilly-s-Yonne
Melleroy
Fontenouilles
Chêne-Arnoult
Charny
La Ferté-Loupière
Senan
Chichery
Cheny
Villiers-s-Tholon
Laduz
Guerchy
Branches
Appoigny
Gurgy
Aillant-s-Tholon
Poilly-s-Tholon
Fleury-la-Vallée
Chambeugle
Perreux
Sommecaise
Les Ormes
Chassy
St-Maurice-Thizouaille
Marchais-Beton
St-Martin-s-Ouanne
St-Denis-s-Ouanne
St-Aubin-Château-Neuf
St-Maurice-le-Vieil
Charbuy
Perrigny
Auxerre
Malicorne
Grandchamp
St-Martin-s-Ocre
Égleny
Lindry
St-Georges-s-Baulche
Le Charme
Champignelles
Villiers-St-Benoît
Merry-la-Vallée
Beauvoir
Villefargeau
Dracy
Parly
Pourrain
Chevannes
Vallan
Champcevrais
Villeneuve-les-Genêts
Tannerre-en-Puisaye
Toucy
Diges
Escamps
Gy-l'Évêque
Jussy
Bléneau
Mézilles
Fontaines
Moulins-s-Ouanne
Lalande
Leugny
Coulangeron
Migé
St-Privé
St-Martin-des-Champs
Ouanne
Merry-Sec
Mouffy
Charentenay
St-Fargeau
Levis
Fontenoy
Sementron
Chastenay
Fontenailles
Courson-les-Carrières
Saints
Lain
Taingy
Molesmes
Lavau
Moutiers-en-Puisaye
St-Sauveur-en-Puisaye
Thury
Fouronnes
Festigny
Ste-Colombe-s-Loing
Ratilly
Sougères-en-Puisaye
Lainsecq
Treigny
Druyes-les-Belles-Fontaines
Arquian
St-Amand-en-Puisaye
Coulanges-s-Yonne
Crain
Andryes
Etais-la-Sauvin
Sainpuits
Dampierre-s-Bouhy
Bouhy
Bitry
St-Vérain
Surgy
Billy-s-Oisy
Oisy
Clamecy
Forêt de Frétoy
Forêt d'Othe
A6
N6
N151
D965
D955
D943
63
82
102
15
16
17

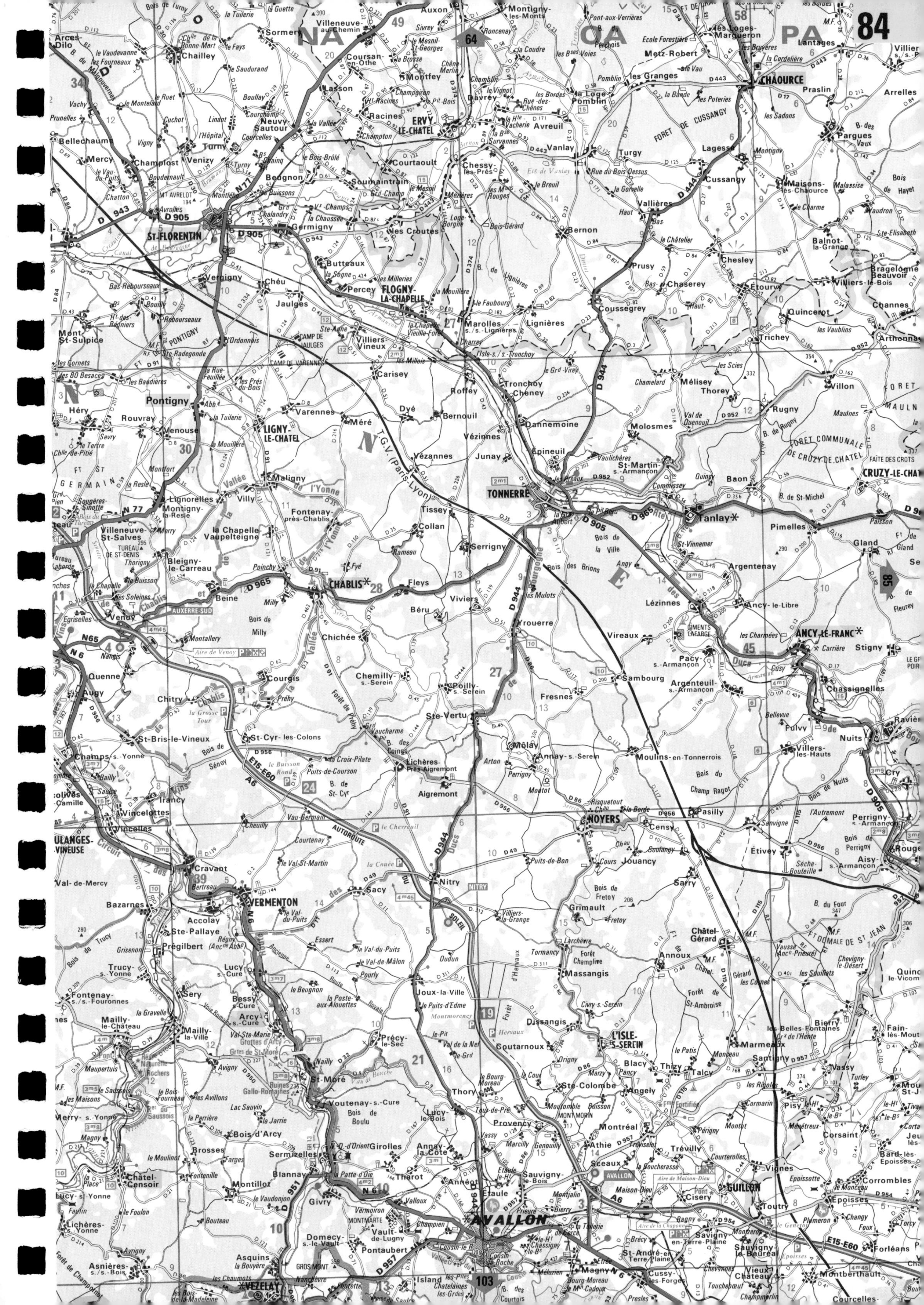

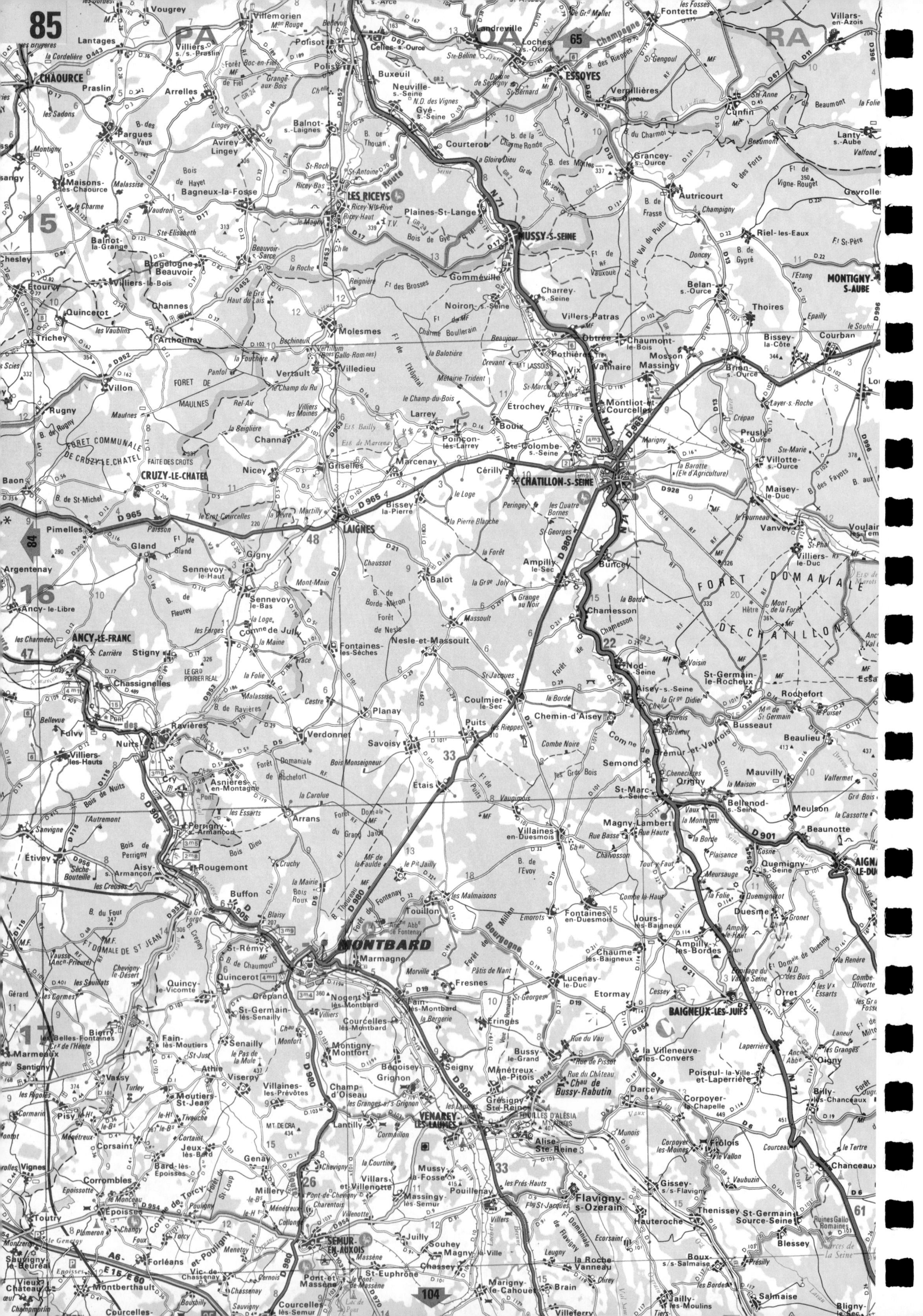

CHAOURCE
Praslin
Lantages
Vougrey
Villemorien
Villiers-s.-Praslin
Arrelles
Pargues
Avirey-Lingey
Balnot-s.-Laignes
Polisot
Polisy
Celles-s.-Ource
Landreville
Loches-s.-Ource
ESSOYES
Fontette
Verpillières-s.-Ource
Cunfin
Villars-en-Azois
Buxeuil
Neuville-s.-Seine
Gyé-s.-Seine
Courteron
Grancey-s.-Ource
Autricourt
Lanty-s.-Aube
Gevrolles
Maisons-lès-Chaource
Bagneux-la-Fosse
LES RICEYS
Plaines-St-Lange
MUSSY-S-SEINE
Riel-les-Eaux
MONTIGNY-S-AUBE
Balnot-la-Grange
Bragelogne-Beauvoir
Villiers-le-Bois
Etourvy
Channes
Quincerot
Trichey
Molesmes
Gomméville
Noiron-s.-Seine
Charrey-s.-Seine
Belan-s.-Ource
Thoires
Arthonnay
Villers-Patras
Obtrée
Chaumont-le-Bois
Pothières
Vix
Vannaire
Mosson
Massingy
Brion-s.-Ource
Bissey-la-Côte
Courban
Villon
Rugny
Vertault
Villedieu
FORET DE MAULNES
Larrey
Etrochey
Montliot-et-Courcelles
Prusly-s.-Ource
Channay
Poinçon-lès-Larrey
Bouix
Ste-Colombe-s.-Seine
Villotte-s.-Ource
Maisey-le-Duc
FORET COMMUNALE DE CRUZY-LE-CHATEL
CRUZY-LE-CHATEL
Nicey
Griselles
Marcenay
Cérilly
CHATILLON-S-SEINE
Baon
Pimelles
Gland
LAIGNES
Bissey-la-Pierre
Vanvey
Villiers-le-Duc
Gigny
Sennevoy-le-Haut
Sennevoy-le-Bas
Ampilly-le-Sec
Buncey
Balot
Argentenay
Ancy-le-Libre
Chamesson
FORET DOMANIALE DE CHATILLON
Massoult
Nesle-et-Massoult
ANCY-LE-FRANC
Stigny
Fontaines-les-Sèches
Nod-s.-Seine
St-Germain-le-Rocheux
Chassignelles
Aisey-s.-Seine
Rochefort
Coulmier-le-Sec
Planay
Chemin-d'Aisey
Busseaut
Ravières
Verdonnet
Savoisy
Puits
Beaulieu
Nuits
Villiers-les-Hauts
Cry
Asnières-en-Montagne
Étais
Semond
Mauvilly
Origny
St-Marc-s.-Seine
Bellenod-s.-Seine
Meulson
Arrans
Perrigny-s.-Armançon
Villaines-en-Duesmois
Magny-Lambert
Beaunotte
Étivey
Aisy-s.-Armançon
Rougemont
Quemigny-s.-Seine
AIGNAY-LE-DUC
Buffon
Touillon
Fontaines-en-Duesmois
Jours-lès-Baigneux
Duesme
MONTBARD
St-Rémy
Marmagne
Chaume-lès-Baigneux
Ampilly-les-Bordes
Quincy-le-Vicomte
Quincerot
Fresnes
Lucenay-le-Duc
Nogent-lès-Montbard
Fain-lès-Montbard
Etormay
BAIGNEUX-LES-JUIFS
Orret
St-Germain-lès-Senailly
Courcelles-lès-Montbard
Eringes
Fain-lès-Moutiers
Senailly
Montigny-Montfort
la Villeneuve-les-Convers
Oigny
Marmeaux
Athie
Viserny
Benoisey
Grignon
Seigny
Bussy-le-Grand
Ménétreux-le-Pitois
Poiseul-la-Ville-et-Laperrière
Vassy
Moutiers-St-Jean
Villaines-les-Prévôtes
Champ-d'Oiseau
Gresigny-Ste-Reine
Darcey
Corpoyer-la-Chapelle
Billy-lès-Chanceaux
Pisy
Lantilly
VENAREY-LES-LAUMES
Alise-Ste-Reine
Frôlois
Corsaint
Jeux-lès-Bard
Genay
Mussy-la-Fosse
Chanceaux
Vignes
Bard-lès-Époisses
Villars-et-Villenotte
Pouillenay
Gissey-s/s-Flavigny
Corrombles
Millery
Massingy-lès-Semur
Flavigny-s-Ozerain
Thenissey
Hauteroche
St-Germain-Source-Seine
Toutry
Époisses
SEMUR-EN-AUXOIS
Juilly
Souhey
Magny-la-Ville
Blessey
Forléans
Chassey
Boux-s/s-Salmaise
Vic-de-Chassenay
Montberthault
St-Euphrône
Pont-et-Massène
Marigny-le-Cahouët
Brain
Salmaise
Courcelles-lès-Semur
Villeferry
Bligny-le-Sec
Jailly-les-Moulins
104
65
84
61

CHATEAUVILLAIN
ARC-EN-BARROIS
AUBERIVE
LANGRES
NOGENT
RECEY-S-OURCE
GRANCEY-LE-CHATEAU-NEUVELLE
SELONGEY
PRAUTHOY
LONGEAU-PERCEY
FONTAINE-FRANÇAISE
IS-S-TILLE
Silvarouvres
Blessonville
Semoutiers-Montsaon
Verbiesles
Luzy-s.-Marne
Sarcey
Louvières
Poulangy
Richebourg
Dinteville
Marnay s.-Marne
Vesaignes-s.-Marne
Thivet
Poinson-lès-Nogent
Latrecey-Ormoy-s.-Aube
Coupray
Cour-l'Évêque
Bugnières
Villiers-s.-Suize
Leffonds
Faverolles
Rolampont
Chauffourt
Veuxhaulles-s.-Aube
Dancevoir
Boudreville
Aubepierre-s.-Aube
Giey-s.-Aujon
Ternat
Ormancey
Marac
Chanoy
Humes-Jorquenay
Charmes
Changey
Bannes
Lignerolles
St-Loup-s.-Aujon
Mardor
St-Ciergues
Champigny-lès-Langres
Peigney
les Goulles
la Chaume
Vauxbons
Perrancey-les-Vieux-Moulins
Rochetaillée
Voisines
Rouvres-sur-Aube
Arbot
Gurgy-la-Ville
Lucey
Faverolles-lès-Lucey
Courcelles-en-Montagne
Noidant-le-Rocheux
Aulnoy-s.-Aube
Bay-s.-Aube
Vitry-en-Montagne
Gurgy-le-Château
Perrogney-les-Fontaines
Rouelles
Leuglay
Buxerolles
Germaines
Chambain
Brennes
Flagey
Bourg
Cohons
Colmier-le-Haut
Colmier-le-Bas
Menesble
Orcevaux
Verseilles-le-Haut
Aprey
Villiers-lès-Aprey
Baissey
Villars-Santenoge
Chaugey
Praslay
Aujeurres
Bure-les-Templiers
Vivey
Montmoyen
Terrefondrée
Poinson-lès-Grancey
Poinsenot
Vaillant
Leuchey
St-Broingt-les-Fosses
Villegusien-le-Lac
Chassigny
St-Broing-les-Moines
Beneuvre
Vals-des-Tilles
Mouilleron
Vesvres-s/s-Chalancey
Vals d'Esnoms
Dommarien
Moitron
Chalancey
Rivière-les-Fosses
Vaux-s/s-Aubigny
Montsaugeon
Choilley-Dardenay
Minot
Bussières
Busserotte-et-Montenaille
Vernois-lès-Vesvres
Isômes
Cusey
Fraignot-et-Vesvrotte
Courlon
Cussey-les-Forges
Boussenois
Étalante
Salives
Avot
Foncegrive
Occey
Echalot
Barjon
Marey-s.-Tille
Sacquenay
le Meix
Avelanges
Chaume-et-Courchamp
Poiseul-lès-Saulx
Poiseul-la-Grange
Léry
Villey-s.-Tille
Crécey-s.-Tille
Orville
Chazeuil
Courtivron
Lamargelle
Moloy
Frénois
Tarsul
Saulx-le-Duc
Diénay
Echevannes
Marcilly-s.-Tille
Til-Châtel
Véronnes
Bourberain
Fontenelle
Villecomte
Vernot
Lux
Pellerey
Poncey-s.-l'Ignon
Gemeaux
Chaignay
Bèze
Licey s.-Vingeanne
Dampierre-et-Flée
Beaumont-s.-Vingeanne
Vaux-Saules
Saussy
Francheville
Pichanges
Champagny
Curtil-St-Seine
Marsannay-le-Bois
Spoy
Blagny-s.-Vingeanne
Noiron-s.-Bèze
FORÊT DE IS-S-TILLE
66
87
105

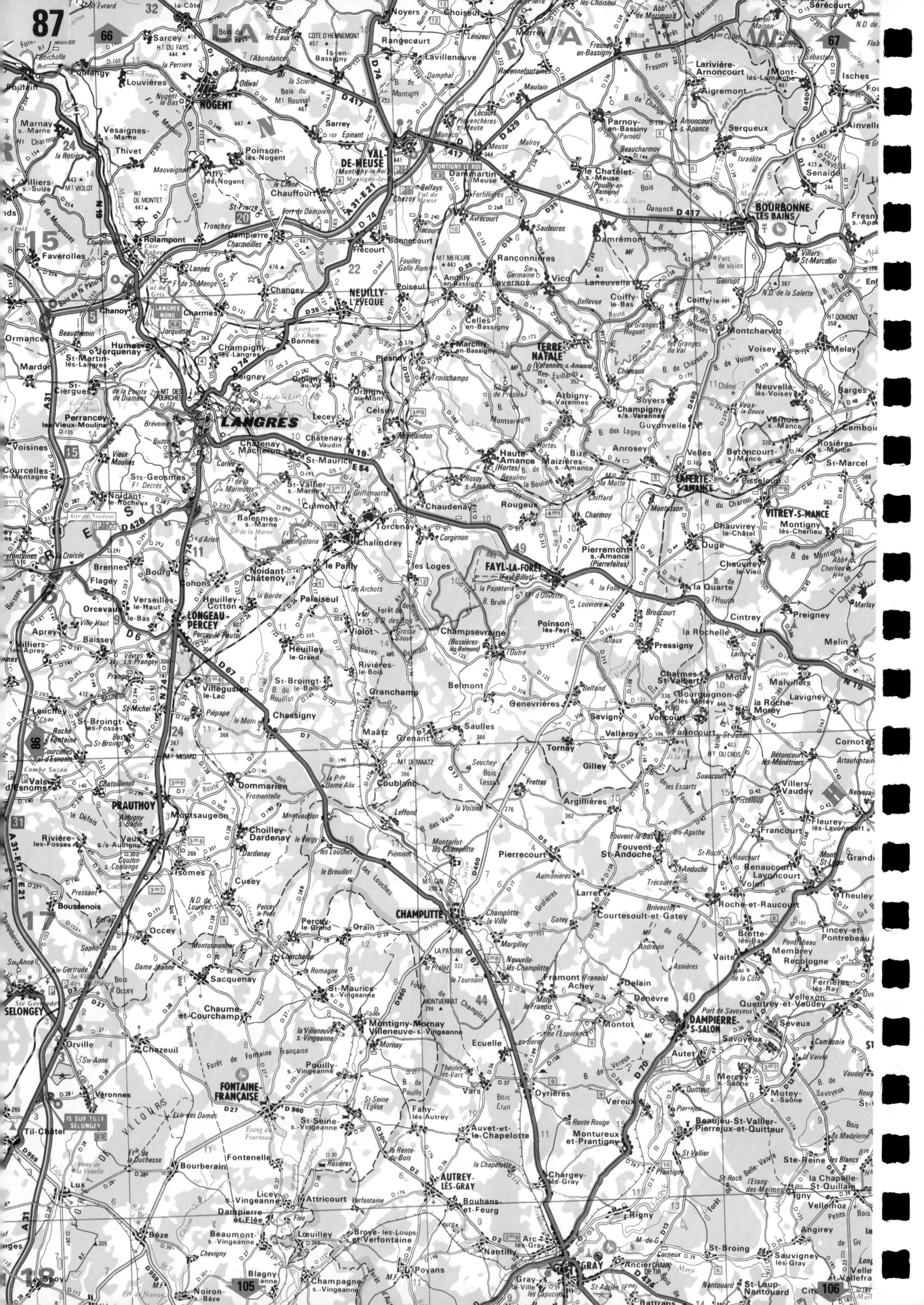

66
67
86
105
106

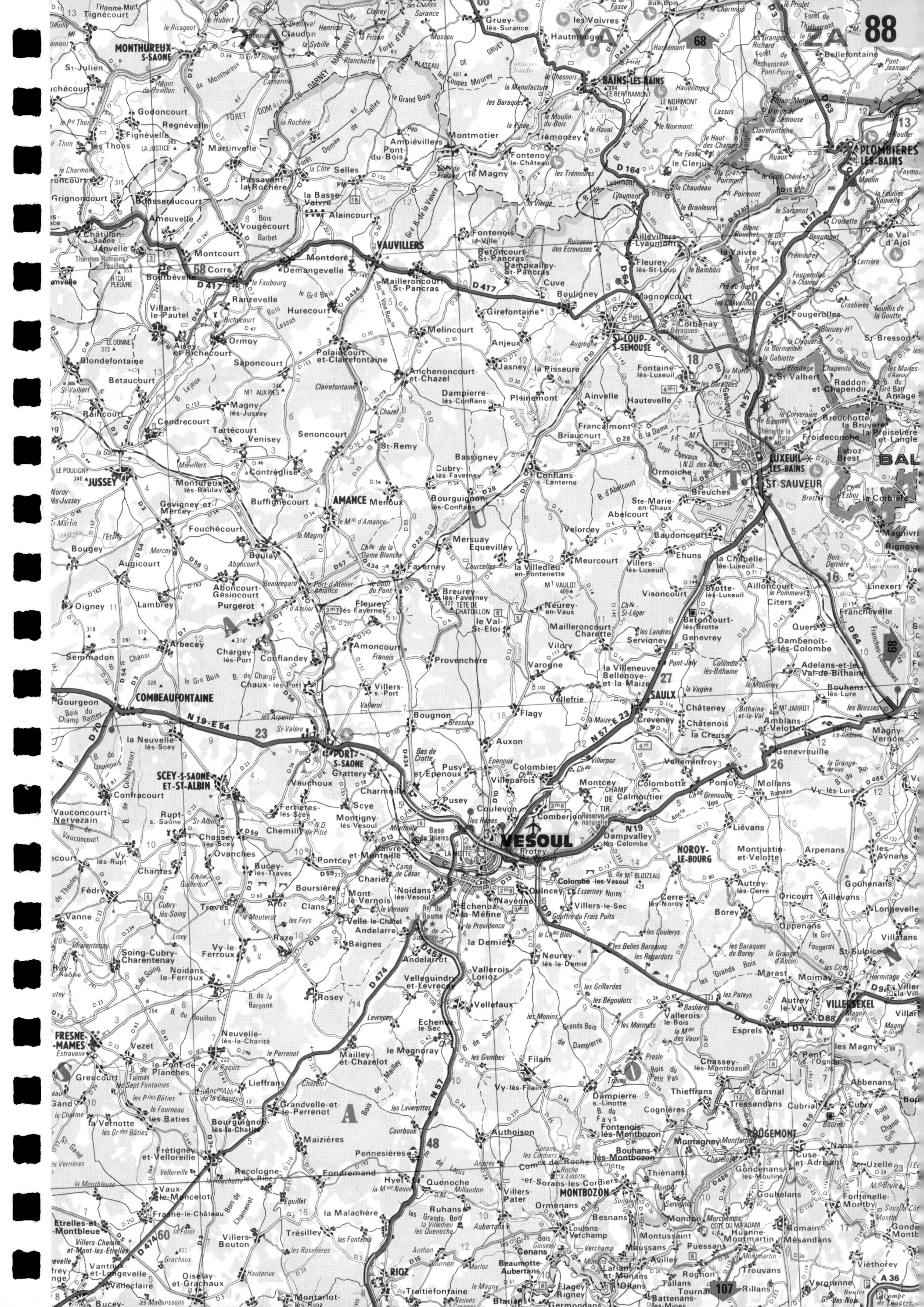
MONTHUREUX-S-SAONE
Tignécourt
Claudon
Gruey-lès-Surance
Hautmougey
les Voivres
Bellefontaine
BAINS-LES-BAINS
PLOMBIERES-LES-BAINS
St-Julien
Godoncourt
Regnévelle
Fignévelle
Martinvelle
Ambiévillers
Pont-du-Bois
Montmotier
Fontenoy-le-Château
Selles
Passavant-la-Rochère
Bousseraucourt
Ameuvelle
Vougécourt
Alaincourt
Châtillon-s-Saône
Jonvelle
Montcourt
Corre
Bourbévelle
Ranzevelle
Montdoré
Demangevelle
VAUVILLERS
Mailleroncourt-St-Pancras
Fontenois-la-Ville
Betoncourt-St-Pancras
Dampvalley-St-Pancras
Cuve
Bouligney
Aillevillers-et-Lyaumont
Fleurey-lès-St-Loup
Magnoncourt
Villars-le-Pautel
Hurecourt
Girefontaine
Melincourt
ST-LOUP-S-SEMOUSE
Corbenay
Fougerolles
Aisey-et-Richecourt
Ormoy
Saponcourt
Polaincourt-et-Clairefontaine
Anchenoncourt-et-Chazel
Anjeux
Jasney
la Pisseure
Fontaine-lès-Luxeuil
Hautevelle
Ainvelle
Plainemont
Dampierre-lès-Conflans
Blondefontaine
Betaucourt
Raincourt
Magny-lès-Jussey
Cendrecourt
Tartécourt
Venisey
Senoncourt
St-Remy
Bassigney
Briaucourt
Francalmont
LUXEUIL-LES-BAINS
ST-SAUVEUR
Froideconche
Breuches
Ormoiche
Conflans-s-Lanterne
Cubry-lès-Faverney
JUSSEY
Montureux-lès-Baulay
Contréglise
Buffignécourt
AMANCE
Menoux
Bourguignon-lès-Conflans
Gevigney-et-Mercey
Fouchécourt
Bougey
Augicourt
Baulay
Faverney
Mersuay
Equevilley
Velorcey
Meurcourt
Baudoncourt
Ste-Marie-en-Chaux
Abelcourt
Villers-lès-Luxeuil
Ehuns
la Chapelle-lès-Luxeuil
Aboncourt-Gésincourt
Purgerot
Lambrey
Oigney
Fleurey-lès-Faverney
Breurey-lès-Faverney
la Villedieu-en-Fontenette
Neurey-en-Vaux
Visoncourt
Brotte-lès-Luxeuil
Aillloncourt
Citers
Linexert
Franchevelle
Arbecey
Chargey-lès-Port
Conflandey
Amoncourt
Provenchère
le Val-St-Eloi
Mailleroncourt-Charette
Vilory
Varogne
Betoncourt-lès-Brotte
Genevrey
Servigney
Quers
Dambenoît-lès-Colombe
Semmadon
Chaux-lès-Port
Villers-s-Port
la Villeneuve-Bellenoye-et-la-Maize
Adelans-et-le-Val-de-Bithaine
Bouhans-lès-Lure
COMBEAUFONTAINE
Gourgeon
Bougnon
Flagy
Vellefrie
SAULX
Châteney
Châtenois
Creveney
la Creuse
Amblans-et-Velotte
Magny-Vernois
la Neuvelle-lès-Scey
PORT-S-SAONE
Auxon
Colombier
Villeparois
Genevreuille
Velleminfroy
Pomoy
Mollans
Vy-lès-Lure
SCEY-S-SAONE ET-ST-ALBIN
Confracourt
Vauchoux
Grattery
Charmoille
Pusy-et-Epenoux
Pusey
Montcey
Colombotte
Calmoutier
Vauconcourt-Nervezain
Rupt-s-Saône
Ferrières-lès-Scey
Chemilly
Scye
Montigny-lès-Vesoul
Coulevon
Comberjon
VESOUL
Frotey-lès-Vesoul
Dampvalley-lès-Colombe
NOROY-LE-BOURG
Liévans
Montjustin-et-Velotte
Arpenans
Chassey-lès-Scey
Ovanches
Vy-lès-Rupt
Chantes
Bucey-lès-Traves
Pontcey
Mont-le-Vernois
Chariez
Noidans-lès-Vesoul
Navenne
Quincey
Colombe-lès-Vesoul
Villers-le-Sec
Cerre-lès-Noroy
Autrey-lès-Cerre
Oricourt
Aillevans
Fédry
Traves
Aroz
Boursières
Clans
Echenoz-la-Méline
Borey
Oppenans
Longevelle
Vanne
Velle-le-Châtel
Andelarre
Baignes
la Demie
Neurey-lès-la-Demie
Villafans
Vy-le-Ferroux
Raze
Soing-Cubry-Charentenay
Noidans-le-Ferroux
Andelarrot
Vallerois-Lorioz
Velleguindry-et-Levrecey
Rosey
Vellefaux
Marast
Moimay
VILLERSEXEL
Autrey-le-Vay
Vallerois-le-Bois
Esprels
FRESNE-ST-MAMES
Vezet
Neuvelle-lès-la-Charité
Echenoz-le-Sec
le Magnoray
Mailley-et-Chazelot
Filain
Chassey-lès-Montbozon
Pont-s-l'Ognon
Greucourt
le Pont-de-Planches
Lieffrans
Vy-lès-Filain
Dampierre-s-Linotte
Thieffrans
Bonnal
Abbenans
Tressandans
Cubrial
Cubry
la Vernotte
les Baties
Bourguignon-lès-la-Charité
Grandvelle-et-le-Perrenot
Authoison
Fontenois-lès-Montbozon
Cognières
Montagney
ROUGEMONT
Nans
Maizières
Pennesières
Bouhans-lès-Montbozon
Frétigney-et-Velloreille
Recologne-lès-Rioz
Fondremand
Hyet
Quenoche
Villers-Pater
Thiénans
Gondenans-les-Moulins
Cuse-et-Adrisans
Uzelle
Vaux-le-Moncelot
Fontenelle-Montby
Fraine-le-Château
la Malachère
Ruhans
MONTBOZON
Ormenans
Besnans
Mondon
Gouhelans
Etrelles-et-la-Montbleue
Villers-Bouton
Trésilley
Loulans-Verchamp
Cenans
Montussaint
Huanne-Montmartin
Romain
Mésandans
Vantoux-et-Longevelle
Oiselay-et-Grachaux
Beaumotte-Aubertans
Maussans
Puessans
Avilley
Trouvans
Viéthorey
Vellelaire
RIOZ
Traitiéfontaine
Montarlot-lès-Rioz
Blarians
Flagey-Rigney
Larians-et-Munans
Tallans
Rognon
Tournans
Rillans
Vergranne
Battenans
Bucey
A 36
N 19-E 54
N 57-E 23
D 417
D 474
D 64
107
68
89

68
Dinozé
Archettes
Docelles
Xamontarupt
Tendon
Rehaupal
Arches
Pouxeux
Eloyes
TETE DES CUVEAUX
Liézey
GERARDMER
Xonrupt-Longemer
Dounoux
Uriménil
Hadol
Uzemain
la Forge
XERTIGNY
Raon-aux-Bois
St-Nabord
St-Amé
Sapois
Rochesson
REMIREMONT
Vagney
Bellefontaine
Dommartin-lès-Remiremont
Vecoux
Thiéfosse
SAULXURES-S.-MOSELOTTE
Cornimont
la Bresse
VENTRON
PLOMBIERES-LES-BAINS
Girmont-Val-d'Ajol
le Val d'Ajol
Rupt-s.-Moselle
BALLONS
Ferdrupt
le Ménil
LE THILLOT
Bussang
Fougerolles
Corravillers
Ramonchamp
Fresse-Moselle
DES
St-Maurice-s.-Moselle
Esmoulières
Beulotte-St-Laurent
Château-Lambert
FAUCOGNEY-ET-LA-MER
BALLON D'ALSACE
Raddon-et-Chapendu
VOSGES
Servance
LUXEUIL-LES-BAINS
ST SAUVEUR
Froideconche
Breuchotte
Ternuay-Melay-et-St-Hilaire
Belfahy
Sewen
Dolleren
Ecromagny
Belmont
Magnivray
Belonchamp
MELISEY
Fresse
Plancher-les-Mines
GIROMAGNY
Lepuix
St-Barthélemy
Auxelles-Haut
Auxelles-Bas
Citers
Linexert
Franchevelle
Quers
St-Germain
la Neuvelle-lès-Lure
Malbouhans
Ronchamp
CHAMPAGNEY
Lachapelle-s/s-Chaux
Froideterre
LURE
Magny-Danigon
Errevet
VALDOIE
OFFEMONT
BELFORT
Roye
Clairegoutte
Frédéric-Fontaine
Echavanne
Chenebier
Genevreuille
Mollans
Vouhenans
Lyoffans
Belverne
Etobon
Chalonvillars
Essert
DANJOUTIN
Moffans-et-Vacheresse
Lomont
Courmont
Chagey
Mandrevillars
NOROY-LE-BOURG
Arpenans
Faymont
Couthenans
HERICOURT
Gouhenans
Athesans-Etroitefontaine
Champey
CHATENOIS-LES-FORGES
Villafans
Mignavillers
Saulnot
Trémoins
Grand-Charmont
VILLERSEXEL
Désandans
Arcey
MONTBELIARD
SOCHAUX
Esprels
Marvelise
Allondans
Ste-Suzanne
ETUPES
Courchaton
Onans
Présentevillers
AUDINCOURT
107

COLMAR
MULHOUSE
BASEL
(BALE)
ALTKIRCH
GUEBWILLER
THANN
CERNAY
ROUFFACH
ENSISHEIM
ILLZACH
WITTENHEIM
HABSHEIM
NEUF-BRISACH
ANDOLSHEIM
WINTZENHEIM
MUNSTER
MASEVAUX
ST-AMARIN
DANNEMARIE
HIRSINGUE
FERRETTE
SIERENTZ
DELLE
GRANDVILLARS
BEAUCOURT
FONTAINE
ROUGEMONT-LE-CHATEAU
SOULTZ-HT-RHIN
Eguisheim
Ingersheim
Turckheim
Kaysersberg
Breisach am Rhein
Vogelgrun
Fessenheim
Blodelsheim
Ottmarsheim
Chalampé
Neuenburg
Kembs
Huningue
St-Louis
Hégenheim
Allschwil
Oberwil
Binningen
Bottmingen
Reinach
Hésingue
Blotzheim
Volgelsheim
Biesheim
Kunheim
Urschenheim
Durrenentzen
Bischwihr
Fortschwihr
Sundhoffen
Horbourg-Wihr
Wettolsheim
Herrlisheim-près-Colmar
Hattstatt
Gueberschwihr
Pfaffenheim
Soultzmatt
Westhalten
Lautenbach
Buhl
Murbach
Issenheim
Raedersheim
Ungersheim
Bollwiller
Pulversheim
Staffelfelden
Wittelsheim
Kingersheim
Richwiller
Pfastatt
Lutterbach
Reiningue
Morschwiller-le-Bas
Brunstatt
Zimmersheim
Eschentzwiller
Dietwiller
Landser
Schlierbach
Kappelen
Helfrantzkirch
Waldighofen
Oberdorf
Grentzingen
Henflingen
Ueberstrass
Seppois-le-Bas
Bisel
Feldbach
Riespach
Durmenach
Werentzhouse
Fislis
Linsdorf
Bettlach
Oltingue
Sondersdorf
Raedersdorf
Biederthal
Rodersdorf
Leymen
Liebenswiller
Pfetterhouse
Durlinsdorf
Liebsdorf
Bonfol
Lugnez
Beurnevésin
Courtelevant
Réchésy
Florimont
Suarce
Friesen
Hindlingen
Largitzen
Mertzen
Fulleren
Hirtzbach
Carspach
Ballersdorf
Montreux-Vieux
Montreux-Jeune
Romagny
Magny
Chavannes-les-Grands
Traubach-le-Haut
Hagenbach
Eglingen
Wolfersdorf
Gommersdorf
Elbach
Guevenatten
Bréchaumont
Bellemagny
Sternenberg
Diefmatten
Burnhaupt-le-Haut
Burnhaupt-le-Bas
Soppe-le-Haut
Soppe-le-Bas
Mortzwiller
Guewenheim
Sentheim
Lauw
Michelbach
Aspach-le-Haut
Aspach-le-Bas
Schweighouse-Thann
Vieux-Thann
Leimbach
Bourbach-le-Haut
Bourbach-le-Bas
Rammersmatt
Roderen
Sickert
Wegscheid
Oderen
Fellering
Husseren-Wesserling
Malmerspach
Mollau
Moosch
Mitzach
Ranspach
Geishouse
Goldbach-Altenbach
Bitschwiller-lès-Thann
Willer-s-Thur
Steinbach
Uffholtz
Wattwiller
Berrwiller
Wuenheim
Hartmannswiller
Jungholtz
Rimbach-près-Guebwiller
Bergholtz
Orschwihr
Gundolsheim
Merxheim
Meyenheim
Munwiller
Réguisheim
Oberentzen
Niederentzen
Biltzheim
Oberhergheim
Niederhergheim
Dessenheim
Heiteren
Balgau
Nambsheim
Rustenhart
Hirtzfelden
Roggenhouse
Munchhouse
Rumersheim-le-Haut
Bantzenheim
Baldersheim
Battenheim
Ruelisheim
Sausheim
Rixheim
Homburg
Petit-Landau
Niffer
Riedisheim
Didenheim
Hochstatt
Galfingue
Heimsbrunn
Bernwiller
Froeningen
Spechbach-le-Haut
Spechbach-le-Bas
Illfurth
Zillisheim
Flaxlanden
Bruebach
Steinbrunn-le-Bas
Steinbrunn-le-Haut
Luemschwiller
Tagolsheim
Walheim
Emlingen
Heiwiller
Obermorschwiller
Wahlbach
Zaessingue
Magstatt-le-Bas
Magstatt-le-Haut
Bartenheim
Stetten
Brinckheim
Rantzwiller
Koetzingue
Waltenheim
Geispitzen
Uffheim
Rosenau
Ranspach-le-Bas
Ranspach-le-Haut
Michelbach-le-Bas
Michelbach-le-Haut
Attenschwiller
Buschwiller
Folgensbourg
Wentzwiller
Neuwiller
Hagenthal-le-Bas
Hagenthal-le-Haut
Schönenbuch
Muespach
Muespach-le-Haut
Roppentzwiller
Steinsoultz
Knoeringue
Berentzwiller
Jettingen
Hundsbach
Hausgauen
Franken
Tagsdorf
Wittersdorf
Schwoben
Willer
Bettendorf
Heimersdorf
Ruederbach
St-Ulrich
Altenach
Strueth
Sept
Manspach
Retzwiller
Valdieu-Lutran
Chavannes-s-l'Etang
Petitefontaine
Lachapelle-s-Rougemont
Romagny s/s-Rougemont
Felon
Angeot
Lagrange
Larivière
Reppe
Fontaine
Lacollonge
Fousse magne
Bessoncourt
Frais
Phaffans
Cunelières
Chèvremont
Fontenelle
Petit-Croix
Novillard
Autrechêne
Bretagne
Brebotte
Grosne
Chavanatte
Vellescot
Recouvrance
Boron
Froidefontaine
Lachat
Le Puix
Lepuix-Neuf
Joncherey
Faverois
Thiancourt
Méziré
Boncourt
Montignez
Buix
Badevel
Fêche-l'Eglise
Lebetain
Grottes
Leval
Wintzenheim
Zimmerbach
Walbach
Gunsbach
Soultzeren
Stosswihr
Luttenbach-près-Munster
Breitenbach
Metzeral
Mittlach
Sondernach
Wasserbourg
Osenbach
Linthal
Soultzbach-les-Bains
Griesbach-au-Val
Eschbach-au-Val
Voegtlinshoffen
Husseren-les-Châteaux
Obermorschwihr
Logelheim
Appenwihr
Wolfgantzen
Weckolsheim
Ste-Croix-en-Plaine
Hettenschlag
Algolsheim
Obersaasheim
Geiswasser
Widensolen
Feldkirch
Bitschwiller
Kruth
Le Markstein
Grd Ballon
Le Hohneck
Col de la Schlucht
Le Valtin
Les Trois Epis
Le Linge
Niedermorschwihr
Vieil Armand
Ballon d'Alsace
Le Thillot
Ihringen
Achkarren
Breisach
Heitersheim
Grissheim
Müllheim
Auggen
Schliengen
Bad Bellingen
Efringen-Kirchen
Weil am Rhein
Lörrach
Mappach
Hertingen
Blansingen
Kleinkems
Huttingen
Istein
Eimeldingen
Märkt
Neuenburg
Steinenstadt
Zienken
Hügelheim
Bamlach
Rheinweiler
Biel
Benken
Therwil
Ettingen
Witterswil
Flüh
Hofstetten
Metzerlen
Burg
Pfeffingen
Landskron
Mariastein
Schach
Bâle-Mulhouse
A 36 E 54-60
A 35 E 25
A 5 E 35
N 66
N 83
N 415
N 466
N 19
D 419
D 432
D 201
D 466
D 52
D 468
D 39
CB
DB
DES
VOSGES
HAUT-RHIN
TERRITOIRE DE BELFORT
FORET DOMANIALE DE LA HARDT
CAMP DE TIR
USINE PEUGEOT
FRONHOLTZ
NIEDERHERGHEIM
ENSISHEIM MEYENHEIM
MULHOUSE-C.
ILE NAPOLEON
MULHOUSE BOURTZWILLER
LUTTERBACH DORNACH
BURNHAUPT
MEYENHEIM
OTTMARSHEIM
RIXHEIM
BARTENHEIM
EFRINGEN KIRCHEN
MULLHEIM NEUENBURG
LADHOF
SEMM
ST-LOUIS
LORRACH
REINACH
69
70
108

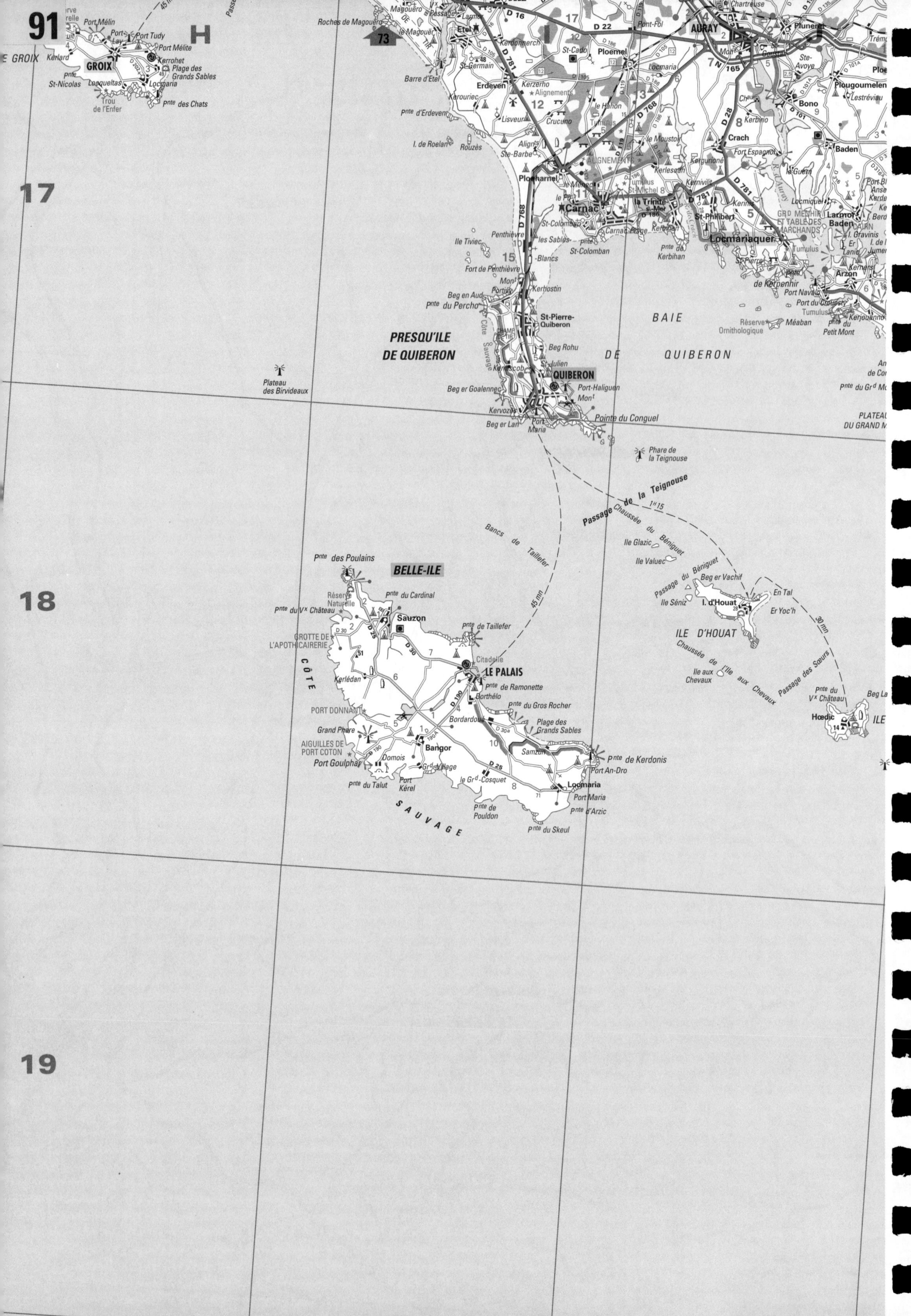
H
17
18
19
73
GROIX
Port Mélin
Port Tudy
Port Mélite
Kerlard
Kerrohet
Plage des Grands Sables
Locmaria
St-Nicolas
Trou de l'Enfer
Pnte des Chats
Roches de Magouëro
Le Magouër
Etel
Lamor
Barre d'Etel
St-Germain
Erdeven
Kerzerho
Alignements
Karouriec
Pnte d'Erdeven
Lisveur
Crucuno
I. de Roelan
Rouzès
Ste-Barbe
Plouharnel
Carnac
St-Colomban
Penthièvre
Ile Tiviec
les Sables-Blancs
Fort de Penthièvre
Kerhostin
Beg en Aud
Pnte du Perch
St-Pierre-Quiberon
PRESQU'ILE DE QUIBERON
Côte Sauvage
Beg Rohu
St-Julien
QUIBERON
Port-Haliguen
Beg er Goalennec
Kervozès
Beg er Lan
Port Maria
Pointe du Conguel
Plateau des Birvideaux
D 16
D 22
D 781
D 768
St-Cado
Ploemel
Pont-Fol
AURAY
Chartreuse
Plunere
Ste-Avoye
Locmaria
Plougoumelen
Bono
Crach
Fort Espagnol
Baden
Le Guern
Larmor Baden
ALIGNEMENTS
Tumulus St-Michel
la Trinité s-Mer
Kerbihan
Kernivilit
St-Philibert
Locmariaquer
GRD MENHIR ET TABLE DES MARCHANDS
St-Pierre
Kerpenhir
Port Navalo
Port du Crouesty
Arzon
Tumulus
Kerjouanno
Pnte du Petit Mont
Réserve Ornithologique
Méaban
BAIE DE QUIBERON
Pnte du Grd Mo
PLATEAU DU GRAND M
Phare de la Teignouse
Passage de la Teignouse
1h15
Bancs de Taillefer
45 mn
Chaussée du Béniguet
Ile Glazic
Ile Valuec
Passage du Béniguet
Beg er Vachif
Ile Séniz
I. d'Houat
En Tal
Er Yoc'h
30 mn
ILE D'HOUAT
Chaussée de l'Ile aux Chevaux
Ile aux Chevaux
Passage des Sœurs
Pnte du Vx Château
Hœdic
Pnte des Poulains
BELLE-ILE
Réserve Naturelle
Pnte du Cardinal
Pnte du Vx Château
Sauzon
Pnte de Taillefer
GROTTE DE L'APOTHICAIRERIE
Citadelle
LE PALAIS
Pnte de Ramonette
Borthélo
Kerlédan
CÔTE SAUVAGE
PORT DONNANT
Pnte du Gros Rocher
Grand Phare
Bordardoue
Plage des Grands Sables
AIGUILLES DE PORT COTON
Bangor
Samzun
Pnte de Kerdonis
Port Goulphar
Domois
Grd Village
Port An-Dro
Pnte du Talut
Port Kérel
le Grd-Cosquet
Locmaria
Port Maria
Pnte d'Arzic
Pnte de Pouldon
Pnte du Skeul
D 25
D 30
D 190

REDON
ST-NICOLAS-DE-REDON
ALLAIRE
GUÉMENÉ-PENFAO
DERVAL
NOZAY
ST-GILDAS-DES-BOIS
Missillac
Guenrouet
Plessé
BLAIN
PONTCHÂTEAU
Bouvron
Fay-de-Bretagne
Héric
Campbon
SAVENAY
MONTOIR-DE-BRETAGNE
Donges
ST-NAZAIRE
PAIMBŒUF
Cordemais
ST-ÉTIENNE-DE-MONTLUC
ORVAULT
LA CHAPELLE-S.-ERDRE
St-Brévin-les-Pins
ST-PÈRE-EN-RETZ
Frossay
Couëron
ST-HERBLAIN
LE PELLERIN
Bouguenais
REZÉ
BOUAYE
PORNIC
Chauvé
Ste-Pazanne
St-Hilaire-de-Chaléons
Arthon-en-Retz
Chéméré
Port-St-Père
St-Mars-de-Coutais
La Chevrolière
la Bernerie-en-Retz
La Plaine-s.-Mer
St-Michel-Chef-Chef
FORÊT DU GÂVRE
FORÊT DE PRINCE
LOIRE
Lac de Grand-Lieu
75
92
109

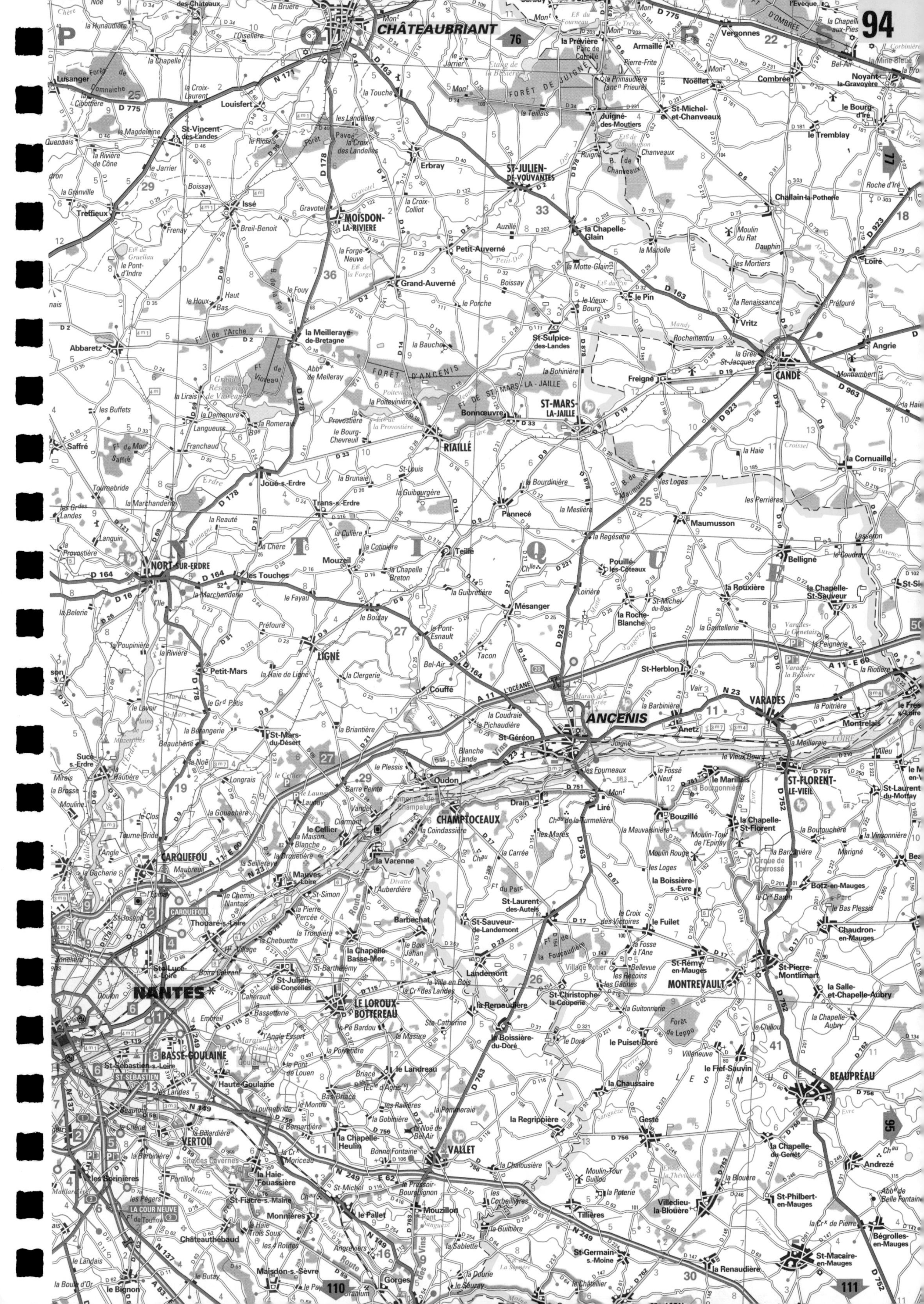

CHÂTEAUBRIANT
76
Lusanger
Forêt de Domnaiche
D 775
Louisfert
St-Vincent-des-Landes
la Magdeleine
Erbray
ST-JULIEN-DE-VOUVANTES
FORÊT DE JUIGNÉ
la Prévière
Armaillé
Vergonnes
Noëllet
Combrée
Noyant-la-Gravoyère
Juigné-des-Moutiers
St-Michel-et-Chanveaux
le Tremblay
Chanveaux
Challain-la-Potherie
Treffieux
Issé
MOISDON-LA-RIVIERE
Petit-Auverné
la Chapelle-Glain
Grand-Auverné
le Pin
Vritz
Abbaretz
la Meilleraye-de-Bretagne
St-Sulpice-des-Landes
FORÊT D'ANCENIS
Freigné
CANDÉ
Angrie
ST-MARS-LA-JAILLE
Bonnœuvre
RIAILLÉ
Saffré
Joué-s.-Erdre
Trans-s.-Erdre
Pannecé
Maumusson
la Cornuaille
NORT-SUR-ERDRE
Mouzeil
Teillé
Pouillé-les-Côteaux
Belligné
les Touches
Mésanger
la Rouxière
la Chapelle-St-Sauveur
LIGNÉ
Petit-Mars
St-Herblon
Couffé
ANCENIS
VARADES
Anetz
St-Géréon
Montrelais
St-Mars-du-Désert
Oudon
ST-FLORENT-LE-VIEIL
CHAMPTOCEAUX
Liré
Drain
Bouzillé
le Cellier
la Chapelle-St-Florent
CARQUEFOU
Mauves-s-Loire
Thouaré-s.-Loire
Barbechat
St-Laurent-des-Autels
le Fuilet
Botz-en-Mauges
Chaudron-en-Mauges
St-Luce-s-Loire
la Chapelle-Basse-Mer
Landemont
St-Rémy-en-Mauges
MONTREVAULT
St-Pierre-Montlimart
NANTES
St-Julien-de-Concelles
LE LOROUX-BOTTEREAU
St-Christophe-la-Couperie
la Salle-et-Chapelle-Aubry
la Boissière-du-Doré
le Puiset-Doré
BASSE-GOULAINE
St-Sébastien-s-Loire
le Landreau
le Fief-Sauvin
BEAUPRÉAU
Haute-Goulaine
la Chaussaire
VERTOU
la Regrippière
Gesté
la Chapelle-Heulin
VALLET
la Chapelle-du-Genêt
Andrezé
les Sorinières
la Haie-Fouassière
St-Fiacre-s.-Maine
Mouzillon
Tillières
Villedieu-la-Blouère
St-Philbert-en-Mauges
Monnières
le Pallet
Châteauthébaud
St-Germain-s.-Moine
Bégrolles-en-Mauges
Maisdon-s.-Sèvre
Gorges
St-Macaire-en-Mauges
la Renaudière
le Bignon
LES MAUGES
A 11 - E 60
N 23
N 249
D 763
D 752
D 923
D 178
D 164
95
77
110
111

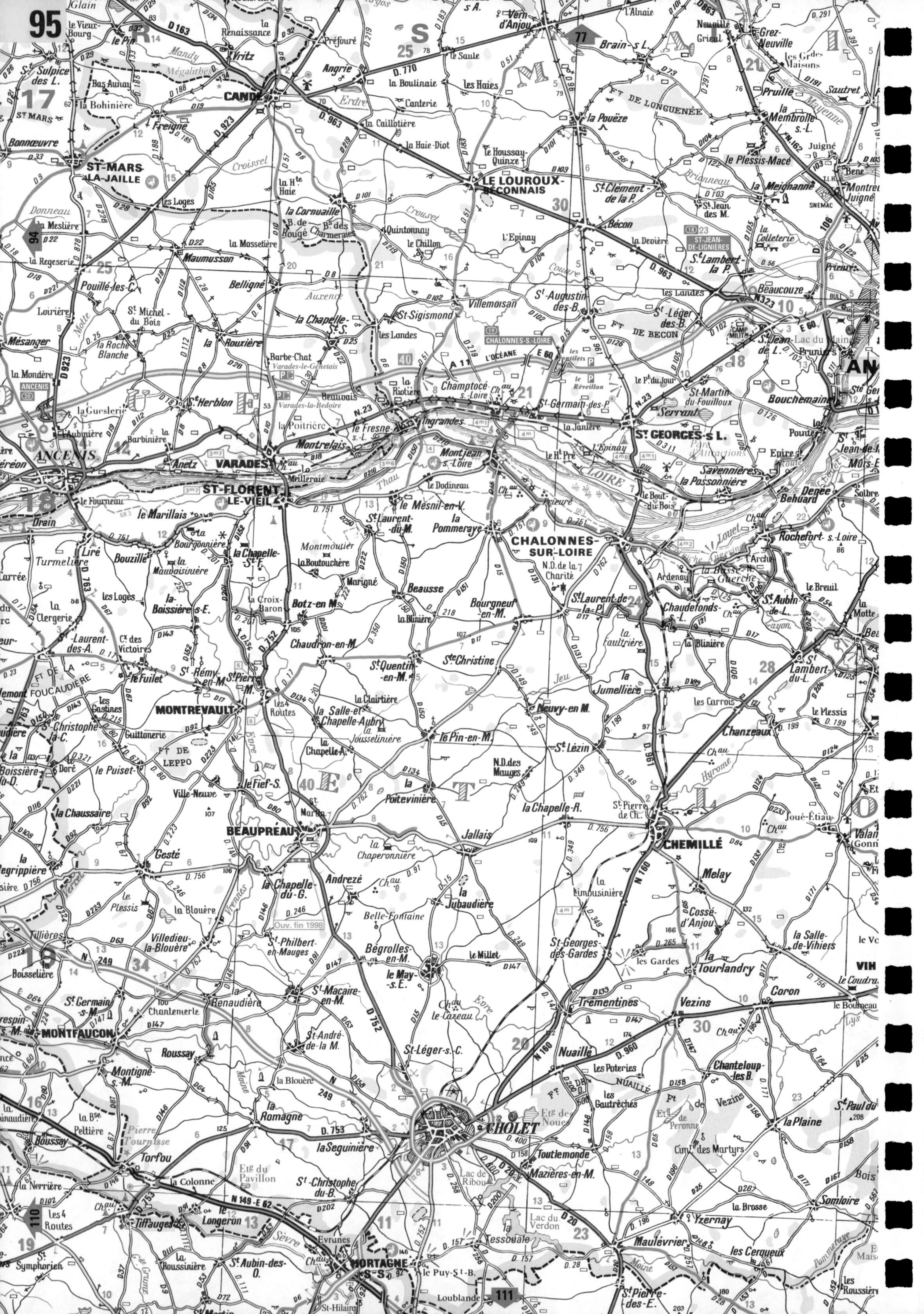
Candé
St-Mars-la-Jaille
Le Louroux-Béconnais
St-Clément-de-la-P.
Bécon
St-Augustin-des-B.
St-Léger-des-B.
St-Sigismond
Villemoisan
Ancenis
Varades
St-Florent-le-Vieil
Montjean-s.-Loire
Champtocé-s.-Loire
St-Germain-des-P.
Ingrandes
St-Georges-s.-L.
Savennières
la Possonnière
Chalonnes-sur-Loire
Rochefort-s.-Loire
Chaudefonds-s.-L.
St-Aubin-de-L.
St-Lambert-du-L.
Chanzeaux
Montrevault
St-Pierre-M.
St-Rémy-en-M.
le Fuilet
Botz-en-M.
Chaudron-en-M.
Beausse
Bourgneuf-en-M.
Ste-Christine
St-Quentin-en-M.
Neuvy-en-M.
St-Lézin
la Jumellière
le Pin-en-M.
la Poitevinière
Jallais
la Chapelle-R.
Chemillé
Melay
Beaupréau
Andrezé
la Jubaudière
Bégrolles-en-M.
le May-s.-E.
St-Macaire-en-M.
St-Philbert-en-Mauges
Villedieu-la-Blouère
St-Georges-des-Gardes
Trémentines
Vezins
Coron
Montfaucon
Roussay
Montigné-s.-M.
la Romagne
Torfou
Cholet
Nuaillé
Toutlemonde
Mazières-en-M.
Tiffauges
le Longeron
Mortagne-s.-S.
la Séguinière
St-Christophe-du-B.
Tessouale
Maulévrier
Yzernay
les Cerqueux
Somloire
St-Paul-du-B.
la Plaine
Chanteloup-les-B.
Cossé-d'Anjou
la Tourlandry
la Salle-de-Vihiers
Bouchemaine
Beaucouzé
St-Jean-de-L.
St-Martin-du-Fouilloux
Serrant
St-Lambert-la-P.
la Meignanne
la Membrolle-s.-L.
Grez-Neuville
Brain-s.-L.
Vern-d'Anjou
la Pouëze
St-Jean-de-Linières
Chalonnes-s.-Loire
Loire
Mayenne
Erdre
Èvre
Hyrôme
Layon
Sèvre
L'Océane
A 11
E 60
N 23
N 160
N 249
D 752
D 963
D 770
111
110
94
77

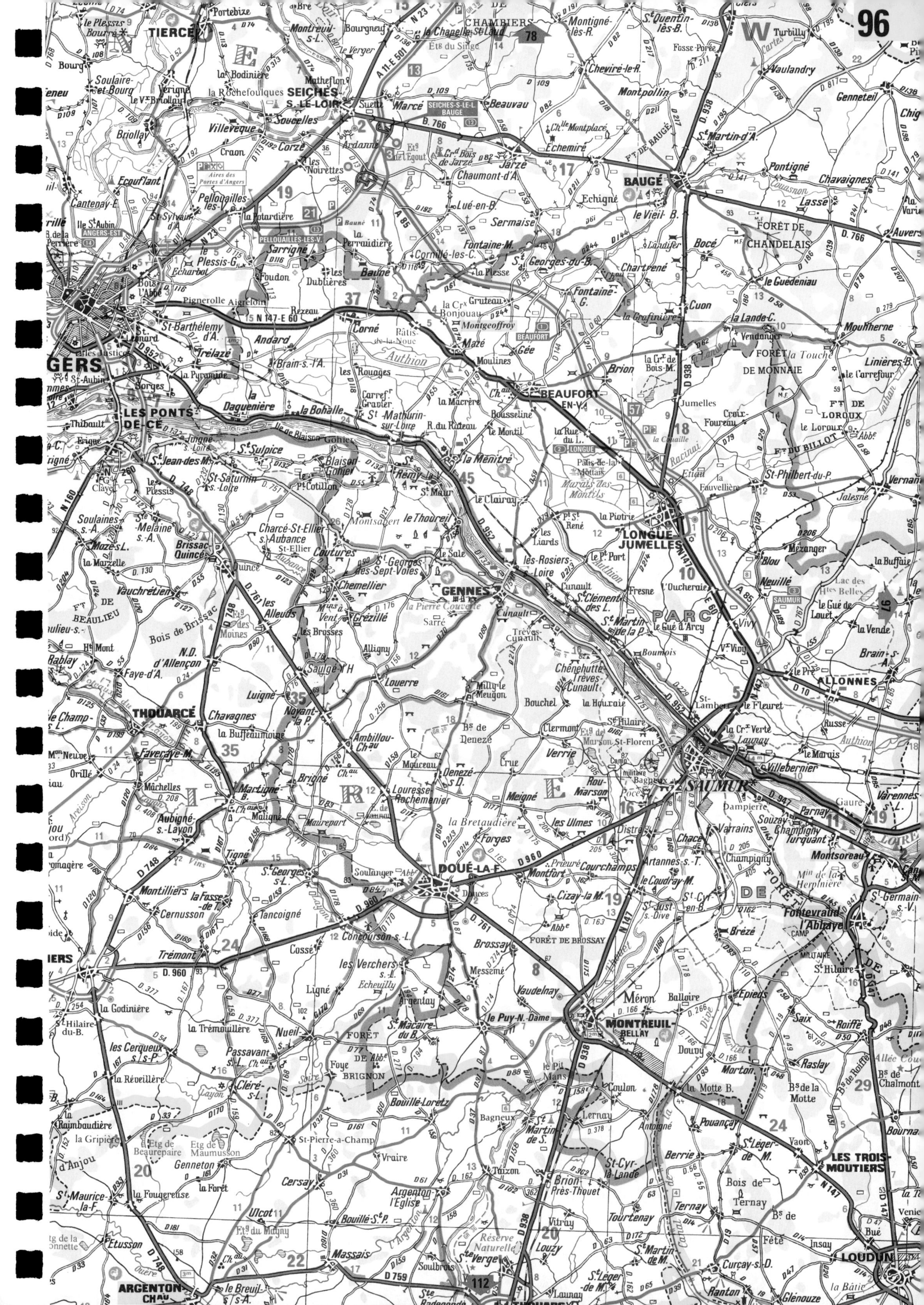

TIERCÉ
SEICHES-S.-LE-LOIR
Montreuil-s.-L.
Bourgneuf
la Chapelle-St-Laud
CHAMBIERS
St Quentin-lès-B.
Montigné-lès-R.
Turbilly
le Plessis-Bourré
Soulaire-et-Bourg
Briollay
Villevêque
Soucelles
Corzé
Marcé
Beauvau
Cheviré-le-R.
Montpollin
Vaulandry
Genneteil
Jarzé
Chaumont-d'A.
Echemiré
BAUGÉ
Pontigné
Chavaignes
Lasse
Écouflant
Pellouailles-les-V.
Sarrigné
Lué-en-B.
Sermaise
Fontaine-M.
Cornillé-les-C.
St Georges-du-B.
Chartrené
le Vieil-B.
Bocé
FORÊT DE CHANDELAIS
le Guédeniau
Cuon
la Lande-C.
Mouliherne
Corné
Andard
Trélazé
Brain-s.-l'A.
Mazé
Gée
Beaufort-en-V.
Brion
Jumelles
Vendanger
FORÊT DE MONNAIE
Linières-B.
LES PONTS-DE-CÉ
la Daguenière
la Bohalle
St Mathurin-sur-Loire
la Ménitré
St Sulpice
St Jean-des-M.
Blaison-Gohier
St Rémy-la-V.
St Maur
le Thoureil
LONGUÉ-JUMELLES
St Philbert-du-P.
Brissac-Quincé
Charcé-St-Ellier-s.-Aubance
Coutures
St Georges-des-Sept-Voies
GENNES
les Rosiers-s.-Loire
Chemellier
Grézillé
Cunault
St Clément-des-L.
St Martin-de-la-P.
Vivy
Allonnes
Vauchrétien
les Alleuds
Bois de Brissac
N.D. d'Allençon
Faye-d'A.
THOUARCÉ
Chavagnes
Luigné
Noyant-la-P.
Louerre
Milly-le-Meugon
Chênehutte-Trêves-Cunault
Faveraye-M.
Martigné-B.
Brigné
Louresse-Rochemenier
Denezé-s.-D.
SAUMUR
Villebernier
Varennes-s.-L.
Aubigné-s.-Layon
Tigné
St Georges-s.-L.
DOUÉ-LA-F.
Meigné
Rou-Marson
les Ulmes
Distré
Varrains
Chacé
Souzay-Champigny
Turquant
Montsoreau
Montilliers
Cernusson
Tancoigné
Concourson-s.-L.
Montfort
Courchamps
Cizay-la-M.
Artannes-s.-T.
le Coudray-M.
St Cyr-en-B.
St Just-s.-Dive
Fontevraud-l'Abbaye
Brézé
Trémont
Cossé
les Verchers-s.-L.
Brossay
FORÊT DE BROSSAY
Vaudelnay
Méron
MONTREUIL-BELLAY
Epieds
Saix
Roiffé
la Godinière
la Trémouillère
Nueil-s.-L.
St Macaire-du-B.
le Puy-N.-Dame
les Cerqueux-s/s-P.
Passavant-s.-L.
Cléré-s.-L.
Bouillé-Loretz
Coulon
la Motte B.
Morton
Raslay
Pouançay
St Léger-de-M.
Vaon
LES TROIS-MOUTIERS
St Pierre-a-Champ
Vraire
Genneton
Cersay
Argenton-l'Eglise
Brion-Près-Thouet
Tourtenay
Ternay
Bouillé-St-P.
Ulcot
Etusson
Massais
Louzy
St Martin-de-M.
Curçay-s.-D.
LOUDUN
ARGENTON-CHÂU
le Breuil-s/s-A.
Soulbrois
Ste Verge
St Léger-de-M.
Glénouze
THOUARS

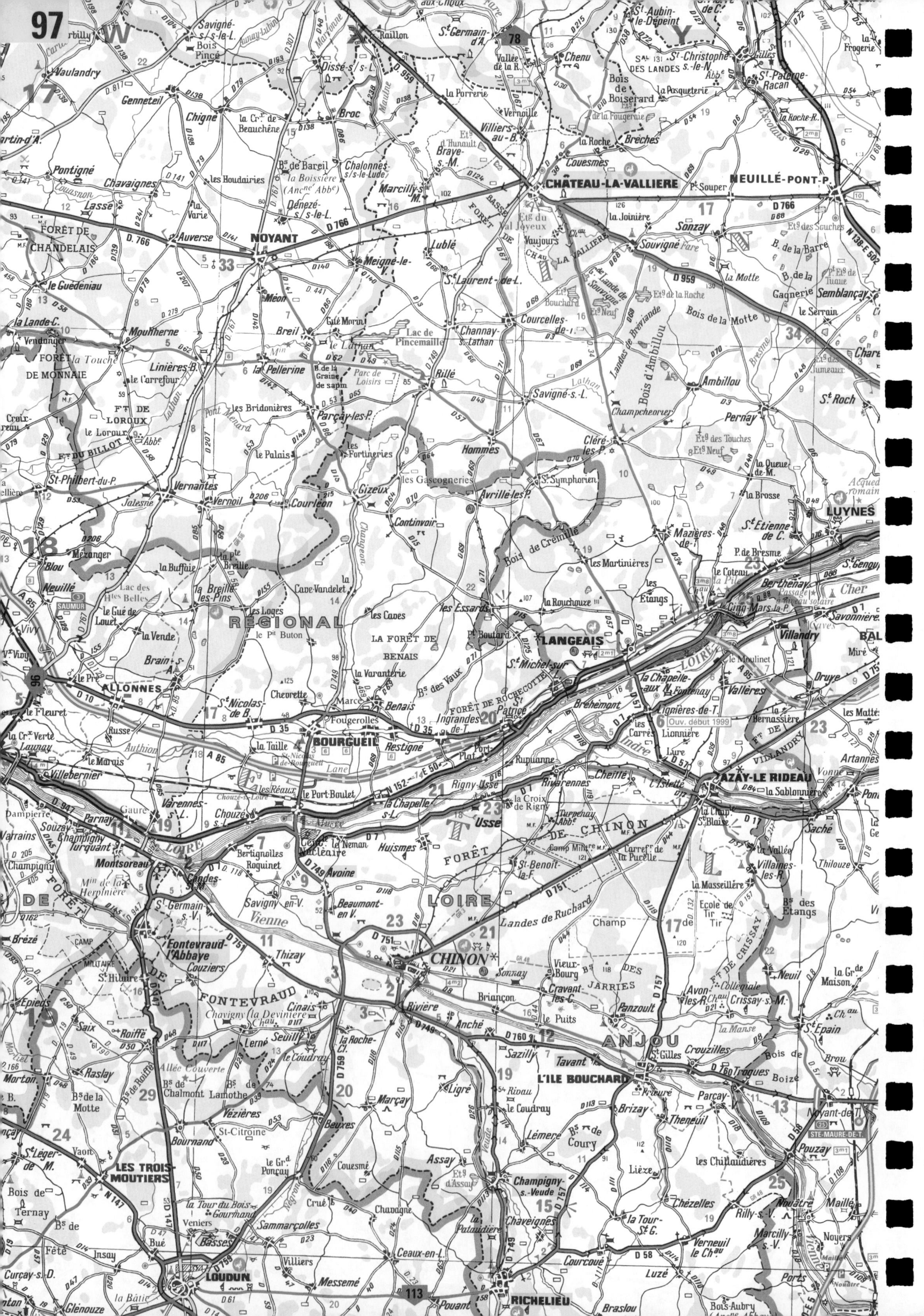
Savigné-s/s-le-L.
Raillon
St Germain-d'A.
78
St Aubin-le-Dépeint
St Christophe-s.-le-N.
St Paterne-Racan
Vaulandry
Genneteil
Chigné
Broc
Villiers-au-B.
Brèches
Pontigné
Chavaignes
Chalonnes-s/s-le-Lude
Braye-s.-M.
Couesmes
CHÂTEAU-LA-VALLIERE
NEUILLÉ-PONT-P.
Lasse
Dénezé-s/s-le-L.
Marcilly-s.-M.
Sonzay
FORÊT DE CHANDELAIS
Auverse
NOYANT
Lublé
Souvigné
Meigné-le-V.
St Laurent-de-L.
le Guédeniau
Méon
Semblançay
Courcelles-de-T.
Channay-s.-Lathan
Bois de la Motte
la Lande-C.
Mouliherne
Breil
Lac de Pincemaille
Linières-B.
la Pellerine
Rillé
Savigné-s.-L.
Ambillou
FORÊT DE MONNAIE
Parçay-les-P.
Pernay
St Roch
le Palais
Hommes
Cléré-les-P.
St Philbert-du-P.
Vernantes
Gizeux
Avrillé-les-P.
St Symphorien
Vernoil
Courléon
Continvoir
LUYNES
Mazières-de-T.
St Etienne-de-C.
Mézanger
Blou
la Breille-les-Pins
Bois de Cremille
les Martinières
Neuillé
Cing-Mars-la-P.
les Essards
RÉGIONAL
les Caves
LA FORÊT DE BENAIS
LANGEAIS
Villandry
la Vende
Brain-s-A.
St Michel-sur-L.
ALLONNES
St Nicolas-de-B.
Benais
Bréhémont
Vallères
Ingrandes-de-T.
Lignières-de-T.
Ouv. début 1999
BOURGUEIL
Restigné
AZAY-LE RIDEAU
Villebernier
Varennes-s.-L.
Chouzé-s.-L.
la Chapelle-s.-L.
Rigny-Ussé
Rivarennes
Cheillé
Parnay
Ussé
DE CHINON
Saché
Montsoreau
Candes-St M.
Avoine
Huismes
FORÊT
LOIRE
Villaines-les-R.
Savigny-en-V.
Beaumont-en-V.
Landes de Ruchard
Fontevraud-l'Abbaye
Thizay
CHINON
Couziers
FONTEVRAUD
Rivière
Cravant-les-C.
Panzoult
Crissay-s.-M.
Neuil
Cinais
Seuilly
Anché
Sazilly
Tavant
ANJOU
Crouzilles
L'ILE BOUCHARD
Troques
Ligré
Marçay
Brizay
Theneuil
Vezières
Bournand
Beuxes
LES TROIS-MOUTIERS
Assay
Lémeré
Pouzay
Champigny-s.-Veude
Chézelles
Noyant-de-T.
Sammarçolles
Chaveignes
la Tour-St G.
Ceaux-en-L.
Verneuil le Chau
LOUDUN
Messemé
Courcoué
Luzé
RICHELIEU
Braslou

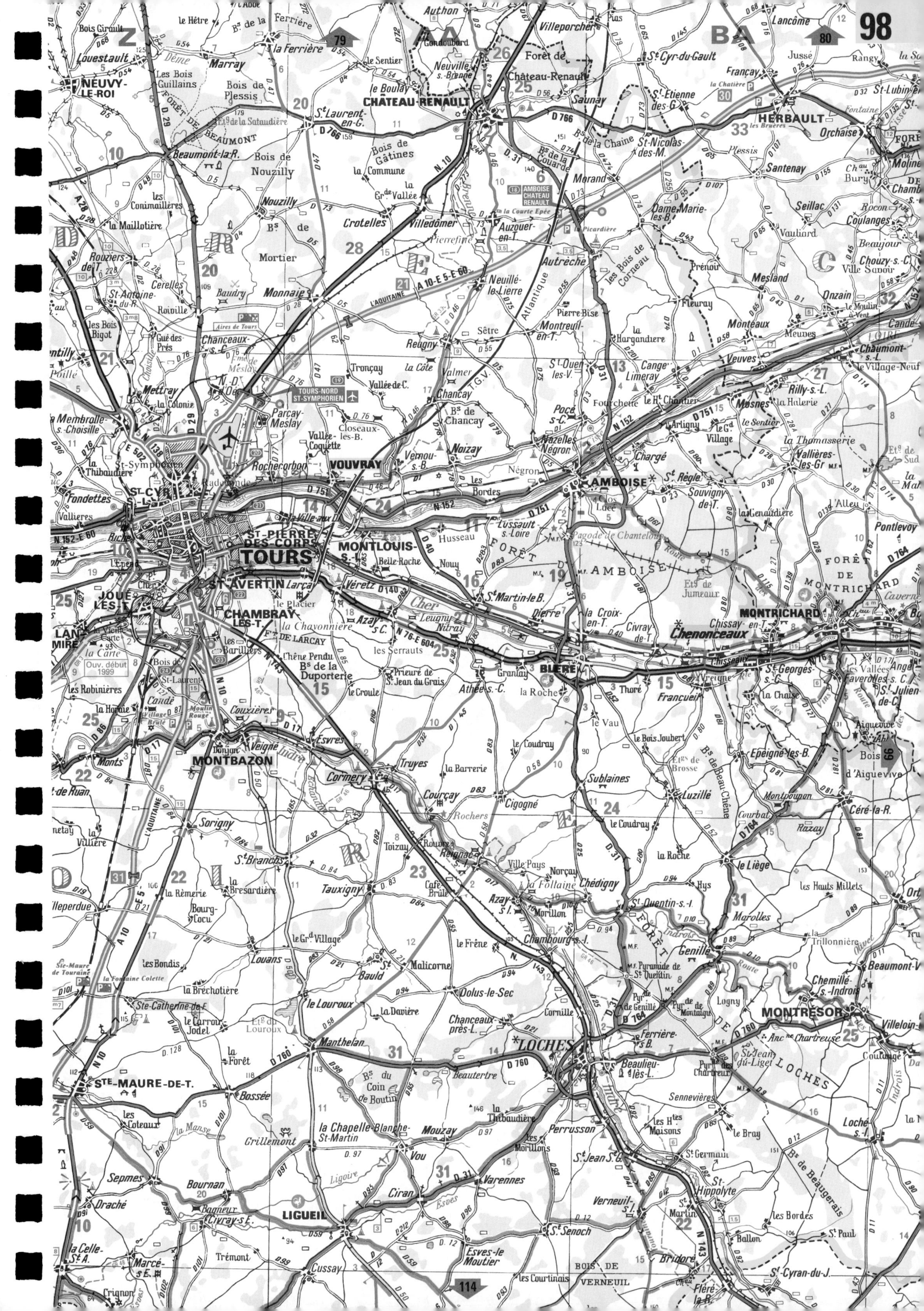

79
80
114
99
Authon
Villeporcher
Lancôme
Bois Girault
le Hêtre
Bs de la Ferrière
la Ferrière
Gondoubard
Forêt de Château-Renault
St Cyr-du-Gault
Jussé
Rangy
Louestault
Marray
le Sentier
Neuville s.-Brenne
Françay
NEUVY-LE-ROI
Les Bois Guillains
Bois de Plessis
le Boulay
CHATEAU-RENAULT
Saunay
St Etienne des-G.
HERBAULT
St-Lubin
St Laurent-en-G.
Orchaise
FORÊT DE BEAUMONT
Beaumont-la-R.
Bois de Gâtines
Bois de Nouzilly
la Commune
Bs de la Chaîne
Bs de la Couarde
St-Nicolas-des-M.
Santenay
Morand
AMBOISE CHATEAU RENAULT
les Conimaillères
Gr de Vallée
Nouzilly
Crotelles
Villedômer
Auzouer-en-T.
Dame-Marie-les-B.
Seillac
Coulanges
la Maillotière
Bs de Mortier
Pierrefitte
Vauliard
Beaujour
Rouziers de-T.
Mortier
Autrèche
Prénou
Chouzy-s.-C.
Ville Sapour
Cerelles
Monnaie
Neuillé-le-Lierre
Les Bois de Corneau
Mesland
St-Antoine-du-R.
Baudry
L'AQUITAINE A 10-E 5-E 60
Atlantique
Onzain
Rouville
Fleuray
Le Moulin-à-Vent
Les Bois Bigot
Aires de Tours
Pierre Bise
Montreuil-en-T.
Monteaux
Meunes
Gué-des-Prés
Chanceaux-s.-C.
Sêtre
la Hargandière
Reugny
Chaumont-s.-L.
Tronçay
la Côte
Valmer
St Ouen-les-V.
Cange
Limeray
Veuves
le Village-Neuf
Poillé
N.-D. d'Oé
Vallée de C.
TOURS-NORD ST-SYMPHORIEN
Chançay
Rilly-s.-L.
Mettray
la Colonie
T.G.V.
Fourchette
le Ht Chantier
Mosnes
la Halerie
Parçay-Meslay
Closeaux-les-B.
Bs de Chançay
Pocé-s.-C.
Artigny
le Gd Village
le Sentier
la Membrolle-s.-Choisille
Vallée Coquette
Noizay
Nazelles-Négron
Chargé
la Thamasserie
la Thibaudière
St-Symphorien
Rochecorbon
VOUVRAY
Vernou-s.-B.
Vallières-les-Gr
les Bordes
Négron
AMBOISE
St Règle
Souvigny-de-T.
Fondettes
ST-CYR-s.-L.
Radegonde
Clos Lucé
Vallières
la Ville-aux-D.
Husseau
Lussault-s.-Loire
la Genaudière
l'Alleu
Pontlevoy
ST-PIERRE-DES-CORPS
MONTLOUIS-S.-L.
Pagode de Chanteloup
TOURS
Belle-Roche
Nouy
FORÊT D'AMBOISE
FORÊT DE MONTRICHARD
Véretz
St Martin-le-B.
Ets de Jumeaux
ST AVERTIN
Larçay
JOUÉ-LES-T.
le Placier
Cher
CHAMBRAY-LES-T.
la Chavonnière
Azay-s.-C.
Leugny
Nitray
Dierré
la Croix-en-T.
Civray-de-T.
Chenonceaux
Chissay-en-T.
MONTRICHARD
la Carte
Ft DE LARCAY
les Barilliers
les Serrauts
Ouv. début 1999
Chêne Pendu
Bs de la Duporterie
Prieuré de St Jean du Grais
Granlay
BLÉRÉ
Chisseaux
St-Georges-s.-C.
les Vallées
Faverolles-s.-C.
St Julien-de-C.
les Robinières
Bois de St-Laurent
Athée-s.-C.
la Roche
Thoré
Francueil
Vreigne
la Chaise
le Croule
Candé
la Horaie
Village Brûlé
Moulin Rouge
Couzières
le Vau
le Bois Joubert
Aiguevive
Bs de Beau Chêne
Bois d'Aiguevive
Monts
Donjon
Veigné
MONTBAZON
Esvres
Indre
Truyes
le Coudray
Ets de Brosse
Epeigné-les-B.
de Ruan
Cormery
la Barrerie
Sublaines
Luzillé
Courçay
Cigogné
Montpoupon
Céré-la-R.
Sorigny
Rochers
le Coudray
Courbat
Razay
la Villière
St Branchs
Toizay
Reignac
la Roche
le Liège
Ville Pays
Norçay
Chédigny
la Rémerie
la Bresardière
Tauxigny
Café Brûlé
la Follaine
Hys
les Hauts Millets
Bourg-Cocu
Azay-s.-I.
Morillon
St Quentin-s.-I.
Marolles
FORÊT
le Gr Village
le Frêne
Chambourg-s.-I.
la Trillonnière
Genillé
les Bondis
Louans
St Bauld
Malicorne
Pyramide de St Quentin
Chemillé-s.-Indrois
Ste-Maure de Touraine
la Fontaine Colette
Beaumont-V.
la Bréchotière
Dolus-le-Sec
Pyr de Genillé
Pyr de Montaigu
Logny
Ste-Catherine-de-F.
le Louroux
la Davière
Chanceaux-près-L.
Cornille
MONTRÉSOR
Villeloin
le Carroi Jodel
Ets du Louroux
LOCHES
Ferrière-s.-B.
Anc ne Chartreuse
St Jean du-Liget
la Forêt
Manthelan
Beaulieu-lès-L.
Pyr des Chartreux
Coulange
STE-MAURE-DE-T.
Bossée
Beautertre
Bs du Coin de Boutin
la Thibaudière
Sennevières
les Coteaux
la Manse
la Chapelle-Blanche-St-Martin
Mouzay
Perrusson
les Hes Maisons
Loché-s.-I.
Grillemont
Vou
les Morillons
le Bray
St Jean St G.
St Germain
Bs de Beaugerais
Sepmes
Bournan
Varennes
St-Hippolyte
Ligoire
Ciran
Drache
Bagneux
Verneuil-s.-I.
St Martin
Les Bordes
LIGUEIL
Civray-s-E.
St Senoch
St Paul
Ballon
la Celle-St-A.
Marcé-s.E.
Trémont
Esves-le Moutier
Bridoré
Cussay
BOIS DE VERNEUIL
les Courtinais
St-Cyran-du-J.
Crignon
Flère-la-R.

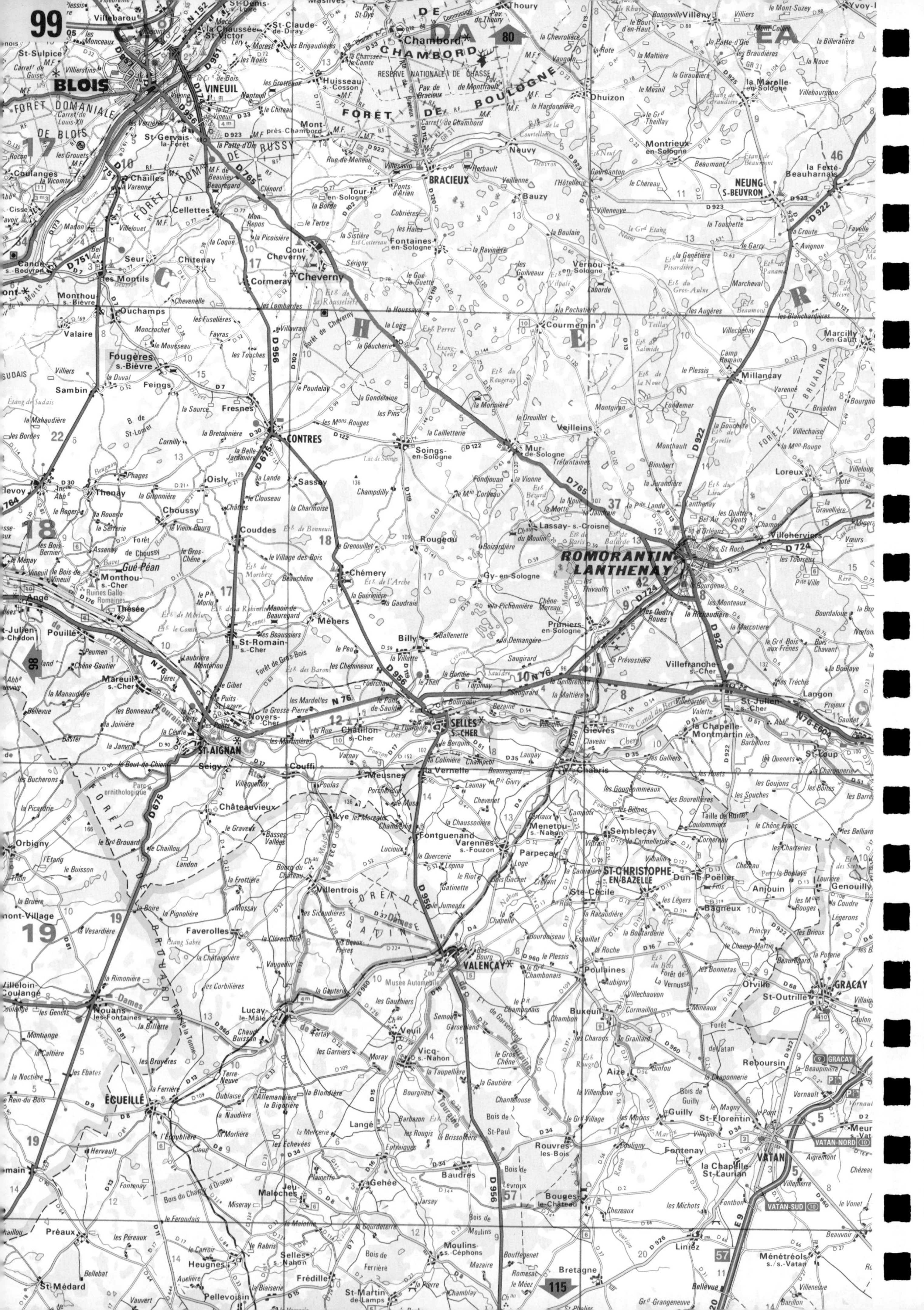
BLOIS
VINEUIL
Villebarou
St-Sulpice
St-Claude-de-Diray
Chambord
CHAMBORD
RESERVE NATIONALE DE CHASSE
FORÊT DE BOULOGNE
FORÊT DOMANIALE DE BLOIS
FORÊT DE RUSSY
Huisseau s.-Cosson
Mont-près-Chambord
St-Gervais-la-Forêt
Thoury
Dhuizon
Montrieux-en-Sologne
La Marolle-en-Sologne
Neuvy
BRACIEUX
Villesavin
Tour-en-Sologne
Bauzy
Chailles
Cellettes
Cour-Cheverny
Cheverny
Fontaines-en-Sologne
Vernou-en-Sologne
NEUNG-S-BEUVRON
la Ferté-Beauharnais
Candé s.-Beuvron
Seur
Chitenay
Cormeray
les Montils
Monthou s.-Bièvre
Ouchamps
Valaire
Fougères s.-Bièvre
Feings
Sambin
Fresnes
CONTRES
Soings-en-Sologne
Mur-de-Sologne
Veilleins
Courmemin
Millancay
Marcilly en-Gault
Thenay
Oisly
Sassay
Choussy
Couddes
Rougeou
Lassay-s.-Croisne
ROMORANTIN-LANTHENAY
Gué-Péan
Monthou-s.-Cher
Thésée
Chémery
Méhers
Gy-en-Sologne
Pruniers-en-Sologne
Pouillé
St-Romain-s.-Cher
Billy
Villefranche-s.-Cher
Mareuil-s.-Cher
Noyers-s.-Cher
ST-AIGNAN
Seigy
Châtillon-s.-Cher
SELLES-S.-CHER
Gièvres
St-Julien-s.-Cher
Langon
la Chapelle-Montmartin
Chabris
Couffi
Meusnes
Châteauvieux
Orbigny
Fontguenand
Varennes-s.-Fouzon
Menetou-s.-Nahon
Parpeçay
Semblecay
ST-CHRISTOPHE-EN-BAZELLE
Dun-le-Poëlier
Ste-Cécile
Villentrois
Faverolles
VALENÇAY
Poulaines
Bagneux
Anjouin
Genouilly
GRACAY
St-Outrille
Orville
Nouans-les-Fontaines
Lucay-le-Mâle
Veuil
Vicq-s.-Nahon
Buxeuil
Aize
Reboursin
ÉCUEILLÉ
Langé
Rouvres-les-Bois
Guilly
St-Florentin
Fontenay
VATAN
la Chapelle-St-Laurian
Baudres
Gehée
Jeu-Maloches
Bouges-le-Château
Préaux
Heugnes
Selles-s.-Nahon
Moulins-s.-Céphons
Linéz
Ménétréols-s./s.-Vatan
St-Médard
Frédille
Pellevoisin
St-Martin-de-Lamps
Bretagne
Bellevue
80
98
115
D 956
D 765
D 922
D 724
N 76
D 960
VATAN-NORD
VATAN-SUD

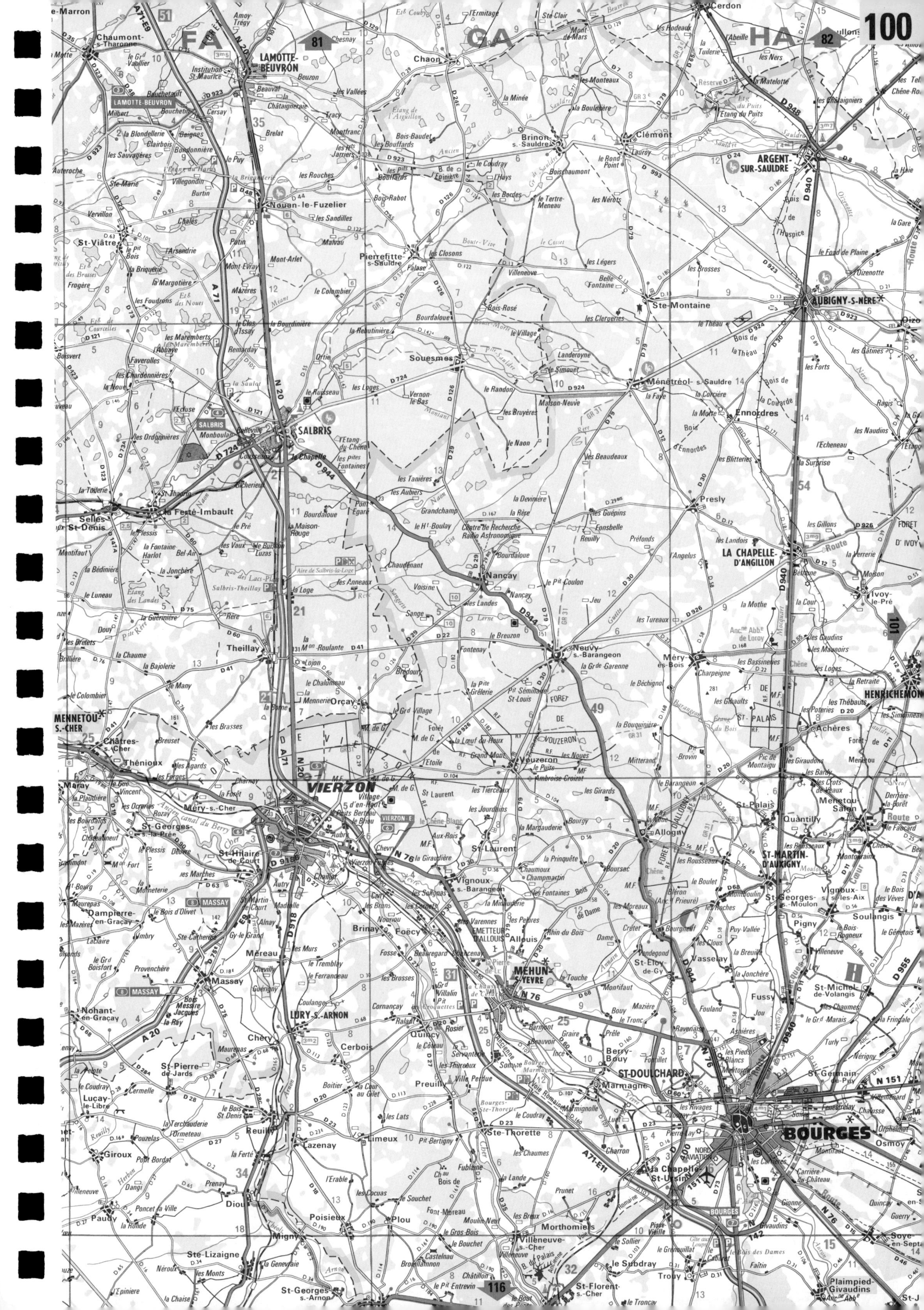

81
82
101
116
LAMOTTE-BEUVRON
Chaumont-s-Tharonne
Chaon
Cerdon
Argent-sur-Sauldre
Brinon-s.-Sauldre
Clémont
Nouan-le-Fuzelier
Pierrefitte-s-Sauldre
St-Viâtre
Aubigny-s-Nère
Ste-Montaine
Souesmes
Ménétréol-s-Sauldre
Ennordres
Salbris
Selles-St-Denis
la Ferté-Imbault
Presly
La Chapelle-d'Angillon
Nançay
Theillay
Neuvy-s.-Barangeon
Méry-ès-Bois
Henrichemont
Mennetou-s.-Cher
Châtres-s.-Cher
Orçay
Vouzeron
Vierzon
Méry-s.-Cher
St-Georges-s.-la-Prée
St-Hilaire-de-Court
Allogny
St-Martin-d'Auxigny
Vignoux-s.-Barangeon
St-Laurent
Foëcy
Mehun-s-Yèvre
Massay
Méreau
Lury-s.-Arnon
Quincy
Nohant-en-Graçay
Cerbois
Preuilly
St-Doulchard
Berry-Bouy
Marmagne
Bourges
Lucay-le-Libre
Reuilly
Limeux
Ste-Thorette
Lazenay
Poisieux
Morthomiers
Villeneuve-s.-Cher
St-Florent-s.-Cher
Plaimpied-Givaudins
Ste-Lizaigne
St-Georges-s.-Arnon
A 71
A 20
N 20
N 76
N 151
D 940

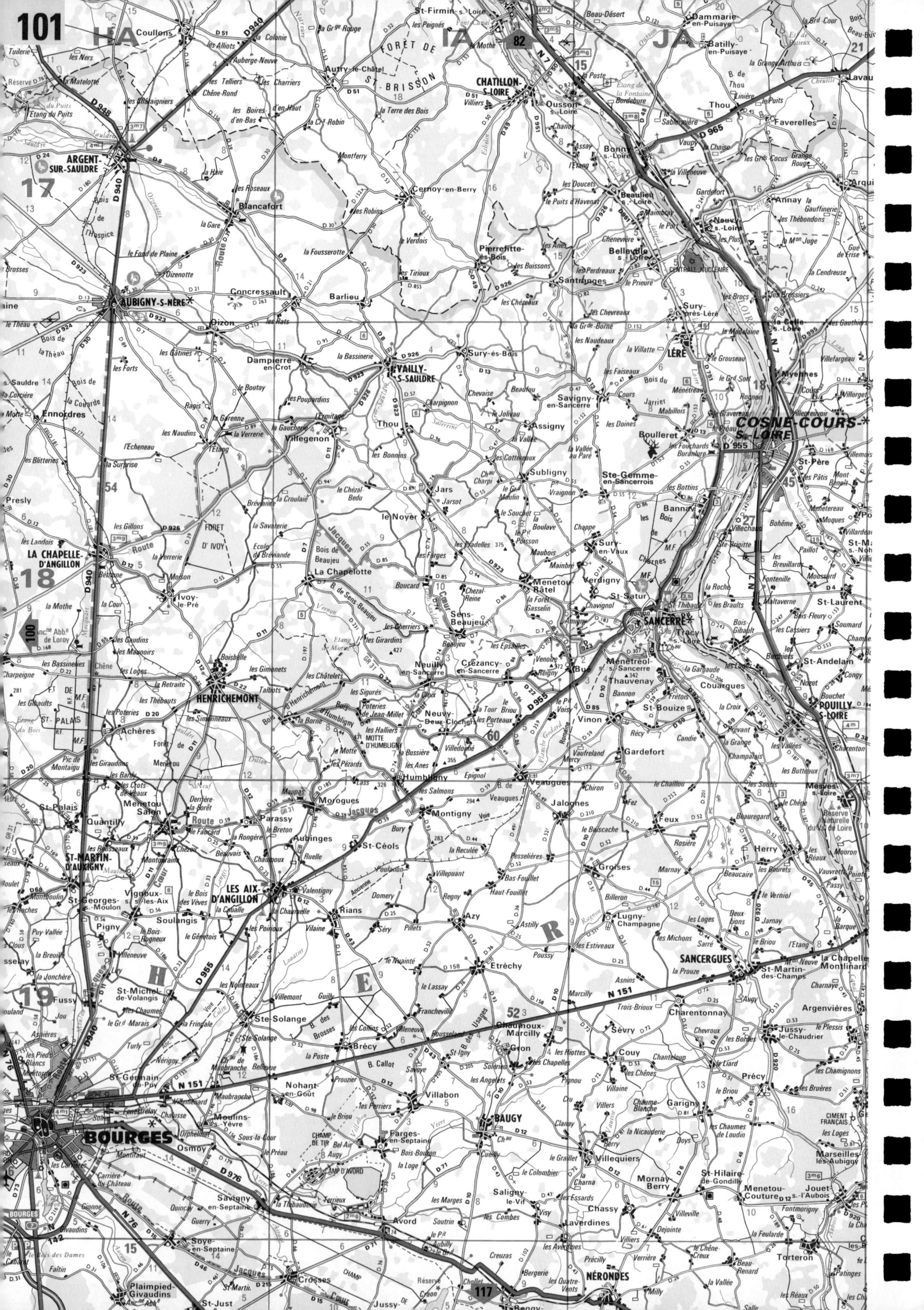
101
Coullons
Argent-sur-Sauldre
Aubigny-s-Nère
Blancafort
Concressault
Barlieu
Oizon
Dampierre-en-Crot
Vailly-s-Sauldre
Autry-le-Châtel
Forêt de St-Brisson
St-Firmin-s-Loire
Châtillon-s-Loire
Ousson-s-Loire
Bonny-s-Loire
Beaulieu-s-Loire
Belleville-s-Loire
Centrale nucléaire
Dammarie-en-Puisaye
Batilly-en-Puisaye
Thou
Faverelles
Annay
Neuvy-s-Loire
Cernoy-en-Berry
Pierrefitte-ès-Bois
Santranges
Sury-près-Léré
Léré
Sury-ès-Bois
Savigny-en-Sancerre
Cosne-Cours-s-Loire
St-Père
Myennes
La Celle-s-Loire
Ennordres
La Chapelle-d'Angillon
Ivoy-le-Pré
Forêt d'Ivoy
La Chapelotte
Jars
Le Noyer
Assigny
Subligny
Ste-Gemme-en-Sancerrois
Bannay
Sury-en-Vaux
Menetou-Râtel
Verdigny
St-Satur
Sancerre
Tracy-s-Loire
Pouilly-s-Loire
St-Andelain
St-Laurent
Sens-Beaujeu
Crezancy-en-Sancerre
Neuilly-en-Sancerre
Henrichemont
Achères
Neuvy-Deux-Clochers
Humbligny
Motte d'Humbligny
Bué
Ménétréol-s-Sancerre
Thauvenay
St-Bouize
Vinon
Gardefort
Veaugues
Jalognes
Feux
Herry
Mesves-s-Loire
Réserve naturelle du Val de Loire
Menetou-Salon
Quantilly
Parassy
Morogues
Aubinges
Montigny
St-Céols
Groises
St-Martin-d'Auxigny
St-Georges-s-Moulon
Vignoux-s-les-Aix
Les Aix-d'Angillon
Rians
Azy
Étréchy
Lugny-Champagne
Sancergues
St-Martin-des-Champs
La Chapelle-Montlinard
Soulangis
Pigny
St-Michel-de-Volangis
Fussy
Ste-Solange
Brécy
Chaumoux-Marcilly
Gron
Couy
Charentonnay
Jussy-le-Chaudrier
Argenvières
Précy
Garigny
St-Germain-du-Puy
Bourges
Moulins-s-Yèvre
Osmoy
Nohant-en-Goût
Villabon
Baugy
Farges-en-Septaine
Camp d'Avord
Villequiers
Mornay-Berry
St-Hilaire-de-Gondilly
Menetou-Couture
Jouet-s-l'Aubois
Marseilles-lès-Aubigny
Savigny-en-Septaine
Avord
Saligny-le-Vif
Chassy
Laverdines
Soye-en-Septaine
Crosses
Nérondes
Torteron
Plaimpied-Givaudins
St-Just
Jussy-Champagne
D 940
D 955
N 151
N 7
N 76
D 976
A 77
82
100
117
HA
IA
JA
H
E
R
17
18
19
21

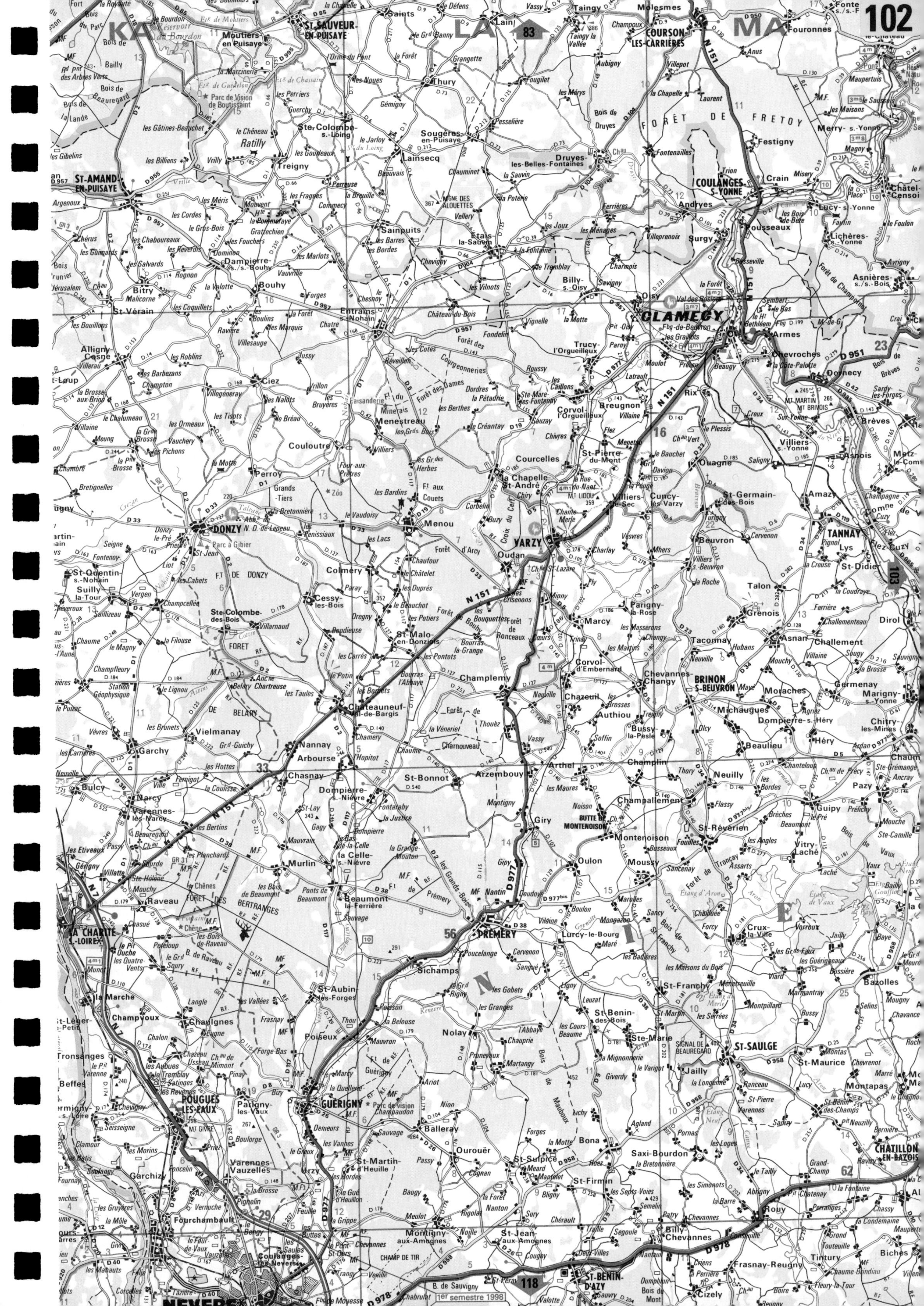
St-Sauveur-en-Puisaye
Moutiers-en-Puisaye
Saints
Thury
Taingy
Molesmes
Courson-les-Carrières
Fouronnes
Ste-Colombe-s.-Loing
Sougères-en-Puisaye
Lainsecq
Treigny
Ratilly
Druyes-les-Belles-Fontaines
Forêt de Fretoy
Festigny
St-Amand-en-Puisaye
Coulanges-s.-Yonne
Crain
Châtel-Censoir
Andryes
Lucy-s.-Yonne
Sainpuits
Etais-la-Sauvin
Surgy
Pousseaux
Lichères-s.-Yonne
Dampierre-s/s.-Bouhy
Bitry
Bouhy
Billy-s.-Oisy
Asnières-s./s.-Bois
St-Vérain
Entrains-s.-Nohain
Clamecy
Armes
Alligny-Cosne
Trucy-l'Orgueilleux
Chevroches
Dornecy
Ciez
Breugnon
Rix
Corvol-l'Orgueilleux
Brèves
Menestreau
Villiers-s.-Yonne
Couloutre
Courcelles
St-Pierre-du-Mont
Ouagne
Asnois
Perroy
La Chapelle-St-André
Cuncy-lès-Varzy
St-Germain-des-Bois
Amazy
Menou
Villiers-le-Sec
Donzy
Varzy
Beuvron
Tannay
Oudan
Colmery
Talon
St-Didier
St-Quentin-s.-Nohain
Suilly-la-Tour
Cessy-les-Bois
Ste-Colombe-des-Bois
Grenois
Marcy
Parigny-la-Rose
Dirol
Asnan
Challement
St-Malo-en-Donziois
Tacconnay
Corvol-d'Embernard
Champlemy
Chevannes-Changy
Brinon-s.-Beuvron
Germenay
Marigny-s.-Yonne
Chazeuil
Authiou
Moraches
Michaugues
Dompierre-s.-Héry
Châteauneuf-Val-de-Bargis
Vielmanay
Garchy
Nannay
Arbourse
Beaulieu
Héry
Chasnay
St-Bonnot
Arzembouy
Arthel
Champlin
Neuilly
Bulcy
Narcy
Dompierre-s.-Nièvre
Pazy
Varennes-lès-Narcy
Giry
Champallement
Guipy
Butte de Montenoison
Montenoison
St-Révérien
Murlin
La Celle-s.-Nièvre
Oulon
Moussy
Vitry-Laché
La Charité-s.-Loire
Raveau
Beaumont-la-Ferrière
Prémery
Lurcy-le-Bourg
Crux-la-Ville
Forêt des Bertranges
Sichamps
Bazolles
St-Aubin-les-Forges
St-Franchy
Champvoux
Chaulgnes
St-Benin-des-Bois
Poiseux
Nolay
Ste-Marie
St-Saulge
St-Maurice
Montapas
Pougues-les-Eaux
Parigny-les-Vaux
Guérigny
Balleray
Jailly
St-Benin-des-Champs
Garchizy
Varennes-Vauzelles
St-Martin-d'Heuille
Urzy
Ourouër
St-Sulpice
Bona
Saxi-Bourdon
Châtillon-en-Bazois
Fourchambault
Montigny-aux-Amognes
St-Jean-aux-Amognes
St-Firmin
Billy-Chevannes
Rouy
Coulanges-lès-Nevers
St-Benin-d'Azy
Frasnay-Reugny
Tintury
Cizely
Nevers
1er semestre 1998

84
Massangis
L'ISLE-S-SEREIN
Coutarnoux
Dissangis
Joux-la-Ville
Précy-le-Sec
Mailly-le-Château
Mailly-la-Ville
Arcy-s-Cure
Séry
Bessy-s-Cure
St-Moré
Voutenay-s-Cure
Lucy-le-Bois
Thory
Angely
Ste-Colombe
Blacy
Thizy
Talcy
Santigny
Marmeaux
Vassy
Pisy
Montréal
Trévilly
Athie
Provency
Sermizelles
Girolles
Annay-la-Côte
Blannay
Givry
Tharot
Annéot
Etaule
Sauvigny-le-Bois
Sceaux
Guillon
Cisery
Toutry
Epoisses
AVALLON
Pontaubert
Island
Domecy-s-le-Vault
Asquins
Vault-de-Lugny
Magny
St-André-en-Terre-Plaine
Savigny-en-Terre-Plaine
Sauvigny-le-Beuréal
Vieux-Château
Montberthault
Cussy-les-Forges
Ste-Magnance
VEZELAY
St-Père
Tharoiseau
Menades
Charmoux
Dornecy
Asnières-s.-s-Bois
Châtel-Censoir
Lichères-s-Yonne
Merry-s-Yonne
Lucy-s-Yonne
Brosses
Montillot
Bois-d'Arcy
Foissy-lès-Vézelay
Pierre-Perthuis
Fontenay-près-Vézelay
Brèves
La Maison-Dieu
Domecy-s-Cure
St-Germain-des-Champs
Marigny-l'Eglise
QUARRE-LES-TOMBES
St-Léger-Vauban
Rouvray
St-Andeux
Bussières
Sincey-lès-Rouvray
Villeneuve
Beauvilliers
Chastellux-s-Cure
St-Aubin-des-Chaumes
Asnois
Metz-le-Comte
Nuars
Bazoches
Amazy
TANNAY
Teigny
Neuffontaines
Empury
Flez-Cuzy
St-Didier
Saizy
Monceaux-le-Comte
Moissy-Moulinot
Anthien
Pouques-Lormes
St-Martin-du-Puy
Chalaux
Dirol
Challement
Ruages
Magny-Lormes
LORMES
Brassy
Dun-les-Places
St-Brisson
St-Agnan
PARC NATUREL REGIONAL DU MORVAN
Champeau-en-Morvan
Germenay
Marigny-s-Yonne
Chitry-les-Mines
CORBIGNY
Cervon
Chaumot
Vauclaix
Gâcogne
Héry
Pazy
Guipy
Mhère
Gouloux
MONTSAUCHE LES SETTONS
Alligny-en-Morvan
Mouron-s-Yonne
Epiry
Sardy-lès-Epiry
Montreuillon
Ouroux-en-Morvan
Moux-en-Morvan
La Collancelle
Bazolles
Montigny-en-Morvan
Blismes
Chaumard
Planchez
Gien-s-Cure
Ménessaire
Achun
Aunay-en-Bazois
Corancy
Châtin
Lavault-de-Frétoy
Cussy-en-Morvan
St-Maurice
Mont-et-Marré
Montapas
Dun-s-Grandry
Chougny
Ougny
St-Péreuse
Dommartin
St-Hilaire-en-Morvan
CHATEAU-CHINON
Anost
CHATILLON-EN-BAZOIS
Tamnay-en-Bazois
Maux
Chateau-Chinon-Campagne
Arleuf
Roussillon-en-Morvan
La Petite-Verrière
Alluy
Sermages
St-Léger-de-Fougeret
Biches
Brinay
MOULINS-ENGILBERT
La Celle-en-Morvan
Fâchin
119
102
A6
E15-E60
N6
D944
D951
D985
D978

BAIGNEUX-LES-JUIFS
VENAREY-LES-LAUMES
Alise-Ste-Reine
Flavigny-s-Ozerain
SEMUR-EN-AUXOIS
Chau de Bussy-Rabutin
ST-SEINE-L'ABBAYE
PRECY S/S-THIL
VITTEAUX
SOMBERNON
SAULIEU
POUILLY-EN-AUXOIS
Châteauneuf
LIERNAIS
ARNAY-LE-DUC
BLIGNY-S-OUCHE
LUCENAY-L'ÉVÊQUE
EPINAC
BEAUNE
Sully
AUTOROUTE DU SOLEIL
BIERRE LES SEMUR
PONT DE PANY
AUBIGNY LES S.
CREANCEY
CIVRY EN M
POUILLY EN A
SOMBERNON PARIS PAR RN6
Aire du Chien Blanc
Aire des Lochères
85
105
120

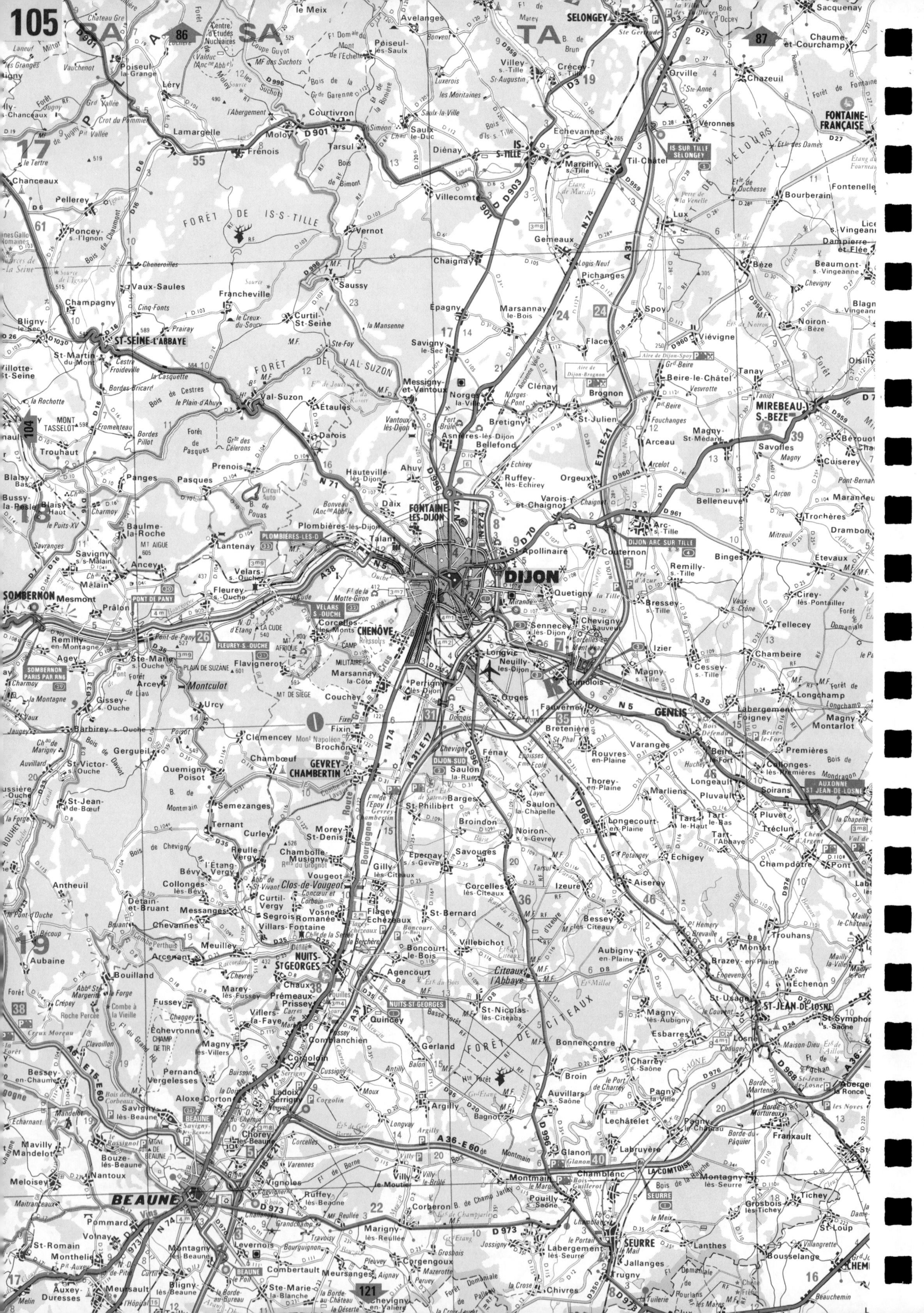
86
87
104
121
SELONGEY
IS-S-TILLE
FONTAINE-FRANÇAISE
MIREBEAU-S.-BEZE
FORÊT DE IS-S-TILLE
FORÊT DE VAL-SUZON
ST-SEINE-L'ABBAYE
SOMBERNON
DIJON
FONTAINE-LES-DIJON
CHENÔVE
GEVREY-CHAMBERTIN
GENLIS
NUITS-ST-GEORGES
Cîteaux l'Abbaye
FORÊT DE CÎTEAUX
ST-JEAN-DE-LOSNE
BEAUNE
SEURRE
Auxonne
Quetigny
Longvic
Talant
Marsannay-la-Côte
Couchey
Fixin
Brochon
Morey-St-Denis
Chambolle-Musigny
Vougeot
Clos-de-Vougeot
Vosne-Romanée
Aloxe-Corton
Savigny-lès-Beaune
Pommard
Volnay
Meursault
Arc-s.-Tille
Is-s-Tille
Til-Châtel
Lux
Bèze
Mirande
Plombières-lès-Dijon
Val-Suzon
Messigny-et-Vantoux
Chevigny-St-Sauveur
Izeure
Aiserey
Brazey-en-Plaine
Auvillars s.-Saône
Pagny-la-Ville
Lechâtelet
Labruyère
Chamblanc
Pouilly-s.-Saône
Corberon
Corgengoux
Combertault
Bligny-lès-Beaune
Chorey-lès-Beaune
Ladoix-Serrigny
Corgoloin
Comblanchien
Premeaux-Prissey
Villers-la-Faye
Magny-lès-Villers
Pernand-Vergelesses
Bouze-lès-Beaune
Nantoux
Meloisey
Mavilly-Mandelot
Bessey-en-Chaume
Saulon-la-Rue
Barges
Broindon
Noiron-s/s-Gevrey
Savouges
Epernay-s.-Gevrey
Gilly-lès-Cîteaux
Flagey-Echézeaux
Boncourt-le-Bois
Agencourt
Quincey
Gerland
Villebichot
St-Bernard
Corcelles-lès-Cîteaux
St-Nicolas-lès-Cîteaux
Bonnencontre
Broin
Charrey-s.-Saône
Esbarres
Magny-lès-Aubigny
Aubigny-en-Plaine
Bessey-lès-Cîteaux
Echigey
Longecourt-en-Plaine
Thorey-en-Plaine
Rouvres-en-Plaine
Varanges
Bretenière
Fauverney
Crimolois
Neuilly-lès-Dijon
Ouges
Fénay
Perrigny-lès-Dijon
Chambeire
Izier
Magny-s.-Tille
Cessey-s.-Tille
Bressey-s.-Tille
Remilly-s.-Tille
Couternon
St-Apollinaire
Varois-et-Chaignot
Orgeux
Ruffey-lès-Echirey
Bellefond
Asnières-lès-Dijon
Norges-la-Ville
Bretigny
Clénay
St-Julien
Brognon
Flacey
Spoy
Vievigne
Beire-le-Châtel
Arceau
Magny-St-Médard
Belleneuve
Binges
Trochères
Drambon
Etevaux
Cirey-lès-Pontailler
Tellecey
Longchamp
Labergement-Foigney
Magny-Montarlot
Premières
Collonges-lès-Premières
Soirans
Pluvet
Tréclun
Champdôtre
Montot
Trouhans
Echenon
St-Symphorien-s.-Saône
Losne
Tichey
Grosbois-lès-Tichey
Bousselange
St-Loup
Lanthes
Jallanges
Trugny
Labergement-lès-Seurre
Chivres
Montagny-lès-Seurre
Franxault
La Comtoise
Glanon
Montmain
Villy-le-Moutier
Argilly
Bagnot
Marigny-lès-Reulée
Meursanges
Ste-Marie-la-Blanche
Chevigny-en-Valière
Levernois
Montagny-lès-Beaune
Ruffey-lès-Beaune
Vignoles
Auxey-Duresses
Monthelie
St-Romain
Baubigny
Bouilland
Fussey
Marey-lès-Fussey
Echevronne
Arcenant
Meuilley
Chevannes
Messanges
Détain-et-Bruant
Collonges-lès-Bévy
Bévy
Reulle-Vergy
Curtil-Vergy
Segrois
Villars-Fontaine
Curley
Ternant
Semezanges
Quemigny-Poisot
Chamboeuf
Clémencey
Gerqueil
St-Victor-s.-Ouche
St-Jean-de-Boeuf
Antheuil
Aubaine
Barbirey-s.-Ouche
Gissey-s.-Ouche
Urcy
Arcey
Ste-Marie-s.-Ouche
Flavignerot
Corcelles-les-Monts
Velars-s.-Ouche
Fleurey-s.-Ouche
Pont-de-Pany
Agey
Remilly-en-Montagne
Mesmont
Prâlon
Mâlain
Savigny-s.-Mâlain
Ancey
Lantenay
Baulme-la-Roche
Blaisy-Haut
Blaisy-Bas
Bussy-la-Pesle
Panges
Pasques
Prenois
Darois
Etaules
Hauteville-lès-Dijon
Ahuy
Daix
Trouhaut
Val-Suzon
Saussy
Curtil-St-Seine
Francheville
Vaux-Saules
Champagny
Bligny-le-Sec
St-Martin-du-Mont
Poncey-s.-l'Ignon
Pellerey
Chanceaux
Lamargelle
Frénois
Moloy
Léry
Poiseul-la-Grange
Courtivron
Tarsul
Saulx-le-Duc
Diénay
Villecomte
Vernot
Chaignay
Epagny
Savigny-le-Sec
Marsannay-le-Bois
Gemeaux
Pichanges
Marcilly-s.-Tille
Echevannes
Crécey-s.-Tille
Villey-s.-Tille
Poiseul-lès-Saulx
Avelanges
le Meix
Orville
Chazeuil
Véronnes
Chaume-et-Courchamp
Sacquenay
Fontenelle
Bourberain
Dampierre-et-Flée
Beaumont-s.-Vingeanne
Blagny-s.-Vingeanne
Noiron-s.-Bèze
Tanay
Savolles
Cuiserey
Marandeuil
Oisilly
Bérouot

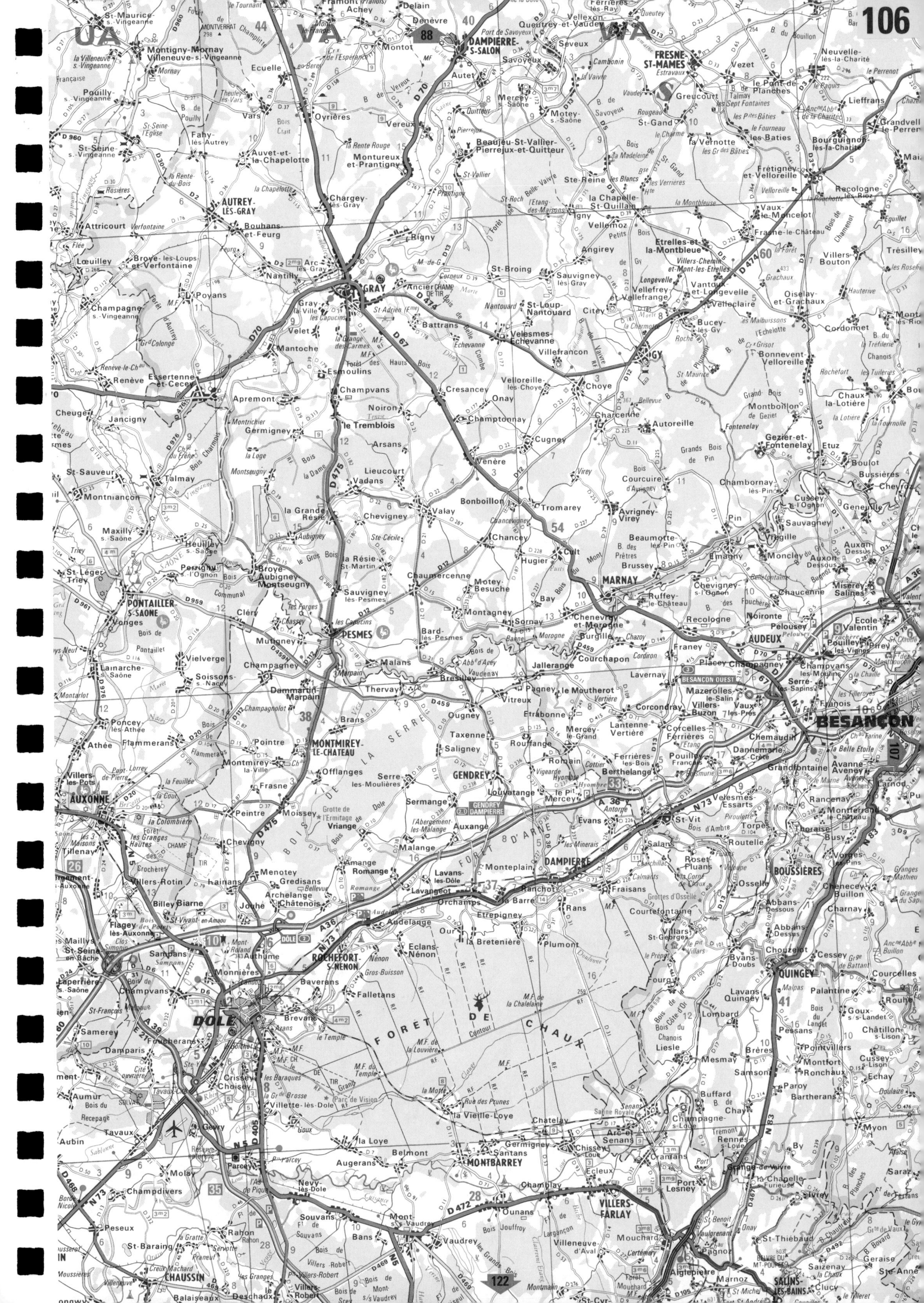
UA
VA
WA
DAMPIERRE-S-SALON
FRESNE ST-MAMES
Montigny-Mornay Villeneuve-s.-Vingeanne
St-Seine-s.-Vingeanne
Beaujeu-St-Vallier-Pierrejux-et-Quitteur
Chargey-lès-Gray
AUTREY-LES-GRAY
GRAY
Arc-lès-Gray
Velesmes-Echevanne
GY
Essertenne-et-Cecey
Champagne-s.-Vingeanne
Mantoche
Apremont
Esmoulins
Champvans
Noiron
le Tremblois
Cresancey
Onay
Champtonnay
Cugney
Choye
Charcenne
Autoreille
Talmay
St-Sauveur
Montmançon
Maxilly-s.-Saône
Heuilley-s.-Saône
Perrigny-s.-l'Ognon
PONTAILLER-S-SAONE
Vonges
Chevigney
Valay
Bonboillon
Tromarey
Chancey
Marnay
Sauvigney-lès-Pesmes
PESMES
Montagney
Sornay
Mutigney
Champagney
Malans
Bresilley
Vitreux
Pagney
Jallerange
Courchapon
Lavernay
AUDEUX
Pouilley-les-Vignes
BESANÇON
Champvans-les-Moulins
Serre-les-Sapins
Franois
BESANCON OUEST
Mazerolles-le-Salin
Corcondray
Montmirey-la-Ville
MONTMIREY-LE-CHATEAU
Offlanges
Serre-les-Moulières
GENDREY
Louvatange
Sermange
Auxange
GENDREY DAMPIERRE
Moissey
Peintre
Frasne
Flammerans
AUXONNE
Athée
Poncey-lès-Athée
Villers-les-Pots
Tillenay
Chevigny
Menotey
Romange
Gredisans
Archelange
Châtenois
Jouhe
Biarne
Billey
Villers-Rotin
Flagey-lès-Auxonne
Lavans-lès-Dole
Orchamps
la Barre
Ranchot
Rans
DAMPIERRE
Monteplain
Evans
St-Vit
Salans
Roset-Fluans
Osselle
BOUSSIÈRES
Torpes
Routelle
Thoraise
Busy
Grandfontaine
Avanne-Aveney
Rancenay
Montferrand-le-Château
Chemaudin
Dannemarie-s-Crète
Pouilley-Français
Velesmes-Essarts
Villars-St-Georges
Byans-s-Doubs
Fourg
QUINGEY
Lombard
Lavans-Quingey
Pessans
Brères
Liesle
Mesmay
Samson
Buffard
Champagne-s-Loue
Chissey-s-Loue
Arc-et-Senans
Cramans
Port-Lesney
Mouchard
VILLERS-FARLAY
Aiglepierre
SALINS-LES-BAINS
Marnoz
Chatelay
Germigney
MONTBARREY
Santans
Belmont
Augerans
la Loye
Champlay
Ounans
Vaudrey
Mont-s-Vaudrey
Souvans
Bans
Nevy-lès-Dole
Rahon
Chaussin
Champdivers
Peseux
St-Baraing
Molay
Parcey
Gevry
Tavaux
Aumur
Damparis
Samerey
Choisey
Crissey
Villette-lès-Dole
Falletans
Brevans
DOLE
Baverans
Monnières
Sampans
Authume
ROCHEFORT-S-NENON
Eclans-Nénon
Our
la Bretenière
Plumont
FORET DE CHAUX
FORÊT D'ARNE
BOIS DE LA SERRE
A 36
A 39
N 73
N 5
D 475
D 67
D 70
D 459
Rochefort
Emagny
Moncley
Chaucenne
Miserey-Salines
Ecole-Valentin
Pelousey
Recologne
Noironte
Franey
Placey
Champagney
Ruffey-le-Château
Chevigney-s-l'Ognon
Beaumotte-lès-Pin
Brussey
Avrigney-Virey
Sauvagney
Pin
Etuz
Boulot
Gezier-et-Fontenelay
Montboillon
Chaux-la-Lotière
Bonnevent-Velloreille
Bucey-lès-Gy
Oiselay-et-Grachaux
Cordonnet
Villers-Bouton
Fretigney-et-Velloreille
Recologne-lès-Rioz
Bourguignon-lès-la-Charité
Etrelles-et-la-Montbleue
Vellefrey-et-Vellefrange
Vantoux-et-Longevelle
Angirey
Vellemoz
la Chapelle-St-Quillain
Sauvigney-lès-Gray
St-Loup-Nantouard
Citey
Velloreille-lès-Choye
St-Broing
Battrans
Montureux-et-Prantigny
Oyrières
Vereux
Ecuelle
Autet
Savoyeux
Seveux
Mercey-s.-Saône
Motey-s.-Saône
Greucourt
Vezet
Neuvelle-lès-la-Charité
Lieffrans
Talmay
Broye-les-Loups-et-Verfontaine
Nantilly
Poyans
Attricourt
Bouhans-et-Feurg
Auvet-et-la-Chapelotte
Fahy-lès-Autrey
Pouilly-s.-Vingeanne
Renève
Cheuge
Jancigny
Broye-Aubigney-Montseugny
Clery
Vielverge
Soissons-s.-Nacey
Lamarche-s.-Saône
Dammartin-Marpain
Thervay
Brans
Ougney
Taxenne
Saligney
Rouffange
Mercey-le-Grand
Romain
Ferrières-les-Bois
Berthelange
Corcelles-Ferrières
Lantenne-Vertière
Villers-Buzon
Etrabonne
le Moutherot
Burgille
Chenevrey-et-Morogne
Bay
Moutherot
Hugier
Cult
Sampans
Champvans
St-Seine-en-Bâche
Saint-Aubin
Abbans-Dessous
Abbans-Dessus
Chouzelot
Cessey
Palantine
Courcelles
Montfort
Ronchaux
Paroy
Bartherans
Echay
Myon
Ivrey
la Chapelle-Furieuse
St-Thiébaud
Pagnoz
Mont-s-Vaudrey
122
88
107

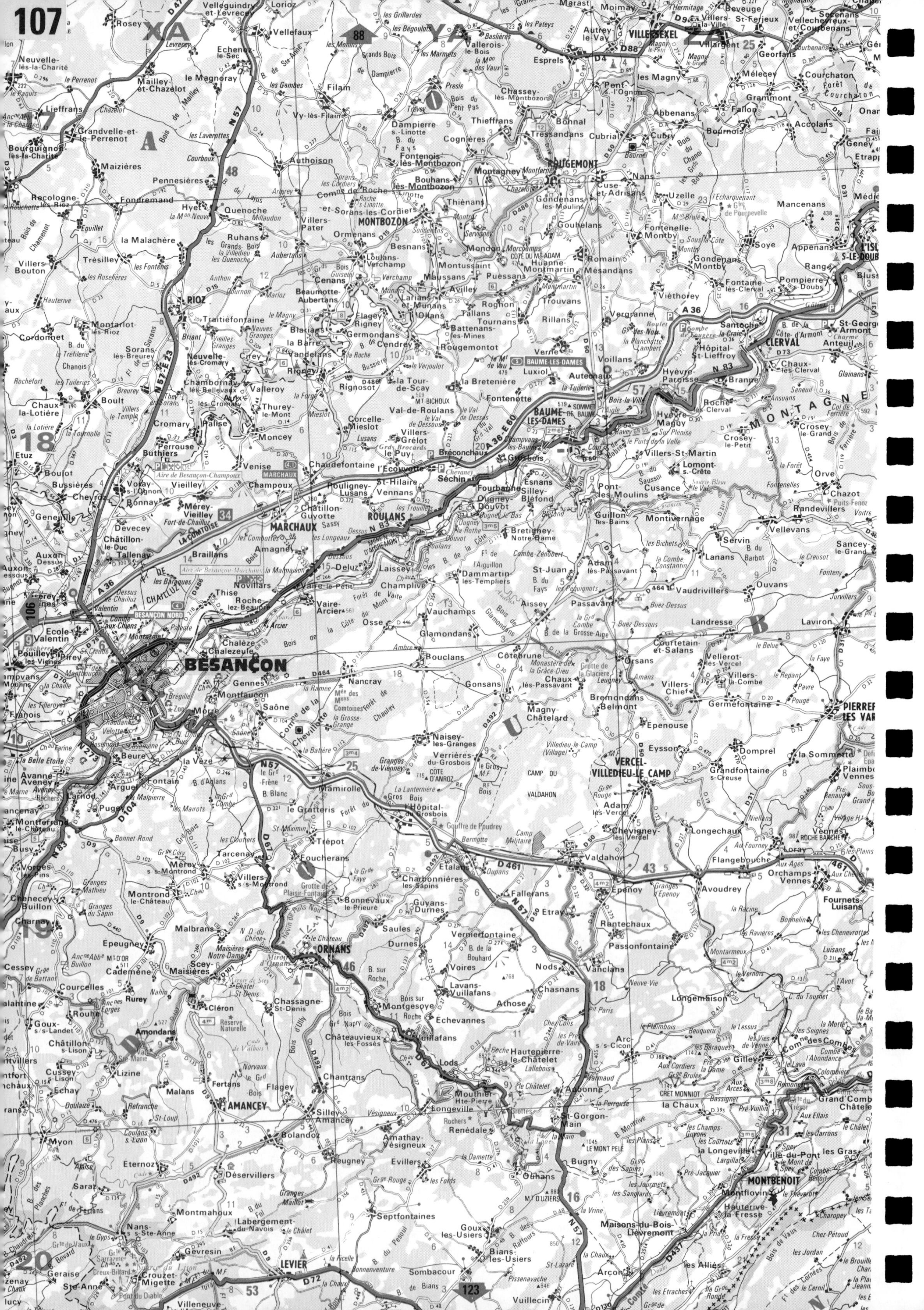
XA
YA
ZA
88
106
123
BESANÇON
VILLERSEXEL
ROUGEMONT
MONTBOZON
RIOZ
MARCHAUX
ROULANS
BAUME-LES-DAMES
CLERVAL
VERCEL-VILLEDIEU-LE CAMP
ORNANS
AMANCEY
LEVIER
MONTBENOIT
PIERREFONTAINE-LES-VARANS
Vellefaux
Filain
Vy-lès-Filain
Authoison
Rosey
Neuvelle-lès-la-Charité
Mailley-et-Chazelot
le Magnoray
Grandvelle-et-le-Perrenot
Maizières
Pennesières
Fondremand
Quenoche
Ruhans
la Malachère
Villers-Bouton
Tresilley
Cenans
Flagey-Rigney
Germondans
Rigney
Rignosot
Valleroy
Thurey-le-Mont
Moncey
Cromary
Buthiers
Venise
Vieilley
Champoux
Chaudefontaine
Bonnay
Devecey
Châtillon-le-Duc
Tallenay
Braillans
Amagney
Novillars
Thise
Roche-lez-Beaupré
Deluz
Laissey
Champlive
Vaire-Arcier
Osse
Vauchamps
Glamondans
Bouclans
Gonsans
Nancray
Gennes
Montfaucon
Saône
Morre
Beure
Arguel
Pugey
Fontain
la Vèze
Mamirolle
le Gratteris
Trépot
Foucherans
Tarcenay
Villers-s-Montrond
Mérey-s-Montrond
Montrond-le-Château
Malbrans
Epeugney
Scey-Maisières
Cademène
Rurey
Cléron
Chassagne-St-Denis
Montgesoye
Vuillafans
Lods
Mouthier-Hte-Pierre
Chantrans
Flagey
Silley-Amancey
Bolandoz
Amathay-Vésigneux
Déservilliers
Eternoz
Myon
Nans-s-Ste-Anne
Septfontaines
Goux-les-Usiers
Bians-les-Usiers
Sombacour
Ouhans
Renédale
Bugny
St-Gorgon-Main
Aubonne
Hautepierre-le-Châtelet
Athose
Chasnans
Nods
Vanclans
Etalans
Fallerans
Etray
Epenoy
Valdahon
Chevigney-lès-Vercel
Adam-lès-Vercel
Grandfontaine-s-Creuse
Epenoucr
Eysson
Dompre l
Orsans
Vellerot-lès-Vercel
Villers-Chief
Passavant
Landresse
Laviron
Vellevans
Servin
Lanans
Ouvans
Vaudrivillers
Guillon-les-Bains
Pont-les-Moulins
Cusance
Villers-St-Martin
Lomont-s-Crête
Chazot
Randevillers
Hyèvre-Paroisse
Hyèvre-Magny
Branne
Autechaux
Voillans
Luxiol
Fontenotte
Rillans
Trouvans
Romain
Mésandans
Huanne-Montmartin
Gouhelans
Gondenans-les-Moulins
Cuse-et-Adrisans
Nans
Uzelle
Fontenelle-Montby
Soye
Gondenans-Montby
Fontaine-lès-Clerval
Pompierre-s-Doubs
Santoche
Hôpital-St-Lieffroy
Chaux-lès-Clerval
Anteuil
Crosey-le-Grand
Crosey-le-Petit
Orve
Sancey-le-Grand
Mancenans
Appenans
Rang
Accolans
Bournois
Fallon
Abbenans
Cubry
Bonnal
Cubrial
Tressandans
Thieffrans
Montagney
Cognières
Fontenois-lès-Montbozon
Dampierre-s-Linotte
Chassey-lès-Montbozon
Esprels
Autrey-le-Vay
Villargent
Georfans
Mélecey
Courchaton
Grammont
Thiénans
Loulans-Verchamp
Besnans
Ormenans
Maussans
Avilley
Rognon
Tallans
Tournans
Battenans-les-Mines
Rougemontot
la Bretenière
Val-de-Roulans
Corcelle-Mieslot
Villers-Grélot
le Puy
Séchin
Vennans
Pouligney-Lusans
Châtillon-Guyotte
Fourbanne
Ougney-Douvot
Esnans
Silley-Bléfond
Bretigney-Notre-Dame
Dammartin-les-Templiers
St-Juan
Adam-lès-Passavant
Aissey
Côtebrune
Chaux-lès-Passavant
Bremondans
Magny-Châtelard
Naisey-les-Granges
Verrières-du-Grosbois
l'Hôpital-du-Grosbois
Charbonnières-les-Sapins
Bonnevaux-le-Prieuré
Guyans-Durnes
Saules
Durnes
Vernierfontaine
Voires
Lavans-Vuillafans
Echevannes
Châteauvieux-les-Fossés
Longeville
Evillers
Arc-s/s-Cicon
Gilley
la Chaux
la Longeville
Ville-du-Pont
Montflovin
Hauterive-la-Fresse
Maisons-du-Bois-Lièvremont
Arçon
Vuillecin
Longemaison
Passonfontaine
Rantechaux
Avoudrey
Flangebouche
Loray
Orchamps-Vennes
Fournets-Luisans
Longechaux
Germéfontaine
Courtetain-et-Salans
Villers-la-Combe
la Sommette
Vennes
Grand'Combe-Châteleu
Les Gras
Gevresin
Crouzet-Migette
Geraise
Ste-Anne
Villeneuve
Labergement-du-Navois
Montmahoux
Sarraz
Alaise
Lizine
Echay
Cussey-s-Lison
Châtillon-s-Lison
Rouhe
Goux-s/s-Landet
Courcelles
Cessey
Charnay
Chenecey-Buillon
Vorges-les-Pins
Busy
Montferrand-le-Château
Larnod
Avanne-Aveney
Franois
Pouilley-les-Vignes
Ecole-Valentin
Auxon-Dessus
Geneuille
Cheyroz
Bussières
Boulot
Etuz
Voray-s-l'Ognon
Mérey-Vieilley
Perrouse
Palise
Aulx-lès-Cromary
Chambornay-lès-Bellevaux
Neuvelle-les-Cromary
Sorans-lès-Breurey
Traitiefontaine
Boult
Chaux-la-Lotière
Cordonnet
Montarlot-lès-Rioz
Recologne-lès-Rioz
Bourguignon-lès-la-Charité
Lieffrans
Montagne
Camp du Valdahon
Fort de Chailluz
Forêt de Chailluz
Aire de Besançon-Champoux
Aire de Besançon-Marchaux
Besançon Nord
La Comtoise
Sommet de Baume
Mt Bichoux
Côte d'Anroz
Le Mont Pelé
Mt d'Uziers
Crêt Monniot
Gouffre de Poudrey
Grotte de Plaisir-Fontaine
Source Bleue
Réserve Naturelle
Pont du Diable
Creux-Billard
Puits-Noir

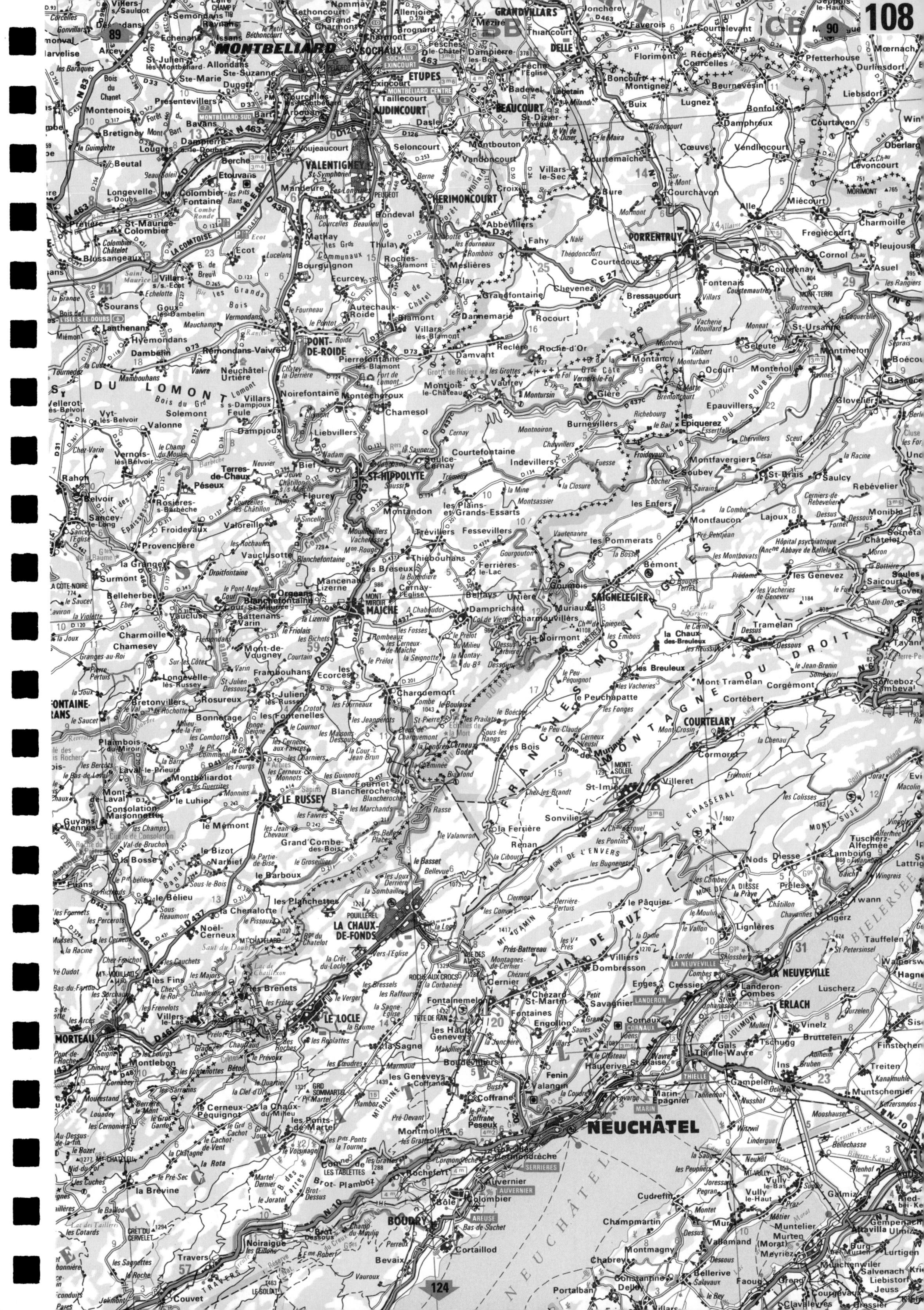

89
90
124
MONTBELIARD
SOCHAUX
ETUPES
AUDINCOURT
VALENTIGNEY
HERIMONCOURT
BEAUCOURT
DELLE
GRANDVILLARS
PORRENTRUY
PONT-DE-ROIDE
ST-HIPPOLYTE
MAICHE
SAIGNELEGIER
St-Ursanne
Tramelan
la Chaux-des-Breuleux
les Breuleux
COURTELARY
St-Imier
LE RUSSEY
LA CHAUX-DE-FONDS
LE LOCLE
MORTEAU
les Brenets
la Brévine
NEUCHÂTEL
LA NEUVEVILLE
ERLACH
BOUDRY
Colombier
Auvernier
Peseux
Valangin
Cernier
Fontainemelon
Bevaix
Cortaillod
Cudrefin
Murten (Morat)
Vully
Ins
Gampelen
Le Landeron
Cressier
Dombresson
Villiers
Sonvilier
Renan
Noirmont
Goumois
DU LOMONT
FRANCHES MONTAGNES
MONTAGNE DU DROIT
LE CHASSERAL
MONT SOLEIL
MONT SUJET
VAL DE RUZ
LAC DE NEUCHÂTEL
BIELERSEE
Couvet
Travers
Noiraigue

BAIE DE BOURGNEUF
ILE DE NOIRMOUTIER
NOIRMOUTIER-EN-L'ILE
l'Herbaudière
Bois de la Chaize
la Guérinière
Barbâtre
l'Epine
le Grand-viel
la Madeleine
Pierre Moine
les Bœufs
CHENAL D'ANJOUBERT
le Cois
Port du Bec
Fromentine
la Barre-de-M.
les Marguerites
N.-D.-de-Monts
le Pont d'Yeu
la Tonnelle
les Amiaux
ST JEAN-DE-MONTS
la Plage
Pt des Demoiselles
Orouet
le Pissot
Sion-s.-l'Océan
Croix-de-Vie
Pilours
ST-GILLES-CROIX-DE-VIE
St Hilaire-de-Riez
le Fenouiller
Givrand
N.D. des Dunes
la Sauzaie
Brétignolles-s.-M.
la Parée
St-Nicolas-de-Brem
Brem-s.-M.
Vairé
la Brardière
l'Ile d'Olonne
St Mathurin
Olonne-s.-Mer
l'Aubraie
Phare des Barges
Château d'O.
LES SABLES-D'OLONNE
Pte de l'Aiguille
Fort St Nicolas
les Barges d'Olonne
la Bernerie-en-Retz
les Moutiers-en-Retz
Prigny
BOURGNEUF-EN-R.
St Cyr
Fresnay-en-R.
St Hilaire-de Ch.
MACHECOUL
St Même-le-T.
la Marne
Paulx
Bouin
les Champs
BEAUVOIR-S.-MER
St Gervais
St Urbain
Châteauneuf
Bois-de-Cené
la Garnache
Sallertaine
CHALLANS
le Perrier
Soullans
Froidfond
Falleron
Touvois
St-Etienne-de-Mer-Morte
St Christophe-du-L.
Commequiers
Apremont
Maché
N.-D. de Riez
Coëx
St Révérend
St-Maixent-s.-Vie
l'Aiguillon-s.-Vie
la Chapelle-H.
la Chaize-Giraud
Landevieille
St Julien-des-L.
LA MOTHE-ACHARD
Ste Foy
Grosbr
Martinet
ILE D'YEU
Port-Joinville
Ker Borny
Ker Bossy
St Sauveur
Port-de-la-Meule
Pierre Tremblante
COTE SAUVAGE
ANSE DES VIEILLES
Pte des Corbeaux
Pte de la Tranche
Pte du Châtelet
Pte du Château
Pte des Chiens-Perrins
Pte Gauthier
Pte de la Cour
19
20
21
22
93

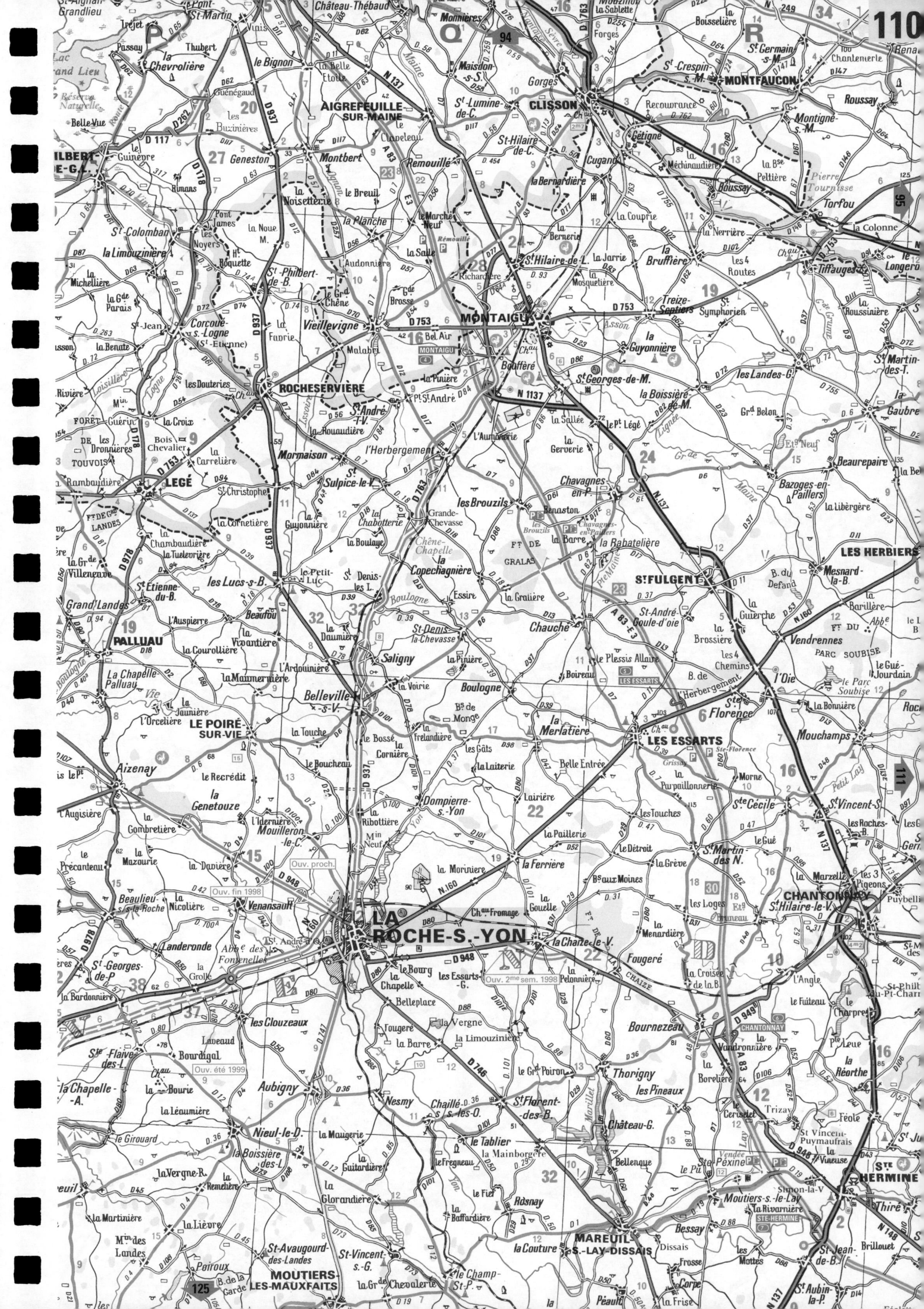
Château-Thébaud
Monnières
Clisson
Gorges
Maisdon-s-S.
St-Lumine-de-C.
AIGREFEUILLE SUR-MAINE
le Bignon
la Chevrolière
Passay
Thubert
Geneston
Montbert
Remouillé
St-Hilaire-de-C.
Cugand
Gétigné
St Crespin-s.-M.
MONTFAUCON
St Germain-s-M.
Roussay
Montigné-s.-M.
Boussay
Torfou
la Colonne
Tiffauges
Longeron
la Bernardière
la Bruffière
St-Hilaire-de-L.
Treize-Septiers
St Symphorien
MONTAIGU
Vieillevigne
St-Philbert-de-B.
Corcoué-s.-Logne
la Limouzinière
St-Colomban
la Benate
ROCHESERVIÈRE
Boufféré
St Georges-de-M.
la Guyonnière
les Landes-G.
la Boissière-de-M.
St Martin-des-T.
la Gaubretière
St-André-T.V.
l'Herbergement
Mormaison
St Sulpice-le-V.
LEGÉ
Touvois
les Brouzils
Chavagnes-en-P.
Bazoges-en-Pailliers
Beaurepaire
la Rabatelière
la Copechagnière
St FULGENT
LES HERBIERS
Mesnard-la-B.
les Lucs-s-B.
St Etienne-du-B.
Grand'Landes
PALLUAU
Beaufou
Chauché
St-Denis-la-Chevasse
St-André-Goule-d'oie
Vendrennes
Saligny
Boulogne
la Chapelle-Palluau
Belleville-s-V.
LE POIRÉ-SUR-VIE
la Merlatière
LES ESSARTS
Ste Florence
l'Oie
Mouchamps
Aizenay
la Genetouze
Mouilleron-le-C.
Dompierre-s.-Yon
la Ferrière
Ste Cécile
St Vincent-S.
Beaulieu-s-la-Roche
Venansault
LA ROCHE-S.-YON
la Chaize-le-V.
Fougeré
St Martin-des N.
CHANTONNAY
St Hilaire-le-V.
Landeronde
St-Georges-de-P.
les Clouzeaux
Bournezeau
Ste-Flaive-des-L.
Aubigny
Nesmy
Chaillé-s.-les-O.
St Florent-des-B.
Thorigny
Château-G.
Nieul-le-D.
la Boissière-des-L.
le Tablier
Rosnay
Ste Pexine
STE HERMINE
Moutiers-s.-le-Lay
Thiré
St-Avaugourd-des-Landes
St-Vincent-s.-G.
MOUTIERS LES-MAUXFAITS
le Champ-St-P.
MAREUIL-S.-LAY-DISSAIS
Bessay
St Jean-de-B.
St Aubin-la-P.
Ouv. proch.
Ouv. fin 1998
Ouv. 2me sem. 1998
Ouv. été 1999

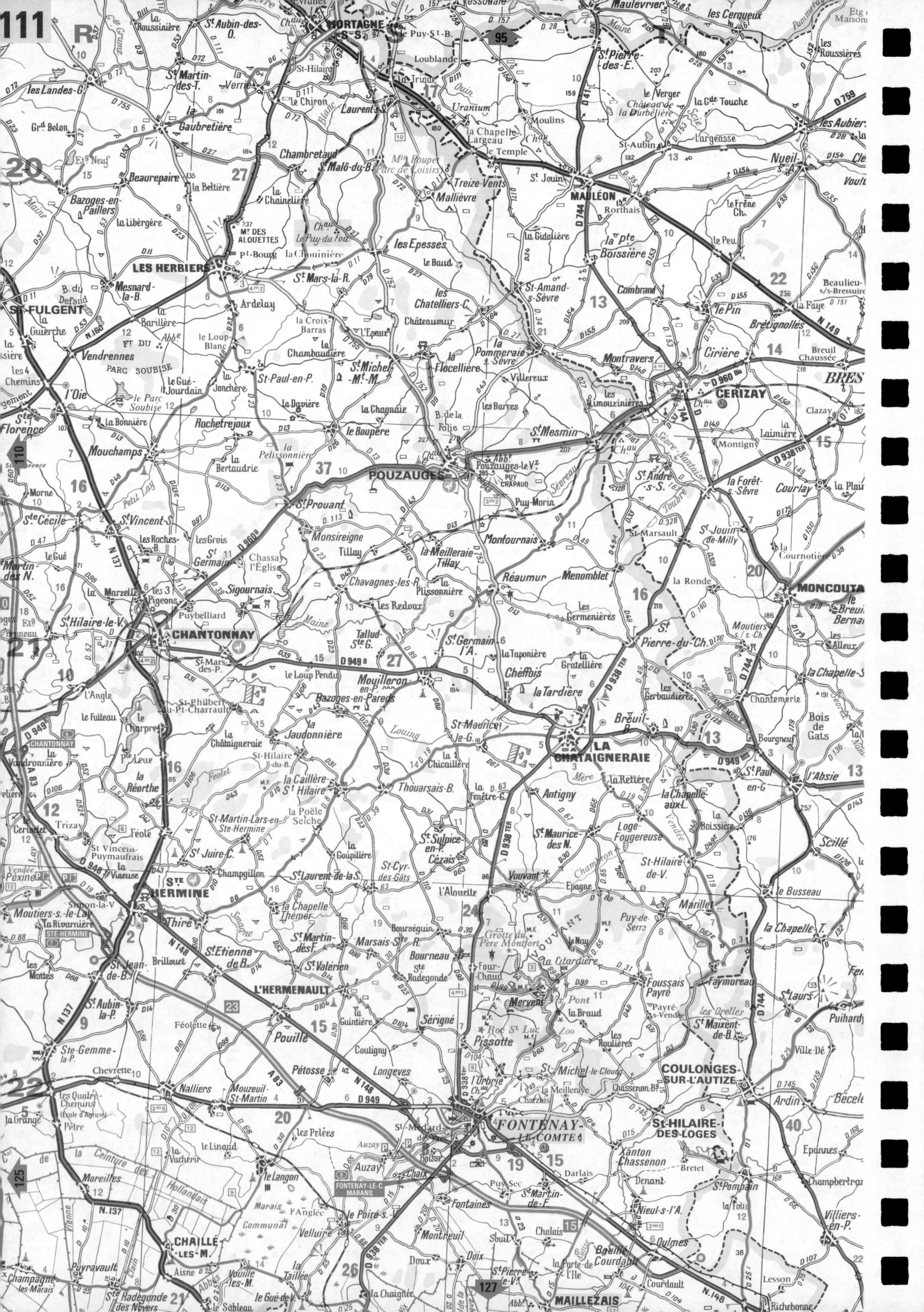

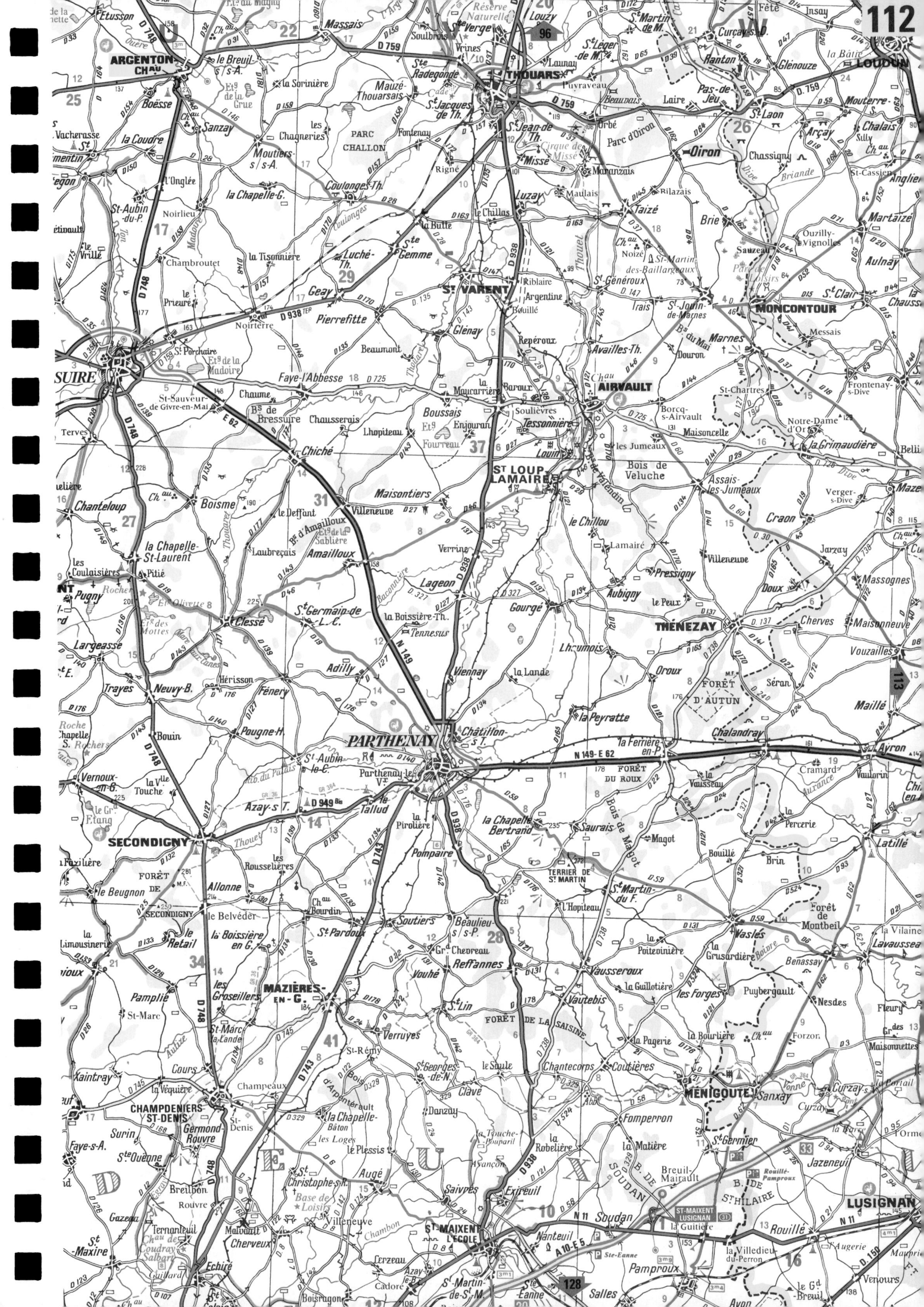

ARGENTON-CHÂU
THOUARS
LOUDUN
BRESSUIRE
AIRVAULT
MONCONTOUR
ST VARENT
ST LOUP LAMAIRÉ
THÉNEZAY
PARTHENAY
SECONDIGNY
MAZIÈRES-EN-G.
CHAMPDENIERS-ST-DENIS
MÉNIGOUTE
LUSIGNAN
ST MAIXENT L'ÉCOLE
ST-MAIXENT LUSIGNAN
Etusson
Massais
Ste Verge
Louzy
Soulbrois
Vrines
le Breuil-s/s-A.
Ste Radegonde
Mauzé-Thouarsais
St Jacques de Th.
St Jean-de Th.
Boësse
Sanzay
la Coudre
Moutiers-s/s-A.
les Chagneries
PARC CHALLON
Fontenay
Coulonges-Th.
la Chapelle-G.
l'Onglée
St-Aubin-du-P.
Noirlieu
Chambroutet
le Prieuré
la Tisonnière
Luché-Th.
Ste Gemme
la Butte
le Chillou
Luzay
Rigné
Missé
Maranzais
Taizé
Brie
Oiron
Parc d'Oiron
Orbé
Puyraveau
Launay
St Léger-de M.
St Martin-de M.
Curçay-s-D.
Ranton
Glénouze
Pas-de-Jeu
Laire
St Laon
Mouterre-s.
Chalais
Arçay
Chassigny
Martaizé
Aulnay
St Clair
Ouzilly-Vignolles
Sauzeau
Frontenay
St-Cassien
Geay
Pierrefitte
Noirterre
St Porchaire
Etg de la Madoire
Beaumont
Glénay
Ribiaire
Argentine
Bouillé
Repéroux
Availles-Th.
St-Généroux
St-Martin-des-Baillargeaux
Irais
St-Jouin-de-Marnes
Marnes
Douron
Messais
Frontenay-s-Dive
Faye-l'Abbesse
Chaume
St-Sauveur-de Givre-en-Mai
Bs de Bressuire
Chausserais
Boussais
Etg Fourreau
Enjouran
la Maucarrière
Barour
Soulièvres
Tessonnière
Louin
Borcq-s-Airvault
Maisoncelle
St-Chartres
Notre-Dame d'Or
la Grimaudière
les Jumeaux
Bois de Veluche
Assais-les-Jumeaux
Terves
Chiché
Lhopiteau
Maisontiers
Villeneuve
Chanteloup
Boismé
le Deffant
Bs d'Amailloux
Etg de la Sablière
Amailloux
le Chillou
Lamairé
Craon
Verger-s-Dive
Jarzay
la Chapelle-St-Laurent
Les Coulaisières
Pitié
Laubreçais
Verrine
Lageon
Pressigny
Villeneuve
Massognes
Doux
Pugny
Etg Olivette
Etg des Mottes
Clessé
St Germain-de-L.C.
la Boissière-Th.
Tennesus
Gourgé
Aubigny
le Peux
Cherves
Maisonneuve
Largeasse
Trayes
Neuvy-B.
Hérisson
Fénery
Adilly
Viennay
la Lande
Lhoumois
Oroux
FORÊT D'AUTUN
Séran
Vouzailles
Maillé
Bouin
Pougne-H.
Châtillon-s/T.
la Peyratte
Chalandray
la Ferrière-en-P.
Ayron
Vernoux-en-G.
la Vlle Touche
St-Aubin-le-C.
Parthenay-le-Vx
FORÊT DU ROUX
Vausseau
Cramard
Vaulorin
le Grd Etang
Azay-s-T.
le Tallud
la Pirolière
la Chapelle Bertrand
Saurais
Bois de Magot
Magot
Percerie
Latillé
la Fuxilière
FORÊT DE SECONDIGNY
le Beugnon
Allonne
les Rousselières
Chau Bourdin
Pompaire
TERRIER DE ST MARTIN
St Martin-du F.
l'Hopiteau
Bouillé
Brin
Forêt de Montbeil
le Belvédère
le Retail
la Boissière en G.
Soutiers
St Pardoux
Beaulieu-s/s-P.
Grd Chevreau
Reffannes
la Poitevinière
Vasles
la Grusardière
Benassay
Lavausseau
la Vilaine
Vausseroux
la Guillotière
les Forges
Puybergault
Nesdes
Fleury
Limousinerie
Pamplie
St-Marc
les Groseillers
Vouhé
St Lin
Vautebis
St-Marc-la-Lande
Verruyes
FORÊT DE LA SAISINE
la Pagerie
la Bourlière
Forzon
Grdes Maisonnettes
Xaintray
Cours
la Véquière
St-Rémy
St-Georges-de-N.
le Saule
Chantecorps
Coutières
Curzay-s-V.
Champeaux
Bois d'Arpentérault
Clavé
Sanxay
Germond-Rouvre
St-Denis
la Chapelle-Bâton
Danzay
Fomperron
Surin
Faye-s-A.
Ste Ouenne
les Loges
le Plessis
la Touche-Pouparil
la Robelière
la Matière
St Germier
Jazeneuil
St Christophe-s-R.
Augé
Avançon
B. de Soudan
Breuil-Mairault
B. de St Hilaire
Rouillé-Pamproux
Breilbon
Rouvre
Base de Loisirs
Saivres
Exireuil
Soudan
la Guitière
Rouillé
Gazeau
Ternanteuil
Chau du Coudray-Salbart
Malvault
Cherveux
Villeneuve
Chambon
Nanteuil
Ste-Eanne
la Villedieu-du-Perron
l'Augerie
St-Maxire
Guillard
Echiré
Cerzeau
Azay-le-B.
Cadoré
St-Martin-de-St-M.
Ste-Eanne
Pamproux
le Gd Breuil
Venours
Boisragon
Salles
Avon
N 149 - E 62
N 149
D 938
D 748
D 743
N 11
A 10-E 5
96
113
128

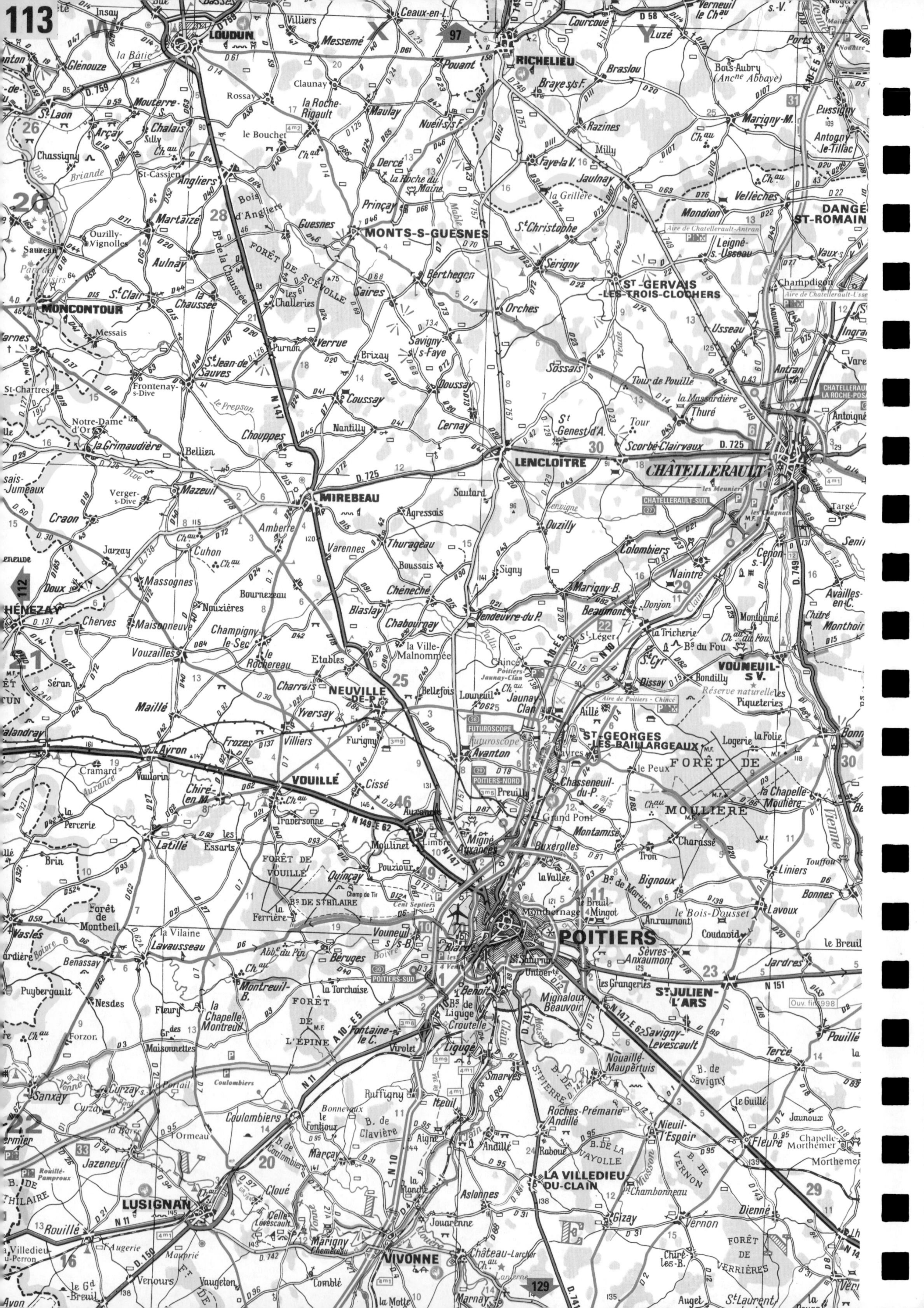
LOUDUN
Insay
Villiers
Messemé
Ceaux-en-L.
97
RICHELIEU
Courcoué
Luzé
Verneuil le Ch.au
Ports
Glenouze
la Bâtie
Pouant
Braslou
Bois-Aubry (Anc.ne Abbaye)
Claunay
Rossay
Braye s/s F.
St-Laon
Mouterre-S.
la Roche-Rigault
Maulay
Nueil-s/s F.
Razines
Marigny-M.
Pussigny
Antogny-le-Tillac
Chalais
Arçay
Sully
le Bouchet
Chassigny
Briande
Dive
St-Cassien
Angliers
Dercé
la Roche du Maine
Faye-la V.
Milly
Jaulnay
Vellèches
DANGÉ ST-ROMAIN
Bois d'Angliers
Martaizé
Prinçay
la Grillère
Mondion
Guesnes
MONTS-S-GUESNES
St-Christophe
Aire de Chatellerault-Antran
Leigné-s.-Usseau
Ouzilly-Vignolles
Sauzeau
Aulnay
FORÊT DE SCÉVOLLE
Sérigny
Vaux-s.-V.
Berthegon
ST-GERVAIS-LES-TROIS-CLOCHERS
Champdigon
MONCONTOUR
St Clair
la Chaussée
les Challeries
Saires
Orches
Usseau
Aire de Chatellerault-Usseau
Messais
Verrue
Purnon
Savigny-s/s-Faye
Brixay
Sossais
Antran
St-Jean-de-Sauves
Frontenay-s-Dive
St-Chartres
Coussay
Doussay
Tour de Pouillé
la Massardière
Thuré
CHATELLERAULT LA ROCHE-POSAY
Antoigné
Le Prepson
N 141
Notre-Dame d'Or
Nantilly
Cernay
St Genest d'A.
Tour
Scorbé-Clairvaux
D. 725
la Grimaudière
Chouppes
Bellien
LENCLOITRE
CHÂTELLERAULT
Mazeuil
Verger-s-Dive
Jumeaux
MIREBEAU
Sautard
les Meuniers
CHATELLERAULT-SUD
Targé
Craon
Amberre
Agressais
Ouzilly
les Chagnats
Jarzay
Cuhon
Varennes
Thurageau
Colombiers
Naintré
Cenon-s.-V.
Senil
112
Doux
Massognes
Boussais
Signy
Availles-en-C.
Bournezeau
Chéneché
Marigny-B.
Donjon
Montgamé
Chitré
Monthoir
HÉNEZAY
Cherves
Nouzières
Maisonneuve
Blaslay
Chabournay
Vendeuvre-du-P.
Beaumont
la Tricherie
Ch.au du Fou
Champigny-le-Sec
le Rochereau
Vouzailles
la Ville-Malnommée
St-Léger
Bs du Fou
Chincé
Poitiers Jaunay-Clan
St-Cyr
VOUNEUIL-S.V.
Etables
Bondilly
Séran
Charrais
NEUVILLE-DE-P.
Bellefois
Louneuil
Jaunay-Clan
Dissay
Aire de Poitiers - Chincé
Réserve naturelle les Piqueteries
Maillé
Yversay
FUTUROSCOPE
Futuroscope
Aillé
ST-GEORGES-LES-BAILLARGEAUX
Logerie
la Folie
Ayron
Frozes
Villiers
Furigny
Avanton
Vayres
FORÊT DE
Cramard
Vaulorin
VOUILLÉ
Cissé
POITIERS-NORD
Chasseneuil-du-P.
le Peux
la Chapelle-Moulière
Chiré-en-M.
Preuilly
Auzance
MOULIÈRE
Traversonne
N 149-E 62
Auxances
Grand Pont
Montamisé
Percerie
Latillé
les Essarts
Moulinet
Migné-Auxances
Buxerolles
Charassé
FORÊT DE VOUILLÉ
Limbre
Tron
Liniers
Touffou
Brin
Quinçay
Pouzioux
la Vallée
Bs de Mortier
Bignoux
Bonnes
Champ de Tir
Bs DE ST-HILAIRE
Cent Septiers
le Breuil-Mingot
Montbernage
Lavoux
Forêt de Montbeil
la Ferrière
le Bois-Dousset
Vasles
la Vilaine
Vouneuil-s-B.
POITIERS
Anraumont
Coudavid
le Breuil
Lavausseau
Abb.e du Pin
Béruges
Biard
St Saturnin
Sèvres-Anxaumont
Jardres
Benassay
Montreuil-B.
POITIERS-SUD
la Torchaise
St-Benoît
Univerté
les Grangeries
ST-JULIEN-L'ARS
N 151
Puybergault
Nesdes
FORÊT DE L'ÉPINE
Bs de Ligugé
Mignaloux-Beauvoir
N 147-E 62
Savigny-Levescault
Fleury
la Chapelle-Montreuil
Croutelle
Pouillé
Forzon
Gr.des Maisonnettes
Fontaine-le C.
Virolet
Ligugé
Clain
Tercé
Nouaillé-Maupertuis
B. de Savigny
Sanxay
Vonne
Curzay-s.-V.
Portail
Coulombiers
N 11
Ruffigny
Iteuil
Smarves
ST-PIERRE
le Guillé
Jaunoux
Curzay
Coulombiers
le Fontioux
Bonnevaux
B. de Clavière
Roches-Prémarie-Andillé
Nieuil-l'Espoir
Fleuré
Chapelle-Morthemer
l'Ormeau
Aigné
Andillé
Rabouë
B. DE LA VAYOLLE
B. DE VERNON
Morthemer
Jazeneuil
Marçay
N 10
LA VILLEDIEU-DU-CLAIN
Rouillé-Pamproux
B. DE ST-HILAIRE
LUSIGNAN
Cloué
Aslonnes
Chambonneau
Rouillé
Celle-Lévescault
Jouarenne
Gizay
Vernon
Dienné
l'Augerie
Marigny Chémereau
Clouère
FORÊT DE VERRIÈRES
Villedieu-du-Perron
Maupriée
VIVONNE
Château-Larcher
Chiré-les-B.
Venours
Vaugeton
Comblé
Lanterne
129
le Gd Breuil
la Motte
Marnay
Auget
St Laurent
Avon

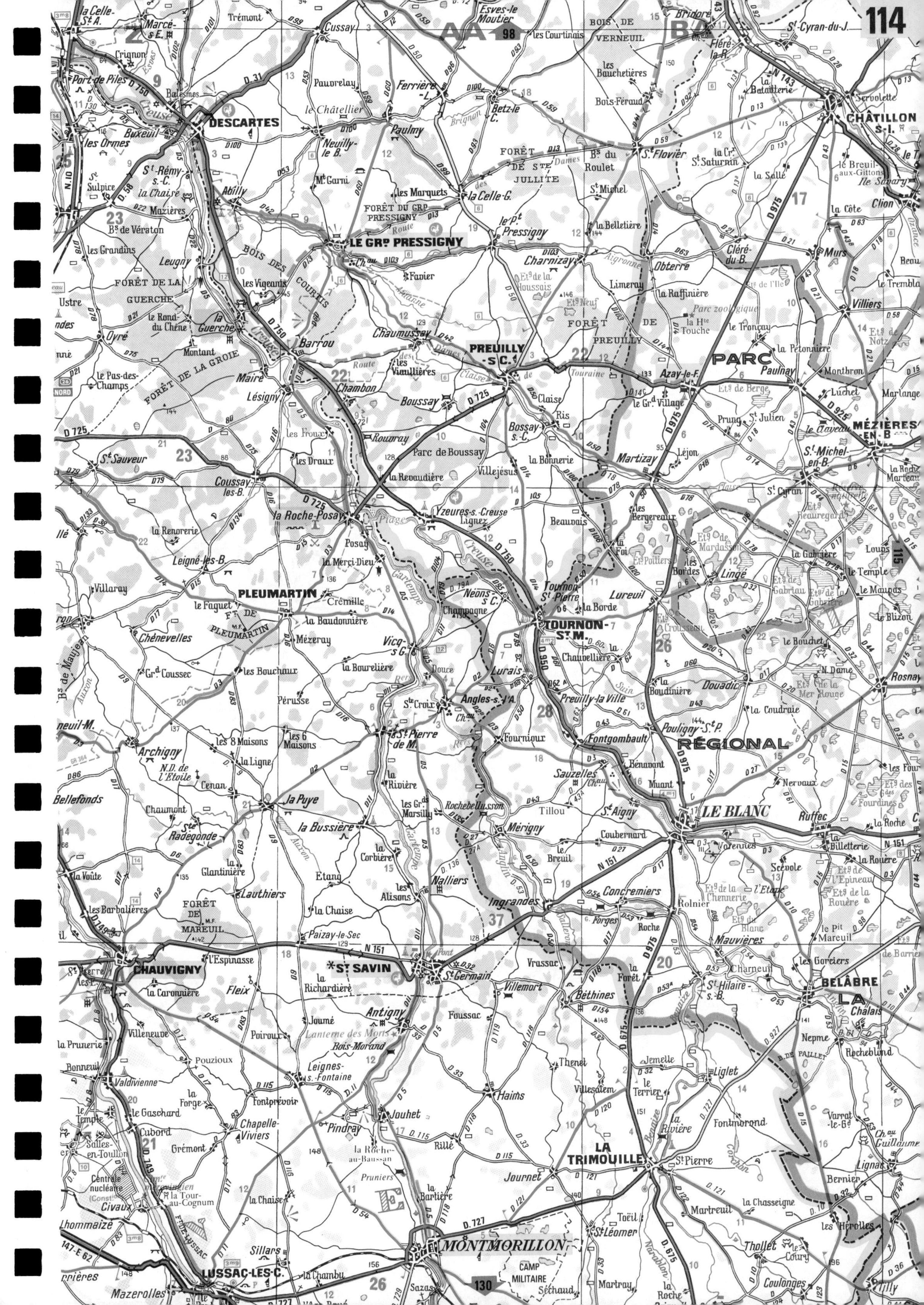
DESCARTES
LE GRD PRESSIGNY
PREUILLY-S C.
CHÂTILLON S-I.
MÉZIÈRES EN B.
PARC
RÉGIONAL
LE BLANC
PLEUMARTIN
TOURNON-St M.
la Roche-Posay
CHAUVIGNY
St SAVIN
LA TRIMOUILLE
MONTMORILLON
LUSSAC-LES-C.
BELÂBRE
Cussay
Esves-le Moutier
Ferrière-L.
Betz-le C.
St Flovier
Paulmy
Neuilly-le B.
Abilly
la Celle-G.
le Pt Pressigny
Charnizay
Obterre
Azay-le-F.
Martizay
Barrou
Chaumussay
Boussay
Yzeures-s.-Creuse
Lésigny
Coussay-les-B.
Leigné-les-B.
Vicq-s-G.
Angles-s.-l'A.
St Pierre de M.
Archigny
la Puye
la Bussière
Mérigny
Fontgombault
Pouligny-St P.
Lureuil
Linge
Douadic
Rosnay
Ruffec
Concremiers
Ingrandes
Nalliers
Lauthiers
Antigny
Leignes-s.-Fontaine
Jouhet
Pindray
Journet
Liglet
Haims
Béthines
Villemort
St Hilaire-s.-B.
Mauvières
Valdivienne
Civaux
Sillars
Mazerolles
Chalais
Rocheblond
Lignac
les Hérolles
Tholllet
Coulonges
CAMP MILITAIRE
FORÊT DE LA GUERCHE
FORÊT DE LA GROIE
FORÊT DE PREUILLY
FORÊT DU GRD PRESSIGNY
FORÊT DE STE JULLITE
FORÊT DE MAREUIL
BOIS DE VERNEUIL
BOIS DES COURTIS
N 143
N 151
D 975
D 750
D 725
98
130
115

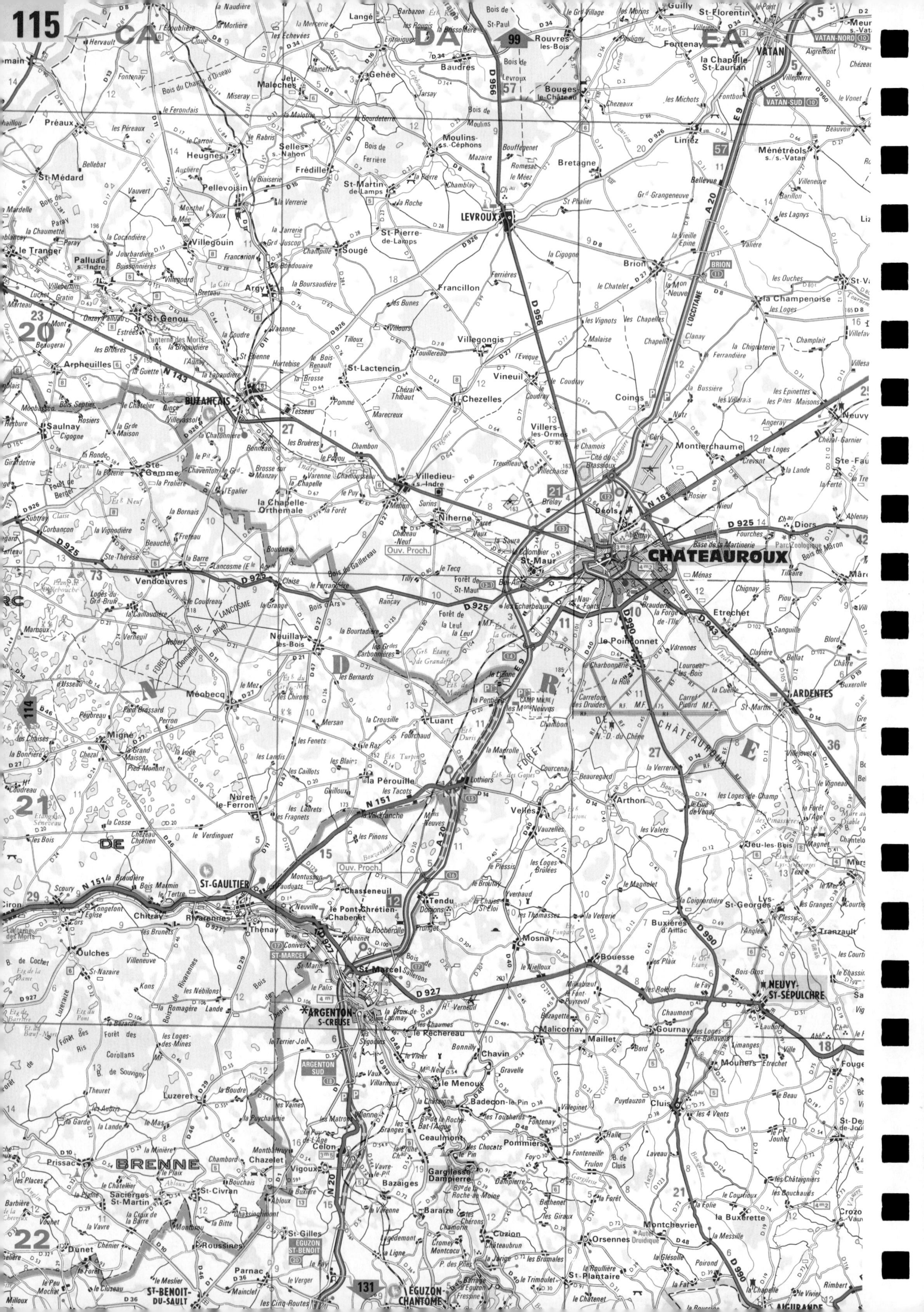
CHÂTEAUROUX
LEVROUX
VATAN
BUZANÇAIS
ARDENTES
ST-GAULTIER
ARGENTON-S-CREUSE
NEUVY-ST-SÉPULCHRE
ÉGUZON-CHANTÔME
ST-BENOÎT-DU-SAULT
AIGURANDE
VATAN-NORD
VATAN-SUD
BRION
ST-MARCEL
ARGENTON SUD
ÉGUZON ST-BENOÎT
BRENNE
FORÊT DE CHÂTEAUROUX
DOMAINE DE LANCOSME
CAMP MILRE
Ouv. Proch.
Déols
Montierchaume
Coings
Villedieu-s.-Indre
St-Maur
Le Poinçonnet
Etrechet
Diors
Niherne
Vineuil
Villegongis
Francillon
Chezelles
St-Lactencin
Argy
Palluau-s.-Indre
St-Genou
Pellevoisin
Heugnes
Selles-s.-Nahon
Frédille
Moulins-s.-Céphons
Bretagne
Liniez
Ménétréols s.-Vatan
Baudres
Rouvres-les-Bois
Bouges-le-Château
Fontenay
Guilly
St-Florentin
Langé
Gehée
Jeu-Maloches
Préaux
St-Médard
Villegouin
Sougé
St-Pierre-de-Lamps
St-Martin-de-Lamps
Arpheuilles
Saulnay
Ste-Gemme
la Chapelle-Orthemale
Vendœuvres
Neuillay-les-Bois
Méobecq
Migné
Nuret-le-Ferron
Luant
la Pérouille
Lothiers
Velles
Arthon
Jeu-les-Bois
Mosnay
Bouesse
Buxières-d'Aillac
Lys-St-Georges
Tendu
Chasseneuil
le Pont-Chrétien-Chabenet
Thenay
Rivarennes
Chitray
Oulches
Luzeret
Prissac
Chazelet
Vigoux
Celon
Bazaiges
Ceaulmont
Gargilesse-Dampierre
Badecon-le-Pin
Pommiers
Cluis
Malicornay
Maillet
Gournay
Mouhers
Orsennes
Montchevrier
la Buxerette
Cuzion
Baraize
St-Gilles
Roussines
Parnac
Dunet
Sacierges-St-Martin
St-Civran
Chavin
le Menoux
le Pêchereau
Tranzault
St-Plantaire
N 143
N 151
N 20
A 20
E 9
D 925
D 926
D 956
D 927
D 990
D 943
L'OCCITANE
99
131
114

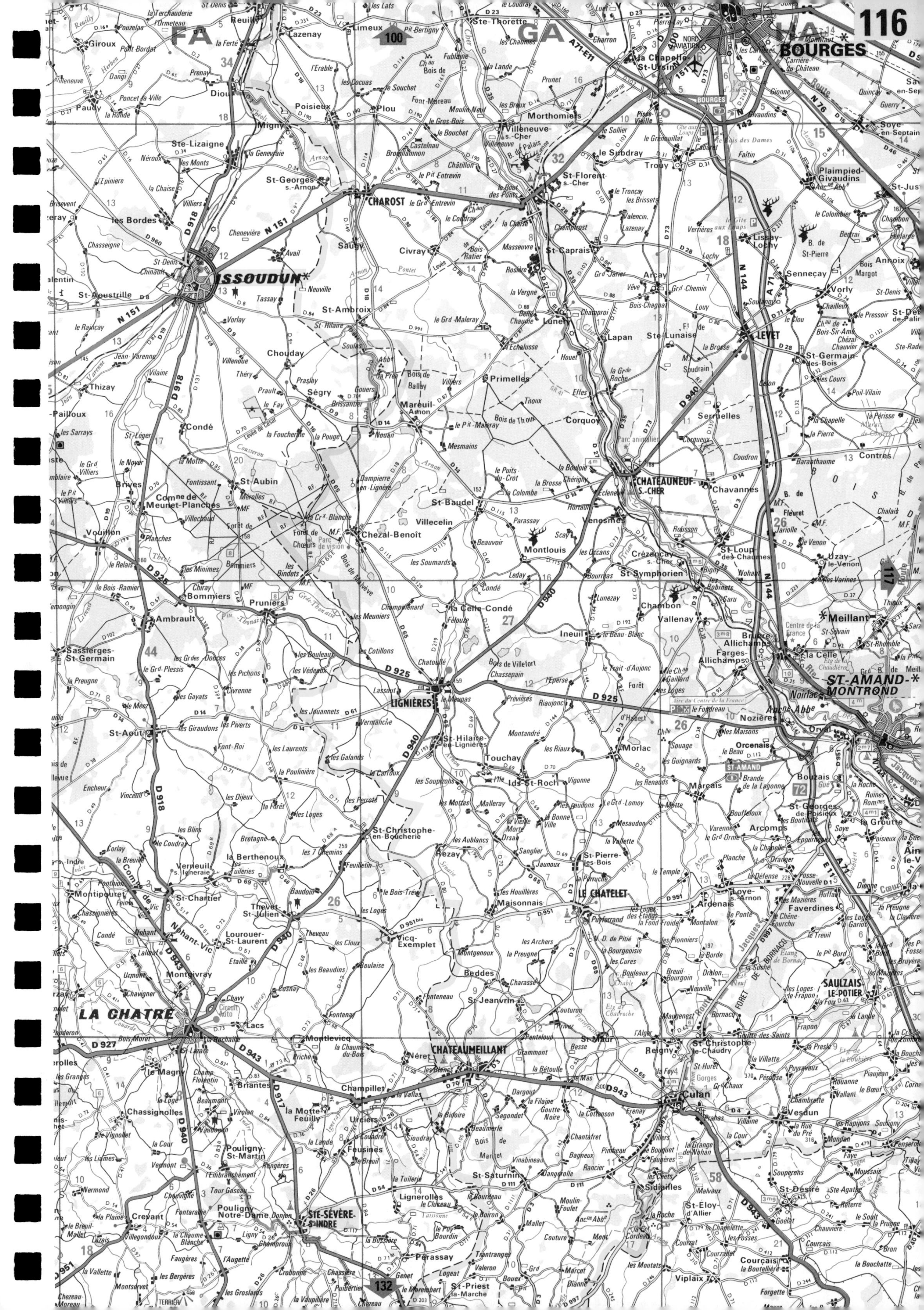
BOURGES
ISSOUDUN
CHAROST
LEVET
CHATEAUNEUF-S.-CHER
LIGNIÈRES
ST-AMAND-MONTROND
LE CHATELET
LA CHATRE
CHATEAUMEILLANT
SAULZAIS-LE-POTIER
STE-SÉVÈRE-S-INDRE
Culan
Meillant
St-Florent-s.-Cher
Mehun
Villeneuve-s.-Cher
Lunery
Primelles
Chezal-Benoît
Montlouis
Vallenay
Orval
Bouzais
Vesdun
Lignerolles
St-Saturnin
St-Christophe-en-Boucherie
Vicq-Exemplet
Ids-St-Roch
Touchay
Ineuil
Condé
Bommiers
Pruniers
Ambrault
St-Aout
Montgivray
Nohant-Vic
Thevet-St-Julien
St-Chartier
Chassignolles
Pouligny-St-Martin
Pouligny-Notre-Dame
Crevant
Champillet
Néret
Beddes
Maisonnais
Ardenais
Faverdines
Arcomps
Marçais
Nozières
Farges-Allichamps
Bruère-Allichamps
Chambon
Crézançay-s.-Cher
St-Symphorien
Venesmes
St-Loup-des-Chaumes
Chavannes
Corquoy
Serruelles
Lapan
Ste-Lunaise
Arçay
St-Caprais
Plaimpied-Givaudins
Lissay-Lochy
Senneçay
St-Germain-des-Bois
Uzay-le-Venon
Trouy
Le Subdray
Morthomiers
La Chapelle-St-Ursin
Ste-Thorette
Limeux
Lazenay
Reuilly
Poisieux
Mareuil-s-Arnon
Ségry
Chouday
St-Ambroix
St-Georges-s.-Arnon
Ste-Lizaigne
Thizay
Vouillon
St-Aubin
Brives
Villecelin
St-Baudel
La Celle-Condé
St-Hilaire-en-Lignières
Morlac
Reigny
St-Christophe-le-Chaudry
Sidiailles
St-Jeanvrin
Urciers
Feusines
La Motte-Feuilly
Briantes
Lacs
Montlevicq
Perassay
St-Priest-la-Marche
Courçais
Viplaix
St-Désiré
D 925
D 940
D 918
D 943
N 151
N 144
A 71
100
117
132

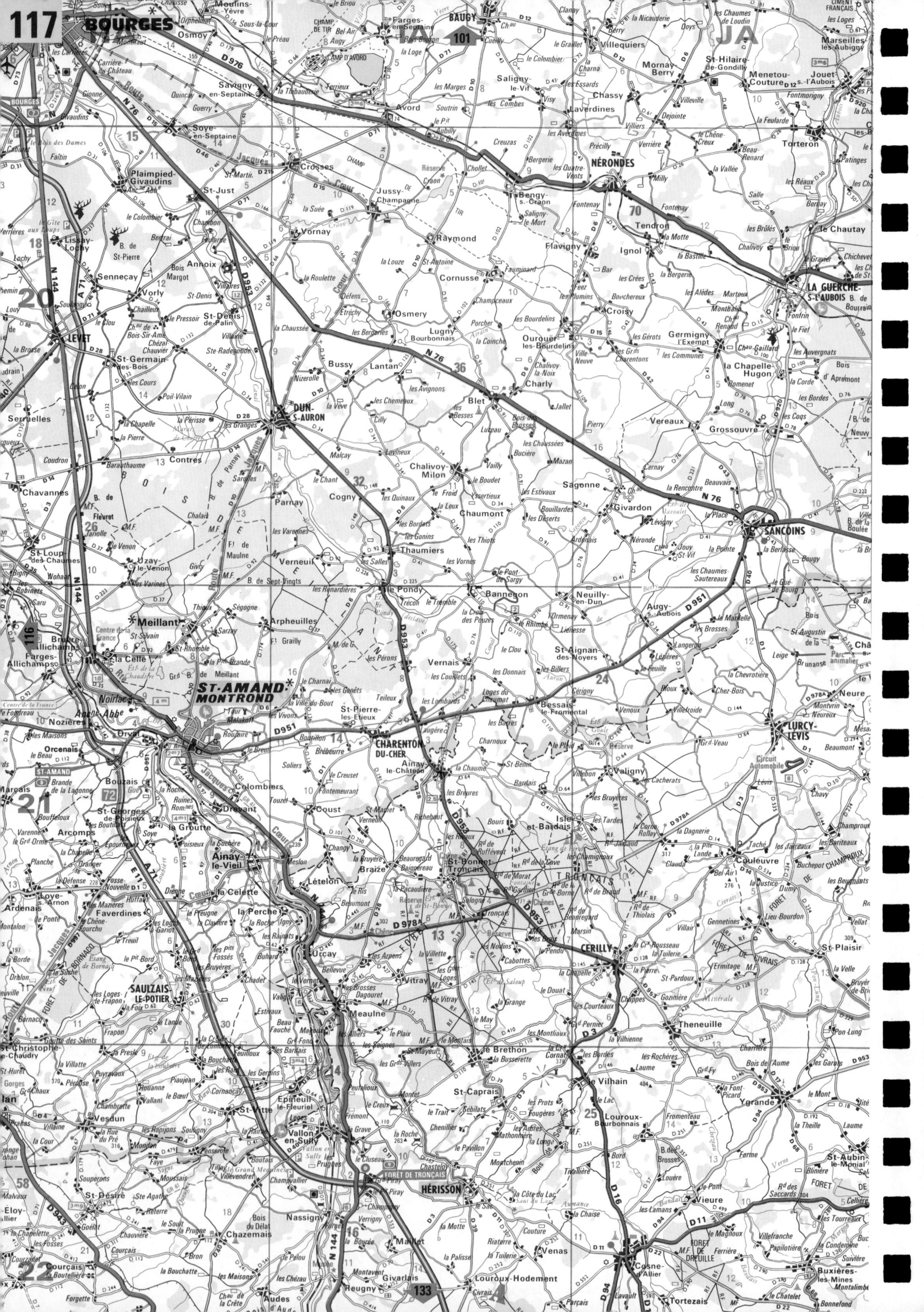
117
BOURGES
Osmoy
Moulins-s.-Yèvre
Sous-la-Tour
Fargessen-Septaine
BAUGY
101
Villequiers
St-Hilaire-de-Gondilly
Menetou-Couture
Jouet-s.-l'Aubois
Marseilles-les-Aubigny
Savigny-en-Septaine
Avord
Saligny-le-Vif
Mornay-Berry
Chassy
Laverdines
Torteron
Soye-en-Septaine
Crosses
Jussy-Champagne
NÉRONDES
Plaimpied-Givaudins
St-Just
Bengy-s.-Craon
Tendron
Vornay
Raymond
Flavigny
Ignol
Le Chautay
Annoix
Cornusse
LA GUERCHE-S.-L'AUBOIS
Senneçay
Vorly
St-Denis-de-Palin
Osmery
Croisy
LEVET
Lugny-Bourbonnais
Ourouer-les-Bourdelins
Germigny-l'Exempt
St-Germain-des-Bois
Bussy
Lantan
Blet
Charly
La Chapelle-Hugon
Serruelles
DUN-S-AURON
Vereaux
Grossouvre
Contres
Chalivoy-Milon
Chavannes
Cogny
Parnay
Sagonne
Givardon
SANCOINS
Uzay-le-Venon
Thaumiers
Verneuil
St-Loup-des-Chaumes
Bannegon
Neuilly-en-Dun
Augy-s.-Aubois
Meillant
Arpheuilles
Bruère-Allichamps
Farges-Allichamps
La Celle
Vernais
St-Aignan-des-Noyers
ST-AMAND-MONTROND
Bessais-le-Fromental
Nozières
Orval
Orcenais
St-Pierre-les-Étieux
CHARENTON-DU-CHER
Ainay-le-Château
LURCY-LÉVIS
Valigny
Bouzais
Colombiers
Drevant
Coust
St-Georges-de-Poisieux
Arcomps
Ainay-le-Vieil
Isle-et-Bardais
Couleuvre
Braize
St-Bonnet-Tronçais
Lételon
La Celette
Ardenais
Faverdines
La Perche
Urçay
Cerilly
St-Plaisir
Vitray
Meaulne
SAULZAIS-LE-POTIER
Theneuille
Le Brethon
Cornat
Le Vilhain
St-Caprais
Ygrande
Epineuil-le-Fleuriel
Vesdun
St-Vitte
Vallon-en-Sully
Louroux-Bourbonnais
St-Aubin-le-Monial
HÉRISSON
St-Désiré
Chazemais
Nassigny
Vieure
Maillet
Venas
Cosne-d'Allier
Buxières-les-Mines
Courçais
Givarlais
Reugny
Louroux-Hodement
Audes
Tortezais
133
116
N 76
D 953
D 951
N 144
A 71
D 976

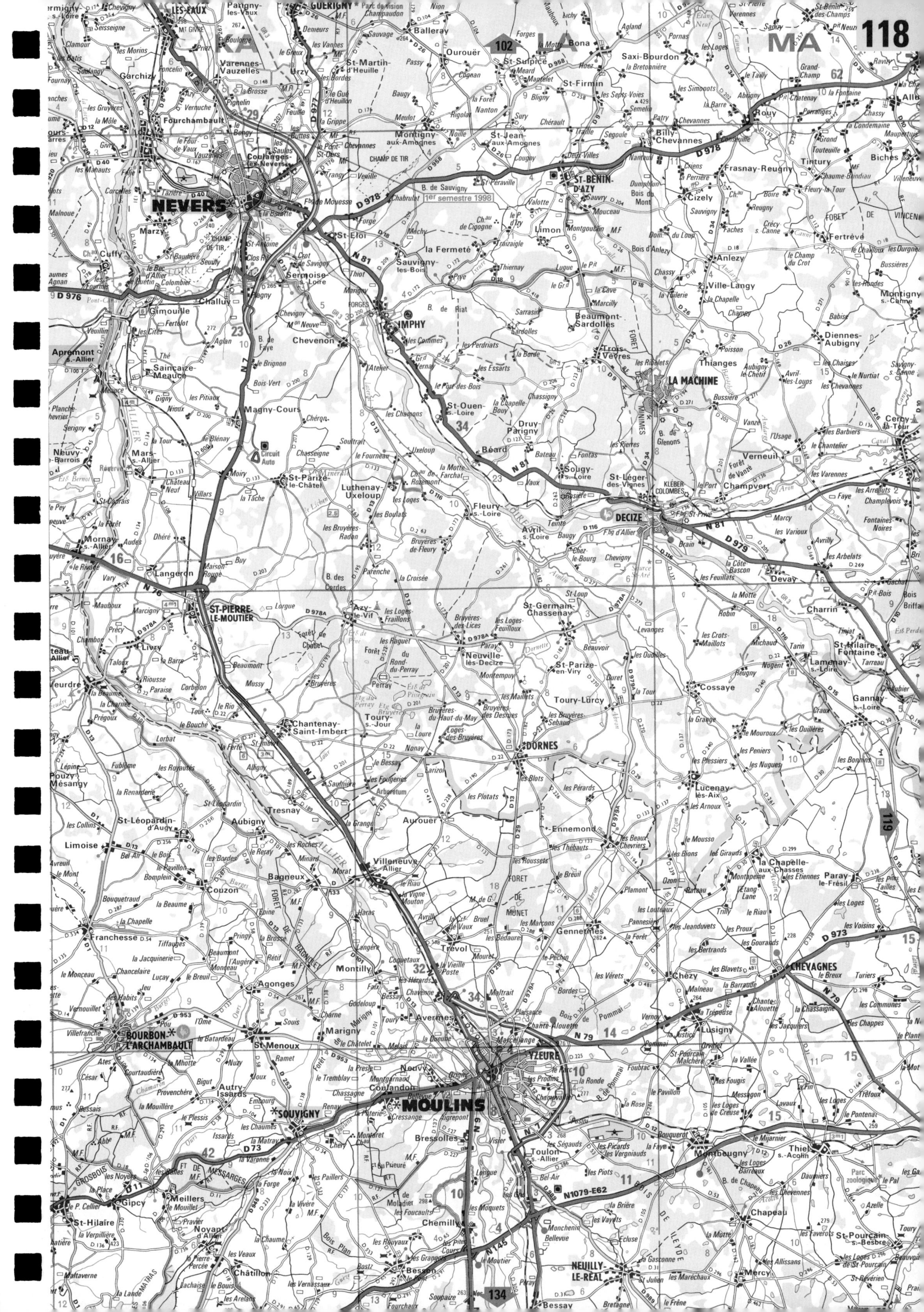
102
NEVERS
Coulanges-lès-Nevers
Fourchambault
Garchizy
Varennes-Vauzelles
Marzy
Challuy
Sermoise-s.-Loire
St-Eloi
IMPHY
Chevenon
Saincaize-Meauce
Magny-Cours
Mars-s.-Allier
St-Parize-le-Châtel
Luthenay-Uxeloup
Langeron
ST-PIERRE-LE-MOUTIER
Chantenay-Saint-Imbert
DORNES
Toury-Lurcy
ST-BENIN-D'AZY
Cizely
LA MACHINE
Thianges
Béard
DECIZE
St-Léger-des-Vignes
Devay
Cossaye
Lucenay-lès-Aix
Lamenay-s.-Loire
Gannay-s.-Loire
Cercy-la-Tour
Verneuil
Champvert
Fleury-s.-Loire
Avril-s.-Loire
St-Germain-Chassenay
Neuville-lès-Decize
Saxi-Bourdon
Billy-Chevannes
Rouy
Frasnay-Reugny
Anlezy
Ville-Langy
Villeneuve-s.-Allier
Bagneux
Couzon
Aubigny
St-Léopardin-d'Augy
Franchesse
Agonges
BOURBON-L'ARCHAMBAULT
St-Menoux
Autry-Issards
SOUVIGNY
MOULINS
YZEURE
Avermes
Trevol
Gennetines
Chevagnes
Chézy
Lusigny
Montbeugny
Toulon-s.-Allier
Bressolles
Chemilly
Chapeau
Thiel-s.-Acolin
NEUILLY-LE-REAL
Besson
Châtillon
Meillers
Gipcy
St-Hilaire
Noyant-d'Allier
St-Pourçain-s.-Besbre
N 7
N 81
N 79
N 145
N1079-E62
D 978
D 973
D 979
D 976
119
134
1er semestre 1998

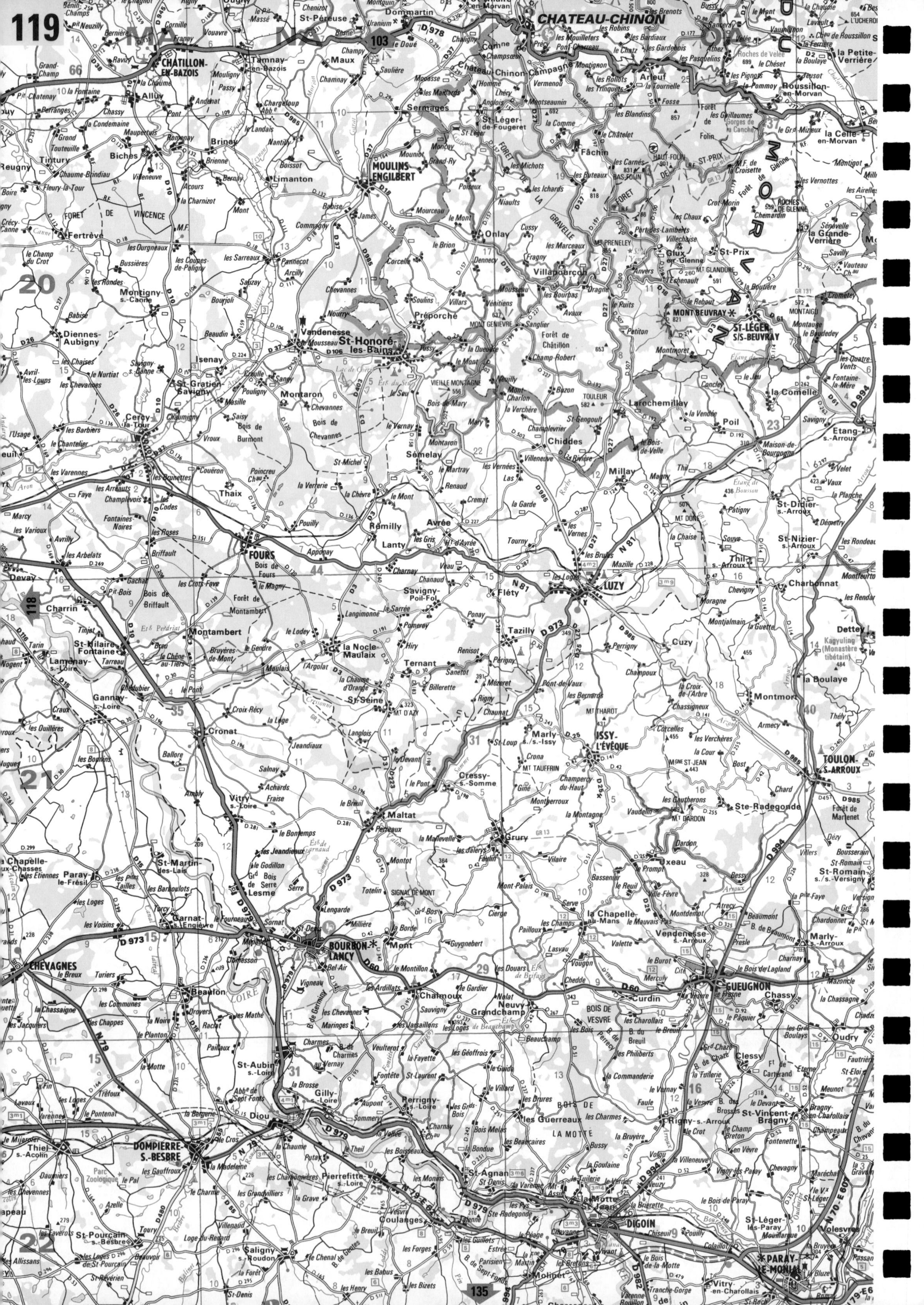
CHATEAU-CHINON
CHATILLON-EN-BAZOIS
MOULINS-ENGILBERT
St-Honoré-les-Bains
Vandenesse
St-Péreuse
Dommartin
Maux
Sermages
Limanton
Biches
Brinay
Alluy
Fertrève
Montigny-s.-Canne
Cercy-la-Tour
Isenay
Montaron
Préporche
Onlay
Villapourçon
Arleuf
Fâchin
Glux-en-Glenne
MONT BEUVRAY
ST-LÉGER S/S-BEUVRAY
Larochemillay
Poil
Millay
Chiddes
Sémelay
Rémilly
Avrée
FOURS
LUZY
Savigny-Poil-Fol
Fléty
Tazilly
la Nocle-Maulaix
Ternant
Montambert
Charrin
Cronat
ISSY-L'ÉVÊQUE
Cressy-s.-Somme
Maltat
Grury
Marly-s.-Issy
TOULON-S-ARROUX
Ste-Radegonde
Uxeau
BOURBON-LANCY
CHEVAGNES
Beaulon
Chalmoux
Grandchamp
GUEUGNON
Neuvy
St-Aubin-s.-Loire
Gilly-s.-Loire
Diou
DOMPIERRE-S.-BESBRE
Thiel-s.-Acolin
Pierrefitte-s.-Loire
Coulanges
DIGOIN
PARAY-LE-MONIAL
Rigny-s.-Arroux
St-Vincent-Bragny
Chassy
Vendenesse-s.-Arroux
la Chapelle-au-Mans
Vitry-s.-Loire
Gannay-s.-Loire
Lamenay-s.-Loire
St-Hilaire-Fontaine
Charbonnat
Dettey
Montmort
Etang-s.-Arroux
St-Didier-s.-Arroux
St-Nizier-s.-Arroux
Thil-s.-Arroux
la Comelle
la Grande-Verrière
St-Prix
Roussillon-en-Morvan
la Petite-Verrière
la Celle-en-Morvan
FORÊT DE VINCENCE
MORVAN
103
118
135
N 81
N 79
D 973
D 994
D 979
D 60
D 985

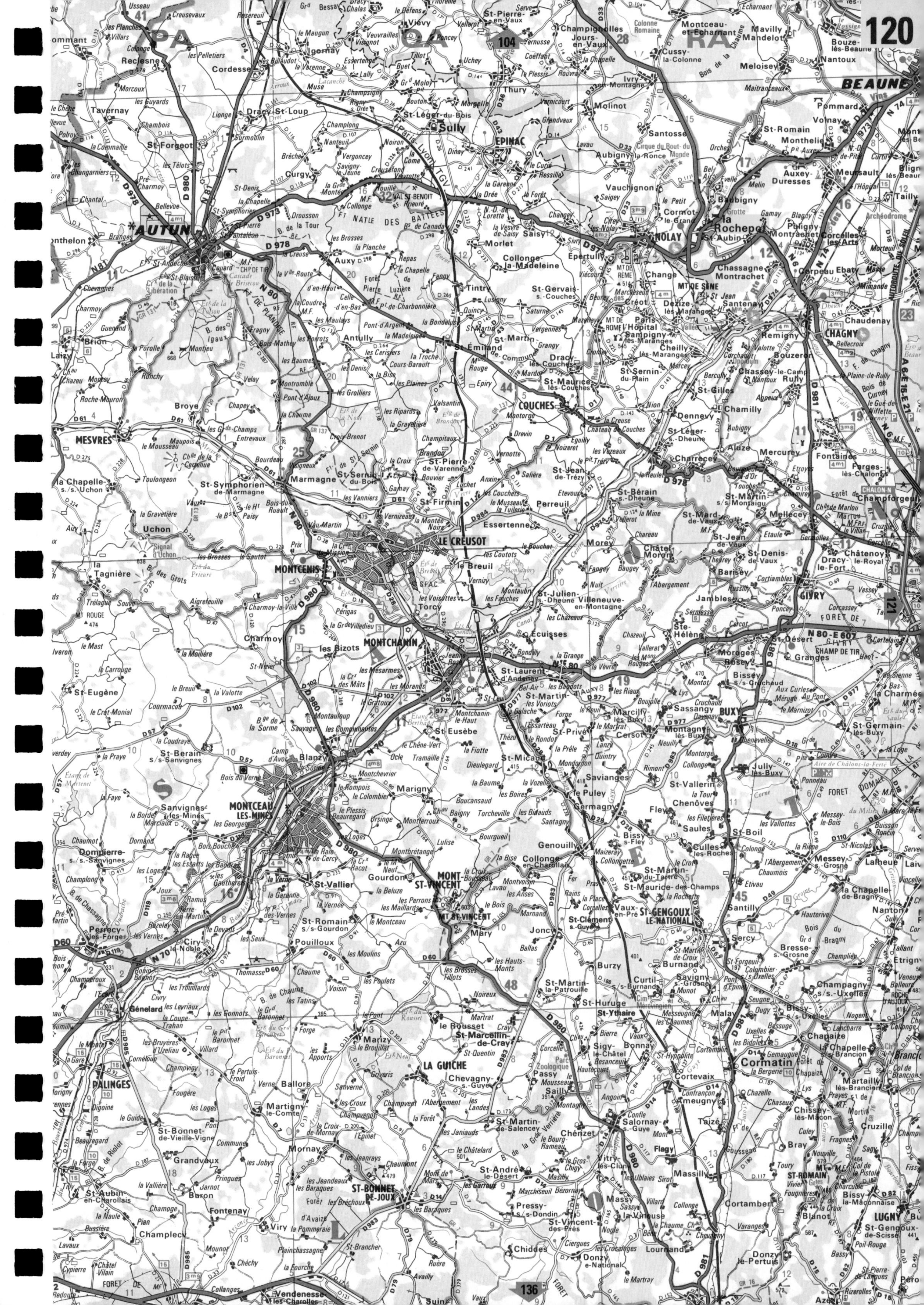
BEAUNE
AUTUN
EPINAC
Sully
NOLAY
la Rochepot
CHAGNY
COUCHES
LE CREUSOT
MONTCENIS
MONTCHANIN
MESVRES
GIVRY
BUXY
MONTCEAU-LES-MINES
MONT-ST-VINCENT
ST-GENGOUX-LE-NATIONAL
LA GUICHE
PALINGES
Cormatin
ST-BONNET-DE-JOUX
LUGNY
Génelard
Uchon
Santenay
Pommard
Volnay
Meursault
Mercurey
Marmagne
St-Symphorien-de-Marmagne
Blanzy
Perrecy-les-Forges
Ciry-le-Noble
Sanvignes-les-Mines
St-Vallier
Gourdon
Toulon-sur-Arroux
Chalon-N
104
136
121

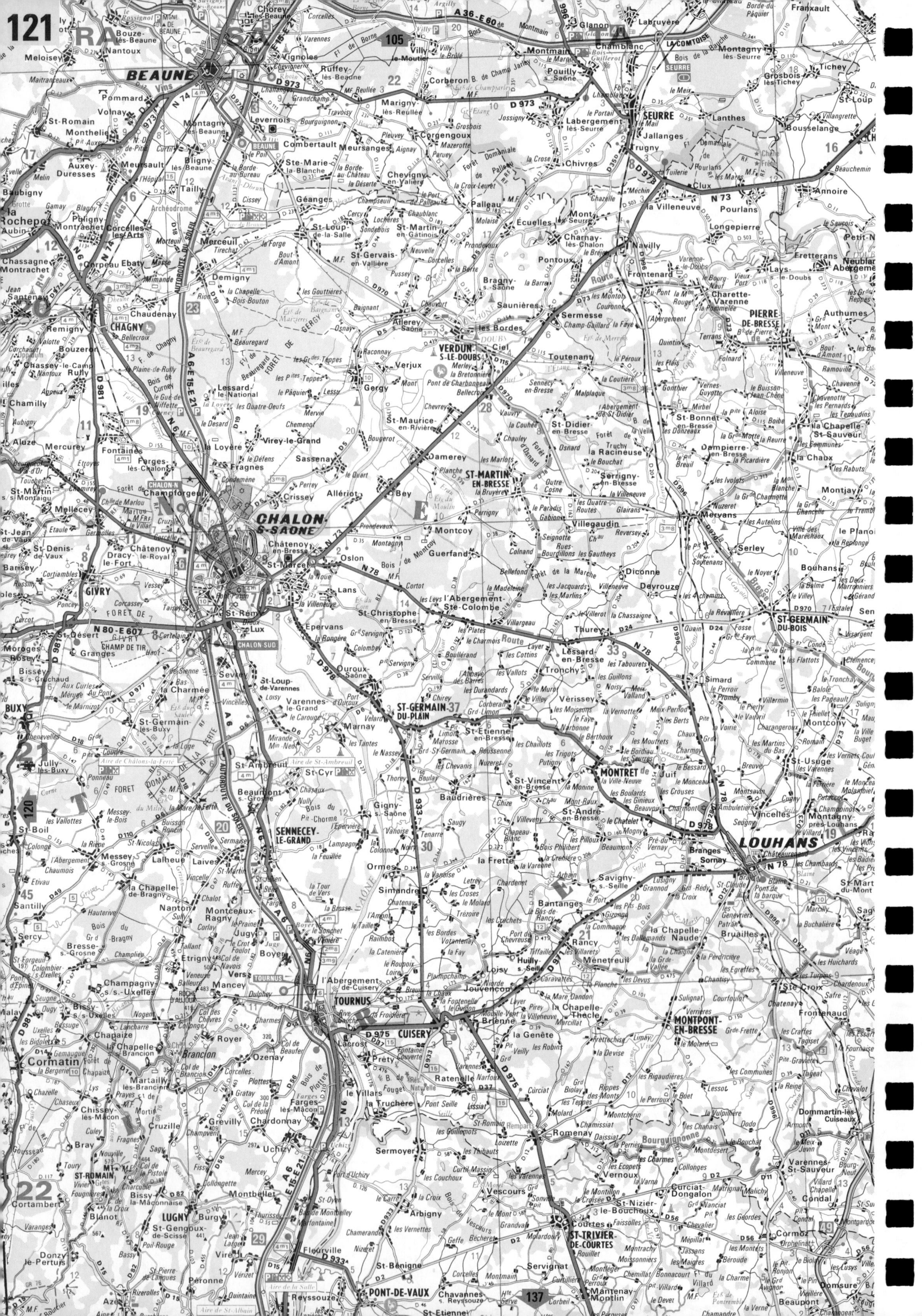

BEAUNE
CHALON-S-SAONE
LOUHANS
TOURNUS
SEURRE
VERDUN-S-LE-DOUBS
PIERRE-DE-BRESSE
ST-GERMAIN-DU-BOIS
ST-GERMAIN-DU-PLAIN
ST-MARTIN-EN-BRESSE
SENNECEY-LE-GRAND
MONTRET
MONTPONT-EN-BRESSE
CUISERY
ST-TRIVIER-DE-COURTES
PONT-DE-VAUX
CHAGNY
GIVRY
BUXY
LUGNY
ST-ROMAIN
Cormatin
Brancion
Chalon-sur-Saône
Mâcon
Nolay
A 36 - E 60
A 6 - E 15 - E 21
AUTOROUTE DU SOLEIL
N 6
N 73
N 78
N 80 - E 607
D 973
D 975
D 970
D 978
D 933
D 996
FORÊT DE GERGY
FORÊT DE GIVRY
CHAMP DE TIR
Aire de Beaune
Aire de Châlons-la-Ferté
Aire de St-Ambreuil
Aire de la Salle
Aire de St-Albain
CHALON SUD
CHALON-N
TOURNUS
105
120
137

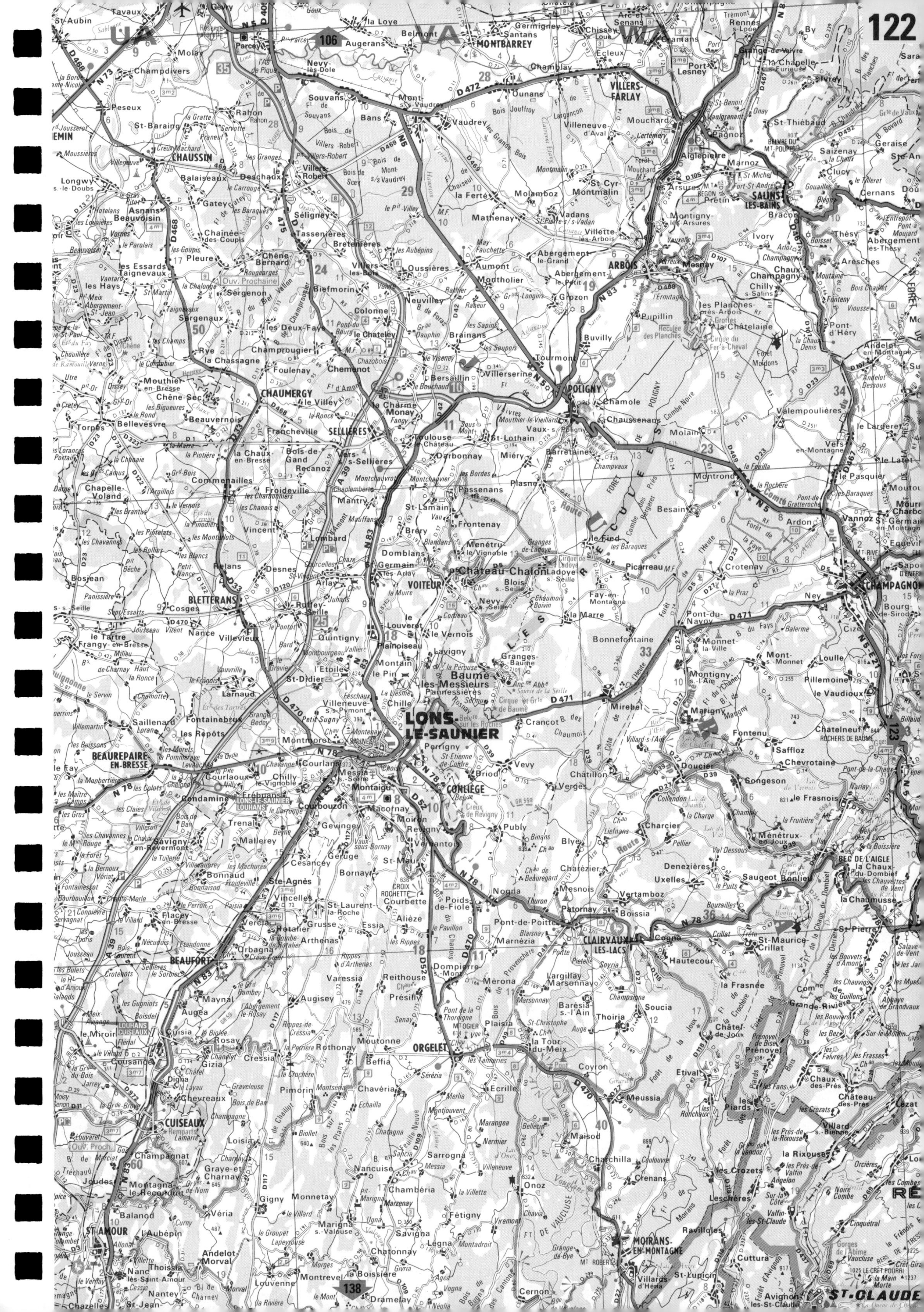
106
138
123
MONTBARREY
VILLERS-FARLAY
SALINS-LES-BAINS
ARBOIS
POLIGNY
CHAUSSIN
CHAUMERGY
SELLIÈRES
BLETTERANS
VOITEUR
Château-Chalon
Baume-les-Messieurs
LONS-LE-SAUNIER
CONLIÈGE
BEAUREPAIRE-EN-BRESSE
BEAUFORT
CUISEAUX
ST-AMOUR
ORGELET
CLAIRVAUX-LES-LACS
MOIRANS-EN-MONTAGNE
CHAMPAGNOLE
BEC DE L'AIGLE
ST-CLAUDE
LOUHANS
Chamblay
Mouchard
Vaudrey
Mont-s/s-Vaudrey
Tourmont
Mirebel
Doucier
Marigny
Saffloz
Pont-du-Navoy
Crotenay
Vevy
Pont-de-Poitte
Marnézia
Dompierre-s.-Mont
Augisey
Rothonay
Chavéria
St-Maurice-Crillat
Prénovel
Les Piards
Ravilloles
Villards-d'Héria
Cuttura
St-Lupicin
Lavans-les-St-Claude
Beffia
Sarrogna
Nancuise
Chambéria
Fétigny
Légna
Savigna
Chatonnay
La Boissière
Dramelay
Gigny
Monnetay
Montrevel
Louvenne
Andelot-Morval
Balanod
Nanc-lès-St-Amour
Thoissia
Nantey
St-Jean
Chazelles
Courlans
Chilly-le-Vignoble
Messia-s.-Sorne
Montaigu
Macornay
Perrigny
Briod
Vernantois
Nogna
Poids-de-Fiole
Publy
Chatillon
Verges
Revigny
Moiron
Gevingey
Trenal
Courbouzon
Frébuans
Condamine
Savigny-en-Revermont
Bonnaud
Flacey-en-Bresse
Cousance
Gizia
Digna
Rosay
Maynal
Augea
Loisia
Champagnat
Graye-et-Charnay
Montagna-le-Reconduit
Véria
L'Aubépin

XA
YA
107
Bolandoz
Amathay-Vésigneux
Renédale
Ouhans
Bugny
MONTBENOIT
Déservillers
Septfontaines
Nans-s-Ste-Anne
Goux-les-Usiers
Bians-les-Usiers
LEVIER
Sombacour
Gevresin
Crouzet-Migette
Ste-Anne
Villeneuve-d'Amont
Chapelle-d'Huin
Vuillecin
Dommartin
Houtaud
Chaffois
PONTARLIER
Doubs
Verrières-de-Joux
Bulle
Bannans
Boujailles
Dompierre-les-Tilleuls
Courvières
Ste-Colombe
Oye-et-Pallet
Frasne
Bouverans
la Rivière-Drugeon
Andelot-en-Montagne
Chapois
Cuvier
Malpas
Montperreux
Vaux-et-Chantegrue
St-Point-Lac
Censeau
Bief-du-Fourg
Bonnevaux
Malbuisson
les Hôpitaux-Vieux
Mignovillard
Labergement-Ste-Marie
St-Antoine
Métabief
Jougne
NOZEROY
Longcochon
Remoray-Boujeons
Longevilles-Mont-d'Or
Rochejean
CHAMPAGNOLE
Sirod
Gillois
Fraroz
Cerniébaud
Rondefontaine
Gellin
Sarrageois
les Pontets
les Villedieu
MOUTHE
Reculfoz
Vallorbe
Ballaigues
Romainmôtier-Envy
Crans
Syam
Bief-des-Maisons
Petite-Chaux
Chaux-Neuve
Châtelblanc
les Chalesmes
Foncine-le-Haut
Foncine-le-Bas
LES PLANCHES-EN-MONTAGNE
Entre-deux-Monts
le Lieu
l'Abbaye
le Sentier
FORÊT DU MONT NOIR
MONT RISOUX
Chapelle-des-Bois
Montricher
ST-LAURENT-EN-GRANDVAUX
Bellefontaine
Bois-d'Amont
VALLÉE DE JOUX
Morbier
MOREZ
Bière
St-George
Gimel
AUBONNE
Rolle
les Rousses
PARC
RÉGIONAL
Prémanon
St-Cergue
Gingins
Chéserex
Trélex
Nyon
Gland
Vich
Coinsins
Begnins
Lamoura
ST-CLAUDE
139
LA DOLE
THONON-LES-BAINS

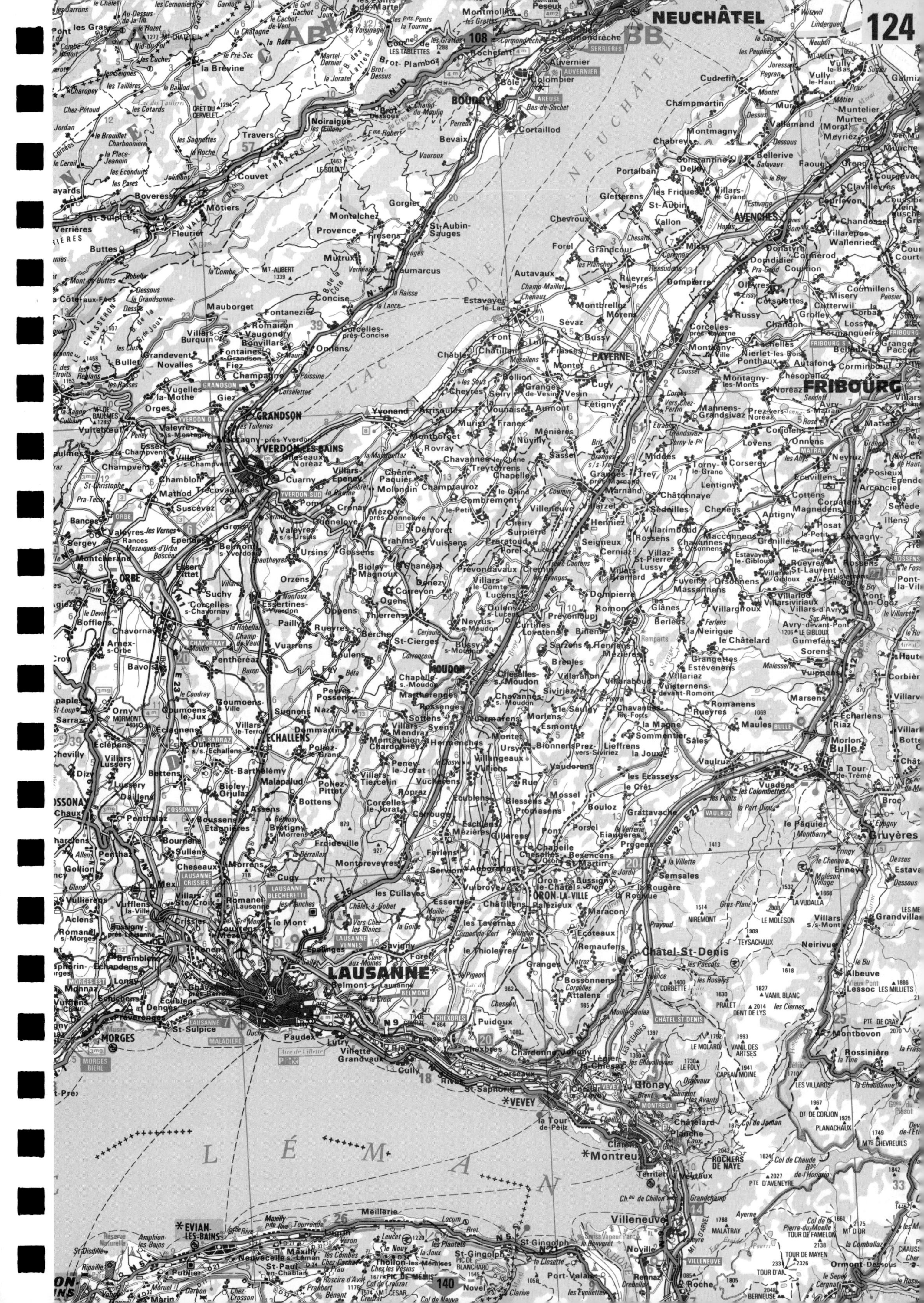
NEUCHÂTEL
LAC DE NEUCHÂTEL
YVERDON-LES-BAINS
GRANDSON
ORBE
ESTAVAYER-le-Lac
PAYERNE
AVENCHES
FRIBOURG
MOUDON
ECHALLENS
ORON-LA-VILLE
LAUSANNE
MORGES
VEVEY
Montreux
Châtel-St-Denis
Bulle
Gruyères
Romont
LÉMAN
EVIAN-LES-BAINS
Villeneuve
St-Gingolph
Fleurier
Couvet
Travers
Boudry
Cortaillod
Bevaix
Sainte-Croix
La Sarraz
Cossonay
Cully
Blonay
Vaulruz
Rossinière
Montbovon
140
108

LES SABLES-D'OLONNE
LUÇON
MAREUIL-S.-LAY-DISSAIS
MOUTIERS-LES-M.
TALMONT-ST-HILAIRE
LA MOTHE-ACHARD
STE-HERMINE
CHAILLÉ-LES-M.
MARANS
l'Aiguillon-s.-Mer
la Faute-s.-Mer
la Tranche-s.-Mer
Longeville-s.-Mer
St-Vincent-sur-J.
Jard s.-M.
Olonne-s.-Mer
Château-d'O.
l'Île-d'Olonne
Vairé
Avrillé
Angles
Triaize
St-Michel-en-l'Herm
Grues
St-Denis-du-Payré
Champagné-les-Marais
Puyravault
Ste-Radegonde-des-Noyers
Nalliers
Mouzeuil-St-Martin
Ste-Gemme-la-Plaine
St-Aubin-la-Plaine
St-Jean-de-Beugné
Thorigny
les Pineaux
Château-Guibert
Moutiers-s.-le-Lay
Ste-Pexine
la Couture
la Bretonnière
Rosnay
Chaillé-s/s-les-Ormeaux
Nesmy
Aubigny
les Clouzeaux
St-Florent-des-Bois
la Boissière-des-Landes
Grosbreuil
Ste-Foy
St-Mathurin
la Chapelle-Achard
Ste-Flaive-des-Loups
St-Cyr-en-Talmondais
Curzon
la Jonchère
St-Benoist-s.-Mer
Moricq
Esnandes
Marsilly
Andilly
Villedoux
Charron
Ars-en-Ré
les Portes-en-Ré
St-Clément-des-Baleines
Loix
PERTUIS BRETON
Fosse de Chevarache
Banc du Grouin du Cou
ANSE DE L'AIGUILLON
MARAIS POIT
Baie de Cayola
Forêt d'Olonne
Phare des Barges
Pte de l'Aiguille
Plage du Veillon
Pte du Payré
Rade de St-Martin
Réserve ornithologique
Réserve naturelle
Ouv. été 1999
N. 137 - E 3
D 949
D 746
N. 137
109
110
111

LA ROCHELLE
*ROCHEFORT
ILE DE RÉ*
ILE
D' OLÉRON*
PERTUIS D' ANTIOCHE
PERTUIS DE MAUMUSSON
RADE DES BASQUES
ANSE DE FOURAS
Rade des Trousses
Ile d'Aix
Fouras
Châtelaillon-Plage
AYTRÉ
*MARENNES
LE CHATEAU-D'OLÉRON
St PIERRE
St MARTIN-de-RÉ
Ste-Marie-de-Ré
St Denis
St Georges
Dolus-d'Oléron
Marennes-Plage
PLATEAU DE CHARDONNIÈRE
Ph. de Chassiron
Rocher d'Antioche
Plateau d'Angoulins
la Grande Plage
127
141

125
111
MARAIS POITEVIN
Triaize
Champagné-les-Marais
Puyravault
CHAILLÉ-LES-M.
Vouillé-les-Marais
Vix
Montreuil
Doix
Chalais
Maillezais
Ste Radegonde des Noyers
le Gué-de-Velluire
l'Ile d'Elle
Maillé
Damvix
St-Sigismond
Ste-Christine
Liez
Arçais
le Vanneau
Pont du Brault
Bas-Bizet
MARANS
Charron
ANSE DE L'AIGUILLON
Réserve ornithologique
Taugon
la Ronde
Esnandes
Villedoux
Andilly
Marsilly
Nieul-s.-Mer
St-Jean-de-Liversay
Courçon
St-Sauveur-d'Aunis
Ferrières
Nuaillé-d'A.
Benon
Forêt de Benon
Mauzé-s.-le-Mignon
St-Hilaire-la-Palud
Amuré
St-Georges-de-Rex
St Xandre
Lagord
Puilboreau
Dompierre-s.-Mer
LA ROCHELLE
Aytré
Angoulins
Châtelaillon-Plage
la Jarne
La Jarrie
Aigrefeuille d'Aunis
Surgères
Vouhé
Puyravault
St-Georges-du-Bois
St-Saturnin-du-Bois
St-Pierre-d'Amilly
Rade des Basques
Ile d'Aix
Fouras
Yves
Ballon
Ciré-d'Aunis
Ardillières
Muron
Vandré
Genouillé
Chervettes
St-Laurent-de-la-Barrière
St-Crépin
Annezay
Breuil-Magné
Ile Madame
ROCHEFORT
Tonnay-Charente
Tonnay-Boutonne
Puy-du-Lac
St-Coutant-le-Grand
Archingeay
Bignay
St-Nazaire-sur-C.
Soubise
Moëze
Échillais
St-Hippolyte
Champdolent
Le Château-d'Oléron
Bourcefranc-le-Chapus
Marennes
Beaugeay
St-Agnant
Trizay
Beurlay
St-Savinien
Romegoux
Ste-Radegonde
la Roche-Courbon
St-Porchaire
Pont-l'Abbé-d'Arnoult
Taillebourg
Annepont
St-Just-Luzac
St-Sulpice-d'Arnoult
St-Vaize
141

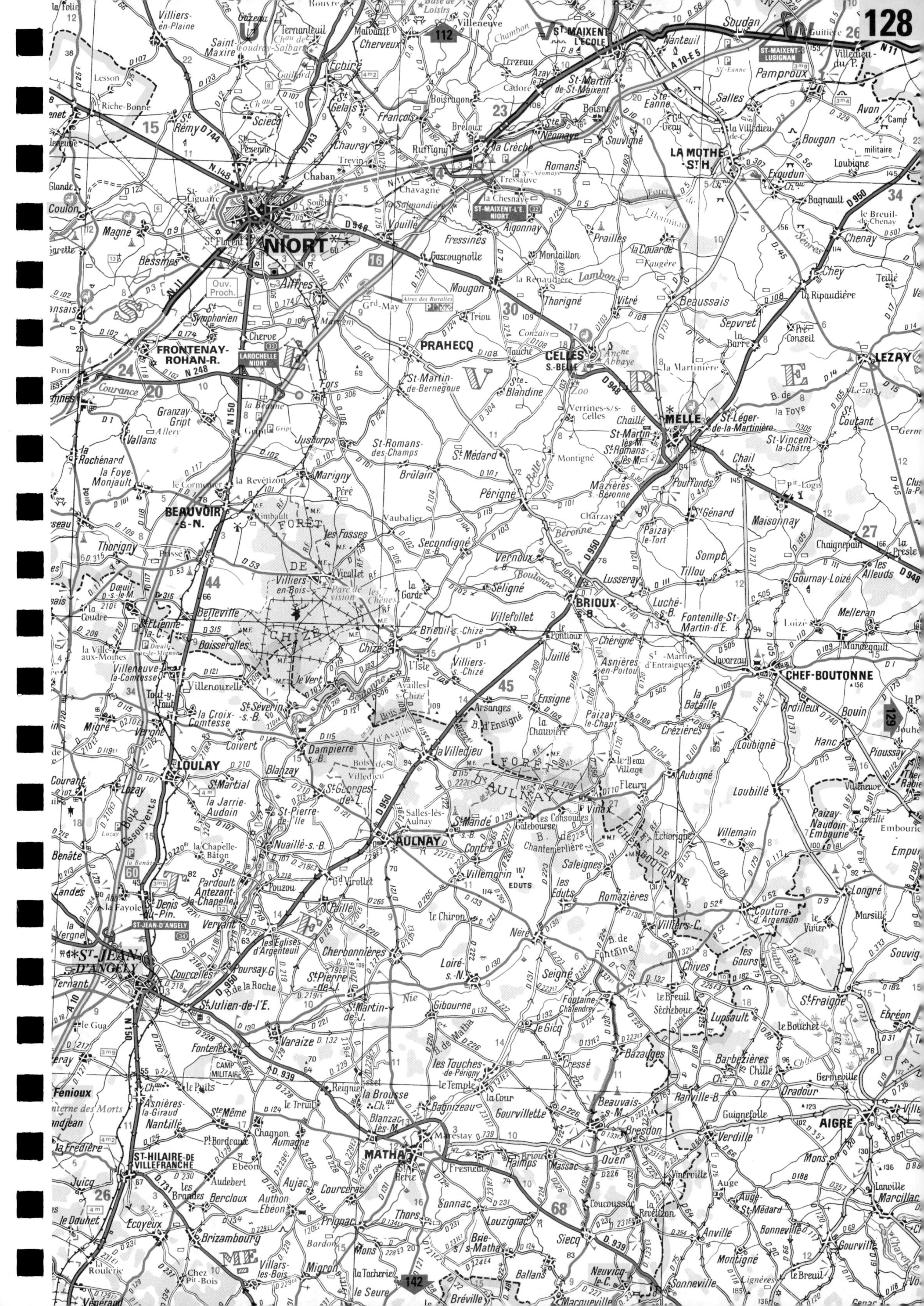

NIORT
St-MAIXENT-L'ÉCOLE
FRONTENAY-ROHAN-R.
PRAHECQ
CELLES-S.-BELLE
MELLE
LA MOTHE-St-H.
LEZAY
BEAUVOIR-s-N.
BRIOUX-S-B.
CHEF-BOUTONNE
LOULAY
AULNAY
St-JEAN-D'ANGÉLY
MATHA
AIGRE
St-HILAIRE-DE-VILLEFRANCHE
FORÊT DE CHIZÉ
FORÊT D'AULNAY
FORÊT DE CHEF-BOUTONNE
Villiers-en-Plaine
Saint-Maxire
Échiré
Cherveux
Chauray
La Crèche
Aiffres
Mougon
Thorigné
Vitré
Beaussais
Sepvret
Pamproux
Soudan
Exoudun
Chenay
Marigny
Brûlain
Périgné
Secondigné-s.-B.
Chizé
Villiers-en-Bois
Vernoux-s.-B.
Séligné
Lusseray
Sompt
Tillou
Juillé
Chérigné
Ensigné
Paizay-le-Chapt
Crézières
Loubigné
Loubillé
Villemain
Couture-d'Argenson
Villiers-C.
Les Gours
Chives
Lupsault
Barbezières
Oradour
Verdille
Bresdon
Massac
St-Ouen
Beauvais-s.-M.
Bazauges
Cressé
Gourvillette
Les Touches-de-Périgny
Sonnac
Thors
Prignac
Brie-s-Matha
Louzignac
Siecq
Neuvicq-le-C.
Sonneville
Ballans
Bréville
Migron
Villars-les-Bois
Brizambourg
Écoyeux
Authon-Ébéon
Bercloux
Aujac
Courcerac
Blanzac-lès-M.
Nantillé
Asnières-la-Giraud
Varaize
Fontenet
St-Julien-de-l'E.
Courcelles
Poursay-G.
Les Églises-d'Argenteuil
Cherbonnières
Loiré-s.-N.
Néré
Seigné
Villemorin
Saleignes
Romazières
Contré
Salles-lès-Aulnay
St-Mandé
Vinax
Fleury
Aubigné
La Villedieu
Dampierre-s.-B.
Blanzay
St-Georges-de-L.
Nuaillé-s.-B.
St-Pierre-de-l'Isle
La Jarrie-Audoin
St-Martial
Lozay
Coivert
Vergné
Migré
La Croix-Comtesse
St-Séverin-s.-B.
Villenouvelle
Villeneuve-la-Comtesse
Boisserolles
Belleville
St-Étienne-la-C.
Dœuil-s-le-M.
Vallans
Granzay-Gript
Magné
Coulon
Bessines
Thorigny
Prissé
St-Martin-de-Bernegoue
Ste-Blandine
St-Romans-des-Champs
St-Médard
Juscorps
Fors
Vouillé
Fressines
Aigonnay
Prailles
La Couarde
Chey
Pouffonds
St-Génard
Maisonnay
Chaignepain
Les Alleuds
Gournay-Loizé
Melleran
Mairé-Levescault
Hanc
Pioussay
Paizay-Naudoin-Embourie
Longré
Souvigné
St-Fraigne
Ébréon
Le Bouchet
Germeville
Marcillac
Gourville
Bonneville
Anville
Auge-St-Médard
Mons

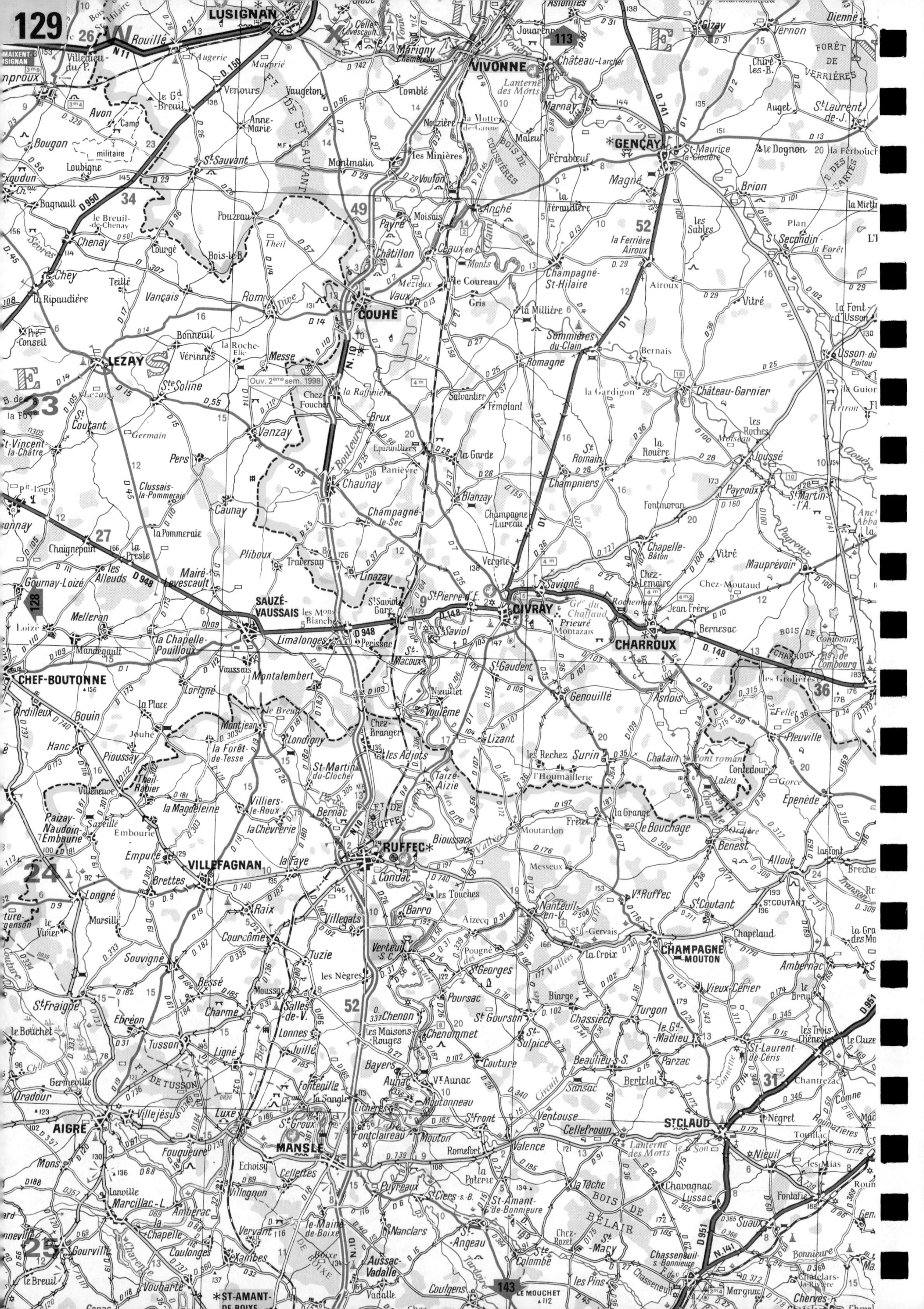
LUSIGNAN
Rouillé
VIVONNE
Château-Larcher
Gizay
Vernon
Dienné
FORÊT DE VERRIÈRES
Lanterne des Morts
Marnay
Vaugeton
Venours
Comblé
St-Laurent-de-J.
GENÇAY
St-Maurice-la-Clouère
le Dognon
Avon
Bougon
Loubigne
St-Sauvant
Montmalin
les Minières
Voulon
Brion
Pouzeau
Payré
Anché
Magné
Chenay
Châtillon
Champagné-St-Hilaire
la Ferrière-Airoux
Chey
Teillé
Vançais
Rom
COUHÉ
Vaux
la Millière
Sommières-du-Clain
la Ripaudière
LEZAY
Bonneuil
Vérinnes
Messe
Romagne
Usson-du-Poitou
Ste-Soline
Château-Garnier
Vanzay
Brux
la Garde
St-Romain
Joussé
Pers
Chaunay
Blanzay
Champniers
Payroux
Caunay
Champagné-le-Sec
Chapelle-Bâton
Vitré
Mauprévoir
Pliboux
Traversay
Linazay
Vergné
Savigné
Mairé-Levescault
SAUZÉ-VAUSSAIS
St-Pierre-d'E.
CIVRAY
Prieuré Montazais
CHARROUX
Gournay-Loizé
Melleran
la Chapelle-Pouilloux
Limalonges
St-Saviol
Bernesac
CHEF-BOUTONNE
Montalembert
St-Gaudent
Genouillé
Asnois
Lorigné
Voulême
Pleuville
Bouin
Londigny
Lizant
Surin
Chatain
Hanc
Pioussay
les Adjots
Taizé-Aizie
Epenède
Villiers-le-Roux
la Magdeleine
Bernac
la Chèvrerie
le Bouchage
Benest
RUFFEC
Bioussac
Alloue
Empuré
VILLEFAGNAN
Condac
Longré
Raix
Villegats
Nanteuil-en-V.
St-Coutant
Courcôme
Tuzie
Verteuil-s.-C.
CHAMPAGNE-MOUTON
Souvigné
Bessé
St-Georges
Ambernac
St-Fraigne
Ebréon
Charmé
Salles-de-V.
Chenon
Poursac
St-Gourson
Chassiecq
Turgon
Vieux-Cérier
Tusson
Lonnes
Juillé
Chenommet
Couture
St-Laurent-de-Céris
Fontenille
Aunac
Moutonneau
Parzac
Chantrezac
AIGRE
Villejésus
Luxé
St-Groux
St-Front
Ventouse
ST-CLAUD
MANSLE
Fontclaireau
Mouton
Cellefrouin
Valence
Nieuil
Fouqueure
Cellettes
Romefort
Lanterne des Morts
Mons
Villognon
Puyréaux
St-Ciers-s.-B.
St-Amant-de-Bonnieure
la Tâche
Chavagnac
Lussac
Marcillac-L.
Ambérac
Vervant
Nanclars
St-Angeau
BOIS DE BELAIR
Suaux
Gourville
Coulonges
Xambes
Aussac-Vadalle
Ste-Colombe
St-Mary
Chasseneuil-s.-Bonnieure
Vouharte
ST-AMANT-DE-BOIXE
Coulgens
LE MOUCHET
les Pins
Margnac
Cherves
Ouv. 2ème sem. 1998
113
128
143

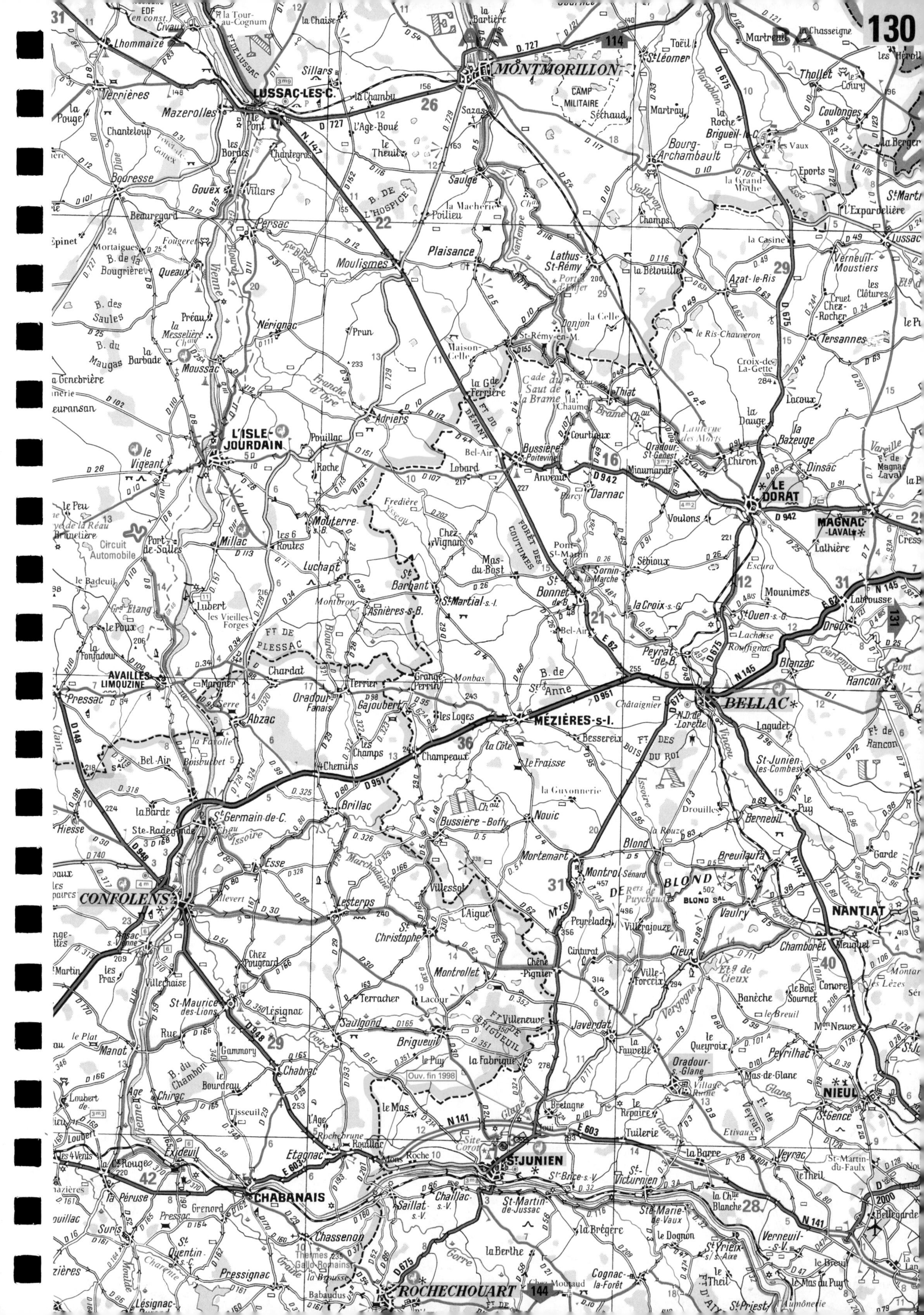
130
MONTMORILLON
LUSSAC-LES-C.
Lhommaizé
Civaux
Sillars
la Chaise
Verrières
Mazerolles
la Pouge
Chanteloup
Gouex
Villars
Persac
Queaux
Moulismes
Plaisance
Saulgé
Lathus-St-Rémy
Bourg-Archambault
St Léomer
Tersannes
Azat-le-Ris
Thollet
Coulonges
Eports
Nérignac
Moussac
Adriers
L'ISLE-JOURDAIN
le Vigeant
Millac
Mouterre-s-B.
Luchapt
St Barbant
St Martial-s.-I.
Asnières-s-B.
Bussière Poitevine
Darnac
Thiat
LE DORAT
Dinsac
MAGNAC-LAVAL
Lathière
St Bonnet-de-B.
Peyrat-de-B.
BELLAC
Blanzac
Rancon
Availles-Limouzine
Pressac
Abzac
Oradour-Fanais
Mézières-s-I.
Brillac
St Germain-de-C.
CONFOLENS
Esse
Lesterps
St Christophe
Bussière-Boffy
Nouic
Mortemart
Montrol-Sénard
Blond
Vaulry
Cieux
Nantiat
Chamboret
Javerdat
Oradour-s-Glane
Nieul
Saulgond
Brigueuil
Chabrac
Chirac
Exideuil
CHABANAIS
Etagnac
Saillat-s.-V.
Chaillac-s.-V.
ST JUNIEN
St Brice-s-V.
St Victurnien
Chassenon
ROCHECHOUART
Cognac-la-Forêt
St Martin-de-Jussac
Verneuil-s.-V.
Veyrac
St Gence
Pressignac
St Quentin-s.-C.
Suris
la Péruse
Lésignac
Ouv. fin 1998
114
131
144

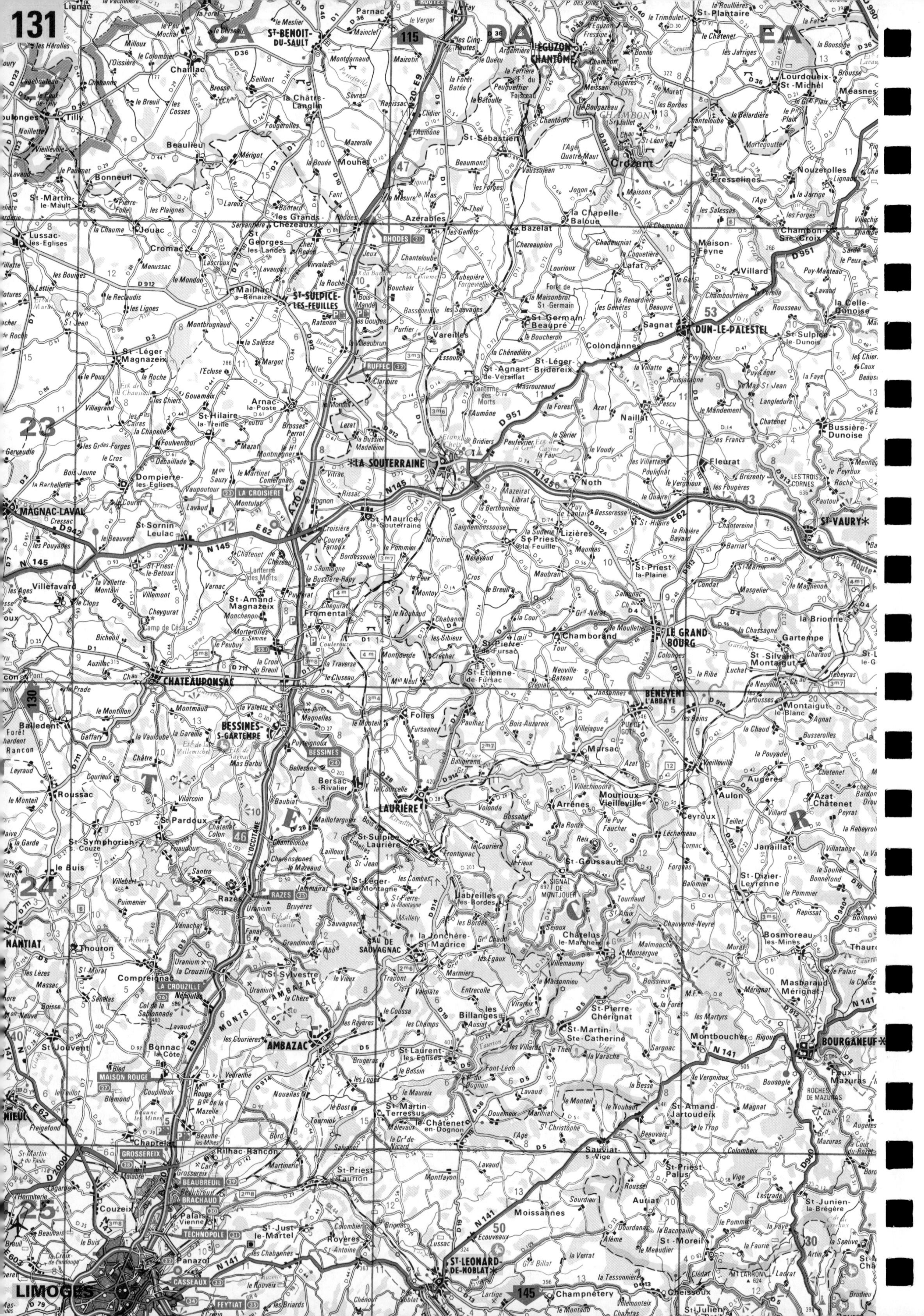

ST-BENOIT-DU-SAULT
Parnac
115
ÉGUZON-CHANTÔME
St-Plantaire
Chaillac
Tilly
Beaulieu
Bonneuil
la Châtre-Langlin
Mouhet
Vaussujean
Crozant
Fresselines
Lourdoueix-St-Michel
Méasnes
Nouzerolles
Lussac-les-Eglises
Jouac
Cromac
St-Georges-les-Landes
les Grands-Chézeaux
Azerables
Bazelat
Maison-Feyne
Chambon-Ste-Croix
Mailhac-s-Benaize
ST-SULPICE-LES-FEUILLES
Vareilles
St-Germain-Beaupré
Sagnat
DUN-LE-PALESTEL
la Celle-Dunoise
St-Léger-Magnazeix
St-Agnant-de-Versillat
St-Léger-Bridereix
Colondannes
St-Sulpice-le-Dunois
Arnac-la-Poste
St-Hilaire-la-Treille
Naillat
Bussière-Dunoise
Dompierre-les-Eglises
LA SOUTERRAINE
Fleurat
MAGNAC-LAVAL
St-Maurice-la-Souterraine
Noth
ST-VAURY
St-Sornin-Leulac
St-Priest-la-Feuille
St-Priest-la-Plaine
Villefavard
St-Amand-Magnazeix
Fromental
LE GRAND BOURG
Chamborand
St-Pierre-de-Fursac
St-Etienne-de-Fursac
Gartempe
St-Silvain-Montaigut
CHÂTEAUPONSAC
BESSINES-S-GARTEMPE
Folles
BÉNÉVENT-L'ABBAYE
Montaigut-le-Blanc
Balledent
Rancon
Roussac
Bersac-s-Rivalier
LAURIÈRE
Marsac
Arrênes
Mourioux-Vieilleville
Vieilleville
Aulon
Augères
Azat-Châtenet
St-Pardoux
St-Symphorien
St-Sulpice-Laurière
Ceyroux
Janaillat
Razès
St-Léger-la-Montagne
St-Goussaud
Jabreilles-les-Bordes
St-Dizier-Leyrenne
NANTIAT
Thouron
la Jonchère-St-Maurice
Châtelus-le-Marcheix
Bosmoreau-les-Mines
Compreignac
St-Sylvestre
Masbaraud-Mérignat
AMBAZAC
les Billanges
St-Pierre-Chérignat
St-Martin-Ste-Catherine
Montboucher
BOURGANEUF
St-Jouvent
Bonnac-la-Côte
St-Laurent-les-Eglises
Faux-Mazuras
St-Martin-Terressus
le Châtenet-en-Dognon
St-Amand-Jartoudeix
Chaptelat
Rilhac-Rancon
St-Priest-Taurion
Sauviat-s-Vige
St-Priest-Palus
Couzeix
Moissannes
Auriat
St-Junien-la-Brégère
St-Just-le-Martel
Royères
ST-LÉONARD-DE-NOBLAT
St-Moreil
LIMOGES
Panazol
Champnétery
Cheissoux
St-Julien

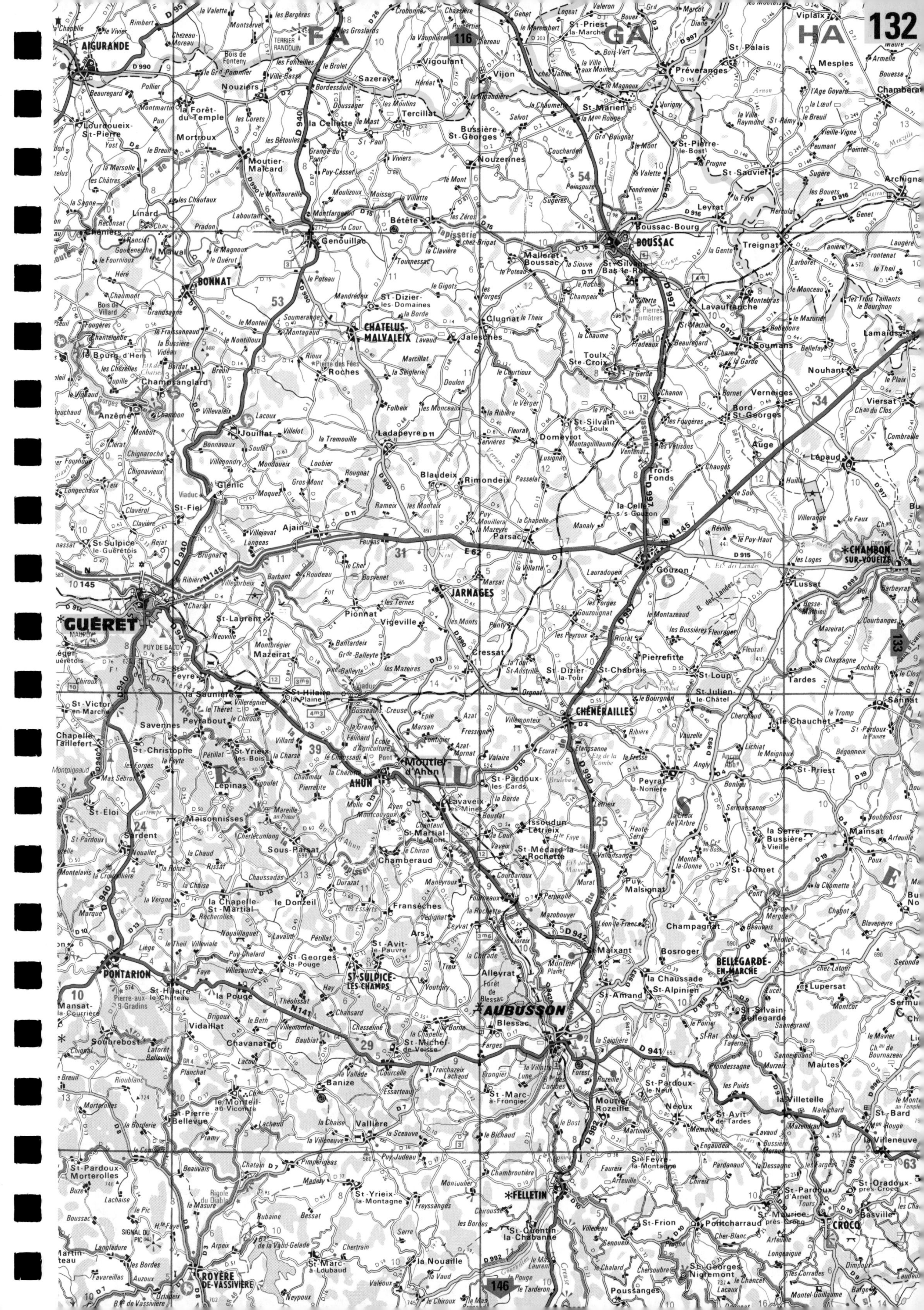
FA
GA
HA
AIGURANDE
Nouziers
Vigoulant
Vijon
Préveranges
St-Priest la-Marche
St-Palais
Mesples
Chambérat
La Forêt-du-Temple
La Cellette
Tercillat
Bussière-St-Georges
St-Marien
St-Pierre-le-Bost
Mortroux
Moutier-Malcard
Nouzerines
St-Sauvier
Archignat
Lourdoueix-St-Pierre
Linard
Bétête
Genouillac
Boussac-Bourg
BOUSSAC
Leyrat
Treignat
Malleret-Boussac
St-Silvain-Bas-le-Roc
BONNAT
St-Dizier-les-Domaines
CHATELUS-MALVALEIX
Clugnat
Jalesches
Lavaufranche
Soumans
Lamaids
Toulx-Ste-Croix
Champsanglard
Roches
Nouhant
Anzême
Jouillat
Ladapeyre
St-Silvain-s/s-Toulx
Domeyrot
Bord-St-Georges
Verneiges
Viersat
Auge
Lépaud
Glénic
Blaudeix
Rimondeix
Trois-Fonds
St-Fiel
Ajain
Parsac
la Celle-s/s-Gouzon
St-Sulpice-le-Guérétois
Gouzon
CHAMBON-SUR-VOUEIZE
GUÉRET
JARNAGES
Pionnat
Vigeville
St-Laurent
Lussat
Mazeirat
Cressat
St-Dizier-la-Tour
St-Chabrais
Pierrefitte
St-Loup
Tardes
Ste-Feyre
St-Hilaire-la-Plaine
Busseau-s-Creuse
St-Julien-le-Châtel
CHÉNÉRAILLES
Savennes
St-Christophe
Peyrabout
St-Yrieix-les-Bois
Moutier-d'Ahun
AHUN
St-Pardoux-les-Cards
Peyrat-la-Nonière
St-Priest
Lépinas
Lavaveix-les-Mines
Issoudun-Létrieix
Mainsat
Maisonnisses
St-Martial-le-Mont
St-Médard-la-Rochette
Sardent
Sous-Parsat
Chamberaud
Puy-Malsignat
St-Domet
La Chapelle-St-Martial
le Donzeil
Fransèches
Champagnat
St-Avit-le-Pauvre
Ars
St-Maixant
Bosroger
BELLEGARDE-EN-MARCHE
PONTARION
St-Georges-la-Pouge
ST-SULPICE-LES-CHAMPS
Alleyrat
St-Alpinien
St-Amand
Lupersat
St-Hilaire-le-Château
AUBUSSON
Blessac
Vidaillat
Soubrebost
Chavanat
St-Michel-de-Veisse
Mautes
Banize
St-Marc-à-Frongier
St-Pardoux-le-Neuf
Moutier-Rozeille
Néoux
St-Avit-de-Tardes
St-Bard
Vallière
St-Pierre-Bellevue
la Villeneuve
St-Pardoux-Morterolles
Ste-Feyre-la-Montagne
St-Yrieix-la-Montagne
FELLETIN
St-Pardoux-d'Arnet
St-Oradoux-près-Crocq
St-Maurice-près-Crocq
CROCQ
Basville
St-Quentin-la-Chabanne
St-Frion
Pontcharraud
St-Marc-à-Loubaud
La Nouaille
ROYÈRE-DE-VASSIVIÈRE
St-Georges-Nigremont
Poussanges
116
146
133
63

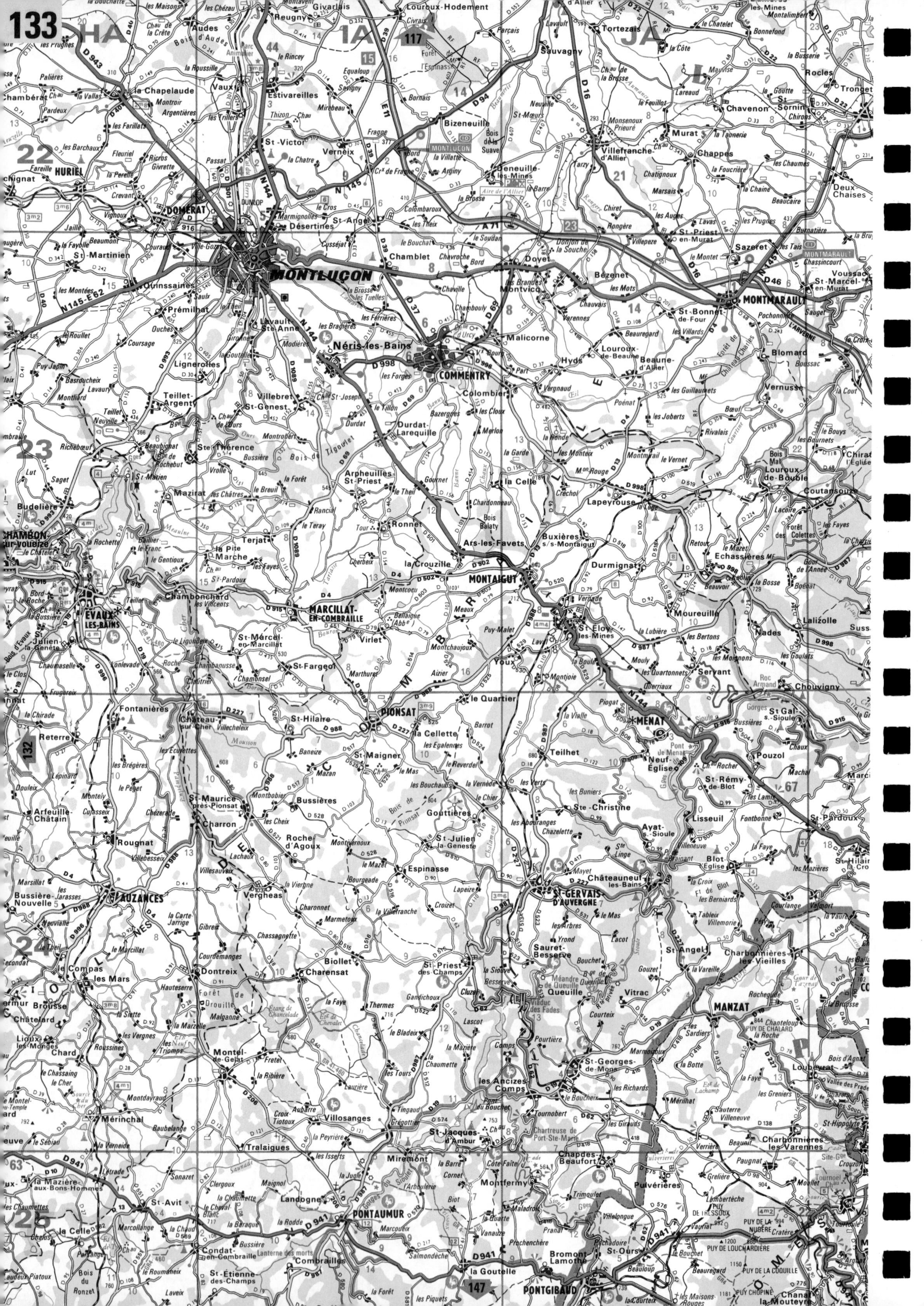

Audes
Givarlais
Reugny
Louroux-Hodement
Tortezais
Sauvagny
la Chapelaude
Vaux
Estivareilles
Bizeneuille
St-Victor
Verneix
Villefranche-d'Allier
Murat
Chappes
Deneuille-les-Mines
Huriel
Domérat
Désertines
St-Angel
Chamblet
Montluçon
Doyet
Bézenet
Montmarault
St-Martinien
Quinssaines
Prémilhat
Lavault-Ste-Anne
Néris-les-Bains
Commentry
Malicorne
Hyds
Beaune-d'Allier
Blomard
Lignerolles
Villebret
Colombier
Vernusse
Teillet-Argenty
St-Genest
Durdat-Larequille
Ste-Thérence
Arpheuilles-St-Priest
la Celle
Louroux-de-Bouble
Mazirat
Lapeyrouse
Coutansouze
Budelière
Terjat
Ronnet
Ars-les-Favets
Buxières s/s-Montaigut
Échassières
Chambon-sur-Voueize
la Crouzille
Montaigut
Durmignat
Chambonchard
Marcillat-en-Combraille
St-Éloy-les-Mines
Moureuille
Évaux-les-Bains
Lalizolle
Nades
St-Marcel-en-Marcillat
Virlet
Youx
St-Fargeol
Servant
Chouvigny
Fontanières
Château-sur-Cher
St-Hilaire
Pionsat
la Cellette
Menat
Reterre
St-Maigner
Teilhet
Neuf-Église
Pouzol
Bussières
St-Rémy-de-Blot
Arfeuille-Châtain
St-Maurice-près-Pionsat
Gouttières
Ste-Christine
Charron
Lisseuil
Rougnat
Roche-d'Agoux
St-Julien-la-Geneste
Ayat-s-Sioule
Espinasse
Blot-l'Église
St-Pardoux
Auzances
Vergheas
St-Gervais-d'Auvergne
Châteauneuf-les-Bains
Saurat-Besserve
St-Angel
Charbonnières-les-Vieilles
Dontreix
Charensat
St-Priest-des-Champs
Queuille
Vitrac
Manzat
Brousse
Viaduc des Fades
Montel-de-Gelat
St-Georges-de-Mons
Loubeyrat
Mérinchal
Villosanges
Les Ancizes-Comps
Tralaigues
St-Jacques-d'Ambur
Charbonnières-les-Varennes
Miremont
Montfermy
Chapdes-Beaufort
Pulvérières
Landogne
St-Avit
Pontaumur
Condat-en-Combraille
Combrailles
Bromont-Lamothe
St-Ours
St-Étienne-des-Champs
la Goutelle
Pontgibaud
Chanat-la-Mouteyre
N 144
N 145
D 998
D 941
A 71
132
147
117

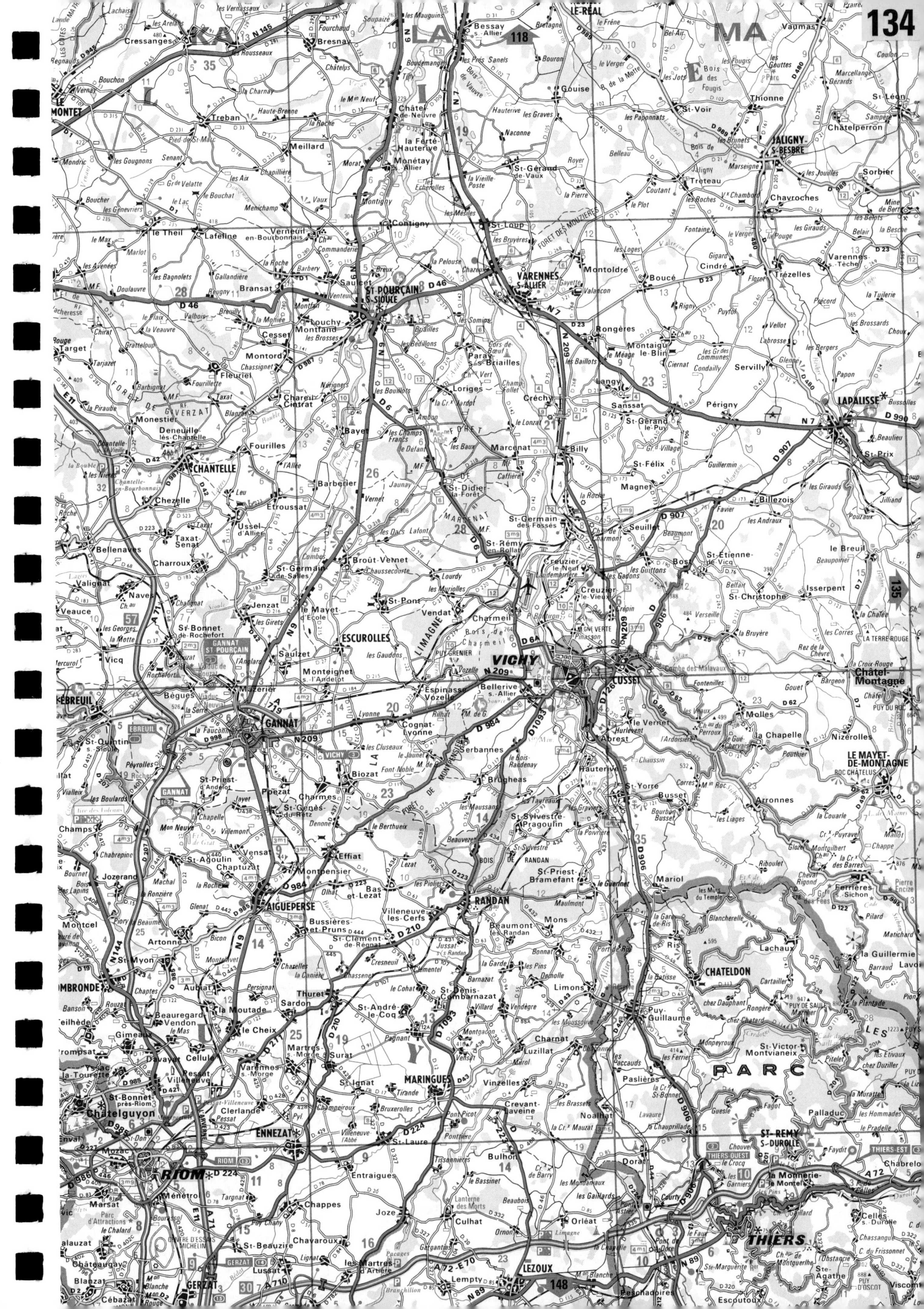

118
135
148
Cressanges
Bresnay
Bessay s-Allier
Le Réal
Vaumas
Montet
Treban
Châtel-de-Neuvre
Meillard
la Ferté-Hauterive
Monétay-s-Allier
St-Gérand-de-Vaux
Thionne
St-Voir
Jaligny-s-Besbre
St-Léon
Châtelperron
Treteau
Sorbier
Chavroches
Le Theil
Lafeline
Verneuil-en-Bourbonnais
Contigny
St-Loup
Varennes-s-Allier
Montoldre
Bouçé
Cindré
Trézelles
Varennes-s-Tèche
Bransat
Saulcet
St-Pourçain-s-Sioule
Louchy-Montfand
Cesset
Rongères
Montaigu-le-Blin
Paray-s-Briailles
Servilly
Lapalisse
Montord
Fleuriet
Loriges
Créchy
Sanssat
Périgny
Chareil-Cintrat
Bayet
Billy
St-Gérand-le-Puy
Monestier
Deneuille-lès-Chantelle
Fourilles
Marcenat
St-Félix
St-Prix
Chantelle
Barberier
St-Didier-la-Forêt
Magnet
Billezois
Chezelle
Etroussat
Ussel-d'Allier
St-Germain-des-Fossés
Seuillet
Taxat-Senat
Bellenaves
St-Rémy-en-Rollat
Charroux
Broût-Vernet
St-Germain-de-Salles
Creuzier-le-Neuf
Bost
St-Etienne-de-Vicq
Le Breuil
Valignat
Naves
Jenzat
St-Pont
Creuzier-le-Vieux
Isserpent
St-Christophe
Veauce
Le Mayet-d'École
Vendat
Charmeil
St-Bonnet-de-Rochefort
Escurolles
Saulzet
Vicq
Monteignet-s-l'Andelot
Vichy
Cusset
Châtel-Montagne
Ébreuil
Bègues
Mazerier
Espinasse-Vozelle
Bellerive-s-Allier
Gannat
Cognat-Lyonne
Le Vernet
Abrest
Molles
La Chapelle
Nizerolles
St-Quintin-s-Sioule
Serbannes
Le Mayet-de-Montagne
St-Priest-d'Andelot
Biozat
Brugheas
Hauterive
Poëzat
Charmes
St-Genès-du-Retz
St-Yorre
Busset
Arronnes
Champs
St-Sylvestre-Pragoulin
Effiat
St-Agoulin
Vensat
Chaptuzat
Montpensier
St-Priest-Bramefant
Mariol
Aigueperse
Bas-et-Lezat
Randan
Montcel
Artonne
Bussières-et-Pruns
Villeneuve-les-Cerfs
St-Clément-de-Régnat
Beaumont-lès-Randan
Mons
St-Myon
Ris
Chateldon
Lachaux
Combronde
Aubiat
Thuret
Sardon
St-Denis-Combarnazat
Limons
Beauregard-Vendon
Gimeaux
La Moutade
Le Cheix
St-André-le-Coq
Puy-Guillaume
Martres-s-Morge
Surat
Charnat
Luzillat
St-Victor-Montvianeix
Davayat
Cellule
Yssac-la-Tourette
Pessat-Villeneuve
Varennes-s-Morge
St-Ignat
Maringues
Vinzelles
Paslières
St-Bonnet-près-Riom
Châtelguyon
Clerlande
Crevant-Laveine
Noalhat
Palladuc
Ennezat
St-Laure
St-Rémy-s-Durolle
Mozac
Riom
Entraigues
Bulhon
Dorat
Ménétrol
Marsat
Chappes
Joze
Culhat
Orléat
Courty
Celles-s-Durolle
St-Beauzire
Chavaroux
Les Martres-d'Artière
Lussat
Thiers
Châteaugay
Lempty
Lezoux
Peschadoires
Escoutoux
Blanzat
Gerzat
Cébazat
Parc

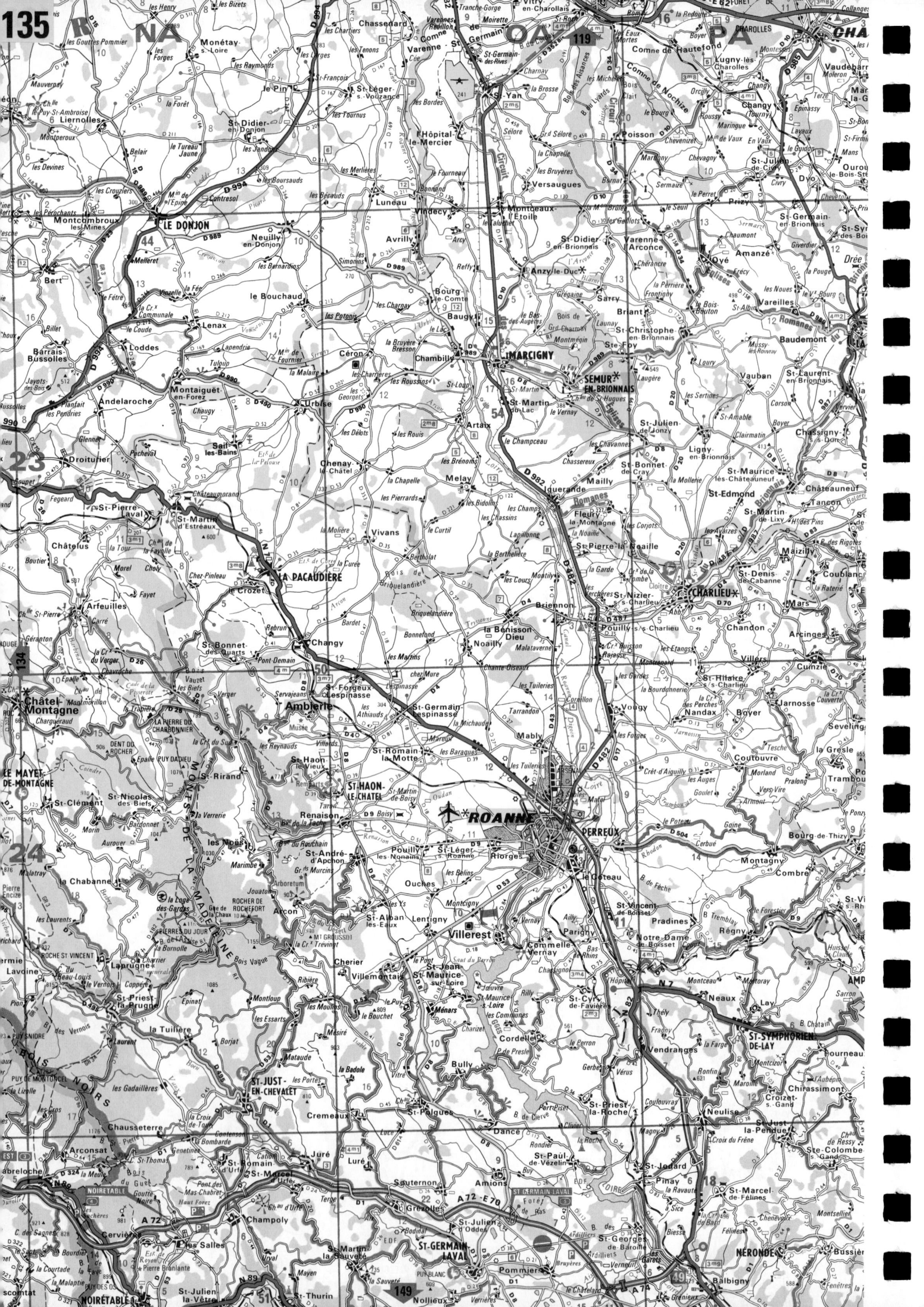

Chassenard
Monétay-s.-Loire
Vitry-en-Charollais
Varenne-St-Germain
St-Germain-des-Rives
St-Yan
Charolles
Lugny-lès-Charolles
Changy
Vaudebarrier
Liernolles
Montperoux
St-Didier-en-Donjon
St-Léger-s.-Vouzance
le Pin
l'Hôpital-le-Mercier
Poisson
St-Julien-de-Civry
Versaugues
Montcombroux-les-Mines
LE DONJON
Neuilly-en-Donjon
Luneau
Vindecy
Montceaux-l'Étoile
Avrilly
St-Didier-en-Brionnais
Varenne-l'Arconce
Prizy
St-Germain-en-Brionnais
Amanzé
Oyé
Bert
le Bouchaud
Anzy-le-Duc
Sarry
Bourg-le-Comte
Baugy
Vareilles
Lenax
Loddes
Barrais-Bussolles
Céron
Chambilly
MARCIGNY
Briant
St-Christophe-en-Brionnais
Baudemont
SEMUR-EN-BRIONNAIS
Montaiguët-en-Forez
Andelaroche
Urbise
Artaix
St-Martin-du-Lac
Vauban
St-Laurent-en-Brionnais
St-Julien-de-Jonzy
Ligny-en-Brionnais
Chassigny-s.-Dun
Sail-les-Bains
Droiturier
Chenay-le-Châtel
Melay
Iguerande
Mailly
St-Bonnet-de-Cray
St-Maurice-lès-Châteauneuf
St-Edmond
Châteauneuf
St-Pierre-Laval
St-Martin-d'Estréaux
Châtelus
Vivans
Fleury-la-Montagne
St-Pierre-la-Noaille
St-Martin-de-Lixy
Tancon
Maizilly
LA PACAUDIÈRE
Le Crozet
St-Denis-de-Cabanne
CHARLIEU
Coublanc
Arfeuilles
Briennon
St-Nizier-s.-Charlieu
Pouilly-s/s-Charlieu
Chandon
Arcinges
Mars
Changy
la Bénisson-Dieu
Noailly
St-Bonnet-des-Quarts
Villers
Cuinzier
St-Hilaire-s.-Charlieu
Châtel-Montagne
St-Forgeux-Lespinasse
Ambierle
St-Germain-Lespinasse
Vougy
Nandax
Boyer
Jarnosse
Sevelinges
Mably
St-Romain-la-Motte
St-Haon-le-Vieux
St-Rirand
LE MAYET-DE-MONTAGNE
St-Nicolas-des-Biefs
St-Clément
ST-HAON-LE-CHÂTEL
Renaison
ROANNE
PERREUX
Coutouvre
la Gresle
Bourg-de-Thizy
les Noës
St-André-d'Apchon
Pouilly-les-Nonains
St-Léger-s.-Roanne
Riorges
le Coteau
Montagny
Combre
la Chabanne
Arcon
Ouches
St-Alban-les-Eaux
Lentigny
Villerest
St-Vincent-de-Boisset
Pradines
Régny
Parigny
Commelle-Vernay
Notre-Dame-de-Boisset
Laprugne
St-Priest-la-Prugne
Cherier
Villemontais
St-Jean-St-Maurice-sur-Loire
St-Cyr-de-Favières
Neaux
Lay
ST-SYMPHORIEN-DE-LAY
Montloup
Ménars
St-Maurice-s.-Loire
la Tuilière
Cordelle
Vendranges
Bully
ST-JUST-EN-CHEVALET
St-Priest-la-Roche
Chirassimont
Neulise
Cremeaux
St-Polgues
Dance
St-Just-la-Pendue
Arconsat
Chausseterre
St-Romain-d'Urfé
St-Marcel-d'Urfé
Juré
Luré
St-Paul-de-Vézelin
St-Jodard
Pinay
St-Marcel-de-Félines
Ste-Colombe-s.-Gand
Souternon
Amions
Grézolles
Champoly
Cervières
les Salles
St-Julien-d'Oddes
ST-GERMAIN-LAVAL
St-Georges-de-Baroille
NÉRONDE
St-Martin-la-Sauveté
Pommiers
Balbigny
NOIRÉTABLE
St-Julien-la-Vêtre
St-Thurin
Nollieux
MONTS DE LA MADELEINE
BOIS NOIRS
A 72 - E 70
N 7
N 82
D 482

134
149

CLUNY
Jalogny
Mazille
Ste-Cécile
Bourgvilain
Clermain
Sologny
Milly-Lamartine
Berzé-la-Ville
Verzé
Igé
Clessé
Senozan
Laizé
Charbonnières
St-Martin-Belle-Roche
MACON NORD
MACON CENTRE
MACON SUD
MACON
Hurigny
Prissé
Davayé
Vergisson
Solutré-Pouilly
Fuissé
Chasselas
Leynes
Vinzelles
Chaintré
Crêches-s.-Saône
Replonges
Feillens
Manziat
Bâgé-le-Châtel
St-Laurent-s.-Saône
Pont-de-Veyle
Varennes-lès-Mâcon
Crottet
Grièges
Cormoranche-s.-Saône
Laiz
Cruzilles-lès-Mépillat
Verosvres
Trivy
Brandon
Ozolles
Matour
Gibles
Trambly
Tramayes
Montmelard
Germolles-s-Grosne
St-Pierre-le-Vieux
St-Christophe
St-Mamert
St-Bonnet-des-Bruyères
Aigueperse
Chauffailles
St-Igny-de-Vers
Monsols
Ouroux
Émeringes
Juliénas
La Chapelle-de-Guinchay
Chénas
Fleurie
Romanèche-Thorins
Thoissey
Avenas
Vauxrenard
Chiroubles
Villié-Morgon
Corcelles-en-Beaujolais
Beaujeu
Propières
Azolette
Belmont-de-la-Loire
Les Écharmeaux
Poule-les-Écharmeaux
Ranchal
Lantignié
Régnié-Durette
Cercié
Belleville
St-Lager
Guéreins
Montmerle-s.-Saône
Charentay
Odenas
St-Étienne-la-Varenne
Le Perréon
Vaux-en-Beaujolais
Lamure-s-Azergues
Claveisolles
Marchampt
Quincié-en-Beaujolais
Cours-la-Ville
Thel
St-Bonnet-le-Troncy
St-Nizier-d'Azergues
Thizy
Marnand
Grandris
Chambost-Allières
Cublize
St-Just-d'Avray
Salle-Arbuissonnas-en-Beaujolais
Blacé
Montmelas-St-Sorlin
Arnas
VILLEFRANCHE-S-SAÔNE
Gleizé
Limas
Cogny
Lacenas
Denicé
Rivolet
Chamelet
Létra
Ste-Paule
Oingt
Ternand
Le Bois-d'Oingt
Theizé
Anse
Pommiers
Trévoux
Reyrieux
St-Didier-de-Formans
Jassans-Riottier
Frans
Savigneux
Messimy-s-Saône
Fareins
Beauregard
Villeneuve
Chaleins
Montceaux
Chaneins
Valeins
Baneins
St-Trivier-s-Moignans
Ambérieux
Lucenay
Morancé
Chessy
Charnay
Bagnols
Légny
Valsonne
St-Appolinaire
Tarare
St-Cyr-de-Valorges
Joux
St-Marcel-l'Éclairé
Pontcharra-s-Turdine
Les Olmes
Sarcey
St-Loup
Dareizé
St-Vérand
St-Forgeux
St-Romain-de-Popey
Bully
L'Arbresle
Châtillon
Chazay-d'Azergues
St-Jean-des-Vignes
Lozanne
Dommartin
Limonest
Les Chères
Neuville-s-Saône
Genay
Massieux
Fleurieu-s-Saône
Ancy
Savigny
Affoux
Violay
Montchal
Villechenève
Sourcieux-les-Mines
Sain-Bel
Bibost
Lentilly
Fleurieux-s-l'Arbresle
Caluire-et-Cuire
Rillieux-la-Pape
Collonges
Fontaines-s-Saône
Rochetaillée-s-Saône
Couzon-au-Mt-d'Or
Albigny-s-Saône
St-Germain-au-Mt-d'Or
Poleymieux-au-Mt-d'Or
Chasselay
Lissieu
Civrieux
Parcieux
Misérieux
Rancé
Toussieux
Ste-Euphémie
Illiat
St-Didier-s-Chalaronne
St-Étienne-s-Chalaronne
Mogneneins
Peyzieux-s-Saône
Genouilleux
Dompierre-s-Chalaronne
Garnerans
Bey
120
121
137
150
151

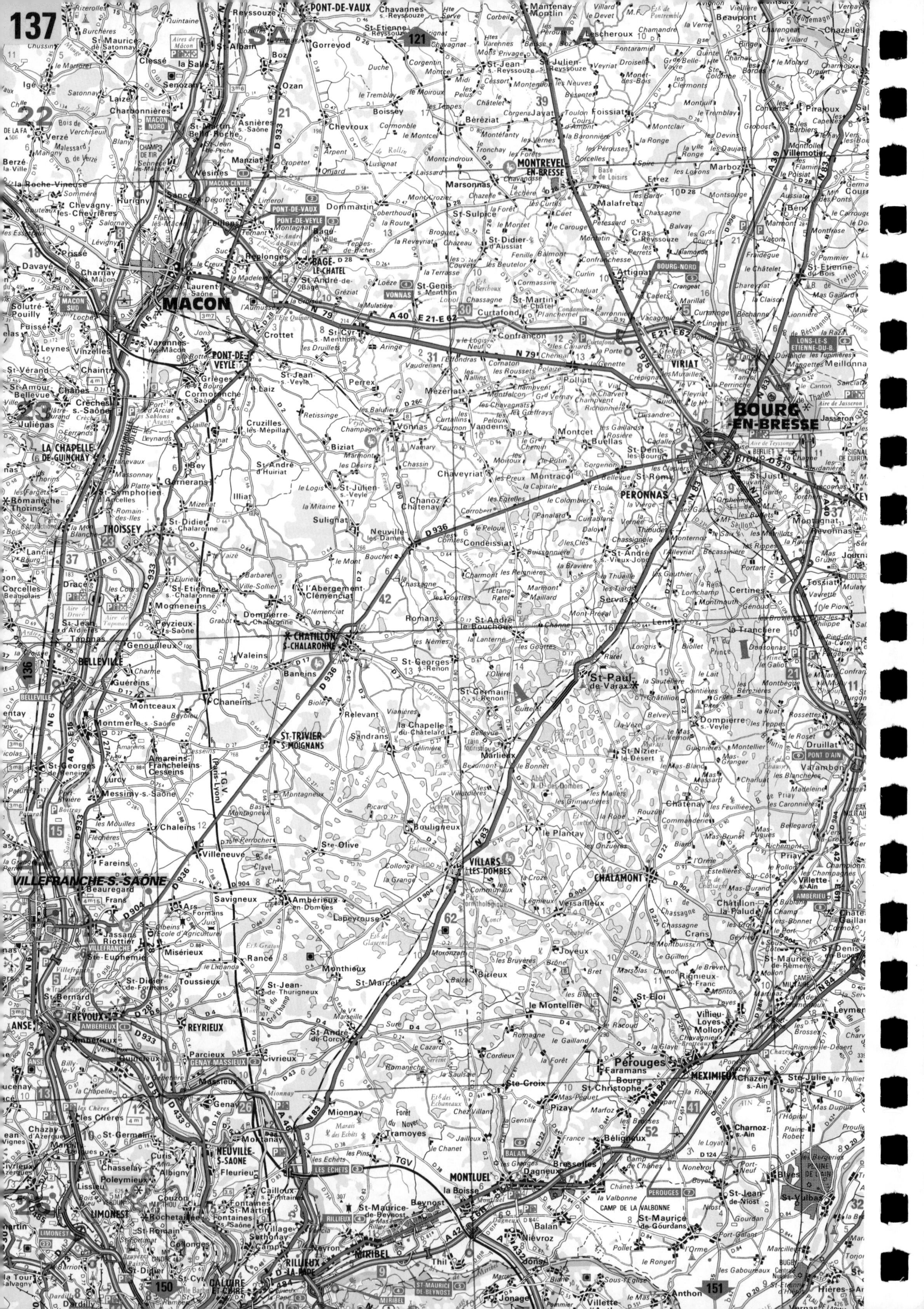

PONT-DE-VAUX
MACON
MONTREVEL-EN-BRESSE
BOURG-EN-BRESSE
PONT-DE-VEYLE
BAGE-LE-CHATEL
VIRIAT
PERONNAS
THOISSEY
LA CHAPELLE-DE-GUINCHAY
BELLEVILLE
CHATILLON-S-CHALARONNE
ST-TRIVIER-S-MOIGNANS
VILLEFRANCHE-S-SAONE
VILLARS-LES-DOMBES
CHALAMONT
TREVOUX
REYRIEUX
NEUVILLE-S-SAONE
LIMONEST
MONTLUEL
MEXIMIEUX
Pérouges
MIRIBEL
RILLIEUX-LA-PAPE
CALUIRE-ET-CUIRE
St-Paul-de-Varax
Vonnas
Romans
Lent
Servas
Montagnat
Druillat
Ambérieux-en-Dombes
Jassans-Riottier
Anse
Genay
Mionnay
Dagneux
Bressolles
Balan
Béligneux
Charnoz-s-Ain
St-Jean-de-Niost
St-Vulbas
Villette
Anthon
Jonage
Dardilly

ST-CLAUDE
HAUT JURA
OYONNAX
NANTUA
BELLEGARDE S-VALSERINE
COLLONGES
FRANGY
SEYSSEL
RUMILLY
RUFFIEUX
ALBENS
CULOZ
VIRIEU-LE-GRAND
CHAMPAGNE-EN-VALROMEY
HAUTEVILLE-LOMPNES
BRÉNOD
AMBÉRIEU-EN-BUGEY
ST-RAMBERT-EN-BUGEY
LAGNIEU
PONT-D'AIN
PONCIN
IZERNORE
TREFFORT-CUISIAT
COLIGNY
ST-JULIEN
ARINTHOD
LES BOUCHOUX
CRET DU NU
LE GRD COLOMBIER
PLATEAU DE RETORD
Tunnel de Chamoise
Aire de Ceignes-Cerdon
Aire de Valleiry
NANTUA HAUTEVILLE-LOMPNES
FRANGY SEYSSEL
2°ch. Ouv. Proch.
Ouv. Proch.
la Balme-les-Grottes
A40
A404
N 504
N 84
D 904
D 992
D 991
D 984
D 436
122
139
152

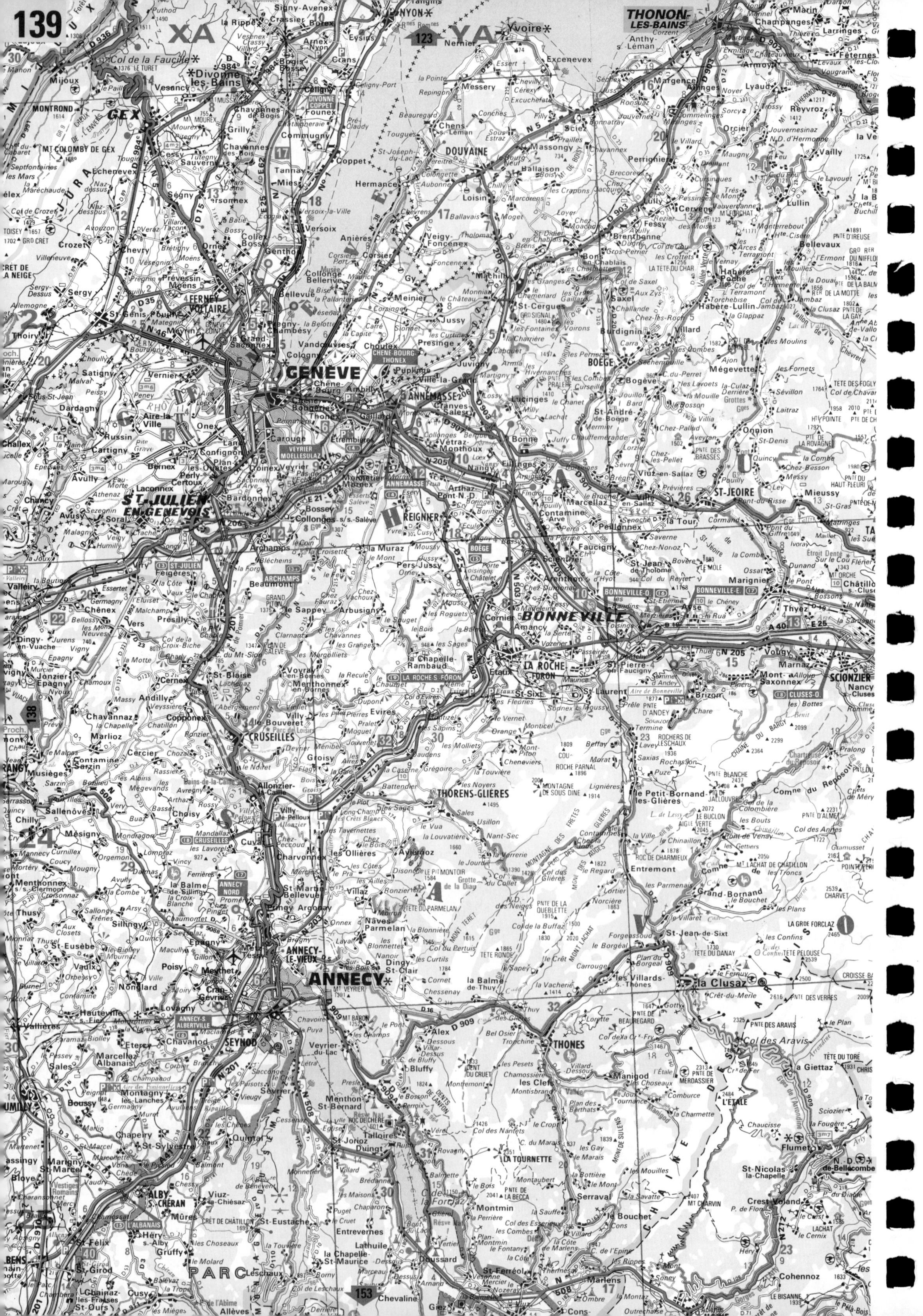
XA
YA
123
THONON-LES-BAINS
NYON
Yvoire
Col de la Faucille
Divonne-les-Bains
GEX
Excenevex
Messery
Douvaine
Sciez
Margencel
Allinges
Hermance
Versoix
Anières
Ferney-Voltaire
St-Genis-Pouilly
GENÈVE
Chêne-Bourg
ANNEMASSE
Carouge
Thônex
Veyrier
ST-JULIEN-EN-GENEVOIS
Bonne
Boëge
Saxel
St-Jeoire
Mieussy
Reignier
Cruseilles
BONNEVILLE
LA ROCHE-S-FORON
St-Pierre-en-Faucigny
Thyez
Marnaz
SCIONZIER
Cluses
THORENS-GLIÈRES
Le Petit-Bornand-les-Glières
Entremont
Grand-Bornand
St-Jean-de-Sixt
La Clusaz
Col des Aravis
ANNECY
ANNECY-LE-VIEUX
Seynod
Veyrier-du-Lac
Talloires
Duingt
Alex
THONES
Manigod
La Giettaz
Flumet
St-Nicolas-la-Chapelle
Crest-Voland
Cohennoz
Alby-s-Chéran
Gruffy
St-Félix
Lathuile
Doussard
Chevaline
St-Ferréol
Marlens
La Tournette
Montmin
Serraval
Le Bouchet
Faverges
PARC
153
138
ARAVIS

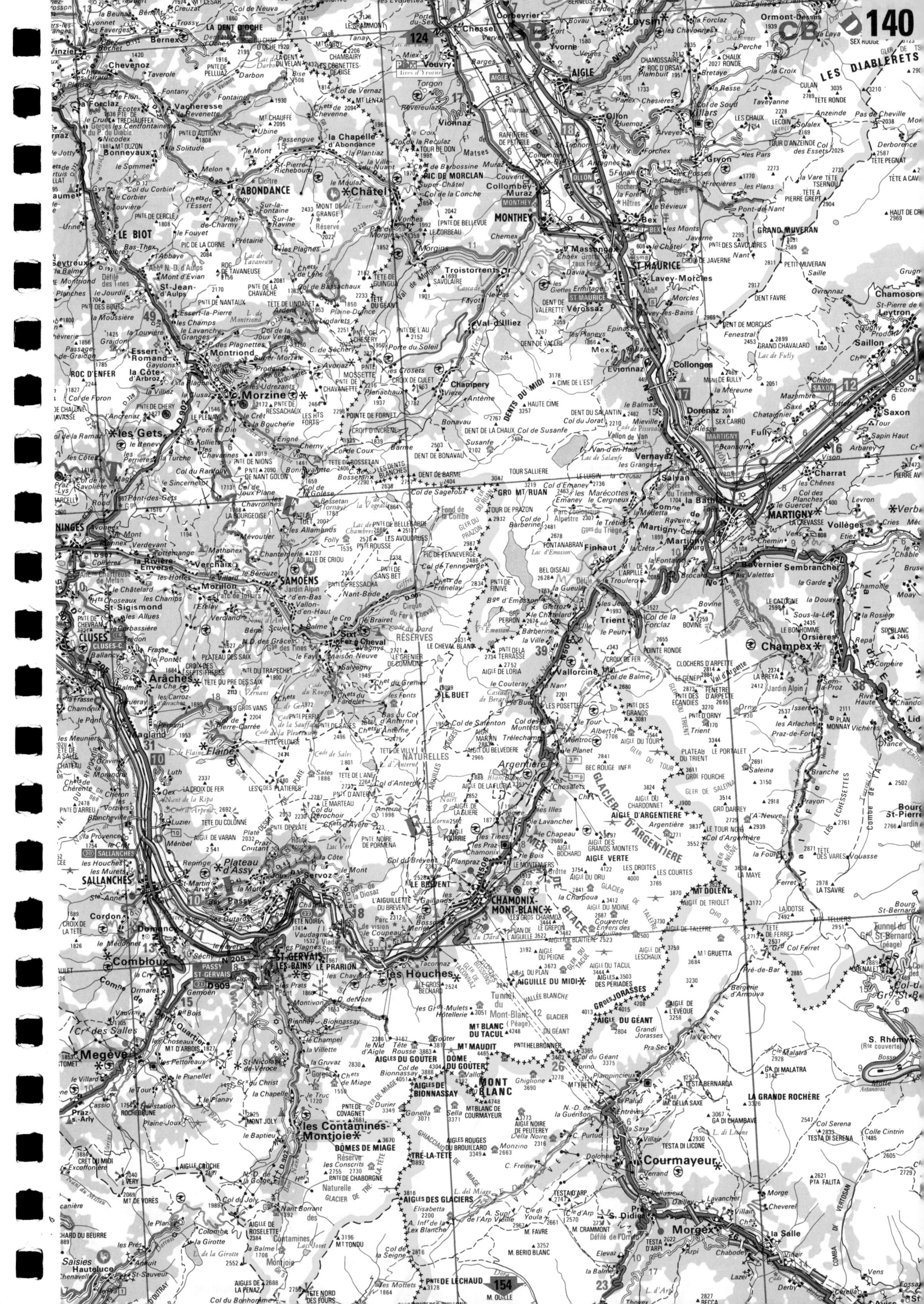
CB
LES DIABLERETS
Leysin
AIGLE
Vouvry
Monthey
Châtel
ABONDANCE
LA DENT D'OCHE
Bernex
Chevenoz
Vacheresse
Bonnevaux
LE BIOT
St-Jean-d'Aulps
Morzine
Les Gets
Avoriaz
Champéry
Val-d'Illiez
Troistorrents
Morgins
St MAURICE
Bex
Villars
Gryon
Ollon
GRAND MUVERAN
DENTS DU MIDI
Collonges
Dorénaz
Vernayaz
Salvan
MARTIGNY
Fully
Saxon
Saillon
Leytron
Chamoson
Charrat
Vollèges
Sembrancher
Orsières
Champex
Trient
Finhaut
Vallorcine
Col de la Forclaz
Col de Balme
Le Buet
Sixt-Fer-à-Cheval
SAMOËNS
Morillon
Taninges
CLUSES
St-Sigismond
Arâches
Flaine
Magland
SALLANCHES
Plateau d'Assy
Passy
Servoz
Combloux
Cordon
Domancy
ST-GERVAIS-LES-BAINS
les Houches
CHAMONIX-MONT-BLANC
Argentière
LE BRÉVENT
AIGUILLE DU MIDI
AIGLE VERTE
AIGLE D'ARGENTIÈRE
MT DOLENT
MER DE GLACE
GLACIER D'ARGENTIÈRE
GRDES JORASSES
AIGLE DU GÉANT
MT BLANC DU TACUL
MONT BLANC
DÔME DU GOÛTER
AIGLES DU GOÛTER
AIGLE DE BIONNASSAY
Tunnel du Mont-Blanc
Megève
les Contamines-Montjoie
DÔMES DE MIAGE
AIGLES DES GLACIERS
Courmayeur
Pré-St-Didier
Morgex
La Salle
LA GRANDE ROCHÈRE
Tunnel du Gd St-Bernard
Col Ferret
S. Rhémy
Bourg-St-Pierre
124
154

MARENNES
Marennes-Plage
Pte de Manson
Pte de Gatseau
Pte aux Herbes
DE MAUMUSSON
Ronce-les-B.
Pte Espagnole
Forêt de la Tremblade
LA TREMBLADE
25
CÔTE SAUVAGE
FORÊT DOMANIALE DE LA COUBRE
Phare de la Coubre
Bonne Anse
Pte de la Coubre
Pte de la Palmyre
la Palmyre
les Mathes
la Fouasse
le Néré
Arvert
Etaules
Dirée
Fouilloux
Avallon
Coux
la Cayenne
Mauzac
Luzac
Arlouan
les Touches
St-Just-Luzac
St-Jean-d'Angle
les Gds Ajots
la Gripperie
St-Symphorien
Blénac
St-Sornin
Nieulle-s.-Seudre
Chatressac
la Brousse
Chaillevette
Mornac-s.-Seudre
Souhe
l'Eguille
la Passe
St-Augustin
Charosson
le Grallet
Breuillet
St-Sulpice-de-Royan
Lafond
Combots
la Palud
la Gde Côte
Courlay-s.-M.
Vaux-s.-M.
St-Palais-s.-M.
Nauzan
Pontaillac
ROYAN
St-Georges-de-D.
Phare de Cordouan
Barre à l'Anglais
Grand Banc
Montrevel
Bernon
les Maries
Brie
Médis
Toussauge
Musson
Trignac
Didonne
Semussac
Serres
de Suzac
Pte de Suzac
Champagne
Courbon
Pont-l'Abbé-d'Arnoult
St-PORCHAIRE
St-Sulpice-d'Arnoult
Plassay
Port d'Envaux
St-Saturnin-de-S.
Conchamp
B. des Héros
Rulon
Ecurat
les Essards
Soulignonne
Nieul-lès-S.
St-Georges-des-C.
les Aiguilles
l'Isleau
Dunjon
Ste-Gemme
les Geais
Nancras
Balanzac
Corme-Royal
la Clisse
Pessines
les Roches
Cadeuil
Chalons
le Gua
Sablonceaux
Dercie
le Breuil
les Chies Blanches
Luchat
Pisany
St-Romain-de-B.
Varzay
Brasseau
le Pinier
Chermignac
Retaud
Thézac
Thénac
SAUJON
le Vivier
la Seudre
les Portiers
Meursac
les Epeaux
le Chay
Corme-Écluse
Montpellier-de-Médillan
Chez-Raynaud
Rioux
les Cinq-Timbres
Thaims
Grézac
la Roche
Jorignac
St-Simon-de-Pellouaille
St-André-de-Lidon
Cravans
Chez-Gombaud
COZES
les Maréchaux
la Merletterie
Chadeniers
GÉMOZAC
la Foy
Bardécille
Brézillas
Liboulas
Théon
Javrezac
les Gorces
Arces
la Bastille
Meschers-s.-Gironde
Grottes
P. Marant
le Colombier
Epargnes
Talmont
Barzan
Chenac
St-Seurin-d'Uzet
les Rimondières
Vallerit
Virollet
Maine-Fleuret
la Vacherie
Rousillon
St-Germain-du-Seudre
Touvent
Boutenac-Touvent
Brie-s/s-Mortagne
Mortagne-s.-Gironde
la Rive
Floirac
Ermitage
Mageloup
Chez Bizet
St-Fort-s.-G.
Lorignac
Tirac
St-Romain-s.-Gironde
St-Dizant-du-Gua
Port-Maubert
les Abaupins
Ste-Ramée
Chez Vieuille
Font-Clair
Conac
Bondut
St-Thomas-de-Conac
St-Sorlin-de-Conac
St-Bonnet-s.-Gironde
Chenine
Port-de-Cônac
Vitrezay
Pte de Grave
Mont U.S.A.
PASSE DE GRAVE
26
le Chevrier
Pt de Verdon
le Logit
le Royannais
le Verdon s.-Mer
Pte de la Chambrette
Soulac-s.-Mer
les Hattes
Vieux Soulac
Neyran
le Jeune Soulac
Banc des Olives
Bancs des Marguerites
Banc de St Vivien
Pte aux Oiseaux
l'Amélie
Lillan
Pointe de la Négade
Talais
Grayan-et-l'Hôpital
le Gurp
les Eyres
Lède du Gurp
Etang de la Barreyre
Dépée
Daugagnan
St-VIVIEN-DE-MÉDOC
Canau
Charmail
Pointe de Richard
la Hourcade
Jau-Dignac-et-Loirac
Dignac
Gaudin
Vensac
Noaillac
Loirac
le Centre
Port-de-Goulée
Valeyrac
Lède de la Canillouse
Montalivet-les-Bs
MARAIS DE LA PERGE
Mayan
Sémian
le Mouva
Courbian
Troussas
Port-de-By
By
Bégadan
Vendays-Montalivet
Sarnac
l'Escapon
Queyrac
Tremblaux
Couquèques
St-Christoly-Médoc
27
40
Lède des Fourgs
Hourcan
Coudessanx
Gaillan-en-Médoc
Civrac-en-M.
Prignac-en-M.
Port de Lamena
Queyzan
GIRONDE
Bourgueyraud
Blaignan
Blanc
la Cardonne
Potensac
St-Yzans-de-Médoc
la Maréchale
Cadourne
Marais de Lespan
LESPARRE-MÉDOC
St-Trélody
Vernous
Ordonnac
Marque
la Bresquette
Forêt du Junca
Escot
Conquillac
St-Germain-d'Esteuil
St-Seurin-de-Cadourne
St-Isidore
le Pin Sec
Plassan
Liard
Artiguillon
St-Gaux
St-Corbian
St-Estèphe
Péris
Naujac-s.-M.
la Prise
Magagnan
Dunes de Brémontier
Marais Belsaneau
Lande de Vignolles
Bois du Plantier
Lugagnac
Vertheuil
Leyssac
Garramey
Meyney
Montrose
Hourtin-Plge
Marais dit Palu
Contaut
Genets
Cartignac
Buradey
Cissac-Médoc
Larrivaux
Lafite
Raff. de Pétrole
le Breuil
Mouton-Rothschild
Landes de la Sausseouse
C. Motouse
Piqueyrot
Lagunan
St-Sauveur
Fonpiqueyre
PAUILLAC
le Philippe
Berdot
Anglade
le Passage
LA VERGNE
le Pas-de-Gourbeuil
St-CIERS-s.-GIRONDE
les Ferrés
LE MARAIS
Port des Callonges
Centrale nucléaire
Braud-et-St-Louis
126
127
155
N 137
N 150
N 215
D 728
D 730
D 732
D 733
D 25

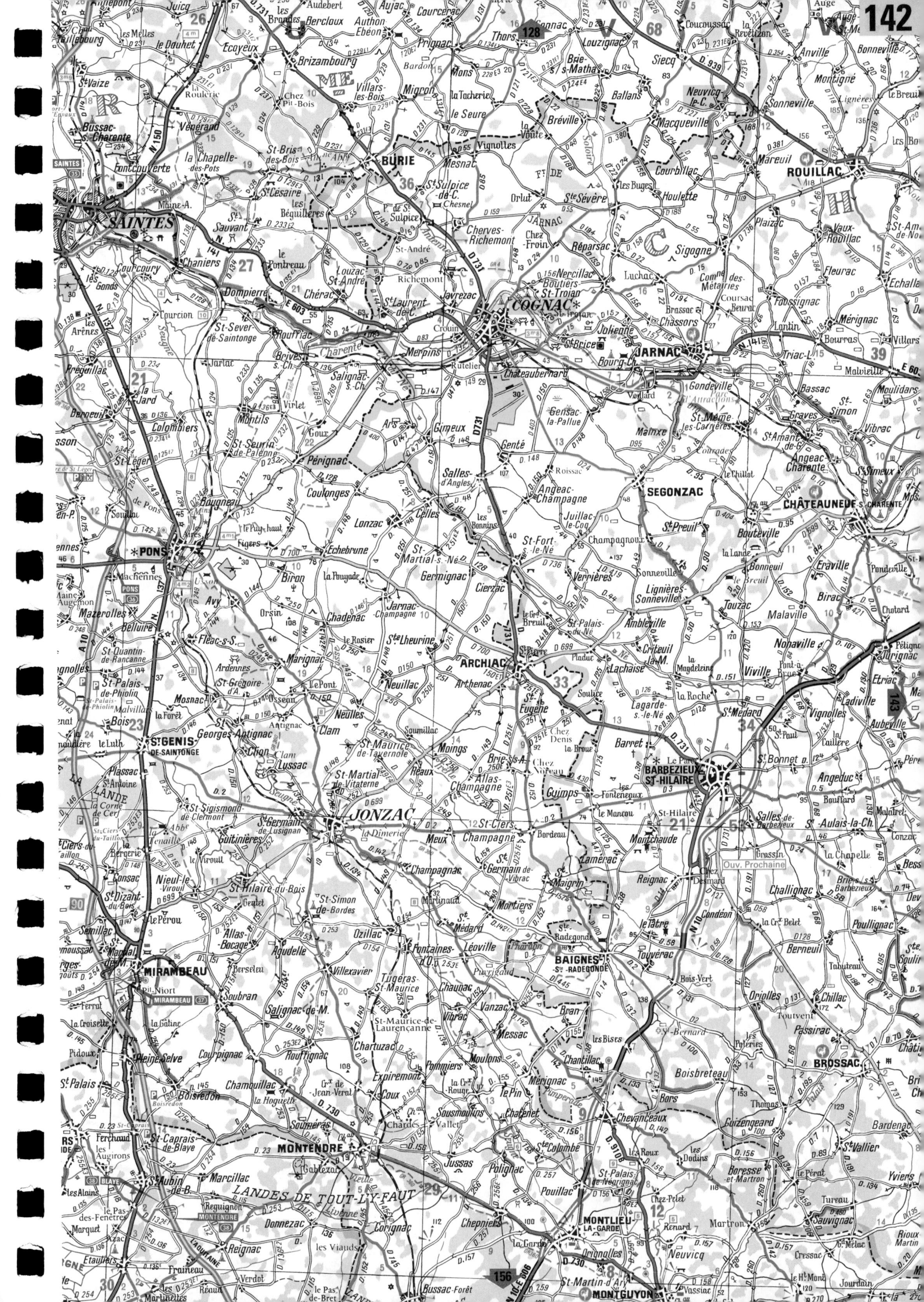

SAINTES
COGNAC
JARNAC
ROUILLAC
BURIE
PONS
ARCHIAC
SEGONZAC
CHÂTEAUNEUF s. CHARENTE
BARBEZIEUX ST-HILAIRE
JONZAC
St GENIS DE-SAINTONGE
MIRAMBEAU
BAIGNES-Ste RADEGONDE
BROSSAC
MONTENDRE
MONTLIEU LA-GARDE
MONTGUYON
LANDES DE TOUT-LY-FAUT
Charente
Juicq
Ecoyeux
Brizambourg
Audebert
Aujac
Courcerac
Authon Ebéon
Prignac
Mons
Thors
Louzignac
Coucoussac
Siecq
Anville
Bonneville
Montigné
Sonneville
Bréville
Macqueville
Neuvicq-le-C.
Mareuil
Ballans
Brie-s-Matha
Migron
Villars-les-Bois
le Seure
Vignolles
Mesnac
St Sulpice-de-C.
St-Bris-des-Bois
St-Césaire
les Béquillères
Chaniers
Courcoury
Dompierre
Chérac
Louzac St-André
Richemont
Javrezac
Cherves-Richemont
Orlut
Ste Sévère
Houlette
Courbillac
Réparsac
Sigogne
Plaizac
Vaux-Rouillac
Fleurac
Foussignac
Mérignac
Nercillac
Boutiers-St-Troian
Julienne
Chassors
St Brice
Bourg-Ch.
Châteaubernard
Merpins
Rouffiac
St-Sever-de-Saintonge
Brives-s.-Ch.
Salignac-s.-Ch.
Gondeville
Triac-L.
Bassac
St-Simon
Graves
Vibrac
Mainxe
St-Même-les-Carrières
Gensac-la-Pallue
Genté
Gimeux
Ars
Montils
Colombiers
St-Seurin-de-Palenne
Pérignac
Coulonges
Salles-d'Angles
Angeac-Champagne
Angeac-Charente
St Simeux
Bougneau
Lonzac
Celles
St-Martial-s.-Né
Juillac-le-Coq
St-Fort-s.-le-Né
Champagnoux
St Preuil
Bouteville
Eraville
Biron
Germignac
Cierzac
Verrières
Lignières-Sonneville
Touzac
Birac
Malaville
Chadenac
Jarnac-Champagne
St-Palais-du-Né
Ambleville
Criteuil-la-M.
Nonaville
Jurignac
Avy
Mazerolles
Belluire
Fléac-s-S.
Marignac
Ste Lheurine
Neuillac
Arthenac
St-Pierre
Lachaise
Viville
St-Quentin-de-Rancanne
St-Palais-de-Phiolin
Mosnac
St Grégoire-d'A.
Neulles
Clam
St Eugène
Lagarde-s.-le-Né
St Médard
Vignolles
Aubeville
St-Georges-Antignac
Clion
Lussac
St-Maurice-de-Tavernole
Moings
Brie-s-A.
Barret
St Bonnet
Plassac
St-Martial-de-Vitaterne
Réaux
Allas-Champagne
Guimps
Angeduc
St-Sigismond-de-Clermont
St Germain-de-Lusignan
Guitinières
Meux
St-Ciers Champagne
Montchaude
St Aulais-la-Ch.
Consac
Nieul-le-Virouil
St Hilaire-du-Bois
Champagnac
St Germain-de-Vibrac
Lamérac
Reignac
Challignac
St Dizant-du-Bois
St-Simon-de-Bordes
Mortiers
St Maigrin
Condéon
Allas-Bocage
Ozillac
St-Médard
Léoville
le Tâtre
Poullignac
Agudelle
Fontaines-d'O.
Touvérac
Berneuil
Villexavier
Tugéras-St-Maurice
Chaunac
Soubran
Salignac-de-M.
St-Maurice-de-Laurençanne
Vibrac
Vanzac
Oriolles
Chillac
Messac
Passirac
Courpignac
Rouffignac
Chartuzac
Pommiers
Moulons
Mérignac
Chantillac
Boisbreteau
Chamouillac
Expiremont
Coux
Le Pin
Chatenet
Bors
Chevanceaux
Guizengeard
Boisredon
Sousmoulins
Soumeras
Bardenac
St-Caprais-de-Blaye
Ste Colombe
Jussas
Polignac
St Vallier
Marcillac
St-Aubin-de-B.
St Palais-de-Négrignac
Boresse-et-Martron
Yviers
Pouillac
Sauvignac
Donnezac
Corignac
Chepniers
Neuvicq
Orignolles
Reignac
Bussac-Forêt
St-Martin-d'Ary
Ouv. Prochaine
D. 731
D. 730
D. 939
N. 141
N. 137
N. 150
N. 10
E 603
A 10
128
143
156

Marcillac-L.
Ambérac
Villognon
Puyréaux
St-Ciers-s.-B.
St-Amant-de-Bonnieure
La Tâche
Chavagnac
Lussac
Bois de Belair
Gourville
Coulonges
Xambes
Nanclars
St-Angeau
St-Mary
Aussac-Vadalle
Ste-Colombe
Chasseneuil-s.-Bonnieure
Suaux
Vouharte
ST-AMANT-DE-BOIXE
Coulgens
Le Mouchet
Les Pins
Genac
Bignac
Montignac-Charente
Villejoubert
Tourriers
Chez-Renard
La Rochette
Quatre-Vaux
Marognac
Cherves-Châtelars
Théâtre gallo-romain
St-Cybardeaux
Jauldes
Le Pont-d'Agris
Taponnat-Fleurignac
Vitrac-St-Vincent
Anais
Agris
Rivières
St-Genis-d'H.
Vars
Churet
La Chignolle
Brie
Champ de la Jauvigère
St-Projet-St-Constant
St-Adjutory
Yvrac-et-Malleyrand
Mazerolles
St-Amant-de-Nouère
Marsac
Neuillac
Echallat
Asnières-s.-Nouère
La Simarde
Champniers
Ouv. Juin 1999
La Rochefoucauld
Marillac-le-Franc
La Braconne
La Ribe
Douzat
Balzac
Les Chauvauds
St-Yrieix-s.-C.
Bunzac
St-Sornin
Rouzède
Villars
Le Pontouvre
Ruelle-s.-Touvre
Camp Militaire
Les Deffends
Rancogne
Vilhonneur
Orgedeuil
Hiersac
Fléac
Le Gond-Pontouvre
Touvre
Magnac
Mornac
Pranzac
La Borderie
Châtain-B.
Moulidars
St-Saturnin
Linars
Trois-Palis
Angoulême
Soyaux
Bois Blanc
St-Paul
Lachaise
Vouthon
Montbron
Champmillon
St-Michel
Nersac
Grottes du Quéroy et de Barroury
Chazelles
Le Mas de Baud
Maranda
Eymouthiers
Sireuil
Mosnac
Pombreton
La Couronne
Ste-Catherine
Garat
L'Age-Martin
St-Germain-de-M.
Marthon
Puymoyen
La Croix
Bouëx
Chez Vincent
Soudat
Roullet-St-Estèphe
Dirac
Boisseau
Sers
Vouzan
L'Agneau
Feuillade
Le Bois Brulé
Vœuil-et-Giget
La Boissière
Forêt de Dirac
Logis-de-Nanteuil
Souffrignac
Varaignes
La Chartoire
Claix
Landolie
Torsac
Massilloux
Dignac
Chêne-Vert
Grassac
La Brechinie
Le Gd Moulin
Teyjat
Mouthiers-s.-Boëme
Pougaud
Beaulieu
Forêt d'Horte
Doumérac
Les Buis
La Chapelle-St-Robert
Javerlhac-la-Chle
Péllignac
Les Coffres
Gersac
Ravgnac
Charras
Mainzac
Le Gd Jilloux
Plassac-Rouffiac
Rouffiac
Fouquebrune
La Marolle
Cloulas
Monchoisi
Ft de la Roche Beaucourt
Le Clédou
Hautefaye
L'Espinasse
Mainfonds
Champagne-Vigny
Voulgezac
Chassagne
Villars
La Garde
Fontroubade
B. de Beaussac
Bécheresse
Chadurie
Voie Romaine
La Mercerie
Magnac-Lavalette-Villars
Le Peyrat
Rozet
Bretanges
Connezac
Lussas-et-Nontronneau
Péreuil
Blanzac-Porcheresse
Gayet
La Meulière
Charmant
Ronsenac
Gardes-le-Pontaroux
Edon
Combiers
Les Graulges
Beaussac
Rudeau-Ladosse
Pérignac
Puypéroux
Juillaguet
Villebois-Lavalette
Blanzaguet
La Rochebeaucourt-et-Argentine
Puyrenier
St-Léger
Chavenat
Nadaillac
Ste-Croix-de-M.
La Vergne
St-Sulpice-de-Mareuil
Champeaux-la-Chapelle-Pommier
Aignes-et-Puypéroux
Apremont
Maillé-Berchie
Mareuil
St-Genis-de-Blanzac
Cressac-St-Genis
Bessac
La Léotardie
Gurat
La Jaufrenie
Fontaine
Beaulieu
Chaveroche
St-Pardoux-de-M.
Vx-Mareuil
Nonac
St-Cybard
Vaux-Lavalette
Champagne-et-Fontaine
Montardy
Beauregard
Deviat
St-Eutrope
Montmoreau-St-Cybard
Lafaiteau
Gout-Rossignol
Rossignol
La Buisson
Monsec
St-Félix-de-B.
Chez le Blais
Vendoire
St-Amant
Courgeac
St-Laurent-de-Belzagot
Cherval
Grenouillier
La Chapelle-Montabourlet
Le Brouillac
Rousselières
Ste-Souline
Nanteuil-Auriac-de-Bourzac
Jovelle
St-Félix
Salles-Lavalette
La Chapelle-Grésignac
Léguillac-de-Cercles
Bourpuneix
St-Martial
Juignac
Bouzac
Auriac-de-Bourzac
Montignac
Bouilhac
La Negrerie
Les Perrotins
St-Laurent-des-Combes
Peudry
Servolle
La Tour Blanche
Bois
Cercles
Rochers
St-Julien-de-B.
Bors
St-Martial-Viveyrol
Le Pontis
Verteillac
Le Breuil
Châtignac
Montignac-le-Coq
Palluaud
Bouteilles-St-Sébastien
Chapdeuil
Passac-et-St-Vivien
Gueyjat
Brie-s/s-Chalais
Montboyer
St-Paul-Lizonne
Lusignac
Bourg-des-Maisons
B. de Fonteillac
St-Just
Pillac
St-Séverin
Coutures
Flayac
Brie
St-Vivien
Fonseigner
Puygironde
Marouatte
Creyssac
Curac
Ste-Marie
Courlac
Bellon
Puychaud
Bertric-Burée
Burée
Celles
Gd-Brassac
Chalais
Orival
St-Romain
Nabinaud
Laprade
Bersac
Pontel
Comberanche-et-Epeluche
Allemans
Monlardit
Rendmion
Puymaurin
St-Martial
Aubeterre-s.-Dronne
Epeluche
Villetoureix
Montagrier
Lisle
St-Christophe
Rouffiac
St-Quentin-de-Ch.
Bourg-du-Bost
La Borie
Lepare
St-Victor
Sérignac
Riou-Martin
St-Avit
Bonnes
St-Antoine-Cumond
Chassaignes
Faye
La Borderie
St-Martial
Beauséjour
Tocane-St-Apre
La Lande
Dourle
Médillac
Bazac
Les Essards
Ramouly
Cumond
Ribérac
St-Méard-de-Drône
Douchapt
Vernode
Lembertie
Puychaud
St-Privat-des-Prés
Fayolles
St-Pardoux-de-Drône
N. 10
N. 141
E 603
N 41
D 939
D 674
D 708
D 951
129
142
157
25
26
27
30
29
61

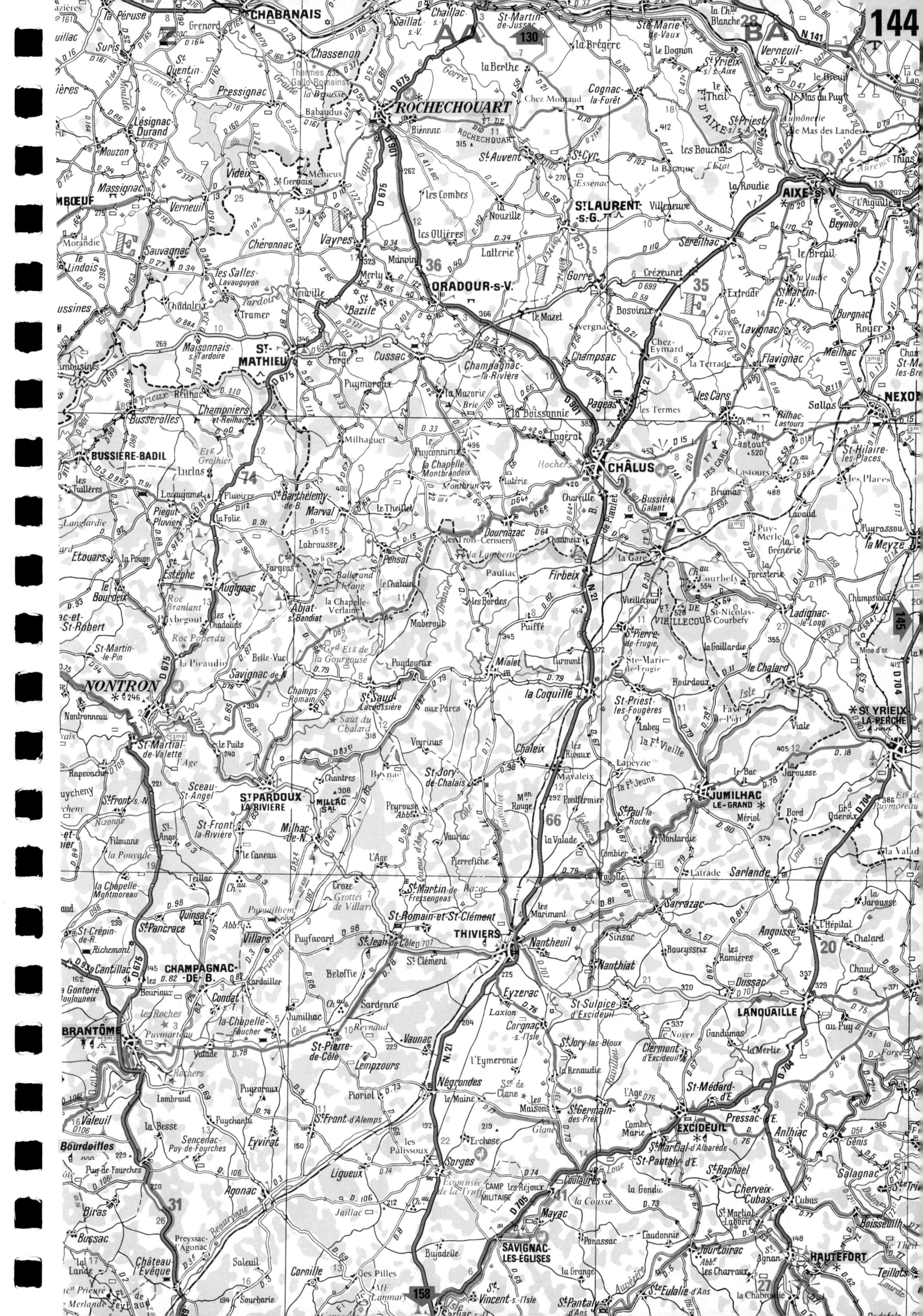
144
145
130
158
AA
BA
CHABANAIS
Chassenon
ROCHECHOUART
St-Martin-de-Jussac
Saillat-s-V.
Chaillac-s-V.
Ste-Marie-de-Vaux
la Brégère
le Dognon
St-Yrieix-s/s-Aixe
Verneuil-s-V.
la Péruse
Grenord
Suris
St-Quentin-s-C.
Pressignac
Lésignac-Durand
Mouzon
Massignac
Videix
Verneuil
Cognac-la-Forêt
la Berthe
St-Auvent
St-Cyr
St-Priest-s-A.
les Bouchauds
AIXE-s-V.
ST-LAURENT-s-G.
Séreilhac
Beynac
Vayres
les Combes
la Nouzille
les Ollières
Chéronnac
Sauvagnac
les Salles-Lavauguyon
Marvin
ORADOUR-s-V.
Gorre
Crézeunet
St-Bazile
Cussac
ST-MATHIEU
Maisonnais-s-Tardoire
Champagnac-la-Rivière
Champsac
Pageas
Flavignac
Les Cars
NEXON
Champniers-et-Reilhac
Busserolles
BUSSIÈRE-BADIL
Luclas
la Chapelle-Montbrandeix
CHÂLUS
Bussière-Galant
Rilhac-Lastours
St-Hilaire-les-Places
Piegut-Pluviers
St-Barthélemy-de-B.
Marval
Dournazac
Firbeix
la Meyze
St-Estèphe
Augignac
Abjat-s-Bandiat
Pensol
Ladignac-le-Long
St-Pierre-de-Frugie
St-Nicolas-Courbefy
Savignac-de-N.
Mialet
NONTRON
la Coquille
St-Saud-Lacoussière
St-Priest-les-Fougères
Le Chalard
ST-YRIEIX-LA-PERCHE
St-Martial-de-Valette
Chaleix
St-Jory-de-Chalais
STPARDOUX-LA-RIVIERE
MILLAC
JUMILHAC-LE-GRAND
St-Paul-la-Roche
St-Front-la-Rivière
Milhac-de-N.
Sarlande
Quinsac
St-Pancrace
Villars
St-Martin-de-Fressengeas
St-Romain-et-St-Clément
THIVIERS
Nantheuil
Sarrazac
Angoisse
CHAMPAGNAC-DE-B.
Cantillac
Condat
St-Jean-de-Côle
Nanthiat
Dussac
LANOUAILLE
BRANTÔME
la-Chapelle-Faucher
St-Pierre-de-Côle
Vaunac
Eyzerac
Corgnac-s-l'Isle
St-Sulpice-d'Excideuil
St-Jory-las-Bloux
Clermont-d'Excideuil
Négrondes
St-Médard-d'E.
EXCIDEUIL
Pressac-d'E.
Anlhiac
Valeuil
Bourdeilles
Eyvirat
St-Front-d'Alemps
Sorges
Ligueux
St-Germain-des-Prés
St-Martial-d'Albarède
St-Pantaly-d'E.
St-Raphael
Cherveix-Cubas
Salagnac
Agonac
Coulaures
Mayac
Biras
Bussac
SAVIGNAC-LES-ÉGLISES
Tourtoirac
HAUTEFORT
Château-l'Évêque
Cornille
St-Vincent-s-l'Isle
Ste-Eulalie-d'Ans

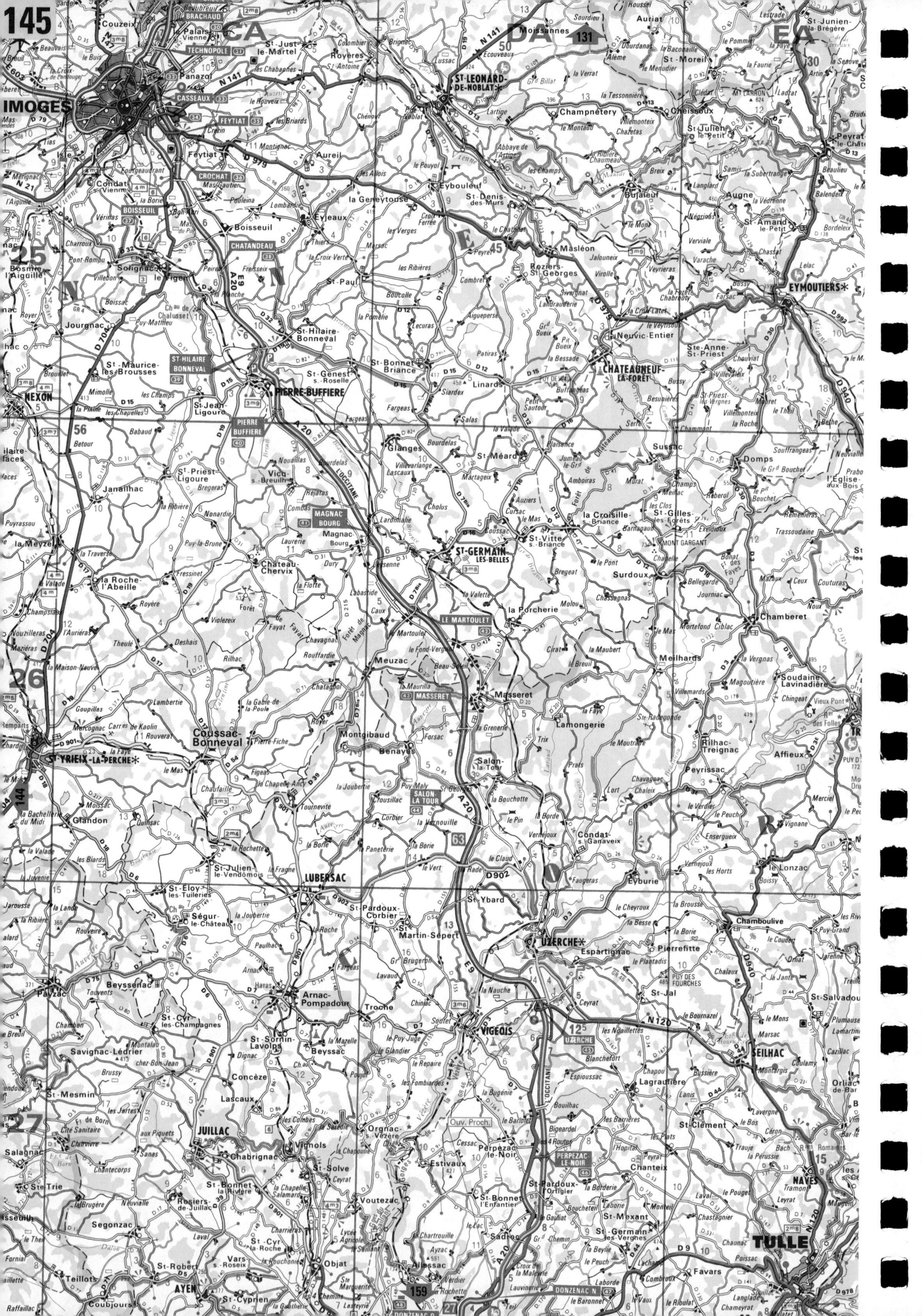
LIMOGES
Couzeix
Panazol
St-Just-le-Martel
Royères
Moissannes
131
St-Léonard-de-Noblat
Auriat
St-Moreil
St-Junien-la-Brégère
Champnetery
Cheissoux
St-Julien-le-Petit
Peyrat-le-Château
Feytiat
Aureil
Eybouleuf
St-Denis-des-Murs
Bujaleuf
Augne
St-Amand-le-Petit
Condat-sur-Vienne
Boisseuil
Eyjeaux
la Geneytouse
Masléon
Roziers-St-Georges
Eymoutiers
Solignac
le Vigen
St-Paul
Jourgnac
St-Hilaire-Bonneval
Neuvic-Entier
Ste-Anne-St-Priest
St-Maurice-les-Brousses
St-Genest-s.-Roselle
St-Bonnet-Briance
Linards
Châteauneuf-la-Forêt
Nexon
Pierre-Buffière
St-Jean-Ligoure
Glanges
St-Méard
Sussac
Domps
St-Priest-Ligoure
Vicq-s.-Breuilh
Janailhac
Magnac-Bourg
la Croisille-s.-Briance
St-Gilles-les-Forêts
St-Germain-les-Belles
St-Vitte-s.-Briance
Surdoux
la Roche-l'Abeille
Château-Chervix
la Porcherie
Chamberet
Meuzac
Meilhards
Masseret
Lamongerie
Coussac-Bonneval
St-Yrieix-la-Perche
Montgibaud
Benayes
Salon-la-Tour
Rilhac-Treignac
Affieux
Peyrissac
Glandon
St-Julien-le-Vendômois
Lubersac
Condat-s.-Ganaveix
Eyburie
le Lonzac
St-Eloy-les-Tuileries
Ségur-le-Château
St-Pardoux-Corbier
St-Ybard
Uzerche
Chamboulive
Pierrefitte
Espartignac
Beyssenac
Arnac-Pompadour
Troche
Vigeois
St-Jal
Seilhac
St-Cyr-les-Champagnes
St-Sornin-Lavolps
Beyssac
Savignac-Lédrier
Concèze
Lagraulière
St-Mesmin
Lascaux
St-Clément
Juillac
Orgnac-s.-Vézère
Vignols
Perpezac-le-Noir
Chabrignac
St-Solve
Estivaux
Chanteix
Naves
St-Bonnet-la-Rivière
Voutezac
St-Pardoux-l'Ortigier
St-Bonnet-l'Enfantier
St-Mexant
Segonzac
Rosiers-de-Juillac
Sadroc
St-Germain-les-Vergnes
Tulle
St-Cyr-la-Roche
Objat
Allassac
Vars-s.-Roseix
St-Robert
Ayen
St-Cyprien
Favars
159
A 20
N 120
D 920
D 940
D 704
D 979
D 901
D 902
N 141

FELLETIN
St-Yrieix-la-Montagne
Royère-de-Vassivière
Lac de Vassivière
Beaumont-du-Lac
Gentioux-Pigerolles
Faux-la-Montagne
Nedde
Peyrelevade
Tarnac
Rempnat
St-Quentin-la-Chabanne
St-Frion
Pontcharraud
St-Pardoux-d'Arnet
St-Maurice-près-Crocq
CROCQ
St-Georges-Nigremont
Poussanges
Magnat-l'Étrange
St-Agnant-près-Crocq
Clairavaux
Malleret
Beissat
Flayat
Féniers
Gioux
Croze
Le Mas-d'Artige
La Courtine
St-Oradoux-de-Chirouze
St-Setiers
Sornac
St-Martial-le-Vieux
Couffy-s.-Sarsonne
Courteix
St-Rémy
Lignareix
Millevaches
Toy-Viam
St-Merd-les-Oussines
Chavanac
St-Sulpice-les-Bois
St-Germain-Lavolps
St-Pardoux-le-Vieux
St-Pardoux-le-Neuf
Aix
Bugeat
Viam
Pérols-sur-Vézère
Alleyrat
Chaveroche
Lacelle
USSEL
St-Fréjoux
Meymac
Ambrugeat
Bonnefond
Gourdon-Murat
Lestards
Veix
Pradines
Grandsaigne
Davignac
Combressol
St-Angel
Mestes
St-Exupéry-les-Roches
Veyrières
Péret-Bel-Air
Maussac
Valiergues
St-Yrieix-le-Déjalat
Chaumeil
Chirac-Bellevue
St-Étienne-la-Geneste
St-Victour
Margerides
Soudeilles
Darnets
Palisse
Ste-Marie-Lapanouze
Roche-le-Peyroux
Liginiac
St-Augustin
Sarran
Égletons
Moustier-Ventadour
Rosiers-d'Égletons
Meyrignac-l'Église
Vitrac-s.-Montane
Corrèze
Neuvic
St-Hilaire-Luc
Lamazière-Basse
Sérandon
Montaignac-St-Hippolyte
Chapelle-Spinasse
Champagnac
St-Hilaire-Foissac
St-Pantaléon-de-Lapleau
Vayrières
Eyrein
Marcouyeux
Le Jardin
Champagnac-la-Noaille
Lafage-sur-Sombre
Lapleau
Latronche
Arches
St-Priest-de-Gimel
Gimel-les-Cascades
Clergoux
Marcillac-la-Croisille
St-Merd-de-Lapleau
Soursac
Sourniac
Chanac-les-Mines
St-Martial-de-Gimel
St-Bonnet-Avalouse
St-Pardoux-la-Croisille
Laval-sur-Luzège
Jaleyrac
PLATEAU DE MILLEVACHES
N 89-E 70
132
147
160

133
PONTAUMUR
St-Avit
Landogne
Montfermy
Pulvérières
Condat-en-Combraille
Combrailles
la Goutelle
PONTGIBAUD
Bromont Lamothe
St-Ours
Giat
Voingt
St-Étienne-des-Champs
St-Hilaire-les-Monges
Cisternes-la-Forêt
Puy St-Gulmier
St-Pierre-le-Chastel
PUY DE DÔME
PARC
Orcines
CHAMALIÈRES
ROYAT
Verneugheol
Sauvagnat
Gelles
Prondines
HERMENT
St-Germain-près-Herment
Tortebesse
Heume-l'Église
Mazaye
Ceyssat
Olby
Nébouzat
St-Genès-Champanelle
Laroche-près-Feyt
Lastic
Briffons
St-Pierre-Roche
St-Bonnet-près-Orcival
ROCHEFORT-MONTAGNE
Orcival
Aurières
Vernines
Aydat
Feyt
EYGURANDE
Monestier-Merlines
BOURG-LASTIC
St-Julien-Puy-Lavèze
Perpezat
Laqueuille
St-Sulpice
Saulzet-le-Froid
Messeix
Avèze
St-Sauves-d'Auvergne
Murat-le-Quaire
Savennes
la Bourboule
Mont-Dore
Murol
St-Nectaire
St-Étienne-aux-Clos
Singles
TAUVES
Chambon-s-Lac
St-Victor-la-Rivière
St-Diéry
Confolent-Port-Dieu
LA TOUR-D'AUVERGNE
PUY DE SANCY
RÉGIONAL
BESSE-ET-ST-ANASTAISE
Larodde
Thalamy
Trémouille-St-Loup
Bagnols
Chastreix
Monestier-Port-Dieu
Labessette
Lac Pavin
Picherande
St-Donat
Cros
Beaulieu
Lanobre
Compains
St-Genès-Champespe
Egliseneuve-d'Entraigues
CHAMPS-S-TARENTAINE-MARCHAL
BORT-LES-ORGUES
Espinchal
St-Alyre-ès-Montagne
la Godivelle
Mazoires
Trémouille
Montboudif
Chanterelle
DES
Antignac
SAIGNES
CONDAT
Montgreleix
St-Amandin
Marcenat
LE CEZALLIER
Lugarde
RIOM-ÈS-MONTAGNES
St-Bonnet-de-Condat
Landeyrat
Pradiers
Vèze
Auzers
Trizac
Apchon
St-Saturnin
Molèdes
161
146
25
26
147

CLERMONT-FERRAND
THIERS
LEZOUX
GERZAT
PONT-DU-CHATEAU
VERTAIZON
COURNON D'AUVERGNE
AUBIÈRE
BEAUMONT
BILLOM
COURPIÈRE
OLLIERGUES
ST-DIER-D'AUVERGNE
CUNLHAT
VIC-LE-COMTE
VEYRE-MONTON
St-Saturnin
CHAMPEIX
ISSOIRE
SAUXILLANGES
ST-AMAND-ROCHE-SAVINE
ST-GERMAIN-LEMBRON
ST-GERMAIN-L'HERM
JUMEAUX
ARDES
AUZON
BLESLE
BRIOUDE
MASSIAC
LIVRADOIS
RÉGIONA
DU
Entraigues
Chappes
Culhat
Orléat
Joze
St-Beauzire
Chavaroux
Lussat
Malintrat
Aulnat
Seychalles
Moissat
Ravel
Bort-l'Étang
Glaine-Montaigut
Sermentizon
Neuville
Bongheat
Espirat
Beauregard-l'Évêque
Chauriat
Dallet
Mezel
Pérignat-ès-Allier
St-Bonnet-lès-Allier
St-Georges-s-Allier
La Roche-Noire
Orcet
Mirefleurs
Busséol
Montmorin
St-Julien-de-Coppel
Fayet-le-Château
Estandeuil
Mauzun
Trézioux
Sauviat
St-Flour
Domaize
Tours-s-Meymont
Ceilloux
Isserteaux
Sallèdes
Pignols
St-Jean-des-Ollières
Manglieu
Sugères
Brousse
Auzelles
St-Babel
Aulhat-St-Privat
Orbeil
Flat
Yronde-et-Buron
St-Yvoine
Plauzat
Coudes
Neschers
Sauvagnat-Ste-Marthe
Chadeleuf
Pardines
Perrier
Meilhaud
Solignat
Vodable
Bergonne
Le Broc
Parentignat
Varennes-s-Usson
Usson
St-Rémy-de-Chargnat
Les Pradeaux
St-Martin-des-Plains
Nonette
Orsonnette
Lamontgie
Bansat
La Chapelle-s-Usson
Chaméane
St-Étienne-s-Usson
St-Genès-la-Tourette
Aix-la-Fayette
Fournols
Echandelys
Condat-lès-Montboissier
St-Éloy-la-Glacière
Églisenenve-des-Liards
St-Quentin-s-Sauxillanges
Vernet-la-Varenne
Champagnat-le-Jeune
Ste-Catherine
Peslières
Valz-s-Châteauneuf
St-Jean-St-Gervais
St-Martin-d'Ollières
Novacelles
St-Bonnet-le-Bourg
Fayet-Ronaye
Doranges
Collanges
Vichel
St-Gervazy
Charbonnier-les-Mines
Ste-Florine
Brassac-les-Mines
Vézézoux
Moriat
Frugères-les-Mines
Lempdes-s-Allagnon
Chambezon
Léotoing
Torsiac
Bournoncle-St-Pierre
St-Géron
Lorlanges
Vergongheon
Azérat
Champagnac-le-Vieux
Chassignolles
St-Vert
Laval-s-Doulon
Cohade
Agnat
Lamothe
Fontannes
Vieille-Brioude
Lavaudieu
St-Laurent-Chabreuges
Paulhac
St-Beauzire
Grenier-Montgon
Espalem
Lubilhac
Cistrières
Connangles
St-Didier-s-Doulon
Berbezit
Vals-le-Chastel
Frugières-le-Pin
Montclard
Sembadel
Madriat
Rentières
Apchat
Mareugheol
Villeneuve
Chalus
Boudes
St-Hérent
Leyvaux
Autrac
Chassagne
Dauzat-s-Vodable
Ternant-les-Eaux
Antoingt
Gignat
Clermont
134
162
149
Ouv. Prochaine
Aire de Lafayette-Lorlanges
Aire de l'Authezat
N 89
N 102
A 71
A 72-E 70
A 75
E 11
D 996
D 212
D 906

135
NOIRÉTABLE
St-Germain-Laval
Boën
Feurs
Néronde
Balbigny
St-Georges-en-Couzan
Montbrison
Ambert
St-Anthème
St-Jean-Soleymieux
St-Just-St-Rambert
St-Bonnet-le-Château
Viverols
Arlanc
Forez
La Chaise-Dieu
Craponne-s-Arzon
Bas-en-Basset
Monistrol-s-Loire
Aurec-s-Loire
Firminy
Ste-Sigolène
Andrézieux-Bouthéon
Montrond-les-Bains
Sury-le-Comtal
Usson-en-Forez
Chalmazel
Sauvain
St-Marcellin-en-Forez
Périgneux
Chambles
Montarcher
Estivareilles
Apinac
Tiranges
Beauzac
Pierre sur Haute
Puy de Loire
148
163

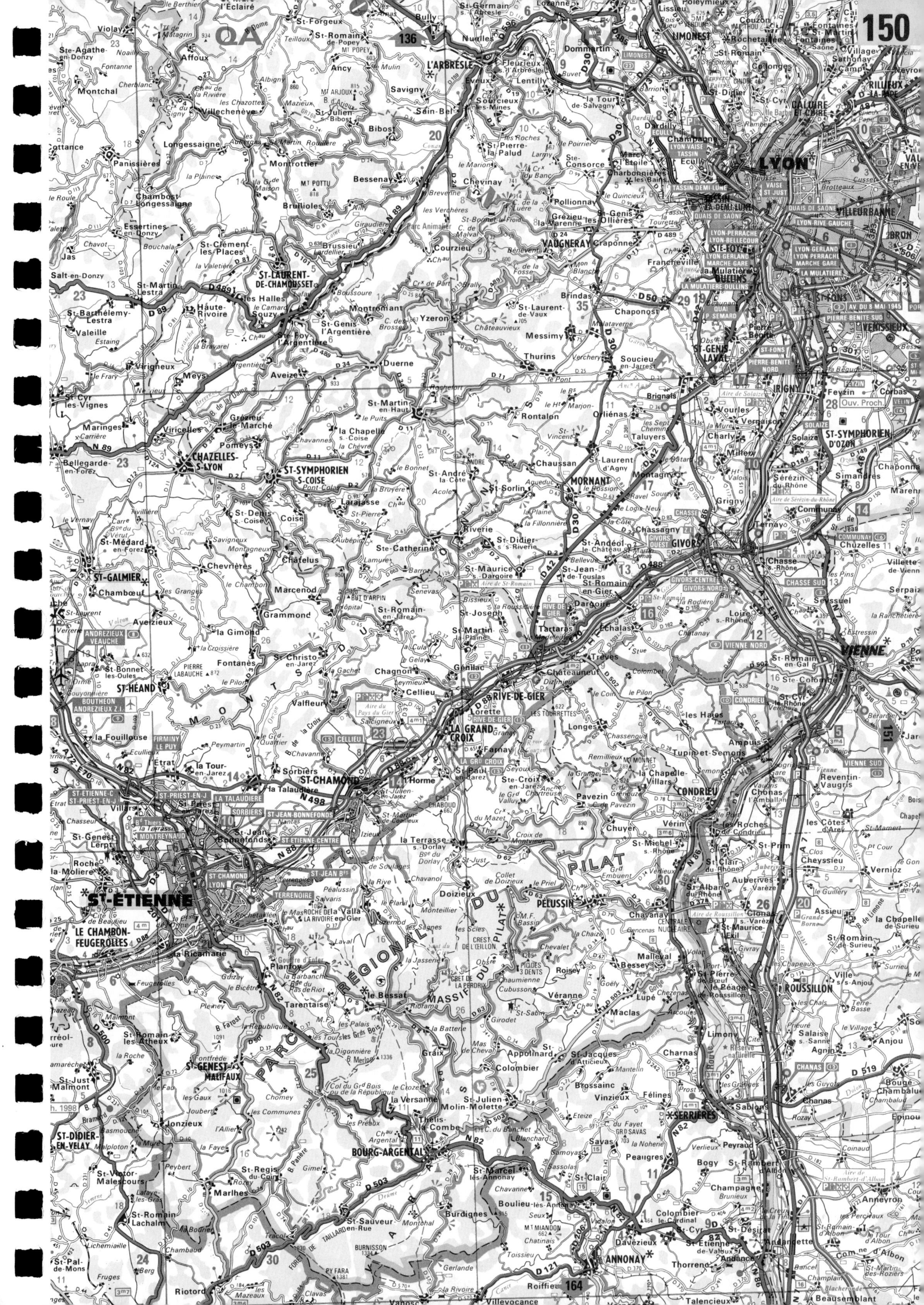
Violay
L'Éclaire
St-Forgeux
Bully
St-Germain s. l'Arbresle
Lozanne
Lissieu
Poleymieux
Couzon
Fontaines s. Saône
St-Romain de Popey
Nuelles
L'ARBRESLE
Dommartin
LIMONEST
Rochetaillée
Ste-Agathe-en-Donzy
Affoux
Ancy
Fleurieux s. l'Arbresle
Lentilly
St-Romain
Collonges
Sathonay
Montchal
Savigny
Éveux
Sourcieux les-Mines
la Tour de-Salvagny
St-Didier
St-Cyr
CALUIRE ET-CUIRE
RILLIEUX LA-PAPE
Villechenève
St-Julien s. Bibost
Sain-Bel
Dardilly
Champagne
Écully
Bibost
St-Pierre-la-Palud
Ste-Consorce
Marcy l'Étoile
Charbonnières les-Bains
LYON
Cottance
Panissières
Longessaigne
Montrottier
Bessenay
Chevinay
Pollionnay
TASSIN LA-DEMI-LUNE
VAISE
VILLEURBANNE
BRON
Chambost-Longessaigne
Brullioles
St-Bonnet-le-Froid
Grézieu-la-Varenne
St-Genis-les-Ollières
Essertines-en-Donzy
Parc Animalier
St-Clément-les-Places
Brussieu
Courzieu
VAUGNERAY
Craponne
STE-FOY
Francheville
Jas
Salt-en-Donzy
St-Martin-Lestra
ST-LAURENT-DE-CHAMOUSSET
Les Halles
Haute-Rivoire
Souzy
St-Barthélemy-Lestra
Valeille
Montromant
Yzeron
St-Laurent-de-Vaux
Brindas
OULLINS
Chaponost
St-Genis-l'Argentière
Ste-Foy-l'Argentière
Messimy
ST-GENIS-LAVAL
Pierre-Bénite
ST-FONS
VÉNISSIEUX
Virigneux
Meys
Aveize
Duerne
Thurins
Soucieu-en-Jarrest
St-Cyr-les-Vignes
Maringes
Viricelles
Grézieu-le-Marché
St-Martin-en-Haut
Rontalon
Brignais
IRIGNY
Feyzin
Corbas
Orliénas
Vourles
Vernaison
Pomeys
CHAZELLES-S-LYON
Bellegarde-en-Forez
ST-SYMPHORIEN-S-COISE
la Chapelle s. Coise
St-André-la-Côte
Chaussan
MORNANT
St-Laurent-d'Agny
Taluyers
Charly
Millery
ST-SYMPHORIEN-D'OZON
Solaize
Larajasse
Montagny
Sérézin-du-Rhône
Simandres
Grigny
Communay
St-Denis-s.-Coise
Coise
Riverie
St-Didier-s-Riverie
Chassagny
GIVORS
Ternay
St-Médard-en-Forez
Chevrières
Châtelus
Ste-Catherine
St-Andéol-le-Château
St-Jean-de-Touslas
Chuzelles
ST-GALMIER
Chambœuf
Marcenod
St-Maurice-s-Dargoire
St-Romain-en-Gier
Chasse-s-Rhône
Villette-de-Vienne
Grammond
St-Romain-en-Jarez
Dargoire
Tartaras
Échalas
Loire-s-Rhône
Seyssuel
Aveizieux
La Gimond
St-Joseph
St-Martin-la-Plaine
VIENNE
Fontanès
St-Christo-en-Jarez
Chagnon
Genilac
Châteauneuf
Trèves
St-Romain-en-Gal
St-Bonnet-les-Oules
ST-HÉAND
Valfleury
Cellieu
RIVE-DE-GIER
Ste-Colombe
St-Cyr-s-Rhône
La Fouillouse
LA GRAND CROIX
Lorette
Longes
Les Haies
Ampuis
L'Étrat
la Tour-en-Jarez
Sorbiers
Farnay
Tupin-et-Semons
ST-CHAMOND
l'Horme
St-Paul-en-Jarez
Ste-Croix-en-Jarez
la Chapelle-Villars
CONDRIEU
Reventin-Vaugris
Villars
St-Priest
la Talaudière
Pavezin
Chonas-l'Amballan
St-Jean-Bonnefonds
Chuyer
Vérin
les Roches-de-Condrieu
les Côtes-d'Arey
St-Genest-Lerpt
la Terrasse-s-Dorlay
St-Michel-s-Rhône
St-Prim
Roche-la-Molière
Doizieux
PILAT
St-Clair-du-Rhône
Cheyssieu
ST-ÉTIENNE
Pélussin
St-Alban-du-Rhône
Auberives-s-Varèze
Vernioz
LE CHAMBON-FEUGEROLLES
Chavanay
Clonas-s-Varèze
Assieu
La Ricamarie
PARC NATUREL RÉGIONAL DU PILAT
St-Maurice-l'Exil
St-Romain-de-Surieu
Planfoy
Roisey
Malleval
Bessey
Le Péage-de-Roussillon
ROUSSILLON
Ville-s-Anjou
Tarentaise
le Bessat
MASSIF DU PILAT
Véranne
Lupé
Maclas
St-Romain-les-Atheux
La Roche
Graix
St-Appolinard
St-Jacques-d'Atticieux
Limony
Salaise-s-Sanne
Anjou
Agnin
ST-GENEST-MALIFAUX
Colombier
Charnas
St-Just-Malmont
Brossainc
Vinzieux
Félines
la Versanne
St-Julien-Molin-Molette
SERRIÈRES
Sablons
Chanas
Bougé-Chambalud
Jonzieux
Thélis-la-Combe
ST-DIDIER-EN-VELAY
BOURG-ARGENTAL
Savas
Peyraud
Peaugres
Bogy
St-Rambert-d'Albon
St-Victor-Malescours
Marlhes
St-Regis-du-Coin
St-Marcel-lès-Annonay
St-Clair
Champagne
St-Romain-Lachalm
Burdignes
Boulieu-lès-Annonay
St-Sauveur-en-Rue
Colombier-le-Cardinal
St-Cyr
St-Désirat
Anneyron
Davézieux
St-Étienne-de-Valoux
Andancette
St-Pal-de-Mons
ANNONAY
Thorrenc
Andance
Riotord
Roiffieux
Villevocance
Beausemblant
Talencieux
Vanosc

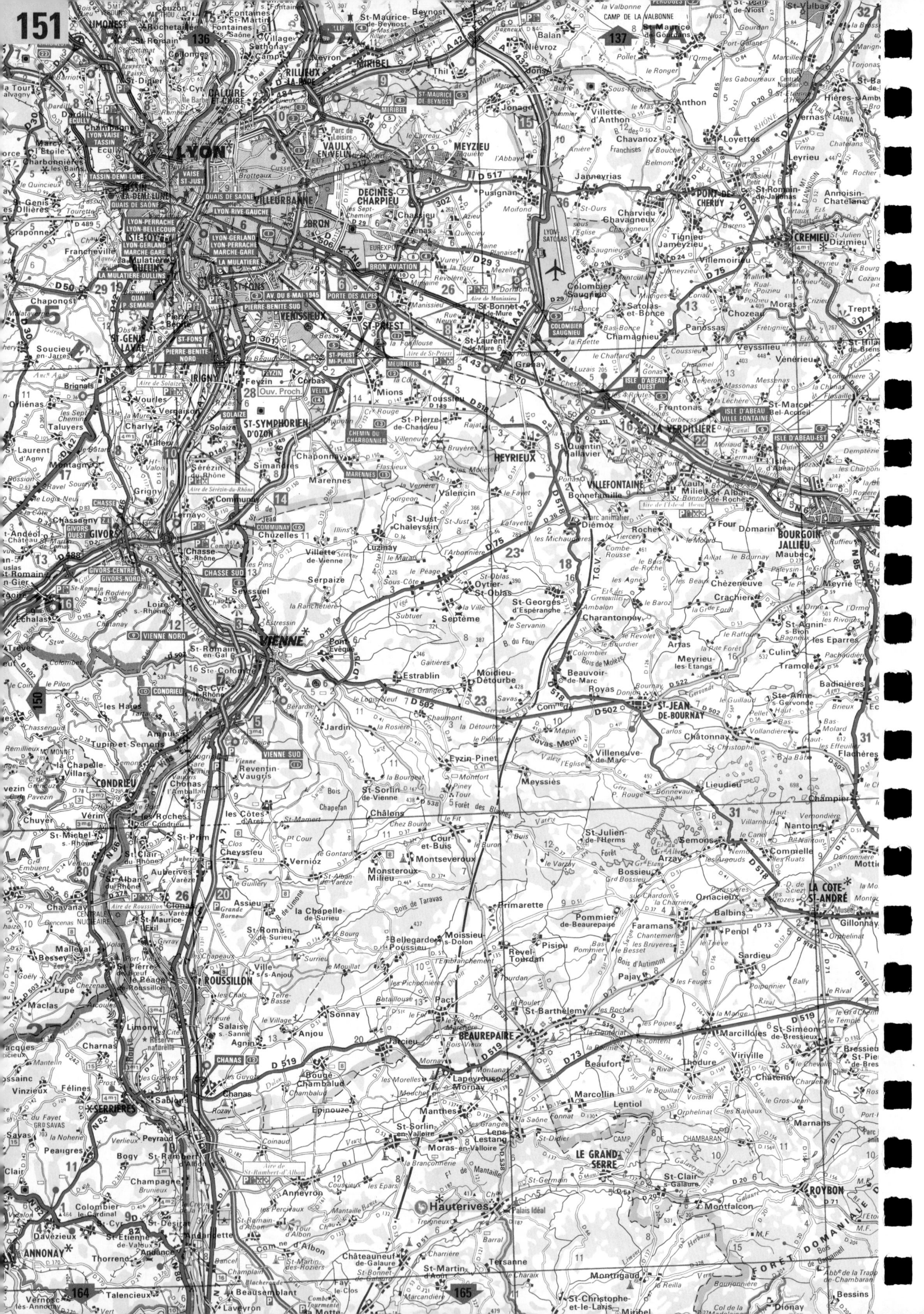
136
137
150
164
165
LYON
VILLEURBANNE
VAISE ST-JUST
QUAIS DE SAÔNE
LYON-RIVE-GAUCHE
LYON-PERRACHE
LYON-BELLECOUR
LYON-GERLAND
MARCHE GARE
LA MULATIÈRE
LA MULATIÈRE-OULLINS
TASSIN-DEMI-LUNE
LYON-VAISE
ECULLY
Limonest
Rochetaillée
Couzon
Fontaines-St-Martin
Fontaines-s-Saône
Collonges
St-Cyr
Caluire et Cuire
Rillieux-la-Pape
Sathonay
Neyron
Miribel
Beynost
St-Maurice-de-Beynost
ST-MAURICE DE-BEYNOST
Balan
Niévroz
Thil
Jons
Jonage
Meyzieu
Décines-Charpieu
Vaulx-en-Velin
Bron
BRON AVIATION
EUREXPO
PORTE DES ALPES
AV. DU 8-MAI-1945
PIERRE-BÉNITE-SUD
PIERRE-BÉNITE-NORD
Vénissieux
St-Fons
St-Priest
ST-PRIEST MI-PLAINE
Aire de St-Priest
Aire de Manissieux
St-Bonnet-de-Mure
St-Laurent-de-Mure
Pusignan
Genas
Chassieu
Colombier-Saugnieu
COLOMBIER SAUGNIEU
LYON SATOLAS
Satolas-et-Bonce
Janneyrias
Villette-d'Anthon
Anthon
Chavanoz
Charvieu-Chavagneux
Pont-de-Chéruy
Tignieu-Jameyzieu
Villemoirieu
Crémieu
Loyettes
Camp de la Valbonne
St-Maurice-de-Gourdans
St-Vulbas
Hières-s-Amby
Vernas
Leyrieu
Annoisin-Chatelans
Dizimieu
Moras
Trept
Chozeau
Panossas
Chamagnieu
Frontonas
Vénérieu
Veyssilieu
ISLE D'ABEAU OUEST
ISLE D'ABEAU VILLE FONTAINE
ISLE D'ABEAU-EST
La Verpillière
St-Marcel-Bel-Accueil
L'Isle-d'Abeau
Villefontaine
Vaulx-Milieu
St-Alban-de-Roche
Bourgoin-Jallieu
Domarin
Four
Ruffieu
Maubec
Grenay
Heyrieux
St-Quentin-Fallavier
Bonnefamille
Diémoz
Valencin
St-Just-Chaleyssin
St-Pierre-de-Chandieu
Toussieu
Mions
Corbas
Feyzin
St-Symphorien-d'Ozon
Simandres
Marennes
MARENNES
Chaponnay
CHEMIN DU CHARBONNIER
Solaize
SOLAIZE
Sérézin-du-Rhône
Aire de Sérézin-du-Rhône
Communay
COMMUNAY
Ternay
Irigny
Vourles
Charly
Millery
Grigny
Brignais
Chaponost
Francheville
Craponne
St-Genis-Laval
Oullins
Pierre-Bénite
Soucieu-en-Jarrez
Orliénas
Taluyers
St-Laurent-d'Agny
Montagny
Chassagny
Givors
GIVORS-CENTRE
GIVORS-NORD
Chasse-s-Rhône
CHASSE SUD
Chuzelles
Villette-de-Vienne
Luzinay
Serpaize
Seyssuel
Loire-s-Rhône
Échalas
Trèves
VIENNE NORD
VIENNE SUD
Vienne
Pont-Évêque
Septème
Oytier-St-Oblas
St-Georges-d'Espéranche
Charantonnay
Artas
Meyrieu-les-Étangs
Châteauvilain
Culin
Tramolé
Les Éparres
St-Agnin-s-Bion
Crachier
Chèzeneuve
Meyrié
Estrablin
Moidieu-Détourbe
Beauvoir-de-Marc
Royas
St-Jean-de-Bournay
Châtonnay
Ste-Anne-s-Gervonde
Badinières
Flachères
Villeneuve-de-Marc
Savas-Mépin
Eyzin-Pinet
Meyssiès
Lieudieu
Champier
Nantoin
Commelle
St-Julien-de-l'Herms
Semons
Arzay
Bossieu
Ornacieux
Balbins
La Côte-St-André
Gillonnay
Penol
Sardieu
Faramans
Pommier-de-Beaurepaire
Pisieu
Revel-Tourdan
Primarette
Moissieu-s-Dolon
Bellegarde-Poussieu
St-Romain-en-Gal
Ste-Colombe
St-Cyr-s-le-Rhône
CONDRIEU
Condrieu
Ampuis
Tupin-et-Semons
Les Haies
Reventin-Vaugris
Chonas-l'Amballan
Les Roches-de-Condrieu
Les Côtes-d'Arey
Jardin
Chaumont
St-Sorlin-de-Vienne
Châlons
Cour-et-Buis
Montseveroux
Monsteroux-Milieu
Vernioz
St-Alban-de-Varèze
Cheyssieu
Auberives-s-Varèze
St-Prim
St-Clair-du-Rhône
St-Alban-du-Rhône
Aire de Roussillon
St-Maurice-l'Exil
Assieu
la Chapelle-de-Surieu
St-Romain-de-Surieu
Roussillon
Le Péage-de-Roussillon
Salaise-s-Sanne
Sonnay
Anjou
Agnin
Jarcieu
Beaurepaire
Pact
St-Barthélemy
Marcilloles
St-Siméon-de-Bressieux
Bressieux
Viriville
Thodure
Beaufort
Marcollin
Lentiol
Lapeyrouse-Mornay
Bougé-Chambalud
Chanas
CHANAS
Sablons
Serrières
Félines
Peaugres
Peyraud
Bogy
St-Rambert-d'Albon
Aire de St-Rambert-d'Albon
Champagne
Anneyron
Manthes
St-Sorlin-en-Valloire
Moras-en-Valloire
Lens-Lestang
Epinouze
Le Grand-Serre
St-Clair-s-Galaure
Roybon
Montfalcon
Hauterives
Palais Idéal
Tersanne
Châteauneuf-de-Galaure
St-Martin-d'Août
Montrigaud
St-Christophe-et-le-Laris
Dionay
Bessins
Chambaran
Forêt Domaniale de Chambaran
Colombier-le-Cardinal
Davézieux
Annonay
Thorrenc
Andance
Andancette
Beausemblant
Laveyron
Talencieux
Vernosc-lès-Annonay
Charnas
Limony
Vinzieux
Maclas
Lupé
Bessey
Malleval
Chavanay
Chuyer
Vérin
St-Michel-s-Rhône
Pélussin
Réserve naturelle
Ile de la Platière
A 7
A 42
A 43
A 46
A 47
A 432
E 70
N 6
N 7
N 82
N 86
D 502
D 517
D 518
D 519
D 522
D 538
D 75
D 73
T.G.V.

BELLEY
LHUIS
MORESTEL
LA TOUR-DU-PIN
YENNE
CHAMBERY
AIX-LES-BAINS
ST-GENIX-S.-GUIERS
LE PONT-DE-BEAUVOISIN
LES ECHELLES
ST-GEOIRE-EN-VALDAINE
VIRIEU
VOIRON
RIVES
LE GRAND-LEMPS
ST-ETIENNE-DE-ST-GEOIRS
TULLINS
ST-EGRÈVE
VINAY
ST-LAURENT-DU-PONT
Aiguebelette-le-Lac
LA MOTTE-SERVOLEX
ALBENS
MEYLAN
DOMÈNE
ST-ISMIER
FONTAINE
PARC RÉGIONAL DU MASSIF DE LA CHARTREUSE
Charavines
Chirens
St-Pierre-de-Chartreuse
Couvt de la Grande-Chartreuse
Abbe de Hautecombe
DENT DU CHAT
MONTAGNE DE L'EPINE
PLAINE DU LIERS
PLAINE DE BIÈVRE
CHAMBARAN
Ouv. début 1999
138
153
166

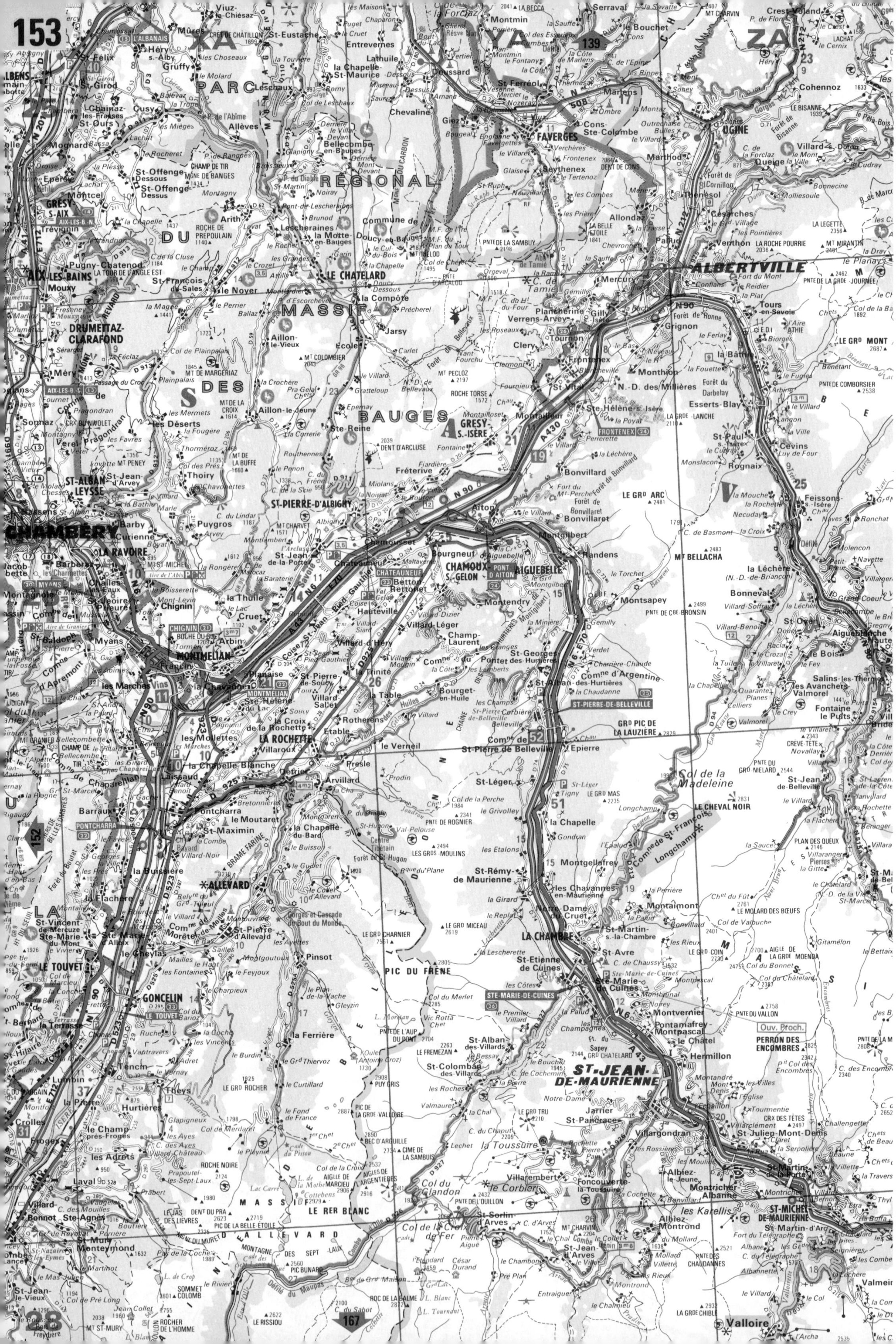

139

PARC RÉGIONAL DU MASSIF DES BAUGES

Viuz-la-Chiésaz
St-Eustache
Mûres
Héry-s.-Alby
Gruffy
St-Félix
St-Girod
Albens
Leschaux
Entrevernes
Lathuile
Doussard
Montmin
Serraval
le Bouchet
Crest-Voland
Cohennoz
Chevaline
Giez
St-Ferréol
Marlens
Faverges
Cons-Ste-Colombe
Ugine
Cusy
Allèves
Bellecombe-en-Bauges
Mognard
St-Offenge-Dessous
St-Offenge-Dessus
Montcel
Grésy-s-Aix
Trévignin
Arith
Lescheraines
la Motte-en-Bauges
Doucy-en-Bauges
Seythenex
Marthod
Thénésol
Césarches
Venthon
Allondaz
Aix-les-Bains
Pugny-Chatenod
Mouxy
St-François-de-Sales
le Noyer
Le Châtelard
la Compôte
Jarsy
École
Albertville
Mercury
Gilly
Plancherine
Verrens-Arvey
Tournon
Grignon
Frontenex
Clery
Tours-en-Savoie
Drumettaz-Clarafond
Aillon-le-Vieux
Méry
Sonnaz
Aillon-le-Jeune
les Déserts
Thoiry
St-Jean-d'Arvey
St-Alban-Leysse
Chambéry
Puygros
Curienne
Barby
La Ravoire
Bauges
Grésy-s.-Isère
Montailleur
Ste-Hélène-s.-Isère
St-Vital
Ste-Reine
Fréterive
St-Pierre-d'Albigny
Monthion
N.-D. des Millières
Esserts-Blay
St-Paul
Rognaix
Cevins
Feissons-s.-Isère
Bonvillard
Bonvillaret
Aiton
Chamousset
Châteauneuf
Bourgneuf
Chamoux-s.-Gelon
Aiguebelle
Randens
Montgilbert
Betton-Bettonet
Montendry
Montsapey
St-Jean-de-la-Porte
la Thuile
Cruet
Arbin
Chignin
Montmélian
Myans
St-Baldoph
Challes-les-Eaux
Barberaz
Hauteville
Villard-Léger
Villard-d'Héry
Champ-Laurent
la Léchère
Bonneval
St-Oyen
Aigueblanche
Salins-les-Thermes
les Avanchers-Valmorel
Fontaine-le-Puits
Planaise
la Chavanne
Ste-Hélène-du-Lac
les Marches
Francin
La Trinité
St-Pierre-de-Soucy
Villard-Sallet
Bourget-en-Huile
St-Georges-des-Hurtières
St-Alban-des-Hurtières
St-Pierre-de-Belleville
Grd Pic de la Lauzière
la Croix de la Rochette
La Rochette
Étable
Rotherens
les Mollettes
Villaroux
le Verneil
Epierre
Com^{ne} de St-Pierre de Belleville
Col de la Madeleine
le Cheval Noir
St-Jean-de-Belleville
la Chapelle-Blanche
Détrier
Arvillard
Presle
St-Léger
Laissaud
Chapareillan
Pontcharra
le Moutaret
St-Maximin
Barraux
la Chapelle-du-Bard
la Chapelle
Montgellafrey
St-Rémy-de-Maurienne
les Chavannes-en-Maurienne
Allevard
la Buissière
Pinsot
Le Touvet
Goncelin
St-Vincent-de-Mercuze
Ste-Marie-d'Alloix
le Cheylas
St-Pierre-d'Allevard
Notre-Dame-du-Cruet
La Chambre
St-Martin-s.-la-Chambre
St-Avre
St-Étienne-de-Cuines
Ste-Marie-de-Cuines
Montaimont
Col de la Madeleine
Pic du Frêne
la Ferrière
St-Alban-des-Villards
St-Colomban-des-Villards
Montvernier
Pontamafrey-Montpascal
le Châtel
Hermillon
St-Jean-de-Maurienne
Jarrier
St-Pancrace
Villargondran
St-Julien-Mont-Denis
Perron des Encombres
Theys
Hurtières
la Pierre
Tencin
Lumbin
Crolles
Froges
les Adrets
Laval
Villard-Bonnot
Ste-Agnès
Revel
Le Versoud
St-Martin-d'Uriage
Col du Glandon
Col de la Croix de Fer
St-Sorlin-d'Arves
St-Jean-d'Arves
Fontcouverte-la-Toussuire
Villarembert
la Toussuire
Albiez-le-Jeune
Albiez-Montrond
Montricher-Albanne
St-Michel-de-Maurienne
St-Martin-d'Arc
Valloire
Massif d'Allevard
Chaîne de Belledonne

152

167

AB
BB
CB
140
168
BEAUFORT
Hauteluce
Saisies
Contamines
Montjoie
AIGLES DES GLACIERS
MT TONDU
Col de la Seigne
PNTE DE LECHAUD
Morgex
la Salle
Avise
la Thuile
Col du Pit St-Bernard
LANCEBRANLETTE
M. PARAMONT
Valgrisanche
TESTA DEL RUTOR
BECCA DU LAC
Rhêmes-Notre-Dame
GRANDE ROUSSE
Bgede Roselend
Cormet de Roselend
LA TERRASSE
LE ROIGNAIS
BOURG-ST-MAURICE
Séez
Montvalezan
Ste-Foy-Tarentaise
Villaroger
les Arcs
Arc 1600
Arc 2000
les Chapelles
Landry
Valezan
Bellentre
AIME
Macôt-la-Plagne
Montgirod
la Plagne
Peisey-Nancroix
MT POURRI
Tignes
Barrage de Tignes
Tignes-le-Lac
Val-d'Isère
TSANTELEINA
Réserve Naturelle de Tignes
MOUTIERS
Montagny
Champagny-en-Vanoise
BOZEL
Planay
Méribel
Courchevel-1850
Pralognan-la-Vanoise
PARC NATIONAL DE LA VANOISE
PNTE DE LA GRANDE CASSE
DÔME DE CHASSEFORÊT
DÔME DE L'ARPONT
LA DENT PARRACHÉE
Col de l'Iseran
Bonneval-Arc
Bessans
LANSLEBOURG-MT-CENIS
Lanslevillard
Termignon
Sollières-Sardières
Col du Mont-Cenis
Lac du Mont-Cenis
AIGLE DE PÉCLET
Val Thorens
les Ménuires
Aussois
Avrieux
Bramans
MODANE
Orelle
St-André
Moncenisio
Novalesa
ROCCIAMELONE
DENT D'AMBIN
AIGLE DE SCOLETTE
Venaus
Mompantero
CHAMP DE TIR
A 43
E 70
N 90
N 6 - E 70
N 566
D 902

141
Dunes de Brémontier
Hourtin-Plage
Lande de Vignolles
Landes de la Sausseouse
Hourtin
Landes de Bré
Landes de Garrigou
ST-LAURENT-MÉDOC
PAUILLAC
Vertheuil
Cissac-Médoc
St-Sauveur
St-Estèphe
St-Julien-Beychevelle
BLAYE
FORÊT DOMANIALE DE CARCANS
ÉTANG DE CARCANS
ÉTANG D'HOURTIN
Carcans-Plage
Carcans
Crohot-des-Cavales
28
Base de plein-air de Bombannes
Maubuisson
Listrac-M.
Moulis-en-M.
Margaux
Soussans
Arcins
Lamarque
CASTELNAU-DE-MÉDOC
Avensan
Brach
Lande de Ludey
Landes de Méogas
LANDE DE TAUSSAC
Lacanau-Océan
Lacanau
ÉTANG DE LACANAU
Ste-Hélène
Salaunes
Saumos
Lande de Lavigne
Bois de Puy-Bacot
FORÊT DOMANIALE DU PORGE
le Porge-Océan
le Porge
le Temple
29
ST-MÉDARD-EN-JALLES
Eysines
CHAMP DE TIR DE SOUGE
Lande des Courtious Brûlés
Bois de Boutas
Bois du Bourgey
Martignas-s-Jalle
MÉRIGNAC
St-Jean-d'Illac
Lège-Cap-Ferret
Arès
Andernos-les-Bains
BASSIN D'ARCACHON
Ile aux Oiseaux
Lanton
AUDENGE
Bois de Lubec
Marcheprime
Croix-d'Hins
Cestas
Canéjan
Léognan
ARCACHON
Pyla-s.-Mer
LA TESTE
Biganos
le Teich
Mios
169
30

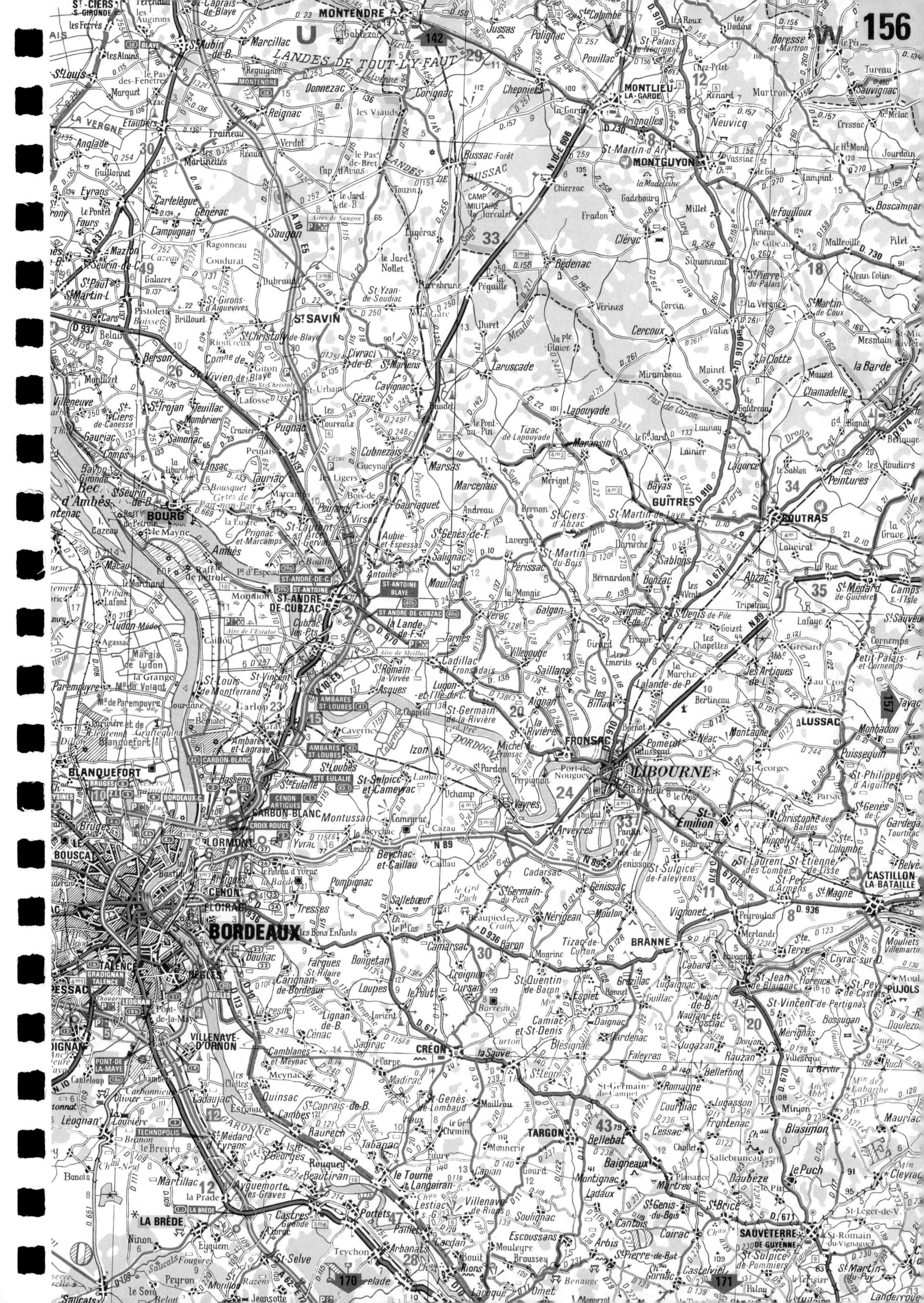

156
U
V
W
142
157
170
171
MONTENDRE
St-Aubin-de-B.
Marcillac
LANDES DE TOUT-Y-FAUT
Donnezac
Corignac
Jussas
Polignac
Pouillac
St-Palais-de-Négrignac
MONTLIEU-LA-GARDE
Orignolles
Neuvicq
Boresse-et-Martron
Sauvignac
Cressac
Reignac
Étauliers
LA VERGNE
Anglade
Eyrans
Cartelègue
Générac
Campugnan
Saugon
Bussac-Forêt
LANDES DE BUSSAC
CAMP MILITAIRE DU Jarculet
Chierzac
St-Martin-d'Ary
MONTGUYON
Clérac
Bédenac
Le Fouilloux
Boscamnant
Mazion
St-Seurin-de-C.
St-Paul
St-Martin-L.
Cars
St-Girons-d'Aiguevives
St-Yzan-de-Soudiac
Péguille
Vérines
Cercoux
St-Martin-de-Coux
ST SAVIN
St-Christoly-de-Blaye
Berson
Civrac-de-B.
St-Mariens
Laruscade
Mirambeau
Moinet
La Clotte
La Barde
Chamadelle
Comne de Blaye
St-Vivien-de-Blaye
Cavignac
Cézac
Lapouyade
Tizac-de-Lapouyade
Maransin
Villeneuve
St-Ciers-de-Canesse
St-Trojan
Teuillac
Mombrier
Gauriac
Samonac
Comps
Pugnac
Cubnezais
Marsas
Marcenais
Bayas
Lagorce
Les Peintures
Bec d'Ambès
BOURG
Lansac
Tauriac
Peujard
Gauriaquet
GUÎTRES
COUTRAS
St-Martin-de-Laye
St-Laurent-d'Arce
St-Gervais
Prignac-et-Marcamps
Aubie-et-Espessas
St-Genès-de-F.
Salignac
Ambès
Périssac
St-Martin-du-Bois
Sablons
Bonzac
Abzac
St-Médard-de-Guizières
Camps-s.-l'Isle
ST-ANDRÉ-DE-CUBZAC
Cubzac-les-Pts
Mouillac
Galgon
Savignac-de-l'I.
St-Denis-de-Pile
Ludon-Médoc
La Lande-de-F.
Tarnes
Vérac
Villegouge
Saillans
Lalande-de-P.
Les Artigues-de-L.
Petit-Palais-et-Cornemps
Parempuyre
St-Louis-de-Montferrand
St-Vincent-de-Paul
Cadillac-en-Fronsadais
Lugon-et-l'Île-du-C.
St-Germain-de-la-Rivière
St-Aignan
La Rivière
Fronsac
Les Billaux
Néac
Montagne
LUSSAC
Montbadon
Puisseguin
Ambarès-et-Lagrave
Blanquefort
Izon
DORDOGNE
St-Loubès
Ste-Eulalie
St-Sulpice-et-Cameyrac
Vayres
LIBOURNE
Pomerol
St-Philippe-d'Aiguille
Carbon-Blanc
Bassens
Montussan
Yvrac
Arveyres
St-Émilion
St-Christophe-des-Bardes
St-Genès-de-C.
Gardegan
LE BOUSCAT
Bruges
LORMONT
Beychac-et-Caillau
Pompignac
St-Sulpice-de-Faleyrens
St-Laurent-des-Combes
St-Étienne-de-Lisse
CASTILLON-LA-BATAILLE
CENON
FLOIRAC
Tresses
Sallebœuf
St-Germain-du-Puch
Génissac
Vignonet
St-Pey-d'Armens
St-Magne
BORDEAUX
Bouliac
Fargues-St-Hilaire
Bonnetan
Camarsac
Baron
Nérigean
Moulon
Tizac-de-Curton
BRANNE
Ste-Terre
Civrac-sur-D.
TALENCE
PESSAC
BÈGLES
Carignan-de-Bordeaux
Loupes
Croignon
Cursan
St-Quentin-de-Baron
Espiet
Grézillac
Lugaignac
St-Jean-de-Blaignac
Ste-Florence
St-Pey-de-Castets
PUJOLS
VILLENAVE-D'ORNON
Latresne
Lignan-de-B.
Cénac
Sadirac
Le Pout
CRÉON
La Sauve
Camiac-et-St-Denis
Daignac
Dardenac
Blésignac
Naujan-et-Postiac
St-Vincent-de-Pertignas
Mérignas
Camblanes-et-Meynac
Quinsac
Cambes
Madirac
St-Caprais-de-B.
St-Genès-de-Lombaud
St-Léon
Faleyras
Jugazan
Rauzan
Bellefond
Romagne
CARONNE
Léognan
Cadaujac
St-Médard-d'Eyrans
Isle-St-Georges
Baurech
Tabanac
Haux
TARGON
Bellebat
Courpiac
Frontenac
Blasimon
Mauriac
Martillac
Ayguemorte-les-Graves
Beautiran
Le Tourne
Langoiran
Capian
Baigneaux
Montignac
Ladaux
Daubèze
Le Puch
Cleyrac
LA BRÈDE
Castres-Gironde
Portets
Lestiac-s.-G.
Villenave-de-Rions
Soulignac
St-Genis-du-Bois
Martres
St-Brice
SAUVETERRE-DE-GUYENNE
St-Romain-du-Vignague
Arbanats
Paillet
Cardan
Escoussans
Arbis
Cantois
Coirac
St-Sulpice-de-Pommiers
St-Pierre-de-Bat
Castelviel
Gornac
St-Martin-du-Puy
St-Selve
Rions
Mouleyre
Broussey
Saucats
Peyron
Jeansotte
Landerrouat

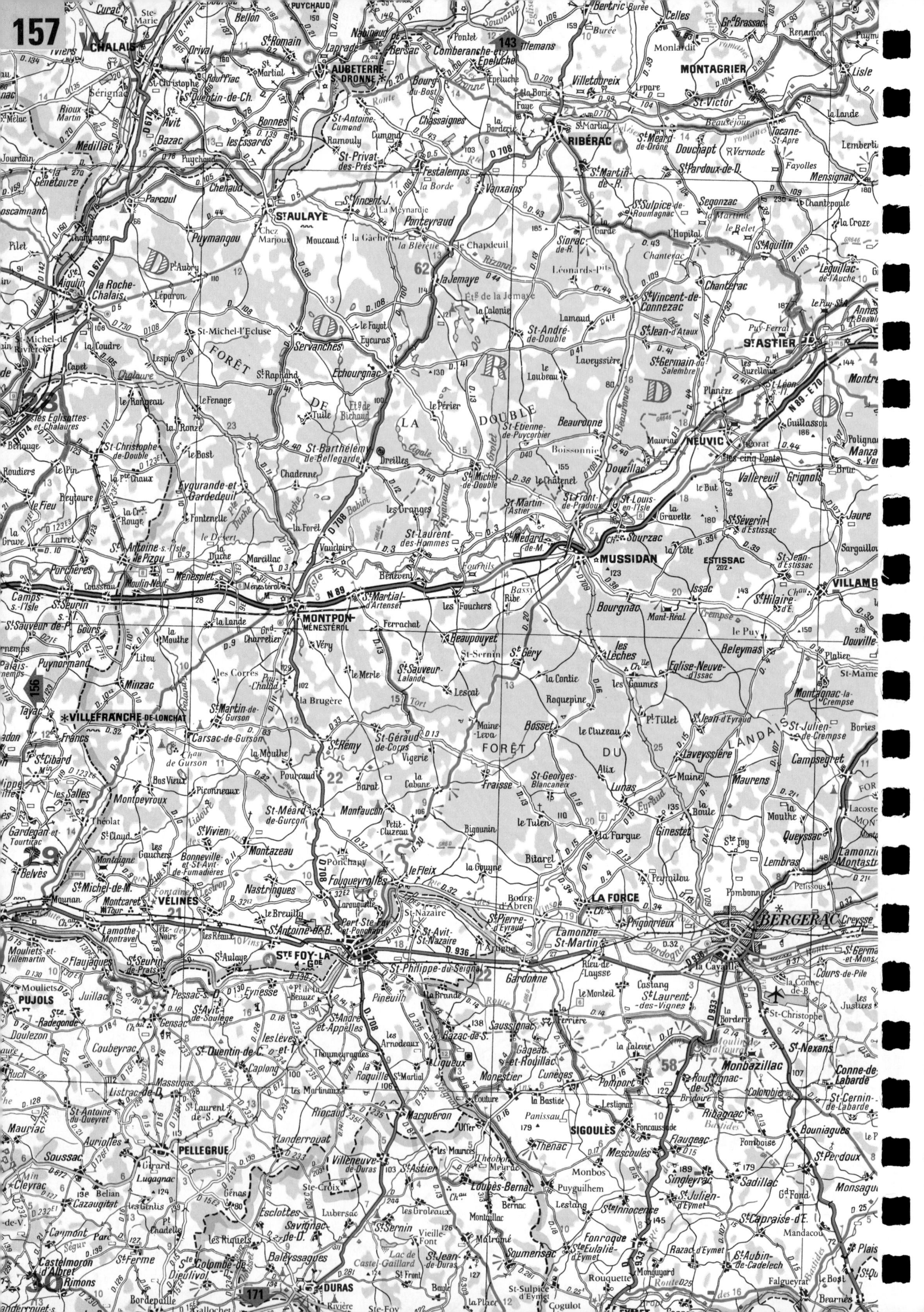
CHALAIS
AUBETERRE-S-DRONNE
Bertric-Burée
Celles
Gd Brassac
MONTAGRIER
Lisle
Villetoureix
RIBÉRAC
St-Victor
Tocane-St-Apre
Douchapt
Festalemps
Vanxains
St AULAYE
Ponteyraud
Parcoul
Puymangou
La Roche-Chalais
St Aigulin
la Jemaye
St-Vincent-de-Connezac
Chantérac
St ASTIER
Servanches
Echourgnac
St-André-de-Double
NEUVIC
FORÊT DE LA DOUBLE
St-Barthélemy-de-Bellegarde
Douzillac
St-Front-de-Pradoux
St-Louis-en-l'Isle
MUSSIDAN
Sourzac
St-Laurent-des-Hommes
St Médard-de-M.
St-Antoine-s-l'Isle
Ménesplet
Porchères
MONTPON-MÉNESTÉROL
St Martial-d'Artenset
Les Fouchers
Beaupouyet
St Géry
Bourgnac
Issac
VILLAMBLARD
Douville
les Lèches
Eglise-Neuve-d'Issac
Beleymas
Montagnac-la-Crempse
*VILLEFRANCHE-DE-LONCHAT
Minzac
St-Martin-de-Gurson
Carsac-de-Gurson
St-Géraud-de-Corps
FORÊT DU LANDAIS
Bosset
St-Jean-d'Eyraud
Laveyssière
Campsegret
Montpeyroux
St-Méard-de-Gurçon
Monfaucon
Fraisse
St-Georges-Blancaneix
Lunas
Maurens
Queyssac
Montazeau
Fougueyrolles
le Fleix
La Force
Prigonrieux
BERGERAC
Vélines
Nastringues
St Antoine-de-B.
STE FOY-LA-Gde
Port-Ste-Foy-et-Ponchapt
St Seurin-de-Prats
Flaujagues
Lamonzie-St-Martin
Gardonne
St-Philippe-du-Seignal
Pineuilh
St Laurent-des-Vignes
Cours-de-Pile
PUJOLS
Pessac-s-D.
Eynesse
St-Quentin-de-C.
Saussignac
Monestier
Cunèges
Pomport
Monbazillac
Rouffignac-de-S.
St-Nexans
Conne-de-Labarde
Ligueux
Margueron
SIGOULÈS
Ribagnac
Flaugeac
Bouniagues
PELLEGRUE
Soussac
Villeneuve-de-Duras
St Astier
Thénac
Mescoules
Singleyrac
Sadillac
St Perdoux
Loubès-Bernac
Ste Innocence
St Julien-d'Eymet
St Capraise-d'E.
Savignac-de-D.
Soumensac
Fonroque
Ste Eulalie-d'Eymet
St Aubin-de-Cadelech
Castelmoron d'Albret
Rimons
Baleyssagues
DURAS
Ste Colombe-de-Duras
St Jean-de-Duras
St-Sulpice-d'Eymet
N 89
D. 708
D. 936

PÉRIGUEUX
Trélissac
Chancelade
Marsac-s.-l'Isle
Coulounieix-Chamiers
Boulazac
Bassilac
Champcevinel
Antonne-et-Trigonant
Escoire
Sarliac-s.-l'Isle
Cubjac
SAVIGNAC-LES-ÉGLISES
Mayac
Sorges
Ligueux
Agonac
Château-l'Évêque
Biras
Bussac
Cornille
Coulaures
St-Pantaly-d'E.
St-Raphaël
Cherveix-Cubas
Tourtoirac
HAUTEFORT
Nailhac
Granges-d'Ans
Gabillou
Brouchaud
Chourgnac
Ste-Eulalie-d'Ans
La Boissière-d'Ans
Le Change
Blis-et-Born
Montagnac-d'Auberoche
Limeyrat
Ajat
Azerat
St-Rabier
THENON
La Bachellerie
Peyrignac
Fossemagne
St-Antoine-d'Auberoche
St-Crépin-d'Auberoche
ST-PIERRE-DE-CHIGNAC
Ste-Marie-de-Chignac
Eyliac
St-Laurent-s.-M.
Atur
Razac-s.-l'Isle
Coursac
N.-D.-de-Sanilhac
Marsaneix
Chalagnac
Creyssensac-et-Pissot
Église-Neuve-de-Vergt
St-Paul-de-Serre
Grun-Bordas
Bourrou
St-Maime-de-Péreyrol
VERGT
Salon
Lacropte
St-Geyrac
Milhac-d'Auberoche
FORÊT BARADE
Bars
Auriac-du-Périgord
Les Farges
MONTIGNAC
Fanlac
Plazac
Rouffignac-St-Cernin-de-Reilhac
St-Félix-de-Reillac-et-Mortemart
Thonac
Valojoulx
Sergeac
St-Léon-s.-V.
Peyzac-le-M.
Fleurac
Mauzens-et-Miremont
Cendrieux
Veyrines-de-Vergt
St-Amand-de-Vergt
St-Michel-de-Villadeix
Fouleix
Beauregard-et-Bassac
St-Martin-des-C.
Clermont-de-Beauregard
St-Félix-de-Villadeix
St-Marcel-du-Périgord
STE-ALVÈRE
Journiac
Savignac-de-M.
Manaurie
Tursac
Tamniès
Marquay
Les Eyzies-de-Tayac
LE BUGUE
Campagne
St-Cirq
Meyrals
Audrix
Limeuil
Paunat
Trémolat
Pezuls
Pressignac-Vicq
Liorac-s.-Louyre
FORÊT DE LIORAC
St-Sauveur
Mouleydier
Cause-de-Clérans
Lalinde
Mauzac-et-Grd-Castang
St-Chamassy
ST-CYPRIEN
Castels
St-André-d'Allas
Beynac-et-Cazenac
Bézenac
LE BUISSON-DE-CADOUIN
Badefols-s.-D.
Pontours
Lanquais
Couze-et-St-Front
Molières
Cadouin
Siorac-en-Périgord
Mouzens
Marnac
Berbiguières
St-Vincent-de-Cosse
La Roque-Gageac
Castelnaud-la-Chapelle
Veyrines-de-Domme
St-Cybranet
Monplaisant
BELVÈS
Sagelat
Carves
St-Pardoux-et-Vielvic
St-Avit-Sénieur
BEAUMONT
Faux
Monsac
Naussannes
Montferrand-du-Périgord
St-Avit-Rivière
Larzac
St-Amand-de-Belvès
St-Laurent-la-Vallée
Daglan
ISSIGEAC
St-Léon-d'Issigeac
Nojals-et-Clottes
Ste-Croix
St-Romain-de-M.
St-Marcory
Salles-de-Belvès
Orliac
St-Pompon
Rampieux
Lolme
Lavalade
Marsalès
Ste-Sabine-Born
St-Cassien
Capdrot
MONPAZIER
Tourliac
Prats-d.-Périgord
Campagnac-les-Quercy
Ste-Radegonde
172
173
159
144

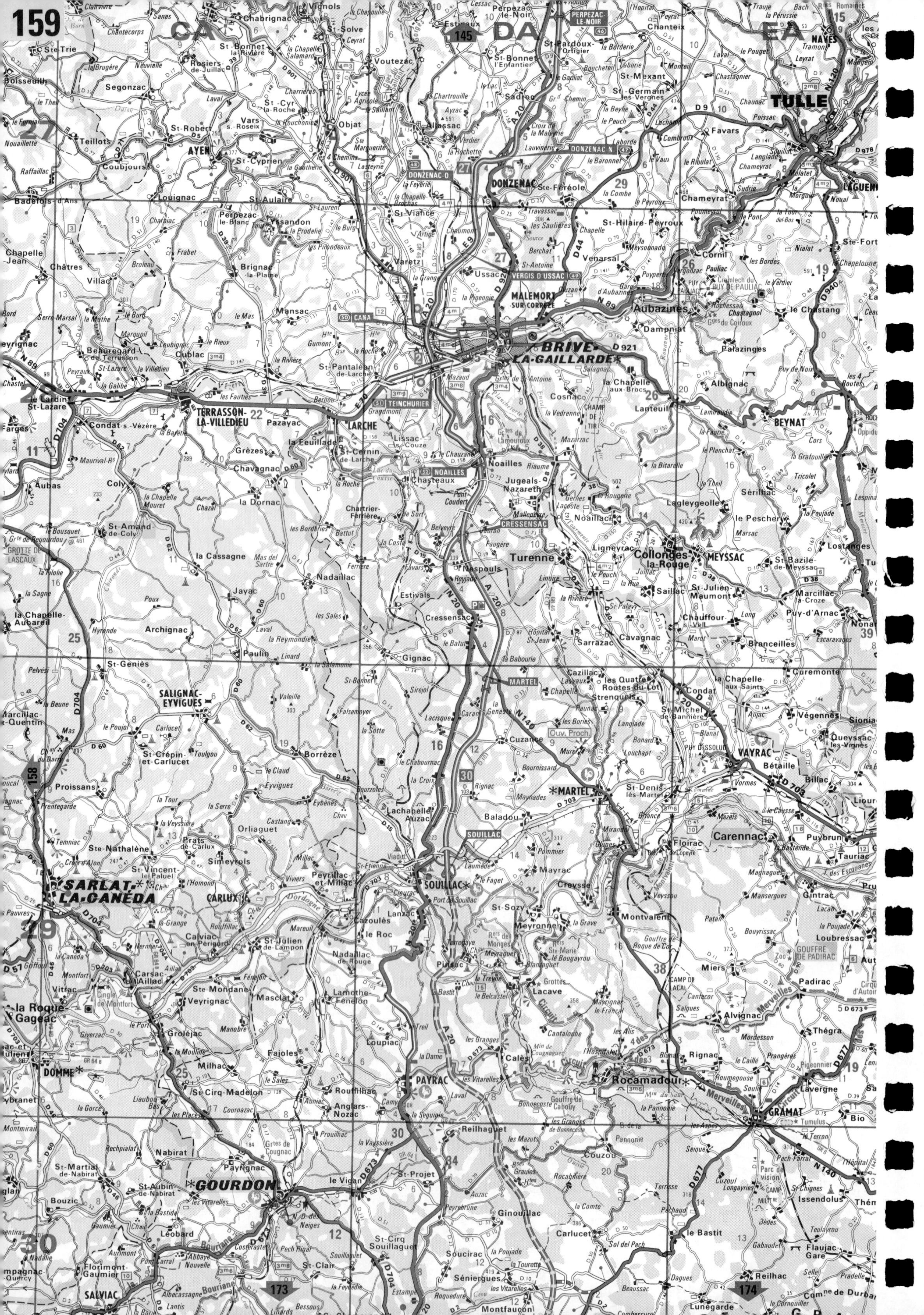
145
173
174
158
TULLE
BRIVE-LA-GAILLARDE
SARLAT-LA-CANÉDA
GOURDON
GRAMAT
DONZENAC
MALEMORT-SUR-CORRÈZE
TERRASSON-LA-VILLEDIEU
LARCHE
AYEN
Aubazines
Collonges-la-Rouge
MEYSSAC
Turenne
BEYNAT
VAYRAC
MARTEL
SOUILLAC
Rocamadour
PAYRAC
DOMME
CARLUX
SALIGNAC-EYVIGUES
SALVIAC
Carennac
Noailles
Cressensac
Objat
Allassac
Vignols
Voutezac
St-Viance
Ussac
Varetz
Mansac
Cublac
Pazayac
Nadaillac
Jayac
Archignac
Paulin
Borrèze
Gignac
Cuzance
Creysse
Montvalent
Meyronne
Lacave
Calès
Padirac
Alvignac
Rignac
Lavergne
Reilhac
Nabirat
Groléjac
Veyrignac
Carsac-Aillac
Vitrac
Proissans
Ste-Nathalène
Orliaguet
Lanzac
Pinsac
Cazoulès
Loupiac
Fajoles
Milhac
Le Vigan
St-Projet
Reilhaguet
Couzou
Carlucet
Séniergues
Montfaucon
Soucirac
Ginouillac
Issendolus
Le Bastit
Flaujac-Gare
Lunegarde
Beaussac
Florimont-Gaumier
Léobard
St-Martial-de-Nabirat
Bouzic
Condat-s.-Vézère
Coly
Aubas
Chavagnac
Grèzes
St-Amand-de-Coly
La Cassagne
St-Geniès
St-Crépin-et-Carlucet
Tulle
Chanteix
Favars
Sadroc
Ste-Féréole
St-Hilaire-Peyroux
Venarsal
Dampniat
Palazinges
Albignac
Lanteuil
Cosnac
Jugeals-Nazareth
Noailhac
Ligneyrac
Lagleygeolle
Sérilhac
Lostanges
Marcillac-la-Croze
Puy-d'Arnac
Branceilles
Curemonte
Sarrazac
Cavagnac
Chauffour-s.-Vell
Saillac
St-Julien-Maumont
Condat
St-Michel-de-Bannière
Végennes
Queyssac-les-Vignes
Bétaille
Billac
Tauriac
Puybrun
Floirac
Strenquels
St-Denis-lès-Martel
Baladou
Mayrac
St-Sozy
Gintrac
Loubressac
Thégra
Miers
GOUFFRE DE PADIRAC
GROTTE DE LASCAUX
Peyrillac-et-Millac
St-Julien-de-Lampon
Calviac-en-Périgord
Ste-Mondane
Masclat
Lamothe-Fénelon
Nadaillac-de-Rouge
Rouffilhac
Anglars-Nozac
St-Cirq-Madelon
St-Cirq-Souillaguet
St-Clair
Prats-de-Carlux
Simeyrols
St-Vincent-le-Paluel
la Roque-Gageac
Beauregard-de-Terrasson
Villac
Châtres
Brignac-la-Plaine
Perpezac-le-Blanc
Yssandon
St-Aulaire
St-Cyprien
Louignac
Segonzac
Chabrignac
St-Robert
Vars-s.-Roseix
St-Cyr-la-Roche
St-Bonnet-la-Rivière
Rosiers-de-Juillac
St-Solve
Estivaux
Perpezac-le-Noir
St-Pardoux-l'Ortigier
St-Bonnet-l'Enfantier
St-Mexant
St-Germain-les-Vergnes
NAVES
LAGUENNE
Chameyrat
Cornil
Le Chastang
St-Pantaléon-de-Larche
Lissac-s.-Couze
St-Cernin-de-Larche
Chasteaux
Chartrier-Ferrière
Estivals
Lachapelle-Auzac
Badefols-d'Ans
Teillots
Coubjours
A 20
N 20
N 89
N 140
D 704

146
LAPLEAU
Champagnac-la-Noaille
Lafage-s-Sombre
Marcillac-la-Croisille
St-Merd-de-Lapleau
Clergoux
Gimel-les-Cascades
St-Priest-de-Gimel
Chanac-les-Mines
St-Bonnet-Avalouse
St-Martial-de-Gimel
St-Pardoux-la-Croisille
Ladignac-s-Rondelles
Espagnac
Pandrignes
Soursac
Laval-s-Luzège
Latronche
Arches
Sourniac
Jaleyrac
Chalvignac
MAURIAC
Brageac
Le Vigean
Salins
Auriac
Bassignac-le-Haut
St-Paul
Gumond
Gros-Chastang
LA ROCHE-CANILLAC
Champagnac-la-Prune
St-Martin-la-Méanne
St-Bazile-de-la-Roche
St-Sylvain
Marc-la-Tour
St-Bonnet-Elvert
Forgès
Darazac
Rilhac-Xaintrie
Chaussenac
Escorailles
Ally
Drugeac
ST-PRIVAT
Servières-le-Château
St-Martial-Entraygues
St-Chamant
Albussac
Neuville
St-Julien-aux-Bois
PLEAUX
Barriac-les-Bosquets
ARGENTAT
Monceaux-s-Dordogne
St-Hilaire-Taurieux
Hautefage
St-Geniez-ô-Merle
St-Cirgues-la-Loutre
St-Christophe-les-Gorges
St-Martin-Cantalès
Besse
St-Martin-Valmeroux
Ste-Eulalie
Chenailler-Mascheix
Sexcles
St-Bonnet-les-Tours-de-Merle
Cros-de-Montvert
Arnac
St-Illide
St-Cirgues-de-Malbert
ST-CERNIN
Goulles
Rouffiac
St-Santin-Cantalès
La Chapelle-St-Géraud
MERCŒUR
Brivezac
Bassignac-le-Bas
Reygade
St-Julien-le-Pèlerin
St-Mathurin-Léobazel
St-Victor
Freix-Anglards
161
Montvert
BEAULIEU-S-DORDOGNE
Camps-St-Mathurin-Léobazel
Nieudan
Ayrens
Teissières-de-Cornet
LAROQUEBROU
St-Étienne-Cantalès
Siran
St-Gérons
Crandelles
Astaillac
Laval-de-Cère
Cahus
Lamativie
Comiac
St-Paul-des-Landes
Gagnac-s-Cère
Biars-s-Cère
Teyssieu
Calviac
Lacapelle-Viescamp
AURILLAC
Ytrac
BRETENOUX
Cornac
Belmont-Bretenoux
Glénat
Sansac-de-Marmiesse
St-Michel-Loubéjou
SOUSCEYRAC
la Ségalassière
Omps
St-Médard-de-Presque
St-Laurent-les-Tours
ST-CÉRÉ
Frayssinhes
St-Saury
Roannes-St-Mary
St-Jean-Lespinasse
Latouille-Lentillac
Roumégoux
Labastide-du-Haut-Mont
ST-MAMET-LA-SALVETAT
St-Vincent-du-Pendit
St-Paul-de-Vern
Senaillac-Latronquière
Parlan
Cayrols
St-Jean-Lagineste
Mayrinhac-Lentour
Ladirat
Bessonies
Bannes
Molières
LATRONQUIÈRE
Gorses
Boisset
Aynac
Leyme
Marcolès
St-Médard-Nicourby
St-Hilaire
St-Julien-de-Toursac
Rouziers
Lacapelle-del-Fraisse
Albiac
Espeyroux
Montet-et-Bouxal
Labathude
Quézac
St-Antoine
Rueyres
St-Maurice-en-Quercy
Sabadel-Latronquière
St-Cirgues
Leynhac
Anglars
Rudelle
LACAPELLE-MARIVAL
Théminettes
St-Étienne-de-Maurs
Calvinet
MAURS
Ste-Colombe
St-Bressou
Prendeignes
Le Bourg
Sonac
St-Simon
175
St-Constant
Cassaniouze
Mourjou

VOLCANS
MONTS DU CANTAL
D'AUVERGNE
VALLÉE DU FALGOUX
PLATEAU DU LIMON
LE CEZALLIER
RIOM-ÈS-MONTAGNES
Cheylade
Allanche
Murat
Le Lioran
Plomb du Cantal
Puy Mary
Salers
Aurillac
Vic-s-Cère
Thiézac
Arpajon sur-Cère
Pierrefort
Chaudes-Aigues
Mur-de-Barrez
Ste-Geneviève-s-Argence
Montsalvy
Laguiole
St-Amans-des-Cots
Neussargues-Moissac
Paulhac
Brezons
Carlat
Raulhac
147
160
175
176

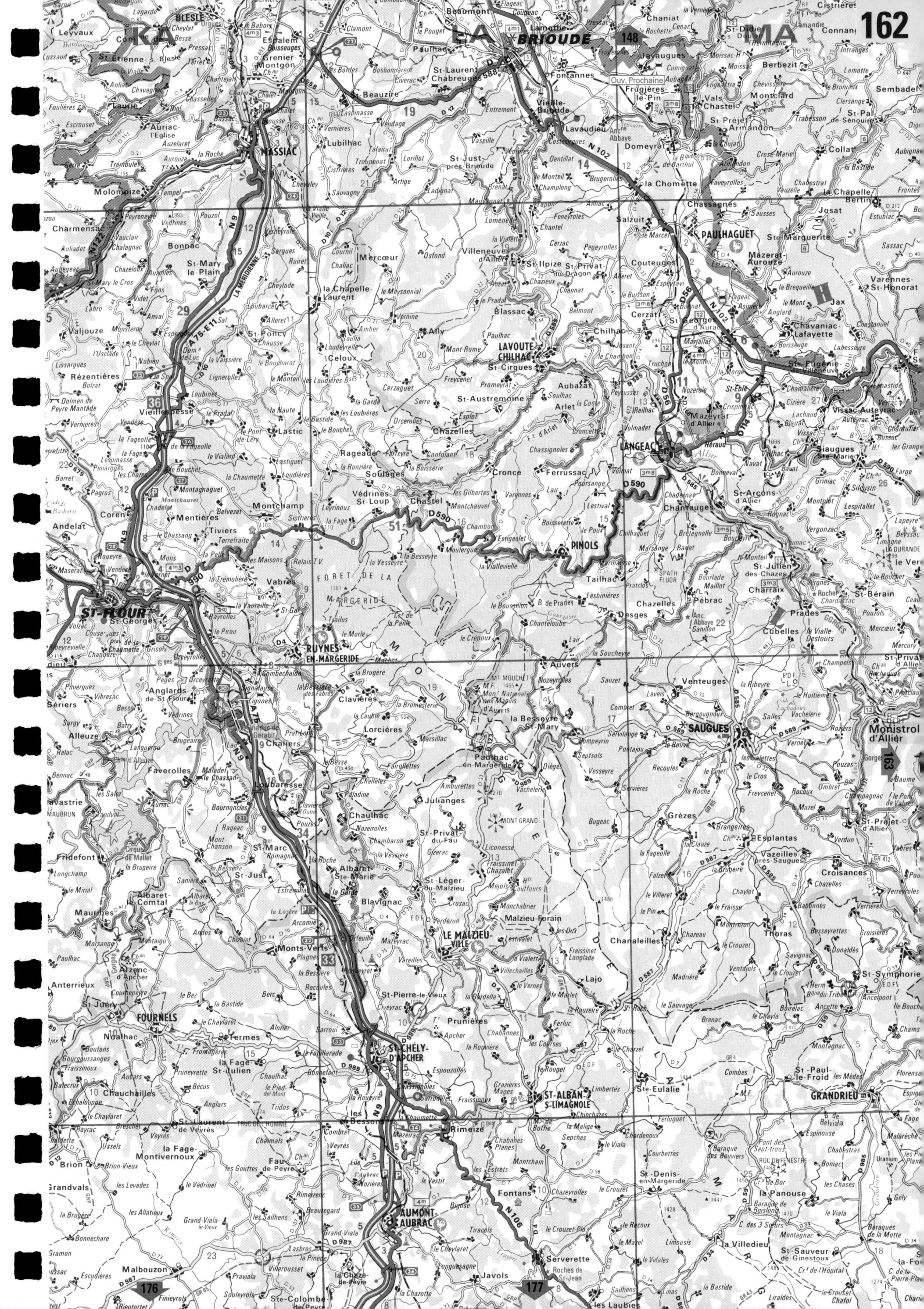
BRIOUDE
148
Ouv. Prochaine
MASSIAC
Blesle
Lempdes
Paulhac
St-Laurent-Chabreuges
Fontannes
Vieille-Brioude
Lavaudieu
Domeyrat
Paulhaguet
St-Just-près-Brioude
Lubilhac
Molompize
La Chomette
Salzuit
Charmensac
Bonnac
St-Mary-le-Plain
Mercœur
Villeneuve-d'Allier
St-Ilpize
Couteuges
Mazerat-Aurouze
St-Privat-du-Dragon
La Chapelle-Laurent
Blassac
Lavoute-Chilhac
Chilhac
Cerzat
St-Georges-d'Aurac
Chavaniac-Lafayette
Allègre
St-Poncy
Celoux
St-Cirgues
Aubazat
St-Austremoine
Mazeyrat-d'Allier
Vieillespesse
Lastic
Chazelles
Arlet
Langeac
Siaugues-Ste-Marie
Rageade
Soulages
Ferrussac
Cronce
Vissac-Auteyrac
Montchamp
Védrines-St-Loup
Chastel
Chanteuges
St-Arcons-d'Allier
Andelat
Coren
Mentières
Tiviers
Pinols
Tailhac
St-Julien-des-Chazes
Charraix
ST-FLOUR
St-Georges
Vabres
Forêt de la Margeride
Desges
Pébrac
Prades
Cubelles
Ruynes-en-Margeride
Auvers
Venteuges
Saugues
Monistrol-d'Allier
Anglards-de-St-Flour
Clavières
Lorcières
Chaliers
la Besseyre-St-Mary
Paulhac-en-Margeride
Alleuze
Faverolles
Loubaresse
Chaulhac
Julianges
Esplantas
Grèzes
St-Préjet-d'Allier
St-Marc
St-Just
Albaret-Ste-Marie
St-Léger-du-Malzieu
Blavignac
Le Malzieu-Ville
Malzieu-Forain
Croisances
Vazeilles-près-Saugues
Albaret-le-Comtal
Chanaleilles
Thoras
Monts-Verts
Arzenc-d'Apcher
Anterrieux
St-Pierre-le-Vieux
Prunières
St-Symphorien
Fournels
Noalhac
St-Chély-d'Apcher
Chauchailles
St-Alban-s-Limagnole
Ste-Eulalie
St-Paul-le-Froid
Grandrieu
St-Laurent-de-Veyrès
la Fage-St-Julien
la Fage-Montivernoux
Rimeize
Fau-de-Peyre
St-Denis-en-Margeride
Fontans
La Panouse
Brion
Grandvals
Aumont-Aubrac
Serverette
St-Sauveur-de-Ginestoux
Malbouzon
Javols
176
177
163
N 102
N 9
A 75
N 106

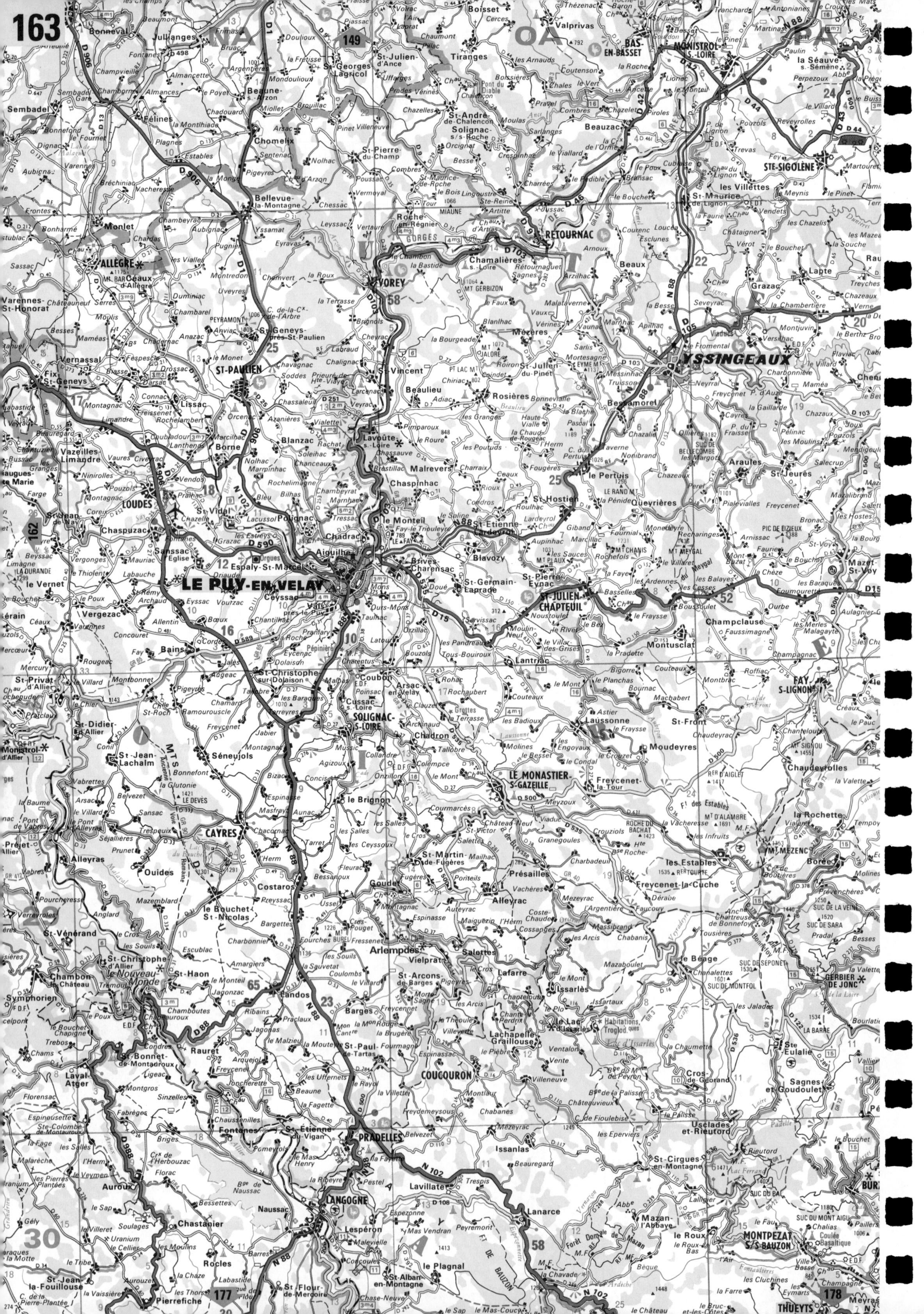
149
Bonneval
Jullianges
Boisset
Valprivas
BAS-EN-BASSET
MONISTROL-S-LOIRE
la Séauve-s.-Sémène
St-Julien-d'Ance
St-Georges-Lagricol
Tiranges
Beaune-s.-Arzon
St-André-de-Chalencon
Solignac-s/s-Roche
Beauzac
Sembadel
Félines
Chomelix
St-Pierre-du-Champ
STE-SIGOLÈNE
Bellevue-la-Montagne
Roche-en-Régnier
RETOURNAC
St-Maurice-de-Lignon
les Villettes
Monlet
ALLÈGRE
Chamalières-s.-Loire
VOREY
MT GERBIZON
Beaux
Grazac
Lapte
Varennes-St-Honorat
St-Geneys-près-St-Paulien
Mézères
YSSINGEAUX
ST-PAULIEN
St-Vincent
Beaulieu
Rosières
St-Julien-du-Pinet
Bessamorel
Fix-St-Geneys
Lissac
Lavoûte-s.-Loire
Araules
Vazeilles-Limandre
Borne
Blanzac
Malrevers
le Pertuis
St-Jeures
LOUDES
Chaspinhac
St-Hostien
Queyrières
Polignac
St-Étienne-Lardeyrol
Chaspuzac
Chadrac
Blavozy
PIC DE LIZIEUX
Sanssac-l'Église
Espaly-St-Marcel
Aiguilhe
Brives-Charensac
St-Germain-Laprade
St-Pierre-Eynac
MT MEYGAL
LE PUY-EN-VELAY
Ceyssac
Vals-près-le-Puy
ST-JULIEN-CHAPTEUIL
Mazet-St-Voy
le Vernet
Vergezac
Bains
Champclause
Montusclat
Lantriac
St-Privat-d'Allier
St-Christophe-sur-Dolaison
Coubon
FAY-S-LIGNON
St-Didier-d'Allier
SOLIGNAC-S-LOIRE
Laussonne
St-Front
Moudeyres
St-Jean-Lachalm
Séneujols
LE MONASTIER-S-GAZEILLE
Freycenet-la-Tour
Chaudeyrolles
le Brignon
CAYRES
la Rochette
Alleyras
Ouides
St-Martin-de-Fugères
Présailles
les Estables
MT MÉZENC
Costaros
Goudet
Alleyrac
Freycenet-la-Cuche
Le Bouchet-St-Nicolas
St-Vénérand
Arlempdes
Salettes
le Béage
St-Christophe-d'Allier
St-Haon
Landos
St-Arcons-de-Barges
Lafarre
Issarlès
GERBIER DE JONC
Chambon-le-Château
Le Nouveau-Monde
Barges
Lachapelle-Graillouse
le Lac d'Issarlès
St-Symphorien
St-Bonnet-de-Montadroux
Rauret
St-Paul-de-Tartas
COUCOURON
Ste-Eulalie
Laval-Atger
Cros-de-Géorand
Sagnes-et-Goudoulet
Fontanes
St-Étienne-du-Vigan
PRADELLES
Issanlas
Usclades-et-Rieutord
Auroux
St-Cirgues-en-Montagne
LANGOGNE
Lavillatte
Chastanier
Lespéron
Lanarce
Mazan-l'Abbaye
MONTPEZAT S/S-BAUZON
Rocles
le Plagnal
St-Alban-en-Montagne
St-Jean-la-Fouillouse
Pierrefiche
St-Flour-de-Mercoire
THUEYTS
30
162
177
178
N 88
N 102
D 906
D 590

ST-DIDIER-EN-VELAY
Jonzieux
BOURG-ARGENTAL
St-Marcel-lès-Annonay
Savas
Peaugres
St-Rambert-d'Albon
Marlhes
St-Regis-du-Coin
St-Sauveur-en-Rue
Burdignes
Boulieu-lès-Annonay
Davézieux
St-Cyr
St-Désirat
Andancette
Anneyron
St-Romain-Lachalm
ANNONAY
Riotord
Vanosc
Villevocance
Roiffieux
Talencieux
Beausemblant
Dunières
Monestier
Vocance
St-Alban-d'Ay
Quintenas
Ardoix
St-Uze
MONTFAUCON-EN-VELAY
St-Julien-Molhesabate
St-Julien-Vocance
St-Romain-d'Ay
ST-VALLIER
St-Barthélemy-de-Vals
Montregard
St-Bonnet-le-Froid
St-Symphorien-de-Mahun
SATILLIEU
Préaux
St-Jeure-d'Ay
Eclassan
Ponsas
Sécheras
Erôme
Gervans
TENCE
le Mas-de-Tence
St-André-en-Vivarais
St-Pierre-s.-Doux
Lalouvesc
Vaudevant
St-Victor
Etables
Cheminas
Lemps
Vion
Larnage
Crozes-Hermitage
TAIN-L'HERMITAGE
Lafarre
Pailharès
ST-FÉLICIEN
Colombier-le-Vieux
Rochepaule
Devesset
le Chambon-s.-Lignon
Bozas
TOURNON S.-RHÔNE
Mauves
St-Barthélemy-le-Plain
St-Jeure-d'Andaure
Boucieu-le-Roi
Arlebosc
Nozières
Empurany
Mars
Labatie-d'Andaure
ST-AGRÈVE
Colombier-le-Jeune
le Crestet
Plats
Glun
Désaignes
LAMASTRE
St-Sylvestre
Châteaubourg
Gilhoc-s.-Ormèze
St-Romain-de-Lerps
Intres
St-Julien-Boutières
Champis
Cornas
ST-PÉRAY
St-Basile
St-Barthélemy-Grozon
Alboussière
Lachapelle-s/s-Chanéac
St-Jean-Roure
St-Prix
Nonières
St-Apollinaire-de-Rias
Guilherand-Granges
Chanéac
ST-MARTIN-DE-VALAMAS
St-Cierge-s/s-le-Cheylard
Boffres
Châteauneuf-de-Vernoux
Jaunac
LE CHEYLARD
St-Julien-Labrousse
St-Jean-Chambre
VERNOUX-EN-VIVARAIS
Toulaud
Soyons
Arcens
Mariac
Accons
St-Michel-d'Aurance
PORTES-LES-VALENCE
St-Barthélemy-le-Meil
Beauvène
Chalencon
Silhac
St-Georges-les-Bains
St-Martial
St-Christol
St-Julien-le-Roux
Gilhac-et-Bruzac
Charmes-s.-Rhône
Dornas
St-Genest-Lachamp
Gluiras
St-Maurice-en-Chalencon
St-Michel-de-Chabrillanoux
St-Andéol-de-Fourchades
St-Fortunat-s.-Eyrieux
St-Laurent-du-Pape
Beauchastel
St-Sauveur-de-Montagut
Lachamp-Raphaël
Marcols-les-Eaux
Albon
ST-PIERREVILLE
Dunières-s.-Eyrieux
LA VOULTE-S-RHÔNE
Mézilhac
St-Etienne-de-Serre
les Ollières-s-Eyrieux
St-Vincent-de-Durfort
St-Cierge-la-Serre
Issamoulenc
Rompon
LORIOL
Livron-s-Drôme
St-Julien-du-Gua
Pranles
Lyas
Laviolle
Ajoux
Pourchères
Creysseilles
Flaviac
le Pouzin
St-Julien-en-St-Alban
LORIOL S-DRÔME
St-Joseph-des-Bancs
Veyras
Coux
PRIVAS
St-Symphorien-s/s-Chomérac
Aizac
Gourdon
St-Priest
Cliousclat
Saulce-s-Rhône
ANTRAIGUES-S.-VOLANE
Genestelle
Alissas
CHOMÉRAC
Baix
Juvinas
St-Etienne-de-Boulogne
Mirmande
Asperjoc
St-Michel-de-Boulogne
St-Lager-Bressac
Chirols
Freyssenet
Rochessauve
St-Bauzile
MONTELIMAR NORD

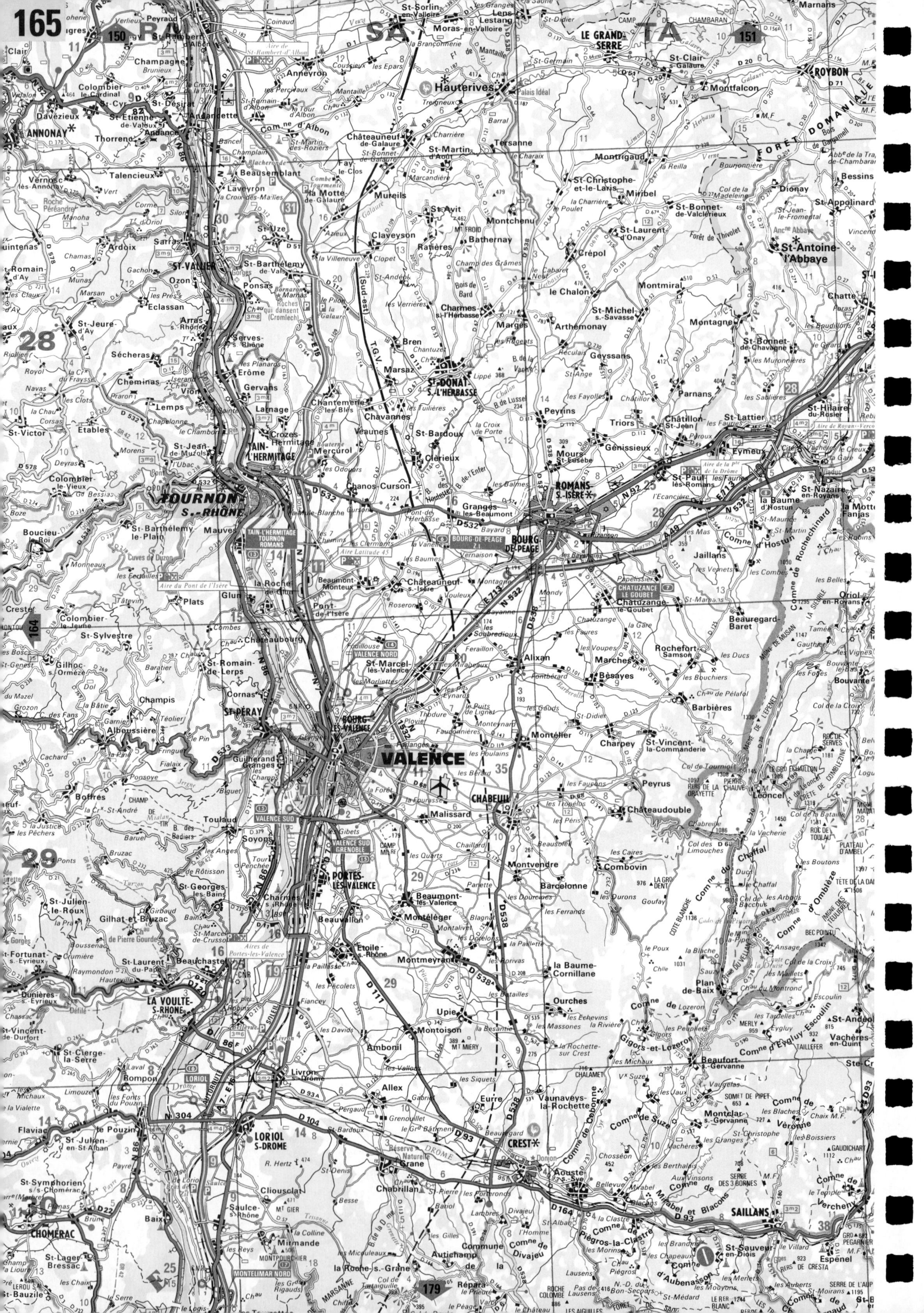

ANNONAY
St-Vallier
Tournon s.-Rhône
Tain-l'Hermitage
Romans s.-Isère
Bourg-de-Péage
Valence
Bourg-lès-Valence
Portes-lès-Valence
St-Péray
Chabeuil
Crest
Loriol s-Drôme
La Voulte-s-Rhône
Livron-s-Drôme
Chomérac
Saillans
Hauterives
St-Donat s.-l'Herbasse
Le Grand Serre
Roybon
St-Antoine-l'Abbaye
St-Marcel-lès-Valence
Montélier
Montmeyran
Étoile-s-Rhône
Beaumont-lès-Valence
Châteauneuf-de-Galaure
St-Rambert-d'Albon
Anneyron
Andance
Clérieux
Alixan
Peyrus
Châteaudouble
Beaufort-s-Gervanne
Aouste-s-Sye
Grane
Allex
Eurre
Upie
Montoison
Le Pouzin
Baix
St-Laurent-du-Pape
Beauchastel
Charmes-s-Rhône
Soyons
Toulaud
Guilherand-Granges
Cornas
Chateaubourg
Glun
Mauves
St-Nazaire-en-Royans
Pont-de-l'Isère
Châteauneuf-s.-Isère
Beaumont-Monteux
T.G.V. (Sud-est)

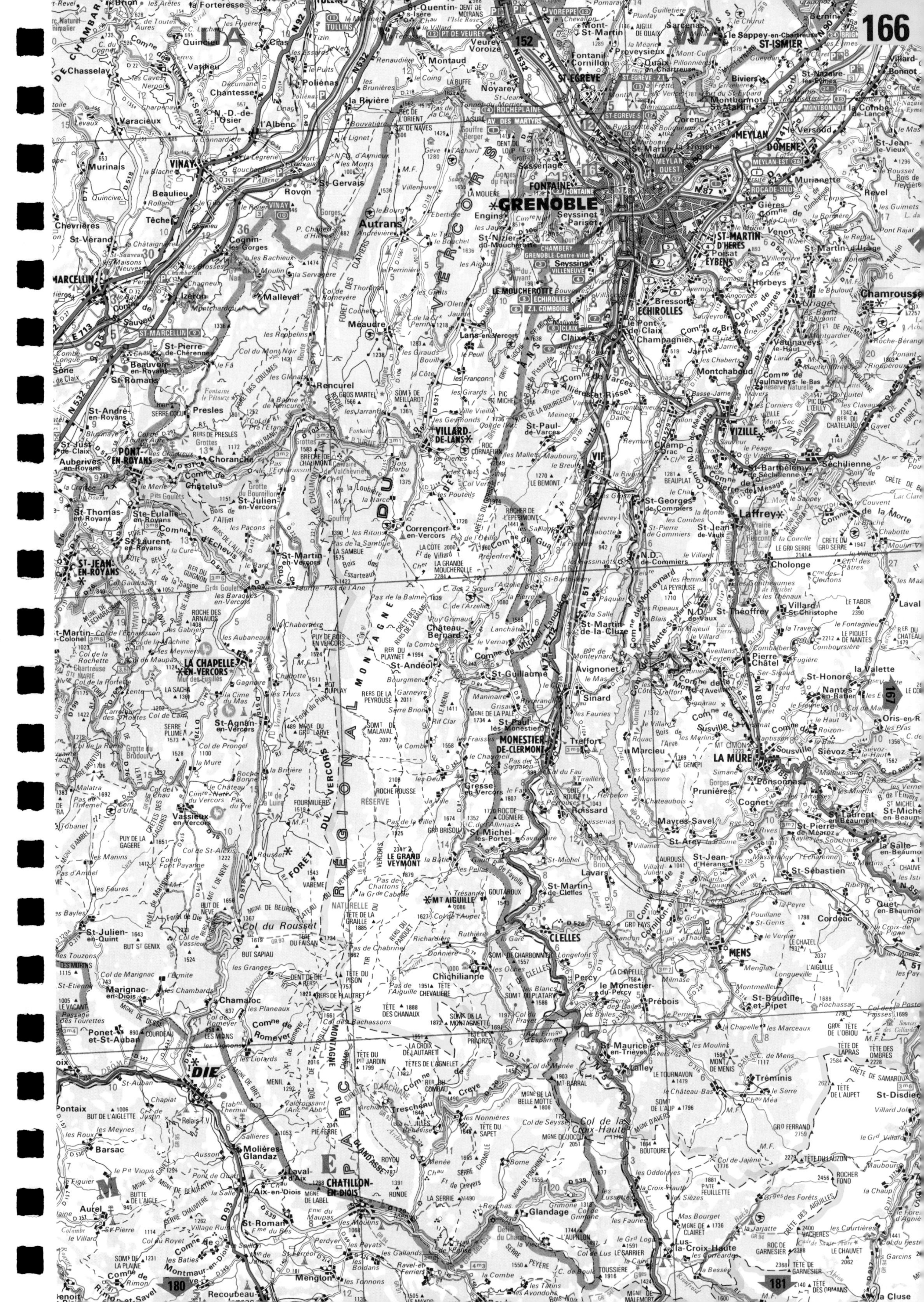
GRENOBLE
St-Egrève
Meylan
Domène
St-Ismier
Voreppe
Fontaine
Seyssinet-Pariset
Seyssins
Échirolles
St-Martin-d'Hères
Eybens
Vizille
Villard-de-Lans
Autrans
Méaudre
Lans-en-Vercors
Corrençon-en-Vercors
Vif
Laffrey
La Mure
Mens
Clelles
Monestier-de-Clermont
La Chapelle-en-Vercors
St-Jean-en-Royans
Pont-en-Royans
Vinay
Die
Chatillon-en-Diois
Lus-la-Croix-Haute
Col de la Croix-Haute
Col du Rousset
Chamrousse
Tullins
Sassenage
Noyarey
Veurey-Voroize
Rencurel
Choranche
St-Julien-en-Vercors
St-Martin-en-Vercors
St-Agnan-en-Vercors
Vassieux-en-Vercors
Gresse-en-Vercors
St-Andéol
St-Guillaume
Château-Bernard
Le Grand Veymont
Mt Aiguille
Chichilianne
Tréminis
Glandage
Prébois
Marignac-en-Diois
Chamaloc
Molières-Glandaz
Laval-d'Aix
Aix-en-Diois
St-Roman
Barsac
Aurel
Menglon
Recoubeau
Ponet-et-St-Auban
PARC NATUREL RÉGIONAL DU VERCORS
FORÊT DU VERCORS
N 75
A 51
N 85
N 532
E 713
180
181
167

153

les Adrets
Laval
Prabert
Prapoutel-les-Sept-Laux
ROCHE NOIRE 2124
Col de la Croix
AIGLE DE MARCIEU
AIGLE DE L'ARGENTIÈRES
LA SAMBUIS
Col du Glandon
Villarembert
le Corbier
Foncouverte-la-Toussuire
Albiez-le-Jeune
Montricher-Albanne
St-Martin-de-la-Porte
Villard-Bonnot
Ste-Agnès
C. des Mouilles
DENT DU PRA 2623
LE JAS DES LIÈVRES
PIC DE LA BELLE-ÉTOILE
MASSIF D'ALLEVARD
LE RER BLANC
PNTE DE L'OUILLON
St-Sorlin-d'Arves
C. d'Arves
MT CHARVIN
Albiez-Montrond
les Karellis
ST-MICHEL-DE-MAURIENNE
St-Martin-d'Arc
Col de Révollat
le Mure
Monteymond
Combe-Lancey
Boutière
Col de la Croix de Fer
Pierre Aigüe
le Chal
St-Jean-d'Arves
le Collet
Fort du Télégraphe
Albane
C. du Télégraphe
Albannette
MONTAGNE DES SEPT LAUX
Pas de la Coche
le Martinot
PIC BUNARD
l'Étendard
César Durand
le Chambon
PNTES DE CHAUDANNES
le Mas-Julien
L. de Crop
le Rivier
Bge du Grd Maison
Pré Plan
Montrond
St-Jean-le-Vieux
Col de Pré Long
SOMMET COLOMB
Défilé du Maupas
Entraigues
Jean Collet
C. du Sabot
ROC DE LA BALME
L. Blanc
L. Tournant
le Chalmieu
le Villard
Valmeinier
Bois de Freydière
ROCHER DE L'HOMME
LE RISSIOU
LA GRDE CHIBLE
Valloire
le Col
Revel
GRDE LANCE DE DOMÈNE
GRD PIC DE BELLEDONNE
CIRQUE DU BOULON
CIMES DE LA COCHETTE
MT FALCON
l'Archa
les Guimets
Pont Rajat
le Molard
la Villette
Vaujany
la Motte
GROS GRENIER
les Verneys
GRDE LANCE D'ALLEMONT
PIC DE L'ETENDARD
CIMES DES TORCHES
Aiguilles d'Arves
L. Longuet
le Verney
Oz
Pourchery
Chet du Sauvage
Col des Prés-Nouveaux
LES AIGUILLES D'ARVES
AIGLE DE L'EPAISSEUR
la Rivine
LA SETA DES PRES
Chet du Rieu-Blanc
le Coumandraut
Bonnenuit
Chamrousse
LE GRD SORBIER
Allemond
le Bessey
DOME DES PITES ROUSSES
PIC BAYLE
PIC DU LAC BLANC
PIC DU MAS-DE-LA-GRAVE
CRX DE CHAMROUSSE
Verney
Sardonne
GLER DE SARENNES
TÊTE DE VALLON
PICS BUFFE D'EN-HAUT
AIGLES DE LA SAUSSA
GLACIER LOMBARD
PNTE D'ARGENTIÈRE
ROUSSES
PNTE DE LA CHA
Plan de Lachat
Camp des Rochilles
Roche-Béranger
B. de Cornillon
Bge de Poutran
la Grd Sure
Rochetaillée
ROMANCHE
PIC DE L'HERPIE
le Perron
Chet d'Arlet
la Buffe
MGNE DU GOLÉON
ROCHE OLVERA
Ponant
Riouperoux
Comne de Livet-et-Gavet
CORNILLON
les Sables
Villard-Reculas
l'Alpe-d'Huez
Col de Sarenne
GALIBIER
GRANDES
Carrand
Col du Galibier
les Mottets
le Clots
RIOUPEROUX
LE GRD GALBERT
Huez
Clavans-le-Haut
Besse
Chet Barthélemy
CIME DU RACHAS
PIC DES TROIS EVÊCHÉS
CRÊTE DU FORT
Oulles
Rassel
CROIX DE CASSINI
le Rosay
la Garde
SAL DE L'HOMME
Clavans-en-Haut-Oisans
le Fay
PLATEAU D'EN-PARIS
Valfroide
GRAND GALIBIER
PNTE DE L'AIGUILLE
Gavet
le Taillefer
LE BOURG-D'OISANS
Armentier
les Cours
le Puys
Mizoën
Singuigneret
Oratoire
le Chazelet
Ventelon
les Hières
L. du Pontet
C. de la Ponsonnière
TÊTE DE CASSILL
Col du Lautaret
les Terrasses
Combe de Malaval
LA GRAVE
Villar-d'Arène
PIC DE L'HOMME
GRDE DE COMBEYNOT
L'AIGUILLETTE
Oulles
le Freney-d'Oisans
Bge du Chambon
le Puy de Poursollet
la Grenonière
Ornon
le Poyat
Auris
PRÉGENTIL
Palud
Mont-de-Lans
Romanche
les Fréaux
E. Chancel
BEC DE L'HOMME
PICS DE COMBEYNOT
le Lauzet
CRÊTE DE BOUFFRIER
LE TAILLEFER
la Poutuire
Villard-Reymond
l'Alpe-de-Mont-de-Lans
LA MEIJE
GLACIER DE LA GIROSE
L. de Combeynot
Couvent
LA TÊTE DE LOUIS XVI
Villard-Notre-Dame
la Faurie
la Fée
l'Aigle
LES MAYES
TÊTE DES FILONS
les Deux Alpes
LE RATEAU
PIC GASPARD
PIC DU LAC-DE-COMBEYNOT
Chabotte
Col d'Ornon
GLER DU MT DE LANS
le Promontoire
l'Alpe-de-Villar-d'Arène
Moulin-Vieux
LE GRD RENAUD
les Gauchoirs
PIC DU D'ORNON
les Ougiers
la Rivoire
Vénosc
LE JANDRI
le Lac du Pave
LE MONÊTIER-LES-BAINS
les Mazoirs
le Suffey
Villelongue
AIGLE DU MIDI
LE ROCHAIL
le Bourg-d'Arud
TÊTE DE LA TOURA
Chet de la Selle
la Selle
TÊTES DU REPLAT
le Châtelleret
GLER DU CLOT DES CAVALES
PICS DE CHAMOISIÈRE
PICS DU CASSET
GRD ARMET
les Bosses
la Danchère
Réserve Naturelle Lac Lauvitel
le Plan-du-Lac
Diable
MIF DU SOREILLER
GLER DU PLARET
LA GRDE RUINE
Planchard
PIC DE NEIGE-CORDIER
Lavaldens
Comne de Chantelouve
Lac du Vallon
AIGLE DE VENOSC
Lanchâtra
LA COCHE
AIGLE DU PLAT-DE-LA-SELLE
le Soreiller
TÊTE DU ROUGET
TÊTE DE CHARRIÈRE
PIC DES AGNEAUX
SOMT DES CLOTTOUS
la Muzelle
St-Christophe-en-Oisans
P. du Diable
le Clot-d'en-Haut
les Daurens
RER DU CHÂTEAU
LE GRD VENT
TÊTE DE LA MURAILLETTE
TÊTE DE LA MARSARE
TÊTE DE LA MAYE
Réserve Naturelle
la Bérarde
LA ROCHE FAURIO
Glacier-Blanc
PNTE DES ARCAS
C. de l'Eychauda
LE TOURET
RER DU LAC
PARC NATIONAL DES ÉCRINS
l'Alpe-du-Pin
Champhorent
LE PIERROUX
les Étages
C. des Ecrins
PNTE DE LA GRDE SAGNE
Valette
Confolens
le Haut
le Bas
Bois
Dourdouillet
le Périer
C. de la Muzelle
RE DE LA MUZELLE
TÊTE DE LAURANOURE
la Lavey
GRDE AIGLE DE BERARDE
BARRE DES ECRINS
Pré de Madame-Carle
Cézanne
Réserve Naturelle
les Everras
LE COIRO
Malissol
Dessous-Roche
TÊTE DES CHETIVES
Valsenestre
PNTE SWAN
PNTE DE BALME-ROUSSE
PIC COOLIDGE
Temple-Ecrins
Oris-en-Rattier
L'ETILLIER
C. de la Dreyre
PIC VERT
L'OISANS
Plan du Carrelet
PNTE DURAND
C. de Plan-Collet
VALBONNAIS
Entraigues
L'ARCANIER
Réserve Naturelle
TÊTE DES FÉTOULES
CIME DE CLOT-CHATEL
PIC DE LA TEMPLE
MT PELVOUX
l'Ailefroide
TÊTE DE LOZA D'AIME
CÔTE BELLE
AIGLE DES MARMES
PNTE DE LA MARIANDE
AIGLE DES ARIAS
la Lavey
TÊTE DU CHERET
Pelvoux
PIC DE VALSENESTRE
Comne de Valjouffrey
TÊTE DE L'ETRET
PNTE DU VALLON DES ÉTAGES
PICS DU SAYS
PNTE DU SÉLÉ
les Verneys
Gragnolet
la Chapelle-en-Valjouffrey
AIGLE D'OLAN
Fond-Turbat
la Pilatte
PIC GUYARD
Comne de Puy-Aillaud
St-Michel-en-Beaumont
LE COLOMBIER
le Chap
le Désert
PIC DES SOUFFLES
PIC D'OLAN
LES ROUIES
GIOBERNEY
PNTE DES BOEUFS-ROUGES
PIC DE CLAPHOUSE
Pelvoux
le Villard
GARGAS
N.-D. de la Salette
CRX DE ROUGNY
les Faures
CIME DU VALLON
PNTE DE LA MUANDE
SOMMET DES BANS
Beassac
Puy-St-Vincent
la Salle-en-Beaumont
CÔTE ROUGE
C. de l'Homme
C. de Pré-Clos
PIC DE TURBAT
C. de Turbat
Chalence
le Pigeonnier
PIC DES AUPILLOUS
les Bans
Ste-Luce
CHAUVET
les Abiandens
la Salette-Fallavaux
PIT CHAPELET
TÊTE DU CLOTONNET
C. de la Vaurze
l'Olan
Gioberney
Clot
Réserve Naturelle
PIC DE BONVOISIN
les Istiers
GRD CHAPELET
les Peines
Villar-Loubière
les Andrieux
Casset
Xavier-Blanc
Narreyroux
Quet-en-Beaumont
les Côtes de Corps
Bge du Sautet
N.-D. des 7 Douleurs
le Pont du Moulin
LE LATON
la Loubière
la Chapelle-en-Valgaudemar
PNTE DE L'AIGLIÈRE
POINTES DE NEYZETS
CRÊTE DE LA PENDINE
CORPS
ROCHE COURBE
GRUN DE ST-MAURICE
le Roux
AIGLE DU MIDI DES ANDRIEUX
les Portes
AIGLE DES MORGES
Vallonpierre
Chabournéou
PNTE DE VERDONNE
CRÊTE DE PRAROL
Salce
Ste-Marguerite
Aspres-lès-Corps
St-Maurice-en-Valgodemard
VALGAUDEMAR
Navette (Village Rne)
PIC DE VALLONPIERRE
SIRAC
Ambel
les Payas
Pellafol
Col des Festreaux
les Reculas
les Prés-Hauts
le Chaup
PIC PETARFI
ST-FIRMIN
le Villard
Beaufin
le Séchier
PIC DE DISDIER
PIC DE PARIÈRES
PUY RIVAROL
PIC DE LA CAVALE
Pas-de-la-Cavale
TÊTE DE SOULAURE
TÊTE DE DOURMILLOUSE
Col des Fosses
St-Jacques-en-Valgodemard
PIC CHAILLOL
LES CHOUCIÈRES VERTES
Lacs de Crupillouse
PNTES DE ROUGNOUX
CRÊTE DE DOURMILLOUSE
Monestier-d'Ambel
Tardivière
LE FAROT
Combardeng
l'Hôpital
MGNE DU BANC-DU-PEYRON
C. de Font-Froide
les Auber
GRDE ROCHE
PIC PIERROUX
les Bandettes
Roafam
PIC DE COLLE-BLANCHE
les Clots
MGNE DE CEDERA
PNTE DES ESTARIS
C. de Freissinières
Dourmillouse
TÊTE DES OMBRES
LE GICON
Défilé de la Souloise
Gicon
le Glaizil
Chauffayer
les Costes
les Courts
Molines-en-Champsaur
VX CHAILLOL
GLER DE L'AUP
les Baumes
AIGLE DE CEDERA
PNTE DES HOMMES
Réserve Naturelle des Estaris
SOMT DROUVET
GRD PINIER
le Palluel
St-Disdier
Aubessagne
Pouillardenc
St-Eusèbe-en-Champsaur
la Motte-en-Champsaur
les Héritières
LE CUCHON
les Gondoins
les Fermons
les Borels
L. Faravel
Villard-Joli
ROC ROUX
MONTAGNE DE FERAUD
la Guinguette
Lacoue
le Villardon
les Infournas
le Roy
PIC DU TOURNOND
Comne de Champoléon
les Martins
ROC D'ALBRANDES
Merlette
Forest-des-Estaris
PIT PINIER
LE TUBA
PIC DE ROCHELAIRE
TÊTE DE CLAUDEL
St-Étienne-en-Dévoluy
Rioupes
le Noyer
les Evarras
Bénévent-et-Charbillac
PIQUEYREL
PNTE DE LA VENASQUE
LE PALASTRE
les Richards
les Veyers
les Estaris
Prapic
ORCIÈRES
ROC BLANC
TÊTE DE COSTE
Agnières-en-Dévoluy
Poligny
ST-BONNET-EN-CHAMPSAUR
Chaillol
les Roranches
la Coche
les Garnauds
les Marches
les Tourengs
Montcheny
la Chaup
PIC PONSON
Col du Noyer
les Forestons
les Combes
la Villette
les Marrons
St-Jean-St-Nicolas
les Usclas
les Audiberts
la Saulce
Superdévoluy
Bruziaud
St-Étienne
Aulagnier
Chantaussel
les Chanets
le Fréne
St-Michel-de-Chaillol
Pont-du-Fossé
Saint-Eyraud
LE CARABRUT
le Forest-d'Agnières
BEC DE L'AIGLE
la Fare-en-Champsaur
les Combettes
Chabottes
Chabottonnes
Archinard
C. des Tourettes
N.-D. du Bois-Vert
St-Julien-en-Champsaur
Buissard
GRANDE AUTANE
PNTE DE LA DIABLÉE
la Serre
Col du Festre
SERRE LACROIX
les Farelles
les Garcins
le Villard
Forest-St-Julien
la Plaine
St-Léger-les-Mélèzes
PITE AUTANE
LE MOURRE-FROID
MGNE D'AUROUZE
SOMMAREL
OBSERVATOIRE (en constn)
PIC PONCON
RER DE LA PALETTE
Col de Rabou
PIC DE GLEIZE
Laye
St-Laurent-du-Cros
Serre Richard
le Villard
les Matherons
les Faix
Ancelle
Cne de Rouannette
LA SOUPA
PIC DE SERRE
TÊTE DE L'HIVERNAL
la Cluse
TÊTE DU CHÂTEAU
Col de Chabanottes
St-Hilaire
les Fareaux
Refuge
PNTE DE FLEURENDON
les Gourniers
TÊTE DE LUCY

166

181

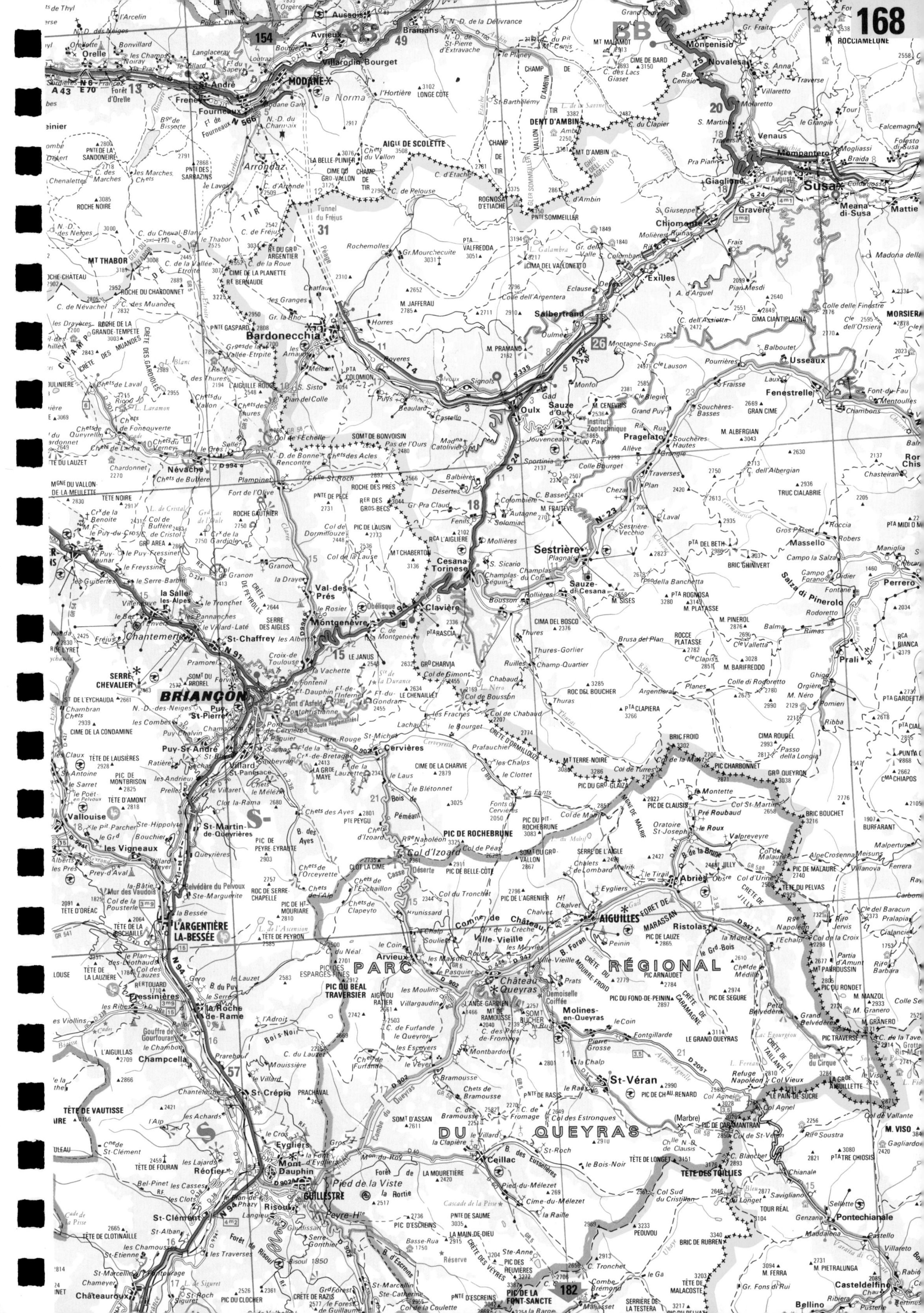
154
49
BB
Modane
Bardonecchia
Oulx
Sestrière
Briançon
Montgenèvre
Clavière
Cesana Torinese
Susa
Exilles
Salbertrand
Chiomonte
Fenestrelle
Pragelato
Usseaux
Perrero
Prali
Névache
Plampinet
Val-des-Prés
La Salle-les-Alpes
St-Chaffrey
Chantemerle
Cervières
Abriès
Aiguilles
Ristolas
Château-Queyras
Molines-en-Queyras
St-Véran
Arvieux
Guillestre
Mont-Dauphin
Vallouise
Les Vigneaux
L'Argentière-la-Bessée
Champcella
St-Crépin
Ceillac
Pontechianale
Casteldelfino
Bellino
Sauze d'Oulx
Sauze di Cesana
Puy-St-André
Puy-St-Pierre
Villard-St-Pancrace
St-Martin-de-Queyrières
Réotier
Risoul
St-Clément
Châteauroux
Freissinières
Villarodin-Bourget
Avrieux
Aussois
Bramans
Orelle
Fourneaux
St-André
Moncenisio
Novalesa
Venaus
Mompantero
Gravere
Meana di-Susa
Mattie
Giaglione
Salza di Pinerolo
Massello
Roure
MT THABOR
MT CHABERTON
PIC DE ROCHEBRUNE
Col d'Izoard
Col du Lautaret
Col de l'Échelle
Col de Montgenèvre
PARC
RÉGIONAL
DU
QUEYRAS
M. VISO
182

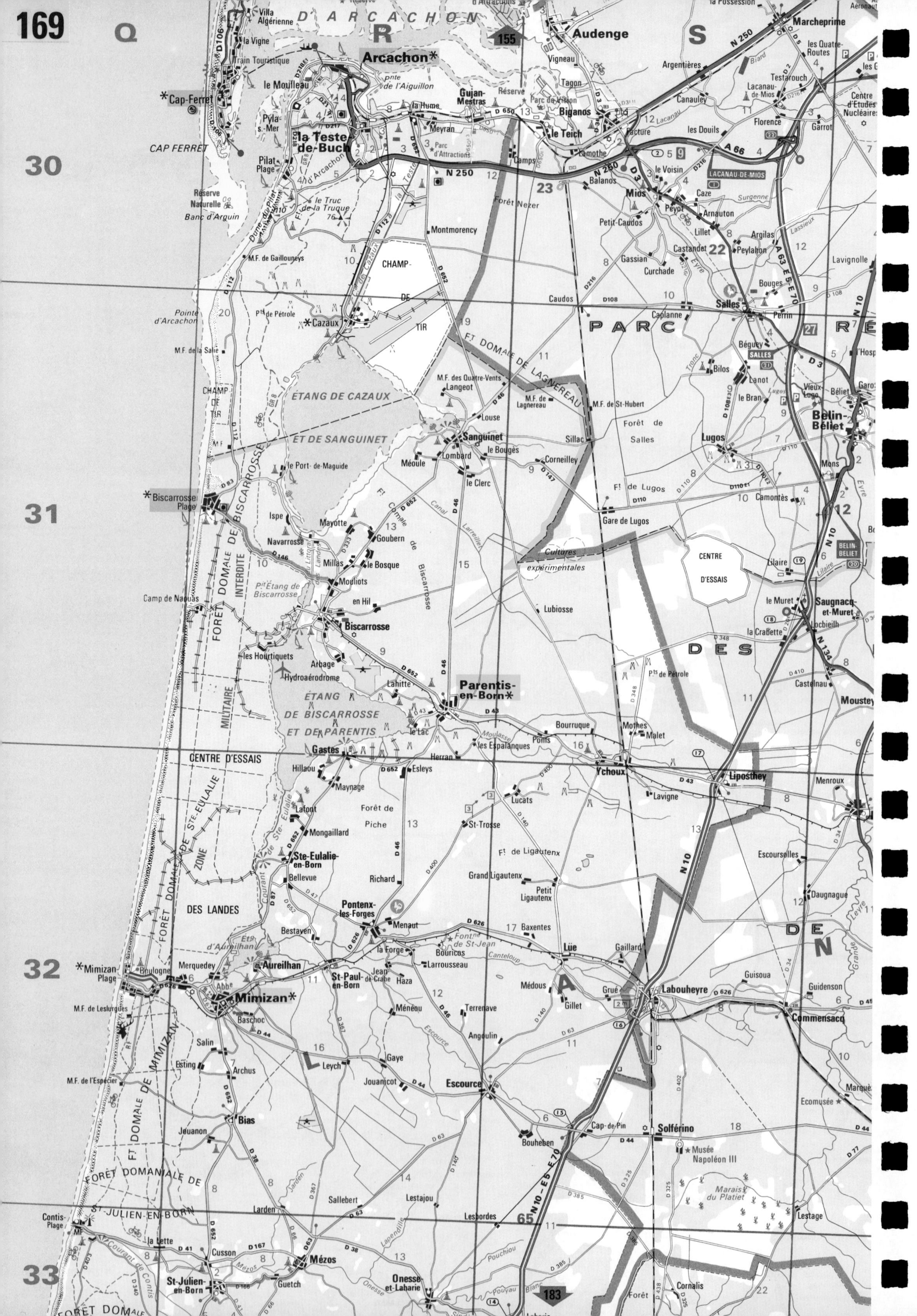
Q
R
S
D'ARCACHON
155
Arcachon*
Audenge
Marcheprime
Cap-Ferret
CAP FERRET
le Moulleau
Pyla-s.-Mer
la Teste-de-Buch
Pilat Plage
Gujan-Mestras
Biganos
le Teich
Mios
Salles
30
Réserve Naturelle
Banc d'Arguin
Dune du Pilat
le Truc de la Truque
Montmorency
CHAMP-DE-TIR
Cazaux
Pointe d'Arcachon
PARC
RÉ
FT DOMALE DE LAGNEREAU
ÉTANG DE CAZAUX ET DE SANGUINET
Sanguinet
Forêt de Salles
Lugos
Belin-Béliet
Biscarrosse Plage
31
FORÊT DOMALE DE BISCARROSSE
ZONE INTERDITE MILITAIRE
Gare de Lugos
Cultures expérimentales
CENTRE D'ESSAIS
Biscarrosse
Saugnacq-et-Muret
DES
Hydroaérodrome
ÉTANG DE BISCARROSSE ET DE PARENTIS
Parentis-en-Born*
Ychoux
Liposthey
CENTRE D'ESSAIS
Gastes
Forêt de Piche
Ste-Eulalie-en-Born
FORÊT DOMALE DE STE-EULALIE
DES LANDES
Pontenx-les-Forges
Lüe
DE
N
Mimizan-Plage
32
Mimizan*
Aureilhan
St-Paul-en-Born
Labouheyre
Commensacq
Escource
Solférino
Musée Napoléon III
Marais du Platiet
FORÊT DOMANIALE DE ST-JULIEN-EN-BORN
FT DOMALE DE MIMIZAN
Bias
Contis-Plage
33
Mézos
St-Julien-en-Born
Onesse-et-Laharie
183

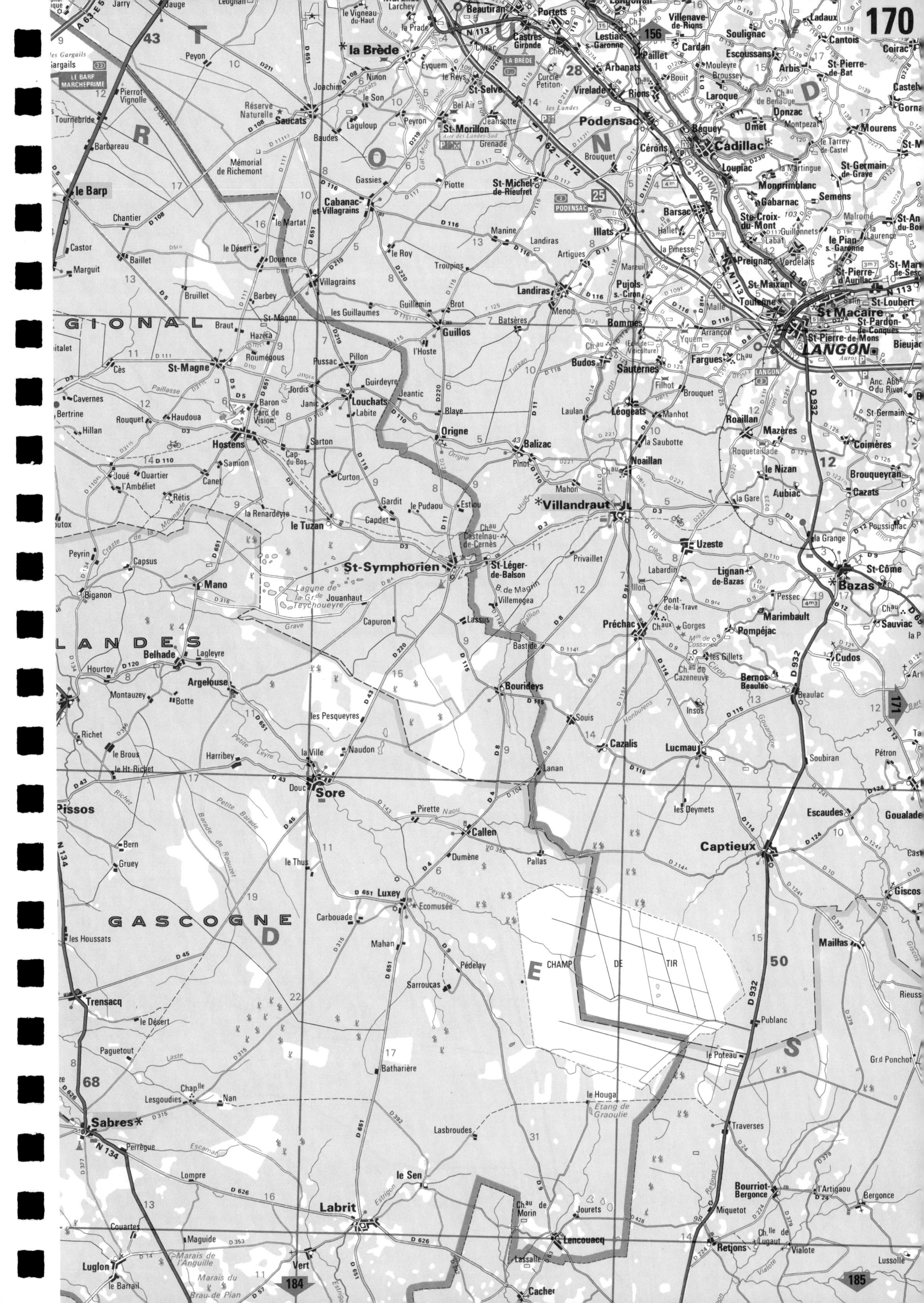

Jarry
Dauge
le Vigneau-du-Haut
Larchey
Beautiran
Portets
Villenave-de-Rions
Ladaux
Cantois
Coirac
la Prade
la Brède
Castres-Gironde
Lestiac-s-Garonne
156
Cardan
Soulignac
Escoussans
Arbis
St-Pierre-de-Bat
Castelv
LE BARP MARCHEPRIME
Peyon
Eyquem
Cérons
Cadillac
Cabanac-et-Villagrains
St-Selve
Virelade
Podensac
Rions
Paillet
Arbanats
Bouit
Laroque
Omet
Donzac
Mourens
Gorna
Gargails
Pierrot-Vignolle
Joachim
Ninon
le Son
Saucats
Réserve Naturelle
Laguloup
Baudes
Peyron
St-Morillon
Aire des Landes-Sud
Jeansotte
Grenade
Bel Air
Brouquet
Loupiac
Montpezat
la Martingue
St-Germain-de-Grave
Tournebride
Barbareau
Mémorial de Richemont
Gassies
Piotte
St-Michel-de-Rieufret
Monprimblanc
Semens
Gabarnac
le Barp
Chantier
le Martat
Manine
Landiras
Barsac
Illats
Ste-Croix-du-Mont
Guillonnets
le Pian-s-Garonne
Malromé
PODENSAC
la Pinesse
Preignac
Verdelais
St-Maixant
Toulenne
St Macaire
St-Pierre-de-Mons
St-Pardon-de-Conques
LANGON
Bieujac
St-Loubert
Castor
Marguit
Baillet
le Désert
Douence
Villagrains
le Roy
Troupins
Artigues
Mareuil
Pujols-s.-Ciron
Bruillet
Barbey
Guillemin
Brot
les Guillaumes
Batsères
Menon
Bommes
Arrançon
Yquem
Fargues
St-Magne
Braut
Hazéra
Guillos
l'Hoste
Budos
Sauternes
Filhot
Brouquet
Anc. Abb. du Rivet
GIONAL
Cès
Roumégous
Pussac
Pillon
Guirdeyre
Jeantic
Blaye
Laulan
Léogeats
Manhot
Roaillan
Mazères
St-Germain
Cavernes
Bertrine
Hillan
Rouquet
Haudoua
Baron
Parc de Vision
Jordis
Janic
Louchats
Labite
Origne
Balizac
la Saubotte
Noaillan
Roquetaillade
Coimères
Hostens
Samion
Cap-du-Bos
Sarton
Curton
Pinot
le Nizan
Aubiac
Brouqueyran
Cazats
Joué
Quartier
l'Ambéliet
Canet
Rétis
la Renardeyre
le Tuzan
Gardit
le Pudaou
Capdet
Estiou
Mahon
Villandraut
la Gare
Uzeste
Poussignac
la Grange
Peyrin
Capsus
Castelnau-de-Cernès
St-Symphorien
St-Léger-de-Balson
Privaillet
Labardin
Lignan-de-Bazas
Bazas
St-Côme
Mano
Biganon
Jouanhaut
Lagune de la Gr. de Teychoueyre
B. de Magrin
Villemegea
Pont-de-la-Trave
Pessec
Marimbault
Sauviac
Capuron
Lassus
Préchac
Gorges
Pompéjac
Cudos
LANDES
Belhade
Lagleyre
Hourtoy
Argelouse
Montauzey
Botte
Bastide
les Gillets
Ch.au de Cazeneuve
Bernos-Beaulac
Beaulac
Bourideys
Souis
Insos
les Pesqueyres
Cazalis
Lucmau
Soubiran
Pétron
Richet
le Brous
Harribey
la Ville
Naudon
le Ht-Richet
Lanan
Pissos
Douc
Sore
Pirette
Callen
les Deymets
Escaudes
Goualade
Bern
Gruey
le Thus
Dumène
Pallas
Captieux
Luxey
Ecomusée
Carbouade
Giscos
GASCOGNE
Mahan
Pédelay
CHAMP DE TIR
Maillas
les Houssats
Sarroucas
Trensacq
le Désert
Publanc
Rieuss
Paguetout
Batharière
le Poteau
Grd Ponchot
Lesgoudies
Nan
le Houga
Etang de Graoulie
Sabres
Perrègue
Lasbroudes
Traverses
Lompre
le Sen
Bourriot-Bergonce
l'Artigaou
Bergonce
Labrit
Chau Morin
Jourets
Miquetot
Courartes
Maguide
Lencouacq
Retjons
Vialote
Luglon
le Barrail
Marais de l'Anguille
Marais du Brau-de-Pian
Vert
Lassalle
Cachen
Lussolle
184
185
171

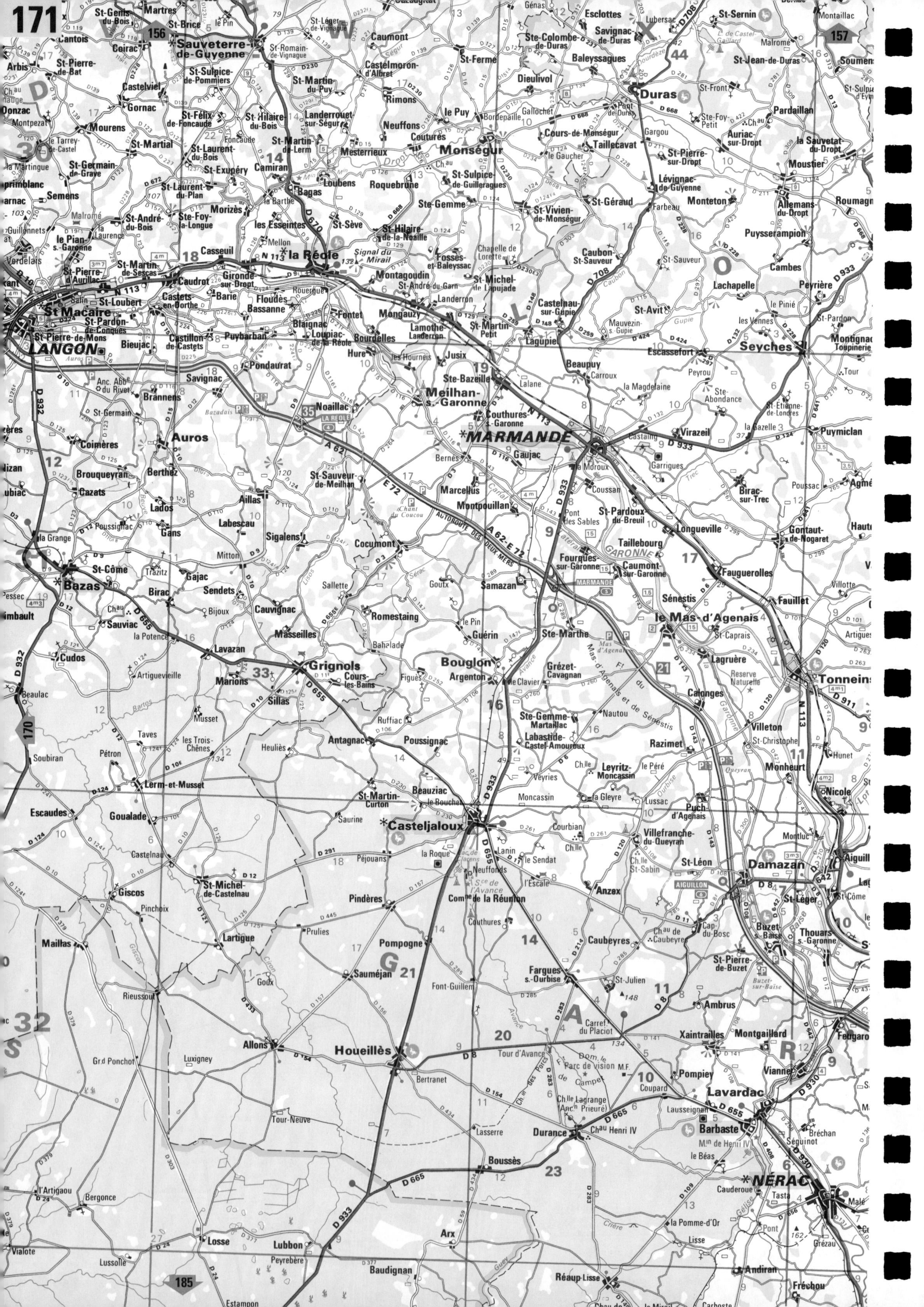
156
157
170
185
Sauveterre-de-Guyenne
St-Brice
Martres
Caumont
St-Ferme
Ste-Colombe-de-Duras
Esclottes
Savignac-de-Duras
Lubersac
St-Sernin
Montaillac
Malromé
St-Jean-de-Duras
Baleyssagues
Dieulivol
Castelmoron-d'Albret
St-Martin-du-Puy
Rimons
Duras
St-Front
Pardaillan
Castelviel
Gornac
St-Félix-de-Foncaude
St-Hilaire-du-Bois
Landerrouet-sur-Ségur
Neuffons
le Puy
Bordepaille
Gallochet
Pont-de-Duras
Ste-Foy-Petit
Auriac-sur-Dropt
La Sauvetat-du-Dropt
Mourens
St-Martial
St-Laurent-du-Bois
St-Martin-de-Lerm
Mesterrieux
Coutures
Monségur
Cours-de-Monségur
Taillecavat
Gargou
St-Pierre-sur-Dropt
Moustier
St-Germain-de-Grave
St-Exupéry
Camiran
Loubens
Roquebrune
St-Sulpice-de-Guilleragues
le Gaucher
Lévignac-de-Guyenne
Semens
St-Laurent-du-Plan
Morizès
la Barthe
Bagas
Ste-Gemme
St-Vivien-de-Monségur
St-Géraud
Farbeau
Monteton
Allemans-du-Dropt
Roumagne
Malromé
St-André-du-Bois
Ste-Foy-la-Longue
les Esseintes
St-Sève
St-Hilaire-de-la-Noaille
Puysserampion
le Pian-s.-Garonne
Verdelais
St-Pierre-d'Aurillac
St-Martin-de-Sescas
Casseuil
Caudrot
Gironde-sur-Dropt
la Réole
Signal du Mirail
Montagoudin
Fossès-et-Baleyssac
Chapelle de Lorette
St-Michel-de-Lapujade
Caubon-St-Sauveur
St-Sauveur
Cambes
Peyrière
St Macaire
St-Loubert
Castets-en-Dorthe
Barie
Floudès
Bassanne
Rouergue
St-André-du-Garn
Landerron
Castelnau-sur-Gupie
Lachapelle
St-Pierre-de-Mons
St-Pardon-de-Conques
Castillon-de-Castets
Puybarban
Blaignac
Fontet
Loupiac-de-la-Réole
Mongauzy
Lamothe-Landerron
St-Martin-Petit
Lagupie
Mauvezin-s.-Gupie
St-Avit
le Piniè
les Vennes
St-Pardoux
LANGON
Bieujac
Pondaurat
Bourdelles
Hure
les Hourneis
Jusix
Escassefort
Seyches
Montignac-Toupinerie
Savignac
Brannens
Anc. Abb. du Rivet
Ste-Bazeille
Lalane
Beaupuy
Carroux
Peyrou
Tour
St-Germain
Noaillac
Meilhan-s.-Garonne
Couthures-s.-Garonne
la Magdelaine
Ste-Abondance
St-Étienne-de-Londres
Auros
Coimères
MARMANDE
Gaujac
Virazeil
la Gazelle
Puymiclan
Bernes
Castaing
Garrigues
Brouqueyran
Berthez
St-Sauveur-de-Meilhan
Marcellus
le Moroux
Coussan
Birac-sur-Trec
Poussac
Agmé
Cazats
Lados
Aillas
Montpouillan
Chant du Coucou
Autoroute des Deux-Mers
Pont des Sables
St-Pardoux-du-Breuil
Longueville
Gontaut-de-Nogaret
la Grange
Poussignac
Gans
Labescau
Sigalens
Cocumont
Taillebourg
GARONNE
Fourques-sur-Garonne
Caumont-sur-Garonne
Fauguerolles
St-Côme
Trazitz
Mitton
Gajac
Sendets
Samazan
Bazas
Birac
Sallette
Goutx
Sénestis
Villotte
Fauillet
Cauvignac
Romestaing
le Pin
le Mas-d'Agenais
St-Caprais
Sauviac
Bijoux
Masseilles
Guérin
Ste-Marthe
Artigues
la Potence
Lavazan
Bahalade
Bouglon
Argenton
Grézet-Cavagnan
Lagruère
Reserve Naturelle
Tonneins
Cudos
Grignols
Cours-les-Bains
Figuès
le Clavier
Calonges
Artiguevieille
Marions
Sillas
Beaulac
Bartos
Musset
Ruffiac
Ste-Gemme-Martaillac
Nautou
Villeton
Labastide-Castel-Amouroux
St-Christophe
Taves
les Trois-Chênes
Heuliès
Antagnac
Poussignac
Razimet
Hunet
Soubiran
Pétron
Leyritz-Moncassin
le Péré
Monheurt
Queyran
Veyries
Lerm-et-Musset
Beauziac
St-Martin-Curton
le Bouchet
Moncassin
la Gleyre
Lussac
Puch-d'Agenais
Nicole
Escaudes
Goualade
Saurine
Casteljaloux
Courbian
Villefranche-du-Queyran
Montluc
Aiguillon
Castelnau
Péjouans
la Roque
Lanin
le Sendat
St-Sabin
St-Léon
Damazan
Neuffonds
Giscos
St-Michel-de-Castelnau
Pindères
Comne de la Réunion
l'Escale
Anzex
AIGUILLON
St-Léger
St-Côme
Pinchoix
Prulies
Couthures
Chau de Caubeyres
Cap-du-Bosc
Buzet-s.-Baïse
Thouars-s.-Garonne
Maillas
Lartigue
Pompogne
Caubeyres
St-Pierre-de-Buzet
Buzet-sur-Baïse
Sauméjan
Goux
Font-Guilhem
Fargues-s.-Ourbise
St-Julien
Rieussou
Ambrus
Carref. du Placiot
Xaintrailles
Montgaillard
Feugarolles
Grd Ponchot
Luxigney
Allons
Houeillès
Tour d'Avance
Dom. le Parc de vision M.F. de Campet
Pompiey
Vianne
Bertranet
Coupard
Lavardac
Chlle Lagrange (Ancn Prieuré)
Lausseignan
Barbaste
Tour-Neuve
Lasserre
Durance
Chau Henri IV
Mln de Henri IV
Bréchan
Séguinot
le Béas
Boussès
NÉRAC
l'Artigaou
Bergonce
Cauderoue
Tasta
Malé
la Pomme-d'Or
Pont
Grézau
Vialote
Losse
Lubbon
Arx
Lisse
Lussolle
Peyrebère
Baudignan
Réaup-Lisse
Andiran
Fréchou
Estampon

Ste-Innocence
St-Julien-d'Eymet
St-Capraise-d'Eymet
Mandacou
Monmarvès
Boisse
St-Léon-d'Issigeac
Larocal
Rampieux
Lolme
St-Romain-de-Monpazier
Ste-Eulalie-d'Eymet
Fonroque
Plaisance
Canterane
Faurilles
Peyrouillers
Razac-d'Eymet
St-Aubin-de-Cadelech
Cavarc
Rocquepine
Ste-Sabine-Born
Lavalade
Marsalès
Rouquette
St-Quentin-du-Dropt
Bom-de-Champs
Tourliac
St-Cassien
Capdrot
Eymet
Serres-et-Montguyard
Moulin-Neuf
Falgueyrat
Ste-Radegonde
Monseyroux
Gaugeac
Monpazier
Queyssel
Cahuzac
St-Dizier
Mazières-Naresse
Parranquet
Lalandusse
Castillonnès
Doudrac
Rayet
Rives
Villeréal
Soulaures
St-Romain
St-Grégoire
Servelaure
Ferrensac
St-Martin-de-Villeréal
Lauzun
St-Nazaire
Douzains
Vergt-de-Biron
Biron
St-Pardoux-Isaac
Bourgougnague
Montauriol
Pompiac
Bournel
St-Étienne-de-Villeréal
St-Colomb-de-Lauzun
Miramont-de-Guyenne
Sérignac-Péboudou
Montaut
Lacapelle-Biron
Lavergne
Maurillac
Born
Dévillac
Bois-Vert
Lamothe-d'Alles
Gervinie
Ségalas
St-Maurice-de-Lestapel
Lougratte
St-Eutrope-de-Born
Laussou
St-Avit
La Sauvetat
Salabès
Cardayres
Seandaillac
Bonnenouvelle
Montignac-de-Lauzun
Carnicot
Armillac
Lagaillardie
Monviel
Brides
Pils
Laures
Paulhiac
St-Sardos-de-Laurenque
Gavaudun
Laperche
Rouffiac
Monbahus
Boudy-de-Beauregard
Roquefaire
Salles
Cuzorn
Pignéra
Moirax
Moulinet
Cancon
Flayac
Monflanquin
Montagnac-s.-Lède
Villebramar
Lassale
Tesquet
St-Barthélemy-d'Agenais
Boisverdun
Tombebœuf
Cahannes
Pech-Redon
Lacaussade
Vauris
Fumel
Tourtrès
Gardelle
Beaugas
Calviac
Monsempron-Libos
Labretonie
St-Pastour
Castelnaud-de-Gratecambe
Labarthe
Monségur
Condezaygues
Montastruc
Verteuil-d'Agenais
St-Pierre-de-Caubel
Pailloles
Savignac-sur-Leyze
St-Aubin
Coulx
La Sauvetat-sur-Lède
St-Vite
Carron
Soubirous
Monclar
Verdegas
Casseneuil
Lédat
Lamothefey
Laval
Ladignac
Salomon
Brugnac
Pinel
Roquebert
Pinel-Hauterive
Septfond
Campagnac
Trentels
St-Georges
Grateloup
Sermet
St-Étienne-de-Fougères
St-Sernin
St-Aignan
Lustrac
Carbonac
Lagarde
Castelmoron-sur-Lot
Ste-Livrade-sur-Lot
La Landette
Bias
Sangruère
St-Marcel
St-Sylvestre-sur-Lot
St-Martin-des-Cailles
Trémons
La Castagnade
Villeneuve-sur-Lot
St-Sulpice-de-Rivelot
La Grâce
N.-D. de Peyragude
Penne-d'Agenais
Cazideroque
Laparade
Fongrave
Allez-et-Cazeneuve
Pujols
Tour
Dausse
Marsac
Gouneau
Le Temple-sur-Lot
Laurier
St-Germain
Granges-s.-Lot
Cazeneuve
Ste-Foy
Chau de Castelgaillard
Valeilles
Anthé
Clairac
Dolmayrac
Ste-Colombe-de-Villeneuve
Montpezat
Bourran
Lafitte-sur-Lot
St-Sardos
Grottes de Lestournelles
Auradou
St-Beauzeil
Brice
Pérignac
Massoulès
Colleignes
Lacépède
St-Médard
Cours
St-Antoine-de-Ficalba
Roquecor
Ste-Radegonde-sur-Lot
St-Vincent
Quittimont
Sembas
Grottes de Fontirou
Parc Zoologique Préhistorique
Hautefage-la-Tour
Massels
St-Amans-du-Pech
Férussac
Galapian
St-Salvy
Castella
Laugnac
Frespech
Blaymont
Lesterne
la Croix-Blanche
Monbalen
Camp Militaire
Cassignas
Lacour
Jarrigue
Prayssas
Loy
St-Avit
Fregimont
Madaillan
Arasse
St-Victor
Laroque-Timbaut
Beauville
Bourg-de-Visa
Gaujac
Lusignan-Petit
Fraisse
Galimas
St-Arnaud
Cauzac
St-Julien
Commanderie de Bajamont
Port-Ste-Marie
Bazens
Artigues
Dondas
Engayrac
Clermont-Dessous
Puy-Masson
Lusignan-Grand
Cardonnet
Franc
Sauvagnas
St-Robert
St-Laurent
St-Cirq
Foulayronnes
Caoulet
St-Xiste
Gandaille
Le Bugat
Meneaux
Béquin
St-Hilaire-de-Lusignan
Monbran
Alary
Pont-du-Casse
Sérignac-s.-Garonne
Colayrac-St-Cirq
La Sauvetat-de-Savères
St-Martin-de-Beauville
Brassac
Goulard
Réserve Naturelle
St-Ferréol
St-Maurin
Bruch
Montesquieu
Brax
Le Passage
Agen
St-Caprais-de-Lerm
Manoir de Pech-Redon
Tayrac
Montjoi
Aire d'Agen Porte d'Aquitaine
Mourrens
la Demi-Lune
Ste-Radegonde
Dolmayrac
Bon-Encontre
Castelculier
Puymirol
Perville
Castelsagrat
St-Loup
Roquefort
Ste-Colombe-en-Bruilhois
Gr.d-Fonds
St-Pierre-de-Clairac
Espiens
St-Pierre-de-Gaubert
Lafox
St-Jean-de-Thurac
Grayssas
St-Clair
Montagnac-s.-Auvignon
Boé
St-Romain-le-Noble
St-Urcisse
Gasques
Pleichac
Estillac
Moirax
Sauveterre-St-Denis
Laspeyres
St-Pierre-de-Malaure
Clermont-Soubiran
Moncaut
Aubiac
Bois-Renaud
Hillac
Fontarède
La Chapelle
Le Sahuc
Layrac
St-Nicolas-de-la-Balerme
Coupet
Calignac
Saumont
St-Sixte
Lamagistère
Golfech
La Lande
Goudourville
St-Vincent-Lespinasse
Collège agricole
Puy-Fort-Eguille
Laplume
Contras
Caudecoste
Donzac
Valence
Centrale nucléaire
Garlies
Goulens
Pommevic
Lartifume
Fieux
Nomdieu
St-Vincent-de-Lamontjoie
Marmont-Pachas
Fals
St-Martial
158
173
186
187

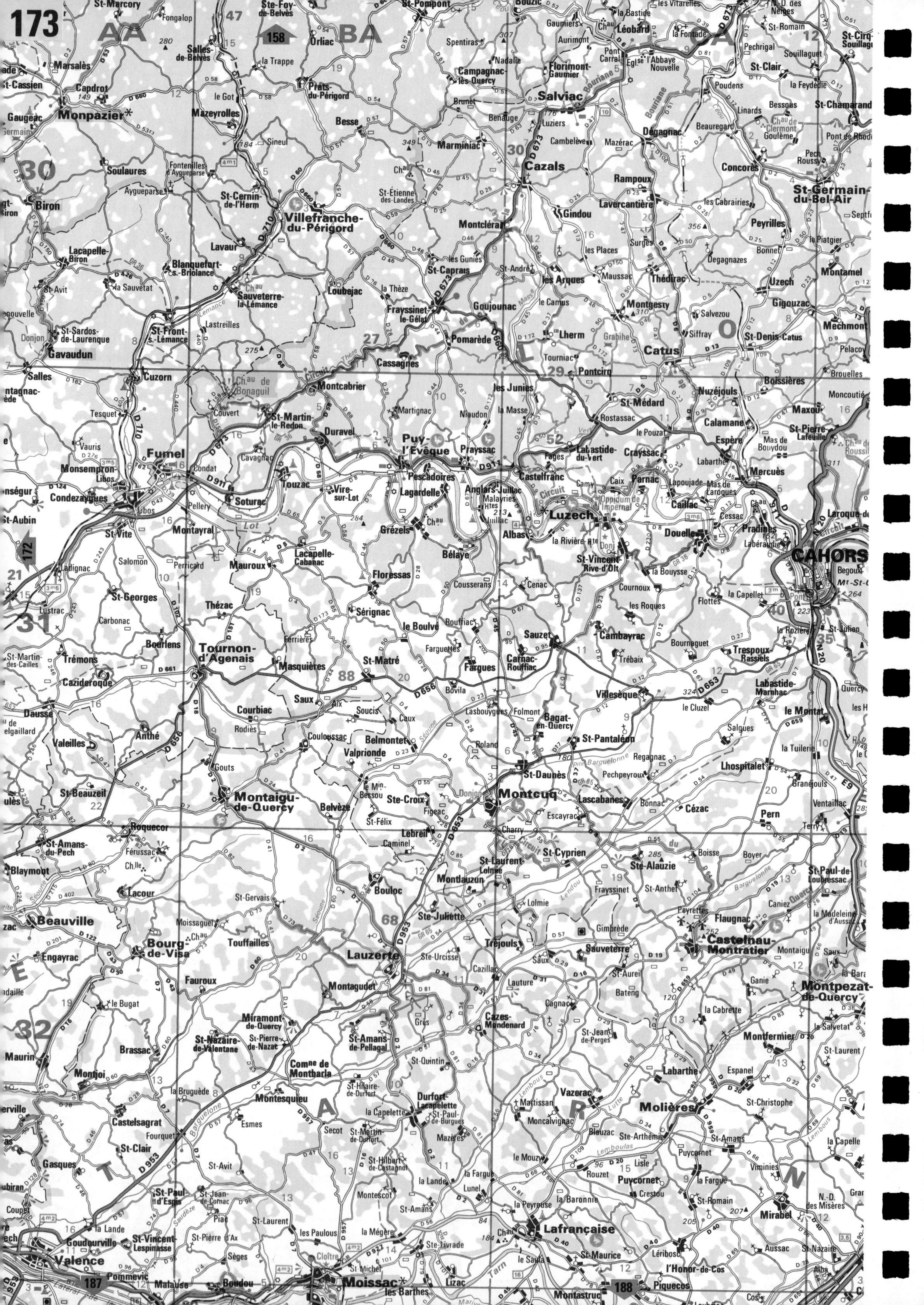

Monpazier
Biron
Villefranche-du-Périgord
Salviac
Cazals
Gindou
Catus
Fumel
Puy-l'Évêque
Prayssac
Luzech
Castelfranc
Douelle
CAHORS
Tournon-d'Agenais
Montaigu-de-Quercy
Montcuq
Lauzerte
Castelnau-Montratier
Montpezat-de-Quercy
Molières
Lafrançaise
Moissac
Valence
Bourg-de-Visa
Beauville
Sauveterre-la-Lémance
Cuzorn
Montcabrier
Duravel
Soturac
Touzac
Mercuès
Pradines
Lhospitalet
Durfort-Lacapelette
Mirabel
Piquecos
Montastruc
Lot
Tarn

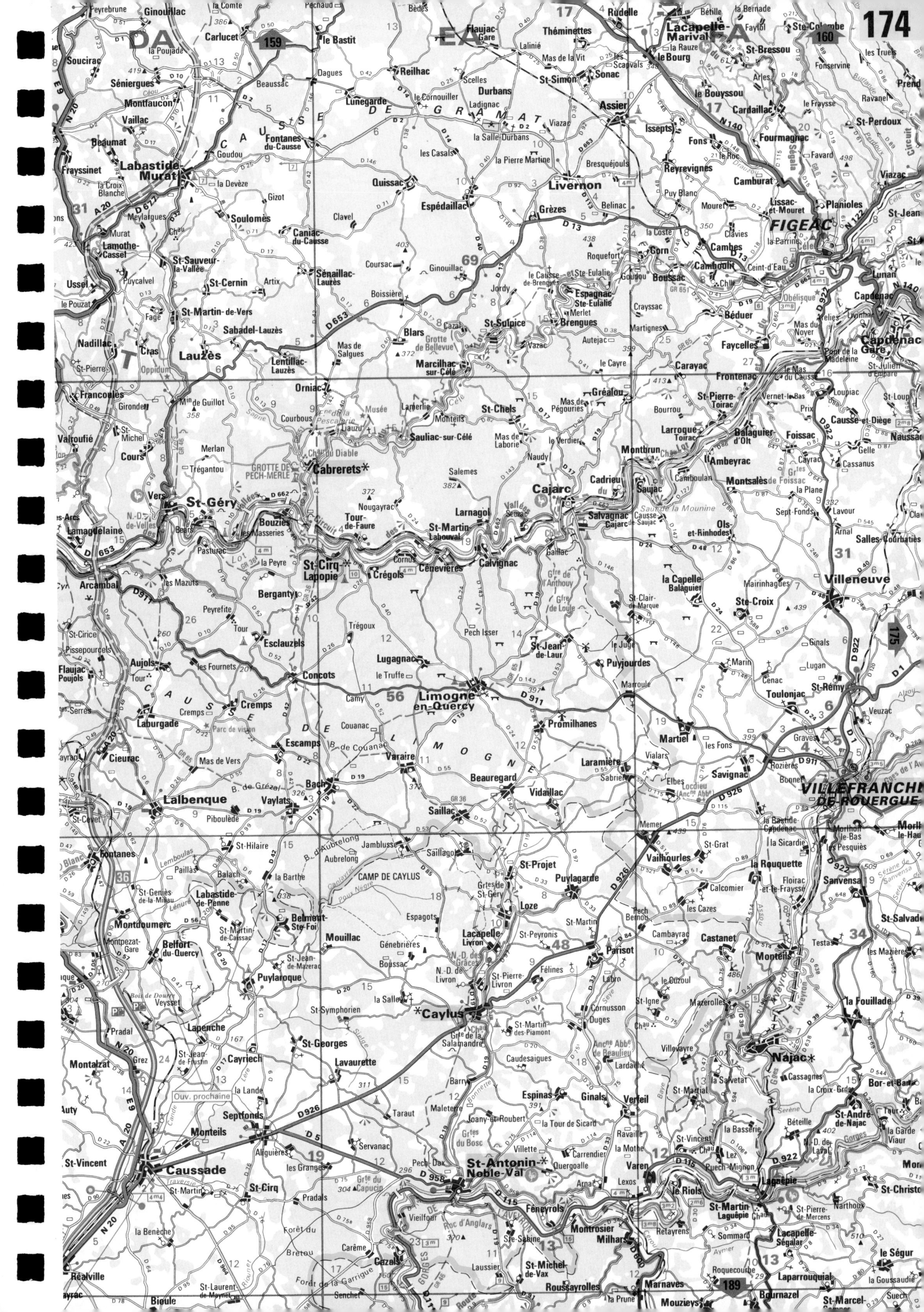

Gramat
Causse de Limogne
Ginouillac
Carlucet
Le Bastit
Flaujac-Gare
Théminettes
Rudelle
Lacapelle-Marival
Souciraс
Sénierguеs
Montfaucon
Reilhac
Lunegarde
Durbans
Assier
Sonac
St-Simon
Cardaillac
Fourmagnac
St-Perdoux
Fons
Vaillac
Beaumat
Fontanes-du-Causse
Labastide-Murat
Frayssinet
Quissac
Espédaillac
Livernon
Reyrevignes
Camburat
Viazac
Figeac
Planioles
Lissac-et-Mouret
Soulomès
Caniac-du-Causse
Grèzes
Corn
Cambes
Camboulit
Boussac
St-Sauveur-la-Vallée
St-Cernin
Sénaillac-Lauzès
Ussel
St-Martin-de-Vers
Sabadel-Lauzès
Blars
St-Sulpice
Brengues
Espagnac-Ste-Eulalie
Béduer
Capdenac
Capdenac-Gare
Faycelles
Nadillac
Lauzès
Lentillac-Lauzès
Marcilhac-sur-Célé
Carayac
Frontenac
Orniac
Gréalou
St-Chels
Sauliac-sur-Célé
St-Pierre-Toirac
Larroque-Toirac
Balaguier-d'Olt
Foissac
Cabrerets
Grotte de Pech-Merle
Cours
Vers
St-Géry
Cajarc
Cadrieu
Saujac
Montbrun
Ambeyrac
Montsalès
Bouziès
Tour-de-Faure
Larnagol
St-Martin-Labouval
Salvagnac-Cajarc
St-Cirq-Lapopie
Crégols
Cénevières
Calvignac
Arcambal
Bergantу
La Capelle-Balaguier
Ste-Croix
Villeneuve
Esclauzels
St-Jean-de-Laur
Puyjourdes
Aujols
Concots
Lugagnac
Limogne-en-Quercy
Toulonjac
St-Rémy
Laburgade
Cremps
Promilhanes
Martiel
Escamps
Cieurac
Varaire
Laramière
Savignac
Villefranche-de-Rouergue
Lalbenque
Vaylats
Bach
Beauregard
Vidaillac
Saillac
Fontanes
Vailhourles
La Rouquette
Sanvensa
Camp de Caylus
St-Projet
Puylagarde
Labastide-de-Penne
Montdoumerc
Belmont-Ste-Foi
Mouillac
Lacapelle-Livron
Loze
Parisot
Castanet
Monteils
Belfort-du-Quercy
Puylaroque
Caylus
La Fouillade
Najac
Lapenche
St-Georges
Lavaurette
Cayriech
Montalzat
Espinas
Ginals
Verfeil
Septfonds
Monteils
Caussade
St-Cirq
St-Antonin-Noble-Val
Varen
Laguépie
St-Martin-Laguépie
Féneyrols
Montrosier
Milhars
Lacapelle-Ségalar
Le Ségur
Cazals
St-Michel-de-Vax
Roussayrolles
Marnaves
Laparrouquial
Réalville
Bioule
Mouzieys
Bournazel
St-Marcel
N 20
A 20
N 140
N 122
D 911
D 926
D 922
D 958
D 653
159
160
175
189
Ouv. prochaine

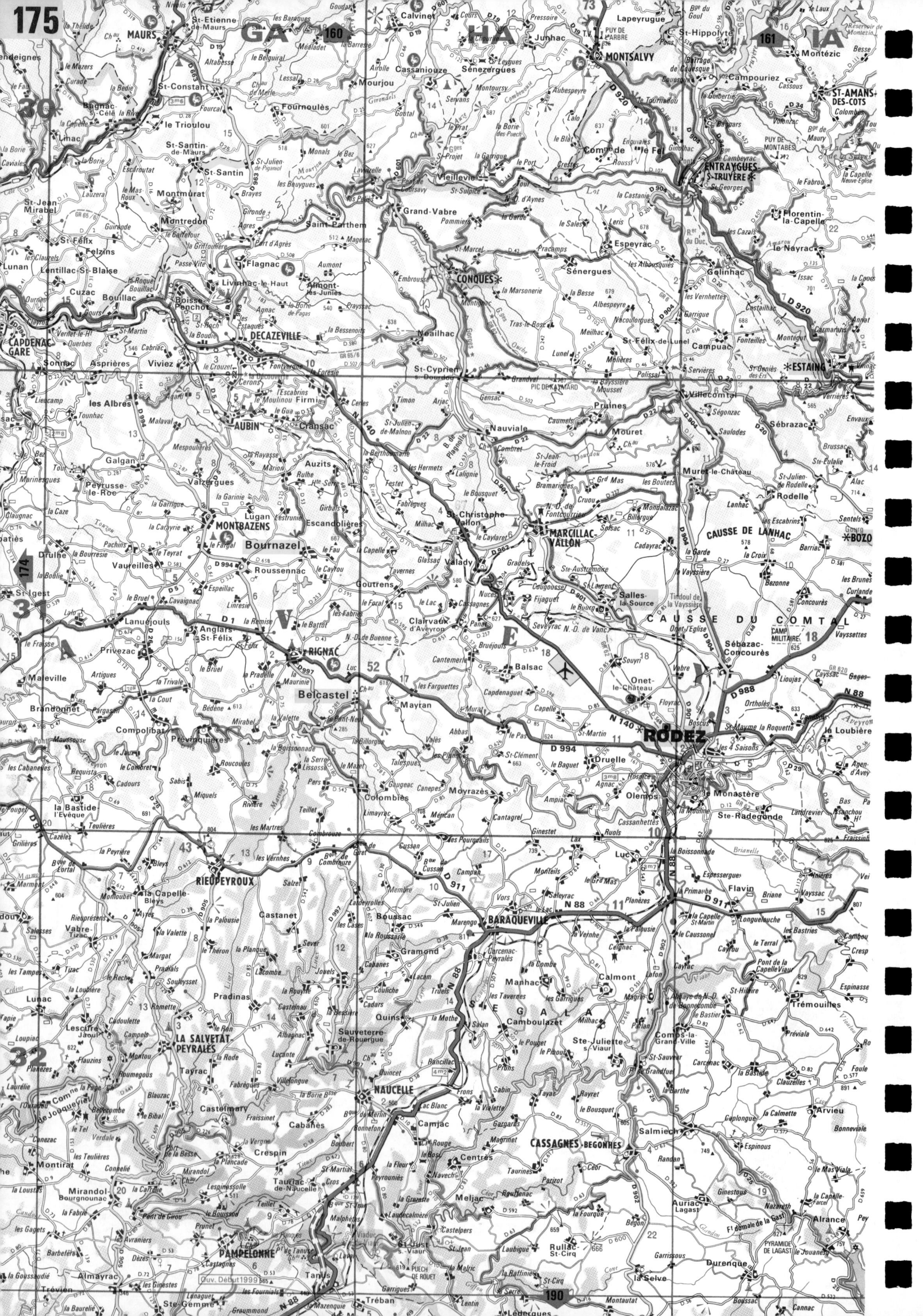
MAURS
St-Etienne-de-Maurs
GA
160
Calvinet
HA
Junhac
Lapeyrugue
MONTSALVY
161
IA
Montézic
St-Hippolyte
Cassaniouze
Sénezergues
Mourjou
St-Constant
Fournoulès
Bagnac-s-Célé
le Trioulou
St-Santin-de-Maurs
St-Santin
Montmurat
Montredon
St-Félix
Felzins
Lunan
Lentillac-St-Blaise
Flagnac
Livinhac-le-Haut
Cuzac
Bouillac
Boisse-Penchot
Aumont
Almont-les-Junies
Saint-Parthem
Grand-Vabre
Vieillevie
Conques
Sénergues
Espeyrac
ENTRAYGUES-S-TRUYÈRE
ST-AMANS-DES-COTS
Florentin-la-Capelle
le Nayrac
Golinhac
Campuac
St-Félix-de-Lunel
ESTAING
DECAZEVILLE
CAPDENAC-GARE
Sonnac
Asprières
Viviez
Firmi
AUBIN
Cransac
St-Cyprien-s-Dourdou
Nauviale
Pruines
Mouret
Villecomtal
Sébrazac
les Albres
Galgan
Valzergues
Auzits
Peyrusse-le-Roc
MONTBAZENS
Lugan
Bournazel
Escandolières
St-Christophe-Vallon
MARCILLAC-VALLON
Muret-le-Château
Rodelle
CAUSSE DE LANHAC
BOZOULS
Drulhe
Vaureilles
Roussennac
Goutrens
Valady
Salles-la-Source
CAUSSE DU COMTAL
Sébazac-Concourès
CAMP MILITAIRE
174
31
Lanuéjouls
Anglars-St-Félix
Privezac
RIGNAC
Clairvaux-d'Aveyron
Balsac
Onet-le-Château
Belcastel
Mayran
RODEZ
Compolibat
Prévinquières
Druelle
Olemps
le Monastère
Ste-Radegonde
la Bastide-l'Évêque
Colombiès
Moyrazès
RIEUPEYROUX
la Capelle-Bleys
Luc
Flavin
BARAQUEVILLE
Castanet
Boussac
Gramond
Manhac
Calmont
Tremouilles
LA SALVETAT-PEYRALÈS
Pradinas
SÉGALA
Camboulazet
Sauveterre-de-Rouergue
Comps-la-Grand-Ville
32
NAUCELLE
Castelmary
Crespin
Camjac
Salmiech
CASSAGNES-BÉGONHES
Arvieu
Centrès
Meljac
Mirandol-Bourgnounac
PAMPELONNE
Rullac-St-Cirq
Durenque
Auriac-Lagast
Alrance
Almayrac
Tanus
Trévien
Ste-Gemme
Tréban
190
Ouv. Début 1999

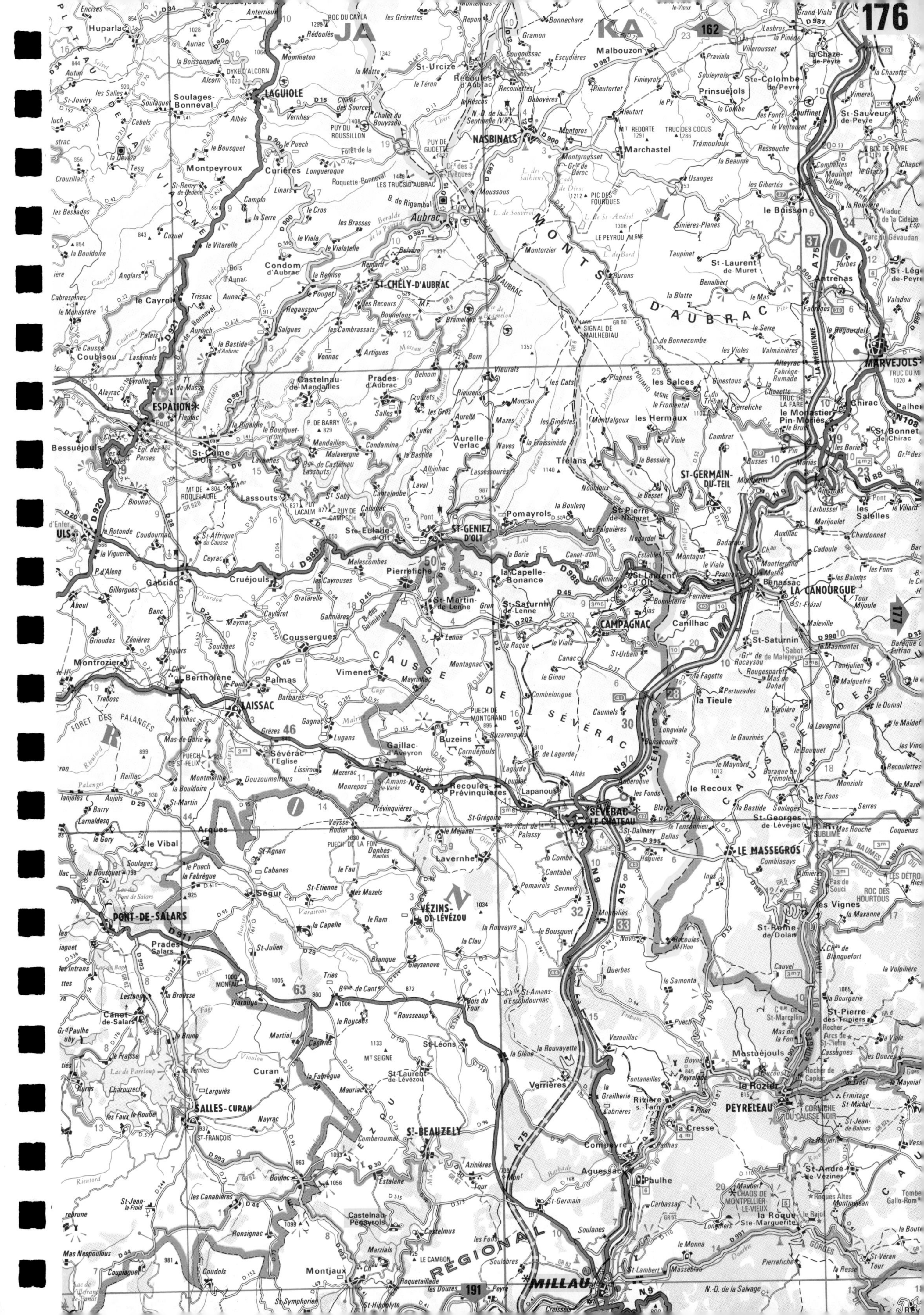
162
177
191
LAGUIOLE
NASBINALS
Malbouzon
Marchastel
MONTS D'AUBRAC
ST-CHÉLY-D'AUBRAC
Aubrac
ESPALION
St-Côme-d'Olt
ST-GENIEZ-D'OLT
MARVEJOLS
LA CANOURGUE
ST-GERMAIN-DU-TEIL
St-Laurent-d'Olt
CAMPAGNAC
LAISSAC
CAUSSE DE SÉVÉRAC
SÉVÉRAC-LE-CHÂTEAU
LE MASSEGROS
PONT-DE-SALARS
VÉZINS-DE-LÉVÉZOU
SALLES-CURAN
ST-BEAUZELY
Le Rozier
PEYRELEAU
MILLAU
Aguessac
Montpeyroux
Soulages-Bonneval
Castelnau-de-Mandailles
Prades-d'Aubrac
Pierrefiche
Coussergues
Palmas
Buzeins
Recoules-Prévinquières
Lapanouse
Ségur
Curan
Verrières
Compeyre
Paulhe
Castelnau-Pégayrols
Montjaux
REGIONAL
FORET DES PALANGES
CHAOS DE MONTPELLIER-LE-VIEUX

162
163
176
192
30
31
32
Serverette
Javols
St-Amans
Estables
Rieutort-de-Randon
Châteauneuf-de-Randon
Pierrefiche
Rocles
St-Flour-de-Mercoire
St-Alban-en-Montagne
Chaudeyrac
Cheylard-l'Évêque
Luc
Laveyrune
La Bastide-Puylaurent
Montbel
Laubert
Pelouse
Le Born
Chastel-Nouvel
Servières
Montrodat
Ribennes
Lachamp
Badaroux
Allenc
Belvezet
Chasseradès
Mende
Chadenet
Bagnols-les-Bains
St-Julien-du-Tournel
Le Bleymard
Lanuéjols
Balsièges
Barjac
Chanac
Esclanèdes
Brenoux
St-Bauzile
St-Étienne-du-Valdonnez
Mas-d'Orcières
Cubières
Cubiérettes
Altier
Pourcharesses
Mont Lozère
Sommet de Finiels
Col de Finiels
Col de Montmirat
Les Bondons
Ste-Énimie
Quézac
Ispagnac
Cocurès
Le Pont-de-Montvert
Fraissinet-de-Lozère
Florac
Bédouès
Montbrun
Laval-du-Tarn
Mas-St-Chély
La Malène
Causse Méjean
Hures-la-Parade
Vebron
Barre-des-Cévennes
St-Laurent-de-Trèves
St-Julien-d'Arpaon
Cassagnas
Vialas
St-Maurice-de-Ventalon
St-Germain-de-Calberte
St-Martin-de-Lansuscle
Le Pompidou
Ste-Croix-Vallée-Française
St-Étienne-Vallée-Française
St-André-de-Valborgne
Meyrueis
Gatuzières
Aven Armand
Mont Aigoual
Lanuéjols
Camprieu
Les Plantiers
Saumane
L'Estréchure
St-Jean-du-Gard
Trèves
Corniche des Cévennes
Cévennes

THUEYTS
VALS-LES-BAINS
AUBENAS
ST-ÉTIENNE-DE-LUGDARÈS
VALGORGE
LE TANARGUE
Col de la Crx de Bauzon
Rocher d'Abraham
Jaujac
Prades
Mercuer
Labégude
Ucel
St-Privat
Vesseaux
Darbres
St-Laurent s/s-Coiron
Mirabel
Lussas
St-Didier-s/s-Aubenas
Lavilledieu
VILLENEUVE-DE-BERG
St-Germain
Vogüé
Lachapelle-s/s-Aubenas
Fons
St-Sernin
Chazeaux
Lentillères
St-Cirgues-de-Prades
La Souche
Laboule
Loubaresse
St-Laurent-les-Bains
Laval-d'Aurelle
Dompnac
Rocles
Tauriers
Joannas
Rocher
Chassiers
LARGENTIÈRE
Sanilhac
Montréal
Uzer
Vinezac
Lanas
St-Maurice-d'Ardèche
Balazuc
Rochecolombe
St-Maurice-d'Ibie
Beaumont
Sablières
St-Mélany
Montselgues
St-André-Lachamp
Vernon
Ribes
Planzolles
Faugères
Thines
Ste-Marguerite-Lafigère
La Garde-Guérin
Pied-de-Borne
Rosières
JOYEUSE
Lablachère
Chauzon
Pradons
Ruoms
Labeaume
Lagorce
St-Pierre-St-Jean
Payzac
St-Alban-Auriolles
Sampzon
VALLON-PONT-D'ARC
Salavas
Grospierres
Chandolas
VILLEFORT
Gravières
Chambonas
Malons-et-Elze
LES VANS
Les Assions
Ponteils-et-Brésis
St-André-Capcèze
Berrias-et-Casteljau
Beaulieu
Banne
Bonnevaux
Malbosquet
Malbosc
GÉNOLHAC
Aujac
Sénéchas
St-Paul-le-Jeune
Bessas
Vagnas
St-Remèze
Labastide-de-Virac
BARJAC
Orgnac-l'Aven
Bordezac
Gagnières
St-André-de-Cruzières
St-Sauveur-de-Cruzières
Courry
BESSÈGES
Chamborigaud
Robiac-Rochessadoule
Meyrannes
St-Brès
ST-AMBROIX
St-Jean-de-Maruéjols-et-Avejan
St-Privat-de-Champclos
Montclus
Issirac
St-Christol-de-Rodières
Portes
St-Julien-des-Points
Ste-Cécile-d'Andorge
Molières-s.-Cèze
St-Victor-de-Malcap
Rochegude
Tharaux
St-André-de-Roquepertuis
Cornillon
Goudargues
Les Mages
St-Denis
Potelières
Rivières
Méjannes-le-Clap
LA GRD COMBE
Laval-Pradel
St-Julien-de-Cassagnas
Rousson
Fons-s.-Lussan
Verfeuil
Salindres
Servas
Navacelles
Bouquet
LUSSAN
St-Martin-de-Valgalgues
Cendras
ALÈS
St-Sébastien-d'Aigrefeuille
St-Privat-des-Vieux
Brouzet-lès-Alès
Seynes
Vallérargues
La Bruguière
Fontarèches
St-Laurent-la-Vernède
Cavillargues
Mons
Méjannes-lès-Alès
St-Jean-du-Pin
St-Christol-lès-Alès
Monteils
St-Just-et-Vacquières
Belvézet
Générargues
Bagard
Corbès
St-Hilaire-de-Brethmas
St-Hippolyte-de-Caton
Euzet
N 102
N 106
N 110
D 104
D 904
D 901
D 579
D 6
164
179
193

164
165
178
195
Rochessauve
St-Bauzile
St-Lager-Bressac
Mirmande
Autichamp
Divajeu
Piégros-la-Clastre
Aubenasson
Les Tourrettes
Cruas
St-Vincent-de-Barrès
St-Martin-s.-Lavezon
la Coucourde
Condillac
Marsanne
Roynac
Puy-St-Martin
Soyans
Francillon-sur-Roubion
Saou
Mornans
Berzème
St-Gineis-en-Coiron
Sceautres
Meysse
Savasse
Sauzet
la Laupie
Bonlieu-s.-Roubion
Cléon-d'Andran
Manas
Charols
Pont-de-Barret
le Poët-Célard
Félines-sur-Rimandoule
Commune
Aubignas
St-Pons
Rochemaure
Ancône
St-Marcel-lès-Sauzet
St-Gervais-sur-Roubion
Rochebaudin
Eyzahut
Salettes
Truinas
Bourdeaux
Alba-la-Romaine
Montélimar
le Teil
Montboucher-sur-Jabron
la Bâtie-Rolland
Châteauneuf-de-Mazenc
la Bégude-de-Mazenc
Souspierre
Comps
Dieulefit
St-Thomé
Valvignères
St-Alban
Puygiron
Espeluche
Portes-en-Valdaine
la Touche
Rochefort-en-Valdaine
le Poët-Laval
Allan
Malataverne
Aleyrac
Montjoux
Viviers
Châteauneuf-du-Rhône
Montjoyer
Roche-St-Secret-Béconne
Salles-sous-Bois
Taulignan
Montbrison
Larnas
St-Montant
Donzère
Réauville
Roussas
Valaurie
les Granges-Gontardes
Grignan
le Pègue
Rousset-les-Vignes
St-Pantaléon-les-Vignes
Chamaret
Grillon
Colonzelle
Valréas
Venterol
La Garde-Adhémar
Chantemerle-lès-Grignan
Pierrelatte
Bourg-St-Andéol
Clansayes
Montségur-sur-Lauzon
Richerenches
St-Paul-Trois-Châteaux
Solérieux
la Baume-de-Transit
Vinsobres
St-Marcel-d'Ardèche
St-Restitut
Visan
St-Maurice-s.-Eygues
Mirabel-aux-Baronnies
St-Martin-d'Ardèche
Lapalud
Bouchet
Tulette
Villedieu
St-Just
Aiguèze
Suze-la-Rousse
Buisson
Lamotte-du-Rhône
Bollène
St-Roman-de-Malegarde
Puyméras
St-Paulet-de-Caisson
Salazac
Pont-St-Esprit
Rochegude
Ste-Cécile-les-Vignes
Roaix
Vaison-la-Romaine
St-Romain-en-Viennois
Mondragon
Lagarde-Paréol
Cairanne
Rasteau
Carsan
St-Alexandre
Uchaux
Crestet
St-Laurent-de-Carnols
St-Michel-d'Euzet
Mornas
Séguret
Sablet
St-Nazaire
St-Gervais
Vénéjan
Sérignan-du-Comtat
Travaillan
Gigondas
Malaucène
St-Étienne-des-Sorts
Piolenc
Bagnols-s.-Cèze
Camaret-s.-Aigues
Violès
Chusclan
Orange
Vacqueyras
Lafare
La Roque-Alric
le Barroux
Sabran
St-Hippolyte-le-Graveyron
Orsan
Codolet
Jonquières
Beaumes-de-Venise
Laudun
Aubignan
Tresques
Caderousse
Connaux
Courthézon
Sarrians
Loriol-du-Comtat
St-Paul-les-Fonts
Gaujac
Montfaucon
Châteauneuf-du-Pape
Mazan
Modène
Caromb

St-Pierre
Montmaur-en-Diois
St-Benoît-en-Diois
Rimon-et-Savel
Barnave
Recoubeau-Jansac
Menglon
Espenel
Chastel-Arnaud
Pennes-le-Sec
Montlaur-en-Diois
Aucelon
Luc-en-Diois
Miscon
La Chaudière
Pradelle
Rochefourchat
Poyols
Beaumont-en-Diois
Beaurières
Lesches-en-Diois
Val-Maravel
Bretté
Jonchères
Volvent
Les Tonils
St-Nazaire-le-Désert
Crupies
Bellegarde-en-Diois
Charens
Les Prés
Montlahuc
St-Dizier-en-Diois
Valdrôme
La Bâtie-des-Fonds
Aspres-sur-Buëch
Bouvières
Gumiane
Chalancon
Establet
La Motte-Chalancon
Rottier
La Charce
Bruis
Ste-Marie
Montmorin
Arnayon
Chaudebonne
Valouse
Cornillon-sur-l'Oule
Cornillac
Pommerol
Villeperdrix
St-May
Rémuzat
St-Ferréol-Trente-Pas
Sahune
Eyroles
Condorcet
Montréal-les-Sources
Verclause
Rosans
Ribeyret
Moydans
L'Épine
Montclus
Serres
Sigottier
La Piarre
Aspremont
Curnier
Arpavon
Les Pilles
Aubres
NYONS
Le Poët-Sigillat
Pelonne
St-André-de-Rosans
Sorbiers
Montjay
Trescléoux
Chanousse
Bellecombe-Tarendol
Lemps
Montferrand-la-Fare
Sainte-Jalle
Montaulieu
St-Sauveur-Gouvernet
Roussieux
Laux-Montaux
Villebois-les-Pins
Étoile-St-Cyrice
Orpierre
Lagrand
Rochebrune
Bésignan
Chauvac
Vercoiran
Ste-Euphémie-s.-Ouvèze
Montguers
Laborel
Ste-Colombe
Bénivay-Ollon
Beauvoisin
Buis-les-Baronnies
St-Auban-s.-l'Ouvèze
Montauban-s.-l'Ouvèze
Barret-le-Bas
Propiac
La Rochette-du-Buis
Comne de Rioms
Izon-la-Bruisse
Ballons
Mérindol-les-Oliviers
La Penne-s.-l'Ouvèze
Le Poët-en-Percip
Mévouillon
Eygalayes
Salérans
Pierrelongue
Eygaliers
Plaisians
Aulan
Vers-s.-Méouge
Lachau
Mollans-s.-Ouvèze
St-Léger-du-Ventoux
Villefranche-le-Château
Séderon
Éourres
Brantes
Barret-de-Lioure
Montfroc
Curel
Savoillan
Montbrun-les-Bains
Les Omergues
Reilhanette
Châteauneuf-Miravail
MONT VENTOUX
Ferrassières
Aurel
Bédoin
Crillon-le-Brave
St-Trinit
Saumane
L'Hospitalet
Flassan
Sault
Revest-du-Bion
Comne de Redortiers
La Rochegiron
Monieux
Mormoiron
Lardiers
MONTAGNE
166
59
64
181
196

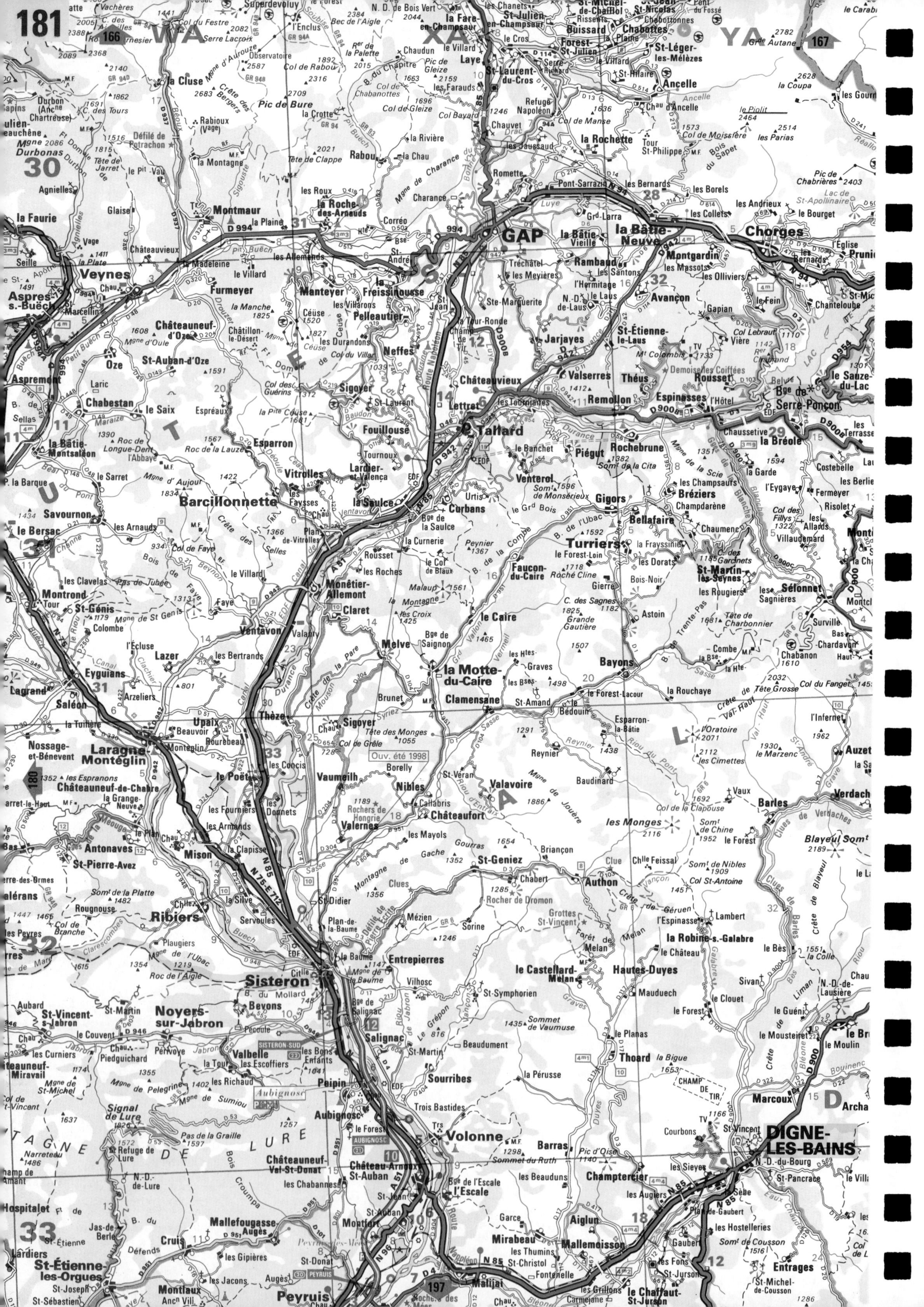
166
167
180
197
Superdevoluy
N. D. de Bois Vert
la Fare-en-Champsaur
St-Julien-en-Champsaur
St-Nicolas
Buissard
Chabottes
Forest-St-Julien
St-Léger-les-Mélèzes
l'Enclus
Serre Lacroix
Observatoire
la Cluse
Pic de Bure
Chaudun
le Villard
Laye
St-Laurent-du-Cros
Ancelle
Refuge Napoléon
Col de Manse
la Rochette
Tour St-Philippe
Col de Moissière
les Parias
la Coupa
Rabioux
Défilé de Potrachon
la Rivière
Rabou
la Chau
Chauvet
les Jaussaud
Romette
Pont-Sarrazin
les Bernards
les Borels
Pic de Chabrières
Lac de St-Apollinaire
Durbon
Mgne Durbonas
30
la Montagne
Agnielles
Montmaur
la Plaine
les Roux
la Roche-des-Arnauds
Charance
Corréo
GAP
la Bâtie-Vieille
la Bâtie-Neuve
Chorges
les Andrieux
le Bourget
les Collets
Grd-Larra
la Faurie
Glaise
Vage
Seille
la Plate
Châteauvieux
la Madeleine
le Villard
les Allemands
St-André
Tréchâtel
les Meyières
Rambaud
les Santons
l'Hermitage
Montgardin
les Massots
les Olliviers
l'Eglise
Prunières
Veynes
Aspres-s.-Buëch
St-Marcellin
Furmeyer
Manteyer
la Freissinouse
Pelleautier
Ste-Marguerite
N.-D.-de-Laus
le Laus
Avançon
Gapian
le Fein
Chanteloube
Céüse
les Villarons
la Tour-Ronde
Châteauneuf-d'Oze
Châtillon-le-Désert
Mgne d'Oule
les Durandons
Neffes
Jarjayes
St-Étienne-le-Laus
Col Lebraut
Vière
Oze
St-Auban-d'Oze
Col du Villar
Mt Colombis
Demoiselles Coiffées
Théus
Rousset
Lac de Serre-Ponçon
le Sauze-du-Lac
Aspremont
Laric
Chabestan
le Saix
Espréaux
Col des Guérins
Sigoyer
St-Laurent
Châteauvieux
Valserres
Remollon
Espinasses
l'Hôtel
Bge de Serre-Ponçon
B. de Sellas
la Pte Céüse
Lettret
les Tourniaires
Tallard
Chaussetive
la Bréole
les Terrasses
la Bâtie-Montsaléon
Roc de Longue-Dent
l'Abbaye
Roc de la Lauze
Esparron
Fouillouse
Tournoux
le Banchet
Piégut
Rochebrune
Mgne de la Scie
Costebelle
P. la Barque
le Sarret
Mgne d'Aujour
Vitrolles
Lardier-et-Valença
Venterol
Somt de la Cita
la Garde
les Champsaurs
Bréziers
l'Eygaye
Fermeyer
Savournon
Barcillonnette
les Faysses
la Saulce
Urtis
Somt de Monsérieux
Curbans
le Grd Bois
Gigors
Champdarène
Risolet
Col des Fillys
les Allards
Villaudemard
le Bersac
les Arnauds
Crête des Selles
Plan-de-Vitrolles
Bge de la Saulce
B. de l'Ubac
Bellafaire
Chaumenc
Col de Faye
la Curnerie
Peynier
B. de la Combe
Turriers
la Frayssinie
le Forest-Loin
Rousset
les Roches
le Col de Blaux
Faucon-du-Caire
Roche Cline
les Dorats
Col des Garcinets
St-Martin-lès-Seynes
Bois de Faye
le Villard
les Clavelas
Pas de Jubéo
Monêtier-Allemont
Malaup
la Montagne
Gierre
Bois-Noir
les Rougiers
les Sagnières
Sélonnet
Montrond
Tour
St-Genis
Mgne de St Genis
Faye
Claret
les Croix
le Caire
C. des Sagnes
Grande Gautière
Astoin
Tête de Charbonnier
Surville
Bas-Chardavon
Colombe
Ventavon
Valauty
Bge de Saignon
l'Écluse
Lazer
les Bertrands
Melve
les Htes-Graves
Bayons
Combe
la Bse-
la Hte-
Chabanon
Eyguians
Arzeliers
la Motte-du-Caire
les Bses-
St-Amand
le Forest-Lacour
la Rouchaye
Crête de Tête Grosse
Col du Fanget
Lagrand
Saléon
Clamensane
Brunet
Bédouin
Esparron-la-Bâtie
Crête de Val-Haut
l'Infernet
Upaix
Beauvoir
Bourebeau
Thèze
Sigoyer
Tête des Monges
Col de Grêle
l'Oratoire
Nossage-et-Bénevent
la Tuilière
Laragne-Montéglin
Reynier
le Marzenc
Auzet
les Cimettes
les Esparons
Châteauneuf-de-Chabre
la Grange-Neuve
le Poët
les Coucis
Ouv. été 1998
Borelly
Vaumeilh
Nibles
St-Véran
Valavoire
Baudinard
Mgne de Jouère
Vaux
Barles
Verdaches
Antonaves
les Fourniers
les Armands
le Plan
Rochers de Hongrie
Callabris
Châteaufort
Valernes
Col de la Clapouse
Somt de Chine
les Monges
le Forest
Clues de Verdaches
Blayeul Somt
St-Pierre-Avez
Mison
la Clapisse
les Mayols
Gourras
Montagne de Gache
St-Geniez
Briançon
Clue
Chlle Feissal
Somt de Nibles
Col St-Antoine
Somt de la Platte
Rougnouse
Col de Branche
Ribiers
la Silve
Servoules
St-Didier
Clues
Chabert
Authon
Rocher de Dromon
Crête de Géruen
Lambert
Mézien
Sorine
Grottes St-Vincent
Forêt de Melan
l'Espinasse
Clues de Barles
Crête de Blayeul
Plan-de-la-Baume
Défilé de Pierre Écrite
la Robine-s.-Galabre
le Château
le Bès
la Colle
Plaugiers
Mgne de l'Ubac
Roc de l'Aigle
la Baume
Mgne de la Baume
Entrepierres
le Castellard-Melan
Hautes-Duyes
Sivan
N.-D.-de-Lausière
Aubard
St-Vincent-s-Jabron
St-Martin
Noyers-sur-Jabron
Sisteron
B. du Mollard
Bevons
Vilhosc
St-Symphorien
Mauduech
le Clouet
le Guéni
Sigoyer
Le Couvent
Pécoule
Bge de Salignac
Salignac
Le Grépon
Sommet de Vaumuse
le Planas
le Mousteiret
le Moulin
les Curniers
Piedguichard
Pervoye
Valbelle
les Escoffiers
Sisteron-Sud
les Bons Enfants
St-Martin
Beaudument
Thoard
la Bigue
Châteauneuf-Miravail
la Tour
les Richaud
Mgne de Pelegrine
Mgne de Sumiou
Aubignosc
Peipin
Sourribes
la Pérusse
Champ de Tir
Marcoux
Archail
Mgne de St-Michel
Col de St-Vincent
Signal de Lure
Trois Bastides
Volonne
Courbons
St-Vincent
Digne-les-Bains
Pas de la Graille
le Forest
Aubignosc
Refuge de Lure
Montagne de Lure
Narreteau
Châteauneuf-Val-St-Donat
Château-Arnoux
St-Auban
Sommet du Ruth
Pic d'Oise
Barras
Champtercier
les Sieyes
N.-D.-du-Bourg
St-Pancrace
N.-D.-de-Lure
les Chabannes
les Beauduns
Bge de l'Escale
l'Escale
Hospitalet
Jas-de-Berle
les Auglers
la Sèbe
Plan-de-Gaubert
Mallefougasse-Augès
Montfort
Garce
Aiglun
les Hostelleries
Somt de Cousson
Gaubert
33
St-Étienne
Lardiers
Cruis
Défends
Mirabeau
Mallemoisson
Les Thumins
St-Christol
les Fons
St-Jurson
Entrages
St-Étienne-les-Orgues
les Gipières
St-Donat
Peyruis
Fontenelle
Malijai
les Grillons
le Chaffaut-St-Jurson
St-Michel-de-Cousson
St-Joseph
les Jacons
Augès
St-Sébastien
Montlaux
Peyruis
Rochers des Mées
Carmejane

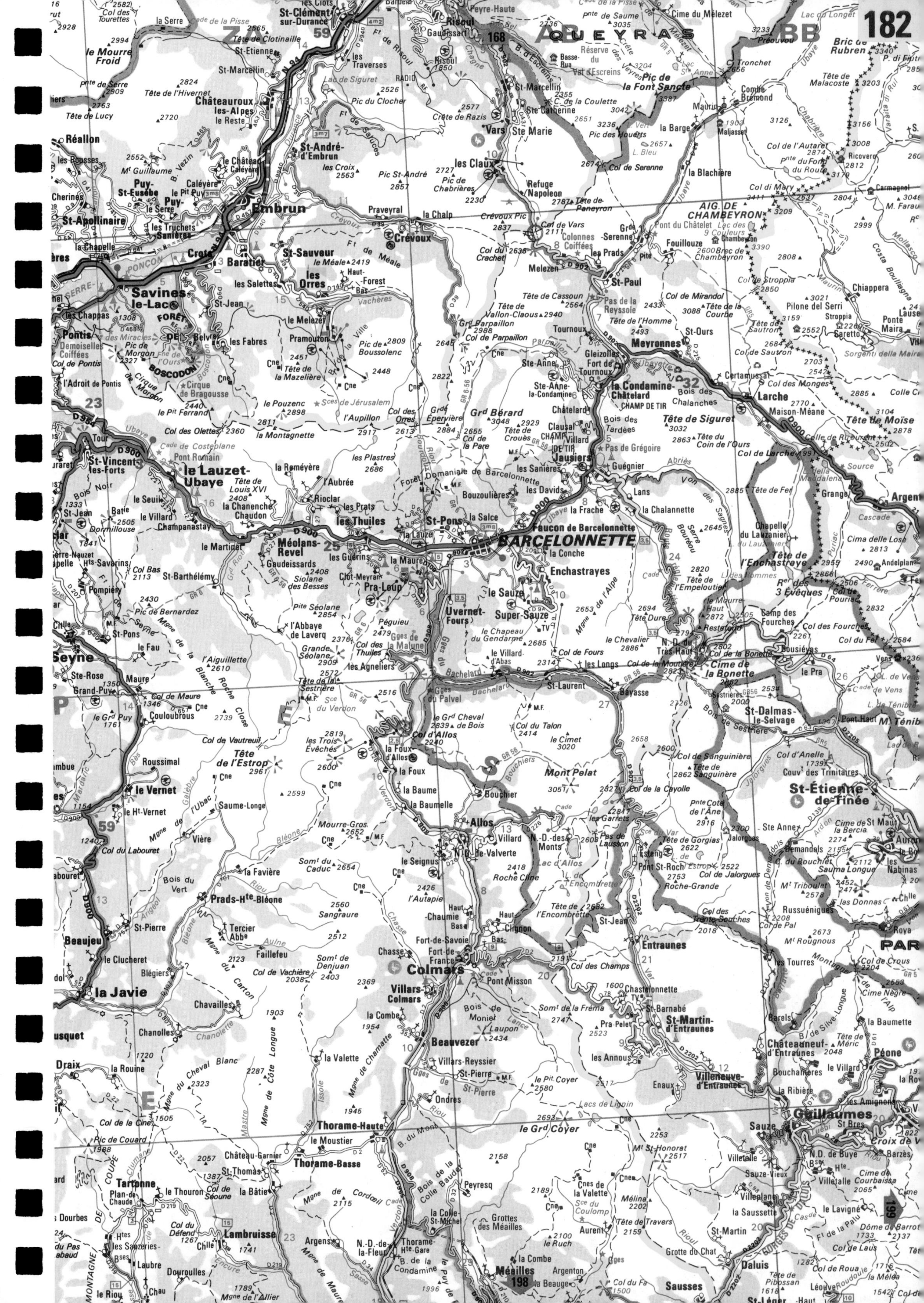
QUEYRAS
St-Clément-sur-Durance
Risoul
Châteauroux-les-Alpes
Réallon
Vars
St-André-d'Embrun
les Claux
Embrun
Crévoux
St-Sauveur
les Orres
Baratier
Savines-le-Lac
AIG. DE CHAMBEYRON
St-Paul
Meyronnes
Larche
la Condamine-Châtelard
Grd Bérard
Tête de Siguret
Jausiers
le Lauzet-Ubaye
Méolans-Revel
les Thuiles
St-Pons
BARCELONNETTE
Faucon de Barcelonnette
Enchastrayes
Pra-Loup
le Sauze
Super-Sauze
Uvernet-Fours
Tête de l'Enchastraye
Cime de la Bonette
Seyne
Col d'Allos
la Foux d'Allos
Tête de l'Estrop
Mont Pelat
St-Étienne-de-Tinée
le Vernet
Allos
St-Dalmas-le-Selvage
Prads-Hte-Bléone
Entraunes
Colmars
Villars-Colmars
St-Martin-d'Entraunes
Beauvezer
la Javie
Beaujeu
Villeneuve-d'Entraunes
Châteauneuf-d'Entraunes
Péone
Guillaumes
Thorame-Haute
Thorame-Basse
Tartonne
Lambruisse
le Grd Coyer
Méailles
Sausses
Daluis
Draix
198
199
168

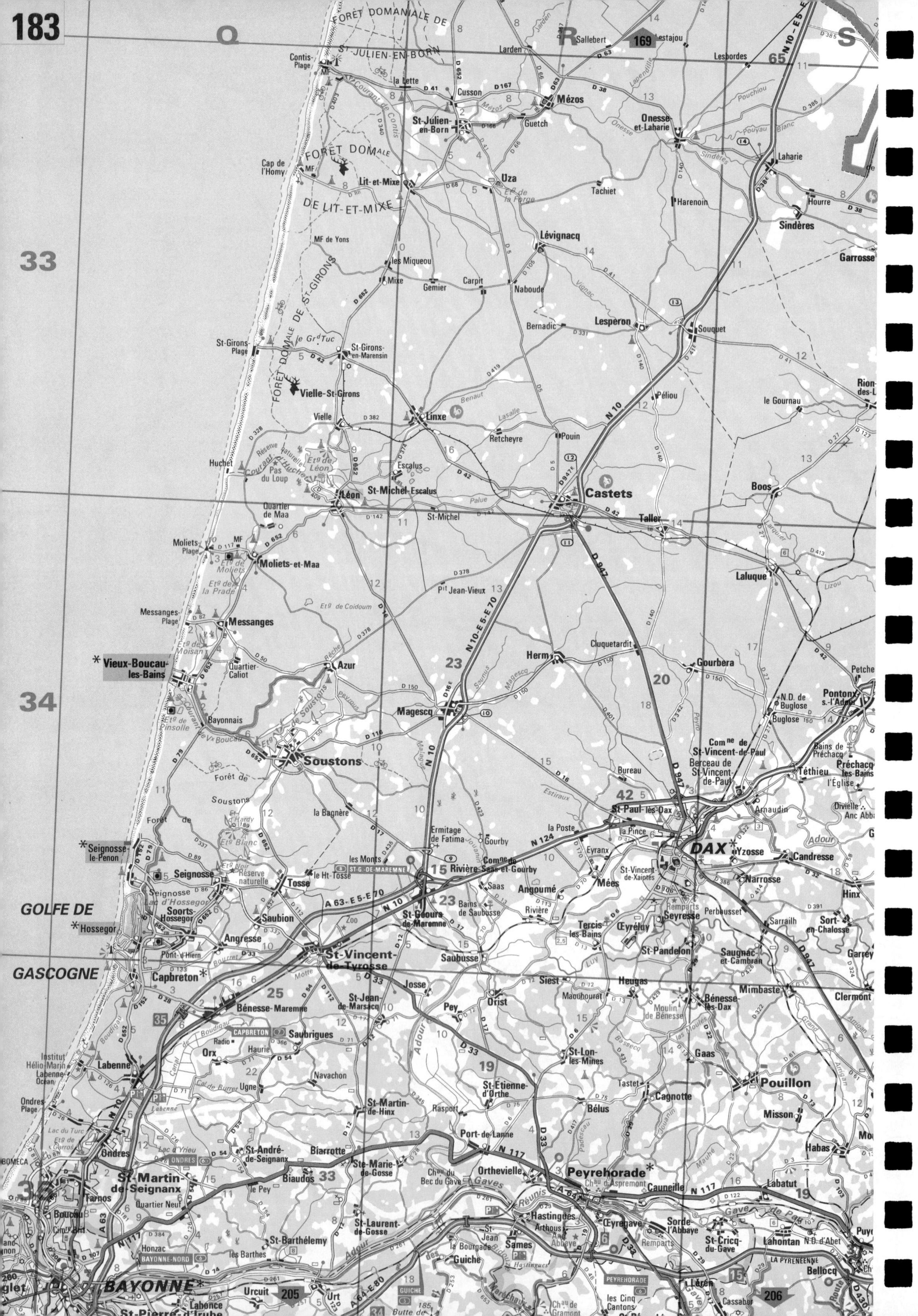
Q
R
S
33
34
169
206
205
FORÊT DOMANIALE DE ST-JULIEN-EN-BORN
Contis-Plage
St-Julien-en-Born
Mézos
Onesse-et-Laharie
Laharie
Lit-et-Mixe
Uza
Lévignacq
Sindères
Lesperon
St-Girons-Plage
St-Girons-en-Marensin
Vielle-St-Girons
Linxe
Castets
Léon
St-Michel-Escalus
Moliets-et-Maa
Messanges
Vieux-Boucau-les-Bains
Azur
Magescq
Soustons
Herm
Gourbera
Seignosse
Tosse
Hossegor
Capbreton
St-Vincent-de-Tyrosse
St-Paul-lès-Dax
DAX
GOLFE DE GASCOGNE
Labenne
Ondres
St-Martin-de-Seignanx
Tarnos
Boucau
BAYONNE
Peyrehorade
Pouillon
Orthevielle
Hastingues
Bénesse-Maremne
Saubrigues
Orx
Biarrotte
Habas
Labatut

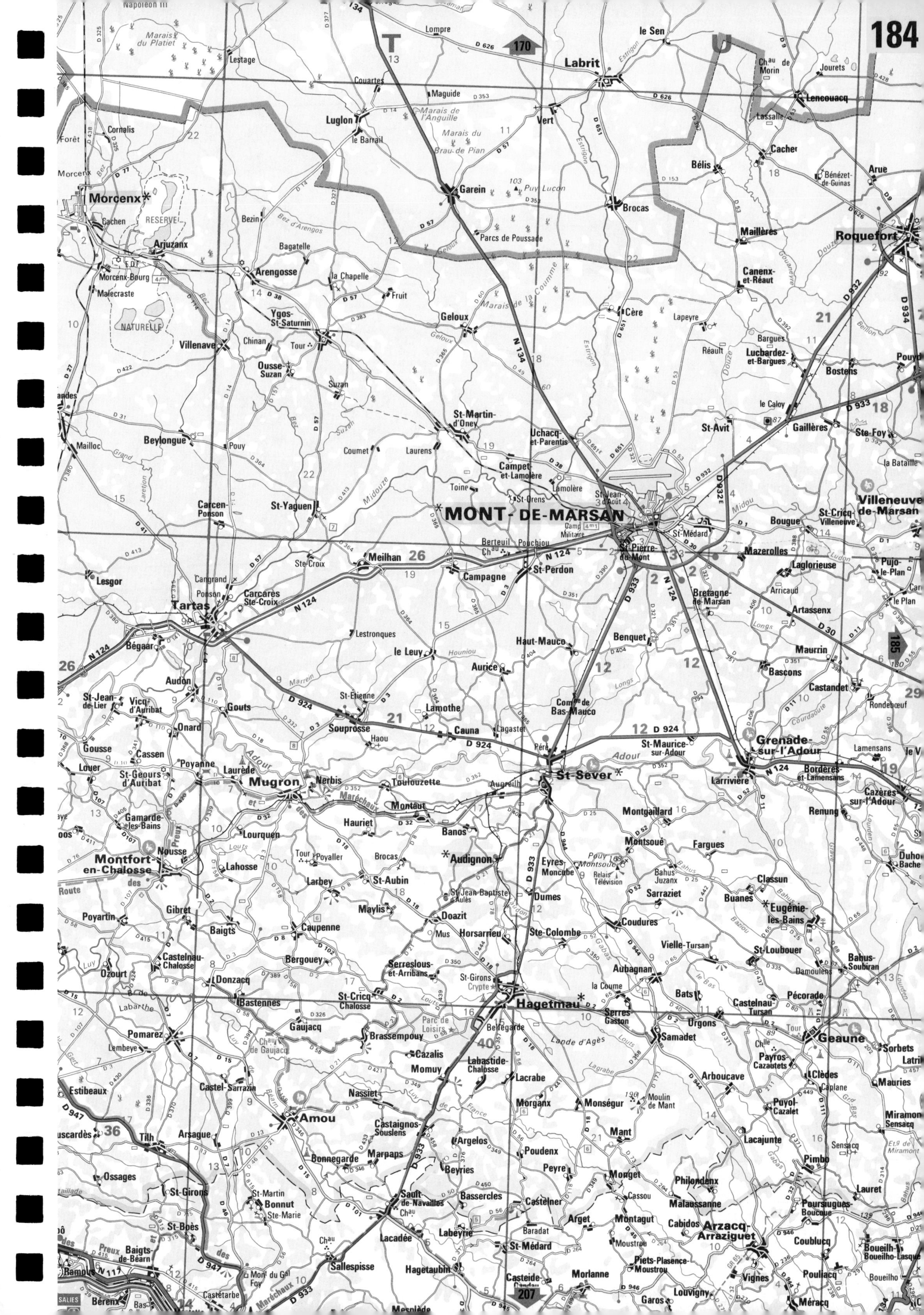
Napoléon III
Marais du Platiet
Lestage
Lompre
T
170
le Sen
Labrit
U
Chau de Morin
Jourets
Courtes
Maguide
D 626
Lencouacq
Lassalle
Cornalis
Luglon
Marais de l'Anguille
Marais du Brau de Pian
Vert
le Barrail
Cacher
Forêt
Bélis
Arue
Morcenx
Bénézet-de-Guinas
Morcenx
Garein
Puy Lucon
RESERVE
Brocas
Gachen
Bezin
Bez d'Arengos
Parcs de Poussade
Maillères
Roquefort
Arjuzanx
Bagatelle
Arengosse
la Chapelle
Canenx-et-Réaut
Morcenx-Bourg
Malecraste
Fruit
NATURELLE
Ygos-St-Saturnin
Geloux
Marais de la Coumme
Cère
Lapeyre
Villenave
Chinan
Tour
Bargues
Lucbardez-et-Bargues
Réault
Bostens
Pouydesseaux
Ousse-Suzan
Suzan
N 134
le Caloy
Gaillères
Ste-Foy
St-Avit
St-Martin-d'Oney
Beylongue
Mailloc
Pouy
Coumet
Laurens
Uchacq-et-Parentis
la Bataille
Campet-et-Lamolère
Lamolère
Villeneuve-de-Marsan
Toine
St-Orens
St-Jean-d'Août
MONT-DE-MARSAN
Carcen-Ponson
St-Yaguen
Camp Militaire
St-Cricq-Villeneuve
Bougue
St-Médard
Berteuil
Pouchiou
St-Pierre-du-Mont
Mazerolles
Meilhan
Ste-Croix
N 124
St-Perdon
Campagne
Laglorieuse
Pujo-le-Plan
Lesgor
Cangrand
Ponson
Carcarès-Ste-Croix
Bretagne-de-Marsan
Arricaud
Le Plan
Tartas
Artassenx
Lestronques
Bégaar
Haut-Mauco
Benquet
Maurrin
le Leuy
Aurice
Bascons
Castandet
Audon
St-Jean-de-Lier
Vicq-d'Auribat
Gouts
St-Etienne
Lamothe
Comte de Bas-Mauco
Rondebœuf
Onard
D 924
Souprosse
Haou
Cauna
Lagastet
St-Maurice-sur-Adour
Grenade-sur-l'Adour
Gousse
Cassen
Péré
Lamensans
Louer
Poyanne
Laurède
Adour
St-Sever
Larrivière
Bordères-et-Lamensans
St-Geours-d'Auribat
Mugron
Nerbis
Toulouzette
Augreilh
Cazères-sur-l'Adour
Montaut
Montgaillard
Renung
Gamarde-les-Bains
Hauriet
Banos
Lourquen
Montsoué
Fargues
Nousse
Tour
Poyaller
Brocas
Audignon
Eyres-Moncube
Montfort-en-Chalosse
Lahosse
Bahus-Juzanx
Classun
Larbey
St-Aubin
St-Jean-Baptiste d'Aulès
Dumes
Sarraziet
Buanes
Eugénie-les-Bains
Poyartin
Gibret
Maylis
Doazit
Baigts
Caupenne
Mus
Horsarrieu
Ste-Colombe
Coudures
Castelnau-Chalosse
Bergouey
Vielle-Tursan
St-Loubouer
Bahus-Soubiran
Ozourt
Serreslous-et-Arribans
Aubagnan
Damoulens
Donzacq
St-Girons
Crypte
la Coume
Bats
Pécorade
Bastennes
St-Cricq-Chalosse
Hagetmau
Castelnau-Tursan
Labarthe
Serres-Gaston
Urgons
Gaujacq
Parc de Loisirs
Pomarez
Brassempouy
Samadet
Geaune
Chau de Gaujacq
Bellegarde
Lande d'Agès
Sorbets
Lembeye
Cazalis
Payros-Cazautets
Momuy
Labastide-Chalosse
Lacrabe
Arboucave
Clèdes
Estibeaux
Castel-Sarrazin
Caplane
Mauries
Nassiet
Morganx
Monségur
Moulin de Mant
Puyol-Cazalet
Amou
Castaignos-Souslens
Miramont-Sensacq
Tilh
Arsague
Mant
Lacajunte
Argelos
Marpaps
Poudenx
Sensacq
Ossages
Bonnegarde
Pimbo
Beyries
Peyre
Monget
St-Girons
Philondenx
Lauret
St-Martin
Bonnut
Ste-Marie
Sault-de-Navailles
Bassercles
Castelner
Cassou
Malaussanne
Poursiugues-Boucoue
Chau
St-Boès
Arget
Montagut
Cabidos
Arzacq-Arraziguet
Coublucq
Baigts-de-Béarn
Lacadée
Labeyrie
Baradat
St-Médard
Moustrou
Boueilh-Boueilho-Lasque
Ramous
Sallespisse
Hagetaubin
Casteide-Candau
Morlanne
Piets-Plasence-Moustrou
Vignes
Pouliacq
Boueilho
Mont du Gal
Foy
Bérenx
Castétarbe
Mesplède
Louvigny
Garos
Méracq
207
185

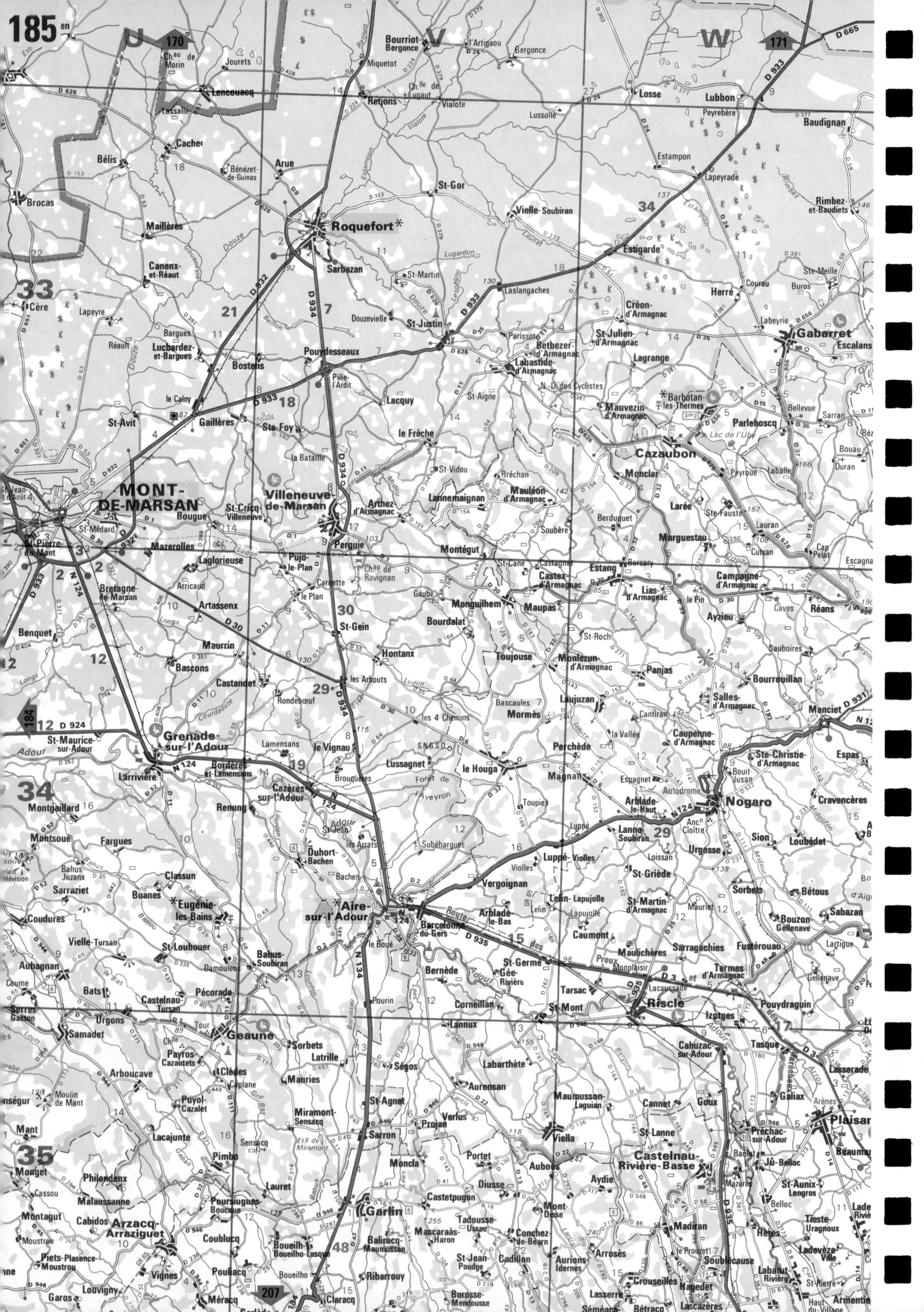

170
171
184
207
U
V
W
33
34
35
Ch.au de Morin
Jourets
Lencouacq
Lassalle
Cacher
Bélis
Brocas
Maillères
Canenx-et-Réaut
Cère
Lapeyre
Réault
Lucbardez-et-Bargues
Bargues
Bostens
le Caloy
St-Avit
Gaillères
Bénézet-de-Guinas
Arue
Roquefort
Sarbazan
Bourriot-Bergonce
l'Artigaou
Bergonce
Miquetot
Retjons
Ch.lle de Lugaut
Vialotte
St-Gor
Lussolle
Losse
Lubbon
Peyrebère
Baudignan
Estampon
Lapeyrade
Rimbez-et-Baudiets
Vielle-Soubiran
Estigarde
Laslangaches
St-Martin
Douzevielle
St-Justin
Pouydesseaux
Pille-l'Ardit
Lacquy
Créon-d'Armagnac
Herré
Couraü
Buros
Ste-Meille
Labeyrie
Gabarret
Escalans
St-Julien-d'Armagnac
Parissot
Betbezer-d'Armagnac
Labastide-d'Armagnac
Lagrange
N.-D. des Cyclistes
St-Aigne
Barbotan-les-Thermes
Mauvezin-d'Armagnac
Parleboscq
Bellevue
Sarran
Lac de l'Uby
Cazaubon
Bouau
Duran
Ste-Foy
le Frêche
la Bataille
MONT-DE-MARSAN
St-Jean-d'Août
St-Médard
St-Pierre-du-Mont
Bougue
St-Cricq-Villeneuve
Villeneuve-de-Marsan
Arthez-d'Armagnac
Perquie
St-Vidou
Bréchan
Lannemaignan
Mauléon-d'Armagnac
Monclar
Larée
Ste-Fauste
Peyrolle
Laballe
Berduguet
Soubère
Marguestau
Lauran
Cutxan
Cap Pelat
Escagna
Mazerolles
Laglorieuse
Pujo-le-Plan
Ch.au de Ravignan
Carrette
Montégut
St-Cane
Castagnet
Castex-d'Armagnac
Estang
Borcary
Campagne-d'Armagnac
Lias-d'Armagnac
le Pin
Caves
Réans
Bretagne-de-Marsan
Arricaud
Artassenx
le Plan
Gaube
Monguilhem
Maupas
Ayzieu
Benquet
Maurrin
St-Gein
Bourdalat
St-Roch
Sauboires
Bascons
Hontanx
Toujouse
Monlezun-d'Armagnac
Panjas
Bourrouillan
Castandet
les Arbouts
Rondebœuf
Bascaules
Mormès
Laujuzan
Salles-d'Armagnac
Cantiran
Manciet
St-Maurice-sur-Adour
Grenade-sur-l'Adour
Lamensans
le Vignau
les 4 Chemins
S.N.G.S.O.
la Vallée
Perchède
Caupenne-d'Armagnac
Ste-Christie-d'Armagnac
Espas
Adour
Larrivière
Bordères-et-Lamensans
Cazères-sur-l'Adour
Lussagnet
Brouquères
Forêt de Laveyron
le Houga
Magnan
Espagnet
Autodrome
Bouit-Jusan
Nogaro
Cravencères
Montgaillard
Renung
St-Jean
les Arrats
Toupies
Arblade-le-Haut
Anc.n Cloître
Lanne-Soubiran
Sion
Loubédat
Montsoué
Fargues
Duhort-Bachen
Subéhargues
Luppé
Luppé-Violles
Violles
Loissan
Urgosse
Bahus-Juzanx
Classun
Bachen
Vergoignan
St-Griède
Sorbets
Bétous
Sarraziet
Buanes
Eugénie-les-Bains
Aire-sur-l'Adour
Barcelonne-du-Gers
Arblade-le-Bas
Lelin-Lapujolle
Lelin
Lapujolle
St-Martin-d'Armagnac
Mauriet
Bouzon-Gellenave
Sabazan
Coudures
Vielle-Tursan
St-Loubouer
le Boué
Caumont
Maulichères
Sarragachies
Fustérouau
Lartigue
Aubagnan
Bahus-Soubiran
Damoulens
Bernède
St-Germé
Gée-Rivière
Preux
Monplaisir
Termes-d'Armagnac
Gellenave
Coume
Bats
Castelnau-Tursan
Pécorade
Pourin
Corneillan
St-Mont
Tarsac
Lacaussade
Riscle
Pouydraguin
Serres-Gaston
Urgons
Samadet
Tour
Geaune
Lannux
Izotges
Tasque
Ch.lle Payros-Cazautets
Sorbets
Latrille
Labarthète
Cahuzac-sur-Adour
Lasserade
Arboucave
Clèdes
Caplane
Ségos
Mauries
Aurensan
Moulin de Mant
Puyol-Cazalet
Miramont-Sensacq
St-Agnet
Maumusson-Laguian
Cannet
Goux
Galiax
Arènes
Plaisance
Mant
Lacajunte
Sensacq
Etg de Miramont
Sarron
Projan
Verlus
Viella
St-Lanne
Préchac-sur-Adour
Beaumarchés
Monget
Pimbo
Portet
Aubous
Castelnau-Rivière-Basse
Baulat
Ju-Belloc
Philondenx
Cassou
Lauret
Moncla
Diusse
Aydie
Mazères
St-Aunix-Lengros
Malaussanne
Poursiugues-Boucoue
Garlin
Castetpugon
Mont-Disse
Madiran
Belloc
Lade-Rivière
Montagut
Cabidos
Arzacq-Arraziguet
Coublucq
Balliracq-Maumusson
Tadousse-Ussau
Mascaraàs-Haron
Conchez-de-Béarn
Hères
Tieste-Uragnoux
Moustrou
Piets-Plasence-Moustrou
Boueilh-Boueilho-Lasque
St-Jean-Poudge
Cadillon
Aurions-Idernes
Arrosès
le Prouzet
Soublecause
Ladevèze-Ville
Vignes
Pouliacq
Boueilho
Ribarrouy
Crouseilles
Labatut-Rivière
St-Pierre
Louvigny
Garos
Méracq
Claracq
Burosse-Mendousse
Lasserre
Hagedet
Séméacq
Bétracq
Lascazères
Haut-Village
Armentieux
Douze
Midour
Ludon
Estampon
Lugardon
Longs
Bahus
Gabas
Louts
Larcis
Bergons
Saget
Arros
Lees
Broussau
Retjons
D 626
D 933
D 932
D 934
D 30
D 924
D 935
D 665
D 931
N 124
N 134

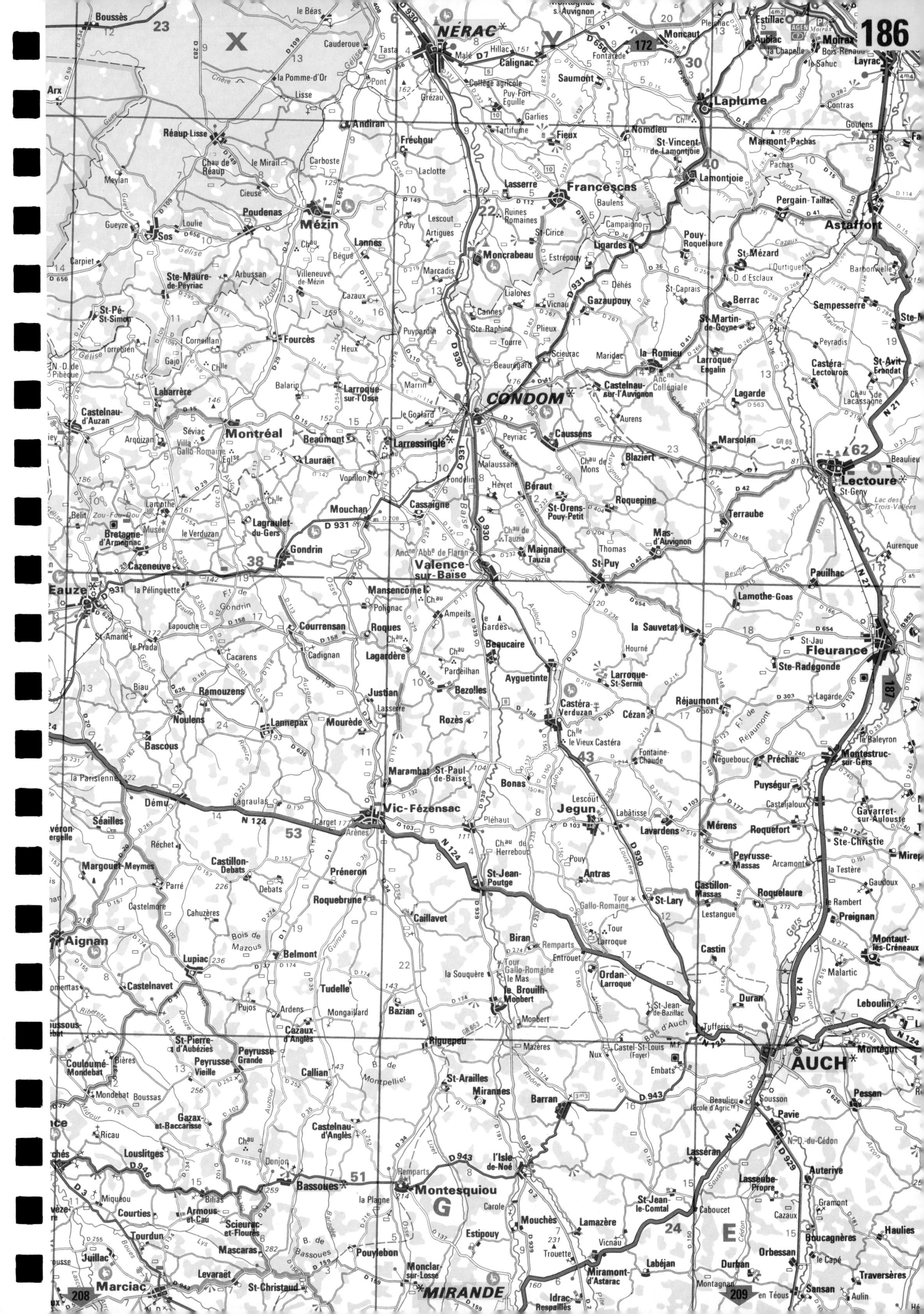
NÉRAC
Moncaut
Estillac
Moirax
Layrac
Boussès
le Béas
Calignac
Fontarède
Aubiac
Tasta
Hillac
Saumont
Laplume
Cauderoue
la Pomme-d'Or
Lisse
Collège agricole
Puy-Fort Eguille
Grézau
Garlies
Tartifume
Andiran
Fieux
Nomdieu
St-Vincent-de-Lamontjoie
Marmont-Pachas
Pachas
Goulens
Contras
Réaup-Lisse
Fréchou
Chau de Réaup
le Mirail
Carboste
Laclotte
Lasserre
Francescas
Lamontjoie
Meylan
Cieuse
Baulens
Pergain-Taillac
Astaffort
Mézin
Poudenas
Loulie
Gueyze
Sos
Lescout
Pouy
Artigues
Ruines Romaines
St-Cirice
Campaigno
Ligardes
Pouy-Roquelaure
St-Mézard
Lannes
Bégué
Moncrabeau
Estrépouy
Carpiet
Ste-Maure-de-Peyriac
Arbussan
Villeneuve-de-Mézin
Marcadis
Dèhés
St-Caprais
N.-D. d'Esclaux
l'Ourtiguet
Barbonvielle
Cazaux
Lialores
Vicnau
Gazaupouy
Berrac
Sempesserre
St-Pé-St-Simon
Cannes
Ste-Raphine
Plieux
St-Martin-de-Goyne
Torrebren
Corneillan
Fourcès
Puypardin
Tourre
Peyradis
Gajo
Heux
Scieurac
Maridac
la Romieu
Larroque-Engalin
Castéra-Lectourois
St-Avit-Frandat
N.-D. de Pibèque
Beauregard
Castelnau-sur-l'Auvignon
Anc. Collégiale
Lagarde
Labarrère
Balarin
Larroque-sur-l'Osse
Marrin
CONDOM
Chau de Lacassagne
Castelnau-d'Auzan
le Goalard
Aurens
Séviac
Villa Gallo-Romaine
Montréal
Beaumont
Larressingle
Peyriac
Caussens
Marsolan
Arquizan
Lauraët
Malaussanne
Chau de Mons
Blaziert
Lectoure
St-Geny
Lac des Trois-Vallées
Beaulieu
Vopillon
Fondelin
Herret
Béraut
Belit
Lamothe
Zou-Fou-Dou
Musée
Mouchan
Cassaigne
St-Orens-Pouy-Petit
Roquepine
Terraube
Bretagne-d'Armagnac
le Verduzan
Lagraulet-du-Gers
Chau de Tauzia
Maignaut-Tauzia
Thomas
Mas-d'Auvignon
Aurenque
Cazeneuve
Gondrin
Anc. Abb. de Flaran
Valence-sur-Baïse
St-Puy
Pauilhac
Eauze
la Pélinguette
Mansencome
Polignac
Lamothe-Goas
Lapouche
Courrensan
Roques
Ampeils
le Gardès
la Sauvetat
St-Amand
le Prada
Cadignan
Lagardère
Beaucaire
Hourné
St-Jau
Fleurance
Cacarens
Pardeilhan
Ayguetinte
Larroque-St-Sernin
Ste-Radegonde
Biau
Ramouzens
Justian
Lasserre
Bezolles
Castéra-Verduzan
Réjaumont
Lagarde
Noulens
Lannepax
Mourède
Rozès
Cézan
Chlle le Vieux Castéra
Bascous
Fontaine-Chaude
F.t de Réjaumont
le Baleyron
Montestruc-sur-Gers
Nègueboue
Préchac
la Parisienne
Marambat
St-Paul-de-Baïse
Bonas
Puységur
Démù
Lagraulas
Vic-Fézensac
Lescout
Jegun
Labâtisse
Castéjaloux
Gavarret-sur-Aulouste
Séailles
Carget
Arènes
Pléhaut
Lavardens
Mérens
Roquefort
Ste-Christie
Réchet
Chau de Herrebouc
Mirepoix
Margouet-Meymes
Castillon-Debats
Préneron
Pouy
Peyrusse-Massas
Arcamont
la Testère
Parré
Debats
St-Jean-Poutge
Antras
Gaudoux
Castelmore
Roquebrune
Castillon-Massas
Roquelaure
Tour Gallo-Romaine
St-Lary
le Rambert
Cahuzères
Lestangue
Preignan
Caillavet
Aignan
Bois de Mazous
Biran
Remparts
Tour Larroque
Castin
Montaut-les-Créneaux
Lupiac
Belmont
Entrouet
Malartic
Castelnavet
la Souquère
Tour Gallo-Romaine
le Mas
Ordan-Larroque
Tudelle
le Brouilh-Monbert
Duran
Leboulin
Pujos
Ardens
Mongaillard
Bazian
St-Jean-de-Bazillac
Monbert
Bois d'Auch
Tufferis
Cazaux-d'Anglès
St-Pierre-d'Aubézies
Riguepeu
Mazères
Nux
Castel-St-Louis (Foyer)
Montégut
Couloumé-Mondebat
Bières
Peyrusse-Grande
Peyrusse-Vieille
Callian
B. de Montpellier
St-Arailles
Mirannes
Embats
AUCH
Mondebat
Boussas
Barran
Beaulieu (École d'Agric.re)
Sousson
Pessan
Gazax-et-Baccarisse
Castelnau-d'Anglès
Pavie
Ricau
N.-D.-du-Cédon
Louslitges
Donjon
Remparts
l'Isle-de-Noé
Lasséran
Auterive
Bassoues
Montesquiou
Lasseube-Propre
Miquéou
Bilias
la Plagne
St-Jean-le-Comtal
Caboucet
Gramont
Courties
Armous-et-Cau
Scieurac-et-Flourès
Carole
Mouchès
Lamazère
Cazaux
Tourdun
Mascaras
B. de Bassoues
Estipouy
Trouette
Vicnau
Bucagnères
Haulies
Orbessan
Juillac
Pouylebon
Monclar-sur-Losse
Labéjan
Durban
le Capé
Levaraët
Miramont-d'Astarac
Traversères
Marciac
St-Christaud
MIRANDE
Montagnan
Idrac-Respaillès
en Téous
Sansan
Aulin
X
Y
G
E
208
209
187
172

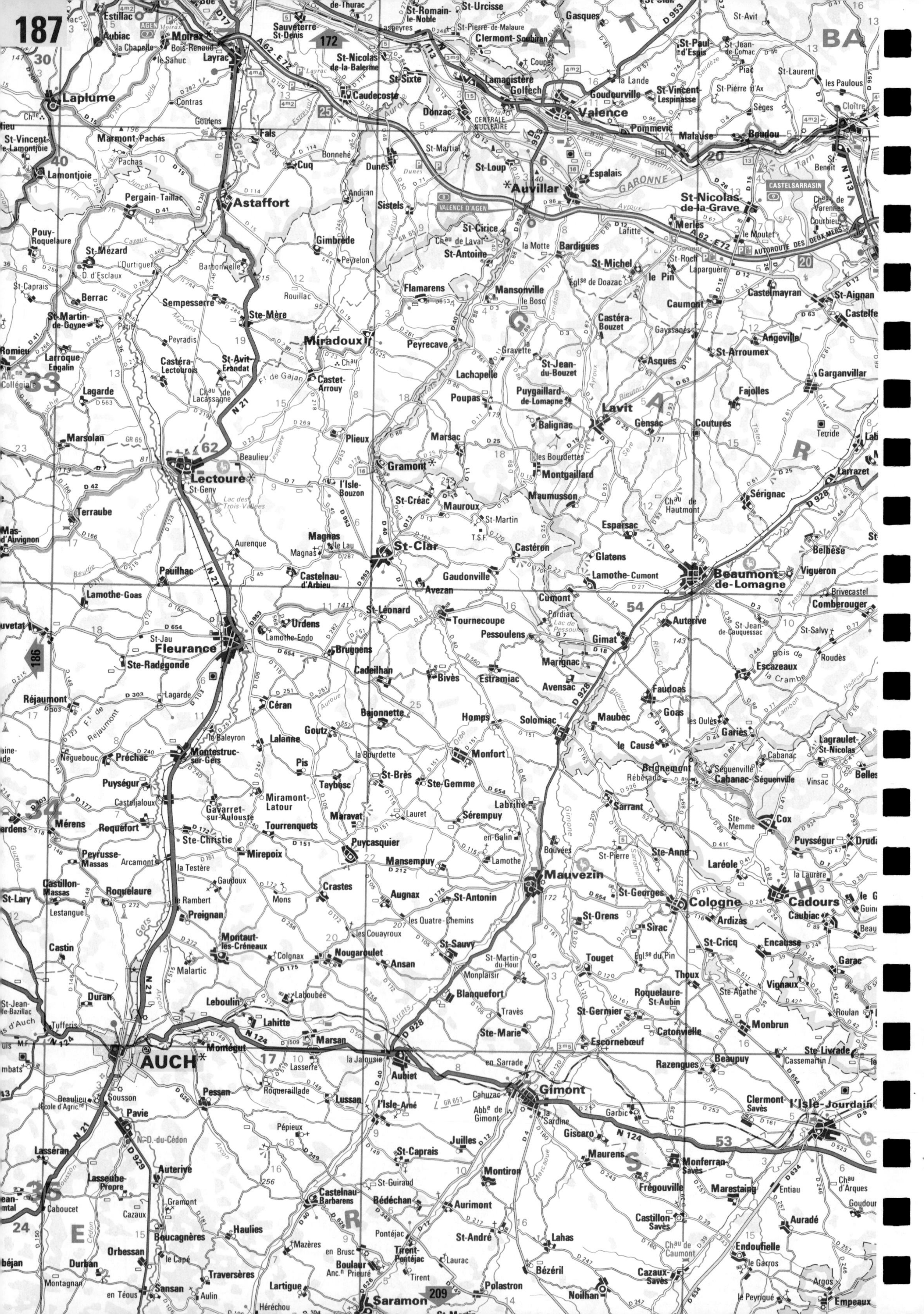
Estillac
Aubiac
Moirax
Layrac
Sauveterre-St-Denis
172
St-Romain-le-Noble
St-Urcisse
Gasques
St-Avit
BA
Laplume
St-Nicolas-de-la-Balerme
St-Sixte
Clermont-Soubiran
Lamagistère
Golfech
Goudourville
St-Vincent-Lespinasse
St-Paul-d'Espis
St-Jean-de-Cornac
Piac
St-Laurent
les Paulous
Caudecoste
Donzac
CENTRALE NUCLÉAIRE
Valence
Pommevic
Malause
Boudou
Moissac
Marmont-Pachas
Fals
St-Vincent-Lamontjoie
Lamontjoie
Cuq
Bonnehé
Dunes
St-Martial
St-Loup
Espalais
Auvillar
GARONNE
CASTELSARRASIN
St-Nicolas-de-la-Grave
Pergain-Taillac
Astaffort
Sistels
VALENCE D'AGEN
Merles
Pouy-Roquelaure
St-Mézard
Gimbrède
St-Cirice
Chau de Laval
St-Antoine
Bardigues
la Motte
Lafitte
le Moutet
AUTOROUTE DES DEUX MERS
A 62 - E 72
St-Caprais
N.-D. d'Esclaux
Barbonvielle
Peyrelon
St-Michel
le Pin
Laparguère
Berrac
Sempesserre
Rouillac
Flamarens
Mansonville
Caumont
Castelmayran
St-Aignan
St-Martin-de-Goyne
Ste-Mère
Castéra-Bouzet
Castelferrus
Romieu
Larroque-Engalin
Peyradis
Miradoux
Peyrecave
Gayssanes
Angeville
Castéra-Lectourois
St-Avit-Frandat
Castet-Arrouy
Lachapelle
St-Jean-du-Bouzet
Asques
St-Arroumex
33
Lagarde
Chau de Lacassagne
Poupas
Puygaillard-de-Lomagne
Lavit
Gensac
Fajolles
Garganvillar
Marsolan
Plieux
Marsac
Balignac
Coutures
Tercide
62
Lectoure
Beaulieu
St-Geny
Lac des Trois-Vallées
Gramont
les Bourdettes
Montgaillard
R
Terraube
l'Isle-Bouzon
St-Créac
Mauroux
Maumusson
Chau de Hautmont
Sérignac
Larrazet
Mas-d'Auvignon
St-Martin
Esparsac
Aurenque
Magnas
le Lau
St-Clar
Castéron
Glatens
Belbèse
Pauilhac
Castelnau-d'Arbieu
Gaudonville
Lamothe-Cumont
Beaumont-de-Lomagne
Vigueron
Lamothe-Goas
Avezan
Cumont
Brivecastel
Comberouger
St-Léonard
Tournecoupe
Pordiac
Lac de Pessoulens
54
Urdens
Lamothe-Endo
Pessoulens
Gimat
Auterive
St-Jean-de-Cauquessac
St-Salvy
St-Jau
Fleurance
186
Brugnens
Cadeilhan
Bivès
Estramiac
Marignac
Escazeaux
Roudès
Ste-Radegonde
Avensac
Faudoas
Réjaumont
Lagarde
Céran
Bajonnette
Homps
Solomiac
Maubec
Goas
les Oulès
Gariès
Lagraulet-St-Nicolas
le Baleyron
Lalanne
Goutz
la Bourdette
Monfort
le Causé
Brignemont
Cabanac-Séguenville
Séguenville
Bellesserre
Néguebouc
Préchac
Montestruc-sur-Gers
Pis
St-Brès
Ste-Gemme
Rébérado
Vinsac
Puységur
Castéljaloux
Gavarret-sur-Aulouste
Miramont-Latour
Taybosc
Labrihe
Sarrant
Ste-Memme
Cox
34
Mérens
Roquefort
Maravat
Lauret
Sérempuy
Puysségur
Drudas
Ste-Christie
Tourrenquets
en-Galin
Bouvées
St-Pierre
Ste-Anne
Peyrusse-Massas
Arcamont
Mirepoix
Puycasquier
Mansempuy
Lamothe
Laréole
la Testère
Mauvezin
la Laurère
Castillon-Massas
Gaudoux
Mons
Crastes
Augnax
St-Antonin
St-Georges
Cologne
Cadours
St-Lary
Roquelaure
Lestangue
le Rambert
Preignan
les Quatre-Chemins
St-Orens
Sirac
Ardizas
Caubiac
les Couayroux
Castin
Montaut-les-Créneaux
Colgnax
Nougaroulet
Ansan
St-Sauvy
St-Cricq
Encausse
Garac
Malartic
St-Martin-du-Hour
Touget
Egl.se du Pin
Monplaisir
Thoux
Vignaux
Ste-Agathe
Duran
Laboubée
Blanquefort
Roquelaure-St-Aubin
Leboulin
Travès
St-Germier
Roulan
St-Jean-le-Bazillac
Lahitte
Monbrun
Tufferis
N 124
Marsan
Ste-Marie
Catonvielle
Montégut
Escorneboeuf
Ste-Livrade
AUCH
17
Lasserre
la Jalousie
Aubiet
en Sarrade
Razengues
Beaupuy
Cassemartin
Sousson
Pessan
Roqueraillade
Cahuzac
Gimont
Clermont-Savès
l'Isle-Jourdain
Beaulieu
Pavie
Lussan
l'Isle-Arné
Abbe de Gimont
la Sardine
Garbic
N.-D.-du-Cédon
Pépieux
Giscaro
53
Lasséran
St-Caprais
Juilles
Maurens
Monferran-Savès
Auterive
Montiron
Chau d'Arques
Lasseube-Propre
St-Guiraud
Frégouville
Marestaing
Entiau
Goudourville
35
Gramont
Castelnau-Barbarens
Bédéchan
Aurimont
Caboucet
Cazaux
Castillon-Savès
Auradé
24
E
Boucagnères
Haulies
St-André
Lahas
R
Pontéjac
Chau de Caumont
Endoufielle
Orbessan
Mazères
Tirent-Pontéjac
le Capé
en Brusc
Laurac
le Garros
Durban
Boulaur
Anc.n Prieuré
Bézéril
Traversères
Tirent
Cazaux-Savès
Montagnan
Lartigue
Polastron
Argos
en Téous
Sansan
Aulin
Saramon
209
Noilhan
le Peyrigué
Empeaux
Hérécbou

173
174
189
210
211
Caussade
St-Cirq
Lafrançaise
Moissac
Castelsarrasin
Montauban
Nègrepelisse
Montricoux
Bruniquel
Réalville
Caussade
Mirabel
Puycornet
Lizac
Montastruc
Albias
Villemade
Meauzac
Labastide-du-Temple
Albefeuille-Lagarde
La Ville-Dieu-du-Temple
St-Etienne-de-Tulmont
Vaïssac
Puygaillard-de-Quercy
Montbeton
Lacourt-St-Pierre
Escatalens
St-Porquier
Cordes-Tolosannes
Lafitte
Montech
Bressols
St-Nauphary
Monclar-de-Quercy
Montdurausse
St-Urcisse
Corbarieu
Reyniès
Villebrumier
Labastide-St-Pierre
Montbartier
Finhan
Mas-Grenier
Monbéqui
Campsas
Orgueil
Nohic
Montgaillard
Salvagnac
Bessens
Dieupentale
Villemur-s-Tarn
Verdun-sur-Garonne
Fronton
Canals
Fabas
Bouillac
Grisolles
Pompignan
Villaudric
Bondigoux
Layrac-sur-Tarn
Mirepoix-sur-Tarn
Rabastens
Aucamville
St-Rustice
Castelnau-d'Estrétefonds
Grenade
Bouloc
Vacquiers
Montjoire
Bessières
Mézens
St-Sulpice
Launac
Larra
St-Jory
St-Sauveur
Cépet
Labastide-St-Sernin
Bazus
Gémil
Montastruc-la-Conseillère
Merville
Lespinasse
Gratentour
Pechbonnieu
Garidech
St-Paul-sur-Save
Daux
Montaigut-sur-Save
Seilh
Gagnac-sur-Garonne
Castelginest
St-Alban
St-Loup Cammas
Lévignac
Aussonne
Fenouillet
Fonbeauzard
Launaguet
Castelmaurou
Gragnague
Verfeil
Mondonville
Beauzelle
Aucamville
Rouffiac-Tolosan
St-Marcel-Paulel
Cornebarrieu
Blagnac
L'Union
Montrabé
Lavalette
Teulat
Lasserre
Mérenvielle
Pibrac
Colomiers
Toulouse
Balma
Pin-Balma
Mons
Gauré
Léguevin
Pujaudran
Flourens
Drémil-Lafage
Vallesvilles
Tournefeuille
La Salvetat-St-Gilles
Quint-Fonsegrives
St-Pierre-de-Lages
Plaisance-du-Touch
Aigrefeuille
Lanta
Fontenilles
Ramonville-St-Agne
St-Orens-de-Gameville
Bonrepos-sur-Aussonnelle
Fonsorbes
Cugnaux
Pechbusque
Auzielle
Ste-Foy-d'Aigrefeuille
Auzeville-Tolosane
Labège
Préserville
Odars
Saiguède
Villeneuve-Tolosane
Garonne
Tarn
Aveyron

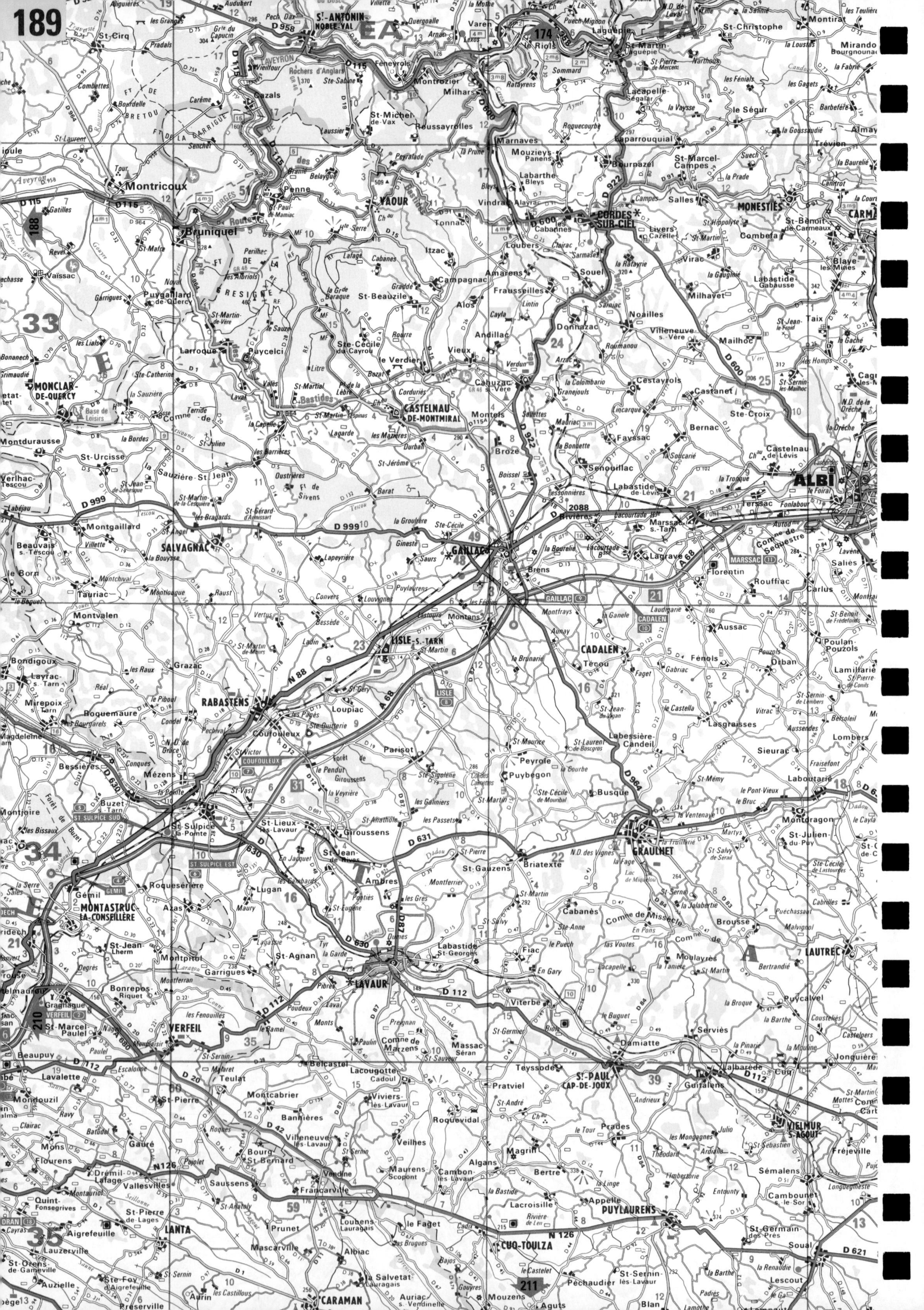
St-Antonin-Noble-Val
St-Cirq
Varen
Laguépie
St-Martin-Laguépie
St-Christophe
Montirat
Mirandol-Bourgnounac
Féneyrols
Montrozier
Milhars
Cazals
St-Michel-de-Vax
Roussayrolles
Lacapelle-Ségalar
le Ségur
Marnaves
Mouzieys-Panens
Laparrouquial
Bournazel
St-Marcel-Campes
Montricoux
Penne
Vaour
Labarthe-Bleys
Vindrac-Alayrac
Salles
Monestiés
Bruniquel
Cordes-sur-Ciel
Tonnac
Itzac
Livers-Cazelles
Combefa
St-Benoît-de-Carmeaux
Blaye-les-Mines
Vaïssac
Campagnac
Amarens
Souel
Virac
Labastide-Gaillac
Puygaillard-de-Quercy
Frausseilles
Milhavet
St-Beauzile
Alos
Noailles
Monclar-de-Quercy
Larroque
Puycelci
Ste-Cécile-du-Cayrou
le Verdier
Vieux
Andillac
Donnazac
Villeneuve-s.-Vère
Mailhoc
Cahuzac-s.-Vère
Cestayrols
Castanet
Ste-Croix
Castelnau-de-Montmiral
Montels
Bernac
Montdurausse
St-Urcisse
Broze
Fayssac
Castelnau-de-Lévis
Albi
Senouillac
Labastide-de-Lévis
Montgaillard
Salvagnac
D 999
Rivières
Marssac-s.-Tarn
Terssac
Gaillac
Brens
Lagrave
Florentin
Rouffiac
Beauvais-s.-Tescou
Tauriac
Montans
Cadalen
Montvalen
Lisle-s.-Tarn
Aussac
Fénols
Orban
Rabastens
Grazac
Couffouleux
Loupiac
Parisot
Labessière-Candeil
Mézens
Peyrole
Puybegon
Busque
Giroussens
Graulhet
St-Sulpice-la-Pointe
Briatexte
St-Gauzens
Ambres
Montastruc-la-Conseillère
Lugan
Azas
Lavaur
St-Agnan
Labastide-St-Georges
Cabanès
Brousse
Moulayrès
Lautrec
Verfeil
Viterbe
Damiatte
Serviès
St-Paul-Cap-de-Joux
Guitalens
Vielmur-s.-Agout
Teulat
Montcabrier
Pratviel
Prades
Magrin
Algans
Bertre
Puylaurens
Lanta
Caraman
Cuq-Toulza
Sémalens
Soual
Lescout
D 621
N 126
D 112
A 68
N 88

Crespin
Tauriac-de-Naucelle
Centrès
Meljac
Rullac St-Cirq
Auriac-Lagast
Alrance
PAMPELONNE
Tanus
St-Just-s.-Viaur
Durenque
Ouv. début 1999
Trébàn
Ste Gemme
Lentin
Ledergues
Villefranche-de-Panat
Moularès
Crespin
Rosières
VALENCE-D'ALBIGEOIS
REQUISTA
Padiès
Faussergues
Connac
VALDERIES
St-Michel-Labadié
Brousse-le-Château
Saussenac
St-Izaire
Montclar
Assac
Cadix
Coupiac
Fraissines
Sérénac
St-Grégoire
Arthès
Lescure
Crespinet
Ambialet
Courris
Trébas
Plaisance
Martrin
Marsal
Cunac
Cambon
St-André
Curvalle
Balaguier-s.-Rance
VILLEFRANCHE-D'ALBIGEOIS
ALBAN
Miolles
ST-SERNIN-S.-RANCE
Mouzieys-Teulet
Massals
Montfranc
Pousthomy
Dénat
Teillet
Paulinet
Combret
Fauch
Ronel
Rayssac
BELMONT-S.-RANCE
St-Salvi-de-Carcaves
Roumégoux
St-Antonin-de-Lacalm
Mont-Roc
Laval-Roquecézière
RÉALMONT
Arifat
Le Masnau-Massuguiès
St-Sever-du-Moustier
St-Pierre-de-Trivisy
Murasson
Sénaux
Escroux
Vénès
MONTREDON-LABESSONNIÉ
Lacaze
LACAUNE
Gijounet
Espérausses
VABRE
Berlats
St-Germier
ROQUECOURBE
Lacrouzette
Ferrières
Burlats
BRASSAC
Lamontélarié
CASTRES
LA SALVETAT-S.-AGOUT
Noailhac
Boissezon
Cambounès
Saix
ANGLÈS
Navès
Viviers-lès-Montagnes
LABRUGUIÈRE
St-Affrique-les-Montagnes
le Rialet
MONTS DE LACAUNE
PARC NATUREL RÉGIONAL DU HAUT-LANGUEDOC

MILLAU
RÉGIONAL
DES
GRANDS - CAUSSES
CAUSSE
St-AFFRIQUE
Vabres l'Abbaye
Roquefort-S.-Soulzon
Tournemire
St-Rome-de-Tarn
St-Rome-de-Cernon
St-Georges-de-Luzençon
Compregnac
Montjaux
Viala-du-Tarn
Ayssènes
le Truel
la Cavalerie
Lapanouse-de-Cernon
CAMP DU LARZAC
l'Hospitalet-du-Larzac
CORNUS
St-Beaulize
Fondamente
Montlaur
Rebourguil
BELMONT-S.-RANCE
CAMARÈS
Sylvanès
Montagnol
Fayet
Brusque
Ceilhes-et-Rocozels
Avène
Roqueredonde
LUNAS
le Bousquet-d'Orb
Graissessac
St-GERVAIS-S.-MARE
St-Étienne-Estréchoux
Lamalou-les-Bains
BÉDARIEUX
MURAT-S.-VÈBRE
LA SALVETAT-S.-AGOUT
Fraisse-s.-Agout
OLARGUES
Mons
St-Martin-de-l'Arcon
Colombières-s.-Orb
le Poujol-s.-Orb
Faugères
Roquessels
Caussiniojouls
Cabrerolles
St-Vincent-d'Olargues
Prémian
St-Étienne-d'Albagnan
Vieussan
Rosis
Castanet-le-Haut
Mélagues
Pézènes-les-Mines
PLATEAU DE GUILHAUMARD
LE CAYLAR
ALZON
LA MÉRIDIENNE
CHAOS DE MONTPELLIER-LE-VIEUX
176
190
212
213

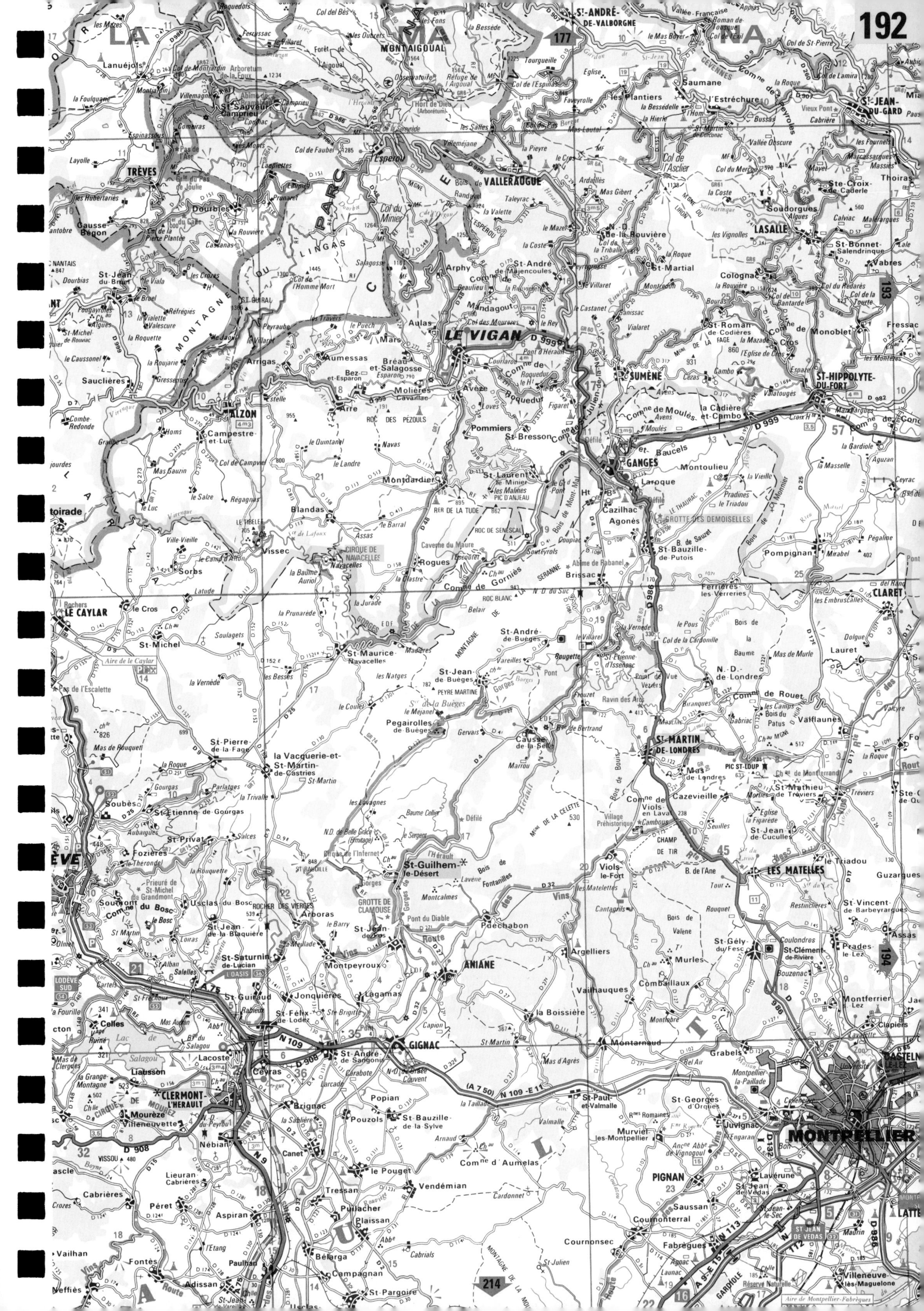
LA MARGERIDE
MONT AIGOUAL
St-ANDRÉ-DE-VALBORGNE
177
Lanuéjols
St-Sauveur-Camprieu
TRÈVES
Dourbies
l'Espérou
VALLERAUGUE
Causse Bégon
St-Jean-du-Bruel
St-JEAN-DU-GARD
Saumane
L'Estréchure
les Plantiers
LASALLE
Sumène
St-HIPPOLYTE-DU-FORT
LE VIGAN
Aulas
Arphy
Mandagout
Molières-Cavaillac
Avèze
Arrigas
Aumessas
ALZON
Sauclières
Campestre-et-Luc
Montdardier
Blandas
Rogues
Vissec
Pommiers
St-Bresson
GANGES
Cazilhac
Agonès
St-Bauzille-de-Putois
Brissac
Pompignan
CLARET
193
LE CAYLAR
St-Michel
St-Maurice-Navacelles
CIRQUE DE NAVACELLES
St-Jean-de-Buèges
Pegairolles-de-Buèges
St-André-de-Buèges
Causse-de-la-Selle
St-MARTIN-DE-LONDRES
N.-D.-de-Londres
PIC ST-LOUP
Valflaunès
St-Pierre-de-la-Fage
la Vacquerie-et-St-Martin-de-Castries
Soubès
St-Étienne-de-Gourgas
St-Privat
Fozières
LODÈVE
St-Guilhem-le-Désert
Viols-le-Fort
LES MATELLES
St-Jean-de-Cuculles
Arboras
Montpeyroux
ANIANE
Puéchabon
Argelliers
St-Gély-du-Fesc
Prades-le-Lez
194
Jonquières
Lagamas
St-Guiraud
St-Félix-de-Lodez
Vailhauquès
Combaillaux
Montferrier-sur-Lez
Celles
Lac du Salagou
GIGNAC
St-André-de-Sangonis
Montarnaud
la Boissière
Grabels
Liausson
Lacoste
Ceyras
CLERMONT-L'HÉRAULT
Mourèze
Villeneuvette
Brignac
Popian
Pouzols
St-Bauzille-de-la-Sylve
St-Paul-et-Valmalle
Murviel-lès-Montpellier
Juvignac
MONTPELLIER
Nébian
Canet
le Pouget
Vendémian
Aumelas
PIGNAN
Lavérune
St-Jean-de-Védas
Cabrières
Péret
Aspiran
Tressan
Puilacher
Plaissan
Saussan
Cournonterral
Fabrègues
Cournonsec
Bélarga
Campagnan
St-Pargoire
Paulhan
Adissan
Fontès
Villeneuve-lès-Maguelone
214

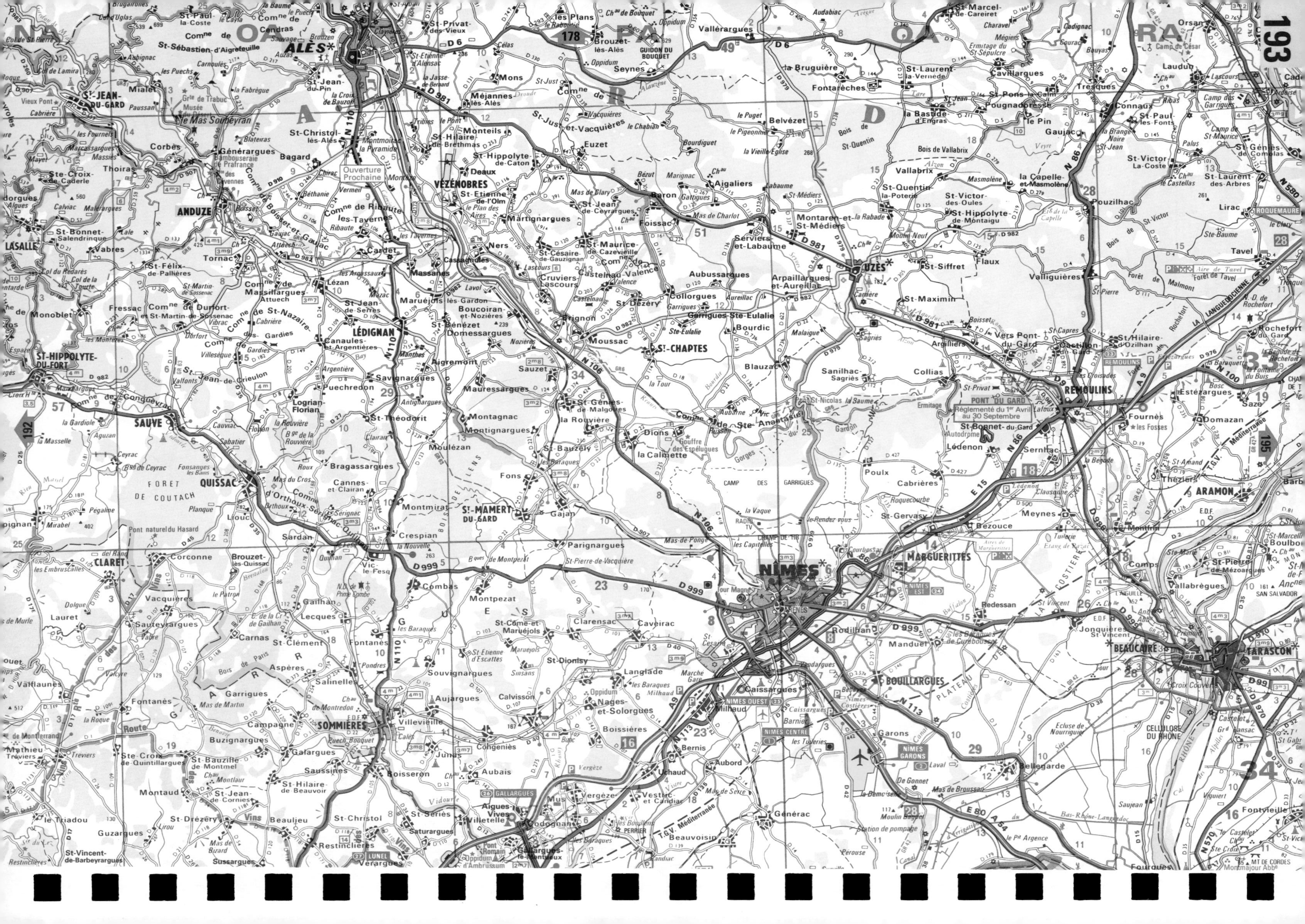
ALÈS
UZÈS
NÎMES
BEAUCAIRE
TARASCON
REMOULINS
SOMMIÈRES
ANDUZE
LÉDIGNAN
QUISSAC
SAUVE
ST-HIPPOLYTE-DU-FORT
MARGUERITTES
BOUILLARGUES
VÉZÉNOBRES
ST-CHAPTES
ST-MAMERT-DU-GARD
CLARET
LASALLE
ST-JEAN-DU-GARD
PONT DU GARD
Réglementé du 1er Avril au 30 Septembre
ARAMON
CAMP DES GARRIGUES
FORET DE COUTACH
N 106
N 110
N 86
N 113
D 999
178
195
192

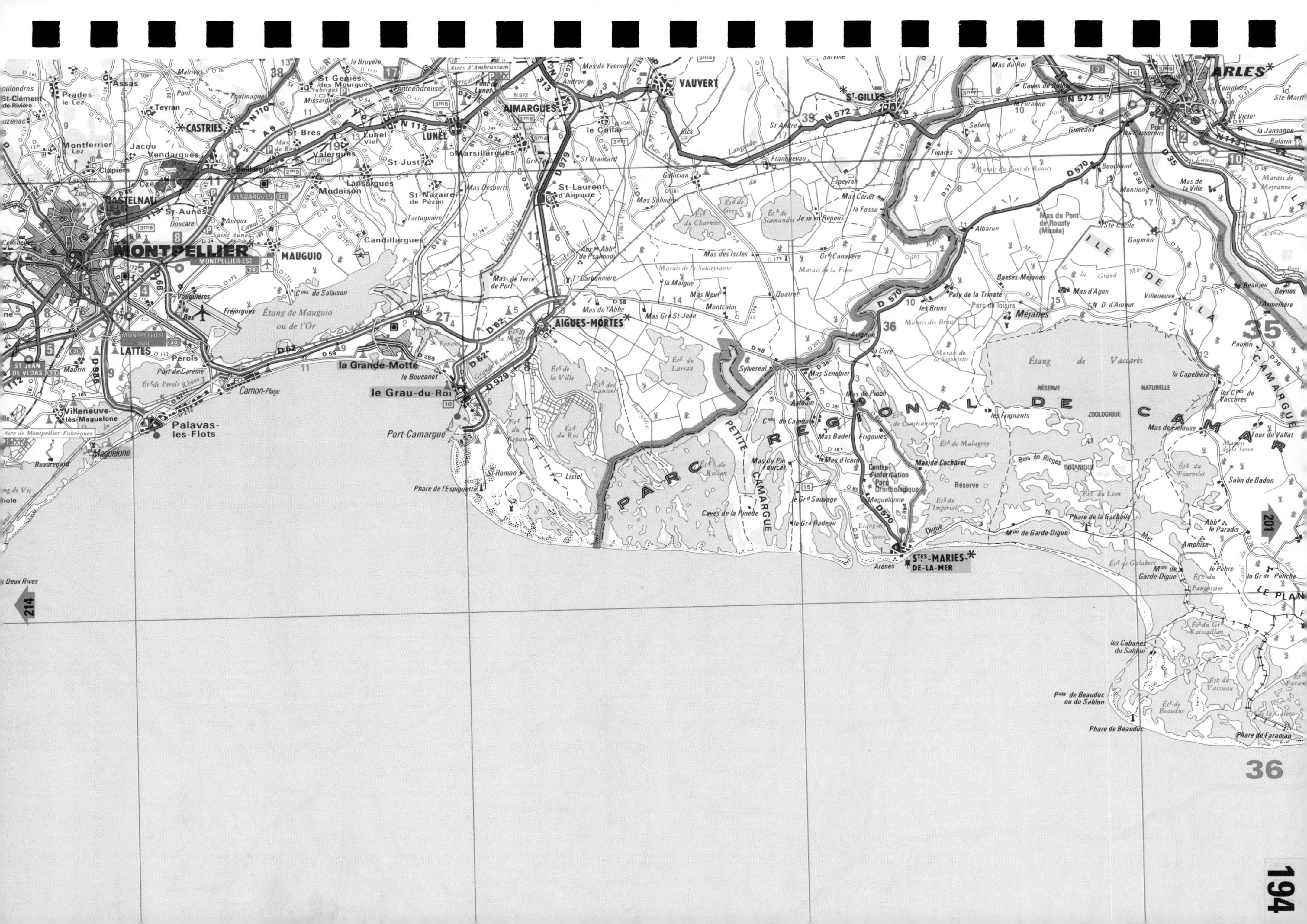

ARLES
ST-GILLES
VAUVERT
AIMARGUES
LUNEL
CASTRIES
MONTPELLIER
MAUGUIO
AIGUES-MORTES
la Grande-Motte
le Grau-du-Roi
Port-Camargue
Palavas-les-Flots
Étang de Mauguio ou de l'Or
ILE DE LA CAMARGUE
PARC RÉGIONAL DE CAMAR
PETITE CAMARGUE
Étang de Vaccarès
STES-MARIES-DE-LA-MER
Phare de l'Espiguette
Phare de Beauduc
Phare de Faraman
35
36
201
214

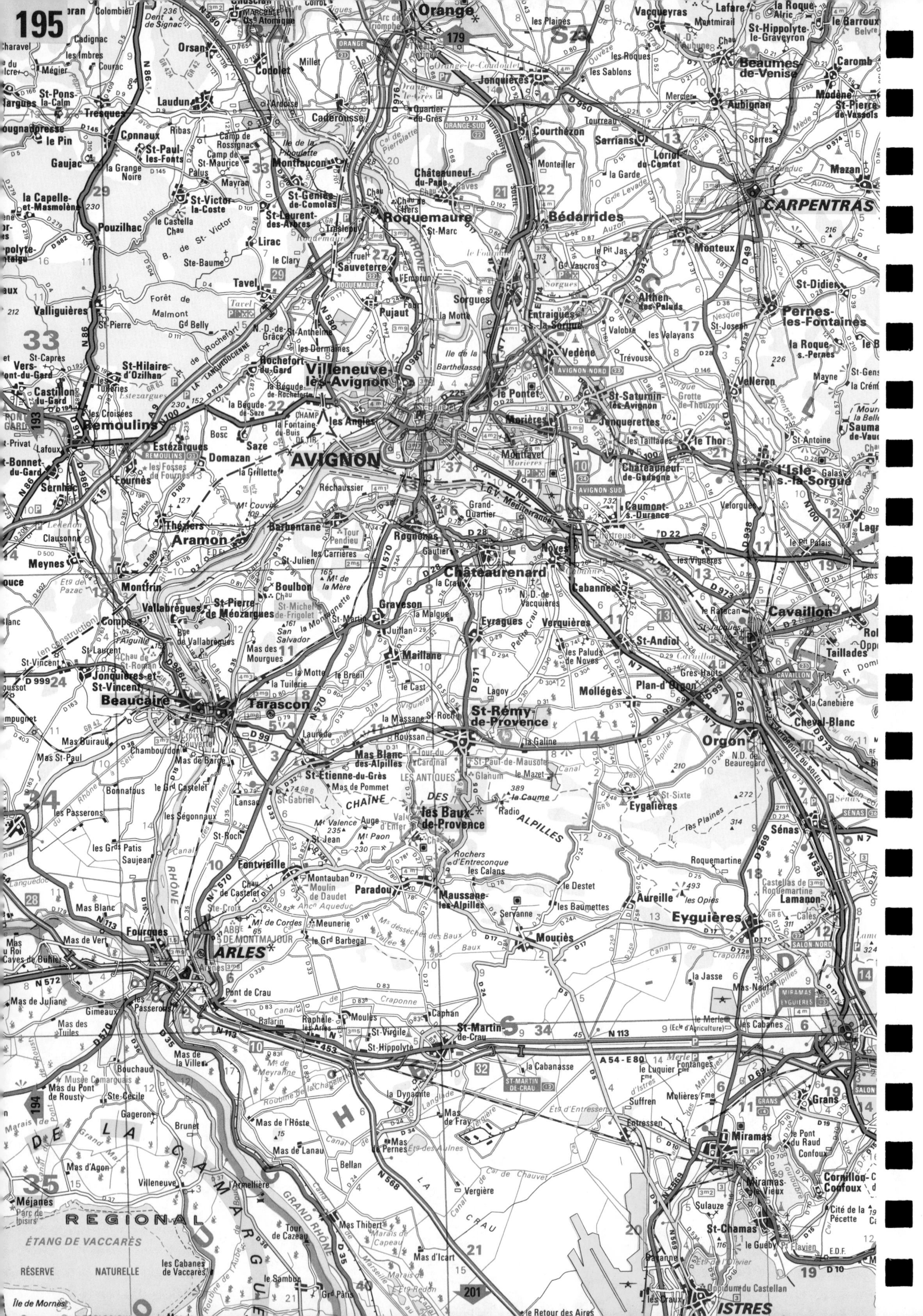

Orange
Arc de Triomphe
Vacqueyras
Lafare
la Roque-Alric
le Barroux
St-Hippolyte-le-Graveyron
Beaumes-de-Venise
Caromb
Modène
St-Pierre-de-Vassols
Aubignan
Mazan
CARPENTRAS
Monteux
Loriol-du-Comtat
Sarrians
Courthezon
Jonquières
Orsan
Codolet
Cadignac
St-Pons-la-Calm
Tresques
Laudun
Connaux
le Pin
St-Paul-les-Fonts
Gaujac
Caderousse
Montfaucon
Châteauneuf-du-Pape
Bédarrides
la Capelle-et-Masmolène
Pouzilhac
St-Victor-la-Coste
St-Geniès-de-Comolas
St-Laurent-des-Arbres
Roquemaure
Lirac
Sauveterre
Tavel
Pujaut
Sorgues
Entraigues-s-la-Sorgue
Althen-des-Paluds
Pernes-les-Fontaines
St-Didier
Valliguières
Forêt de Malmont
Vers-Pont-du-Gard
St-Hilaire-d'Ozilhan
Castillon-du-Gard
Rochefort-du-Gard
Villeneuve-lès-Avignon
Vedène
Velleron
le Pontet
St-Saturnin-lès-Avignon
Jonquerettes
Remoulins
Estézargues
Domazan
Saze
les Angles
AVIGNON
Morières
Montfavet
le Thor
l'Isle-s-la-Sorgue
Fournès
Sernhac
Théziers
Aramon
Barbentane
Rognonas
Châteaurenard
Noves
Caumont-s-Durance
Châteauneuf-de-Gadagne
Meynes
Montfrin
Vallabrègues
Boulbon
St-Pierre-de-Mézoargues
Graveson
Eyragues
Verquières
Cabannes
Cavaillon
St-Andiol
Comps
Jonquières-et-St-Vincent
Beaucaire
Tarascon
Maillane
St-Rémy-de-Provence
Mollégès
Plan-d'Orgon
Orgon
Cheval-Blanc
Taillades
Mas Blanc-des-Alpilles
St-Étienne-du-Grès
LES ANTIQUES
Glanum
CHAÎNE DES ALPILLES
les Baux-de-Provence
Eygalières
Sénas
Fontvieille
Paradou
Maussane-les-Alpilles
Mouriès
Aureille
Eyguières
Lamanon
Fourques
ARLES
Pont de Crau
Raphèle-lès-Arles
St-Martin-de-Crau
Miramas
Miramas-le-Vieux
Grans
Cornillon-Confoux
St-Chamas
ISTRES
CAMARGUE
ÉTANG DE VACCARÈS
RÉSERVE NATURELLE
GRAND RHÔNE
RHÔNE
LA CRAU
Méjanes
Mas Thibert
N 113
A 54 - E 80
AUTOROUTE DU SOLEIL
201

Bédoin
Crillon-le-Brave
Flassan
Aurel
Sault
St-Trinit
Revest-du-Bion
Redortiers
la Rochegiron
Saumane
l'Hospitalet
Lardiers
Mormoiron
Monieux
Villes-s-Auzon
Banon
St-Christol
Montsalier
Ongles
Blauvac
Malemort-du-Comtat
Méthamis
Simiane-la-Rotonde
Lagarde-d'Apt
Revest-des-Brousses
Limans
Vénasque
Murs
Lioux
St-Saturnin-lès-Apt
Oppedette
Aubenas-les-Alpes
Vachères
Rustrel
Gignac
Fontaine-de-Vaucluse
Gordes
Roussillon
Gargas
Villars
St-Michel-l'Observatoire
Reillanne
Viens
APT
Caseneuve
Cabrières-d'Avignon
St-Pantaléon
Goult
Saignon
St-Martin-de-Castillon
Céreste
Montjustin
Villemus
Beaumettes
Maubec
Oppède
Ménerbes
Lacoste
Bonnieux
Buoux
Sivergues
Castellet
Auribeau
Vitrolles
Montfuron
Pierrevert
PARC RÉGIONAL DU LUBÉRON
MONTAGNE DU LUBÉRON
Cabrières-d'Aigues
Peypin-d'Aigues
La Motte-d'Aigues
la Bastide-des-Jourdans
Vaugines
Cucuron
Mérindol
Puget
Lauris
Puyvert
Lourmarin
St-Martin-de-la-Brasque
Grambois
Sannes
Beaumont-de-Pertuis
Cadenet
Ansouis
la Tour-d'Aigues
Mallemort
Charleval
la Roque-d'Anthéron
Villelaure
Pertuis
la Bastidonne
Mirabeau
Alleins
St-Estève-Janson
St-Paul-lès-Durance
Vernègues
Lambesc
Rognes
le Puy-Ste-Réparade
Peyrolles-en-Provence
Jouques
Salon-de-Provence
Pélissanne
St-Cannat
Meyrargues
Venelles
Lançon-Provence
Éguilles
Vauvenargues
Coudoux
St-Marc-Jaumegarde
la Fare-les-Oliviers
Ventabren
AIX-EN-PROVENCE
Le Tholonet
St-Antonin-s.-Bayon
Puyloubier
Beaurecueil
Velaux
Châteauneuf

DIGNE-LES-BAINS
FORCALQUIER
Volonne
Château-Arnoux
St-Auban
Châteauneuf Val-St-Donat
l'Escale
Malijai
Peyruis
les Mées
Mallefougasse-Augès
Cruis
St-Étienne-les-Orgues
Montlaux
Ongles
Revest-St-Martin
Fontienne
Sigonce
Lurs
Limans
Pierrerue
Mane
Niozelles
la Brillanne
Oraison
Le Castellet
Entrevennes
Puimichel
St-Jeannet
Estoublon
Bras-d'Asse
St-Julien-d'Asse
Mézel
Châteauredon
Beynes
Entrages
Chaffaut-St-Jurson
Mallemoisson
Aiglun
Mirabeau
Champtercier
Brunet
Puimoisson
Moustiers-Ste-Marie
St-Jurs
Riez
Roumoules
Valensole
Manosque
Volx
Villeneuve
St-Maime
Dauphin
St-Martin-les-Eaux
Villemus
Pierrevert
Ste-Tulle
Corbières
Gréoux-les-Bains
St-Martin-de-Brômes
Allemagne-en-Provence
Montagnac-Montpezat
Ste-Croix-de-Verdon
Esparron-de-Verdon
Quinson
St-Laurent-du-Verdon
Baudinard-sur-Verdon
Artignosc-sur-Verdon
Bauduen
Aiguines
les Salles-sur-Verdon
Vinon-sur-Verdon
St-Paul-lès-Durance
Ginasservis
St-Julien
la Verdière
Montmeyan
Régusse
Moissac-Bellevue
Aups
Rians
Artigues
Esparron
St-Martin
Varages
Tavernes
Fox-Amphoux
Villecroze
Salernes
Sillans-la-Cascade
Barjols
Pontevès
Cotignac
Entrecasteaux
Brue-Auriac
Seillons-Sce-d'Argens
Pourrières
Ollières
Châteauvert
Correns
Montfort-sur-Argens
PARC
DU
196
202
203

182
199
200
Thorame-Basse
Tartonne
Lambruisse
Clumanc
St-Lions
Chaudon-Norante
St-Jacques
Barrême
Moriez
St-André-les-Alpes
La Mure-Argens
Allons
Le Fugeret
Méailles
Annot
Braux
Castellet-lès-Sausses
Sausses
St-Benoît
Daluis
St-Léger
Puget-Théniers
Entrevaux
Angles
Vergons
St-Julien-du-Verdon
Senez
Blieux
Demandolx
Ubraye
Val-de-Chalvagne
Amirat
Collongues
Les Mujouls
Soleilhas
St-Auban
Briançonnet
Gars
Le Mas
CASTELLANE
la Garde
Peyroules
Rougon
Valderoure
Séranon
Caille
Andon
la Palud-sur-Verdon
Trigance
le Bourguet
Châteauvieux
la Martre
Brenon
Bargème
la Bastide
la Roque-Esclapon
Escragnolles
Comps-sur-Artuby
Mons
St-Vallier-de-Thiey
Cabris
Spéracèdes
St-Cézaire-s-Siagne
Seillans
Fayence
Tourrettes
Callian
Montauroux
Ampus
Montferrat
Châteaudouble
Callas
Bargemon
Claviers
Tourtour
Figanières
DRAGUIGNAN
Flayosc
Lorgues
Trans-en-Provence
la Motte
le Muy
St-Paul-en-Forêt
Bagnols-en-Forêt
les Adrets-de-l'Estérel
Les Arcs
Puget-s-Argens
MILITAIRE
DE
CANJUERS
N 202
N 85
D 562

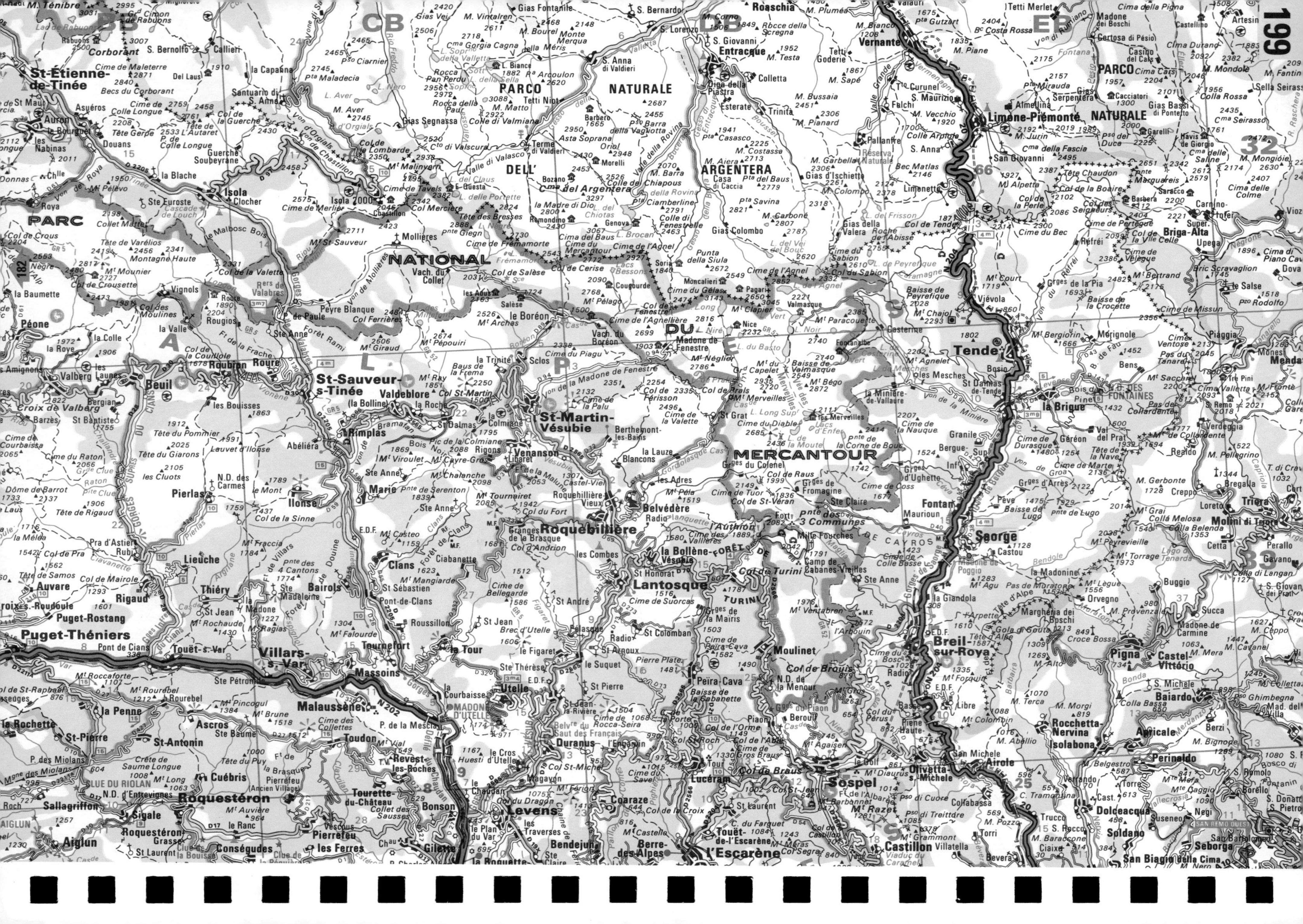

PARCO NATURALE
Limone-Piemonte
Vernante
Entracque
ARGENTERA
PARCO NATURALE DELL' ARGENTERA
Tende
La Brigue
Saorge
Breil-sur-Roya
Sospel
MERCANTOUR
PARC NATIONAL DU MERCANTOUR
St-Martin-Vésubie
Belvédère
Roquebillière
Lantosque
Lucéram
l'Escarène
Levens
St-Sauveur-s-Tinée
Isola
Isola 2000
St-Étienne-de-Tinée
Beuil
Valberg
Péone
Puget-Théniers
Villars-s-Var
Touët-s-Var
Roquestéron
Malaussène
Utelle
Clans
Ilonse
Rimplas
Valdeblore
Roubion
Roure
Pierlas
Lieuche
Bairols
Tournefort
Massoins
Pigna
Triora
Airole
Olivetta
Castillon
Fontan
Moulinet
Peira-Cava
Coaraze
Bendejun
Berre-des-Alpes
Touët-de-l'Escarène

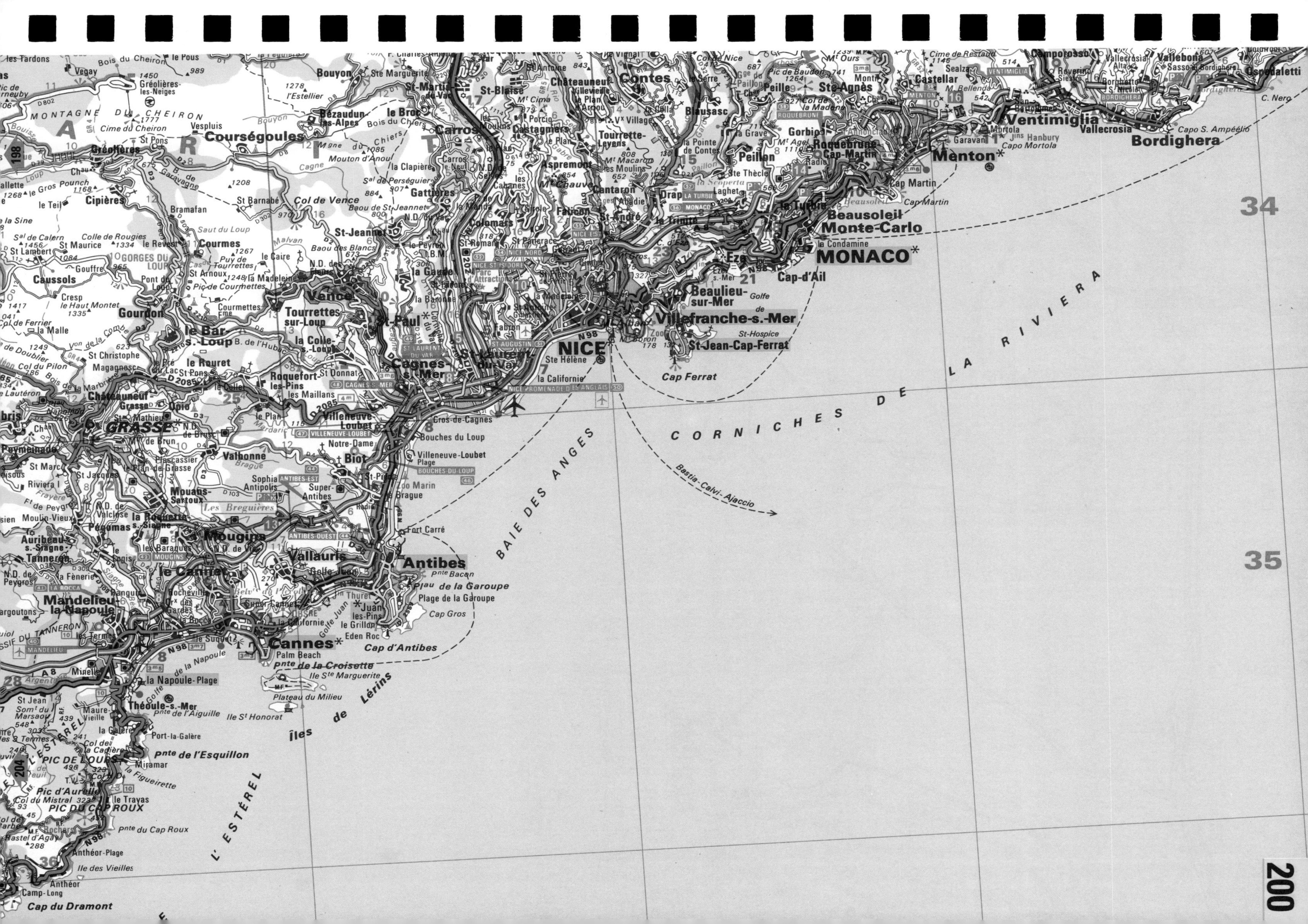
34
35
Bordighera
Capo S. Ampeglio
Vallecrosia
Ventimiglia
Capo Mortola
Menton
Cap Martin
Roquebrune-Cap-Martin
Beausoleil
Monte-Carlo
MONACO
la Condamine
Cap-d'Ail
Èze
Beaulieu-sur-Mer
Villefranche-s.-Mer
St-Jean-Cap-Ferrat
Cap Ferrat
St-Hospice
CORNICHES DE LA RIVIERA
Bastia-Calvi-Ajaccio
NICE
Ste Hélène
la Californie
BAIE DES ANGES
St-Laurent-du-Var
Cagnes-s.-Mer
Cros-de-Cagnes
Villeneuve-Loubet
Villeneuve-Loubet Plage
Bouches du Loup
Antibes
Cap Gros
Plage de la Garoupe
Cap d'Antibes
Juan-les-Pins
Golfe Juan
Vallauris
Cannes
Palm Beach
pnte de la Croisette
Ile Ste Marguerite
Plateau du Milieu
Ile St Honorat
Îles de Lérins
L'ESTÉREL
pnte de l'Esquillon
Théoule-s.-Mer
Mandelieu-la-Napoule
la Napoule-Plage
le Trayas
pnte du Cap Roux
PIC DU CAP ROUX
Anthéor-Plage
Cap du Dramont
GRASSE
Mougins
Valbonne
Sophia Antipolis
Biot
Vence
St-Paul
Tourrettes-sur-Loup
la Colle-s.-Loup
Roquefort-les-Pins
le Bar-s.-Loup
Gourdon
Courmes
Coursegoules
Gréolières
Cipières
Caussols
MONTAGNE DU CHEIRON
Col de Vence
Carros
Gattières
Contes
Drap
Peillon
Peille
Ste-Agnès
Castellar
Châteauneuf
Tourrette-Levens
Aspremont
St-Blaise
Bouyon
Bézaudun-les-Alpes
le Broc
St-Martin-du-Var
le Cannet
Pégomas
Auribeau-s.-Siagne
198
204

195
194
36
37
le Grd Barbegal
Mouriès
Lamanon
St-Martin
Vernègues
Cazan
Lambesc
Aurons
Badasset
Salon-de-Provence
Pélissanne
la Barben
Parc zoologique
Lançon-Provence
St-Symphorien
la Fare-les-Oliviers
Coudoux
les Guignes
Calissane
Cornillon-Confoux
Champ de Tir
Grans
Miramas
Miramas-le-Vieux
St-Chamas
le Pont du Raud
Confoux
Cité de la Pécette
Sulauze
le Gueby
Flavien
Moyroux
Mauran
St-Estève
la Suzanne
N.D. de Caderot
Berre-l'Étang
l'Agneau
Rognac
Vitrolles
la Pointe
Marignane
Pte Bourdigue
Plage de Jaï
St-Victoret
le Pas des Lanciers
Gignac-la-Nerthe
Bricard
les Tourels
Châteauneuf-les-Martigues
la Mède
Radio-Phare
Ensuès-la-Redonne
le Rouet
Niolon
Méjean
Carry-le-Rouet
Sausset-les-Pins
Tamaris
la Couronne
Carro
Cap Couronne
St-Julien
Chaîne de l'Estaque
les Ventrons
Cité de Lavéra
Port Pétrolier de Lavéra
Martigues
N.-D.-des-Marins
Roseron
St-Mitre-les-Remparts
Istres
Oppidum du Castellan
les Craux
Rassuen
Lavalduc
St-Blaise
Étang de Berre
Anse de Ranquet
Varage
St-Pierre
Lauron
Pte de Bonnieu
Ponteau
Port de Ponteau
Golfe de Fos
Port-de-Bouc
Fos-s-Mer
Port de Fos
Pte de St-Gervais
les Carabins
Valin
Rnes Romaines
les Arcades
Raffinerie
Solmer
Usine Aciers
Atochem
Terminal méthanier
I.C.I.
le Retour des Aires
Entressen
Suffren
Molières Fme
Fontanges Fme
le Luquier Fme
la Cabanasse
la Jasse
Mas-Neuf
le Merle
les Cabanes
St-Martin-de-Crau
St-Hippolyte
St-Virgile
Caphan
Moulès
Raphèle-lès-Arles
Balarin
Mas de Meyranne
la Dynamite
Mas de Fray
Mas de Pernes
Mas de l'Hoste
Mas de Lanau
Bellan
Vergière
La Crau
Armellière
Mas Thibert
Tour de Cazeau
Mas d'Icart
le Sambuc
Grd Pâtis
Tour du Vallat
le Pt Pâtis
Grd Boisviel
Badon
le Radeau
Bergerie
le Relai
la Porcelette
Peaudure
Chartrouse
la Louisiane
Grd Badon
le Vedeau
Campane Mas
l'Eysselle
la Bélugue
Faraman
Salins du Midi
Salin de Giraud
Bois François Mas
Port-St-Louis-du-Rhône
Phare de Faraman
Plage d'Arles
They de Roustan
They de la Gracieuse
Grand Rhône
Île de Planier
Miramas Lygueres
Salon-Nord
Salon Centre
St-Martin-de-Crau
Martigues Nord
Martigues Sud Lavéra
Martigues Centre
La Mède Ouest
La Mède Est
Carry
Le Rove Marseille Ports Nord
Gignac
A54-E80
A7-E714
E80
N113
N568
N569
N268
N544
N545
A55
D5
D9
D10

Somt de Malacoste
Pont Mirabeau
Jouques
N.D. de Consolation
Pt St-Paul
Rognes
le Puy-Ste-Réparade
la Cride
Peyrolles-en-Provence
Meyrargues
St-Canadet
Jas d'Amour
CHAINE DE LA TRÉVARESSE
Traconnade
St-Antonin
Rians
St-Antoine
BOIS DU MONT-MAJOR
Notre-Dame
Artigues
Esparron
St-Cannat
Grd St-Jean
Font-Rousse
Venelles
les Logis
la Campane
Concors
Mgne des Ubacs
Colline de St-Pierre
Puyricard
Camaïsse
la Calade
les Logissons
LES PLATANES
Lambruisse
Bois de la Gardiole
le Puits de Rians
Éguilles
T.G.V. Méditerranée
Vauvenargues
St-Marc-Jaumegarde
Tour de César
Pain de Munition Oppidum
Le Puits d'Arlon
Ventabren
les Bons Fils
les Granettes
Celony
AIX-EN-PROVENCE
Bge de Bimont
Ste-Victoire
MGNE STE VICTOIRE
la Croix de Provence
Pic des Mouches
Ermitage St-Ser
Puyloubier
Bois de Pourrières
Dme Capitaine d'Anjou
les Hermentaires
Pourrières
St-Pancrace
le Tholonet
le Canet
Beaurecueil
St-Antonin-s.-Bayon
CHATEAUNEUF-LE-ROUGE
Châteauneuf-le-Rouge
Meyreuil
Palette
Paradou
Meynes
la Mérindolle
les Milles
AIX-CENTRE
AIX-EST
AIX OUEST
LES MILLES
St-Hilaire
Ollières
Saragousse
la Tour d'Arbois
Luynes
LUYNES GARDANNE
la Lagremeuse
BOUC-BEL-AIR
la Barque
le Plan
Rousset
Pourcieux
Barcelone
Roquefeuille
Lacombe
Réservoir de Réaltor
Chaîne de Vitrolles
Vitrolles
la Mounine
Bouc-Bel-Air
Chapus
Gardanne
Fuveau
les Michels
Peynier
Trets
Mt Aurélien
St-Maximin-la-Ste-Baume
les Puits
Calas
Cassole
VITROLLES Centre Commercial
Champouse
Plaines d'Arbois
Cabriès
la Salle
Biver
les Moulières
Gréasque
Belcodène
Provence
MARIGNANE
LES PENNES
le Plan de Campagne
la Malle
Simiane-Collongue
Mimet
St-Germain
Col Ste-Anne
la Valentine
St-Jean du Puy
Kierbon
Mgne de Regagnas
la Riperte
les Adrets
les Pennes-Mirabeau
la Vaulne
les Peyrets
les Caillols
BOUC-BEL-AIR-GARDANNE
PLAN DE CAMPAGNE
Pilon du Roi
St-Savournin
N.D. des Anges
Cadolive
Mt Julien
la Pomme
le Pigeonnier
Bouilladisse
Aubagne-Neuve
Peypin
Auriol
PAS DE TRETS
Min de Redon
St-Zacharie
Rougiers
Nans-les-Pins
Plan des Pennes
Septèmes-les-Vallons
Grde Étoile
CHAINE DE L'ÉTOILE
la Destrousse
N.D. d'Orgnon
Jas de Rhodes
la Nerthe
Cadeneaux
la Gavotte
St-Antoine
ST-ANTOINE HOPITAL NORD
Grtes Loubière
la Montade
les Logis Neuf
Roquevaire
Lascours
Pérus
Rove
l'Estaque
Anse de l'Estaque
la Batarelle
Aygalades
AYGALADES
Gémenos
Plan-de-Cuques
Allauch
Croix-Rouge
Ret du Garlaban
Pont de l'Étoile
Tête de Roussargue
Hôtellerie
Plan-d'Aups-Ste-Baume
ST PILON
CHAINE DE LA SAINTE BAUME
le Latay
Tête de Masson
Rade de Marseille
MARSEILLE
les Olives
les Trois Lucs
St-Julien
la Treille
Ouv. Proch.
St-Jean-de-Garguier
St-Pierre-lès-Aubagnes
Pic de Bertagne
Roque Forcade
PONT DE L'ÉTOILE
AUBAGNE NORD
AUBAGNE
St-Lazare
St-Barnabé
la Valentine
les Caillols
les Camoins
Éoures
Aubagne
Parc de St-Pons
Riboux
Signes
Île Ratonneau
la Plaine
N.D. de la Garde
St-Marcel
ST-MARCEL
LA VALENTINE
la Penne-s.-Huveaune
AUBAGNE-SUD
AUBAGNE EST
Mt Cruvelier
Coulin
Cuges-les-Pins
Parc d'Attractions
Circuit Auto
Pt de Frioul
Chau d'If
Rade d'Endoume
Pomègues
Ste-Marguerite
Bonneveine
Chaîne de St-Cyr
Mt Carpiagne
CAMP MILITAIRE
Vaufrèges
CARNOUX
Carnoux-en-Provence
le Pit Rouvière
Roquefort
Col de l'Ange
le Camp
la Bégude
Ste-Anne du Castellet
Grd Caunet
Propriano
Ajaccio
Bastia
la Madrague
Mt Rose
Montredon
la Cayolle
Mazargues
le Redon
Luminy
Col de la Gineste
les Fourniers
Pas d'Ouillier
LA BÉDOULE
Roquefort-la-Bédoule
Laouque
le Brulat
Rocher de l'Aigle
Cap Croisette
Île Tiboulen
Île Maire
Mne de Marseilleveyre
les Goudes
Sormiou
Morgiou
les Baumettes
Ft Dome de Port-Miou
Cassis
la Gardiole
N.D. de Bon Voyage
CASSIS
Ceyreste
LES LECQUES
Plaines Baronnes
le Castellet
le Beausset
LES CALANQUES
CAP CANAILLE
LA CIOTAT
La Cadière-d'Azur
St-Cyr-s.-Mer
LE CASTELLET
N.D. du Vieux-Beausset
Île de Jarre
Île Calseraigne
Cal. d'En-Vau
Cal. de Port-Pin
Sémaphore
La Ciotat
les Lecques
les Baumelles
le Plan
Ste-Anne d'Évenos
Grd Canadeau
Évenos
Île de Riou
N.D. de la Garde
Anse de Figuerolles
Île Verte
Cap de l'Aigle
la Madrague
le Port d'Alon
Pte du Deffend
BANDOL
LE GROS CERVEAU
Ollioules
CAMP LAURENT
Bandol
Île de Bendor
Zoo
Pte de la Cride
les Playes
Sanary-s.-Mer
Six-Fours-les-Plages
Observatoire de la Mer
le Brusc
Chau
Iles des Embiez
Roche-Blanche

Varages
Tavernes
St-Martin
les Annelles
Barjols
Pontevès
le Pigeonnier
Brue-Auriac
Notre-Dame
St-Estève
Seillons-Sce-d'Argens
Bras
St-Étienne
St-Maximin-la-Ste-Baume
Tourves
Mazaugues
la Roquebrussanne
Signes
Amphoux
Fox-Amphoux
le Logis
Fabrègues
les Cabanons
Sillans-la-Cascade
Salernes
Cotignac
N.D. de Grâce
Bois de Correns
Châteauvert
les Faisses
Correns
Montfort-sur-Argens
Miraval
N.D. d'Espérance
Carcès
Lac de Carcès
le Val
Vins-sur-Caramy
St-Vincent
Cabasse
BRIGNOLES
la Celle
Camps-la-Source
Montagne de la Loube
Bois de Garéoult
les Moulières
Garéoult
Forcalqueiret
Ste-Anastasie-s.-Issole
Besse-sur-Issole
Néoules
Rocbaron
Carnoules
Pignans
Puget-Ville
Méounes-les-Montrieux
Belgentier
Cuers
Solliès-Toucas
Solliès-Pont
Solliès-Ville
la Farlède
le Revest-les-Eaux
Ollioules
la Valette-du-Var
la Crau
Hyères
TOULON
la Seyne-sur-Mer
la Garde
le Pradet
Carqueiranne
St-Mandrier-sur-Mer
Presqu'île de St-Mandrier
Cap Sicié
N.D. du Mai
Six-Fours
les Sablettes
Tamaris
Cap Brun
Cap Cépet
Golfe de Giens
Presqu'île de Giens
Giens
la Madrague
Île de Porquerolles
Porquerolles
Tourtour
Villecroze
Ampus
Entrecasteaux
St-Antonin-du-Var
Lorgues
Flayosc
le Thoronet
ABBE DU THORONET
Taradeau
Vidauban
le Luc
le Cannet-des-Maures
Flassans-sur-Issole
Gonfaron
les Mayons
Collobrières
Pierrefeu-du-Var
la Londe-les-Maures
Bormes-les-Mimosas
Le Lavandou
Cavalière
Cap Bénat
RADE D'HYERES
MASSIF DES MAURES
PARC NATIONAL DE PORT-CROS
Île de Port-Cros
A8 LA PROVENÇALE
N7
N97
N98

Callas
Claviers
Col de Boussague
N.D. des Selves
Terrassonnes
Bois de
198
l'Ermite
Lac de St-Cassien
les Marjeris
N.D. de Peygros
la Fènerie
Mandelieu-la-Napoule
le Cannet
les Quatre Chemins
B. du Prignonet
St-Paul-en-Forêt
Forêt Royale
Mine de Garrot
les Margoutons
Castel de Guiol
MASSIF DU TANNERON
les Termes
Cannes
Palm Beach
DRAGUIGNAN
Bagnols-en-Forêt
B. du Rouet
St-Denis
St-Antoine
B. de Bagnols
le Planestel
les Adrets-de-l'Estérel
les Baraques
Minelle
la Napoule-Plage
Théoule-s.-Mer
Plateau du Milieu
Ile St Honorat
la Colle du Rouet
Gorges
Pic de la Gardiette
Malpasset
St-Michel d'Esclans
B. de Malvoisin
CHAMP DE TIR
Observatoire
Vinaigre
St Jean
Somt du Marsaou
Maure-Vieille
Pnte de l'Aiguille
Port-la-Galère
la Galère
Col de la Cadière
Col des Suvières
PIC DE L'OURS
Miramar
Pnte de l'Esquillon
Îles
la Motte
B. de Ralayson
le Capitou
la Figueirette
la Marchandise
le Canaver
Camp de la Lègue
N.D. de Jérusalem
Pic d'Aurelle
Col du Mistral
PIC DU CAP ROUX
le Trayas
le Muy
Puget-Argens
Camp de Caïs
la Tour de-Mare
Valescure
Col de Belle-Barbe
le Rastel d'Agay
Pnte du Cap Roux
MASSIF DE L'ESTÉREL
Anthéor-Plage
Ile des Vieilles
les Preyres
Rocher de Roquebrune
Roquebrune-s.-Argens
Fréjus
St-Raphaël
le Dramont
Agay
Anthéor
Camp-Long
Cap du Dramont
N.D. de Pitié
Somt du Peynier
le Clos
Fréjus-Plage
Boulouris
Ile d'Or
le Lion de Mer
Golfe de Fréjus
FORÊT DES ARCS
Col de Valdingarde
Vieux-Revest
la Bastide Rouge
la Mère
Villepey
St-Aygulf
MAURES
Peigros
Col de Gratteloup
la Gaillarde
le Revest
le Lissandre
Pointe de la Calle
Col de Bougnon
les Issambres
Pnte des Issambres
Val-d'Esquières
San-Peire-sur-Mer
Camp-Long
Valaury
La Moure
Plan-de-la-Tour
Baie de Bougnon
Col de Vignon
Sémaphore
la Nartelle
Prat-Bourdin
Pnte des Sardinaux
la Garde-Freinet
St-Preire
Hte Suane
Ste-Maxime
les Vernades
les Mûres
Guerre Vieille
Golfe de St-Tropez
Beauvallon
Pnte de Rabiou
St-Pons-les-Mûres
Grimaud
N.D. de la Queste
Port-Grimaud
Marines de Cogolin
St-Tropez
Cap de St-Tropez
les Salins
Pnte de Gapon
Bestagne
la Capilla
Plage de Tahiti
Cogolin
St-Marc
B. de Faucon
Giégi
Gassin
Radio
Salagru
Anse de Pampelonne
les Guiols
la Croix-Valmer
Moulins de Paillas
Ramatuelle
Môle
Montjean
la Bouillabaisse
Col de Collebasse
l'Escalet
Cap Camarat
Baie de Bon-Porté
les Pradels
Sylvabelle
Baie de Cavalaire
St-Michel
Cap Cartaya
Rayol-Canadel-s.-Mer
Col du Canadel
Cavalaire-s.-Mer
Cap Cavalaire
Cap Lardier
Pramousquier
Pnte de la Chappe
CORNICHE DES MAURES
CORNICHE DE L'ESTÉREL
2h
1h30
Pnte du Castellas
Pnte de Calle Rousse
Pnte de l'Arête
Île du Levant
Grand-Avis
Héliopolis
Grd Cap
Maupertuis
D'HYÈRES
200

O
P
35
36
37
Côte d'Argent
Biarritz
BAYONNE
Anglet
St-Jean-de-Luz
Hendaye
Fuenterrabia
Irun
Ciboure
Urrugne
Bidart
Guéthary
Ustaritz
Espelette
Cambo-les-Bains
Hasparren
La Rhune
Sare
Ascain
Ainhoa
Dancharia
Vera-de-Bidasoa
Lesaca
Echalar
Urdax
Zugarramurdi
Bidarray
Louhossoa
Itxassou
St-Martin-de-Seignanx
Ondres
Boucau
Tarnos
St-Pierre-d'Irube
Mouguerre
Villefranque
Arcangues
Bassussarry
Arbonne
Ahetze
St-Pée-sur-Nivelle
Ossès
St-Martin-d'Arrossa
Irouléguy
St-Étienne-de-Baïgorry
St-Jean-Pied-de-Port
Arnéguy
Valcarlos
Roncesvalles
Burguete
Aldudes
Urepel
Banca
Maya del Baztán
Elizondo (Baztán)
Erratzu
Arizcun
Santesteban
Sumbilla
Navarte (Bértiz-Arana)
Ituren
Elgorriaga
Zubieta
Donamaria
Oiz
Labayen
Saldias
Erasun
Aranaz
Yanci
Puerto de Velate
Lanz
Olagüe (Anue)
Linzoáin (Erro)
Eugui
Urtasun
Vallée des Aldudes
Valle del Baztán
Montes de Bidasoa
Cinqo Villas
Col d'Ibardin
Col de St-Ignace
Col de Lizuniaga
Col des 3 Bornes
Col d'Ispéguy
Puerto de Ibañeta
Pas de Roland
Col des Veaux
Cabo Higuer (Cap du Figuier)

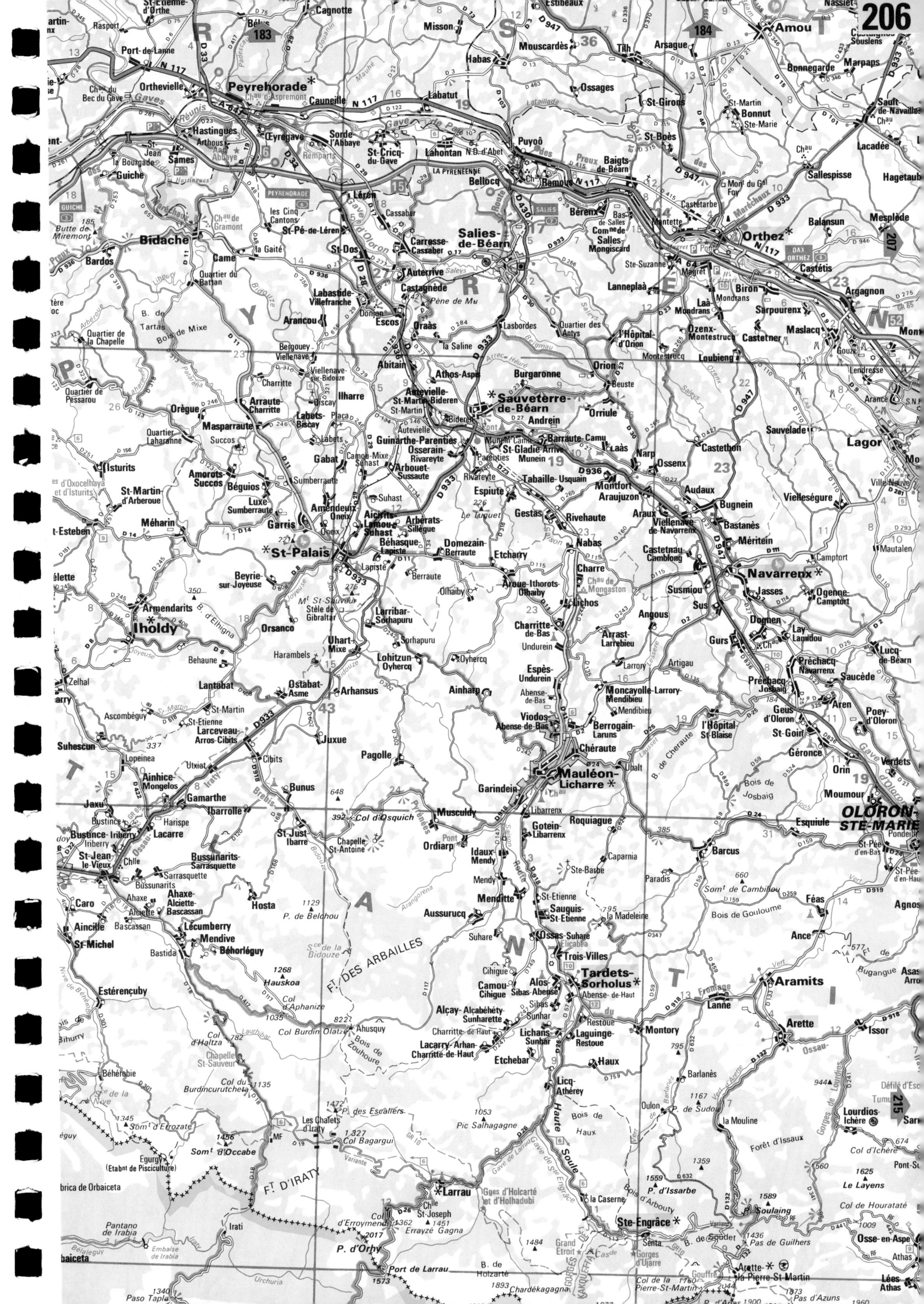

183
184
207
215
Peyrehorade
Port-de-Lanne
Orthevielle
Cagnotte
Misson
Habas
Mouscardès
Tilh
Arsague
Amou
Bonnegarde
Marpaps
Ossages
St-Girons
Bonnut
Sault-de-Navailles
Lacadée
Sallespisse
Hagetaubin
Cauneille
Labatut
Œyregave
Sorde-l'Abbaye
St-Cricq-du-Gave
Lahontan
Puyoô
Baigts-de-Béarn
St-Boès
Hastingues
Sames
Guiche
Bidache
Bardos
Came
Léren
Cassaber
Carresse-Cassaber
St-Pé-de-Léren
St-Dos
Salies-de-Béarn
Bellocq
Ramous
Bérenx
Orthez
Castétis
Argagnon
Mesplède
Balansun
l'Auterrive
Castagnède
Labastide-Villefranche
Escos
Oraàs
Arancou
Lanneplaà
Biron
Sarpourenx
Maslacq
Castetner
Ozenx-Montestrucq
l'Hôpital-d'Orion
Orion
Loubieng
Bergouey-Viellenave
Abitain
Athos-Aspis
Burgaronne
Sauveterre-de-Béarn
Andrein
Orriule
Charritte
Arraute-Charritte
Labets-Biscay
Ilharre
Orègue
Masparraute
Guinarthe-Parenties
Osserain-Rivareyte
Barraute-Camu
St-Gladie-Arrive-Munein
Laàs
Narp
Ossenx
Castetbon
Sauvelade
Lagor
Isturits
Amorots-Succos
Béguios
Luxe-Sumberraute
St-Martin-d'Arberoue
Méharin
Garris
Gabat
Arbouet-Sussaute
Amendeuix-Oneix
Aïcirits
Arbérats-Sillègue
Espiute
Tabaille-Usquain
Montfort
Araujuzon
Audaux
Bugnein
Viellesègure
Gestas
Rivehaute
Araux
Viellenave-de-Navarrenx
Bastanès
Méritein
St-Palais
Béhasque-Lapiste
Domezain-Berraute
Etcharry
Nabas
Castetnau-Camblong
Navarrenx
Beyrie-sur-Joyeuse
Aroue-Ithorots-Olhaiby
Charre
Lichos
Susmiou
Sus
Jasses
Ogenne-Camptort
Armendarits
Iholdy
Orsanco
Larribar-Sorhapuru
Charritte-de-Bas
Angous
Dognen
Lay-Lamidou
Arrast-Larrebieu
Gurs
Préchacq-Navarrenx
Lucq-de-Béarn
Uhart-Mixe
Lohitzun-Oyhercq
Harambels
Ostabat-Asme
Arhansus
Lantabat
Ainharp
Espès-Undurein
Moncayolle-Larrory-Mendibieu
Préchacq-Josbaig
Saucède
Geus-d'Oloron
Aren
Poey-d'Oloron
St-Goin
Zelhal
Suhescun
Larceveau-Arros-Cibits
Juxue
Pagolle
Viodos-Abense-de-Bas
Berrogain-Laruns
l'Hôpital-St-Blaise
Chéraute
Mauléon-Licharre
Garindein
Géronce
Orin
Verdets
Moumour
Aïnhice-Mongelos
Gamarthe
Ibarrolle
Bunus
Musculdy
Jaxu
Bustince-Iriberry
Lacarre
St-Just-Ibarre
Ordiarp
Gotein-Libarrenx
Roquiague
Esquiule
Oloron-Ste-Marie
St-Jean-le-Vieux
Bussunarits-Sarrasquette
Col d'Osquich
Idaux-Mendy
Barcus
Caro
Aincille
St-Michel
Ahaxe-Alciette-Bascassan
Hosta
Mendy
Menditte
Sauguis-St-Étienne
Féas
Lécumberry
Mendive
Béhorléguy
Aussurucq
Ossas-Suhare
Ance
Trois-Villes
Tardets-Sorholus
Aramits
Estérençuby
Camou-Cihigue
Alos-Sibas-Abense
Alçay-Alçabéhéty-Sunharette
Lanne
Arette
Issor
Col d'Aphanize
Col Burdin Olatze
Ahusquy
F.t des Arbailles
Lichans-Sunhar
Laguinge-Restoue
Montory
Lacarry-Arhan-Charritte-de-Haut
Etchebar
Haux
Licq-Athérey
Lourdios-Ichère
Les Chalets d'Iraty
Col Bagargui
Pic Salhagagne
F.t d'Iraty
Larrau
Ste-Engrâce
P. d'Orhy
Port de Larrau
Arette-la-Pierre-St-Martin
Osse-en-Aspe
Lées-Athas

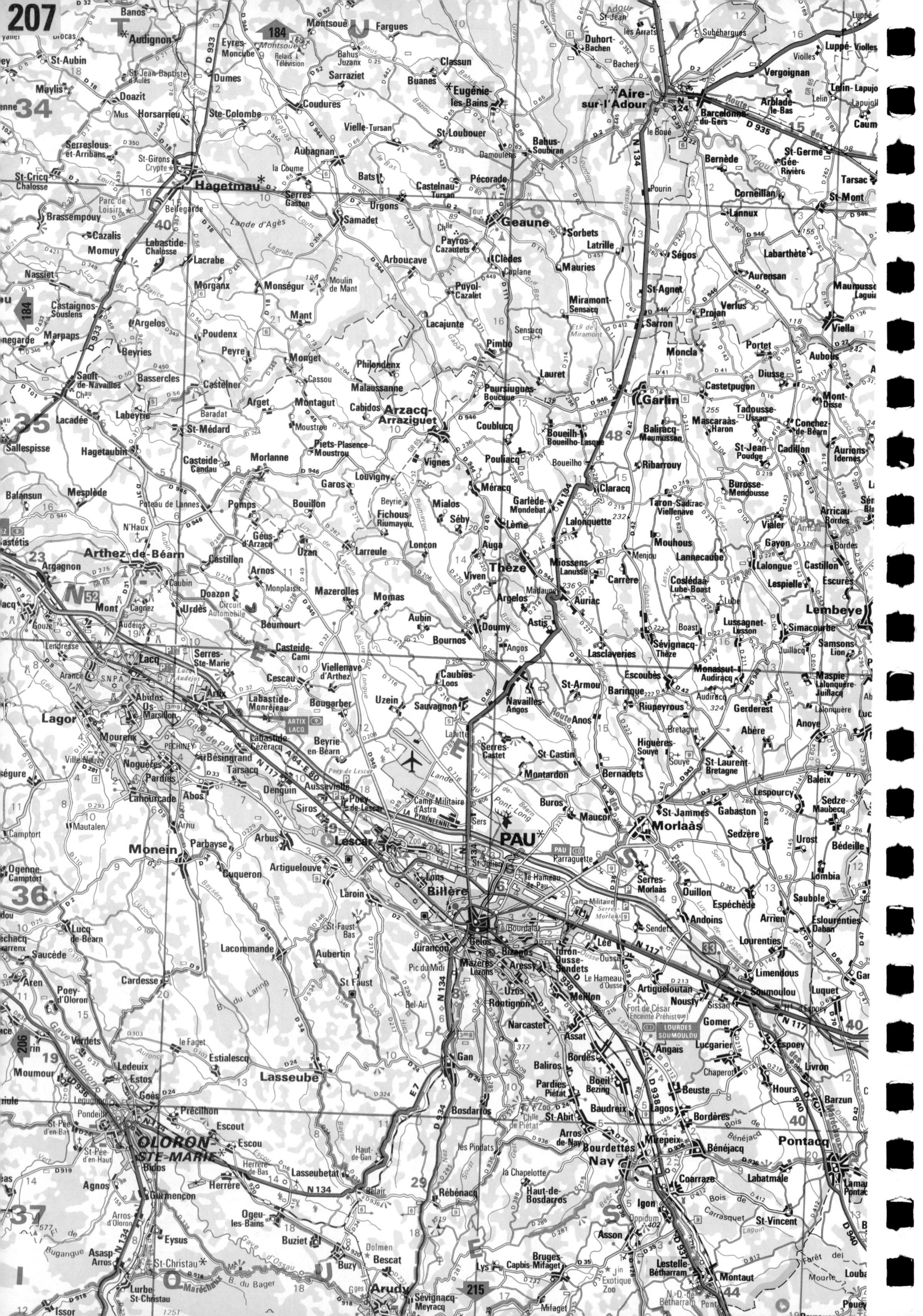
184
Banos
Audignon
Montsoué
Fargues
Eyres-Moncube
Duhort-Bachen
Subéhargues
Luppé-Violles
St-Aubin
St-Jean-Baptiste d'Aulès
Dumes
Bahus-Juzanx
Classun
Maylis
Doazit
Sarraziet
Buanes
Eugénie-les-Bains
Aire-sur-l'Adour
Vergoignan
Arblade-le-Bas
Barcelonne-du-Gers
Coudures
Horsarrieu
Ste-Colombe
Vielle-Tursan
St-Loubouer
Bahus-Soubiran
Serreslous-et-Arribans
Aubagnan
St-Germé
Gée-Rivière
Tarsac
St-Girons Crypte
St-Cricq-Chalosse
Hagetmau
Bats
Pécorade
Bernède
Corneillan
St-Mont
Brassempouy
Serres-Gaston
Urgons
Castelnau-Tursan
Samadet
Geaune
Lannux
Cazalis
Momuy
Labastide-Chalosse
Lacrabe
Payros-Cazautets
Sorbets
Latrille
Ségos
Labarthète
Nassiet
Arboucave
Clèdes
Mauries
Aurensan
Morganx
Monségur
Moulin de Mant
Puyol-Cazalet
Miramont-Sensacq
St-Agnet
Maumusson-Laguian
Castaignos-Souslens
Mant
Lacajunte
Sarron
Projan
Verlus
Viella
Argelos
Marpaps
Poudenx
Sensacq
Pimbo
Moncla
Portet
Aubous
Beyries
Peyre
Monget
Philondenx
Lauret
Diusse
Sault-de-Navailles
Bassercles
Castelner
Malaussanne
Poursiugues-Boucoue
Garlin
Castetpugon
Mont-Disse
Labeyrie
Arget
Montagut
Cabidos
Arzacq-Arraziguet
Lacadée
St-Médard
Coublucq
Boueilh-Boueilho-Lasque
Baliracq-Maumusson
Mascaraàs-Haron
Tadousse-Ussau
Conchez-de-Béarn
Sallespisse
Hagetaubin
Piets-Plasence-Moustrou
Vignes
St-Jean-Poudge
Cadillon
Aurions-Idernes
Casteide-Candau
Morlanne
Pouliacq
Ribarrouy
Louvigny
Garos
Méracq
Claracq
Burosse-Mendousse
Balansun
Mesplède
Pomps
Bouillon
Mialos
Garlède-Mondebat
Taron-Sadirac-Viellenave
Arricau-Bordes
Fichous-Riumayou
Séby
Lème
Lalonquette
Vialer
Arthez-de-Béarn
Castillon
Géus-d'Arzacq
Uzan
Larreule
Loncon
Auga
Mouhous
Lannecaube
Gayon
Argagnon
Arnos
Thèze
Miossens-Lanusse
Carrère
Cosledaà-Lube-Boast
Lalongue
Castillon
Escurès
Doazon
Monplaisir
Mazerolles
Momas
Lespielle
Mont
Cagnez
Urdès
Circuit Automobile
Argelos
Auriac
Lembeye
Boumourt
Aubin
Doumy
Astis
Lussagnet-Lusson
Simacourbe
Bournos
Sévignacq-Thèze
Samsons-Lion
Lacq
Serres-Ste-Marie
Casteide-Cami
Lasclaveries
Escoubès
Monassut-Audiracq
Maspie-Lalonquère-Juillacq
Abidos
Os-Marsillon
Artix
Cescau
Viellenave d'Arthez
Caubios-Loos
St-Armou
Barinque
Lagor
Labastide-Monréjeau
Bougarber
Uzein
Sauvagnon
Navailles-Angos
Riupeyrous
Gerderest
Anoye
Mourenx
Labastide-Cézéracq
Beyrie-en-Béarn
Serres-Castet
Anos
Abère
Higuères-Souye
St-Laurent-Bretagne
Noguères
Bésingrand
Tarsacq
St-Castin
Montardon
Bernadets
Baleix
Pardies
Abos
Denguin
Aussevielle
Poey-de-Lescar
Lahourcade
Siros
Buros
Maucor
St-Jammes
Morlaàs
Gabaston
Lespourcy
Sedze-Maubecq
Monein
Parbayse
Arbus
Lescar
PAU
Sedzère
Urost
Bédeille
Artiguelouve
Lons
Parraguette
Serres-Morlaàs
Ouillon
Cuqueron
Laroin
Billère
Espéchède
Saubole
Lombia
Lucq-de-Béarn
St-Faust-Bas
Bourdalat
Andoins
Arrien
Eslourenties-Daban
Lacommande
Jurançon
Gelos
Bizanos
Lée
Sendets
Lourenties
Saucède
Aubertin
Mazères-Lezons
Aressy
Idron-Ousse-Sendets
Limendous
Cardesse
St Faust
Uzos
Rontignon
Meillon
Artigueloutan
Nousty
Soumoulou
Luquet
Poey-d'Oloron
Narcastet
Assat
Gomer
Espoey
Verdets
Estialescq
Gan
Lucgarier
Livron
Moumour
Ledeux
Estos
Lasseube
Baliros
Bordes
Angaïs
Beuste
Hours
Barzun
Goès
Précilhon
Bosdarros
Pardies-Piétat
Boeil-Bezing
Baudreix
Lagos
Bordères
Escout
St-Abit
Arros-de-Nay
Bourdettes
Mirepeix
Bénéjacq
Pontacq
OLORON-STE-MARIE
Escou
Haut-de-Gan
Nay
Coarraze
Labatmale
Bidos
Herrère
Lasseubetat
Rébénacq
Haut-de-Bosdarros
Igon
St-Vincent
Agnos
Gurmençon
Ogeu-les-Bains
Arros-d'Oloron
Buziet
Asson
Eysus
Asasp-Arros
Buzy
Bescat
Bruges-Capbis-Mifaget
Lestelle-Bétharram
Montaut
Lurbe-St-Christau
Arudy
Sévignacq-Meyracq
215
Mifaget
Issor

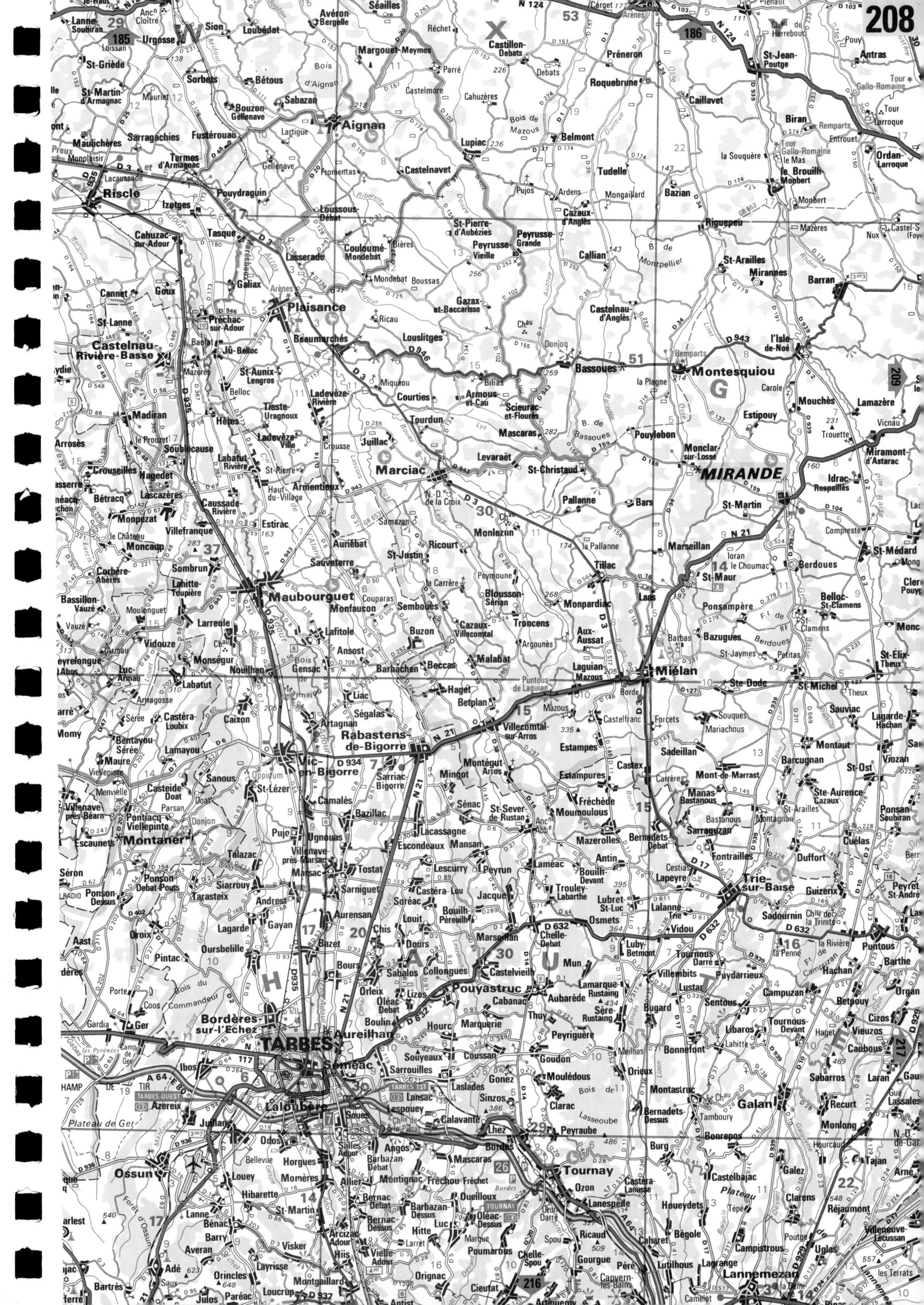

185
186
209
216
217
Lanne-Soubiran
Sion
Loubédat
Avéron-Bergelle
Séailles
Castillon-Debats
Préneron
Roquebrune
St-Jean-Poutge
Antras
Urgosse
St-Griède
Sorbets
Bétous
Margouët-Meymes
Parré
Castelmore
Cahuzères
Caillavet
St-Martin-d'Armagnac
Bouzon-Gellenave
Sabazan
Aignan
Lupiac
Belmont
Biran
Maulichères
Sarragachies
Fustérouau
Termes-d'Armagnac
Castelnavet
Tudelle
la Souquère
Ordan-Larroque
Le Brouilh-Monbert
Riscle
Izotges
Pouydraguin
Loussous-Débat
Pujos
Ardens
Mongaillard
Bazian
Cazaux-d'Anglès
Riguepeu
Tasque
Cahuzac-sur-Adour
Lasserade
Couloumé-Mondebat
St-Pierre-d'Aubézies
Peyrusse-Grande
Peyrusse-Vieille
Callian
St-Arailles
Mirannes
Barran
Galiax
Goux
Cannet
Plaisance
Gazax-et-Baccarisse
Castelnau-d'Anglès
St-Lanne
Préchac-sur-Adour
Castelnau-Rivière-Basse
Jû-Belloc
Beaumarchés
Louslitges
Bassoues
Montesquiou
l'Isle-de-Noé
St-Aunix-Lengros
Ladevèze-Rivière
Courties
Armous-et-Cau
Scieurac-et-Flourès
Madiran
Hères
Tieste-Uragnoux
Ladevèze-Ville
Tourdun
Mascaras
Pouylebon
Estipouy
Mouchès
Lamazère
Arrosès
Soublecause
Juillac
Marciac
Levaraët
St-Christaud
Monclar-sur-Losse
MIRANDE
Miramont-d'Astarac
Crouseilles
Hagedet
Labatut-Rivière
Armentieux
Idrac-Respaillès
Bétracq
Lascazères
Caussade-Rivière
Pallanne
Bars
St-Martin
Monpezat
Estirac
Villefranque
Moncaup
Auriébat
Monlezun
Ricourt
St-Justin
la Pallanne
Marseillan
St-Médard
Sombrun
Corbère-Abères
Lahitte-Toupière
Sauveterre
Tillac
St-Maur
Berdoues
Maubourguet
Monfaucon
Sembouès
Blousson-Sérian
Monpardiac
Laas
Ponsampère
Belloc-St-Clamens
Bassillon-Vauzé
Larreule
Lafitole
Buzon
Cazaux-Villecomtal
Troncens
Aux-Aussat
Bazugues
Vidouze
Monségur
Ansost
Nouilhan
Gensac
Barbachen
Beccas
Malabat
Laguian-Mazous
Miélan
Ste-Dode
St-Michel
St-Elix-Theux
Labatut
Liac
Hagét
Betplan
Armagosse
Castéra-Loubix
Caixon
Ségalas
Artagnan
Rabastens-de-Bigorre
Villecomtal-sur-Arros
Estampes
Sadeillan
Sauviac
Lagarde-Hachan
Bentayou-Sérée
Lamayou
Vic-en-Bigorre
Sarriac-Bigorre
Montégut-Arros
Castex
Montaut
Barcugnan
Maure
Sanous
St-Lézer
Mingot
Estampures
Mont-de-Marrast
St-Ost
Viozan
Casteide-Doat
Camalès
Sénac
Fréchède
Moumoulous
Manas-Bastanous
Ste-Aurence-Cazaux
Villenave-près-Béarn
Pontiacq-Viellepinte
Bazillac
St-Sever-de-Rustan
Sarraguzan
Ponsan-Soubiran
Escaunets
Montaner
Pujo
Ugnouas
Lacassagne
Escondeaux
Mansan
Mazerolles
Bernadets-Debat
Cuélas
Talazac
Villenave-près-Marsac
Marsac
Tostat
Lescurry
Peyrun
Lamèac
Antin
Fontrailles
Duffort
Séron
Ponson-Debat-Pouts
Siarrouy
Sarniguet
Castéra-Lou
Jacque
Bouilh-Devant
Lapeyre
Trie-sur-Baïse
Guizerix
Ponson-Dessus
Tarasteix
Andrest
Soréac
Trouley-Labarthe
Lubret-St-Luc
Lalanne-Trie
Sadournin
Lagarde
Gayan
Aurensan
Louit
Bouilh-Péreuilh
Osmets
Vidou
Oroix
Bazet
Chis
Dours
Marseillan
Chelle-Debat
Luby-Betmont
Puntous
Aast
Pintac
Oursbelille
Bours
Sabalos
Collongues
Castelvieilh
Mun
Tournous-Darré
Villembits
Puydarrieux
Barthe
Hachan
Orleix
Oléac-Debat
Lizos
Pouyastruc
Cabanac
Aubarède
Lamarque-Rustaing
Sère-Rustaing
Lustar
Sentous
Campuzan
Organ
Betpouy
Porte
Coos
Ger
Bordères-sur-l'Echez
TARBES
Aureilhan
Boulin
Hourc
Marquerie
Thuy
Bugard
Peyriguère
Libaros
Tournous-Devant
Cizos
Vieuzos
Caubous
Ibos
Séméac
Souyeaux
Sarrouilles
Coussan
Goudon
Bonnefont
Orieux
Laslades
Gonez
Mouledous
Montastruc
Sabarros
Laran
Azereix
Laloubère
Lansac
Soues
Lespouey
Sinzos
Clarac
Bernadets-Dessus
Galan
Recurt
Juillan
Odos
Calavanté
Lhez
Peyraube
Bonrepos
Monlong
Ossun
Horgues
Angos
Salles-Adour
Barbazan-Debat
Mascaras
Bordes
Tournay
Burg
Castelbajac
Galez
Tajan
Louey
Momères
Allier
Montignac
Fréchou-Fréchet
Ozon
Castéra-Lanusse
Clarens
Hibarette
Bernac-Debat
Oueilloux
Lanespède
Houeydets
Réjaumont
Lanne
Bénac
St-Martin
Barbazan-Dessus
Oléac-Dessus
Bégole
Barry
Bernac-Dessus
Luc
Ricaud
Caharet
Campistrous
Uglas
Averan
Visker
Arcizac-Adour
Hitte
Marque
Poumarous
Chelle-Spou
Gourgue
Péré
Lutilhous
Lagrange
Adé
Orincles
Layrisse
Hiis
Vielle-Adour
Orignac
Capvern-les-Bains
Lannemezan
Bartrès
Julos
Paréac
Loucrup
Montgaillard
Cieutat
TARBES-EST
TARBES-OUEST
Plateau de Ger
Forêt d'Ossun
Bois du Commandeur
Bois d'Aignan
Bois de Mazous

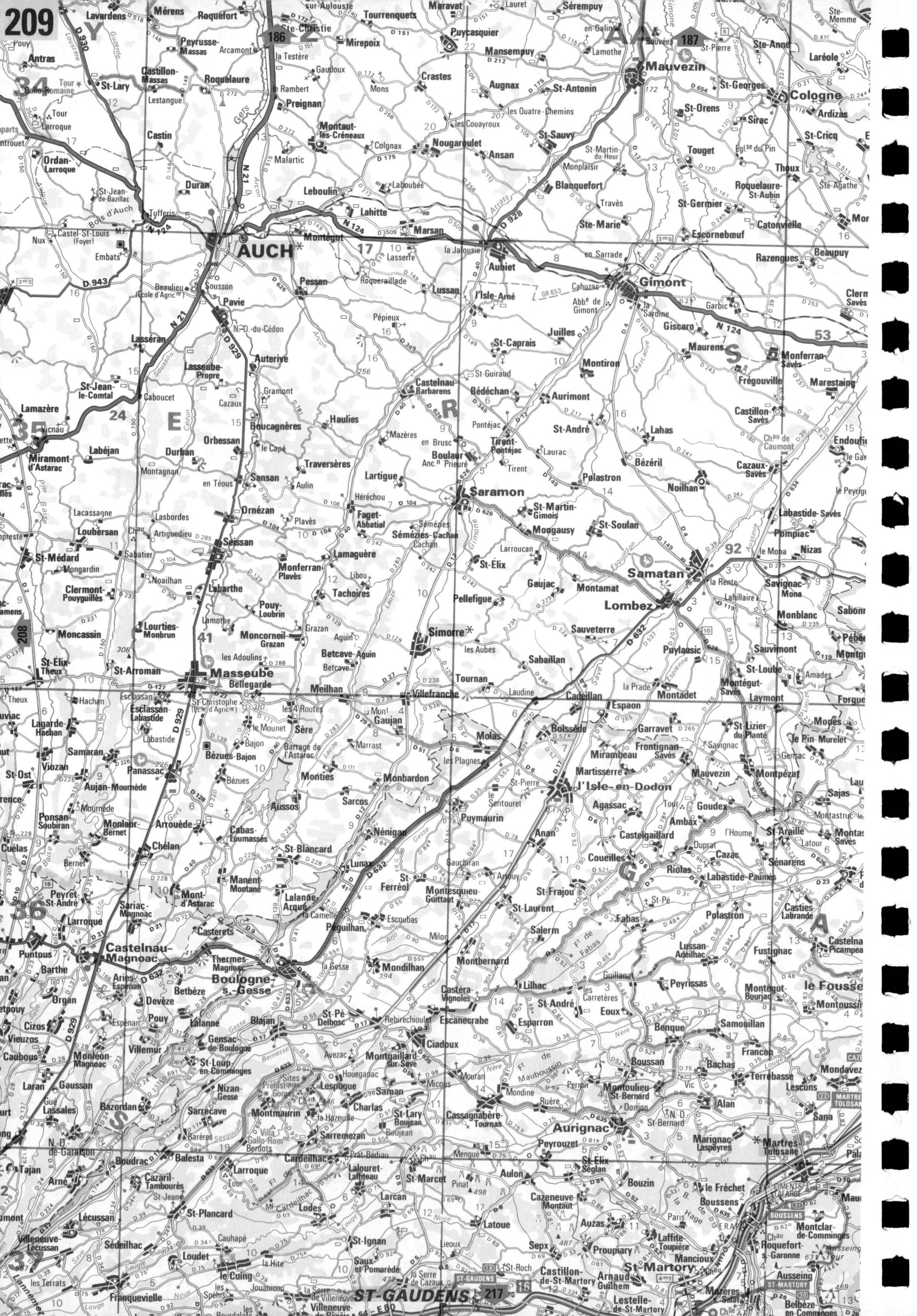
Lavardens
Mérens
Roquefort
Ste-Christie
Tourrenquets
Maravat
Lauret
Sérempuy
186
187
Peyrusse-Massas
Arcamont
Mirepoix
Puycasquier
Mansempuy
Lamothe
Mauvezin
Ste-Anne
Laréole
Antras
Castillon-Massas
Roquelaure
Crastes
Augnax
St-Antonin
St-Georges
Cologne
St-Lary
Preignan
St-Orens
Sirac
Ardizas
Montaut-les-Créneaux
Nougaroulet
Ansan
St-Sauvy
Touget
St-Cricq
Castin
Colgnax
Ordan-Larroque
Malartic
Blanquefort
Thoux
Duran
Leboulin
Roquelaure-St-Aubin
Lahitte
St-Germier
Travès
Ste-Marie
Catonvielle
Marsan
Escornebœuf
AUCH
Montégut
Lasserre
Aubiet
Gimont
Razengues
Beaupuy
Embats
Pessan
Roquelaillade
Lussan
l'Isle-Arné
Sousson
Pavie
Giscaro
Maurens
Juilles
St-Caprais
Montiron
Monferran-Savès
Frégouville
Marestaing
Lasséran
Auterive
Lasseube-Propre
St-Jean-le-Comtal
Castelnau-Barbarens
Bédéchan
Aurimont
Castillon-Savès
Lamazère
Boucagnères
Haulies
Pontéjac
St-André
Lahas
Miramont-d'Astarac
Labéjan
Durban
Orbessan
Traversères
Tirent-Pontéjac
Bézéril
Cazaux-Savès
Lartigue
Boulaur
Polastron
Noilhan
Sansan
Saramon
St-Martin-Gimois
Labastide-Savès
Ornézan
Faget-Abbatial
Mongausy
St-Soulan
Loubersan
Seissan
Sémézies-Cachan
Pompiac
St-Médard
Lamaguère
St-Élix
Samatan
Nizas
Monferran-Plavès
Clermont-Pouyguillès
Labarthe
Tachoires
Gaujac
Montamat
Lombez
Savignac-Mona
Pouy-Loubrin
Pellefigue
Monblanc
Lourties-Monbrun
Moncassin
Moncorneil-Grazan
Simorre
Sauveterre
Sauvimont
Betcave-Aguin
Sabaillan
Puylausic
St-Loube
St-Élix-Theux
St-Arroman
Masseube
Meilhan
Tournan
Montégut-Savès
Montadet
Espaon
Cadeillan
Laymont
Esclassan-Labastide
Villefranche
Gaujan
Sère
Boissède
Garravet
Lagarde-Hachan
Molas
Mirambeau
Frontignan-Savès
St-Lizier-du-Planté
Samaran
Bézues-Bajon
Monties
Monbardon
Martisserre
l'Isle-en-Dodon
Mauvezin
Montpézat
Panassac
Viozan
Aujan-Mournède
Sarcos
Aussos
Puymaurin
Agassac
Goudex
Ponsan-Soubiran
Monlaur-Bernet
Arrouède
Cabas-Loumassès
Nénigan
Anan
Castelgaillard
Ambax
St-Araille
Chélan
St-Blancard
Coueilles
Riolas
Labastide-Paumès
Sénarens
Lunax
St-Ferréol
Manent-Montané
Mont-d'Astarac
Lalanne-Arqué
Montesquieu-Guittaut
St-Frajou
St-Laurent
Polastron
Peyret-St-André
Sariac-Magnoac
Castelnau-Magnoac
Puntous
Casterets
Péguilhan
Escoubas
Salerm
Fabas
Fustignac
Lussan-Adeilhac
Castelnau-Picampeau
Thermes-Magnoac
Boulogne-s.-Gesse
Mondilhan
Montbernard
Lilhac
Peyrissas
Montégut-Bourjac
le Fousseret
Montoussin
Barthe
Aries-Espénan
Betbèze
Castéra-Vignoles
St-André
Eoux
Samouillan
Devèze
Pouy
Lalanne
Blajan
St-Pé-Delbosc
Escanecrabe
Esparron
Benque
Gensac-de-Boulogne
Ciadoux
Boussan
Francon
Mondavezan
Villemur
St-Loup-en-Comminges
Montgaillard-sur-Save
Bachas
Terrebasse
Laran
Gaussan
Nizan-Gesse
Lespugue
Saman
Montoulieu-St-Bernard
Lescuns
Bazordan
Sarrecave
Charlas
Cassagnabère-Tournas
Alan
Montmaurin
St-Lary-Boujean
Aurignac
Sana
Sarremezan
Marignac-Laspeyres
Martres-Tolosane
Balesta
Cardeilhac
Peyrouzet
St-Élix-Séglan
Boudrac
Larroque
Lalouret-Laffiteau
St-Marcet
Aulon
Bouzin
le Fréchet
Arné
Cazaril-Tambourès
Larcan
Cazeneuve-Montaut
Boussens
St-Plancard
Lodes
Latoue
Auzas
Montclar-de-Comminges
Lécussan
St-Ignan
Sepx
Proupiary
Laffite-Toupière
Mancioux
Roquefort-s-Garonne
Villeneuve-Lécussan
Sédeilhac
Loudet
Saux-et-Pomarède
St-Roch
Castillon-de-St-Martory
St-Martory
Arnaud-Guilhem
Le Cuing
Franquevielle
ST-GAUDENS
Lestelle-de-St-Martory
Mazères
Ausseing
Belbèze-en-Comminges

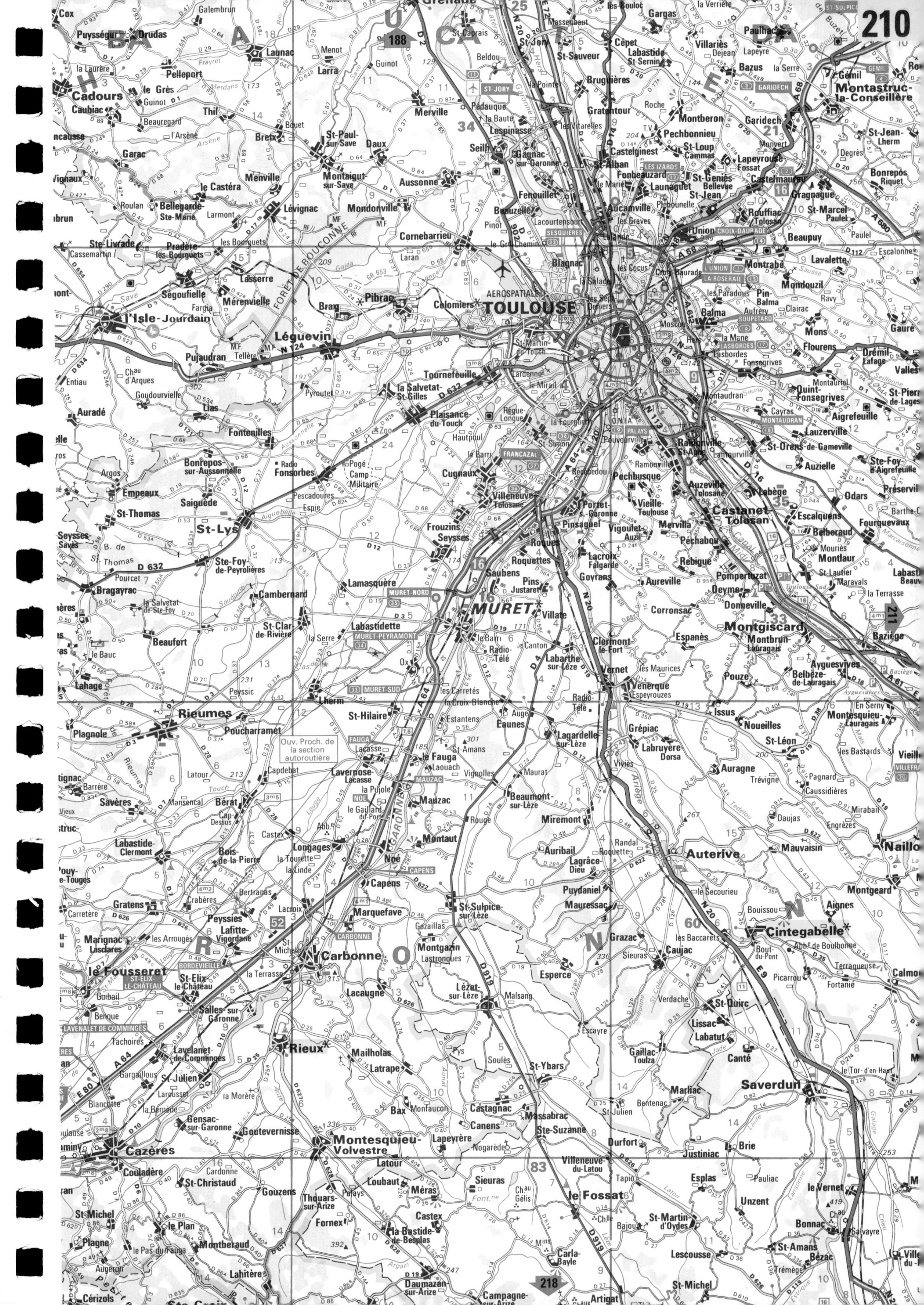

Cadours
Launac
Grenade
Montastruc-la-Conseillère
Merville
Daux
St-Paul-sur-Save
Seilh
Gratentour
Castelginest
Pechbonnieu
Montberon
Garidech
St-Sauveur
Bruguières
Cépet
Fenouillet
Aucamville
L'Union
Castelmaurou
St-Jean
Gragnague
Lévignac
Mondonville
Aussonne
Cornebarrieu
Blagnac
Pibrac
Colomiers
TOULOUSE
Balma
l'Isle-Jourdain
Léguevin
Pujaudran
Tournefeuille
Plaisance-du-Touch
Fonsorbes
St-Lys
Cugnaux
Villeneuve-Tolosane
Portet-s-Garonne
Ramonville-St-Agne
Castanet-Tolosan
Labège
Quint-Fonsegrives
Flourens
Escalquens
Frouzins
Seysses
Roques
Roquettes
Saubens
MURET
Lamasquère
Labastidette
Montgiscard
Baziège
Rieumes
Lherm
Eaunes
Lagardelle-sur-Lèze
Vernet
Venerque
Longages
Noé
Carbonne
Capens
Marquefave
St-Sulpice-sur-Lèze
Auterive
Cintegabelle
le Fousseret
Cazères
Rieux
Montesquieu-Volvestre
Lézat-sur-Lèze
St-Ybars
Saverdun
le Fossat
Daumazan-sur-Arize
Carla-Bayle
A 64
A 61
A 68
N 20
N 124
188
211
218

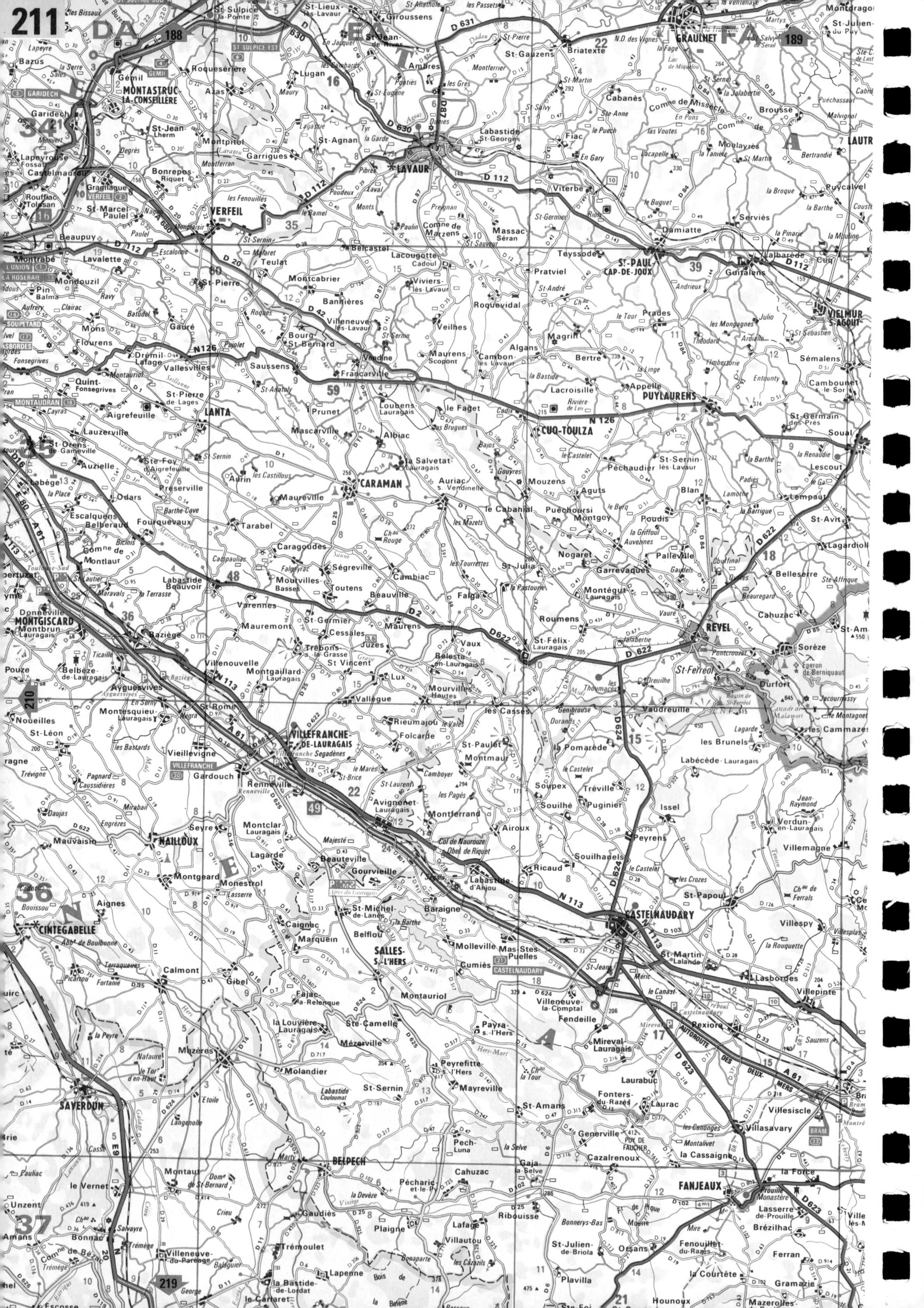
188
189
210
219
St-Sulpice-la-Pointe
St-Lieux-lès-Lavaur
Giroussens
GRAULHET
Montdragon
St-Julien-du-Puy
St-Jean-de-Rives
Briatexte
St-Gauzens
Gémil
MONTASTRUC-LA-CONSEILLÈRE
Roquesérière
Azas
Lugan
Ambres
Garidech
St-Jean-Lherm
Montpitol
St-Agnan
Labastide-St-Georges
Cabanès
Brousse
Fiac
LAVAUR
Garrigues
Lapeyrouse-Fossat
Castelmaurou
Bonrepos-Riquet
Gragnague
Viterbe
Rouffiac-Tolosan
St-Marcel-Paulel
VERFEIL
Massac-Séran
Damiatte
Serviès
Beaupuy
Belcastel
Lacougotte-Cadoul
Teyssode
ST-PAUL-CAP-DE-JOUX
Guitalens
Montrabé
Lavalette
Teulat
Pratviel
VIELMUR-S-AGOUT
Mondouzil
St-Pierre
Montcabrier
Viviers-lès-Lavaur
Bannières
Roquevidal
Prades
Pin-Balma
Villeneuve-lès-Lavaur
Veilhes
Mons
Gauré
Bourg-St-Bernard
Flourens
Maurens-Scopont
Cambon-lès-Lavaur
Algans
Magrin
Bertre
Sémalens
Drémil-Lafage
Vallesvilles
Saussens
Vendine
Francarville
Lacroisille
Appelle
PUYLAURENS
Cambounet-le-Sor
Quint-Fonsegrives
St-Pierre-de-Lages
Loubens-Lauragais
le Faget
LANTA
Aigrefeuille
Prunet
Mascarville
CUQ-TOULZA
St-Germain-des-Prés
Soual
Lauzerville
St-Orens-de-Gameville
Albiac
Auzielle
Ste-Foy-d'Aigrefeuille
La Salvetat-Lauragais
St-Sernin-lès-Lavaur
Péchaudier
Lescout
Labège
Aurin
Préserville
CARAMAN
Auriac-s-Vendinelle
Mouzens
Aguts
Blan
Odars
Maureville
le Cabanial
Puéchoursi
Montgey
Lempaut
Escalquens
Belberaud
Fourquevaux
Tarabel
Poudis
St-Avit
Caragoudes
Nogaret
Palleville
Lagardiolle
Montlaur
Ségreville
Cambiac
St-Julia
Garrevaques
Belleserre
Labastide-Beauvoir
Mourvilles-Basses
Toutens
Beauville
Falga
Montégut-Lauragais
Cahuzac
Donneville
MONTGISCARD
Varennes
Roumens
REVEL
Montbrun-Lauragais
Baziège
Mauremont
St-Germier
Cessales
Maurens
St-Félix-Lauragais
Sorèze
Ticaille
Belbèze-de-Lauragais
Trébons-la-Grasse
Juzes
Vaux
Belesta-en-Lauragais
St-Ferréol
Villenouvelle
Montgaillard-Lauragais
St Vincent
Lux
Durfort
Ayguesvives
Mourvilles-Hautes
Vallègue
Montesquieu-Lauragais
St-Rome
les Cassés
Vaudreuille
Noueilles
Rieumajou
Folcarde
les Cammazes
St-Léon
VILLEFRANCHE-DE-LAURAGAIS
Vieillevigne
St-Paulet
la Pomarède
les Brunels
Labécède-Lauragais
Montmaur
Gardouch
Renneville
Tréville
Soupex
Souilhé
Puginier
Issel
Avignonet-Lauragais
Montferrand
Airoux
Verdun-en-Lauragais
Seyre
Montclar-Lauragais
Peyrens
Mauvaisin
NAILLOUX
Villemagne
Beauteville
Lagarde
Gourvieille
Labastide-d'Anjou
Ricaud
Souilhanels
Montgeard
Monestrol
St-Papoul
Aignes
St-Michel-de-Lanès
Baraigne
CASTELNAUDARY
CINTEGABELLE
Caignac
Marquein
Belflou
Villespy
Molleville
Mas-Stes-Puelles
SALLES-S-L'HERS
Cumiès
St-Martin-Lalande
Calmont
Gibel
Lasbordes
Villepinte
Montauriol
Villeneuve-la-Comptal
Fendeille
Fajac-la-Relenque
Ste-Camelle
Payra-s-l'Hers
Pexiora
La Louvière-Lauragais
Mézerville
Mireval-Lauragais
Mazères
Molandier
Peyrefitte-s-l'Hers
Mayreville
Lauraguel
SAVERDUN
St-Sernin
Fonters-du-Razès
Laurac
St-Amans
Villesiscle
Generville
Villasavary
Cazalrenoux
la Cassaigne
BELPECH
Montaut
Cahuzac
Pécharic-et-le-Py
FANJEAUX
le Vernet
Prouille
Lasserre-de-Prouille
Gaudiès
Ribouisse
Brézilhac
Plaigne
Lafage
Salvayre
Villautou
Orsans
Fenouillet-du-Razès
Villeneuve-du-Paréage
St-Julien-de-Briola
Tréinoulet
Ferran
Lapenne
Plavilla
la Courtète
La Bastide-de-Lordat
Gramazie
le Carlaret
Hounoux
Mazerolles
AUTOROUTE DES DEUX-MERS

190
213
221
CASTRES
MAZAMET
CARCASSONNE
LACAUNE
BRASSAC
ANGLÈS
LA SALVETAT S.-AGOUT
LABRUGUIÈRE
ROQUECOURBE
MONTREDON-LABESSONNIÉ
VABRE
DOURGNE
SAISSAC
ALZONNE
MONTRÉAL
MAS-CABARDÈS
CONQUES S.-ORBIEL
PEYRIAC-MINERVOIS
OLONZAC
CAPENDU
ST-AMANS-SOULT
MONTS DE LACAUNE
PARC REGIONAL
FORET DE MONTAUD
MONTAGNE NOIRE
FORET DE NORE
PIC DE NORE
ROC DE PEYREMAUX
LES CAUSSES
Commune de Montfa
Comne de Montpinier
Comne de Castelnau-de-Brassac
Comne du Margnes
Comne de Viane
Comne de Lasfaillades
Vénès
St-Germier
Lacrouzette
Burlats
Lagarrigue
Noailhac
Boissezon
Saix
Navès
Viviers-lès-Montagnes
St-Affrique-les-Montagnes
Verdalle
Escoussens
Massaguel
Aiguefonde
Aussillon
Pont de Larn
Bout-du-Pont-de-Larn
Rouairoux
Sauveterre
Lacabarède
Labastide-Rouairoux
Albine
Espérausses
Berlats
Gijounet
Lamontélarié
Cambounès
Le Rialet
le Vintrou
Arfons
Laprade
les Martys
Pradelles-Cabardès
Castans
Lespinassière
Cassagnoles
Ferrals-les-Montagnes
Boisset
Lacombe
Fontiers-Cabardès
Cuxac-Cabardès
Caudebronde
Miraval-Cabardès
Labastide-Esparbairenque
Roquefère
Cabrespine
Les Ilhes
Villanière
Villardonnel
Fournes-Cabardès
Trassanel
Limousis
Lastours
Salsigne
Sallèles-Cabardès
Caunes-Minervois
Trausse
Félines-Minervois
La Livinière
Cesseras
Siran
Villeneuve-Minervois
Montolieu
Brousses-et-Villaret
Fraisse-Cabardès
Aragon
Moussoulens
Ventenac-Cabardès
Villegailhenc
Villemoustaussou
Pezens
Ste-Eulalie
Pennautier
Villesèquelande
Caux-et-Sauzens
Villarzel-Cabardès
Bagnoles
Villalier
Malves-en-Minervois
Bouilhonnac
Villedubert
Trèbes
Berriac
Rustiques
Badens
Aigues-Vives
Puichéric
St-Frichoux
La Redorte
Rieux-Minervois
Azille
Homps
Laure-Minervois
Castelnau-d'Aude
Escales
Roquecourbe-Minervois
Blomac
Marseillette
St-Couat-d'Aude
Montbrun-des-Corbières
Conilhac-Corbières
Douzens
Moux
Fontcouverte
Barbaira
Floure
Fontiès-d'Aude
Montirat
Comigne
Palaja
Cazilhac
Cavanac
Leuc
Couffoulens
Preixan
Roullens
Alairac
Lavalette
Arzens
Villarzel-du-Razès
Cailhau
Cailhavel
Raissac-s.-Lampy
St-Martin-le-Vieil
Carlipa
CARCASSONNE OUEST
CARCASSONNE EST
Aire des Corbières
Monze
Pradelles-en-Val
N.D. de Consolation
Fabrezan
Camplong
CHAMP DE TIR

191
190
212
223
Peux-et-Couffouleux
Avène
Mélagues
Joncels
LUNAS
Lavalette
Graissessac
Camplong
Le Bousquet-d'Orb
Lamalou-les-Bains
Hérépian
BÉDARIEUX
MURAT-S.-VÈBRE
LA SALVETAT-S.-AGOUT
Fraisse-s.-Agout
St-Vincent-d'Olargues
OLARGUES
St-Martin-de-l'Arçon
Mons
Colombières-s.-Orb
Vieussan
Roquebrun
St-Nazaire-de-Ladarez
Cabrerolles
Caussiniojouls
Faugères
Roquessels
Laurens
Autignac
Gabian
Fouzilhon
Pouzolles
Margon
Magalas
Puissalicon
Coulobres
Espondeilhan
St-Geniès-de-Fontedit
Causses-et-Veyran
Cessenon-s.-Orb
MURVIEL-LES-BEZIERS
Pailhès
Puimisson
Thézan-lès-Béziers
Corneilhan
Lieuran-lès-Béziers
Bassan
Boujan-s.-Libron
Prémian
St-Étienne-d'Albagnan
Riols
ST-PONS-DE-THOMIÈRES
Courniou
Berlou
Ferrières-Poussarou
Pardailhan
Prades-s.-Vernazobre
ST-CHINIAN
Pierrerue
Cazedarnes
Cébazan
Assignan
St-Jean-de-Minervois
Villespassans
Cazouls-lès-Béziers
Puisserguier
Creissan
Maraussan
Lignan-s.-Orb
BÉZIERS
Vélieux
Minerve
La Caunette
Aigne
Agel
Aigues-Vives
Cruzy
Montouliers
Quarante
Maureilhan
Montady
CAPESTANG
Colombiers
Villeneuve-lès-Béziers
Azillanet
Bize-Minervois
Argeliers
Poilhes
Montels
Ouveillan
Mailhac
Beaufort
OLONZAC
Oupia
Pouzols-Minervois
Ste-Valière
GINESTAS
Mirepeisset
Nissan-lez-Ensérune
Sauvian
Sérignan
Lespignan
Vendres
Paraza
Argens-Minervois
Roubia
Ventenac-en-Minervois
Sallèles-d'Aude
Cuxac-d'Aude
COURSAN
Salles-d'Aude
Fleury
Tourouzelle
Canet
Raissac-d'Aude
St-Marcel-s.-Aude
St-Nazaire-d'Aude
Marcorignan
Moussan
Villedaigne
Névian
LÉZIGNAN-CORBIÈRES
NARBONNE
Cruscades
Montredon-Corbières
Vinassan
Armissan
Ornaisons
Luc-s.-Orbieu
Bizanet
Boutenac
Ferrals-les-Corbières
Les Cabanes-de-Fleury
St-Pierre-s.-Mer
Narbonne Plage
Bages
LANGUEDOC

192
194
St-Guilhem-le-Désert
Aniane
Gignac
St-André-de-Sangonis
Clermont-l'Hérault
Lac du Salagou
Montpeyroux
Puéchabon
Argelliers
Viols-le-Fort
Les Matelles
St-Gély-du-Fesc
St-Clément-de-Rivière
Montferrier-Lez
Clapiers
Vailhauquès
La Boissière
Montarnaud
Grabels
Montpellier
St-Georges-d'Orques
St-Paul-et-Valmalle
Juvignac
Murviel-lès-Montpellier
Pignan
Lavérune
St-Jean-de-Védas
Saussan
Cournonterral
Cournonsec
Fabrègues
Villeneuve-lès-Maguelone
Maguelone
Mireval
Vic-la-Gardiole
Étang de Vic
Frontignan
Montbazin
Gigean
Poussan
Villeveyrac
Balaruc-le-Vieux
Balaruc-les-Bains
Bouzigues
Loupian
Mèze
Sète
Fort St-Pierre
Bassin de Thau
Marseillan
Marseillan-Plage
Pinet
Pomérols
Florensac
Montagnac
Pézenas
Castelnau-de-Guers
St-Thibéry
Bessan
Agde
Vias
Le Grau d'Agde
Cap d'Agde
Fort Brescou
Rochelongue
Portiragnes
Sérignan-Plage
Redoute Plage
Farinette Plage
Servian
Roujan
Caux
Nizas
Paulhan
Aspiran
Canet
Brignac
Nébian
Péret
Cabrières
Fontès
Adissan
Usclas-d'Hérault
St-Pons-de-Mauchiens
St-Pargoire
Campagnan
Bélarga
Plaissan
Puilacher
Tressan
Le Pouget
Vendémian
Pouzols
St-Bauzille-de-la-Sylve
Popian
Montagne de la Moure
Aire de Montpellier-Fabrègues
Aire de Béziers-Montblanc
A 75
A 9 - E 15
N 109
N 113
N 112
N 9

PAU
Billère
Lons
Lescar
Jurançon
Gelos
Bizanos
Mazères-Lezons
Idron
Lée
Artigueloutan
Nousty
Soumoulou
Limendous
Oloron-Ste-Marie
Lasseube
Lasseubetat
Herrère
Escout
Précilhon
Goès
Ledeuix
Estialescq
Lacommande
Aubertin
Cuqueron
Artiguelouve
Laroin
Cardesse
Verdets
Moumour
Orin
Gurmençon
Agnos
Asasp-Arros
Eysus
Ogeu-les-Bains
Buziet
Buzy
Bescat
Arudy
Sévignacq-Meyracq
Ste-Colome
Izeste
Louvie-Juzon
Castet
Bielle
Bilhères
Gère-Bélesten
Aste-Béon
Louvie-Soubiron
Béost
Laruns
Eaux-Bonnes
Gourette
Les-Eaux-Chaudes
Gan
Bosdarros
Rébénacq
Narcastet
Rontignon
Uzos
Meillon
Assat
Bordes
Baliros
Pardies-Piétat
Baudreix
Lagos
Beuste
Bordères
Bénéjacq
Pontacq
Mirepeix
Nay
Bourdettes
Arros-de-Nay
St-Abit
Coarraze
Igon
Asson
Bruges-Capbis-Mifaget
Lestelle-Bétharram
Montaut
St-Pé-de-Bigorre
Lys
Arthez-d'Asson
Ferrières
Arbéost
Argelès-Gazost
Arras-en-Lavedan
Aucun
Arrens-Marsous
Estaing
Cauterets
Col d'Aubisque
Pic de Ger
Pic du Midi d'Ossau
PARC NATIONAL DES PYRÉNÉES
Balaïtous
Vignemale
Lurbe-St-Christau
Escot
Sarrance
Lourdios-Ichère
Bedous
Osse-en-Aspe
Accous
Lées-Athas
Lescun
Cette-Eygun
Etsaut
Borce
Urdos
Col du Somport
Candanchú
Canfranc-Estación
Canfranc
Col du Pourtalet
El Formigal
Sallent-de-Gallego
Lanuza
Escarrilla
Panticosa
Baños de Panticosa
El Pueyo-de-Jaca
Tramacastilla-de-Tena
Piedrafita-de-Jaca
Vallée d'Aspe
Vallée d'Ossau
Forêt de Très Crouts
Grottes de Bétharram

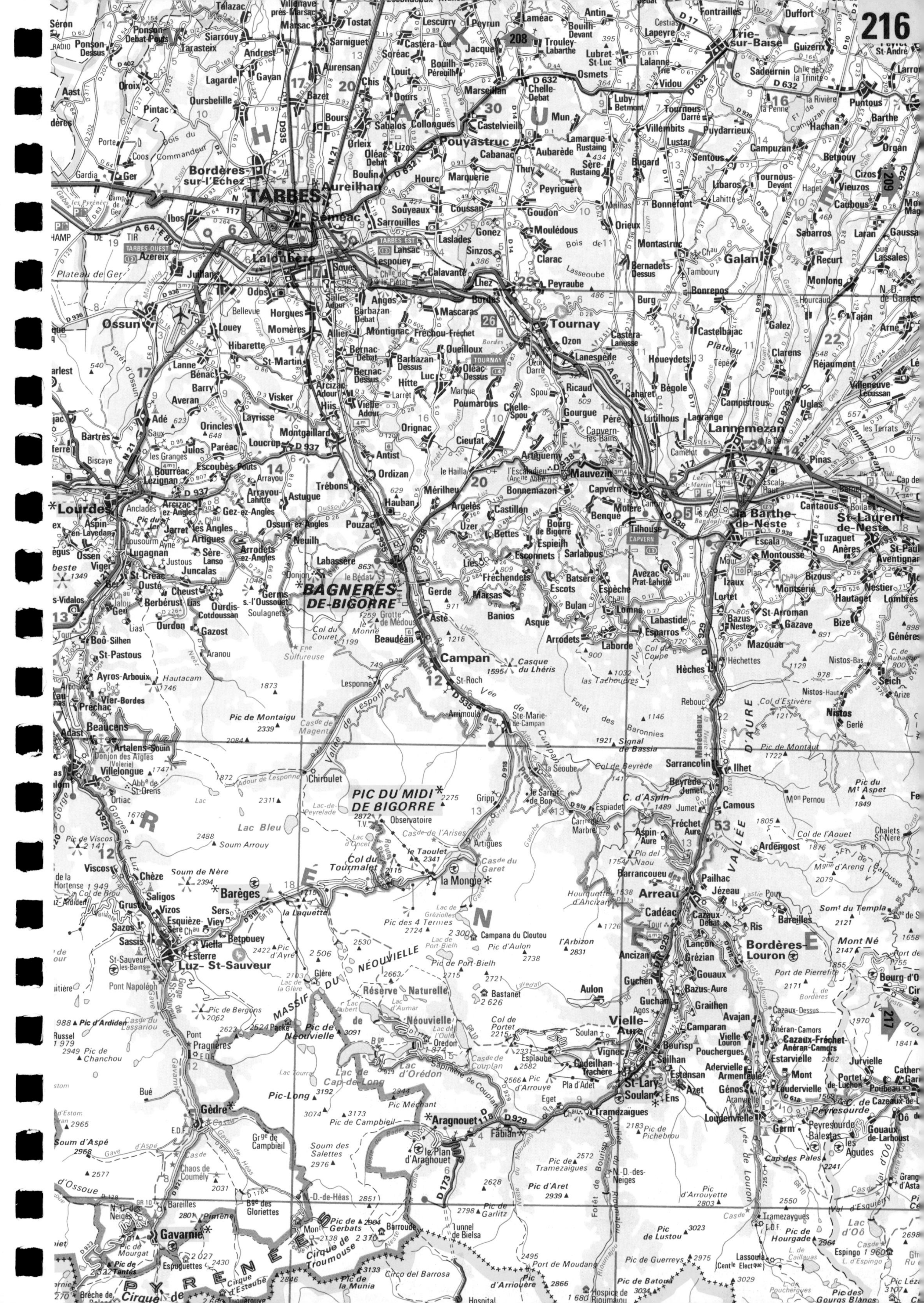
TARBES
Lourdes
BAGNÈRES-DE-BIGORRE
PIC DU MIDI DE BIGORRE
Lannemezan
Tournay
Campan
Barèges
Luz-St-Sauveur
Gavarnie
Gèdre
Arreau
Vielle-Aure
St-Lary-Soulan
Aragnouet
Sarrancolin
La Barthe-de-Neste
St-Laurent-de-Neste
Bordères-Louron
Loudenvielle
Col du Tourmalet
La Mongie
Lac Bleu
MASSIF DU NÉOUVIELLE
Réserve Naturelle
Pic-Long
Cirque de Troumouse
Cirque de Gavarnie
PYRÉNÉES
VALLÉE D'AURE
Galan
Pouyastruc
Ossun
Aureilhan
Séméac
Laloubère
Trie-sur-Baïse
Capvern
Mauvezin
Col d'Aspin
Tunnel de Bielsa
217

Trie-sur-Baïse
Castelnau-Magnoac
Boulogne-s.-Gesse
Lannemezan
St-GAUDENS
Montréjeau
St-Laurent-de-Neste
La Barthe-de-Neste
St-Bertrand-de-Comminges
Mauléon-Barousse
Barbazan
Aspet
Aurignac
St-Martory
Salies-du-Salat
Bagnères-de-Luchon
St-Béat
Bordères-Louron
Superbagnères
Col de Peyresourde
Col de Portet-d'Aspet
Col de Menté
Port de Balès
Pic de Maubermé
Bosost
Les
Canejan
Arrés
Vilamós
Arròs y Vila
las Bordas
Vilach
Betlan
Hospice de France
Valentine
Miramont-de-Comminges
Montespan
Mazères-sur-Salat
Montsaunès
Cier-de-Luchon
Marignac
Fos
Melles
Arlos
Chaum
Cierp-Gaud
Sauveterre-de-Comminges
Encausse-les-Thermes
Cazères
Galan
Montréjeau
Loudenvielle
Germ
Génos
Valle d'Aran

Labastide-Clermont
Longages
Noé
Auribail
Lagrâce-Dieu
Auterive
Sénarens
Pouy-de-Touges
Bois-de-la-Pierre
Capens
Puydaniel
Mauressac
Castelnau-Picampeau
Gratens
Peyssies
Lafitte-Vigordane
Marquefave
St-Sulpice-sur-Lèze
Cintagabelle
Fustignac
Marignac-Lasclares
Carbonne
Montgazin
Grazac
Caujac
le Fousseret
St-Elix-le-Château
Lacaugne
Lézat-sur-Lèze
Esperce
Montoussin
Salles-sur-Garonne
St-Quirc
Lissac
Labatut
Mondavezan
Lavelanet-de-Comminges
Rieux
Mailholas
Latrape
St-Ybars
Gaillac-Toulza
Canté
Lescuns
St-Julien
Marliac
Saverdun
Sana
Bax
Castagnac
Massabrac
Martres-Tolosane
Gensac-sur-Garonne
Gouteverniss
Montesquieu-Volvestre
Canens
Lapeyrère
Ste-Suzanne
Durfort
Brie
Palaminy
Cazères
Latour
Villeneuve-du-Latou
Couladère
St-Christaud
Gouzens
Thouars-sur-Arize
Loubaut
Méras
Sieuras
le Fossat
Esplas
Unzent
Mauran
Montclar-de-Comminges
St-Michel
le Plan
Fornex
Castex
La Bastide-de-Besplas
St-Martin-d'Oydes
Roquefort-s-Garonne
Plagne
Montberaud
Carla-Bayle
Lescousse
Ausseing
Lahitère
Daumazan-sur-Arize
Belbèze-en-Comminges
Cérizols
Ste-Croix-Volvestre
Montbrun-Bocage
Campagne-sur-Arize
Artigat
Cassagne
Escoulis
Castéras
Lanoux
Fabas
Marsoulas
Tourtouse
Montfa
les Bordes-sur-Arize
Pailhès
Madière
Mérigon
Sabarat
Monesple
Betchat
Bédeille
Camarade
Touille
Bagert
Lasserre
Montardit
Mauvezin-de-Ste-Croix
le Mas-d'Azil
Gabre
Montégut-Plantaurel
Artix
la Bastide-du-Salat
Barjac
Contrazy
Rieubach
Lacave
Mercenac
Taurignan-Castet
le Saret
Allières
Loubens
Caumont
Clermont
Durban-sur-Arize
Suzan
Prat-Bonrepaux
Lorp-Sentaraille
Gajan
Montgauch
St-Lizier
Lescure
Rimont
Castelnau-Durban
Cadarcet
Larbont
la Bastide-de-Sérou
Montels
Cazavet
Montjoie-en-Couserans
ST-GIRONS
Nescus
Alzen
Montégut-en-Couserans
Esplas-de-Sérou
Montagagne
Balaguères
Moulis
Eycheil
Sentenac-de-Sérou
Serres-sur-Arget
Burret
Bénac
Arrout
Engomer
Lacourt
Rivèrenert
Brassac
Audressein
Cescau
Erp
Soulan
le Bosc
Castillon-en-Couserans
Alos
Biert
Boussenac
Massat
Bethmale
Uchentein
Soueix-Rogalle
Aleu
Saurat
Oust
le Port
Bédeilhac-et-Aynat
Rabat-les-Trois-Seigneurs
Seix
Ercé
Gourbit
Ustou
Couflens
Aulus-les-Bains
Illier-et-Laramade
Suc-et-Sentenac
Auzat
Vicdessos
Orus
Mt Valier
Pic de Fonta
Pic de Montaud
Pic de Certescans
Pic Rouge de Bassiès
Cap de Ruhos
Pico de Moredo
220

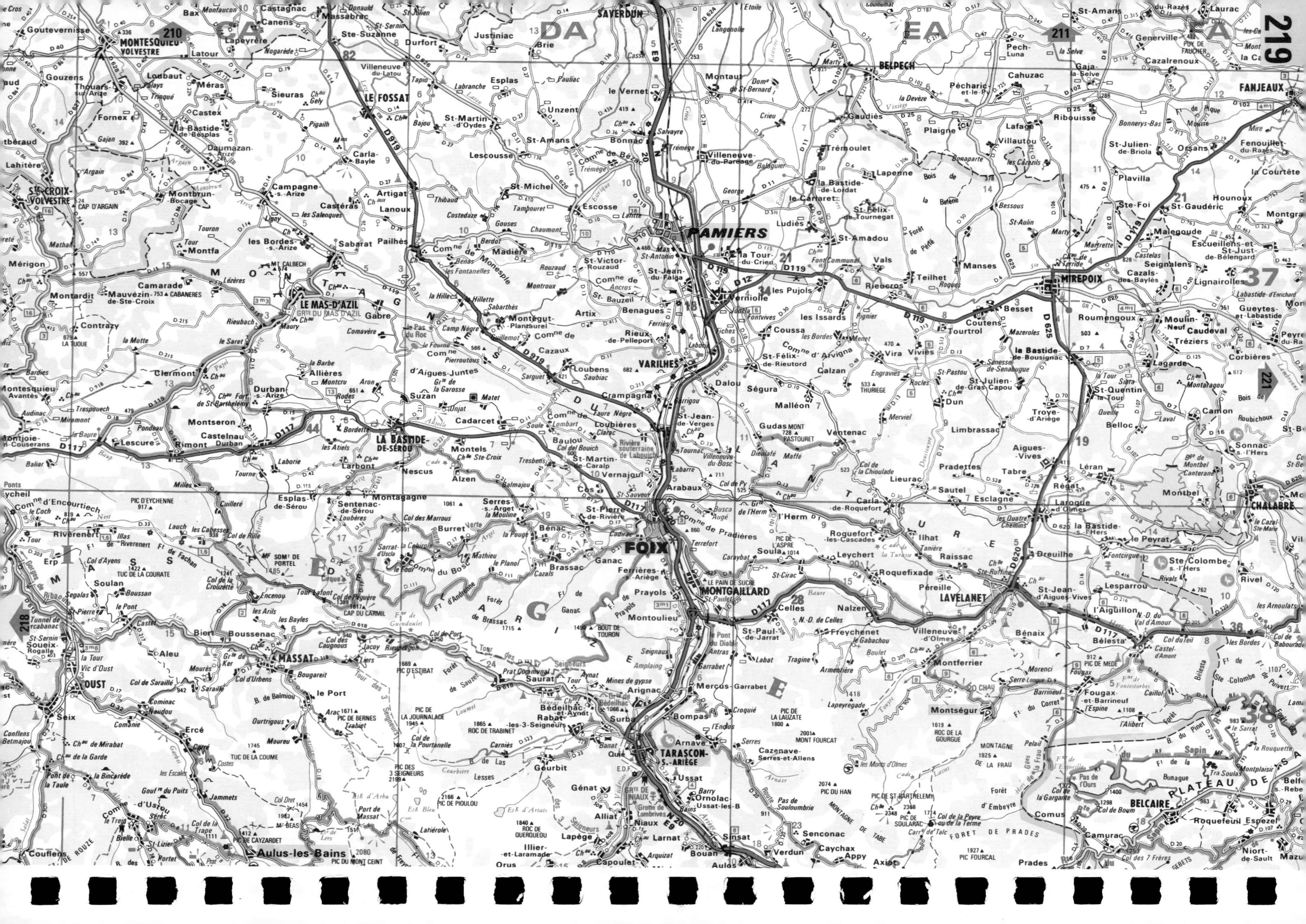

210
211
221
218
MONTESQUIEU-VOLVESTRE
SAVERDUN
BELPECH
FANJEAUX
LE FOSSAT
STE-CROIX-VOLVESTRE
PAMIERS
MIREPOIX
LE MAS-D'AZIL
VARILHES
LA BASTIDE-DE-SÉROU
CHALABRE
FOIX
MONTGAILLARD
LAVELANET
MASSAT
OUST
TARASCON-S.-ARIÈGE
Montségur
BELCAIRE
Aulus-les-Bains
D 919
D 119
D 625
D 117
D 620
E9

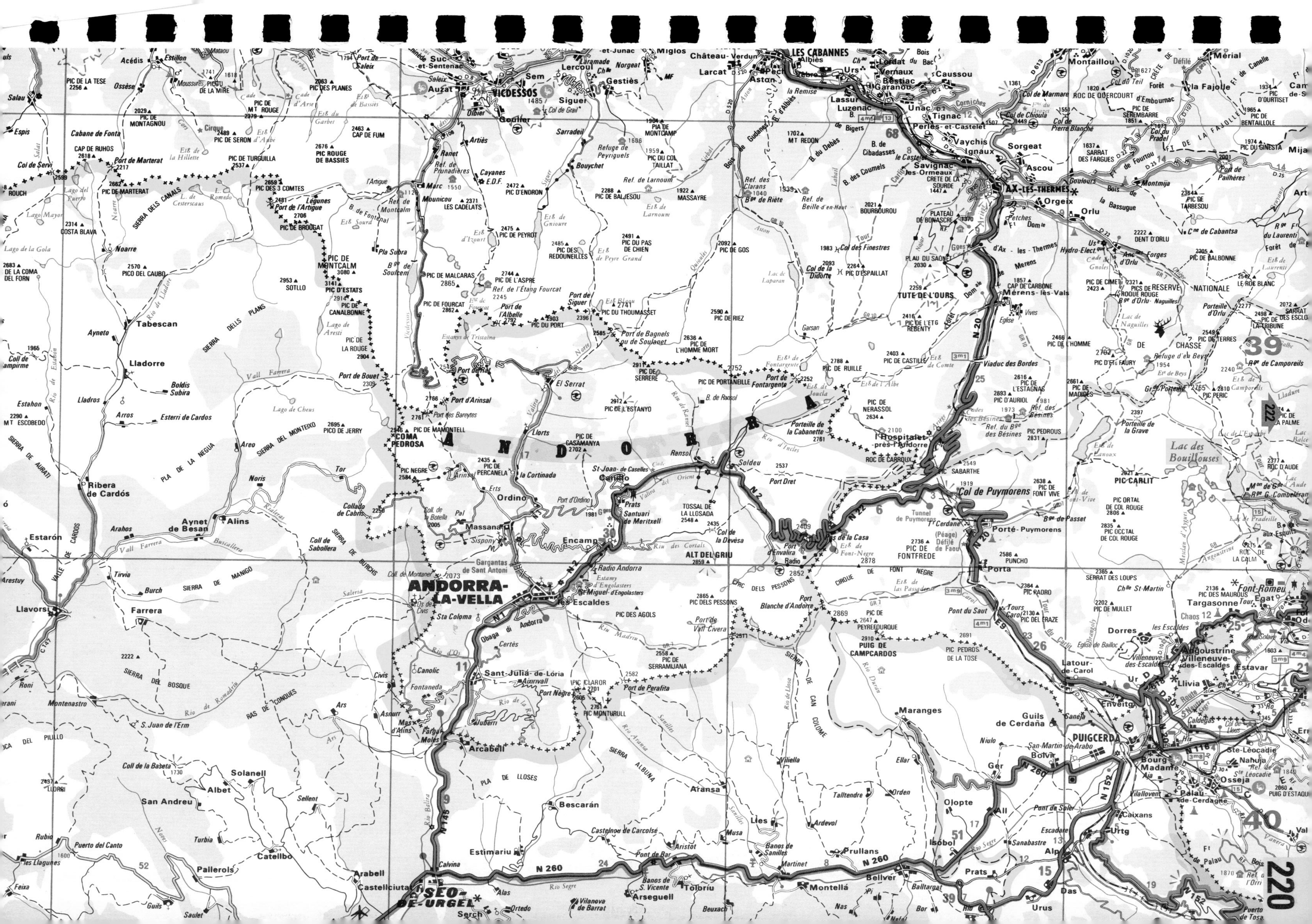
ANDORRA-LA-VELLA
A N D O R R A
PUIGCERDA
SEO-DE-URGEL
AX-LES-THERMES
LES CABANNES
VICDESSOS
Encamp
Ordino
Massana
Canillo
Escaldes
Sant-Julià-de-Lòria
Llivia
Bourg-Madame
Latour-de-Carol
Col de Puymorens
PIC CARLIT
Lac des Bouillouses
Font-Romeu
PIC DE MONTCALM
PIC D'ESTATS
COMA PEDROSA
Soldeu
Ribera de Cardós
Llavorsi
Bellver
N 20
N 260
N 145
N 152
39
40
222

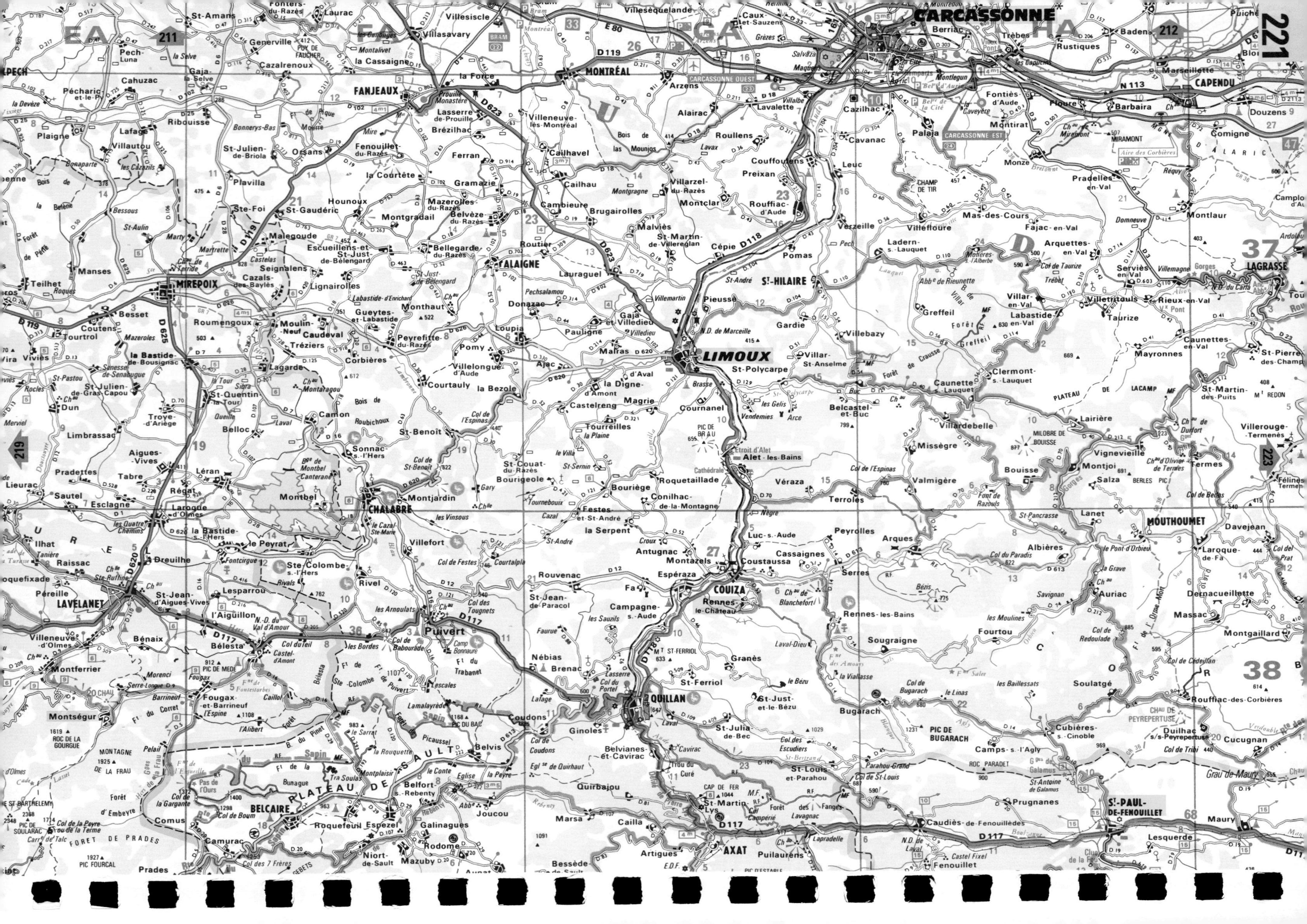
211
212
219
223
37
38
CARCASSONNE
CAPENDU
LAGRASSE
MOUTHOUMET
ST-PAUL-DE-FENOUILLET
MONTRÉAL
FANJEAUX
ST-HILAIRE
LIMOUX
ALAIGNE
COUIZA
QUILLAN
AXAT
CHALABRE
Puivert
MIREPOIX
LAVELANET
BELCAIRE
PIC DE BUGARACH
PLATEAU DE SAULT
Alet-les-Bains
Rennes-les-Bains
Espéraza
Bugarach
Trèbes
Arques
Montségur
Bélesta
Prades
Comus

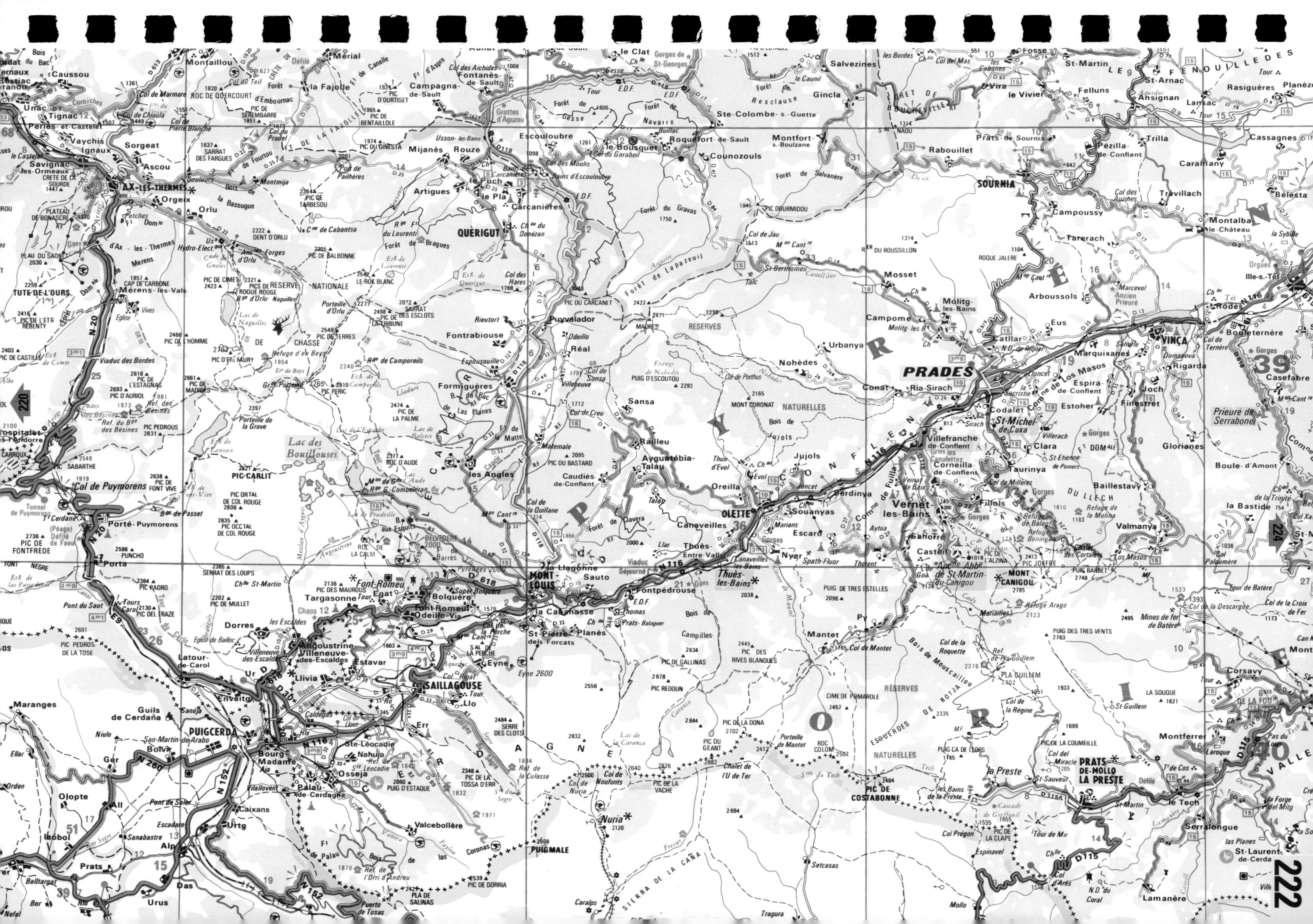

PRADES
PRATS-DE-MOLLO-LA PRESTE
Vinça
Ille-s.-Têt
Montalba-le-Château
Caramany
SOURNIA
Mosset
Molitg-les-Bains
Eus
Villefranche-de-Conflent
Vernet-les-Bains
MONT CANIGOU
OLETTE
Thuès-les-Bains
MONT-LOUIS
Font-Romeu
Bolquère
SAILLAGOUSE
PUIGCERDA
Bourg-Madame
AX-LES-THERMES
QUÈRIGUT
Formiguères
les Angles
Lac des Bouillouses
Porté-Puymorens
Col de Puymorens
PIC DE COSTABONNE
PUIGMALE
Nuria
Llivia
Latour-de-Carol
Osséja
Err
Eyne
Planès
Sauto
Fontpédrouse
Corneilla-de-Conflent
Casteil
Mantet
Py
Sahorre
Taurinya
Codalet
Clara
Fillols
Serralongue
Lamanère
le Tech
Montferrer
Corsavy
224
220

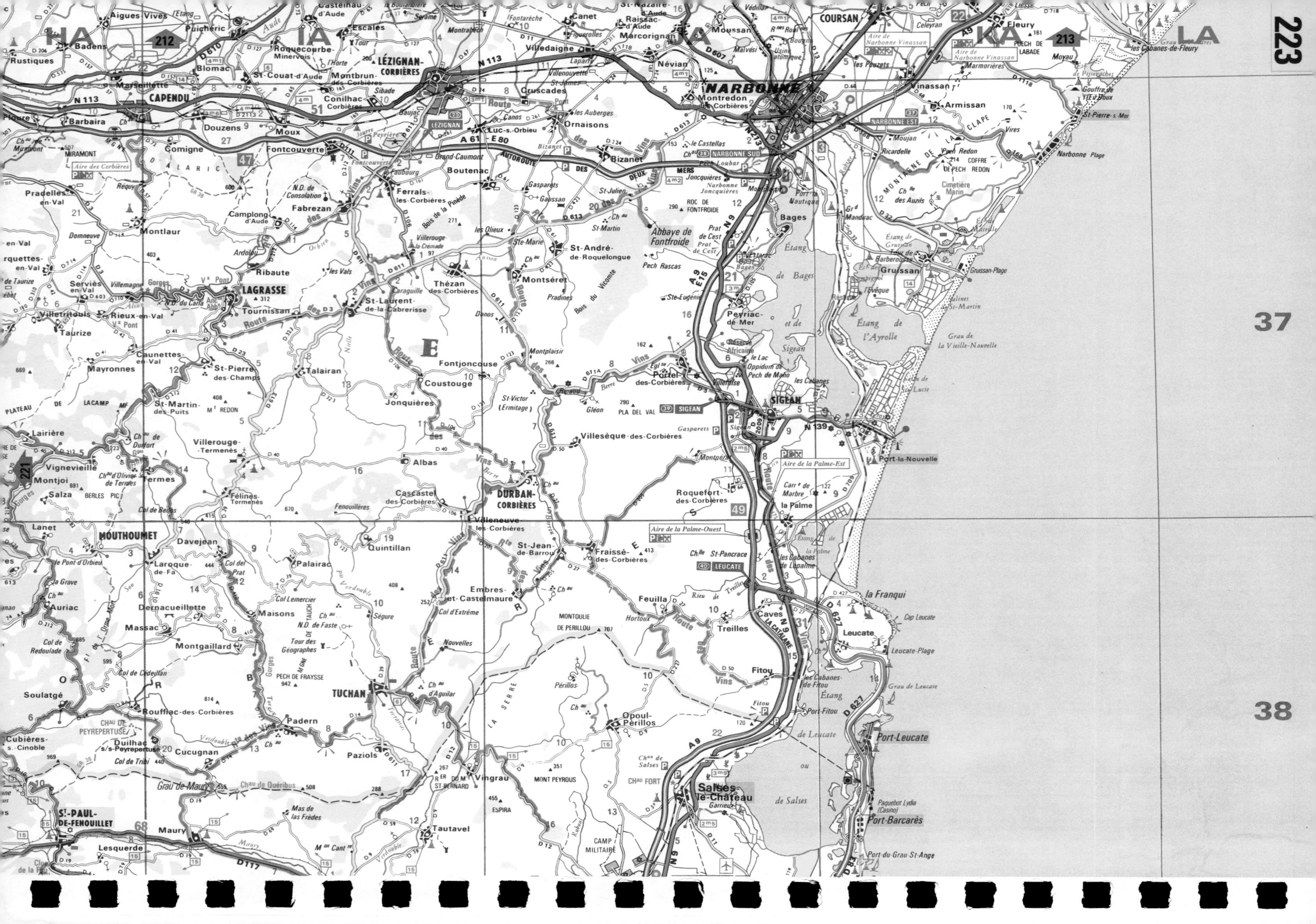
37
38
NARBONNE
COURSAN
LÉZIGNAN-CORBIÈRES
CAPENDU
SIGEAN
DURBAN-CORBIÈRES
TUCHAN
LAGRASSE
MOUTHOUMET
ST-PAUL-DE-FENOUILLET
Gruissan
Leucate
Port-Leucate
Port-Barcarès
Port-la-Nouvelle
Salses-le-Château
Fitou
Bages
Peyriac-de-Mer
Fleury
Armissan
Vinassan
Bizanet
Ornaisons
Thézan-des-Corbières
Fontjoncouse
Coustouge
Albas
Cascastel-des-Corbières
Villeneuve-les-Corbières
St-Jean-de-Barrou
Embres-et-Castelmaure
Feuilla
Treilles
Roquefort-des-Corbières
Fraissé-des-Corbières
Villesèque-des-Corbières
Portel-des-Corbières
Opoul-Périllos
Vingrau
Tautavel
Paziols
Padern
Cucugnan
Maury
Abbaye de Fontfroide
Étang de Bages et de Sigean
Étang de Leucate ou de Salses
213
212
221

39
40
CÔTE VERMEILLE
PERPIGNAN
Rivesaltes
St-Laurent-de-la-Salanque
Canet-en-Roussillon
St-Cyprien-Plage
Argelès-s.-Mer
Elne
Collioure
Port-Vendres
Banyuls-s.-Mer
Cerbère
Cap de l'Abeille
Port-Bou
Llansa
le Boulou
le Perthus
la Junquera
Céret
Amélie-les-Bains-Palalda
Arles-s.-Tech
Prats-de-Mollo-la-Preste
Thuir
Ille-s.-Têt
Millas
Vinça
Estagel
Latour-de-France
St-Estève
Toulouges
Bompas
Baixas
Cabestany
Ponteilla
Trouillas
Banyuls-dels-Aspres
St-Génis-des-Fontaines
Sorède
Laroque-des-Albères
Maureillas-Las-Illas
Reynès
St-Laurent-de-Cerdans
Coustouges
Serralongue
Montferrer
Corsavy
Prieuré de Serrabona
Bouleternère
Rodès
Montner
Cases-de-Pène
Espira-de-l'Agly
Peyrestortes
Pia
Claira
Torreilles
St-Hippolyte
Villelongue-de-la-Salanque
Ste-Marie
St-Nazaire
Alénya
Théza
Saleilles
Villeneuve-de-la-Raho
Bages
Montescot
Ortaffa
Palau-del-Vidre
St-André
Brouilla
Villemolaque
Passa
Tresserre
Fourques
Llauro
Tordères
Calmeilles
Oms
Taillet
Montauriol
Caixas
Castelnou
Ste-Colombe-de-la-Commanderie
Camélas
Corbère
Corbère-les-Cabanes
St-Michel-de-Llotes
Casefabre
Boule-d'Amont
la Bastide
Glorianes
Rigarda
Finestret
Joch
Valmanya
Baillestavy
Marquixanes
Espira-de-Conflent
Estoher
Tarerach
Trévillach
Caramany
Montalba-le-Château
Cassagnes
Bélesta
Planèzes
Rasiguères
Lansac
Ansignan
Trilla
St-Arnac
Pézilla-de-Conflent
Felluns
St-Martin
Calce
Pézilla-la-Rivière
Villeneuve-la-Rivière
Corneilla-la-Rivière
St-Féliu-d'Amont
St-Féliu-d'Avall
Néfiach
le Soler
Canohès
Pollestres
Llupia
Terrats
Vivès
St-Jean-Pla-de-Corts
Montbolo
St-Marsal
Taulis
Espolla
Rabos
Vilamaniscle
Colera
Molinas
Requesens
Cantallops
Agullana
Darnius
Massanet de Cabrenys
A 9
N 9
N 114
N 116
D 612
D 618
D 115
A 7 - E 15
N II
PIC NEULOS
PUIG DEL TOURN
ROC DE FRANCE
Tour Madeloc
Réserve Naturelle
le Barcarès
Canet-Plage
Argelès-Plage
Vallespir
Aspres

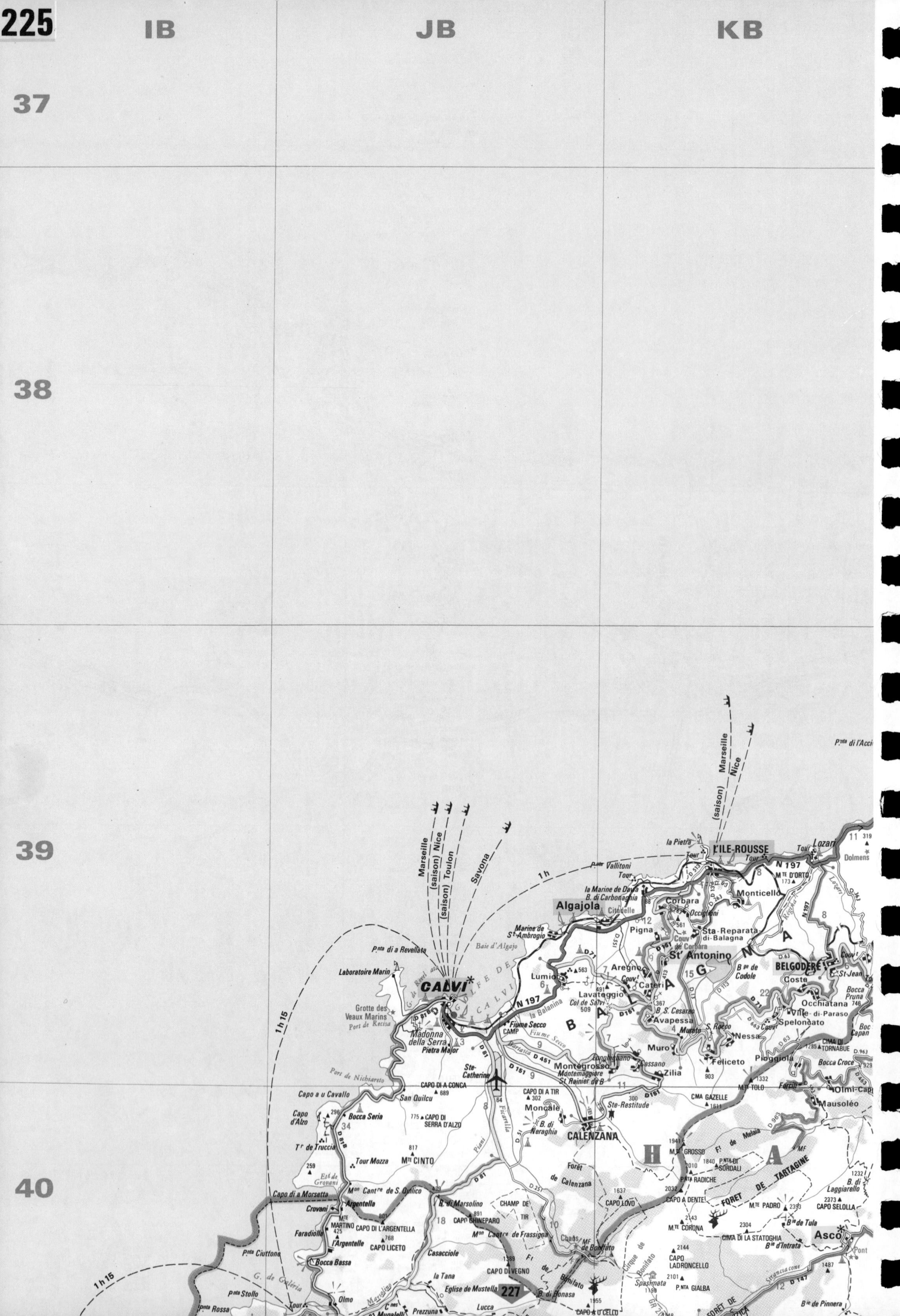
IB
JB
KB
37
38
39
40
Pnta di l'Acci
Marseille
(saison)
Nice
Toulon
Savona
1 h
1 h 15
la Pietra
L'ILE-ROUSSE
Lozari
Tour
N 197
Pnta Vallitoni
Dolmens
Mte D'ORTO
la Marine de Davia
B. di Carbonaghia
Monticello
Algajola
Citadelle
Corbara
Occiglioni
Marine de St Ambrogio
Pigna
Sta-Reparata di-Balagna
Couv. de Corbara
Pnta di a Revellata
Baie d'Algajo
St Antonino
BELGODERE
St-Jean
Laboratoire Marin
CALVI
GOLFE DE CALVI
Lumio
Aregno
Cateri
B de Codole
Costa
Occhiatana
Bocca Pruna
Grotte des Veaux Marins
Port de Recisa
Lavatoggio
Col de Salvi
B. S. Cesareo
Avapessa
Ville-di-Paraso
Spelonçato
Madonna della Serra
Pietra Major
Fiume Secco
CAMP
Muro
Nessa
Feliceto
Pioggiola
CIMA DI TORNABUE
Bocca Croce
Port de Nichiareto
Ste-Catherine
Montegrosso
Montemaggiore
St Reinier de B
Cassano
Zilia
Mte TOLO
Olmi-Cap
Mausoléo
Capo a u Cavallo
CAPO DI A CONCA
San Quilcu
CAPO DI A TIR
Moncale
Ste-Restitude
CMA GAZELLE
Capo d'Alzo
Bocca Seria
CAPO DI SERRA D'ALZO
B. di Neraghia
CALENZANA
Tr de Truccia
Tour Mozza
Mte CINTO
Forêt de Calenzana
Mte GROSSO
Ft de Melaja
Pnta DI SORDALI
Pnta RADICHE
Etg de Crovani
Mon Cantre de S. Quilico
Capo di a Morsetta
Argentella
Crovani
B. di Marsolino
CHAMP DE TIR
CAPO GHINEPARO
CAPO LOVO
CAPO A DENTE
FORET DE TARTAGINE
Mte PADRO
B. di Laggiarello
CAPO SELOLLA
Mte MARTINO
CAPO DI L'ARGENTELLA
Faradiollo
l'Argentelle
CAPO LICETO
Mon Cantre de Frassiga
Chaos de Bonifato
Mte CORONA
CIMA DI LA STATOGHIA
Bte de Tula
Bie d'Intrata
Asco
Pnta Ciuttone
Bocca Bassa
Casacciole
CAPO DI VEGNO
Cirque de Bonifato
CAPO LADRONCELLO
Pont
G. de Galéria
Pnta Stollo
Pnta Rossa
la Tana
Eglise de Mustella
227
B. di Bonasa
Spasimata
P.NTA GIALBA
FORET DE
Olmo
Lucca
Prezzuna
CAPO A U CELLU
Bie de Pinnera
D 147

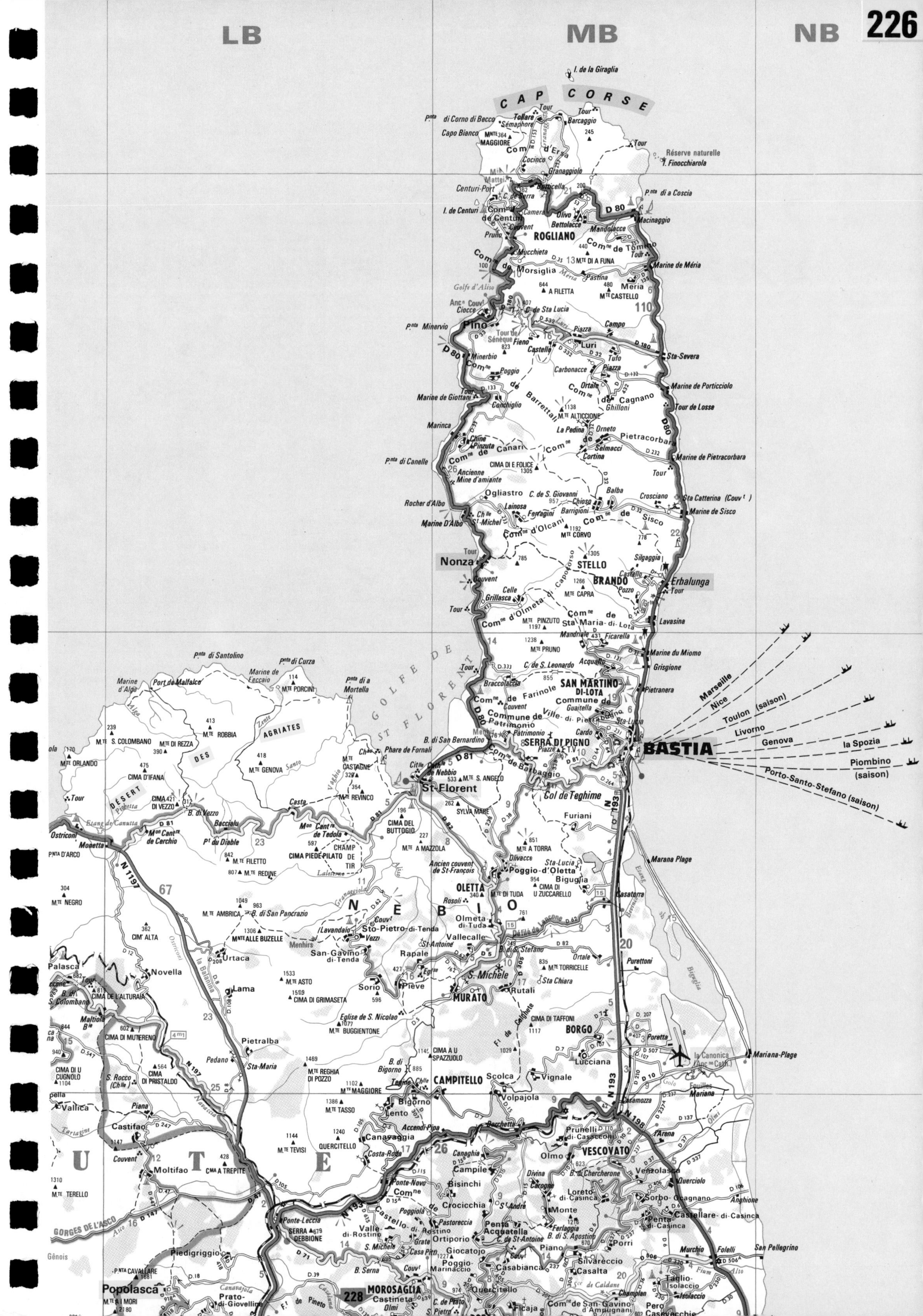

LB
MB
NB
I. de la Giraglia
CAP CORSE
Tollare
Sémaphore
Barcaggio
Capo Bianco
MAGGIORE
Comne d'Ersa
Cocinco
Granaggiolo
Réserve naturelle
I. Finocchiarola
Centuri-Port
Botticella
I. de Centuri
Comne de Centuri
Pruno
ROGLIANO
Pnta di a Coscia
Macinaggio
Olivo
Bettolacce
Mandolacce
Comne de Tomino
Mucchieta
Comne de Morsiglia
MTE DI A FUNA
Golfe d'Aliso
Pastina
Marine de Méria
Méria
A FILETTA
MTE CASTELLO
Pnta Minervio
Pino
C. de Sta Lucia
Campo
Tour de Sénèque
Fieno
Castello
Luri
Piazza
Sta-Severa
Minerbio
Comne de Barrettali
Poggio
Carbonacce
Tufo
Marine de Giottani
Conchiglio
Ortale
Comne de Cagnano
Marine de Porticciolo
Ghilloni
MTE ALTICCIONE
Tour de Losse
Marinca
La Pedina
Orneto
Chine
Pinzuta
Comne de Canari
Comne de Pietracorbara
Selmacci
Cortina
Pnta di Canelle
Marine de Pietracorbara
CIMA DI E FOLICE
Ancienne Mine d'amiante
Ogliastro
C. de S. Giovanni
Balba
Crosciano
Sta Catterina (Couvt)
Chioso
Barrigioni
Marine de Sisco
Rocher d'Albo
Lainosa
Ferragini
Marine D'Albo
Comne d'Olcani
Comne de Sisco
MTE CORVO
Nonza
Couvent
STELLO
BRANDO
Silgaggia
Castello
Erbalunga
Celle
Grillasca
Comne d'Olmeta-di-Capocorso
MTE CAPRA
Pozzo
Comne de Sta Maria-di-Lota
MTE PINZUTO
Lavasina
Mandriale
Ficarella
MTE PRUNO
Marine du Miomo
C. de S. Leonardo
Acquatella
Grisgione
Pnta di Santolino
Pnta di Curza
Marine de Feccaio
MTE PORCINI
Pnta di a Mortella
GOLFE DE ST FLORENT
Braccolaccia
SAN MARTINO DI-LOTA
Pietranera
Marine d'Alga
Port de Malfalco
Comne de Farinole
Couvent
Commune de Guaitella
Commune de Ville-di-Pietrabugno
Commune de Patrimonio
Sta-Lucia
Marseille
Nice
Toulon (saison)
Livorno
Genova
la Spezia
Piombino (saison)
Porto-Santo-Stefano (saison)
M.TE ROBBIA
DES AGRIATES
DÉSERT DES AGRIATES
M.TE S. COLOMBANO
M.TE DI REZZA
M.TE ORLANDO
M.TE GENOVA
M.TE CASTAGNE
Phare de Fornali
B. di San Bernardino
Patrimonio
Cardo
SERRA DI PIGNO
BASTIA
CIMA D'IFANA
St-Florent
Cathle de Nebbio
M.TE S. ANGELO
Comne de Barbaggio
M.TE REVINCO
Col de Teghime
Tour
CIMA DI VEZZO
B. di Vezzo
Casta
SYLVA MARE
Ostriconi
Baccialu
Mon Cantre de Tedola
CIMA DEL BUTTOGIO
Furiani
Monetta
Mon Cantre de Cerchio
Pt du Diable
CHAMP DE TIR
M.TE A MAZZOLA
M.TE A TORRA
PNTA D'ARCO
M.TE FILETTO
CIMA PIEDE PILATO
Olivacce
Marana Plage
M.TE REDINE
Ancien couvent de St-François
Poggio-d'Oletta
Sta-Lucia
Biguglia
N 1197
OLETTA
M.TE DI TUDA
CIMA DI U ZUCCARELLO
Casatorra
M.TE NEGRO
Rosoli
M.TE AMBRICA
B. di San Pancrazio
NEBBIO
Olmeta-di-Tuda
Défilé de Lancone
CIM' ALTA
M.TE ALLE BUZELLE
Lavandaio
Sto-Pietro-di-Tenda
Vezzi
Menhirs
Vallecalle
St-Antoine
B. di S. Stefano
Palasca
Urtaca
San-Gavino-di-Tenda
Rapale
Ortale
Purettoni
Novella
M.TE ASTO
Eglise
S. Michele
M.TE TORRICELLE
Sta Chiara
Lama
CIMA DI GRIMASETA
Sorio
Pieve
MURATO
Rutali
B. di S. Colombano
CIMA DE L'ALTURAIA
la Bafanina
Eglise de S. Nicolao
CIMA DI TAFFONI
M.TE BUGGIENTONE
CIMA DI MUTERENO
BORGO
Poretta
Pietralba
CIMA A U SPAZZUOLO
Lucciana
la Canonica (Anc. Cathle)
Mariana-Plage
Pedano
Sta-Maria
M.TE REGHIA DI POZZO
B. di Bigorno
CIMA DI PRISTALDO
CIMA DI U CUGNOLO
S. Rocco (Chlle)
CAMPITELLO
Scolca
Vignale
M.TE MAGGIORE
Volpajola
Fouilles Mariana
Valiica
Piana
M.TE TASSO
Bigorno
Lento
Casamozza
Accendi-Pipa
Prunelli-di-Casacconi
Castifao
Canavaggia
QUERCITELLO
M.TE TEVISI
Costa-Roda
Arena
Couvent
UTE
Moltifao
CMA A TREPITE
Canaghia
Campile
Olmo
VESCOVATO
Venzolasca
M.TE TERELLO
B. di Chercherone
Ponte-Novo
Bisinchi
Divina
Carogne
Loreto-di-Casinca
Querciolo
Comne de Castello-di-Rostino
Crocicchia
St-André
Monte
Sorbo-Ocagnano
Anghione
GORGES DE L'ASCO
Ponte-Leccia
Poggiola
Pastoreccia
Penta-Acquatella
Ferlaggia
Penta-di-Casinca
Castellare-di-Casinca
SERRA DEBBIONE
Valle-di-Rostino
Ortiporio
C. de St-Antoine
B. di S. Agostino
Porri
Génois
Grate
Piedigriggio
S. Michele
Casa Pitti
Giocatojo
Piano
Murchio
Folelli
San Pellegrino
Poggio-Marinaccio
Casabianca
Silvareccio
PNTA CAVALLARE
B. Serna
Couvt
Casalta
Popolasca
Canavajola
MOROSAGLIA
Quercitello
Scre de Caldane
Taglio-Isolaccio
M.TE A I MORI
Prato-di-Giovellina
Fl de Pineto
228
Castineta
Olmi
C. de Prato
S. Pietro
Ficaja
Comne de San-Gavino-d'Ampugnani
Champlan
Pero-Casevecchie
Isolaccio

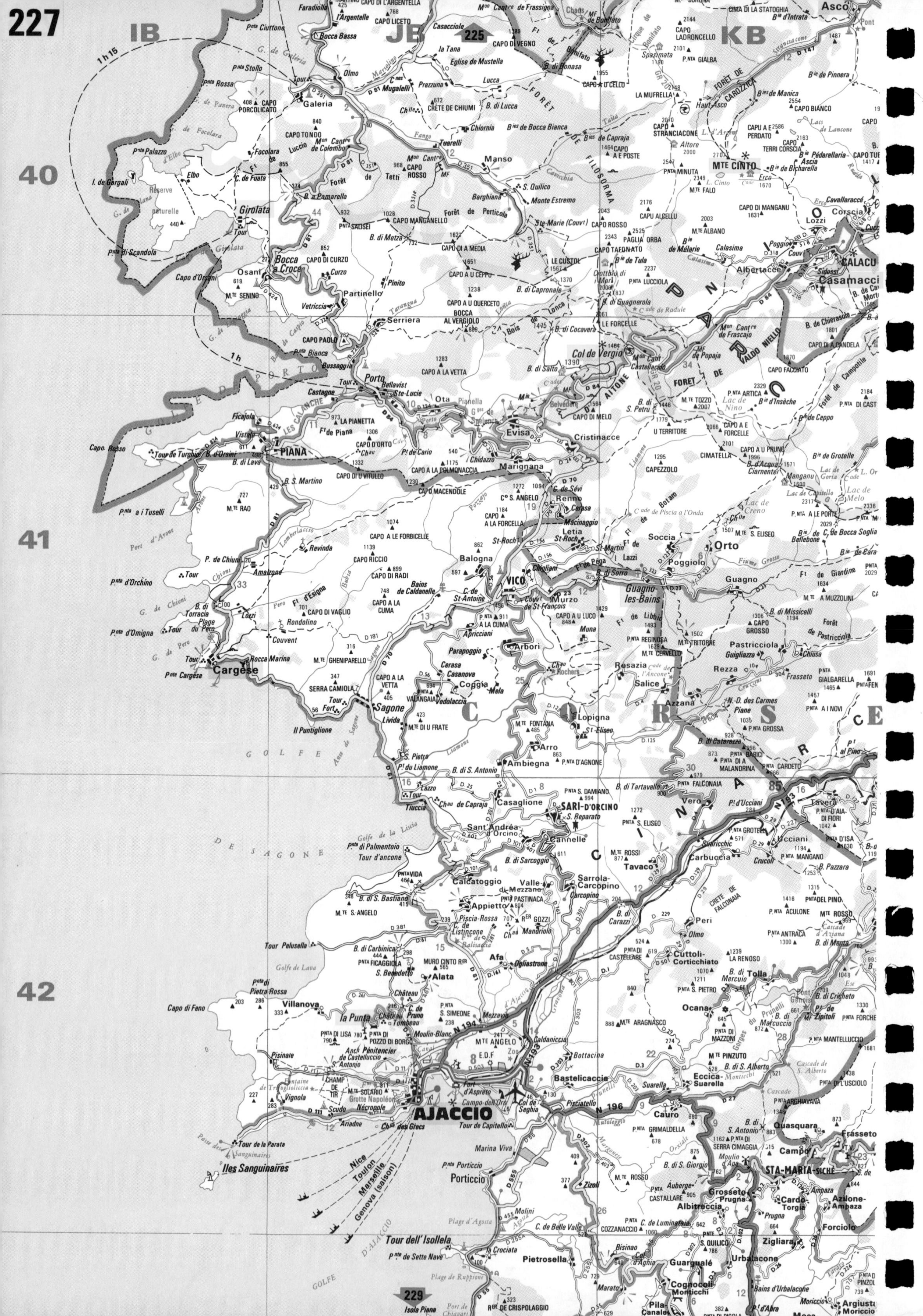
IB
JB
KB
225
40
41
42
229
Galeria
Girolata
Osani
Bocca a Croce
Partinello
Serriera
Porto
Ota
Evisa
Piana
Capo Rosso
Cargèse
Sagone
Vico
Coggia
Cristinacce
Marignana
Col de Vergio
Mte Cinto
Calacuccia
Casamaccioli
Albertacce
Lozzi
Corscia
Soccia
Orto
Poggiolo
Guagno
Guagno-les-Bains
Murzo
Letia
Renno
Balogna
Arbori
Salice
Azzana
Rezza
Pastricciola
Lopigna
Arro
Ambiegna
Casaglione
Sari-d'Orcino
Cannelle
Calcatoggio
Sarrola-Carcopino
Tavaco
Vero
Ucciani
Carbuccia
Appietto
Alata
Villanova
Afa
Peri
Cuttoli-Corticchiato
Tolla
Ocana
Ajaccio
Bastelicaccia
Eccica-Suarella
Cauro
Quasquara
Frasseto
Campo
Sta-Maria-Siché
Grosseto-Prugna
Albitreccia
Cardo-Torgia
Azilone-Ampaza
Forciolo
Zigliara
Urbalacone
Guargualé
Cognocoli-Monticchi
Pietrosella
Porticcio
Tour de la Parata
Iles Sanguinaires
Golfe de Sagone
Golfe de Lava
Golfe de Porto
Forêt de Filosorma
Forêt d'Aitone
Forêt de Valdo Niello
Forêt de Libbio
Forêt de Pastricciola
Parc
Corse
Nice
Toulon
Marseille
Genova (saison)
Isola Piana
N 193
N 194
N 196

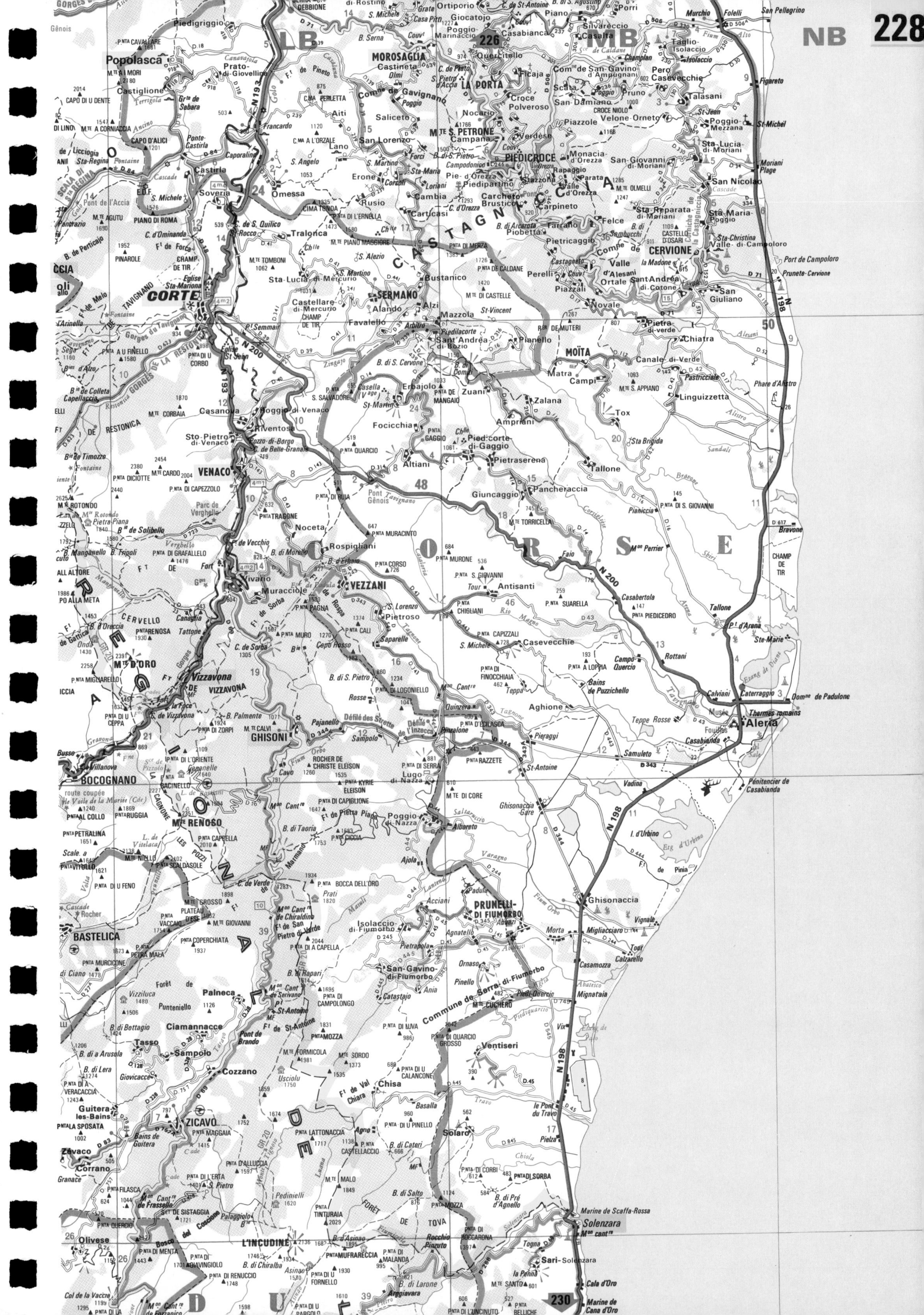

NB
228
LB
MB
Popolasca
Piedigriggio
Castiglione
Prato-di-Giovellina
Castirla
Soveria
Omessa
Morosaglia
La Porta
Piedicroce
Cervione
Corte
Sermano
Bustanico
Alando
Mazzola
Venaco
Riventosa
Poggio-di-Venaco
Casanova
Erbajolo
Focicchia
Altiani
Pietraserena
Giuncaggio
Pancheraccia
Tallone
Moïta
Zalana
Linguizzetta
Canale-di-Verde
Chiatra
Vezzani
Rospigliani
Noceta
Vivario
Muracciole
Antisanti
Casevecchie
Aghione
Aléria
Ghisoni
Vizzavona
Bocognano
Poggio-di-Nazza
Lugo-di-Nazza
Ghisonaccia
Prunelli-di-Fiumorbo
Isolaccio-di-Fiumorbo
San-Gavino-di-Fiumorbo
Serra-di-Fiumorbo
Ventiseri
Chisa
Solaro
Solenzara
Sari-Solenzara
Bastelica
Palneca
Ciamannacce
Cozzano
Zicavo
Guitera-les-Bains
Olivese
L'Incudine
CASTAGNICCIA
CORSE
RÉGION
N 193
N 200
N 198
230
226

IB
JB
KB
43
44
45
227
Tour dell' Isollela
Pietrosella
Isola Piana
Coti-Chiavari
Acqua Doria
Marmontaja
Capo di Muro
Capo Nero
Serra-di-Ferro
Porto Pollo
Filitosa
Sollacaro
OLMETO
Casalabriva
PETRETO-BICCHISANO
Propriano
Viggianello
Marseille
Toulon
(saison)
GOLFE
VALINCO
Capo Lauroso
Portigliolo
Belvédère
Campomoro
Commune de Belvédère Campomoro
SARTENE
Bilia
Grossa
Giuncheto
Granace
Arbellara
Fozzano
Sta-Maria-Figaniella
Tizzano
Cap de Zivia
Golfe de Roccapina
I. des Moines
Iles Bruzzi
Monacia-d'Aullène
N 196

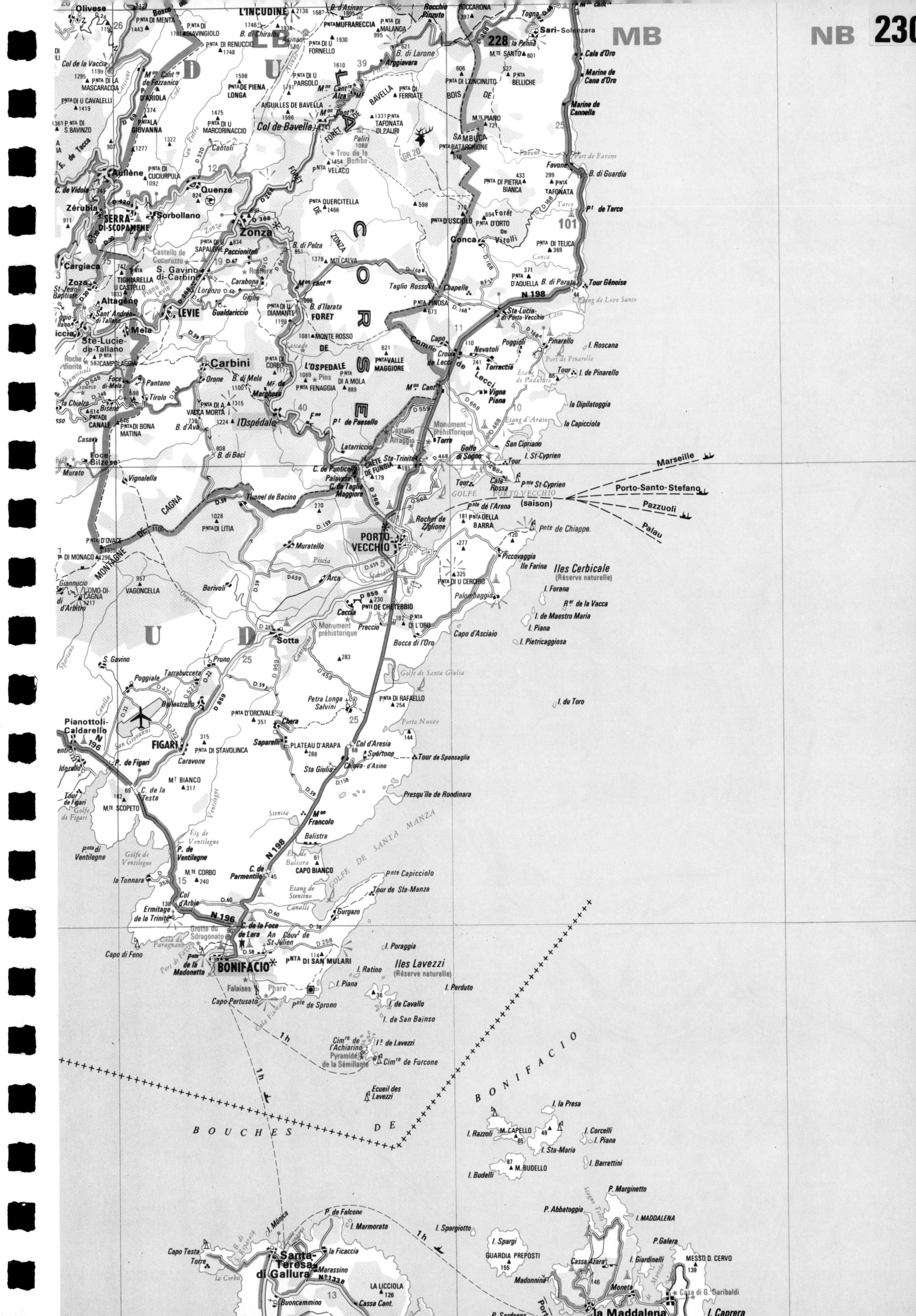
MB
NB
L'INCUDINE
Col de Bavella
AIGUILLES DE BAVELLA
Sari-Solenzara
Cala d'Oro
Marine de Cana d'Oro
Marine de Cannella
Favone
B. di Guardia
Pt de Tarco
Aullène
Quenza
Zérubia
SERRA-DI-SCOPAMENE
Sorbollano
Zonza
B. di Pelza
Conca
Cargiaca
Zoza
Altagène
S. Gavino di-Carbini
LEVIE
Carbini
Ste-Lucie-de-Tallano
Mela
Chapelle
Tour Génoise
Ste-Lucia-di-Porto-Vecchio
Pinarello
I. Roscana
I. de Pinarello
Nevatoli
Torraccia
Vigna Piana
la Dipilatoggia
la Capicciola
L'OSPEDALE
FORET
MONTE ROSSO
l'Ospédale
Pt de Paesello
Castello d'Araggio
Torre
Golfo di Sogno
San Cipriano
I. St-Cyprien
Cala Rossa
Pnte St-Cyprien
Marseille
Porto-Santo-Stefano
Pazzuoli
Palau
(saison)
GOLFE PORTO VECCHIO
Tunnel de Bacino
CAGNA
MONTAGNE DE CAGNA
PORTO-VECCHIO
Rocher de Ziglione
Pnte de l'Arena
Pnte de Chiappe
Piccovaggia
Iles Cerbicale
(Réserve naturelle)
Ile Farina
I. Forana
Rer de la Vacca
I. de Maestro Maria
I. Piana
I. Pietricaggiosa
Palombaggia
Capo d'Asciaio
Bocca di l'Oro
Muratello
Arca
Ceccia
Monument préhistorique
Sotta
Figari
Pianottoli-Caldarello
P. de Figari
Chera
Saparelli
PLATEAU D'ARAPA
Col d'Aresia
Tour de Sponsaglia
Sta Giulia
Presqu'île de Rondinara
I. du Toro
Porto Nuovo
Golfe de Santa Giulia
M. Francolo
Balistra
GOLFE DE SANTA MANZA
CAPO BIANCO
Pnte Capicciolo
Tour de Sta-Manza
P. de Ventilegne
Golfe de Ventilegne
la Tonnara
Ermitage de la Trinité
Col d'Arbia
C. de Parmentile
C. de la Foce de Lera
Gurgazo
Capo di Feno
BONIFACIO
Pnte DI SAN MULARI
Iles Lavezzi
(Réserve naturelle)
I. Ratino
I. Piana
I. Perduto
Falaises
Phare
Capo Pertusato
Pnte de Sprono
I. de Cavallo
I. de San Bainso
Cimre de l'Achiarino
Pyramide de la Sémillante
Is de Lavezzi
Cimre de Furcone
Ecueil des Lavezzi
BOUCHES DE BONIFACIO
1h
I. la Presa
I. Razzoli
M. CAPELLO
I. Corcelli
I. Piana
I. Sta-Maria
I. Barrettini
I. Budelli
M. BUDELLO
P. Marginetto
P. Abbatoggia
I. MADDALENA
P.Galera
I. Giardinelli
MESSO D. CERVO
I. Spargiotto
I. Spargi
GUARDIA PREPOSTI
Cassa Azara
Moneta
Madonnina
Casa di G. Garibaldi
la Maddalena
I. Caprera
P. Sardegna
P. de Falcone
I. Monica
I. Marmorata
Capo Testa
Torre
Santa-Teresa di Gallura
la Ficaccia
Marassino
LA LICCIOLA
Buoncammino
Cassa Cant.

banlieue de paris

ST-DENIS
LA COURNEUVE
LE BOURGET
LE BLANC-MESNIL
Drancy
Le Blanc-Mesnil
Aulnay-sous-Bois
Rougemont
LA COURNEUVE
les 4000 Nord
les 4000 Sud
Fort de l'Est
Stade de France
Aubervilliers la Courneuve
Paris-Campagne
DRANCY
Montfort
les Quatre Routes
La Courneuve 8 Mai 1945
le Pt Drancy
la Muette
le Village Parisien
Terre St-Blaise
la Poudrette
la Plaine Stade de France
AUBERVILLIERS
Fort d'Aubervilliers
les Courtillières
Avicenne
les 6 Routes
LES PAVILLONS-S/S-BOIS
la Plaine St-Denis
Cimetière Parisien de Pantin
BOBIGNY
Préfecture
Bobigny Pablo Picasso
la Fourche
la Basoche
PANTIN
Quatre-Chemins
BONDY
Pte de la Chapelle
Pte d'Aubervilliers
Pte de la Villette
Parc de la Villette
Bobigny-Pantin-Raymond Queneau
Noisy-le-Sec
Eglise de Pantin
Petit Pantin l'Avenir
les Bas Pays
ROMAINVILLE
NOISY-LE-SEC
Merlan
Pte de Pantin
Hoche
LE PRÉ-ST-GERVAIS
la Seigneurerie
Fort de Romainville
Pylônes
Fort de Noisy
C. Commercial Rosny 2
Rosny-Bois-Perrier
les Marnaudes
VILLEMON
Gare du Nord
Pte Chaumont
Robert Debré
Parc des Buttes-Chaumont
LES LILAS
Mairie des Lilas
les Grds Champs
Gare de l'Est
Pte du Pré-St-Gervais
Pte des Lilas
la Boissière
ROSNY-S/S.-BOIS
le Plateau d'Avron
St-Louis
Malassis
BAGNOLET
Fort de Rosny C.N.I.R.
Rosny-sous-Bois
Place de la République
Pte de Bagnolet
la Noue
les 7 Chemins
St-Antoine
Musée les Ruffins
NEUILLY-PLAISANCE
Gallieni
Mairie de Montreuil
Cimetière du Père-Lachaise
la Croix-de-Chavaux
MONTREUIL
PARC DES BEAUMONT
Tillemont
la Maltournée
Hôtel de Ville
Robespierre
Croix-de-Chavaux
Val-de-Fontenay
Place de la Bastille
Opéra
Pte de Montreuil
Blay Foldex
FONTENAY-S/S.-BOIS
Place de la Nation
Nation
Pte de Vincennes
VINCENNES
les Rigollots
Rond-Point du Mt-Leclerc
Château de Vincennes
Fontenay-s-Bois
Jardin des Plantes
Gare de Lyon
Bégin
Château
Fort de Vincennes
Fort de Nogent
Pte de St-Mandé
LE PERREUX-S.-MARNE
Gare d'Austerlitz
Salpêtrière
Lac de Saint-Mandé
NOGENT-S.-MARNE
P.O.P.-B.
Gare de Bercy
ST-MANDÉ
Parc Floral
Lac des Minimes
la Pitié
Musée
Pte Dorée
Sous-Préfecture
Jardin Tropical
Rocher
Zoo
Institut National des Sports
Pyramide
Pavillon Baltard
Pte de Charenton
Embarcadère
BOIS DE VINCENNES
Place d'Italie
Pte de Bercy
Lac Daumesnil
Pte de la Gare
Vélodrome
PARC DE LOISIRS DU TREMBLAY
Bd Masséna
Liberté
Hippodrome de Vincennes
Ferme G. Ville
Polangis
Golf
CHAMPIGNY-S.-MARNE
Pte de Vitry
Centre Commercial
le Plant
Pte d'Ivry
CHARENTON-LE-PONT
ST-MAURICE
Arborétum
Joinville-le-Pont
Fourchette de Champigny
Pte de Choisy
Esquirol
JOINVILLE-LE-PONT
Monument
Temple
IVRY-S.-SEINE
Mairie d'Ivry
Ivry-Port
Charentonneau
le Maroc
Cimetière
MAISONS-ALFORT
Ecole Vétérinaire
Tour
Bicêtre
Parisien Kremlin
Fort de Charenton
Maisons-Alfort Stade
KREMLIN-BICÊTRE
Pasteur
Villejuif Léo Lagrange
Charles Foix
ALFORTVILLE
le Parc-de-St-Maur
Fort de Bicêtre
Fort d'Ivry
St-Maur Créteil
le Parc
les Barmonts
les Malassis
Vitry-S.-Seine
le Port à l'Anglais
Maisons-Alfort-Alfortville
Maisons-Alfort-les-Juilliottes
Place J. Moulin
Musée
Paul-Brousse
Villejuif-Paul Vaillant-Couturier
Vert de Maisons
Créteil-l'Echat
Henri Mondor
ST-MAUR-DES-FOSSÉS
le Mn de Saquet
Centrale Thermique de Vitry
Ile St-Pierre
Temple
la Varenne-St-Hilaire
Hôpital Spécialisé
VITRY-S.-SEINE
Centrale
le Vert-de-Maisons
Université Paris XII
Chenevier
CRÉTEIL
la Pie

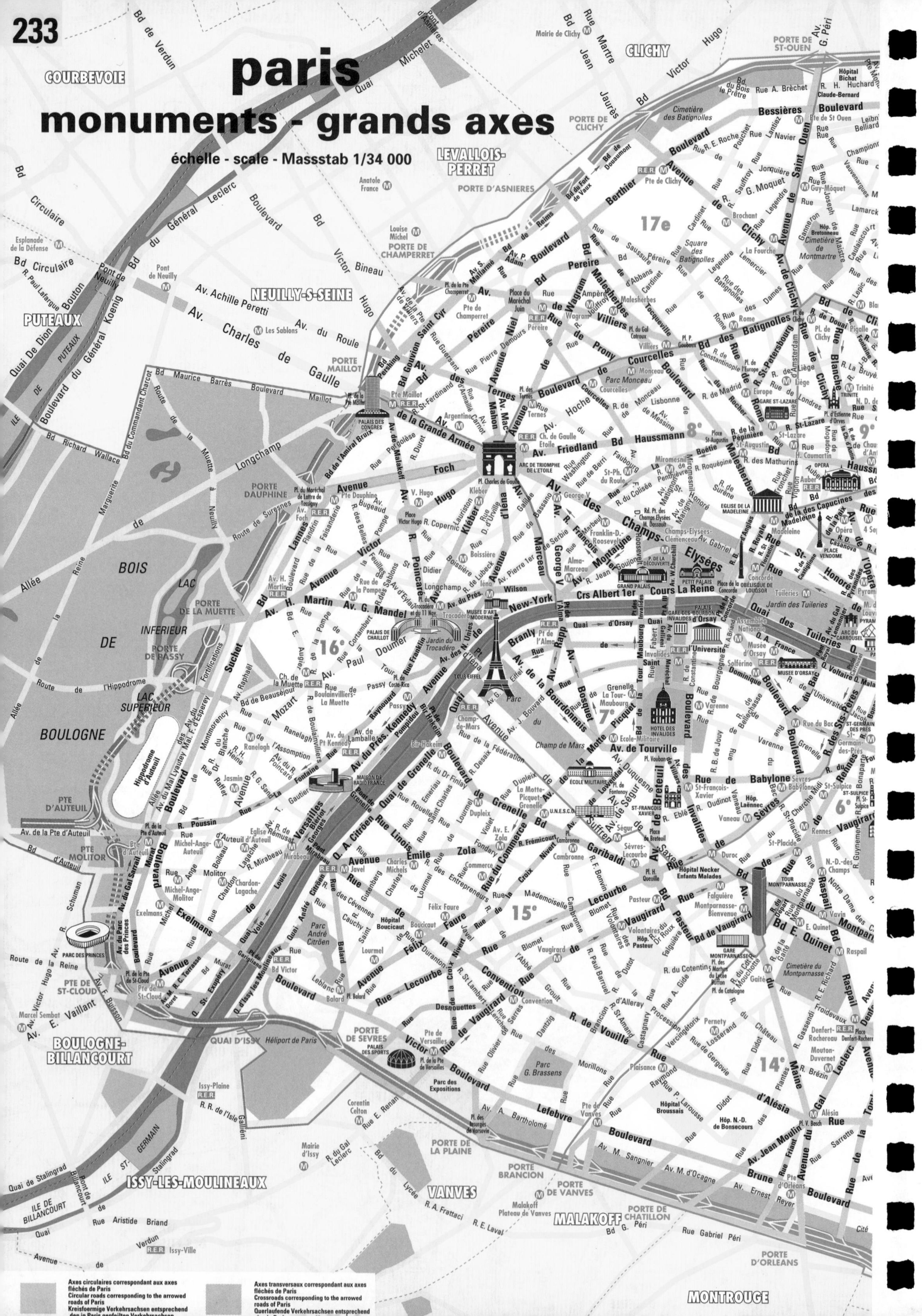
paris
monuments - grands axes
échelle - scale - Massstab 1/34 000
COURBEVOIE
PUTEAUX
LEVALLOIS-PERRET
NEUILLY-S-SEINE
CLICHY
BOIS DE BOULOGNE
BOULOGNE-BILLANCOURT
ISSY-LES-MOULINEAUX
VANVES
MALAKOFF
MONTROUGE
ILE DE BILLANCOURT
PORTE DE ST-OUEN
PORTE DE CLICHY
PORTE D'ASNIERES
PORTE DE CHAMPERRET
PORTE MAILLOT
PORTE DAUPHINE
PORTE DE LA MUETTE
PORTE DE PASSY
PTE D'AUTEUIL
PTE MOLITOR
PTE DE ST-CLOUD
PORTE DE SEVRES
PORTE DE LA PLAINE
PORTE BRANCION
PORTE DE VANVES
PORTE DE CHATILLON
PORTE D'ORLEANS
17e
8e
9e
16e
7e
6e
15e
14e
LAC INFERIEUR
LAC SUPERIEUR
Hippodrome d'Auteuil
PALAIS DES CONGRES
ARC DE TRIOMPHE DE L'ETOILE
PALAIS DE CHAILLOT
TOUR EIFFEL
MUSEE D'ART MODERNE
MAISON DE RADIO FRANCE
ECOLE MILITAIRE
U.N.E.S.C.O.
HOTEL DES INVALIDES
GRAND PALAIS
PETIT PALAIS
P. DE LA DECOUVERTE
PALAIS BOURBON
MUSEE D'ORSAY
EGLISE DE LA MADELEINE
OPERA
GARE ST-LAZARE
TOUR MONTPARNASSE
GARE MONTPARNASSE
PARC DES PRINCES
PALAIS DES SPORTS
Jardin des Tuileries
Champ de Mars
Parc Monceau
Cimetière des Batignolles
Cimetière de Montmartre
Cimetière du Montparnasse
Parc André Citroën
Parc G. Brassens
Parc des Expositions
Héliport de Paris
QUAI D'ISSY
Av. des Champs-Elysées
Av. de la Grande Armée
Av. Foch
Bd Périphérique
Axes circulaires correspondant aux axes fléchés de Paris
Circular roads corresponding to the arrowed roads of Paris
Kreisfoermige Verkehrsachsen entsprechend den in Paris gepfeilten Verkehrsachsen
Axes transversaux correspondant aux axes fléchés de Paris
Crossroads corresponding to the arrowed roads of Paris
Querlaufende Verkehrsachsen entsprechend

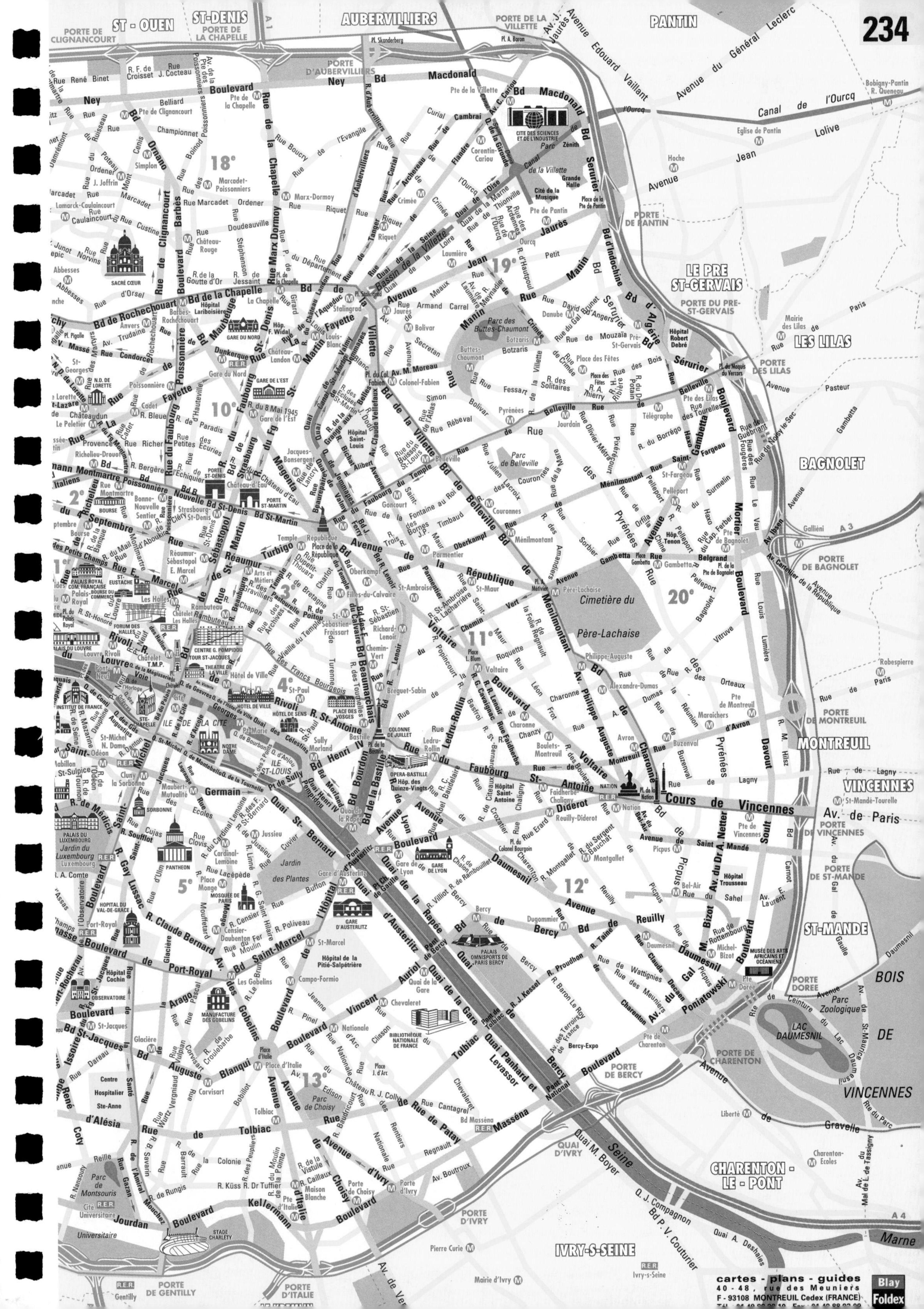

cartes - plans - guides
40 - 48, rue des Meuniers
F - 93108 MONTREUIL Cedex (FRANCE)
Blay Foldex

bordeaux
Les Chartrons
Quai des Chartrons
Croiseur Colbert
Jardin Botanique
JARDIN PUBLIC
Muséum d'Hist. Nat.
Place Longchamps
Archives Départem.
Cours de Verdun
Crs Xavier Arnozan
Musée d'Art Contemporain
Hôtel Fenwick
Bourse Maritime
Place Lainé
Allées de Chartres
ESPLANADE DES QUINCONCES
Mont des Girondins
Embarcadère Bateaux Fluv.
Quai Louis XVIII
Allées de Tourny
Cours G. Clemenceau
Place de Tourny
Palais Gallien (ruines)
Rue Fondaudège
Hôtel de Police
St-Seurin
Place des Martyrs de la Résist.
Grand Théatre
Place de la Comédie
Crs du Chapeau Rouge
Crs de l'Intendance
Place Gambetta
Pte Dijeaux
Place de la Bourse
Musée des Douanes
Quai d'Escale Paquebots
Quai Richelieu
Pte de Cailhau
Pont de Pierre
LA GARONNE
Place de Bir-Hakeim
Porte des Salinières (ou de Bourgogne)
Cours d'Alsace et Lorraine
Cathédrale St-André
Hôtel de Ville
Musée des Beaux-Arts
Tr Pey-Berland
Mériadeck
Esplanade Charles de Gaulle
Préfecture
Rue G. Bonnac
Hôtel des Postes
Cours du Mal Juin
Palais de Justice
Ec. Nat. de la Magistrature
Musée d'Aquitaine
Cours Pasteur
Cours Victor Hugo
Lycée M. Montaigne
Cours d'Albert
Hôpital St-André
Cours de la Libération
Cours Aristide Briand
Porte d'Aquitaine
Place de la Victoire
Fac. Méd. et Pharm.
Marché des Capucins
St-Michel
Quai de la Grave
Quai de la Monnaie
Porte de la Monnaie
Quai Sainte Croix
Conserv. Régional de Musique
Ec. des Bx Arts
Cours de la Marne
Lycée Technique Gustave Eiffel
Ecole de Santé des Armées
Cours de l'Argonne
Cours de la Somme
Cours de Pessac
Rue de Saint Genès
Lycée Fr. Magendie
Caserne Boudet
Grand Séminaire
Caserne St-Nicolas
Quai des Queyries
Jardin des Queyries
Caserne Niel
Chantiers Navals
H.B.M. Paul Boncour
Ancienne Gare d'Orléans
Pl. de Stalingrad

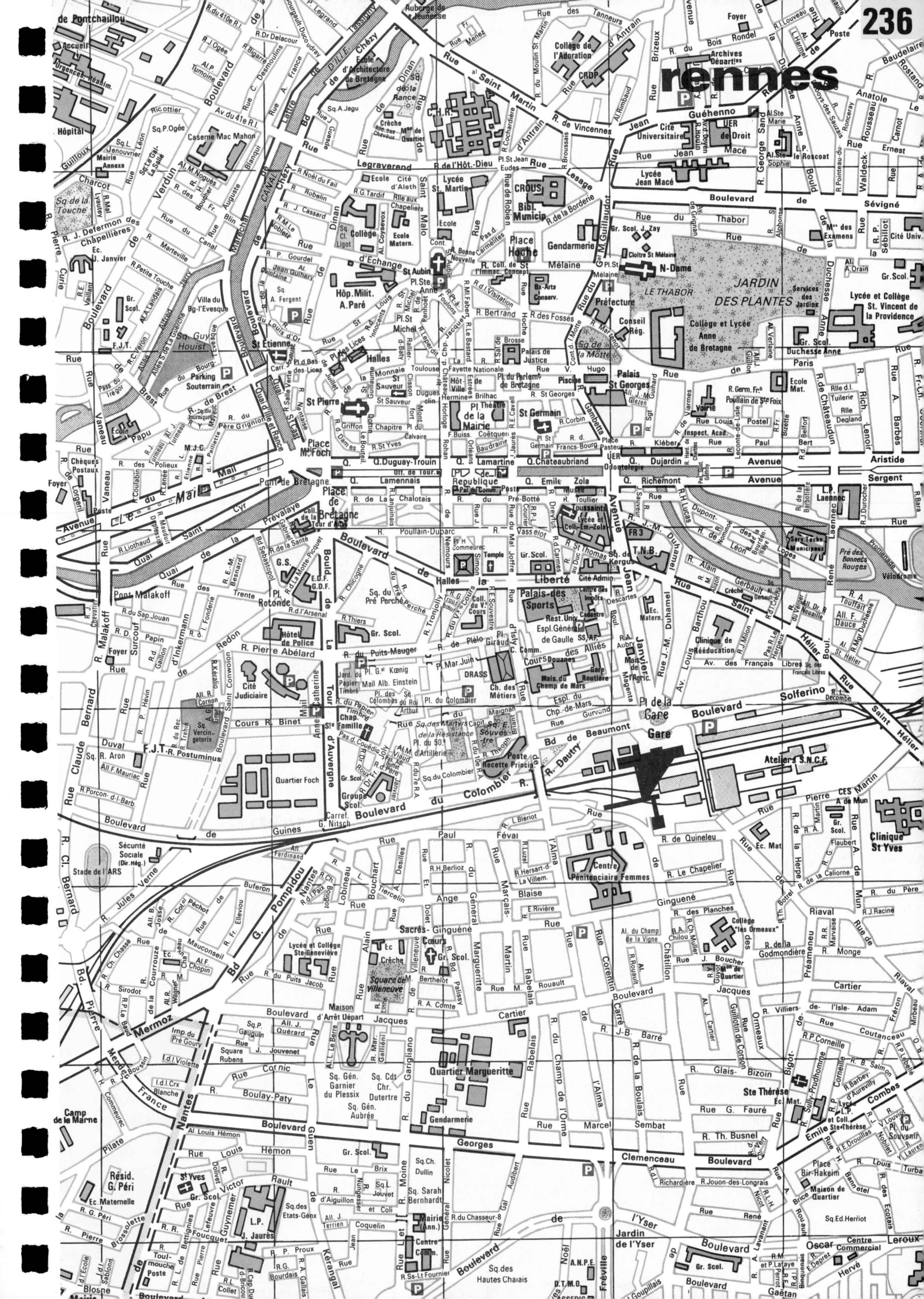
rennes
de Pontchaillou
Hôpital
Caserne Mac Mahon
Sq. de la Touche
Mairie Annexe
École d'Architecture de Bretagne
Sq. de la Rance
C.H.R.
Collège de l'Adoration
CRDP
Archives Départles
Cité Universitaire
UER de Droit
Lycée Jean Macé
Lycée St. Martin
CROUS
Bibl. Municip.
Place Hoche
Gendarmerie
Cloître St Mélaine
N-Dame
JARDIN DES PLANTES
LE THABOR
Préfecture
Conseil Rég.
Collège et Lycée Anne de Bretagne
Lycée et Collège St. Vincent de la Providence
Sq. de la Motte
Palais de Justice
Hôp. Milit. A. Paré
St Aubin
St Etienne
Sq. Guy Houist
Halles
St Sauveur
St Pierre
Pl. de la Mairie
Théâtre
St Germain
Palais St Georges
Piscine
Place Mal Foch
Q. Duguay-Trouin
Q. Lamartine
Q. Chateaubriand
Q. Dujardin
Q. Lamennais
République
Q. Emile Zola
Q. Richemont
Avenue Aristide Sergent
Pont de Bretagne
Place de Bretagne
Le Mail
Quai Saint Cyr
Pont Malakoff
Boulevard de la Liberté
Palais des Sports
Cité Judiciaire
Hôtel de Police
Sq. du Pré Perché
Cours des Alliés
Gare Routière
Mais. du Champ de Mars
DRASS
Ch. des Métiers
Sq. Vercingetorix
Quartier Foch
Boulevard de Beaumont
Gare
Ateliers S.N.C.F.
Poste Recette Princip.
Boulevard du Colombier
Boulevard Solferino
T.N.B.
Clinique de Rééducation
Vélodrome
Pré des Bonnets Rouges
Centre Pénitenciaire Femmes
Clinique St Yves
Stade de l'ARS
Sécurité Sociale
Collège "les Ormeaux"
Lycée et Collège Ste-Geneviève
Square de Villeneuve
Sacrés-Cœurs
Quartier Margueritte
Gendarmerie
Sq. Gén. Garnier du Plessix
Boulevard Georges Clemenceau
Boulevard Jacques Cartier
Ste Thérèse
Place Bir Hakeim
Camp de la Marne
Résid. G. Péri
St Yves
L.P. J. Jaurès
Jardin de l'Yser
Boulevard de l'Yser
Sq. des Hautes Chalais
Boulevard Oscar Leroux
Centre Commercial

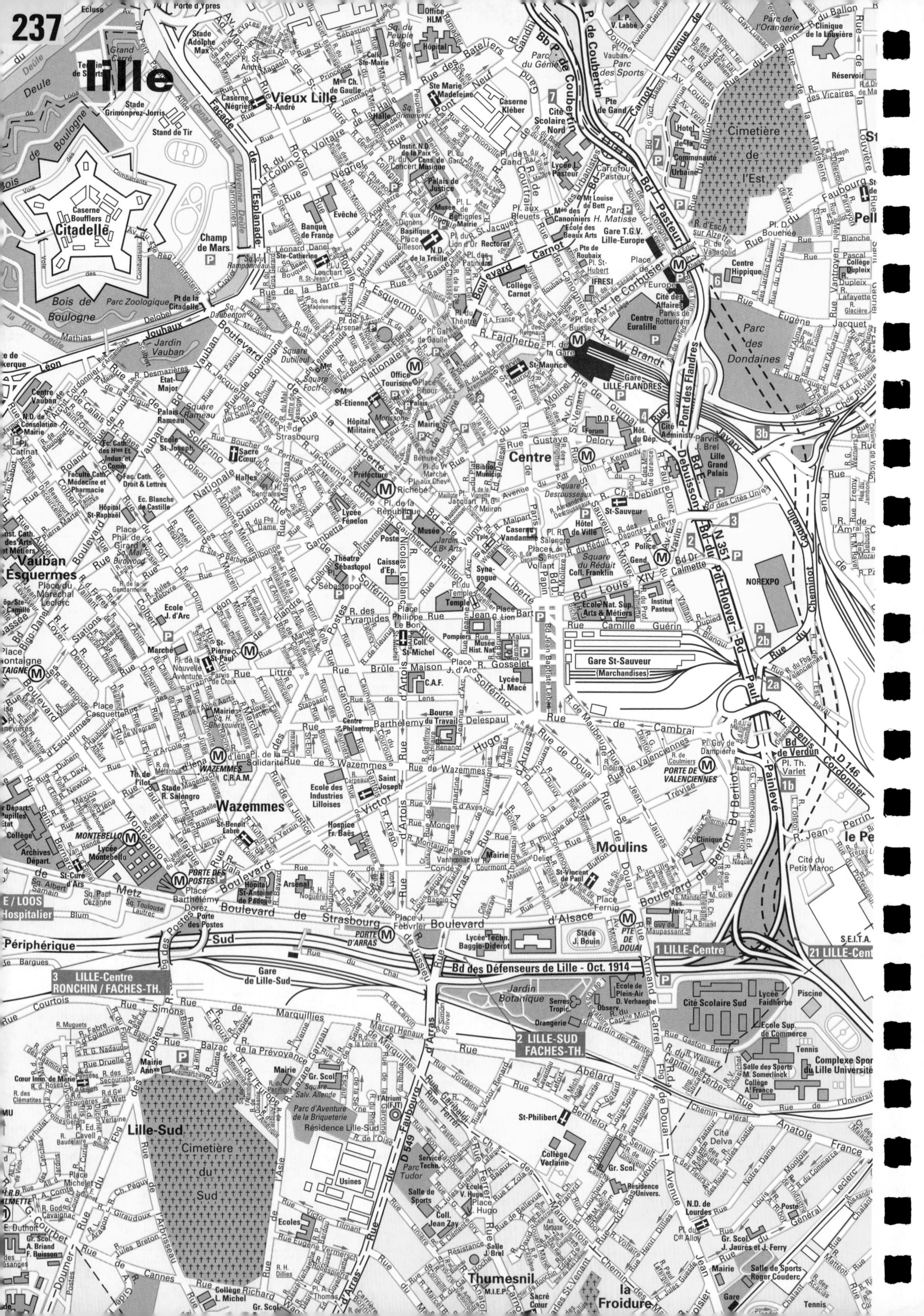
237
lille
Vieux Lille
Citadelle
Bois de Boulogne
Parc Zoologique
Jardin Vauban
Champ de Mars
Cimetière de l'Est
Parc des Dondaines
Centre
Centre Euralille
Gare T.G.V. Lille-Europe
Gare LILLE-FLANDRES
Lille Grand Palais
NOREXPO
Gare St-Sauveur (Marchandises)
Vauban Esquermes
Wazemmes
Moulins
PORTE DE VALENCIENNES
PORTE DES POSTES
PORTE D'ARRAS
PTE DE DOUAI
Périphérique
Bd des Défenseurs de Lille - Oct. 1914
Gare de Lille-Sud
Jardin Botanique
1 LILLE-Centre
2 LILLE-SUD FACHES-TH.
3 LILLE-Centre RONCHIN / FACHES-TH.
21 LILLE-Cent
Lille-Sud
Cimetière du Sud
Thumesnil
la Froidure
Boulevard de Strasbourg
Boulevard de la Liberté
Rue Nationale
Rue Solférino
Boulevard Vauban
Boulevard Carnot
Bd Louis XIV
Rue de Cambrai
Rue de Douai
D 549
D 146
N 351
Cité du Petit Maroc
Complexe Sports du Lille Université
Cité Scolaire Sud
Stade J. Bouin
Lycée Baggio-Diderot

montpellier
la Pompignane
BASSIN DE LA POMPIGNANE
LEZ
Antigone
Piscine Olympique
Aiguerelles
Résidence Plein Sud
Résidence Parc-à-Ballon
Lycée Technique Jean Mermoz
Lycée Joffre
le Polygone
Comédie
Gares
CENTRE Historique
Gambetta
les Arceaux
ESPLANADE CHARLES DE GAULLE
JARDIN DU CHAMP DE MARS
PROMENADE DU PEYROU
JARDIN DES PLANTES
Cité Mion
Cité Maury
Clos Gasc
Avenue de Palavas
Boulevard Louis Blanc
Bould Pasteur
Bould Ledru-Rollin
Cours Gambetta
Avenue Dubout
Chemin des Moulares
Hôpital Général
Gare des Marchandises
Lycée G. Clemenceau
Caserne Guilleminot
Ecole d'Application de l'Infanterie
H.L.M. Chemin des Chasseurs

nice
Echangeur de Nice-Nord
Châteauneuf
Autoroute A8
Viaduc Vallon des Fleurs
Tunnel du Cap de Croix
Tunnel de la Baume
Viaduc de la Banquière
CAP-DE-CROIX
Hôpital Psych. Ste-Marie
Monastère Ste-Claire
LE RAY
Cité Gravier
Stade Léo Lagrange
Parc Orangini
Quatre Chins
St-MAURICE
Brancolar
C.H.R. Pasteur
Abbaye de St-Pons
U.E.R. Médecine
Centre Ant. Lacassagne
Arènes
PARC PUBLIC
Musée Matisse
Monastère N.-D. de Cimiez
Thermes Romains
Faculté des Sciences
CIMIEZ
Cité Univers.
ROQUEBILLIÈRE
Gare de Marchandises
Abattoirs
Gare St-Roch
Maison d'Arrêt
Stade Munal Vauban
Caserne Riquier
Palais des Expos
Carabacel
Cons. de Musique
Musée M. Chagall
Gare de Prov.
St-ETIENNE
Gare Nice-Ville
Camp Long
"Acropolis"
Centre Comcial
Gare
RIQUIER
Castel des 2 Rois
Musée
LEP les Palmiers
Lympia
BASSIN LYMPIA
BASSIN DES AMIRAUX
BASSIN DU COMMERCE
CLUB NAUT.
Phare
Cimetière
Table d'Orientation
le Château
Tour Bellanda
Pointe Rauba Capeu
Pointe des Ponchettes
Castel Plage
Opéra Plage
Ruhl Plage
Blue Beach
Quai des Etats Unis
Anglais
la Buffa
Musée Masséna
JARDIN ALBERT Ier
ESPACE MASSENA
Lycée Masséna
Cath.
Hôtel de V.
Boulevard Gambetta
Av. Jean Médecin
Bd Victor Hugo
Boulevard Raimbaldi
Av. Malausséna
Bd Joseph Garnier
Bd de Cessole
Av. Borriglione
Bd Pasteur
Route de Turin
Av. des Diables Bleus
Bd de l'Armée des Alpes
Bd Stalingrad
Grand Sémin.
N.-D. du Perpetuel Secours

nantes
GARE DE NANTES
GARE DE L'ÉTAT
Cimetière de Miséricorde
JARDIN DES PLANTES
Cathédrale St. Pierre
Bras de la Madeleine
BEAULIEU
ÎLE - DE - NANTES
Bras de Pirmil
Hôpital Général
ST. JACQUES

toulouse
les Minimes
Gare de Raynal
le Raisin
Ateliers Municipaux
AEROSPATIALE ST-ÉLOI
Futur Hôtel du Département
Canal de Brienne
Boulevard Lascrosses
Cité Administrative
Palais des Sports
Centre Commercial Compans
Jardins
Compans Cafarelli
E.D.F. G.D.F.
Gare Routière
Gare Matabiau
MARENGO SNCF
Place Marengo
Matabiau
Place Roquelaine
Lycée St Sernin
St Sernin
Université des Sciences Sociales
Pl. J. d'Arc
Allées Jean Jaurès
JEAN JAURÈS
Boulevard de Strasbourg
Place du Capitole
CAPITOLE
H. de Ville
Théâtre
les Jacobins
Lycée Fermat
St Aubin
ENSEEIHT
Université Annexe
Hospice St Joseph de la Grave
Pont des Catalans
Chaussée du Bazacle
Pont Neuf
Hôtel Dieu St-Jacques
Musée de la Médecine
ESQUIROL
Cath St Etienne
Préfecture
Allées Fr. Verdier
GRAND ROND
Jardin Royal
St Etienne
ST-CYPRIEN RÉPUBLIQUE
Rue de la République
Av. Etienne Billères
St Cyprien
LA GARONNE
PRAIRIE DES FILTRES
Allées Jules Guesde
Jardin Botanique
Jardin des Plantes
Allées Fr. Mistral
Muséum
Grande-Rue St Michel
Place Lafourcade
le Busca
Parc et Foire Exposition
Maison des Congrès
Piscines
Hôtel Régional
Lycée d'Etat Berthelot
St Michel
Maison d'Arrêt
Jardin d'Acclimatation
Allée des Demoiselles
Pont St Michel
Pont Pierre de Coubertin
Bd des Récollets
Bd. Delacourtie
Croix-de-Pierre
I.U.F.M.
Cimetière

strasbourg

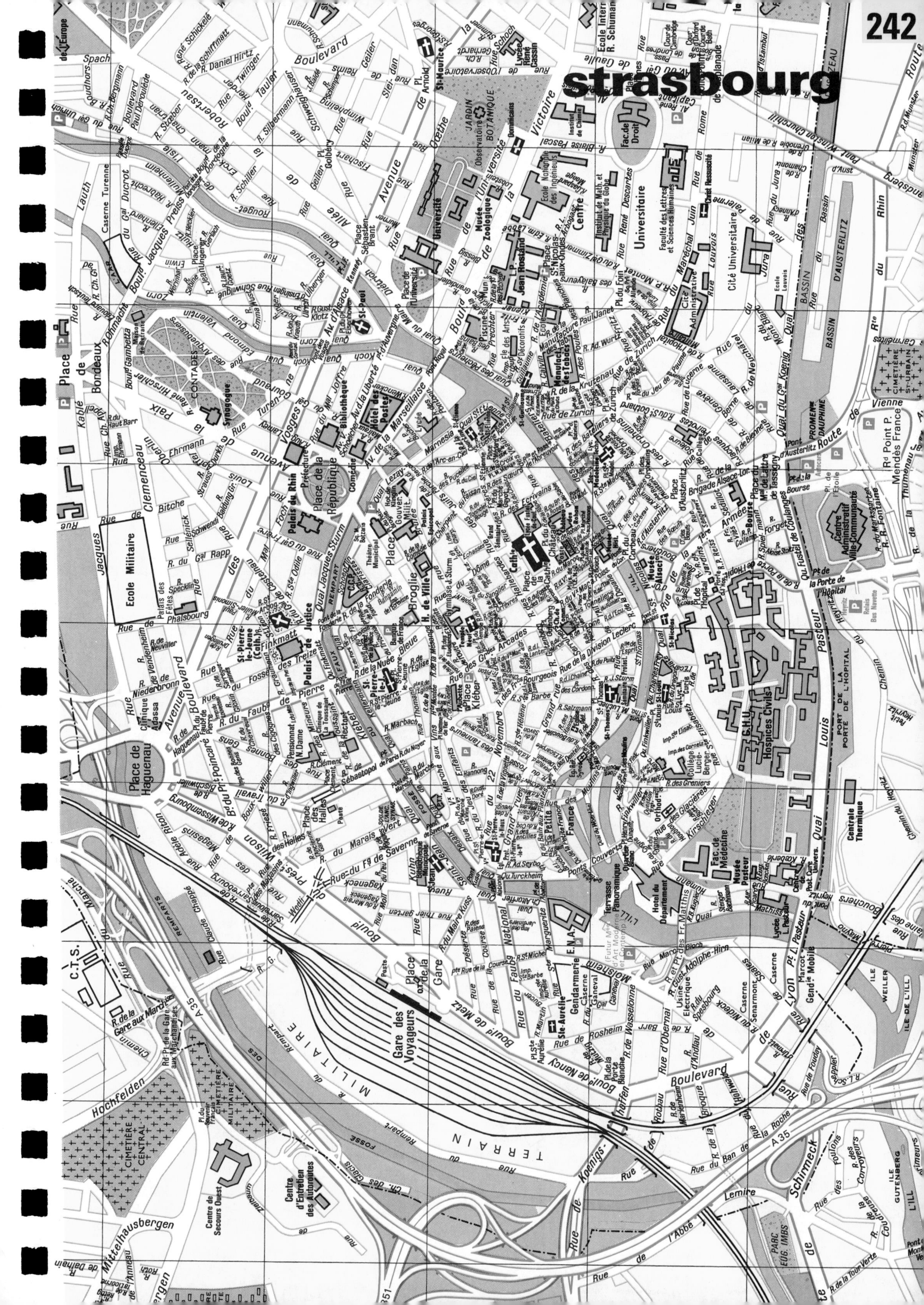

Jardin Botanique
Observatoire
Université
Musée Zoologique
Centre Universitaire
Cité Universitaire
Fac. de Droit
Institut de Chimie
Lycée René Cassin
St-Maurice
St-Paul
Place de l'Université
Place Sébastien Brant
Allée de la Robertsau
Boulevard Tauler
Avenue de la Paix
Contades
Synagogue
Place de Bordeaux
Caserne Turenne
Ecole Militaire
Palais du Rhin
Place de la République
Préfecture
Bibliothèque
Hôtel des Postes
Comédie
Théâtre Municipal
Place Broglie
H. de Ville
Cathédrale
Place de la Cathédrale
Château des Rohan
Musée Alsacien
Place Kléber
Palais de Justice
Place de Haguenau
Rue de la Division Leclerc
Grand' Rue
Rue des Grandes Arcades
Ponts Couverts
Terrasse Panoramique
Hôtel du Département
Fac. de Médecine
Musée Pasteur
C.H.U. Hospices Civils
Quai Louis Pasteur
Port de l'Hôpital
Centrale Thermique
Centre Administratif Ville-Communauté
Place d'Austerlitz
Bassin d'Austerlitz
Promenade Dauphine
Cimetière St-Urbain
Route du Rhin
Gare des Voyageurs
Place de la Gare
Terrain Militaire
Boulevard de Metz
Boulevard de Nancy
Boulevard de Lyon
Gendarmerie Caserne
Ste-Aurélie
Cimetière Central
Centre de Secours Ouest
Centre d'Entretien des Autoroutes
C.T.S.
Gare aux Marchandises
Hochfelden
Mittelhausbergen
Schirmeck
A 35
Ile Weiler
Ile de l'Ill
Ile Gutenberg
Parc Eug. Imbs
Route de Vienne
Place de l'Etoile
Rue de Rosheim
Rue de Wasselonne
Rue d'Obernai
Rue du Faubourg National
Rue du 22 Novembre
E.N.A.
Rue de l'Abbé Lemire

Lyon
LA CROIX ROUSSE
4e Ar
1er Ar
2e Ar
6e Ar
7e Ar
SERIN
FOURVIÈRE
LA SARRA
ST JUST
ST IRÉNÉE
PERRACHE
LA MOUCHE
LES BROTTEAUX
GUILLOTIÈRE
GRAND TROU
PARC DE LA TÊTE D'OR
FLEUVE
LE RHÔNE
LA SAÔNE
Place Bellecour
Place Carnot
Gare de Perrache
Gare de la Part-Dieu
Gare de la Guillotière
Gare des Brotteaux
Lycée Diderot
Jardin des Chartreux
Tunnel Routier
Théâtres Romains
Hôpital Debrousse
Caserne Sergt Blandan
Nouveau Cimetière de la Guillotière
Ancien Cimet. de la Guillotière
Fort Montluc
Hôtel de Police
Quartier Général Frère
Atelier de Construction de Lyon
Etablissement Régional du Matériel de Lyon
Marché de Gros
Stade Bouliste Ed. Herriot
Préfecture
Halles
Centre Commercial
Vélodrome
Interpol
Cours Gambetta
Cours Lafayette
Cours Vitton
Boulevard de la Croix Rousse
Avenue Berthelot
Avenue Jean Jaurès
Route de Vienne
Boulevard des Etats-Unis

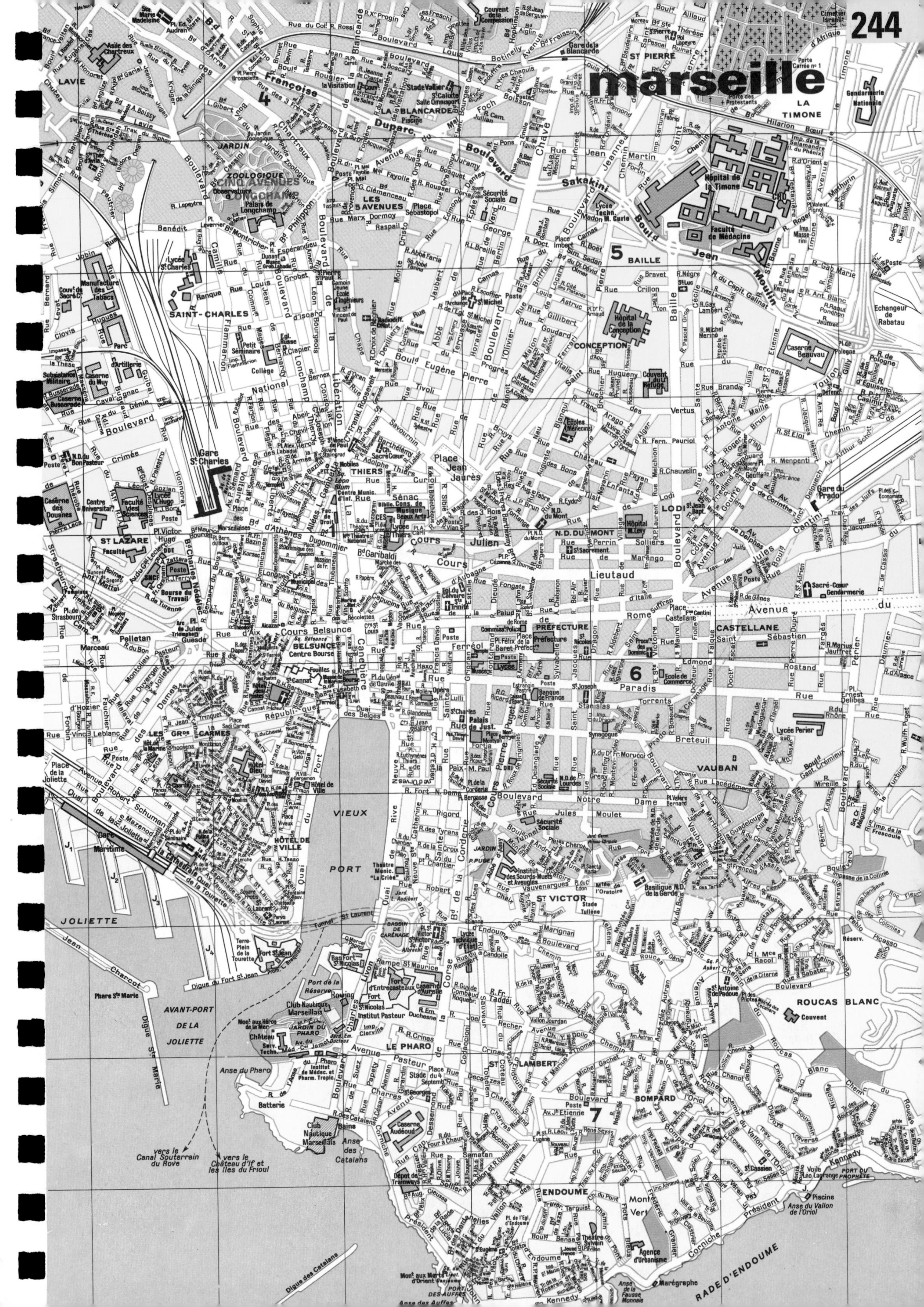
marseille
LA TIMONE
ST PIERRE
LA BLANCARDE
LAVIE
LES 5 AVENUES
SAINT-CHARLES
BAILLE
CONCEPTION
THIERS
LODI
N.D. DU MONT
PRÉFECTURE
CASTELLANE
BELSUNCE
LES GRDS CARMES
ST LAZARE
VAUBAN
HÔTEL DE VILLE
VIEUX PORT
ST VICTOR
JOLIETTE
LE PHARO
ROUCAS BLANC
BOMPARD
ENDOUME
ST LAMBERT
AVANT-PORT DE LA JOLIETTE
RADE D'ENDOUME
Gare St Charles
Gare Maritime
Hôpital de la Timone
Hôpital de la Conception
Basilique N.D. de la Garde
Fort St Jean
Fort St Nicolas
Palais de Longchamp
Jardin Zoologique
Phare Ste Marie
Digue Ste Marie
Anse des Catalans
Anse du Pharo
vers le Canal Souterrain du Rove
vers le Château d'If et les Iles du Frioul
Canebière
Cours Julien
Avenue du Prado
Boulevard Baille
Boulevard Chave
Rue de Rome
Gare du Prado
Cimetière St Pierre
Caserne Beauvau
Lycée Perier
Club Nautique Marseillais

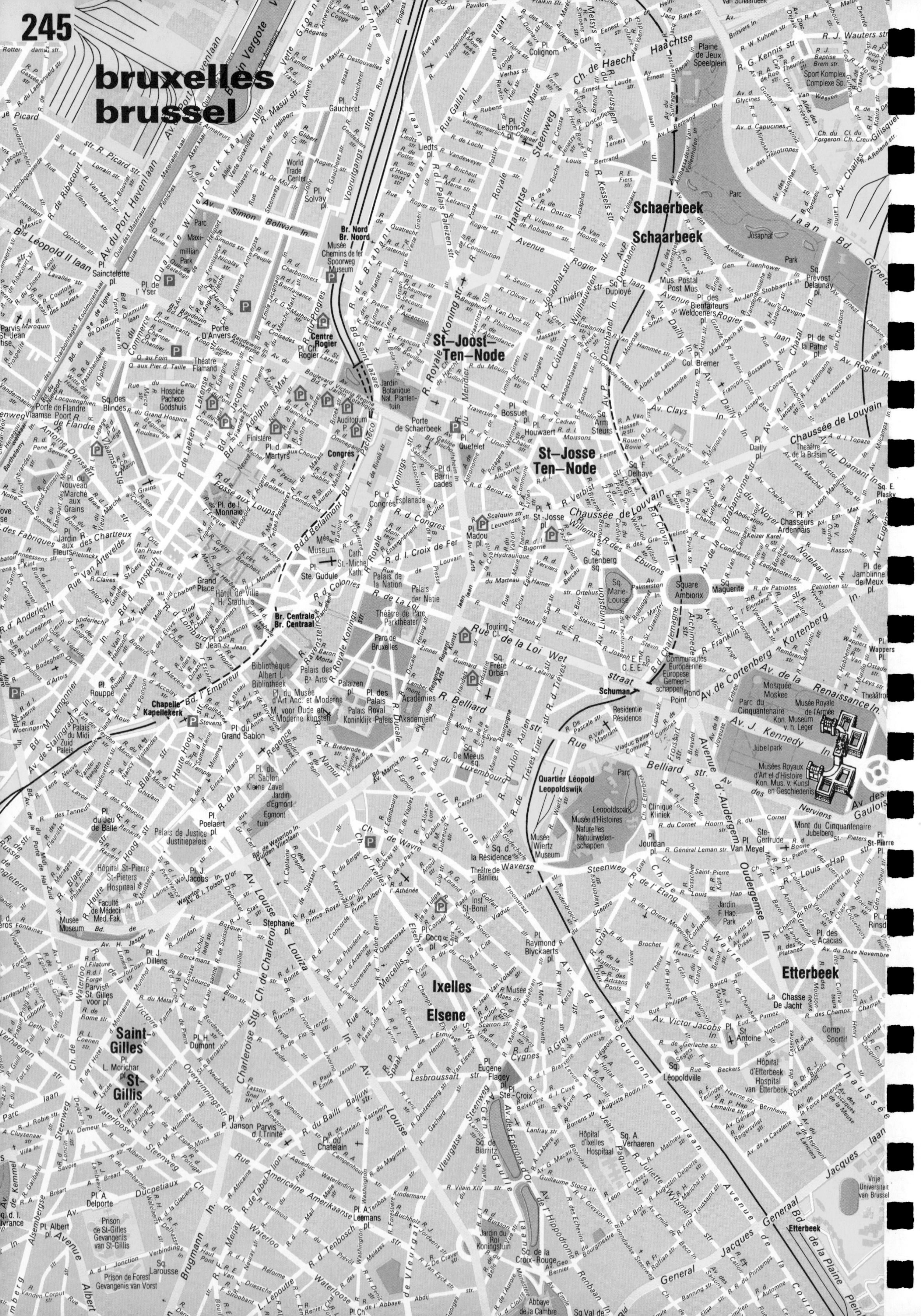
bruxelles
brussel
Schaerbeek
Schaarbeek
St-Joost-Ten-Node
St-Josse Ten-Node
Ixelles
Elsene
Saint-Gilles
St-Gillis
Etterbeek
Br. Nord
Br. Noord
Br. Centrale
Br. Centraal
Grand Place
Hôtel de Ville
H. Stadhuis
Parc de Bruxelles
Palais Royal
Koninklijk Paleis
Palais de Justice
Justitiepaleis
Square Ambiorix
Sq. Marie-Louise
Quartier Léopold
Leopoldswijk
Leopoldspark
Musée d'Histoires Naturelles
Natuurwetenschappen
Jubelpark
Parc du Cinquantenaire
Mosquée
Moskee
Musée Royale de l'Armée
Kon. Museum v.h. Leger
Musées Royaux d'Art et d'Histoire
Kon. Mus. v. Kunst en Geschiedenis
Prison de St-Gilles
Gevangenis van St-Gillis
Prison de Forest
Gevangenis van Vorst
Vrije Universiteit van Brussel
Jardin Botanique
Nat. Plantentuin
Cath. St.-Michel
Ste. Gudule
Congrès
Centre Rogier
Schuman
Rond Point
Chaussée de Louvain
Chaussée de Wavre
Avenue Louise
Louizalaan
Bd. Saint Lazare
Av. J. Kennedy
Rue de la Loi
Wetstraat
R. Belliard
Belliard str.
Josaphat Park
Plaine de Jeux
Speelplein
World Trade Center
Théâtre Flamand
Bibliothèque Albert I.
Albert I. Bibliotheek
Musée Wiertz
Hôpital St-Pierre
St-Pieters Hospitaal
Hôpital d'Etterbeek
Hôpital d'Ixelles
Pl. Eugene Flagey
Abbaye de la Cambre
Jardin du Roi
Koningstuin
Sq. de la Croix-Rouge
Pl. du Jeu de Balle
Pl. Poelaert
Pl. du Grand Sablon
Pl. du Petit Sablon
Kleine Zavel
Pl. Stephanie
Pl. Rouppe
Pl. Madou
Pl. Liedts
Pl. Colignom
Pl. Dailly
Pl. Jourdan
Sq. Léopoldville
La Chasse
De Jacht
Mont du Cinquantenaire
Jubelberg
Palais de la Nation
Palais des Beaux Arts
Théâtre de Parc
Parktheater
Porte de Schaerbeek
Porte de Flandre
Vlaamse Poort
Porte d'Anvers
Chapelle
Kapellekerk
Parvis St-Jean
Sq. Prevost Delaunay
Mus. Postal
Post Mus.
Sport Komplex
Complex Sp.

INDEX DES COMMUNES
TOWN INDEX - VERZEICHNIS DER GEMEINDEN
GEMEENTE-LIJST - INDICE DEI COMUNI

FRANCE

44	ABBARETZ	C Chef-lieu de canton	77	P 17
Département	Nom	S Sous-préfecture	Page	Coordonnées
		P Préfecture		

01 Ain
02 Aisne
03 Allier
04 Alpes-de-Haute-Provence
05 Alpes (Hautes)
06 Alpes-Maritimes
07 Ardèche
08 Ardennes
09 Ariège
10 Aube
11 Aude
12 Aveyron
13 Bouches-du-Rhône
14 Calvados
15 Cantal
16 Charente
17 Charente-Maritime
18 Cher
19 Corrèze
2A Corse du Sud
2B Corse (Haute)
21 Côte-d'Or
22 Côtes-d'Armor
23 Creuse
24 Dordogne
25 Doubs
26 Drôme
27 Eure
28 Eure-et-Loir
29 Finistère
30 Gard
31 Garonne (Haute)
32 Gers
33 Gironde
34 Hérault
35 Ille-et-Vilaine
36 Indre
37 Indre-et-Loire
38 Isère
39 Jura
40 Landes
41 Loir-et-Cher
42 Loire
43 Loire (Haute)
44 Loire-Atlantique
45 Loiret
46 Lot
47 Lot-et-Garonne
48 Lozère
49 Maine-et-Loire
50 Manche
51 Marne
52 Marne (Haute)
53 Mayenne
54 Meurthe-et-Moselle
55 Meuse
56 Morbihan
57 Moselle
58 Nièvre
59 Nord
60 Oise
61 Orne
62 Pas-de-Calais
63 Puy-de-Dôme
64 Pyrénées-Atlantiques
65 Pyrénées (Hautes)
66 Pyrénées-Orientales
67 Rhin (Bas)
68 Rhin (Haut)
69 Rhône
70 Saône (Haute)
71 Saône-et-Loire
72 Sarthe
73 Savoie
74 Savoie (Haute)
75 Paris
76 Seine-Maritime
77 Seine-et-Marne
78 Yvelines
79 Deux-Sèvres
80 Somme
81 Tarn
82 Tarn-et-Garonne
83 Var
84 Vaucluse
85 Vendée
86 Vienne
87 Vienne (Haute)
88 Vosges
89 Yonne
90 Belfort (Territoire de)
91 Essonne
92 Hauts-de-Seine
93 Seine-Saint-Denis
94 Val-de-Marne
95 Val-d'Oise

A

Dép.	Nom		Page		
4	AAST		208	W	36
55	ABAINVILLE		67	VA	13
59	ABANCOURT		18	KA	5
60	ABANCOURT		25	EA	8
54	ABAUCOURT		46	YA	11
5	ABAUCOURT HAUTECOURT		45	VA	10
5	ABBANS DESSOUS		106	WA	19
25	ABBANS DESSUS		106	WA	19
44	ABBARETZ		94	P	17
02	ABBECOURT		27	KA	8
60	ABBECOURT		26	GA	9
5	ABBENANS		107	ZA	17
0	ABBEVILLE	S	15	EA	6
1	ABBEVILLE LA RIVIERE		61	GA	14
54	ABBEVILLE LES CONFLANS		45	WA	10
60	ABBEVILLE ST LUCIEN		26	GA	8
25	ABBEVILLERS		108	BB	18
34	ABEILHAN		214	LA	35
0	ABELCOURT		88	YA	16
4	ABERE		207	V	36
01	ABERGEMENT CLEMENCIAT, L'		137	SA	23
71	ABERGEMENT DE CUISERY, L'		121	SA	21
01	ABERGEMENT DE VAREY, L'		138	UA	24
39	ABERGEMENT LA RONCE		105	UA	19
9	ABERGEMENT LE GRAND		122	VA	20
9	ABERGEMENT LE PETIT		122	VA	20
9	ABERGEMENT LES THESY		123	XA	20
71	ABERGEMENT STE COLOMBE, L'		121	SA	21
64	ABIDOS		207	T	36
37	ABILLY		114	Z	20
4	ABITAIN		206	S	36
4	ABJAT SUR BANDIAT		144	AA	26
62	ABLAIN ST NAZAIRE		17	IA	5
80	ABLAINCOURT PRESSOIR		27	JA	7
62	ABLAINZEVELLE		17	IA	6
51	ABLANCOURT		43	QA	12
5	ABLEIGES		39	FA	10
8	ABLEUVENETTES, LES		68	YA	14
8	ABLIS		61	EA	13
14	ABLON		23	X	9
94	ABLON SUR SEINE		40	HA	12
42	ABOEN		149	OA	27
54	ABONCOURT		67	XA	14
7	ABONCOURT		46	YA	10
0	ABONCOURT GESINCOURT		88	XA	16
57	ABONCOURT SUR SEILLE		46	YA	12
74	ABONDANCE	C	140	AB	23
28	ABONDANT		38	CA	12
64	ABOS		207	U	36
57	ABRESCHVILLER		69	CB	12
3	ABREST		133	LA	24
8	ABRETS, LES		152	VA	26
05	ABRIES		168	BB	29
59	ABSCON		18	LA	5
79	ABSIE, L'		111	U	21
16	ABZAC		130	Z	24
3	ABZAC		156	V	28
5	ACCOLANS		107	ZA	17
9	ACCOLAY		84	NA	17
07	ACCONS		164	QA	29
64	ACCOUS	C	215	T	37
57	ACHAIN		47	ZA	11
7	ACHEN		48	CB	11
7	ACHENHEIM		70	EB	13
8	ACHERES		101	HA	18
78	ACHERES		39	FA	11
77	ACHERES LA FORET		62	IA	14
02	ACHERY		28	LA	8
80	ACHEUX EN AMIENOIS	C	17	HA	6
0	ACHEUX EN VIMEU		15	EA	6
2	ACHEVILLE		17	JA	5
0	ACHEY		87	VA	17
62	ACHICOURT		17	IA	5
62	ACHIET LE GRAND		17	JA	6
62	ACHIET LE PETIT		17	IA	6
58	ACHUN		103	MA	19
0	ACHY		25	FA	8
5	ACIGNE		76	P	15
27	ACLOU		37	Z	10
27	ACON		38	BA	12
62	ACQ		17	IA	5
14	ACQUEVILLE		36	U	11
0	ACQUEVILLE		33	O	8
7	ACQUIGNY		38	BA	10
2	ACQUIN WESTBECOURT		7	GA	3
02	ACY		28	LA	9
60	ACY EN MULTIEN		41	JA	10
08	ACY ROMANCE		29	PA	9
57	ADAINCOURT		47	ZA	11
8	ADAINVILLE		39	EA	12
25	ADAM LES PASSAVANT		107	YA	18
25	ADAM LES VERCEL		107	YA	19
67	ADAMSWILLER		48	CB	11
65	ADAST		216	W	37
65	ADE		216	W	37
57	ADELANGE		47	AB	11
70	ADELANS ET LE VAL DE BITHAINE		89	ZA	16
65	ADERVIELLE POUCHERGUES		216	Y	38
79	ADILLY		112	V	21
62	ADINFER		17	IA	5
34	ADISSAN		214	LA	35
16	ADJOTS, LES		129	X	24
45	ADON		82	JA	16
38	ADRETS, LES		153	XA	27
83	ADRETS DE L'ESTEREL, LES		198	AB	35
86	ADRIERS		130	AA	23
2A	AFA		227	JB	42
19	AFFIEUX		145	EA	26
54	AFFLEVILLE		45	WA	10
69	AFFOUX		136	QA	25
54	AFFRACOURT		68	XA	13
62	AFFRINGUES		7	FA	3
31	AGASSAC		209	AA	36
34	AGDE	C	214	LA	36
34	AGEL		213	JA	36
47	AGEN	P	172	Z	32
12	AGEN D'AVEYRON		175	IA	31
21	AGENCOURT		105	SA	19
80	AGENVILLE		16	FA	6
80	AGENVILLERS		16	FA	5
60	AGEUX, LES		26	IA	9
52	AGEVILLE		66	UA	15
21	AGEY		104	RA	18
2B	AGHIONE		228	MB	41
54	AGINCOURT		46	YA	12
47	AGME		171	Y	31
47	AGNAC		172	Y	30
43	AGNAT		148	LA	27
50	AGNEAUX		34	R	10
60	AGNETZ		26	HA	9
62	AGNEZ LES DUISANS		17	IA	5
02	AGNICOURT ET SECHELLES		28	OA	8
62	AGNIERES		17	IA	5
05	AGNIERES EN DEVOLUY		167	WA	30
38	AGNIN		151	SA	27
64	AGNOS		215	T	37
62	AGNY		17	IA	5
50	AGON COUTAINVILLE		34	P	11
24	AGONAC		144	Z	27
34	AGONES		192	NA	33
03	AGONGES		118	KA	21
65	AGOS VIDALOS		215	W	37
16	AGRIS		143	Y	25
17	AGUDELLE		142	U	27
12	AGUESSAC		176	KA	32
02	AGUILCOURT		29	OA	9
81	AGUTS		211	FA	35
14	AGY		35	T	10
64	AHAXE ALCIETTE BASCASSAN		206	R	37
64	AHETZE		205	P	36
88	AHEVILLE		68	YA	14
53	AHUILLE		77	S	15
23	AHUN	C	132	FA	24
21	AHUY		105	SA	18
59	AIBES		19	OA	5
25	AIBRE		89	AB	17
64	AICIRITS CAMOU SUHAST		206	S	36
79	AIFFRES		128	U	23
30	AIGALIERS		193	PA	33
61	AIGLE, L'	C	37	Z	12
08	AIGLEMONT		29	RA	7
39	AIGLEPIERRE		122	WA	20
27	AIGLEVILLE		38	CA	11
04	AIGLUN		197	XA	33
06	AIGLUN		200	BB	34
32	AIGNAN	C	186	X	34
21	AIGNAY LE DUC	C	85	RA	17
34	AIGNE		213	IA	36
72	AIGNE		78	X	15
14	AIGNERVILLE		35	S	9
31	AIGNES		210	DA	36
16	AIGNES ET PUYPEROUX		143	X	26
80	AIGNEVILLE		15	DA	6
51	AIGNY		43	PA	11
79	AIGONNAY		128	V	23
16	AIGRE	C	129	W	25
31	AIGREFEUILLE		210	DA	35
17	AIGREFEUILLE D'AUNIS	C	127	S	24
44	AIGREFEUILLE SUR MAINE	C	110	Q	19
30	AIGREMONT		193	OA	33
52	AIGREMONT		87	WA	15
78	AIGREMONT		39	FA	11
89	AIGREMONT		84	NA	16
73	AIGUEBELETTE LE LAC		152	WA	26
73	AIGUEBELLE	C	153	YA	26
73	AIGUEBLANCHE		153	ZA	26
81	AIGUEFONDE		212	GA	35
63	AIGUEPERSE	C	134	KA	24
69	AIGUEPERSE		136	OA	23
09	AIGUES JUNTES		219	DA	37
30	AIGUES MORTES	C	194	PA	35
09	AIGUES VIVES		219	EA	37
11	AIGUES VIVES		212	HA	36
30	AIGUES VIVES		193	PA	34
34	AIGUES VIVES		213	JA	36
30	AIGUEZE		179	QA	32
43	AIGUILHE		163	NA	28
05	AIGUILLES	C	168	BB	30
47	AIGUILLON		171	Y	32
09	AIGUILLON, L'		221	FA	38
85	AIGUILLON SUR MER, L'		125	O	23
85	AIGUILLON SUR VIE, L'		109	O	21
83	AIGUINES		197	YA	34
36	AIGURANDE	C	132	EA	22
07	AILHON		178	PA	30
45	AILLANT SUR MILLERON		82	JA	16
89	AILLANT SUR THOLON	C	83	LA	16
33	AILLAS		171	W	31
42	AILLEUX		149	OA	25
70	AILLEVANS		89	ZA	17
10	AILLEVILLE		65	RA	14
70	AILLEVILLERS ET LYAUMONT		88	YA	16
52	AILLIANVILLE		67	UA	14
72	AILLIERES BEAUVOIR		59	X	13
73	AILLON LE JEUNE		153	XA	26
73	AILLON LE VIEUX		153	XA	26
70	AILLONCOURT		89	ZA	16
27	AILLY		38	CA	10
80	AILLY LE HAUT CLOCHER	C	16	FA	6
80	AILLY SUR NOYE	C	26	HA	7
80	AILLY SUR SOMME		16	GA	7
30	AIMARGUES	C	194	PA	34
73	AIME	C	154	AB	26
03	AINAY LE CHATEAU		117	IA	21
18	AINAY LE VIEIL		117	HA	21
64	AINCILLE		206	R	37
95	AINCOURT		39	EA	10
55	AINCREVILLE		30	TA	9
54	AINGERAY		45	XA	12
88	AINGEVILLE		67	WA	14
52	AINGOULAINCOURT		66	UA	13
64	AINHARP		206	S	36
64	AINHICE MONGELOS		206	R	36
64	AINHOA		205	P	36
70	AINVELLE		88	YA	16
88	AINVELLE		87	WA	15
80	AIRAINES		16	FA	6
14	AIRAN		36	W	10
08	AIRE		29	PA	9
40	AIRE SUR L'ADOUR	C	185	V	34
62	AIRE SUR LA LYS	C	8	HA	3
50	AIREL		34	R	10
34	AIRES, LES		213	KA	35
60	AIRION		26	HA	9
62	AIRON NOTRE DAME		15	DA	4
62	AIRON ST VAAST		15	EA	4
11	AIROUX		211	EA	36
79	AIRVAULT	C	112	W	20
21	AISEREY		105	TA	19
70	AISEY ET RICHECOURT		88	XA	16
21	AISEY SUR SEINE		85	RA	16
02	AISONVILLE ET BERNOVILLE		18	MA	7
25	AISSEY		107	YA	18
21	AISY SOUS THÍL		104	PA	18
89	AISY SUR ARMANCON		85	PA	17
2B	AITI		228	LB	40
73	AITON		153	YA	26
19	AIX		146	HA	26
59	AIX		18	LA	4
18	AIX D'ANGILLON, LES	C	101	HA	19
26	AIX EN DIOIS		166	UA	30
62	AIX EN ERGNY		7	FA	4
62	AIX EN ISSART		16	EA	4
10	AIX EN OTHE	C	64	NA	14
13	AIX EN PROVENCE	S	202	VA	35
63	AIX LA FAYETTE		148	MA	26
73	AIX LES BAINS	C	152	WA	25
62	AIX NOULETTE		17	IA	4
87	AIXE SUR VIENNE	C	144	BA	25
07	AIZAC		164	PA	30
52	AIZANVILLE		66	SA	15
36	AIZE		99	EA	19
80	AIZECOURT LE BAS		17	KA	6
80	AIZECOURT LE HAUT		17	JA	6
02	AIZELLES		28	NA	9
85	AIZENAY		110	P	21
27	AIZIER		23	Z	9
02	AIZY JOUY		28	MA	9
11	AJAC		221	GA	37
2A	AJACCIO	P	227	JB	42
23	AJAIN		132	FA	23
24	AJAT		158	BA	28
57	AJONCOURT		46	YA	11
27	AJOU		37	AA	11
07	AJOUX		164	OA	30
11	ALAIGNE	C	221	FA	37
02	ALAINCOURT		28	LA	7
70	ALAINCOURT		88	XA	15
57	ALAINCOURT LA COTE		46	YA	11
11	ALAIRAC		221	GA	37
31	ALAN		209	AA	36
2B	ALANDO		228	LB	40
2A	ALATA		227	JB	42
07	ALBA LA ROMAINE		179	QA	30
81	ALBAN	C	190	HA	33
48	ALBARET LE COMTAL		162	KA	29
48	ALBARET STE MARIE		162	LA	29
11	ALBAS		223	IA	37
46	ALBAS		173	CA	31
67	ALBE		70	DB	14
82	ALBEFEUILLE LAGARDE		188	CA	33
38	ALBENC, L'		152	UA	27
73	ALBENS	C	152	WA	25
15	ALBEPIERRE BREDONS		161	JA	28
66	ALBERE, L'		224	JA	40
80	ALBERT	C	17	IA	6
2B	ALBERTACCE		227	KB	40
73	ALBERTVILLE	S	153	ZA	26
57	ALBESTROFF	C	47	BB	11
81	ALBI	P	189	GA	33
31	ALBIAC		211	EA	35
46	ALBIAC		160	EA	30
82	ALBIAS		188	DA	33
11	ALBIERES		221	HA	38
09	ALBIES		220	EA	38
73	ALBIEZ LE JEUNE		153	YA	27
73	ALBIEZ MONTROND		167	YA	28
19	ALBIGNAC		159	EA	28
69	ALBIGNY SUR SAONE		137	SA	25
81	ALBINE		212	HA	35
2A	ALBITRECCIA		227	KB	42
07	ALBON		164	QA	29
26	ALBON		151	SA	27
07	ALBOUSSIERE		164	RA	29
12	ALBRES, LES		175	GA	31
19	ALBUSSAC		159	EA	28
74	ALBY SUR CHERAN	C	139	XA	25
64	ALCAY ALCABEHETY SUNHARETTE		206	S	37
64	ALDUDES		205	O	37
62	ALEMBON		7	EA	3
61	ALENCON	P	58	X	13
66	ALENYA		224	JA	39
2B	ALERIA		228	MB	41
30	ALES	S	178	OA	32
11	ALET LES BAINS		221	GA	37
62	ALETTE		7	EA	4
09	ALEU		219	CA	38
74	ALEX		139	YA	25
53	ALEXAIN		57	T	14
26	ALEYRAC		179	SA	31
94	ALFORTVILLE	C	40	HA	12
2B	ALGAJOLA		225	JB	39
81	ALGANS		211	EA	35
68	ALGOLSHEIM		90	EB	15
57	ALGRANGE	C	32	XA	9
39	ALIEZE		122	VA	21
34	ALIGNAN DU VENT		214	LA	35
08	ALINCOURT		29	PA	9
62	ALINCTHUN		7	EA	3
21	ALISE STE REINE		85	QA	17
07	ALISSAS		179	RA	30
69	ALIX		136	RA	24
26	ALIXAN		165	SA	29
27	ALIZAY		24	BA	9
54	ALLAIN		67	WA	13
80	ALLAINES		17	JA	6
28	ALLAINES MERVILLIERS		61	FA	14
28	ALLAINVILLE		38	CA	12
78	ALLAINVILLE		61	FA	13
56	ALLAIRE	C	93	M	17
54	ALLAMONT		45	WA	10
54	ALLAMPS		67	WA	13
26	ALLAN		179	RA	31
15	ALLANCHE	C	161	JA	27
08	ALLAND'HUY ET SAUSSEUIL		29	OA	8
88	ALLARMONT		69	BB	13
17	ALLAS BOCAGE		142	U	27
17	ALLAS CHAMPAGNE		142	V	26
24	ALLAS LES MINES		158	BA	29
19	ALLASSAC		159	DA	27
13	ALLAUCH	C	202	VA	36
30	ALLEGRE		178	PA	32
43	ALLEGRE	C	163	NA	28
13	ALLEINS		196	TA	34
04	ALLEMAGNE EN PROVENCE		197	XA	34
51	ALLEMANCHE LAUNAY ET SOYER		64	NA	12
24	ALLEMANS		143	Y	27
47	ALLEMANS DU DROPT		171	X	30
02	ALLEMANT		28	MA	9
51	ALLEMANT		42	NA	12
38	ALLEMOND		167	XA	28
80	ALLENAY		15	DA	6
48	ALLENC		177	MA	31
25	ALLENJOIE		89	BB	17
59	ALLENNES LES MARAIS		9	JA	4
67	ALLENWILLER		49	DB	12
21	ALLEREY		104	QA	19
71	ALLEREY SUR SAONE		121	SA	20
71	ALLERIOT		121	SA	20
80	ALLERY		16	EA	6
24	ALLES SUR DORDOGNE		158	AA	29
49	ALLEUDS, LES		96	U	18
79	ALLEUDS, LES		129	W	23
08	ALLEUX, LES		30	RA	9
15	ALLEUZE		162	KA	29
38	ALLEVARD	C	153	XA	27
74	ALLEVES		153	XA	25
26	ALLEX		165	SA	30
43	ALLEYRAC		163	OA	29
43	ALLEYRAS		163	NA	29
19	ALLEYRAT		146	GA	26
23	ALLEYRAT		132	GA	24
47	ALLEZ ET CAZENEUVE		172	Z	31
51	ALLIANCELLES		44	SA	12
09	ALLIAT		219	DA	38
10	ALLIBAUDIERES		64	OA	13
52	ALLICHAMPS		66	SA	13
65	ALLIER		216	X	37
09	ALLIERES		218	CA	37
25	ALLIES, LES		124	ZA	20
58	ALLIGNY COSNE		102	KA	18
58	ALLIGNY EN MORVAN		103	PA	19
22	ALLINEUC		54	J	14
74	ALLINGES		139	ZA	23
18	ALLOGNY		100	GA	19
25	ALLONDANS		89	AB	17
73	ALLONDAZ		153	YA	25
54	ALLONDRELLE LA MALMAISON		31	VA	8
60	ALLONNE		26	FA	9
79	ALLONNE		112	U	21
28	ALLONNES		61	DA	14
49	ALLONNES	C	97	W	18
72	ALLONNES	C	78	X	15
04	ALLONS		198	ZA	33
47	ALLONS		171	W	32
80	ALLONVILLE		16	HA	7
74	ALLONZIER LA CAILLE		139	XA	24
04	ALLOS		182	AB	32
62	ALLOUAGNE		8	HA	4
16	ALLOUE		129	Y	24
18	ALLOUIS		100	GA	19
76	ALLOUVILLE BELLEFOSSE		24	Z	8
73	ALLUES, LES		154	ZA	27
78	ALLUETS LE ROI, LES		39	FA	11
58	ALLUY		103	MA	19
28	ALLUYES		60	CA	14
15	ALLY		160	GA	28
43	ALLY		162	LA	28
81	ALMAYRAC		175	GA	32
61	ALMENECHES		58	X	12
12	ALMONT LES JUNIES		175	GA	30
09	ALOS		218	BA	38
81	ALOS		189	EA	33
64	ALOS SIBAS ABENSE		206	S	37
21	ALOXE CORTON		105	SA	19
12	ALPUECH		161	JA	30
62	ALQUINES		7	FA	3
12	ALRANCE		175	IA	32
57	ALSTING		47	BB	10
2A	ALTAGENE		230	KB	43
67	ALTECKENDORF		49	EB	12
68	ALTENACH		90	CB	17
67	ALTENHEIM		49	DB	12
84	ALTHEN DES PALUDS		195	SA	33
2B	ALTIANI		228	LB	41
48	ALTIER		177	NA	31
19	ALTILLAC		160	EA	29
68	ALTKIRCH	S	90	CB	17
67	ALTORF		70	EB	13
57	ALTRIPPE		47	AB	11
57	ALTVILLER		47	AB	10
67	ALTWILLER		47	BB	11
71	ALUZE		120	RA	20
46	ALVIGNAC		159	EA	29
76	ALVIMARE		23	Z	8
09	ALZEN		219	DA	37
2B	ALZI		228	LB	40
57	ALZING		47	ZA	10
30	ALZON	C	192	LA	33
11	ALZONNE	C	212	GA	36
70	AMAGE		89	ZA	16
08	AMAGNE		29	QA	8
25	AMAGNEY		107	XA	18

79 AMAILLOUX 112 V 21
10 AMANCE 65 QA 14
54 AMANCE 46 YA 12
70 AMANCE C 88 XA 16
25 AMANCEY C 107 XA 19
74 AMANCY 139 YA 24
39 AMANGE 106 VA 19
35 AMANLIS 76 P 15
55 AMANTY 67 VA 13
57 AMANVILLERS 45 XA 10
71 AMANZE 135 PA 23
01 AMAREINS FRANCHELEINS
CESSEINS 137 SA 24
81 AMARENS 189 FA 33
25 AMATHAY VESIGNEUX 107 YA 20
14 AMAYE SUR ORNE 35 U 10
14 AMAYE SUR SEULLES 35 T 10
58 AMAZY 102 MA 18
88 AMBACOURT 68 XA 14
33 AMBARES ET LAGRAVE 156 U 29
31 AMBAX 209 AA 36
87 AMBAZAC C 131 CA 24
38 AMBEL 167 WA 29
27 AMBENAY 37 Z 11
16 AMBERAC 129 W 25
01 AMBERIEU EN BUGEY C 138 UA 24
69 AMBERIEUX 136 RA 24
01 AMBERIEUX EN DOMBES 137 SA 24
16 AMBERNAC 129 Y 24
86 AMBERRE 113 X 21
63 AMBERT S 149 NA 26
33 AMBES 156 U 28
12 AMBEYRAC 174 FA 31
81 AMBIALET 190 HA 33
2A AMBIEGNA 227 JB 41
42 AMBIERLE 135 NA 24
70 AMBIEVILLERS 88 XA 15
37 AMBILLOU 97 Y 18
49 AMBILLOU CHATEAU 96 V 18
74 AMBILLY 139 YA 23
60 AMBLAINVILLE 39 FA 10
70 AMBLANS ET VELOTTE 89 ZA 17
02 AMBLENY 27 KA 9
01 AMBLEON 152 VA 25
62 AMBLETEUSE 7 DA 3
16 AMBLEVILLE 142 V 26
95 AMBLEVILLE 39 EA 10
14 AMBLIE 35 U 9
08 AMBLIMONT 30 TA 8
41 AMBLOY 79 AA 16
08 AMBLY FLEURY 29 QA 9
55 AMBLY SUR MEUSE 44 UA 11
37 AMBOISE C 98 BA 18
56 AMBON 92 L 17
26 AMBONIL 165 SA 29
51 AMBONNAY 43 PA 10
52 AMBONVILLE 66 SA 14
36 AMBRAULT 116 FA 21
81 AMBRES 189 EA 34
62 AMBRICOURT 16 GA 4
02 AMBRIEF 28 LA 9
51 AMBRIERES 65 SA 12
53 AMBRIERES LES VALLEES C 57 T 13
62 AMBRINES 17 HA 5
01 AMBRONAY 138 UA 24
19 AMBRUGEAT 146 FA 26
76 AMBRUMESNIL 24 AA 7
47 AMBRUS 171 X 32
01 AMBUTRIX 138 UA 24
27 AMECOURT 25 EA 9
55 AMEL SUR L'ETANG 45 VA 10
57 AMELECOURT 47 ZA 11
66 AMELIE LES BAINS PALALDA 224 IA 40
64 AMENDEUIX ONEIX 206 R 36
54 AMENONCOURT 69 AB 12
95 AMENUCOURT 39 DA 10
62 AMES 8 HA 4
62 AMETTES 8 HA 4
71 AMEUGNY 120 RA 22
88 AMEUVELLE 88 XA 15
14 AMFREVILLE 36 V 10
50 AMFREVILLE 33 Q 9
27 AMFREVILLE LA CAMPAGNE C 37 AA 10
76 AMFREVILLE LA MI VOIE 24 BA 9
27 AMFREVILLE LES CHAMPS 24 CA 9
76 AMFREVILLE LES CHAMPS 24 AA 8
27 AMFREVILLE SOUS LES MONTS 24 CA 9
27 AMFREVILLE SUR ITON 38 BA 10
59 AMFROIPRET 19 NA 5
80 AMIENS P 16 GA 7
02 AMIFONTAINE 29 OA 9
50 AMIGNY 34 R 10
02 AMIGNY ROUY 28 LA 8
77 AMILLIS 41 KA 12
28 AMILLY 60 CA 13
45 AMILLY C 82 IA 15
42 AMIONS 135 OA 25
06 AMIRAT 198 AB 33
68 AMMERSCHWIHR 69 DB 15
68 AMMERZWILLER 90 CB 17
72 AMNE 78 W 15
57 AMNEVILLE 32 XA 10
70 AMONCOURT 88 XA 16
25 AMONDANS 107 XA 19
70 AMONT ET EFFRENEY 89 ZA 16
64 AMOROTS SUCCOS 206 R 36
40 AMOU C 184 T 35
21 AMPILLY LE SEC 85 QA 16
21 AMPILLY LES BORDES 85 RA 17
69 AMPLEPUIS C 136 PA 24
62 AMPLIER 16 HA 6
53 AMPOIGNE 77 S 16
77 AMPONVILLE 62 HA 14
2B AMPRIANI 228 MB 41
69 AMPUIS 150 RA 26
83 AMPUS 203 YA 35
79 AMURE 127 T 23
60 AMY 27 JA 8
16 ANAIS 129 X 24
17 ANAIS 127 S 23
31 ANAN 209 AA 36
64 ANCE 206 T 37
76 ANCEAUMEVILLE 24 BA 8
61 ANCEINS 37 Y 11
05 ANCELLE 181 YA 30
55 ANCEMONT 44 UA 10
44 ANCENIS S 94 R 18
55 ANCERVILLE C 66 SA 12
57 ANCERVILLE 47 ZA 11
54 ANCERVILLER 69 BB 13
21 ANCEY 105 SA 18
08 ANCHAMPS 20 RA 7
37 ANCHE 97 X 19
86 ANCHE 129 X 23
70 ANCHENONCOURT ET CHAZEL 88 XA 16
02 ANCIENVILLE 41 KA 10
70 ANCIER 106 VA 18
72 ANCINNES 58 X 14

65 ANCIZAN 216 Y 38
63 ANCIZES COMPS, LES 133 JA 24
26 ANCONE 179 RA 30
76 ANCOURT 24 BA 7
76 ANCOURTEVILLE
SUR HERICOURT 23 Z 8
76 ANCRETIEVILLE ST VICTOR 24 AA 8
76 ANCRETTEVILLE SUR MER 23 Y 7
50 ANCTEVILLE 34 Q 10
14 ANCTOVILLE 35 T 10
50 ANCTOVILLE SUR BOSCQ 56 P 11
69 ANCY 136 OA 25
89 ANCY LE FRANC C 85 PA 16
89 ANCY LE LIBRE 84 OA 16
57 ANCY SUR MOSELLE 45 XA 10
80 ANDAINVILLE 25 EA 7
07 ANDANCE 150 RA 27
26 ANDANCETTE 150 RA 27
49 ANDARD 96 U 18
27 ANDE 38 CA 10
80 ANDECHY 27 IA 8
22 ANDEL 54 L 13
02 ANDELAIN 28 LA 8
03 ANDELAROCHE 135 NA 23
70 ANDELARRE 88 XA 17
70 ANDELARROT 88 XA 17
15 ANDELAT 162 KA 28
90 ANDELNANS 89 BB 17
52 ANDELOT BLANCHEVILLE C 66 UA 14
39 ANDELOT EN MONTAGNE 123 XA 20
39 ANDELOT MORVAL 122 UA 22
78 ANDELU 39 EA 11
27 ANDELYS, LES S 38 DA 10
55 ANDERNAY 44 SA 12
33 ANDERNOS LES BAINS 155 R 30
54 ANDERNY 31 WA 9
01 ANDERT ET CONDON 152 VA 25
60 ANDEVILLE 39 GA 10
49 ANDIGNE 77 T 17
81 ANDILLAC 189 FA 33
17 ANDILLY 125 R 23
54 ANDILLY 45 WA 12
74 ANDILLY 139 XA 24
95 ANDILLY 40 GA 11
52 ANDILLY EN BASSIGNY 87 VA 15
47 ANDIRAN 186 X 33
67 ANDLAU 70 DB 13
64 ANDOINS 207 V 36
68 ANDOLSHEIM C 90 DB 15
06 ANDON 198 AB 34
45 ANDONVILLE 61 FA 14
70 ANDORNAY 89 ZA 17
53 ANDOUILLE 77 T 14
35 ANDOUILLE NEUVILLE 76 P 14
81 ANDOUQUE 190 GA 33
64 ANDREIN 206 S 36
62 ANDRES 7 FA 2
65 ANDREST 208 W 36
78 ANDRESY C 39 FA 11
49 ANDREZE 95 S 19
77 ANDREZEL 62 JA 12
42 ANDREZIEUX BOUTHEON 149 PA 26
89 ANDRYES 83 MA 17
30 ANDUZE C 193 OA 33
65 ANERES 217 Y 37
28 ANET C 38 DA 11
44 ANETZ 94 R 18
64 ANGAIS 207 V 36
41 ANGE 99 CA 18
16 ANGEAC CHAMPAGNE 142 V 26
16 ANGEAC CHARENTE 142 W 26
08 ANGECOURT 30 SA 8
16 ANGEDUC 142 W 26
89 ANGELY 84 OA 17
90 ANGEOT 90 BB 17
49 ANGERS P 95 U 18
14 ANGERVILLE 36 W 10
91 ANGERVILLE 61 FA 14
76 ANGERVILLE BAILLEUL 23 Y 8
76 ANGERVILLE L'ORCHER 23 X 8
27 ANGERVILLE LA CAMPAGNE 38 BA 11
76 ANGERVILLE LA MARTEL 23 Y 7
91 ANGERVILLIERS 61 FA 13
82 ANGEVILLE 187 BA 33
57 ANGEVILLERS 32 XA 9
50 ANGEY 56 Q 12
60 ANGICOURT 26 HA 9
76 ANGIENS 24 AA 7
70 ANGIREY 106 WA 18
60 ANGIVILLERS 26 HA 9
33 ANGLADE 156 T 28
15 ANGLARDS DE SALERS 161 HA 28
15 ANGLARDS DE ST FLOUR 162 KA 29
46 ANGLARS 160 EA 30
46 ANGLARS JUILLAC 173 BA 31
46 ANGLARS NOZAC 159 CA 29
12 ANGLARS ST FELIX 175 GA 31
01 ANGLEFORT 138 WA 24
88 ANGLEMONT 68 AB 13
04 ANGLES 198 ZA 33
81 ANGLES C 212 HA 35
85 ANGLES 125 Q 22
30 ANGLES, LES 195 RA 33
65 ANGLES, LES 216 W 37
66 ANGLES, LES 222 FA 39
19 ANGLES SUR CORREZE, LES 146 EA 27
86 ANGLES SUR L'ANGLIN 114 AA 21
76 ANGLESQUEVILLE L'ESNEVAL 23 X 8
76 ANGLESQUEVILLE
LA BRAS LONG 24 Z 7
64 ANGLET C 205 P 35
17 ANGLIERS 127 S 23
86 ANGLIERS 113 X 20
51 ANGLURE C 64 NA 13
71 ANGLURE SOUS DUN 136 PA 23
51 ANGLUZELLES ET COURCELLES 64 NA 12
24 ANGOISSE 144 BA 27
54 ANGOMONT 69 BB 13
65 ANGOS 216 X 37
16 ANGOULEME P 143 X 26
17 ANGOULINS 126 R 24
40 ANGOUME 183 R 34
64 ANGOUS 206 T 36
66 ANGOUSTRINE VILLENEUVE
DES ESCALDES 222 FA 40
14 ANGOVILLE 36 U 11
50 ANGOVILLE AU PLAIN 34 R 9
50 ANGOVILLE SUR AY 34 P 10
62 ANGRES 17 IA 4
40 ANGRESSE 183 O 34
49 ANGRIE 95 S 17
14 ANGUERNY 36 U 9
02 ANGUILCOURT LE SART 28 LA 8
60 ANGY 26 HA 9
64 ANHAUX 205 Q 37
59 ANHIERS 18 KA 4
34 ANIANE C 192 MA 34
59 ANICHE 18 LA 5

14 ANISY 36 U 10
02 ANIZY LE CHATEAU C 28 MA 8
70 ANJEUX 88 YA 16
38 ANJOU 151 SA 27
36 ANJOUIN 99 EA 19
90 ANJOUTEY 89 BB 16
65 ANLA 217 Z 37
58 ANLEZY 118 MA 20
24 ANLHIAC 144 BA 27
58 ANNAY 83 JA 17
62 ANNAY 17 JA 4
89 ANNAY LA COTE 84 NA 17
89 ANNAY SUR SEREIN 84 OA 16
14 ANNEBAULT 36 W 10
74 ANNECY P 139 YA 24
74 ANNECY LE VIEUX C 139 XA 24
08 ANNELLES 29 QA 9
74 ANNEMASSE C 139 YA 23
89 ANNEOT 84 NA 17
17 ANNEPONT 127 T 25
62 ANNEQUIN 8 IA 4
24 ANNESSE ET BEAULIEU 157 Z 28
77 ANNET SUR MARNE 40 IA 11
59 ANNEUX 18 KA 6
76 ANNEVILLE AMBOURVILLE 24 AA 9
50 ANNEVILLE EN SAIRE 33 Q 8
52 ANNEVILLE LA PRAIRIE 66 TA 14
50 ANNEVILLE SUR MER 34 P 10
76 ANNEVILLE SUR SCIE 24 BA 7
26 ANNEYRON 151 SA 27
17 ANNEZAY 127 T 24
62 ANNEZIN 8 IA 4
59 ANNOEULLIN 9 JA 4
39 ANNOIRE 121 UA 20
02 ANNOIS 27 KA 8
38 ANNOISIN CHATELANS 151 UA 25
18 ANNOIX 117 HA 20
07 ANNONAY C 150 RA 27
52 ANNONVILLE 66 UA 13
04 ANNOT C 198 AB 33
76 ANNOUVILLE VILMESNIL 23 Y 8
89 ANNOUX 84 OA 17
50 ANNOVILLE 34 P 11
59 ANOR 19 OA 6
64 ANOS 207 V 36
71 ANOST 103 OA 19
88 ANOULD 69 BB 14
54 ANOUX 45 WA 10
64 ANOYE 208 W 36
76 ANQUETIERVILLE 23 Z 8
52 ANROSEY 87 VA 16
16 ANSAC SUR VIENNE 130 Z 24
60 ANSACQ 26 HA 9
32 ANSAN 187 AA 34
54 ANSAUVILLE 45 WA 12
60 ANSAUVILLERS 26 HA 8
69 ANSE C 136 RA 24
60 ANSERVILLE 39 GA 10
66 ANSIGNAN 222 HA 38
65 ANSOST 208 X 35
84 ANSOUIS 196 UA 34
59 ANSTAING 9 KA 4
47 ANTAGNAC 171 W 31
15 ANTERRIEUX 162 KA 29
25 ANTEUIL 107 ZA 18
17 ANTEZANT LA CHAPELLE 128 U 24
47 ANTHE 173 AA 31
54 ANTHELUPT 68 ZA 12
51 ANTHENAY 42 NA 10
08 ANTHENY 29 PA 7
21 ANTHEUIL 104 RA 19
60 ANTHEUIL PORTES 27 IA 9
58 ANTHIEN 103 NA 18
38 ANTHON 151 TA 25
74 ANTHY SUR LEMAN 139 ZA 22
06 ANTIBES C 200 CB 35
65 ANTICHAN 217 Z 37
31 ANTICHAN DE FRONTIGNES 217 Z 38
15 ANTIGNAC 147 HA 27
31 ANTIGNAC 217 Z 38
85 ANTIGNY 111 T 21
86 ANTIGNY 114 AA 22
21 ANTIGNY LA VILLE 104 QA 19
57 ANTILLY 46 YA 10
60 ANTILLY 41 JA 10
65 ANTIN 208 X 36
2B ANTISANTI 228 MB 41
65 ANTIST 216 X 37
37 ANTOGNY LE TILLAC 113 Z 20
49 ANTOIGNE 96 W 19
61 ANTOIGNY 58 V 13
63 ANTOINGT 148 KA 26
05 ANTONAVES 181 WA 32
24 ANTONNE ET TRIGONANT 158 AA 28
92 ANTONY S 40 GA 12
07 ANTRAIGUES SUR VOLANE C 164 OA 30
35 ANTRAIN C 56 P 13
86 ANTRAN 113 Y 20
09 ANTRAS 217 AA 38
32 ANTRAS 186 Y 34
48 ANTRENAS 176 LA 30
11 ANTUGNAC 221 GA 38
71 ANTULLY 120 QA 20
76 ANVEVILLE 24 Z 8
16 ANVILLE 128 W 25
62 ANVIN 16 GA 4
02 ANY MARTIN RIEUX 29 PA 7
63 ANZAT LE LUGUET 147 KA 27
57 ANZELING 47 ZA 10
23 ANZEME 132 EA 23
47 ANZEX 171 X 32
59 ANZIN C 18 MA 5
62 ANZIN ST AUBIN 17 IA 5
71 ANZY LE DUC 135 OA 23
38 AOSTE 152 VA 26
51 AOUGNY 42 NA 10
08 AOUSTE 29 PA 7
26 AOUSTE SUR SYE 165 TA 30
88 AOUZE 67 WA 13
57 APACH 32 ZA 9
63 APCHAT 148 KA 27
15 APCHON 161 IA 27
42 APINAC 149 OA 27
81 APPELLE 211 FA 35
61 APPENAI SOUS BELLEME 59 Z 14
25 APPENANS 107 ZA 18
68 APPENWIHR 90 DB 15
50 APPEVILLE 34 O 9
27 APPEVILLE ANNEBAULT 23 Z 9
2A APPIETTO 227 JB 42
60 APPILLY 27 KA 8
89 APPOIGNY 83 MA 16
38 APPRIEU 152 VA 27
09 APPY 219 EA 38
01 APREMONT 138 VA 23
08 APREMONT 44 SA 10
60 APREMONT 40 HA 10
70 APREMONT 106 VA 18

73 APREMONT 153 XA 26
85 APREMONT 109 O 21
55 APREMONT LA FORET 45 VA 11
18 APREMONT SUR ALLIER 118 KA 20
52 APREY 86 TA 16
84 APT S 196 UA 33
09 ARABAUX 219 DA 37
74 ARACHES 140 AB 24
65 ARAGNOUET 216 X 38
11 ARAGON 212 GA 36
64 ARAMITS C 206 T 37
30 ARAMON C 195 RA 33
01 ARANC 138 VA 24
64 ARANCOU 206 R 35
01 ARANDAS 138 VA 25
38 ARANDON 152 UA 25
64 ARAUJUZON 206 S 36
43 ARAULES 163 PA 28
64 ARAUX 206 T 36
33 ARBANATS 156 U 30
31 ARBAS 217 AA 37
70 ARBECEY 88 XA 16
2A ARBELLARA 229 KB 43
01 ARBENT 138 VA 23
65 ARBEOST 215 V 37
64 ARBERATS SILLEGUE 206 S 36
01 ARBIGNIEU 152 VA 25
01 ARBIGNY 121 SA 22
52 ARBIGNY SOUS VARENNES 87 VA 16
73 ARBIN 153 XA 26
33 ARBIS 170 V 30
32 ARBLADE LE BAS 185 V 34
32 ARBLADE LE HAUT 185 W 34
39 ARBOIS C 122 WA 20
31 ARBON 217 Z 37
64 ARBONNE 205 P 35
77 ARBONNE LA FORET 62 IA 13
34 ARBORAS 192 MA 34
2A ARBORI 227 JB 41
52 ARBOT 86 SA 16
25 ARBOUANS 108 AB 17
40 ARBOUCAVE 207 U 35
64 ARBOUET SUSSAUTE 206 S 36
58 ARBOURSE 102 KA 18
66 ARBOUSSOLS 222 HA 39
69 ARBRESLE, L' C 136 RA 25
35 ARBRISSEL 76 Q 15
64 ARBUS 207 U 36
74 ARBUSIGNY 139 YA 24
52 ARC EN BARROIS C 65 SA 15
25 ARC ET SENANS 106 WA 19
70 ARC LES GRAY 106 VA 18
25 ARC SOUS CICON 107 YA 19
25 ARC SOUS MONTENOT 123 XA 20
21 ARC SUR TILLE 105 TA 18
33 ARCACHON C 169 R 30
79 ARCAIS 127 T 23
46 ARCAMBAL 174 DA 31
64 ARCANGUES 205 P 35
18 ARCAY 116 GA 20
86 ARCAY 112 W 20
21 ARCEAU 105 TA 18
21 ARCENANT 105 SA 19
07 ARCENS 164 PA 29
17 ARCES 141 S 26
89 ARCES DILO 64 MA 15
21 ARCEY 105 SA 18
25 ARCEY 89 AB 17
04 ARCHAIL 181 YA 32
74 ARCHAMPS 139 XA 23
39 ARCHELANGE 106 VA 19
15 ARCHES 146 GA 27
88 ARCHES 68 ZA 15
88 ARCHETTES 68 ZA 15
17 ARCHIAC C 142 V 26
24 ARCHIGNAC 159 CA 28
03 ARCHIGNAT 132 HA 22
86 ARCHIGNY 114 Z 21
17 ARCHINGEAY 127 T 24
02 ARCHON 29 OA 7
42 ARCINGES 135 PA 23
33 ARCINS 155 T 28
51 ARCIS LE PONSART 42 NA 10
10 ARCIS SUR AUBE C 65 PA 13
65 ARCIZAC ADOUR 216 X 37
65 ARCIZAC EZ ANGLES 216 W 37
65 ARCIZANS AVANT 215 W 37
65 ARCIZANS DESSUS 216 W 37
18 ARCOMPS 116 HA 21
25 ARCON 123 YA 20
42 ARCON 135 NA 24
21 ARCONCEY 104 QA 19
72 ARCONNAY 58 X 13
63 ARCONSAT 135 NA 25
10 ARCONVILLE 65 RA 14
83 ARCS, LES 203 ZA 35
94 ARCUEIL C 40 HA 12
02 ARCY STE RESTITUE 41 LA 10
89 ARCY SUR CURE 84 NA 17
28 ARDELLES 60 BA 13
28 ARDELU 61 FA 14
18 ARDENAIS 116 HA 21
72 ARDENAY SUR MERIZE 79 Y 15
65 ARDENGOST 216 Y 38
36 ARDENTES C 115 EA 21
63 ARDES C 148 KA 27
08 ARDEUIL ET MONTFAUXELLES 43 RA 10
31 ARDIEGE 217 Z 37
69 ARDILLATS, LES 136 QA 23
79 ARDILLEUX 128 W 24
17 ARDILLIERES 127 S 24
79 ARDIN 111 U 22
32 ARDIZAS 187 BA 34
07 ARDOIX 164 RA 28
39 ARDON 122 WA 21
45 ARDON 81 EA 16
76 ARDOUVAL 24 CA 7
62 ARDRES C 7 FA 2
2B AREGNO 225 KB 39
41 AREINES 80 BA 16
64 AREN 206 T 36
40 ARENGOSSE 184 T 33
74 ARENTHON 139 YA 24
33 ARES 155 R 30
39 ARESCHES 122 WA 20
64 ARESSY 207 V 36
64 ARETTE 206 T 37
23 ARFEUILLE CHATAIN 133 HA 24
03 ARFEUILLES 135 NA 23
81 ARFONS 212 GA 35
64 ARGAGNON 207 T 35
14 ARGANCHY 35 T 10
10 ARGANCON 65 RA 14
57 ARGANCY 46 YA 10
09 ARGEIN 218 BA 38
65 ARGELES 216 X 37
65 ARGELES GAZOST S 215 V 37
66 ARGELES SUR MER C 224 JA 39

11 ARGELIERS 213 JA 3
34 ARGELLIERS 192 MA 34
40 ARGELOS 184 T 35
64 ARGELOS 207 V 35
40 ARGELOUSE 170 T 3
14 ARGENCES 36 V 1
11 ARGENS MINERVOIS 213 IA 3
18 ARGENT SUR SAULDRE C 82 HA 17
61 ARGENTAN S 58 W 12
19 ARGENTAT C 160 FA 28
89 ARGENTENAY 84 OA 16
95 ARGENTEUIL S 39 GA 1
89 ARGENTEUIL SUR ARMANCON 84 OA 1
05 ARGENTIERE LA BESSEE, L' C 168 ZA 2
77 ARGENTIERES 63 JA 12
73 ARGENTINE 153 YA 26
47 ARGENTON 171 W 31
79 ARGENTON CHATEAU C 112 U 2
79 ARGENTON L'EGLISE 96 V 1
53 ARGENTON NOTRE DAME 77 T 1
36 ARGENTON SUR CREUSE C 115 DA 21
53 ARGENTRE C 77 T 15
35 ARGENTRE DU PLESSIS C 76 R 15
18 ARGENVIERES 101 JA 19
28 ARGENVILLIERS 59 AA 1
51 ARGERS 44 SA 1
64 ARGET 207 U 3
90 ARGIESANS 89 AB 17
70 ARGILLIERES 87 VA 17
30 ARGILLIERS 193 QA 33
21 ARGILLY 105 SA 1
01 ARGIS 138 VA 2
2A ARGIUSTA MORICCIO 229 KB 4
80 ARGOEUVES 16 GA 7
29 ARGOL 51 D 14
74 ARGONAY 139 XA 24
50 ARGOUGES 56 Q 13
80 ARGOULES 16 EA
76 ARGUEIL C 25 DA
25 ARGUEL 107 XA 1
80 ARGUEL 25 EA 7
31 ARGUENOS 217 Z 38
31 ARGUT DESSOUS 217 Z 38
36 ARGY 115 CA 2
64 ARHANSUS 206 S 3
65 ARIES ESPENAN 209 Y 3
81 ARIFAT 190 GA 34
09 ARIGNAC 219 DA 38
39 ARINTHOD C 138 VA 22
73 ARITH 153 XA 25
40 ARJUZANX 184 S 3
63 ARLANC C 149 NA 2
39 ARLAY 122 VA 2
07 ARLEBOSC 164 RA 28
43 ARLEMPDES 163 OA 29
13 ARLES S 195 RA 34
66 ARLES SUR TECH C 224 IA 4
43 ARLET 162 LA 2
58 ARLEUF 103 OA 1
59 ARLEUX C 18 KA 5
62 ARLEUX EN GOHELLE 17 JA 5
31 ARLOS 217 Z 38
49 ARMAILLE 94 R 16
60 ARMANCOURT 27 JA
80 ARMANCOURT 27 IA
54 ARMAUCOURT 46 YA 1
59 ARMBOUTS CAPPEL 8 HA 2
89 ARMEAU 83 LA 15
64 ARMENDARITS 206 R 36
65 ARMENTEULE 216 Y 3
59 ARMENTIERES C 9 JA
77 ARMENTIERES EN BRIE 41 KA 1
27 ARMENTIERES SUR AVRE 37 AA 12
02 ARMENTIERES SUR OURCQ 41 LA 10
32 ARMENTIEUX 208 W 35
58 ARMES 102 MA 18
47 ARMILLAC 172 Y 3
11 ARMISSAN 223 KA 3
01 ARMIX 138 VA 2
32 ARMOUS ET CAU 208 X 35
74 ARMOY 139 ZA 23
15 ARNAC 160 GA 28
87 ARNAC LA POSTE 131 CA 2
19 ARNAC POMPADOUR 145 CA 2
12 ARNAC SUR DOURDOU 191 JA 3
72 ARNAGE 78 X 16
52 ARNANCOURT 66 SA 14
69 ARNAS 136 RA 24
31 ARNAUD GUILHEM 217 AA 37
09 ARNAVE 219 DA 3
54 ARNAVILLE 45 XA 1
21 ARNAY LE DUC C 104 OA 1
21 ARNAY SOUS VITTEAUX 104 QA 18
26 ARNAYON 180 UA 31
65 ARNE 217 Y 37
64 ARNEGUY 205 O 3
59 ARNEKE 8 HA
08 ARNICOURT 29 QA
27 ARNIERES SUR ITON 38 BA 11
64 ARNOS 207 U 35
95 ARNOUVILLE LES GONESSE 40 HA 11
78 ARNOUVILLE LES MANTES 39 EA 11
88 AROFFE 67 WA 1
39 AROMAS 138 VA 2
53 ARON 57 U 1
64 AROUE ITHOROTS OLHAIBY 206 S 36
70 AROZ 88 XA 17
30 ARPAILLARGUES ET AUREILLAC 193 OA 33
91 ARPAJON C 62 GA 1
91 ARPAJON C 62 GA 1
15 ARPAJON SUR CERE C 161 HA 2
26 ARPAVON 180 UA 31
70 ARPENANS 89 ZA 17
18 ARPHEUILLES 117 HA 21
36 ARPHEUILLES 115 CA 20
03 ARPHEUILLES ST PRIEST 133 IA 2
30 ARPHY 192 MA 3
53 ARQUENAY 77 U 1
11 ARQUES 221 HA 38
12 ARQUES 176 JA 32
62 ARQUES C 8 GA 3
46 ARQUES, LES 173 CA 3
76 ARQUES LA BATAILLE 24 BA
11 ARQUETTES EN VAL 221 HA 3
80 ARQUEVES 17 HA 6
58 ARQUIAN 83 JA 17
54 ARRACOURT C 46 ZA 12
56 ARRADON 92 K 17
57 ARRAINCOURT 47 ZA 1
91 ARRANCOURT 61 GA 1
02 ARRANCY 28 NA
55 ARRANCY SUR CRUSNE 31 VA 9
21 ARRANS 85 PA 17
62 ARRAS P 17 IA 5
65 ARRAS EN LAVEDAN 215 V 3
07 ARRAS SUR RHONE 164 RA 2
64 ARRAST LARREBIEU 206 S 3
64 ARRAUTE CHARRITTE 206 R 36

54	ARRAYE ET HAN		46	YA	11
65	ARRAYOU LAHITTE		216	W	37
30	ARRE		192	MA	33
65	ARREAU	C	216	Y	38
10	ARRELLES		85	PA	15
10	ARREMBECOURT		65	RA	13
23	ARRENES		131	DA	24
65	ARRENS MARSOUS		215	V	38
88	ARRENTES DE CORCIEUX		69	BB	15
10	ARRENTIERES		65	RA	14
80	ARREST		15	DA	6
08	ARREUX		29	RA	7
57	ARRIANCE		47	ZA	11
64	ARRICAU BORDES		207	W	35
64	ARRIEN		207	V	36
09	ARRIEN EN BETHMALE		218	BA	38
30	ARRIGAS		192	MA	33
51	ARRIGNY		65	RA	12
2A	ARRO		227	JB	41
65	ARRODETS		216	X	37
65	ARRODETS EZ ANGLES		216	W	37
14	ARROMANCHES LES BAINS		35	T	9
03	ARRONNES		133	MA	24
95	ARRONVILLE		39	FA	10
64	ARROS DE NAY		215	V	37
64	ARROSES		208	W	35
28	ARROU		60	BA	15
32	ARROUEDE		209	Z	36
09	ARROUT		218	BA	38
57	ARRY		46	XA	11
80	ARRY		15	EA	5
16	ARS		142	U	26
23	ARS		132	FA	24
17	ARS EN RE	C	125	P	23
57	ARS LAQUENEXY		46	YA	10
63	ARS LES FAVETS		133	IA	23
01	ARS SUR FORMANS		137	SA	24
57	ARS SUR MOSELLE	C	45	XA	10
33	ARSAC		155	T	29
43	ARSAC EN VELAY		163	OA	29
40	ARSAGUE		184	S	35
70	ARSANS		106	VA	18
10	ARSONVAL		65	RA	14
39	ARSURE ARSURETTE		123	XA	21
39	ARSURES, LES		122	WA	20
60	ARSY		27	IA	9
54	ART SUR MEURTHE		46	YA	12
65	ARTAGNAN		208	X	36
08	ARTAISE LE VIVIER		30	SA	8
71	ARTAIX		135	OA	23
65	ARTALENS SOUIN		216	W	38
37	ARTANNES SUR INDRE		97	Z	18
49	ARTANNES SUR THOUET		96	W	19
38	ARTAS		151	TA	26
40	ARTASSENX		184	U	34
01	ARTEMARE		138	VA	25
02	ARTEMPS		27	KA	7
45	ARTENAY	C	81	FA	15
74	ARTHAZ PONT NOTRE DAME		139	YA	23
58	ARTHEL		102	LA	19
26	ARTHEMONAY		165	TA	28
17	ARTHENAC		142	V	26
39	ARTHENAS		122	VA	21
81	ARTHES		190	GA	33
40	ARTHEZ D'ARMAGNAC		185	V	33
64	ARTHEZ D'ASSON		215	V	37
64	ARTHEZ DE BEARN	C	207	T	35
72	ARTHEZE		78	V	16
95	ARTHIES		39	EA	10
36	ARTHON		115	EA	21
44	ARTHON EN RETZ		93	N	19
89	ARTHONNAY		85	PA	15
42	ARTHUN		149	OA	25
09	ARTIGAT		218	CA	37
83	ARTIGNOSC SUR VERDON		197	XA	34
31	ARTIGUE		217	Z	38
64	ARTIGUELOUTAN		207	V	36
64	ARTIGUELOUVE		207	U	36
65	ARTIGUEMY		216	X	37
09	ARTIGUES		222	FA	39
11	ARTIGUES		221	GA	38
65	ARTIGUES		216	W	37
83	ARTIGUES		202	WA	35
33	ARTIGUES DE LUSSAC, LES		156	W	29
33	ARTIGUES PRES BORDEAUX		156	U	29
41	ARTINS		79	Z	16
09	ARTIX		219	DA	37
64	ARTIX		207	U	36
67	ARTOLSHEIM		70	EB	14
02	ARTONGES		42	MA	11
63	ARTONNE		134	KA	24
59	ARTRES		18	MA	5
68	ARTZENHEIM		70	EB	15
64	ARUDY	C	215	U	37
40	ARUE		185	V	33
17	ARVERT		141	R	25
33	ARVEYRES		156	V	29
12	ARVIEU		175	IA	32
05	ARVIEUX		168	AB	30
09	ARVIGNA		219	EA	37
73	ARVILLARD		153	XA	27
41	ARVILLE		60	AA	15
77	ARVILLE		62	HA	14
80	ARVILLERS		26	IA	7
40	ARX		171	W	32
64	ARZACQ ARRAZIGUET	C	207	U	35
56	ARZAL		92	M	17
29	ARZANO	C	73	H	16
38	ARZAY		151	TA	27
58	ARZEMBOUY		102	LA	19
48	ARZENC D'APCHER		162	KA	29
48	ARZENC DE RANDON		177	MA	30
11	ARZENS		221	GA	37
51	ARZILLIERES NEUVILLE		65	RA	12
56	ARZON		91	J	17
57	ARZVILLER		69	CB	12
64	ASASP ARROS		215	T	37
64	ASCAIN		205	P	36
64	ASCARAT		205	Q	37
67	ASCHBACH		50	GB	11
45	ASCHERES LE MARCHE		61	FA	15
2B	ASCO		225	KB	40
09	ASCOU		220	EA	39
45	ASCOUX		62	GA	15
06	ASCROS		199	BB	33
08	ASFELD	C	29	OA	9
86	ASLONNES		113	Y	22
58	ASNAN		102	MA	18
39	ASNANS BEAUVOISIN		122	UA	20
14	ASNELLES		35	U	9
27	ASNIERES		37	Y	10
14	ASNIERES EN BESSIN		35	S	9
21	ASNIERES EN MONTAGNE		85	PA	16
79	ASNIERES EN POITOU		128	V	24
17	ASNIERES LA GIRAUD		128	U	25
21	ASNIERES LES DIJON		105	TA	18
89	ASNIERES SOUS BOIS		84	MA	17
86	ASNIERES SUR BLOUR		130	AA	23
16	ASNIERES SUR NOUERE		143	W	25
95	ASNIERES SUR OISE		40	HA	10
01	ASNIERES SUR SAONE		137	SA	22
92	ASNIERES SUR SEINE	C	40	GA	11
72	ASNIERES SUR VEGRE		78	V	16
58	ASNOIS		103	MA	18
86	ASNOIS		129	Y	24
57	ASPACH		69	BB	12
68	ASPACH		90	CB	17
68	ASPACH LE BAS		90	CB	16
68	ASPACH LE HAUT		90	CB	16
30	ASPERES		193	OA	34
07	ASPERJOC		164	PA	30
31	ASPET	C	217	AA	37
65	ASPIN AURE		216	Y	38
65	ASPIN EN LAVEDAN		216	W	37
34	ASPIRAN		214	LA	35
05	ASPREMONT		180	WA	31
06	ASPREMONT		200	CB	34
61	ASPRES, LES		37	Z	12
05	ASPRES LES CORPS		167	XA	29
05	ASPRES SUR BUECH	C	180	WA	31
31	ASPRET SARRAT		217	Z	37
12	ASPRIERES		175	GA	30
65	ASQUE		216	X	37
33	ASQUES		156	U	29
82	ASQUES		187	AA	33
89	ASQUINS		84	NA	17
81	ASSAC		190	HA	33
80	ASSAINVILLERS		26	IA	8
79	ASSAIS LES JUMEAUX		112	W	21
34	ASSAS		193	OA	34
64	ASSAT		207	V	36
37	ASSAY		97	X	19
53	ASSE LE BERENGER		77	V	14
72	ASSE LE BOISNE		58	W	14
72	ASSE LE RIBOUL		78	X	14
10	ASSENAY		64	OA	14
10	ASSENCIERES		65	PA	14
57	ASSENONCOURT		47	AB	12
44	ASSERAC		92	M	18
59	ASSEVENT		19	OA	5
80	ASSEVILLERS		27	JA	7
46	ASSIER		174	EA	30
38	ASSIEU		151	SA	27
34	ASSIGNAN		213	JA	36
18	ASSIGNY		101	IA	18
76	ASSIGNY		15	CA	6
07	ASSIONS, LES		178	PA	31
02	ASSIS SUR SERRE		28	MA	8
64	ASSON		215	V	37
67	ASSWILLER		48	CB	11
47	ASTAFFORT	C	187	Z	33
19	ASTAILLAC		160	EA	29
65	ASTE		216	X	37
64	ASTE BEON		215	U	37
07	ASTET		178	OA	30
53	ASTILLE		77	S	15
64	ASTIS		207	V	35
09	ASTON		220	EA	38
65	ASTUGUE		216	W	37
21	ATHEE		106	UA	19
53	ATHEE		76	S	16
37	ATHEE SUR CHER		98	AA	18
70	ATHESANS ETROITEFONTAINE		89	ZA	17
21	ATHIE		85	PA	17
89	ATHIE		84	OA	17
54	ATHIENVILLE		46	ZA	12
62	ATHIES		17	JA	5
80	ATHIES		27	JA	7
02	ATHIES SOUS LAON		28	NA	8
51	ATHIS		42	OA	11
61	ATHIS DE L'ORNE	C	57	U	12
91	ATHIS MONS	C	40	HA	12
64	ATHOS ASPIS		206	S	36
25	ATHOSE		107	YA	19
95	ATTAINVILLE		40	HA	10
52	ATTANCOURT		66	SA	13
62	ATTAQUES, LES		7	FA	2
68	ATTENSCHWILLER		90	DB	17
59	ATTICHES		9	KA	4
60	ATTICHY	C	27	KA	9
01	ATTIGNAT		137	TA	23
73	ATTIGNAT ONCIN		152	WA	26
88	ATTIGNEVILLE		67	WA	13
08	ATTIGNY	C	29	QA	9
88	ATTIGNY		67	XA	15
57	ATTILLONCOURT		46	ZA	12
02	ATTILLY		27	KA	7
62	ATTIN		15	EA	4
54	ATTON		46	XA	11
45	ATTRAY		61	GA	15
70	ATTRICOURT		87	UA	17
24	ATUR		158	Z	28
40	AUBAGNAN		184	U	34
13	AUBAGNE	C	202	VA	36
21	AUBAINE		104	RA	19
30	AUBAIS		193	PA	34
65	AUBAREDE		208	X	36
24	AUBAS		158	BA	28
43	AUBAZAT		162	LA	28
19	AUBAZINES		159	DA	28
57	AUBE		46	YA	11
61	AUBE		37	Z	12
76	AUBEGUIMONT		25	EA	7
07	AUBENAS	C	178	QA	30
04	AUBENAS LES ALPES		196	VA	33
26	AUBENASSON		165	TA	30
59	AUBENCHEUL AU BAC		18	KA	5
02	AUBENCHEUL AUX BOIS		18	LA	6
02	AUBENTON	C	29	PA	7
77	AUBEPIERRE OZOUER LE REPOS		63	JA	12
52	AUBEPIERRE SUR AUBE		86	SA	16
39	AUBEPIN, L'		122	UA	22
59	AUBERCHICOURT		18	KA	5
80	AUBERCOURT		26	HA	7
78	AUBERGENVILLE	C	39	EA	11
51	AUBERIVE		43	QA	10
52	AUBERIVE	C	86	TA	16
38	AUBERIVES EN ROYANS		166	UA	28
38	AUBERIVES SUR VAREZE		150	RA	27
76	AUBERMESNIL AUX ERABLES		25	DA	7
76	AUBERMESNIL BEAUMAIS		24	BA	7
59	AUBERS		9	JA	4
64	AUBERTIN		207	U	36
14	AUBERVILLE		36	W	9
76	AUBERVILLE LA CAMPAGNE		23	Z	8
76	AUBERVILLE LA MANUEL		23	Z	7
76	AUBERVILLE LA RENAULT		23	Y	8
93	AUBERVILLIERS	C	40	HA	11
10	AUBETERRE		64	OA	13
16	AUBETERRE SUR DRONNE	C	143	X	27
16	AUBEVILLE		142	W	26
27	AUBEVOYE		38	CA	10
33	AUBIAC		170	V	31
47	AUBIAC		172	Z	32
63	AUBIAT		134	KA	24
33	AUBIE ET ESPESSAS		156	U	28
63	AUBIERE	C	148	KA	25
79	AUBIERS, LES		111	U	20
32	AUBIET		209	AA	35
84	AUBIGNAN		195	TA	33
07	AUBIGNAS		179	RA	30
35	AUBIGNE		75	P	14
79	AUBIGNE		128	W	24
72	AUBIGNE RACAN		78	X	17
49	AUBIGNE SUR LAYON		96	U	19
04	AUBIGNOSC		181	XA	32
03	AUBIGNY		118	KA	21
14	AUBIGNY		36	V	11
79	AUBIGNY		112	W	21
80	AUBIGNY		26	HA	7
85	AUBIGNY		110	Q	21
59	AUBIGNY AU BAC		18	KA	5
02	AUBIGNY AUX KAISNES		27	KA	7
62	AUBIGNY EN ARTOIS	C	17	IA	5
02	AUBIGNY EN LAONNOIS		28	NA	9
21	AUBIGNY EN PLAINE		105	TA	19
21	AUBIGNY LA RONCE		120	RA	20
08	AUBIGNY LES POTHEES		29	OA	7
21	AUBIGNY LES SOMBERNON		104	RA	18
18	AUBIGNY SUR NERE	C	82	HA	17
51	AUBILLY		42	NA	10
12	AUBIN	C	175	GA	31
64	AUBIN		207	U	35
62	AUBIN ST VAAST		16	FA	5
18	AUBINGES		101	IA	19
08	AUBONCOURT VAUZELLES		29	OA	8
25	AUBONNE		107	YA	19
30	AUBORD		193	PA	34
54	AUBOUE		45	XA	10
64	AUBOUS		207	V	35
26	AUBRES		180	TA	31
55	AUBREVILLE		44	TA	10
08	AUBRIVES		20	RA	6
62	AUBROMETZ		16	GA	5
59	AUBRY DU HAINAUT		18	LA	5
61	AUBRY EN EXMES		58	W	12
61	AUBRY LE PANTHOU		36	X	11
68	AUBURE		69	CB	14
30	AUBUSSARGUES		193	PA	33
23	AUBUSSON	S	132	GA	24
61	AUBUSSON		57	U	12
63	AUBUSSON D'AUVERGNE		148	MA	25
80	AUBVILLERS		26	HA	8
59	AUBY		17	KA	4
22	AUCALEUC		55	N	13
31	AUCAMVILLE		188	DA	34
82	AUCAMVILLE		188	BA	34
09	AUCAZEIN		217	AA	38
26	AUCELON		180	UA	30
50	AUCEY LA PLAINE		56	O	13
32	AUCH	P	209	Z	35
62	AUCHEL	C	8	HA	4
80	AUCHONVILLERS		17	IA	6
62	AUCHY AU BOIS		8	HA	4
60	AUCHY LA MONTAGNE		26	GA	8
62	AUCHY LES HESDIN		16	FA	4
62	AUCHY LES MINES		8	IA	4
59	AUCHY LEZ ORCHIES		18	KA	4
65	AUCUN	C	215	V	37
64	AUDAUX		206	T	36
39	AUDELANGE		106	VA	19
52	AUDELONCOURT		67	VA	15
62	AUDEMBERT		7	EA	2
33	AUDENGE	C	155	S	30
50	AUDERVILLE		33	N	8
03	AUDES		117	HA	22
25	AUDEUX	C	106	WA	18
45	AUDEVILLE		62	GA	14
29	AUDIERNE		71	C	15
02	AUDIGNICOURT		27	KA	9
59	AUDIGNIES		19	NA	5
40	AUDIGNON		184	T	34
02	AUDIGNY		28	MA	7
25	AUDINCOURT	C	89	BB	17
62	AUDINCTHUN		7	GA	4
62	AUDINGHEN		7	DA	2
40	AUDON		184	S	34
50	AUDOUVILLE LA HUBERT		33	R	9
62	AUDREHEM		7	FA	3
09	AUDRESSEIN		218	BA	38
62	AUDRESSELLES		7	DA	3
14	AUDRIEU		35	T	10
24	AUDRIX		158	AA	29
62	AUDRUICQ	C	7	FA	2
54	AUDUN LE ROMAN	C	32	WA	9
57	AUDUN LE TICHE		32	XA	9
67	AUENHEIM		50	GB	12
78	AUFFARGIS		39	FA	12
76	AUFFAY		24	BA	8
77	AUFFERVILLE		62	IA	14
78	AUFFREVILLE BRASSEUIL		39	EA	11
08	AUFLANCE		31	UA	8
64	AUGA		207	U	35
56	AUGAN		74	M	16
08	AUGE		29	PA	7
23	AUGE		132	GA	23
79	AUGE		112	V	22
16	AUGE ST MEDARD		128	W	25
39	AUGEA		122	UA	22
60	AUGER ST VINCENT		40	JA	10
39	AUGERANS		122	VA	20
23	AUGERES		131	EA	24
63	AUGEROLLES		148	MA	25
77	AUGERS EN BRIE		63	LA	12
45	AUGERVILLE LA RIVIERE		62	HA	14
70	AUGICOURT		88	WA	16
24	AUGIGNAC		144	Z	26
09	AUGIREIN		217	AA	38
39	AUGISEY		122	VA	22
63	AUGNAT		148	KA	27
32	AUGNAX		187	AA	34
87	AUGNE		145	EA	25
57	AUGNY		46	XA	10
61	AUGUAISE		37	Z	12
02	AUGY		28	MA	9
89	AUGY		84	MA	16
18	AUGY SUR AUBOIS		117	JA	21
17	AUJAC		128	U	25
30	AUJAC		178	OA	31
32	AUJAN MOURNEDE		209	Y	36
30	AUJARGUES		193	OA	34
52	AUJEURRES		86	TA	16
46	AUJOLS		174	DA	31
26	AULAN		180	UA	32
30	AULAS		192	MA	33
63	AULHAT ST PRIVAT		148	LA	26
2A	AULLENE		230	LB	43
63	AULNAT		148	KA	25
10	AULNAY		65	QA	13
17	AULNAY	C	128	V	24
86	AULNAY		113	X	20
51	AULNAY L'AITRE		43	QA	11
45	AULNAY LA RIVIERE		62	HA	14
93	AULNAY SOUS BOIS	C	40	HA	11
27	AULNAY SUR ITON		38	BA	11
51	AULNAY SUR MARNE		43	PA	11
78	AULNAY SUR MAULDRE		39	EA	11
72	AULNEAUX, LES		59	Y	13
88	AULNOIS		67	WA	14
55	AULNOIS EN PERTHOIS		66	TA	12
02	AULNOIS SOUS LAON		28	MA	8
57	AULNOIS SUR SEILLE		46	YA	11
77	AULNOY		41	KA	11
59	AULNOY LEZ VALENCIENNES		18	MA	5
52	AULNOY SUR AUBE		86	SA	16
59	AULNOYE AYMERIES		19	NA	5
23	AULON		131	EA	24
31	AULON		217	AA	37
65	AULON		216	X	38
09	AULOS		219	EA	38
80	AULT	C	15	DA	6
09	AULUS LES BAINS		219	CA	38
70	AULX LES CROMARY		107	XA	18
17	AUMAGNE		128	U	25
76	AUMALE	C	25	EA	7
80	AUMATRE		15	EA	7
34	AUMELAS		214	MA	35
51	AUMENANCOURT		29	OA	9
62	AUMERVAL		16	HA	4
34	AUMES		214	MA	35
30	AUMESSAS		192	MA	33
57	AUMETZ		32	XA	9
50	AUMEVILLE LESTRE		33	Q	8
39	AUMONT		122	VA	20
80	AUMONT		26	FA	7
48	AUMONT AUBRAC	C	162	LA	30
60	AUMONT EN HALATTE		40	IA	10
88	AUMONTZEY		69	AB	14
39	AUMUR		106	UA	19
16	AUNAC		129	X	24
11	AUNAT		222	FA	38
58	AUNAY EN BAZOIS		103	MA	19
61	AUNAY LES BOIS		59	X	13
28	AUNAY SOUS AUNEAU		61	EA	13
28	AUNAY SOUS CRECY		60	CA	12
14	AUNAY SUR ODON	C	35	T	11
28	AUNEAU	C	61	EA	13
60	AUNEUIL	C	26	FA	9
61	AUNOU LE FAUCON		58	W	12
61	AUNOU SUR ORNE		58	X	12
76	AUPPEGARD		24	BA	7
83	AUPS	C	203	YA	35
14	AUQUAINVILLE		37	X	10
76	AUQUEMESNIL		15	CA	7
32	AURADE		210	BA	35
47	AURADOU		172	AA	31
31	AURAGNE		210	DA	36
56	AURAY	C	73	J	17
08	AURE		43	RA	10
43	AUREC SUR LOIRE	C	149	PA	27
87	AUREIL		145	CA	25
40	AUREILHAN		169	R	32
65	AUREILHAN	C	208	X	36
13	AUREILLE		195	SA	34
26	AUREL		166	UA	30
84	AUREL		180	UA	32
12	AURELLE VERLAC		176	JA	31
32	AURENSAN		207	V	35
65	AURENSAN		208	X	36
31	AUREVILLE		210	DA	35
11	AURIAC		221	HA	38
19	AURIAC		160	GA	28
64	AURIAC		207	V	35
24	AURIAC DU PERIGORD		158	BA	28
15	AURIAC L'EGLISE		162	KA	27
12	AURIAC LAGAST		175	IA	32
47	AURIAC SUR DROPT		171	X	30
31	AURIAC SUR VENDINELLE		211	EA	35
23	AURIAT		131	DA	25
31	AURIBAIL		210	CA	36
84	AURIBEAU		196	UA	34
06	AURIBEAU SUR SIAGNE		200	BB	35
40	AURICE		184	T	34
65	AURIEBAT		208	X	35
63	AURIERES		147	JA	25
31	AURIGNAC	C	209	AA	36
15	AURILLAC	P	161	HA	29
32	AURIMONT		209	AA	35
31	AURIN		211	EA	35
13	AURIOL		202	VA	36
33	AURIOLLES		157	W	30
64	AURIONS IDERNES		207	W	35
38	AURIS		167	XA	28
13	AURONS		196	TA	34
33	AUROS	C	171	W	31
03	AUROUER		118	LA	21
48	AUROUX		163	NA	30
81	AUSSAC		189	FA	34
16	AUSSAC VADALLE		143	X	25
31	AUSSEING		218	BA	37
64	AUSSEVIELLE		207	U	36
81	AUSSILLON		212	GA	35
73	AUSSOIS		154	AB	27
31	AUSSON		217	Z	37
08	AUSSONCE		29	PA	9
31	AUSSONNE		188	CA	34
32	AUSSOS		209	Z	36
64	AUSSURUCQ		206	S	37
41	AUTAINVILLE		80	CA	16
25	AUTECHAUX		107	YA	18
25	AUTECHAUX ROIDE		108	AB	18
02	AUTELS, LES		29	PA	7
14	AUTELS ST BAZILE, LES		36	X	11
28	AUTELS VILLEVILLON, LES		60	BA	14
31	AUTERIVE	C	210	DA	36
32	AUTERIVE		209	Z	35
82	AUTERIVE		187	AA	34
64	AUTERRIVE		206	S	35
70	AUTET		87	VA	17
60	AUTEUIL		26	FA	9
78	AUTEUIL		39	EA	11
64	AUTEVIELLE ST MARTIN BIDEREN		206	S	36
08	AUTHE		30	SA	9
28	AUTHEUIL		80	CA	15
61	AUTHEUIL		59	Z	13
27	AUTHEUIL AUTHOUILLET		38	CA	10
60	AUTHEUIL EN VALOIS		41	KA	10
80	AUTHEUX		16	GA	6
27	AUTHEVERNES		39	DA	10
63	AUTHEZAT		148	KA	26
14	AUTHIE		35	U	10
80	AUTHIE		17	HA	6
80	AUTHIEULE		16	HA	6
27	AUTHIEUX, LES		38	CA	11
61	AUTHIEUX DU PUITS, LES		37	Y	12
14	AUTHIEUX PAPION, LES		36	W	10
76	AUTHIEUX RATIEVILLE		24	BA	8
14	AUTHIEUX SUR CALONNE, LES		37	X	9
76	AUTHIEUX SUR LE PORT ST OUEN, LES		24	BA	9
58	AUTHIOU		102	LA	18
70	AUTHOISON		88	XA	17
04	AUTHON		181	XA	32
41	AUTHON		79	AA	17
28	AUTHON DU PERCHE	C	59	AA	14
17	AUTHON EBEON		128	U	25
91	AUTHON LA PLAINE		61	FA	13
27	AUTHOU		37	Z	10
80	AUTHUILLE		17	IA	6
39	AUTHUME		106	VA	19
71	AUTHUMES		121	UA	20
26	AUTICHAMP		165	SA	30
34	AUTIGNAC		213	KA	35
76	AUTIGNY		24	AA	7
88	AUTIGNY LA TOUR		67	WA	13
52	AUTIGNY LE GRAND		66	TA	13
52	AUTIGNY LE PETIT		66	TA	13
62	AUTINGUES		7	FA	3
46	AUTOIRE		159	EA	29
70	AUTOREILLE		106	WA	18
78	AUTOUILLET		39	EA	11
43	AUTRAC		148	KA	27
38	AUTRANS		166	VA	28
37	AUTRECHE		79	BA	17
90	AUTRECHENE		90	BB	17
60	AUTRECHES		27	KA	9
08	AUTRECOURT ET POURRON		30	SA	8
55	AUTRECOURT SUR AIRE		44	TA	11
02	AUTREMENCOURT		28	NA	8
54	AUTREPIERRE		69	AB	12
02	AUTREPPES		28	NA	7
76	AUTRETOT		24	Z	8
02	AUTREVILLE		27	LA	8
88	AUTREVILLE		67	WA	13
55	AUTREVILLE ST LAMBERT		30	TA	8
52	AUTREVILLE SUR LA RENNE		66	SA	15
54	AUTREVILLE SUR MOSELLE		46	XA	11
54	AUTREY		67	XA	13
88	AUTREY		68	AB	14
70	AUTREY LE VAY		89	ZA	17
70	AUTREY LES CERRE		88	YA	17
70	AUTREY LES GRAY	C	87	VA	17
21	AUTRICOURT		85	RA	15
08	AUTRUCHE		30	SA	9
45	AUTRUY SUR JUINE		61	FA	14
08	AUTRY		43	SA	10
03	AUTRY ISSARDS		118	KA	22
45	AUTRY LE CHATEL		82	IA	17
71	AUTUN	S	120	PA	20
82	AUTY		174	DA	32
06	AUVARE		199	BB	33
51	AUVE		43	RA	11
91	AUVERNAUX		62	HA	13
43	AUVERS		162	LA	29
50	AUVERS		34	Q	9
72	AUVERS LE HAMON		77	V	16
72	AUVERS SOUS MONTFAUCON		78	W	15
91	AUVERS ST GEORGES		62	GA	13
95	AUVERS SUR OISE	C	39	GA	10
49	AUVERSE		97	W	17
70	AUVET ET LA CHAPELOTTE		87	VA	17
82	AUVILLAR	C	187	AA	33
14	AUVILLARS		36	X	10
21	AUVILLARS SUR SAONE		105	TA	19
08	AUVILLERS LES FORGES		29	OA	7
76	AUVILLIERS		25	DA	7
45	AUVILLIERS EN GATINAIS		82	HA	15
32	AUX AUSSAT		208	X	35
50	AUXAIS		34	O	10
39	AUXANGE		106	VA	19
21	AUXANT		104	RA	19
90	AUXELLES BAS		89	AB	16
90	AUXELLES HAUT		89	AB	16
89	AUXERRE	P	83	MA	16
21	AUXEY DURESSES		104	RA	19
62	AUXI LE CHATEAU	C	16	GA	5
10	AUXON		64	NA	15
70	AUXON		88	YA	17
25	AUXON DESSOUS		107	XA	18
25	AUXON DESSUS		107	XA	18
21	AUXONNE	C	106	UA	19
45	AUXY		62	HA	15
71	AUXY		120	QA	20
88	AUZAINVILLIERS		67	WA	14
23	AUZANCES	C	133	HA	24
31	AUZAS		217	AA	37
09	AUZAT		220	DA	38
63	AUZAT SUR ALLIER		148	LA	26
85	AUZAY		111	S	22
76	AUZEBOSC		24	Z	8
63	AUZELLES		148	MA	26
15	AUZERS		161	HA	27
04	AUZET		181	YA	32
31	AUZEVILLE TOLOSANE		210	DA	35
31	AUZIELLE		210	DA	35
12	AUZITS		175	GA	31
43	AUZON	C	148	LA	27
37	AUZOUER EN TOURAINE		79	AA	17
76	AUZOUVILLE AUBERBOSC		23	Z	8
76	AUZOUVILLE L'ESNEVAL		24	AA	8
76	AUZOUVILLE SUR RY		24	CA	9
76	AUZOUVILLE SUR SAANE		24	AA	7
86	AVAILLES EN CHATELLERAULT		113	Z	21
86	AVAILLES LIMOUZINE	C	130	Z	24
35	AVAILLES SUR SEICHE		76	R	15
79	AVAILLES THOUARSAIS		112	V	20
65	AVAJAN		216	Y	38
89	AVALLON	S	84	OA	17
73	AVANCHERS VALMOREL, LES		153	ZA	26
05	AVANCON		181	YA	31
08	AVANCON		29	PA	9
25	AVANNE AVENEY		107	XA	19
10	AVANT LES MARCILLY		64	MA	13
10	AVANT LES RAMERUPT		65	PA	13
86	AVANTON		113	X	21
2B	AVAPESSA		225	KB	39
41	AVARAY		80	DA	16
08	AVAUX		29	OA	9
69	AVEIZE		150	QA	25
42	AVEIZIEUX		150	PA	26
21	AVELANGES		86	SA	17
80	AVELESGES		16	FA	7
59	AVELIN		9	KA	4
80	AVELUY		17	IA	6
69	AVENAS		136	RA	23
14	AVENAY		35	U	10
51	AVENAY VAL D'OR		42	OA	10
34	AVENE		191	KA	34
38	AVENIERES, LES		152	VA	26
32	AVENSAC		187	AA	34
33	AVENSAN		155	T	28
65	AVENTIGNAN		217	Y	37
65	AVERAN		216	W	37
62	AVERDOINGT		17	HA	5
41	AVERDON		80	CA	17
03	AVERMES		118	LA	21
95	AVERNES		39	EA	10
61	AVERNES SOUS EXMES		58	X	12

61	AVERNES ST GOURGON		37	Y 11
32	AVERON BERGELLE		185	W 34
53	AVERTON		58	V 14
59	AVESNELLES		19	OA 6
62	AVESNES		7	FA 4
80	AVESNES CHAUSSOY		25	EA 7
76	AVESNES EN BRAY		25	EA 9
72	AVESNES EN SAOSNOIS		59	Y 14
76	AVESNES EN VAL		15	CA 7
62	AVESNES LE COMTE	C	17	HA 5
59	AVESNES LE SEC		18	LA 5
59	AVESNES LES AUBERT		18	LA 5
62	AVESNES LES BAPAUME		17	JA 6
59	AVESNES SUR HELPE	S	19	NA 6
44	AVESSAC		93	N 17
72	AVESSE		78	V 15
65	AVEUX		217	Z 37
65	AVEZAC PRAT LAHITTE		216	Y 37
32	AVEZAN		187	AA 34
30	AVEZE		192	MA 33
63	AVEZE		147	IA 26
72	AVEZE		59	Z 14
74	AVIERNOZ		139	YA 24
84	AVIGNON	P	195	RA 33
39	AVIGNON LES ST CLAUDE		122	WA 22
38	AVIGNONET		166	VA 29
31	AVIGNONET LAURAGAIS		211	EA 36
54	AVILLERS		31	WA 9
88	AVILLERS		68	YA 14
55	AVILLERS STE CROIX		45	WA 11
25	AVILLEY		107	YA 18
60	AVILLY ST LEONARD		40	HA 10
62	AVION	C	17	JA 4
55	AVIOTH		31	UA 8
49	AVIRE		77	T 16
10	AVIREY LINGEY		85	PA 15
27	AVIRON		38	BA 11
51	AVIZE	C	42	OA 11
55	AVOCOURT		44	TA 10
37	AVOINE		97	X 19
61	AVOINE		58	W 12
72	AVOISE		78	V 16
67	AVOLSHEIM		70	DB 13
77	AVON		62	IA 13
79	AVON		129	W 22
10	AVON LA PEZE		64	MA 13
37	AVON LES ROCHES		97	Y 19
62	AVONDANCE		16	FA 4
18	AVORD		101	IA 19
21	AVOSNES		104	RA 18
21	AVOT		86	SA 17
25	AVOUDREY		107	ZA 19
54	AVRAINVILLE		45	XA 12
88	AVRAINVILLE		68	YA 13
91	AVRAINVILLE		62	GA 13
50	AVRANCHES	S	56	Q 12
88	AVRANVILLE		67	VA 13
60	AVRECHY		26	HA 9
58	AVREE		119	NA 20
76	AVREMESNIL		24	AA 7
73	AVRESSIEUX		152	VA 26
10	AVREUIL		84	OA 15
54	AVRICOURT		69	AB 12
57	AVRICOURT		69	AB 12
60	AVRICOURT		27	JA 8
73	AVRIEUX		168	AB 28
70	AVRIGNEY VIREY		106	WA 18
60	AVRIGNY		27	IA 9
54	AVRIL		32	XA 9
58	AVRIL SUR LOIRE		118	LA 20
49	AVRILLE		95	U 17
85	AVRILLE		125	P 22
37	AVRILLE LES PONCEAUX		97	X 18
03	AVRILLY		135	OA 23
27	AVRILLY		38	BA 11
61	AVRILLY		57	T 13
62	AVROULT		8	GA 3
17	AVY		142	U 26
59	AWOINGT		18	LA 6
09	AX LES THERMES	C	220	EA 39
11	AXAT	C	221	GA 38
09	AXIAT		219	EA 38
51	AY	C	42	OA 10
57	AY SUR MOSELLE		46	YA 10
63	AYAT SUR SIOULE		133	JA 24
63	AYDAT		147	JA 26
64	AYDIE		208	W 35
64	AYDIUS		215	U 37
88	AYDOILLES		68	ZA 14
19	AYEN	C	159	CA 27
80	AYENCOURT		26	IA 8
62	AYETTE		17	IA 5
66	AYGUATEBIA TALAU		222	GA 39
33	AYGUEMORTE LES GRAVES		156	U 30
31	AYGUESVIVES		210	DA 35
32	AYGUETINTE		186	Y 34
64	AYHERRE		205	R 36
73	AYN		152	WA 26
46	AYNAC		160	EA 29
47	AYNANS, LES		89	ZA 17
15	AYRENS		160	GA 29
86	AYRON		112	W 21
65	AYROS ARBOUIX		216	W 37
74	AYSE		139	ZA 24
12	AYSSENES		191	IA 33
17	AYTRE	C	126	R 23
08	AYVELLES, LES		30	RA 8
65	AYZAC OST		215	W 37
32	AYZIEU		185	W 34
55	AZANNES ET SOUMAZANNES		31	UA 9
31	AZAS		189	EA 34
23	AZAT CHATENET		131	EA 24
87	AZAT LE RIS		130	BA 23
79	AZAY LE BRULE		112	V 22
36	AZAY LE FERRON		114	BA 20
37	AZAY LE RIDEAU	C	97	Y 18
37	AZAY SUR CHER		98	AA 18
37	AZAY SUR INDRE		98	AA 19
79	AZAY SUR THOUET		112	V 21
41	AZE		79	BA 16
53	AZE		77	T 16
71	AZE		120	RA 22
54	AZELOT		68	YA 13
23	AZERABLES		131	DA 22
54	AZERAILLES		68	AB 13
24	AZERAT		158	BA 28
43	AZERAT		148	LA 27
65	AZEREIX		208	W 36
65	AZET		216	Y 38
50	AZEVILLE		33	Q 9
34	AZILLANET		213	IA 36
11	AZILLE		212	IA 36
2A	AZILONE AMPAZA		227	KB 42
62	AZINCOURT		16	FA 4
69	AZOLETTE		136	OA 23
57	AZOUDANGE		69	AB 12
40	AZUR		183	Q 34
18	AZY		101	IA 19
58	AZY LE VIF		118	LA 21
02	AZY SUR MARNE		41	LA 11
2A	AZZANA		227	KB 41

B

55	BAALON		30	TA 9
08	BAALONS		30	RA 8
34	BABEAU BOULDOUX		213	JA 35
60	BABOEUF		27	KA 8
77	BABY		63	LA 13
54	BACCARAT	C	69	AB 13
45	BACCON		80	DA 16
46	BACH		174	DA 31
59	BACHANT		19	NA 5
31	BACHAS		209	AA 36
24	BACHELLERIE, LA		158	BA 28
60	BACHIVILLERS		39	FA 9
31	BACHOS		217	Z 38
59	BACHY		9	LA 4
50	BACILLY		56	Q 12
51	BACONNES		43	PA 10
53	BACONNIERE, LA		77	S 14
60	BACOUEL		26	HA 8
80	BACOUEL SUR SELLE		26	GA 7
57	BACOURT		47	ZA 11
27	BACQUEPUIS		38	BA 10
27	BACQUEVILLE		25	CA 9
76	BACQUEVILLE EN CAUX	C	24	BA 7
15	BADAILHAC		161	IA 29
48	BADAROUX		177	MA 31
36	BADECON LE PIN		115	DA 22
24	BADEFOLS D'ANS		144	BA 27
24	BADEFOLS SUR DORDOGNE		158	AA 29
56	BADEN		91	J 17
11	BADENS		212	HA 36
25	BADEVEL		90	BB 17
38	BADINIERES		151	UA 26
88	BADMENIL AUX BOIS		68	ZA 14
54	BADONVILLER	C	69	BB 13
55	BADONVILLIERS GERAUVILLIERS		67	VA 13
67	BAERENDORF		48	CB 11
57	BAERENTHAL		48	EB 11
88	BAFFE, LA		68	ZA 14
63	BAFFIE		149	NA 26
30	BAGARD		193	OA 33
33	BAGAS		171	W 30
46	BAGAT EN QUERCY		173	CA 31
01	BAGE LA VILLE		137	SA 23
01	BAGE LE CHATEL	C	137	SA 23
09	BAGERT		218	BA 37
11	BAGES		223	JA 37
66	BAGES		224	JA 39
31	BAGIRY		217	Z 37
46	BAGNAC SUR CELE		175	GA 30
89	BAGNEAUX		64	MA 14
77	BAGNEAUX SUR LOING		62	IA 14
65	BAGNERES DE BIGORRE	S	216	X 37
31	BAGNERES DE LUCHON	C	217	Z 38
02	BAGNEUX		27	LA 9
03	BAGNEUX		118	KA 21
36	BAGNEUX		99	EA 19
51	BAGNEUX		64	NA 13
54	BAGNEUX		67	WA 13
92	BAGNEUX	C	40	GA 12
10	BAGNEUX LA FOSSE		85	PA 15
17	BAGNIZEAU		128	V 25
11	BAGNOLES		212	HA 36
61	BAGNOLES DE L'ORNE		58	U 13
93	BAGNOLET	C	40	HA 11
63	BAGNOLS		147	IA 26
69	BAGNOLS		136	RA 24
83	BAGNOLS EN FORET		198	AB 35
48	BAGNOLS LES BAINS		177	MA 31
30	BAGNOLS SUR CEZE	C	179	RA 32
21	BAGNOT		105	TA 19
35	BAGUER MORVAN		55	O 13
35	BAGUER PICAN		55	P 13
66	BAHO		224	JA 39
40	BAHUS SOUBIRAN		185	V 34
28	BAIGNEAUX		61	EA 15
33	BAIGNEAUX		156	V 30
41	BAIGNEAUX		80	CA 16
70	BAIGNES		88	XA 17
16	BAIGNES STE RADEGONDE	C	142	V 27
21	BAIGNEUX LES JUIFS	C	85	RA 17
28	BAIGNOLET		61	DA 14
40	BAIGTS		184	T 34
64	BAIGTS DE BEARN		206	S 35
34	BAILLARGUES		193	OA 34
35	BAILLE		56	O 14
28	BAILLEAU ARMENONVILLE		61	DA 13
28	BAILLEAU L'EVEQUE		60	CA 13
28	BAILLEAU LE PIN		60	CA 14
66	BAILLESTAVY		222	HA 39
95	BAILLET EN FRANCE		40	GA 10
59	BAILLEUL	C	8	IA 3
61	BAILLEUL		58	W 12
80	BAILLEUL		16	EA 6
72	BAILLEUL, LE		78	V 16
62	BAILLEUL AUX CORNAILLES		17	HA 5
27	BAILLEUL LA VALLEE		37	Y 10
60	BAILLEUL LE SOC		26	IA 9
62	BAILLEUL LES PERNES		8	HA 4
76	BAILLEUL NEUVILLE		25	CA 7
62	BAILLEUL SIR BERTHOULT		17	JA 5
60	BAILLEUL SUR THERAIN		26	GA 9
62	BAILLEULMONT		17	IA 5
62	BAILLEULVAL		17	IA 5
60	BAILLEVAL		26	HA 9
76	BAILLOLET		25	CA 7
41	BAILLOU		79	AA 15
60	BAILLY		27	JA 9
78	BAILLY		39	FA 11
52	BAILLY AUX FORGES		66	SA 13
76	BAILLY EN RIVIERE		15	CA 7
10	BAILLY LE FRANC		65	RA 13
77	BAILLY ROMAINVILLIERS		40	JA 11
35	BAIN DE BRETAGNE	C	75	P 16
62	BAINCTHUN		7	EA 3
62	BAINGHEN		7	FA 3
43	BAINS		163	NA 28
88	BAINS LES BAINS	C	88	YA 15
35	BAINS SUR OUST		75	N 16
54	BAINVILLE AUX MIROIRS		68	YA 13
88	BAINVILLE AUX SAULES		68	XA 14
54	BAINVILLE SUR MADON		67	XA 13
06	BAIROLS		199	CB 33
35	BAIS		76	Q 15
53	BAIS	C	58	V 14
59	BAISIEUX		9	LA 4
52	BAISSEY		86	TA 16
59	BAIVES		19	PA 6
07	BAIX		164	RA 30
66	BAIXAS		224	JA 39
80	BAIZIEUX		17	HA 6
51	BAIZIL, LE		42	NA 11
47	BAJAMONT		172	Z 32
32	BAJONNETTE		187	AA 34
62	BAJUS		17	HA 4
09	BALACET		217	AA 38
46	BALADOU		159	DA 29
60	BALAGNY SUR THERAIN		40	GA 9
09	BALAGUERES		218	BA 38
12	BALAGUIER D'OLT		174	FA 31
12	BALAGUIER SUR RANCE		190	IA 33
39	BALAISEAUX		122	UA 21
08	BALAIVES ET BUTZ		30	RA 8
01	BALAN		137	TA 25
08	BALAN		30	SA 8
39	BALANOD		122	UA 22
64	BALANSUN		206	T 35
17	BALANZAC		141	S 25
34	BALARUC LE VIEUX		214	NA 35
34	BALARUC LES BAINS		214	MA 35
80	BALATRE		27	JA 8
35	BALAZE		76	R 14
07	BALAZUC		178	QA 31
42	BALBIGNY		149	PA 25
38	BALBINS		151	TA 27
67	BALBRONN		70	DB 13
67	BALDENHEIM		70	EB 14
68	BALDERSHEIM		90	DB 16
50	BALEINE, LA		56	Q 11
64	BALEIX		207	W 36
52	BALESMES SUR MARNE		87	UA 16
31	BALESTA		217	Z 37
47	BALEYSSAGUES		171	X 30
68	BALGAU		90	EB 15
08	BALHAM		29	PA 9
82	BALIGNAC		187	AA 33
10	BALIGNICOURT		65	QA 13
27	BALINES		38	BA 12
62	BALINGHEM		7	FA 2
64	BALIRACQ MAUMUSSON		207	V 35
64	BALIROS		207	V 36
33	BALIZAC		170	U 31
91	BALLAINVILLIERS		62	GA 12
74	BALLAISON		139	YA 23
37	BALLAN MIRE	C	98	Z 18
91	BALLANCOURT SUR ESSONNE		62	HA 13
17	BALLANS		142	V 25
08	BALLAY		30	RA 9
87	BALLEDENT		131	BA 24
53	BALLEE		77	U 15
58	BALLERAY		102	LA 19
14	BALLEROY	C	35	S 10
68	BALLERSDORF		90	CB 17
88	BALLEVILLE		67	WA 14
17	BALLON		127	S 24
72	BALLON	C	78	X 14
26	BALLONS		180	VA 32
71	BALLORE		120	QA 22
53	BALLOTS		76	R 16
77	BALLOY		63	KA 13
31	BALMA		210	DA 35
73	BALME, LA		152	WA 25
39	BALME D'EPY, LA		138	UA 22
74	BALME DE SILLINGY, LA		139	XA 24
74	BALME DE THUY, LA		139	YA 24
38	BALME LES GROTTES, LA		138	UA 25
10	BALNOT LA GRANGE		85	PA 15
10	BALNOT SUR LAIGNES		85	PA 15
2A	BALOGNA		227	JB 41
21	BALOT		85	QA 16
12	BALSAC		175	HA 31
68	BALSCHWILLER		90	CB 17
48	BALSIEGES		177	LA 31
68	BALTZENHEIM		70	EB 15
16	BALZAC		143	X 25
59	BAMBECQUE		8	HA 2
57	BAMBIDERSTROFF		47	ZA 10
88	BAN DE LAVELINE		69	BB 14
88	BAN DE SAPT		69	BB 14
57	BAN ST MARTIN, LE		46	XA 10
88	BAN SUR MEURTHE		69	BB 14
48	BANASSAC		176	KA 31
64	BANCA		205	Q 37
02	BANCIGNY		29	OA 7
62	BANCOURT		17	JA 6
83	BANDOL		202	WA 37
01	BANEINS		137	SA 24
24	BANEUIL		158	Z 29
56	BANGOR		91	I 18
65	BANIOS		216	X 37
23	BANIZE		132	FA 24
29	BANNALEC	C	72	G 15
25	BANNANS		123	YA 20
18	BANNAY		101	JA 18
51	BANNAY		42	NA 11
57	BANNAY		47	ZA 10
07	BANNE		178	PA 31
18	BANNEGON		117	IA 21
46	BANNES		160	FA 29
51	BANNES		42	OA 12
52	BANNES		87	UA 16
53	BANNES		77	V 15
14	BANNEVILLE LA CAMPAGNE		36	V 10
14	BANNEVILLE SUR AJON		35	U 10
81	BANNIERES		211	EA 35
55	BANNONCOURT		44	UA 11
77	BANNOST VILLEGAGNON		63	KA 12
08	BANOGNE RECOUVRANCE		29	OA 8
04	BANON	C	196	VA 33
40	BANOS		184	T 34
39	BANS		122	VA 20
63	BANSAT		148	LA 26
71	BANTANGES		121	TA 21
59	BANTEUX		18	KA 6
95	BANTHELU		39	EA 10
55	BANTHEVILLE		30	TA 9
59	BANTIGNY		18	KA 5
59	BANTOUZELLE		18	KA 6
68	BANTZENHEIM		90	DB 16
90	BANVILLARS		89	AB 17
14	BANVILLE		35	U 9
61	BANVOU		57	U 12
66	BANYULS DELS ASPRES		224	JA 39
66	BANYULS SUR MER		224	KA 40
89	BAON		84	OA 16
76	BAONS LE COMTE		24	AA 8
62	BAPAUME	C	17	JA 6
19	BAR		145	EA 27
55	BAR LE DUC	P	44	TA 12
08	BAR LES BUZANCY		30	SA 9
10	BAR SUR AUBE	S	65	RA 14
06	BAR SUR LOUP, LE	C	200	BB 34
10	BAR SUR SEINE	C	65	QA 15
49	BARACE		77	U 17
11	BARAIGNE		211	EA 36
36	BARAIZE		115	DA 22
62	BARALLE		17	KA 5
12	BARAQUEVILLE	C	175	HA 32
62	BARASTRE		17	JA 6
05	BARATIER		182	ZA 31
65	BARBACHEN		208	X 35
2B	BARBAGGIO		226	MB 39
11	BARBAIRA		221	HA 37
08	BARBAISE		29	RA 8
54	BARBAS		69	BB 13
47	BARBASTE		171	X 32
85	BARBATRE		109	M 20
31	BARBAZAN	C	217	Z 37
65	BARBAZAN DEBAT		216	X 37
65	BARBAZAN DESSUS		216	X 37
44	BARBECHAT		94	Q 18
13	BARBEN, LA		201	TA 35
13	BARBENTANE		195	RA 33
73	BARBERAZ		153	XA 26
10	BARBEREY ST SULPICE		64	OA 14
03	BARBERIER		133	LA 23
14	BARBERY		36	V 11
60	BARBERY		40	IA 10
14	BARBEVILLE		35	T 10
77	BARBEY		63	KA 14
88	BARBEY SEROUX		69	BB 15
16	BARBEZIERES		128	W 24
16	BARBEZIEUX ST HILAIRE	C	142	V 26
26	BARBIERES		165	TA 29
21	BARBIREY SUR OUCHE		104	RA 18
77	BARBIZON		62	IA 13
51	BARBONNE FAYEL		64	NA 12
54	BARBONVILLE		68	YA 13
25	BARBOUX, LE		108	AB 19
10	BARBUISE		64	MA 13
08	BARBY		29	PA 8
73	BARBY		153	XA 26
27	BARC		37	AA 10
66	BARCARES, LE		224	KA 38
26	BARCELONNE		165	TA 29
32	BARCELONNE DU GERS		185	V 34
04	BARCELONNETTE	S	182	AB 31
57	BARCHAIN		69	BB 12
05	BARCILLONNETTE	C	181	WA 31
32	BARCUGNAN		208	Y 36
64	BARCUS		206	T 37
77	BARCY		41	JA 11
42	BARD		149	OA 26
21	BARD LE REGULIER		104	PA 19
21	BARD LES EPOISSES		85	PA 17
70	BARD LES PESMES		106	VA 18
17	BARDE, LA		156	W 28
16	BARDENAC		142	W 27
82	BARDIGUES		187	AA 33
45	BARDON, LE		80	DA 16
64	BARDOS		206	R 35
24	BARDOU		158	Z 30
76	BARDOUVILLE		24	AA 9
65	BAREGES		216	W 38
65	BAREILLES		216	Y 38
67	BAREMBACH		69	CB 13
31	BAREN		217	Z 38
76	BARENTIN		24	AA 8
50	BARENTON	C	57	S 13
02	BARENTON BUGNY		28	MA 8
02	BARENTON CEL		28	MA 8
02	BARENTON SUR SERRE		28	MA 8
39	BARESIA SUR L'AIN		122	VA 22
50	BARFLEUR		33	R 8
83	BARGEME		198	ZA 34
83	BARGEMON		198	ZA 35
21	BARGES		105	TA 19
43	BARGES		163	NA 29
70	BARGES		87	WA 16
60	BARGNY		41	JA 10
33	BARIE		171	W 30
27	BARILS, LES		37	AA 12
64	BARINQUE		207	V 36
54	BARISEY AU PLAIN		67	WA 13
54	BARISEY LA COTE		67	WA 13
02	BARISIS		28	LA 8
71	BARIZEY		120	RA 21
09	BARJAC		218	BA 37
30	BARJAC	C	178	PA 32
48	BARJAC		177	LA 31
83	BARJOLS	C	203	XA 35
21	BARJON		86	SA 17
28	BARJOUVILLE		60	DA 13
04	BARLES		181	YA 32
65	BARLEST		216	W 37
80	BARLEUX		27	JA 7
18	BARLIEU		82	IA 17
62	BARLIN	C	17	IA 4
62	BARLY		17	HA 5
80	BARLY		16	GA 5
28	BARMAINVILLE		61	FA 14
07	BARNAS		178	PA 30
26	BARNAVE		166	UA 30
71	BARNAY		104	PA 19
14	BARNEVILLE LA BERTRAN		23	X 9
50	BARNEVILLE CARTERET	C	33	O 9
27	BARNEVILLE SUR SEINE		24	AA 9
61	BAROCHE SOUS LUCE, LA		57	U 13
54	BAROCHES, LES		45	WA 10
76	BAROMESNIL		15	CA 6
30	BARON		193	PA 33
33	BARON		156	V 29
60	BARON		40	IA 10
71	BARON		120	PA 22
14	BARON SUR ODON		35	U 10
57	BARONVILLE		47	AB 11
14	BAROU EN AUGE		36	W 11
10	BAROVILLE		65	RA 14
33	BARP, LE		170	T 30
27	BARQUET		37	AA 11
67	BARR	C	70	DB 13
03	BARRAIS BUSSOLLES		135	NA 23
32	BARRAN		208	Y 35
65	BARRANCOUEU		216	Y 38
04	BARRAS		181	XA 32
64	BARRAUTE CAMU		206	S 36
38	BARRAUX		153	XA 27
81	BARRE		191	JA 34
39	BARRE, LA		106	VA 19
70	BARRE, LA		107	YA 18
85	BARRE DE MONTS, LA		109	N 20
50	BARRE DE SEMILLY, LA		35	S 10
48	BARRE DES CEVENNES	C	177	MA 32
27	BARRE EN OUCHE, LA		37	Z 11
04	BARREME	C	198	YA 33
16	BARRET		142	V 26
26	BARRET DE LIOURE		180	VA 32
05	BARRET LE BAS		180	VA 32
39	BARRETAINE		122	VA 20
2B	BARRETTALI		226	MB 38
15	BARRIAC LES BOSQUETS		160	GA 28
16	BARRO		129	X 24
37	BARROU		114	AA 20
84	BARROUX, LE		179	TA 32
65	BARRY		216	W 37
82	BARRY D'ISLEMADE		188	CA 33
24	BARS		158	BA 28
32	BARS		208	X 35
26	BARSAC		166	UA 30
33	BARSAC		170	V 30
57	BARST		47	AB 10
25	BART		108	AB 17
68	BARTENHEIM		90	DB 17
65	BARTHE		209	Y 36
65	BARTHE DE NESTE, LA	C	216	Y 37
54	BARTHELEMONT LES BAUZEMONT		46	ZA 12
25	BARTHERANS		106	WA 19
82	BARTHES, LES		188	BA 33
65	BARTRES		216	W 37
27	BARVILLE		37	Y 10
61	BARVILLE		59	Y 13
88	BARVILLE		67	WA 13
45	BARVILLE EN GATINAIS		62	HA 15
17	BARZAN		141	S 26
64	BARZUN		207	W 36
02	BARZY EN THIERACHE		18	NA 6
02	BARZY SUR MARNE		42	MA 10
43	BAS EN BASSET	C	149	OA 27
63	BAS ET LEZAT		133	LA 24
59	BAS LIEU		19	OA 6
40	BAS MAUCO		184	U 34
40	BASCONS		184	U 34
32	BASCOUS		186	X 34
54	BASLIEUX		31	WA 9
51	BASLIEUX LES FISMES		28	NA 9
51	BASLIEUX SOUS CHATILLON		42	NA 10
14	BASLY		36	U 9
16	BASSAC		142	W 26
34	BASSAN		213	LA 36
33	BASSANNE		171	W 30
44	BASSE GOULAINE	C	94	Q 19
57	BASSE HAM		32	YA 9
57	BASSE RENTGEN		32	YA 9
88	BASSE SUR LE RUPT		89	AB 15
70	BASSE VAIVRE, LA		88	XA 15
59	BASSEE, LA	C	9	JA 4
67	BASSEMBERG		69	CB 14
14	BASSENEVILLE		36	V 10
33	BASSENS		156	U 29
73	BASSENS		152	WA 26
40	BASSERCLES		184	T 35
86	BASSES		97	X 19
62	BASSEUX		17	IA 5
77	BASSEVELLE		41	LA 11
15	BASSIGNAC		146	HA 27
19	BASSIGNAC LE BAS		160	EA 28
19	BASSIGNAC LE HAUT		160	FA 28
70	BASSIGNEY		88	YA 16
24	BASSILAC		158	AA 28
64	BASSILLON VAUZE		208	W 35
57	BASSING		47	AB 11
02	BASSOLES AULERS		28	LA 8
52	BASSONCOURT		67	VA 15
89	BASSOU		83	MA 16
32	BASSOUES		208	X 35
51	BASSU		43	RA 11
51	BASSUET		43	RA 12
48	BASSURELS		177	MA 32
64	BASSUSSARRY		205	P 35
74	BASSY		138	WA 24
64	BASTANES		206	T 36
2A	BASTELICA	C	226	KB 42
2A	BASTELICACCIA		227	JB 42
40	BASTENNES		184	T 35
2B	BASTIA	P	226	MB 39
66	BASTIDE, LA		224	IA 39
83	BASTIDE, LA		198	AB 34
64	BASTIDE CLAIRENCE, LA	C	205	Q 36
30	BASTIDE D'ENGRAS, LA		193	QA 33
09	BASTIDE DE BESPLAS, LA		218	CA 37
09	BASTIDE DE BOUSIGNAC, LA		219	EA 37
09	BASTIDE DE LORDAT, LA		219	EA 37
09	BASTIDE DE SEROU, LA	C	218	CA 37
84	BASTIDE DES JOURDANS, LA		196	VA 34
09	BASTIDE DU SALAT, LA		218	BA 37
12	BASTIDE L'EVEQUE, LA		175	GA 31
12	BASTIDE PRADINES, LA		191	KA 33
48	BASTIDE PUYLAURENT, LA		177	NA 30
12	BASTIDE SOLAGES, LA		190	HA 33
09	BASTIDE SUR L'HERS, LA		221	FA 38
84	BASTIDONNE, LA		196	VA 34
46	BASTIT, LE		159	EA 30
23	BASVILLE		132	HA 25
79	BATAILLE, LA		128	W 24
26	BATHERNAY		165	SA 28
73	BATHIE, LA		153	ZA 26
26	BATIE DES FONDS, LA		180	VA 31
38	BATIE DIVISIN, LA		152	VA 26
38	BATIE MONTGASCON, LA		152	VA 26
05	BATIE MONTSALEON, LA		181	WA 31
05	BATIE NEUVE, LA	C	181	YA 30
26	BATIE ROLLAND, LA		179	SA 30
05	BATIE VIEILLE, LA		181	XA 30
70	BATIES, LES		88	WA 17
54	BATILLY		45	XA 10
61	BATILLY		58	V 12
45	BATILLY EN GATINAIS		62	HA 16
45	BATILLY EN PUISAYE		82	JA 17
40	BATS		184	U 34
65	BATSERE		216	X 37
25	BATTENANS LES MINES		107	YA 18
25	BATTENANS VARIN		108	AB 19
68	BATTENHEIM		90	DB 16
88	BATTEXEY		68	YA 13
54	BATTIGNY		67	XA 13
70	BATTRANS		106	VA 18
44	BATZ SUR MER		92	L 18
67	BATZENDORF		49	EB 12
21	BAUBIGNY		120	RA 20
73	BAUCHE, LA		152	WA 26
56	BAUD	C	73	J 16
51	BAUDEMENT		64	NA 13
71	BAUDEMONT		135	PA 23
40	BAUDIGNAN		185	W 33
55	BAUDIGNECOURT		66	UA 13
83	BAUDINARD SUR VERDON		197	XA 34
70	BAUDONCOURT		88	YA 16
55	BAUDONVILLIERS		44	SA 12
50	BAUDRE		34	R 10
52	BAUDRECOURT		66	SA 13
57	BAUDRECOURT		47	ZA 11
64	BAUDREIX		207	V 36
55	BAUDREMONT		44	UA 11
36	BAUDRES		99	DA 19
28	BAUDREVILLE		61	FA 14
50	BAUDREVILLE		34	P 9
88	BAUDRICOURT		67	XA 14
71	BAUDRIERES		121	SA 21
83	BAUDUEN		197	YA 34
49	BAUGE	C	96	W 17
18	BAUGY	C	101	IA 19
60	BAUGY		27	IA 9
71	BAUGY		135	OA 23
70	BAULAY		88	XA 16

Dép.	Commune		Page	Carreau
45	BAULE		81	EA 16
44	BAULE ESCOUBLAC, LA	C	92	L 18
21	BAULME LA ROCHE		105	SA 18
91	BAULNE		62	HA 13
02	BAULNE EN BRIE		42	MA 11
55	BAULNY		44	SA 10
35	BAULON		75	N 15
09	BAULOU		219	DA 37
74	BAUME, LA		140	ZA 23
26	BAUME CORNILLANE, LA		165	TA 29
26	BAUME D'HOSTUN, LA		165	TA 28
26	BAUME DE TRANSIT, LA		179	SA 31
25	BAUME LES DAMES	C	107	YA 18
39	BAUME LES MESSIEURS		87	VA 17
49	BAUNE		96	V 17
50	BAUPTE		34	Q 9
14	BAUQUAY		35	T 11
33	BAURECH		156	U 30
35	BAUSSAINE, LA		75	O 14
59	BAUVIN		9	JA 4
27	BAUX DE BRETEUIL, LES		37	AA 11
13	BAUX DE PROVENCE, LES		195	SA 34
27	BAUX STE CROIX, LES		38	BA 11
54	BAUZEMONT		46	ZA 12
41	BAUZY		80	DA 17
25	BAVANS		89	AB 17
59	BAVAY	C	19	NA 5
80	BAVELINCOURT		17	HA 6
14	BAVENT		36	V 10
39	BAVERANS		106	VA 19
90	BAVILLIERS		89	AB 17
59	BAVINCHOVE		8	HA 3
62	BAVINCOURT		17	IA 5
31	BAX		210	CA 36
70	BAY		106	WA 18
52	BAY SUR AUBE		86	TA 16
24	BAYAC		158	Z 29
52	BAYARD SUR MARNE		66	TA 13
33	BAYAS		156	V 28
29	BAYE		72	G 16
51	BAYE		42	NA 11
88	BAYECOURT		68	ZA 14
10	BAYEL		66	RA 14
80	BAYENCOURT		17	IA 6
62	BAYENGHEM LES EPERLECQUES		7	FA 3
62	BAYENGHEM LES SENINGHEM		7	FA 3
16	BAYERS		129	X 24
03	BAYET		133	LA 23
14	BAYEUX	S	35	T 9
54	BAYON	C	68	YA 13
33	BAYON SUR GIRONDE		156	T 28
64	BAYONNE	S	205	Q 35
04	BAYONS		181	XA 31
08	BAYONVILLE		30	SA 9
54	BAYONVILLE SUR MAD		45	XA 11
80	BAYONVILLERS		27	IA 7
16	BAZAC		143	W 27
36	BAZAIGES		115	DA 22
54	BAZAILLES		31	WA 9
78	BAZAINVILLE		39	EA 12
51	BAZANCOURT		29	PA 9
60	BAZANCOURT		25	EA 8
89	BAZARNES		84	MA 17
33	BAZAS	C	170	V 31
17	BAZAUGES		128	V 24
88	BAZEGNEY		68	YA 14
08	BAZEILLES		30	SA 8
55	BAZEILLES SUR OTHAIN		31	UA 8
23	BAZELAT		131	DA 23
78	BAZEMONT		39	EA 11
47	BAZENS		172	Y 32
80	BAZENTIN		17	IA 6
14	BAZENVILLE		35	U 9
65	BAZET		208	W 36
87	BAZEUGE, LA		130	BA 23
32	BAZIAN		186	Y 34
60	BAZICOURT		26	IA 9
31	BAZIEGE		210	DA 35
88	BAZIEN		68	AB 13
65	BAZILLAC		208	X 36
27	BAZINCOURT SUR EPTE		39	EA 9
55	BAZINCOURT SUR SAULX		44	TA 12
62	BAZINGHEN		7	DA 3
76	BAZINVAL		15	DA 6
28	BAZOCHE GOUET, LA		60	AA 15
58	BAZOCHES		103	NA 18
61	BAZOCHES AU HOULME		36	V 11
28	BAZOCHES EN DUNOIS		60	DA 15
77	BAZOCHES LES BRAY		63	KA 13
45	BAZOCHES LES GALLERANDES		61	FA 14
28	BAZOCHES LES HAUTES		61	EA 15
78	BAZOCHES SUR GUYONNE		39	EA 12
61	BAZOCHES SUR HOENE	C	59	Y 13
45	BAZOCHES SUR LE BETZ		63	JA 15
02	BAZOCHES SUR VESLES		28	MA 9
50	BAZOGE, LA		57	S 12
72	BAZOGE, LA		78	X 15
53	BAZOGE MONTPINCON, LA		57	U 14
85	BAZOGES EN PAILLERS		110	R 20
85	BAZOGES EN PAREDS		111	S 21
88	BAZOILLES ET MENIL		67	XA 14
88	BAZOILLES SUR MEUSE		67	VA 14
58	BAZOLLES		103	MA 19
57	BAZONCOURT		46	YA 10
14	BAZOQUE, LA		35	S 10
61	BAZOQUE, LA		57	U 12
27	BAZOQUES		37	Z 10
65	BAZORDAN		209	Y 36
53	BAZOUGE DE CHEMERE, LA		77	U 15
53	BAZOUGE DES ALLEUX, LA		77	T 14
35	BAZOUGE DU DESERT, LA		56	R 13
53	BAZOUGERS		77	U 15
35	BAZOUGES LA PEROUSE		56	P 13
72	BAZOUGES SUR LE LOIR		78	V 17
59	BAZUEL		18	MA 6
32	BAZUGUES		208	Y 35
31	BAZUS		188	DA 34
65	BAZUS AURE		216	Y 38
65	BAZUS NESTE		216	Y 37
07	BEAGE, LE		163	OA 29
80	BEALCOURT		16	GA 5
62	BEALENCOURT		16	GA 4
58	BEARD		118	LA 20
76	BEAUBEC LA ROSIERE		25	DA 8
71	BEAUBERY		136	QA 22
50	BEAUBIGNY		33	O 9
27	BEAUBRAY		37	AA 11
30	BEAUCAIRE	C	195	RA 34
32	BEAUCAIRE		186	Y 34
80	BEAUCAMPS LE JEUNE		25	EA 7
80	BEAUCAMPS LE VIEUX		25	EA 7
59	BEAUCAMPS LIGNY		9	JA 4
35	BEAUCE		76	R 14
65	BEAUCENS		216	W 37
84	BEAUCET, LE		196	TA 33
31	BEAUCHALOT		217	AA 37
95	BEAUCHAMP	C	39	GA 11
50	BEAUCHAMPS		56	O 11
80	BEAUCHAMPS		15	DA 6
45	BEAUCHAMPS SUR HUILLARD		82	HA 15
07	BEAUCHASTEL		164	RA 29
28	BEAUCHE		37	AA 12
41	BEAUCHENE		79	BA 15
61	BEAUCHENE		57	T 12
77	BEAUCHERY ST MARTIN		63	LA 12
55	BEAUCLAIR		30	TA 9
50	BEAUCOUDRAY		34	R 11
90	BEAUCOURT	C	90	BB 17
80	BEAUCOURT EN SANTERRE		27	IA 7
80	BEAUCOURT SUR L'ANCRE		17	IA 6
80	BEAUCOURT SUR L'HALLUE		17	HA 6
49	BEAUCOUZE		95	T 17
38	BEAUCROISSANT		152	UA 27
65	BEAUDEAN		216	X 37
60	BEAUDEDUIT		26	FA 8
59	BEAUDIGNIES		18	MA 5
62	BEAUDRICOURT		17	HA 5
61	BEAUFAI		37	Y 12
72	BEAUFAY		59	Y 14
50	BEAUFICEL		57	S 12
27	BEAUFICEL EN LYONS		25	DA 9
38	BEAUFIN		167	XA 29
31	BEAUFORT		210	BA 35
34	BEAUFORT		213	IA 36
38	BEAUFORT		151	TA 27
39	BEAUFORT	C	122	UA 22
59	BEAUFORT		19	OA 5
73	BEAUFORT	C	154	ZA 25
62	BEAUFORT BLAVINCOURT		17	HA 5
55	BEAUFORT EN ARGONNE		30	TA 9
80	BEAUFORT EN SANTERRE		26	IA 7
49	BEAUFORT EN VALLEE	C	96	V 18
26	BEAUFORT SUR GERVANNE		165	TA 29
85	BEAUFOU		110	P 20
14	BEAUFOUR DRUVAL		36	W 10
88	BEAUFREMONT		67	WA 14
47	BEAUGAS		172	Z 31
17	BEAUGEAY		127	S 25
45	BEAUGENCY	C	80	DA 16
60	BEAUGIES SOUS BOIS		27	KA 8
04	BEAUJEU		182	YA 32
69	BEAUJEU	C	136	RA 23
70	BEAUJEU ST VALLIER PIERREJUX ET QUITTEUR		87	VA 17
61	BEAULANDAIS		57	U 13
62	BEAULENCOURT		17	JA 6
07	BEAULIEU		178	PA 31
14	BEAULIEU		35	T 11
15	BEAULIEU		147	HA 26
21	BEAULIEU		85	RA 16
34	BEAULIEU		193	OA 34
36	BEAULIEU		131	CA 22
38	BEAULIEU		166	UA 28
43	BEAULIEU		163	OA 28
58	BEAULIEU		102	MA 18
61	BEAULIEU		37	Z 12
63	BEAULIEU		148	LA 27
55	BEAULIEU EN ARGONNE		44	TA 11
60	BEAULIEU LES FONTAINES		27	JA 8
37	BEAULIEU LES LOCHES		98	BA 19
85	BEAULIEU SOUS LA ROCHE		110	P 21
79	BEAULIEU SOUS PARTHENAY		112	V 22
19	BEAULIEU SUR DORDOGNE	C	159	EA 29
49	BEAULIEU SUR LAYON		95	U 18
45	BEAULIEU SUR LOIRE		82	JA 17
06	BEAULIEU SUR MER		200	DB 34
53	BEAULIEU SUR OUDON		76	S 15
16	BEAULIEU SUR SONNETTE		129	Y 24
03	BEAULON		119	MA 21
14	BEAUMAIS		36	W 11
32	BEAUMARCHES		208	W 35
46	BEAUMAT		174	DA 30
02	BEAUME		29	PA 7
05	BEAUME, LA		180	VA 30
88	BEAUMENIL		69	AB 14
62	BEAUMERIE ST MARTIN		16	EA 4
84	BEAUMES DE VENISE	C	179	TA 32
14	BEAUMESNIL		35	S 11
27	BEAUMESNIL	C	37	Z 11
84	BEAUMETTES		196	TA 34
80	BEAUMETZ		16	GA 6
62	BEAUMETZ LES AIRE		8	GA 4
62	BEAUMETZ LES CAMBRAI		17	JA 6
62	BEAUMETZ LES LOGES	C	17	IA 5
07	BEAUMONT		178	PA 31
19	BEAUMONT		146	EA 27
24	BEAUMONT	C	158	Z 30
32	BEAUMONT		186	X 33
43	BEAUMONT		148	LA 27
54	BEAUMONT		45	WA 11
63	BEAUMONT	C	148	KA 25
74	BEAUMONT		139	XA 24
86	BEAUMONT		113	Y 21
89	BEAUMONT		83	MA 16
82	BEAUMONT DE LOMAGNE	C	187	BA 33
84	BEAUMONT DE PERTUIS		196	VA 34
77	BEAUMONT DU GATINAIS		62	HA 15
87	BEAUMONT DU LAC		146	EA 25
84	BEAUMONT DU VENTOUX		179	TA 32
08	BEAUMONT EN ARGONNE		30	SA 8
14	BEAUMONT EN AUGE		36	X 10
02	BEAUMONT EN BEINE		27	KA 8
59	BEAUMONT EN CAMBRESIS		18	LA 6
26	BEAUMONT EN DIOIS		180	UA 30
55	BEAUMONT EN VERDUNOIS (VILLAGE RUINE)		44	UA 10
37	BEAUMONT EN VERON		97	X 19
50	BEAUMONT HAGUE	C	33	O 8
80	BEAUMONT HAMEL		17	IA 6
58	BEAUMONT LA FERRIERE		102	KA 19
37	BEAUMONT LA RONCE		79	Z 17
76	BEAUMONT LE HARENG		24	CA 8
27	BEAUMONT LE ROGER	C	37	Z 10
28	BEAUMONT LES AUTELS		60	AA 14
60	BEAUMONT LES NONAINS		26	FA 9
63	BEAUMONT LES RANDAN		133	LA 24
26	BEAUMONT LES VALENCE		165	SA 29
26	BEAUMONT MONTEUX		165	SA 28
53	BEAUMONT PIED DE BOEUF		77	U 16
72	BEAUMONT PIED DE BOEUF		79	Y 16
58	BEAUMONT SARDOLLES		118	LA 20
72	BEAUMONT SUR DEME		79	Z 17
71	BEAUMONT SUR GROSNE		121	SA 21
31	BEAUMONT SUR LEZE		210	CA 36
95	BEAUMONT SUR OISE	C	40	GA 10
72	BEAUMONT SUR SARTHE	C	58	X 14
51	BEAUMONT SUR VESLE		43	PA 10
21	BEAUMONT SUR VINGEANNE		105	UA 18
37	BEAUMONT VILLAGE		98	BA 19
27	BEAUMONTEL		37	AA 10
70	BEAUMOTTE AUBERTANS		107	YA 18
70	BEAUMOTTE LES PIN		106	WA 18
51	BEAUNAY		42	NA 11
21	BEAUNE	S	121	SA 20
03	BEAUNE D'ALLIER		133	JA 23
45	BEAUNE LA ROLANDE	C	82	HA 15
43	BEAUNE SUR ARZON		149	NA 27
21	BEAUNOTTE		85	RA 17
01	BEAUPONT		121	TA 22
24	BEAUPOUYET		157	X 29
49	BEAUPREAU	C	95	S 19
31	BEAUPUY		188	DA 34
32	BEAUPUY		209	BA 35
47	BEAUPUY		171	X 31
82	BEAUPUY		188	BA 34
80	BEAUQUESNE		16	HA 6
59	BEAURAIN		18	MA 5
62	BEAURAINS		17	JA 5
60	BEAURAINS LES NOYON		27	JA 8
62	BEAURAINVILLE		16	FA 4
13	BEAURECUEIL		202	VA 35
01	BEAUREGARD		136	RA 24
46	BEAUREGARD		174	EA 31
26	BEAUREGARD BARET		165	TA 29
24	BEAUREGARD DE TERRASSON		159	CA 28
24	BEAUREGARD ET BASSAC		158	Z 29
63	BEAUREGARD L'EVEQUE		148	LA 25
63	BEAUREGARD VENDON		134	KA 24
38	BEAUREPAIRE	C	151	SA 27
60	BEAUREPAIRE		40	IA 9
76	BEAUREPAIRE		23	X 8
85	BEAUREPAIRE		110	R 20
71	BEAUREPAIRE EN BRESSE	C	122	UA 21
59	BEAUREPAIRE SUR SAMBRE		19	NA 6
02	BEAUREVOIR		18	LA 6
26	BEAURIERES		180	VA 30
02	BEAURIEUX		28	NA 9
59	BEAURIEUX		19	OA 5
24	BEAURONNE		157	Y 28
26	BEAUSEMBLANT		165	SA 28
55	BEAUSITE		44	TA 11
06	BEAUSOLEIL	C	200	DB 34
24	BEAUSSAC		143	Y 26
79	BEAUSSAIS		128	V 23
76	BEAUSSAULT		25	DA 8
49	BEAUSSE		95	S 18
83	BEAUSSET, LE	C	202	WA 37
31	BEAUTEVILLE		211	EA 36
77	BEAUTHEIL		41	KA 12
33	BEAUTIRAN		156	U 30
02	BEAUTOR		28	LA 8
76	BEAUTOT		24	BA 8
61	BEAUVAIN		58	V 12
60	BEAUVAIS	P	26	GA 9
17	BEAUVAIS SUR MATHA		128	V 25
81	BEAUVAIS SUR TESCOU		188	DA 33
80	BEAUVAL		16	HA 6
76	BEAUVAL EN CAUX		24	BA 7
26	BEAUVALLON		165	SA 29
49	BEAUVAU		96	V 17
07	BEAUVENE		164	QA 29
71	BEAUVERNOIS		122	UA 20
04	BEAUVEZER		182	ZA 32
31	BEAUVILLE		211	EA 35
47	BEAUVILLE	C	172	AA 32
28	BEAUVILLIERS		61	DA 14
41	BEAUVILLIERS		80	CA 16
89	BEAUVILLIERS		103	OA 18
50	BEAUVOIR		56	P 12
60	BEAUVOIR		26	HA 8
77	BEAUVOIR		63	JA 12
89	BEAUVOIR		83	LA 16
38	BEAUVOIR DE MARC		151	TA 26
76	BEAUVOIR EN LYONS		25	DA 8
38	BEAUVOIR EN ROYANS		166	UA 28
85	BEAUVOIR SUR MER	C	109	N 20
79	BEAUVOIR SUR NIORT	C	128	U 23
62	BEAUVOIR WAVANS		16	GA 5
62	BEAUVOIS		16	GA 5
59	BEAUVOIS EN CAMBRESIS		18	LA 6
02	BEAUVOIS EN VERMANDOIS		27	KA 7
26	BEAUVOISIN		180	TA 32
30	BEAUVOISIN		193	PA 34
43	BEAUX		163	OA 28
43	BEAUZAC		149	OA 27
31	BEAUZELLE		188	CA 34
47	BEAUZIAC		171	W 31
57	BEBING		69	BB 12
68	BEBLENHEIM		70	DB 15
76	BEC DE MORTAGNE		23	Y 8
27	BEC HELLOUIN, LE		37	Z 10
27	BEC THOMAS, LE		38	BA 10
32	BECCAS		208	X 35
79	BECELEUF		111	U 22
54	BECHAMPS		45	WA 10
35	BECHEREL	C	75	N 14
16	BECHERESSE		143	W 26
57	BECHY		46	YA 11
49	BECON LES GRANITS		95	T 17
80	BECORDEL BECOURT		17	IA 6
62	BECOURT		7	FA 3
02	BECQUIGNY		18	MA 6
80	BECQUIGNY		26	IA 8
34	BEDARIEUX	C	213	KA 35
84	BEDARRIDES	C	195	SA 33
18	BEDDES		116	GA 21
32	BEDECHAN		209	AA 35
35	BEDEE		75	N 14
09	BEDEILHAC ET AYNAT		219	DA 38
09	BEDEILLE		218	BA 37
64	BEDEILLE		207	W 36
17	BEDENAC		156	V 28
84	BEDOIN		180	TA 32
48	BEDOUES		177	MA 31
64	BEDOUS		215	T 37
46	BEDUER		174	FA 30
18	BEFFES		102	KA 19
39	BEFFIA		122	VA 22
08	BEFFU ET LE MORTHOMME		30	SA 9
40	BEGAAR		184	S 34
33	BEGADAN		141	S 27
56	BEGANNE		92	M 17
22	BEGARD	C	53	I 12
33	BEGLES	C	156	U 29
88	BEGNECOURT		68	YA 14
65	BEGOLE		216	Y 37
49	BEGROLLES EN MAUGES		95	S 19
26	BEGUDE DE MAZENC, LA		179	SA 31
03	BEGUES		134	KA 24
33	BEGUEY		170	V 30
64	BEGUIOS		206	R 36
62	BEHAGNIES		17	JA 6
64	BEHASQUE LAPISTE		206	S 36
80	BEHEN		15	EA 6
80	BEHENCOURT		17	HA 6
60	BEHERICOURT		27	KA 8
55	BEHONNE		44	TA 12
64	BEHORLEGUY		206	R 37
78	BEHOUST		39	EA 11
57	BEHREN LES FORBACH	C	47	BB 10
49	BEHUARD		95	T 18
56	BEIGNON		75	M 15
72	BEILLE		59	Y 15
89	BEINE		84	NA 16
51	BEINE NAUROY	C	43	PA 10
67	BEINHEIM		50	GB 11
21	BEIRE LE CHATEL		105	TA 18
21	BEIRE LE FORT		105	TA 19
23	BEISSAT		146	GA 25
36	BELABRE	C	114	BA 22
21	BELAN SUR OURCE		85	RA 15
34	BELARGA		214	MA 35
46	BELAYE		173	BA 31
31	BELBERAUD		210	DA 35
82	BELBESE		187	BA 33
76	BELBEUF		38	AA 9
31	BELBEZE DE LAURAGAIS		210	DA 35
31	BELBEZE EN COMMINGES		218	BA 37
11	BELCAIRE	C	221	FA 38
12	BELCASTEL		175	GA 31
81	BELCASTEL		211	EA 35
11	BELCASTEL ET BUC		221	GA 37
13	BELCODENE		202	VA 35
09	BELESTA		221	FA 38
66	BELESTA		224	IA 39
31	BELESTA EN LAURAGAIS		211	EA 35
24	BELEYMAS		157	Y 29
70	BELFAHY		89	AB 16
25	BELFAYS		108	BB 19
11	BELFLOU		211	EA 36
61	BELFONDS		58	X 12
90	BELFORT	P	89	BB 17
46	BELFORT DU QUERCY		174	DA 32
11	BELFORT SUR REBENTY		221	FA 38
53	BELGEARD		57	U 14
83	BELGENTIER		203	XA 36
2B	BELGODERE	C	225	KB 39
40	BELHADE		170	T 31
28	BELHOMERT GUEHOUVILLE		60	BA 13
25	BELIEU, LE		108	AB 19
01	BELIGNEUX		137	TA 25
33	BELIN BELIET	C	169	T 31
40	BELIS		184	U 33
87	BELLAC	S	130	BA 24
04	BELLAFAIRE		181	YA 31
59	BELLAING		18	LA 5
80	BELLANCOURT		16	FA 6
57	BELLANGE		47	ZA 11
61	BELLAVILLIERS		59	Y 13
95	BELLAY EN VEXIN, LE		39	FA 10
60	BELLE EGLISE		40	GA 10
62	BELLE ET HOULLEFORT		7	EA 3
22	BELLE ISLE EN TERRE	C	53	H 13
02	BELLEAU		41	LA 10
54	BELLEAU		46	YA 12
33	BELLEBAT		156	V 30
62	BELLEBRUNE		7	EA 3
19	BELLECHASSAGNE		146	GA 26
89	BELLECHAUME		83	MA 15
39	BELLECOMBE		138	WA 23
73	BELLECOMBE EN BAUGES		153	XA 25
26	BELLECOMBE TARENDOL		180	UA 31
21	BELLEFOND		105	TA 18
33	BELLEFOND		156	V 30
86	BELLEFONDS		114	Z 21
39	BELLEFONTAINE		123	XA 22
50	BELLEFONTAINE		57	S 12
88	BELLEFONTAINE		89	ZA 15
95	BELLEFONTAINE		40	HA 10
67	BELLEFOSSE		69	CB 13
30	BELLEGARDE		193	QA 34
32	BELLEGARDE		209	Z 35
45	BELLEGARDE	C	82	HA 15
81	BELLEGARDE		190	GA 33
11	BELLEGARDE DU RAZES		221	FA 37
26	BELLEGARDE EN DIOIS		180	UA 31
42	BELLEGARDE EN FOREZ		150	PA 26
23	BELLEGARDE EN MARCHE	C	132	GA 24
38	BELLEGARDE POUSSIEU		151	SA 27
31	BELLEGARDE STE MARIE		188	BA 34
01	BELLEGARDE SUR VALSERINE	C	138	WA 23
25	BELLEHERBE		108	AB 18
68	BELLEMAGNY		90	CB 17
61	BELLEME	C	59	Z 13
03	BELLENAVES		134	KA 23
76	BELLENCOMBRE	C	24	CA 8
21	BELLENEUVE		105	TA 18
02	BELLENGLISE		18	KA 7
14	BELLENGREVILLE		36	V 10
76	BELLENGREVILLE		24	BA 7
21	BELLENOD SUR SEINE		85	RA 17
21	BELLENOT SOUS POUILLY		104	QA 18
73	BELLENTRE		154	AB 26
55	BELLERAY		44	UA 10
03	BELLERIVE SUR ALLIER		133	LA 24
42	BELLEROCHE		136	QA 23
57	BELLES FORETS		47	BB 12
81	BELLESSERRE		211	FA 35
31	BELLESSERRE		187	BA 34
02	BELLEU		28	LA 9
80	BELLEUSE		26	FA 8
74	BELLEVAUX		139	ZA 23
71	BELLEVESVRE		122	UA 20
54	BELLEVILLE		46	XA 12
69	BELLEVILLE	C	136	RA 24
79	BELLEVILLE		128	U 23
76	BELLEVILLE EN CAUX		24	BA 8
08	BELLEVILLE ET CHATILLON SUR BAR		30	SA 9
18	BELLEVILLE SUR LOIRE		82	JA 17
76	BELLEVILLE SUR MER		15	BA 6
55	BELLEVILLE SUR MEUSE		44	UA 10
85	BELLEVILLE SUR VIE		110	Q 21
43	BELLEVUE LA MONTAGNE		149	NA 27
01	BELLEY	S	152	VA 25
01	BELLEYDOUX		138	WA 23
02	BELLICOURT		18	LA 6
61	BELLIERE, LA		58	W 12
76	BELLIERE, LA		25	DA 8
01	BELLIGNAT		138	VA 23
44	BELLIGNE		94	S 18
59	BELLIGNIES		19	NA 5
89	BELLIOLE, LA		63	KA 15
09	BELLOC		221	FA 37
32	BELLOC ST CLAMENS		208	Y 35
64	BELLOCQ		206	S 35
16	BELLON		143	X 27
62	BELLONNE		17	KA 5
77	BELLOT		41	LA 11
14	BELLOU		36	X 11
61	BELLOU EN HOULME		57	U 12
61	BELLOU LE TRICHARD		59	Z 14
61	BELLOU SUR HUISNE		59	Z 13
60	BELLOY		27	IA 8
95	BELLOY EN FRANCE		40	HA 10
80	BELLOY EN SANTERRE		27	JA 7
80	BELLOY ST LEONARD		26	FA 7
80	BELLOY SUR SOMME		16	GA 6
17	BELLUIRE		142	U 26
76	BELMESNIL		24	BA 7
25	BELMONT		107	YA 19
32	BELMONT		186	X 34
38	BELMONT		152	UA 26
39	BELMONT		122	VA 20
52	BELMONT		87	VA 16
67	BELMONT		69	CB 13
69	BELMONT		136	RA 25
70	BELMONT		89	ZA 16
46	BELMONT BRETENOUX		160	FA 29
42	BELMONT DE LA LOIRE	C	136	QA 23
88	BELMONT LES DARNEY		67	XA 15
01	BELMONT LUTHEZIEU		138	VA 25
46	BELMONT STE FOI		174	DA 32
88	BELMONT SUR BUTTANT		69	AB 14
12	BELMONT SUR RANCE	C	191	IA 34
88	BELMONT SUR VAIR		67	WA 14
73	BELMONT TRAMONET		152	VA 26
46	BELMONTET		173	BA 31
70	BELONCHAMP		89	ZA 16
11	BELPECH	C	219	EA 37
55	BELRAIN		44	UA 11
88	BELRUPT		68	XA 15
55	BELRUPT EN VERDUNOIS		44	UA 10
40	BELUS		183	R 35
08	BELVAL		29	RA 7
50	BELVAL		34	Q 11
88	BELVAL		69	CB 13
08	BELVAL BOIS DES DAMES		30	TA 9
51	BELVAL EN ARGONNE		44	SA 11
51	BELVAL SOUS CHATILLON		42	NA 10
06	BELVEDERE		199	DB 33
2A	BELVEDERE CAMPOMORO		229	JB 44
70	BELVERNE		89	AB 17
24	BELVES	C	158	BA 29
33	BELVES DE CASTILLON		157	W 29
82	BELVEZE		173	BA 31
11	BELVEZE DU RAZES		221	FA 37
30	BELVEZET		193	QA 33
48	BELVEZET		177	NA 30
11	BELVIANES ET CAVIRAC		221	GA 38
11	BELVIS		221	FA 38
25	BELVOIR		108	AB 18
56	BELZ	C	73	I 17
27	BEMECOURT		37	AA 11
09	BENAC		219	DA 38
65	BENAC		216	W 37
09	BENAGUES		219	DA 37
37	BENAIS		97	X 18
54	BENAMENIL		68	AB 13
76	BENARVILLE		23	Y 8
86	BENASSAY		112	W 22
17	BENATE, LA		128	U 24
02	BENAY		28	LA 7
19	BENAYES		145	DA 26
06	BENDEJUN		199	CB 34
68	BENDORF		90	CB 17
64	BENEJACQ		215	V 37
14	BENERVILLE SUR MER		36	W 9
40	BENESSE LES DAX		183	S 35
40	BENESSE MAREMNE		183	Q 35
16	BENEST		129	Y 24
57	BENESTROFF		47	AB 11
76	BENESVILLE		24	AA 7
85	BENET		128	T 22
21	BENEUVRE		86	SA 17
05	BENEVENT ET CHARBILLAC		167	XA 30
23	BENEVENT L'ABBAYE	C	131	DA 24
55	BENEY EN WOEVRE		45	WA 11
67	BENFELD	C	70	EB 14
18	BENGY SUR CRAON		117	IA 20
62	BENIFONTAINE		17	JA 4
57	BENING LES ST AVOLD		47	BB 10
42	BENISSON DIEU, LA		135	OA 23
26	BENIVAY OLLON		180	TA 32
78	BENNECOURT		38	DA 11
76	BENNETOT		23	Z 8
54	BENNEY		68	YA 13
68	BENNWIHR		70	DB 15
29	BENODET		72	E 16
21	BENOISEY		85	QA 17
50	BENOITVILLE		33	O 8
17	BENON		127	T 23
01	BENONCES		138	UA 25
14	BENOUVILLE		36	V 10
76	BENOUVILLE		23	X 8
31	BENQUE		209	AA 36
31	BENQUE DESSOUS ET DESSUS		217	Z 38
65	BENQUE		216	X 37
40	BENQUET		184	U 34
64	BENTAYOU SEREE		208	W 36
01	BENY		137	UA 23
14	BENY BOCAGE, LE	C	35	S 11
14	BENY SUR MER		35	U 9
01	BEON		138	WA 25
89	BEON		83	LA 15
64	BEOST		215	U 37
31	BERAT		210	BA 36
32	BERAUT		186	Y 33
65	BERBERUST LIAS		216	W 37
43	BERBEZIT		162	MA 27
24	BERBIGUIERES		158	BA 29
10	BERCENAY EN OTHE		64	NA 14
25	BERCHE		108	AB 18
28	BERCHERES LES PIERRES		60	DA 13
28	BERCHERES ST GERMAIN		60	DA 13
28	BERCHERES SUR VESGRE		38	DA 11
62	BERCK	C	15	DA 4
17	BERCLOUX		128	U 25
61	BERD'HUIS		59	Z 14
32	BERDOUES		208	Y 35
59	BERELLES		19	OA 5
27	BERENGEVILLE LA CAMPAGNE		38	BA 10
68	BERENTZWILLER		90	DB 17
64	BERENX		206	S 35
01	BEREZIAT		137	TA 22
72	BERFAY		79	Z 15
67	BERG		48	CB 11
57	BERG SUR MOSELLE		32	YA 9
46	BERGANTY		174	DA 31
67	BERGBIETEN		70	DB 13
24	BERGERAC	S	157	Y 29
10	BERGERES		65	RA 14
51	BERGERES LES VERTUS		42	OA 11
51	BERGERES SOUS MONTMIRAIL		42	MA 11
71	BERGESSERIN		136	QA 22
68	BERGHEIM		70	DB 14
68	BERGHOLTZ		90	CB 16
68	BERGHOLTZZELL		90	CB 15
80	BERGICOURT		26	FA 7
08	BERGNICOURT		29	PA 9
63	BERGONNE		148	KA 26
40	BERGOUEY		184	T 34
64	BERGOUEY VIELLENAVE		206	R 35
62	BERGUENEUSE		16	GA 4
59	BERGUES	C	8	HA 2
02	BERGUES SUR SAMBRE		18	NA 6

22 BERHET 53 H 12
57 BERIG VINTRANGE 47 AB 11
50 BERIGNY 35 S 10
61 BERJOU 35 U 11
59 BERLAIMONT C 19 NA 5
02 BERLANCOURT 28 NA 7
60 BERLANCOURT 27 KA 8
81 BERLATS 190 IA 34
62 BERLENCOURT LE CAUROY 16 HA 5
62 BERLES AU BOIS 17 IA 5
62 BERLES MONCHEL 17 HA 5
08 BERLIERE, LA 30 SA 8
57 BERLING 48 CB 12
02 BERLISE 29 OA 8
34 BERLOU 213 JA 35
59 BERMERAIN 18 MA 5
51 BERMERICOURT 29 OA 9
59 BERMERIES 19 NA 5
57 BERMERING 47 AB 11
80 BERMESNIL 25 EA 7
62 BERMICOURT 16 GA 4
90 BERMONT 90 BB 17
76 BERMONVILLE 23 Z 8
16 BERNAC 129 X 24
81 BERNAC 189 FA 33
65 BERNAC DEBAT 216 X 37
65 BERNAC DESSUS 216 X 37
64 BERNADETS 207 V 36
65 BERNADETS DEBAT 208 Y 36
65 BERNADETS DESSUS 208 Y 36
85 BERNARD, LE 125 Q 22
85 BERNARDIERE, LA 110 Q 19
67 BERNARDSWILLER 70 DB 13
67 BERNARDVILLE 70 DB 14
80 BERNATRE 16 FA 5
80 BERNAVILLE C 16 GA 6
27 BERNAY S 37 Z 10
72 BERNAY 78 W 15
80 BERNAY EN PONTHIEU 15 EA 5
17 BERNAY ST MARTIN 127 T 24
77 BERNAY VILBERT 63 JA 12
56 BERNE 73 H 15
54 BERNECOURT 45 WA 11
32 BERNEDE 185 V 34
44 BERNERIE EN RETZ, LA 109 N 19
80 BERNES 18 KA 7
95 BERNES SUR OISE 40 GA 10
14 BERNESQ 35 S 9
16 BERNEUIL 142 W 27
17 BERNEUIL 142 T 26
80 BERNEUIL 16 GA 6
87 BERNEUIL 130 BA 24
60 BERNEUIL EN BRAY 26 FA 9
60 BERNEUIL SUR AISNE 27 JA 9
76 BERNEVAL LE GRAND 15 BA 6
62 BERNEVILLE 17 IA 5
74 BERNEX 140 AB 22
27 BERNIENVILLE 38 BA 10
76 BERNIERES 23 Y 8
14 BERNIERES D'AILLY 36 W 11
14 BERNIERES LE PATRY 57 T 12
14 BERNIERES SUR MER 36 U 9
27 BERNIERES SUR SEINE 38 CA 10
62 BERNIEULLES 7 EA 4
38 BERNIN 152 WA 27
30 BERNIS 193 PA 34
67 BERNOLSHEIM 49 EB 12
10 BERNON 84 OA 15
33 BERNOS BEAULAC 170 V 31
02 BERNOT 28 MA 7
89 BERNOUIL 84 NA 16
27 BERNOUVILLE 39 EA 9
68 BERNWILLER 90 CB 17
80 BERNY EN SANTERRE 27 JA 7
02 BERNY RIVIERE 27 KA 9
28 BEROU LA MULOTIERE 38 BA 12
32 BERRAC 187 Z 33
06 BERRE DES ALPES 199 DB 34
13 BERRE L'ETANG C 201 TA 35
11 BERRIAC 212 HA 36
07 BERRIAS ET CASTELJAU 178 PA 31
56 BERRIC 92 L 17
86 BERRIE 96 W 19
29 BERRIEN 52 F 13
02 BERRIEUX 28 NA 9
64 BERROGAIN LARUNS 206 S 36
51 BERRU 42 PA 10
68 BERRWILLER 90 CB 16
02 BERRY AU BAC 28 NA 9
18 BERRY BOUY 100 GA 19
05 BERSAC, LE 181 WA 31
87 BERSAC SUR RIVALIER 131 CA 24
39 BERSAILLIN 122 VA 20
59 BERSEE 18 KA 4
59 BERSILLIES 19 OA 5
33 BERSON 156 U 28
67 BERSTETT 49 EB 12
67 BERSTHEIM 49 EB 12
03 BERT 135 NA 23
80 BERTANGLES 16 GA 6
02 BERTAUCOURT EPOURDON 28 LA [illegible]
80 BERTEAUCOURT LES DAMES 16 GA 6
80 BERTEAUCOURT LES THENNES 26 HA 7
76 BERTHEAUVILLE 23 Z 7
60 BERTHECOURT 26 GA 9
86 BERTHEGON 113 X 20
25 BERTHELANGE 106 WA 19
57 BERTHELMING 47 BB 12
59 BERTHEN 8 IA 3
37 BERTHENAY 97 Y 18
02 BERTHENICOURT 28 LA 7
27 BERTHENONVILLE 39 EA 10
36 BERTHENOUX, LA 116 FA 21
33 BERTHEZ 171 V 31
12 BERTHOLENE 176 JA 31
27 BERTHOUVILLE 37 Z 10
63 BERTIGNAT 149 NA 26
10 BERTIGNOLLES 65 QA 15
62 BERTINCOURT C 17 JA 6
08 BERTONCOURT 29 OA 8
54 BERTRAMBOIS 69 BB 12
80 BERTRANCOURT 17 IA 6
57 BERTRANGE 32 YA 9
81 BERTRE 211 FA 35
65 BERTREN 217 Z 37
76 BERTREVILLE 23 Z 7
76 BERTREVILLE ST OUEN 24 BA 7
24 BERTRIC BUREE 143 Y 27
54 BERTRICHAMPS 69 AB 13
02 BERTRICOURT 29 OA 9
76 BERTRIMONT 24 BA 8
88 BERTRIMOUTIER 69 CB 14
59 BERTRY 18 LA 6
89 BERU 84 NA 16
86 BERUGES 113 X 22
10 BERULLE 64 MA 14
72 BERUS 58 W 14
76 BERVILLE 24 AA 8
95 BERVILLE 39 FA 10
27 BERVILLE EN ROUMOIS 37 AA 9
27 BERVILLE LA CAMPAGNE 38 AA 11
27 BERVILLE SUR MER 23 Y 9
76 BERVILLE SUR SEINE 24 AA 9
57 BERVILLER EN MOSELLE 47 AB 10
71 BERZE LA VILLE 136 RA 22
71 BERZE LE CHATEL 136 RA 22
07 BERZEME 179 QA 30
51 BERZIEUX 43 SA 10
02 BERZY LE SEC 28 LA 9
08 BESACE, LA 30 SA 8
39 BESAIN 122 WA 21
25 BESANCON P 107 XA 19
26 BESAYES 165 TA 29
64 BESCAT 215 U 37
26 BESIGNAN 180 UA 32
64 BESINGRAND 207 U 36
50 BESLON 56 R 11
02 BESME 27 KA 8
02 BESMONT 29 OA 7
70 BESNANS 107 YA 18
44 BESNE 93 N 18
50 BESNEVILLE 33 P 9
02 BESNY ET LOIZY 28 MA 8
16 BESSAC 143 W 27
18 BESSAIS LE FROMENTAL 117 IA 21
43 BESSAMOREL 163 OA 28
34 BESSAN 214 LA 36
95 BESSANCOURT 39 GA 11
73 BESSANS 154 BB 27
07 BESSAS 178 PA 31
42 BESSAT, LE 150 QA 27
85 BESSAY 125 R 22
03 BESSAY SUR ALLIER 118 LA 22
15 BESSE 160 HA 28
16 BESSE 129 W 24
24 BESSE 173 BA 30
38 BESSE 167 YA 28
63 BESSE ET ST ANASTAISE C 147 JA 26
72 BESSE SUR BRAYE 79 Z 16
83 BESSE SUR ISSOLE C 203 YA 36
11 BESSEDE DE SAULT 221 GA 38
30 BESSEGES C 178 OA 32
69 BESSENAY 150 QA 25
82 BESSENS 188 CA 33
09 BESSET 219 EA 37
42 BESSEY 150 RA 27
21 BESSEY EN CHAUME 104 RA 19
21 BESSEY LA COUR 104 RA 19
21 BESSEY LES CITEAUX 105 TA 19
43 BESSEYRE ST MARY, LA 162 LA 29
31 BESSIERES 188 DA 34
79 BESSINES 128 U 23
87 BESSINES SUR GARTEMPE C 131 CA 24
38 BESSINS 165 UA 28
03 BESSON 118 LA 22
90 BESSONCOURT 90 BB 17
46 BESSONIES 160 GA 29
48 BESSONS, LES 162 LA 30
12 BESSUEJOULS 176 IA 31
10 BESSY 64 OA 13
89 BESSY SUR CURE 84 NA 17
09 BESTIAC 220 EA 38
46 BETAILLE 159 EA 29
70 BETAUCOURT 88 WA 16
65 BETBEZE 209 Z 36
40 BETBEZER D'ARMAGNAC 185 V 33
32 BETCAVE AGUIN 209 Z 35
09 BETCHAT 218 BA 37
23 BETETE 132 FA 22
60 BETHANCOURT EN VALOIS 41 JA 9
02 BETHANCOURT EN VAUX 27 KA 8
55 BETHELAINVILLE 44 TA 10
95 BETHEMONT LA FORET 40 GA 10
59 BETHENCOURT 18 LA 6
80 BETHENCOURT SUR MER 15 DA 6
80 BETHENCOURT SUR SOMME 27 JA 7
51 BETHENIVILLE 29 OA 9
51 BETHENY 42 OA 9
55 BETHINCOURT 44 TA 10
86 BETHINES 114 AA 22
60 BETHISY ST MARTIN 41 JA 9
60 BETHISY ST PIERRE 41 JA 9
09 BETHMALE 218 BA 38
51 BETHON 64 MA 12
72 BETHON 58 W 14
25 BETHONCOURT 89 AB 17
62 BETHONSART 17 HA 5
28 BETHONVILLIERS 59 AA 14
90 BETHONVILLIERS 90 BB 17
62 BETHUNE S 8 IA 4
10 BETIGNICOURT 65 QA 13
77 BETON BAZOCHES 41 LA 12
70 BETONCOURT LES BROTTE 88 YA 16
70 BETONCOURT ST PANCRAS 88 YA 16
70 BETONCOURT SUR MANCE 87 WA 16
32 BETOUS 185 W 34
32 BETPLAN 208 X 36
65 BETPOUEY 216 W 38
65 BETPOUY 208 Y 36
64 BETRACQ 208 W 35
67 BETSCHDORF 49 FB 11
54 BETTAINVILLERS 32 WA 9
52 BETTANCOURT LA FERREE 66 SA 12
51 BETTANCOURT LA LONGUE 44 SA 12
57 BETTANGE 47 ZA 10
01 BETTANT 138 UA 24
57 BETTBORN 48 BB 12
88 BETTEGNEY ST BRICE 68 YA 14
57 BETTELAINVILLE 46 YA 10
80 BETTEMBOS 25 EA 7
80 BETTENCOURT RIVIERE 16 FA 6
80 BETTENCOURT ST OUEN 16 GA 6
68 BETTENDORF 90 DB 17
65 BETTES 216 X 37
76 BETTEVILLE 24 AA 8
59 BETTIGNIES 19 OA 5
57 BETTING LES ST AVOLD 47 AB 10
68 BETTLACH 90 DB 17
35 BETTON C 75 P 14
73 BETTON BETTONET 153 YA 26
88 BETTONCOURT 68 XA 14
59 BETTRECHIES 19 NA 5
57 BETTVILLER 48 DB 10
67 BETTWILLER 48 CB 11
60 BETZ C 41 JA 10
37 BETZ LE CHATEAU 114 AA 20
62 BEUGIN 17 HA 4
62 BEUGNATRE 17 JA 6
02 BEUGNEUX 41 LA 10
59 BEUGNIES 19 OA 6
89 BEUGNON 84 NA 15
79 BEUGNON, LE 112 U 21
62 BEUGNY 17 JA 6
06 BEUIL 199 BB 33
88 BEULAY, LE 69 BB 14
70 BEULOTTE ST LAURENT 89 AB 16
25 BEURE 107 XA 19
10 BEUREY 65 QA 14
21 BEUREY BAUGUAY 104 QA 19
55 BEUREY SUR SAULX 44 SA 12
63 BEURIERES 149 NA 27
21 BEURIZOT 104 QA 18
17 BEURLAY 127 S 25
52 BEURVILLE 66 SA 14
62 BEUSSENT 7 EA 4
64 BEUSTE 207 V 36
25 BEUTAL 108 AB 18
62 BEUTIN 15 EA 4
02 BEUVARDES 41 MA 10
54 BEUVEILLE 31 VA 9
54 BEUVEZIN 67 XA 13
14 BEUVILLERS 37 X 10
54 BEUVILLERS 32 WA 9
59 BEUVRAGES 18 MA 5
80 BEUVRAIGNES 27 IA 8
62 BEUVREQUEN 7 EA 3
50 BEUVRIGNY 35 S 11
58 BEUVRON 102 MA 18
14 BEUVRON EN AUGE 36 W 10
59 BEUVRY LA FORET 18 LA 4
57 BEUX 46 YA 11
86 BEUXES 97 X 19
29 BEUZEC CAP SIZUN 71 C 15
27 BEUZEVILLE C 23 Y 9
50 BEUZEVILLE AU PLAIN 33 O 9
50 BEUZEVILLE LA BASTILLE 33 Q 9
76 BEUZEVILLE LA GRENIER 23 Y 8
76 BEUZEVILLE LA GUERARD 23 Z 8
76 BEUZEVILLETTE 23 Y 8
38 BEVENAIS 152 UA 27
70 BEVEUGE 89 ZA 17
28 BEVILLE LE COMTE 61 EA 13
59 BEVILLERS 18 LA 6
04 BEVONS 181 WA 32
21 BEVY 105 SA 19
01 BEY 137 SA 23
71 BEY 121 SA 20
54 BEY SUR SEILLE 46 YA 12
33 BEYCHAC ET CAILLAU 156 U 29
40 BEYLONGUE 184 S 33
87 BEYNAC 144 BA 25
24 BEYNAC ET CAZENAC 158 BA 29
19 BEYNAT C 159 EA 28
04 BEYNES 197 YA 33
78 BEYNES 39 EA 11
01 BEYNOST 137 SA 25
65 BEYREDE JUMET 216 Y 38
57 BEYREN LES SIERCK 32 YA 9
64 BEYRIE EN BEARN 207 U 36
64 BEYRIE SUR JOYEUSE 206 R 36
40 BEYRIES 184 T 35
19 BEYSSAC 145 CA 27
19 BEYSSENAC 145 CA 27
81 BEZ, LE 212 HA 35
30 BEZ ET ESPARON 192 MA 33
09 BEZAC 219 DA 37
77 BEZALLES 63 LA 12
76 BEZANCOURT 25 DA 9
54 BEZANGE LA GRANDE 46 ZA 12
57 BEZANGE LA PETITE 68 AB 12
51 BEZANNES 42 OA 10
06 BEZAUDUN LES ALPES 200 CB 34
26 BEZAUDUN SUR BINE 180 TA 30
54 BEZAUMONT 46 XA 11
21 BEZE 105 UA 18
24 BEZENAC 158 BA 29
03 BEZENET 133 JA 23
32 BEZERIL 209 AA 35
34 BEZIERS S 213 LA 36
62 BEZINGHEM 7 EA 4
31 BEZINS GARRAUX 217 Z 38
11 BEZOLE, LA 221 FA 37
32 BEZOLLES 186 Y 34
95 BEZONS C 39 GA 11
55 BEZONVAUX (VILLAGE RUINE) 45 VA 10
30 BEZOUCE 193 QA 33
21 BEZOUOTTE 105 UA 18
27 BEZU LA FORET 25 DA 9
02 BEZU LE GUERY 41 LA 11
27 BEZU ST ELOI 39 EA 9
02 BEZU ST GERMAIN 41 LA 10
32 BEZUES BAJON 209 Z 36
62 BIACHE ST VAAST 17 JA 5
80 BIACHES 17 JA 7
25 BIANS LES USIERS 123 YA 20
86 BIARD 113 X 22
39 BIARNE 106 UA 19
80 BIARRE 27 JA 8
64 BIARRITZ C 205 P 35
40 BIARROTTE 183 Q 35
46 BIARS SUR CERE 160 EA 29
40 BIAS 169 R 32
47 BIAS 172 Z 31
40 BIAUDOS 183 Q 35
57 BIBICHE 47 ZA 9
67 BIBLISHEIM 49 FB 11
69 BIBOST 150 OA 25
02 BICHANCOURT 27 KA 8
58 BICHES 119 MA 20
57 BICKENHOLTZ 48 CB 12
54 BICQUELEY 67 WA 12
64 BIDACHE C 206 R 35
64 BIDARRAY 205 Q 36
64 BIDART 205 P 35
57 BIDESTROFF 47 AB 11
57 BIDING 47 AB 10
07 BIDON 179 QA 31
64 BIDOS 215 T 37
88 BIECOURT 67 XA 14
68 BIEDERTHAL 90 DB 18
25 BIEF 108 AB 18
39 BIEF DES MAISONS 123 XA 21
39 BIEF DU FOURG 123 XA 20
39 BIEFMORIN 122 VA 20
62 BIEFVILLERS LES BAPAUME 17 JA 6
64 BIELLE 215 U 37
80 BIENCOURT 15 EA 6
55 BIENCOURT SUR ORGE 66 UA 13
60 BIENVILLE 27 JA 9
54 BIENVILLE LA PETITE 46 ZA 12
62 BIENVILLERS AU BOIS 17 IA 5
08 BIERMES 29 QA 9
60 BIERMONT 27 IA 8
53 BIERNE C 77 U 16
59 BIERNE 8 HA 2
21 BIERRE LES SEMUR 104 PA 18
89 BIERRY LES BELLES FONTAINES 85 PA 17
09 BIERT 219 CA 38
76 BIERVILLE 24 CA 8
68 BIESHEIM 90 EB 15
52 BIESLES 66 UA 15
67 BIETLENHEIM 49 FB 12
33 BIEUJAC 171 V 31
02 BIEUXY 27 LA 9
56 BIEUZY 73 I 15
50 BIEVILLE 35 S 10
14 BIEVILLE BEUVILLE 36 V 10
14 BIEVILLE QUETIEVILLE 36 W 10
02 BIEVRES 28 NA 9
08 BIEVRES 31 UA 8
91 BIEVRES C 40 GA 12
88 BIFFONTAINE 69 AB 14
33 BIGANOS 169 S 30
16 BIGNAC 143 W 25
56 BIGNAN 74 K 16
17 BIGNAY 127 T 24
14 BIGNE, LA 35 T 11
08 BIGNICOURT 29 OA 9
51 BIGNICOURT SUR MARNE 43 RA 12
51 BIGNICOURT SUR SAULX 43 RA 12
44 BIGNON, LE 110 P 19
53 BIGNON DU MAINE, LE 77 T 15
45 BIGNON MIRABEAU, LE 63 JA 15
86 BIGNOUX 113 Y 21
2B BIGORNO 226 LB 40
53 BIGOTTIERE, LA 57 S 14
2B BIGUGLIA 226 MB 39
76 BIHOREL 24 BA 9
62 BIHUCOURT 17 JA 6
64 BILHERES 215 U 37
2A BILIA 229 KB 44
38 BILIEU 152 VA 27
19 BILLAC 159 EA 29
28 BILLANCELLES 60 CA 13
80 BILLANCOURT 27 JA 7
87 BILLANGES, LES 131 DA 24
33 BILLAUX, LES 156 V 29
35 BILLE 76 R 14
39 BILLECUL 123 XA 21
64 BILLERE C 207 U 36
21 BILLEY 106 UA 19
03 BILLEZOIS 133 MA 23
01 BILLIAT 138 WA 24
73 BILLIEME 152 WA 25
31 BILLIERE 216 Y 38
56 BILLIERS 92 L 17
56 BILLIO 74 K 16
63 BILLOM C 148 LA 25
03 BILLY 133 LA 23
14 BILLY 36 V 10
41 BILLY 99 DA 18
62 BILLY BERCLAU 9 JA 4
58 BILLY CHEVANNES 118 MA 20
51 BILLY LE GRAND 43 PA 10
21 BILLY LES CHANCEAUX 85 RA 17
62 BILLY MONTIGNY 17 JA 4
55 BILLY SOUS MANGIENNES 31 VA 9
02 BILLY SUR AISNE 28 LA 9
58 BILLY SUR OISY 83 LA 17
02 BILLY SUR OURCQ 41 LA 10
67 BILWISHEIM 49 EB 12
68 BILTZHEIM 90 DB 15
62 BIMONT 7 FA 4
51 BINARVILLE 44 SA 10
41 BINAS 80 DA 16
67 BINDERNHEIM 70 EB 14
21 BINGES 105 TA 18
22 BINIC 54 K 12
57 BINING 48 CB 11
50 BINIVILLE 33 P 9
31 BINOS 217 Z 38
51 BINSON ET ORQUIGNY 42 NA 10
46 BIO 159 EA 29
38 BIOL 152 UA 26
73 BIOLLE, LA 152 WA 25
63 BIOLLET 133 IA 24
50 BION 57 S 12
57 BIONCOURT 46 YA 12
54 BIONVILLE 69 BB 13
57 BIONVILLE SUR NIED 47 ZA 10
06 BIOT 200 CB 35
74 BIOT, LE C 140 AB 23
82 BIOULE 188 DA 33
16 BIOUSSAC 129 X 24
03 BIOZAT 133 LA 24
16 BIRAC 142 W 26
33 BIRAC 171 V 31
47 BIRAC SUR TREC 171 X 31
32 BIRAN 186 Y 34
24 BIRAS 144 Z 27
64 BIRIATOU 205 O 36
01 BIRIEUX 137 TA 24
67 BIRKENWALD 49 DB 12
17 BIRON 142 U 26
24 BIRON 172 AA 30
64 BIRON 206 T 35
40 BISCARROSSE 169 R 31
67 BISCHHEIM C 49 FB 12
67 BISCHHOLTZ 48 EB 11
67 BISCHOFFSHEIM 70 EB 13
68 BISCHWIHR 70 DB 15
67 BISCHWILLER C 49 FB 12
68 BISEL 90 CB 17
2B BISINCHI 228 MB 40
55 BISLEE 44 UA 11
67 BISSERT 47 BB 11
51 BISSEUIL 42 OA 10
21 BISSEY LA COTE 85 RA 16
21 BISSEY LA PIERRE 85 QA 16
71 BISSEY SOUS CRUCHAUD 120 RA 21
59 BISSEZEELE 8 HA 2
14 BISSIERES 36 W 10
71 BISSY LA MACONNAISE 120 RA 22
71 BISSY SOUS UXELLES 120 RA 22
71 BISSY SUR FLEY 120 RA 21
57 BISTEN EN LORRAINE 47 ZA 10
57 BISTROFF 47 AB 11
57 BITCHE C 48 DB 10
58 BITRY 83 KA 17
60 BITRY 27 KA 9
67 BITSCHHOFFEN 48 EB 11
68 BITSCHWILLER LES THANN 90 CB 16
32 BIVES 187 AA 34
38 BIVIERS 152 WA 27
50 BIVILLE 33 O 8
76 BIVILLE LA BAIGNARDE 24 BA 8
76 BIVILLE LA RIVIERE 24 AA 7
76 BIVILLE SUR MER 15 CA 6
61 BIVILLIERS 59 Z 13
11 BIZANET 223 JA 37
64 BIZANOS 207 V 36
52 BIZE 87 VA 16
65 BIZE 217 Y 37
11 BIZE MINERVOIS 213 JA 36
03 BIZENEUILLE 133 IA 22
01 BIZIAT 137 SA 23
38 BIZONNES 152 UA 26
25 BIZOT, LE 108 AB 19
71 BIZOTS, LES 120 OA 21
61 BIZOU 59 Z 13
65 BIZOUS 217 Y 37
69 BLACE 136 RA 24
60 BLACOURT 25 EA 9
76 BLACQUEVILLE 24 AA 8
51 BLACY 43 QA 12
89 BLACY 84 OA 17
67 BLAESHEIM 70 EB 13
31 BLAGNAC 210 CA 35
08 BLAGNY 30 TA 8
21 BLAGNY SUR VINGEANNE 105 UA 18
33 BLAIGNAC 171 W 30
33 BLAIGNAN 141 S 27
44 BLAIN C 93 O 17
60 BLAINCOURT LES PRECY 40 HA 10
10 BLAINCOURT SUR AUBE 65 OA 13
76 BLAINVILLE CREVON 24 CA 8
54 BLAINVILLE SUR L'EAU 68 ZA 13
50 BLAINVILLE SUR MER 34 P 10
14 BLAINVILLE SUR ORNE 36 V 10
62 BLAIRVILLE 17 IA 5
51 BLAISE SOUS ARZILLIERES 65 QA 12
49 BLAISON GOHIER 96 V 18
52 BLAISY 66 SA 14
21 BLAISY BAS 104 RA 18
21 BLAISY HAUT 104 RA 18
31 BLAJAN 209 Z 36
25 BLAMONT 108 BB 18
54 BLAMONT C 69 BB 13
81 BLAN 211 FA 35
36 BLANC, LE S 114 BA 21
93 BLANC MESNIL, LE C 40 HA 11
18 BLANCAFORT 82 HA 17
21 BLANCEY 104 QA 18
60 BLANCFOSSE 26 GA 8
57 BLANCHE EGLISE 47 AB 12
08 BLANCHEFOSSE ET BAY 29 PA 7
67 BLANCHERUPT 69 CB 13
28 BLANDAINVILLE 60 CA 14
30 BLANDAS 192 MA 33
38 BLANDIN 152 UA 26
53 BLANDOUET 77 V 15
77 BLANDY 62 JA 13
91 BLANDY 62 GA 14
62 BLANGERVAL BLANGERMONT 16 GA 5
14 BLANGY LE CHATEAU C 37 X 10
80 BLANGY SOUS POIX 26 FA 7
76 BLANGY SUR BRESLE C 15 DA 7
62 BLANGY SUR TERNOISE 16 GA 4
80 BLANGY TRONVILLE 26 HA 7
89 BLANNAY 84 NA 17
21 BLANOT 104 PA 19
71 BLANOT 120 RA 22
32 BLANQUEFORT 187 AA 34
33 BLANQUEFORT C 156 T 29
47 BLANQUEFORT SUR BRIOLANCE 173 AA 30
43 BLANZAC 163 NA 28
87 BLANZAC 130 BA 23
17 BLANZAC LES MATHA 128 V 25
16 BLANZAC PORCHERESSE C 143 W 26
16 BLANZAGUET ST CYBARD 143 Y 26
63 BLANZAT 148 KA 25
86 BLANZAY 129 X 23
17 BLANZAY SUR BOUTONNE 128 U 24
55 BLANZEE 45 VA 10
71 BLANZY 120 QA 21
08 BLANZY LA SALONNAISE 29 PA 9
02 BLANZY LES FISMES 28 MA 9
60 BLARGIES 25 EA 8
25 BLARIANS 107 YA 18
59 BLARINGHEM 8 HA 3
46 BLARS 174 EA 30
78 BLARU 38 BA 10
33 BLASIMON 156 W 30
86 BLASLAY 113 X 21
43 BLASSAC 162 LA 28
23 BLAUDEIX 132 FA 23
06 BLAUSASC 200 DB 34
84 BLAUVAC 196 TA 33
30 BLAUZAC 193 PA 33
48 BLAVIGNAC 162 LA 29
43 BLAVOZY 163 OA 28
14 BLAY 35 S 10
33 BLAYE S 155 T 28
81 BLAYE LES MINES 189 GA 33
47 BLAYMONT 172 AA 32
32 BLAZIERT 186 Y 33
52 BLECOURT 66 TA 13
59 BLECOURT 18 KA 5
89 BLEIGNY LE CARREAU 84 NA 16
54 BLEMEREY 68 AB 13
88 BLEMEREY 67 XA 14
62 BLENDECQUES 8 GA 3
89 BLENEAU C 83 JA 17
77 BLENNES 63 KA 14
54 BLENOD LES PONT A MOUSSON 45 XA 11
54 BLENOD LES TOUL 67 WA 13
62 BLEQUIN 7 FA 3
02 BLERANCOURT 27 KA 8
37 BLERE C 98 AA 18
35 BLERUAIS 75 N 15
33 BLESIGNAC 156 V 29
43 BLESLE C 148 KA 27
51 BLESME 43 RA 12
02 BLESMES 41 MA 11
23 BLESSAC 132 GA 24
21 BLESSEY 85 RA 17
52 BLESSONVILLE 66 SA 15
62 BLESSY 8 GA 4
18 BLET 117 IA 20
39 BLETTERANS C 122 UA 21
88 BLEURVILLE 67 XA 15
28 BLEURY 61 EA 13
88 BLEVAINCOURT 67 VA 15
72 BLEVES 59 Y 13
48 BLEYMARD, LE C 177 NA 31
60 BLICOURT 26 FA 8
67 BLIENSCHWILLER 70 DB 14
57 BLIES EBERSING 48 CB 10
57 BLIES GUERSVILLER 48 CB 10
57 BLIESBRUCK 48 CB 10
04 BLIEUX 198 YA 33
10 BLIGNICOURT 65 QA 13
10 BLIGNY 65 RA 14
51 BLIGNY 42 NA 10
21 BLIGNY LE SEC 104 RA 18
21 BLIGNY LES BEAUNE 121 SA 20
21 BLIGNY SUR OUCHE C 104 RA 19
60 BLINCOURT 26 IA 9
62 BLINGEL 16 GA 4
24 BLIS ET BORN 158 AA 28
58 BLISMES 103 NA 19
68 BLODELSHEIM 90 EB 16
41 BLOIS P 80 CA 17
39 BLOIS SUR SEILLE 122 VA 21
11 BLOMAC 212 IA 36
03 BLOMARD 133 JA 23

08 BLOMBAY 29 QA 7
87 BLOND 130 BA 24
70 BLONDEFONTAINE 88 WA 16
14 BLONVILLE SUR MER 36 W 9
76 BLOSSEVILLE 24 AA 7
50 BLOSVILLE 33 Q 9
63 BLOT L'EGLISE 133 JA 24
68 BLOTZHEIM 90 DB 17
49 BLOU 96 W 18
32 BLOUSSON SERIAN 208 X 35
50 BLOUTIERE, LA 56 R 11
74 BLOYE 138 WA 25
74 BLUFFY 139 YA 25
52 BLUMERAY 66 SA 14
25 BLUSSANGEAUX 108 AB 18
25 BLUSSANS 107 ZA 18
39 BLYE 122 VA 21
01 BLYES 137 UA 25
14 BO, LE 35 U 11
93 BOBIGNY P 40 HA 11
22 BOBITAL 55 N 13
76 BOCASSE, LE 24 BA 8
49 BOCE 96 W 17
2A BOCOGNANO C 226 KB 41
88 BOCQUEGNEY 68 YA 14
61 BOCQUENCE 37 Y 11
22 BODEO, LE 53 J 14
29 BODILIS 52 E 13
47 BOE 172 Z 32
61 BOECE 59 Y 13
74 BOEGE C 139 ZA 23
64 BOEIL BEZING 207 V 36
42 BOEN C 149 OA 25
67 BOERSCH 70 DB 13
59 BOESCHEPE 8 IA 3
59 BOESEGHEM 8 HA 3
67 BOESENBIESEN 70 EB 14
45 BOESSE 62 HA 14
79 BOESSE 112 U 20
72 BOESSE LE SEC 59 Z 15
89 BOEURS EN OTHE 64 NA 15
62 BOFFLES 16 GA 5
07 BOFFRES 164 RA 29
74 BOGEVE 139 ZA 23
08 BOGNY SUR MEUSE 29 RA 7
07 BOGY 150 RA 27
02 BOHAIN EN VERMANDOIS C 18 MA 6
56 BOHAL 74 L 16
49 BOHALLE, LA 96 U 18
29 BOHARS 51 C 13
01 BOHAS MEYRIAT RIGNAT 138 UA 23
91 BOIGNEVILLE 62 HA 14
45 BOIGNY SUR BIONNE 81 FA 15
78 BOINVILLE EN MANTOIS 39 EA 11
55 BOINVILLE EN WOEVRE 45 VA 10
78 BOINVILLE LE GAILLARD 61 EA 13
78 BOINVILLIERS 39 DA 11
62 BOIRY BECQUERELLE 17 JA 5
62 BOIRY NOTRE DAME 17 JA 5
62 BOIRY ST MARTIN 17 IA 5
62 BOIRY STE RICTRUDE 17 IA 5
17 BOIS 142 T 26
73 BOIS, LE 153 ZA 26
27 BOIS ANZERAY 37 Z 11
27 BOIS ARNAULT 37 Z 12
62 BOIS BERNARD 17 JA 5
92 BOIS COLOMBES C 40 GA 11
39 BOIS D AMONT 123 XA 22
78 BOIS D'ARCY 39 FA 12
89 BOIS D'ARCY 84 NA 17
76 BOIS D'ENNEBOURG 24 CA 9
69 BOIS D'OINGT, LE C 136 QA 24
85 BOIS DE CENE 109 O 20
88 BOIS DE CHAMP 69 AB 14
39 BOIS DE GAND 122 VA 20
31 BOIS DE LA PIERRE 210 BA 36
59 BOIS GRENIER 9 JA 3
76 BOIS GUILBERT 25 CA 8
76 BOIS GUILLAUME C 24 BA 9
27 BOIS HELLAIN, LE 37 Y 9
76 BOIS HEROULT 25 CA 8
91 BOIS HERPIN 62 GA 14
76 BOIS HIMONT 23 Z 8
27 BOIS JEROME ST OUEN 39 DA 10
76 BOIS L'EVEQUE 24 CA 9
27 BOIS LE ROI 38 CA 11
77 BOIS LE ROI 62 IA 13
02 BOIS LES PARGNY 28 MA 7
27 BOIS NORMAND PRES LYRE 37 Z 11
17 BOIS PLAGE EN RE, LE 125 Q 23
76 BOIS ROBERT, LE 24 BA 7
71 BOIS STE MARIE 136 PA 23
80 BOISBERGUES 16 GA 6
16 BOISBRETEAU 142 V 27
45 BOISCOMMUN 82 HA 15
62 BOISDINGHEM 7 FA 3
77 BOISDON 63 KA 12
27 BOISEMONT 38 DA 9
95 BOISEMONT 39 FA 11
28 BOISGASSON 80 BA 15
35 BOISGERVILLY 75 N 14
62 BOISJEAN 15 EA 4
80 BOISLE, LE 16 FA 5
62 BOISLEUX AU MONT 17 IA 5
62 BOISLEUX ST MARC 17 JA 5
79 BOISME 112 U 21
54 BOISMONT 31 WA 9
80 BOISMONT 15 EA 6
45 BOISMORAND 82 IA 16
27 BOISNEY 37 Z 10
17 BOISREDON 142 U 27
50 BOISROGER 34 P 10
76 BOISSAY 25 CA 8
24 BOISSE 158 Z 30
01 BOISSE, LA 137 SA 25
12 BOISSE PENCHOT 175 GA 30
41 BOISSEAU 80 CA 16
45 BOISSEAUX 61 FA 14
31 BOISSEDE 209 AA 36
61 BOISSEI LA LANDE 58 W 12
79 BOISSEROLLES 128 U 24
34 BOISSERON 193 OA 34
15 BOISSET 160 GA 29
34 BOISSET 212 IA 36
43 BOISSET 149 OA 27
30 BOISSET ET GAUJAC 193 OA 33
42 BOISSET LES MONTROND 149 PA 26
27 BOISSET LES PREVANCHES 38 CA 11
42 BOISSET ST PRIEST 149 OA 26
78 BOISSETS 39 DA 11
77 BOISSETTES 62 IA 13
87 BOISSEUIL 145 CA 25
24 BOISSEUILH 144 BA 27
01 BOISSEY 137 SA 22
14 BOISSEY 36 W 11
27 BOISSEY LE CHATEL 37 AA 10
81 BOISSEZON 212 HA 35
39 BOISSIA 122 WA 21
14 BOISSIERE, LA 36 X 10
27 BOISSIERE, LA 38 CA 11
34 BOISSIERE, LA 192 MA 34
39 BOISSIERE, LA 122 VA 22
53 BOISSIERE, LA 76 S 16
24 BOISSIERE D'ANS, LA 158 AA 28
85 BOISSIERE DE MONTAIGU, LA 110 R 20
85 BOISSIERE DES LANDES, LA 125 Q 22
44 BOISSIERE DU DORE, LA 94 R 19
78 BOISSIERE ECOLE, LA 61 DA 12
79 BOISSIERE EN GATINE, LA 112 U 22
49 BOISSIERE SUR EVRE, LA 94 R 18
30 BOISSIERES 193 PA 34
46 BOISSIERES 173 CA 31
77 BOISSISE LA BERTRAND 62 IA 13
77 BOISSISE LE ROI 62 IA 13
77 BOISSY AUX CAILLES 62 HA 14
28 BOISSY EN DROUAIS 38 CA 12
60 BOISSY FRESNOY 41 JA 10
95 BOISSY L'AILLERIE 39 FA 10
91 BOISSY LA RIVIERE 61 GA 14
27 BOISSY LAMBERVILLE 37 Z 10
60 BOISSY LE BOIS 39 FA 9
77 BOISSY LE CHATEL 41 KA 11
91 BOISSY LE CUTTE 62 GA 13
51 BOISSY LE REPOS 42 MA 11
91 BOISSY LE SEC 61 FA 13
28 BOISSY LES PERCHE 37 AA 12
61 BOISSY MAUGIS 59 Z 13
78 BOISSY MAUVOISIN 38 DA 11
78 BOISSY SANS AVOIR 39 EA 11
91 BOISSY SOUS ST YON 61 GA 13
94 BOISSY ST LEGER C 40 HA 12
35 BOISTRUDAN 76 Q 15
28 BOISVILLE LA ST PERE 61 EA 14
50 BOISYVON 56 R 12
61 BOITRON 59 X 13
77 BOITRON 41 LA 11
25 BOLANDOZ 107 XA 20
29 BOLAZEC 53 G 13
76 BOLBEC C 23 Y 8
84 BOLLENE C 179 RA 32
06 BOLLENE VESUBIE, LA 199 DB 33
50 BOLLEVILLE 33 P 9
76 BOLLEVILLE 23 Z 8
59 BOLLEZEELE 8 GA 2
68 BOLLWILLER 90 CB 16
52 BOLOGNE 66 TA 14
01 BOLOZON 138 UA 23
66 BOLQUERE 222 FA 40
67 BOLSENHEIM 70 EB 13
77 BOMBON 63 JA 13
33 BOMMES 170 U 30
36 BOMMIERS 116 FA 21
09 BOMPAS 219 DA 38
66 BOMPAS 224 JA 39
62 BOMY 8 GA 4
47 BON ENCONTRE 172 Z 32
58 BONA 102 LA 19
09 BONAC IRAZEIN 217 AA 38
32 BONAS 186 Y 34
70 BONBOILLON 106 VA 18
28 BONCE 60 DA 14
53 BONCHAMP LES LAVAL 77 T 15
02 BONCOURT 29 OA 8
27 BONCOURT 38 CA 11
28 BONCOURT 38 DA 11
54 BONCOURT 45 WA 10
21 BONCOURT LE BOIS 105 SA 19
55 BONCOURT SUR MEUSE 45 VA 12
45 BONDAROY 62 GA 14
25 BONDEVAL 108 BB 18
31 BONDIGOUX 188 DA 34
48 BONDONS, LES 177 MA 31
91 BONDOUFLE 62 HA 12
59 BONDUES 9 KA 3
93 BONDY C 40 HA 11
63 BONGHEAT 148 LA 25
68 BONHOMME, LE 69 CB 14
2A BONIFACIO C 230 LB 45
60 BONLIER 26 GA 9
39 BONLIEU 122 WA 21
26 BONLIEU SUR ROUBION 179 SA 30
64 BONLOC 205 R 36
09 BONNAC 219 DA 37
15 BONNAC 162 KA 28
87 BONNAC LA COTE 131 CA 24
25 BONNAL 88 YA 17
89 BONNARD 83 MA 15
23 BONNAT C 132 FA 23
39 BONNAUD 122 UA 21
25 BONNAY 107 XA 18
71 BONNAY 120 RA 22
80 BONNAY 17 HA 7
74 BONNE 139 YA 23
14 BONNEBOSQ 36 X 10
52 BONNECOURT 87 VA 15
45 BONNEE 82 HA 16
38 BONNEFAMILLE 151 TA 26
61 BONNEFOI 59 Z 12
19 BONNEFOND 146 FA 26
65 BONNEFONT 208 Y 36
39 BONNEFONTAINE 122 WA 21
40 BONNEGARDE 184 T 35
02 BONNEIL 41 LA 11
78 BONNELLES 61 FA 12
35 BONNEMAIN 55 O 13
14 BONNEMAISON 35 U 11
65 BONNEMAZON 216 X 37
21 BONNENCONTRE 105 TA 19
16 BONNES 143 X 27
86 BONNES 113 Z 21
02 BONNESVALYN 41 LA 10
55 BONNET 66 UA 13
72 BONNETABLE C 59 Y 14
25 BONNETAGE 108 AB 19
33 BONNETAN 156 U 29
16 BONNEUIL 142 W 26
36 BONNEUIL 131 CA 22
95 BONNEUIL EN FRANCE 40 HA 11
60 BONNEUIL EN VALOIS 41 JA 9
60 BONNEUIL LES EAUX 26 GA 8
86 BONNEUIL MATOURS 113 Z 21
94 BONNEUIL SUR MARNE C 40 HA 12
28 BONNEVAL C 60 CA 14
43 BONNEVAL 149 NA 27
73 BONNEVAL 153 ZA 26
73 BONNEVAL SUR ARC 154 BB 27
25 BONNEVAUX 123 YA 21
30 BONNEVAUX 178 OA 31
74 BONNEVAUX 140 AB 23
25 BONNEVAUX LE PRIEURE 107 YA 19
41 BONNEVEAU 79 AA 16
70 BONNEVENT VELLOREILLE 106 WA 18
16 BONNEVILLE 128 W 25
74 BONNEVILLE S 139 YA 24
80 BONNEVILLE 16 GA 6
50 BONNEVILLE, LA 33 Q 9
27 BONNEVILLE APTOT 37 Z 10
24 BONNEVILLE ET ST AVIT DE FUMADIERES 157 X 29
14 BONNEVILLE LA LOUVET 37 Y 9
27 BONNEVILLE SUR ITON, LA 38 BA 11
14 BONNEVILLE SUR TOUQUES 23 X 9
60 BONNIERES 25 FA 8
62 BONNIERES 16 GA 5
78 BONNIERES SUR SEINE C 39 DA 11
84 BONNIEUX C 196 UA 34
62 BONNINGUES LES ARDRES 7 FA 3
62 BONNINGUES LES CALAIS 7 EA 2
14 BONNOEIL 36 V 11
44 BONNOEUVRE 94 Q 17
64 BONNUT 184 T 35
45 BONNY SUR LOIRE 82 JA 17
56 BONO 91 J 17
65 BONREPOS 208 Y 36
31 BONREPOS RIQUET 188 DA 34
31 BONREPOS SUR AUSSONNELLE 210 BA 35
74 BONS EN CHABLAIS 139 YA 23
14 BONS TASSILLY 36 V 11
76 BONSECOURS 24 BA 9
61 BONSMOULINS 59 Z 12
06 BONSON 199 CB 34
42 BONSON 149 PA 26
73 BONVILLARD 153 YA 26
73 BONVILLARET 153 YA 26
54 BONVILLER 46 ZA 12
60 BONVILLERS 26 HA 8
88 BONVILLET 67 XA 15
02 BONY 18 KA 6
33 BONZAC 156 V 28
55 BONZEE 45 VA 10
65 BOO SILHEN 216 W 37
67 BOOFZHEIM 70 EB 14
40 BOOS 183 S 33
76 BOOS C 24 CA 9
67 BOOTZHEIM 70 EB 14
22 BOQUEHO 54 J 13
12 BOR ET BAR 174 FA 32
60 BORAN SUR OISE 40 HA 10
64 BORCE 215 U 38
23 BORD ST GEORGES 132 GA 23
33 BORDEAUX P 156 U 29
45 BORDEAUX EN GATINAIS 62 HA 15
76 BORDEAUX ST CLAIR 23 X 8
64 BORDERES 207 V 36
40 BORDERES ET LAMENSANS 184 U 34
65 BORDERES LOURON C 216 Y 38
65 BORDERES SUR L'ECHEZ C 208 W 36
64 BORDES 207 V 36
65 BORDES 216 X 37
36 BORDES, LES 116 FA 20
45 BORDES, LES 82 HA 16
71 BORDES, LES 121 SA 20
89 BORDES, LES 63 LA 15
10 BORDES AUMONT, LES 64 OA 14
31 BORDES DE RIVIERE 217 Z 37
09 BORDES SUR ARIZE, LES 218 CA 37
09 BORDES SUR LEZ, LES 218 BA 38
30 BORDEZAC 178 OA 32
17 BORDS 127 T 25
07 BOREE 163 PA 29
17 BORESSE ET MARTRON 142 W 27
60 BOREST 40 IA 10
70 BOREY 88 YA 17
2B BORGO C 226 MB 39
83 BORMES LES MIMOSAS 203 YA 37
31 BORN, LE 188 DA 33
48 BORN, LE 177 MA 30
76 BORNAMBUSC 23 Y 8
39 BORNAY 122 VA 21
07 BORNE 178 OA 30
43 BORNE 163 NA 28
60 BORNEL 39 GA 10
90 BORON 90 BB 17
59 BORRE 8 IA 3
24 BORREZE 159 CA 29
16 BORS (canton de BAIGNES) 142 V 27
16 BORS (canton de MONTMOREAU) 143 X 27
63 BORT L'ETANG 148 LA 25
19 BORT LES ORGUES C 147 HA 27
54 BORVILLE 68 ZA 13
09 BOSC, LE 219 DA 38
34 BOSC, LE 192 LA 34
27 BOSC BENARD COMMIN 24 AA 9
27 BOSC BENARD CRESCY 24 AA 9
76 BOSC BERENGER 24 CA 8
76 BOSC BORDEL 25 CA 8
76 BOSC EDELINE 25 CA 8
76 BOSC GUERARD ST ADRIEN 24 BA 8
76 BOSC HYONS 25 DA 9
76 BOSC LE HARD 24 BA 8
76 BOSC MESNIL 25 CA 8
61 BOSC RENOULT, LE 37 Y 11
27 BOSC RENOULT EN OUCHE 37 Z 11
27 BOSC RENOULT EN ROUMOIS 24 AA 9
27 BOSC ROGER EN ROUMOIS, LE 37 AA 9
76 BOSC ROGER SUR BUCHY 25 CA 8
17 BOSCAMNANT 157 W 28
64 BOSDARROS 207 U 36
27 BOSGOUET 24 AA 9
27 BOSGUERARD DE MARCOUVILLE 37 AA 10
71 BOSJEAN 122 UA 21
87 BOSMIE L'AIGUILLE 145 CA 25
02 BOSMONT SUR SERRE 28 NA 7
23 BOSMOREAU LES MINES 131 EA 24
27 BOSNORMAND 37 AA 9
80 BOSQUEL 26 GA 7
27 BOSQUENTIN 25 DA 9
27 BOSROBERT 37 AA 10
23 BOSROGER 132 GA 24
10 BOSSANCOURT 65 RA 14
37 BOSSAY SUR CLAISE 114 AA 20
25 BOSSE, LA 108 AB 19
72 BOSSE, LA 59 Z 14
35 BOSSE DE BRETAGNE, LA 75 P 16
37 BOSSEE 98 Z 19
67 BOSSENDORF 49 EB 12
24 BOSSET 157 Y 29
08 BOSSEVAL ET BRIANCOURT 30 SA 7
74 BOSSEY 139 YA 23
38 BOSSIEU 151 TA 27
33 BOSSUGAN 156 W 29
08 BOSSUS LES RUMIGNY 29 PA 7
03 BOST 133 MA 23
40 BOSTENS 184 U 33
76 BOSVILLE 23 Z 7
90 BOTANS 90 BB 17
29 BOTMEUR 52 F 13
29 BOTSORHEL 52 G 13
27 BOTTEREAUX, LES 37 Z 11
49 BOTZ EN MAUGES 95 S 18
45 BOU 81 FA 16
78 BOUAFLE 39 FA 11
27 BOUAFLES 38 CA 10
09 BOUAN 219 DA 38
44 BOUAYE C 93 P 19
62 BOUBERS LES HESMOND 16 FA 4
62 BOUBERS SUR CANCHE 16 GA 5
60 BOUBIERS 39 EA 10
13 BOUC BEL AIR 202 UA 35
32 BOUCAGNERES 209 Z 35
64 BOUCAU 205 Q 35
03 BOUCE 133 MA 23
61 BOUCE 58 W 12
16 BOUCHAGE, LE 129 Y 24
38 BOUCHAGE, LE 152 VA 26
59 BOUCHAIN C 18 LA 5
53 BOUCHAMPS LES CRAON 76 S 16
03 BOUCHAUD, LE 135 NA 23
80 BOUCHAVESNES BERGEN 17 JA 6
49 BOUCHEMAINE 95 T 18
57 BOUCHEPORN 47 AB 10
26 BOUCHET 179 SA 32
74 BOUCHET, LE 139 YA 25
43 BOUCHET ST NICOLAS, LE 163 NA 29
27 BOUCHEVILLIERS 25 EA 9
80 BOUCHOIR 27 IA 7
80 BOUCHON 16 FA 6
55 BOUCHON SUR SAULX, LE 66 TA 12
39 BOUCHOUX, LES C 138 WA 23
51 BOUCHY ST GENEST 64 MA 12
07 BOUCIEU LE ROI 164 RA 28
25 BOUCLANS 107 YA 19
30 BOUCOIRAN ET NOZIERES 193 PA 33
08 BOUCONVILLE 43 RA 10
55 BOUCONVILLE SUR MADT 45 WA 11
02 BOUCONVILLE VAUCLAIR 28 NA 9
60 BOUCONVILLERS 39 FA 10
54 BOUCQ 45 WA 12
63 BOUDES 148 KA 26
76 BOUDEVILLE 24 AA 8
82 BOUDOU 187 BA 33
31 BOUDRAC 217 Z 37
21 BOUDREVILLE 86 SA 15
47 BOUDY DE BEAUREGARD 172 Z 30
02 BOUE 18 NA 6
44 BOUEE 93 O 18
64 BOUEILH BOUEILHO LASQUE 207 V 35
76 BOUELLES 25 DA 8
72 BOUER 59 Z 15
53 BOUERE 77 U 16
53 BOUESSAY 77 U 16
36 BOUESSE 115 EA 21
16 BOUEX 143 Y 26
35 BOUEXIERE, LA 76 O 14
95 BOUFFEMONT 40 GA 11
85 BOUFFERE 110 Q 20
02 BOUFFIGNEREUX 28 NA 9
80 BOUFFLERS 16 FA 5
41 BOUFFRY 80 BA 15
80 BOUGAINVILLE 26 FA 7
64 BOUGARBER 207 U 36
38 BOUGE CHAMBALUD 151 SA 27
36 BOUGES LE CHATEAU 99 EA 19
70 BOUGEY 88 WA 16
78 BOUGIVAL 39 GA 11
28 BOUGLAINVAL 60 DA 13
77 BOUGLIGNY 62 IA 14
47 BOUGLON C 171 W 31
17 BOUGNEAU 142 U 26
70 BOUGNON 88 XA 17
79 BOUGON 128 W 22
40 BOUGUE 184 U 33
44 BOUGUENAIS 93 P 19
14 BOUGY 35 U 10
45 BOUGY LEZ NEUVILLE 81 FA 15
71 BOUHANS 121 UA 21
70 BOUHANS ET FEURG 87 VA 17
70 BOUHANS LES LURE 89 ZA 17
70 BOUHANS LES MONTBOZON 88 YA 17
17 BOUHET 127 S 23
21 BOUHEY 104 RA 19
58 BOUHY 83 KA 17
65 BOUILH DEVANT 208 X 36
65 BOUILH PEREUILH 208 X 36
11 BOUILHONNAC 212 HA 36
12 BOUILLAC 175 GA 30
24 BOUILLAC 158 AA 30
82 BOUILLAC 188 BA 34
13 BOUILLADISSE, LA 202 VA 36
80 BOUILLANCOURT EN SERY 15 DA 6
80 BOUILLANCOURT LA BATAILLE 26 HA 8
60 BOUILLANCY 41 JA 10
21 BOUILLAND 104 RA 19
30 BOUILLARGUES C 193 OA 34
76 BOUILLE, LA 24 AA 9
79 BOUILLE LORETZ 96 V 19
49 BOUILLE MENARD 76 S 16
79 BOUILLE ST PAUL 96 V 19
22 BOUILLIE, LA 54 L 13
64 BOUILLON 207 U 35
61 BOUILLON, LE 58 X 13
54 BOUILLONVILLE 45 WA 11
10 BOUILLY C 64 OA 14
51 BOUILLY 42 NA 10
45 BOUILLY EN GATINAIS 62 GA 15
79 BOUIN 129 W 24
85 BOUIN 109 N 20
62 BOUIN PLUMOISON 16 FA 5
11 BOUISSE 221 HA 37
21 BOUIX 85 OA 16
25 BOUJAILLES 123 XA 20
34 BOUJAN SUR LIBRON 213 LA 36
10 BOULAGES 64 OA 13
88 BOULAINCOURT 67 XA 14
77 BOULANCOURT 62 HA 14
57 BOULANGE 32 XA 9
32 BOULAUR 209 Z 35
37 BOULAY, LE 79 AA 17
45 BOULAY LES BARRES 81 EA 15
53 BOULAY LES IFS 58 W 13
27 BOULAY MORIN, LE 38 BA 10
57 BOULAY MOSELLE S 47 ZA 10
71 BOULAYE, LA 119 PA 21
24 BOULAZAC 158 AA 28
13 BOULBON 195 RA 34
26 BOULC 180 VA 30
66 BOULE D'AMONT 224 IA 39
66 BOULETERNERE 224 IA 39
77 BOULEURS 41 JA 11
51 BOULEUSE 42 NA 10
33 BOULIAC 156 U 29
07 BOULIEU LES ANNONAY 150 RA 27
01 BOULIGNEUX 137 SA 24
70 BOULIGNEY 88 YA 16
55 BOULIGNY 31 WA 9
65 BOULIN 208 X 36
60 BOULLARRE 41 KA 10
28 BOULLAY LES DEUX EGLISES, LE 60 CA 12
91 BOULLAY LES TROUX 61 FA 12
28 BOULLAY MIVOYE, LE 60 CA 12
28 BOULLAY THIERRY, LE 60 DA 12
18 BOULLERET 101 JA 18
27 BOULLEVILLE 23 Y 9
31 BOULOC 188 CA 34
82 BOULOC 173 BA 32
85 BOULOGNE 110 O 21
92 BOULOGNE BILLANCOURT S 40 GA 11
60 BOULOGNE LA GRASSE 27 IA 8
31 BOULOGNE SUR GESSE C 209 Z 36
59 BOULOGNE SUR HELPE 19 NA 6
62 BOULOGNE SUR MER S 7 DA 3
72 BOULOIRE C 79 Z 15
14 BOULON 36 U 10
70 BOULOT 107 XA 18
66 BOULOU, LE 224 JA 39
70 BOULT 107 XA 18
08 BOULT AUX BOIS 30 SA 9
51 BOULT SUR SUIPPE 29 OA 9
46 BOULVE, LE 173 BA 31
08 BOULZICOURT 30 RA 8
64 BOUMOURT 207 U 35
24 BOUNIAGUES 157 Z 30
85 BOUPERE, LE 111 S 21
62 BOUQUEHAULT 7 EA 3
27 BOUQUELON 23 Y 9
80 BOUQUEMAISON 16 HA 5
55 BOUQUEMONT 44 UA 11
30 BOUQUET 178 PA 32
27 BOUQUETOT 24 AA 9
95 BOUQUEVAL 40 HA 11
10 BOURANTON 65 PA 14
91 BOURAY SUR JUINE 62 GA 13
68 BOURBACH LE BAS 90 BB 16
68 BOURBACH LE HAUT 90 BB 16
21 BOURBERAIN 87 UA 17
70 BOURBEVELLE 88 XA 16
03 BOURBON L'ARCHAMBAULT C 118 KA 21
71 BOURBON LANCY C 119 NA 21
52 BOURBONNE LES BAINS C 87 WA 15
63 BOURBOULE, LA 147 IA 26
59 BOURBOURG C 8 GA 2
22 BOURBRIAC C 53 I 13
17 BOURCEFRANC LE CHAPUS 126 R 25
39 BOURCIA 138 UA 22
08 BOURCQ 30 RA 9
76 BOURDAINVILLE 24 AA 8
40 BOURDALAT 185 V 34
73 BOURDEAU 152 WA 25
26 BOURDEAUX C 179 TA 30
24 BOURDEILLES 144 Z 27
24 BOURDEIX, LE 144 Z 26
33 BOURDELLES 171 W 30
79 BOURDET, LE 127 T 23
30 BOURDIC 193 PA 33
28 BOURDINIERE ST LOUP, LA 60 DA 14
80 BOURDON 16 FA 6
57 BOURDONNAY 69 AB 12
78 BOURDONNE 39 DA 12
52 BOURDONS SUR ROGNON 66 UA 14
62 BOURECQ 8 HA 4
02 BOURESCHES 41 LA 10
86 BOURESSE 130 Z 22
62 BOURET SUR CANCHE 16 GA 5
55 BOUREUILLES 44 SA 10
33 BOURG C 156 U 28
52 BOURG 87 UA 16
46 BOURG, LE 160 FA 30
27 BOURG ACHARD 24 AA 9
86 BOURG ARCHAMBAULT 130 BA 22
42 BOURG ARGENTAL C 150 OA 27
27 BOURG BEAUDOUIN 24 CA 9
29 BOURG BLANC 51 C 13
67 BOURG BRUCHE 69 CB 14
16 BOURG CHARENTE 142 V 25
23 BOURG D'HEM, LE 132 EA 23
49 BOURG D'IRE, LE 94 S 17
38 BOURG D'OISANS, LE C 167 XA 28
31 BOURG D'OUEIL 217 Y 38
65 BOURG DE BIGORRE 216 X 37
26 BOURG DE PEAGE C 165 SA 28
39 BOURG DE SIROD 123 XA 21
69 BOURG DE THIZY 135 PA 24
82 BOURG DE VISA C 173 AA 32
35 BOURG DES COMPTES 75 O 15
24 BOURG DES MAISONS 143 Y 27
24 BOURG DU BOST 143 X 27
76 BOURG DUN, LE 24 AA 7
01 BOURG EN BRESSE P 137 UA 23
02 BOURG ET COMIN 28 MA 9
08 BOURG FIDELE 29 OA 7
49 BOURG L'EVEQUE 76 S 16
92 BOURG LA REINE C 40 GA 12
63 BOURG LASTIC C 147 HA 26
71 BOURG LE COMTE 135 OA 23
72 BOURG LE ROI 58 X 14
26 BOURG LES VALENCE C 165 SA 29
66 BOURG MADAME 222 FA 40
90 BOURG SOUS CHATELET 90 BB 16
07 BOURG ST ANDEOL C 179 RA 31
31 BOURG ST BERNARD 211 EA 35
01 BOURG ST CHRISTOPHE 137 TA 25
61 BOURG ST LEONARD, LE 58 X 12
73 BOURG ST MAURICE C 154 AB 26
52 BOURG STE MARIE 67 VA 14
57 BOURGALTROFF 47 AB 11
23 BOURGANEUF C 131 EA 24
35 BOURGBARRE 75 P 15
14 BOURGEAUVILLE 36 W 10
18 BOURGES P 101 HA 19
93 BOURGET, LE C 40 HA 11
73 BOURGET DU LAC, LE 152 WA 26
73 BOURGET EN HUILE 153 YA 26
67 BOURGHEIM 70 DB 13
59 BOURGHELLES 9 LA 4
24 BOURGNAC 157 Y 28
17 BOURGNEUF 126 R 23
73 BOURGNEUF 153 YA 26
49 BOURGNEUF EN MAUGES 95 S 18
44 BOURGNEUF EN RETZ C 109 O 19
53 BOURGNEUF LA FORET, LE 76 S 14
51 BOURGOGNE C 29 OA 9
38 BOURGOIN JALLIEU C 151 TA 26
53 BOURGON 76 R 14
88 BOURGONCE, LA 69 AB 14
47 BOURGOUGNAGUE 172 Y 30
27 BOURGTHEROULDE INFREVILLE C 24 AA 9
14 BOURGUEBUS C 36 V 10
37 BOURGUEIL C 97 X 18
50 BOURGUENOLLES 56 Q 12
83 BOURGUET, LE 198 ZA 34
25 BOURGUIGNON 108 AB 18
70 BOURGUIGNON LES CONFLANS 88 XA 16
70 BOURGUIGNON LES LA CHARITE 88 XA 17

70 BOURGUIGNON LES MOREY 87 VA 16
02 BOURGUIGNON SOUS COUCY 27 KA 8
02 BOURGUIGNON SOUS MONTBAVIN 28 MA 8
10 BOURGUIGNONS 65 PA 15
71 BOURGVILAIN 136 RA 22
33 BOURIDEYS 170 U 31
11 BOURIEGE 221 GA 37
11 BOURIGEOLE 221 FA 37
65 BOURISP 216 Y 38
47 BOURLENS 173 AA 31
62 BOURLON 18 KA 5
52 BOURMONT C 67 VA 14
27 BOURNAINVILLE FAVEROLLES 37 Y 10
37 BOURNAN 98 Z 19
86 BOURNAND 97 W 19
12 BOURNAZEL 175 GA 31
81 BOURNAZEL 189 FA 33
85 BOURNEAU 111 S 22
47 BOURNEL 172 Z 30
27 BOURNEVILLE 23 Z 9
85 BOURNEZEAU 110 R 21
24 BOURNIQUEL 158 AA 29
25 BOURNOIS 107 ZA 17
43 BOURNONCLE ST PIERRE 148 LA 27
62 BOURNONVILLE 7 EA 3
64 BOURNOS 207 U 35
90 BOUROGNE 89 BB 17
47 BOURRAN 172 Y 31
41 BOURRE 99 CA 18
65 BOURREAC 216 W 37
82 BOURRET 188 BA 33
40 BOURRIOT BERGONCE 170 V 32
77 BOURRON MARLOTTE 62 IA 14
24 BOURROU 158 Z 28
32 BOURROUILLAN 185 W 34
62 BOURS 16 HA 4
65 BOURS 208 X 36
51 BOURSAULT 42 NA 10
41 BOURSAY 79 AA 15
57 BOURSCHEID 48 CB 12
22 BOURSEUL 55 M 13
80 BOURSEVILLE 15 DA 6
70 BOURSIERES 88 XA 17
59 BOURSIES 17 KA 6
62 BOURSIN 7 EA 3
60 BOURSONNE 41 KA 10
27 BOURTH 37 AA 12
62 BOURTHES 7 FA 4
76 BOURVILLE 24 AA 7
60 BOURY EN VEXIN 39 EA 10
57 BOUSBACH 47 BB 10
59 BOUSBECQUE 9 KA 3
33 BOUSCAT, LE C 156 T 29
59 BOUSIES 18 MA 6
59 BOUSIGNIES 18 LA 4
59 BOUSIGNIES SUR ROC 19 PA 5
11 BOUSQUET, LE 222 GA 39
34 BOUSQUET D'ORB, LE 191 KA 34
12 BOUSSAC 175 HA 32
23 BOUSSAC C 132 GA 23
46 BOUSSAC 174 FA 30
35 BOUSSAC, LA 56 P 13
23 BOUSSAC BOURG 132 GA 22
79 BOUSSAIS 112 V 20
31 BOUSSAN 209 AA 36
37 BOUSSAY 114 AA 20
44 BOUSSAY 110 R 19
57 BOUSSE 32 YA 9
72 BOUSSE 78 W 16
21 BOUSSELANGE 121 UA 20
09 BOUSSENAC 219 CA 38
21 BOUSSENOIS 86 TA 17
31 BOUSSENS 217 AA 37
70 BOUSSERAUCOURT 88 XA 15
47 BOUSSES 171 X 32
57 BOUSSEVILLER 48 DB 10
21 BOUSSEY 104 OA 18
80 BOUSSICOURT 26 IA 8
25 BOUSSIERES C 106 WA 19
59 BOUSSIERES EN CAMBRESIS 18 LA 6
59 BOUSSIERES SUR SAMBRE 19 NA 5
59 BOUSSOIS 19 OA 5
74 BOUSSY 139 XA 25
91 BOUSSY ST ANTOINE 62 HA 12
57 BOUST 32 YA 9
57 BOUSTROFF 47 AB 11
81 BOUT DU PONT DE LARN 212 HA 35
08 BOUTANCOURT 30 RA 8
60 BOUTAVENT 25 EA 8
02 BOUTEILLE, LA 28 OA 7
24 BOUTEILLES ST SEBASTIEN 143 X 27
11 BOUTENAC 223 IA 37
17 BOUTENAC TOUVENT 141 T 26
60 BOUTENCOURT 25 EA 9
91 BOUTERVILLIERS 61 FA 13
16 BOUTEVILLE 142 W 26
16 BOUTIERS ST TROJAN 142 V 25
77 BOUTIGNY 41 JA 11
28 BOUTIGNY PROUAIS 39 DA 12
91 BOUTIGNY SUR ESSONNE 62 HA 13
80 BOUTTENCOURT 15 DA 7
50 BOUTTEVILLE 33 R 9
31 BOUTX 217 Z 38
80 BOUVAINCOURT SUR BRESLE 15 DA 6
51 BOUVANCOURT 28 NA 9
26 BOUVANTE 165 TA 29
62 BOUVELINGHEM 7 FA 3
08 BOUVELLEMONT 30 RA 8
25 BOUVERANS 123 YA 20
38 BOUVESSE QUIRIEU 152 UA 25
26 BOUVIERES 180 TA 31
59 BOUVIGNIES 18 KA 4
62 BOUVIGNY BOYEFFLES 17 IA 4
28 BOUVILLE 60 CA 14
76 BOUVILLE 24 AA 8
91 BOUVILLE 62 GA 13
80 BOUVINCOURT EN VERMANDOIS 27 KA 7
59 BOUVINES 9 KA 4
60 BOUVRESSE 25 EA 8
44 BOUVRON 93 O 18
54 BOUVRON 45 WA 12
21 BOUX SOUS SALMAISE 85 RA 17
88 BOUXIERES AUX BOIS 68 YA 14
54 BOUXIERES AUX CHENES 46 YA 12
54 BOUXIERES AUX DAMES 46 YA 12
54 BOUXIERES SOUS FROIDMONT 46 XA 11
88 BOUXURULLES 68 YA 14
67 BOUXWILLER C 48 DB 11
68 BOUXWILLER 90 DB 17
51 BOUY 43 PA 10
10 BOUY LUXEMBOURG 65 PA 13
10 BOUY SUR ORVIN 63 MA 13
06 BOUYON 200 CB 34
46 BOUYSSOU, LE 174 FA 30
18 BOUZAIS 117 HA 21
52 BOUZANCOURT 66 SA 14
54 BOUZANVILLE 67 XA 14
21 BOUZE LES BEAUNE 104 RA 19
63 BOUZEL 148 LA 25
88 BOUZEMONT 68 YA 14
71 BOUZERON 120 RA 20
24 BOUZIC 159 CA 30
46 BOUZIES 174 DA 31
34 BOUZIGUES 214 MA 35
49 BOUZILLE 94 R 18
31 BOUZIN 217 AA 37
80 BOUZINCOURT 17 IA 6
32 BOUZON GELLENAVE 185 W 34
57 BOUZONVILLE C 47 ZA 9
45 BOUZONVILLE AUX BOIS 62 GA 15
51 BOUZY 42 PA 10
45 BOUZY LA FORET 82 HA 16
55 BOVEE SUR BARBOURE 67 VA 12
35 BOVEL 75 N 15
80 BOVELLES 26 GA 7
80 BOVES C 26 HA 7
55 BOVIOLLES 44 UA 12
62 BOYAVAL 16 GA 4
62 BOYELLES 17 JA 5
42 BOYER 135 PA 24
71 BOYER 121 SA 21
01 BOYEUX ST JEROME 138 UA 24
45 BOYNES 62 HA 15
01 BOZ 137 SA 22
07 BOZAS 164 RA 28
73 BOZEL C 154 AB 27
12 BOZOULS C 175 IA 31
55 BRABANT LE ROI 44 SA 11
55 BRABANT SUR MEUSE 44 UA 10
33 BRACH 155 S 28
52 BRACHAY 66 SA 13
80 BRACHES 26 HA 7
76 BRACHY 24 AA 7
41 BRACIEUX C 80 DA 17
39 BRACON 122 WA 20
76 BRACQUEMONT 15 BA 7
76 BRACQUETUIT 24 BA 8
76 BRADIANCOURT 25 CA 8
50 BRAFFAIS 56 R 12
30 BRAGASSARGUES 193 OA 33
31 BRAGAYRAC 210 BA 35
15 BRAGEAC 160 GA 28
10 BRAGELOGNE BEAUVOIR 85 PA 15
71 BRAGNY SUR SAONE 121 TA 20
25 BRAILLANS 107 XA 18
80 BRAILLY CORNEHOTTE 16 FA 5
21 BRAIN 104 QA 18
49 BRAIN SUR ALLONNES 97 W 18
49 BRAIN SUR L'AUTHION 96 U 18
49 BRAIN SUR LONGUENEE 95 T 17
39 BRAINANS 122 VA 20
02 BRAINE C 28 MA 9
44 BRAINS 93 O 19
72 BRAINS SUR GEE 78 W 15
53 BRAINS SUR LES MARCHES 76 R 16
50 BRAINVILLE 34 P 10
54 BRAINVILLE 45 WA 10
52 BRAINVILLE SUR MEUSE 67 VA 14
60 BRAISNES 27 IA 9
03 BRAIZE 117 IA 21
54 BRALLEVILLE 68 YA 13
11 BRAM 212 GA 36
73 BRAMANS 168 AB 28
76 BRAMETOT 24 AA 7
65 BRAMEVAQUE 217 Z 37
17 BRAN 142 V 27
19 BRANCEILLES 159 EA 28
89 BRANCHES 83 LA 16
02 BRANCOURT EN LAONNOIS 28 LA 8
02 BRANCOURT LE GRAND 18 LA 6
56 BRANDERION 73 I 16
55 BRANDEVILLE 31 UA 9
56 BRANDIVY 73 J 16
2B BRANDO C 226 MB 38
71 BRANDON 136 QA 22
12 BRANDONNET 175 GA 31
51 BRANDONVILLERS 65 OA 13
71 BRANGES 121 TA 21
38 BRANGUES 152 VA 25
89 BRANNAY 63 KA 14
25 BRANNE 107 ZA 18
33 BRANNE C 156 V 29
33 BRANNENS 171 V 31
30 BRANOUX LES TAILLADES 178 OA 32
39 BRANS 106 VA 19
03 BRANSAT 134 KA 23
51 BRANSCOURT 42 NA 10
77 BRANSLES 62 JA 15
84 BRANTES 180 UA 32
88 BRANTIGNY 68 YA 14
24 BRANTOME C 144 Z 27
14 BRANVILLE 36 W 9
50 BRANVILLE HAGUE 33 O 8
55 BRAQUIS 45 VA 10
83 BRAS 203 XA 35
04 BRAS D'ASSE 197 XA 33
55 BRAS SUR MEUSE 44 UA 10
12 BRASC 190 IA 33
02 BRASLES 41 LA 10
37 BRASLOU 113 Y 20
29 BRASPARTS 52 E 14
09 BRASSAC 219 DA 38
81 BRASSAC C 212 HA 35
82 BRASSAC 173 AA 32
63 BRASSAC LES MINES 148 LA 27
40 BRASSEMPOUY 184 T 35
60 BRASSEUSE 40 IA 10
58 BRASSY 103 OA 18
80 BRASSY 26 FA 7
54 BRATTE 46 YA 12
33 BRAUD ET ST LOUIS 141 T 27
55 BRAUVILLIERS 66 TA 13
04 BRAUX 198 AB 33
10 BRAUX 65 QA 13
21 BRAUX 104 QA 18
52 BRAUX LE CHATEL 66 SA 15
51 BRAUX ST REMY 44 SA 11
51 BRAUX STE COHIERE 44 SA 10
31 BRAX 210 CA 35
47 BRAX 172 Z 32
27 BRAY 37 AA 10
71 BRAY 120 RA 22
59 BRAY DUNES 8 HA 2
45 BRAY EN VAL 82 HA 16
95 BRAY ET LU 39 EA 10
80 BRAY LES MAREUIL 16 EA 6
02 BRAY ST CHRISTOPHE 27 KA 7
77 BRAY SUR SEINE C 63 KA 13
80 BRAY SUR SOMME C 17 IA 7
02 BRAYE 28 LA 9
02 BRAYE EN LAONNOIS 28 MA 9
02 BRAYE EN THIERACHE 29 OA 7
37 BRAYE SOUS FAYE 113 Y 20
37 BRAYE SUR MAULNE 97 X 17
21 BRAZEY EN MORVAN 104 PA 19
21 BRAZEY EN PLAINE 105 TA 19
35 BREAL SOUS MONTFORT 75 O 15
35 BREAL SOUS VITRE 76 R 15
95 BREANCON 39 FA 10
77 BREAU 63 JA 13
30 BREAU ET SALAGOSSE 192 MA 33
76 BREAUTE 23 Y 8
51 BREBAN 65 QA 13
62 BREBIERES 17 JA 5
90 BREBOTTE 90 BB 17
35 BRECE 76 Q 15
53 BRECE 57 T 13
50 BRECEY C 56 R 12
56 BRECH 73 J 16
88 BRECHAINVILLE 67 VA 14
28 BRECHAMPS 60 DA 12
68 BRECHAUMONT 90 BB 17
37 BRECHES 97 Y 17
25 BRECONCHAUX 107 YA 18
50 BRECTOUVILLE 35 S 11
02 BRECY 41 LA 10
18 BRECY 101 IA 19
08 BRECY BRIERES 30 RA 9
33 BREDE, LA C 156 U 30
53 BREE 77 U 14
17 BREE LES BAINS, LA 126 O 24
61 BREEL 58 U 12
01 BREGNIER CORDON 152 VA 26
60 BREGY 40 JA 10
57 BREHAIN 47 ZA 11
54 BREHAIN LA VILLE 32 WA 9
50 BREHAL C 56 P 11
56 BREHAN 74 K 15
22 BREHAND 54 L 13
37 BREHEMONT 97 Y 18
55 BREHEVILLE 31 UA 9
57 BREIDENBACH 48 DB 10
49 BREIL 97 X 18
72 BREIL SUR MERIZE, LE 79 Y 15
06 BREIL SUR ROYA C 199 EB 33
49 BREILLE LES PINS, LA 97 W 18
80 BREILLY 16 GA 7
57 BREISTROFF LA GRANDE 32 YA 9
67 BREITENAU 69 DB 14
67 BREITENBACH 69 DB 14
68 BREITENBACH HAUT RHIN 90 CB 15
29 BRELES 51 B 13
22 BRELIDY 53 I 12
85 BREM SUR MER 109 O 21
54 BREMENIL 69 BB 13
62 BREMES 7 FA 2
54 BREMONCOURT 68 YA 13
25 BREMONDANS 107 YA 19
76 BREMONTIER MERVAL 25 DA 8
14 BREMOY 35 T 11
21 BREMUR ET VAUROIS 85 RA 16
26 BREN 165 SA 28
11 BRENAC 221 GA 38
34 BRENAS 191 LA 34
63 BRENAT 148 LA 26
01 BRENAZ 138 WA 24
02 BRENELLE 28 MA 9
46 BRENGUES 174 EA 30
52 BRENNES 86 TA 16
29 BRENNILIS 52 F 14
01 BRENOD C 138 VA 24
83 BRENON 198 ZA 34
60 BRENOUILLE 26 HA 9
48 BRENOUX 177 MA 31
01 BRENS 152 VA 25
81 BRENS 189 FA 33
74 BRENTHONNE 139 ZA 23
02 BRENY 41 LA 10
04 BREOLE, LA 181 YA 31
25 BRERES 106 WA 19
39 BRERY 122 VA 21
17 BRESDON 128 V 25
25 BRESEUX, LES 108 AB 18
70 BRESILLEY 106 VA 18
80 BRESLE 17 HA 6
60 BRESLES 26 GA 9
03 BRESNAY 134 LA 22
61 BRESOLETTES 59 Z 12
88 BRESSE, LA 89 BB 15
71 BRESSE SUR GROSNE 120 RA 21
21 BRESSEY SUR TILLE 105 TA 18
38 BRESSIEUX 151 UA 27
01 BRESSOLLES 137 TA 25
03 BRESSOLLES 118 LA 22
82 BRESSOLS 188 CA 33
38 BRESSON 166 WA 28
79 BRESSUIRE S 111 U 20
29 BREST S 51 C 14
27 BRESTOT 24 Z 9
36 BRETAGNE 115 EA 20
90 BRETAGNE 90 BB 17
32 BRETAGNE D'ARMAGNAC 186 X 33
40 BRETAGNE DE MARSAN 184 U 34
27 BRETAGNOLLES 38 CA 11
45 BRETEAU 82 JA 17
35 BRETEIL 75 O 14
21 BRETENIERE 105 TA 19
25 BRETENIERE, LA 107 YA 18
39 BRETENIERE, LA 106 VA 19
39 BRETENIERES 122 VA 20
46 BRETENOUX C 160 EA 29
27 BRETEUIL C 37 AA 11
60 BRETEUIL C 26 GA 8
61 BRETHEL 37 Z 12
52 BRETHENAY 66 TA 14
03 BRETHON, LE 117 IA 22
25 BRETIGNEY 108 AB 17
25 BRETIGNEY NOTRE DAME 107 YA 18
79 BRETIGNOLLES 111 T 20
85 BRETIGNOLLES SUR MER 109 O 21
21 BRETIGNY 105 TA 18
27 BRETIGNY 37 Z 10
60 BRETIGNY 27 KA 8
91 BRETIGNY SUR ORGE C 62 GA 12
61 BRETONCELLES 59 AA 13
85 BRETONNIERE, LA 125 R 22
25 BRETONVILLERS 108 AB 19
26 BRETTE 180 UA 30
72 BRETTE LES PINS 78 Y 16
68 BRETTEN 90 CB 16
16 BRETTES 129 W 24
50 BRETTEVILLE 33 P 8
76 BRETTEVILLE DU GRAND CAUX 23 Y 8
14 BRETTEVILLE L'ORGUEILLEUSE 35 U 10
14 BRETTEVILLE LE RABET 36 V 11
76 BRETTEVILLE ST LAURENT 24 AA 7
50 BRETTEVILLE SUR AY 34 P 10
14 BRETTEVILLE SUR DIVES 36 W 11
14 BRETTEVILLE SUR LAIZE C 36 V 11
14 BRETTEVILLE SUR ODON 36 U 10
57 BRETTNACH 47 ZA 10
31 BRETX 188 BA 34
70 BREUCHES 88 YA 16
70 BREUCHOTTE 89 ZA 16
58 BREUGNON 102 LA 18
51 BREUIL 28 NA 9
80 BREUIL 27 JA 7
03 BREUIL, LE 133 MA 23
51 BREUIL, LE 42 MA 11
69 BREUIL, LE 136 QA 25
71 BREUIL, LE 120 QA 21
85 BREUIL BARRET 111 T 21
79 BREUIL BERNARD, LE 111 U 21
78 BREUIL BOIS ROBERT 39 EA 11
14 BREUIL EN AUGE, LE 36 X 10
14 BREUIL EN BESSIN, LE 35 S 10
17 BREUIL LA REORTE 127 T 24
60 BREUIL LE SEC 26 HA 9
60 BREUIL LE VERT 26 HA 9
17 BREUIL MAGNE 127 S 24
79 BREUIL SOUS ARGENTON, LE 112 U 20
63 BREUIL SUR COUZE, LE 148 LA 26
87 BREUILAUFA 130 BA 24
24 BREUILH 158 Z 28
17 BREUILLET 141 R 25
91 BREUILLET 61 GA 13
27 BREUILPONT 38 DA 11
70 BREUREY LES FAVERNEY 88 XA 16
67 BREUSCHWICKERSHEIM 70 EB 13
52 BREUVANNES EN BASSIGNY 67 VA 15
51 BREUVERY SUR COOLE 43 PA 11
50 BREUVILLE 33 P 8
55 BREUX 31 UA 8
91 BREUX JOUY 61 GA 13
27 BREUX SUR AVRE 38 BA 12
41 BREVAINVILLE 80 CA 15
78 BREVAL 38 DA 11
50 BREVANDS 34 R 9
39 BREVANS 106 VA 19
14 BREVEDENT, LE 37 X 10
58 BREVES 103 MA 18
78 BREVIAIRES, LES 39 EA 12
10 BREVIANDES 64 OA 14
14 BREVIERE, LA 36 X 11
14 BREVILLE 36 V 10
16 BREVILLE 142 V 25
50 BREVILLE SUR MER 56 P 11
80 BREVILLERS 16 HA 5
62 BREVILLIERS 16 FA 5
70 BREVILLIERS 89 AB 17
08 BREVILLY 30 TA 8
10 BREVONNES 65 QA 14
62 BREXENT ENOCQ 15 EA 4
25 BREY ET MAISON DU BOIS 123 YA 21
49 BREZE 96 W 19
05 BREZIERS 181 YA 31
11 BREZILHAC 221 FA 37
38 BREZINS 152 UA 27
28 BREZOLLES C 38 BA 12
15 BREZONS 161 JA 29
05 BRIANCON S 168 ZA 29
06 BRIANCONNET 198 AB 34
21 BRIANNY 104 QA 18
71 BRIANT 135 PA 23
36 BRIANTES 116 FA 22
45 BRIARE C 82 IA 17
45 BRIARRES SUR ESSONNE 62 HA 14
59 BRIASTRE 18 MA 6
81 BRIATEXTE 189 FA 34
52 BRIAUCOURT 66 TA 14
70 BRIAUCOURT 88 YA 16
52 BRICON 66 SA 15
28 BRICONVILLE 60 CA 13
50 BRICQUEBEC C 33 P 9
50 BRICQUEBOSQ 33 P 8
14 BRICQUEVILLE 35 S 9
50 BRICQUEVILLE LA BLOUETTE 56 Q 11
50 BRICQUEVILLE SUR MER 56 P 11
45 BRICY 81 EA 15
73 BRIDES LES BAINS 154 ZA 27
73 BRIDOIRE, LA 152 WA 26
37 BRIDORE 114 BA 20
02 BRIE 28 MA 8
09 BRIE 210 DA 36
16 BRIE 143 X 25
35 BRIE 76 P 15
79 BRIE 112 W 20
80 BRIE 27 JA 7
77 BRIE COMTE ROBERT C 40 IA 12
38 BRIE ET ANGONNES 166 WA 28
17 BRIE SOUS ARCHIAC 142 V 26
16 BRIE SOUS BARBEZIEUX 142 W 27
16 BRIE SOUS CHALAIS 143 W 27
17 BRIE SOUS MATHA 128 V 25
17 BRIE SOUS MORTAGNE 141 T 26
29 BRIEC C 72 E 15
10 BRIEL SUR BARSE 65 PA 14
35 BRIELLES 76 R 15
71 BRIENNE 121 SA 22
10 BRIENNE LA VIEILLE 65 QA 13
10 BRIENNE LE CHATEAU C 65 QA 13
08 BRIENNE SUR AISNE 29 OA 9
42 BRIENNON 135 OA 23
89 BRIENON SUR ARMANCON C 83 MA 15
91 BRIERES LES SCELLES 61 GA 13
79 BRIEUIL SUR CHIZE 128 V 24
08 BRIEULLES SUR BAR 30 SA 9
55 BRIEULLES SUR MEUSE 30 TA 9
61 BRIEUX 36 W 11
54 BRIEY S 32 XA 10
63 BRIFFONS 147 IA 25
34 BRIGNAC 214 MA 35
56 BRIGNAC 74 L 15
19 BRIGNAC LA PLAINE 159 CA 28
69 BRIGNAIS 150 RA 26
95 BRIGNANCOURT 39 FA 10
49 BRIGNE 96 U 19
31 BRIGNEMONT 187 AA 34
29 BRIGNOGAN PLAGE 51 D 12
83 BRIGNOLES S 203 XA 36
30 BRIGNON 193 PA 33
43 BRIGNON, LE 163 NA 29
06 BRIGUE, LA 199 EB 33
86 BRIGUEIL LE CHANTRE 130 BA 22
16 BRIGUEUIL 130 AA 24
91 BRIIS SOUS FORGES 61 GA 12
16 BRILLAC 130 AA 24
04 BRILLANNE, LA 197 WA 33
10 BRILLECOURT 65 QA 13
50 BRILLEVAST 33 Q 8
59 BRILLON 18 LA 4
55 BRILLON EN BARROIS 44 TA 12
62 BRIMEUX 16 EA 4
51 BRIMONT 29 OA 9
54 BRIN SUR SEILLE 46 YA 12
18 BRINAY 100 GA 19
58 BRINAY 119 NA 20
68 BRINCKHEIM 90 DB 17
69 BRINDAS 150 RA 25
22 BRINGOLO 53 J 13
58 BRINON SUR BEUVRON C 102 MA 18
18 BRINON SUR SAULDRE 81 GA 17
39 BRIOD 122 VA 21
49 BRIOLLAY 96 U 17
01 BRION 138 VA 23
36 BRION 115 EA 20
38 BRION 152 UA 27
48 BRION 162 KA 30
49 BRION 96 V 18
71 BRION 120 PA 20
86 BRION 129 Y 22
89 BRION 83 MA 15
79 BRION PRES THOUET 96 V 19
21 BRION SUR OURCE 85 RA 16
27 BRIONNE C 37 Z 10
23 BRIONNE, LA 131 EA 23
01 BRIORD 152 UA 25
72 BRIOSNE LES SABLES 59 Y 14
60 BRIOT 25 FA 8
41 BRIOU 80 DA 16
43 BRIOUDE S 148 LA 27
79 BRIOUX SUR BOUTONNE C 128 V 23
61 BRIOUZE C 58 U 12
80 BRIQUEMESNIL FLOXICOURT 26 FA 7
08 BRIQUENAY 30 SA 9
64 BRISCOUS 205 Q 35
73 BRISON ST INNOCENT 152 WA 25
34 BRISSAC 192 NA 33
49 BRISSAC QUINCE 96 U 18
49 BRISSARTHE 77 U 16
02 BRISSAY CHOIGNY 28 LA 8
02 BRISSY HAMEGICOURT 28 LA 7
19 BRIVE LA GAILLARDE S 159 DA 28
36 BRIVES 116 FA 20
43 BRIVES CHARENSAC 163 OA 28
17 BRIVES SUR CHARENTE 142 U 25
19 BRIVEZAC 160 EA 28
50 BRIX 33 P 8
55 BRIXEY AUX CHANOINES 67 WA 13
17 BRIZAMBOURG 128 U 25
37 BRIZAY 97 Y 19
55 BRIZEAUX 44 TA 11
74 BRIZON 139 ZA 24
49 BROC 97 X 17
06 BROC, LE 200 CB 34
63 BROC, LE 148 KA 26
40 BROCAS 184 U 33
21 BROCHON 105 SA 19
80 BROCOURT 25 EA 7
27 BROGLIE C 37 Y 11
25 BROGNARD 89 BB 17
08 BROGNON 19 PA 7
21 BROGNON 105 TA 18
21 BROIN 105 TA 19
21 BROINDON 105 TA 19
39 BROISSIA 138 UA 22
60 BROMBOS 25 FA 8
45 BROMEILLES 62 HA 14
12 BROMMAT 161 IA 29
63 BROMONT LA MOTHE 147 JA 25
69 BRON C 151 SA 25
57 BRONVAUX 45 XA 10
22 BROONS C 55 M 14
67 BROQUE, LA 69 CB 13
60 BROQUIERS 25 EA 8
12 BROQUIES 190 IA 33
16 BROSSAC C 142 W 27
07 BROSSAINC 150 RA 27
49 BROSSAY 96 V 19
77 BROSSE MONTCEAUX 63 KA 14
89 BROSSES 84 NA 17
27 BROSVILLE 38 BA 10
70 BROTTE LES LUXEUIL 88 YA 16
70 BROTTE LES RAY 87 WA 17
28 BROU C 60 BA 14
77 BROU SUR CHANTEREINE 40 IA 11
50 BROUAINS 57 S 12
35 BROUALAN 56 P 13
14 BROUAY 35 U 10
24 BROUCHAUD 158 BA 28
80 BROUCHY 27 KA 8
57 BROUCK 47 ZA 10
59 BROUCKERQUE 8 GA 2
57 BROUDERDORFF 69 CB 12
28 BROUE 38 DA 12
55 BROUENNES 30 TA 8
32 BROUILH MONBERT, LE 186 Y 34
66 BROUILLA 224 JA 39
51 BROUILLET 42 NA 10
33 BROUQUEYRAN 170 V 31
23 BROUSSE 133 HA 24
63 BROUSSE 148 LA 26
81 BROUSSE 189 FA 34
17 BROUSSE, LA 128 V 25
12 BROUSSE LE CHATEAU 190 IA 33
11 BROUSSES ET VILLARET 212 GA 36
52 BROUSSEVAL 66 SA 13
55 BROUSSEY EN BLOIS 67 VA 12
55 BROUSSEY RAULECOURT 45 WA 12
51 BROUSSY LE GRAND 42 NA 12
51 BROUSSY LE PETIT 42 NA 12
03 BROUT VERNET 133, LA 23
88 BROUVELIEURES C 69 AB 14
54 BROUVILLE 69 AB 13
57 BROUVILLER 48 CB 12
91 BROUY 62 GA 14
30 BROUZET LES ALES 178 PA 32
30 BROUZET LES QUISSAC 193 OA 34
85 BROUZILS, LES 110 Q 20
59 BROXEELE 8 GA 3
71 BROYE 120 PA 20
70 BROYE AUBIGNEY MONTSEUGNY 106 VA 18
70 BROYE LES LOUPS ET VERFONTAINE 106 UA 18
51 BROYES 42 NA 12
60 BROYES 26 HA 8
81 BROZE 189 FA 33
88 BRU 68 AB 14
71 BRUAILLES 121 TA 21
62 BRUAY LA BUISSIERE C 16 HA 4
59 BRUAY SUR L'ESCAUT 18 MA 5
35 BRUC SUR AFF 75 N 16
80 BRUCAMPS 16 FA 6
47 BRUCH 172 Y 32
50 BRUCHEVILLE 33 R 9
14 BRUCOURT 36 W 10
83 BRUE AURIAC 203 WA 35
68 BRUEBACH 90 DB 16
78 BRUEIL EN VEXIN 39 EA 11
18 BRUERE ALLICHAMPS 116 HA 21
72 BRUERE SUR LOIR, LA 78 Y 17
85 BRUFFIERE, LA 110 R 20
11 BRUGAIROLLES 221 GA 37
63 BRUGERON, LE 149 NA 25
33 BRUGES 156 T 29
64 BRUGES CAPBIS MIFAGET 215 V 37
03 BRUGHEAS 133 LA 24
47 BRUGNAC 172 Y 31

32	BRUGNENS		187	Z	34
51	BRUGNY VAUDANCOURT		42	NA	11
30	BRUGUIERE, LA		178	QA	32
31	BRUGUIERES		188	CA	34
59	BRUILLE LEZ MARCHIENNES		18	KA	5
59	BRUILLE ST AMAND		18	MA	4
05	BRUIS		180	VA	31
79	BRULAIN		128	V	23
35	BRULAIS, LES		75	N	16
57	BRULANGE		47	ZA	11
53	BRULATTE, LA		76	S	15
54	BRULEY		45	WA	12
61	BRULLEMAIL		59	Y	12
69	BRULLIOLES		150	OA	25
72	BRULON	C	78	V	15
67	BRUMATH	C	49	EB	12
02	BRUMETZ		41	KA	10
02	BRUNEHAMEL		29	PA	7
28	BRUNELLES		59	AA	14
11	BRUNELS, LES		211	FA	36
62	BRUNEMBERT		7	FA	3
59	BRUNEMONT		18	KA	5
04	BRUNET		197	XA	33
82	BRUNIQUEL		189	EA	33
91	BRUNOY	C	62	HA	12
68	BRUNSTATT		90	DB	16
76	BRUNVILLE		15	CA	6
60	BRUNVILLERS LA MOTTE		26	HA	8
12	BRUSQUE		191	JA	34
04	BRUSQUET, LE		181	YA	32
70	BRUSSEY		106	WA	18
69	BRUSSIEU		150	QA	25
51	BRUSSON		43	RA	12
22	BRUSVILY		55	N	13
80	BRUTELLES		15	DA	6
54	BRUVILLE		45	WA	10
86	BRUX		129	X	23
70	BRUYERE, LA		89	ZA	16
88	BRUYERES	C	68	AB	14
02	BRUYERES ET MONTBERAULT		28	MA	8
91	BRUYERES LE CHATEL		61	GA	13
02	BRUYERES SUR FERE		41	LA	10
95	BRUYERES SUR OISE		40	HA	10
02	BRUYS		42	MA	10
35	BRUZ	C	75	O	15
59	BRY		18	MA	5
94	BRY SUR MARNE	C	40	HA	11
62	BRYAS		16	HA	4
28	BU		38	DA	12
14	BU SUR ROUVRES, LE		36	V	11
50	BUAIS		57	S	13
40	BUANES		184	U	34
61	BUBERTRE		59	Z	12
56	BUBRY		73	I	15
78	BUC		39	GA	12
90	BUC		89	AB	17
60	BUCAMPS		26	GA	8
14	BUCEELS		35	T	10
10	BUCEY EN OTHE		64	NA	14
70	BUCEY LES GY		106	WA	18
70	BUCEY LES TRAVES		88	XA	17
78	BUCHELAY		39	EA	11
10	BUCHERES		64	OA	14
57	BUCHY		46	YA	11
76	BUCHY	C	25	CA	8
02	BUCILLY		29	OA	7
62	BUCQUOY		17	IA	6
02	BUCY LE LONG		28	LA	9
45	BUCY LE ROI		81	FA	15
02	BUCY LES CERNY		28	MA	8
02	BUCY LES PIERREPONT		28	OA	8
45	BUCY ST LIPHARD		81	EA	15
23	BUDELIERE		133	HA	23
57	BUDING		32	YA	9
57	BUDLING		32	YA	9
33	BUDOS		170	U	31
18	BUE		101	JA	18
27	BUEIL		38	DA	11
37	BUEIL EN TOURAINE		144	Z	27
01	BUELLAS		137	TA	23
68	BUETHWILLER		90	CB	17
25	BUFFARD		106	WA	19
71	BUFFIERES		136	QA	22
70	BUFFIGNECOURT		88	XA	16
21	BUFFON		85	PA	17
11	BUGARACH		221	HA	38
65	BUGARD		208	Y	36
19	BUGEAT	C	146	FA	26
64	BUGNEIN		206	T	36
59	BUGNICOURT		18	KA	5
52	BUGNIERES		86	TA	15
25	BUGNY		107	YA	20
24	BUGUE, LE	C	158	AA	29
67	BUHL		50	GB	11
68	BUHL		90	CB	15
57	BUHL LORRAINE		48	CB	12
95	BUHY		39	EA	10
60	BUICOURT		25	EA	8
80	BUIGNY L'ABBE		16	FA	6
80	BUIGNY LES GAMACHES		15	DA	6
80	BUIGNY ST MACLOU		16	EA	6
02	BUIRE		19	OA	7
62	BUIRE AU BOIS		16	GA	5
80	BUIRE COURCELLES		17	KA	7
62	BUIRE LE SEC		16	EA	5
80	BUIRE SUR L'ANCRE		17	IA	6
02	BUIRONFOSSE		19	NA	6
87	BUIS, LE		131	CA	24
26	BUIS LES BARONNIES	C	180	TA	32
27	BUIS SUR DAMVILLE		38	BA	11
05	BUISSARD		167	XA	30
38	BUISSE, LA		152	VA	27
38	BUISSIERE, LA		153	XA	27
84	BUISSON		179	SA	32
48	BUISSON, LE		176	KA	30
51	BUISSON, LE		43	RA	12
24	BUISSON DE CADOUIN, LE	C	158	AA	29
54	BUISSONCOURT		46	YA	12
62	BUISSY		17	KA	5
87	BUJALEUF		145	DA	25
65	BULAN		216	X	37
22	BULAT PESTIVIEN		53	H	13
58	BULCY		102	KA	19
56	BULEON		74	K	15
88	BULGNEVILLE	C	67	WA	14
63	BULHON		134	LA	25
28	BULLAINVILLE		60	DA	14
25	BULLE		123	YA	20
62	BULLECOURT		17	JA	5
60	BULLES		26	HA	9
54	BULLIGNY		67	WA	13
78	BULLION		61	FA	12
28	BULLOU		60	CA	14
42	BULLY		135	OA	24
69	BULLY		136	QA	25
76	BULLY		25	CA	7
62	BULLY LES MINES	C	17	IA	4
08	BULSON		30	SA	8
88	BULT		68	AB	14
65	BUN		215	V	38
21	BUNCEY		85	QA	16
62	BUNEVILLE		16	HA	5
91	BUNO BONNEVAUX		62	HA	14
64	BUNUS		206	R	36
16	BUNZAC		143	Y	25
84	BUOUX		196	UA	34
67	BURBACH		48	CB	11
01	BURBANCHE, LA		138	VA	25
62	BURBURE		8	HA	4
38	BURCIN		152	UA	27
14	BURCY		35	T	11
77	BURCY		62	HA	14
42	BURDIGNES		150	QA	27
74	BURDIGNIN		139	ZA	23
55	BURE		66	UA	13
61	BURE		59	Y	13
21	BURE LES TEMPLIERS		86	SA	16
02	BURELLES		28	NA	7
54	BURES		46	ZA	12
61	BURES		59	Y	13
76	BURES EN BRAY		25	CA	7
14	BURES LES MONTS		35	S	11
91	BURES SUR YVETTE		39	GA	12
53	BURET, LE		77	U	16
27	BUREY		38	AA	11
55	BUREY EN VAUX		67	VA	13
55	BUREY LA COTE		67	VA	13
65	BURG		216	Y	37
31	BURGALAYS		217	Z	38
64	BURGARONNE		206	S	36
31	BURGAUD, LE		188	BA	34
25	BURGILLE		106	WA	18
87	BURGNAC		144	BA	25
71	BURGY		121	SA	22
17	BURIE	C	142	U	25
54	BURIVILLE		68	AB	13
81	BURLATS		212	GA	35
57	BURLIONCOURT		46	ZA	11
71	BURNAND		120	RA	21
25	BURNEVILLERS		108	BB	18
68	BURNHAUPT LE BAS		90	CB	16
68	BURNHAUPT LE HAUT		90	CB	16
64	BUROS		207	V	36
64	BUROSSE MENDOUSSE		207	V	35
09	BURRET		219	DA	38
61	BURSARD		58	X	13
54	BURTHECOURT AUX CHENES		68	YA	13
57	BURTONCOURT		46	YA	10
60	BURY		26	HA	9
07	BURZET	C	163	PA	30
71	BURZY		120	RA	21
62	BUS		17	JA	6
80	BUS LA MESIERE		27	IA	8
80	BUS LES ARTOIS		17	HA	6
27	BUS ST REMY		39	DA	10
68	BUSCHWILLER		90	DB	17
59	BUSIGNY		18	MA	6
41	BUSLOUP		80	BA	16
62	BUSNES		8	HA	4
81	BUSQUE		189	FA	34
24	BUSSAC		144	Z	27
17	BUSSAC FORET		156	V	28
17	BUSSAC SUR CHARENTE		142	T	25
88	BUSSANG		89	AB	16
79	BUSSEAU, LE		111	U	21
21	BUSSEAUT		85	RA	16
63	BUSSEOL		148	LA	25
24	BUSSEROLLES		144	Z	26
21	BUSSEROTTE ET MONTENAILLE		86	SA	17
03	BUSSET		133	MA	24
02	BUSSIARES		41	LA	10
45	BUSSIERE, LA		82	IA	16
86	BUSSIERE, LA		114	AA	21
24	BUSSIERE BADIL	C	144	Z	26
87	BUSSIERE BOFFY		130	AA	24
23	BUSSIERE DUNOISE		131	EA	23
87	BUSSIERE GALANT		144	BA	26
23	BUSSIERE NOUVELLE		133	HA	24
87	BUSSIERE POITEVINE		130	AA	23
23	BUSSIERE ST GEORGES		132	FA	22
21	BUSSIERE SUR OUCHE, LA		104	RA	19
21	BUSSIERES		86	SA	17
42	BUSSIERES		135	PA	25
63	BUSSIERES		133	JA	24
70	BUSSIERES		107	YA	18
71	BUSSIERES		136	RA	23
77	BUSSIERES		41	KA	11
89	BUSSIERES		103	OA	18
63	BUSSIERES ET PRUNS		133	IA	24
52	BUSSON		66	UA	14
80	BUSSU		17	JA	7
64	BUSSUNARITS SARRASQUETTE		206	R	37
80	BUSSUS BUSSUEL		16	FA	6
18	BUSSY		117	IA	20
60	BUSSY		27	JA	8
42	BUSSY ALBIEUX		149	OA	25
89	BUSSY EN OTHE		83	MA	15
21	BUSSY LA PESLE		104	RA	18
58	BUSSY LA PESLE		102	LA	18
51	BUSSY LE CHATEAU		43	QA	10
21	BUSSY LE GRAND		85	QA	17
51	BUSSY LE REPOS		43	RA	11
89	BUSSY LE REPOS		83	KA	15
80	BUSSY LES DAOURS		26	HA	7
80	BUSSY LES POIX		26	FA	7
51	BUSSY LETTREE		43	PA	12
77	BUSSY ST GEORGES		40	IA	11
77	BUSSY ST MARTIN		40	IA	11
67	BUST		48	CB	11
2B	BUSTANICO		228	LB	40
64	BUSTINCE IRIBERRY		206	R	37
67	BUSWILLER		49	EB	12
25	BUSY		107	XA	19
70	BUTHIERS		107	XA	18
77	BUTHIERS		62	HA	14
76	BUTOT		24	BA	8
76	BUTOT VENESVILLE		23	Z	7
95	BUTRY SUR OISE		39	GA	10
89	BUTTEAUX		84	NA	15
67	BUTTEN		48	CB	11
80	BUVERCHY		27	JA	7
39	BUVILLY		122	WA	20
36	BUXERETTE, LA		115	EA	22
21	BUXEROLLES		86	SA	16
86	BUXEROLLES		113	Y	21
10	BUXEUIL		85	OA	15
36	BUXEUIL		99	EA	19
86	BUXEUIL		114	Z	20
36	BUXIERES D'AILLAC		115	EA	21
52	BUXIERES LES CLEFMONT		67	UA	15
03	BUXIERES LES MINES		117	JA	22
52	BUXIERES LES VILLIERS		66	SA	15
55	BUXIERES SOUS LES COTES		45	VA	11
63	BUXIERES SOUS MONTAIGUT		133	JA	23
10	BUXIERES SUR ARCE		65	QA	15
71	BUXY	C	120	RA	21
59	BUYSSCHEURE		8	GA	3
09	BUZAN		217	AA	38
36	BUZANCAIS	C	115	CA	20
02	BUZANCY		28	LA	9
08	BUZANCY	C	30	SA	9
12	BUZEINS		176	JA	31
47	BUZET SUR BAISE		171	X	32
31	BUZET SUR TARN		188	DA	34
64	BUZIET		215	U	37
34	BUZIGNARGUES		193	OA	34
65	BUZON		208	X	35
64	BUZY		215	U	37
55	BUZY DARMONT		45	VA	10
25	BY		122	WA	20
25	BYANS SUR DOUBS		106	WA	19

C

65	CABANAC		208	X	36
31	CABANAC CAZAUX		217	Z	37
33	CABANAC ET VILLAGRAINS		170	U	30
31	CABANAC SEGUENVILLE		187	BA	34
66	CABANASSE, LA		222	GA	40
12	CABANES		175	GA	32
81	CABANES		189	FA	34
31	CABANIAL, LE		211	EA	35
13	CABANNES		195	SA	34
09	CABANNES, LES	C	220	EA	38
81	CABANNES, LES		189	FA	33
33	CABARA		156	V	29
17	CABARIOT		127	S	24
32	CABAS LOUMASSES		209	Z	36
83	CABASSE		203	YA	35
66	CABESTANY		224	JA	39
64	CABIDOS		207	U	35
14	CABOURG	C	36	W	9
46	CABRERETS		174	EA	31
34	CABREROLLES		213	KA	35
11	CABRESPINE		212	HA	36
30	CABRIERES		193	QA	33
34	CABRIERES		214	LA	35
84	CABRIERES D'AIGUES		196	UA	34
84	CABRIERES D'AVIGNON		196	TA	33
13	CABRIES		202	UA	35
06	CABRIS		198	BB	34
94	CACHAN	C	40	GA	12
40	CACHEN		184	U	33
80	CACHY		26	HA	7
81	CADALEN	C	189	FA	34
09	CADARCET		219	DA	37
33	CADARSAC		156	V	29
33	CADAUJAC		156	U	30
65	CADEAC		216	Y	38
32	CADEILHAN		187	AA	34
65	CADEILHAN TRACHERE		216	Y	38
32	CADEILLAN		209	AA	35
25	CADEMENE		107	XA	19
56	CADEN		92	M	17
84	CADENET	C	196	UA	34
84	CADEROUSSE		195	RA	33
83	CADIERE D'AZUR, LA		202	WA	37
30	CADIERE ET CAMBO, LA		192	NA	33
33	CADILLAC	C	170	V	30
33	CADILLAC EN FRONSADAIS		156	V	29
64	CADILLON		207	V	35
81	CADIX		190	HA	33
13	CADOLIVE		202	VA	36
31	CADOURS	C	187	BA	34
46	CADRIEU		174	EA	31
14	CAEN	P	36	V	10
59	CAESTRE		8	IA	3
62	CAFFIERS		7	EA	3
81	CAGNAC LES MINES		189	GA	33
2B	CAGNANO		226	MB	38
06	CAGNES SUR MER	C	200	CB	34
62	CAGNICOURT		17	JA	5
59	CAGNONCLES		18	LA	5
40	CAGNOTTE		183	R	35
14	CAGNY		36	V	10
80	CAGNY		26	GA	7
14	CAHAGNES		35	T	10
14	CAHAGNOLLES		35	T	10
27	CAHAIGNES		39	DA	10
61	CAHAN		35	U	11
65	CAHARET		216	Y	37
80	CAHON		15	EA	6
46	CAHORS	P	173	DA	31
46	CAHUS		160	FA	29
11	CAHUZAC		219	EA	37
47	CAHUZAC		172	Z	30
81	CAHUZAC		211	FA	35
32	CAHUZAC SUR ADOUR		208	W	35
81	CAHUZAC SUR VERE		189	FA	33
31	CAIGNAC		211	EA	36
30	CAILAR, LE		193	PA	34
11	CAILHAU		221	GA	37
11	CAILHAVEL		221	GA	37
11	CAILLA		221	GA	38
46	CAILLAC		173	CA	31
32	CAILLAVET		186	Y	34
06	CAILLE		198	AB	34
85	CAILLERE ST HILAIRE, LA		111	S	21
76	CAILLEVILLE		24	Z	7
02	CAILLOUEL CREPIGNY		27	KA	8
27	CAILLOUET ORGEVILLE		38	CA	11
69	CAILLOUX SUR FONTAINES		137	SA	25
76	CAILLY		24	CA	8
27	CAILLY SUR EURE		38	BA	10
14	CAINE, LA		35	U	11
84	CAIRANNE		179	SA	32
04	CAIRE, LE		181	XA	31
14	CAIRON		35	U	10
60	CAISNES		27	KA	8
30	CAISSARGUES		193	PA	34
80	CAIX		27	IA	7
66	CAIXAS		224	IA	39
65	CAIXON		208	W	36
46	CAJARC	C	174	EA	31
2B	CALACUCCIA	C	227	KB	40
62	CALAIS	S	7	EA	2
46	CALAMANE		173	CA	31
56	CALAN		73	H	16
22	CALANHEL		53	H	13
65	CALAVANTE		208	X	36
2A	CALCATOGGIO		227	JB	42
66	CALCE		224	IA	38
2B	CALENZANA	C	225	JB	40
24	CALES		158	AA	29
46	CALES		159	DA	29
47	CALIGNAC		172	Y	32
61	CALIGNY		57	U	12
22	CALLAC	C	53	H	13
83	CALLAS	C	198	ZA	35
40	CALLEN		170	U	32
76	CALLENGEVILLE		25	DA	7
27	CALLEVILLE		37	AA	10
76	CALLEVILLE LES DEUX EGLISES		24	BA	8
32	CALLIAN		208	X	35
83	CALLIAN		198	AB	35
66	CALMEILLES		224	IA	39
12	CALMELS ET LE VIALA		191	IA	33
30	CALMETTE, LA		193	PA	33
12	CALMONT		175	HA	32
31	CALMONT		210	DA	36
70	CALMOUTIER		88	YA	17
42	CALOIRE		149	PA	27
47	CALONGES		171	X	31
62	CALONNE RICOUART		17	HA	4
62	CALONNE SUR LA LYS		8	IA	4
22	CALORGUEN		55	N	13
62	CALOTTERIE, LA		15	EA	4
69	CALUIRE ET CUIRE	C	151	SA	25
2B	CALVI	S	225	JB	39
46	CALVIAC		160	FA	29
24	CALVIAC EN PERIGORD		159	CA	29
46	CALVIGNAC		174	EA	31
15	CALVINET		160	HA	30
30	CALVISSON		193	PA	34
09	CALZAN		219	EA	37
65	CAMALES		208	W	36
09	CAMARADE		218	CA	37
12	CAMARES	C	191	JA	34
84	CAMARET SUR AIGUES		179	SA	32
29	CAMARET SUR MER		51	C	14
33	CAMARSAC		156	V	29
46	CAMBAYRAC		173	CA	31
14	CAMBE, LA		35	S	9
31	CAMBERNARD		210	BA	35
50	CAMBERNON		34	Q	10
33	CAMBES		156	U	30
46	CAMBES		174	FA	30
47	CAMBES		171	X	30
14	CAMBES EN PLAINE		36	U	10
2B	CAMBIA		228	LB	40
31	CAMBIAC		211	EA	35
11	CAMBIEURE		221	GA	37
62	CAMBLAIN CHATELAIN		17	HA	4
62	CAMBLAIN L'ABBE		17	IA	5
33	CAMBLANES ET MEYNAC		156	U	30
62	CAMBLIGNEUL		17	IA	5
64	CAMBO LES BAINS		205	Q	36
81	CAMBON		190	GA	33
34	CAMBON ET SALVERGUES		213	JA	35
81	CAMBON LES LAVAUR		211	EA	35
12	CAMBOULAZET		175	HA	32
46	CAMBOULIT		174	FA	30
81	CAMBOUNES		212	HA	35
81	CAMBOUNET SUR LE SOR		211	FA	35
22	CAMBOUT, LE		74	L	15
59	CAMBRAI	S	18	LA	5
14	CAMBREMER	C	36	W	10
62	CAMBRIN	C	8	IA	4
80	CAMBRON		15	EA	6
60	CAMBRONNE LES CLERMONT		26	HA	9
60	CAMBRONNE LES RIBECOURT		27	JA	8
46	CAMBURAT		174	FA	30
64	CAME		206	R	35
66	CAMELAS		224	IA	39
02	CAMELIN		27	KA	8
61	CAMEMBERT		36	X	11
50	CAMETOURS		34	Q	10
33	CAMIAC ET ST DENIS		156	V	29
62	CAMIERS		7	DA	4
33	CAMIRAN		171	W	30
12	CAMJAC		175	HA	32
22	CAMLEZ		53	H	12
81	CAMMAZES, LES		211	FA	36
56	CAMOEL		92	M	17
09	CAMON		221	FA	37
80	CAMON		26	HA	7
56	CAMORS		73	J	16
64	CAMOU CIHIGUE		206	S	37
65	CAMOUS		216	Y	38
11	CAMPAGNA DE SAULT		223	FA	38
12	CAMPAGNAC	C	176	KA	31
81	CAMPAGNAC		189	EA	33
24	CAMPAGNAC LES QUERCY		173	BA	30
34	CAMPAGNAN		214	MA	35
24	CAMPAGNE		158	AA	29
34	CAMPAGNE		193	OA	34
40	CAMPAGNE		184	T	34
60	CAMPAGNE		27	JA	8
32	CAMPAGNE D'ARMAGNAC		185	W	34
62	CAMPAGNE LES BOULONNAIS		7	FA	4
62	CAMPAGNE LES GUINES		7	FA	3
62	CAMPAGNE LES HESDIN	C	16	EA	5
62	CAMPAGNE LES WARDRECQUES		8	HA	3
09	CAMPAGNE SUR ARIZE		218	CA	37
11	CAMPAGNE SUR AUDE		221	GA	38
14	CAMPAGNOLLES		35	S	11
65	CAMPAN	C	216	X	37
2B	CAMPANA		228	MB	40
14	CAMPANDRE VALCONGRAIN		35	T	11
65	CAMPARAN		216	Y	38
44	CAMPBON		93	N	18
14	CAMPEAUX		35	S	11
60	CAMPEAUX		25	EA	8
35	CAMPEL		75	N	15
56	CAMPENEAC		74	M	15
30	CAMPESTRE ET LUC		192	LA	33
40	CAMPET ET LAMOLERE		184	T	33
59	CAMPHIN EN CAREMBAULT		9	JA	4
59	CAMPHIN EN PEVELE		9	LA	4
2B	CAMPI		228	MB	41
62	CAMPIGNEULLES LES GRANDES		15	EA	4
62	CAMPIGNEULLES LES PETITES		15	EA	4
14	CAMPIGNY		35	T	10
27	CAMPIGNY		23	Z	9
2B	CAMPILE		228	MB	40
65	CAMPISTROUS		216	Y	37
2B	CAMPITELLO	C	226	MB	39
34	CAMPLONG		191	KA	34
11	CAMPLONG D'AUDE		223	IA	37
76	CAMPNEUSEVILLE		25	DA	7
2A	CAMPO		227	KB	42
66	CAMPOME		222	HA	39
12	CAMPOURIEZ		175	IA	30
66	CAMPOUSSY		222	HA	39
60	CAMPREMY		26	GA	8
50	CAMPROND		34	Q	10
80	CAMPS EN AMIENOIS		26	FA	7
83	CAMPS LA SOURCE		203	XA	36
19	CAMPS ST MATHURIN LEOBAZEL		160	FA	29
11	CAMPS SUR L'AGLY		221	HA	38
33	CAMPS SUR L'ISLE		157	W	28
82	CAMPSAS		188	CA	33
24	CAMPSEGRET		157	Y	29
12	CAMPUAC		175	IA	30
33	CAMPUGNAN		156	U	28
65	CAMPUZAN		208	Y	36
11	CAMURAC		221	FA	38
2B	CANALE DI VERDE		228	MB	41
82	CANALS		188	CA	34
80	CANAPLES		16	GA	6
27	CANAPPEVILLE		38	BA	10
14	CANAPVILLE		23	X	9
61	CANAPVILLE		37	X	11
2B	CANARI		226	MB	38
30	CANAULES ET ARGENTIERES		193	OA	33
2B	CANAVAGGIA		226	LB	40
66	CANAVEILLES		222	GA	39
35	CANCALE	C	55	O	12
14	CANCHY		35	S	9
80	CANCHY		16	FA	5
47	CANCON	C	172	Z	31
80	CANDAS		16	GA	6
49	CANDE	C	95	S	17
41	CANDE SUR BEUVRON		80	CA	17
37	CANDES ST MARTIN		97	W	19
34	CANDILLARGUES		194	OA	35
60	CANDOR		27	JA	8
40	CANDRESSE		183	S	34
76	CANEHAN		15	CA	6
33	CANEJAN		155	T	30
31	CANENS		210	CA	36
40	CANENX ET REAUT		184	U	33
11	CANET		213	JA	36
34	CANET		214	MA	35
12	CANET DE SALARS		176	IA	32
66	CANET EN ROUSSILLON	C	224	KA	39
62	CANETTEMONT		16	HA	5
37	CANGEY		98	BA	18
46	CANIAC DU CAUSSE		174	DA	30
22	CANIHUEL		53	I	14
48	CANILHAC		176	KA	31
50	CANISY	C	34	R	10
62	CANLERS		16	GA	4
60	CANLY		27	IA	9
60	CANNECTANCOURT		27	JA	8
2A	CANNELLE		227	JB	42
06	CANNES	C	200	BB	35
77	CANNES ECLUSE		63	JA	14
30	CANNES ET CLAIRAN		193	OA	33
80	CANNESSIERES		15	EA	7
32	CANNET		208	W	35
06	CANNET, LE	C	200	BB	35
83	CANNET DES MAURES, LE		203	YA	36
60	CANNY SUR MATZ		27	IA	8
60	CANNY SUR THERAIN		25	EA	8
66	CANOHES		224	IA	39
48	CANOURGUE, LA	C	176	LA	31
76	CANOUVILLE		23	Z	7
59	CANTAING SUR ESCAUT		18	KA	6
65	CANTAOUS		217	Y	37
06	CANTARON		200	DB	34
09	CANTE		210	DA	36
76	CANTELEU		24	BA	9
62	CANTELEUX		16	GA	5
14	CANTELOUP		36	V	10
50	CANTELOUP		33	Q	8
33	CANTENAC		156	T	28
49	CANTENAY EPINARD		96	U	17
27	CANTIERS		39	DA	10
80	CANTIGNY		26	HA	8
24	CANTILLAC		144	Z	27
59	CANTIN		18	KA	5
12	CANTOIN		161	JA	29
33	CANTOIS		156	V	30
50	CANVILLE LA ROCQUE		34	P	9
76	CANVILLE LES DEUX EGLISES		24	AA	7
76	CANY BARVILLE	C	23	Z	7
27	CAORCHES ST NICOLAS		37	Z	10
22	CAOUENNEC LANVEZEAC		53	H	12
80	CAOURS		16	EA	6
06	CAP D'AIL		200	DB	34
40	CAPBRETON		183	Q	35
46	CAPDENAC		174	FA	30
12	CAPDENAC GARE	C	175	FA	30
24	CAPDROT		173	AA	30
59	CAPELLE		18	MA	5
02	CAPELLE, LA	C	19	OA	6
12	CAPELLE BALAGUIER, LA		174	FA	31
12	CAPELLE BLEYS, LA		175	GA	32
12	CAPELLE BONANCE, LA		176	KA	31
30	CAPELLE ET MASMOLENE, LA		193	QA	33
62	CAPELLE FERMONT		17	IA	5
62	CAPELLE LES BOULOGNE, LA		7	EA	3
27	CAPELLE LES GRANDS		37	Y	10
62	CAPELLE LES HESDIN		16	FA	5
11	CAPENDU	C	223	IA	37
31	CAPENS		210	CA	36
34	CAPESTANG	C	213	JA	36
33	CAPIAN		156	V	30
59	CAPINGHEM		9	JA	3
33	CAPLONG		157	X	29
09	CAPOULET ET JUNAC		219	DA	38
57	CAPPEL		47	BB	10
59	CAPPELLE BROUCK		8	GA	2
59	CAPPELLE EN PEVELE		9	KA	4
59	CAPPELLE LA GRANDE		8	HA	2
80	CAPPY		17	IA	7
33	CAPTIEUX	C	170	V	32
65	CAPVERN		216	X	37
31	CARAGOUDES		211	EA	35
31	CARAMAN	C	211	EA	35
66	CARAMANY		224	IA	39
29	CARANTEC		52	F	12
50	CARANTILLY		34	R	10
46	CARAYAC		174	FA	30
49	CARBAY		76	R	16
81	CARBES		212	GA	35
2A	CARBINI		230	LB	43
33	CARBON BLANC	C	156	U	29
31	CARBONNE	C	210	CA	36
2A	CARBUCCIA		227	KB	42
14	CARCAGNY		35	T	10
09	CARCANIERES		222	FA	39
33	CARCANS		155	R	28
40	CARCARES STE CROIX		184	T	34
11	CARCASSONNE	P	212	HA	36
40	CARCEN PONSON		184	S	33
83	CARCES		203	YA	35
2B	CARCHETO BRUSTICO		228	MB	40
46	CARDAILLAC		174	FA	30
33	CARDAN		156	V	30
31	CARDEILHAC		217	Z	37
64	CARDESSE		207	T	36
30	CARDET		193	OA	33
2A	CARDO TORGIA		227	KB	42
80	CARDONNETTE		16	HA	6
80	CARDONNOIS, LE		26	HA	8
14	CARDONVILLE		34	R	9
35	CARDROC		75	O	14
53	CARELLES		57	S	13
62	CARENCY		17	IA	5
46	CARENNAC		159	EA	29
50	CARENTAN	C	34	R	9
56	CARENTOIR		75	N	16
2A	CARGESE		227	IB	41
2A	CARGIACA		230	KB	43

29	CARHAIX PLOUGUER	C	53	G	14
08	CARIGNAN	C	30	TA	8
33	CARIGNAN DE BORDEAUX		156	U	29
89	CARISEY		84	NA	16
09	CARLA BAYLE		218	CA	37
09	CARLA DE ROQUEFORT		219	EA	37
09	CARLARET, LE		219	EA	37
15	CARLAT		161	IA	29
34	CARLENCAS ET LEVAS		213	KA	35
60	CARLEPONT		27	KA	8
57	CARLING		47	AB	10
11	CARLIPA		212	GA	36
46	CARLUCET		159	DA	30
81	CARLUS		189	GA	33
24	CARLUX	C	159	CA	29
62	CARLY		7	EA	3
81	CARMAUX	C	189	GA	33
56	CARNAC		91	I	17
46	CARNAC ROUFFIAC		173	CA	31
30	CARNAS		193	OA	34
61	CARNEILLE, LA		57	U	12
50	CARNET		56	Q	13
77	CARNETIN		40	IA	11
50	CARNEVILLE		33	Q	8
59	CARNIERES	C	18	LA	6
59	CARNIN		9	JA	4
22	CARNOET		53	G	14
83	CARNOULES		203	YA	36
13	CARNOUX EN PROVENCE		202	VA	36
80	CARNOY		17	IA	6
56	CARO		74	M	16
64	CARO		206	R	37
84	CAROMB		179	TA	32
84	CARPENTRAS	S	195	TA	33
2B	CARPINETO		228	MB	40
14	CARPIQUET		35	U	10
50	CARQUEBUT		33	O	9
44	CARQUEFOU	C	94	Q	18
83	CARQUEIRANNE		203	XA	37
80	CARREPUIS		27	JA	8
64	CARRERE		207	V	35
64	CARRESSE CASSABER		206	S	35
78	CARRIERES SOUS POISSY		39	FA	11
78	CARRIERES SUR SEINE		39	GA	11
06	CARROS	C	200	CB	34
61	CARROUGES	C	58	V	13
13	CARRY LE ROUET		201	TA	36
33	CARS		156	T	28
87	CARS, LES		144	BA	25
24	CARSAC AILLAC		159	CA	29
24	CARSAC DE GURSON		157	X	29
30	CARSAN		179	RA	32
27	CARSIX		37	Z	10
68	CARSPACH		90	CB	17
33	CARTELEGUE		156	U	28
2B	CARTICASI		228	LB	40
59	CARTIGNIES		19	NA	6
80	CARTIGNY		17	KA	7
14	CARTIGNY L'EPINAY		35	S	10
24	CARVES		158	BA	29
14	CARVILLE		35	S	11
76	CARVILLE LA FOLLETIERE		24	AA	8
76	CARVILLE POT DE FER		24	Z	8
62	CARVIN	C	9	JA	4
2B	CASABIANCA		228	MB	40
2A	CASAGLIONE		227	JB	42
2A	CASALABRIVA		229	KB	43
2B	CASALTA		228	MB	40
2B	CASAMACCIOLI		227	KB	40
2B	CASANOVA		228	LB	41
11	CASCASTEL DES CORBIERES		223	IA	37
66	CASEFABRE		224	IA	39
84	CASENEUVE		196	VA	33
66	CASES DE PENE		224	JA	38
2B	CASEVECCHIE		228	MB	41
31	CASSAGNABERE TOURNAS		209	AA	36
48	CASSAGNAS		177	NA	32
31	CASSAGNE		218	BA	37
24	CASSAGNE, LA		159	CA	28
46	CASSAGNES		173	BA	30
66	CASSAGNES		224	IA	39
12	CASSAGNES BEGONHES	C	175	HA	32
30	CASSAGNOLES		193	PA	33
34	CASSAGNOLES		212	IA	36
32	CASSAIGNE		186	Y	33
11	CASSAIGNE, LA		211	FA	36
11	CASSAIGNES		221	GA	38
15	CASSANIOUZE		160	HA	30
59	CASSEL	C	8	HA	3
40	CASSEN		184	S	34
47	CASSENEUIL		172	Z	31
11	CASSES, LES		211	EA	36
33	CASSEUIL		171	W	30
47	CASSIGNAS		172	AA	32
13	CASSIS		202	VA	36
44	CASSON		93	P	18
12	CASSUEJOULS		161	JA	30
29	CAST		72	E	14
31	CASTAGNAC		210	CA	36
31	CASTAGNEDE		217	AA	37
64	CASTAGNEDE		206	S	35
06	CASTAGNIERS		200	CB	34
40	CASTAIGNOS SOUSLENS		184	T	35
40	CASTANDET		185	V	34
12	CASTANET		175	GA	32
81	CASTANET		189	FA	33
82	CASTANET		174	FA	32
34	CASTANET LE HAUT		191	JA	34
31	CASTANET TOLOSAN	C	210	DA	35
11	CASTANS		212	HA	36
64	CASTEIDE CAMI		207	U	36
64	CASTEIDE CANDAU		207	U	35
64	CASTEIDE DOAT		208	W	36
66	CASTEIL		222	HA	39
40	CASTEL SARRAZIN		184	T	35
65	CASTELBAJAC		216	Y	37
31	CASTELBIAGUE		217	AA	37
47	CASTELCULIER		172	Z	32
82	CASTELFERRUS		187	BA	33
46	CASTELFRANC		173	CA	31
31	CASTELGAILLARD		209	AA	36
31	CASTELGINEST		188	DA	34
47	CASTELJALOUX	C	171	W	32
47	CASTELLA		172	Z	32
04	CASTELLANE	S	198	ZA	34
06	CASTELLAR		200	DB	34
04	CASTELLARD MELAN, LE		181	XA	32
2B	CASTELLARE DI CASINCA		228	MB	40
2B	CASTELLARE DI MERCURIO		228	LB	40
84	CASTELLET		196	VA	34
04	CASTELLET, LE		197	XA	33
83	CASTELLET, LE		202	WA	36
04	CASTELLET LES SAUSSES		198	AB	33
2B	CASTELLO DI ROSTINO		226	LB	40
12	CASTELMARY		175	GA	32
31	CASTELMAUROU		188	DA	34
82	CASTELMAYRAN		187	BA	33
33	CASTELMORON D'ALBRET		171	W	30
47	CASTELMORON SUR LOT	C	172	Y	31
32	CASTELNAU BARBARENS		209	Z	35
40	CASTELNAU CHALOSSE		184	S	34
32	CASTELNAU D'ANGLES		208	X	35
32	CASTELNAU D'ARBIEU		187	Z	33
11	CASTELNAU D'AUDE		212	IA	36
32	CASTELNAU D'AUZAN		186	X	33
31	CASTELNAU D'ESTRETEFONDS		188	CA	34
81	CASTELNAU DE BRASSAC		190	HA	34
34	CASTELNAU DE GUERS		214	LA	35
81	CASTELNAU DE LEVIS		189	FA	33
12	CASTELNAU DE MANDAILLES		176	JA	31
33	CASTELNAU DE MEDOC	C	155	S	28
81	CASTELNAU DE MONTMIRAL	C	189	EA	33
09	CASTELNAU DURBAN		218	CA	37
34	CASTELNAU LE LEZ	C	214	NA	35
65	CASTELNAU MAGNOAC	C	209	Y	36
46	CASTELNAU MONTRATIER	C	173	CA	32
12	CASTELNAU PEGAYROLS		176	JA	32
31	CASTELNAU PICAMPEAU		209	BA	36
65	CASTELNAU RIVIERE BASSE	C	208	W	35
47	CASTELNAU SUR GUPIE		171	X	30
32	CASTELNAU SUR L'AUVIGNON		186	Y	33
40	CASTELNAU TURSAN		184	U	34
30	CASTELNAU VALENCE		193	PA	33
47	CASTELNAUD DE GRATECAMBE		172	Z	31
24	CASTELNAUD LA CHAPELLE		158	BA	29
11	CASTELNAUDARY	C	211	FA	36
32	CASTELNAVET		186	X	34
40	CASTELNER		207	U	35
66	CASTELNOU		224	IA	39
11	CASTELRENG		221	GA	37
24	CASTELS		158	BA	29
82	CASTELSAGRAT		173	AA	32
82	CASTELSARRASIN	S	188	BA	33
65	CASTELVIEILH		208	X	36
33	CASTELVIEL		171	V	30
31	CASTERA, LE		188	BA	34
82	CASTERA BOUZET		187	AA	33
65	CASTERA LANUSSE		216	X	37
32	CASTERA LECTOUROIS		187	Z	33
65	CASTERA LOU		208	X	36
64	CASTERA LOUBIX		208	W	36
32	CASTERA VERDUZAN		186	Y	34
31	CASTERA VIGNOLES		209	AA	36
09	CASTERAS		218	CA	37
65	CASTERETS		209	Z	36
32	CASTERON		187	AA	33
64	CASTET		215	U	37
32	CASTET ARROUY		187	Z	33
64	CASTETBON		206	T	36
64	CASTETIS		206	T	35
64	CASTETNAU CAMBLONG		206	T	36
64	CASTETNER		206	T	35
64	CASTETPUGON		207	V	35
40	CASTETS	C	183	R	33
33	CASTETS EN DORTHE		171	V	30
09	CASTEX		218	CA	37
32	CASTEX		208	X	36
32	CASTEX D'ARMAGNAC		185	V	34
31	CASTIES LABRANDE		209	BA	36
2B	CASTIFAO		226	LB	40
2B	CASTIGLIONE		228	LB	40
06	CASTILLON		199	DB	34
14	CASTILLON		35	T	10
65	CASTILLON		216	X	37
64	CASTILLON (Canton D'ARTHEZ DE BEARN)		207	U	35
64	CASTILLON (Canton DE LEMBEYE)		208	W	35
33	CASTILLON DE CASTETS		171	W	31
31	CASTILLON DE LARBOUST		217	Y	38
31	CASTILLON DE ST MARTORY		217	AA	37
32	CASTILLON DEBATS		186	X	34
30	CASTILLON DU GARD		193	QA	33
14	CASTILLON EN AUGE		36	W	11
09	CASTILLON EN COUSERANS	C	218	BA	38
33	CASTILLON LA BATAILLE	C	156	W	29
32	CASTILLON MASSAS		187	Z	34
32	CASTILLON SAVES		209	AA	35
47	CASTILLONNES	C	172	Z	30
14	CASTILLY		35	S	9
32	CASTIN		187	Z	34
2B	CASTINETA		228	LB	40
2B	CASTIRLA		228	LB	40
02	CASTRES		28	LA	7
81	CASTRES	S	212	GA	35
33	CASTRES GIRONDE		156	U	30
34	CASTRIES	C	193	OA	34
59	CATEAU CAMBRESIS, LE	C	18	MA	6
02	CATELET, LE	C	18	LA	6
76	CATELIER, LE		24	BA	7
76	CATENAY		25	CA	8
60	CATENOY		26	HA	9
2B	CATERI		225	KB	39
31	CATHERVIELLE		217	Y	38
60	CATHEUX		26	GA	8
60	CATIGNY		27	JA	8
60	CATILLON FUMECHON		26	HA	8
59	CATILLON SUR SAMBRE		18	MA	6
66	CATLLAR		222	HA	39
32	CATONVIELLE		187	AA	34
59	CATTENIERES		18	LA	6
57	CATTENOM	C	32	YA	9
50	CATTEVILLE		33	P	9
46	CATUS	C	173	CA	30
50	CATZ		33	R	9
47	CAUBEYRES		171	X	32
31	CAUBIAC		187	BA	34
64	CAUBIOS LOOS		207	U	36
47	CAUBON ST SAUVEUR		171	X	30
31	CAUBOUS		217	Y	38
65	CAUBOUS		209	Y	36
81	CAUCALIERES		212	GA	35
62	CAUCHIE, LA		17	IA	5
62	CAUCHY A LA TOUR		17	HA	4
62	CAUCOURT		17	HA	4
56	CAUDAN		73	H	16
76	CAUDEBEC EN CAUX	C	24	Z	8
76	CAUDEBEC LES ELBEUF	C	38	BA	9
11	CAUDEBRONDE		212	GA	36
47	CAUDECOSTE		172	Z	32
11	CAUDEVAL		221	FA	37
66	CAUDIES DE CONFLENT		222	GA	39
66	CAUDIES DE FENOUILLEDES		221	HA	38
33	CAUDROT		171	W	30
59	CAUDRY		18	LA	6
60	CAUFFRY		26	HA	9
27	CAUGE		38	BA	11
31	CAUJAC		210	DA	36
02	CAULAINCOURT		27	KA	7
76	CAULE STE BEUVE, LE		25	DA	7
80	CAULIERES		26	FA	7
59	CAULLERY		18	LA	6
22	CAULNES	C	75	N	14
02	CAUMONT		27	KA	8
09	CAUMONT		218	BA	37
27	CAUMONT		24	AA	9
32	CAUMONT		185	W	34
33	CAUMONT		157	W	30
62	CAUMONT		16	FA	5
82	CAUMONT		187	AA	33
14	CAUMONT L'EVENTE	C	35	T	10
84	CAUMONT SUR DURANCE		195	SA	33
47	CAUMONT SUR GARONNE		171	X	31
14	CAUMONT SUR ORNE		35	U	11
40	CAUNA		184	T	34
79	CAUNAY		129	X	23
40	CAUNEILLE		183	R	35
11	CAUNES MINERVOIS		212	HA	36
34	CAUNETTE, LA		213	IA	36
11	CAUNETTE SUR LAUQUET		221	HA	37
11	CAUNETTES EN VAL		223	IA	37
40	CAUPENNE		184	T	34
32	CAUPENNE D'ARMAGNAC		185	W	34
51	CAURE, LA		42	NA	11
22	CAUREL		73	J	14
51	CAUREL		42	PA	9
2A	CAURO		227	KB	42
59	CAUROIR		18	LA	6
08	CAUROY		29	OA	9
51	CAUROY LES HERMONVILLE		28	NA	9
82	CAUSE, LE		187	AA	34
24	CAUSE DE CLERANS		158	Z	29
82	CAUSSADE	C	174	DA	32
65	CAUSSADE RIVIERE		208	W	35
30	CAUSSE BEGON		192	LA	33
34	CAUSSE DE LA SELLE		192	MA	34
12	CAUSSE ET DIEGE		174	FA	31
32	CAUSSENS		186	Y	33
34	CAUSSES ET VEYRAN		213	KA	35
34	CAUSSINIOJOULS		213	KA	35
06	CAUSSOLS		200	BB	34
09	CAUSSOU		220	EA	38
65	CAUTERETS		215	V	38
27	CAUVERVILLE EN ROUMOIS		23	Z	9
14	CAUVICOURT		36	V	11
33	CAUVIGNAC		171	W	31
60	CAUVIGNY		40	GA	9
14	CAUVILLE		35	U	11
76	CAUVILLE		23	X	8
34	CAUX		214	LA	35
11	CAUX ET SAUZENS		212	GA	36
47	CAUZAC		172	AA	32
46	CAVAGNAC		159	DA	28
84	CAVAILLON	C	195	TA	34
83	CAVALAIRE SUR MER		204	ZA	37
12	CAVALERIE, LA		191	KA	33
22	CAVAN		53	H	12
11	CAVANAC		221	HA	37
47	CAVARC		172	Z	30
30	CAVEIRAC		193	PA	34
11	CAVES		223	JA	38
33	CAVIGNAC		156	U	28
50	CAVIGNY		34	R	10
30	CAVILLARGUES		178	QA	32
80	CAVILLON		16	FA	7
62	CAVRON ST MARTIN		16	FA	4
09	CAYCHAX		219	EA	38
80	CAYEUX EN SANTERRE		26	IA	7
80	CAYEUX SUR MER		15	DA	5
34	CAYLAR, LE	C	192	LA	34
82	CAYLUS	C	174	EA	32
82	CAYRAC		174	DA	32
43	CAYRES	C	163	NA	29
82	CAYRIECH		174	DA	32
12	CAYROL, LE		176	IA	30
15	CAYROLS		160	GA	29
31	CAZAC		209	AA	36
33	CAZALIS		170	U	31
40	CAZALIS		184	T	35
11	CAZALRENOUX		211	FA	36
46	CAZALS	C	173	CA	30
82	CAZALS		174	EA	32
09	CAZALS DES BAYLES		221	FA	37
31	CAZARIL LASPENES		217	Z	38
31	CAZARIL TAMBOURES		217	Z	37
65	CAZARILH		217	Z	38
33	CAZATS		170	V	31
32	CAZAUBON	C	185	W	33
33	CAZAUGITAT		157	W	30
31	CAZAUNOUS		217	Z	37
09	CAZAUX		219	DA	37
32	CAZAUX D'ANGLES		186	X	34
65	CAZAUX DEBAT		216	Y	38
65	CAZAUX FRECHET ANERAN CAMORS		217	Y	38
31	CAZAUX LAYRISSE		217	Z	38
32	CAZAUX SAVES		209	AA	35
32	CAZAUX VILLECOMTAL		208	X	35
09	CAZAVET		218	BA	37
31	CAZEAUX DE LARBOUST		217	Y	38
34	CAZEDARNES		213	KA	36
09	CAZENAVE SERRES ET ALLENS		219	EA	38
32	CAZENEUVE		186	X	33
31	CAZENEUVE MONTAUT		217	AA	37
31	CAZERES	C	210	BA	36
40	CAZERES SUR L'ADOUR		185	V	34
82	CAZES MONDENARD		173	CA	32
34	CAZEVIEILLE		192	NA	34
47	CAZIDEROQUE		173	AA	31
11	CAZILHAC		221	HA	37
34	CAZILHAC		192	NA	33
46	CAZILLAC		159	DA	29
24	CAZOULES		159	DA	29
34	CAZOULS D'HERAULT		214	LA	35
34	CAZOULS LES BEZIERS		213	KA	36
61	CEAUCE		57	T	13
36	CEAULMONT		115	DA	22
50	CEAUX		56	O	12
43	CEAUX D'ALLEGRE		163	NA	28
86	CEAUX EN COUHE		129	X	23
86	CEAUX EN LOUDUN		97	X	19
34	CEBAZAN		213	JA	36
63	CEBAZAT		148	KA	25
52	CEFFONDS		65	RA	13
01	CEIGNES		138	VA	24
34	CEILHES ET ROCOZELS		191	KA	34
05	CEILLAC		168	AB	30
63	CEILLOUX		148	MA	26
54	CEINTREY		68	YA	13
18	CELETTE, LA		117	HA	21
41	CELLE		79	AA	16
03	CELLE, LA		133	JA	23
18	CELLE, LA		117	HA	21
63	CELLE, LA		133	HA	25
83	CELLE, LA		203	XA	36
18	CELLE CONDE, LA		116	GA	21
23	CELLE DUNOISE, LA		131	EA	23
71	CELLE EN MORVAN		119	PA	20
37	CELLE GUENAND, LA		114	AA	20
78	CELLE LES BORDES, LA		61	FA	12
51	CELLE SOUS CHANTEMERLE, LA		64	NA	12
23	CELLE SOUS GOUZON, LA		132	GA	23
02	CELLE SOUS MONTMIRAIL, LA		41	MA	11
37	CELLE ST AVANT, LA		98	Z	19
78	CELLE ST CLOUD, LA	C	39	GA	11
89	CELLE ST CYR, LA		83	LA	15
58	CELLE SUR LOIRE, LA		101	JA	18
77	CELLE SUR MORIN, LA		41	JA	12
58	CELLE SUR NIEVRE, LA		102	KA	19
16	CELLEFROUIN		129	Y	25
09	CELLES		219	EA	38
15	CELLES		161	JA	28
17	CELLES		142	U	26
24	CELLES		143	Y	27
34	CELLES		192	LA	34
52	CELLES EN BASSIGNY		87	VA	16
02	CELLES LES CONDE		42	MA	11
86	CELLES LEVESCAULT		113	X	22
02	CELLES SUR AISNE		28	MA	9
79	CELLES SUR BELLE	C	128	V	23
63	CELLES SUR DUROLLE		134	MA	25
10	CELLES SUR OURCE		65	OA	15
88	CELLES SUR PLAINE		69	BB	13
23	CELLETTE, LA		132	FA	22
63	CELLETTE, LA		133	IA	24
16	CELLETTES		129	X	25
41	CELLETTES		80	CA	17
44	CELLIER, LE		94	Q	18
07	CELLIER DU LUC		177	NA	30
42	CELLIEU		150	OA	26
63	CELLULE		134	KA	24
36	CELON		115	DA	22
15	CELOUX		162	LA	28
52	CELSOY		87	UA	16
77	CELY		62	HA	13
70	CEMBOING		87	WA	16
60	CEMPUIS		26	FA	8
33	CENAC		156	U	29
24	CENAC ET ST JULIEN		158	BA	29
70	CENANS		107	YA	18
30	CENDRAS		178	OA	32
63	CENDRE, LE		148	KA	25
70	CENDRECOURT		88	XA	16
25	CENDREY		107	YA	18
24	CENDRIEUX		158	AA	29
46	CENEVIERES		174	EA	31
11	CENNE MONESTIES		212	GA	36
33	CENON	C	156	U	29
86	CENON SUR VIENNE		113	Y	21
39	CENSEAU		123	XA	20
21	CENSEREY		104	PA	19
89	CENSY		84	OA	17
76	CENT ACRES, LES		24	BA	7
12	CENTRES		175	HA	32
2B	CENTURI		226	MB	38
69	CENVES		136	RA	23
31	CEPET		188	DA	34
11	CEPIE		221	GA	37
45	CEPOY		82	IA	15
32	CERAN		187	Z	34
72	CERANS FOULLETOURTE		78	W	16
66	CERBERE		224	KA	40
18	CERBOIS		100	FA	19
69	CERCIE		136	RA	24
74	CERCIER		139	XA	24
24	CERCLES		143	Y	27
45	CERCOTTES		81	FA	15
17	CERCOUX		156	V	28
61	CERCUEIL, LE		58	W	12
58	CERCY LA TOUR		119	MA	20
01	CERDON		138	UA	24
45	CERDON		82	HA	17
40	CERE		184	U	33
37	CERE LA RONDE		98	BA	18
37	CERELLES		79	Z	17
50	CERENCES		56	Q	11
04	CERESTE		196	VA	34
66	CERET	S	224	IA	40
59	CERFONTAINE		19	OA	5
42	CERGNE, LE		136	PA	23
95	CERGY	C	39	FA	11
03	CERILLY	C	117	JA	21
21	CERILLY		85	QA	16
89	CERILLY		64	MA	14
61	CERISE		58	X	13
52	CERISIERES		66	TA	14
89	CERISIERS	C	64	MA	15
80	CERISY		26	IA	7
61	CERISY BELLE ETOILE		57	T	12
80	CERISY BULEUX		15	EA	6
50	CERISY LA FORET		35	S	10
50	CERISY LA SALLE	C	34	Q	11
79	CERIZAY	C	111	T	20
09	CERIZOLS		218	BA	37
02	CERIZY		28	LA	7
76	CERLANGUE, LA		23	Y	8
39	CERNANS		123	XA	20
14	CERNAY		37	Y	11
28	CERNAY		60	CA	13
68	CERNAY	C	90	CB	16
86	CERNAY		113	X	20
51	CERNAY EN DORMOIS		43	RA	10
25	CERNAY L'EGLISE		108	BB	18
78	CERNAY LA VILLE		61	FA	12
51	CERNAY LES REIMS		42	OA	10
77	CERNEUX		41	LA	12
74	CERNEX		139	XA	24
39	CERNIEBAUD		123	XA	21
08	CERNION		29	QA	7
39	CERNON		122	VA	22
51	CERNON		43	PA	11
60	CERNOY		26	HA	9
45	CERNOY EN BERRY		82	IA	17
49	CERNUSSON		96	U	19
91	CERNY		62	GA	13
02	CERNY EN LAONNOIS		28	MA	9
02	CERNY LES BUCY		28	MA	8
71	CERON		135	OA	23
33	CERONS		170	V	30
14	CERQUEUX		37	Y	11
49	CERQUEUX DE MAULEVRIER, LES		95	T	20
49	CERQUEUX SOUS PASSAVANT, LES		96	U	19
70	CERRE LES NOROY		88	YA	17
34	CERS		214	LA	36
79	CERSAY		96	U	19
02	CERSEUIL		28	MA	9
71	CERSOT		120	RA	21
88	CERTILLEUX		67	WA	14
01	CERTINES		137	TA	23
74	CERVENS		139	ZA	23
05	CERVIERES		168	AB	29
42	CERVIERES		135	NA	25
54	CERVILLE		46	YA	12
2B	CERVIONE	C	228	MB	40
58	CERVON		103	NA	19
43	CERZAT		162	MA	28
39	CESANCEY		122	VA	21
73	CESARCHES		153	ZA	25
45	CESARVILLE DOSSAINVILLE		62	GA	14
09	CESCAU		218	BA	38
64	CESCAU		207	U	36
14	CESNY AUX VIGNES OUEZY		36	W	10
14	CESNY BOIS HALBOUT		36	U	11
33	CESSAC		156	V	30
31	CESSALES		211	EA	35
55	CESSE		30	TA	8
34	CESSENON SUR ORB		213	KA	35
73	CESSENS		138	WA	25
34	CESSERAS		212	IA	36
03	CESSET		134	KA	23
27	CESSEVILLE		38	BA	10
25	CESSEY		106	WA	19
21	CESSEY SUR TILLE		105	TA	18
02	CESSIERES		28	MA	8
38	CESSIEU		152	UA	26
77	CESSON		62	IA	13
35	CESSON SEVIGNE	C	76	P	15
77	CESSOY EN MONTOIS		63	KA	13
01	CESSY		139	XA	23
58	CESSY LES BOIS		102	KA	18
33	CESTAS		155	T	30
81	CESTAYROLS		189	FA	33
61	CETON		59	Z	14
64	CETTE EYGUN		215	U	38
73	CEVINS		153	ZA	26
34	CEYRAS		214	LA	35
63	CEYRAT		147	KA	25
13	CEYRESTE		202	VA	36
23	CEYROUX		131	DA	24
43	CEYSSAC		163	NA	28
63	CEYSSAT		147	JA	25
01	CEYZERIAT	C	137	UA	23
01	CEYZERIEU		138	WA	25
33	CEZAC		156	U	28
46	CEZAC		173	CA	31
85	CEZAIS		111	S	21
32	CEZAN		186	Y	34
42	CEZAY		149	OA	25
15	CEZENS		161	JA	29
39	CEZIA		138	VA	22
89	CEZY		83	LA	15
16	CHABANAIS	C	130	Z	25
03	CHABANNE, LA		135	NA	24
05	CHABESTAN		181	WA	31
26	CHABEUIL	C	165	SA	29
89	CHABLIS	C	84	NA	16
38	CHABONS		152	UA	27
05	CHABOTTES		167	YA	30
86	CHABOURNAY		113	X	21
16	CHABRAC		130	Z	24
63	CHABRELOCHE		134	MA	25
19	CHABRIGNAC		145	CA	27
26	CHABRILLAN		165	SA	30
36	CHABRIS		99	EA	18
49	CHACE		96	W	19
10	CHACENAY		65	QA	15
02	CHACRISE		28	LA	9
63	CHADELEUF		148	KA	26
17	CHADENAC		142	U	26
48	CHADENET		177	MA	31
43	CHADRAC		163	NA	28
43	CHADRON		163	OA	29
16	CHADURIE		143	X	26
26	CHAFFAL, LE		165	TA	29
04	CHAFFAUT ST JURSON, LE		197	YA	33
25	CHAFFOIS		123	YA	20
70	CHAGEY		89	AB	17
42	CHAGNON		150	QA	26
08	CHAGNY		30	RA	8
71	CHAGNY	C	120	RA	20
72	CHAHAIGNES		79	Y	16
61	CHAHAINS		58	W	13
21	CHAIGNAY		105	TA	18
27	CHAIGNES		38	DA	11
79	CHAIL		128	W	23
36	CHAILLAC		131	CA	22
87	CHAILLAC SUR VIENNE		130	AA	25
53	CHAILLAND	C	57	S	14
85	CHAILLE LES MARAIS	C	111	S	22
85	CHAILLE SOUS LES ORMEAUX		110	Q	21
41	CHAILLES		80	CA	17
17	CHAILLEVETTE		141	R	25
02	CHAILLEVOIS		28	MA	8
89	CHAILLEY		64	NA	15
55	CHAILLON		45	VA	11
61	CHAILLOUE		58	X	12
77	CHAILLY EN BIERE		62	IA	13
77	CHAILLY EN BRIE		41	KA	12
45	CHAILLY EN GATINAIS		82	HA	15
57	CHAILLY LES ENNERY		46	YA	10
21	CHAILLY SUR ARMANCON		104	QA	18
74	CHAINAZ LES FRASSES		153	XA	25
39	CHAINEE DES COUPIS		122	UA	20
45	CHAINGY		81	EA	16
71	CHAINTRE		136	RA	23
77	CHAINTREAUX		62	JA	14
51	CHAINTRIX BIERGES		42	OA	11
10	CHAISE, LA		65	RA	14
50	CHAISE BAUDOUIN, LA		56	R	12
43	CHAISE DIEU, LA	C	149	NA	27
27	CHAISE DIEU DU THEIL		37	Z	12
85	CHAIX		111	S	22
85	CHAIZE GIRAUD, LA		109	O	21
85	CHAIZE LE VICOMTE, LA		110	Q	21
11	CHALABRE	C	221	FA	37
24	CHALAGNAC		158	Z	28
42	CHALAIN D'UZORE		149	OA	25
42	CHALAIN LE COMTAL		149	PA	26
55	CHALAINES		67	VA	13
16	CHALAIS	C	143	W	27
36	CHALAIS		114	BA	22
86	CHALAIS		112	W	20
01	CHALAMONT	C	137	TA	24
68	CHALAMPE		90	EB	16
52	CHALANCEY		86	TA	17
26	CHALANCON		180	UA	31
86	CHALANDRAY		112	W	21
02	CHALANDRY		28	MA	8
08	CHALANDRY ELAIRE		30	RA	8
61	CHALANGE, LE		59	X	13
87	CHALARD, LE		144	BA	26
77	CHALAUTRE LA GRANDE		63	MA	13
77	CHALAUTRE LA PETITE		63	LA	13
58	CHALAUX		103	OA	18
01	CHALEINS		137	SA	24
24	CHALEIX		144	AA	26
07	CHALENCON		164	QA	29
39	CHALESMES, LES		123	XA	21
45	CHALETTE SUR LOING	C	82	IA	15
10	CHALETTE SUR VOIRE		65	OA	13
01	CHALEY		138	VA	24
25	CHALEZE		107	XA	18
25	CHALEZEULE		107	XA	18
15	CHALIERS		162	KA	29
77	CHALIFERT		40	IA	11
54	CHALIGNY		67	XA	12
15	CHALINARGUES		161	JA	28

52 CHALINDREY 87 UA 16
18 CHALIVOY MILON 117 IA 20
49 CHALLAIN LA POTHERIE 95 S 17
85 CHALLANS C 109 O 20
58 CHALLEMENT 103 MA 18
08 CHALLERANGE 30 RA 9
01 CHALLES 138 UA 23
72 CHALLES 79 Y 15
73 CHALLES LES EAUX 153 XA 26
28 CHALLET 60 DA 13
01 CHALLEX 139 XA 23
16 CHALLIGNAC 142 W 27
74 CHALLONGES 138 WA 24
58 CHALLUY 118 KA 20
77 CHALMAISON 63 LA 13
42 CHALMAZEL 149 NA 25
71 CHALMOUX 119 NA 21
91 CHALO ST MARS 61 FA 13
26 CHALON, LE 165 TA 28
71 CHALON SUR SAONE S 121 SA 20
49 CHALONNES SOUS LE LUDE 97 X 17
49 CHALONNES SUR LOIRE C 95 T 18
38 CHALONS 151 SA 26
53 CHALONS DU MAINE 77 T 14
51 CHALONS EN CHAMPAGNE P 43 OA 11
51 CHALONS SUR VESLE 42 NA 9
70 CHALONVILLARS 89 AB 17
91 CHALOU MOULINEUX 61 FA 13
51 CHALTRAIT 42 NA 11
63 CHALUS 148 KA 26
87 CHALUS C 144 BA 26
15 CHALVIGNAC 160 GA 27
52 CHALVRAINES 67 UA 14
33 CHAMADELLE 156 W 28
88 CHAMAGNE 68 YA 13
38 CHAMAGNIEU 151 TA 25
63 CHAMALIERES C 147 KA 25
43 CHAMALIERES SUR LOIRE 163 OA 28
26 CHAMALOC 166 UA 29
60 CHAMANT 40 IA 10
91 CHAMARANDE 62 GA 13
52 CHAMARANDES CHOIGNES 66 TA 15
26 CHAMARET 179 SA 31
42 CHAMBA, LA 149 NA 25
21 CHAMBAIN 86 SA 16
21 CHAMBEIRE 105 UA 18
49 CHAMBELLAY 77 T 17
42 CHAMBEON 149 PA 25
03 CHAMBERAT 132 HA 22
23 CHAMBERAUD 132 FA 24
19 CHAMBERET 145 EA 26
39 CHAMBERIA 122 VA 22
73 CHAMBERY P 152 WA 26
89 CHAMBEUGLE 83 KA 16
43 CHAMBEZON 148 KA 27
71 CHAMBILLY 135 OA 23
27 CHAMBLAC 37 Z 11
21 CHAMBLANC 105 TA 19
39 CHAMBLAY 122 VA 20
42 CHAMBLES 149 PA 27
03 CHAMBLET 133 IA 23
54 CHAMBLEY BUSSIERES C 45 WA 11
60 CHAMBLY 40 GA 10
21 CHAMBOEUF 105 SA 19
42 CHAMBOEUF 150 PA 26
61 CHAMBOIS 58 X 12
21 CHAMBOLLE MUSIGNY 105 SA 19
17 CHAMBON 127 S 24
18 CHAMBON 116 GA 21
30 CHAMBON 178 OA 32
37 CHAMBON 114 AA 20
07 CHAMBON, LE 164 PA 29
42 CHAMBON FEUGEROLLES, LE C 150 PA 27
45 CHAMBON LA FORET 82 GA 15
48 CHAMBON LE CHATEAU 163 MA 29
23 CHAMBON STE CROIX 131 EA 23
41 CHAMBON SUR CISSE 80 CA 17
63 CHAMBON SUR DOLORE 148 MA 26
63 CHAMBON SUR LAC 147 JA 26
43 CHAMBON SUR LIGNON, LE 164 PA 28
23 CHAMBON SUR VOUEIZE C 132 HA 23
07 CHAMBONAS 178 PA 31
23 CHAMBONCHARD 133 HA 23
42 CHAMBONIE, LA 149 NA 25
23 CHAMBORAND 131 DA 23
27 CHAMBORD 37 Z 11
41 CHAMBORD 80 DA 17
87 CHAMBORET 130 BA 24
30 CHAMBORIGAUD 178 OA 32
70 CHAMBORNAY LES BELLEVAUX 107 XA 18
70 CHAMBORNAY LES PIN 106 WA 18
60 CHAMBORS 39 EA 10
69 CHAMBOST ALLIERES 136 OA 24
69 CHAMBOST LONGESSAIGNE 150 QA 25
19 CHAMBOULIVE 145 EA 27
78 CHAMBOURCY 39 FA 11
37 CHAMBOURG SUR INDRE 98 AA 19
27 CHAMBRAY 38 CA 10
37 CHAMBRAY LES TOURS C 98 Z 18
73 CHAMBRE, LA C 153 YA 27
51 CHAMBRECY 42 NA 10
50 CHAMBRES, LES 56 Q 12
85 CHAMBRETAUD 111 S 20
57 CHAMBREY 46 ZA 12
52 CHAMBRONCOURT 66 UA 14
02 CHAMBRY 28 MA 8
77 CHAMBRY 41 JA 11
63 CHAMEANE 148 LA 26
69 CHAMELET 136 OA 24
51 CHAMERY 42 OA 10
25 CHAMESEY 108 AB 19
25 CHAMESOL 108 BB 18
21 CHAMESSON 85 OA 16
19 CHAMEYRAT 159 EA 27
77 CHAMIGNY 41 KA 11
71 CHAMILLY 120 RA 20
53 CHAMMES 77 U 15
39 CHAMOLE 122 WA 20
74 CHAMONIX MONT BLANC C 140 BB 24
17 CHAMOUILLAC 142 U 27
02 CHAMOUILLE 28 MA 9
52 CHAMOUILLEY 66 TA 13
73 CHAMOUSSET 153 YA 26
89 CHAMOUX 103 NA 18
73 CHAMOUX SUR GELON C 153 YA 26
10 CHAMOY 64 OA 15
21 CHAMP D'OISEAU 85 PA 17
61 CHAMP DE LA PIERRE, LE 58 V 12
27 CHAMP DOLENT 38 BA 11
14 CHAMP DU BOULT 57 S 12
61 CHAMP HAUT 37 Y 12
73 CHAMP LAURENT 153 YA 26
88 CHAMP LE DUC 69 AB 14
38 CHAMP PRES FROGES, LE 153 XA 27
85 CHAMP ST PERE, LE 125 Q 22
10 CHAMP SUR BARSE 65 QA 14
38 CHAMP SUR DRAC 166 WA 28
49 CHAMP SUR LAYON, LE 96 U 18

15 CHAMPAGNAC 146 HA 27
17 CHAMPAGNAC 142 U 27
24 CHAMPAGNAC DE BELAIR C 144 Z 27
19 CHAMPAGNAC LA NOAILLE 146 FA 27
19 CHAMPAGNAC LA PRUNE 159 EA 28
87 CHAMPAGNAC LA RIVIERE 144 AA 25
43 CHAMPAGNAC LE VIEUX 148 MA 27
23 CHAMPAGNAT 132 GA 24
71 CHAMPAGNAT 122 UA 22
63 CHAMPAGNAT LE JEUNE 148 LA 26
07 CHAMPAGNE 150 RA 27
17 CHAMPAGNE 127 S 25
28 CHAMPAGNE 39 DA 12
72 CHAMPAGNE 78 X 15
69 CHAMPAGNE AU MONT D'OR 150 RA 25
01 CHAMPAGNE EN VALROMEY C 138 VA 24
24 CHAMPAGNE ET FONTAINE 143 Y 27
86 CHAMPAGNE LE SEC 129 X 23
85 CHAMPAGNE LES MARAIS 125 R 22
16 CHAMPAGNE MOUTON C 129 Y 24
86 CHAMPAGNE ST HILAIRE 129 Y 23
39 CHAMPAGNE SUR LOUE 106 WA 19
95 CHAMPAGNE SUR OISE 40 GA 10
77 CHAMPAGNE SUR SEINE 62 JA 13
21 CHAMPAGNE SUR VINGEANNE 106 UA 18
16 CHAMPAGNE VIGNY 143 W 26
73 CHAMPAGNEUX 152 VA 26
25 CHAMPAGNEY 106 WA 19
39 CHAMPAGNEY 106 VA 18
70 CHAMPAGNEY C 89 AB 16
38 CHAMPAGNIER 166 WA 28
39 CHAMPAGNOLE C 122 WA 21
17 CHAMPAGNOLLES 141 T 26
21 CHAMPAGNY 104 RA 18
73 CHAMPAGNY EN VANOISE 154 AB 27
71 CHAMPAGNY SOUS UXELLES 120 RA 21
58 CHAMPALLEMENT 102 MA 19
74 CHAMPANGES 124 ZA 22
51 CHAMPAUBERT 42 NA 11
05 CHAMPCELLA 168 ZA 30
77 CHAMPCENEST 63 LA 12
61 CHAMPCERIE 58 V 12
50 CHAMPCERVON 56 O 12
24 CHAMPCEVINEL 158 Z 28
89 CHAMPCEVRAIS 83 JA 16
50 CHAMPCEY 56 Q 12
43 CHAMPCLAUSE 163 PA 28
91 CHAMPCUEIL 62 HA 13
79 CHAMPDENIERS ST DENIS C 112 U 22
77 CHAMPDEUIL 62 IA 12
42 CHAMPDIEU 149 OA 26
39 CHAMPDIVERS 122 UA 21
17 CHAMPDOLENT 127 T 24
01 CHAMPDOR 138 VA 24
21 CHAMPDOTRE 105 UA 19
88 CHAMPDRAY 69 AB 15
21 CHAMPEAU EN MORVAN 103 PA 18
35 CHAMPEAUX 76 Q 15
50 CHAMPEAUX 56 P 12
77 CHAMPEAUX 62 JA 13
61 CHAMPEAUX, LES 36 X 11
24 CHAMPEAUX
ET LA CHAPELLE POMMIER 143 Z 26
61 CHAMPEAUX SUR SARTHE 59 Y 13
63 CHAMPEIX C 148 KA 26
27 CHAMPENARD 38 CA 10
36 CHAMPENOISE, LA 115 EA 20
54 CHAMPENOUX 46 YA 12
53 CHAMPEON 57 U 14
63 CHAMPETIERES 149 NA 26
70 CHAMPEY 89 AB 17
54 CHAMPEY SUR MOSELLE 46 XA 11
72 CHAMPFLEUR 58 X 13
10 CHAMPFLEURY 64 OA 12
51 CHAMPFLEURY 42 OA 10
71 CHAMPFORGEUIL 121 RA 20
53 CHAMPFREMONT 58 W 13
01 CHAMPFROMIER 138 WA 23
53 CHAMPGENETEUX 57 U 14
51 CHAMPGUYON 42 MA 12
28 CHAMPHOL 60 DA 13
80 CHAMPIEN 27 JA 8
38 CHAMPIER 151 UA 26
49 CHAMPIGNE 77 U 17
89 CHAMPIGNELLES 83 KA 16
51 CHAMPIGNEUL CHAMPAGNE 42 PA 11
08 CHAMPIGNEUL SUR VENCE 30 RA 8
08 CHAMPIGNEULLE 30 SA 9
54 CHAMPIGNEULLES 46 XA 12
52 CHAMPIGNEULLES
EN BASSIGNY 67 VA 15
10 CHAMPIGNOL LEZ MONDEVILLE 65 RA 15
21 CHAMPIGNOLLES 104 OA 19
27 CHAMPIGNOLLES 37 AA 11
51 CHAMPIGNY 42 OA 10
89 CHAMPIGNY 63 KA 14
41 CHAMPIGNY EN BEAUCE 80 CA 16
27 CHAMPIGNY LA FUTELAYE 38 CA 11
86 CHAMPIGNY LE SEC 113 X 21
52 CHAMPIGNY LES LANGRES 87 UA 16
52 CHAMPIGNY SOUS VARENNES 87 VA 16
10 CHAMPIGNY SUR AUBE 64 OA 13
94 CHAMPIGNY SUR MARNE C 40 HA 12
37 CHAMPIGNY SUR VEUDE 97 Y 19
36 CHAMPILLET 116 FA 22
51 CHAMPILLON 42 OA 10
07 CHAMPIS 164 RA 29
91 CHAMPLAN 40 GA 12
91 CHAMPLAT ET BOUJACOURT 42 NA 10
89 CHAMPLAY 83 LA 15
71 CHAMPLECY 120 PA 22
58 CHAMPLEMY 102 LA 18
08 CHAMPLIN 29 PA 7
58 CHAMPLIN 102 LA 19
70 CHAMPLITTE C 87 VA 17
25 CHAMPLIVE 107 YA 18
89 CHAMPLOST 84 MA 15
16 CHAMPMILLON 143 W 26
91 CHAMPMOTTEUX 62 GA 14
87 CHAMPNETERY 145 DA 25
55 CHAMPNEUVILLE 44 UA 10
16 CHAMPNIERS 143 X 25
86 CHAMPNIERS 129 Y 23
87 CHAMPNIERS ET REILHAC 144 Z 25
05 CHAMPOLEON 167 YA 30
42 CHAMPOLY 135 NA 25
61 CHAMPOSOULT 36 X 11
55 CHAMPOUGNY 67 VA 13
45 CHAMPOULET 82 JA 17
25 CHAMPOUX 107 YA 18
21 CHAMPRENAULT 104 RA 18
50 CHAMPREPUS 56 Q 11
72 CHAMPROND 59 Z 15
28 CHAMPROND EN GATINE 60 BA 13
28 CHAMPROND EN PERCHET 59 AA 14
39 CHAMPROUGIER 122 VA 20
02 CHAMPS 27 LA 8
61 CHAMPS 59 Z 13

63 CHAMPS 134 KA 24
50 CHAMPS DE LOSQUE, LES 34 R 10
22 CHAMPS GERAUX, LES 55 N 13
24 CHAMPS ROMAIN 144 AA 26
77 CHAMPS SUR MARNE C 40 IA 11
15 CHAMPS SUR TARENTAINE
MARCHAL C 147 IA 27
89 CHAMPS SUR YONNE 84 MA 16
87 CHAMPSAC 144 AA 25
23 CHAMPSANGLARD 132 EA 23
61 CHAMPSECRET 57 U 12
28 CHAMPSERU 61 DA 13
52 CHAMPSEVRAINE 87 VA 16
04 CHAMPTERCIER 197 XA 33
49 CHAMPTEUSSESUR BACONNE 77 T 17
49 CHAMPTOCE SUR LOIRE 95 S 18
49 CHAMPTOCEAUX C 94 Q 18
70 CHAMPTONNAY 106 VA 18
89 CHAMPVALLON 83 LA 15
39 CHAMPVANS 106 VA 19
70 CHAMPVANS 106 VA 18
25 CHAMPVANS LES MOULINS 106 WA 19
58 CHAMPVERT 118 MA 20
51 CHAMPVOISY 42 MA 10
58 CHAMPVOUX 102 KA 19
38 CHAMROUSSE 167 WA 28
89 CHAMVRES 83 LA 15
48 CHANAC C 177 LA 31
19 CHANAC LES MINES 160 EA 27
43 CHANALEILLES 162 MA 29
38 CHANAS 151 SA 27
63 CHANAT LA MOUTEYRE 147 JA 25
01 CHANAY 138 WA 24
73 CHANAZ 138 WA 25
37 CHANCAY 98 AA 18
35 CHANCE 76 O 15
21 CHANCEAUX 85 RA 17
37 CHANCEAUX PRES LOCHES 98 AA 19
37 CHANCEAUX SUR CHOISILLE 79 Z 17
24 CHANCELADE 158 Z 28
52 CHANCENAY 44 SA 12
70 CHANCEY 106 VA 18
39 CHANCIA 138 VA 23
61 CHANDAI 37 Z 12
07 CHANDOLAS 178 PA 31
42 CHANDON 135 PA 23
07 CHANEAC 164 PA 29
01 CHANEINS 137 SA 24
71 CHANES 136 RA 23
53 CHANGE 77 T 15
71 CHANGE 120 RA 20
72 CHANGE 78 X 15
24 CHANGE, LE 158 AA 28
52 CHANGEY 87 UA 15
77 CHANGIS SUR MARNE 41 KA 11
42 CHANGY 135 NA 23
51 CHANGY 43 RA 12
71 CHANGY 135 PA 22
43 CHANIAT 148 MA 27
17 CHANIERS 142 U 25
21 CHANNAY 85 PA 16
37 CHANNAY SUR LATHAN 97 X 17
10 CHANNES 85 PA 15
63 CHANONAT 148 KA 25
26 CHANOS CURSON 165 SA 28
05 CHANOUSSE 180 VA 31
52 CHANOY 87 UA 16
01 CHANOZ CHATENAY 137 SA 23
45 CHANTEAU 81 FA 15
45 CHANTECOQ 83 JA 15
79 CHANTECORPS 112 V 22
54 CHANTEHEUX 68 ZA 13
19 CHANTEIX 145 DA 27
03 CHANTELLE C 134 KA 23
27 CHANTELOUP 38 BA 11
35 CHANTELOUP 75 P 15
50 CHANTELOUP 56 Q 11
79 CHANTELOUP 112 U 21
77 CHANTELOUP EN BRIE 40 IA 11
49 CHANTELOUP LES BOIS 95 T 19
78 CHANTELOUP LES VIGNES 39 FA 11
38 CHANTELOUVE 167 XA 29
51 CHANTEMERLE 64 MA 12
26 CHANTEMERLE LES BLES 165 SA 28
26 CHANTEMERLE LES GRIGNAN 179 SA 31
17 CHANTEMERLE SUR LA SOIE 127 T 24
58 CHANTENAY ST IMBERT 118 KA 21
72 CHANTENAY VILLEDIEU 78 V 16
35 CHANTEPIE 75 P 15
24 CHANTERAC 157 Y 28
55 CHANTERAINE 44 UA 12
15 CHANTERELLE 147 JA 27
70 CHANTES 88 WA 17
38 CHANTESSE 152 UA 27
43 CHANTEUGES 162 MA 28
16 CHANTILLAC 142 V 27
60 CHANTILLY C 40 HA 10
85 CHANTONNAY C 111 S 21
88 CHANTRAINE 68 ZA 14
52 CHANTRAINES 66 TA 14
25 CHANTRANS 107 XA 19
53 CHANTRIGNE 57 U 13
61 CHANU 57 T 12
57 CHANVILLE 47 ZA 11
49 CHANZEAUX 95 T 18
41 CHAON 81 GA 17
54 CHAOUILLEY 67 XA 13
10 CHAOURCE C 85 PA 15
02 CHAOURSE 29 OA 8
71 CHAPAIZE 120 RA 22
38 CHAPAREILLAN 153 XA 27
63 CHAPDES BEAUFORT 133 JA 25
24 CHAPDEUIL 143 Y 27
03 CHAPEAU 118 MA 22
74 CHAPEIRY 139 XA 25
51 CHAPELAINE 65 OA 13
03 CHAPELAUDE, LA 133 HA 22
03 CHAPELLE, LA 133 MA 24
08 CHAPELLE, LA 30 SA 7
16 CHAPELLE, LA 129 W 25
73 CHAPELLE, LA 153 YA 27
85 CHAPELLE ACHARD, LA 110 P 21
63 CHAPELLE AGNON, LA 148 MA 26
53 CHAPELLE ANTHENAISE, LA 77 T 15
71 CHAPELLE AU MANS, LA 119 OA 21
61 CHAPELLE AU MOINE, LA 57 T 12
53 CHAPELLE AU RIBOUL, LA 57 U 14
24 CHAPELLE AUBAREIL, LA 158 BA 28
88 CHAPELLE AUX BOIS, LA 68 YA 15
19 CHAPELLE AUX BROCS, LA 159 DA 28
03 CHAPELLE AUX CHASSES, LA 118 MA 21
72 CHAPELLE AUX CHOUX, LA 78 X 17
35 CHAPELLE AUX FILTZMEENS, LA 55 O 13
85 CHAPELLE AUX LYS, LA 111 T 21
37 CHAPELLE AUX NAUX, LA 97 Y 18
19 CHAPELLE AUX SAINTS, LA 159 EA 29
23 CHAPELLE BALOUE, LA 131 DA 22
44 CHAPELLE BASSE MER, LA 94 Q 18

79 CHAPELLE BATON, LA 112 V 22
86 CHAPELLE BATON, LA 129 Y 23
27 CHAPELLE BAYVEL, LA 37 Y 10
43 CHAPELLE BERTIN, LA 162 MA 27
79 CHAPELLE BERTRAND, LA 112 V 21
61 CHAPELLE BICHE, LA 57 T 12
22 CHAPELLE BLANCHE, LA 75 N 14
73 CHAPELLE BLANCHE, LA 153 XA 27
37 CHAPELLE BLANCHE
ST MARTIN, LA 98 AA 19
35 CHAPELLE BOUEXIC, LA 75 O 15
56 CHAPELLE CARO, LA 74 L 16
50 CHAPELLE CECELIN, LA 56 R 12
35 CHAPELLE CHAUSSEE, LA 75 O 14
53 CHAPELLE CRAONNAISE, LA 77 S 16
74 CHAPELLE D'ABONDANCE, LA 140 AB 23
15 CHAPELLE D'ALAGNON, LA 161 JA 28
72 CHAPELLE D'ALIGNE, LA 78 V 16
61 CHAPELLE D'ANDAINE, LA 57 U 13
18 CHAPELLE D'ANGILLON, LA C 100 HA 18
59 CHAPELLE
D'ARMENTIERES, LA 9 JA 3
28 CHAPELLE D'AUNAINVILLE, LA 61 EA 13
43 CHAPELLE D'AUREC, LA 149 PA 27
25 CHAPELLE D'HUIN 123 YA 20
71 CHAPELLE DE BRAGNY, LA 120 RA 21
35 CHAPELLE DE BRAIN, LA 75 O 16
71 CHAPELLE DE GUINCHAY, LA C 136 RA 23
38 CHAPELLE DE LA TOUR, LA 152 UA 26
69 CHAPELLE DE MARDORE, LA 136 QA 24
38 CHAPELLE DE SURIEU, LA 151 SA 27
25 CHAPELLE DES BOIS 123 XA 21
35 CHAPELLE DES FOUGERETZ, LA 75 O 14
44 CHAPELLE DES MARAIS, LA 92 M 18
17 CHAPELLE DES POTS, LA 142 U 25
88 CHAPELLE
DEVANT BRUYERES, LA 69 AB 14
38 CHAPELLE DU BARD, LA 153 XA 27
72 CHAPELLE DU BOIS, LA 59 Z 14
27 CHAPELLE DU BOIS
DES FAULX, LA 38 BA 10
76 CHAPELLE DU BOURGAY, LA 24 BA 7
01 CHAPELLE DU CHATELARD, LA 137 SA 24
49 CHAPELLE DU GENET, LA 95 S 19
35 CHAPELLE DU LOU, LA 75 N 14
71 CHAPELLE DU MONT
DE FRANCE, LA 136 OA 22
73 CHAPELLE DU MONT
DU CHAT, LA 152 WA 25
28 CHAPELLE DU NOYER, LA 80 CA 15
50 CHAPELLE EN JUGER, LA 34 R 10
42 CHAPELLE EN LAFAYE, LA 149 OA 26
60 CHAPELLE EN SERVAL, LA 40 HA 10
05 CHAPELLE
EN VALGAUDEMAR, LA 167 YA 29
26 CHAPELLE EN VERCORS, LA C 166 UA 29
95 CHAPELLE EN VEXIN, LA 39 EA 10
41 CHAPELLE ENCHERIE, LA 80 BA 16
14 CHAPELLE ENGERBOLD, LA 35 T 11
35 CHAPELLE ERBREE, LA 76 R 15
24 CHAPELLE FAUCHER, LA 144 Z 27
51 CHAPELLE FELCOURT, LA 43 RA 11
28 CHAPELLE FORAINVILLIERS, LA 38 DA 12
28 CHAPELLE FORTIN, LA 59 AA 12
56 CHAPELLE GACELINE, LA 75 N 16
79 CHAPELLE GAUDIN, LA 112 U 20
72 CHAPELLE GAUGAIN, LA 79 Z 16
27 CHAPELLE GAUTHIER, LA 37 Y 11
77 CHAPELLE GAUTHIER, LA 63 JA 13
43 CHAPELLE GENESTE, LA 148 MA 27
44 CHAPELLE GLAIN, LA 94 R 17
24 CHAPELLE GONAGUET, LA 144 Z 27
24 CHAPELLE GRESIGNAC, LA 143 Y 27
28 CHAPELLE GUILLAUME 59 AA 15
27 CHAPELLE HARENG, LA 37 Y 10
14 CHAPELLE HAUTE GRUE, LA 36 X 11
85 CHAPELLE HERMIER, LA 109 O 21
44 CHAPELLE HEULIN, LA 94 Q 19
18 CHAPELLE HUGON, LA 117 JA 20
49 CHAPELLE HULLIN, LA 76 R 16
72 CHAPELLE HUON, LA 79 Z 16
77 CHAPELLE IGER, LA 63 JA 12
35 CHAPELLE JANSON, LA 76 R 14
77 CHAPELLE LA REINE, LA C 62 IA 14
51 CHAPELLE LASSON, LA 64 NA 12
44 CHAPELLE LAUNAY, LA 93 N 18
15 CHAPELLE LAURENT, LA 162 LA 28
70 CHAPELLE LES LUXEUIL, LA 88 YA 16
63 CHAPELLE MARCOUSSE, LA 148 KA 26
24 CHAPELLE MONTABOURLET, LA 143 Y 27
87 CHAPELLE MONTBRANDEIX, LA 144 AA 26
02 CHAPELLE MONTHODON, LA 42 MA 11
61 CHAPELLE MONTLIGEON, LA 59 Z 13
18 CHAPELLE MONTLINARD, LA 101 JA 19
41 CHAPELLE MONTMARTIN, LA 99 EA 18
24 CHAPELLE MONTMOREAU, LA 144 Z 27
86 CHAPELLE MONTREUIL, LA 113 X 22
86 CHAPELLE MOULIERE, LA 113 Z 21
77 CHAPELLE MOUTILS, LA 41 LA 12
71 CHAPELLE NAUDE, LA 44 TA 12
22 CHAPELLE NEUVE, LA 53 H 13
56 CHAPELLE NEUVE, LA 73 J 16
45 CHAPELLE ONZERAIN, LA 80 DA 15
36 CHAPELLE ORTHEMALE, LA 115 DA 20
85 CHAPELLE PALLUAU, LA 110 P 21
79 CHAPELLE POUILLOUX, LA 129 W 23
61 CHAPELLE PRES SEES, LA 58 X 13
77 CHAPELLE RABLAIS, LA 63 JA 13
53 CHAPELLE RAINSOUIN, LA 77 U 15
74 CHAPELLE RAMBAUD, LA 139 YA 24
27 CHAPELLE REANVILLE, LA 38 CA 10
49 CHAPELLE ROUSSELIN, LA 95 T 19
28 CHAPELLE ROYALE 60 BA 15
61 CHAPELLE SOUEF, LA 59 Z 14
71 CHAPELLE SOUS BRANCION, LA 120 RA 22
71 CHAPELLE SOUS DUN, LA 136 PA 23
51 CHAPELLE SOUS ORBAIS, LA 42 NA 11
71 CHAPELLE SOUS UCHON, LA 120 PA 20
19 CHAPELLE SPINASSE 146 FA 27
58 CHAPELLE ST ANDRE, LA 102 LA 18
35 CHAPELLE ST AUBERT, LA 76 O 14
72 CHAPELLE ST AUBIN, LA 78 X 15
79 CHAPELLE ST ETIENNE, LA 111 U 21
49 CHAPELLE ST FLORENT, LA 94 R 18
72 CHAPELLE ST FRAY, LA 78 X 15
19 CHAPELLE ST GERAUD, LA 160 FA 28
24 CHAPELLE ST JEAN, LA 158 BA 28
49 CHAPELLE ST LAUD, LA 77 V 17
79 CHAPELLE ST LAURENT, LA 112 U 21
36 CHAPELLE ST LAURIAN, LA 99 EA 19
10 CHAPELLE ST LUC, LA C 64 OA 14
23 CHAPELLE ST MARTIAL, LA 132 FA 24
73 CHAPELLE ST MARTIN, LA 152 WA 26
41 CHAPELLE ST MARTIN
EN PLAINE, LA 80 CA 16
74 CHAPELLE ST MAURICE, LA 139 YA 25
45 CHAPELLE ST MESMIN 81 EA 16
76 CHAPELLE ST OUEN, LA 25 DA 8

70 CHAPELLE ST QUILLAIN, LA 87 WA 17
72 CHAPELLE ST REMY, LA 59 Y 15
44 CHAPELLE ST SAUVEUR, LA 95 S 18
71 CHAPELLE ST SAUVEUR, LA 121 UA 20
45 CHAPELLE ST SEPULCRE, LA 82 JA 15
77 CHAPELLE ST SULPICE, LA 63 KA 13
18 CHAPELLE ST URSIN, LA 100 GA 19
45 CHAPELLE SUR AVEYRON, LA 82 JA 16
02 CHAPELLE SUR CHEZY, LA 41 LA 11
69 CHAPELLE SUR COISE, LA 150 QA 26
76 CHAPELLE SUR DUN, LA 24 AA 7
44 CHAPELLE SUR ERDRE, LA C 93 P 18
39 CHAPELLE SUR FURIEUSE, LA 122 WA 20
37 CHAPELLE SUR LOIRE, LA 97 X 19
89 CHAPELLE SUR OREUSE, LA 63 LA 14
49 CHAPELLE SUR OUDON, LA 77 S 17
63 CHAPELLE SUR USSON, LA 145 EA 26
23 CHAPELLE TAILLEFERT, LA 132 EA 24
71 CHAPELLE THECLE, LA 121 TA 22
85 CHAPELLE THEMER, LA 111 S 22
79 CHAPELLE THIREUIL, LA 111 U 22
35 CHAPELLE THOUARAULT, LA 75 O 15
50 CHAPELLE UREE, LA 56 R 12
10 CHAPELLE VALLON 64 OA 13
89 CHAPELLE VAUPELTEIGNE, LA 84 NA 16
41 CHAPELLE VENDOMOISE, LA 80 CA 17
41 CHAPELLE VICOMTESSE, LA 79 BA 15
61 CHAPELLE VIEL, LA 37 Z 12
42 CHAPELLE VILLARS, LA 150 RA 26
86 CHAPELLE VIVIERS 114 Z 22
39 CHAPELLE VOLAND 122 UA 20
14 CHAPELLE YVON, LA 37 Y 10
73 CHAPELLES, LES 154 AB 26
77 CHAPELLES BOURBON, LES 40 JA 12
45 CHAPELON 82 IA 15
18 CHAPELOTTE, LA 101 IA 18
78 CHAPET 39 FA 11
39 CHAPOIS 123 XA 20
69 CHAPONNAY 151 SA 26
69 CHAPONOST 150 RA 25
03 CHAPPES 133 JA 22
08 CHAPPES 29 PA 8
10 CHAPPES 65 PA 14
63 CHAPPES 134 LA 25
87 CHAPTELAT 131 CA 24
63 CHAPTUZAT 134 KA 24
38 CHARANCIEU 152 VA 26
38 CHARANTONNAY 151 TA 26
38 CHARAVINES 152 VA 27
08 CHARBOGNE 29 QA 8
71 CHARBONNAT 119 OA 21
63 CHARBONNIER LES MINES 148 LA 27
28 CHARBONNIERES 60 AA 14
71 CHARBONNIERES 137 SA 22
69 CHARBONNIERES LES BAINS 150 RA 25
25 CHARBONNIERES LES SAPINS 107 YA 19
63 CHARBONNIERES
LES VARENNES 133 JA 24
63 CHARBONNIERES LES VIEILLES 133 JA 24
89 CHARBUY 83 MA 16
26 CHARCE, LA 180 UA 31
49 CHARCE ST ELLIER
SUR AUBANCE 96 U 18
70 CHARCENNE 106 WA 18
53 CHARCHIGNE 57 U 13
39 CHARCHILLA 122 VA 22
39 CHARCIER 122 WA 21
23 CHARD 133 HA 24
08 CHARDENY 30 RA 9
55 CHARDOGNE 44 TA 12
71 CHARDONNAY 121 SA 22
03 CHAREIL CINTRAT 134 KA 23
21 CHARENCEY 104 RA 18
39 CHARENCY 123 XA 21
54 CHARENCY VEZIN 31 VA 9
26 CHARENS 180 VA 31
63 CHARENSAT 133 IA 24
69 CHARENTAY 136 RA 24
89 CHARENTENAY 83 MA 17
37 CHARENTILLY 97 Z 18
18 CHARENTON DU CHER C 117 IA 21
94 CHARENTON LE PONT C 40 HA 11
18 CHARENTONNAY 101 JA 19
38 CHARETTE 138 UA 25
71 CHARETTE 121 TA 20
54 CHAREY 45 WA 11
39 CHAREZIER 122 VA 21
37 CHARGE 98 BA 18
70 CHARGEY LES GRAY 87 VA 17
70 CHARGEY LES PORT 88 XA 16
70 CHARIEZ 88 XA 17
21 CHARIGNY 104 QA 18
58 CHARITE SUR LOIRE, LA C 102 KA 19
01 CHARIX 138 WA 23
31 CHARLAS 209 Z 36
13 CHARLEVAL 196 UA 34
27 CHARLEVAL 25 CA 9
51 CHARLEVILLE 42 MA 12
08 CHARLEVILLE MEZIERES P 30 RA 7
57 CHARLEVILLE SOUS BOIS 47 ZA 10
42 CHARLIEU C 135 PA 23
02 CHARLY C 41 LA 11
18 CHARLY 117 IA 20
69 CHARLY 150 RA 26
57 CHARLY ORADOUR 46 YA 10
16 CHARMANT 143 X 26
25 CHARMAUVILLERS 108 BB 19
16 CHARME 129 X 24
39 CHARME, LA 122 VA 20
45 CHARME, LE 83 KA 16
71 CHARMEE, LA 121 SA 21
03 CHARMEIL 133 LA 23
02 CHARMEL, LE 42 MA 10
15 CHARMENSAC 162 KA 28
77 CHARMENTRAY 40 IA 11
02 CHARMES 28 LA 8
03 CHARMES 133 LA 24
21 CHARMES 105 UA 18
52 CHARMES 87 UA 16
88 CHARMES C 68 YA 13
52 CHARMES EN L'ANGLE 66 SA 14
54 CHARMES LA COTE 67 WA 12
52 CHARMES LA GRANDE 66 SA 13
70 CHARMES ST VALBERT 87 VA 16
26 CHARMES SUR L'HERBASSE 165 SA 28
07 CHARMES SUR RHONE 165 SA 29
25 CHARMOILLE 108 AB 19
70 CHARMOILLE 88 XA 17
54 CHARMOIS 68 ZA 13
90 CHARMOIS 89 BB 17
88 CHARMOIS DEVANT BRUYERES 68 ZA 14
88 CHARMOIS L'ORGUEILLEUX 68 YA 15
51 CHARMONT 44 SA 11
95 CHARMONT 39 EA 10
45 CHARMONT EN BEAUCE 61 GA 14
10 CHARMONT SOUS BARBUISE 65 PA 13
51 CHARMONTOIS, LES 43 SA 11
10 CHARMOY 64 MA 13

71	CHARMOY		120	PA	21
89	CHARMOY		83	MA	15
07	CHARNAS		150	RA	27
63	CHARNAT		133	LA	24
25	CHARNAY		107	XA	19
69	CHARNAY		136	RA	25
71	CHARNAY LES CHALON		121	TA	20
71	CHARNAY LES MACON		136	RA	23
38	CHARNECLES		152	VA	27
37	CHARNIZAY		114	AA	20
39	CHARNOD		138	VA	23
08	CHARNOIS		20	SA	6
01	CHARNOZ SUR AIN		137	TA	25
21	CHARNY		104	QA	18
77	CHARNY		40	IA	11
89	CHARNY	C	83	KA	16
10	CHARNY LE BACHOT		64	OA	13
55	CHARNY SUR MEUSE	C	44	UA	10
71	CHAROLLES	S	120	PA	22
26	CHAROLS		179	SA	30
28	CHARONVILLE		60	CA	14
18	CHAROST	C	116	GA	20
55	CHARPENTRY		44	TA	10
26	CHARPEY		165	TA	29
28	CHARPONT		38	CA	12
25	CHARQUEMONT		108	BB	19
86	CHARRAIS		113	X	21
43	CHARRAIX		162	MA	28
16	CHARRAS		143	Y	26
28	CHARRAY		80	CA	15
64	CHARRE		206	S	36
71	CHARRECEY		120	RA	20
21	CHARREY SUR SAONE		105	TA	19
21	CHARREY SUR SEINE		85	QA	15
58	CHARRIN		119	MA	21
64	CHARRITTE DE BAS		206	S	36
17	CHARRON		125	R	23
23	CHARRON		133	IA	24
03	CHARROUX		134	KA	23
86	CHARROUX	C	129	Y	23
95	CHARS		39	FA	10
45	CHARSONVILLE		80	DA	15
28	CHARTAINVILLIERS		60	DA	13
02	CHARTEVES		41	MA	10
72	CHARTRE SUR LE LOIR, LA	C	79	Z	16
49	CHARTRENE		96	W	17
28	CHARTRES	P	60	DA	13
35	CHARTRES DE BRETAGNE		75	O	15
77	CHARTRETTES		62	IA	13
19	CHARTRIER FERRIERE		159	DA	28
77	CHARTRONGES		41	LA	12
17	CHARTUZAC		142	U	27
38	CHARVIEU CHAVAGNEUX		151	TA	25
74	CHARVONNEX		139	XA	24
63	CHAS		148	LA	25
10	CHASEREY		84	OA	15
85	CHASNAIS		125	R	22
25	CHASNANS		107	YA	19
58	CHASNAY		102	KA	19
35	CHASNE SUR ILLET		76	P	14
43	CHASPINHAC		163	OA	28
43	CHASPUZAC		163	NA	28
63	CHASSAGNE		148	KA	26
39	CHASSAGNE, LA		122	UA	20
21	CHASSAGNE MONTRACHET		120	RA	20
25	CHASSAGNE ST DENIS		107	XA	19
43	CHASSAGNES		162	MA	28
69	CHASSAGNY		150	RA	26
24	CHASSAIGNES		143	X	27
39	CHASSAL		138	WA	22
28	CHASSANT		60	BA	14
72	CHASSE		58	X	13
38	CHASSE SUR RHONE		151	SA	26
50	CHASSEGUEY		56	R	12
71	CHASSELAS		136	RA	23
38	CHASSELAY		152	UA	27
69	CHASSELAY		136	RA	25
02	CHASSEMY		28	LA	9
03	CHASSENARD		119	OA	22
36	CHASSENEUIL		115	DA	21
86	CHASSENEUIL DU POITOU		113	Y	21
16	CHASSENEUIL SUR BONNIEURE		129	Y	25
16	CHASSENON		130	AA	25
48	CHASSERADES		177	NA	30
21	CHASSEY		104	QA	18
55	CHASSEY BEAUPRE		66	UA	13
71	CHASSEY LE CAMP		120	RA	20
70	CHASSEY LES MONTBOZON		88	YA	17
70	CHASSEY LES SCEY		88	XA	17
16	CHASSIECQ		129	Y	24
07	CHASSIERS		178	PA	30
69	CHASSIEU		151	SA	25
89	CHASSIGNELLES		85	PA	16
38	CHASSIGNIEU		152	VA	26
36	CHASSIGNOLLES		116	FA	22
43	CHASSIGNOLLES		148	MA	27
52	CHASSIGNY		87	UA	16
71	CHASSIGNY SOUS DUN		135	PA	23
72	CHASSILLE		78	W	15
16	CHASSORS		142	V	25
18	CHASSY		101	JA	19
71	CHASSY		119	OA	21
89	CHASSY		83	LA	16
19	CHASTANG, LE		159	EA	28
48	CHASTANIER		163	NA	30
19	CHASTEAUX		159	DA	28
43	CHASTEL		162	LA	28
26	CHASTEL ARNAUD		165	TA	30
48	CHASTEL NOUVEL		177	MA	30
15	CHASTEL SUR MURAT		161	JA	28
89	CHASTELLUX SUR CURE		103	NA	18
63	CHASTREIX		147	IA	26
85	CHATAIGNERAIE, LA	C	111	T	21
86	CHATAIN		129	Y	24
28	CHATAINCOURT		38	CA	12
88	CHATAS		69	BB	14
71	CHATEAU		136	RA	22
04	CHATEAU ARNOUX ST AUBAN		197	XA	33
38	CHATEAU BERNARD		166	VA	29
57	CHATEAU BREHAIN		47	ZA	11
39	CHATEAU CHALON		122	VA	21
87	CHATEAU CHERVIX		145	CA	26
58	CHATEAU CHINON (Campagne)		103	OA	19
58	CHATEAU CHINON (Ville)	S	103	OA	19
61	CHATEAU D'ALMENECHES, LE		58	X	12
17	CHATEAU D'OLERON, LE	C	126	R	25
85	CHATEAU D'OLONNE		125	O	22
39	CHATEAU DES PRES		122	WA	22
72	CHATEAU DU LOIR	C	97	Y	17
01	CHATEAU GAILLARD		137	UA	24
86	CHATEAU GARNIER		129	Y	23
53	CHATEAU GONTIER	S	77	T	16
85	CHATEAU GUIBERT		110	R	21
59	CHATEAU L'ABBAYE		10	MA	4
24	CHATEAU L'EVEQUE		144	Z	27
72	CHATEAU L'HERMITAGE		78	X	16
37	CHATEAU LA VALLIERE	C	97	Y	17
77	CHATEAU LANDON	C	62	IA	15
86	CHATEAU LARCHER		113	Y	22
08	CHATEAU PORCIEN	C	29	PA	8
37	CHATEAU RENAULT	C	79	AA	17
57	CHATEAU ROUGE		47	ZA	9
57	CHATEAU SALINS	S	47	ZA	11
03	CHATEAU SUR ALLIER		118	KA	21
63	CHATEAU SUR CHER		133	HA	24
27	CHATEAU SUR EPTE		39	DA	10
02	CHATEAU THIERRY	S	41	LA	10
09	CHATEAU VERDUN		220	DA	38
05	CHATEAU VILLE VIEILLE		168	AB	30
57	CHATEAU VOUE		47	AB	11
16	CHATEAUBERNARD		142	V	26
77	CHATEAUBLEAU		63	KA	13
07	CHATEAUBOURG		165	SA	29
35	CHATEAUBOURG	C	76	Q	15
44	CHATEAUBRIANT	S	94	Q	16
26	CHATEAUDOUBLE		165	TA	29
83	CHATEAUDOUBLE		198	ZA	35
28	CHATEAUDUN	S	80	CA	15
04	CHATEAUFORT		181	XA	32
78	CHATEAUFORT		39	GA	12
63	CHATEAUGAY		148	KA	25
35	CHATEAUGIRON	C	76	P	15
29	CHATEAULIN	S	72	E	14
18	CHATEAUMEILLANT	C	116	GA	22
21	CHATEAUNEUF		104	RA	19
42	CHATEAUNEUF		150	RA	26
71	CHATEAUNEUF		135	PA	23
73	CHATEAUNEUF		153	XA	26
85	CHATEAUNEUF		109	O	20
06	CHATEAUNEUF D'ENTRAUNES		182	BB	32
35	CHATEAUNEUF D'ILLE ET VILAINE	C	55	O	13
05	CHATEAUNEUF D'OZE		181	WA	31
26	CHATEAUNEUF DE BORDETTE		179	TA	31
05	CHATEAUNEUF DE CHABRE		181	WA	32
84	CHATEAUNEUF DE GADAGNE		195	SA	33
26	CHATEAUNEUF DE GALAURE		151	SA	27
48	CHATEAUNEUF DE RANDON	C	177	MA	30
07	CHATEAUNEUF DE VERNOUX		164	RA	29
29	CHATEAUNEUF DU FAOU	C	72	F	14
84	CHATEAUNEUF DU PAPE		195	SA	33
26	CHATEAUNEUF DU RHONE		179	RA	31
28	CHATEAUNEUF EN THYMERAIS	C	60	CA	13
06	CHATEAUNEUF GRASSE		200	BB	34
87	CHATEAUNEUF LA FORET	C	145	DA	25
13	CHATEAUNEUF LE ROUGE		202	VA	35
63	CHATEAUNEUF LES BAINS		133	JA	24
13	CHATEAUNEUF LES MARTIGUES	C	201	TA	36
04	CHATEAUNEUF MIRAVAIL		180	WA	32
16	CHATEAUNEUF SUR CHARENTE	C	142	W	26
18	CHATEAUNEUF SUR CHER	C	116	GA	20
26	CHATEAUNEUF SUR ISERE		165	SA	28
45	CHATEAUNEUF SUR LOIRE	C	81	GA	16
49	CHATEAUNEUF SUR SARTHE	C	77	U	17
58	CHATEAUNEUF VAL DE BARGIS		102	LA	18
04	CHATEAUNEUF VAL ST DONAT		181	WA	32
06	CHATEAUNEUF VILLEVIEILLE		200	CB	34
87	CHATEAUPONSAC	C	131	CA	23
04	CHATEAUREDON		197	YA	33
13	CHATEAURENARD	C	195	SA	34
45	CHATEAURENARD	C	82	JA	15
05	CHATEAUROUX LES ALPES		182	ZA	30
36	CHATEAUROUX	P	115	EA	20
44	CHATEAUTHEBAUD		94	Q	19
83	CHATEAUVERT		203	XA	35
05	CHATEAUVIEUX		181	XA	31
41	CHATEAUVIEUX		99	CA	19
83	CHATEAUVIEUX		198	ZA	34
25	CHATEAUVIEUX LES FOSSES		107	YA	19
38	CHATEAUVILAIN		152	UA	26
52	CHATEAUVILLAIN	C	86	SA	15
74	CHATEL		140	AB	23
73	CHATEL, LE		153	YA	27
89	CHATEL CENSOIR		84	MA	17
08	CHATEL CHEHERY		30	SA	9
39	CHATEL DE JOUX		122	WA	22
03	CHATEL DE NEUVRE		134	LA	22
89	CHATEL GERARD		84	OA	17
03	CHATEL MONTAGNE		135	NA	24
71	CHATEL MORON		120	RA	21
57	CHATEL ST GERMAIN		45	XA	10
88	CHATEL SUR MOSELLE	C	68	ZA	14
17	CHATELAILLON PLAGE		126	R	24
53	CHATELAIN		77	U	16
39	CHATELAINE, LA		122	WA	20
49	CHATELAIS		77	S	16
23	CHATELARD		133	HA	24
73	CHATELARD, LE	C	153	XA	25
22	CHATELAUDREN	C	54	J	13
39	CHATELAY		106	VA	19
25	CHATELBLANC		123	XA	21
63	CHATELDON	C	133	MA	24
18	CHATELET, LE	C	116	GA	21
77	CHATELET EN BRIE, LE	C	62	IA	13
52	CHATELET SUR MEUSE, LE		87	VA	15
08	CHATELET SUR RETOURNE, LE		29	PA	9
08	CHATELET SUR SORMONNE, LE		29	OA	7
28	CHATELETS, LES		60	BA	12
39	CHATELEY, LE		122	VA	20
63	CHATELGUYON		134	KA	24
51	CHATELIER, LE		44	SA	11
21	CHATELLENOT		104	QA	19
86	CHATELLERAULT	S	113	Y	20
35	CHATELLIER, LE		56	Q	13
61	CHATELLIER, LE		57	U	12
85	CHATELLIERS CHATEAUMUR, LES		111	S	20
28	CHATELLIERS NOTRE DAME, LES		60	BA	14
39	CHATELNEUF		122	WA	21
42	CHATELNEUF		149	OA	26
03	CHATELPERRON		134	MA	22
51	CHATELRAOULD ST LOUVENT		43	QA	12
03	CHATELUS		135	NA	23
38	CHATELUS		166	UA	28
42	CHATELUS		150	QA	26
23	CHATELUS LE MARCHEIX		131	DA	24
23	CHATELUS MALVALEIX	C	132	FA	23
01	CHATENAY		137	TA	24
28	CHATENAY		61	FA	14
38	CHATENAY		151	TA	27
71	CHATENAY		136	QA	23
95	CHATENAY EN FRANCE		40	HA	10
52	CHATENAY MACHERON		87	UA	16
92	CHATENAY MALABRY	C	40	GA	12
77	CHATENAY SUR SEINE		63	KA	13
52	CHATENAY VAUDIN		87	UA	16
17	CHATENET		142	V	27
87	CHATENET EN DOGNON, LE		131	DA	24
70	CHATENEY		88	YA	17
39	CHATENOIS		106	VA	19
67	CHATENOIS		70	DB	14
70	CHATENOIS		88	YA	17
88	CHATENOIS	C	67	WA	14
90	CHATENOIS LES FORGES	C	89	AB	17
45	CHATENOY		82	HA	16
77	CHATENOY		62	IA	14
71	CHATENOY EN BRESSE		121	SA	21
71	CHATENOY LE ROYAL		120	RA	21
16	CHATIGNAC		143	W	27
91	CHATIGNONVILLE		61	FA	13
03	CHATILLON		118	KA	22
39	CHATILLON		122	WA	21
69	CHATILLON		136	RA	25
86	CHATILLON		129	X	23
92	CHATILLON	C	40	GA	12
45	CHATILLON COLIGNY	C	82	JA	16
58	CHATILLON EN BAZOIS	C	103	MA	19
26	CHATILLON EN DIOIS	C	166	UA	30
28	CHATILLON EN DUNOIS		60	BA	15
01	CHATILLON EN MICHAILLE		138	WA	23
35	CHATILLON EN VENDELAIS		76	R	14
25	CHATILLON GUYOTTE		107	YA	18
77	CHATILLON LA BORDE		62	JA	13
01	CHATILLON LA PALUD		137	TA	24
25	CHATILLON LE DUC		107	XA	18
45	CHATILLON LE ROI		61	FA	14
02	CHATILLON LES SONS		28	NA	7
55	CHATILLON SOUS LES COTES		45	VA	10
26	CHATILLON ST JEAN		165	TA	28
51	CHATILLON SUR BROUE		65	RA	13
01	CHATILLON SUR CHALARONNE	C	137	SA	24
41	CHATILLON SUR CHER		99	DA	18
74	CHATILLON SUR CLUSES		139	ZA	24
53	CHATILLON SUR COLMONT		57	T	14
36	CHATILLON SUR INDRE	C	114	BA	20
25	CHATILLON SUR LISON		107	XA	19
45	CHATILLON SUR LOIRE	C	82	IA	17
51	CHATILLON SUR MARNE	C	42	NA	10
51	CHATILLON SUR MORIN		42	MA	12
02	CHATILLON SUR OISE		28	LA	7
88	CHATILLON SUR SAONE		88	WA	15
21	CHATILLON SUR SEINE	C	85	QA	16
79	CHATILLON SUR THOUET		112	V	21
58	CHATIN		103	NA	19
38	CHATONNAY		151	TA	26
39	CHATONNAY		122	VA	22
52	CHATONRUPT SOMMERMONT		66	TA	13
78	CHATOU	C	39	GA	11
36	CHATRE, LA	S	116	FA	21
36	CHATRE LANGLIN, LA		131	CA	22
10	CHATRES		64	NA	13
24	CHATRES		159	CA	28
77	CHATRES		40	JA	12
53	CHATRES LA FORET		77	U	15
41	CHATRES SUR CHER		100	FA	18
51	CHATRICES		44	SA	11
55	CHATTANCOURT		44	TA	10
38	CHATTE		165	UA	28
26	CHATUZANGE LE GOUBET		165	TA	28
25	CHAUCENNE		106	WA	18
48	CHAUCHAILLES		162	KA	29
85	CHAUCHE		110	Q	20
23	CHAUCHET, LE		132	GA	24
10	CHAUCHIGNY		64	OA	13
77	CHAUCONIN NEUFMONTIERS		40	JA	11
02	CHAUDARDES		28	NA	9
26	CHAUDEBONNE		180	TA	31
49	CHAUDEFONDS SUR LAYON		95	T	18
25	CHAUDEFONTAINE		107	YA	18
51	CHAUDEFONTAINE		43	SA	10
52	CHAUDENAY		87	VA	16
71	CHAUDENAY		120	RA	20
21	CHAUDENAY LA VILLE		104	RA	19
21	CHAUDENAY LE CHATEAU		104	RA	19
54	CHAUDENEY SUR MOSELLE		45	WA	12
15	CHAUDES AIGUES	C	161	KA	29
48	CHAUDEYRAC		177	NA	30
43	CHAUDEYROLLES		163	PA	29
26	CHAUDIERE, LA		180	TA	30
28	CHAUDON		60	DA	12
04	CHAUDON NORANTE		198	YA	33
10	CHAUDREY		65	PA	13
49	CHAUDRON EN MAUGES		95	S	18
02	CHAUDUN		27	LA	9
71	CHAUFFAILLES	C	136	PA	23
05	CHAUFFAYER		167	XA	30
88	CHAUFFECOURT		68	YA	14
10	CHAUFFOUR LES BAILLY		65	PA	14
91	CHAUFFOUR LES ETRECHY		61	GA	13
19	CHAUFFOUR SUR VELL		159	EA	28
28	CHAUFFOURS		60	CA	13
52	CHAUFFOURT		87	UA	15
77	CHAUFFRY		41	KA	12
78	CHAUFOUR LES BONNIERES		38	DA	11
72	CHAUFOUR NOTRE DAME		78	W	15
21	CHAUGEY		86	SA	16
58	CHAULGNES		102	KA	19
48	CHAULHAC		162	LA	29
50	CHAULIEU		57	S	12
63	CHAULME, LA		149	OA	26
80	CHAULNES	C	27	JA	7
31	CHAUM		217	Z	38
58	CHAUMARD		103	OA	19
21	CHAUME, LA		86	SA	16
21	CHAUME ET COURCHAMP		87	UA	17
21	CHAUME LES BAIGNEUX		85	QA	17
19	CHAUMEIL		146	FA	26
70	CHAUMERCENNE		106	VA	18
39	CHAUMERGY	C	122	VA	20
77	CHAUMES EN BRIE		62	JA	12
10	CHAUMESNIL		65	RA	14
18	CHAUMONT		117	IA	20
52	CHAUMONT	P	66	TA	15
61	CHAUMONT		37	Y	11
74	CHAUMONT		138	WA	24
89	CHAUMONT		63	KA	14
49	CHAUMONT D'ANJOU		96	V	17
55	CHAUMONT DEVANT DAMVILLERS		31	UA	9
60	CHAUMONT EN VEXIN	C	39	FA	10
52	CHAUMONT LA VILLE		67	VA	15
21	CHAUMONT LE BOIS		85	RA	16
63	CHAUMONT LE BOURG		149	NA	26
08	CHAUMONT PORCIEN	C	29	PA	8
55	CHAUMONT SUR AIRE		44	UA	11
41	CHAUMONT SUR LOIRE		80	BA	17
41	CHAUMONT SUR THARONNE		81	FA	17
95	CHAUMONTEL		40	HA	10
58	CHAUMOT		103	MA	19
89	CHAUMOT		63	KA	15
88	CHAUMOUSEY		68	YA	14
18	CHAUMOUX MARCILLY		101	IA	19
37	CHAUMUSSAY		114	AA	20
39	CHAUMUSSE, LA		122	WA	21
51	CHAUMUZY		42	NA	10
17	CHAUNAC		142	V	27
86	CHAUNAY		129	X	23
02	CHAUNY	C	27	LA	8
79	CHAURAY		128	U	22
63	CHAURIAT		148	LA	25
23	CHAUSSADE, LA		132	GA	24
49	CHAUSSAIRE, LA		94	R	19
69	CHAUSSAN		150	RA	26
76	CHAUSSEE, LA		24	BA	7
86	CHAUSSEE, LA		113	X	20
28	CHAUSSEE D'IVRY, LA		38	DA	11
41	CHAUSSEE ST VICTOR, LA		80	CA	17
51	CHAUSSEE SUR MARNE, LA		43	QA	11
80	CHAUSSEE TIRANCOURT, LA		16	GA	6
15	CHAUSSENAC		160	GA	28
39	CHAUSSENANS		122	WA	20
42	CHAUSSETERRE		135	NA	24
39	CHAUSSIN	C	122	UA	20
80	CHAUSSOY EPAGNY		26	GA	7
45	CHAUSSY		61	FA	14
95	CHAUSSY		39	EA	10
18	CHAUTAY, LE		117	JA	20
26	CHAUVAC		180	VA	32
44	CHAUVE		93	N	19
55	CHAUVENCY LE CHATEAU		31	UA	8
55	CHAUVENCY ST HUBERT		31	UA	8
35	CHAUVIGNE		56	Q	13
86	CHAUVIGNY	C	114	Z	22
41	CHAUVIGNY DU PERCHE		80	BA	15
27	CHAUVINCOURT PROVEMONT		39	DA	10
70	CHAUVIREY LE CHATEL		87	WA	16
70	CHAUVIREY LE VIEIL		87	WA	16
55	CHAUVONCOURT		45	VA	11
95	CHAUVRY		40	GA	10
21	CHAUX		105	SA	19
90	CHAUX		89	BB	16
25	CHAUX, LA		107	ZA	20
61	CHAUX, LA		58	V	12
71	CHAUX, LA		121	UA	20
39	CHAUX CHAMPAGNY		122	WA	20
39	CHAUX DES CROTENAY		123	XA	21
39	CHAUX DES PRES		122	WA	22
39	CHAUX DU DOMBIEF, LA		122	WA	21
39	CHAUX EN BRESSE, LA		122	UA	20
70	CHAUX LA LOTIERE		107	XA	18
25	CHAUX LES CLERVAL		107	ZA	18
25	CHAUX LES PASSAVANT		107	YA	19
70	CHAUX LES PORT		88	XA	16
25	CHAUX NEUVE		123	XA	21
07	CHAUZON		178	PA	31
15	CHAVAGNAC		161	JA	28
24	CHAVAGNAC		159	CA	28
35	CHAVAGNE		75	O	15
49	CHAVAGNES		96	U	18
85	CHAVAGNES EN PAILLERS		110	Q	20
85	CHAVAGNES LES REDOUX		111	S	21
49	CHAVAIGNES		97	W	17
19	CHAVANAC		146	FA	26
23	CHAVANAT		132	FA	24
90	CHAVANATTE		90	CB	17
42	CHAVANAY		150	RA	27
10	CHAVANGES	C	65	OA	13
43	CHAVANIAC LAFAYETTE		162	MA	28
74	CHAVANNAZ		139	XA	24
70	CHAVANNE		89	AB	17
73	CHAVANNE, LA		153	XA	26
18	CHAVANNES		116	HA	20
26	CHAVANNES		165	SA	28
73	CHAVANNES EN MAURIENNE, LES		153	YA	27
90	CHAVANNES LES GRANDS		90	BB	17
68	CHAVANNES SUR L'ETANG		90	BB	17
01	CHAVANNES SUR REYSSOUZE		121	SA	22
01	CHAVANNES SUR SURAN		138	UA	23
74	CHAVANOD		139	XA	25
38	CHAVANOZ		151	TA	25
63	CHAVAROUX		148	LA	25
80	CHAVATTE, LA		27	IA	7
37	CHAVEIGNES		97	Y	19
88	CHAVELOT		68	ZA	14
16	CHAVENAT		143	X	26
78	CHAVENAY		39	FA	11
60	CHAVENCON		39	FA	10
03	CHAVENON		133	JA	22
39	CHAVERIA		122	VA	22
19	CHAVEROCHE		146	GA	26
01	CHAVEYRIAT		137	TA	23
02	CHAVIGNON		28	MA	9
02	CHAVIGNY		28	LA	9
54	CHAVIGNY		67	XA	12
27	CHAVIGNY BAILLEUL		38	BA	11
92	CHAVILLE	C	39	GA	12
36	CHAVIN		115	DA	22
02	CHAVONNE		28	MA	9
01	CHAVORNAY		138	WA	25
51	CHAVOT COURCOURT		43	QA	11
50	CHAVOY		56	Q	12
03	CHAVROCHES		134	MA	22
25	CHAY		106	WA	19
17	CHAY, LA		141	S	26
69	CHAZAY D'AZERGUES		136	RA	25
48	CHAZE DE PEYRE, LA		162	LA	30
49	CHAZE HENRY		76	R	16
49	CHAZE SUR ARGOS		77	S	17
07	CHAZEAUX		178	PA	30
36	CHAZELET		115	CA	22
15	CHAZELLES		162	LA	28
16	CHAZELLES		143	Y	26
39	CHAZELLES		122	UA	22
43	CHAZELLES		162	MA	28
54	CHAZELLES SUR ALBE		69	AB	13
42	CHAZELLES SUR LAVIEU		149	OA	26
42	CHAZELLES SUR LYON	C	150	QA	26
03	CHAZEMAIS		117	HA	22
21	CHAZEUIL		87	UA	17
58	CHAZEUIL		102	LA	18
01	CHAZEY BONS		138	VA	25
01	CHAZEY SUR AIN		137	TA	25
21	CHAZILLY		104	OA	19
25	CHAZOT		107	ZA	18
45	CHECY	C	81	FA	16
37	CHEDIGNY		98	BA	19
79	CHEF BOUTONNE	C	128	W	24
50	CHEF DU PONT		33	Q	9
88	CHEF HAUT		67	XA	14
49	CHEFFES		77	U	17
85	CHEFFOIS		111	T	21
14	CHEFFREVILLE TONNENCOURT		37	X	11
50	CHEFRESNE, LE		56	R	11
08	CHEHERY		30	SA	8
01	CHEIGNIEU LA BALME		138	VA	25
37	CHEILLE		97	Y	18
71	CHEILLY LES MARANGES		120	RA	20
31	CHEIN DESSUS		217	AA	37
87	CHEISSOUX		145	DA	25
63	CHEIX, LE		134	KA	24
44	CHEIX EN RETZ		93	O	19
32	CHELAN		209	Z	36
62	CHELERS		17	HA	5
38	CHELIEU		152	VA	26
65	CHELLE DEBAT		208	X	36
65	CHELLE SPOU		216	X	37
60	CHELLES		27	KA	9
77	CHELLES	C	40	IA	11
35	CHELUN		76	R	16
25	CHEMAUDIN		106	WA	19
53	CHEMAZE		77	T	16
49	CHEMELLIER		96	V	18
39	CHEMENOT		122	VA	21
44	CHEMERE		93	O	19
53	CHEMERE LE ROI		77	U	15
41	CHEMERY		99	DA	18
57	CHEMERY LES DEUX		47	ZA	9
08	CHEMERY SUR BAR		30	SA	8
39	CHEMILLA		138	VA	22
49	CHEMILLE	C	95	T	19
37	CHEMILLE SUR DEME		79	Z	17
37	CHEMILLE SUR INDROIS		98	BA	19
61	CHEMILLI		59	Y	14
03	CHEMILLY		118	LA	22
70	CHEMILLY		88	XA	17
89	CHEMILLY SUR SEREIN		84	NA	16
89	CHEMILLY SUR YONNE		83	MA	16
39	CHEMIN	C	121	UA	20
51	CHEMIN, LE		44	SA	11
21	CHEMIN D'AISEY		85	QA	16
07	CHEMINAS		164	RA	28
51	CHEMINON		44	SA	12
57	CHEMINOT		46	XA	11
72	CHEMIRE EN CHARNIE		78	V	15
72	CHEMIRE LE GAUDIN		78	W	16
49	CHEMIRE SUR SARTHE		77	U	16
59	CHEMY		9	JA	4
17	CHENAC ST SEURIN D'UZET		141	T	26
19	CHENAILLER MASCHEIX		160	EA	28
25	CHENALOTTE, LA		108	AB	19
69	CHENAS		136	RA	23
24	CHENAUD		157	X	28
51	CHENAY		29	OA	9
72	CHENAY		58	X	13
79	CHENAY		129	W	23
71	CHENAY LE CHATEL		135	OA	23
10	CHENE, LE		65	PA	13
89	CHENE ARNOULT		83	KA	16
39	CHENE BERNARD		122	VA	20
74	CHENE EN SEMINE		138	WA	24
39	CHENE SEC		122	UA	20
70	CHENEBIER		89	AB	17
25	CHENECEY BUILLON		107	XA	19
86	CHENECHE		113	X	21
14	CHENEDOLLE		35	T	11
61	CHENEDOUIT		58	V	12
49	CHENEHUTTE TREVES CUNAULT		96	V	18
69	CHENELETTE		136	QA	23
23	CHENERAILLES	C	132	GA	24
42	CHENEREILLES		149	OA	26
43	CHENEREILLES		163	PA	28
86	CHENEVELLES		114	Z	21
54	CHENEVIERES		68	ZA	13
70	CHENEVREY ET MOROGNE		106	WA	18
74	CHENEX		139	XA	24
89	CHENEY		84	OA	16
54	CHENICOURT		46	YA	11
54	CHENIERES		31	WA	9
23	CHENIERS		132	EA	23
51	CHENIERS		43	PA	11
49	CHENILLE CHANGE		77	T	16
88	CHENIMENIL		68	AB	15
27	CHENNEBRUN		37	AA	12
10	CHENNEGY		64	NA	14
95	CHENNEVIERES LES LOUVRES		40	IA	10
94	CHENNEVIERES SUR MARNE	C	40	HA	12
57	CHENOIS		47	ZA	11
77	CHENOISE		63	KA	12
16	CHENOMMET		129	X	24
16	CHENON		129	X	24
37	CHENONCEAUX		98	BA	18
77	CHENOU		62	IA	14
21	CHENOVE	C	105	SA	18
71	CHENOVES		120	RA	21
74	CHENS SUR LEMAN		139	YA	23
72	CHENU		97	Y	17
89	CHENY		83	MA	15
17	CHEPNIERS		142	V	27
60	CHEPOIX		26	HA	8
51	CHEPPE, LA		43	QA	11
51	CHEPPES LA PRAIRIE		43	OA	11
55	CHEPPY		44	TA	10
91	CHEPTAINVILLE		62	GA	13
51	CHEPY		43	QA	11
80	CHEPY		15	DA	6
17	CHERAC		142	U	25
53	CHERANCE		76	S	16
72	CHERANCE		58	X	14
64	CHERAUTE		206	S	36
17	CHERBONNIERES		128	U	24
50	CHERBOURG	S	33	P	8
95	CHERENCE		39	DA	10
50	CHERENCE LE HERON		56	R	12
50	CHERENCE LE ROUSSEL		57	S	12
59	CHERENG		9	KA	4
69	CHERES, LES		136	RA	25
02	CHERET		28	MA	8
62	CHERIENNES		16	FA	5
42	CHERIER		135	OA	24
79	CHERIGNE		128	V	24
50	CHERIS, LES		56	R	12
72	CHERISAY		58	X	14
57	CHERISEY		46	YA	11
28	CHERISY		38	DA	12
62	CHERISY		17	JA	5
71	CHERIZET		120	QA	22
17	CHERMIGNAC		141	T	25
88	CHERMISEY		67	VA	13
02	CHERMIZY AILLES		28	NA	8
87	CHERONNAC		144	Z	25
27	CHERONVILLIERS		37	AA	12
89	CHEROY	C	63	KA	14
49	CHERRE		77	U	16
72	CHERRE		59	Z	14
72	CHERREAU		59	Z	14
35	CHERRUEIX		55	P	12
24	CHERVAL		143	Y	27
24	CHERVEIX CUBAS		144	BA	27
86	CHERVES		112	W	21
16	CHERVES CHATELARS		143	Y	25
16	CHERVES RICHEMONT		142	V	25
17	CHERVETTES		127	T	24
79	CHERVEUX		112	U	22
10	CHERVEY		65	QA	15
51	CHERVILLE		42	PA	11
18	CHERY		100	FA	19
02	CHERY CHARTREUVE		42	MA	10
02	CHERY LES POUILLY		28	MA	8
02	CHERY LES ROZOY		29	OA	8

10 CHESLEY 84 OA 15
78 CHESNAY, LE C 39 GA 12
08 CHESNE, LE C 30 RA 8
27 CHESNE, LE 38 AA 11
08 CHESNOIS AUBONCOURT 29 QA 8
57 CHESNY 46 YA 10
74 CHESSENAZ 138 WA 24
69 CHESSY 136 RA 25
77 CHESSY 40 IA 11
10 CHESSY LES PRES 84 OA 15
89 CHEU 84 NA 15
21 CHEUGE 106 UA 18
65 CHEUST 216 W 37
14 CHEUX 35 U 10
03 CHEVAGNES C 119 MA 21
71 CHEVAGNY LES CHEVRIERES 136 RA 23
71 CHEVAGNY SUR GUYE 120 QA 22
35 CHEVAIGNE 75 P 14
53 CHEVAIGNE DU MAINE 57 U 13
72 CHEVAIN, LE 58 X 13
84 CHEVAL BLANC 195 TA 34
74 CHEVALINE 153 YA 25
44 CHEVALLERAIS, LA 93 P 17
17 CHEVANCEAUX 142 V 27
21 CHEVANNAY 104 RA 18
21 CHEVANNES 105 SA 19
45 CHEVANNES 63 JA 15
89 CHEVANNES 83 MA 16
91 CHEVANNES 62 HA 13
58 CHEVANNES CHANGY 102 LA 18
02 CHEVENNES 28 NA 7
58 CHEVENON 118 KA 20
74 CHEVENOZ 140 AB 23
41 CHEVERNY 80 DA 17
08 CHEVEUGES 30 SA 8
08 CHEVIERES 30 SA 9
70 CHEVIGNEY 106 VA 18
25 CHEVIGNEY LES VERCEL 107 YA 19
25 CHEVIGNEY SUR L'OGNON 106 WA 18
39 CHEVIGNY 106 VA 19
21 CHEVIGNY EN VALIERE 121 SA 20
21 CHEVIGNY ST SAUVEUR 105 TA 18
01 CHEVILLARD 138 VA 24
72 CHEVILLE 78 V 15
52 CHEVILLON C 66 TA 13
89 CHEVILLON 83 KA 16
45 CHEVILLON SUR HUILLARD 82 IA 15
25 CHEVILLOTTE, LA 107 XA 19
45 CHEVILLY 81 FA 15
94 CHEVILLY LARUE C 40 HA 12
69 CHEVINAY 150 RA 25
60 CHEVINCOURT 27 JA 8
49 CHEVIRE LE ROUGE 96 V 17
77 CHEVRAINVILLIERS 62 IA 14
39 CHEVREAUX 122 UA 22
02 CHEVREGNY 28 MA 9
90 CHEVREMONT 90 BB 17
16 CHEVRERIE, LA 129 X 24
02 CHEVRESIS MONCEAU 28 MA 7
78 CHEVREUSE C 39 FA 12
50 CHEVREVILLE 56 R 12
60 CHEVREVILLE 41 JA 10
74 CHEVRIER 138 WA 24
38 CHEVRIERES 166 UA 28
42 CHEVRIERES 150 QA 26
60 CHEVRIERES 27 IA 9
58 CHEVROCHES 102 MA 18
44 CHEVROLIERE, LA 110 P 19
39 CHEVROTAINE 122 WA 21
01 CHEVROUX 137 SA 22
25 CHEVROZ 107 XA 18
77 CHEVRU 41 KA 12
01 CHEVRY 139 XA 23
50 CHEVRY 34 R 11
77 CHEVRY COSSIGNY 40 IA 12
77 CHEVRY EN SEREINE 63 JA 14
45 CHEVRY SOUS LE BIGNON 63 JA 15
79 CHEY 128 W 23
15 CHEYLADE 162 KA 28
07 CHEYLARD, LE C 164 OA 29
48 CHEYLARD L'EVEQUE 177 NA 30
38 CHEYLAS, LE 153 XA 27
38 CHEYSSIEU 151 SA 27
18 CHEZAL BENOIT 116 FA 20
65 CHEZE 216 W 38
22 CHEZE, LA C 74 K 15
03 CHEZELLE 134 KA 23
36 CHEZELLES 115 DA 20
37 CHEZELLES 97 Y 19
38 CHEZENEUVE 151 TA 26
01 CHEZERY FORENS 138 WA 23
03 CHEZY 118 MA 21
02 CHEZY EN ORXOIS 41 KA 10
02 CHEZY SUR MARNE 41 LA 11
2B CHIATRA 228 MB 41
79 CHICHE 112 V 21
14 CHICHEBOVILLE 36 V 10
89 CHICHEE 84 NA 16
89 CHICHERY 83 MA 16
51 CHICHEY 42 NA 12
38 CHICHILIANNE 166 VA 29
57 CHICOURT 47 ZA 11
58 CHIDDES 119 OA 20
71 CHIDDES 120 OA 22
63 CHIDRAC 148 KA 26
02 CHIERRY 41 LA 11
57 CHIEULLES 46 YA 10
49 CHIGNE 97 W 17
73 CHIGNIN 153 XA 26
02 CHIGNY 19 NA 7
51 CHIGNY LES ROSES 42 OA 10
89 CHIGY 63 MA 14
43 CHILHAC 162 LA 28
16 CHILLAC 142 W 27
39 CHILLE 122 VA 21
45 CHILLEURS AUX BOIS 81 GA 15
79 CHILLOU, LE 112 W 21
08 CHILLY 29 QA 7
74 CHILLY 139 XA 24
80 CHILLY 27 IA 7
39 CHILLY LE VIGNOBLE 122 VA 21
91 CHILLY MAZARIN C 40 GA 12
39 CHILLY SUR SALINS 122 WA 20
38 CHIMILIN 152 VA 26
73 CHINDRIEUX 138 WA 25
37 CHINON S 97 X 19
80 CHIPILLY 17 IA 7
16 CHIRAC 130 Z 24
48 CHIRAC 176 LA 31
19 CHIRAC BELLEVUE 146 GA 26
42 CHIRASSIMONT 135 PA 24
03 CHIRAT L'EGLISE 133 KA 23
86 CHIRE EN MONTREUIL 113 X 21
38 CHIRENS 152 VA 27
80 CHIRMONT 26 HA 8
07 CHIROLS 178 PA 30
69 CHIROUBLES 136 RA 23
60 CHIRY OURSCAMPS 27 JA 8

65 CHIS 208 X 36
2B CHISA 228 LB 42
41 CHISSAY EN TOURAINE 98 BA 18
37 CHISSEAUX 98 BA 18
39 CHISSERIA 138 VA 22
71 CHISSEY EN MORVAN 104 PA 19
71 CHISSEY LES MACON 120 RA 22
39 CHISSEY SUR LOUE 122 WA 20
41 CHITENAY 80 CA 17
36 CHITRAY 115 CA 21
89 CHITRY 84 NA 16
58 CHITRY LES MINES 103 MA 18
17 CHIVES 128 W 24
21 CHIVRES 121 TA 20
02 CHIVRES EN LAONNOIS 28 NA 8
02 CHIVRES VAL 28 LA 9
02 CHIVY LES ETOUVELLES 28 MA 8
79 CHIZE 128 U 24
62 CHOCQUES 8 IA 4
52 CHOILLEY DARDENAY 87 UA 17
78 CHOISEL 61 FA 12
52 CHOISEUL 67 VA 15
39 CHOISEY 106 UA 19
59 CHOISIES 19 OA 5
74 CHOISY 139 XA 24
60 CHOISY AU BAC 27 JA 9
77 CHOISY EN BRIE 41 KA 12
60 CHOISY LA VICTOIRE 26 IA 9
94 CHOISY LE ROI C 40 HA 12
49 CHOLET S 95 S 19
38 CHOLONGE 166 WA 29
52 CHOLOY MENILLOT 45 WA 12
43 CHOMELIX 149 NA 27
07 CHOMERAC C 164 RA 30
43 CHOMETTE, LA 162 MA 27
38 CHONAS L'AMBALLAN 150 RA 26
55 CHONVILLE MALAUMONT 45 VA 12
08 CHOOZ 20 RA 6
60 CHOQUEUSE LES BENARDS 26 FA 8
38 CHORANCHE 166 UA 28
21 CHOREY 105 SA 19
05 CHORGES C 181 YA 30
14 CHOUAIN 35 T 10
36 CHOUDAY 116 FA 20
41 CHOUE 79 AA 15
58 CHOUGNY 103 NA 19
51 CHOUILLY 42 OA 11
86 CHOUPPES 113 X 20
24 CHOURGNAC 144 BA 27
41 CHOUSSY 99 CA 18
03 CHOUVIGNY 133 KA 23
39 CHOUX 138 WA 23
45 CHOUX, LES 82 IA 16
02 CHOUY 41 LA 10
37 CHOUZE SUR LOIRE 97 X 19
25 CHOUZELOT 106 WA 19
41 CHOUZY SUR CISSE 80 CA 17
70 CHOYE 106 WA 18
38 CHOZEAU 151 TA 25
45 CHUELLES 83 JA 15
08 CHUFFILLY ROCHE 30 RA 9
80 CHUIGNES 27 IA 7
80 CHUIGNOLLES 27 IA 7
28 CHUISNES 60 BA 13
30 CHUSCLAN 179 RA 32
42 CHUYER 150 RA 26
38 CHUZELLES 151 SA 26
31 CIADOUX 209 Z 36
2A CIAMANNACCE 228 LB 42
64 CIBOURE 205 P 36
76 CIDEVILLE 24 AA 8
71 CIEL 121 TA 20
31 CIER DE LUCHON 217 Z 38
31 CIER DE RIVIERE 217 Z 37
02 CIERGES 42 MA 10
55 CIERGES SOUS MONTFAUCON 30 TA 9
31 CIERP GAUD 217 Z 38
27 CIERREY 38 CA 11
17 CIERZAC 142 V 26
46 CIEURAC 174 DA 31
65 CIEUTAT 216 X 37
87 CIEUX 130 BA 24
58 CIEZ 102 KA 18
37 CIGOGNE 98 AA 18
02 CILLY 28 NA 7
37 CINAIS 97 X 19
03 CINDRE 133 MA 23
37 CINQ MARS LA PILE 97 Y 18
60 CINQUEUX 26 HA 9
31 CINTEGABELLE C 210 DA 36
14 CINTHEAUX 36 V 10
27 CINTRAY 37 AA 12
28 CINTRAY 60 CA 13
35 CINTRE 75 O 15
70 CINTREY 87 WA 16
13 CIOTAT, LA C 202 VA 37
06 CIPIERES 200 BB 34
61 CIRAL 58 W 13
37 CIRAN 98 AA 19
88 CIRCOURT 68 YA 14
88 CIRCOURT SUR MOUZON 67 VA 14
17 CIRE D'AUNIS 127 S 24
31 CIRES 217 Y 38
60 CIRES LES MELLO 40 HA 9
70 CIREY 107 XA 18
52 CIREY LES MAREILLES 66 UA 14
21 CIREY LES PONTAILLER 105 UA 18
52 CIREY SUR BLAISE 66 SA 14
54 CIREY SUR VEZOUZE C 69 BB 13
52 CIRFONTAINES EN AZOIS 66 SA 15
52 CIRFONTAINES EN ORNOIS 66 UA 13
79 CIRIERE 111 T 20
36 CIRON 115 CA 21
71 CIRY LE NOBLE 120 PA 21
02 CIRY SALSOGNE 28 LA 9
61 CISAI ST AUBIN 37 Y 12
89 CISERY 84 OA 17
33 CISSAC MEDOC 141 S 27
86 CISSE 113 X 21
63 CISTERNES LA FORET 147 IA 25
43 CISTRIERES 148 MA 27
80 CITERNE 16 EA 6
70 CITERS 89 ZA 16
70 CITEY 106 WA 18
11 CITOU 212 HA 36
77 CITRY 41 LA 11
86 CIVAUX 114 Z 22
42 CIVENS 149 PA 25
27 CIVIERES 39 DA 10
33 CIVRAC DE BLAYE 156 U 28
33 CIVRAC EN MEDOC 141 S 27
33 CIVRAC SUR DORDOGNE 156 W 29
18 CIVRAY 116 GA 20
86 CIVRAY C 129 X 23
37 CIVRAY DE TOURAINE 98 BA 18
37 CIVRAY SUR ESVES 98 Z 19
01 CIVRIEUX 137 SA 24
69 CIVRIEUX D'AZERGUES 136 RA 25

28 CIVRY 60 DA 15
21 CIVRY EN MONTAGNE 104 RA 18
78 CIVRY LA FORET 39 DA 11
80 CIZANCOURT 27 JA 7
49 CIZAY LA MADELEINE 96 V 19
01 CIZE 138 UA 23
39 CIZE 122 WA 21
58 CIZELY 118 MA 20
65 CIZOS 209 Y 36
02 CLACY ET THIERRET 28 MA 8
24 CLADECH 158 BA 29
66 CLAIRA 224 JA 38
47 CLAIRAC 172 Y 31
23 CLAIRAVAUX 146 GA 25
78 CLAIREFONTAINE EN YVELINES 61 FA 12
61 CLAIREFOUGERE 57 T 12
70 CLAIREGOUTTE 89 AB 17
59 CLAIRFAYTS 19 OA 6
02 CLAIRFONTAINE 19 OA 6
62 CLAIRMARAIS 8 GA 3
60 CLAIROIX 27 JA 9
12 CLAIRVAUX D'AVEYRON 175 HA 31
39 CLAIRVAUX LES LACS C 122 WA 21
80 CLAIRY SAULCHOIX 26 GA 7
76 CLAIS 25 DA 7
16 CLAIX 143 W 26
38 CLAIX 166 VA 28
17 CLAM 142 U 26
51 CLAMANGES 42 OA 12
92 CLAMART C 40 GA 12
02 CLAMECY 28 LA 9
58 CLAMECY S 102 MA 18
04 CLAMENSANE 181 XA 31
21 CLAMEREY 104 QA 18
06 CLANS 199 CB 33
70 CLANS 88 XA 17
26 CLANSAYES 179 SA 31
55 CLAON, LE 44 SA 10
12 CLAPIER, LE 191 KA 34
34 CLAPIERS 192 NA 34
66 CLARA 222 HA 39
31 CLARAC 217 Z 37
65 CLARAC 208 X 36
64 CLARACQ 207 V 35
74 CLARAFOND 138 WA 24
14 CLARBEC 36 X 10
65 CLARENS 216 Y 37
30 CLARENSAC 193 PA 34
04 CLARET 181 XA 31
34 CLARET C 192 NA 34
62 CLARQUES 8 GA 3
59 CLARY C 18 LA 6
40 CLASSUN 184 U 34
02 CLASTRES 28 LA 7
76 CLASVILLE 23 Z 7
11 CLAT, LE 222 GA 38
88 CLAUDON 67 XA 15
15 CLAUX, LE 161 IA 28
38 CLAVANS EN HAUT OISANS 167 XA 28
79 CLAVE 112 V 22
69 CLAVEISOLLES 136 QA 24
17 CLAVETTE 127 S 23
26 CLAVEYSON 165 SA 28
15 CLAVIERES 162 LA 29
83 CLAVIERS 198 ZA 35
27 CLAVILLE 38 BA 10
76 CLAVILLE MOTTEVILLE 24 BA 8
08 CLAVY WARBY 29 OA 7
85 CLAYE, LA 125 Q 22
77 CLAYE SOUILLY C 40 IA 11
35 CLAYES 75 O 14
78 CLAYES SOUS BOIS, LES 39 FA 12
71 CLAYETTE, LA C 136 PA 23
54 CLAYEURES 68 ZA 13
14 CLECY 35 U 11
29 CLEDEN CAP SIZUN 71 B 15
29 CLEDEN POHER 72 G 14
29 CLEDER 52 E 12
40 CLEDES 207 U 35
67 CLEEBOURG 49 FB 11
88 CLEFCY 69 BB 14
52 CLEFMONT C 67 VA 15
49 CLEFS 78 W 17
74 CLEFS, LES 139 YA 25
56 CLEGUER 73 H 16
56 CLEGUEREC C 73 I 15
38 CLELLES C 166 VA 29
21 CLEMENCEY 105 SA 19
63 CLEMENSAT 148 KA 26
54 CLEMERY 46 YA 11
18 CLEMONT 82 GA 17
21 CLENAY 105 TA 18
62 CLENLEU 7 EA 4
76 CLEON 24 BA 9
26 CLEON D'ANDRAN 179 SA 30
42 CLEPPE 149 PA 25
17 CLERAC 156 V 28
36 CLERE DU BOIS 114 BA 20
37 CLERE LES PINS 97 Y 18
49 CLERE SUR LAYON 96 U 19
76 CLERES C 24 BA 8
10 CLEREY 65 PA 14
88 CLEREY LA COTE 67 WA 13
54 CLEREY SUR BRENON 67 XA 13
19 CLERGOUX 160 FA 27
26 CLERIEUX 165 SA 28
89 CLERIMOIS, LES 63 MA 14
88 CLERJUS, LE 78 YA 15
63 CLERLANDE 134 KA 24
71 CLERMAIN 136 QA 22
09 CLERMONT 218 CA 37
40 CLERMONT 183 S 35
60 CLERMONT S 26 HA 9
74 CLERMONT 138 WA 24
72 CLERMONT CREANS 78 W 16
24 CLERMONT D'EXCIDEUIL 144 BA 27
47 CLERMONT DE BEAUREGARD 158 Z 29
47 CLERMONT DESSOUS 172 Y 32
55 CLERMONT EN ARGONNE C 44 TA 10
63 CLERMONT FERRAND P 148 KA 25
34 CLERMONT L'HERAULT C 214 LA 35
31 CLERMONT LE FORT 210 DA 35
02 CLERMONT LES FERMES 29 OA 8
32 CLERMONT POUYGUILLES 209 Y 35
32 CLERMONT SAVES 209 BA 35
32 CLERMONT SOUBIRAN 172 AA 32
11 CLERMONT SUR LAUQUET 221 HA 37
25 CLERON 107 XA 19
62 CLERQUES 7 FA 3
25 CLERVAL C 107 ZA 18
21 CLERY 106 VA 18
73 CLERY 153 YA 26
95 CLERY EN VEXIN 39 EA 10
55 CLERY GRAND 30 TA 9
55 CLERY PETIT 30 TA 9
45 CLERY ST ANDRE C 81 EA 16
80 CLERY SUR SOMME 17 JA 6
51 CLESLES 64 NA 13

71 CLESSE 137 SA 22
79 CLESSE 112 U 21
71 CLESSY 119 OA 22
62 CLETY 8 GA 3
88 CLEURIE 89 AB 15
76 CLEUVILLE 23 Z 8
14 CLEVILLE 36 W 10
76 CLEVILLE 23 Z 8
28 CLEVILLIERS 60 CA 13
33 CLEYRAC 157 W 30
01 CLEYZIEU 138 UA 24
88 CLEZENTAINE 68 ZA 13
92 CLICHY C 40 GA 11
93 CLICHY SOUS BOIS 40 HA 11
67 CLIMBACH 49 FB 11
52 CLINCHAMP 67 UA 14
14 CLINCHAMPS SUR ORNE 36 U 10
17 CLION 142 U 26
36 CLION 114 CA 20
26 CLIOUSCLAT 165 SA 30
76 CLIPONVILLE 23 Z 8
08 CLIRON 29 RA 7
17 CLISSE, LA 141 T 25
44 CLISSON C 110 Q 19
50 CLITOURPS 33 Q 8
29 CLOHARS CARNOET 72 G 16
29 CLOHARS FOUESNANT 72 E 16
29 CLOITRE PLEYBEN, LE 52 F 14
29 CLOITRE ST THEGONNEC, LE 52 F 13
21 CLOMOT 104 OA 19
38 CLONAS SUR VAREZE 150 RA 27
77 CLOS FONTAINE 63 JA 12
17 CLOTTE, LA 156 W 28
57 CLOUANGE 32 XA 10
86 CLOUE 113 X 22
85 CLOUZEAUX, LES 110 P 21
28 CLOYES SUR LE LOIR C 80 CA 15
51 CLOYES SUR MARNE 43 RA 12
39 CLUCY 122 WA 20
23 CLUGNAT 132 GA 23
36 CLUIS 115 EA 22
04 CLUMANC 198 YA 33
71 CLUNY C 120 RA 22
74 CLUSAZ, LA 139 ZA 24
05 CLUSE, LA 181 WA 30
25 CLUSE ET MIJOUX, LA 124 ZA 20
74 CLUSES C 140 ZA 24
66 CLUSES, LES 224 JA 40
79 CLUSSAIS LA POMMERAIE 129 W 23
71 CLUX 121 TA 20
22 COADOUT 53 I 13
06 COARAZE 199 DB 34
64 COARRAZE 215 V 37
29 COAT MEAL 51 C 13
22 COATASCORN 53 I 12
22 COATREVEN 53 H 12
26 COBONNE 165 TA 30
59 COBRIEUX 9 LA 4
61 COCHERE, LA 58 X 12
77 COCHEREL 41 KA 11
57 COCHEREN 47 BB 10
10 COCLOIS 65 PA 13
80 COCQUEREL 16 FA 6
47 COCUMONT 171 W 31
48 COCURES 177 MA 31
66 CODALET 222 HA 39
30 CODOGNAN 193 PA 34
30 CODOLET 179 RA 32
35 COESMES 76 Q 16
22 COETLOGON 74 L 15
22 COETMIEUX 54 L 13
02 COEUVRES ET VALSERY 27 KA 9
85 COEX 109 O 21
2A COGGIA 227 JB 41
35 COGLES 56 Q 13
39 COGNA 122 WA 21
16 COGNAC S 142 V 25
87 COGNAC LA FORET 144 AA 25
03 COGNAT LYONNE 133 LA 24
72 COGNERS 79 Z 16
38 COGNET 166 WA 29
70 COGNIERES 88 YA 17
73 COGNIN C 152 WA 26
38 COGNIN LES GORGES 166 UA 28
2A COGNOCOLI MONTICCHI 229 KB 43
18 COGNY 117 IA 20
69 COGNY 136 RA 24
83 COGOLIN 204 ZA 36
43 COHADE 148 LA 27
73 COHENNOZ 153 ZA 25
22 COHINIAC 53 J 13
52 COHONS 87 UA 16
52 COIFFY LE BAS 87 VA 16
52 COIFFY LE HAUT 87 WA 16
80 COIGNEUX 17 HA 6
78 COIGNIERES 39 FA 12
50 COIGNY 34 Q 9
33 COIMERES 170 V 31
57 COIN LES CUVRY 46 YA 11
57 COIN SUR SEILLE 46 XA 11
45 COINCES 81 EA 15
88 COINCHES 69 BB 14
54 COINCOURT 68 AB 12
02 COINCY 41 LA 10
57 COINCY 46 YA 10
36 COINGS 115 EA 20
02 COINGT 29 OA 7
33 COIRAC 156 V 30
69 COISE 150 QA 26
73 COISE ST JEAN PIED GAUTHIER 153 XA 26
39 COISERETTE 138 WA 23
70 COISEVAUX 89 AB 17
39 COISIA 138 VA 23
80 COISY 16 GA 6
17 COIVERT 128 U 24
60 COIVREL 26 IA 8
51 COIZARD JOCHES 42 NA 11
47 COLAYRAC ST CIRQ 172 Z 32
62 COLEMBERT 7 EA 3
01 COLIGNY C 138 UA 22
80 COLINCAMPS 17 IA 6
89 COLLAN 84 NA 16
58 COLLANCELLE, LA 103 MA 19
15 COLLANDRES 161 IA 27
27 COLLANDRES QUINCARNON 37 AA 11
63 COLLANGES 148 KA 27
43 COLLAT 162 MA 27
06 COLLE SUR LOUP, LA 200 CB 34
77 COLLEGIEN 40 IA 11
89 COLLEMIERS 63 KA 14
59 COLLERET 19 OA 5
48 COLLET DE DEZE, LE 178 OA 32
27 COLLETOT 23 Z 9
76 COLLEVILLE 23 Y 7
14 COLLEVILLE MONTGOMERY 36 V 9
14 COLLEVILLE SUR MER 35 S 9
30 COLLIAS 193 QA 33
02 COLLIGIS CRANDELAIN 28 MA 9

57 COLLIGNY 46 YA 10
62 COLLINE BEAUMONT 15 EA 5
22 COLLINEE C 74 L 14
66 COLLIOURE 224 KA 39
83 COLLOBRIERES C 203 YA 36
71 COLLONGE EN CHAROLLAIS 120 QA 21
71 COLLONGE LA MADELEINE 120 QA 20
01 COLLONGES C 138 WA 23
69 COLLONGES AU MONT D'OR 137 SA 25
19 COLLONGES LA ROUGE 159 DA 28
21 COLLONGES LES BEVY 105 SA 19
21 COLLONGES LES PREMIERES 105 UA 19
74 COLLONGES SOUS SALEVE 139 YA 23
06 COLLONGUES 198 BB 33
65 COLLONGUES 208 X 36
29 COLLOREC 52 F 14
30 COLLORGUES 193 PA 33
68 COLMAR P 90 DB 15
04 COLMARS C 182 ZA 32
57 COLMEN 47 ZA 9
58 COLMERY 102 LA 18
76 COLMESNIL MANNEVILLE 24 BA 7
54 COLMEY 31 VA 9
52 COLMIER LE BAS 86 SA 16
52 COLMIER LE HAUT 86 SA 16
30 COLOGNAC 192 NA 33
32 COLOGNE C 187 BA 34
06 COLOMARS 200 CB 34
38 COLOMBE 152 UA 27
41 COLOMBE, LA 80 CA 16
50 COLOMBE, LA 56 R 11
10 COLOMBE LA FOSSE 66 RA 14
10 COLOMBE LE SEC 66 RA 14
70 COLOMBE LES VESOUL 88 YA 17
14 COLOMBELLES 36 V 10
92 COLOMBES C 40 GA 11
54 COLOMBEY LES BELLES C 67 WA 13
52 COLOMBEY
LES DEUX EGLISES 66 SA 14
03 COLOMBIER 133 IA 23
21 COLOMBIER 104 RA 19
24 COLOMBIER 157 Y 30
42 COLOMBIER 150 RA 27
70 COLOMBIER 88 YA 17
71 COLOMBIER EN BRIONNAIS 135 PA 22
25 COLOMBIER FONTAINE 108 AB 18
07 COLOMBIER LE CARDINAL 150 RA 27
07 COLOMBIER LE JEUNE 164 RA 28
07 COLOMBIER LE VIEUX 164 RA 28
69 COLOMBIER SAUGNIEU 151 TA 25
14 COLOMBIERES 35 S 9
34 COLOMBIERES SUR ORB 213 JA 35
17 COLOMBIERS 142 U 26
18 COLOMBIERS 117 HA 21
34 COLOMBIERS 213 KA 36
61 COLOMBIERS 58 W 13
86 COLOMBIERS 113 Y 21
53 COLOMBIERS DU PLESSIS 57 S 13
14 COLOMBIERS SUR SEULLES 35 U 9
12 COLOMBIES 175 HA 31
70 COLOMBOTTE 88 YA 17
50 COLOMBY 33 P 9
14 COLOMBY SUR THAON 36 U 10
31 COLOMIERS 210 CA 35
01 COLOMIEU 152 VA 25
61 COLONARD CORUBERT 59 Z 13
23 COLONDANNES 131 DA 23
02 COLONFAY 28 NA 7
39 COLONNE 122 VA 20
26 COLONZELLE 179 SA 31
56 COLPO 74 K 16
88 COLROY LA GRANDE 69 CB 14
67 COLROY LA ROCHE 69 CB 13
28 COLTAINVILLE 61 DA 13
15 COLTINES 161 JA 28
24 COLY 159 CA 28
34 COMBAILLAUX 192 NA 34
30 COMBAS 193 OA 34
38 COMBE DE LANCEY, LA 166 WA 28
70 COMBEAUFONTAINE C 88 WA 16
81 COMBEFA 189 FA 33
24 COMBERANCHE ET EPELUCHE 143 X 27
70 COMBERJON 88 YA 17
82 COMBEROUGER 187 BA 34
21 COMBERTAULT 121 SA 20
34 COMBES 213 KA 35
25 COMBES, LES 107 ZA 19
16 COMBIERS 143 Y 26
21 COMBLANCHIEN 105 SA 19
80 COMBLES C 17 JA 6
55 COMBLES EN BARROIS 44 TA 12
35 COMBLESSAC 75 N 16
45 COMBLEUX 81 FA 16
61 COMBLOT 59 Z 13
74 COMBLOUX 140 AB 24
27 COMBON 37 AA 10
35 COMBOURG C 55 O 13
35 COMBOURTILLE 76 R 14
26 COMBOVIN 165 TA 29
63 COMBRAILLES 133 IA 25
79 COMBRAND 111 T 20
14 COMBRAY 35 U 11
42 COMBRE 135 PA 24
49 COMBREE 94 R 16
28 COMBRES 60 BA 14
55 COMBRES SOUS LES COTES 45 VA 10
19 COMBRESSOL 146 GA 26
12 COMBRET 190 IA 34
45 COMBREUX 82 GA 15
88 COMBRIMONT 69 CB 14
29 COMBRIT 71 E 16
63 COMBRONDE C 134 KA 24
77 COMBS LA VILLE C 62 IA 12
71 COMELLE, LA 119 OA 20
46 COMIAC 160 FA 29
11 COMIGNE 223 IA 37
59 COMINES 9 KA 3
29 COMMANA 52 F 13
21 COMMARIN 104 RA 18
61 COMMEAUX 58 W 12
38 COMMELLE 151 TA 27
42 COMMELLE VERNAY 135 OA 24
39 COMMENAILLES 122 UA 20
02 COMMENCHON 27 KA 8
40 COMMENSACQ 169 T 32
03 COMMENTRY C 133 IA 23
95 COMMENY 39 FA 10
85 COMMEQUIERS 109 O 21
53 COMMER 57 T 14
55 COMMERCY S 45 VA 12
72 COMMERVEIL 59 Y 14
14 COMMES 35 T 9
39 COMMUNAILLES
EN MONTAGNE 123 XA 21
69 COMMUNAY 151 SA 26
63 COMPAINS 147 JA 27
76 COMPAINVILLE 25 DA 8
77 COMPANS 40 IA 11

23 COMPAS, LE 133 HA 24
51 COMPERTRIX 43 PA 11
12 COMPEYRE 176 KA 32
60 COMPIEGNE S 27 JA 9
89 COMPIGNY 63 LA 14
12 COMPOLIBAT 175 GA 31
73 COMPOTE, LA 153 YA 26
12 COMPREGNAC 191 JA 33
87 COMPREIGNAC 131 CA 24
26 COMPS 179 TA 31
30 COMPS 195 RA 34
33 COMPS 156 T 28
12 COMPS LA GRAND VILLE 175 IA 32
83 COMPS SUR ARTUBY C 198 ZA 34
62 COMTE, LA 17 HA 4
11 COMUS 221 FA 38
41 CONAN 80 CA 16
01 CONAND 138 UA 25
66 CONAT 222 HA 39
2A CONCA 230 MB 43
29 CONCARNEAU C 72 F 16
02 CONCEVREUX 28 NA 9
19 CONCEZE 145 CA 27
27 CONCHES EN OUCHE C 38 AA 11
77 CONCHES SUR GONDOIRE 40 IA 11
64 CONCHEZ DE BEARN 207 V 35
62 CONCHIL LE TEMPLE 15 EA 5
60 CONCHY LES POTS 27 IA 8
62 CONCHY SUR CANCHE 16 GA 5
46 CONCORES 173 CA 30
56 CONCORET 75 M 15
46 CONCOTS 174 DA 31
30 CONCOULES 177 OA 31
49 CONCOURSON SUR LAYON 96 V 19
36 CONCREMIERS 114 BA 21
18 CONCRESSAULT 82 IA 17
41 CONCRIERS 80 DA 16
16 CONDAC 129 X 24
71 CONDAL 121 UA 22
01 CONDAMINE 138 VA 24
39 CONDAMINE 122 UA 21
04 CONDAMINE CHATELARD, LA 182 AB 31
15 CONDAT C 147 IA 27
46 CONDAT 159 EA 29
63 CONDAT EN COMBRAILLE 133 IA 25
63 CONDAT LES MONTBOISSIER 148 MA 26
19 CONDAT SUR GANAVEIX 145 DA 26
24 CONDAT SUR TRINCOU 144 Z 27
24 CONDAT SUR VEZERE 159 CA 28
87 CONDAT SUR VIENNE 145 CA 25
36 CONDE 116 FA 20
02 CONDE EN BRIE C 42 MA 11
80 CONDE FOLIE 16 FA 6
08 CONDE LES AUTRY 44 SA 10
08 CONDE LES HERPY 29 PA 8
57 CONDE NORTHEN 47 ZA 10
77 CONDE STE LIBIAIRE 40 JA 11
02 CONDE SUR AISNE 28 MA 9
61 CONDE SUR HUISNE 59 AA 13
14 CONDE SUR IFS 36 W 11
27 CONDE SUR ITON 38 AA 11
59 CONDE SUR L'ESCAUT C 18 MA 4
51 CONDE SUR MARNE 42 PA 11
14 CONDE SUR NOIREAU C 35 U 11
27 CONDE SUR RISLE 23 Z 9
61 CONDE SUR SARTHE 58 W 13
14 CONDE SUR SEULLES 35 T 10
02 CONDE SUR SUIPPE 29 OA 9
78 CONDE SUR VESGRE 39 DA 12
50 CONDE SUR VIRE 35 S 10
61 CONDEAU 59 AA 13
95 CONDECOURT 39 FA 11
01 CONDEISSIAT 137 TA 23
16 CONDEON 142 V 27
39 CONDES 138 VA 23
52 CONDES 66 TA 15
62 CONDETTE 7 DA 3
47 CONDEZAYGUES 173 AA 31
26 CONDILLAC 179 SA 30
32 CONDOM S 186 Y 33
12 CONDOM D'AUBRAC 176 JA 30
26 CONDORCET 180 TA 31
02 CONDREN 28 LA 8
69 CONDRIEU C 150 RA 26
70 CONFLANDEY 88 XA 16
54 CONFLANS EN JARNISY C 45 WA 10
78 CONFLANS STE HONORINE C 39 FA 11
72 CONFLANS SUR ANILLE 79 Z 15
70 CONFLANS SUR LANTERNE 88 YA 16
45 CONFLANS SUR LOING 82 JA 15
51 CONFLANS SUR SEINE 64 MA 13
16 CONFOLENS S 130 Z 24
19 CONFOLENT PORT DIEU 147 HA 26
01 CONFORT 138 WA 23
70 CONFRACOURT 88 WA 17
01 CONFRANCON 137 TA 23
72 CONGE SUR ORNE 78 X 14
30 CONGENIES 193 PA 34
91 CONGERVILLE THIONVILLE 61 FA 14
77 CONGIS SUR THEROUANNE 41 JA 11
53 CONGRIER 76 R 16
51 CONGY 42 NA 11
28 CONIE MOLITARD 60 DA 15
11 CONILHAC CORBIERES 223 IA 37
11 CONILHAC DE LA MONTAGNE 221 GA 37
73 CONJUX 152 WA 25
72 CONLIE C 78 W 15
39 CONLIEGE C 122 VA 21
12 CONNAC 190 IA 33
43 CONNANGLES 148 MA 27
51 CONNANTRAY VAUREFROY 42 OA 12
51 CONNANTRE 42 OA 12
30 CONNAUX 195 RA 33
24 CONNE DE LABARDE 157 Z 29
27 CONNELLES 38 CA 10
72 CONNERRE 79 Y 15
24 CONNEZAC 143 Y 26
02 CONNIGIS 42 MA 11
44 CONQUEREUIL 93 O 17
12 CONQUES C 175 HA 30
11 CONQUES SUR ORBIEL C 212 HA 36
29 CONQUET, LE 51 B 14
30 CONQUEYRAC 193 OA 33
54 CONS LA GRANDVILLE 31 VA 9
74 CONS STE COLOMBE 153 YA 25
17 CONSAC 142 U 27
06 CONSEGUDES 200 BB 34
55 CONSENVOYE 31 UA 9
52 CONSIGNY 66 UA 14
25 CONSOLATION MAISONNETTES 108 AB 19
80 CONTALMAISON 17 IA 6
74 CONTAMINE SARZIN 139 XA 24
74 CONTAMINE SUR ARVE 139 YA 23
74 CONTAMINES MONTJOIE, LES 140 AB 25
51 CONTAULT 43 RA 11
80 CONTAY 17 HA 6
39 CONTE 123 XA 21
06 CONTES C 200 DB 34
62 CONTES 16 FA 4
02 CONTESCOURT 27 KA 7
53 CONTEST 57 T 14
14 CONTEVILLE 36 V 10
27 CONTEVILLE 23 Y 9
60 CONTEVILLE 26 FA 8
76 CONTEVILLE 25 DA 8
80 CONTEVILLE 16 FA 5
62 CONTEVILLE EN TERNOIS 16 GA 4
62 CONTEVILLE LES BOULOGNE 7 EA 3
57 CONTHIL 47 AB 11
49 CONTIGNE 77 U 16
03 CONTIGNY 134 LA 22
72 CONTILLY 59 Y 13
37 CONTINVOIR 97 X 18
80 CONTOIRE 26 IA 8
09 CONTRAZY 218 CA 37
17 CONTRE 128 V 24
80 CONTRE 26 FA 7
70 CONTREGLISE 88 XA 16
76 CONTREMOULINS 23 Y 8
18 CONTRES 117 HA 20
41 CONTRES C 99 DA 18
08 CONTREUVE 30 RA 9
01 CONTREVOZ 138 VA 25
88 CONTREXEVILLE 67 WA 14
50 CONTRIERES 34 Q 11
55 CONTRISSON 44 SA 12
80 CONTY C 26 GA 7
57 CONTZ LES BAINS 32 YA 9
01 CONZIEU 152 VA 25
51 COOLE 43 QA 12
51 COOLUS 43 PA 11
85 COPECHAGNIERE, LA 110 O 20
74 COPPONEX 139 XA 24
14 COQUAINVILLIERS 36 X 10
62 COQUELLES 7 EA 2
24 COQUILLE, LA 144 AA 26
28 CORANCEZ 60 DA 14
58 CORANCY 103 OA 19
29 CORAY 72 F 15
28 CORBARA 225 KB 39
82 CORBARIEU 188 CA 33
69 CORBAS 151 SA 26
62 CORBEHEM 17 KA 5
51 CORBEIL 65 OA 13
60 CORBEIL CERF 39 GA 9
91 CORBEIL ESSONNES C 62 HA 12
45 CORBEILLES 82 HA 15
73 CORBEL 152 WA 27
38 CORBELIN 152 VA 26
70 CORBENAY 88 YA 16
02 CORBENY 28 NA 9
66 CORBERE 224 IA 39
64 CORBERE ABERES 208 W 35
66 CORBERE LES CABANES 224 IA 39
21 CORBERON 121 SA 20
30 CORBES 193 OA 33
80 CORBIE C 17 HA 7
70 CORBIERE, LA 89 ZA 16
04 CORBIERES 197 WA 34
11 CORBIERES 221 FA 37
58 CORBIGNY C 103 NA 18
14 CORBON 36 W 10
61 CORBON 59 Z 13
01 CORBONOD 138 WA 24
91 CORBREUSE 61 FA 13
25 CORCELLE MIESLOT 107 YA 18
01 CORCELLES 138 VA 24
69 CORCELLES EN BEAUJOLAIS 136 RA 23
25 CORCELLES FERRIERES 106 WA 19
21 CORCELLES LES ARTS 120 RA 20
21 CORCELLES LES CITEAUX 105 TA 19
21 CORCELLES LES MONTS 105 SA 18
88 CORCIEUX C 69 BB 14
25 CORCONDRAY 106 WA 19
30 CORCONNE 193 OA 34
44 CORCOUE SUR LOGNE 110 P 20
02 CORCY 41 KA 10
38 CORDEAC 166 WA 29
14 CORDEBUGLE 37 Y 10
42 CORDELLE 135 OA 24
44 CORDEMAIS 93 O 18
81 CORDES SUR CIEL C 189 FA 33
82 CORDES TOLOSANNES 188 BA 33
71 CORDESSE 104 PA 19
14 CORDEY 36 V 11
74 CORDON 140 ZA 24
70 CORDONNET 107 XA 18
15 COREN 162 KA 28
38 CORENC 166 WA 28
63 CORENT 148 KA 26
51 CORFELIX 42 NA 11
21 CORGENGOUX 121 SA 20
24 CORGNAC SUR L'ISLE 144 AA 27
21 CORGOLOIN 105 SA 19
17 CORIGNAC 142 U 27
22 CORLAY C 53 J 14
01 CORLIER 138 VA 24
28 CORMAINVILLE 61 DA 15
01 CORMARANCHE EN BUGEY 138 VA 24
71 CORMATIN 120 RA 22
17 CORME ECLUSE 141 S 26
17 CORME ROYAL 141 T 25
27 CORMEILLES C 37 Y 10
60 CORMEILLES 26 GA 8
95 CORMEILLES EN PARISIS C 40 GA 11
95 CORMEILLES EN VEXIN 39 FA 10
14 CORMELLES LE ROYAL 36 V 10
41 CORMENON 79 AA 15
41 CORMERAY 80 CA 17
37 CORMERY 98 AA 18
72 CORMES 59 Z 14
51 CORMICY 28 NA 9
27 CORMIER, LE 38 CA 11
14 CORMOLAIN 35 S 10
62 CORMONT 7 EA 4
51 CORMONTREUIL 42 OA 10
01 CORMORANCHE SUR SAONE 137 SA 23
21 CORMOT LE GRAND 120 RA 20
51 CORMOYEUX 42 NA 10
01 CORMOZ 121 TA 22
46 CORN 174 FA 30
46 CORNAC 160 FA 29
89 CORNANT 63 KA 15
07 CORNAS 165 SA 29
08 CORNAY 30 SA 9
49 CORNE 96 V 18
31 CORNEBARRIEU 188 CA 34
34 CORNEILHAN 213 KA 36
66 CORNEILLA DE CONFLENT 222 HA 39
66 CORNEILLA DEL VERCOL 224 JA 39
66 CORNEILLA LA RIVIERE 224 IA 39
32 CORNEILLAN 185 V 34
27 CORNEUIL 38 BA 11
27 CORNEVILLE LA FOUQUETIERE 37 Z 10
27 CORNEVILLE SUR RISLE 23 Z 9
74 CORNIER 139 YA 24
19 CORNIL 159 EA 28
26 CORNILLAC 180 UA 31
24 CORNILLE 144 AA 27
35 CORNILLE 76 O 15
49 CORNILLE LES CAVES 96 V 17
30 CORNILLON 178 QA 32
13 CORNILLON CONFOUX 201 TA 35
38 CORNILLON EN TRIEVES 166 WA 29
26 CORNILLON SUR L'OULE 180 UA 31
88 CORNIMONT 89 BB 15
39 CORNOD 138 VA 23
70 CORNOT 87 WA 17
49 CORNUAILLE, LA 95 S 17
12 CORNUS C 191 KA 33
18 CORNUSSE 117 IA 20
27 CORNY 38 DA 9
08 CORNY MACHEROMENIL 29 QA 8
57 CORNY SUR MOSELLE 46 XA 11
21 CORON 95 T 19
49 CORON 95 T 19
85 CORPE 125 R 22
21 CORPEAU 120 RA 20
21 CORPOYER LA CHAPELLE 85 RA 17
38 CORPS C 167 XA 29
35 CORPS NUDS 75 P 15
45 CORQUILLEROY 82 IA 15
18 CORQUOY 116 GA 20
2A CORRANO 226 KB 42
70 CORRAVILLERS 89 AB 16
70 CORRE 88 XA 16
38 CORRENCON EN VERCORS 166 VA 28
83 CORRENS 203 XA 35
19 CORREZE C 146 FA 27
51 CORRIBERT 42 NA 11
51 CORROBERT 42 MA 11
21 CORROMBLES 85 PA 17
32 CORRONSAC 210 DA 35
51 CORROY 42 OA 12
21 CORSAINT 85 PA 17
66 CORSAVY 224 IA 40
2B CORSCIA 227 KB 40
44 CORSEPT 93 N 18
22 CORSEUL 55 N 13
71 CORTAMBERT 120 RA 22
2B CORTE S 228 LB 40
71 CORTEVAIX 120 RA 22
45 CORTRAT 82 IA 16
28 CORVEES LES YYS, LES 60 BA 14
01 CORVEISSIAT 138 UA 23
58 CORVOL D'EMBERNARD 102 LA 18
58 CORVOL L'ORGUEILLEUX 102 LA 18
49 CORZE 96 U 17
09 COS 219 DA 37
39 COSGES 122 UA 21
64 COSLEDAA LUBE BOAST 207 V 35
53 COSMES 77 S 16
19 COSNAC 159 DA 28
58 COSNE COURS SUR LOIRE S 101 JA 18
03 COSNE D'ALLIER 118 JA 22
54 COSNES ET ROMAIN 31 VA 8
50 COSQUEVILLE 33 O 8
58 COSSAYE 118 MA 21
49 COSSE D'ANJOU 95 T 19
53 COSSE EN CHAMPAGNE 77 V 15
53 COSSE LE VIVIEN C 77 S 15
14 COSSESSEVILLE 35 U 11
67 COSSWILLER 49 DB 12
2B COSTA 225 KB 39
43 COSTAROS 163 NA 29
05 COSTES, LES 167 XA 30
12 COSTES GOZON, LES 191 JA 33
70 COTE, LA 89 ZA 17
73 COTE D'AIME, LA 154 AB 26
73 COTE D'ARBROZ, LA 140 AB 23
42 COTE EN COUZAN, LA 149 NA 25
38 COTE ST ANDRE, LA C 151 UA 27
42 COTEAU, LE 135 OA 24
25 COTEBRUNE 107 YA 19
38 COTES D'AREY, LES 151 SA 26
38 COTES DE CORPS, LES 167 WA 29
2A COTI CHIAVARI 229 JB 43
83 COTIGNAC C 203 XA 35
42 COTTANCE 150 PA 25
80 COTTENCHY 26 HA 7
76 COTTEVRARD 24 CA 8
14 COTTUN 35 T 10
79 COUARDE, LA 128 V 23
17 COUARDE SUR MER, LA 126 Q 23
18 COUARGUES 101 JA 18
77 COUBERT 62 IA 12
33 COUBEYRAC 157 W 29
12 COUBISOU 176 IA 30
24 COUBJOURS 159 CA 27
58 COUBLANC 87 UA 17
71 COUBLANC 135 PA 23
38 COUBLEVIE 152 VA 27
64 COUBLUCQ 207 V 35
43 COUBON 163 NA 29
93 COUBRON 40 IA 11
71 COUCHES C 120 QA 20
21 COUCHEY 105 SA 18
26 COUCOURDE, LA 179 RA 30
07 COUCOURON C 163 OA 29
08 COUCY 29 QA 8
02 COUCY LA VILLE 28 LA 8
02 COUCY LE CHATEAU AUFFRIQUE C 28 LA 8
02 COUCY LES EPPES 28 NA 8
41 COUDDES 99 CA 18
61 COUDEHARD 36 X 11
59 COUDEKERQUE 8 HA 2
59 COUDEKERQUE BRANCHE C 8 HA 2
63 COUDES 148 KA 26
50 COUDEVILLE SUR MER 56 P 11
11 COUDONS 221 GA 38
13 COUDOUX 202 UA 35
27 COUDRAY 25 DA 9
45 COUDRAY 62 HA 14
53 COUDRAY 77 T 16
28 COUDRAY, LE 60 DA 13
28 COUDRAY AU PERCHE 59 AA 14
49 COUDRAY MACOUARD, LE 96 W 19
91 COUDRAY MONTCEAUX, LE 62 HA 13
14 COUDRAY RABUT 23 X 9
60 COUDRAY ST GERMER, LE C 25 EA 9
60 COUDRAY SUR THELLE, LE 39 GA 9
79 COUDRE, LA 112 U 20
28 COUDRECEAU 60 AA 14
72 COUDRECIEUX 79 Z 15
27 COUDRES 38 CA 11
45 COUDROY 82 HA 16
65 COUDUN 27 JA 9
40 COUDURES 184 U 34
31 COUEILLES 209 AA 36
44 COUERON 93 O 19
37 COUESMES 97 Y 17
53 COUESMES VAUCE 57 T 13
44 COUFFE 94 O 18
41 COUFFI 99 DA 19
11 COUFFOULENS 221 GA 37
19 COUFFY SUR SARSONNE 146 GA 26
09 COUFLENS 218 BA 38
81 COUFOULEUX 189 EA 34
86 COUHE C 129 X 23
77 COUILLY PONT AUX DAMES 40 JA 11
62 COUIN 17 HA 6
11 COUIZA C 221 GA 38
31 COULADERE 218 BA 37
72 COULAINES 78 X 15
03 COULANDON 118 LA 22
89 COULANGERON 83 MA 17
03 COULANGES 119 NA 22
41 COULANGES 80 CA 17
89 COULANGES LA VINEUSE C 84 MA 17
58 COULANGES LES NEVERS 118 KA 20
89 COULANGES SUR YONNE C 83 MA 17
72 COULANS SUR GEE 78 W 15
24 COULAURES 144 AA 27
03 COULEUVRE 117 JA 21
70 COULEVON 88 YA 17
16 COULGENS 143 X 25
61 COULIMER 59 Y 13
80 COULLEMELLE 26 HA 8
62 COULLEMONT 17 HA 5
45 COULLONS 82 HA 17
61 COULMER 37 X 12
21 COULMIER LE SEC 85 QA 16
45 COULMIERS 80 DA 15
34 COULOBRES 213 LA 35
62 COULOGNE 7 FA 2
60 COULOISY 27 KA 9
72 COULOMBIERS 58 X 14
86 COULOMBIERS 113 X 22
14 COULOMBS 35 U 10
28 COULOMBS 60 DA 12
77 COULOMBS EN VALOIS 41 KA 10
62 COULOMBY 7 FA 3
77 COULOMMES 41 JA 11
08 COULOMMES ET MARQUENY 29 RA 9
51 COULOMMES LA MONTAGNE 42 OA 10
77 COULOMMIERS C 41 KA 12
41 COULOMMIERS LA TOUR 80 BA 16
79 COULON 128 T 23
14 COULONCES 35 S 11
61 COULONCES 36 W 11
61 COULONCHE, LA 57 U 12
72 COULONGE 78 X 17
16 COULONGES 129 W 25
17 COULONGES 142 U 26
86 COULONGES 130 BA 22
02 COULONGES COHAN 42 MA 10
61 COULONGES LES SABLONS 59 AA 13
79 COULONGES SUR L'AUTIZE C 111 T 22
61 COULONGES SUR SARTHE 59 Y 13
79 COULONGES THOUARSAIS 112 V 20
80 COULONVILLERS 16 FA 6
32 COULOUME MONDEBAT 208 X 35
24 COULOUNIEIX CHAMIERS 158 Z 28
89 COULOURS 64 MA 14
58 COULOUTRE 102 KA 18
50 COULOUVRAY BOISBENATRE 56 R 12
14 COULVAIN 35 T 11
47 COULX 172 Y 31
57 COUME 47 ZA 10
11 COUNOZOULS 222 GA 39
62 COUPELLE NEUVE 16 FA 4
62 COUPELLE VIEILLE 7 FA 4
14 COUPESARTE 36 X 10
51 COUPETZ 43 PA 12
51 COUPEVILLE 43 RA 11
12 COUPIAC 190 IA 33
52 COUPRAY 86 SA 15
02 COUPRU 41 LA 11
53 COUPTRAIN C 58 V 13
77 COUPVRAY 40 JA 11
33 COUQUEQUES 141 S 27
41 COUR CHEVERNY 80 DA 17
38 COUR ET BUIS 151 SA 27
52 COUR L'EVEQUE 86 SA 15
45 COUR MARIGNY, LA 82 IA 16
25 COUR ST MAURICE 108 AB 18
41 COUR SUR LOIRE 80 CA 17
91 COURANCES 62 HA 13
17 COURANT 128 U 24
21 COURBAN 85 RA 16
61 COURBE, LA 58 V 12
28 COURBEHAYE 61 DA 14
27 COURBEPINE 37 Z 10
02 COURBES 28 LA 8
54 COURBESSEAUX 46 ZA 12
39 COURBETTE 122 VA 21
53 COURBEVEILLE 77 S 15
92 COURBEVOIE C 40 GA 11
47 COURBIAC 173 BA 31
16 COURBILLAC 142 V 25
02 COURBOIN 41 MA 11
39 COURBOUZON 122 VA 21
41 COURBOUZON 80 DA 16
03 COURCAIS 116 HA 22
37 COURCAY 98 AA 18
72 COURCEBOEUFS 59 Y 15
80 COURCELETTE 17 IA 6
17 COURCELLES 128 U 24
25 COURCELLES 107 XA 19
45 COURCELLES 62 GA 15
54 COURCELLES 67 XA 14
58 COURCELLES 102 LA 18
90 COURCELLES 90 CB 17
80 COURCELLES AU BOIS 17 IA 6
57 COURCELLES CHAUSSY 47 ZA 10
37 COURCELLES DE TOURAINE 97 X 17
55 COURCELLES EN BARROIS 44 UA 11
77 COURCELLES EN BASSEE 63 KA 13
52 COURCELLES EN MONTAGNE 86 TA 16
60 COURCELLES EPAYELLES 26 IA 8
21 COURCELLES FREMOY 103 PA 18
72 COURCELLES LA FORET 78 W 16
62 COURCELLES LE COMTE 17 IA 6
60 COURCELLES LES GISORS 39 EA 10
62 COURCELLES LES LENS 17 KA 4
21 COURCELLES LES MONTBARD 85 QA 17
25 COURCELLES LES MONTBELIARD 108 AB 17
21 COURCELLES LES SEMUR 104 PA 18
51 COURCELLES SAPICOURT 42 NA 10
88 COURCELLES SOUS CHATENOIS 67 WA 14
80 COURCELLES SOUS MOYENCOURT 26 FA 7
80 COURCELLES SOUS THOIX 26 FA 8
55 COURCELLES SUR AIRE 44 TA 11
52 COURCELLES SUR BLAISE 66 SA 13
57 COURCELLES SUR NIED 46 YA 10
27 COURCELLES SUR SEINE 38 CA 10
02 COURCELLES SUR VESLES 28 MA 9
95 COURCELLES SUR VIOSNE 39 FA 10
10 COURCELLES SUR VOIRE 65 QA 13
51 COURCEMAIN 64 OA 12
72 COURCEMONT 59 Y 14
17 COURCERAC 128 U 25
51 COURCERAULT 59 Z 13
10 COURCEROY 63 LA 13
77 COURCHAMP 63 LA 12
02 COURCHAMPS 41 LA 10
49 COURCHAMPS 96 V 19
25 COURCHAPON 106 WA 18
70 COURCHATON 89 ZA 17
59 COURCHELETTES 17 KA 5
53 COURCITE 58 V 14
72 COURCIVAL 59 Y 14
16 COURCOME 129 X 24
17 COURCON C 127 T 23
37 COURCOUE 97 Y 19
91 COURCOURONNES 62 HA 12
17 COURCOURY 142 T 25
70 COURCUIRE 106 WA 18
14 COURCY 36 W 11
50 COURCY 34 Q 11
51 COURCY 29 OA 9
45 COURCY AUX LOGES 81 GA 15
27 COURDEMANCHE 38 CA 12
72 COURDEMANCHE 79 Z 16
51 COURDEMANGES 43 QA 12
95 COURDIMANCHE 39 FA 11
91 COURDIMANCHE SUR ESSONNE 62 HA 13
31 COURET 217 AA 37
72 COURGAINS 59 X 14
16 COURGEAC 143 W 27
72 COURGENARD 59 Z 14
89 COURGENAY 64 MA 14
78 COURGENT 39 DA 11
61 COURGEON 59 Z 13
61 COURGEOUT 59 Y 13
89 COURGIS 84 NA 16
51 COURGIVAUX 42 MA 12
63 COURGOUL 147 KA 26
51 COURJEONNET 42 NA 11
16 COURLAC 143 X 27
51 COURLANDON 28 NA 9
39 COURLANS 122 VA 21
39 COURLAOUX 122 UA 21
79 COURLAY 111 U 21
49 COURLEON 97 X 18
21 COURLON 86 SA 17
89 COURLON SUR YONNE 63 KA 14
01 COURMANGOUX 137 UA 23
51 COURMAS 42 NA 10
02 COURMELLES 28 LA 9
41 COURMEMIN 99 DA 18
61 COURMENIL 58 X 12
06 COURMES 200 BB 34
02 COURMONT 42 MA 10
70 COURMONT 89 AB 17
11 COURNANEL 221 GA 37
93 COURNEUVE, LA C 40 HA 11
34 COURNIOU 213 IA 35
63 COURNOLS 147 KA 26
56 COURNON 75 N 16
63 COURNON D'AUVERGNE C 148 KA 25
34 COURNONSEC 214 NA 35
34 COURNONTERRAL 214 NA 35
16 COURONNE, LA C 143 X 26
55 COUROUVRE 44 UA 11
77 COURPALAY 63 JA 12
33 COURPIAC 156 V 30
63 COURPIERE C 148 MA 25
17 COURPIGNAC 142 U 27
77 COURQUETAINE 62 IA 12
32 COURRENSAN 186 X 34
62 COURRIERES C 17 JA 4
81 COURRIS 190 HA 33
30 COURRY 178 PA 32
46 COURS 174 DA 31
47 COURS 172 Z 32
79 COURS 112 U 22
56 COURS, LE 74 L 16
33 COURS DE MONSEGUR 171 X 30
24 COURS DE PILE 157 Z 29
69 COURS LA VILLE 136 PA 24
33 COURS LES BAINS 171 W 31
18 COURS LES BARRES 102 KA 19
24 COURSAC 158 Z 28
11 COURSAN C 213 KA 36
10 COURSAN EN OTHE 64 NA 15
06 COURSEGOULES C 200 BB 34
62 COURSET 7 EA 3
14 COURSEULLES SUR MER 35 U 9
14 COURSON 56 R 11
89 COURSON LES CARRIERES C 83 MA 17
91 COURSON MONTELOUP 61 GA 13
77 COURTACON 41 LA 12
51 COURTAGNON 42 OA 10
28 COURTALAIN 60 BA 15
10 COURTAOULT 84 NA 15
11 COURTAULY 221 FA 37
68 COURTAVON 90 CB 18
25 COURTEFONTAINE 108 BB 18
39 COURTEFONTAINE 106 WA 19
27 COURTEILLES 38 BA 12
19 COURTEIX 146 HA 26
90 COURTELEVANT 90 CB 17
80 COURTEMANCHE 26 HA 8
45 COURTEMAUX 83 JA 15
51 COURTEMONT 43 RA 10
02 COURTEMONT VARENNES 42 MA 10
45 COURTEMPIERRE 62 IA 15
38 COURTENAY 152 UA 25
45 COURTENAY C 83 KA 15
10 COURTENOT 65 PA 14
10 COURTERANGES 65 PA 14
10 COURTERON 85 QA 15
01 COURTES 121 TA 22
70 COURTESOULT ET GATEY 87 VA 17
25 COURTETAIN ET SALANS 107 ZA 19
11 COURTETE, LA 221 FA 37
60 COURTEUIL 40 HA 10
84 COURTHEZON 195 SA 33
51 COURTHIEZY 42 MA 10
32 COURTIES 208 X 35
60 COURTIEUX 27 KA 9
72 COURTILLERS 77 V 16
50 COURTILS 56 Q 12
23 COURTINE, LA C 146 GA 25
51 COURTISOLS 43 QA 11
21 COURTIVRON 86 SA 17
89 COURTOIN 63 KA 15
89 COURTOIS SUR YONNE 63 LA 14
61 COURTOMER C 59 Y 12
77 COURTOMER 63 JA 12
14 COURTONNE LA MEURDRAC 37 Y 10
14 COURTONNE LES DEUX EGLISES 37 Y 10
02 COURTRIZY ET FUSSIGNY 28 NA 8
77 COURTRY 40 IA 11

14 COURVAUDON 35 T 11
25 COURVIERES 123 XA 20
51 COURVILLE 42 MA 10
28 COURVILLE SUR EURE C 60 CA 13
69 COURZIEU 150 QA 25
39 COUSANCE 122 UA 22
55 COUSANCES LES FORGES 66 TA 12
55 COUSANCES LES TRICONVILLE 44 UA 12
59 COUSOLRE 19 OA 5
09 COUSSA 219 EA 37
87 COUSSAC BONNEVAL 145 CA 26
65 COUSSAN 208 X 36
86 COUSSAY 113 X 20
86 COUSSAY LES BOIS 114 Z 20
10 COUSSEGREY 84 OA 15
12 COUSSERGUES 176 JA 31
88 COUSSEY C 67 VA 13
18 COUST 117 IA 21
11 COUSTAUSSA 221 GA 38
11 COUSTOUGE 223 IA 37
66 COUSTOUGES 224 IA 40
50 COUTANCES S 34 Q 11
03 COUTANSOUZE 133 KA 23
89 COUTARNOUX 84 OA 17
77 COUTENCON 63 KA 13
09 COUTENS 219 EA 37
61 COUTERNE 57 U 13
21 COUTERNON 105 TA 18
43 COUTEUGES 162 MA 28
77 COUTEVROULT 41 JA 11
70 COUTHENANS 89 AB 17
47 COUTHURES SUR GARONNE 171 X 31
59 COUTICHES 18 KA 4
79 COUTIERES 112 W 22
42 COUTOUVRE 135 PA 24
33 COUTRAS C 156 W 28
16 COUTURE 129 X 24
62 COUTURE, LA 8 IA 4
85 COUTURE, LA 125 R 22
27 COUTURE BOUSSEY, LA 38 CA 11
79 COUTURE D'ARGENSON 128 W 24
41 COUTURE SUR LOIR 79 Z 16
62 COUTURELLE 17 HA 5
24 COUTURES 143 Y 27
33 COUTURES 171 W 30
49 COUTURES 96 V 18
82 COUTURES 187 BA 33
50 COUVAINS 35 S 10
61 COUVAINS 37 Z 11
12 COUVERTOIRADE, LA 191 LA 33
55 COUVERTPUIS 66 UA 13
10 COUVIGNON 65 RA 14
50 COUVILLE 33 P 8
55 COUVONGES 44 TA 12
02 COUVRELLES 28 MA 9
02 COUVRON ET AUMENCOURT 28 MA 8
51 COUVROT 43 QA 12
07 COUX 164 RA 30
17 COUX 142 U 27
24 COUX ET BIGAROQUE 158 AA 29
18 COUY 101 JA 19
35 COUYERE, LA 76 P 16
24 COUZE ET ST FRONT 158 Z 29
87 COUZEIX 131 CA 25
37 COUZIERS 97 W 19
03 COUZON 118 KA 21
69 COUZON AU MONT D'OR 137 SA 25
46 COUZOU 159 DA 30
31 COX 187 BA 34
60 COYE LA FORET 40 HA 10
62 COYECQUES 8 GA 4
02 COYOLLES 41 KA 10
39 COYRIERE 138 WA 23
39 COYRON 122 VA 22
54 COYVILLER 68 YA 13
17 COZES C 141 S 26
2A COZZANO 228 LB 42
56 CRACH 91 J 17
38 CRACHIER 151 TA 26
89 CRAIN 83 MA 17
57 CRAINCOURT 46 YA 11
42 CRAINTILLEUX 149 PA 26
88 CRAINVILLIERS 67 WA 14
02 CRAMAILLE 41 MA 10
39 CRAMANS 122 WA 20
51 CRAMANT 42 OA 11
17 CRAMCHABAN 127 T 23
61 CRAMENIL 58 V 12
60 CRAMOISY 40 HA 10
80 CRAMONT 16 FA 6
09 CRAMPAGNA 219 DA 37
74 CRAN GEVRIER 139 XA 24
10 CRANCEY 64 MA 13
39 CRANCOT 122 VA 21
15 CRANDELLES 160 GA 29
72 CRANNES EN CHAMPAGNE 78 W 15
01 CRANS 137 TA 24
39 CRANS 123 XA 21
12 CRANSAC 175 GA 31
54 CRANTENOY 68 YA 13
74 CRANVES SALES 139 YA 23
53 CRAON C 76 S 16
86 CRAON 112 W 21
02 CRAONNE C 28 NA 9
02 CRAONNELLE 28 NA 9
60 CRAPEAUMESNIL 27 JA 8
69 CRAPONNE 150 RA 25
43 CRAPONNE SUR ARZON C 149 NA 27
38 CRAS 152 UA 27
46 CRAS 174 DA 30
01 CRAS SUR REYSSOUZE 137 TA 23
67 CRASTATT 49 DB 12
32 CRASTES 187 Z 34
27 CRASVILLE 38 BA 10
50 CRASVILLE 33 Q 8
76 CRASVILLE LA MALLET 24 Z 7
76 CRASVILLE LA ROCQUEFORT 24 AA 7
83 CRAU, LA C 203 XA 37
90 CRAVANCHE 89 AB 17
17 CRAVANS 141 T 26
45 CRAVANT 80 DA 16
89 CRAVANT 84 NA 17
37 CRAVANT LES COTEAUX 97 Y 19
32 CRAVENCERES 185 W 34
78 CRAVENT 38 DA 11
46 CRAYSSAC 173 CA 31
59 CRAYWICK 8 GA 2
17 CRAZANNES 127 T 25
72 CRE 96 V 17
50 CREANCES 34 P 10
21 CREANCEY 104 RA 19
21 CRECEY SUR TILLE 86 TA 17
79 CRECHE 128 V 22
71 CRECHES SUR SAONE 136 RA 23
65 CRECHETS 217 Z 37
03 CRECHY 133 LA 23
02 CRECY AU MONT 28 LA 9
28 CRECY COUVE 60 CA 12

80 CRECY EN PONTHIEU C 16 EA 5
77 CRECY LA CHAPELLE C 41 JA 11
02 CRECY SUR SERRE C 28 MA 8
56 CREDIN 74 K 15
46 CREGOLS 174 EA 31
77 CREGY LES MEAUX 41 JA 11
57 CREHANGE 47 ZA 11
22 CREHEN 55 M 13
60 CREIL C 40 HA 10
34 CREISSAN 213 JA 36
12 CREISSELS 191 KA 33
62 CREMAREST 7 EA 3
42 CREMEAUX 135 NA 24
80 CREMERY 27 JA 7
38 CREMIEU C 151 UA 25
74 CREMPIGNY BONNEGUETE 138 WA 24
46 CREMPS 174 DA 31
39 CRENANS 122 WA 22
10 CRENEY PRES TROYES 64 OA 14
53 CRENNES SUR FRAUBEE 58 V 13
33 CREON C 156 U 29
40 CREON D'ARMAGNAC 185 W 33
71 CREOT 120 RA 20
21 CREPAND 85 PA 17
54 CREPEY 67 XA 13
26 CREPOL 165 TA 28
14 CREPON 35 U 9
02 CREPY 28 MA 8
62 CREPY 16 GA 4
60 CREPY EN VALOIS C 41 JA 10
62 CREQUY 16 FA 4
34 CRES, LE 194 OA 35
70 CRESANCEY 106 VA 18
10 CRESANTIGNES 64 OA 15
50 CRESNAYS, LES 56 R 12
30 CRESPIAN 193 OA 33
78 CRESPIERES 39 FA 11
12 CRESPIN 175 GA 32
59 CRESPIN 18 MA 4
81 CRESPIN 190 GA 33
81 CRESPINET 190 GA 33
10 CRESPY LE NEUF 65 RA 13
16 CRESSAC ST GENIS 143 W 27
03 CRESSANGES 134 KA 22
23 CRESSAT 132 FA 23
17 CRESSE 128 V 24
12 CRESSE, LA 176 KA 32
46 CRESSENSAC 159 DA 28
14 CRESSERONS 36 V 9
14 CRESSEVEUILLE 36 W 10
39 CRESSIA 122 UA 22
01 CRESSIN ROCHEFORT 152 WA 25
60 CRESSONSACQ 26 HA 9
76 CRESSY 24 BA 8
80 CRESSY OMENCOURT 27 JA 8
71 CRESSY SUR SOMME 119 NA 21
26 CREST C 165 SA 30
63 CREST, LE 148 KA 25
73 CREST VOLAND 139 ZA 25
63 CRESTE 148 KA 26
84 CRESTET 179 TA 32
07 CRESTET, LE 164 RA 28
27 CRESTOT 38 AA 10
94 CRETEIL P 40 HA 12
50 CRETTEVILLE 34 Q 9
14 CREULLY C 35 U 9
80 CREUSE 26 GA 7
70 CREUSE, LA 88 YA 17
71 CREUSOT, LE C 120 QA 20
57 CREUTZWALD 47 AB 10
03 CREUZIER LE NEUF 133 LA 23
03 CREUZIER LE VIEUX 133 LA 23
70 CREVANS ET LA CHAPELLE LES GRANGES 89 ZA 17
36 CREVANT 116 FA 22
63 CREVANT LAVEINE 133 LA 24
54 CREVECHAMPS 68 YA 13
14 CREVECOEUR EN AUGE 36 W 10
77 CREVECOEUR EN BRIE 41 JA 12
60 CREVECOEUR LE GRAND C 26 FA 8
60 CREVECOEUR LE PETIT 26 HA 8
59 CREVECOEUR SUR L'ESCAUT 18 LA 6
70 CREVENEY 88 YA 17
54 CREVIC 46 ZA 12
35 CREVIN 75 P 15
05 CREVOUX 182 ZA 31
38 CREYS MEPIEU 152 VA 25
24 CREYSSAC 143 Z 27
24 CREYSSE 157 Z 29
46 CREYSSE 159 DA 29
07 CREYSSEILLES 164 OA 30
24 CREYSSENSAC ET PISSOT 158 Z 28
18 CREZANCAY SUR CHER 116 GA 20
02 CREZANCY 42 MA 11
18 CREZANCY EN SANCERRE 101 IA 18
79 CREZIERES 128 V 24
54 CREZILLES 67 WA 13
14 CRICQUEBOEUF 23 X 9
14 CRICQUEVILLE EN AUGE 36 W 10
14 CRICQUEVILLE EN BESSIN 35 S 9
76 CRIEL SUR MER 15 CA 6
60 CRILLON 25 FA 8
84 CRILLON LE BRAVE 180 TA 32
21 CRIMOLOIS 105 TA 18
54 CRION 46 ZA 12
76 CRIQUE, LA 24 BA 8
76 CRIQUEBEUF EN CAUX 23 X 7
27 CRIQUEBEUF LA CAMPAGNE 38 BA 10
27 CRIQUEBEUF SUR SEINE 24 BA 9
76 CRIQUETOT L'ESNEVAL C 23 X 8
76 CRIQUETOT LE MAUCONDUIT 23 Z 7
76 CRIQUETOT SUR LONGUEVILLE 24 BA 7
76 CRIQUETOT SUR OUVILLE 24 AA 8
76 CRIQUIERS 25 EA 8
77 CRISENOY 62 IA 13
60 CRISOLLES 27 KA 8
37 CRISSAY SUR MANSE 97 Y 19
72 CRISSE 78 W 14
39 CRISSEY 106 UA 19
71 CRISSEY 121 SA 21
2A CRISTINACCE 227 JB 41
14 CRISTOT 35 T 10
16 CRITEUIL LA MAGDELEINE 142 V 26
76 CRITOT 24 CA 8
2B CROCE 228 MB 40
59 CROCHTE 8 HA 2
2B CROCICCHIA 228 MB 40
23 CROCQ C 132 HA 25
60 CROCQ, LE 26 GA 8
14 CROCY 36 W 11
67 CROETTWILLER 50 GB 11
33 CROIGNON 156 V 29
43 CROISANCES 162 MA 29
62 CROISETTE 16 GA 5
44 CROISIC, LE C 92 L 18
27 CROISILLE, LA 38 BA 11
87 CROISILLE SUR BRIANCE, LA 145 DA 26
14 CROISILLES 35 U 11

28 CROISILLES 60 DA 12
61 CROISILLES 37 X 12
62 CROISILLES C 17 JA 5
54 CROISMARE 68 ZA 12
14 CROISSANVILLE 36 W 10
77 CROISSY BEAUBOURG 40 IA 12
60 CROISSY SUR CELLE 26 GA 8
78 CROISSY SUR SEINE 39 GA 11
56 CROISTY, LE 73 H 15
18 CROISY 117 JA 20
76 CROISY SUR ANDELLE 25 CA 9
27 CROISY SUR EURE 38 CA 11
59 CROIX 9 KA 3
90 CROIX 108 BB 18
08 CROIX AUX BOIS, LA 27 KA 9
88 CROIX AUX MINES, LA 69 CB 14
50 CROIX AVRANCHIN, LA 56 O 13
47 CROIX BLANCHE, LA 172 Z 32
59 CROIX CALUYAU 18 MA 6
17 CROIX CHAPEAU 127 S 24
17 CROIX COMTESSE, LA 128 U 24
73 CROIX DE LA ROCHETTE, LA 153 XA 26
28 CROIX DU PERCHE, LA 60 BA 14
77 CROIX EN BRIE, LA 63 KA 13
51 CROIX EN CHAMPAGNE, LA 43 RA 10
62 CROIX EN TERNOIS 16 GA 5
37 CROIX EN TOURAINE, LA 98 AA 18
02 CROIX FONSOMMES 18 LA 7
56 CROIX HELLEAN, LA 74 L 15
76 CROIX MARE 24 AA 8
80 CROIX MOLIGNEAUX 27 KA 7
27 CROIX ST LEUFROY, LA 38 CA 10
87 CROIX SUR GARTEMPE, LA 130 BA 23
02 CROIX SUR OURCQ, LA 41 LA 10
06 CROIX SUR ROUDOULE, LA 198 BB 33
83 CROIX VALMER, LA 204 ZA 36
56 CROIXANVEC 73 J 15
76 CROIXDALLE 25 CA 7
53 CROIXILLE, LA 76 R 14
80 CROIXRAULT 26 FA 7
42 CROIZET SUR GAND 135 PA 24
38 CROLLES 153 WA 27
50 CROLLON 56 Q 13
87 CROMAC 131 CA 23
70 CROMARY 107 XA 18
71 CRONAT 119 NA 21
43 CRONCE 162 LA 28
53 CROPTE, LA 77 U 15
76 CROPUS 24 BA 7
30 CROS 192 NA 33
63 CROS 147 IA 26
34 CROS, LE 172 LA 34
07 CROS DE GEORAND 164 OA 29
15 CROS DE MONTVERT 160 GA 28
15 CROS DE RONESQUE 161 IA 29
25 CROSEY LE GRAND 107 ZA 18
25 CROSEY LE PETIT 107 ZA 18
72 CROSMIERES 78 W 16
91 CROSNE 40 HA 12
44 CROSSAC 93 N 18
18 CROSSES 117 IA 20
27 CROSVILLE LA VIEILLE 38 AA 10
50 CROSVILLE SUR DOUVE 33 Q 9
76 CROSVILLE SUR SCIE 24 BA 7
37 CROTELLES 79 AA 17
39 CROTENAY 122 WA 21
27 CROTH 38 CA 11
80 CROTOY, LE 15 DA 5
05 CROTS 182 ZA 31
45 CROTTES EN PITHIVERAIS 61 FA 15
01 CROTTET 137 SA 23
35 CROUAIS, LE 75 N 14
14 CROUAY 35 T 10
14 CROUPTE, LA 37 X 11
64 CROUSEILLES 208 W 35
86 CROUTELLE 113 X 22
10 CROUTES, LES 84 NA 15
60 CROUTOY 27 KA 9
61 CROUTTES 36 X 11
02 CROUTTES SUR MARNE 41 LA 11
02 CROUY 28 LA 9
60 CROUY EN THELLE 40 HA 10
80 CROUY ST PIERRE 16 FA 6
41 CROUY SUR COSSON 80 DA 17
77 CROUY SUR OURCQ 41 KA 10
25 CROUZET, LE 123 XA 21
25 CROUZET MIGETTE 123 XA 20
63 CROUZILLE, LA 133 IA 23
37 CROUZILLES 97 Y 19
23 CROZANT 131 DA 22
23 CROZE 146 GA 25
26 CROZES HERMITAGE 165 SA 28
01 CROZET 139 XA 23
42 CROZET, LE 135 NA 23
39 CROZETS, LES 122 WA 22
29 CROZON C 51 C 14
36 CROZON SUR VAUVRE 115 EA 22
07 CRUAS 179 RA 30
28 CRUCEY VILLAGES 60 BA 12
41 CRUCHERAY 80 BA 16
12 CRUEJOULS 176 JA 31
73 CRUET 153 XA 26
21 CRUGEY 104 RA 19
51 CRUGNY 42 NA 10
56 CRUGUEL 74 L 16
04 CRUIS 197 WA 33
61 CRULAI 37 Z 12
26 CRUPIES 180 TA 30
02 CRUPILLY 19 NA 7
11 CRUSCADES 223 IA 37
74 CRUSEILLES C 139 XA 24
54 CRUSNES 32 WA 9
30 CRUVIERS LASCOURS 193 PA 33
58 CRUX LA VILLE 102 MA 19
71 CRUZILLE 120 RA 22
01 CRUZILLES LES MEPILLAT 137 SA 23
34 CRUZY 213 JA 36
89 CRUZY LE CHATEL C 85 PA 16
89 CRY 85 PA 16
43 CUBELLES 162 MA 28
48 CUBIERES 177 NA 31
11 CUBIERES SUR CINOBLE 221 HA 38
48 CUBIERETTES 177 NA 31
24 CUBJAC 144 AA 27
19 CUBLAC 159 CA 28
69 CUBLIZE 136 QA 24
33 CUBNEZAIS 156 U 28
25 CUBRIAL 107 ZA 17
25 CUBRY 107 ZA 17
70 CUBRY LES FAVERNEY 88 XA 16
33 CUBZAC LES PONTS 156 U 29
77 CUCHARMOY 63 KA 13
51 CUCHERY 42 NA 10
62 CUCQ 15 DA 4
11 CUCUGNAN 223 IA 38
84 CUCURON 196 UA 34
33 CUDOS 170 V 31
89 CUDOT 83 KA 15

06 CUEBRIS 199 BB 33
32 CUELAS 208 Y 36
83 CUERS C 203 XA 36
02 CUFFIES 28 LA 9
18 CUFFY 118 KA 20
85 CUGAND 110 Q 19
13 CUGES LES PINS 202 WA 36
31 CUGNAUX 210 CA 35
70 CUGNEY 106 WA 18
02 CUGNY 27 KA 9
35 CUGUEN 55 P 13
31 CUGURON 217 Y 37
86 CUHON 113 X 21
60 CUIGNIERES 26 HA 9
60 CUIGY EN BRAY 25 EA 9
53 CUILLE 76 R 15
62 CUINCHY 8 IA 4
59 CUINCY 17 KA 5
31 CUING, LE 217 Z 37
42 CUINZIER 135 PA 24
02 CUIRIEUX 28 NA 8
02 CUIRY HOUSSE 41 MA 9
02 CUIRY LES CHAUDARDES 28 NA 9
02 CUIRY LES IVIERS 29 OA 7
51 CUIS 42 OA 11
60 CUISE LA MOTTE 27 JA 9
71 CUISEAUX C 122 UA 22
21 CUISEREY 105 UA 18
71 CUISERY C 121 SA 22
39 CUISIA 122 UA 22
61 CUISSAI 58 W 13
02 CUISSY ET GENY 28 NA 9
55 CUISY 44 TA 10
77 CUISY 40 IA 11
02 CUISY EN ALMONT 27 LA 9
18 CULAN 116 HA 22
21 CULETRE 104 QA 19
14 CULEY LE PATRY 35 U 11
63 CULHAT 134 LA 25
38 CULIN 151 TA 26
71 CULLES LES ROCHES 120 RA 21
14 CULLY 35 U 10
52 CULMONT 87 UA 16
01 CULOZ 138 WA 25
70 CULT 106 WA 18
48 CULTURES 177 LA 31
51 CUMIERES 42 OA 10
55 CUMIERES LE MORT HOMME 44 TA 10
11 CUMIES 211 EA 36
82 CUMONT 187 AA 34
81 CUNAC 190 GA 33
58 CUNCY LES VARZY 102 MA 18
24 CUNEGES 157 Y 29
55 CUNEL 30 TA 9
90 CUNELIERES 90 BB 17
10 CUNFIN 85 RA 15
63 CUNLHAT C 148 MA 26
49 CUON 96 W 17
51 CUPERLY 43 OA 10
47 CUQ 187 Z 33
81 CUQ 211 FA 35
81 CUQ TOULZA C 211 FA 35
64 CUQUERON 207 U 36
16 CURAC 143 W 27
12 CURAN 176 JA 32
04 CURBANS 181 XA 31
71 CURBIGNY 136 PA 23
86 CURCAY SUR DIVE 96 W 20
80 CURCHY 27 JA 7
01 CURCIAT DONGALON 121 TA 22
14 CURCY SUR ORNE 35 U 11
71 CURDIN 119 OA 21
04 CUREL 180 VA 32
52 CUREL 66 TA 13
19 CUREMONTE 159 EA 29
72 CURES 78 W 15
59 CURGIES 18 MA 5
71 CURGY 120 QA 20
73 CURIENNE 153 XA 26
12 CURIERES 176 JA 30
69 CURIS AU MONT D'OR 136 RA 25
21 CURLEY 105 SA 19
80 CURLU 17 JA 6
52 CURMONT 66 SA 14
26 CURNIER 180 TA 31
33 CURSAN 156 V 29
01 CURTAFOND 137 TA 23
71 CURTIL SOUS BUFFIERES 136 QA 22
71 CURTIL SOUS BURNAND 120 RA 21
21 CURTIL ST SEINE 105 SA 18
21 CURTIL VERGY 105 SA 19
81 CURVALLE 190 HA 33
86 CURZAY SUR VONNE 112 W 22
85 CURZON 125 Q 22
25 CUSANCE 107 ZA 18
25 CUSE ET ADRISANS 107 ZA 18
52 CUSEY 87 UA 17
15 CUSSAC 161 JA 29
87 CUSSAC 144 AA 25
33 CUSSAC FORT MEDOC 155 T 28
43 CUSSAC SUR LOIRE 163 NA 29
10 CUSSANGY 84 OA 15
37 CUSSAY 114 AA 20
03 CUSSET C 133 MA 24
21 CUSSEY LES FORGES 86 TA 17
25 CUSSEY SUR L'OGNON 107 XA 18
25 CUSSEY SUR LISON 107 XA 19
14 CUSSY 35 T 9
71 CUSSY EN MORVAN 103 PA 19
21 CUSSY LA COLONNE 104 RA 19
21 CUSSY LE CHATEL 104 RA 19
89 CUSSY LES FORGES 103 OA 18
54 CUSTINES 46 XA 12
74 CUSY 153 XA 25
02 CUTRY 27 KA 9
54 CUTRY 31 WA 9
60 CUTS 27 KA 8
57 CUTTING 47 AB 11
2A CUTTOLI CORTICCHIATO 227 KB 42
39 CUTTURA 122 WA 22
74 CUVAT 139 XA 24
70 CUVE 88 YA 16
60 CUVERGNON 41 JA 10
14 CUVERVILLE 36 V 10
27 CUVERVILLE 38 CA 9
76 CUVERVILLE 23 X 8
76 CUVERVILLE SUR YERES 15 CA 6
50 CUVES 56 R 12
52 CUVES 66 UA 15
39 CUVIER 123 XA 20
59 CUVILLERS 18 LA 5
60 CUVILLY 27 IA 8
57 CUVRY 46 YA 11
11 CUXAC CABARDES 212 GA 36
11 CUXAC D'AUDE 213 KA 36
60 CUY 27 JA 8
89 CUY 63 LA 14
76 CUY ST FIACRE 25 EA 8

46 CUZAC 175 GA 30
46 CUZANCE 159 DA 29
01 CUZIEU 138 VA 25
42 CUZIEU 149 PA 26
36 CUZION 115 DA 22
47 CUZORN 173 AA 31
71 CUZY 119 OA 21
02 CYS LA COMMUNE 28 MA 9
59 CYSOING C 9 KA 4

D

91 D'HUISON LONGUEVILLE 62 GA 13
57 DABO 69 CB 12
67 DACHSTEIN 70 EB 13
45 DADONVILLE 62 GA 14
24 DAGLAN 158 BA 30
01 DAGNEUX 137 TA 25
77 DAGNY 41 KA 12
02 DAGNY LAMBERCY 29 OA 7
55 DAGONVILLE 44 UA 12
49 DAGUENIERE, LA 96 U 18
67 DAHLENHEIM 70 EB 13
33 DAIGNAC 156 V 29
08 DAIGNY 30 SA 8
52 DAILLANCOURT 66 SA 14
52 DAILLECOURT 67 VA 15
62 DAINVILLE C 17 IA 5
55 DAINVILLE BERTHELEVILLE 67 VA 13
21 DAIX 105 SA 18
57 DALEM 47 ZA 10
57 DALHAIN 47 ZA 11
67 DALHUNDEN 50 GB 12
63 DALLET 148 KA 25
02 DALLON 28 LA 7
09 DALOU 219 DA 37
57 DALSTEIN 47 ZA 9
06 DALUIS 198 AB 33
88 DAMAS AUX BOIS 68 ZA 13
88 DAMAS ET BETTEGNEY 68 YA 14
47 DAMAZAN C 171 X 32
67 DAMBACH 48 EB 11
67 DAMBACH LA VILLE 70 DB 14
25 DAMBELIN 108 AB 18
25 DAMBENOIS 89 BB 17
70 DAMBENOIT LES COLOMBE 89 ZA 16
88 DAMBLAIN 67 VA 15
14 DAMBLAINVILLE 36 W 11
28 DAMBRON 61 EA 15
27 DAME MARIE 38 BA 12
61 DAME MARIE 59 Z 14
37 DAME MARIE LES BOIS 80 BA 17
54 DAMELEVIERES 68 YA 13
60 DAMERAUCOURT 25 FA 8
71 DAMEREY 121 SA 20
51 DAMERY 42 NA 10
80 DAMERY 27 IA 7
56 DAMGAN 92 L 17
81 DAMIATTE 189 FA 34
61 DAMIGNY 58 X 13
55 DAMLOUP 45 VA 10
02 DAMMARD 41 KA 10
28 DAMMARIE 60 DA 14
45 DAMMARIE EN PUISAYE 82 JA 17
77 DAMMARIE LES LYS 62 IA 13
45 DAMMARIE SUR LOING 82 JA 16
55 DAMMARIE SUR SAULX 66 TA 13
77 DAMMARTIN EN GOELE C 40 IA 10
78 DAMMARTIN EN SERVE 39 DA 11
25 DAMMARTIN LES TEMPLIERS 106 VA 18
39 DAMMARTIN MARPAIN 106 VA 19
52 DAMMARTIN SUR MEUSE 87 VA 15
77 DAMMARTIN SUR TIGEAUX 41 JA 12
59 DAMOUSIES 19 OA 5
08 DAMOUZY 29 RA 7
39 DAMPARIS 122 UA 20
10 DAMPIERRE 65 QA 13
14 DAMPIERRE 35 S 11
39 DAMPIERRE C 106 WA 19
52 DAMPIERRE 87 UA 15
51 DAMPIERRE AU TEMPLE 43 QA 11
76 DAMPIERRE EN BRAY 25 DA 8
71 DAMPIERRE EN BRESSE 121 TA 20
45 DAMPIERRE EN BURLY 82 HA 16
18 DAMPIERRE EN CROT 101 IA 18
18 DAMPIERRE EN GRACAIS 100 FA 19
21 DAMPIERRE EN MONTAGNE 104 QA 18
78 DAMPIERRE EN YVELINES 39 FA 12
21 DAMPIERRE ET FLEE 105 UA 18
51 DAMPIERRE LE CHATEAU 43 SA 11
25 DAMPIERRE LES BOIS 90 BB 17
70 DAMPIERRE LES CONFLANS 88 YA 16
58 DAMPIERRE SOUS BOUHY 83 KA 17
28 DAMPIERRE SOUS BROU 60 BA 14
76 DAMPIERRE ST NICOLAS 24 CA 7
28 DAMPIERRE SUR AVRE 38 BA 12
17 DAMPIERRE SUR BOUTONNE 128 U 24
25 DAMPIERRE SUR LE DOUBS 108 AB 17
70 DAMPIERRE SUR LINOTTE 88 YA 17
51 DAMPIERRE SUR MOIVRE 43 QA 11
70 DAMPIERRE SUR SALON C 87 VA 17
25 DAMPJOUX 89 AB 16
02 DAMPLEUX 41 KA 10
77 DAMPMART 40 IA 11
19 DAMPNIAT 159 DA 28
25 DAMPRICHARD 108 BB 19
27 DAMPS, LES 38 BA 9
27 DAMPSMESNIL 39 DA 10
70 DAMPVALLEY LES COLOMBE 88 YA 17
70 DAMPVALLEY ST PANCRAS 88 YA 16
54 DAMPVITOUX 45 WA 11
52 DAMREMONT 87 VA 15
27 DAMVILLE C 38 BA 11
55 DAMVILLERS C 31 UA 9
85 DAMVIX 127 T 23
42 DANCE 135 OA 25
61 DANCE 59 AA 14
52 DANCEVOIR 86 SA 15
76 DANCOURT 25 DA 7
80 DANCOURT POPINCOURT 27 IA 8
28 DANCY 60 DA 14
14 DANESTAL 36 W 10
86 DANGE ST ROMAIN C 113 Z 20
28 DANGEAU 60 CA 14
28 DANGERS 60 CA 13
72 DANGEUL 58 X 14
67 DANGOLSHEIM 70 DB 13
27 DANGU 39 EA 10
50 DANGY 34 R 11
02 DANIZY 28 LA 8
90 DANJOUTIN C 89 BB 17
57 DANNE ET QUATRE VENTS 49 DB 12
57 DANNELBOURG 48 CB 12
25 DANNEMARIE 108 BB 18
68 DANNEMARIE C 90 CB 17
78 DANNEMARIE 39 DA 12
25 DANNEMARIE SUR CRETE 106 WA 19
89 DANNEMOINE 84 OA 16

Dép.	Commune		Page	Carreau	
91	DANNEMOIS		62	HA	13
62	DANNES		7	DA	4
55	DANNEVOUX		30	TA	9
14	DANVOU LA FERRIERE		35	T	11
41	DANZE		79	BA	16
53	DAON		77	T	16
29	DAOULAS	C	51	D	14
80	DAOURS		26	HA	7
19	DARAZAC		160	FA	28
39	DARBONNAY		122	VA	20
07	DARBRES		178	QA	30
21	DARCEY		85	OA	17
33	DARDENAC		156	V	29
27	DARDEZ		38	BA	10
69	DARDILLY		150	RA	25
69	DAREIZE		136	OA	24
60	DARGIES		26	FA	8
80	DARGNIES		15	DA	6
42	DARGOIRE		150	RA	26
52	DARMANNES		66	TA	14
87	DARNAC		130	AA	23
76	DARNETAL	C	24	BA	9
19	DARNETS		146	GA	27
88	DARNEY	C	67	XA	15
88	DARNEY AUX CHENES		67	WA	14
88	DARNIEULLES		68	YA	14
21	DAROIS		105	SA	18
77	DARVAULT		62	IA	14
45	DARVOY		81	FA	16
25	DASLE		89	BB	17
67	DAUBENSAND		70	EB	14
27	DAUBEUF LA CAMPAGNE		38	BA	10
27	DAUBEUF PRES VATTEVILLE		38	CA	10
76	DAUBEUF SERVILLE		23	Y	8
33	DAUBEZE		156	W	30
67	DAUENDORF		48	EB	11
09	DAUMAZAN SUR ARIZE		218	CA	37
49	DAUMERAY		77	U	16
04	DAUPHIN		197	WA	33
47	DAUSSE		172	AA	31
31	DAUX		188	CA	34
63	DAUZAT SUR VODABLE		148	KA	26
63	DAVAYAT		134	KA	24
71	DAVAYE		136	RA	23
11	DAVEJEAN		223	IA	38
80	DAVENESCOURT		26	IA	8
07	DAVEZIEUX		150	RA	27
19	DAVIGNAC		146	FA	26
10	DAVREY		84	OA	15
78	DAVRON		39	FA	11
40	DAX	S	183	R	34
14	DEAUVILLE		36	W	9
30	DEAUX		193	PA	33
42	DEBATS RIVIERE D'ORPRA		149	OA	25
12	DECAZEVILLE	C	175	GA	30
59	DECHY		18	KA	5
69	DECINES CHARPIEU	C	151	SA	25
58	DECIZE	C	118	LA	20
46	DEGAGNAC		173	CA	30
72	DEGRE		78	W	15
72	DEHAULT		59	Z	14
59	DEHERIES		18	LA	6
67	DEHLINGEN		48	CB	11
88	DEINVILLERS		68	ZA	13
70	DELAIN		87	VA	17
62	DELETTES		8	GA	4
60	DELINCOURT		39	EA	10
90	DELLE	C	90	BB	17
57	DELME	C	47	ZA	11
55	DELOUZE ROSIERES		67	VA	13
60	DELUGE, LE		39	FA	9
55	DELUT		31	UA	9
25	DELUZ		107	YA	18
04	DEMANDOLX		198	ZA	34
55	DEMANGE AUX EAUX		67	UA	13
70	DEMANGEVELLE		88	XA	16
74	DEMI QUARTIER		140	AB	25
70	DEMIE, LA		88	YA	17
71	DEMIGNY		121	SA	20
14	DEMOUVILLE		36	V	10
32	DEMU		186	X	34
80	DEMUIN		26	HA	7
59	DENAIN	C	18	LA	5
81	DENAT		190	GA	34
53	DENAZE		77	S	16
49	DENEE		95	T	18
76	DENESTANVILLE		24	BA	7
03	DENEUILLE LES CHANTELLE		134	KA	23
03	DENEUILLE LES MINES		133	JA	22
54	DENEUVRE		69	AB	13
70	DENEVRE		87	VA	17
49	DENEZE SOUS DOUE		96	V	19
49	DENEZE SOUS LE LUDE		97	X	17
39	DENEZIERES		122	WA	21
64	DENGUIN		207	U	36
69	DENICE		136	RA	24
62	DENIER		17	HA	5
88	DENIPAIRE		69	BB	14
62	DENNEBROEUCQ		7	GA	4
50	DENNEVILLE		34	P	9
71	DENNEVY		120	RA	20
90	DENNEY		89	BB	17
28	DENONVILLE		61	EA	13
57	DENTING		47	ZA	10
36	DEOLS		115	EA	20
88	DERBAMONT		68	YA	14
86	DERCE		113	X	20
76	DERCHIGNY		15	CA	7
02	DERCY		28	MA	8
11	DERNACUEILLETTE		223	IA	38
80	DERNANCOURT		17	IA	6
44	DERVAL	C	93	P	17
07	DESAIGNES		164	QA	29
25	DESANDANS		89	AB	17
37	DESCARTES	C	114	Z	20
39	DESCHAUX, LE		122	UA	20
14	DESERT, LE		35	T	11
03	DESERTINES		133	IA	22
53	DESERTINES		57	S	13
73	DESERTS, LES		153	XA	26
25	DESERVILLERS		107	XA	20
43	DESGES		162	LA	28
74	DESINGY		138	WA	24
45	DESMONTS		62	HA	14
39	DESNES		122	UA	21
57	DESSELING		47	BB	12
68	DESSENHEIM		90	DB	15
39	DESSIA		138	VA	22
88	DESTORD		68	AB	14
13	DESTROUSSE, LA		202	VA	36
57	DESTRY		47	ZA	11
62	DESVRES	C	7	EA	3
21	DETAIN ET BRUANT		104	RA	19
73	DETRIER		153	XA	27
14	DETROIT, LE		36	V	11
71	DETTEY		119	PA	20
67	DETTWILLER		49	DB	12
95	DEUIL LA BARRE		40	GA	11
02	DEUILLET		28	LA	8
59	DEULEMONT		9	JA	3
03	DEUX CHAISES		133	KA	22
53	DEUX EVAILLES		77	U	14
39	DEUX FAYS, LES		122	VA	20
14	DEUX JUMEAUX		35	S	9
15	DEUX VERGES		161	KA	29
08	DEUX VILLES, LES		30	TA	8
54	DEUXVILLE		68	ZA	12
58	DEVAY		118	MA	20
25	DEVECEY		107	XA	18
07	DEVESSET		164	QA	28
65	DEVEZE		209	Z	36
16	DEVIAT		143	W	27
47	DEVILLAC		172	AA	30
08	DEVILLE		29	RA	7
76	DEVILLE LES ROUEN		24	BA	9
80	DEVISE		27	JA	7
71	DEVROUZE		121	TA	21
88	DEYCIMONT		68	AB	14
31	DEYME		210	DA	35
88	DEYVILLERS		68	ZA	14
50	DEZERT, LE		34	R	10
71	DEZIZE LES MARANGES		120	RA	20
77	DHUISY		41	KA	11
02	DHUIZEL		28	MA	9
41	DHUIZON		80	DA	17
21	DIANCEY		104	QA	19
57	DIANE CAPELLE		69	BB	12
77	DIANT		63	JA	14
54	DIARVILLE		68	XA	13
71	DICONNE		121	TA	21
89	DICY		83	KA	15
68	DIDENHEIM		90	CB	16
26	DIE	S	166	UA	30
57	DIEBLING		47	BB	10
67	DIEBOLSHEIM		70	EB	14
67	DIEDENDORF		47	BB	11
67	DIEFFENBACH AU VAL		69	DB	14
67	DIEFFENBACH LES WOERTH		49	FB	11
67	DIEFFENTHAL		70	DB	14
68	DIEFMATTEN		90	CB	16
69	DIEME		136	QA	24
67	DIEMERINGEN		48	CB	11
38	DIEMOZ		151	TA	26
21	DIENAY		86	TA	17
15	DIENNE		161	IA	28
86	DIENNE		113	Y	22
58	DIENNES AUBIGNY		119	MA	20
10	DIENVILLE		65	OA	14
76	DIEPPE	S	24	BA	7
55	DIEPPE SOUS DOUAUMONT		45	VA	10
37	DIERRE		98	AA	18
10	DIERREY ST JULIEN		64	NA	14
10	DIERREY ST PIERRE		64	NA	14
57	DIESEN		47	AB	10
68	DIETWILLER		90	DB	17
60	DIEUDONNE		40	GA	10
55	DIEUE SUR MEUSE		44	UA	10
26	DIEULEFIT	C	179	TA	31
33	DIEULIVOL		171	X	30
54	DIEULOUARD	C	45	XA	11
82	DIEUPENTALE		188	CA	34
57	DIEUZE	C	47	AB	12
62	DIEVAL		17	HA	4
57	DIFFEMBACH LES HELLIMER		47	AB	11
89	DIGES		83	LA	16
39	DIGNA		122	UA	22
16	DIGNAC		143	X	26
11	DIGNE D'AMONT, LA		221	GA	37
11	DIGNE D'AVAL, LA		221	GA	37
04	DIGNE LES BAINS	P	181	YA	32
88	DIGNONVILLE		68	ZA	14
28	DIGNY		60	BA	13
71	DIGOIN	C	119	OA	22
50	DIGOSVILLE		33	P	8
50	DIGULLEVILLE		33	O	8
21	DIJON	P	105	TA	18
45	DIMANCHEVILLE		62	HA	14
67	DIMBSTHAL		49	DB	12
59	DIMECHAUX		19	OA	5
59	DIMONT		19	OA	5
22	DINAN	S	55	N	13
35	DINARD	C	55	N	12
29	DINEAULT		72	E	14
35	DINGE		55	O	14
67	DINGSHEIM		49	EB	12
74	DINGY EN VUACHE		139	XA	24
74	DINGY ST CLAIR		139	YA	24
88	DINOZE		68	ZA	15
87	DINSAC		130	BA	23
67	DINSHEIM		70	DB	13
52	DINTEVILLE		85	RA	15
34	DIO ET VALQUIERES		191	KA	34
38	DIONAY		165	TA	28
30	DIONS		193	PA	33
36	DIORS		115	EA	20
03	DIOU		119	NA	22
36	DIOU		100	FA	19
16	DIRAC		143	X	26
29	DIRINON		51	D	13
58	DIROL		103	MA	18
89	DISSANGIS		84	OA	17
86	DISSAY		113	Y	21
72	DISSAY SOUS COURCILLON		79	Y	17
72	DISSE SOUS BALLON		59	X	14
72	DISSE SOUS LE LUDE		97	X	17
49	DISTRE		96	W	19
57	DISTROFF		32	YA	9
64	DIUSSE		207	V	35
26	DIVAJEU		165	SA	30
60	DIVES		27	JA	8
14	DIVES SUR MER		36	W	9
62	DIVION	C	17	HA	4
01	DIVONNE LES BAINS		139	XA	22
89	DIXMONT		63	LA	15
38	DIZIMIEU		151	UA	25
51	DIZY		42	OA	10
02	DIZY LE GROS		29	OA	8
40	DOAZIT		184	T	34
64	DOAZON		207	U	35
88	DOCELLES		68	AB	15
17	DOEUIL SUR LE MIGNON		128	U	23
64	DOGNEN		206	T	36
88	DOGNEVILLE		68	ZA	14
62	DOHEM		8	GA	3
02	DOHIS		29	PA	7
59	DOIGNIES		17	KA	6
80	DOINGT		17	JA	7
24	DOISSAT		158	BA	30
38	DOISSIN		152	UA	26
85	DOIX		111	T	22
42	DOIZIEUX		150	QA	27
35	DOL DE BRETAGNE	C	55	O	13
88	DOLAINCOURT		67	WA	14
10	DOLANCOURT		65	RA	14
54	DOLCOURT		67	XA	13
39	DOLE	S	106	UA	19
02	DOLIGNON		29	OA	7
68	DOLLEREN		89	BB	16
72	DOLLON		79	Z	15
89	DOLLOT		63	KA	14
47	DOLMAYRAC		172	Z	31
22	DOLO		54	M	13
38	DOLOMIEU		152	VA	26
17	DOLUS D'OLERON		126	O	24
37	DOLUS LE SEC		98	AA	19
57	DOLVING		47	BB	12
08	DOM LE MESNIL		30	RA	8
35	DOMAGNE		76	O	15
63	DOMAIZE		148	MA	25
35	DOMALAIN		76	R	15
74	DOMANCY		140	AB	24
38	DOMARIN		151	TA	26
80	DOMART EN PONTHIEU	C	16	GA	6
80	DOMART SUR LA LUCE		26	HA	7
89	DOMATS		63	KA	15
30	DOMAZAN		195	RA	33
88	DOMBASLE DEVANT DARNEY		67	XA	15
55	DOMBASLE EN ARGONNE		44	TA	10
88	DOMBASLE EN XAINTOIS		67	XA	14
54	DOMBASLE SUR MEURTHE		46	YA	12
52	DOMBLAIN		66	SA	13
39	DOMBLANS		122	VA	21
55	DOMBRAS		31	UA	9
88	DOMBROT LE SEC		67	WA	15
88	DOMBROT SUR VAIR		67	WA	14
89	DOMECY SUR CURE		103	NA	18
89	DOMECY SUR LE VAULT		84	NA	17
60	DOMELIERS		26	GA	8
38	DOMENE	C	166	WA	28
03	DOMERAT	C	133	HA	22
80	DOMESMONT		16	GA	6
30	DOMESSARGUES		193	PA	33
73	DOMESSIN		152	WA	26
54	DOMEVRE EN HAYE	C	45	XA	12
88	DOMEVRE SOUS MONTFORT		67	XA	14
88	DOMEVRE SUR AVIERE		68	ZA	14
88	DOMEVRE SUR DURBION		68	ZA	14
54	DOMEVRE SUR VEZOUZE		69	AB	13
43	DOMEYRAT		162	MA	27
23	DOMEYROT		132	GA	23
64	DOMEZAIN BERRAUTE		206	S	36
88	DOMFAING		69	AB	14
67	DOMFESSEL		48	CB	11
60	DOMFRONT		26	IA	8
61	DOMFRONT	C	57	T	12
72	DOMFRONT EN CHAMPAGNE		78	W	15
54	DOMGERMAIN		67	WA	12
35	DOMINELAIS, LA		75	P	16
80	DOMINOIS		16	EA	5
50	DOMJEAN		35	S	11
54	DOMJEVIN		68	AB	13
88	DOMJULIEN		67	XA	14
80	DOMLEGER LONGVILLERS		16	FA	6
35	DOMLOUP		76	P	15
54	DOMMARIE EULMONT		67	XA	13
52	DOMMARIEN		87	UA	17
54	DOMMARTEMONT		46	YA	12
01	DOMMARTIN		137	SA	23
25	DOMMARTIN		123	YA	20
58	DOMMARTIN		103	NA	19
69	DOMMARTIN		136	RA	25
80	DOMMARTIN		26	HA	7
88	DOMMARTIN AUX BOIS		68	YA	14
51	DOMMARTIN DAMPIERRE		43	SA	10
54	DOMMARTIN LA CHAUSSEE		45	WA	11
55	DOMMARTIN LA MONTAGNE		45	VA	11
10	DOMMARTIN LE COQ		65	QA	13
52	DOMMARTIN LE FRANC		66	SA	13
52	DOMMARTIN LE ST PERE		66	SA	13
71	DOMMARTIN LES CUISEAUX		121	UA	22
88	DOMMARTIN LES REMIREMONT		89	AB	15
54	DOMMARTIN LES TOUL		45	WA	12
88	DOMMARTIN LES VALLOIS		67	XA	14
51	DOMMARTIN LETTREE		43	PA	12
54	DOMMARTIN SOUS AMANCE		46	YA	12
51	DOMMARTIN SOUS HANS		43	RA	10
88	DOMMARTIN SUR VRAINE		67	WA	14
51	DOMMARTIN VARIMONT		43	RA	11
55	DOMMARY BARONCOURT		31	WA	9
24	DOMME	C	159	CA	29
08	DOMMERY		29	QA	8
02	DOMMIERS		27	KA	9
57	DOMNON LES DIEUZE		47	AB	11
95	DOMONT	C	40	GA	11
88	DOMPAIRE	C	68	YA	14
55	DOMPCEVRIN		44	UA	11
60	DOMPIERRE		26	HA	8
61	DOMPIERRE		57	U	12
88	DOMPIERRE		68	ZA	14
55	DOMPIERRE AUX BOIS		45	VA	11
80	DOMPIERRE BECQUINCOURT		17	JA	7
35	DOMPIERRE DU CHEMIN		76	R	14
21	DOMPIERRE EN MORVAN		104	PA	18
87	DOMPIERRE LES EGLISES		131	CA	23
71	DOMPIERRE LES ORMES		136	QA	22
25	DOMPIERRE LES TILLEULS		123	YA	20
71	DOMPIERRE SOUS SANVIGNES		120	PA	21
80	DOMPIERRE SUR AUTHIE		16	FA	5
03	DOMPIERRE SUR BESBRE	C	119	MA	22
01	DOMPIERRE SUR CHALARONNE		137	SA	23
17	DOMPIERRE SUR CHARENTE		142	U	25
59	DOMPIERRE SUR HELPE		19	NA	6
58	DOMPIERRE SUR HERY		102	MA	18
17	DOMPIERRE SUR MER		126	R	23
39	DOMPIERRE SUR MONT		122	VA	22
58	DOMPIERRE SUR NIEVRE		102	LA	19
01	DOMPIERRE SUR VEYLE		137	TA	24
85	DOMPIERRE SUR YON		110	O	21
07	DOMPNAC		178	OA	30
25	DOMPREL		107	ZA	19
51	DOMPREMY		43	RA	12
54	DOMPRIX		31	WA	9
87	DOMPS		145	EA	26
88	DOMPTAIL		68	AB	13
54	DOMPTAIL EN L'AIR		68	YA	13
02	DOMPTIN		41	LA	11
80	DOMQUEUR		16	FA	6
55	DOMREMY LA CANNE		31	VA	9
88	DOMREMY LA PUCELLE		67	VA	13
52	DOMREMY LANDEVILLE		66	TA	14
01	DOMSURE		121	UA	22
88	DOMVALLIER		67	XA	14
80	DOMVAST		16	FA	5
59	DON		9	JA	4
11	DONAZAC		221	GA	37
08	DONCHERY		30	SA	8
88	DONCIERES		68	AB	13
55	DONCOURT AUX TEMPLIERS		45	WA	10
54	DONCOURT LES CONFLANS		45	XA	10
54	DONCOURT LES LONGUYON		31	WA	9
52	DONCOURT SUR MEUSE		67	VA	15
47	DONDAS		172	AA	32
44	DONGES		93	N	18
52	DONJEUX		66	TA	14
57	DONJEUX		46	YA	11
03	DONJON, LE	C	135	NA	23
14	DONNAY		35	U	11
81	DONNAZAC		189	FA	33
57	DONNELAY		47	AB	12
28	DONNEMAIN ST MAMES		60	CA	15
77	DONNEMARIE DONTILLY	C	63	KA	13
10	DONNEMENT		65	QA	13
67	DONNENHEIM		49	EB	12
45	DONNERY		81	FA	16
31	DONNEVILLE		210	DA	35
33	DONNEZAC		142	U	27
23	DONTREIX		133	IA	24
51	DONTRIEN		43	OA	10
50	DONVILLE LES BAINS		56	P	11
33	DONZAC		170	V	30
82	DONZAC		172	AA	32
40	DONZACQ		184	T	34
23	DONZEIL, LE		132	FA	24
19	DONZENAC	C	159	DA	27
26	DONZERE		179	RA	31
58	DONZY	C	102	KA	18
71	DONZY LE NATIONAL		120	QA	22
71	DONZY LE PERTUIS		120	RA	22
63	DORANGES		148	MA	27
90	DORANS		90	BB	17
63	DORAT		134	MA	25
87	DORAT, LE	C	130	BA	23
61	DORCEAU		59	AA	13
45	DORDIVES		62	IA	15
63	DORE L'EGLISE		149	NA	27
53	DOREE, LA		57	S	13
02	DORENGT		18	NA	6
67	DORLISHEIM		70	DB	13
51	DORMANS	C	42	MA	10
77	DORMELLES		63	JA	14
24	DORNAC, LA		159	CA	28
07	DORNAS		164	OA	29
58	DORNECY		103	MA	18
58	DORNES	C	118	LA	21
57	DORNOT		45	XA	10
66	DORRES		222	FA	40
01	DORTAN		138	VA	23
10	DOSCHES		65	PA	14
10	DOSNON		65	PA	12
67	DOSSENHEIM KOCHERSBERG		49	EB	12
67	DOSSENHEIM SUR ZINSEL		49	DB	12
36	DOUADIC		114	BA	21
59	DOUAI	S	17	KA	5
27	DOUAINS		38	CA	11
29	DOUARNENEZ	C	71	D	15
55	DOUAUMONT		44	UA	10
25	DOUBS		123	YA	20
72	DOUCELLES		58	X	14
24	DOUCHAPT		143	Y	27
02	DOUCHY		27	KA	7
45	DOUCHY		83	KA	15
62	DOUCHY LES AYETTE		17	IA	5
59	DOUCHY LES MINES		18	LA	5
39	DOUCIER		122	WA	21
73	DOUCY EN BAUGES		153	YA	25
62	DOUDEAUVILLE		7	EA	4
76	DOUDEAUVILLE		25	EA	8
27	DOUDEAUVILLE EN VEXIN		25	DA	9
80	DOUDELAINVILLE		15	EA	6
76	DOUDEVILLE	C	24	AA	7
47	DOUDRAC		172	Z	30
77	DOUE		41	KA	11
49	DOUE LA FONTAINE	C	96	V	19
46	DOUELLE		173	CA	31
17	DOUHET, LE		128	U	25
72	DOUILLET		58	W	14
80	DOUILLY		27	KA	7
52	DOULAINCOURT SAUCOURT	C	66	TA	14
55	DOULCON		30	TA	9
52	DOULEVANT LE CHATEAU	C	66	SA	13
52	DOULEVANT LE PETIT		66	SA	13
33	DOULEZON		157	W	29
59	DOULIEU, LE		8	IA	3
80	DOULLENS	C	16	HA	6
08	DOUMELY BEGNY		29	PA	8
64	DOUMY		207	U	35
88	DOUNOUX		68	ZA	15
30	DOURBIES		192	LA	33
35	DOURDAIN		76	Q	14
91	DOURDAN	C	61	FA	13
62	DOURGES		17	JA	4
81	DOURGNE	C	212	GA	35
62	DOURIEZ		16	EA	5
59	DOURLERS		19	OA	5
81	DOURN, LE		190	HA	33
87	DOURNAZAC		144	AA	26
39	DOURNON		123	XA	20
65	DOURS		208	X	36
74	DOUSSARD		139	YA	25
86	DOUSSAY		113	X	20
74	DOUVAINE	C	139	YA	23
24	DOUVILLE		157	Z	28
14	DOUVILLE EN AUGE		36	W	10
27	DOUVILLE SUR ANDELLE		24	CA	9
76	DOUVREND		24	CA	7
01	DOUVRES		138	UA	24
14	DOUVRES LA DELIVRANDE	C	36	U	9
62	DOUVRIN	C	9	JA	4
08	DOUX		29	OA	8
79	DOUX		112	W	21
28	DOUY		80	CA	15
77	DOUY LA RAMEE		41	JA	10
47	DOUZAINS		172	Z	30
16	DOUZAT		143	W	25
24	DOUZE, LA		158	AA	28
11	DOUZENS		223	IA	37
24	DOUZILLAC		157	Y	28
08	DOUZY		30	SA	8
50	DOVILLE		34	P	9
39	DOYE		123	XA	21
03	DOYET		133	JA	23
14	DOZULE	C	36	W	10
69	DRACE		136	RA	23
37	DRACHE		98	Z	19
67	DRACHENBRONN BIRLENBACH		49	FB	11
89	DRACY		83	LA	16
71	DRACY LE FORT		120	RA	21
71	DRACY LES COUCHES		120	QA	20
71	DRACY ST LOUP		120	PA	20
50	DRAGEY RONTHON		56	O	12
83	DRAGUIGNAN	S	198	ZA	35
49	DRAIN		94	R	18
04	DRAIX		182	YA	32
08	DRAIZE		29	PA	8
21	DRAMBON		105	UA	18
39	DRAMELAY		122	VA	22
93	DRANCY	C	40	HA	11
06	DRAP		200	DB	34
02	DRAVEGNY		42	MA	10
91	DRAVEIL	C	62	HA	12
21	DREE		104	RA	18
44	DREFFEAC		93	N	17
31	DREMIL LAFAGE		210	DA	35
29	DRENNEC, LE		51	D	13
80	DREUIL LES AMIENS		26	GA	7
09	DREUILHE		219	EA	38
28	DREUX	S	38	CA	12
18	DREVANT		117	HA	21
08	DRICOURT		29	QA	9
80	DRIENCOURT		17	KA	6
59	DRINCHAM		8	GA	2
62	DROCOURT		17	JA	5
78	DROCOURT		39	EA	10
27	DROISY		38	BA	12
74	DROISY		138	WA	24
03	DROITURIER		135	NA	23
02	DROIZY		28	LA	9
01	DROM		138	UA	23
80	DROMESNIL		25	EA	7
76	DROSAY		24	Z	7
51	DROSNAY		65	RA	13
41	DROUE	C	80	BA	15
28	DROUE SUR DROUETTE		61	EA	12
35	DROUGES		76	Q	16
51	DROUILLY		43	QA	12
10	DROUPT ST BASLE		64	OA	13
10	DROUPT STE MARIE		64	OA	13
54	DROUVILLE		46	ZA	12
62	DROUVIN LE MARAIS		17	IA	4
87	DROUX		130	BA	23
52	DROYES		65	RA	13
14	DRUBEC		36	X	10
80	DRUCAT		16	EA	6
27	DRUCOURT		37	Y	10
31	DRUDAS		187	BA	34
12	DRUELLE		175	HA	31
15	DRUGEAC		160	HA	28
01	DRUILLAT		137	UA	24
12	DRULHE		175	GA	31
67	DRULINGEN	C	48	CB	11
73	DRUMETTAZ CLARAFOND	C	153	XA	26
67	DRUSENHEIM		50	FB	12
58	DRUY PARIGNY		118	LA	20
37	DRUYE		97	Z	18
89	DRUYES LES BELLES FONTAINES		83	LA	17
45	DRY		81	EA	16
22	DUAULT		53	H	14
50	DUCEY	C	56	Q	12
76	DUCLAIR	C	24	AA	9
14	DUCY STE MARGUERITE		35	T	10
69	DUERNE		150	QA	25
21	DUESME		85	RA	17
32	DUFFORT		208	Y	36
93	DUGNY		40	HA	11
55	DUGNY SUR MEUSE		44	UA	10
40	DUHORT BACHEN		185	V	34
11	DUILHAC SOUS PEYREPERTUSE		221	HA	38
74	DUINGT		139	YA	25
62	DUISANS		17	IA	5
73	DULLIN		152	WA	26
40	DUMES		184	U	34
09	DUN		219	EA	37
23	DUN LE PALESTEL	C	131	EA	23
36	DUN LE POELIER		99	EA	19
58	DUN LES PLACES		103	OA	18
18	DUN SUR AURON	C	117	IA	20
58	DUN SUR GRANDRY		103	NA	19
55	DUN SUR MEUSE	C	30	TA	9
72	DUNEAU		79	Y	15
82	DUNES		187	AA	33
36	DUNET		115	CA	22
25	DUNG		89	AB	17
43	DUNIERES		164	PA	28
07	DUNIERES SUR EYRIEUX		164	RA	29
59	DUNKERQUE	S	8	GA	2
67	DUNTZENHEIM		49	EB	12
67	DUPPIGHEIM		70	EB	13
32	DURAN		187	Z	34
47	DURANCE		171	X	32
06	DURANUS		199	CB	33
27	DURANVILLE		37	Z	10
47	DURAS	C	171	X	30
46	DURAVEL		173	BA	31
32	DURBAN		209	Z	35
11	DURBAN CORBIERES	C	223	JA	37
09	DURBAN SUR ARIZE		218	CA	37
46	DURBANS		174	EA	30
61	DURCET		57	U	12
03	DURDAT LAREQUILLE		133	IA	23
72	DUREIL		78	V	16
12	DURENQUE		175	IA	32
09	DURFORT		210	DA	36
81	DURFORT		211	FA	35
30	DURFORT ET ST MARTIN DE SOSSENAC		193	OA	33
82	DURFORT LACAPELETTE		173	BA	32
68	DURLINSDORF		90	CB	17
68	DURMENACH		90	DB	17
63	DURMIGNAT		133	JA	23
25	DURNES		107	YA	19
67	DURNINGEN		49	EB	12
67	DURRENBACH		49	FB	11
68	DURRENENTZEN		70	DB	15
67	DURSTEL		48	CB	11
49	DURTAL	C	77	V	17
63	DURTOL		148	KA	25
02	DURY		27	KA	7
62	DURY		17	JA	5
80	DURY		26	GA	7
24	DUSSAC		144	BA	27
67	DUTTLENHEIM		70	EB	13
60	DUVY		40	JA	10
55	DUZEY		31	VA	9
89	DYE		84	NA	16
71	DYO		135	PA	22

E

Dép.	Commune		Page	Carreau	
35	EANCE		76	R	16
95	EAUBONNE	C	40	GA	11
80	EAUCOURT SUR SOMME		16	FA	6
31	EAUNES		210	CA	36
64	EAUX BONNES		215	U	38
10	EAUX PUISEAUX		64	NA	15
32	EAUZE	C	186	X	34
21	EBATY		120	RA	20
59	EBBLINGHEM		8	HA	3
67	EBERBACH SELTZ		50	GB	11
67	EBERSHEIM		70	EB	14
67	EBERSMUNSTER		70	EB	14
57	EBERSVILLER		32	YA	9
57	EBLANGE		47	ZA	10
02	EBOULEAU		28	NA	8
16	EBREON		129	W	24
03	EBREUIL	C	134	KA	24

08 ECAILLE, L' 29 PA 9
59 ECAILLON 18 KA 5
76 ECALLES ALIX 24 AA 8
27 ECAQUELON 24 Z 9
27 ECARDENVILLE LA CAMPAGNE 37 AA 10
27 ECARDENVILLE SUR EURE 38 CA 10
50 ECAUSSEVILLE 33 Q 9
27 ECAUVILLE 38 BA 10
2A ECCICA SUARELLA 227 KB 42
59 ECCLES 19 OA 5
69 ECHALAS 150 RA 26
16 ECHALLAT 143 W 25
01 ECHALLON 138 WA 23
21 ECHALOT 86 SA 17
61 ECHALOU 57 U 12
63 ECHANDELYS 148 MA 26
21 ECHANNAY 104 RA 18
91 ECHARCON 62 HA 13
03 ECHASSIERES 133 JA 23
61 ECHAUFFOUR 37 Y 12
70 ECHAVANNE 89 AB 17
25 ECHAY 107 XA 19
17 ECHEBRUNE 142 U 26
08 ECHELLE, L' 29 OA 7
80 ECHELLE ST AURIN, L' 27 IA 8
73 ECHELLES, LES C 152 WA 27
10 ECHEMINES 64 NA 13
49 ECHEMIRE 96 V 17
25 ECHENANS 89 AB 17
70 ECHENANS
SOUS MONT VAUDOIS 89 AB 17
52 ECHENAY 66 UA 13
01 ECHENEVEX 139 XA 23
21 ECHENON 105 UA 19
70 ECHENOZ LA MELINE 88 XA 17
70 ECHENOZ LE SEC 88 XA 17
21 ECHEVANNES 86 TA 17
25 ECHEVANNES 107 YA 19
26 ECHEVIS 166 UA 28
21 ECHEVRONNE 105 SA 19
21 ECHIGEY 105 TA 19
17 ECHILLAIS 127 S 25
45 ECHILLEUSES 62 HA 14
62 ECHINGHEN 7 DA 3
79 ECHIRE 112 U 22
38 ECHIROLLES C 166 WA 28
77 ECHOUBOULAINS 63 JA 13
24 ECHOURGNAC 157 X 28
67 ECKARTSWILLER 49 DB 12
67 ECKBOLSHEIM 70 EB 13
67 ECKWERSHEIM 49 EB 12
59 ECLAIBES 19 OA 5
51 ECLAIRES 44 SA 11
10 ECLANCE 65 RA 14
39 ECLANS NENON 106 VA 19
52 ECLARON BRAUCOURT
STE LIVIERE C 66 SA 13
07 ECLASSAN 164 RA 28
39 ECLEUX 122 WA 20
62 ECLIMEUX 16 GA 5
38 ECLOSE 152 UA 26
80 ECLUSIER VAUX 17 IA 7
28 ECLUZELLES 38 DA 12
08 ECLY 29 PA 8
42 ECOCHE 136 PA 23
62 ECOIVRES 16 GA 5
73 ECOLE 153 XA 26
25 ECOLE VALENTIN 107 XA 18
51 ECOLLEMONT 65 RA 12
72 ECOMMOY C 78 X 16
50 ECOQUENEAUVILLE 33 Q 9
61 ECORCEI 37 Z 12
25 ECORCES, LES 108 AB 19
61 ECORCHES 36 W 11
08 ECORDAL 29 QA 8
72 ECORPAIN 79 Z 15
27 ECOS C 39 DA 10
25 ECOT 108 AB 18
52 ECOT LA COMBE 66 UA 14
42 ECOTAY L'OLME 149 OA 26
61 ECOUCHE C 58 W 12
95 ECOUEN C 40 HA 11
49 ECOUFLANT 96 U 17
27 ECOUIS 25 DA 9
62 ECOURT ST QUENTIN 18 KA 5
62 ECOUST ST MEIN 17 JA 5
55 ECOUVIEZ 31 UA 8
25 ECOUVOTTE, L' 107 YA 18
17 ECOYEUX 128 U 25
62 ECQUEDECQUES 8 HA 4
62 ECQUES 8 GA 3
27 ECQUETOT 38 BA 10
78 ECQUEVILLY 39 FA 11
76 ECRAINVILLE 23 X 8
14 ECRAMMEVILLE 35 S 9
77 ECRENNES, LES 63 JA 13
76 ECRETTEVILLE LES BAONS 23 Z 8
76 ECRETTEVILLE SUR MER 23 Y 7
51 ECRIENNES 43 RA 12
39 ECRILLE 122 VA 22
70 ECROMAGNY 89 ZA 16
28 ECROSNES 61 EA 13
54 ECROUVES 45 WA 12
76 ECTOT L'AUBER 24 AA 8
76 ECTOT LES BAONS 24 AA 8
51 ECUEIL 42 OA 10
36 ECUEILLE C 99 CA 19
59 ECUELIN 19 NA 5
70 ECUELLE 87 VA 17
71 ECUELLES 121 TA 20
77 ECUELLES 62 JA 14
49 ECUILLE 77 U 17
62 ECUIRES 15 EA 4
71 ECUISSES 120 OA 21
50 ECULLEVILLE 33 O 8
69 ECULLY 150 RA 25
16 ECURAS 143 Z 25
17 ECURAT 141 T 25
25 ECURCEY 108 AB 18
55 ECUREY EN VERDUNOIS 31 UA 9
62 ECURIE 17 IA 5
51 ECURY LE REPOS 42 OA 12
51 ECURY SUR COOLE C 43 PA 11
21 ECUTIGNY 104 RA 19
60 ECUVILLY 27 JA 8
29 EDERN 72 E 15
16 EDON 143 Y 26
17 EDUTS, LES 128 V 24
59 EECKE 8 IA 3
63 EFFIAT 133 LA 24
52 EFFINCOURT 66 UA 13
02 EFFRY 19 OA 7
66 EGAT 222 FA 40
89 EGLENY 83 LA 16
19 EGLETONS C 146 FA 27
77 EGLIGNY 63 KA 13
68 EGLINGEN 90 CB 17
19 EGLISE AUX BOIS, L' 145 EA 26
24 EGLISE NEUVE D'ISSAC 157 Y 29
24 EGLISE NEUVE DE VERGT 158 Z 28
63 EGLISENEUVE
D'ENTRAIGUES 147 JA 27
63 EGLISENEUVE DES LIARDS 148 LA 26
63 EGLISENEUVE PRES BILLOM 148 LA 25
17 EGLISES D'ARGENTEUIL, LES 128 U 24
63 EGLISOLLES 149 NA 26
33 EGLISOTTES
ET CHALAURES, LES 157 W 28
91 EGLY 62 GA 13
77 EGREVILLE 63 JA 14
89 EGRISELLES
LE BOCAGE 63 KA 15
45 EGRY 62 HA 15
57 EGUELSHARDT 48 DB 11
90 EGUENIGUE 89 BB 17
17 EGUILLE, L' 141 S 25
13 EGUILLES 202 UA 35
21 EGUILLY 104 QA 18
10 EGUILLY SOUS BOIS 65 QA 15
68 EGUISHEIM 90 CB 15
36 EGUZON CHANTOME C 131 DA 22
70 EHUNS 88 YA 16
67 EICHHOFFEN 70 DB 13
57 EINCHEVILLE 47 AB 11
54 EINVAUX 68 ZA 13
54 EINVILLE AU JARD 46 ZA 12
55 EIX 45 VA 10
08 ELAN 30 RA 8
78 ELANCOURT 39 FA 12
68 ELBACH 90 CB 17
76 ELBEUF C 24 BA 9
76 ELBEUF EN BRAY 25 DA 9
76 ELBEUF SUR ANDELLE 25 CA 9
60 ELENCOURT 25 FA 8
59 ELESMES 19 OA 5
76 ELETOT 23 Y 7
62 ELEU DIT LEAUWETTE 9 JA 4
59 ELINCOURT 18 LA 6
60 ELINCOURT
STE MARGUERITE 27 JA 8
51 ELISE DAUCOURT 44 SA 10
76 ELLECOURT 25 EA 7
29 ELLIANT 72 F 15
14 ELLON 35 T 10
66 ELNE C 224 JA 39
62 ELNES 7 GA 3
90 ELOIE 89 BB 17
74 ELOISE 138 WA 24
88 ELOYES 89 AB 15
67 ELSENHEIM 70 DB 14
57 ELVANGE 47 ZA 10
56 ELVEN C 74 L 16
57 ELZANGE 32 YA 9
25 EMAGNY 106 WA 18
27 EMALLEVILLE 38 BA 10
78 EMANCE 61 EA 13
27 EMANVILLE 37 AA 10
76 EMANVILLE 24 AA 8
54 EMBERMENIL 68 AB 12
11 EMBRES ET CASTELMAURE 223 JA 38
80 EMBREVILLE 15 DA 6
05 EMBRUN C 182 ZA 30
62 EMBRY 16 FA 4
77 EMERAINVILLE 40 IA 12
59 EMERCHICOURT 18 LA 5
69 EMERINGES 136 RA 23
60 EMEVILLE 41 KA 9
14 EMIEVILLE 36 V 10
68 EMLINGEN 90 DB 17
59 EMMERIN 9 KA 4
50 EMONDEVILLE 33 Q 9
31 EMPEAUX 210 BA 35
07 EMPURANY 164 RA 28
16 EMPURE 129 W 24
58 EMPURY 103 NA 18
32 ENCAUSSE 187 BA 34
31 ENCAUSSE LES THERMES 217 Z 37
04 ENCHASTRAYES 182 AB 31
57 ENCHENBERG 48 DB 11
09 ENCOURTIECH 218 BA 38
32 ENDOUFIELLE 209 BA 35
60 ENENCOURT LE SEC 39 FA 9
60 ENENCOURT LEAGE 39 EA 9
52 ENFONVELLE 88 WA 16
47 ENGAYRAC 172 AA 32
10 ENGENTE 65 RA 14
45 ENGENVILLE 62 GA 14
95 ENGHIEN LES BAINS C 40 GA 11
38 ENGINS 166 VA 28
02 ENGLANCOURT 19 NA 7
80 ENGLEBELMER 17 IA 6
59 ENGLEFONTAINE 18 MA 5
14 ENGLESQUEVILLE EN AUGE 23 X 9
14 ENGLESQUEVILLE LA PERCEE 35 S 9
59 ENGLOS 9 JA 3
09 ENGOMER 218 BA 38
12 ENGUIALES 175 HA 30
62 ENGUINEGATTE 8 GA 4
67 ENGWILLER 48 EB 11
80 ENNEMAIN 27 JA 7
57 ENNERY 46 YA 10
95 ENNERY 39 GA 10
59 ENNETIERES EN WEPPES 9 JA 3
59 ENNEVELIN 9 KA 4
63 ENNEZAT C 134 KA 24
18 ENNORDRES 100 HA 18
62 ENQUIN LES MINES 8 GA 4
62 ENQUIN SUR BAILLONS 7 EA 4
65 ENS 216 Y 38
79 ENSIGNE 128 V 24
68 ENSISHEIM C 90 DB 16
13 ENSUES LA REDONNE 201 TA 36
04 ENTRAGES 197 YA 33
38 ENTRAIGUES 167 XA 29
63 ENTRAIGUES 134 LA 25
84 ENTRAIGUES
SUR LA SORGUE 195 SA 33
58 ENTRAINS SUR NOHAIN 102 LA 18
53 ENTRAMMES 77 T 15
57 ENTRANGE 32 XA 9
06 ENTRAUNES 182 AB 32
12 ENTRAYGUES SUR TRUYERE C 175 IA 30
88 ENTRE DEUX EAUX 69 BB 14
38 ENTRE DEUX GUIERS 152 WA 27
39 ENTRE DEUX MONTS 123 XA 21
83 ENTRECASTEAUX 203 YA 35
84 ENTRECHAUX 179 TA 32
74 ENTREMONT 139 ZA 24
73 ENTREMONT LE VIEUX 152 WA 26
04 ENTREPIERRES 181 XA 32
04 ENTREVAUX C 198 AB 33
04 ENTREVENNES 197 XA 33
74 ENTREVERNES 139 YA 25
67 ENTZHEIM 70 EB 13
63 ENVAL 133 KA 24
66 ENVEIGT 222 FA 40
76 ENVERMEU C 24 CA 7
76 ENVRONVILLE 23 Z 8
05 EOURRES 180 VA 32
31 EOUX 209 AA 36
10 EPAGNE 65 QA 13
80 EPAGNE EPAGNETTE 16 FA 6
02 EPAGNY 27 LA 9
21 EPAGNY 105 TA 18
74 EPAGNY 139 XA 24
27 EPAIGNES 37 Y 9
14 EPANEY 36 V 11
79 EPANNES 128 T 23
02 EPARCY 29 OA 7
55 EPARGES, LES 45 VA 10
17 EPARGNES 141 S 26
38 EPARRES, LES 151 UA 26
80 EPAUMESNIL 25 EA 7
02 EPAUX BEZU 41 LA 10
28 EPEAUTROLLES 60 CA 14
80 EPECAMPS 16 GA 6
27 EPEGARD 37 AA 10
80 EPEHY 18 KA 6
37 EPEIGNE LES BOIS 98 BA 18
37 EPEIGNE SUR DEME 79 Z 17
80 EPENANCOURT 27 JA 7
16 EPENEDE 129 Y 24
25 EPENOUSE 107 ZA 19
25 EPENOY 107 YA 19
51 EPENSE 44 SA 11
42 EPERCIEUX ST PAUL 149 PA 25
62 EPERLECQUES 8 GA 3
51 EPERNAY S 42 OA 11
21 EPERNAY SOUS GEVREY 105 SA 19
28 EPERNON 61 DA 12
61 EPERRAIS 59 Z 13
73 EPERSY 153 XA 25
71 EPERTULLY 120 RA 20
71 EPERVANS 121 SA 21
85 EPESSES, LES 111 S 20
25 EPEUGNEY 107 XA 19
67 EPFIG 70 DB 14
41 EPIAIS 80 CA 16
95 EPIAIS LES LOUVRES 40 HA 11
95 EPIAIS RHUS 39 FA 10
02 EPIEDS 41 LA 10
27 EPIEDS 38 CA 11
49 EPIEDS 96 W 19
45 EPIEDS EN BEAUCE 80 DA 15
73 EPIERRE 153 YA 27
54 EPIEZ SUR CHIERS 31 VA 9
55 EPIEZ SUR MEUSE 67 VA 13
71 EPINAC C 120 QA 20
88 EPINAL P 68 ZA 14
27 EPINAY 37 Z 11
95 EPINAY CHAMPLATREUX 40 HA 10
61 EPINAY LE COMTE, L' 57 T 13
91 EPINAY SOUS SENART C 40 HA 12
76 EPINAY SUR DUCLAIR 24 AA 8
14 EPINAY SUR ODON 35 T 10
91 EPINAY SUR ORGE 62 GA 12
93 EPINAY SUR SEINE C 40 GA 11
05 EPINE, L' 180 VA 31
51 EPINE, L' 43 QA 11
85 EPINE, L' 109 M 20
02 EPINE AUX BOIS, L' 41 LA 11
89 EPINEAU LES VOVES 83 MA 15
72 EPINEU LE CHEVREUIL 78 W 15
89 EPINEUIL 84 OA 16
18 EPINEUIL LE FLEURIEL 117 IA 22
60 EPINEUSE 26 HA 9
53 EPINEUX LE SEGUIN 78 V 15
35 EPINIAC 55 P 13
55 EPINONVILLE 30 TA 9
26 EPINOUZE 151 SA 27
62 EPINOY 18 KA 5
58 EPIRY 103 NA 19
77 EPISY 62 IA 14
52 EPIZON 66 UA 13
80 EPLESSIER 26 FA 7
54 EPLY 46 YA 11
21 EPOISSES 85 PA 17
78 EPONE 39 EA 11
10 EPOTHEMONT 65 RA 13
76 EPOUVILLE 23 X 8
51 EPOYE 43 PA 9
59 EPPE SAUVAGE 19 PA 6
02 EPPES 28 NA 8
80 EPPEVILLE 27 KA 7
57 EPPING 48 DB 10
76 EPRETOT 23 Y 8
76 EPREVILLE 23 Y 8
27 EPREVILLE EN LIEUVIN 37 Z 10
27 EPREVILLE EN ROUMOIS 24 AA 9
27 EPREVILLE
PRES LE NEUBOURG 37 AA 10
14 EPRON 36 V 10
62 EPS 16 GA 4
41 EPUISAY 79 AA 16
80 EQUANCOURT 17 KA 6
14 EQUEMAUVILLE 23 X 9
80 EQUENNES ERAMECOURT 26 FA 7
50 EQUEURDREVILLE
HAINNEVILLE C 33 P 8
70 EQUEVILLEY 88 YA 16
39 EQUEVILLON 123 XA 21
62 EQUIHEN PLAGE 7 DA 3
50 EQUILLY 56 Q 11
62 EQUIRRE 16 GA 4
95 ERAGNY 39 FA 11
60 ERAGNY SUR EPTE 25 EA 9
14 ERAINES 36 V 11
16 ERAVILLE 142 W 26
2B ERBAJOLO 228 LB 41
54 ERBEVILLER SUR AMEZULE 46 ZA 12
44 ERBRAY 94 Q 17
35 ERBREE 76 R 15
09 ERCE 219 CA 38
35 ERCE EN LAMEE 75 P 16
35 ERCE PRES LIFFRE 76 P 14
45 ERCEVILLE 61 FA 14
80 ERCHES 27 IA 7
80 ERCHEU 27 JA 8
59 ERCHIN 18 KA 5
57 ERCHING 48 CB 10
67 ERCKARTSWILLER 48 DB 11
80 ERCOURT 15 EA 6
60 ERCUIS 40 GA 10
56 ERDEVEN 91 I 17
22 EREAC 74 M 14
67 ERGERSHEIM 70 EB 13
80 ERGNIES 16 FA 6
62 ERGNY 7 FA 4
29 ERGUE GABERIC 72 E 15
62 ERIN 16 GA 4
21 ERINGES 85 QA 17
59 ERINGHEM 8 HA 2
55 ERIZE LA BRULEE 44 UA 11
55 ERIZE LA PETITE 44 TA 11
55 ERIZE ST DIZIER 44 UA 12
02 ERLON 28 NA 7
02 ERLOY 19 NA 7
60 ERMENONVILLE 40 IA 10
28 ERMENONVILLE LA GRANDE 60 CA 14
28 ERMENONVILLE LA PETITE 60 CA 14
76 ERMENOUVILLE 24 AA 7
95 ERMONT C 40 GA 11
53 ERNEE C 57 S 14
60 ERNEMONT BOUTAVENT 25 EA 8
76 ERNEMONT LA VILLETTE 25 EA 9
76 ERNEMONT SUR BUCHY 25 CA 8
14 ERNES 36 W 11
57 ERNESTVILLER 47 BB 10
55 ERNEVILLE AUX BOIS 44 UA 12
67 ERNOLSHEIM BRUCHE 70 EB 13
67 ERNOLSHEIM LES SAVERNE 49 DB 12
62 ERNY ST JULIEN 8 GA 4
26 EROME 165 SA 28
80 ERONDELLE 16 FA 6
2B ERONE 228 LB 40
50 EROUDEVILLE 33 Q 9
09 ERP 218 BA 38
60 ERQUERY 26 HA 9
59 ERQUINGHEM LE SEC 9 JA 4
59 ERQUINGHEM LYS 9 JA 3
60 ERQUINVILLERS 26 HA 9
22 ERQUY 54 L 12
66 ERR 222 FA 40
59 ERRE 18 LA 5
70 ERREVET 89 AB 17
54 ERROUVILLE 31 WA 9
2B ERSA 226 MB 37
67 ERSTEIN C 70 EB 13
57 ERSTROFF 47 AB 11
45 ERVAUVILLE 63 JA 15
62 ERVILLERS 17 JA 6
10 ERVY LE CHATEL C 84 NA 15
65 ESBAREICH 217 Z 38
21 ESBARRES 105 TA 19
77 ESBLY 40 JA 11
70 ESBOZ BREST 89 ZA 16
65 ESCALA 216 Y 37
40 ESCALANS 185 W 33
04 ESCALE, L' 197 XA 33
11 ESCALES 212 IA 36
62 ESCALLES 7 EA 2
31 ESCALQUENS 210 DA 35
60 ESCAMES 25 EA 8
46 ESCAMPS 174 DA 31
89 ESCAMPS 83 MA 16
12 ESCANDOLIERES 175 GA 31
31 ESCANECRABE 209 AA 36
51 ESCARDES 42 MA 12
06 ESCARENE, L' C 199 DB 34
59 ESCARMAIN 18 MA 5
66 ESCARO 222 GA 39
47 ESCASSEFORT 171 X 31
82 ESCATALENS 188 BA 33
59 ESCAUDAIN 18 LA 5
33 ESCAUDES 170 V 32
59 ESCAUDOEUVRES 18 LA 5
65 ESCAUNETS 208 W 36
59 ESCAUTPONT 18 MA 4
82 ESCAZEAUX 187 BA 34
67 ESCHAU 70 EB 13
67 ESCHBACH 49 FB 11
68 ESCHBACH AU VAL 90 CB 15
67 ESCHBOURG 49 DB 12
68 ESCHENTZWILLER 90 DB 16
57 ESCHERANGE 32 XA 9
60 ESCHES 39 GA 10
57 ESCHWILLER 48 CB 11
09 ESCLAGNE 219 EA 37
80 ESCLAINVILLERS 26 HA 8
48 ESCLANEDES 177 LA 31
32 ESCLASSAN LABASTIDE 209 Z 36
46 ESCLAUZELS 174 DA 31
76 ESCLAVELLES 25 CA 8
51 ESCLAVOLLES LUREY 64 MA 13
88 ESCLES 68 YA 15
60 ESCLES ST PIERRE 25 EA 7
47 ESCLOTTES 157 X 30
59 ESCOBECQUES 9 JA 4
62 ESCOEUILLES 7 FA 3
24 ESCOIRE 158 AA 28
89 ESCOLIVES STE CAMILLE 84 MA 16
08 ESCOMBRES ET LE CHESNOIS 30 TA 8
65 ESCONDEAUX 208 X 36
65 ESCONNETS 216 X 37
15 ESCORAILLES 160 HA 28
32 ESCORNEBOEUF 187 AA 34
28 ESCORPAIN 38 CA 12
64 ESCOS 206 S 35
09 ESCOSSE 219 DA 37
64 ESCOT 215 T 37
65 ESCOTS 216 X 37
64 ESCOU 215 U 37
64 ESCOUBES 207 V 36
65 ESCOUBES POUTS 216 W 37
31 ESCOULIS 218 BA 37
11 ESCOULOUBRE 222 GA 39
40 ESCOURCE 169 R 32
33 ESCOUSSANS 156 V 30
81 ESCOUSSENS 212 GA 35
64 ESCOUT 215 U 37
63 ESCOUTOUX 148 MA 25
14 ESCOVILLE 36 V 10
06 ESCRAGNOLLES 198 AB 34
45 ESCRENNES 61 GA 15
45 ESCRIGNELLES 82 JA 16
81 ESCROUX 190 IA 34
11 ESCUEILLENS ET ST JUST
DE BELENGARD 221 FA 37
64 ESCURES 207 W 35
03 ESCUROLLES C 133 LA 23
76 ESLETTES 24 BA 8
88 ESLEY 67 XA 14
64 ESLOURENTIES DABAN 207 W 36
77 ESMANS 63 JA 14
80 ESMERY HALLON 27 KA 8
70 ESMOULIERES 89 AB 16
70 ESMOULINS 106 VA 18
17 ESNANDES 125 R 23
25 ESNANS 107 YA 18
59 ESNES 18 LA 6
55 ESNES EN ARGONNE 44 TA 10
89 ESNON 83 MA 15
52 ESNOUVEAUX 66 UA 15
19 ESPAGNAC 160 FA 27
46 ESPAGNAC STE EULALIE 174 EA 30
82 ESPALAIS 187 AA 33
43 ESPALEM 148 KA 27
12 ESPALION C 176 IA 31
43 ESPALY ST MARCEL 163 NA 28
31 ESPANES 210 DA 36
32 ESPAON 209 AA 36
05 ESPARRON 181 WA 31
31 ESPARRON 209 AA 36
83 ESPARRON 202 WA 35
04 ESPARRON DE VERDON 197 XA 34
65 ESPARROS 216 Y 37
82 ESPARSAC 187 AA 33
19 ESPARTIGNAC 145 DA 27
32 ESPAS 185 W 34
60 ESPAUBOURG 25 EA 9
65 ESPECHE 216 X 37
64 ESPECHEDE 207 V 36
46 ESPEDAILLAC 174 EA 30
64 ESPELETTE C 205 Q 36
26 ESPELUCHE 179 SA 31
26 ESPENEL 165 TA 30
81 ESPERAUSSE 190 HA 34
11 ESPERAZA 221 GA 38
31 ESPERCE 210 CA 36
46 ESPERE 173 CA 31
64 ESPES UNDUREIN 206 S 36
12 ESPEYRAC 175 HA 30
46 ESPEYROUX 160 FA 30
11 ESPEZEL 221 FA 38
65 ESPIEILH 216 X 37
47 ESPIENS 172 Y 32
33 ESPIET 156 V 29
82 ESPINAS 174 EA 32
15 ESPINASSE 161 JA 29
63 ESPINASSE 148 MA 25
03 ESPINASSE VOZELLE 133 LA 24
05 ESPINASSES 181 YA 31
63 ESPINCHAL 147 JA 27
14 ESPINS 36 U 11
66 ESPIRA DE CONFLENT 222 HA 39
66 ESPIRA DE L'AGLY 224 JA 38
63 ESPIRAT 148 LA 25
64 ESPIUTE 206 S 36
43 ESPLANTAS 162 MA 29
09 ESPLAS 219 DA 37
09 ESPLAS DE SEROU 219 CA 38
64 ESPOEY 207 V 36
34 ESPONDEILHAN 213 LA 35
70 ESPRELS 88 YA 17
14 ESQUAY NOTRE DAME 35 U 10
14 ESQUAY SUR SEULLES 35 T 9
02 ESQUEHERIES 19 NA 6
59 ESQUELBECQ 8 HA 2
60 ESQUENNOY 26 GA 8
59 ESQUERCHIN 17 JA 5
62 ESQUERDES 8 GA 3
29 ESQUIBIEN 71 C 15
65 ESQUIEZE SERE 216 W 38
64 ESQUIULE 206 T 37
16 ESSARDS, LES 143 X 27
17 ESSARDS, LES 141 T 25
37 ESSARDS, LES 97 X 18
39 ESSARDS TAIGNEVAUX, LES 122 UA 20
21 ESSAROIS 85 RA 16
62 ESSARS 8 IA 4
27 ESSARTS, LES 38 BA 11
41 ESSARTS, LES 79 Z 16
85 ESSARTS, LES C 110 R 21
78 ESSARTS LE ROI, LES 39 FA 12
51 ESSARTS LE VICOMTE, LES 64 MA 12
51 ESSARTS LES SEZANNE, LES 42 MA 12
61 ESSAY 58 X 13
16 ESSE 130 Z 24
35 ESSE 76 Q 15
88 ESSEGNEY 68 YA 14
33 ESSEINTES, LES 171 W 30
90 ESSERT 89 AB 17
74 ESSERT ROMAND 140 AB 23
80 ESSERTAUX 26 GA 7
71 ESSERTENNE 120 QA 20
70 ESSERTENNE ET CECEY 106 UA 18
42 ESSERTINES EN CHATELNEUF 149 OA 26
42 ESSERTINES EN DONZY 150 PA 25
73 ESSERTS BLAY 153 ZA 26
39 ESSERVAL COMBE 123 XA 21
39 ESSERVAL TARTRE 123 XA 20
21 ESSEY 104 QA 19
54 ESSEY ET MAIZERAIS 45 WA 11
54 ESSEY LA COTE 68 ZA 13
54 ESSEY LES NANCY 46 YA 12
39 ESSIA 122 VA 21
02 ESSIGNY LE GRAND 28 LA 7
02 ESSIGNY LE PETIT 18 LA 7
02 ESSISES 41 LA 11
02 ESSOMES SUR MARNE 41 LA 11
14 ESSON 35 U 11
10 ESSOYES C 85 OA 15
60 ESSUILES 26 GA 9
48 ESTABLES 177 MA 30
43 ESTABLES, LES 163 OA 29
26 ESTABLET 180 UA 31
31 ESTADENS 217 AA 37
66 ESTAGEL 224 IA 38
12 ESTAING C 175 IA 30
65 ESTAING 215 V 38
59 ESTAIRES 8 IA 3
46 ESTAL 160 FA 29
32 ESTAMPES 208 X 36
65 ESTAMPURES 208 X 36
31 ESTANCARBON 217 AA 37
63 ESTANDEUIL 148 LA 25
32 ESTANG 185 W 34
65 ESTARVIELLE 217 Y 38
66 ESTAVAR 222 FA 40
63 ESTEIL 148 LA 26
31 ESTENOS 217 Z 38
65 ESTENSAN 216 Y 38
64 ESTERENCUBY 206 R 37
51 ESTERNAY C 42 MA 12
65 ESTERRE 216 W 38
62 ESTEVELLES 17 JA 4
76 ESTEVILLE 24 BA 8
30 ESTEZARGUES 195 RA 33
64 ESTIALESCQ 207 U 36
40 ESTIBEAUX 184 S 35
40 ESTIGARDE 185 W 33
47 ESTILLAC 172 Z 32
32 ESTIPOUY 208 Y 35
65 ESTIRAC 208 W 35
10 ESTISSAC C 64 NA 14
19 ESTIVALS 159 DA 28
03 ESTIVAREILLES 133 IA 22
42 ESTIVAREILLES 149 OA 27
19 ESTIVAUX 145 DA 27
66 ESTOHER 222 HA 39
64 ESTOS 207 T 36
04 ESTOUBLON 197 YA 33
91 ESTOUCHES 61 GA 14
59 ESTOURMEL 18 LA 6
76 ESTOUTEVILLE ECALLES 25 CA 8
45 ESTOUY 62 GA 14
38 ESTRABLIN 151 SA 26
32 ESTRAMIAC 187 AA 34
08 ESTREBAY 29 PA 7
80 ESTREBOEUF 15 DA 6

30 ESTRECHURE, L' 177 NA 32
62 ESTREE 16 EA 4
62 ESTREE BLANCHE 8 GA 4
62 ESTREE CAUCHY 17 IA 5
62 ESTREE WAMIN 16 HA 5
62 ESTREELLES 7 EA 4
02 ESTREES 18 LA 6
59 ESTREES 18 KA 5
80 ESTREES DENIECOURT 27 JA 7
14 ESTREES LA CAMPAGNE 36 V 11
80 ESTREES LES CRECY 16 FA 5
80 ESTREES MONS 27 JA 7
60 ESTREES ST DENIS C 26 IA 9
80 ESTREES SUR NOYE 26 GA 7
88 ESTRENNES 67 XA 14
59 ESTREUX 18 MA 5
59 ESTRUN 18 LA 5
14 ESTRY 35 T 11
37 ESVES LE MOUTIER 98 AA 19
37 ESVRES 98 AA 18
59 ESWARS 18 LA 5
73 ETABLE 153 XA 26
07 ETABLES 164 RA 28
22 ETABLES SUR MER C 54 K 12
16 ETAGNAC 130 Z 25
76 ETAIMPUIS 24 BA 8
55 ETAIN C 45 VA 10
62 ETAING 17 JA 5
76 ETAINHUS 23 Y 8
21 ETAIS 85 QA 16
89 ETAIS LA SAUVIN 83 LA 17
25 ETALANS 107 YA 19
21 ETALANTE 86 RA 17
08 ETALLE 29 QA 7
76 ETALLEVILLE 24 AA 7
80 ETALON 27 JA 7
76 ETALONDES 15 CA 6
91 ETAMPES S 61 GA 13
02 ETAMPES SUR MARNE 41 LA 11
50 ETANG BERTRAND, L' 33 P 9
78 ETANG LA VILLE, L' 39 FA 11
71 ETANG SUR ARROUX 119 PA 20
21 ETANG VERGY, L' 105 SA 19
57 ETANGS, LES 46 YA 10
62 ETAPLES C 7 DA 4
89 ETAULE 84 OA 17
17 ETAULES 141 R 25
21 ETAULES 105 SA 18
33 ETAULIERS 142 T 27
74 ETAUX 139 YA 24
02 ETAVES ET BOCQUIAUX 18 LA 7
60 ETAVIGNY 41 JA 10
64 ETCHARRY 206 S 36
64 ETCHEBAR 206 S 37
08 ETEIGNIERES 29 QA 7
68 ETEIMBES 90 BB 17
56 ETEL 73 I 17
80 ETELFAY 27 IA 8
74 ETERCY 139 XA 25
25 ETERNOZ 107 XA 20
62 ETERPIGNY 17 JA 5
80 ETERPIGNY 27 JA 7
14 ETERVILLE 36 U 10
21 ETEVAUX 105 UA 18
59 ETH 18 MA 5
50 ETIENVILLE 33 Q 9
89 ETIGNY 63 LA 15
28 ETILLEUX, LES 59 AA 14
80 ETINEHEM 17 IA 7
91 ETIOLLES 62 HA 12
39 ETIVAL 122 WA 22
88 ETIVAL CLAIREFONTAINE 69 BB 14
72 ETIVAL LES LE MANS 78 X 15
89 ETIVEY 85 PA 17
70 ETOBON 89 AB 17
51 ETOGES 42 NA 11
39 ETOILE, L' 122 VA 21
80 ETOILE, L' 16 FA 6
05 ETOILE ST CYRICE 180 VA 32
26 ETOILE SUR RHONE 165 SA 29
55 ETON 45 VA 10
21 ETORMAY 85 QA 17
24 ETOUARS 144 Z 26
10 ETOURVY 84 PA 15
76 ETOUTTEVILLE 24 Z 8
25 ETOUVANS 108 AB 18
02 ETOUVELLES 28 MA 8
14 ETOUVY 35 S 11
60 ETOUY 26 HA 9
25 ETRABONNE 106 WA 19
25 ETRAPPE 107 ZA 17
42 ETRAT, L' 150 OA 26
25 ETRAY 107 YA 19
55 ETRAYE 31 UA 9
02 ETREAUPONT 19 OA 7
36 ETRECHET 115 EA 21
18 ETRECHY 101 IA 19
51 ETRECHY 42 OA 11
91 ETRECHY C 61 GA 13
14 ETREHAM 35 T 9
02 ETREILLERS 27 KA 7
80 ETREJUST 16 FA 7
35 ETRELLES 76 R 15
70 ETRELLES ET LA MONTBLEUSE 106 WA 18
10 ETRELLES SUR AUBE 64 NA 13
74 ETREMBIERES 139 YA 23
27 ETREPAGNY C 25 DA 9
39 ETREPIGNEY 106 VA 19
08 ETREPIGNY 30 RA 8
02 ETREPILLY 41 LA 10
77 ETREPILLY 41 JA 11
51 ETREPY 43 RA 12
76 ETRETAT 23 X 8
02 ETREUX 18 MA 6
54 ETREVAL 67 XA 13
27 ETREVILLE 23 Z 9
01 ETREZ 137 TA 23
16 ETRIAC 142 W 26
49 ETRICHE 77 U 17
80 ETRICOURT MANANCOURT 17 JA 6
71 ETRIGNY 121 SA 21
21 ETROCHEY 85 QA 16
59 ETROEUNGT 19 NA 6
03 ETROUSSAT 134 KA 23
62 ETRUN 17 IA 5
64 ETSAUT 215 U 38
67 ETTENDORF 49 EB 12
57 ETTING 48 CB 11
90 ETUEFFONT 89 BB 16
25 ETUPES C 89 BB 17
27 ETURQUERAYE 23 Z 9
79 ETUSSON 96 U 20
70 ETUZ 107 XA 18
57 ETZLING 47 BB 10
76 EU C 15 DA 6
52 EUFFIGNEIX 66 SA 15
40 EUGENIE LES BAINS 184 U 34
08 EUILLY ET LOMBUT 30 TA 8
54 EULMONT 46 YA 12
31 EUP 217 Z 38
26 EURRE 165 SA 30
52 EURVILLE BIENVILLE 66 SA 13
66 EUS 222 HA 39
54 EUVEZIN 45 WA 11
55 EUVILLE 45 VA 12
51 EUVY 42 OA 12
30 EUZET 193 PA 33
72 EVAILLE 79 Z 16
39 EVANS 106 WA 19
88 EVAUX ET MENIL 68 YA 14
23 EVAUX LES BAINS C 133 HA 23
60 EVE 40 IA 10
78 EVECQUEMONT 39 FA 11
83 EVENOS 203 WA 37
02 EVERGNICOURT 29 OA 9
77 EVERLY 63 LA 13
90 EVETTE SALBERT 89 AB 17
69 EVEUX 136 RA 25
74 EVIAN LES BAINS C 124 ZA 22
08 EVIGNY 29 RA 7
25 EVILLERS 107 YA 20
62 EVIN MALMAISON 17 KA 4
74 EVIRES 139 YA 24
2A EVISA 227 JB 41
01 EVOSGES 138 VA 24
22 EVRAN C 55 N 13
57 EVRANGE 32 YA 8
14 EVRECY C 35 U 10
55 EVRES 44 TA 11
27 EVREUX P 38 BA 11
60 EVRICOURT 27 JA 8
56 EVRIGUET 74 L 15
53 EVRON C 77 U 14
89 EVRY 63 LA 14
91 EVRY P 62 HA 12
77 EVRY GREGY SUR YERRE 62 IA 12
74 EXCENEVEX 139 YA 22
24 EXCIDEUIL C 144 BA 27
08 EXERMONT 30 SA 9
16 EXIDEUIL 130 Z 25
25 EXINCOURT 89 AB 17
79 EXIREUIL 112 V 22
61 EXMES C 58 X 12
79 EXOUDUN 128 W 22
17 EXPIREMONT 142 U 27
38 EYBENS C 166 WA 28
87 EYBOULEUF 145 DA 25
19 EYBURIE 145 DA 26
09 EYCHEIL 218 BA 38
38 EYDOCHE 152 UA 27
26 EYGALAYES 180 VA 32
13 EYGALIERES 195 SA 34
26 EYGALIERS 180 UA 32
05 EYGLIERS 168 AB 30
26 EYGLUY ESCOULIN 165 TA 29
05 EYGUIANS 181 WA 31
13 EYGUIERES C 195 SA 34
19 EYGURANDE C 147 HA 26
24 EYGURANDE ET GARDEDEUIL 157 X 28
87 EYJEAUX 145 CA 25
24 EYLIAC 158 AA 28
24 EYMET C 172 Y 30
26 EYMEUX 165 TA 28
16 EYMOUTHIERS 143 Z 26
87 EYMOUTIERS C 145 EA 25
66 EYNE 222 FA 40
33 EYNESSE 157 X 29
13 EYRAGUES 195 SA 34
33 EYRANS 156 T 28
19 EYREIN 146 FA 27
40 EYRES MONCUBE 184 U 34
26 EYROLES 180 TA 31
33 EYSINES 155 T 29
25 EYSSON 107 ZA 19
64 EYSUS 215 U 37
24 EYVIRAT 144 Z 27
67 EYWILLER 48 CB 11
26 EYZAHUT 179 SA 30
24 EYZERAC 144 AA 27
24 EYZIES DE TAYAC SIREUIL, LES 158 BA 29
38 EYZIN PINET 151 SA 26
95 EZANVILLE 40 HA 11
06 EZE 200 DB 34
27 EZY SUR EURE 38 CA 11

F

11 FA 221 GA 38
09 FABAS 218 BA 37
31 FABAS 209 AA 36
82 FABAS 188 CA 34
07 FABRAS 178 PA 30
34 FABREGUES 214 NA 35
11 FABREZAN 223 IA 37
59 FACHES THUMESNIL 9 KA 4
58 FACHIN 119 OA 20
48 FAGE MONTIVERNOUX, LA 162 KA 30
48 FAGE ST JULIEN, LA 162 KA 29
31 FAGET, LE 211 EA 35
32 FAGET ABBATIAL 209 Z 35
51 FAGNIERES 43 PA 11
08 FAGNON 29 RA 7
70 FAHY LES AUTREY 87 UA 17
57 FAILLY 46 YA 10
25 FAIMBE 107 ZA 17
21 FAIN LES MONTBARD 85 QA 17
21 FAIN LES MOUTIERS 85 PA 17
27 FAINS 38 CA 11
28 FAINS LA FOLIE 61 DA 14
55 FAINS VEEL 44 TA 12
08 FAISSAULT 29 QA 8
11 FAJAC EN VAL 221 HA 37
11 FAJAC LA RELENQUE 211 EA 36
46 FAJOLES 159 CA 29
11 FAJOLLE, LA 223 FA 38
82 FAJOLLES 187 BA 33
08 FALAISE 30 RA 9
14 FALAISE C 36 V 11
78 FALAISE, LA 39 EA 11
57 FALCK 47 AB 10
33 FALEYRAS 156 V 29
31 FALGA 211 EA 35
15 FALGOUX, LE 161 IA 28
06 FALICON 200 CB 34
68 FALKWILLER 90 CB 17
76 FALLENCOURT 25 DA 7
25 FALLERANS 107 YA 19
85 FALLERON 109 O 20
39 FALLETANS 106 VA 19
70 FALLON 107 ZA 17
80 FALOISE, LA 26 HA 8
47 FALS 187 Z 33
80 FALVY 27 JA 7
59 FAMARS 18 MA 5
62 FAMECHON 17 HA 6
80 FAMECHON 26 FA 7
57 FAMECK C 32 XA 9
14 FAMILLY 37 Y 11
62 FAMPOUX 17 JA 5
11 FANJEAUX C 221 FA 37
24 FANLAC 158 BA 28
29 FAOU, LE C 52 E 14
22 FAOUET, LE 53 I 12
56 FAOUET, LE C 73 G 15
01 FARAMANS 137 TA 24
38 FARAMANS 151 TA 27
62 FARBUS 17 JA 5
27 FARCEAUX 38 DA 9
05 FARE EN CHAMPSAUR, LA 167 XA 30
13 FARE LES OLIVIERS, LA 201 TA 35
57 FAREBERSVILLER 47 BB 10
01 FAREINS 136 RA 24
77 FAREMOUTIERS 41 KA 12
01 FARGES 138 WA 23
24 FARGES, LES 158 BA 28
18 FARGES ALLICHAMPS 116 HA 21
18 FARGES EN SEPTAINE 101 IA 19
71 FARGES LES CHALON 120 RA 20
71 FARGES LES MACON 121 SA 22
33 FARGUES 170 V 31
40 FARGUES 184 U 34
46 FARGUES 173 BA 31
33 FARGUES ST HILAIRE 156 U 29
47 FARGUES SUR OURBISE 171 X 32
52 FARINCOURT 87 VA 16
2B FARINOLE 226 MB 39
83 FARLEDE, LA 203 XA 37
42 FARNAY 150 RA 26
57 FARSCHVILLER 47 BB 10
72 FATINES 78 Y 15
27 FATOUVILLE GRESTAIN 23 Y 9
15 FAU, LE 161 IA 28
48 FAU DE PEYRE 162 KA 30
81 FAUCH 190 GA 34
74 FAUCIGNY 139 YA 24
70 FAUCOGNEY ET LA MER C 89 ZA 16
88 FAUCOMPIERRE 68 AB 15
84 FAUCON 180 TA 32
04 FAUCON DE BARCELONNETTE 182 AB 31
04 FAUCON DU CAIRE 181 XA 31
88 FAUCONCOURT 68 ZA 14
02 FAUCOUCOURT 28 MA 8
82 FAUDOAS 187 AA 34
31 FAUGA, LE 210 CA 36
07 FAUGERES 178 PA 31
34 FAUGERES 213 KA 35
14 FAUGUERNON 37 X 10
47 FAUGUEROLLES 171 X 31
47 FAUILLET 171 X 31
14 FAULQ, LE 37 Y 10
57 FAULQUEMONT C 47 AB 11
54 FAULX 46 YA 12
59 FAUMONT 18 KA 4
62 FAUQUEMBERGUES C 7 GA 4
05 FAURIE, LA 180 WA 30
24 FAURILLES 172 Z 30
82 FAUROUX 173 BA 32
81 FAUSSERGUES 190 HA 33
85 FAUTE SUR MER, LA 125 Q 23
21 FAUVERNEY 105 TA 18
27 FAUVILLE 38 BA 11
76 FAUVILLE EN CAUX C 23 Z 8
08 FAUX 29 QA 8
24 FAUX 158 Z 29
51 FAUX FRESNAY 64 OA 12
23 FAUX LA MONTAGNE 146 FA 25
23 FAUX MAZURAS 131 EA 24
51 FAUX VESIGNEUL 43 OA 12
10 FAUX VILLECERF 64 NA 14
2B FAVALELLO 228 LB 41
19 FAVARS 159 EA 27
49 FAVERAYE MACHELLES 96 U 18
18 FAVERDINES 117 HA 21
45 FAVERELLES 83 JA 17
74 FAVERGES C 153 YA 25
38 FAVERGES DE LA TOUR 152 VA 26
70 FAVERNEY 88 XA 16
90 FAVEROIS 90 BB 17
02 FAVEROLLES 41 KA 10
15 FAVEROLLES 162 KA 29
28 FAVEROLLES 61 DA 12
36 FAVEROLLES 99 CA 19
52 FAVEROLLES 86 TA 15
61 FAVEROLLES 58 V 12
80 FAVEROLLES 27 IA 8
51 FAVEROLLES ET COEMY 42 NA 10
27 FAVEROLLES LA CAMPAGNE 37 AA 11
21 FAVEROLLES LES LUCEY 86 SA 16
41 FAVEROLLES SUR CHER 98 BA 18
39 FAVIERE, LA 123 XA 21
28 FAVIERES 60 CA 13
54 FAVIERES 67 XA 13
77 FAVIERES 40 JA 12
80 FAVIERES 15 EA 5
51 FAVRESSE 43 RA 12
62 FAVREUIL 17 JA 6
78 FAVRIEUX 39 DA 11
27 FAVRIL, LE 37 Z 10
28 FAVRIL, LE 60 BA 13
59 FAVRIL, LE 18 NA 6
61 FAY 59 Y 12
72 FAY 78 W 15
80 FAY 27 JA 7
71 FAY, LE 121 UA 21
45 FAY AUX LOGES 81 GA 15
44 FAY DE BRETAGNE 93 O 18
39 FAY EN MONTAGNE 122 WA 21
26 FAY LE CLOS 165 SA 28
60 FAY LES ETANGS 39 FA 10
10 FAY LES MARCILLY 64 MA 13
77 FAY LES NEMOURS 62 IA 14
60 FAY ST QUENTIN, LE 26 GA 9
43 FAY SUR LIGNON C 163 PA 29
46 FAYCELLES 174 FA 30
41 FAYE 80 BA 16
16 FAYE, LA 129 X 24
49 FAYE D'ANJOU 96 U 18
79 FAYE L'ABBESSE 112 V 20
37 FAYE LA VINEUSE 113 Y 20
79 FAYE SUR ARDIN 112 U 22
60 FAYEL, LE 27 IA 9
83 FAYENCE C 198 AB 35
02 FAYET 28 LA 7
12 FAYET 191 JA 34
63 FAYET LE CHATEAU 148 LA 25
63 FAYET RONAYE 148 MA 27
52 FAYL LA FORET C 87 VA 16
70 FAYMONT 89 ZA 17
85 FAYMOREAU 111 T 22
52 FAYS 66 TA 13
88 FAYS 68 AB 14
10 FAYS LA CHAPELLE 64 OA 15
81 FAYSSAC 189 FA 33
64 FEAS 206 T 37
62 FEBVIN PALFART 8 GA 4
76 FECAMP C 23 Y 7
59 FECHAIN 18 KA 5
90 FECHE L'EGLISE 90 BB 17
54 FECOCOURT 67 XA 13
70 FEDRY 88 WA 17
67 FEGERSHEIM 70 EB 13
44 FEGREAC 93 N 17
74 FEIGERES 139 XA 24
60 FEIGNEUX 41 JA 10
59 FEIGNIES 19 NA 5
01 FEILLENS 137 SA 23
41 FEINGS 99 CA 18
61 FEINGS 59 Z 13
35 FEINS 75 P 14
45 FEINS EN GATINAIS 82 JA 16
73 FEISSONS SUR ISERE 153 ZA 26
73 FEISSONS SUR SALINS 154 ZA 26
61 FEL 58 X 12
2B FELCE 228 MB 40
68 FELDBACH 90 CB 17
68 FELDKIRCH 90 DB 16
2B FELICETO 225 KB 39
07 FELINES 150 RA 27
43 FELINES 149 NA 27
34 FELINES MINERVOIS 212 IA 36
26 FELINES SUR RIMANDOULE 179 TA 30
11 FELINES TERMENES 223 IA 37
59 FELLERIES 19 OA 6
68 FELLERING 90 BB 16
23 FELLETIN C 132 GA 25
66 FELLUNS 222 HA 38
90 FELON 90 BB 16
46 FELZINS 175 GA 30
59 FENAIN 18 LA 5
21 FENAY 105 TA 19
11 FENDEILLE 211 FA 36
79 FENERY 112 U 21
57 FENETRANGE C 48 BB 11
49 FENEU 95 T 17
82 FENEYROLS 174 EA 32
23 FENIERS 146 GA 25
17 FENIOUX 128 U 25
79 FENIOUX 111 U 22
54 FENNEVILLER 69 BB 13
81 FENOLS 189 FA 34
85 FENOUILLER, LE 109 O 21
31 FENOUILLET 188 CA 34
66 FENOUILLET 221 HA 38
11 FENOUILLET DU RAZES 221 FA 37
08 FEPIN 20 RA 6
44 FERCE 76 Q 16
72 FERCE SUR SARTHE 78 W 16
88 FERDRUPT 89 AB 16
02 FERE, LA C 28 LA 8
51 FERE CHAMPENOISE C 42 OA 12
02 FERE EN TARDENOIS C 42 MA 10
51 FEREBRIANGES 42 NA 11
08 FEREE, LA 29 PA 7
56 FEREL 92 M 17
62 FERFAY 8 HA 4
77 FERICY 62 JA 13
59 FERIN 18 KA 5
50 FERMANVILLE 33 Q 8
58 FERMETE, LA 118 LA 20
01 FERNEY VOLTAIRE C 139 XA 23
63 FERNOEL 146 HA 25
45 FEROLLES 81 GA 16
77 FEROLLES ATTILLY 40 IA 12
59 FERON 19 OA 6
62 FERQUES 7 EA 3
11 FERRALS LES CORBIERES 223 IA 37
34 FERRALS LES MONTAGNES 212 IA 36
11 FERRAN 221 FA 37
26 FERRASSIERES 180 VA 32
35 FERRE, LE 56 Q 13
47 FERRENSAC 172 Z 30
65 FERRERE 217 Y 38
06 FERRES, LES 199 CB 34
68 FERRETTE C 90 DB 17
10 FERREUX QUINCEY 64 MA 13
22 FERRIERE, LA 74 L 15
37 FERRIERE, LA 79 Z 17
38 FERRIERE, LA 153 XA 27
85 FERRIERE, LA 110 Q 21
86 FERRIERE AIROUX, LA 129 Y 23
61 FERRIERE AU DOYEN, LA 59 Y 12
61 FERRIERE AUX ETANGS, LA 57 U 12
61 FERRIERE BECHET, LA 58 X 13
61 FERRIERE BOCHARD, LA 58 W 13
49 FERRIERE DE FLEE, LA 77 S 16
79 FERRIERE EN PARTHENAY, LA 112 W 21
52 FERRIERE ET LAFOLIE 66 TA 13
14 FERRIERE HARANG, LA 35 S 11
59 FERRIERE LA GRANDE 19 OA 5
59 FERRIERE LA PETITE 19 OA 5
37 FERRIERE LARCON 114 AA 20
37 FERRIERE SUR BEAULIEU 98 BA 19
27 FERRIERE SUR RISLE, LA 37 AA 11
17 FERRIERES 127 S 23
45 FERRIERES C 62 JA 15
50 FERRIERES 57 S 13
54 FERRIERES 68 YA 13
60 FERRIERES 26 HA 8
65 FERRIERES 215 V 37
77 FERRIERES EN BRIE 40 IA 12
80 FERRIERES 26 GA 7
81 FERRIERES 190 HA 34
76 FERRIERES EN BRAY 25 EA 9
27 FERRIERES HAUT CLOCHER 38 BA 11
61 FERRIERES LA VERRERIE 59 Y 12
25 FERRIERES LE LAC 108 BB 18
25 FERRIERES LES BOIS 106 WA 19
70 FERRIERES LES RAY 87 WA 17
70 FERRIERES LES SCEY 88 XA 17
34 FERRIERES LES VERRERIES 192 NA 34
34 FERRIERES POUSSAROU 213 JA 35
27 FERRIERES ST HILAIRE 37 Z 11
15 FERRIERES ST MARY 161 KA 28
09 FERRIERES SUR ARIEGE 219 DA 38
03 FERRIERES SUR SICHON 133 MA 24
43 FERRUSSAC 162 LA 28
25 FERTANS 107 XA 19
39 FERTE, LA 122 VA 20
91 FERTE ALAIS, LA C 62 HA 13
41 FERTE BEAUHARNAIS, LA 81 EA 17
72 FERTE BERNARD, LA C 59 Z 14
02 FERTE CHEVRESIS, LA 28 MA 7
61 FERTE FRENEL, LA C 37 Y 11
77 FERTE GAUCHER, LA C 41 LA 12
03 FERTE HAUTERIVE, LA 134 LA 22
41 FERTE IMBAULT, LA 100 FA 18
89 FERTE LOUPIERE, LA 83 LA 16
61 FERTE MACE, LA C 58 V 13
02 FERTE MILON, LA 41 KA 10
77 FERTE SOUS JOUARRE, LA C 41 KA 11
45 FERTE ST AUBIN, LA C 81 FA 16
41 FERTE ST CYR, LA 81 EA 17
76 FERTE ST SAMSON, LA 25 DA 8
08 FERTE SUR CHIERS, LA 30 TA 8
28 FERTE VIDAME, LA C 60 AA 12
28 FERTE VILLENEUIL, LA 80 CA 15
58 FERTREVE 119 MA 20
50 FERVACHES 34 R 11
14 FERVAQUES 36 X 11
80 FESCAMPS 27 IA 8
25 FESCHES LE CHATEL 89 BB 17
02 FESMY LE SART 18 MA 6
76 FESQUES 25 DA 7
28 FESSANVILLIERS MATTANVILLIERS 38 BA 12
68 FESSENHEIM 90 EB 16
67 FESSENHEIM LE BAS 49 EB 12
25 FESSEVILLERS 89 BB 16
70 FESSEY, LES 89 ZA 16
74 FESSY 139 ZA 23
24 FESTALEMPS 143 X 27
11 FESTES ET ST ANDRE 221 GA 38
02 FESTIEUX 28 NA 8
51 FESTIGNY 42 NA 10
89 FESTIGNY 83 MA 17
62 FESTUBERT 8 IA 4
21 FETE, LE 104 OA 19
74 FETERNES 139 ZA 22
39 FETIGNY 122 VA 22
78 FEUCHEROLLES 39 FA 11
62 FEUCHY 17 JA 5
47 FEUGAROLLES 171 Y 32
50 FEUGERES 34 Q 10
10 FEUGES 64 OA 13
27 FEUGUEROLLES 38 BA 10
14 FEUGUEROLLES BULLY 36 U 10
11 FEUILLA 223 JA 38
16 FEUILLADE 143 Y 26
24 FEUILLADE, LA 159 CA 28
29 FEUILLEE, LA 52 F 13
80 FEUILLERES 17 JA 7
50 FEUILLIE, LA 34 Q 10
76 FEUILLIE, LA 25 DA 9
25 FEULE 108 AB 18
60 FEUQUIERES 25 EA 8
80 FEUQUIERES EN VIMEU 15 DA 6
42 FEURS C 149 PA 25
36 FEUSINES 116 FA 22
18 FEUX 101 JA 19
57 FEVES 46 XA 10
57 FEY 46 XA 11
54 FEY EN HAYE 45 XA 11
19 FEYT 147 HA 25
87 FEYTIAT 145 CA 25
69 FEYZIN 151 SA 26
81 FIAC 189 FA 34
2B FICAJA 228 MB 40
62 FICHEUX 17 IA 5
64 FICHOUS RIUMAYOU 207 U 35
27 FIDELAIRE, LE 37 AA 11
39 FIED, LE 122 WA 21
49 FIEF SAUVIN, LE 94 R 19
80 FIEFFES MONTRELET 16 GA 6
62 FIEFS 16 GA 4
62 FIENNES 7 EA 3
80 FIENVILLERS 16 GA 6
14 FIERVILLE BRAY 36 V 10
50 FIERVILLE LES MINES 33 P 9
14 FIERVILLE LES PARCS 37 X 10
33 FIEU, LE 157 W 28
02 FIEULAINE 28 LA 7
47 FIEUX 186 Y 33
83 FIGANIERES 198 ZA 35
2A FIGARI C 230 LB 44
31 FIGAROL 217 AA 37
46 FIGEAC S 174 FA 30
88 FIGNEVELLE 88 WA 15
80 FIGNIERES 26 IA 8
02 FILAIN 28 MA 9
70 FILAIN 88 YA 17
72 FILLE 78 X 16
54 FILLIERES 31 WA 9
62 FILLIEVRES 16 GA 5
74 FILLINGES 139 YA 23
66 FILLOLS 222 HA 39
57 FILSTROFF 47 ZA 9
88 FIMENIL 68 AB 14
66 FINESTRET 222 HA 39
82 FINHAN 188 BA 33
80 FINS 17 KA 6
25 FINS, LES 108 AB 19
27 FIQUEFLEUR EQUAINVILLE 23 Y 9
24 FIRBEIX 144 AA 26
14 FIRFOL 37 Y 10
12 FIRMI 175 GA 31
42 FIRMINY C 149 PA 27
68 FISLIS 90 DB 17
51 FISMES C 28 MA 9
38 FITILIEU 152 VA 26
11 FITOU 223 JA 38
60 FITZ JAMES 26 HA 9
43 FIX ST GENEYS 163 MA 28
57 FIXEM 32 YA 9
21 FIXIN 104 QA 19
21 FLACEY 105 TA 18
28 FLACEY 60 CA 15
71 FLACEY EN BRESSE 122 UA 21
38 FLACHERE, LA 153 XA 27
38 FLACHERES 151 UA 26
78 FLACOURT 39 DA 11
89 FLACY 64 MA 14
25 FLAGEY 107 XA 19
52 FLAGEY 86 TA 16
21 FLAGEY ECHEZEAUX 105 SA 19
21 FLAGEY LES AUXONNE 106 UA 19
25 FLAGEY RIGNEY 107 YA 18
12 FLAGNAC 175 GA 30
70 FLAGY 88 YA 17
71 FLAGY 120 RA 22
77 FLAGY 63 JA 14
08 FLAIGNES HAVYS 29 QA 7
54 FLAINVAL 68 ZA 12
50 FLAMANVILLE 33 O 8
76 FLAMANVILLE 24 AA 8
32 FLAMARENS 187 AA 33
02 FLAMENGRIE, LA 19 OA 6
59 FLAMENGRIE, LA 19 NA 5
76 FLAMETS FRETILS 25 DA 7
21 FLAMMERANS 106 UA 19
52 FLAMMERECOURT 66 TA 14
27 FLANCOURT CATELON 24 AA 9
25 FLANGEBOUCHE 107 ZA 19
84 FLASSAN 196 TA 33
83 FLASSANS SUR ISSOLE 203 YA 36
55 FLASSIGNY 31 UA 9

57 FLASTROFF 47 ZA 9
63 FLAT 148 LA 26
80 FLAUCOURT 17 JA 7
24 FLAUGEAC 157 Y 30
46 FLAUGNAC 173 CA 32
46 FLAUJAC GARE 174 EA 30
46 FLAUJAC POUJOLS 174 DA 31
33 FLAUJAGUES 157 W 29
59 FLAUMONT WAUDRECHIES 19 OA 6
30 FLAUX 193 QA 33
60 FLAVACOURT 25 EA 9
07 FLAVIAC 164 RA 30
87 FLAVIGNAC 144 BA 25
21 FLAVIGNEROT 105 SA 18
18 FLAVIGNY 117 JA 20
51 FLAVIGNY 42 OA 11
02 FLAVIGNY LE GRAND ET BEAURAIN 28 MA 7
54 FLAVIGNY SUR MOSELLE 68 YA 13
21 FLAVIGNY SUR OZERAIN 85 QA 17
12 FLAVIN 175 IA 32
02 FLAVY LE MARTEL 27 KA 8
60 FLAVY LE MELDEUX 27 KA 8
01 FLAXIEU 138 WA 25
68 FLAXLANDEN 90 DB 17
23 FLAYAT 146 HA 25
83 FLAYOSC 203 YA 35
16 FLEAC 143 W 26
17 FLEAC SUR SEUGNE 142 U 26
72 FLECHE, LA S 78 W 16
62 FLECHIN 8 GA 4
60 FLECHY 26 GA 8
21 FLEE 104 PA 18
72 FLEE 79 Y 16
08 FLEIGNEUX 30 SA 7
57 FLEISHEIM 48 CB 12
86 FLEIX 114 Z 22
24 FLEIX, LE 157 X 29
36 FLERE LA RIVIERE 114 BA 20
61 FLERS C 57 U 12
62 FLERS 16 GA 5
80 FLERS 17 JA 6
59 FLERS EN ESCREBIEUX 17 KA 4
80 FLERS SUR NOYE 26 GA 7
59 FLESQUIERES 18 KA 6
80 FLESSELLES 16 GA 6
57 FLETRANGE 47 ZA 10
59 FLETRE 8 IA 3
58 FLETY 119 NA 21
15 FLEURAC 142 W 25
24 FLEURAC 158 BA 28
32 FLEURANCE C 187 Z 34
23 FLEURAT 131 EA 23
62 FLEURBAIX 9 JA 3
61 FLEURE 58 W 12
86 FLEURE 113 Y 22
25 FLEUREY 108 AB 18
70 FLEUREY LES FAVERNEY 88 XA 16
70 FLEUREY LES LAVONCOURT 87 WA 17
70 FLEUREY LES ST LOUP 88 YA 16
21 FLEUREY SUR OUCHE 105 SA 18
69 FLEURIE 136 RA 23
03 FLEURIEL 134 KA 23
69 FLEURIEU SUR SAONE 137 SA 25
69 FLEURIEUX SUR L'ARBRESLE 136 RA 25
35 FLEURIGNE 76 R 14
60 FLEURINES 40 IA 10
71 FLEURVILLE 121 SA 22
02 FLEURY 41 KA 10
11 FLEURY 213 KA 36
50 FLEURY 56 Q 11
57 FLEURY 46 YA 11
60 FLEURY 39 FA 10
62 FLEURY 16 GA 4
80 FLEURY 26 GA 7
55 FLEURY DEVANT DOUAUMONT 44 UA 10
77 FLEURY EN BIERE 62 IA 13
27 FLEURY LA FORET 25 DA 9
71 FLEURY LA MONTAGNE 135 OA 23
51 FLEURY LA RIVIERE 42 NA 10
89 FLEURY LA VALLEE 83 LA 16
45 FLEURY LES AUBRAIS C 81 FA 15
91 FLEURY MEROGIS 62 HA 12
27 FLEURY SUR ANDELLE C 25 CA 9
58 FLEURY SUR LOIRE 118 LA 20
14 FLEURY SUR ORNE 36 V 10
08 FLEVILLE 30 SA 9
54 FLEVILLE DEVANT NANCY 68 YA 12
54 FLEVILLE LIXIERES 45 WA 10
57 FLEVY 46 YA 10
78 FLEXANVILLE 39 EA 11
67 FLEXBOURG 70 DB 13
71 FLEY 120 RA 21
89 FLEYS 84 NA 16
58 FLEZ CUZY 103 MA 18
08 FLIGNY 29 PA 7
54 FLIN 68 AB 13
59 FLINES LES MORTAGNE 10 MA 4
59 FLINES LEZ RACHES 18 KA 4
78 FLINS NEUVE EGLISE 39 DA 11
78 FLINS SUR SEINE 39 FA 11
27 FLIPOU 24 CA 9
54 FLIREY 45 WA 11
80 FLIXECOURT 16 FA 6
08 FLIZE C 30 RA 8
85 FLOCELLIERE, LA 111 S 20
57 FLOCOURT 47 ZA 11
76 FLOCQUES 15 CA 6
89 FLOGNY LA CHAPELLE C 84 NA 15
08 FLOING 30 SA 8
17 FLOIRAC 141 T 26
33 FLOIRAC C 156 U 29
46 FLOIRAC 159 DA 29
48 FLORAC S 177 MA 31
57 FLORANGE C 32 XA 9
88 FLOREMONT 68 YA 14
34 FLORENSAC C 214 MA 36
51 FLORENT EN ARGONNE 44 SA 10
39 FLORENTIA 138 UA 22
81 FLORENTIN 189 FA 33
12 FLORENTIN LA CAPELLE 175 IA 30
46 FLORESSAS 173 BA 31
90 FLORIMONT 90 CB 17
24 FLORIMONT GAUMIER 173 CA 30
62 FLORINGHEM 16 HA 4
17 FLOTTE, LA 126 Q 23
50 FLOTTEMANVILLE 33 Q 9
50 FLOTTEMANVILLE HAGUE 33 O 8
33 FLOUDES 171 W 30
11 FLOURE 221 HA 37
31 FLOURENS 210 DA 35
59 FLOURSIES 19 OA 5
59 FLOYON 19 NA 6
73 FLUMET 139 ZA 25
02 FLUQUIERES 27 KA 7
80 FLUY 26 FA 7
55 FOAMEIX ORNEL 45 VA 10
2A FOCE 230 KB 43
2B FOCICCHIA 228 LB 41
18 FOECY 100 GA 19
22 FOEIL, LE 54 J 13
08 FOISCHES 20 RA 6
12 FOISSAC 174 FA 31
30 FOISSAC 193 PA 33
01 FOISSIAT 137 TA 22
21 FOISSY 104 QA 19
89 FOISSY LES VEZELAY 103 NA 18
89 FOISSY SUR VANNE 64 MA 14
09 FOIX P 219 DA 38
31 FOLCARDE 211 EA 36
02 FOLEMBRAY 27 LA 8
68 FOLGENSBOURG 90 DB 17
29 FOLGOET, LE 51 D 13
50 FOLIE, LA 35 S 10
80 FOLIES 27 IA 7
57 FOLKLING 47 BB 10
78 FOLLAINVILLE DENNEMONT 39 EA 11
87 FOLLES 131 DA 24
76 FOLLETIERE, LA 24 AA 8
14 FOLLETIERE ABENON, LA 37 Y 11
27 FOLLEVILLE 37 Y 10
80 FOLLEVILLE 26 HA 8
50 FOLLIGNY 56 Q 12
57 FOLSCHVILLER 47 AB 10
88 FOMEREY 68 YA 14
79 FOMPERRON 112 W 22
31 FONBEAUZARD 188 DA 34
21 FONCEGRIVE 86 TA 17
80 FONCHES FONCHETTE 27 JA 7
39 FONCINE LE BAS 123 XA 21
39 FONCINE LE HAUT 123 XA 21
62 FONCQUEVILLERS 17 IA 6
12 FONDAMENTE 191 KA 34
37 FONDETTES 98 Z 18
70 FONDREMAND 107 XA 18
47 FONGRAVE 172 Y 31
76 FONGUEUSEMARE 23 X 8
24 FONROQUE 157 Y 30
07 FONS 178 PA 30
30 FONS 193 PA 33
46 FONS 174 FA 30
30 FONS SUR LUSSAN 178 PA 32
02 FONSOMMES 18 LA 7
31 FONSORBES 210 CA 35
66 FONT ROMEU ODEILLO VIA 222 FA 40
25 FONTAIN 107 XA 19
10 FONTAINE 65 RA 14
38 FONTAINE C 166 VA 28
90 FONTAINE C 90 BB 17
59 FONTAINE AU BOIS 18 MA 6
59 FONTAINE AU PIRE 18 LA 6
27 FONTAINE BELLENGER 38 CA 10
60 FONTAINE BONNELEAU 26 GA 8
60 FONTAINE CHAALIS 40 IA 10
17 FONTAINE CHALENDRAY 128 V 24
53 FONTAINE COUVERTE 76 R 16
84 FONTAINE DE VAUCLUSE 196 TA 33
51 FONTAINE DENIS NUISY 64 NA 12
76 FONTAINE EN BRAY 25 DA 8
51 FONTAINE EN DORMOIS 43 RA 10
14 FONTAINE ETOUPEFOUR 35 U 10
77 FONTAINE FOURCHES 63 LA 13
21 FONTAINE FRANCAISE C 87 UA 17
49 FONTAINE GUERIN 96 V 17
14 FONTAINE HENRY 35 U 9
27 FONTAINE HEUDEBOURG 38 CA 10
27 FONTAINE L'ABBE 37 Z 10
62 FONTAINE L'ETALON 16 FA 5
89 FONTAINE LA GAILLARDE 63 LA 14
28 FONTAINE LA GUYON 60 CA 13
27 FONTAINE LA LOUVET 37 Y 10
76 FONTAINE LA MALLET 23 X 8
91 FONTAINE LA RIVIERE 61 GA 14
27 FONTAINE LA SORET 37 Z 10
60 FONTAINE LAVAGANNE 25 FA 8
76 FONTAINE LE BOURG 24 BA 8
86 FONTAINE LE COMTE 113 X 22
76 FONTAINE LE DUN C 24 AA 7
14 FONTAINE LE PIN 36 V 11
77 FONTAINE LE PORT 62 IA 13
73 FONTAINE LE PUITS 153 ZA 26
80 FONTAINE LE SEC 16 EA 7
61 FONTAINE LES BASSETS 36 W 11
62 FONTAINE LES BOULANS 16 GA 4
80 FONTAINE LES CAPPY 27 IA 7
02 FONTAINE LES CLERCS 27 KA 7
25 FONTAINE LES CLERVAL 107 ZA 18
41 FONTAINE LES COTEAUX 79 AA 16
62 FONTAINE LES CROISILLES 17 JA 5
21 FONTAINE LES DIJON C 105 SA 18
10 FONTAINE LES GRES 64 NA 13
62 FONTAINE LES HERMANS 8 HA 4
70 FONTAINE LES LUXEUIL 88 YA 16
28 FONTAINE LES RIBOUTS 60 CA 12
02 FONTAINE LES VERVINS 28 OA 7
10 FONTAINE MACON 63 MA 13
49 FONTAINE MILON 96 V 17
02 FONTAINE NOTRE DAME 28 LA 7
59 FONTAINE NOTRE DAME 18 KA 6
41 FONTAINE RAOUL 80 BA 15
28 FONTAINE SIMON 60 BA 13
27 FONTAINE SOUS JOUY 38 CA 10
80 FONTAINE SOUS MONTDIDIER 26 HA 8
76 FONTAINE SOUS PREAUX 24 BA 9
60 FONTAINE ST LUCIEN 26 GA 8
72 FONTAINE ST MARTIN, LA 78 W 16
51 FONTAINE SUR AY 42 OA 10
80 FONTAINE SUR MAYE 16 FA 5
80 FONTAINE SUR SOMME 16 FA 6
02 FONTAINE UTERTE 18 LA 7
77 FONTAINEBLEAU S 62 IA 13
39 FONTAINEBRUX 122 UA 21
71 FONTAINES 120 RA 20
85 FONTAINES 111 S 22
89 FONTAINES 83 LA 17
17 FONTAINES D'OZILLAC 142 U 27
21 FONTAINES EN DUESMOIS 85 OA 17
41 FONTAINES EN SOLOGNE 80 DA 17
21 FONTAINES LES SECHES 85 QA 16
55 FONTAINES ST CLAIR 30 TA 9
69 FONTAINES ST MARTIN 137 SA 25
52 FONTAINES SUR MARNE 66 TA 13
69 FONTAINES SUR SAONE 137 SA 25
77 FONTAINS 63 JA 13
06 FONTAN 199 EB 33
30 FONTANES 193 OA 34
34 FONTANES 193 OA 34
42 FONTANES 150 QA 26
46 FONTANES 174 DA 32
48 FONTANES 163 NA 30
11 FONTANES DE SAULT 223 FA 38
46 FONTANES DU CAUSSE 174 DA 30
15 FONTANGES 161 HA 28
21 FONTANGY 104 PA 18
23 FONTANIERES 133 HA 24
38 FONTANIL CORNILLON 152 VA 27
43 FONTANNES 162 LA 27
48 FONTANS 162 LA 30
30 FONTARECHES 178 QA 32
16 FONTCLAIREAU 129 X 25
11 FONTCOUVERTE 223 IA 37
17 FONTCOUVERTE 142 T 25
73 FONTCOUVERTE LA TOUSSUIRE 153 YA 27
76 FONTELAYE, LA 24 AA 8
61 FONTENAI LES LOUVETS 58 W 13
61 FONTENAI SUR ORNE 58 W 12
77 FONTENAILLES 63 JA 13
89 FONTENAILLES 83 MA 17
27 FONTENAY 39 DA 10
36 FONTENAY 99 EA 19
50 FONTENAY 57 S 12
71 FONTENAY 120 PA 22
76 FONTENAY 23 X 8
88 FONTENAY 68 ZA 14
92 FONTENAY AUX ROSES C 40 GA 12
10 FONTENAY DE BOSSERY 63 MA 13
95 FONTENAY EN PARISIS 40 HA 10
85 FONTENAY LE COMTE S 111 T 22
78 FONTENAY LE FLEURY 39 FA 11
14 FONTENAY LE MARMION 36 V 10
14 FONTENAY LE PESNEL 35 U 10
91 FONTENAY LE VICOMTE 62 HA 13
91 FONTENAY LES BRIIS 61 GA 12
78 FONTENAY MAUVOISIN 39 DA 11
89 FONTENAY PRES CHABLIS 84 NA 16
89 FONTENAY PRES VEZELAY 103 NA 18
94 FONTENAY SOUS BOIS C 40 HA 11
89 FONTENAY SOUS FOURONNES 84 MA 17
78 FONTENAY ST PERE 39 EA 11
28 FONTENAY SUR CONIE 61 EA 14
28 FONTENAY SUR EURE 60 CA 13
45 FONTENAY SUR LOING 62 IA 15
50 FONTENAY SUR MER 33 O 9
72 FONTENAY SUR VEGRE 78 V 16
60 FONTENAY TORCY 25 EA 8
77 FONTENAY TRESIGNY 40 JA 12
02 FONTENELLE 19 NA 6
21 FONTENELLE 87 UA 17
90 FONTENELLE 90 BB 17
35 FONTENELLE, LA 56 P 13
41 FONTENELLE, LA 79 BA 15
02 FONTENELLE EN BRIE 41 MA 11
25 FONTENELLE MONTBY 107 ZA 18
25 FONTENELLES, LES 108 AB 19
14 FONTENERMONT 56 R 12
17 FONTENET 128 U 24
16 FONTENILLE 129 X 24
79 FONTENILLE ST MARTIN D'ENTRAIGUES 128 W 23
31 FONTENILLES 210 BA 35
70 FONTENOIS LA VILLE 88 YA 15
70 FONTENOIS LES MONTBOZON 88 YA 17
25 FONTENOTTE 107 YA 18
89 FONTENOUILLES 83 KA 16
02 FONTENOY 27 KA 9
89 FONTENOY 83 LA 17
54 FONTENOY LA JOUTE 68 AB 13
88 FONTENOY LE CHATEAU 88 YA 15
54 FONTENOY SUR MOSELLE 45 XA 12
39 FONTENU 122 WA 21
57 FONTENY 47 ZA 11
11 FONTERS DU RAZES 211 FA 36
34 FONTES 214 LA 35
33 FONTET 171 W 30
10 FONTETTE 65 RA 15
49 FONTEVRAUD L'ABBAYE 97 W 19
36 FONTGOMBAULT 114 AA 21
36 FONTGUENAND 99 DA 19
04 FONTIENNE 197 WA 33
11 FONTIERS CABARDES 212 GA 36
11 FONTIES D'AUDE 221 HA 37
11 FONTJONCOUSE 223 IA 37
57 FONTOY C 32 XA 9
66 FONTPEDROUSE 222 GA 40
66 FONTRABIOUSE 222 FA 39
65 FONTRAILLES 208 Y 36
10 FONTVANNES 64 NA 14
13 FONTVIEILLE 195 RA 34
57 FORBACH S 47 BB 10
83 FORCALQUEIRET 203 XA 36
04 FORCALQUIER S 197 WA 33
53 FORCE 77 T 15
11 FORCE, LA 221 FA 37
24 FORCE, LA C 157 Y 29
54 FORCELLES SOUS GUGNEY 67 XA 13
54 FORCELLES ST GORGON 67 XA 13
80 FORCEVILLE 17 HA 6
80 FORCEVILLE EN VIMEU 16 EA 6
52 FORCEY 66 UA 14
2A FORCIOLO 227 KB 42
74 FORCLAZ, LA 140 AB 23
59 FOREST EN CAMBRESIS 18 MA 6
80 FOREST L'ABBAYE 16 EA 5
29 FOREST LANDERNEAU, LA 51 D 13
80 FOREST MONTIERS 15 EA 5
05 FOREST ST JULIEN 167 XA 30
59 FOREST SUR MARQUE 9 KA 3
02 FORESTE 27 KA 7
51 FORESTIERE, LA 64 MA 12
61 FORET AUVRAY, LA 58 V 12
16 FORET DE TESSE, LA 129 X 24
27 FORET DU PARC, LA 38 CA 11
23 FORET DU TEMPLE, LA 132 FA 22
29 FORET FOUESNANT, LA 72 E 16
27 FORET LA FOLIE 38 DA 10
91 FORET LE ROI, LA 61 FA 13
91 FORET STE CROIX, LA 62 GA 13
79 FORET SUR SEVRE, LA 111 T 21
77 FORFRY 40 JA 10
88 FORGE, LA 89 AB 15
17 FORGES 127 S 24
19 FORGES 160 EA 28
49 FORGES 96 V 19
61 FORGES 58 X 13
77 FORGES 63 JA 13
56 FORGES, LES 74 K 15
79 FORGES, LES 112 W 22
88 FORGES, LES 68 ZA 14
35 FORGES LA FORET 76 Q 16
91 FORGES LES BAINS 61 FA 12
76 FORGES LES EAUX C 25 DA 8
55 FORGES SUR MEUSE 44 UA 10
31 FORGUES 209 BA 35
63 FORIE, LA 149 NA 26
21 FORLEANS 85 PA 17
14 FORMENTIN 36 X 10
60 FORMERIE C 25 EA 8
14 FORMIGNY 35 S 9
66 FORMIGUERES 222 FA 39
09 FORNEX 218 CA 37
79 FORS 128 U 23
67 FORSTFELD 50 GB 11
67 FORSTHEIM 48 EB 11
39 FORT DU PLASNE 123 XA 21
67 FORT LOUIS 50 GB 12
80 FORT MAHON PLAGE 15 DA 5
59 FORT MARDYCK 8 GA 2
27 FORT MOVILLE 23 Y 9
41 FORTAN 79 AA 16
62 FORTEL EN ARTOIS 16 GA 5
38 FORTERESSE, LA 152 UA 27
68 FORTSCHWIHR 70 DB 15
31 FOS 217 Z 38
34 FOS 213 KA 35
13 FOS SUR MER 201 SA 35
09 FOSSAT, LE C 218 CA 37
08 FOSSE 30 SA 9
41 FOSSE 80 CA 17
66 FOSSE 222 HA 38
76 FOSSE, LE 25 DA 8
10 FOSSE CORDUAN, LA 64 MA 13
49 FOSSE DE TIGNE, LA 96 U 19
24 FOSSEMAGNE 158 BA 28
80 FOSSEMANANT 26 GA 7
95 FOSSES 40 HA 10
79 FOSSES, LES 128 U 23
33 FOSSES ET BALEYSSAC 171 W 30
60 FOSSEUSE 39 GA 10
62 FOSSEUX 17 HA 5
57 FOSSIEUX 46 YA 11
02 FOSSOY 41 MA 10
76 FOUCARMONT 25 DA 7
76 FOUCART 23 Z 8
50 FOUCARVILLE 33 R 9
80 FOUCAUCOURT EN SANTERRE 27 IA 7
80 FOUCAUCOURT HORS NESLE 15 EA 7
55 FOUCAUCOURT SUR THABAS 44 TA 11
70 FOUCHECOURT 88 XA 16
88 FOUCHECOURT 88 WA 15
25 FOUCHERANS 107 XA 19
39 FOUCHERANS 106 UA 19
10 FOUCHERES 65 PA 14
89 FOUCHERES 63 KA 14
55 FOUCHERES AUX BOIS 66 TA 12
45 FOUCHEROLLES 63 JA 15
67 FOUCHY 69 CB 14
27 FOUCRAINVILLE 38 CA 11
67 FOUDAY 69 CB 13
80 FOUENCAMPS 26 HA 7
29 FOUESNANT C 72 E 16
62 FOUFFLIN RICAMETZ 16 HA 5
54 FOUG 45 WA 12
31 FOUGARON 217 AA 37
09 FOUGAX ET BARRINEUF 221 FA 38
49 FOUGERE 78 V 17
85 FOUGERE 110 R 21
35 FOUGERES S 56 R 14
41 FOUGERES SUR BIEVRE 99 CA 18
56 FOUGERETS, LES 75 M 16
36 FOUGEROLLES 115 EA 22
70 FOUGEROLLES 89 ZA 16
53 FOUGEROLLES DU PLESSIS 57 S 13
24 FOUGUEYROLLES 157 X 29
12 FOUILLADE, LA 174 FA 32
60 FOUILLEUSE 26 HA 9
05 FOUILLOUSE 181 XA 31
42 FOUILLOUSE, LA 150 PA 26
17 FOUILLOUX, LE 156 W 28
60 FOUILLOY 25 EA 7
80 FOUILLOY 26 HA 7
77 FOUJU 62 IA 13
52 FOULAIN 86 TA 15
60 FOULANGUES 40 GA 10
47 FOULAYRONNES 172 Z 32
27 FOULBEC 23 Y 9
57 FOULCREY 69 BB 12
24 FOULEIX 158 Z 29
39 FOULENAY 122 VA 20
57 FOULIGNY 47 ZA 10
14 FOULOGNES 35 S 10
16 FOUQUEBRUNE 143 X 26
60 FOUQUENIES 26 FA 9
62 FOUQUEREUIL 8 IA 4
60 FOUQUEROLLES 26 GA 9
80 FOUQUESCOURT 27 IA 7
16 FOUQUEURE 129 W 25
27 FOUQUEVILLE 38 AA 10
62 FOUQUIERES LES BETHUNE 8 IA 4
62 FOUQUIERES LES LENS 17 JA 4
38 FOUR 151 TA 26
17 FOURAS 126 R 24
25 FOURBANNE 107 YA 18
25 FOURCATIER ET MAISON NEUVE 123 YA 21
32 FOURCES 186 X 33
58 FOURCHAMBAULT 102 KA 19
14 FOURCHES 36 W 11
80 FOURCIGNY 25 EA 7
02 FOURDRAIN 28 MA 8
80 FOURDRINOY 16 GA 7
25 FOURG 106 WA 19
27 FOURGES 39 DA 10
25 FOURGS, LES 124 ZA 20
03 FOURILLES 134 KA 23
46 FOURMAGNAC 174 FA 30
27 FOURMETOT 23 Z 9
59 FOURMIES 19 OA 6
89 FOURNAUDIN 64 MA 14
42 FOURNEAUX 135 PA 24
50 FOURNEAUX 35 S 11
73 FOURNEAUX 168 AB 28
14 FOURNEAUX LE VAL 36 V 11
48 FOURNELS C 162 KA 29
30 FOURNES 195 RA 33
11 FOURNES CABARDES 212 HA 36
59 FOURNES EN WEPPES 9 JA 4
14 FOURNET, LE 36 X 10
25 FOURNET BLANCHEROCHE 108 AB 19
25 FOURNETS LUISANS 107 ZA 19
14 FOURNEVILLE 23 X 9
60 FOURNIVAL 26 HA 9
63 FOURNOLS 148 MA 26
15 FOURNOULES 175 GA 30
89 FOURONNES 83 MA 17
30 FOURQUES 195 RA 34
66 FOURQUES 224 IA 39
47 FOURQUES SUR GARONNE 171 X 31
78 FOURQUEUX 39 FA 11
31 FOURQUEVAUX 210 DA 35
33 FOURS 156 T 28
58 FOURS C 119 NA 20
27 FOURS EN VEXIN 39 DA 10
11 FOURTOU 221 HA 38
85 FOUSSAIS PAYRE 111 T 22
90 FOUSSEMAGNE 90 BB 17
31 FOUSSERET, LE C 210 BA 36
16 FOUSSIGNAC 142 W 25
70 FOUVENT ST ANDOCHE 87 VA 17
34 FOUZILHON 213 LA 35
57 FOVILLE 46 YA 11
83 FOX AMPHOUX 203 XA 35
79 FOYE MONJAULT, LA 128 U 23
34 FOZIERES 192 LA 34
2A FOZZANO 229 KB 43
71 FRAGNES 121 SA 20
70 FRAHIER ET CHATEBIER 89 AB 17
21 FRAIGNOT ET VESVROTTE 86 SA 17
08 FRAILLICOURT 29 PA 8
54 FRAIMBOIS 68 ZA 13
88 FRAIN 67 WA 15
90 FRAIS 90 BB 17
39 FRAISANS 106 WA 19
54 FRAISNES EN SAINTOIS 67 XA 13
24 FRAISSE 157 X 29
11 FRAISSE CABARDES 212 GA 36
11 FRAISSE DES CORBIERES 223 JA 38
34 FRAISSE SUR AGOUT 213 JA 35
42 FRAISSES 149 PA 27
81 FRAISSINES 190 HA 33
48 FRAISSINET DE FOURQUES 177 MA 32
48 FRAISSINET DE LOZERE 177 NA 31
88 FRAIZE C 69 BB 14
10 FRALIGNES 65 QA 14
28 FRAMBOISIERE, LA 60 BA 13
25 FRAMBOUHANS 108 AB 19
62 FRAMECOURT 16 GA 5
80 FRAMERVILLE RAINECOURT 27 IA 7
80 FRAMICOURT 15 EA 6
70 FRAMONT 87 VA 17
52 FRAMPAS 66 SA 13
70 FRANCALMONT 88 YA 16
57 FRANCALTROFF 47 AB 11
31 FRANCARVILLE 211 EA 35
60 FRANCASTEL 26 GA 8
41 FRANCAY 80 BA 17
31 FRANCAZAL 218 BA 38
47 FRANCESCAS C 186 Y 33
03 FRANCHESSE 118 KA 21
08 FRANCHEVAL 30 TA 8
70 FRANCHEVELLE 89 ZA 16
21 FRANCHEVILLE 105 SA 18
27 FRANCHEVILLE 37 AA 12
39 FRANCHEVILLE 122 VA 20
51 FRANCHEVILLE 43 QA 11
54 FRANCHEVILLE 45 WA 12
61 FRANCHEVILLE 58 W 12
69 FRANCHEVILLE 150 RA 25
08 FRANCHEVILLE, LA 30 RA 8
60 FRANCIERES 27 IA 9
80 FRANCIERES 16 FA 6
36 FRANCILLON 115 DA 20
26 FRANCILLON SUR ROUBION 179 TA 30
02 FRANCILLY SELENCY 27 KA 7
73 FRANCIN 153 XA 26
74 FRANCLENS 138 WA 24
79 FRANCOIS 128 U 22
31 FRANCON 209 AA 36
54 FRANCONVILLE 68 ZA 13
95 FRANCONVILLE C 40 GA 11
46 FRANCOULES 174 DA 31
70 FRANCOURT 87 WA 17
28 FRANCOURVILLE 61 EA 13
33 FRANCS 157 W 29
37 FRANCUEIL 98 BA 18
25 FRANEY 106 WA 18
74 FRANGY C 138 WA 24
71 FRANGY EN BRESSE 122 UA 21
68 FRANKEN 90 DB 17
80 FRANLEU 15 DA 6
25 FRANOIS 107 XA 19
31 FRANQUEVIELLE 217 Z 37
02 FRANQUEVILLE 28 NA 7
27 FRANQUEVILLE 37 Z 10
80 FRANQUEVILLE 16 FA 6
76 FRANQUEVILLE ST PIERRE 24 BA 9
01 FRANS 136 RA 24
80 FRANSART 27 IA 7
23 FRANSECHES 132 FA 24
80 FRANSU 16 FA 6
80 FRANSURES 26 GA 8
80 FRANVILLERS 17 HA 6
21 FRANXAULT 105 UA 19
88 FRAPELLE 69 BB 14
57 FRAQUELFING 69 BB 12
39 FRAROZ 123 XA 21
58 FRASNAY REUGNY 118 MA 20
25 FRASNE 123 YA 20
39 FRASNE 106 VA 19
70 FRASNE LE CHATEAU 106 WA 18
39 FRASNEE, LA 122 WA 22
39 FRASNOIS, LE 122 WA 21
59 FRASNOY 18 MA 5
2A FRASSETO 227 KB 42
57 FRAUENBERG 48 CB 10
81 FRAUSSEILLES 189 FA 33
10 FRAVAUX 65 RA 14
81 FRAYSSE, LE 190 HA 33
46 FRAYSSINET 174 DA 30
46 FRAYSSINET LE GELAT 173 BA 30
46 FRAYSSINHES 160 FA 29
28 FRAZE 60 BA 14
76 FREAUVILLE 25 CA 7
88 FREBECOURT 67 VA 13
39 FREBUANS 122 UA 21
40 FRECHE, LE 185 V 33
65 FRECHEDE 208 X 36
80 FRECHENCOURT 17 HA 6
65 FRECHENDETS 216 X 37
31 FRECHET, LE 217 AA 37
65 FRECHET AURE 216 Y 38
47 FRECHOU 186 Y 33
65 FRECHOU FRECHET 216 X 37
52 FRECOURT 87 UA 15
70 FREDERIC FONTAINE 89 AB 17
17 FREDIERE, LA 128 U 25
36 FREDILLE 115 DA 20
47 FREGIMONT 172 Y 32
32 FREGOUVILLE 209 AA 35
22 FREHEL 54 M 12
49 FREIGNE 94 R 17
05 FREISSINIERES 168 ZA 30
05 FREISSINOUSE, LA 181 XA 31
57 FREISTROFF 47 ZA 9
15 FREIX ANGLARDS 160 HA 28
81 FREJAIROLLES 190 GA 33
81 FREJEVILLE 212 GA 35
83 FREJUS C 204 AB 35
68 FRELAND 69 CB 14
59 FRELINGHIEN 9 JA 3
95 FREMAINVILLE 39 EA 10
95 FREMECOURT 39 FA 10
54 FREMENIL 68 AB 13
55 FREMEREVILLE SOUS LES COTES 45 VA 12
57 FREMERY 47 ZA 12
57 FREMESTROFF 47 AB 11
62 FREMICOURT 17 JA 6

88 FREMIFONTAINE 69 AB 14
80 FREMONTIERS 26 FA 7
54 FREMONVILLE 69 BB 12
76 FRENAYE, LA 23 Z 8
62 FRENCQ 7 EA 4
88 FRENELLE LA GRANDE 67 XA 14
88 FRENELLE LA PETITE 67 XA 14
61 FRENES 57 T 12
76 FRENEUSE 24 BA 9
78 FRENEUSE 39 DA 11
27 FRENEUSE SUR RISLE 37 Z 10
73 FRENEY 168 AB 28
38 FRENEY D'OISANS, LE 167 XA 28
60 FRENICHES 27 JA 8
21 FRENOIS 86 SA 17
88 FRENOIS 68 XA 14
14 FRENOUVILLE 36 V 10
95 FREPILLON 40 GA 10
76 FRESLES 25 CA 7
61 FRESNAIE FAYEL, LA 37 X 11
35 FRESNAIS, LA 55 O 12
10 FRESNAY 65 RA 14
44 FRESNAY EN RETZ 109 O 20
28 FRESNAY L'EVEQUE 61 EA 14
28 FRESNAY LE COMTE 60 DA 14
28 FRESNAY LE GILMERT 60 DA 13
76 FRESNAY LE LONG 24 BA 8
61 FRESNAY LE SAMSON 36 X 11
72 FRESNAY SUR SARTHE C 58 W 14
61 FRESNAYE AU SAUVAGE, LA 58 V 12
72 FRESNAYE
SUR CHEDOUET, LA C 58 X 13
27 FRESNE, LE 38 BA 11
51 FRESNE, LE 43 RA 11
14 FRESNE CAMILLY, LE 35 U 10
27 FRESNE CAUVERVILLE 37 Y 10
27 FRESNE L'ARCHEVEQUE 38 CA 9
14 FRESNE LA MERE 36 W 11
76 FRESNE LE PLAN 24 CA 9
60 FRESNE LEGUILLON 39 FA 10
50 FRESNE PORET, LE 57 S 12
70 FRESNE ST MAMES C 88 WA 17
44 FRESNE SUR LOIRE, LE 95 S 18
60 FRESNEAUX
MONTCHEVREUIL 39 FA 9
02 FRESNES 28 LA 8
21 FRESNES 85 OA 17
41 FRESNES 99 CA 18
89 FRESNES 84 OA 16
94 FRESNES C 40 GA 12
55 FRESNES AU MONT 44 UA 11
57 FRESNES EN SAULNOIS 47 ZA 11
02 FRESNES EN TARDENOIS 42 MA 10
55 FRESNES EN WOEVRE C 45 VA 10
62 FRESNES LES MONTAUBAN 17 JA 5
51 FRESNES LES REIMS 29 OA 9
80 FRESNES MAZANCOURT 27 JA 7
52 FRESNES SUR APANCE 87 WA 15
59 FRESNES SUR ESCAUT 18 MA 4
77 FRESNES SUR MARNE 40 IA 11
80 FRESNES TILLOLOY 15 EA 6
80 FRESNEVILLE 25 EA 7
27 FRESNEY 38 CA 11
14 FRESNEY LE PUCEUX 36 U 10
14 FRESNEY LE VIEUX 36 U 11
62 FRESNICOURT LE DOLMEN 17 IA 4
60 FRESNIERES 27 JA 8
54 FRESNOIS LA MONTAGNE 31 VA 9
62 FRESNOY 16 GA 5
62 FRESNOY ANDAINVILLE 25 EA 7
80 FRESNOY AU VAL 26 FA 7
80 FRESNOY EN CHAUSSEE 26 IA 7
62 FRESNOY EN GOHELLE 17 JA 5
60 FRESNOY EN THELLE 40 GA 10
76 FRESNOY FOLNY 25 DA 7
60 FRESNOY LA RIVIERE 41 JA 9
10 FRESNOY LE CHATEAU 65 PA 14
02 FRESNOY LE GRAND 18 LA 6
60 FRESNOY LE LUAT 40 IA 10
80 FRESNOY LES ROYE 27 IA 7
47 FRESPECH 172 AA 32
76 FRESQUIENNES 24 BA 8
30 FRESSAC 193 OA 33
59 FRESSAIN 18 KA 5
02 FRESSANCOURT 28 LA 8
70 FRESSE 89 AB 16
88 FRESSE SUR MOSELLE 89 AB 16
23 FRESSELINES 131 EA 22
80 FRESSENNEVILLE 15 DA 6
59 FRESSIES 18 KA 5
62 FRESSIN 16 FA 4
79 FRESSINES 128 V 23
60 FRESTOY VAUX, LE 26 IA 8
50 FRESVILLE 33 Q 9
73 FRETERIVE 153 YA 26
41 FRETEVAL 80 BA 16
62 FRETHUN 7 EA 2
70 FRETIGNEY ET VELLOREILLE 88 WA 17
28 FRETIGNY 60 BA 14
59 FRETIN 9 KA 4
77 FRETOY 41 KA 12
60 FRETOY LE CHATEAU 27 JA 8
38 FRETTE, LA 152 UA 27
71 FRETTE, LA 121 TA 21
95 FRETTE SUR SEINE, LA 39 GA 11
80 FRETTECUISSE 15 EA 7
80 FRETTEMEULE 15 DA 6
71 FRETTERANS 121 UA 20
08 FRETY, LE 29 PA 7
76 FREULLEVILLE 24 CA 7
62 FREVENT 16 GA 5
76 FREVILLE 24 AA 8
88 FREVILLE 67 VA 14
45 FREVILLE DU GATINAIS 82 HA 15
62 FREVILLERS 17 HA 5
62 FREVIN CAPELLE 17 IA 5
57 FREYBOUSE 47 AB 11
43 FREYCENET LA CUCHE 163 OA 29
43 FREYCENET LA TOUR 163 OA 29
09 FREYCHENET 219 EA 38
57 FREYMING MERLEBACH C 47 AB 10
07 FREYSSENET 164 QA 30
28 FRIAIZE 60 BA 13
14 FRIARDEL 37 Y 11
80 FRIAUCOURT 15 DA 6
54 FRIAUVILLE 45 WA 10
57 FRIBOURG 47 BB 12
80 FRICAMPS 26 FA 7
76 FRICHEMESNIL 24 BA 8
80 FRICOURT 17 IA 6
15 FRIDEFONT 162 KA 29
67 FRIEDOLSHEIM 49 DB 12
02 FRIERES FAILLOUEL 27 LA 8
68 FRIESEN 90 CB 17
67 FRIESENHEIM 70 EB 14
51 FRIGNICOURT 43 RA 12
80 FRISE 17 JA 7
80 FRIVILLE ESCARBOTIN C 15 DA 6
88 FRIZON 68 YA 14
76 FROBERVILLE 23 X 8
60 FROCOURT 26 FA 9
68 FROENINGEN 90 CB 17
67 FROESCHWILLER 48 EB 11
38 FROGES 153 WA 27
80 FROHEN LE GRAND 16 GA 5
80 FROHEN LE PETIT 16 GA 5
67 FROHMUHL 48 CB 11
70 FROIDECONCHE 89 ZA 16
90 FROIDEFONTAINE 90 BB 17
02 FROIDESTREES 19 OA 7
70 FROIDETERRE 89 ZA 16
25 FROIDEVAUX 108 BB 18
39 FROIDEVILLE 122 VA 20
85 FROIDFOND 109 O 20
02 FROIDMONT COHARTILLE 28 NA 8
55 FROIDOS 44 TA 10
60 FROISSY C 26 GA 8
21 FROLOIS 85 RA 17
54 FROLOIS 68 XA 13
08 FROMELENNES 20 SA 6
59 FROMELLES 9 JA 4
87 FROMENTAL 131 CA 23
51 FROMENTIERES 42 NA 11
53 FROMENTIERES 77 T 16
55 FROMEREVILLE LES VALLONS 44 TA 10
55 FROMEZEY 45 VA 10
77 FROMONT 62 HA 14
08 FROMY 30 TA 8
52 FRONCLES 66 TA 14
31 FRONSAC 217 Z 38
33 FRONSAC C 156 V 29
33 FRONTENAC 156 V 30
46 FRONTENAC 174 FA 31
71 FRONTENARD 121 TA 20
69 FRONTENAS 136 RA 24
71 FRONTENAUD 121 UA 22
71 FRONTENAY 122 VA 21
79 FRONTENAY ROHAN ROHAN C 128 U 23
73 FRONTENEX 153 YA 26
34 FRONTIGNAN C 214 NA 35
31 FRONTIGNAN
DE COMMINGES 217 Z 38
31 FRONTIGNAN SAVES 209 AA 36
31 FRONTON C 188 CA 34
38 FRONTONAS 151 TA 26
52 FRONVILLE 66 TA 13
44 FROSSAY 93 O 19
70 FROTEY LES LURE 89 ZA 17
70 FROTEY LES VESOUL 88 YA 17
54 FROUARD 46 XA 12
95 FROUVILLE 39 GA 10
31 FROUZINS 210 CA 35
54 FROVILLE 68 YA 13
80 FROYELLES 16 FA 5
86 FROZES 113 X 21
80 FRUCOURT 16 EA 6
43 FRUGERES LES MINES 148 LA 27
62 FRUGES C 8 GA 4
43 FRUGIERES LE PIN 162 MA 27
28 FRUNCE 60 CA 13
76 FRY 25 DA 8
25 FUANS 108 ZA 19
77 FUBLAINES 41 JA 11
04 FUGERET, LE 198 AB 33
49 FUILET, LE 94 R 18
66 FUILLA 222 HA 39
71 FUISSE 136 RA 23
10 FULIGNY 65 RA 14
68 FULLEREN 90 CB 17
76 FULTOT 24 AA 7
89 FULVY 85 PA 16
08 FUMAY C 20 RA 6
47 FUMEL C 173 AA 31
14 FUMICHON 37 Y 10
67 FURCHHAUSEN 49 DB 12
67 FURDENHEIM 49 EB 12
2B FURIANI 226 MB 39
05 FURMEYER 181 WA 31
21 FUSSEY 105 SA 19
18 FUSSY 100 HA 19
32 FUSTEROUAU 185 W 34
31 FUSTIGNAC 209 AA 36
55 FUTEAU 44 SA 10
13 FUVEAU 202 VA 35
72 FYE 58 W 14

G

40 GAAS 183 S 35
33 GABARNAC 170 V 30
40 GABARRET C 185 W 33
64 GABASTON 207 V 36
64 GABAT 206 S 36
34 GABIAN 213 LA 35
24 GABILLOU 158 BA 28
09 GABRE 218 CA 37
12 GABRIAC 176 IA 31
48 GABRIAC 177 NA 32
48 GABRIAS 177 LA 31
61 GACE C 37 Y 12
56 GACILLY, LA C 75 N 16
58 GACOGNE 103 NA 19
95 GADANCOURT 39 EA 10
27 GADENCOURT 38 CA 11
35 GAEL 75 M 15
24 GAGEAC ET ROUILLAC 157 Y 29
46 GAGNAC SUR CERE 160 FA 30
31 GAGNAC SUR GARONNE 188 CA 34
30 GAGNIERES 178 OA 32
93 GAGNY C 40 HA 11
35 GAHARD 76 P 14
30 GAILHAN 193 OA 34
81 GAILLAC C 189 EA 33
12 GAILLAC D'AVEYRON 176 JA 31
31 GAILLAC TOULZA 210 DA 36
65 GAILLAGOS 215 V 37
33 GAILLAN EN MEDOC 141 S 27
74 GAILLARD 139 YA 23
27 GAILLARD
BOIS CRESSENVILLE 25 CA 9
76 GAILLARDE, LA 24 AA 7
76 GAILLEFONTAINE 25 DA 8
40 GAILLERES 184 U 33
27 GAILLON C 38 CA 10
78 GAILLON SUR MONTCIENT 39 FA 11
76 GAINNEVILLE 23 X 8
11 GAJA ET VILLEDIEU 221 GA 37
11 GAJA LA SELVE 221 FA 37
33 GAJAC 171 W 31
09 GAJAN 218 BA 37
30 GAJAN 193 PA 33
87 GAJOUBERT 130 AA 24
62 GALAMETZ 16 GA 5
65 GALAN C 208 Y 36
47 GALAPIAN 172 Y 32
34 GALARGUES 193 OA 34
2B GALERIA 227 JB 40
09 GALEY 217 AA 38
65 GALEZ 216 Y 37
68 GALFINGUE 90 CB 16
12 GALGAN 175 GA 31
33 GALGON 156 V 29
32 GALIAX 208 W 35
31 GALIE 217 Z 37
11 GALINAGUES 221 FA 38
28 GALLARDON 61 EA 13
30 GALLARGUES LE MONTUEUX 193 PA 34
60 GALLET, LE 26 FA 8
78 GALLUIS 39 EA 12
80 GAMACHES C 15 DA 6
27 GAMACHES EN VEXIN 39 DA 10
40 GAMARDE LES BAINS 184 S 34
64 GAMARTHE 206 R 36
78 GAMBAIS 39 EA 12
78 GAMBAISEUIL 39 EA 12
67 GAMBSHEIM 50 FB 12
64 GAN 207 U 36
09 GANAC 219 DA 38
04 GANAGOBIE 197 WA 33
76 GANCOURT ST ETIENNE 25 EA 8
61 GANDELAIN 58 W 13
02 GANDELU 41 KA 10
57 GANDRANGE 32 XA 10
34 GANGES C 192 NA 33
03 GANNAT C 134 KA 24
03 GANNAY SUR LOIRE 119 MA 21
60 GANNES 26 HA 8
33 GANS 171 V 31
31 GANTIES 217 AA 37
76 GANZEVILLE 23 Y 7
05 GAP P 181 XA 30
80 GAPENNES 16 FA 5
61 GAPREE 59 X 12
31 GARAC 187 BA 34
78 GARANCIERES 39 EA 11
28 GARANCIERES EN BEAUCE 61 FA 13
28 GARANCIERES EN DROUAIS 38 CA 12
09 GARANOU 220 EA 38
16 GARAT 143 X 26
14 GARCELLES SECQUEVILLE 36 V 10
92 GARCHES C 39 GA 11
58 GARCHIZY 102 KA 19
58 GARCHY 102 KA 18
13 GARDANNE C 202 VA 35
04 GARDE, LA 198 ZA 34
38 GARDE, LA 167 XA 28
83 GARDE, LA 203 XA 37
26 GARDE ADHEMAR, LA 179 RA 31
83 GARDE FREINET, LA 204 ZA 36
18 GARDEFORT 101 JA 18
33 GARDEGAN ET TOURTIRAC 157 W 29
65 GARDERES 208 W 36
16 GARDES LE PONTAROUX 143 Y 26
11 GARDIE 221 GA 37
24 GARDONNE 157 Y 29
31 GARDOUCH 211 EA 36
40 GAREIN 184 T 33
27 GARENCIERES 38 CA 11
92 GARENNE COLOMBES, LA C 40 GA 11
27 GARENNES SUR EURE 38 CA 11
78 GARENTREVILLE 62 HA 14
83 GAREOULT 203 XA 36
82 GARGANVILLAR 187 BA 33
31 GARGAS 188 DA 34
84 GARGAS 196 UA 33
78 GARGENVILLE 39 EA 11
95 GARGES LES GONESSE C 40 HA 11
36 GARGILESSE DAMPIERRE 115 DA 22
31 GARIDECH 188 DA 34
82 GARIES 187 BA 34
18 GARIGNY 101 JA 19
31 GARIN 216 Y 38
64 GARINDEIN 206 S 36
29 GARLAN 52 F 13
64 GARLEDE MONDEBAT 207 V 35
64 GARLIN C 207 V 35
30 GARN, LE 178 QA 32
85 GARNACHE, LA 109 O 20
03 GARNAT SUR ENGIEVRE 119 MA 21
28 GARNAY 60 DA 12
01 GARNERANS 137 SA 23
30 GARONS 193 OA 34
64 GAROS 207 U 35
32 GARRAVET 209 AA 36
57 GARREBOURG 69 CB 12
81 GARREVAQUES 211 FA 35
40 GARREY 183 S 34
81 GARRIC, LE 190 GA 33
30 GARRIGUES 193 OA 34
34 GARRIGUES 193 OA 34
81 GARRIGUES 189 EA 34
30 GARRIGUES STE EULALIE 193 PA 33
40 GARROSSE 183 S 33
06 GARS 198 AB 34
23 GARTEMPE 131 EA 23
28 GAS 61 EA 13
27 GASNY 39 DA 10
82 GASQUES 172 AA 32
83 GASSIN 204 ZA 36
14 GAST, LE 56 R 12
40 GASTES 169 R 31
53 GASTINES 76 R 15
77 GASTINS 63 KA 12
28 GASVILLE OISEME 61 DA 13
39 GATEY 122 UA 20
50 GATHEMO 57 S 12
50 GATTEVILLE LE PHARE 33 R 8
06 GATTIERES 200 CB 34
48 GATUZIERES 177 MA 32
45 GAUBERTIN 62 HA 15
85 GAUBRETIERE, LA 110 R 20
62 GAUCHIN LEGAL 17 HA 4
62 GAUCHIN VERLOINGT 16 GA 5
02 GAUCHY 28 LA 7
27 GAUCIEL 38 CA 11
28 GAUDAINE, LA 59 AA 14
06 GAUDE, LA 200 CB 34
60 GAUDECHART 25 FA 8
65 GAUDENT 217 Z 37
62 GAUDIEMPRE 17 HA 5
09 GAUDIES 219 EA 37
32 GAUDONVILLE 187 AA 33
27 GAUDREVILLE LA RIVIERE 38 BA 11
24 GAUGEAC 172 AA 30
30 GAUJAC 193 QA 33
32 GAUJAC 209 AA 35
47 GAUJAC 171 X 31
40 GAUJACQ 184 T 35
32 GAUJAN 209 Z 36
41 GAULT PERCHE, LE 60 AA 15
51 GAULT SOIGNY, LE 42 MA 12
28 GAULT ST DENIS, LE 60 DA 14
31 GAURE 210 DA 35
33 GAURIAC 156 T 28
33 GAURIAGUET 156 U 28
65 GAUSSAN 209 Y 36
22 GAUSSON 54 K 14
61 GAUVILLE 37 Z 11
80 GAUVILLE 25 EA 7
27 GAUVILLE LA CAMPAGNE 38 BA 10
65 GAVARNIE 216 W 39
32 GAVARRET SUR AULOUSTE 187 Z 34
47 GAVAUDUN 172 AA 30
2B GAVIGNANO 228 LB 40
57 GAVISSE 32 YA 9
50 GAVRAY C 56 O 11
44 GAVRE, LE 93 O 17
62 GAVRELLE 17 JA 5
56 GAVRES 73 H 17
14 GAVRUS 35 U 10
65 GAYAN 208 W 36
51 GAYE 42 NA 12
64 GAYON 207 V 35
32 GAZAUPOUY 186 Y 33
65 GAZAVE 216 Y 37
32 GAZAX ET BACCARISSE 208 X 35
78 GAZERAN 61 EA 12
65 GAZOST 216 W 37
71 GEANGES 121 SA 20
40 GEAUNE C 207 U 35
17 GEAY 127 T 25
79 GEAY 112 V 20
65 GEDRE 216 W 38
49 GEE 96 V 18
32 GEE RIVIERE 185 V 34
50 GEFFOSSES 34 P 10
14 GEFOSSE FONTENAY 33 R 9
36 GEHEE 99 DA 19
68 GEISHOUSE 90 BB 16
68 GEISPITZEN 90 DB 17
67 GEISPOLSHEIM C 70 EB 13
68 GEISWASSER 90 EB 15
67 GEISWILLER 49 DB 12
54 GELACOURT 69 AB 13
10 GELANNES 64 MA 13
54 GELAUCOURT 67 XA 13
28 GELLAINVILLE 60 DA 13
54 GELLENONCOURT 46 ZA 12
63 GELLES 147 IA 25
25 GELLIN 123 YA 21
64 GELOS 207 U 36
40 GELOUX 184 T 33
57 GELUCOURT 47 AB 12
88 GELVECOURT ET ADOMPT 68 YA 14
61 GEMAGES 59 Z 14
88 GEMAINGOUTTE 69 CB 14
65 GEMBRIE 217 Z 37
21 GEMEAUX 86 TA 17
13 GEMENOS 202 VA 36
45 GEMIGNY 81 EA 15
31 GEMIL 188 DA 34
88 GEMMELAINCOURT 67 XA 14
25 GEMONVAL 89 ZA 17
54 GEMONVILLE 67 WA 13
17 GEMOZAC C 141 T 26
16 GENAC 143 W 25
95 GENAINVILLE 39 EA 10
69 GENAS 151 SA 25
09 GENAT 219 DA 38
21 GENAY 85 PA 17
69 GENAY 137 SA 25
86 GENCAY C 129 Y 22
88 GENDREVILLE 67 WA 14
39 GENDREY C 106 VA 19
49 GENE 77 T 17
82 GENEBRIERES 188 DA 33
59 GENECH 9 KA 4
71 GENELARD 120 PA 21
30 GENERAC 193 QA 34
33 GENERAC 156 U 28
30 GENERARGUES 193 OA 33
65 GENEREST 217 Y 37
11 GENERVILLE 211 FA 36
61 GENESLAY 57 U 13
53 GENEST ST ISLE, LE 77 S 15
07 GENESTELLE 164 QA 30
44 GENESTON 110 P 19
71 GENETE, LA 121 TA 22
17 GENETOUZE, LA 157 W 28
85 GENETOUZE, LES 110 P 21
50 GENETS 56 P 12
61 GENETTES, LES 59 Z 12
25 GENEUILLE 107 XA 18
61 GENEVRAIE, LA 37 Y 12
77 GENEVRAYE, LA 62 IA 14
70 GENEVREUILLE 89 ZA 17
70 GENEVREY 88 YA 16
52 GENEVRIERES 87 VA 16
52 GENEVROYE, LA 66 TA 14
25 GENEY 107 ZA 17
87 GENEYTOUSE, LA 145 DA 25
95 GENICOURT 39 FA 10
55 GENICOURT SUR MEUSE 44 UA 11
42 GENILAC 150 RA 26
37 GENILLE 98 BA 19
24 GENIS 144 BA 27
33 GENISSAC 156 V 29
26 GENISSIEUX 165 TA 28
21 GENLIS C 105 TA 19
25 GENNES 107 XA 19
49 GENNES C 96 V 18
62 GENNES IVERGNY 16 FA 5
53 GENNES SUR GLAIZE 77 T 16
35 GENNES SUR SEICHE 76 R 15
49 GENNETEIL 97 W 17
03 GENNETINES 118 LA 21
79 GENNETON 96 U 19
14 GENNEVILLE 23 X 9
92 GENNEVILLIERS C 40 GA 11
39 GENOD 138 VA 22
30 GENOLHAC C 178 OA 31
31 GENOS 217 Z 37
65 GENOS 216 Y 38
16 GENOUILLAC 129 Z 25
23 GENOUILLAC 132 FA 23
17 GENOUILLE 127 T 24
86 GENOUILLE 129 Y 24
01 GENOUILLEUX 136 RA 24
18 GENOUILLY 99 EA 19
71 GENOUILLY 120 QA 21
33 GENSAC 157 W 29
65 GENSAC 208 W 35
82 GENSAC 187 AA 33
31 GENSAC DE BOULOGNE 209 Z 36
16 GENSAC LA PALLUE 142 V 26
31 GENSAC SUR GARONNE 210 BA 36
16 GENTE 142 V 26
80 GENTELLES 26 HA 7
94 GENTILLY 40 HA 12
23 GENTIOUX PIGEROLLES C 146 FA 25
60 GENVRY 27 JA 8
70 GEORFANS 89 ZA 17
01 GEOVREISSET 138 VA 23
01 GEOVREISSIAT 138 VA 23
50 GER 57 T 12
64 GER 208 W 36
65 GER 216 W 37
39 GERAISE 123 XA 20
88 GERARDMER C 89 BB 15
10 GERAUDOT 65 PA 14
73 GERBAIX 152 WA 26
88 GERBAMONT 89 AB 15
57 GERBECOURT 47 ZA 11
54 GERBECOURT
ET HAPLEMONT 68 YA 13
88 GERBEPAL 69 BB 14
60 GERBEROY 25 EA 8
54 GERBEVILLER C 68 ZA 13
55 GERCOURT
ET DRILLANCOURT 30 TA 9
02 GERCY 28 NA 7
65 GERDE 216 X 37
64 GERDEREST 207 V 36
64 GERE BELESTEN 215 U 37
02 GERGNY 19 OA 7
21 GERGUEIL 104 RA 19
71 GERGY 121 SA 20
21 GERLAND 105 SA 19
65 GERM 217 Y 38
01 GERMAGNAT 138 UA 23
71 GERMAGNY 120 RA 21
02 GERMAINE 27 KA 8
51 GERMAINE 42 OA 10
52 GERMAINES 86 SA 16
28 GERMAINVILLE 38 DA 12
52 GERMAINVILLIERS 67 VA 15
52 GERMAY 66 UA 13
25 GERMEFONTAINE 107 ZA 19
58 GERMENAY 103 MA 18
17 GERMIGNAC 142 V 26
39 GERMIGNEY 122 VA 20
70 GERMIGNEY 106 VA 18
28 GERMIGNONVILLE 61 EA 14
51 GERMIGNY 42 NA 10
89 GERMIGNY 84 NA 15
45 GERMIGNY DES PRES 81 GA 16
77 GERMIGNY L'EVEQUE 41 JA 11
18 GERMIGNY L'EXEMPT 117 JA 20
77 GERMIGNY SOUS COULOMBS 41 KA 10
58 GERMIGNY SUR LOIRE 102 KA 19
51 GERMINON 42 PA 11
54 GERMINY 67 XA 13
52 GERMISAY 66 UA 13
71 GERMOLLES SUR GROSNE 136 RA 23
79 GERMOND ROUVRE 112 U 22
25 GERMONDANS 107 YA 18
08 GERMONT 30 SA 9
54 GERMONVILLE 68 YA 13
65 GERMS SUR L'OUSSOUET 216 W 37
08 GERNELLE 30 SA 7
02 GERNICOURT 28 NA 9
64 GERONCE 206 T 36
76 GERPONVILLE 23 Z 7
14 GERROTS 36 W 10
67 GERSTHEIM 70 EB 13
67 GERTWILLER 70 DB 13
39 GERUGE 122 VA 21
26 GERVANS 165 SA 28
76 GERVILLE 23 X 8
55 GERY 44 UA 12
63 GERZAT C 148 KA 25
53 GESNES 77 T 15
55 GESNES EN ARGONNE 30 TA 9
72 GESNES LE GANDELIN 58 W 14
08 GESPUNSART 29 RA 7
64 GESTAS 206 S 36
49 GESTE 94 R 19
56 GESTEL 73 H 16
09 GESTIES 220 DA 38
53 GESVRES 58 W 14
77 GESVRES LE CHAPITRE 40 JA 11
44 GETIGNE 110 R 19
74 GETS, LES 140 AB 23
65 GEU 216 W 37
67 GEUDERTHEIM 49 FB 12
64 GEUS D'ARZACQ 207 U 35
64 GEUS D'OLORON 206 T 36
35 GEVEZE 75 O 14
70 GEVIGNEY ET MERCEY 88 XA 16
55 GEVILLE 45 VA 12
39 GEVINGEY 122 VA 21
25 GEVRESIN 123 XA 20
21 GEVREY CHAMBERTIN C 105 SA 19
21 GEVROLLES 85 RA 15
39 GEVRY 106 VA 19
01 GEX S 139 XA 23
26 GEYSSANS 165 TA 28
65 GEZ 215 W 37
65 GEZ EZ ANGLES 216 W 37
80 GEZAINCOURT 16 GA 6
70 GEZIER ET FONTENELAY 106 WA 18
54 GEZONCOURT 45 XA 11
2B GHISONACCIA 228 MB 42
2B GHISONI C 228 LB 41
59 GHISSIGNIES 18 MA 5
59 GHYVELDE 8 HA 2
63 GIAT 147 HA 25
54 GIBEAUMEIX 67 WA 13
31 GIBEL 211 EA 36
02 GIBERCOURT 28 LA 7
14 GIBERVILLE 36 V 10
71 GIBLES 136 QA 23
17 GIBOURNE 128 V 24
40 GIBRET 184 S 34
17 GICQ, LE 128 V 24
45 GIDY 81 EA 15
61 GIEL COURTEILLES 58 V 12
45 GIEN C 82 IA 17
58 GIEN SUR CURE 103 OA 19
38 GIERES 166 WA 28
73 GIETTAZ, LA 139 ZA 25
50 GIEVILLE 35 S 11
41 GIEVRES 99 EA 18
52 GIEY SUR AUJON 86 TA 16
74 GIEZ 153 YA 25
91 GIF SUR YVETTE C 39 GA 12
51 GIFFAUMONT CHAMPAUBERT 65 RA 13
34 GIGEAN 214 NA 35
34 GIGNAC C 192 MA 34
46 GIGNAC 159 DA 28
84 GIGNAC 196 VA 33
13 GIGNAC LA NERTHE 201 TA 36
63 GIGNAT 148 KA 26
88 GIGNEVILLE 67 WA 15
88 GIGNEY 68 YA 14
39 GIGNY 122 UA 22
89 GIGNY 85 PA 16
51 GIGNY BUSSY 65 OA 12
71 GIGNY SUR SAONE 121 SA 21

84 GIGONDAS 179 SA 32
04 GIGORS 181 XA 31
26 GIGORS ET LOZERON 165 TA 29
46 GIGOUZAC 173 CA 30
81 GIJOUNET 190 IA 34
68 GILDWILLER 90 CB 17
06 GILETTE 199 CB 34
07 GILHAC ET BRUZAC 164 RA 29
07 GILHOC SUR ORMEZE 164 RA 29
52 GILLANCOURT 66 SA 14
52 GILLAUME 66 UA 13
28 GILLES 38 DA 11
25 GILLEY 107 ZA 19
52 GILLEY 87 VA 17
39 GILLOIS 123 XA 21
38 GILLONNAY 151 UA 27
21 GILLY LES CITEAUX 105 SA 19
73 GILLY SUR ISERE 153 YA 26
71 GILLY SUR LOIRE 119 NA 22
60 GILOCOURT 41 JA 9
82 GIMAT 187 AA 34
32 GIMBREDE 187 Z 33
63 GIMEAUX 134 KA 24
55 GIMECOURT 44 UA 11
19 GIMEL LES CASCADES 146 EA 27
16 GIMEUX 142 U 26
42 GIMOND, LA 150 OA 26
32 GIMONT C 209 AA 35
58 GIMOUILLE 118 KA 20
61 GINAI 58 X 12
82 GINALS 174 EA 32
83 GINASSERVIS 197 WA 34
80 GINCHY 17 JA 6
11 GINCLA 222 GA 38
55 GINCREY 45 VA 10
46 GINDOU 173 CA 30
11 GINESTAS C 213 JA 36
24 GINESTET 157 Y 29
67 GINGSHEIM 49 EB 12
11 GINOLES 221 GA 38
46 GINOUILLAC 159 DA 30
46 GINTRAC 159 EA 29
2B GIOCATOJO 228 MB 40
51 GIONGES 42 OA 11
15 GIOU DE MAMOU 161 HA 29
23 GIOUX 146 GA 25
03 GIPCY 118 KA 22
46 GIRAC 159 EA 29
88 GIRANCOURT 68 YA 14
54 GIRAUMONT 45 WA 10
60 GIRAUMONT 27 JA 9
55 GIRAUVOISIN 45 VA 12
88 GIRCOURT LES VIEVILLE 68 YA 14
88 GIRECOURT SUR DURBION 68 ZA 14
70 GIREFONTAINE 88 YA 16
77 GIREMOUTIERS 41 KA 11
15 GIRGOLS 161 HA 28
54 GIRIVILLER 68 ZA 13
88 GIRMONT 68 ZA 14
88 GIRMONT VAL D'AJOL 89 ZA 15
45 GIROLLES 82 IA 15
89 GIROLLES 84 NA 17
90 GIROMAGNY C 89 AB 16
01 GIRON 138 WA 23
88 GIRONCOURT SUR VRAINE 67 WA 14
33 GIRONDE SUR DROPT 171 W 30
08 GIRONDELLE 29 OA 7
77 GIRONVILLE 62 HA 14
91 GIRONVILLE SUR ESSONNE 62 HA 14
85 GIROUARD, LE 125 P 22
81 GIROUSSENS 189 EA 34
36 GIROUX 100 FA 19
58 GIRY 102 LA 19
27 GISAY LA COUDRE 37 Z 11
32 GISCARO 209 AA 35
33 GISCOS 171 V 32
27 GISORS C 39 EA 9
12 GISSAC 191 JA 34
21 GISSEY LE VIEIL 104 OA 18
21 GISSEY SOUS FLAVIGNY 85 RA 17
21 GISSEY SUR OUCHE 104 RA 18
89 GISY LES NOBLES 63 LA 14
2B GIUNCAGGIO 228 MB 41
2A GIUNCHETO 229 KB 44
18 GIVARDON 118 KA 20
03 GIVARLAIS 117 IA 22
62 GIVENCHY EN GOHELLE 17 JA 5
62 GIVENCHY LE NOBLE 17 HA 5
62 GIVENCHY LES LA BASSEE 8 IA 4
27 GIVERNY 38 DA 10
27 GIVERVILLE 37 Z 10
08 GIVET C 20 SA 6
08 GIVONNE 30 SA 8
69 GIVORS C 150 RA 26
45 GIVRAINES 62 HA 15
85 GIVRAND 109 O 21
55 GIVRAUVAL 44 UA 12
85 GIVRE, LE 125 Q 22
17 GIVREZAC 141 T 26
08 GIVRON 29 PA 8
08 GIVRY 29 QA 9
71 GIVRY C 120 RA 21
89 GIVRY 84 NA 17
51 GIVRY EN ARGONNE C 44 SA 11
51 GIVRY LES LOISY 42 NA 11
51 GIZAUCOURT 43 RA 10
86 GIZAY 113 Y 22
37 GIZEUX 97 X 18
39 GIZIA 122 UA 22
02 GIZY 28 NA 8
50 GLACERIE, LA 33 P 8
59 GLAGEON 19 OA 6
60 GLAIGNES 40 JA 10
63 GLAINE MONTAIGUT 148 LA 25
08 GLAIRE 30 SA 8
05 GLAIZIL, LE 167 XA 30
25 GLAMONDANS 107 YA 18
02 GLAND 41 MA 10
89 GLAND 85 PA 16
26 GLANDAGE 166 VA 30
87 GLANDON 145 CA 26
46 GLANES 160 FA 29
87 GLANGES 145 DA 26
51 GLANNES 43 QA 12
21 GLANON 105 TA 19
14 GLANVILLE 36 W 9
82 GLATENS 187 AA 33
50 GLATIGNY 34 P 9
57 GLATIGNY 46 YA 10
60 GLATIGNY 25 EA 9
25 GLAY 108 BB 18
69 GLEIZE 136 RA 24
56 GLENAC 75 N 16
15 GLENAT 160 GA 29
79 GLENAY 113 Y 20
23 GLENIC 132 FA 23
02 GLENNES 28 NA 9
86 GLENOUZE 112 W 20
25 GLERE 108 BB 18
76 GLICOURT 15 CA 7
27 GLISOLLES 38 BA 11
80 GLISY 26 HA 7
22 GLOMEL 73 H 14
54 GLONVILLE 68 AB 13
66 GLORIANES 222 HA 39
14 GLOS 37 X 10
61 GLOS LA FERRIERE 37 Z 11
27 GLOS SUR RISLE 37 Z 10
07 GLUIRAS 164 QA 29
26 GLUN 165 SA 28
58 GLUX EN GLENNE 119 OA 20
82 GOAS 187 AA 34
50 GODEFROY, LA 56 Q 12
60 GODENVILLERS 26 HA 8
76 GODERVILLE C 23 Y 8
59 GODEWAERSVELDE 8 IA 3
61 GODISSON 37 X 12
63 GODIVELLE, LA 147 JA 27
88 GODONCOURT 88 WA 15
67 GOERLINGEN 48 CB 12
67 GOERSDORF 49 FB 11
64 GOES 207 T 36
57 GOETZENBRUCK 48 DB 11
59 GOEULZIN 18 KA 5
52 GOGNEY 69 BB 12
59 GOGNIES CHAUSSEE 19 OA 5
50 GOHANNIERE, LA 56 R 12
28 GOHORY 60 CA 14
57 GOIN 46 YA 11
60 GOINCOURT 26 FA 9
60 GOLANCOURT 27 KA 8
88 GOLBEY 68 ZA 14
68 GOLDBACH ALTENBACH 90 CB 16
82 GOLFECH 172 AA 32
12 GOLINHAC 175 IA 30
50 GOLLEVILLE 33 P 9
41 GOMBERGEAN 80 BA 17
57 GOMELANGE 47 ZA 10
22 GOMENE 74 L 14
64 GOMER 207 V 36
91 GOMETZ LA VILLE 61 GA 12
91 GOMETZ LE CHATEL 61 GA 12
62 GOMIECOURT 17 JA 6
62 GOMMECOURT 17 IA 6
78 GOMMECOURT 39 DA 10
59 GOMMEGNIES 18 NA 5
22 GOMMENEC'H 53 J 12
68 GOMMERSDORF 90 CB 17
28 GOMMERVILLE 61 FA 14
76 GOMMERVILLE 23 Y 8
21 GOMMEVILLE 85 OA 15
08 GOMONT 29 PA 8
38 GONCELIN C 153 XA 27
52 GONCOURT 67 VA 14
16 GOND PONTOUVRE, LE C 143 X 25
59 GONDECOURT 9 JA 4
25 GONDENANS LES MOULINS 107 YA 18
25 GONDENANS MONTBY 107 ZA 18
16 GONDEVILLE 142 V 26
54 GONDRECOURT AIX 45 WA 10
55 GONDRECOURT LE CHATEAU C 67 VA 13
21 GONDREVILLE 82 IA 15
54 GONDREVILLE 45 XA 12
60 GONDREVILLE 41 JA 10
57 GONDREXANGE 69 BB 12
54 GONDREXON 69 AB 12
32 GONDRIN 186 X 33
17 GONDS, LES 142 T 25
95 GONESSE C 40 HA 11
65 GONEZ 208 X 36
83 GONFARON 203 YA 36
50 GONFREVILLE 34 Q 10
76 GONFREVILLE CAILLOT 23 Y 8
76 GONFREVILLE L'ORCHER C 23 X 8
61 GONFRIERE, LA 37 Y 12
62 GONNEHEM 8 IA 4
59 GONNELIEU 18 KA 6
76 GONNETOT 24 AA 7
50 GONNEVILLE 33 O 8
14 GONNEVILLE EN AUGE 36 V 10
76 GONNEVILLE LA MALLET 23 X 8
14 GONNEVILLE SUR HONFLEUR 23 X 9
14 GONNEVILLE SUR MER 36 W 9
76 GONNEVILLE SUR SCIE 24 BA 7
25 GONSANS 107 YA 19
47 GONTAUD DE NOGARET 171 X 31
24 GONTERIE BOULOUNEIX, LA 144 Z 27
76 GONZEVILLE 24 AA 7
40 GOOS 184 S 34
06 GORBIO 200 DB 34
54 GORCY 31 VA 8
84 GORDES C 196 TA 33
80 GORENFLOS 16 FA 6
44 GORGES 110 Q 19
50 GORGES 34 O 10
80 GORGES 16 GA 6
59 GORGUE, LA 8 IA 3
88 GORHEY 68 YA 14
33 GORNAC 171 V 30
34 GORNIES 192 MA 33
87 GORRE 144 AA 25
01 GORREVOD 137 SA 22
53 GORRON C 57 T 13
46 GORSES 160 FA 29
57 GORZE 45 XA 10
62 GOSNAY 8 IA 4
35 GOSNE 76 O 14
57 GOSSELMING 47 BB 12
64 GOTEIN LIBARRENX 206 S 37
67 GOTTENHOUSE 49 DB 12
67 GOTTESHEIM 49 DB 12
77 GOUAIX 63 LA 13
33 GOUALADE 171 V 32
22 GOUAREC C 73 I 14
65 GOUAUX 216 Y 38
31 GOUAUX DE LARBOUST 217 Y 38
31 GOUAUX DE LUCHON 217 Z 38
50 GOUBERVILLE 33 Q 8
76 GOUCHAUPRE 15 CA 7
30 GOUDARGUES 178 QA 32
02 GOUDELANCOURT LES BERRIEUX 28 NA 9
02 GOUDELANCOURT LES PIERREPONT 28 NA 8
22 GOUDELIN 53 J 13
43 GOUDET 163 NA 29
31 GOUDEX 209 AA 36
65 GOUDON 208 X 36
82 GOUDOURVILLE 173 AA 32
29 GOUESNACH 72 E 16
35 GOUESNIERE, LA 55 O 12
29 GOUESNOU 51 C 13
86 GOUEX 130 Z 22
29 GOUEZEC 72 E 14
67 GOUGENHEIM 49 EB 12
25 GOUHELANS 107 YA 18
70 GOUHENANS 89 ZA 17
28 GOUILLONS 61 EA 14
03 GOUISE 134 LA 22
46 GOUJOUNAC 173 BA 30
27 GOULAFRIERE, LA 37 Y 11
61 GOULET 58 W 12
29 GOULIEN 71 C 15
09 GOULIER 220 DA 39
19 GOULLES 160 FA 28
21 GOULLES, LES 86 SA 16
58 GOULOUX 103 OA 19
84 GOULT 196 TA 34
29 GOULVEN 51 D 12
25 GOUMOIS 108 BB 18
14 GOUPILLIERES 35 U 11
27 GOUPILLIERES 37 AA 10
76 GOUPILLIERES 24 BA 8
78 GOUPILLIERES 39 EA 11
55 GOURAINCOURT 31 VA 9
22 GOURAY, LE 54 L 14
40 GOURBERA 183 R 34
50 GOURBESVILLE 33 Q 9
09 GOURBIT 219 DA 38
60 GOURCHELLES 25 EA 7
31 GOURDAN POLIGNAN 217 Z 37
15 GOURDIEGES 161 JA 29
06 GOURDON 200 BB 34
07 GOURDON 164 QA 30
46 GOURDON S 159 CA 30
71 GOURDON 120 QA 21
19 GOURDON MURAT 146 FA 26
50 GOURFALEUR 34 R 10
51 GOURGANCON 42 OA 12
79 GOURGE 112 V 21
70 GOURGEON 88 WA 16
65 GOURGUE 216 X 37
56 GOURHEL 74 M 15
56 GOURIN C 72 G 15
29 GOURLIZON 71 D 15
36 GOURNAY 115 EA 21
76 GOURNAY EN BRAY C 25 EA 9
27 GOURNAY LE GUERIN 37 AA 12
79 GOURNAY LOIZE 128 W 23
60 GOURNAY SUR ARONDE 27 IA 9
93 GOURNAY SUR MARNE 40 IA 11
33 GOURS 157 W 29
16 GOURS, LES 128 W 24
11 GOURVIEILLE 211 EA 36
16 GOURVILLE 129 W 25
17 GOURVILLETTE 128 V 25
55 GOUSSAINCOURT 67 VA 13
28 GOUSSAINVILLE 38 DA 12
95 GOUSSAINVILLE C 40 HA 11
02 GOUSSANCOURT 42 MA 10
40 GOUSSE 184 S 34
78 GOUSSONVILLE 39 EA 11
14 GOUSTRANVILLE 36 W 10
24 GOUT ROSSIGNOL 143 Y 27
63 GOUTELLE, LA 147 IA 25
31 GOUTEVERNISSE 210 BA 36
12 GOUTRENS 175 HA 31
40 GOUTS 184 T 34
27 GOUTTIERES 37 AA 11
63 GOUTTIERES 133 IA 24
32 GOUTZ 187 Z 34
77 GOUVERNES 40 IA 11
62 GOUVES 17 IA 5
50 GOUVETS 56 R 11
60 GOUVIEUX 40 HA 10
27 GOUVILLE 38 AA 11
50 GOUVILLE SUR MER 34 P 10
14 GOUVIX 36 V 11
32 GOUX 208 W 35
25 GOUX LES DAMBELIN 108 AB 18
25 GOUX LES USIERS 107 YA 20
25 GOUX SOUS LANDET 107 XA 19
02 GOUY 18 LA 6
76 GOUY 24 BA 9
62 GOUY EN ARTOIS 17 IA 5
62 GOUY EN TERNOIS 16 HA 5
60 GOUY LES GROSEILLERS 26 GA 8
62 GOUY SERVINS 17 IA 4
62 GOUY SOUS BELLONNE 17 KA 5
62 GOUY ST ANDRE 16 FA 5
95 GOUZANGREZ 39 FA 10
59 GOUZEAUCOURT 18 KA 6
31 GOUZENS 218 BA 37
23 GOUZON 132 GA 23
35 GOVEN 75 O 15
54 GOVILLER 67 XA 13
67 GOXWILLER 70 DB 13
80 GOYENCOURT 27 IA 8
31 GOYRANS 210 CA 35
34 GRABELS 214 NA 35
18 GRACAY C 99 EA 19
22 GRACE UZEL 74 K 14
22 GRACES 53 I 13
33 GRADIGNAN C 156 T 30
52 GRAFFIGNY CHEMIN 67 VA 14
12 GRAGNAGUE 188 DA 34
50 GRAIGNES 34 R 10
65 GRAILHEN 216 Y 38
76 GRAIMBOUVILLE 23 Y 8
62 GRAINCOURT LES HAVRINCOURT 18 KA 6
27 GRAINVILLE 25 CA 9
76 GRAINVILLE LA TEINTURIERE 23 Z 7
14 GRAINVILLE LANGANNERIE 36 V 11
14 GRAINVILLE SUR ODON 35 U 10
76 GRAINVILLE SUR RY 24 CA 9
76 GRAINVILLE YMAUVILLE 23 Y 8
61 GRAIS, LE 58 V 12
12 GRAISSAC 161 JA 30
34 GRAISSESSAC 191 KA 34
42 GRAIX 150 QA 27
46 GRAMAT C 159 EA 29
11 GRAMAZIE 221 FA 37
84 GRAMBOIS 196 VA 34
42 GRAMMOND 150 QA 26
70 GRAMMONT 107 ZA 17
12 GRAMOND 175 HA 32
82 GRAMONT 187 AA 33
2A GRANACE 229 KB 43
21 GRANCEY LE CHATEAU NEUVELLE C 86 TA 17
21 GRANCEY SUR OURCE 85 QA 15
88 GRAND 67 VA 13
01 GRAND ABERGEMENT, LE 138 VA 24
44 GRAND AUVERNE 94 Q 17
74 GRAND BORNAND, LE 139 ZA 24
23 GRAND BOURG, LE C 131 DA 23
24 GRAND BRASSAC 143 Y 27
27 GRAND CAMP 37 Z 11
76 GRAND CAMP 23 Z 8
80 GRAND CELLAND, LE 56 R 12
56 GRAND CHAMP C 73 J 16
25 GRAND CHARMONT 89 AB 17
30 GRAND COMBE, LA K 178 OA 32
01 GRAND CORENT 138 UA 23
76 GRAND COURONNE C 24 BA 9
42 GRAND CROIX, LA C 150 RA 26
54 GRAND FAILLY 31 VA 9
59 GRAND FAYT 19 NA 6
59 GRAND FORT PHILIPPE 7 FA 2
35 GRAND FOUGERAY C 75 O 16
80 GRAND LAVIERS 16 EA 6
38 GRAND LEMPS, LE C 152 UA 27
72 GRAND LUCE, LE C 79 Y 16
16 GRAND MADIEU, LE 129 Y 24
37 GRAND PRESSIGNY, LE C 114 AA 20
76 GRAND QUEVILLY C 24 BA 9
02 GRAND ROZOY 41 LA 10
62 GRAND RULLECOURT 17 HA 5
26 GRAND SERRE, LE C 151 TA 27
12 GRAND VABRE 175 HA 30
02 GRAND VERLY 18 MA 7
17 GRAND VILLAGE PLAGE, LE 126 R 25
25 GRAND'COMBE CHATELEU 107 ZA 20
25 GRAND'COMBE DES BOIS 108 AB 19
85 GRAND'LANDES 110 P 20
14 GRANDCAMP MAISY 35 S 9
27 GRANDCHAIN 37 Z 10
08 GRANDCHAMP 29 OA 8
52 GRANDCHAMP 87 UA 16
72 GRANDCHAMP 58 X 14
78 GRANDCHAMP 39 DA 12
89 GRANDCHAMP 83 KA 16
14 GRANDCHAMP LE CHATEAU 36 W 10
44 GRANDCHAMPS DES FONTAINES 93 P 18
76 GRANDCOURT 15 DA 7
80 GRANDCOURT 17 IA 6
88 GRANDE FOSSE, LA 69 CB 14
34 GRANDE MOTTE, LA 194 OA 35
77 GRANDE PAROISSE, LA 63 JA 13
70 GRANDE RESIE, LA 106 VA 18
39 GRANDE RIVIERE 122 WA 22
59 GRANDE SYNTHE C 8 GA 2
71 GRANDE VERRIERE, LA 119 PA 20
70 GRANDECOURT 87 WA 17
08 GRANDES ARMOISES, LES 30 SA 8
10 GRANDES CHAPELLES, LES 64 OA 13
51 GRANDES LOGES, LES 43 PA 10
76 GRANDES VENTES, LES 24 CA 7
63 GRANDEYROLLES 148 KA 26
25 GRANDFONTAINE 106 WA 19
67 GRANDFONTAINE 69 CB 13
25 GRANDFONTAINE SUR CREUSE 107 ZA 19
60 GRANDFRESNOY 27 IA 9
08 GRANDHAM 30 SA 9
17 GRANDJEAN 128 U 25
02 GRANDLUP ET FAY 28 NA 8
08 GRANDPRE C 30 SA 9
77 GRANDPUITS BAILLY CARROIS 63 JA 13
48 GRANDRIEU C 162 MA 29
02 GRANDRIEUX 29 PA 7
63 GRANDRIF 149 NA 26
69 GRANDRIS 136 QA 24
60 GRANDRU 27 KA 8
88 GRANDRUPT 69 BB 14
88 GRANDRUPT DE BAINS 68 YA 15
87 GRANDS CHEZEAUX, LES 131 CA 22
19 GRANDSAIGNE 146 FA 26
63 GRANDVAL 148 MA 26
48 GRANDVALS 162 KA 30
71 GRANDVAUX 120 PA 22
70 GRANDVELLE ET LE PERRENOT 88 XA 17
90 GRANDVILLARS C 90 BB 17
10 GRANDVILLE 65 PA 13
08 GRANDVILLE, LA 29 RA 7
88 GRANDVILLERS 68 AB 14
60 GRANDVILLERS AUX BOIS 26 IA 9
27 GRANDVILLIERS 38 BA 12
60 GRANDVILLIERS C 25 FA 8
26 GRANE 165 SA 30
11 GRANES 221 GA 38
52 GRANGCHAMP 87 UA 17
25 GRANGE, LA 108 AB 18
39 GRANGE DE VAIVRE 122 WA 20
45 GRANGERMONT 62 HA 14
10 GRANGES, LES 84 OA 15
71 GRANGES 120 RA 21
24 GRANGES D'ANS 158 BA 28
26 GRANGES GONTARDES, LES 179 RA 31
70 GRANGES LA VILLE 89 ZA 17
70 GRANGES LE BOURG 89 ZA 17
91 GRANGES LE ROI, LES 61 FA 13
26 GRANGES LES BEAUMONT 165 SA 28
25 GRANGES NARBOZ 123 YA 20
51 GRANGES SUR AUBE 64 NA 13
39 GRANGES SUR BAUME 122 VA 21
47 GRANGES SUR LOT 172 Y 31
88 GRANGES SUR VOLOGNE 69 AB 15
25 GRANGETTES, LES 123 YA 20
14 GRANGUES 36 W 10
73 GRANIER 154 AB 26
38 GRANIEU 152 VA 26
13 GRANS 201 TA 35
50 GRANVILLE C 56 P 11
79 GRANZAY GRIPT 128 U 23
07 GRAS 178 QA 31
25 GRAS, LES 107 ZA 20
16 GRASSAC 143 Y 26
06 GRASSE S 200 BB 34
67 GRASSENDORF 49 EB 12
47 GRATELOUP 172 Y 31
31 GRATENS 210 BA 36
31 GRATENTOUR 188 CA 34
80 GRATIBUS 26 HA 8
50 GRATOT 34 P 10
51 GRATREUIL 43 RA 10
80 GRATTEPANCHE 26 GA 7
25 GRATTERIS, LE 107 XA 19
70 GRATTERY 88 XA 17
30 GRAU DU ROI, LE 194 OA 35
24 GRAULGES, LES 143 Y 26
81 GRAULHET C 189 FA 34
51 GRAUVES 42 OA 11
76 GRAVAL 25 DA 7
05 GRAVE, LA C 167 YA 28
59 GRAVELINES C 8 GA 2
53 GRAVELLE, LA 76 S 15
54 GRAVELOTTE 45 XA 10
14 GRAVERIE, LA 35 S 11
27 GRAVERON SEMERVILLE 38 BA 10
16 GRAVES ST AMANT 142 W 26
13 GRAVESON 195 RA 34
07 GRAVIERES 178 OA 31
27 GRAVIGNY 38 BA 11
77 GRAVON 63 KA 13
70 GRAY C 106 VA 18
70 GRAY LA VILLE 106 VA 18
33 GRAYAN ET L'HOPITAL 141 R 26
39 GRAYE ET CHARNAY 122 UA 22
14 GRAYE SUR MER 35 U 9
47 GRAYSSAS 172 AA 32
31 GRAZAC 210 DA 36
43 GRAZAC 163 PA 28
81 GRAZAC 189 EA 34
53 GRAZAY 57 U 14
46 GREALOU 174 EA 31
13 GREASQUE 202 VA 35
80 GREBAULT MESNIL 15 EA 6
80 GRECOURT 27 JA 8
39 GREDISANS 106 VA 19
56 GREE ST LAURENT, LA 74 L 15
72 GREEZ SUR ROC 59 AA 15
11 GREFFEIL 221 HA 37
76 GREGES 24 BA 7
57 GREMECEY 46 ZA 12
60 GREMEVILLERS 25 EA 8
55 GREMILLY 31 UA 9
76 GREMONVILLE 24 AA 8
31 GRENADE C 188 CA 34
40 GRENADE SUR L'ADOUR C 184 U 34
21 GRENAND LES SOMBERNON 104 RA 18
52 GRENANT 87 UA 16
38 GRENAY 151 TA 26
62 GRENAY 17 IA 4
67 GRENDELBRUCH 69 DB 13
45 GRENEVILLE EN BEAUCE 61 GA 14
42 GRENIER MONTGON 148 KA 27
57 GRENING 47 BB 11
38 GRENOBLE P 166 VA 28
58 GRENOIS 102 MA 18
14 GRENTHEVILLE 36 V 10
68 GRENTZINGEN 90 DB 17
76 GRENY 15 CA 6
06 GREOLIERES 200 BB 34
04 GREOUX LES BAINS 197 WA 34
31 GREPIAC 210 DA 36
31 GRES, LE 187 BA 34
21 GRESIGNY STE REINE 85 QA 17
73 GRESIN 152 VA 26
42 GRESLE, LA 135 PA 24
38 GRESSE EN VERCORS 166 VA 29
78 GRESSEY 39 DA 11
67 GRESSWILLER 70 DB 13
77 GRESSY 40 IA 11
73 GRESY SUR AIX C 153 XA 25
73 GRESY SUR ISERE C 153 YA 26
77 GRETZ ARMAINVILLIERS 40 IA 12
70 GREUCOURT 88 WA 17
76 GREUVILLE 24 AA 7
88 GREUX 67 VA 13
17 GREVE SUR MIGNON, LA 127 T 23
50 GREVILLE HAGUE 33 O 8
62 GREVILLERS 17 JA 6
71 GREVILLY 121 SA 22
60 GREZ 25 FA 8
72 GREZ, LE 78 V 14
53 GREZ EN BOUERE C 77 U 16
49 GREZ NEUVILLE 95 T 17
77 GREZ SUR LOING 62 IA 14
17 GREZAC 141 S 26
46 GREZELS 173 BA 31
24 GREZES 159 CA 28
43 GREZES 162 MA 29
46 GREZES 174 EA 30
48 GREZES 177 LA 31
47 GREZET CAVAGNAN 171 X 31
65 GREZIAN 216 Y 38
69 GREZIEU LA VARENNE 150 RA 25
69 GREZIEU LE MARCHE 150 OA 26
42 GREZIEUX LE FROMENTAL 149 PA 26
33 GREZILLAC 156 V 29
49 GREZILLE 96 V 18
42 GREZOLLES 135 OA 25
02 GRICOURT 28 LA 7
01 GRIEGES 137 SA 23
67 GRIES 49 FB 12
68 GRIESBACH AU VAL 90 CB 15
67 GRIESHEIM PRES MOLSHEIM 70 EB 13
67 GRIESHEIM SUR SOUFFEL 49 EB 12
26 GRIGNAN C 179 SA 31
76 GRIGNEUSEVILLE 24 BA 8
24 GRIGNOLS 157 Y 28
33 GRIGNOLS C 171 W 31
21 GRIGNON 85 QA 17
73 GRIGNON 153 YA 26
88 GRIGNONCOURT 88 WA 15
62 GRIGNY 16 FA 5
69 GRIGNY 150 RA 26
91 GRIGNY C 62 HA 12
44 GRIGONNAIS, LA 93 P 17
84 GRILLON 179 SA 31
01 GRILLY 139 XA 23
55 GRIMAUCOURT EN WOEVRE 45 VA 10
55 GRIMAUCOURT PRES SAMPIGNY 44 UA 12
83 GRIMAUD C 204 ZA 36
86 GRIMAUDIERE, LA 112 W 20
89 GRIMAULT 84 OA 17
14 GRIMBOSQ 35 U 10
50 GRIMESNIL 34 Q 11
54 GRIMONVILLER 67 XA 13
62 GRINCOURT LES PAS 17 HA 6
57 GRINDORFF 32 ZA 9
17 GRIPPERIE ST SYMPHORIEN, LA 141 S 25
54 GRIPPORT 68 YA 13
54 GRISCOURT 45 XA 11
21 GRISELLES 85 QA 16
45 GRISELLES 82 JA 15
02 GRISOLLES 41 LA 10
82 GRISOLLES C 188 CA 34
95 GRISY LES PLATRES 39 FA 10
77 GRISY SUISNES 62 IA 12
77 GRISY SUR SEINE 63 LA 13
24 GRIVES 158 BA 30
80 GRIVESNES 26 HA 8
80 GRIVILLERS 27 IA 8
08 GRIVY LOISY 30 RA 9
62 GROFFLIERS 15 DA 5
59 GROISE, LA 18 NA 6
18 GROISES 101 JA 19
01 GROISSIAT 138 VA 23
74 GROISY 139 YA 24
56 GROIX C 91 H 17
24 GROLEJAC 159 CA 29
18 GRON 101 IA 19
89 GRON 63 LA 14
02 GRONARD 28 NA 7
19 GROS CHASTANG 160 FA 28
57 GROS REDERCHING 48 CB 10
27 GROS THEIL, LE 37 AA 10
57 GROSBLIEDERSTROFF 47 BB 10
25 GROSBOIS 107 YA 18
21 GROSBOIS EN MONTAGNE 104 RA 18
21 GROSBOIS LES TICHEY 121 UA 20
85 GROSBREUIL 125 P 22
79 GROSEILLERS, LES 112 U 22

95 GROSLAY 40 GA 11
01 GROSLEE 152 VA 25
27 GROSLEY SUR RISLE 37 AA 11
90 GROSMAGNY 89 BB 16
90 GROSNE 90 BB 17
07 GROSPIERRES 178 PA 31
78 GROSROUVRE 39 EA 12
54 GROSROUVRES 45 WA 12
2A GROSSA 229 KB 44
2A GROSSETO PRUGNA 227 KB 42
27 GROSSOEUVRE 38 BA 11
18 GROSSOUVRE 117 JA 20
57 GROSTENQUIN C 47 AB 11
50 GROSVILLE 33 O 8
80 GROUCHES LUCHUEL 16 HA 5
02 GROUGIS 18 MA 7
18 GROUTTE, LA 117 HA 21
39 GROZON 122 VA 20
76 GRUCHET LE VALASSE 23 Y 8
76 GRUCHET ST SIMEON 24 AA 7
85 GRUES 125 Q 22
88 GRUEY LES SURANCE 68 YA 15
74 GRUFFY 139 XA 25
49 GRUGE L'HOPITAL 76 R 16
02 GRUGIES 28 LA 7
76 GRUGNY 24 BA 8
11 GRUISSAN 223 KA 37
76 GRUMESNIL 25 EA 8
24 GRUN BORDAS 158 Z 28
57 GRUNDVILLER 47 BB 11
80 GRUNY 27 JA 7
71 GRURY 119 NA 21
59 GRUSON 9 KA 4
39 GRUSSE 122 VA 21
68 GRUSSENHEIM 70 DB 15
65 GRUST 216 W 38
08 GRUYERES 29 QA 8
17 GUA, LE 141 S 25
38 GUA, LE 166 VA 28
2A GUAGNO 227 KB 41
28 GUAINVILLE 38 DA 11
62 GUARBECQUE 8 HA 4
2A GUARGUALE 229 KB 43
65 GUCHAN 216 Y 38
65 GUCHEN 216 Y 38
09 GUDAS 219 EA 37
52 GUDMONT VILLIERS 66 TA 14
17 GUE D'ALLERE 127 S 23
08 GUE D'HOSSUS 20 QA 6
61 GUE DE LA CHAINE, LE 59 Y 14
28 GUE DE LONGROI, LE 61 EA 13
85 GUE DE VELLUIRE, LE 127 S 22
57 GUEBENHOUSE 47 BB 10
68 GUEBERSCHWIHR 90 CB 15
57 GUEBESTROFF 47 AB 11
57 GUEBLANGE LES DIEUZE 47 AB 12
57 GUEBLING 47 AB 11
68 GUEBWILLER S 90 CB 16
72 GUECELARD 78 X 16
49 GUEDENIAU, LE 96 W 17
56 GUEGON 74 L 15
50 GUEHEBERT 34 O 11
56 GUEHENNO 74 K 16
56 GUELTAS 74 K 15
62 GUEMAPPE 17 JA 5
68 GUEMAR 70 DB 14
44 GUEMENE PENFAO C 93 O 17
56 GUEMENE SUR SCORFF C 73 I 15
62 GUEMPS 7 FA 2
57 GUENANGE 32 YA 9
29 GUENGAT 71 D 15
56 GUENIN 73 J 16
22 GUENROC 75 N 14
44 GUENROUET 93 N 17
57 GUENVILLER 47 AB 10
61 GUEPREI 36 W 11
56 GUER C 75 N 16
44 GUERANDE C 92 L 18
77 GUERARD 41 JA 12
80 GUERBIGNY 27 IA 8
37 GUERCHE, LA 114 Z 20
35 GUERCHE DE BRETAGNE, LA C 76 R 15
18 GUERCHE SUR L'AUBOIS, LA C 117 JA 20
77 GUERCHEVILLE 62 HA 14
89 GUERCHY 83 LA 16
01 GUEREINS 136 RA 24
23 GUERET P 132 EA 23
71 GUERFAND 121 SA 21
58 GUERIGNY C 102 KA 19
47 GUERIN 171 W 31
85 GUERINIERE, LA 109 M 20
29 GUERLESQUIN 53 G 13
57 GUERMANGE 47 AB 12
77 GUERMANTES 40 IA 11
56 GUERN 73 I 15
27 GUERNANVILLE 37 AA 11
78 GUERNES 39 DA 11
56 GUERNO, LE 92 L 17
27 GUERNY 39 EA 10
14 GUERON 35 T 10
27 GUEROULDE, LA 37 AA 12
55 GUERPONT 44 UA 12
61 GUERQUESALLES 36 X 11
71 GUERREAUX, LES 119 OA 22
57 GUERSTLING 47 ZA 9
57 GUERTING 47 AB 10
76 GUERVILLE 15 DA 6
78 GUERVILLE C 39 EA 11
80 GUESCHART 16 FA 5
59 GUESNAIN 18 KA 5
86 GUESNES 113 X 20
57 GUESSLING HEMERING 47 AB 11
64 GUETHARY 205 P 35
80 GUEUDECOURT 17 JA 6
71 GUEUGNON C 119 OA 21
76 GUEURES 24 AA 7
76 GUEUTTEVILLE 24 AA 8
76 GUEUTTEVILLE LES GRES 24 AA 7
51 GUEUX 42 NA 10
68 GUEVENATTEN 90 CB 17
68 GUEWENHEIM 90 CB 16
11 GUEYTES ET LABASTIDE 221 FA 37
88 GUGNECOURT 68 AB 14
54 GUGNEY 67 XA 13
88 GUGNEY AUX AULX 68 YA 14
91 GUIBEVILLE 62 GA 13
27 GUICHAINVILLE 38 BA 11
64 GUICHE 206 R 35
71 GUICHE, LA C 120 QA 22
35 GUICHEN C 75 O 15
29 GUICLAN 52 F 13
56 GUIDEL 72 H 16
72 GUIERCHE, LA 78 X 15
60 GUIGNECOURT 26 FA 9
80 GUIGNEMICOURT 26 GA 7
35 GUIGNEN 75 O 16
77 GUIGNES 62 JA 12
45 GUIGNEVILLE 61 GA 14
91 GUIGNEVILLE SUR ESSONNE 62 HA 13
02 GUIGNICOURT 29 OA 9
08 GUIGNICOURT SUR VENCE 30 RA 8
62 GUIGNY 16 FA 5
50 GUILBERVILLE 35 S 11
29 GUILER SUR GOYEN 71 D 15
29 GUILERS 51 C 13
07 GUILHERAND GRANGES 165 SA 29
33 GUILLAC 156 V 29
56 GUILLAC 74 L 16
80 GUILLAUCOURT 26 IA 7
06 GUILLAUMES C 182 BB 33
80 GUILLEMONT 17 JA 6
03 GUILLERMIE, LA 133 MA 24
91 GUILLERVAL 61 FA 14
05 GUILLESTRE C 168 AB 30
28 GUILLEVILLE 61 EA 14
56 GUILLIERS 74 L 15
29 GUILLIGOMARC'H 73 H 15
89 GUILLON C 84 OA 17
25 GUILLON LES BAINS 107 YA 18
28 GUILLONVILLE 61 EA 15
33 GUILLOS 170 U 31
36 GUILLY 99 EA 19
45 GUILLY 81 GA 16
76 GUILMECOURT 15 CA 6
29 GUILVINEC C 71 D 16
29 GUIMAEC 52 G 12
29 GUIMILIAU 52 E 13
16 GUIMPS 142 V 26
64 GUINARTHE PARENTIES 206 S 36
08 GUINCOURT 30 RA 8
52 GUINDRECOURT AUX ORMES 66 TA 13
52 GUINDRECOURT SUR BLAISE 66 SA 14
62 GUINECOURT 16 GA 5
62 GUINES C 7 FA 2
22 GUINGAMP S 53 I 13
57 GUINGLANGE 47 ZA 10
57 GUINKIRCHEN 47 ZA 10
57 GUINZELING 47 BB 11
29 GUIPAVAS C 51 D 13
35 GUIPEL 75 O 14
29 GUIPRONVEL 51 C 13
35 GUIPRY 75 O 16
58 GUIPY 102 MA 19
95 GUIRY EN VEXIN 39 EA 10
60 GUISCARD C 27 KA 8
56 GUISCRIFF 72 G 15
02 GUISE C 28 MA 7
27 GUISENIERS 38 DA 10
50 GUISLAIN, LE 34 R 11
29 GUISSENY 51 C 12
62 GUISY 16 FA 5
81 GUITALENS 211 FA 35
2A GUITERA LES BAINS 226 KB 42
17 GUITINIERES 142 U 27
78 GUITRANCOURT 39 EA 11
33 GUITRES C 156 V 28
27 GUITRY 39 DA 10
22 GUITTE 75 N 14
02 GUIVRY 27 KA 8
80 GUIZANCOURT 26 FA 7
16 GUIZENGEARD 142 W 27
65 GUIZERIX 208 Y 36
33 GUJAN MESTRAS 169 R 30
67 GUMBRECHTSHOFFEN 48 EB 11
10 GUMERY 63 LA 13
26 GUMIANE 180 UA 31
42 GUMIERES 149 OA 26
19 GUMOND 160 FA 28
67 GUNDERSHOFFEN 48 EB 11
68 GUNDOLSHEIM 90 DB 16
67 GUNGWILLER 48 CB 11
68 GUNSBACH 90 CB 15
67 GUNSTETT 49 FB 11
57 GUNTZVILLER 69 CB 12
02 GUNY 27 LA 8
31 GURAN 217 Z 38
16 GURAT 143 X 27
77 GURCY LE CHATEL 63 KA 13
89 GURGY 83 MA 16
21 GURGY LA VILLE 86 SA 16
21 GURGY LE CHATEAU 86 SA 16
64 GURMENCON 215 U 37
64 GURS 206 T 36
22 GURUNHUEL 53 I 13
60 GURY 27 JA 8
55 GUSSAINVILLE 45 VA 10
59 GUSSIGNIES 19 NA 5
78 GUYANCOURT 39 FA 12
25 GUYANS DURNES 107 YA 19
25 GUYANS VENNES 108 ZA 19
02 GUYENCOURT 28 NA 9
80 GUYENCOURT SAULCOURT 18 KA 6
80 GUYENCOURT SUR NOYE 26 HA 7
85 GUYONNIERE, LA 110 O 20
52 GUYONVELLE 87 VA 16
34 GUZARGUES 192 NA 34
70 GY C 106 WA 18
41 GY EN SOLOGNE 99 DA 18
89 GY L'EVEQUE 83 MA 16
45 GY LES NONAINS 82 JA 15
54 GYE 67 WA 12
10 GYE SUR SEINE 85 QA 15

H

62 HABARCQ 17 IA 5
40 HABAS 183 S 35
74 HABERE LULLIN 139 ZA 23
74 HABERE POCHE 139 ZA 23
27 HABIT, L' 38 CA 11
54 HABLAINVILLE 68 AB 13
61 HABLOVILLE 58 V 12
57 HABOUDANGE 47 ZA 11
68 HABSHEIM C 90 DB 16
65 HACHAN 208 Y 36
52 HACOURT 67 VA 14
27 HACQUEVILLE 39 DA 9
60 HADANCOURT
LE HAUT CLOCHER 39 EA 10
88 HADIGNY LES VERRIERES 68 ZA 14
88 HADOL 68 ZA 15
67 HAEGEN 49 DB 12
88 HAGECOURT 68 YA 14
65 HAGEDET 208 W 35
57 HAGEN 32 YA 9
68 HAGENBACH 90 CB 17
68 HAGENTHAL LE BAS 90 DB 17
68 HAGENTHAL LE HAUT 90 DB 17
32 HAGET 208 X 36
64 HAGETAUBIN 207 T 35
40 HAGETMAU C 184 U 34
54 HAGEVILLE 45 WA 11
88 HAGNEVILLE ET RONCOURT 67 WA 14
08 HAGNICOURT 29 QA 8
57 HAGONDANGE 46 YA 10
67 HAGUENAU S 49 FB 12
44 HAIE FOUASSIERE, LA 94 Q 19
53 HAIE TRAVERSAINE, LA 57 T 14
69 HAIES, LES 150 RA 26
54 HAIGNEVILLE 68 YA 13
88 HAILLAINVILLE 68 ZA 13
33 HAILLAN, LE 155 T 29
80 HAILLES 26 HA 7
62 HAILLICOURT 17 IA 4
17 HAIMPS 128 V 25
86 HAIMS 114 AA 22
60 HAINVILLERS 27 IA 8
55 HAIRONVILLE 44 TA 12
62 HAISNES 9 JA 4
61 HALEINE 57 U 13
62 HALINGHEN 7 EA 4
80 HALLENCOURT C 16 FA 6
59 HALLENNES
LEZ HAUBOURDIN 9 JA 4
57 HALLERING 47 ZA 10
69 HALLES, LES 150 OA 25
55 HALLES SOUS LES COTES 30 TA 9
52 HALLIGNICOURT 66 SA 12
62 HALLINES 8 GA 3
80 HALLIVILLERS 26 GA 8
76 HALLOTIERE, LA 25 DA 8
54 HALLOVILLE 69 BB 13
80 HALLOY 25 FA 8
62 HALLOY 17 HA 6
80 HALLOY LES PERNOIS 16 GA 6
80 HALLU 27 JA 7
59 HALLUIN 9 KA 3
64 HALSOU 205 O 36
57 HALSTROFF 32 ZA 9
80 HAM C 27 KA 7
50 HAM, LE 33 Q 9
53 HAM, LE 58 U 13
62 HAM EN ARTOIS 8 HA 4
08 HAM LES MOINES 29 RA 7
57 HAM SOUS VARSBERG 47 AB 10
08 HAM SUR MEUSE 20 RA 6
14 HAMARS 35 U 11
57 HAMBACH 47 BB 10
53 HAMBERS 57 U 14
62 HAMBLAIN LES PRES 17 JA 5
50 HAMBYE 56 Q 11
59 HAMEL 17 KA 5
60 HAMEL, LE 26 FA 8
80 HAMEL, LE 26 IA 7
80 HAMELET 26 HA 7
50 HAMELIN 56 R 13
62 HAMELINCOURT 17 JA 5
62 HAMES BOUCRES 7 EA 2
54 HAMMEVILLE 67 XA 13
55 HAMONVILLE 45 WA 12
10 HAMPIGNY 65 RA 13
57 HAMPONT 47 ZA 11
54 HAN DEVANT PIERREPONT 31 VA 9
55 HAN LES JUVIGNY 31 UA 9
55 HAN SUR MEUSE 45 VA 11
57 HAN SUR NIED 47 ZA 11
79 HANC 128 W 24
28 HANCHES 61 DA 12
80 HANCOURT 27 KA 7
67 HANDSCHUHEIM 70 EB 13
80 HANGARD 26 HA 7
67 HANGENBIETEN 70 EB 13
80 HANGEST EN SANTERRE 26 IA 7
80 HANGEST SUR SOMME 16 FA 6
57 HANGVILLER 48 CB 12
60 HANNACHES 25 EA 9
02 HANNAPES 18 MA 6
08 HANNAPPES 29 PA 7
62 HANNESCAMPS 17 IA 6
57 HANNOCOURT 47 ZA 11
08 HANNOGNE ST MARTIN 30 SA 8
08 HANNOGNE ST REMY 29 PA 8
55 HANNONVILLE
SOUS LES COTES 45 VA 11
54 HANNONVILLE SUZEMONT 45 WA 10
76 HANOUARD, LE 23 Z 7
51 HANS 43 RA 10
59 HANTAY 9 JA 4
29 HANVEC 52 E 14
57 HANVILLER 48 DB 10
60 HANVOILE 25 FA 8
62 HAPLINCOURT 17 JA 6
02 HAPPENCOURT 27 KA 7
28 HAPPONVILLIERS 60 BA 14
02 HARAMONT 41 KA 10
08 HARAUCOURT 30 SA 8
54 HARAUCOURT 46 YA 12
57 HARAUCOURT SUR SEILLE 46 ZA 12
62 HARAVESNES 16 GA 5
95 HARAVILLIERS 39 FA 10
80 HARBONNIERES 27 IA 7
54 HARBOUEY 69 BB 13
76 HARCANVILLE 24 AA 8
88 HARCHECHAMP 67 WA 13
02 HARCIGNY 29 OA 7
27 HARCOURT 37 AA 10
08 HARCY 29 OA 7
88 HARDANCOURT 68 ZA 13
53 HARDANGES 57 U 14
80 HARDECOURT AUX BOIS 17 JA 6
27 HARDENCOURT COCHEREL 38 CA 11
59 HARDIFORT 8 HA 3
62 HARDINGHEN 7 EA 3
50 HARDINVAST 33 P 8
60 HARDIVILLERS 26 GA 8
60 HARDIVILLERS EN VEXIN 39 FA 9
78 HARDRICOURT 39 EA 11
27 HARENGERE, LA 38 BA 10
88 HAREVILLE 67 XA 14
76 HARFLEUR 23 X 8
57 HARGARTEN AUX MINES 47 ZA 10
78 HARGEVILLE 39 EA 11
02 HARGICOURT 18 KA 6
80 HARGICOURT 26 HA 8
08 HARGNIES 20 RA 6
59 HARGNIES 19 NA 5
02 HARLY 28 LA 7
88 HARMONVILLE 67 WA 13
22 HARMOYE, LA 53 J 14
62 HARNES C 17 JA 4
88 HAROL 68 YA 14
54 HAROUE C 68 YA 13
80 HARPONVILLE 17 HA 6
57 HARPRICH 47 AB 11
27 HARQUENCY 38 DA 10
57 HARREBERG 69 CB 12
52 HARREVILLE
LES CHANTEURS 67 VA 14
08 HARRICOURT 30 SA 9
88 HARSAULT 68 YA 15
67 HARSKIRCHEN 48 BB 11
02 HARTENNES ET TAUX 41 LA 10
68 HARTMANNSWILLER 90 CB 16
57 HARTZVILLER 69 CB 12
55 HARVILLE 45 WA 10
02 HARY 28 OA 7
57 HASELBOURG 69 CB 12
59 HASNON 18 LA 4
64 HASPARREN C 205 Q 36
57 HASPELSCHIEDT 48 DB 10
59 HASPRES 18 LA 5
40 HASTINGUES 206 R 35
54 HATRIZE 45 WA 10
67 HATTEN 50 GB 11
80 HATTENCOURT 27 JA 7
76 HATTENVILLE 23 Y 8
57 HATTIGNY 69 BB 12
67 HATTMATT 49 DB 12
68 HATTSTATT 90 CB 15
65 HAUBAN 216 X 37
59 HAUBOURDIN C 9 JA 4
57 HAUCONCOURT 46 YA 10
60 HAUCOURT 25 FA 8
62 HAUCOURT 17 JA 5
76 HAUCOURT 25 EA 8
02 HAUCOURT, LE 18 LA 7
54 HAUCOURT MOULAINE 31 WA 9
55 HAUDAINVILLE 44 UA 10
55 HAUDIOMONT 45 VA 10
60 HAUDIVILLERS 26 GA 9
54 HAUDONVILLE 68 ZA 13
08 HAUDRECY 29 RA 7
76 HAUDRICOURT 25 EA 7
59 HAULCHIN 18 LA 5
32 HAULIES 209 Z 35
08 HAULME 29 RA 7
55 HAUMONTPRES SAMOGNEUX
(VILLAGE RUINE) 31 UA 9
40 HAURIET 184 T 34
68 HAUSGAUEN 90 DB 17
76 HAUSSEZ 25 DA 8
51 HAUSSIGNEMONT 43 RA 12
51 HAUSSIMONT 43 PA 12
54 HAUSSONVILLE 68 YA 13
59 HAUSSY 18 LA 5
57 HAUT CLOCHER 47 BB 12
22 HAUT CORLAY, LE 53 J 14
64 HAUT DE BOSDARROS 215 V 37
70 HAUT DU THEM
CHATEAU LAMBERT, LE 89 AB 16
59 HAUT LIEU 19 NA 6
62 HAUT LOQUIN 7 FA 3
40 HAUT MAUCO 184 U 34
65 HAUTAGET 217 Y 37
80 HAUTBOS 25 EA 8
52 HAUTE AMANCE 87 VA 16
62 HAUTE AVESNES 17 IA 5
05 HAUTE BEAUME, LA 180 VA 30
61 HAUTE CHAPELLE, LA 57 T 12
60 HAUTE EPINE 26 FA 8
44 HAUTE GOULAINE 94 Q 19
95 HAUTE ISLE 39 EA 10
57 HAUTE KONTZ 32 YA 9
77 HAUTE MAISON, LA 41 KA 11
69 HAUTE RIVOIRE 150 QA 25
57 HAUTE VIGNEULLES 47 ZA 10
62 HAUTECLOQUE 16 GA 5
39 HAUTECOUR 122 WA 22
73 HAUTECOUR 153 ZA 26
01 HAUTECOURT ROMANECHE 138 UA 23
19 HAUTEFAGE 160 FA 28
47 HAUTEFAGE LA TOUR 172 Z 32
24 HAUTEFAYE 143 Y 26
77 HAUTEFEUILLE 41 JA 12
71 HAUTEFOND 135 PA 22
60 HAUTEFONTAINE 27 KA 9
24 HAUTEFORT C 144 BA 27
73 HAUTELUCE 154 ZA 25
25 HAUTEPIERRE LE CHATELET 107 YA 19
03 HAUTERIVE 133 LA 24
61 HAUTERIVE 58 X 13
89 HAUTERIVE 83 MA 16
25 HAUTERIVE LA FRESSE 107 ZA 20
26 HAUTERIVES 151 SA 27
21 HAUTEROCHE 85 RA 17
04 HAUTES DUYES 181 YA 32
08 HAUTES RIVIERES, LES 30 SA 7
47 HAUTESVIGNES 171 Y 31
70 HAUTEVELLE 88 YA 16
02 HAUTEVESNES 41 KA 10
02 HAUTEVILLE 28 MA 7
08 HAUTEVILLE 29 PA 8
51 HAUTEVILLE 65 RA 12
62 HAUTEVILLE 17 IA 5
73 HAUTEVILLE 153 YA 26
78 HAUTEVILLE, LA 39 DA 12
50 HAUTEVILLE LA GUICHARD 34 Q 10
21 HAUTEVILLE LES DIJON 105 SA 18
01 HAUTEVILLE LOMPNES C 138 VA 24
74 HAUTEVILLE SUR FIER 139 XA 24
50 HAUTEVILLE SUR MER 56 P 11
02 HAUTION 28 NA 7
59 HAUTMONT C 19 OA 5
88 HAUTMOUGEY 68 YA 15
76 HAUTOT L'AUVRAY 24 Z 7
76 HAUTOT LE VATOIS 23 Z 8
76 HAUTOT ST SULPICE 24 Z 8
76 HAUTOT SUR MER 24 BA 7
76 HAUTOT SUR SEINE 24 AA 9
55 HAUTS DE CHEE, LES 44 TA 11
50 HAUTTEVILLE BOCAGE 33 Q 9
51 HAUTVILLERS 42 OA 10
80 HAUTVILLERS OUVILLE 16 EA 6
27 HAUVILLE 24 AA 9
08 HAUVINE 29 QA 9
33 HAUX 156 U 30
64 HAUX 206 S 37
57 HAVANGE 32 XA 9
28 HAVELU 38 DA 12
59 HAVELUY 18 LA 5
80 HAVERNAS 16 GA 6
59 HAVERSKERQUE 8 HA 3
76 HAVRE, LE S 23 X 9
62 HAVRINCOURT 18 KA 6
94 HAY LES ROSES, L' S 40 HA 12
57 HAYANGE C 32 XA 9
08 HAYBES 20 RA 6
76 HAYE, LA 25 DA 9
88 HAYE, LA 68 YA 15
27 HAYE AUBREE, LA 24 Z 9
50 HAYE BELLEFOND, LA 34 R 11
50 HAYE D'ECTOT, LA 33 O 9
27 HAYE DE CALLEVILLE, LA 37 AA 10
27 HAYE DE ROUTOT, LA 24 Z 9
50 HAYE DU PUITS, LA C 34 P 9
27 HAYE DU THEIL, LA 37 AA 10
27 HAYE LE COMTE, LA 38 BA 10
27 HAYE MALHERBE, LA 38 BA 10
50 HAYE PESNEL, LA C 56 Q 12
27 HAYE ST SYLVESTRE, LA 37 Z 11
57 HAYES 46 YA 10
41 HAYES, LES 79 AA 16
59 HAYNECOURT 18 KA 5
39 HAYS, LES 122 UA 20
59 HAZEBROUCK C 8 HA 3
57 HAZEMBOURG 47 BB 11
95 HEAULME, LE 39 FA 10
50 HEAUVILLE 33 O 8
27 HEBECOURT 25 EA 9
80 HEBECOURT 26 GA 7
50 HEBECREVON 34 R 10
76 HEBERVILLE 24 AA 7
62 HEBUTERNE 17 IA 6
65 HECHES 216 Y 37
68 HECKEN 90 CB 17
27 HECMANVILLE 37 Z 10
27 HECOURT 38 DA 11
60 HECOURT 25 EA 8
59 HECQ 18 MA 5
27 HECTOMARE 38 AA 10
80 HEDAUVILLE 17 IA 6
35 HEDE C 75 O 14
95 HEDOUVILLE 39 GA 10
67 HEGENEY 49 FB 11
68 HEGENHEIM 90 DB 17
67 HEIDOLSHEIM 70 EB 14
68 HEIDWILLER 90 CB 17
67 HEILIGENBERG 70 DB 13
67 HEILIGENSTEIN 70 DB 13
54 HEILLECOURT 46 YA 12
60 HEILLES 26 GA 9
80 HEILLY 17 HA 6
51 HEILTZ L'EVEQUE 43 RA 12
51 HEILTZ LE HUTIER 43 RA 12
51 HEILTZ LE MAURUPT C 44 SA 12
68 HEIMERSDORF 90 CB 17
68 HEIMSBRUNN 90 CB 16
57 HEINING LES BOUZONVILLE 47 ZA 9
55 HEIPPES 44 UA 11
68 HEITEREN 90 EB 15
68 HEIWILLER 90 DB 17
59 HELESMES 18 LA 5
64 HELETTE 205 R 36
62 HELFAUT 8 GA 3
68 HELFRANTZKIRCH 90 DB 17
56 HELLEAN 74 L 15
57 HELLERING LES FENETRANGE 48 BB 12
50 HELLEVILLE 33 O 8
57 HELLIMER 47 BB 11
61 HELOUP 58 W 13
57 HELSTROFF 47 ZA 10
59 HEM 9 KA 3
80 HEM HARDINVAL 16 GA 6
59 HEM LENGLET 18 KA 5
80 HEM MONACU 17 JA 6
50 HEMEVEZ 33 Q 9
60 HEMEVILLERS 27 IA 9
57 HEMILLY 47 ZA 10
57 HEMING 69 BB 12
22 HEMONSTOIR 74 K 14
54 HENAMENIL 46 ZA 12
22 HENANBIHEN 54 L 13
22 HENANSAL 54 L 13
64 HENDAYE C 205 O 36
62 HENDECOURT
LES CAGNICOURT 17 JA 5
62 HENDECOURT LES RANSART 17 IA 5
80 HENENCOURT 17 HA 6
68 HENFLINGEN 90 CB 17
22 HENGOAT 53 I 12
67 HENGWILLER 49 DB 12
62 HENIN BEAUMONT C 17 JA 4
62 HENIN SUR COJEUL 17 JA 5
62 HENINEL 17 JA 5
56 HENNEBONT C 73 H 16
88 HENNECOURT 68 YA 14
55 HENNEMONT 45 VA 10
62 HENNEVEUX 7 EA 3
88 HENNEZEL 67 XA 15
27 HENNEZIS 38 DA 10
22 HENON 54 K 13
60 HENONVILLE 39 FA 10
76 HENOUVILLE 24 AA 9
18 HENRICHEMONT C 101 HA 18
57 HENRIDORFF 48 CB 12
57 HENRIVILLE 47 BB 10
62 HENU 17 HA 6
29 HENVIC 52 F 12
57 HERANGE 48 CB 12
41 HERBAULT C 80 BA 17
80 HERBECOURT 17 JA 7
62 HERBELLES 8 GA 3
85 HERBERGEMENT, L' 110 Q 20
08 HERBEUVAL 31 UA 8
55 HERBEUVILLE 45 VA 11
78 HERBEVILLE 39 FA 11
54 HERBEVILLER 69 AB 13
38 HERBEYS 166 WA 28
85 HERBIERS, LES C 111 S 20
44 HERBIGNAC C 92 M 18
62 HERBINGHEN 7 EA 3
10 HERBISSE 64 OA 12
67 HERBITZHEIM 48 CB 11
95 HERBLAY C 39 GA 11
67 HERBSHEIM 70 EB 14
53 HERCE 57 S 13
60 HERCHIES 26 FA 9
60 HERELLE, LA 26 HA 8
50 HERENGUERVILLE 34 P 11
34 HEREPIAN 213 KA 35
65 HERES 208 W 35
59 HERGNIES 18 MA 4
88 HERGUGNEY 68 YA 13
44 HERIC 93 P 18
62 HERICOURT 16 GA 5
70 HERICOURT C 89 AB 17
76 HERICOURT EN CAUX 24 Z 8
60 HERICOURT SUR THERAIN 25 EA 8
77 HERICY 62 IA 13
02 HERIE, LA 29 OA 7
02 HERIE LA VIEVILLE, LE 28 MA 7
54 HERIMENIL 68 ZA 13
25 HERIMONCOURT C 108 BB 18
59 HERIN 18 LA 5
80 HERISSART 17 HA 6
03 HERISSON C 117 JA 22
80 HERLEVILLE 27 IA 7
62 HERLIERE, LA 17 IA 5
59 HERLIES 9 JA 4
62 HERLIN LE SEC 16 HA 5
62 HERLINCOURT 16 GA 5
62 HERLY 7 FA 4
80 HERLY 27 JA 7
40 HERM 183 R 34
09 HERM, L' 219 EA 38
76 HERMANVILLE 24 BA 7
14 HERMANVILLE SUR MER 36 V 9
48 HERMAUX, LES 176 KA 31

62 HERMAVILLE 17 IA 5
77 HERME 63 LA 13
57 HERMELANGE 69 BB 12
62 HERMELINGHEN 7 EA 3
85 HERMENAULT, L' C 111 S 22
63 HERMENT C 147 HA 25
78 HERMERAY 61 EA 12
60 HERMES 26 GA 9
76 HERMEVILLE 23 X 8
55 HERMEVILLE EN WOEVRE 45 VA 10
62 HERMIES 17 KA 6
73 HERMILLON 153 YA 27
62 HERMIN 17 HA 4
35 HERMITAGE, L' 75 O 15
22 HERMITAGE LORGE, L' 54 J 14
37 HERMITES, LES 79 Z 17
61 HERMITIERE, L' 59 Z 14
14 HERMIVAL LES VAUX 37 X 10
51 HERMONVILLE 29 OA 9
62 HERNICOURT 16 GA 4
57 HERNY 47 ZA 11
76 HERON, LE 25 CA 9
76 HERONCHELLES 25 CA 8
95 HEROUVILLE 39 GA 10
14 HEROUVILLE ST CLAIR C 36 V 10
14 HEROUVILLETTE 36 V 10
88 HERPELMONT 69 AB 14
51 HERPONT 43 RA 11
08 HERPY L'ARLESIENNE 29 PA 8
27 HERQUEVILLE 38 CA 10
50 HERQUEVILLE 33 O 8
31 HERRAN 217 AA 38
40 HERRE 185 W 33
64 HERRERE 215 U 37
59 HERRIN 9 JA 4
67 HERRLISHEIM 49 FB 12
68 HERRLISHEIM PRES COLMAR 90 DB 15
18 HERRY 101 JA 19
54 HERSERANGE C 31 WA 8
62 HERSIN COUPIGNY 17 IA 4
57 HERTZING 69 BB 12
62 HERVELINGHEN 7 EA 2
80 HERVILLY 18 KA 7
58 HERY 102 MA 18
89 HERY 84 MA 16
74 HERY SUR ALBY 139 XA 25
59 HERZEELE 8 HA 2
80 HESBECOURT 18 KA 7
80 HESCAMPS 25 EA 8
62 HESDIGNEUL LES BETHUNE 8 IA 4
62 HESDIGNEUL LES BOULOGNE 7 EA 3
62 HESDIN C 16 FA 5
62 HESDIN L'ABBE 7 EA 3
68 HESINGUE 90 EB 17
62 HESMOND 16 FA 4
57 HESSE 69 BB 12
67 HESSENHEIM 70 EB 14
57 HESTROFF 47 ZA 10
59 HESTRUD 19 OA 5
62 HESTRUS 16 HA 4
60 HETOMESNIL 26 FA 8
57 HETTANGE GRANDE 32 XA 9
68 HETTENSCHLAG 90 DB 15
27 HEUBECOURT HARICOURT 39 DA 10
62 HEUCHIN C 16 GA 4
80 HEUCOURT CROQUOISON 16 EA 7
27 HEUDEBOUVILLE 38 CA 10
27 HEUDICOURT 25 EA 9
80 HEUDICOURT 18 KA 6
55 HEUDICOURT SOUS LES COTES 45 WA 11
27 HEUDREVILLE EN LIEUVIN 37 Y 10
27 HEUDREVILLE SUR EURE 38 BA 10
40 HEUGAS 183 R 35
76 HEUGLEVILLE SUR SCIE 24 BA 7
36 HEUGNES 115 CA 20
61 HEUGON 37 Y 11
50 HEUGUEVILLE SUR SIENNE 34 P 11
52 HEUILLEY COTTON 87 UA 16
52 HEUILLEY LE GRAND 87 UA 16
21 HEUILLEY SUR SAONE 106 UA 18
14 HEULAND 36 W 10
63 HEUME L'EGLISE 147 IA 25
27 HEUNIERE, LA 38 CA 10
27 HEUQUEVILLE 38 CA 9
76 HEUQUEVILLE 23 X 8
62 HEURINGHEM 8 GA 3
76 HEURTEAUVILLE 24 AA 9
14 HEURTEVENT 36 X 11
50 HEUSSE 57 S 13
51 HEUTREGIVILLE 29 PA 9
80 HEUZECOURT 16 GA 6
55 HEVILLIERS 66 UA 12
38 HEYRIEUX C 151 TA 26
62 HEZECQUES 8 GA 4
56 HEZO, LE 92 K 17
65 HIBARETTE 216 W 37
38 HIERES SUR AMBY 151 UA 25
08 HIERGES 20 RA 6
80 HIERMONT 16 FA 5
17 HIERS BROUAGE 126 R 25
16 HIERSAC C 143 W 25
16 HIESSE 130 Z 24
50 HIESVILLE 33 R 9
14 HIEVILLE 36 W 11
64 HIGUERES SOUYE 207 V 36
65 HIIS 216 X 37
57 HILBESHEIM 48 CB 12
22 HILLION 54 K 13
67 HILSENHEIM 70 EB 14
57 HILSPRICH 47 BB 11
02 HINACOURT 28 LA 7
57 HINCKANGE 47 ZA 10
67 HINDISHEIM 70 EB 13
68 HINDLINGEN 90 CB 17
62 HINGES 8 IA 4
22 HINGLE, LE 55 N 13
67 HINSBOURG 48 DB 11
67 HINSINGEN 47 BB 11
40 HINX 183 S 34
67 HIPSHEIM 70 EB 13
35 HIREL 55 O 12
67 HIRSCHLAND 48 CB 11
68 HIRSINGUE C 90 CB 17
02 HIRSON C 19 OA 7
68 HIRTZBACH 90 CB 17
68 HIRTZFELDEN 90 DB 16
31 HIS 217 AA 37
65 HITTE 216 X 37
67 HOCHFELDEN C 49 EB 12
68 HOCHSTATT 90 CB 16
67 HOCHSTETT 49 EB 12
50 HOCQUIGNY 56 O 12
62 HOCQUINGHEN 7 FA 3
60 HODENC EN BRAY 25 FA 9
60 HODENC L'EVEQUE 26 GA 9
76 HODENG AU BOSC 25 EA 7
76 HODENG HODENGER 25 DA 8
95 HODENT 39 EA 10
56 HOEDIC 91 J 18
67 HOENHEIM 49 FB 12
67 HOERDT 49 FB 12
54 HOEVILLE 46 ZA 12
67 HOFFEN 50 FB 11
27 HOGUES, LES 25 CA 9
14 HOGUETTE, LA 36 V 11
67 HOHATZENHEIM 49 EB 12
67 HOHENGOEFT 49 DB 12
67 HOHFRANKENHEIM 49 EB 12
68 HOHROD 90 CB 15
67 HOHWALD, LE 69 DB 13
57 HOLACOURT 47 ZA 11
57 HOLLING 47 ZA 10
02 HOLNON 27 KA 7
59 HOLQUE 8 GA 2
67 HOLTZHEIM 70 EB 13
68 HOLTZWIHR 70 DB 15
57 HOLVING 47 BB 11
80 HOMBLEUX 27 JA 7
02 HOMBLIERES 28 LA 7
68 HOMBOURG 90 DB 16
57 HOMBOURG BUDANGE 32 YA 9
57 HOMBOURG HAUT 47 AB 10
61 HOME CHAMONDOT, L' 59 Z 13
54 HOMECOURT C 45 XA 10
57 HOMMARTING 48 CB 12
57 HOMMERT 69 CB 12
37 HOMMES 97 X 18
50 HOMMET D'ARTHENAY, LE 34 R 10
11 HOMPS 213 IA 36
32 HOMPS 187 AA 34
59 HON HERGIES 19 NA 5
60 HONDAINVILLE 26 GA 9
59 HONDEGHEM 8 HA 3
77 HONDEVILLIERS 41 LA 11
27 HONDOUVILLE 38 BA 10
59 HONDSCHOOTE C 8 HA 2
14 HONFLEUR C 23 X 9
27 HONGUEMARE GUENOUVILLE 24 AA 9
59 HONNECHY 18 MA 6
59 HONNECOURT SUR ESCAUT 18 KA 6
82 HONOR DE COS, L' 173 CA 32
57 HONSKIRCH 47 BB 11
40 HONTANX 185 V 34
57 HOPITAL, L' 47 AB 10
29 HOPITAL CAMFROUT 52 D 14
64 HOPITAL D'ORION, L' 206 S 35
25 HOPITAL DU GROSBOIS, L' 107 YA 19
42 HOPITAL LE GRAND, L' 149 PA 26
71 HOPITAL LE MERCIER, L' 135 OA 22
42 HOPITAL SOUS ROCHEFORT, L' 149 OA 25
64 HOPITAL ST BLAISE, L' 206 T 36
25 HOPITAL ST LIEFFROY, L' 107 ZA 18
25 HOPITAUX NEUFS, LES 123 ZA 21
25 HOPITAUX VIEUX, LES 123 ZA 21
68 HORBOURG WIHR 90 DB 15
59 HORDAIN 18 LA 5
08 HORGNE, LA 30 RA 8
65 HORGUES 216 W 37
42 HORME, L' 150 QA 26
59 HORNAING 18 LA 5
80 HORNOY LE BOURG C 26 FA 7
53 HORPS, LE C 57 U 13
40 HORSARRIEU 184 T 34
55 HORVILLE EN ORNOIS 67 UA 13
27 HOSMES, L' 38 BA 12
04 HOSPITALET, L' 197 WA 33
12 HOSPITALET DU LARZAC, L' 191 KA 33
09 HOSPITALET PRES L'ANDORRE, L' 220 EA 39
64 HOSTA 206 R 37
57 HOSTE 47 BB 10
33 HOSTENS 170 T 31
01 HOSTIAS 138 VA 24
26 HOSTUN 165 TA 28
14 HOTELLERIE, L' 37 Y 10
49 HOTELLERIE DE FLEE, L' 77 S 16
01 HOTONNES 138 VA 24
14 HOTOT EN AUGE 36 W 10
14 HOTTOT LES BAGUES 35 T 10
57 HOTTVILLER 48 DB 10
14 HOUBLONNIERE, LA 36 X 10
74 HOUCHES, LES 140 AB 25
62 HOUCHIN 17 IA 4
62 HOUDAIN C 17 HA 4
59 HOUDAIN LEZ BAVAY 19 NA 5
78 HOUDAN C 39 DA 12
60 HOUDANCOURT 27 IA 9
55 HOUDELAINCOURT 66 UA 13
54 HOUDELMONT 67 XA 13
54 HOUDEMONT 46 XA 12
76 HOUDETOT 24 AA 7
08 HOUDILCOURT 29 OA 9
54 HOUDREVILLE 67 XA 13
88 HOUECOURT 67 WA 14
47 HOUEILLES C 171 W 32
50 HOUESVILLE 34 Q 9
27 HOUETTEVILLE 38 BA 10
88 HOUEVILLE 67 WA 14
65 HOUEYDETS 216 Y 37
32 HOUGA, LE 185 V 34
78 HOUILLES C 39 GA 11
27 HOULBEC COCHEREL 38 CA 10
27 HOULBEC PRES LE GROS THEIL 37 AA 10
08 HOULDIZY 29 RA 7
16 HOULETTE 142 V 25
14 HOULGATE 36 W 9
62 HOULLE 8 GA 3
76 HOULME, LE 24 BA 8
17 HOUMEAU, L' 126 R 23
11 HOUNOUX 221 FA 37
59 HOUPLIN ANCOISNE 9 JA 4
59 HOUPLINES 9 JA 3
76 HOUPPEVILLE 24 BA 8
76 HOUQUETOT 23 Y 8
65 HOURC 208 X 36
51 HOURGES 42 NA 9
64 HOURS 207 V 36
33 HOURTIN 155 R 28
02 HOURY 28 NA 7
41 HOUSSAY 79 AA 16
53 HOUSSAY 77 T 16
27 HOUSSAYE, LA 37 AA 11
76 HOUSSAYE BERANGER, LA 24 BA 8
77 HOUSSAYE EN BRIE, LA 41 JA 12
53 HOUSSEAU BRETIGNOLLES, LE 57 U 13
68 HOUSSEN 70 DB 15
88 HOUSSERAS 69 AB 14
02 HOUSSET 28 NA 7
54 HOUSSEVILLE 67 XA 13
88 HOUSSIERE, LA 69 BB 14
60 HOUSSOYE, LA 25 FA 9
25 HOUTAUD 123 YA 20
59 HOUTKERQUE 8 IA 2
50 HOUTTEVILLE 34 Q 9
27 HOUVILLE EN VEXIN 38 CA 9
28 HOUVILLE LA BRANCHE 61 DA 13
62 HOUVIN HOUVIGNEUL 16 HA 5
28 HOUX 61 DA 13
59 HOYMILLE 8 HA 2
25 HUANNE MONTMARTIN 107 YA 18
62 HUBERSENT 7 EA 4
14 HUBERT FOLIE 36 V 10
50 HUBERVILLE 33 Q 8
62 HUBY ST LEU 16 FA 5
80 HUCHENNEVILLE 16 EA 6
62 HUCLIER 16 HA 4
62 HUCQUELIERS C 7 FA 4
50 HUDIMESNIL 56 P 11
54 HUDIVILLER 68 ZA 13
29 HUELGOAT C 52 F 14
27 HUEST 38 CA 11
45 HUETRE 81 EA 15
38 HUEZ 167 XA 28
70 HUGIER 106 WA 18
76 HUGLEVILLE EN CAUX 24 AA 8
49 HUILLE 77 V 17
52 HUILLIECOURT 67 VA 14
71 HUILLY SUR SEILLE 121 TA 21
51 HUIRON 43 QA 12
37 HUISMES 97 X 19
50 HUISNES SUR MER 56 O 12
41 HUISSEAU EN BEAUCE 79 BA 16
41 HUISSEAU SUR COSSON 80 DA 17
45 HUISSEAU SUR MAUVES 81 EA 16
53 HUISSERIE, L' 77 T 15
62 HULLUCH 17 JA 4
57 HULTEHOUSE 69 CB 12
51 HUMBAUVILLE 65 QA 12
52 HUMBECOURT 66 SA 13
62 HUMBERCAMPS 17 IA 5
80 HUMBERCOURT 17 HA 5
62 HUMBERT 7 FA 4
52 HUMBERVILLE 66 UA 14
18 HUMBLIGNY 101 IA 18
62 HUMEROEUILLE 16 GA 4
52 HUMES JORQUENAY 87 UA 16
62 HUMIERES 16 GA 5
68 HUNAWIHR 70 DB 14
57 HUNDLING 47 BB 10
68 HUNDSBACH 90 DB 17
68 HUNINGUE C 90 EB 17
67 HUNSPACH 50 FB 11
57 HUNTING 32 YA 9
31 HUOS 217 Z 37
12 HUPARLAC 161 IA 30
80 HUPPY 15 EA 6
88 HURBACHE 69 BB 14
33 HURE 171 W 31
70 HURECOURT 88 XA 16
48 HURES LA PARADE 177 LA 32
03 HURIEL C 133 HA 22
71 HURIGNY 136 RA 23
38 HURTIERES 153 XA 27
67 HURTIGHEIM 49 EB 12
68 HUSSEREN LES CHATEAUX 90 DB 15
68 HUSSEREN WESSERLING 90 BB 16
54 HUSSIGNY GODBRANGE 31 WA 9
50 HUSSON 57 S 13
67 HUTTENDORF 49 EB 12
67 HUTTENHEIM 70 EB 14
03 HYDS 133 JA 23
25 HYEMONDANS 108 AB 18
80 HYENCOURT LE GRAND 27 JA 7
50 HYENVILLE 34 P 11
83 HYERES C 203 XA 37
70 HYET 107 XA 18
25 HYEVRE MAGNY 107 ZA 18
25 HYEVRE PAROISSE 107 ZA 18
88 HYMONT 68 XA 14

I

64 IBARROLLE 206 R 37
57 IBIGNY 69 BB 12
65 IBOS 208 W 36
67 ICHTRATZHEIM 70 EB 13
77 ICHY 62 HA 14
64 IDAUX MENDY 206 S 36
32 IDRAC RESPAILLES 208 Y 35
64 IDRON OUSSE SENDETS 207 V 36
18 IDS ST ROCH 116 GA 21
35 IFFENDIC 75 N 15
35 IFFS, LES 75 O 14
14 IFS 36 V 10
76 IFS, LES 25 CA 7
61 IGE 59 Y 14
71 IGE 136 RA 22
80 IGNAUCOURT 26 IA 7
09 IGNAUX 220 EA 39
54 IGNEY 69 AB 12
88 IGNEY 68 ZA 14
18 IGNOL 117 JA 20
70 IGNY 106 WA 18
91 IGNY 39 GA 12
51 IGNY COMBLIZY 42 NA 11
64 IGON 215 V 37
71 IGORNAY 104 OA 19
27 IGOVILLE 24 BA 9
71 IGUERANDE 135 OA 23
64 IHOLDY C 206 R 36
56 ILE AUX MOINES 92 J 17
37 ILE BOUCHARD, L' C 97 Y 19
17 ILE D'AIX 126 R 24
56 ILE D'ARZ 92 K 17
85 ILE D'ELLE, L' 127 S 23
56 ILE D'HOUAT 91 J 18
85 ILE D'OLONNE, L' 125 O 22
85 ILE D'YEU, L' C 109 M 22
29 ILE DE BATZ 52 E 12
22 ILE DE BREHAT 54 J 11
29 ILE DE SEIN 71 B 17
29 ILE MOLENE 51 B 12
2B ILE ROUSSE, L' C 225 KB 39
93 ILE ST DENIS, L' 40 GA 11
29 ILE TUDY 71 E 16
64 ILHARRE 206 S 36
09 ILHAT 219 EA 38
11 ILHES, LES 212 HA 36
65 ILHET 216 Y 38
65 ILHEU 217 Z 37
57 ILLANGE 32 YA 9
09 ILLARTEIN 217 AA 38
33 ILLATS 170 U 30
66 ILLE-SUR-TET 224 IA 39
27 ILLEVILLE SUR MONTFORT 24 Z 9
68 ILLFURTH 90 CB 17
68 ILLHAEUSERN 70 DB 14
01 ILLIAT 137 SA 23
09 ILLIER ET LARAMADE 219 DA 38
28 ILLIERS COMBRAY C 60 CA 14
27 ILLIERS L'EVEQUE 38 CA 11
59 ILLIES 9 JA 4
22 ILLIFAUT 74 M 15
67 ILLKIRCH GRAFFENSTADEN C 70 FB 13
76 ILLOIS 25 EA 7
52 ILLOUD 67 VA 14
08 ILLY 30 SA 7
68 ILLZACH C 90 DB 16
06 ILONSE 199 CB 33
76 IMBLEVILLE 24 AA 8
08 IMECOURT 30 SA 9
57 IMLING 69 BB 12
58 IMPHY C 118 LA 20
08 INAUMONT 29 PA 8
27 INCARVILLE 38 BA 10
76 INCHEVILLE 15 DA 6
59 INCHY 18 MA 6
62 INCHY EN ARTOIS 17 KA 6
62 INCOURT 16 GA 5
25 INDEVILLERS 108 BB 18
44 INDRE 93 P 19
18 INEUIL 116 GA 21
05 INFOURNAS, LES 167 XA 30
67 INGENHEIM 49 EB 12
68 INGERSHEIM 70 DB 15
62 INGHEM 8 GA 3
57 INGLANGE 32 YA 9
67 INGOLSHEIM 50 FB 11
76 INGOUVILLE 24 Z 7
36 INGRANDES 114 AA 21
49 INGRANDES 95 S 18
86 INGRANDES 113 Z 20
37 INGRANDES DE TOURAINE 97 X 18
45 INGRANNES 81 GA 15
45 INGRE C 81 EA 16
56 INGUINIEL 73 I 15
67 INGWILLER 48 DB 11
01 INJOUX GENISSIAT 138 WA 24
67 INNENHEIM 70 EB 13
01 INNIMOND 152 VA 25
55 INOR 30 TA 8
57 INSMING 47 BB 11
57 INSVILLER 47 BB 11
76 INTRAVILLE 15 CA 7
07 INTRES 164 QA 29
28 INTREVILLE 61 FA 14
45 INTVILLE LA GUETARD 61 GA 14
80 INVAL BOIRON 25 EA 7
62 INXENT 7 EA 4
56 INZINZAC LOCHRIST 73 I 16
55 IPPECOURT 44 TA 11
57 IPPLING 47 BB 10
61 IRAI 59 Z 12
79 IRAIS 112 W 20
89 IRANCY 84 MA 16
55 IRE LE SEC 31 UA 9
69 IRIGNY C 151 SA 26
64 IRISSARRY 205 R 36
80 IRLES 17 IA 6
35 IRODOUER 75 N 14
02 IRON 18 MA 6
64 IROULEGUY 205 Q 37
27 IRREVILLE 38 CA 10
29 IRVILLAC 52 D 14
52 IS EN BASSIGNY 87 UA 15
21 IS SUR TILLE C 86 TA 17
62 ISBERGUES 8 HA 4
88 ISCHES 87 WA 15
45 ISDES 81 GA 17
58 ISENAY 119 NA 20
50 ISIGNY LE BUAT C 56 R 12
14 ISIGNY SUR MER C 34 R 9
89 ISLAND 103 NA 18
87 ISLE 145 CA 25
95 ISLE ADAM, L' C 40 GA 10
32 ISLE ARNE, L' 209 AA 35
10 ISLE AUBIGNY 65 PA 13
10 ISLE AUMONT 64 OA 14
32 ISLE BOUZON, L' 187 Z 33
38 ISLE D'ABEAU, L' 151 TA 26
16 ISLE D'ESPAGNAC, L' 143 X 26
32 ISLE DE NOE, L' 208 Y 35
31 ISLE EN DODON, L' C 209 AA 36
03 ISLE ET BARDAIS 117 JA 21
32 ISLE JOURDAIN, L' C 210 BA 35
86 ISLE JOURDAIN, L' C 130 Z 23
33 ISLE ST GEORGES 156 U 30
84 ISLE SUR LA SORGUE, L' C 195 TA 33
25 ISLE SUR LE DOUBS, L' C 107 ZA 18
51 ISLE SUR MARNE 65 RA 12
89 ISLE SUR SEREIN, L' C 84 OA 17
14 ISLES BARDEL, LES 36 V 11
77 ISLES LES MELDEUSES 41 KA 11
77 ISLES LES VILLENOY 40 JA 11
51 ISLES SUR SUIPPE 29 PA 9
55 ISLETTES, LES 44 SA 10
76 ISNEAUVILLE 24 BA 9
06 ISOLA 199 CB 32
2B ISOLACCIO DI FIUMORBO 228 LB 42
52 ISOMES 87 UA 17
48 ISPAGNAC 177 MA 31
64 ISPOURE 205 R 37
62 ISQUES 7 DA 3
24 ISSAC 157 Y 28
07 ISSAMOULENC 164 QA 29
08 ISSANCOURT ET RUMEL 30 SA 7
07 ISSANLAS 163 OA 30
25 ISSANS 89 AB 17
09 ISSARDS, LES 219 EA 37
07 ISSARLES 163 OA 29
44 ISSE 94 O 17
51 ISSE 43 PA 10
11 ISSEL 211 FA 36
46 ISSENDOLUS 159 EA 30
67 ISSENHAUSEN 49 EB 12
68 ISSENHEIM 90 CB 16
46 ISSEPTS 174 FA 30
03 ISSERPENT 133 MA 23
63 ISSERTEAUX 148 LA 26
24 ISSIGEAC C 158 Z 30
30 ISSIRAC 178 QA 32
63 ISSOIRE S 148 LA 26
64 ISSOR 215 T 37
78 ISSOU 39 EA 11
36 ISSOUDUN S 116 FA 20
23 ISSOUDUN LETRIEIX 132 GA 24
31 ISSUS 210 DA 36
71 ISSY L'EVEQUE C 119 OA 21
92 ISSY LES MOULINEAUX C 40 GA 11
13 ISTRES S 201 SA 35
51 ISTRES ET BURY, LES 42 OA 11
64 ISTURITS 206 R 36
02 ITANCOURT 28 LA 7
86 ITEUIL 113 X 22
67 ITTENHEIM 49 EB 12
67 ITTERSWILLER 70 DB 14
91 ITTEVILLE 62 HA 13
64 ITXASSOU 205 Q 36
81 ITZAC 189 EA 33
62 IVERGNY 16 HA 5
77 IVERNY 40 JA 11
02 IVIERS 29 PA 7
27 IVILLE 38 AA 10
60 IVORS 41 KA 10
39 IVORY 122 WA 20
18 IVOY LE PRE 101 HA 18
39 IVREY 122 WA 20
21 IVRY EN MONTAGNE 104 RA 19
27 IVRY LA BATAILLE 38 DA 11
60 IVRY LE TEMPLE 39 FA 10
94 IVRY SUR SEINE C 40 HA 12
59 IWUY 18 LA 5
65 IZAOURT 217 Z 37
31 IZAUT DE L'HOTEL 217 AA 37
65 IZAUX 216 Y 37
53 IZE 58 V 14
38 IZEAUX 152 UA 27
62 IZEL LES EQUERCHIN 17 JA 5
62 IZEL LES HAMEAUX 17 HA 5
01 IZENAVE 138 VA 24
01 IZERNORE C 138 VA 23
38 IZERON 166 UA 28
64 IZESTE 215 U 37
21 IZEURE 105 TA 19
21 IZIER 105 TA 18
01 IZIEU 152 VA 26
33 IZON 156 U 29
26 IZON LA BRUISSE 180 VA 32
32 IZOTGES 185 W 34

J

77 JABLINES 40 IA 11
87 JABREILLES LES BORDES 131 DA 24
15 JABRUN 161 JA 29
73 JACOB BELLECOMBETTE 152 WA 26
34 JACOU 193 OA 34
65 JACQUE 208 X 36
95 JAGNY SOUS BOIS 40 HA 10
77 JAIGNES 41 KA 11
26 JAILLANS 165 TA 28
49 JAILLE YVON, LA 77 T 16
54 JAILLON 45 XA 12
58 JAILLY 102 MA 19
21 JAILLY LES MOULINS 104 RA 18
88 JAINVILLOTTE 67 WA 14
23 JALESCHES 132 FA 23
15 JALEYRAC 160 HA 27
03 JALIGNY SUR BESBRE C 134 MA 22
49 JALLAIS 95 S 19
21 JALLANGES 121 TA 20
28 JALLANS 60 CA 15
57 JALLAUCOURT 47 ZA 11
25 JALLERANGE 106 WA 18
18 JALOGNES 101 IA 19
71 JALOGNY 136 RA 22
51 JALONS 42 PA 11
71 JAMBLES 120 RA 21
78 JAMBVILLE 39 EA 10
60 JAMERICOURT 39 FA 9
55 JAMETZ 31 UA 9
87 JANAILHAC 145 CA 26
23 JANAILLAT 131 EA 24
21 JANCIGNY 106 UA 18
08 JANDUN 29 OA 8
38 JANNEYRIAS 151 TA 25
44 JANS 93 P 17
14 JANVILLE 36 W 10
28 JANVILLE C 61 FA 14
60 JANVILLE 27 JA 9
91 JANVILLE SUR JUINE 62 GA 13
51 JANVILLIERS 42 MA 11
51 JANVRY 42 NA 10
91 JANVRY 61 GA 12
35 JANZE C 76 Q 15
38 JARCIEU 151 SA 27
17 JARD, LA 142 U 26
85 JARD SUR MER 125 P 22
38 JARDIN 151 SA 26
19 JARDIN, LE 146 FA 27
86 JARDRES 113 Z 22
45 JARGEAU C 81 GA 16
05 JARJAYES 181 XA 31
88 JARMENIL 68 ZA 15
16 JARNAC C 142 V 25
17 JARNAC CHAMPAGNE 142 U 25
23 JARNAGES C 132 FA 23
17 JARNE, LA 126 R 23
69 JARNIOUX 136 RA 24
42 JARNOSSE 135 PA 24
54 JARNY 45 WA 10
65 JARRET 216 W 37
38 JARRIE 166 WA 28
17 JARRIE, LA C 127 S 24
17 JARRIE AUDOUIN, LA 128 U 24
73 JARRIER 153 YA 27
18 JARS 101 IA 18
73 JARSY 153 YA 26
54 JARVILLE LA MALGRANGE C 46 YA 12
49 JARZE 96 V 17
42 JAS 150 PA 25
70 JASNEY 88 YA 16
01 JASSANS RIOTTIER 136 RA 24
10 JASSEINES 65 QA 13
01 JASSERON 137 UA 23
64 JASSES 206 T 36
64 JATXOU 205 Q 36
33 JAU DIGNAC ET LOIRAC 141 S 27
10 JAUCOURT 65 RA 14
85 JAUDONNIERE, LA 111 S 21
28 JAUDRAIS 60 BA 13
07 JAUJAC 178 PA 30
16 JAULDES 143 X 25
89 JAULGES 84 NA 15
02 JAULGONNE 41 MA 10
37 JAULNAY 113 Y 20
77 JAULNES 63 LA 13
54 JAULNY 45 WA 11
60 JAULZY 27 KA 9
07 JAUNAC 164 QA 29
86 JAUNAY CLAN 113 Y 21
24 JAURE 157 Z 28
04 JAUSIERS 182 AB 31
60 JAUX 27 JA 9
72 JAUZE 59 Y 14
43 JAVAUGUES 162 MA 27
35 JAVENE 76 R 14
87 JAVERDAT 130 AA 24
24 JAVERLHAC ET LA CHAPELLE ST ROBERT 143 Z 26
10 JAVERNANT 64 OA 14

04 JAVIE, LA C 182 YA 32
48 JAVOLS 162 LA 30
16 JAVREZAC 142 V 25
53 JAVRON LES CHAPELLES 58 V 13
43 JAX 162 MA 28
64 JAXU 206 R 37
24 JAYAC 159 CA 28
01 JAYAT 137 TA 22
86 JAZENEUIL 112 W 22
17 JAZENNES 141 T 26
02 JEANCOURT 18 KA 7
54 JEANDELAINCOURT 46 YA 11
54 JEANDELIZE 45 WA 10
88 JEANMENIL 68 AB 14
42 JEANSAGNIERE 149 NA 25
02 JEANTES 29 OA 7
68 JEBSHEIM 70 DB 15
32 JEGUN C 186 Y 34
24 JEMAYE, LA 157 X 28
59 JENLAIN 18 MA 5
03 JENZAT 134 KA 23
88 JESONVILLE 68 XA 15
10 JESSAINS 65 OA 14
67 JETTERSWILLER 49 DB 12
68 JETTINGEN 90 DB 17
36 JEU LES BOIS 115 EA 21
36 JEU MALOCHES 99 DA 19
78 JEUFOSSE 38 DA 11
10 JEUGNY 64 OA 15
59 JEUMONT 19 OA 5
39 JEURRE 138 VA 22
21 JEUX LES BARD 85 PA 17
88 JEUXEY 68 ZA 14
54 JEVONCOURT 68 YA 13
54 JEZAINVILLE 45 XA 11
65 JEZEAU 216 Y 38
07 JOANNAS 178 PA 30
63 JOB 149 NA 26
50 JOBOURG 33 O 8
66 JOCH 222 HA 39
54 JOEUF 45 XA 10
50 JOGANVILLE 33 Q 9
89 JOIGNY C 83 LA 15
08 JOIGNY SUR MEUSE 27 KA 7
52 JOINVILLE C 66 TA 13
94 JOINVILLE LE PONT C 40 HA 11
51 JOISELLE 41 MA 12
59 JOLIMETZ 18 MA 5
54 JOLIVET 68 ZA 12
69 JONAGE 151 TA 25
34 JONCELS 191 KA 34
85 JONCHERE, LA 125 Q 22
87 JONCHERE ST MAURICE, LA 131 DA 24
26 JONCHERES 180 UA 30
90 JONCHEREY 90 BB 17
52 JONCHERY 66 TA 15
51 JONCHERY SUR SUIPPE 43 QA 10
51 JONCHERY SUR VESLE 42 NA 9
02 JONCOURT 18 LA 6
10 JONCREUIL 65 RA 13
71 JONCY 120 QA 21
73 JONGIEUX 152 WA 25
27 JONQUERETS DE LIVET 37 Z 11
84 JONQUERETTES 195 SA 33
51 JONQUERY 42 NA 10
11 JONQUIERES 223 IA 37
34 JONQUIERES 192 MA 34
60 JONQUIERES 27 IA 9
81 JONQUIERES 189 GA 34
84 JONQUIERES 179 SA 32
30 JONQUIERES ST VINCENT 193 QA 34
69 JONS 151 TA 25
08 JONVAL 30 RA 8
70 JONVELLE 88 WA 15
55 JONVILLE EN WOEVRE 45 WA 10
17 JONZAC S 142 U 26
74 JONZIER EPAGNY 139 XA 24
42 JONZIEUX 150 QA 27
54 JOPPECOURT 31 WA 9
14 JORT 36 W 11
88 JORXEY 68 YA 14
43 JOSAT 162 MA 28
63 JOSERAND 134 KA 24
41 JOSNES 80 DA 16
40 JOSSE 183 R 35
56 JOSSELIN C 74 L 15
77 JOSSIGNY 40 IA 11
15 JOU SOUS MONJOU 161 IA 29
87 JOUAC 131 CA 23
02 JOUAIGNES 42 MA 9
89 JOUANCY 84 OA 17
77 JOUARRE 41 KA 11
78 JOUARS PONTCHARTRAIN 39 FA 12
54 JOUAVILLE 45 XA 10
84 JOUCAS 196 TA 33
11 JOUCOU 221 FA 38
71 JOUDES 122 UA 22
54 JOUDREVILLE 31 WA 9
61 JOUE DU BOIS 58 V 13
61 JOUE DU PLAIN 58 W 12
72 JOUE EN CHARNIE 78 V 15
72 JOUE L'ABBE 78 X 15
37 JOUE LES TOURS C 98 Z 18
44 JOUE SUR ERDRE 94 Q 17
18 JOUET SUR L'AUBOIS 101 JA 19
21 JOUEY 104 QA 19
25 JOUGNE 123 ZA 21
39 JOUHE 106 VA 19
86 JOUHET 114 AA 22
23 JOUILLAT 132 FA 23
13 JOUQUES 202 VA 35
81 JOUQUEVIEL 175 GA 32
87 JOURGNAC 145 CA 25
01 JOURNANS 137 UA 23
86 JOURNET 114 AA 22
24 JOURNIAC 158 AA 29
62 JOURNY 7 FA 3
21 JOURS EN VAUX 104 RA 19
21 JOURS LES BAIGNEUX 85 RA 17
15 JOURSAC 161 JA 28
86 JOUSSE 129 Y 23
71 JOUVENCON 121 TA 21
69 JOUX 136 OA 25
89 JOUX LA VILLE 84 NA 17
28 JOUY 60 DA 13
89 JOUY 63 JA 14
57 JOUY AUX ARCHES 46 XA 10
55 JOUY EN ARGONNE 44 TA 10
78 JOUY EN JOSAS 39 GA 12
45 JOUY EN PITHIVERAIS 61 GA 15
77 JOUY LE CHATEL 63 KA 12
95 JOUY LE MOUTIER C 39 FA 11
45 JOUY LE POTIER 81 EA 16
51 JOUY LES REIMS 42 OA 10
78 JOUY MAUVOISIN 39 DA 11
60 JOUY SOUS THELLE 25 FA 9
27 JOUY SUR EURE 38 CA 10
77 JOUY SUR MORIN 41 LA 12

07 JOYEUSE C 178 PA 31
01 JOYEUX 137 TA 24
63 JOZE 134 LA 25
32 JU BELLOC 208 W 35
14 JUAYE MONDAYE 35 T 10
88 JUBAINVILLE 67 WA 13
49 JUBAUDIERE, LA 95 S 19
53 JUBLAINS 57 U 14
29 JUCH, LE 71 D 15
33 JUGAZAN 156 V 29
19 JUGEALS NAZARETH 159 DA 28
22 JUGON LES LACS C 54 M 13
71 JUGY 121 SA 21
17 JUICQ 128 U 25
71 JUIF 121 TA 21
16 JUIGNAC 143 X 27
44 JUIGNE DES MOUTIERS 94 R 17
49 JUIGNE SUR LOIRE 96 U 18
72 JUIGNE SUR SARTHE 77 V 16
27 JUIGNETTES 37 Z 11
19 JUILLAC C 145 CA 27
32 JUILLAC 208 X 35
33 JUILLAC 157 W 29
16 JUILLAC LE COQ 142 V 26
16 JUILLAGUET 143 X 26
65 JUILLAN 208 W 36
16 JUILLE 129 X 24
72 JUILLE 58 X 14
79 JUILLE 128 V 24
21 JUILLENAY 104 PA 18
32 JUILLES 209 AA 35
50 JUILLEY 56 Q 13
21 JUILLY 85 OA 17
77 JUILLY 40 IA 11
66 JUJOLS 222 GA 39
01 JUJURIEUX 138 UA 24
48 JULIANGES 162 LA 29
69 JULIENAS 136 RA 23
16 JULIENNE 142 V 25
43 JULLIANGES 149 NA 27
69 JULLIE 136 RA 23
50 JULLOUVILLE 56 P 12
89 JULLY 85 PA 16
71 JULLY LES BUXY 120 RA 21
10 JULLY SUR SARCE 65 PA 15
65 JULOS 216 W 37
55 JULVECOURT 44 TA 10
78 JUMEAUVILLE 39 EA 11
63 JUMEAUX C 148 LA 27
80 JUMEL 26 HA 7
27 JUMELLES 38 CA 11
49 JUMELLIERE, LA 95 T 18
02 JUMENCOURT 28 LA 8
76 JUMIEGES 24 AA 9
02 JUMIGNY 28 NA 9
24 JUMILHAC LE GRAND C 144 BA 26
30 JUNAS 193 OA 34
89 JUNAY 84 OA 16
65 JUNCALAS 216 W 37
68 JUNGHOLTZ 90 CB 16
15 JUNHAC 161 HA 30
46 JUNIES, LES 173 CA 31
08 JUNIVILLE C 29 QA 9
72 JUPILLES 79 Y 16
64 JURANCON 207 U 36
45 JURANVILLE 82 HA 15
42 JURE 135 NA 25
16 JURIGNAC 142 W 26
14 JURQUES 35 T 11
31 JURVIELLE 217 Y 38
57 JURY 46 YA 10
79 JUSCORPS 128 U 23
47 JUSIX 171 W 31
15 JUSSAC C 161 HA 29
88 JUSSARUPT 69 AB 14
17 JUSSAS 142 V 27
51 JUSSECOURT MINECOURT 43 RA 12
70 JUSSEY C 88 WA 16
02 JUSSY 27 LA 8
57 JUSSY 46 XA 10
89 JUSSY 83 MA 16
18 JUSSY CHAMPAGNE 117 IA 20
18 JUSSY LE CHAUDRIER 101 JA 19
32 JUSTIAN 186 X 34
08 JUSTINE HERBIGNY 29 PA 8
09 JUSTINIAC 210 DA 36
77 JUTIGNY 63 KA 13
88 JUVAINCOURT 67 XA 14
10 JUVANCOURT 66 SA 15
10 JUVANZE 65 QA 14
49 JUVARDEIL 77 U 17
57 JUVELIZE 47 AB 12
34 JUVIGNAC 214 NA 35
53 JUVIGNE 76 S 14
60 JUVIGNIES 26 FA 8
02 JUVIGNY 28 LA 9
51 JUVIGNY 43 PA 11
74 JUVIGNY 139 YA 23
55 JUVIGNY EN PERTHOIS 66 TA 13
50 JUVIGNY LE TERTRE C 57 S 12
61 JUVIGNY SOUS ANDAINE C 57 U 13
55 JUVIGNY SUR LOISON 31 UA 9
61 JUVIGNY SUR ORNE 58 W 12
14 JUVIGNY SUR SEULLES 35 T 10
57 JUVILLE 46 YA 11
07 JUVINAS 164 PA 30
02 JUVINCOURT ET DAMARY 28 NA 9
91 JUVISY SUR ORGE C 62 HA 12
54 JUVRECOURT 46 ZA 12
64 JUXUE 206 R 36
10 JUZANVIGNY 65 RA 13
52 JUZENNECOURT C 66 SA 14
31 JUZES 211 EA 35
31 JUZET D'IZAUT 217 Z 38
31 JUZET DE LUCHON 217 Z 38
78 JUZIERS 39 EA 11

K

57 KALHAUSEN 48 CB 11
67 KALTENHOUSE 49 FB 12
57 KANFEN 32 XA 9
68 KAPPELEN 90 DB 17
57 KAPPELKINGER 47 BB 11
68 KATZENTHAL 69 CB 15
67 KAUFFENHEIM 50 GB 11
68 KAYSERSBERG C 69 CB 15
57 KEDANGE SUR CANNER 32 YA 9
67 KEFFENACH 49 FB 11
68 KEMBS 90 DB 17
57 KEMPLICH 47 ZA 9
57 KERBACH 47 BB 10
22 KERBORS 53 I 12
22 KERFOT 53 J 12
56 KERFOURN 74 J 15
29 KERGLOFF 52 G 14
56 KERGRIST 73 J 15
22 KERGRIST MOELOU 53 H 14
22 KERIEN 53 I 13
29 KERLAZ 71 D 15
57 KERLING LES SIERCK 32 YA 9
29 KERLOUAN 51 D 12
22 KERMARIA SULARD 53 H 12
22 KERMOROC'H 53 I 12
56 KERNASCLEDEN 73 H 15
29 KERNILIS 51 D 13
29 KERNOUES 51 D 13
22 KERPERT 53 I 13
57 KERPRICH AUX BOIS 47 BB 12
29 KERSAINT PLABENNEC 51 D 13
67 KERTZFELD 70 EB 13
56 KERVIGNAC 73 I 16
67 KESKASTEL 48 BB 11
67 KESSELDORF 50 GB 11
67 KIENHEIM 49 EB 12
68 KIENTZHEIM 69 CB 15
59 KILLEM 8 HA 2
67 KILSTETT 49 FB 12
67 KINDWILLER 48 EB 11
68 KINGERSHEIM 90 DB 16
67 KINTZHEIM 70 DB 14
68 KIRCHBERG 89 BB 16
67 KIRCHHEIM 49 DB 12
67 KIRRBERG 48 CB 12
67 KIRRWILLER BOSSELSHAUSEN 49 DB 12
57 KIRSCH LES SIERCK 32 ZA 9
57 KIRSCHNAUMEN 32 ZA 9
57 KIRVILLER 47 BB 11
57 KLANG 32 YA 9
67 KLEINGOEFT 49 DB 12
68 KNOERINGUE 90 DB 17
67 KNOERSHEIM 49 DB 12
57 KNUTANGE 32 XA 9
57 KOENIGSMACKER 32 YA 9
68 KOESTLACH 90 CB 17
68 KOETZINGUE 90 DB 17
55 KOEUR LA GRANDE 44 UA 11
55 KOEUR LA PETITE 45 VA 11
67 KOGENHEIM 70 EB 14
67 KOLBSHEIM 70 EB 13
67 KRAUTERGERSHEIM 70 EB 13
67 KRAUTWILLER 49 EB 12
94 KREMLIN BICETRE, LE C 40 HA 12
67 KRIEGSHEIM 49 FB 12
68 KRUTH 90 BB 15
68 KUNHEIM 90 EB 15
57 KUNTZIG 32 YA 9
67 KURTZENHOUSE 49 FB 12
67 KUTTOLSHEIM 49 DB 12
67 KUTZENHAUSEN 49 FB 11

L

64 LAA MONDRANS 206 T 35
32 LAAS 208 X 35
45 LAAS 62 GA 15
64 LAAS 206 S 36
01 LABALME 138 VA 24
33 LABARDE 155 T 28
68 LABAROCHE 69 CB 15
32 LABARRERE 186 X 33
32 LABARTHE 209 Z 35
82 LABARTHE 173 CA 32
81 LABARTHE BLEYS 189 FA 33
31 LABARTHE INARD 217 AA 37
31 LABARTHE RIVIERE 217 Z 37
31 LABARTHE SUR LEZE 210 CA 35
32 LABARTHETE 207 V 35
65 LABASSERE 216 X 37
65 LABASTIDE 216 Y 37
31 LABASTIDE BEAUVOIR 210 DA 35
47 LABASTIDE CASTEL AMOUROUX 171 X 31
64 LABASTIDE CEZERACQ 207 U 36
40 LABASTIDE CHALOSSE 184 T 35
31 LABASTIDE CLERMONT 210 BA 36
11 LABASTIDE D'ANJOU 211 EA 36
40 LABASTIDE D'ARMAGNAC 185 V 33
81 LABASTIDE DE LEVIS 189 FA 33
82 LABASTIDE DE PENNE 174 DA 32
07 LABASTIDE DE VIRAC 178 QA 31
81 LABASTIDE DENAT 190 GA 34
46 LABASTIDE DU HAUT MONT 160 GA 29
82 LABASTIDE DU TEMPLE 188 BA 33
46 LABASTIDE DU VERT 173 CA 31
11 LABASTIDE EN VAL 221 HA 37
11 LABASTIDE ESPARBAIRENQUE 212 HA 36
81 LABASTIDE GABAUSSE 189 FA 33
46 LABASTIDE MARNHAC 173 CA 31
64 LABASTIDE MONREJEAU 207 U 36
46 LABASTIDE MURAT C 174 DA 30
31 LABASTIDE PAUMES 209 AA 36
81 LABASTIDE ROUAIROUX 212 IA 35
32 LABASTIDE SAVES 209 BA 35
81 LABASTIDE ST GEORGES 189 EA 34
82 LABASTIDE ST PIERRE 188 CA 33
31 LABASTIDE ST SERNIN 188 DA 34
07 LABASTIDE SUR BESORGUES 164 PA 30
64 LABASTIDE VILLEFRANCHE 206 R 35
31 LABASTIDETTE 210 CA 35
46 LABATHUDE 160 FA 30
07 LABATIE D'ANDAURE 164 QA 28
64 LABATMALE 215 V 37
09 LABATUT 210 DA 36
40 LABATUT 183 S 35
64 LABATUT 208 W 36
65 LABATUT RIVIERE 208 W 35
95 LABBEVILLE 39 GA 10
07 LABEAUME 178 PA 31
11 LABECEDE LAURAGAIS 211 FA 36
31 LABEGE 210 DA 35
07 LABEGUDE 178 PA 30
32 LABEJAN 209 Y 35
40 LABENNE 183 Q 35
25 LABERGEMENT DU NAVOIS 107 XA 20
21 LABERGEMENT FOIGNEY 105 UA 18
21 LABERGEMENT LES AUXONNE 105 UA 19
21 LABERGEMENT LES SEURRE 121 TA 20
25 LABERGEMENT STE MARIE 123 YA 21
60 LABERLIERE 27 IA 8
33 LABESCAU 171 W 31
15 LABESSERETTE 161 HA 30
63 LABESSETTE 147 HA 26
81 LABESSIERE CANDEIL 189 FA 34
64 LABETS BISCAY 206 R 36
55 LABEUVILLE 45 WA 10
62 LABEUVRIERE 8 IA 4
64 LABEYRIE 207 T 35
07 LABLACHERE 178 PA 31
80 LABOISSIERE EN SANTERRE 27 IA 8
60 LABOISSIERE EN THELLE 39 GA 9
65 LABORDE 216 X 37
26 LABOREL 180 VA 32
60 LABOSSE 25 EA 9
40 LABOUHEYRE 169 S 32
81 LABOULBENE 190 GA 34
07 LABOULE 178 PA 30
24 LABOUQUERIE 158 AA 30
82 LABOURGADE 187 BA 33
62 LABOURSE 17 IA 4
81 LABOUTARIE 189 FA 34
47 LABRETONIE 172 Y 31
32 LABRIHE 187 AA 34
40 LABRIT C 170 U 32
31 LABROQUERE 217 Z 37
45 LABROSSE 62 HA 14
15 LABROUSSE 161 HA 29
62 LABROYE 16 FA 5
81 LABRUGUIERE C 212 GA 35
21 LABRUYERE 105 TA 19
60 LABRUYERE 26 HA 9
31 LABRUYERE DORSA 210 DA 36
54 LABRY 45 WA 10
46 LABURGADE 174 DA 31
07 LAC D'ISSARLES, LE 163 OA 29
39 LAC DES ROUGES TRUITES 123 XA 21
81 LACABAREDE 212 IA 35
64 LACADEE 207 T 35
40 LACAJUNTE 207 U 35
12 LACALM 161 JA 29
46 LACAM D'OURCET 160 FA 29
33 LACANAU 155 R 29
21 LACANCHE 104 OA 19
15 LACAPELLE BARRES 161 IA 29
47 LACAPELLE BIRON 173 AA 30
46 LACAPELLE CABANAC 173 BA 31
15 LACAPELLE DEL FRAISSE 160 HA 29
82 LACAPELLE LIVRON 174 EA 32
46 LACAPELLE MARIVAL C 160 FA 30
81 LACAPELLE PINET 190 HA 33
81 LACAPELLE SEGALAR 174 FA 32
15 LACAPELLE VIESCAMP 160 GA 29
64 LACARRE 206 R 37
64 LACARRY ARHAN CHARITTE DE HAUT 206 S 37
65 LACASSAGNE 208 X 36
31 LACAUGNE 210 CA 36
81 LACAUNE C 190 IA 34
47 LACAUSSADE 172 AA 31
09 LACAVE 218 BA 37
46 LACAVE 159 DA 29
81 LACAZE 190 HA 34
19 LACELLE 146 EA 26
69 LACENAS 136 RA 24
47 LACEPEDE 172 Y 31
16 LACHAISE 142 V 26
55 LACHALADE 44 SA 10
57 LACHAMBRE 47 AB 10
48 LACHAMP 177 LA 30
07 LACHAMP RAPHAEL 164 PA 29
47 LACHAPELLE 171 X 30
54 LACHAPELLE 69 AB 13
80 LACHAPELLE 26 FA 7
82 LACHAPELLE 187 AA 33
60 LACHAPELLE AUX POTS 25 FA 9
46 LACHAPELLE AUZAC 159 DA 29
52 LACHAPELLE EN BLAISY 66 SA 14
07 LACHAPELLE GRAILLOUSE 163 OA 29
07 LACHAPELLE SOUS AUBENAS 178 QA 30
07 LACHAPELLE SOUS CHANEAC 164 PA 29
90 LACHAPELLE SOUS CHAUX 89 AB 16
60 LACHAPELLE SOUS GERBEROY 25 EA 8
90 LACHAPELLE SOUS ROUGEMONT 90 BB 16
60 LACHAPELLE ST PIERRE 40 GA 10
69 LACHASSAGNE 136 RA 24
26 LACHAU 180 VA 32
55 LACHAUSSEE 45 WA 11
60 LACHAUSSEE DU BOIS D'ECU 26 GA 8
63 LACHAUX 133 MA 24
60 LACHELLE 27 IA 9
51 LACHY 42 NA 12
90 LACOLLONGE 90 BB 17
11 LACOMBE 212 GA 36
64 LACOMMANDE 207 U 36
34 LACOSTE 214 LA 35
84 LACOSTE 196 TA 34
81 LACOUGOTTE CADOUL 211 EA 35
82 LACOUR 173 AA 32
21 LACOUR D'ARCENAY 104 PA 18
09 LACOURT 218 BA 38
82 LACOURT ST PIERRE 188 CA 33
64 LACQ 207 T 36
40 LACQUY 185 V 33
40 LACRABE 207 U 35
62 LACRES 7 EA 4
81 LACROISILLE 211 FA 35
12 LACROIX BARREZ 161 IA 29
31 LACROIX FALGARDE 210 CA 35
60 LACROIX ST OUEN 27 JA 9
55 LACROIX SUR MEUSE 45 VA 11
24 LACROPTE 158 AA 28
71 LACROST 121 SA 22
81 LACROUZETTE 190 GA 34
36 LACS 116 FA 21
23 LADAPEYRE 132 FA 23
33 LADAUX 156 V 30
11 LADERN SUR LAUQUET 221 HA 37
32 LADEVEZE RIVIERE 208 W 35
32 LADEVEZE VILLE 208 W 35
87 LADIGNAC LE LONG 144 BA 26
19 LADIGNAC SUR RONDELLES 160 EA 27
15 LADINHAC 161 HA 30
46 LADIRAT 160 FA 29
16 LADIVILLE 142 W 26
21 LADOIX SERRIGNY 105 SA 19
45 LADON 82 HA 15
33 LADOS 171 V 31
39 LADOYE SUR SEILLE 122 VA 21
89 LADUZ 83 LA 16
11 LAFAGE 219 EA 37
19 LAFAGE SUR SOMBRE 146 FA 27
84 LAFARE 179 SA 32
07 LAFARRE 164 QA 28
43 LAFARRE 163 OA 29
23 LAFAT 131 DA 23
52 LAFAUCHE 67 UA 14
03 LAFELINE 134 KA 23
52 LAFERTE SUR AMANCE C 87 VA 16
52 LAFERTE SUR AUBE 66 RA 15
15 LAFEUILLADE EN VEZIE 161 HA 29
02 LAFFAUX 28 LA 9
31 LAFFITE TOUPIERE 217 AA 37
38 LAFFREY 166 WA 28
65 LAFITOLE 208 X 35
82 LAFITTE 188 BA 33
47 LAFITTE SUR LOT 172 Y 31
31 LAFITTE VIGORDANE 210 BA 36
47 LAFOX 172 Z 32
82 LAFRANCAISE C 173 CA 32
60 LAFRAYE 26 GA 9
80 LAFRESGUIMONT ST MARTIN 25 EA 7
57 LAFRIMBOLLE 69 BB 13
34 LAGAMAS 192 MA 34
09 LAGARDE 221 FA 37
31 LAGARDE 211 EA 36
32 LAGARDE 187 Z 33
57 LAGARDE 69 AB 12
65 LAGARDE 208 W 36
84 LAGARDE D'APT 196 VA 33
19 LAGARDE ENVAL 159 EA 28
32 LAGARDE HACHAN 209 Y 36
84 LAGARDE PAREOL 179 SA 32
16 LAGARDE SUR LE NE 142 V 26
46 LAGARDELLE 173 BA 31
31 LAGARDELLE SUR LEZE 210 CA 36
32 LAGARDERE 186 X 34
81 LAGARDIOLLE 211 FA 35
47 LAGARRIGUE 172 Y 32
81 LAGARRIGUE 212 GA 35
79 LAGEON 112 V 21
51 LAGERY 42 NA 10
19 LAGLEYGEOLLE 159 EA 28
40 LAGLORIEUSE 184 U 34
84 LAGNES 195 TA 33
54 LAGNEY 45 WA 12
62 LAGNICOURT MARCEL 17 JA 6
01 LAGNIEU C 138 UA 24
60 LAGNY 27 JA 8
60 LAGNY LE SEC 40 IA 10
77 LAGNY SUR MARNE C 40 IA 11
64 LAGOR C 207 T 36
07 LAGORCE 178 QA 31
33 LAGORCE 156 V 28
17 LAGORD 126 R 23
64 LAGOS 207 V 36
31 LAGRACE DIEU 210 CA 36
05 LAGRAND 180 WA 31
40 LAGRANGE 185 W 33
65 LAGRANGE 216 Y 37
90 LAGRANGE 90 BB 17
11 LAGRASSE C 223 IA 37
32 LAGRAULET DU GERS 186 X 33
31 LAGRAULET ST NICOLAS 187 BA 34
19 LAGRAULIERE 145 DA 27
81 LAGRAVE 189 FA 33
47 LAGRUERE 171 X 31
19 LAGUENNE C 159 EA 27
82 LAGUEPIE 174 FA 32
32 LAGUIAN MAZOUS 208 X 35
64 LAGUINGE RESTOUE 206 S 37
12 LAGUIOLE C 176 JA 30
47 LAGUPIE 171 X 30
31 LAHAGE 210 BA 35
32 LAHAS 209 AA 35
55 LAHAYMEIX 44 UA 11
55 LAHAYVILLE 45 WA 11
55 LAHEYCOURT 44 SA 11
31 LAHITERE 218 BA 37
32 LAHITTE 187 Z 34
65 LAHITTE TOUPIERE 208 W 35
64 LAHONCE 205 Q 35
64 LAHONTAN 206 S 35
40 LAHOSSE 184 T 34
64 LAHOURCADE 207 T 36
80 LAHOUSSOYE 17 HA 7
08 LAIFOUR 20 RA 7
53 LAIGNE 77 S 16
17 LAIGNE, LA 127 T 23
72 LAIGNE EN BELIN 78 X 16
35 LAIGNELET 56 R 14
21 LAIGNES C 85 QA 16
60 LAIGNEVILLE 40 HA 9
02 LAIGNY 28 NA 7
35 LAILLE 75 O 15
89 LAILLY 64 MA 14
45 LAILLY EN VAL 81 EA 16
55 LAIMONT 44 TA 11
89 LAIN 83 LA 17
10 LAINES AUX BOIS 64 OA 14
39 LAINS 122 UA 22
89 LAINSECQ 83 LA 17
78 LAINVILLE 39 EA 10
25 LAIRE 89 AB 17
62 LAIRES 8 GA 4
11 LAIRIERE 221 HA 37
85 LAIROUX 125 R 22
12 LAISSAC C 176 JA 31
73 LAISSAUD 153 XA 27
25 LAISSEY 107 YA 18
54 LAITRE SOUS AMANCE 46 YA 12
71 LAIVES 121 SA 21
54 LAIX 31 WA 9
01 LAIZ 137 SA 23
71 LAIZE 136 RA 22
14 LAIZE LA VILLE 36 U 10
71 LAIZY 120 PA 20
48 LAJO 162 LA 29
39 LAJOUX 139 XA 22
61 LALACELLE 58 V 13
89 LALANDE 83 LA 17
33 LALANDE DE POMEROL 156 V 29
60 LALANDE EN SON 25 EA 9
60 LALANDELLE 25 FA 9
47 LALANDUSSE 172 Y 30
32 LALANNE 187 Z 34
65 LALANNE 209 Z 36
32 LALANNE ARQUE 209 Z 36
65 LALANNE TRIE 208 Y 36
67 LALAYE 69 CB 14
81 LALBAREDE 211 FA 35
46 LALBENQUE C 174 DA 31
61 LALEU 59 Y 13
80 LALEU 16 FA 7
07 LALEVADE D'ARDECHE 178 PA 30
71 LALHEUE 120 RA 21
24 LALINDE C 158 Z 29
03 LALIZOLLE 133 KA 23
59 LALLAING 18 KA 5
35 LALLEU 76 P 16
38 LALLEY 166 VA 30
01 LALLEYRIAT 138 WA 23
08 LALOBBE 29 OA 8
54 LALOEUF 67 XA 13
64 LALONGUE 207 V 35
64 LALONQUETTE 207 V 35
65 LALOUBERE C 208 W 36
31 LALOURET LAFFITEAU 217 Z 37
07 LALOUVESC 164 QA 28
40 LALUQUE 183 S 34
2B LAMA 226 LB 39
90 LAMADELEINE VAL DES ANGES 89 BB 16
46 LAMAGDELAINE 174 DA 31
82 LAMAGISTERE 172 AA 32
32 LAMAGUERE 209 Z 35
03 LAMAIDS 132 HA 23
34 LAMALOU LES BAINS 213 KA 35
52 LAMANCINE 66 TA 14
66 LAMANERE 222 HA 40

13	LAMANON		195	TA	34
88	LAMARCHE	C	67	WA	15
21	LAMARCHE SUR SAONE		105	SA	19
21	LAMARGELLE		86	SA	17
80	LAMARONDE		26	FA	7
33	LAMARQUE		155	T	28
65	LAMARQUE PONTACQ		215	W	37
65	LAMARQUE RUSTAING		208	X	36
31	LAMASQUERE		210	CA	35
07	LAMASTRE	C	164	QA	29
54	LAMATH		68	ZA	13
46	LAMATIVIE		160	FA	29
64	LAMAYOU		208	W	36
32	LAMAZERE		208	Y	35
19	LAMAZIERE BASSE		146	GA	27
19	LAMAZIERE HAUTE		146	HA	25
57	LAMBACH		48	DB	11
22	LAMBALLE	C	54	L	13
59	LAMBERSART		9	KA	3
50	LAMBERVILLE		35	S	10
76	LAMBERVILLE		24	AA	7
13	LAMBESC	C	196	TA	34
28	LAMBLORE		60	AA	12
62	LAMBRES		8	HA	4
59	LAMBRES LES DOUAI		17	KA	5
70	LAMBREY		88	WA	16
04	LAMBRUISSE		198	ZA	33
65	LAMEAC		208	X	36
60	LAMECOURT		26	HA	9
30	LAMELOUZE		178	OA	32
58	LAMENAY SUR LOIRE		119	MA	21
16	LAMERAC		142	V	27
08	LAMETZ		30	RA	8
81	LAMILLARIE		189	GA	34
76	LAMMERVILLE		24	BA	7
72	LAMNAY		59	Z	15
19	LAMONGERIE		145	DA	26
81	LAMONTELARIE		212	IA	35
63	LAMONTGIE		148	LA	26
47	LAMONTJOIE		186	Y	33
24	LAMONZIE MONTASTRUC		157	Z	29
24	LAMONZIE ST MARTIN		157	Y	29
60	LAMORLAYE		40	HA	10
55	LAMORVILLE		45	VA	11
40	LAMOTHE		184	T	34
43	LAMOTHE		148	LA	27
82	LAMOTHE CAPDEVILLE		188	CA	33
46	LAMOTHE CASSEL		174	DA	30
82	LAMOTHE CUMONT		187	AA	33
52	LAMOTHE EN BLAISY		66	SA	14
46	LAMOTHE FENELON		159	CA	29
32	LAMOTHE GOAS		187	Z	34
33	LAMOTHE LANDERRON		171	W	30
24	LAMOTHE MONTRAVEL		157	W	29
41	LAMOTTE BEUVRON	C	81	FA	17
80	LAMOTTE BREBIERE		26	HA	7
80	LAMOTTE BULEUX		16	EA	5
84	LAMOTTE DU RHONE		179	RA	32
80	LAMOTTE WARFUSEE		26	IA	7
55	LAMOUILLY		30	TA	8
39	LAMOURA		123	XA	22
29	LAMPAUL GUIMILIAU		52	E	13
29	LAMPAUL PLOUARZEL		51	B	13
29	LAMPAUL PLOUDALMEZEAU		51	B	13
67	LAMPERTHEIM		49	EB	12
67	LAMPERTSLOCH		49	FB	11
69	LAMURE SUR AZERGUES	C	136	QA	24
25	LANANS		107	ZA	18
07	LANARCE		163	OA	30
29	LANARVILY		51	D	13
07	LANAS		178	QA	31
41	LANCE		80	BA	17
80	LANCHERES		15	DA	6
80	LANCHES ST HILAIRE		16	GA	6
02	LANCHY		27	KA	7
69	LANCIE		136	RA	23
22	LANCIEUX		55	M	12
41	LANCOME		80	BA	17
08	LANCON		44	SA	10
65	LANCON		216	Y	38
13	LANCON PROVENCE		201	TA	35
01	LANCRANS		138	WA	23
57	LANDANGE		69	BB	12
59	LANDAS		18	LA	4
56	LANDAUL		73	J	16
88	LANDAVILLE		67	WA	14
35	LANDAVRAN		76	Q	14
49	LANDE CHASLES, LA		96	W	17
50	LANDE D'AIROU, LA		56	Q	12
33	LANDE DE FRONSAC, LA		156	U	29
61	LANDE DE GOULT, LA		58	W	13
61	LANDE DE LOUGE, LA		58	V	12
61	LANDE PATRY, LA		57	T	12
27	LANDE ST LEGER, LA		23	Y	9
61	LANDE ST SIMEON, LA		57	U	12
14	LANDE SUR DROME, LA		35	S	10
61	LANDE SUR EURE, LA		59	AA	13
35	LANDEAN		56	R	13
22	LANDEBAERON		53	I	12
22	LANDEBIA		54	M	13
22	LANDEC, LA		55	M	13
54	LANDECOURT		68	ZA	13
29	LANDEDA		51	C	13
22	LANDEHEN		54	L	13
29	LANDELEAU		72	F	14
28	LANDELLES		60	CA	13
14	LANDELLES ET COUPIGNY		35	S	11
49	LANDEMONT		94	R	18
27	LANDEPEREUSE		37	Z	11
29	LANDERNEAU	C	51	D	13
85	LANDERONDE		110	P	21
33	LANDERROUAT		157	X	30
33	LANDERROUET SUR SEGUR		171	W	30
67	LANDERSHEIM		49	DB	12
17	LANDES		128	U	24
85	LANDES GENUSSON, LES		110	R	20
41	LANDES LE GAULOIS		80	BA	17
14	LANDES SUR AJON		35	U	10
76	LANDES VIEILLES ET NEUVES		25	DA	7
56	LANDEVANT		73	I	16
29	LANDEVENNEC		51	D	14
85	LANDEVIEILLE		109	O	21
15	LANDEYRAT		161	JA	27
02	LANDIFAY ET BERTAIGNEMONT		28	MA	7
61	LANDIGOU		57	U	12
27	LANDIN, LE		24	AA	9
33	LANDIRAS		170	U	30
61	LANDISACQ		57	T	12
29	LANDIVISIAU	C	52	E	13
53	LANDIVY	C	57	S	13
63	LANDOGNE		133	IA	25
31	LANDORTHE		217	AA	37
43	LANDOS		163	NA	29
02	LANDOUZY LA COUR		29	OA	7
02	LANDOUZY LA VILLE		29	OA	7
17	LANDRAIS		127	S	24
44	LANDREAU, LE		94	Q	19
59	LANDRECIES	C	18	NA	6
55	LANDRECOURT LEMPIRE		44	UA	10
54	LANDREMONT		46	XA	11
54	LANDRES		31	WA	9
08	LANDRES ET ST GEORGES		30	SA	9
25	LANDRESSE		107	ZA	18
62	LANDRETHUN LE NORD		7	EA	3
62	LANDRETHUN LES ARDRES		7	FA	3
29	LANDREVARZEC		72	E	15
10	LANDREVILLE		65	QA	15
08	LANDRICHAMPS		20	SA	6
02	LANDRICOURT		28	LA	8
51	LANDRICOURT		66	SA	12
57	LANDROFF		47	AB	11
73	LANDRY		154	AB	26
68	LANDSER		90	DB	17
29	LANDUDAL		72	E	15
29	LANDUDEC		71	D	15
35	LANDUJAN		75	N	14
29	LANDUNVEZ		51	B	13
65	LANESPEDE		216	X	37
56	LANESTER	C	73	H	16
11	LANET		221	HA	38
52	LANEUVELLE		87	VA	16
54	LANEUVELOTTE		46	YA	12
54	LANEUVEVILLE AUX BOIS		68	AB	12
54	LANEUVEVILLE DERRIERE FOUG		45	WA	12
54	LANEUVEVILLE DEVANT BAYON		68	YA	13
54	LANEUVEVILLE DEVANT NANCY		46	YA	12
57	LANEUVEVILLE EN SAULNOIS		47	ZA	11
57	LANEUVEVILLE LES LORQUIN		69	BB	12
52	LANEUVILLE AU PONT		66	SA	12
55	LANEUVILLE AU RUPT		45	VA	12
55	LANEUVILLE SUR MEUSE		30	TA	9
60	LANEUVILLEROY		26	IA	9
22	LANFAINS		54	J	14
54	LANFROICOURT		46	YA	12
35	LANGAN		75	O	14
22	LANGAST		74	K	14
57	LANGATTE		47	BB	12
36	LANGE		99	DA	19
43	LANGEAC	C	162	MA	28
37	LANGEAIS	C	97	Y	18
67	LANGENSOULTZBACH		49	FB	11
58	LANGERON		118	KA	20
45	LANGESSE		82	IA	16
28	LANGEY		80	BA	15
30	LANGLADE		193	PA	34
88	LANGLEY		68	YA	14
22	LANGOAT		53	H	12
56	LANGOELAN		73	I	15
48	LANGOGNE	C	163	NA	30
33	LANGOIRAN		156	U	30
29	LANGOLEN		72	F	15
33	LANGON	S	170	V	31
35	LANGON		75	O	16
41	LANGON		99	EA	18
85	LANGON, LE		111	S	22
56	LANGONNET		73	H	15
35	LANGOUET		75	O	14
22	LANGOURLA		74	L	14
52	LANGRES	S	87	UA	16
22	LANGROLAY SUR RANCE		55	N	13
14	LANGRUNE SUR MER		36	V	9
22	LANGUEDIAS		55	M	13
22	LANGUENAN		55	N	13
22	LANGUEUX	C	54	K	13
80	LANGUEVOISIN QUIQUERY		27	JA	7
56	LANGUIDIC		73	I	16
57	LANGUIMBERG		47	BB	12
03	LANGY		133	MA	23
35	LANHELIN		55	O	13
55	LANHERES		45	VA	10
29	LANHOUARNEAU		52	D	13
29	LANILDUT		51	B	13
57	LANING		47	AB	11
22	LANISCAT		73	I	14
02	LANISCOURT		28	MA	8
22	LANLEFF		53	J	12
22	LANLOUP		53	J	12
22	LANMERIN		53	H	12
29	LANMEUR	C	52	G	12
22	LANMODEZ		53	I	11
65	LANNE		216	W	37
64	LANNE EN BARETOUS		206	T	37
32	LANNE SOUBIRAN		185	W	34
29	LANNEANOU		52	G	13
22	LANNEBERT		53	J	12
64	LANNECAUBE		207	V	35
29	LANNEDERN		52	F	14
33	LANNEMAIGNAN		185	V	33
65	LANNEMEZAN	C	216	Y	37
32	LANNEPAX		186	X	34
64	LANNEPLAA		206	S	35
28	LANNERAY		60	CA	15
47	LANNES		186	X	33
29	LANNEUFFRET		52	D	13
29	LANNILIS	C	51	C	13
22	LANNION	S	53	H	12
59	LANNOY	C	9	KA	3
60	LANNOY CUILLERE		25	EA	8
32	LANNUX		207	V	35
2B	LANO		228	LB	40
15	LANOBRE		147	HA	27
24	LANOUAILLE	C	144	BA	27
56	LANOUEE		74	L	15
09	LANOUX		218	CA	37
24	LANQUAIS		158	Z	29
52	LANQUES SUR ROGNON		66	UA	15
76	LANQUETOT		23	Y	8
22	LANRELAS		74	M	14
35	LANRIGAN		55	P	13
22	LANRIVAIN		53	I	14
29	LANRIVOARE		51	C	13
22	LANRODEC		53	J	13
71	LANS		121	SA	21
38	LANS EN VERCORS		166	VA	28
33	LANSAC		156	U	28
65	LANSAC		208	X	36
66	LANSAC		222	HA	38
34	LANSARGUES		194	OA	35
73	LANSLEBOURG MONT CENIS	C	154	BB	27
73	LANSLEVILLARD		154	BB	27
31	LANTA	C	211	EA	35
64	LANTABAT		206	R	36
10	LANTAGES		65	PA	15
18	LANTAN		117	IA	20
54	LANTEFONTAINE		45	WA	10
01	LANTENAY		138	VA	24
21	LANTENAY		105	SA	18
25	LANTENNE VERTIERE		106	WA	19
70	LANTENOT		89	ZA	16
70	LANTERNE ET LES ARMONTS, LA		89	ZA	16
19	LANTEUIL		159	DA	28
25	LANTHENANS		108	AB	18
21	LANTHES		121	TA	20
14	LANTHEUIL		35	U	10
22	LANTIC		54	J	12
69	LANTIGNIE		136	RA	23
56	LANTILLAC		74	K	15
21	LANTILLY		85	QA	17
33	LANTON		155	S	30
06	LANTOSQUE	C	199	DB	33
43	LANTRIAC		163	OA	28
58	LANTY		119	NA	20
52	LANTY SUR AUBE		85	RA	15
30	LANUEJOLS		177	LA	32
48	LANUEJOLS		177	MA	31
12	LANUEJOULS		175	GA	31
22	LANVALLAY		55	N	13
56	LANVAUDAN		73	I	16
22	LANVELLEC		53	G	12
56	LANVENEGEN		72	G	15
29	LANVEOC		51	C	14
22	LANVOLLON	C	53	J	12
46	LANZAC		159	DA	29
02	LAON	P	28	MA	8
28	LAONS		38	BA	12
03	LAPALISSE	C	133	MA	23
84	LAPALUD		179	RA	32
18	LAPAN		116	GA	20
12	LAPANOUSE		176	KA	31
12	LAPANOUSE DE CERNON		191	KA	33
47	LAPARADE		172	Y	31
81	LAPARROUQUIAL		174	FA	32
09	LAPEGE		219	DA	38
82	LAPENCHE		174	DA	32
09	LAPENNE		219	EA	37
50	LAPENTY		57	S	13
47	LAPERCHE		172	Y	30
21	LAPERRIERE SUR SAONE		106	UA	19
65	LAPEYRE		208	Y	36
31	LAPEYRERE		210	CA	36
01	LAPEYROUSE		137	SA	24
63	LAPEYROUSE		133	JA	23
31	LAPEYROUSE FOSSAT		188	DA	34
26	LAPEYROUSE MORNAY		151	SA	27
15	LAPEYRUGUE		161	HA	30
19	LAPLEAU	C	160	GA	27
47	LAPLUME	C	172	Z	32
68	LAPOUTROIE	C	69	CB	15
33	LAPOUYADE		156	V	28
02	LAPPION		29	OA	8
11	LAPRADE		212	GA	35
16	LAPRADE		143	X	27
03	LAPRUGNE		135	NA	24
63	LAPS		148	LA	26
43	LAPTE		163	PA	28
62	LAPUGNOY		8	HA	4
57	LAQUENEXY		46	YA	10
63	LAQUEUILLE		147	IA	26
05	LARAGNE MONTEGLIN	C	181	WA	32
69	LARAJASSE		150	QA	26
46	LARAMIERE		174	EA	31
65	LARAN		209	Y	36
40	LARBEY		184	T	34
09	LARBONT		218	CA	37
60	LARBROYE		27	JA	8
31	LARCAN		217	Z	37
09	LARCAT		220	DA	38
37	LARCAY		98	AA	18
64	LARCEVEAU ARROS CIBITS		206	R	36
53	LARCHAMP		57	S	14
61	LARCHAMP		57	T	12
77	LARCHANT		62	IA	14
04	LARCHE		182	BB	31
19	LARCHE	C	159	CA	28
39	LARDERET, LE		123	XA	20
05	LARDIER ET VALENCA		181	XA	31
04	LARDIERS		197	WA	33
24	LARDIN ST LAZARE, LE		159	CA	28
91	LARDY		62	GA	13
32	LAREE		185	W	33
31	LAREOLE		187	BA	34
79	LARGEASSE		112	U	21
07	LARGENTIERE	S	178	PA	31
39	LARGILLAY MARSONNAY		122	VA	22
68	LARGITZEN		90	CB	17
02	LARGNY SUR AUTOMNE		41	KA	10
70	LARIANS ET MUNANS		107	YA	18
90	LARIVIERE		90	BB	17
52	LARIVIERE ARNONCOURT		87	WA	15
56	LARMOR BADEN		91	J	17
56	LARMOR PLAGE		73	H	16
26	LARNAGE		165	SA	28
46	LARNAGOL		174	EA	31
07	LARNAS		179	QA	31
09	LARNAT		219	DA	38
39	LARNAUD		122	UA	21
25	LARNOD		107	XA	19
19	LAROCHE PRES FEYT		147	HA	25
89	LAROCHE ST CYDROINE		83	MA	15
58	LAROCHEMILLAY		119	OA	20
63	LARODDE		147	HA	26
64	LAROIN		207	U	36
54	LARONXE		68	AB	13
33	LAROQUE		170	V	30
34	LAROQUE		192	NA	33
09	LAROQUE D'OLMES		219	EA	37
11	LAROQUE DE FA		223	IA	38
66	LAROQUE DES ALBERES		224	JA	40
46	LAROQUE DES ARCS		173	DA	31
47	LAROQUE TIMBAUT	C	172	AA	32
15	LAROQUEBROU	C	160	GA	29
15	LAROQUEVIEILLE		161	HA	28
59	LAROUILLIES		19	OA	6
31	LARRA		188	CA	34
64	LARRAU		206	S	37
82	LARRAZET		187	BA	33
56	LARRE		74	L	16
61	LARRE		58	X	13
32	LARRESSINGLE		186	Y	33
64	LARRESSORE		205	Q	36
70	LARRET		87	VA	17
64	LARREULE		207	U	35
65	LARREULE		208	W	35
21	LARREY		85	QA	16
64	LARRIBAR SORHAPURU		206	S	36
74	LARRINGES		139	ZA	22
40	LARRIVIERE		184	U	34
39	LARRIVOIRE		138	WA	23
31	LARROQUE		217	Z	37
65	LARROQUE		209	Y	36
81	LARROQUE		189	EA	33
32	LARROQUE ENGALIN		187	Z	33
32	LARROQUE ST SERNIN		186	Y	34
32	LARROQUE SUR L'OSSE		186	X	33
46	LARROQUE TOIRAC		174	FA	31
32	LARTIGUE		209	Z	35
33	LARTIGUE		171	W	32
64	LARUNS	C	215	U	37
33	LARUSCADE		156	V	28
24	LARZAC		158	BA	30
51	LARZICOURT		65	RA	12
30	LASALLE	C	192	NA	33
11	LASBORDES		211	FA	36
46	LASCABANES		173	CA	31
19	LASCAUX		145	CA	27
65	LASCAZERES		208	W	35
15	LASCELLE		161	IA	28
64	LASCLAVERIES		207	V	35
81	LASFAILLADES		212	HA	35
81	LASGRAISSES		189	FA	34
65	LASLADES		208	X	36
65	LASSALES		209	Y	36
53	LASSAY LES CHATEAUX	C	57	U	13
41	LASSAY SUR CROISNE		99	DA	18
49	LASSE		96	W	17
64	LASSE		206	R	37
32	LASSERADE		208	W	35
32	LASSERAN		209	Z	35
09	LASSERRE		218	BA	37
31	LASSERRE		210	BA	35
47	LASSERRE		186	Y	33
64	LASSERRE		208	W	35
11	LASSERRE DE PROUILLE		221	FA	37
64	LASSEUBE	C	207	U	36
32	LASSEUBE PROPRE		209	Z	35
64	LASSEUBETAT		215	U	37
10	LASSICOURT		65	QA	13
60	LASSIGNY	C	27	JA	8
14	LASSON		35	U	10
89	LASSON		84	NA	15
12	LASSOUTS		176	JA	31
09	LASSUR		220	EA	38
14	LASSY		35	T	11
35	LASSY		75	O	15
95	LASSY		40	HA	10
15	LASTIC		162	KA	28
63	LASTIC		147	IA	25
11	LASTOURS		212	HA	36
60	LATAULE		27	IA	8
39	LATET, LE		123	XA	20
39	LATETTE, LA		123	XA	21
74	LATHUILE		139	YA	25
86	LATHUS ST REMY		130	AA	23
86	LATILLE		112	W	21
02	LATILLY		41	LA	10
31	LATOUE		217	AA	37
46	LATOUILLE LENTILLAC		160	FA	29
31	LATOUR		218	CA	37
66	LATOUR BAS ELNE		224	KA	39
66	LATOUR DE CAROL		222	FA	40
66	LATOUR DE FRANCE	C	224	IA	38
55	LATOUR EN WOEVRE		45	WA	10
31	LATRAPE		210	CA	36
52	LATRECEY ORMOY SUR AUBE		86	SA	15
33	LATRESNE		156	U	29
40	LATRILLE		207	V	35
19	LATRONCHE		160	GA	27
46	LATRONQUIERE	C	160	FA	29
60	LATTAINVILLE		39	EA	10
34	LATTES	C	194	OA	35
62	LATTRE ST QUENTIN		17	IA	5
65	LAU BALAGNAS		216	W	37
67	LAUBACH		48	EB	11
48	LAUBERT		177	MA	30
48	LAUBIES, LES		177	LA	30
10	LAUBRESSEL		65	PA	14
53	LAUBRIERES		76	R	15
80	LAUCOURT		27	IA	8
57	LAUDREFANG		47	AB	10
30	LAUDUN		179	RA	32
47	LAUGNAC		172	Z	32
32	LAUJUZAN		185	W	34
50	LAULNE		34	O	10
57	LAUMESFELD		47	ZA	9
31	LAUNAC		188	BA	34
31	LAUNAGUET		188	DA	34
27	LAUNAY		37	Z	10
53	LAUNAY VILLIERS		76	S	15
08	LAUNOIS SUR VENCE		29	QA	8
02	LAUNOY		41	LA	10
57	LAUNSTROFF		32	ZA	9
26	LAUPIE, LA		179	SA	30
11	LAURABUC		211	FA	36
11	LAURAC		211	FA	36
07	LAURAC EN VIVARAIS		178	PA	31
32	LAURAET		186	X	33
11	LAURAGUEL		221	GA	37
11	LAURE MINERVOIS		212	HA	36
40	LAUREDE		184	T	34
22	LAURENAN		74	L	14
34	LAURENS		213	KA	35
46	LAURESSES		160	GA	30
34	LAURET		192	NA	34
40	LAURET		207	V	35
15	LAURIE		162	KA	27
87	LAURIERE	C	131	DA	24
84	LAURIS		196	UA	34
34	LAUROUX		191	LA	34
43	LAUSSONNE		163	OA	29
47	LAUSSOU		172	AA	30
68	LAUTENBACH		90	CB	15
68	LAUTENBACHZELL		90	CB	15
67	LAUTERBOURG	C	50	HB	11
86	LAUTHIERS		114	Z	21
31	LAUTIGNAC		209	BA	36
81	LAUTREC	C	189	GA	34
68	LAUW		90	BB	16
59	LAUWIN PLANQUE		17	JA	5
26	LAUX MONTAUX		180	VA	32
56	LAUZACH		92	L	17
82	LAUZERTE	C	173	BA	32
31	LAUZERVILLE		210	DA	35
46	LAUZES	C	174	DA	30
04	LAUZET UBAYE, LE	C	182	ZA	31
47	LAUZUN	C	172	Y	30
60	LAVACQUERIE		26	FA	8
38	LAVAL		153	XA	27
53	LAVAL	P	77	T	15
48	LAVAL ATGER		163	NA	29
26	LAVAL D'AIX		166	UA	30
07	LAVAL D'AURELLE		178	OA	30
46	LAVAL DE CERE		160	FA	29
48	LAVAL DU TARN		177	LA	31
77	LAVAL EN BRIE		63	JA	13
02	LAVAL EN LAONNOIS		28	MA	8
25	LAVAL LE PRIEURE		108	AB	19
08	LAVAL MORENCY		29	QA	7
30	LAVAL PRADEL		178	OA	32
12	LAVAL ROQUECEZIERE		190	IA	34
30	LAVAL ST ROMAN		178	QA	32
43	LAVAL SUR DOULON		148	MA	27
19	LAVAL SUR LUZEGE		160	GA	27
51	LAVAL SUR TOURBE		43	RA	10
88	LAVAL SUR VOLOGNE		68	AB	14
24	LAVALADE		172	AA	30
38	LAVALDENS		167	WA	29
11	LAVALETTE		221	GA	37
31	LAVALETTE		210	DA	35
34	LAVALETTE		191	LA	34
55	LAVALLEE		44	UA	12
39	LAVANCIA EPERCY		138	VA	23
83	LAVANDOU, LE		203	ZA	37
39	LAVANGEOT		106	VA	19
51	LAVANNES		29	PA	9
39	LAVANS LES DOLE		106	VA	19
39	LAVANS LES ST CLAUDE		138	WA	22
25	LAVANS QUINGEY		106	WA	19
39	LAVANS SUR VALOUSE		138	VA	23
25	LAVANS VUILLAFANS		107	YA	19
02	LAVAQUERESSE		19	NA	7
47	LAVARDAC	C	171	X	32
32	LAVARDENS		186	Y	34
41	LAVARDIN		79	AA	16
72	LAVARDIN		78	W	15
72	LAVARE		79	Z	15
38	LAVARS		166	VA	29
15	LAVASTRIE		162	KA	29
2B	LAVATOGGIO		225	JB	39
10	LAVAU		64	OA	14
89	LAVAU		83	JA	17
44	LAVAU SUR LOIRE		93	N	18
43	LAVAUDIEU		162	LA	27
23	LAVAUFRANCHE		132	GA	23
58	LAVAULT DE FRETOY		103	OA	19
03	LAVAULT STE ANNE		133	IA	23
24	LAVAUR		173	BA	30
81	LAVAUR	C	189	EA	34
82	LAVAURETTE		174	EA	32
86	LAVAUSSEAU		112	W	22
23	LAVAVEIX LES MINES		132	FA	24
33	LAVAZAN		171	W	31
15	LAVEISSENET		161	JA	28
15	LAVEISSIERE		161	JA	28
09	LAVELANET	C	219	EA	38
31	LAVELANET DE COMMINGES		210	BA	36
88	LAVELINE DEVANT BRUYERES		69	AB	14
88	LAVELINE DU HOUX		68	AB	15
72	LAVENAY		79	Z	16
62	LAVENTIE	C	8	IA	3
32	LAVERAET		208	X	35
46	LAVERCANTIERE		173	CA	30
18	LAVERDINES		101	IA	19
46	LAVERGNE		159	EA	29
47	LAVERGNE		172	Y	31
72	LAVERNAT		78	Y	16
25	LAVERNAY		106	WA	19
12	LAVERNHE		176	JA	32
31	LAVERNOSE LACASSE		210	CA	36
52	LAVERNOY		87	VA	15
60	LAVERRIERE		26	FA	8
02	LAVERSINE		27	KA	9
60	LAVERSINES		26	GA	9
34	LAVERUNE		214	NA	35
26	LAVEYRON		165	SA	28
07	LAVEYRUNE		177	NA	30
24	LAVEYSSIERE		157	Y	29
42	LAVIEU		149	OA	26
80	LAVIEVILLE		17	IA	6
15	LAVIGERIE		161	IA	28
87	LAVIGNAC		144	BA	25
70	LAVIGNEY		87	WA	16
39	LAVIGNY		122	VA	21
07	LAVILLATTE		163	OA	30
52	LAVILLE AUX BOIS		66	TA	15
07	LAVILLEDIEU		178	OA	30
52	LAVILLENEUVE		87	VA	15
60	LAVILLETERTRE		39	FA	10
55	LAVINCOURT		44	TA	12
07	LAVIOLLE		164	PA	30
25	LAVIRON		107	ZA	18
82	LAVIT	C	187	AA	33
03	LAVOINE		135	NA	24
70	LAVONCOURT		87	WA	17
01	LAVOURS		138	WA	25
43	LAVOUTE CHILHAC	C	162	LA	28
43	LAVOUTE SUR LOIRE		163	NA	28
86	LAVOUX		113	Z	21
55	LAVOYE		44	TA	11
80	LAWARDE MAUGER L'HORTOY		26	GA	8
54	LAXOU	C	46	XA	12
42	LAY		135	PA	24
64	LAY LAMIDOU		206	T	36
54	LAY ST CHRISTOPHE		46	YA	12
54	LAY ST REMY		45	WA	12
05	LAYE		181	XA	30
32	LAYMONT		209	AA	35
47	LAYRAC		172	Z	32
31	LAYRAC SUR TARN		188	DA	34
65	LAYRISSE		216	W	37
71	LAYS SUR LE DOUBS		121	TA	20
29	LAZ		72	F	15
18	LAZENAY		100	FA	19
05	LAZER		181	WA	31
80	LEALVILLERS		17	HA	6
14	LEAUPARTIE		36	W	10
01	LEAZ		138	WA	24
90	LEBETAIN		90	BB	17
54	LEBEUVILLE		68	YA	13
62	LEBIEZ		16	FA	4
32	LEBOULIN		187	Z	34
46	LEBREIL		173	BA	32
62	LEBUCQUIERE		17	JA	6
14	LECAUDE		36	X	10
2A	LECCI		230	LB	43
59	LECELLES		18	LA	4
52	LECEY		87	UA	16
21	LECHATELET		105	TA	19
62	LECHELLE		17	JA	6
77	LECHELLE		63	LA	13
73	LECHERE, LA		153	ZA	26
24	LECHES, LES		157	Y	29
59	LECLUSE		17	KA	5
35	LECOUSSE		56	R	14
30	LECQUES		193	OA	34
39	LECT		138	VA	22
32	LECTOURE	C	187	Z	33
64	LECUMBERRY		206	R	37
31	LECUSSAN		217	Y	37
81	LEDAS ET PENTHIES		190	HA	33
47	LEDAT		172	Z	31
30	LEDENON		193	OA	33
12	LEDERGUES		190	HA	33
59	LEDERZEELE		8	GA	3
64	LEDEUIX		207	T	36
30	LEDIGNAN	C	193	OA	33
62	LEDINGHEM		7	FA	3
59	LEDRINGHEM		8	HA	2
64	LEE		207	V	36
59	LEERS		9	LA	3
64	LEES ATHAS		215	T	38
62	LEFAUX		7	EA	4
14	LEFFARD		36	V	11
08	LEFFINCOURT		29	OA	9
52	LEFFONDS		86	TA	15
59	LEFFRINCKOUCKE		8	HA	2
62	LEFOREST	C	17	KA	4
31	LEGE		217	Z	38

44 LEGE C 110 P 20
33 LEGE CAP FERRET 155 R 29
88 LEGEVILLE ET BONFAYS 68 YA 14
60 LEGLANTIERS 26 HA 9
39 LEGNA 122 VA 22
69 LEGNY 136 RA 24
31 LEGUEVIN C 210 CA 35
24 LEGUILLAC DE CERCLES 143 Y 27
24 LEGUILLAC DE L'AUCHE 157 Z 28
22 LEHON 55 N 13
86 LEIGNE LES BOIS 114 Z 21
86 LEIGNE SUR USSEAU 113 Y 20
86 LEIGNES SUR FONTAINE 114 AA 22
42 LEIGNEUX 149 OA 25
68 LEIMBACH 90 CB 16
54 LEINTREY 69 AB 12
01 LELEX 139 XA 23
32 LELIN LAPUJOLLE 185 V 34
57 LELLING 47 AB 11
54 LEMAINVILLE 68 YA 13
67 LEMBACH 49 FB 11
57 LEMBERG 48 DB 11
64 LEMBEYE C 207 W 35
24 LEMBRAS 157 Y 29
02 LEME 28 NA 7
64 LEME 207 V 35
54 LEMENIL MITRY 68 YA 13
37 LEMERE 97 Y 19
88 LEMMECOURT 67 WA 14
55 LEMMES 44 UA 10
57 LEMONCOURT 46 YA 11
81 LEMPAUT 211 FA 35
43 LEMPDES SUR ALLAGNON 148 LA 27
63 LEMPDES 148 KA 25
02 LEMPIRE 18 KA 6
07 LEMPS 164 RA 28
26 LEMPS 180 UA 31
63 LEMPTY 148 LA 25
24 LEMPZOURS 144 AA 27
57 LEMUD 46 YA 11
39 LEMUY 123 XA 20
14 LENAULT 35 T 11
03 LENAX 135 NA 23
86 LENCLOITRE C 113 Y 20
40 LENCOUACQ 184 U 33
57 LENGELSHEIM 48 DB 10
50 LENGRONNE 56 Q 11
51 LENHARREE 42 OA 12
57 LENING 47 AB 11
29 LENNON 72 F 14
54 LENONCOURT 46 YA 12
62 LENS S 17 JA 4
26 LENS LESTANG 151 SA 27
01 LENT 137 TA 24
39 LENT 123 XA 21
42 LENTIGNY 135 OA 24
46 LENTILLAC LAUZES 174 DA 30
46 LENTILLAC ST BLAISE 175 GA 30
07 LENTILLERES 178 PA 30
10 LENTILLES 65 RA 13
69 LENTILLY 136 RA 25
38 LENTIOL 151 TA 27
2B LENTO 226 LB 40
46 LEOBARD 159 CA 30
33 LEOGEATS 170 U 31
33 LEOGNAN 156 T 30
82 LEOJAC 188 CA 33
40 LEON 183 O 33
26 LEONCEL 165 TA 29
43 LEOTOING 148 KA 27
45 LEOUVILLE 61 FA 14
17 LEOVILLE 142 V 27
88 LEPANGES SUR VOLOGNE 68 AB 14
23 LEPAUD 132 HA 23
73 LEPIN LE LAC 152 WA 26
23 LEPINAS 132 FA 24
62 LEPINE 15 EA 5
08 LEPRON LES VALLEES 29 QA 7
90 LEPUIX 89 AB 16
90 LEPUIX NEUF 90 CB 17
09 LERAN 221 FA 37
09 LERCOUL 220 DA 38
18 LERE C 101 JA 18
64 LEREN 206 S 35
42 LERIGNEUX 149 OA 26
33 LERM ET MUSSET 171 V 31
37 LERNE 97 X 19
55 LEROUVILLE 45 VA 12
88 LERRAIN 68 YA 15
21 LERY 86 SA 17
27 LERY 38 BA 9
02 LERZY 19 NA 7
80 LESBOEUFS 17 JA 6
53 LESBOIS 57 T 13
64 LESCAR C 207 U 36
74 LESCHAUX 139 XA 25
02 LESCHELLES 19 NA 6
73 LESCHERAINES 153 XA 25
39 LESCHERES 122 WA 22
52 LESCHERES
SUR LE BLAISERON 66 SA 14
77 LESCHEROLLES 41 LA 12
01 LESCHEROUX 121 TA 22
77 LESCHES 40 JA 11
26 LESCHES EN DIOIS 180 VA 30
22 LESCOUET GOUAREC 73 I 14
09 LESCOUSSE 219 DA 37
81 LESCOUT 211 FA 35
64 LESCUN 215 T 38
31 LESCUNS 209 BA 36
09 LESCURE 218 CA 37
81 LESCURE D'ALBIGEOIS 190 GA 33
12 LESCURE JAOUL 175 GA 32
65 LESCURRY 208 X 36
59 LESDAIN 18 LA 6
02 LESDINS 28 LA 7
02 LESGES 28 MA 9
40 LESGOR 184 S 34
16 LESIGNAC DURAND 144 Z 25
77 LESIGNY 40 IA 12
86 LESIGNY 114 Z 20
22 LESLAY, LE 53 J 13
71 LESME 119 NA 21
54 LESMENILS 46 XA 11
10 LESMONT 65 OA 13
29 LESNEVEN C 51 D 13
33 LESPARRE MEDOC S 141 S 27
09 LESPARROU 221 FA 38
07 LESPERON 163 NA 30
40 LESPERON 183 R 33
62 LESPESSES 8 HA 4
64 LESPIELLE 207 V 35
34 LESPIGNAN 213 KA 36
31 LESPINASSE 188 CA 34
11 LESPINASSIERE 212 HA 36
62 LESPINOY 16 EA 4
31 LESPITEAU 217 AA 37
65 LESPOUEY 208 X 36
64 LESPOURCY 207 V 36
31 LESPUGUE 209 Z 36
66 LESQUERDE 221 HA 38
02 LESQUIELLES ST GERMAIN 18 MA 7
59 LESQUIN 9 KA 4
16 LESSAC 130 Z 24
71 LESSARD EN BRESSE 121 TA 21
14 LESSARD ET LE CHENE 36 X 10
71 LESSARD LE NATIONAL 121 SA 20
50 LESSAY C 34 P 10
57 LESSE 47 ZA 11
88 LESSEUX 69 CB 14
57 LESSY 46 XA 10
76 LESTANVILLE 24 AA 7
19 LESTARDS 146 EA 26
64 LESTELLE BETHARRAM 215 V 37
31 LESTELLE DE ST MARTORY 217 AA 37
16 LESTERPS 130 AA 24
33 LESTIAC SUR GARONNE 156 U 30
41 LESTIOU 80 DA 16
12 LESTRADE ET THOUELS 190 IA 33
50 LESTRE 33 Q 8
62 LESTREM 8 IA 4
08 LETANNE 30 TA 8
03 LETELON 117 IA 21
28 LETHUIN 61 EA 14
2A LETIA 227 JB 41
69 LETRA 136 QA 24
54 LETRICOURT 46 YA 11
27 LETTEGUIVES 25 CA 9
05 LETTRET 181 XA 31
62 LEUBRINGHEN 7 EA 2
11 LEUC 221 GA 37
15 LEUCAMP 161 HA 29
11 LEUCATE 223 KA 38
52 LEUCHEY 86 TA 16
91 LEUDEVILLE 62 GA 13
77 LEUDON EN BRIE 41 LA 12
21 LEUGLAY 86 RA 16
86 LEUGNY 114 Z 20
89 LEUGNY 83 LA 17
29 LEUHAN 72 F 15
02 LEUILLY SOUS COUCY 28 LA 9
62 LEULINGHEM 8 GA 3
62 LEULINGHEN BERNES 7 EA 3
52 LEURVILLE 66 UA 14
02 LEURY 28 LA 9
67 LEUTENHEIM 50 GB 11
91 LEUVILLE SUR ORGE 62 GA 12
51 LEUVRIGNY 42 NA 10
40 LEUY, LE 184 T 34
02 LEUZE 29 PA 7
28 LEVAINVILLE 61 EA 13
59 LEVAL 19 NA 5
90 LEVAL 90 BB 16
92 LEVALLOIS PERRET C 40 GA 11
53 LEVARE 57 S 13
52 LEVECOURT 67 VA 15
06 LEVENS C 199 CB 34
02 LEVERGIES 28 LA 7
21 LEVERNOIS 121 SA 20
28 LEVES 60 DA 13
33 LEVES
ET THOUMEYRAGUES, LES 157 X 29
28 LEVESVILLE LA CHENARD 61 EA 14
18 LEVET C 116 HA 20
2A LEVIE C 230 LB 43
25 LEVIER C 123 XA 20
31 LEVIGNAC 188 BA 34
47 LEVIGNAC DE GUYENNE 171 X 30
40 LEVIGNACQ 183 R 33
60 LEVIGNEN 41 JA 10
10 LEVIGNY 65 RA 14
89 LEVIS 83 LA 17
78 LEVIS ST NOM 39 FA 12
55 LEVONCOURT 44 UA 12
68 LEVONCOURT 90 CB 16
36 LEVROUX C 115 DA 20
59 LEWARDE 18 KA 5
54 LEXY 31 WA 8
57 LEY 68 AB 12
09 LEYCHERT 219 EA 38
46 LEYME 160 FA 29
68 LEYMEN 90 DB 17
01 LEYMENT 137 UA 24
71 LEYNES 136 RA 23
15 LEYNHAC 160 GA 30
54 LEYR 46 YA 12
23 LEYRAT 132 GA 22
38 LEYRIEU 151 UA 25
47 LEYRITZ MONCASSIN 171 X 31
01 LEYSSARD 138 VA 23
15 LEYVAUX 148 KA 27
57 LEYVILLER 47 BB 11
31 LEZ 217 Z 38
59 LEZ FONTAINE 19 OA 5
30 LEZAN 193 OA 33
22 LEZARDRIEUX C 53 I 12
39 LEZAT 123 XA 22
09 LEZAT SUR LEZE 210 CA 36
79 LEZAY C 129 W 23
59 LEZENNES 9 KA 4
52 LEZEVILLE 66 UA 13
57 LEZEY 47 AB 12
65 LEZIGNAN 216 W 37
11 LEZIGNAN CORBIERES C 213 IA 36
34 LEZIGNAN LA CEBE 214 LA 35
49 LEZIGNE 77 V 17
42 LEZIGNEUX 149 OA 26
89 LEZINNES 84 OA 16
63 LEZOUX C 148 LA 25
60 LHERAULE 25 FA 9
31 LHERM 210 CA 35
46 LHERM 173 CA 30
51 LHERY 42 NA 10
65 LHEZ 208 X 36
86 LHOMMAIZE 114 Z 22
72 LHOMME 79 Z 16
01 LHOPITAL 138 WA 24
57 LHOR 47 BB 11
46 LHOSPITALET 173 CA 31
79 LHOUMOIS 112 W 21
01 LHUIS C 152 VA 25
10 LHUITRE 65 PA 13
02 LHUYS 42 MA 9
65 LIAC 208 X 36
60 LIANCOURT C 26 HA 9
80 LIANCOURT FOSSE 27 JA 7
60 LIANCOURT ST PIERRE 39 FA 10
08 LIART 29 PA 7
32 LIAS 210 BA 35
32 LIAS D'ARMAGNAC 185 W 34
34 LIAUSSON 214 LA 35
65 LIBAROS 208 Y 36
62 LIBERCOURT 17 JA 4
60 LIBERMONT 27 JA 8
33 LIBOURNE S 156 V 29
21 LICEY SUR VINGEANNE 87 UA 17
64 LICHANS SUNHAR 206 S 37
16 LICHERES 129 X 24
89 LICHERES PRES AIGREMONT 84 NA 16
89 LICHERES SUR YONNE 84 MA 17
64 LICHOS 206 S 36
67 LICHTENBERG 48 DB 11
80 LICOURT 27 JA 7
64 LICQ ATHEREY 206 S 37
62 LICQUES 7 FA 3
02 LICY CLIGNON 41 LA 10
57 LIDREZING 47 AB 11
68 LIEBENSWILLER 90 DB 17
68 LIEBSDORF 90 CB 17
25 LIEBVILLERS 108 AB 18
57 LIEDERSCHIEDT 48 DB 10
70 LIEFFRANS 88 XA 17
37 LIEGE, LE 98 BA 19
57 LIEHON 46 YA 11
62 LIENCOURT 17 HA 5
68 LIEPVRE 69 CB 14
80 LIERAMONT 17 KA 6
80 LIERCOURT 16 FA 6
62 LIERES 8 HA 4
69 LIERGUES 136 RA 24
21 LIERNAIS C 104 PA 19
03 LIERNOLLES 135 NA 22
02 LIERVAL 28 MA 9
60 LIERVILLE 39 FA 10
65 LIES 216 X 37
25 LIESLE 106 WA 19
02 LIESSE NOTRE DAME 28 NA 8
59 LIESSIES 19 OA 6
50 LIESVILLE SUR DOUVE 34 Q 9
62 LIETTRES 8 GA 4
59 LIEU ST AMAND 18 LA 5
06 LIEUCHE 199 BB 33
70 LIEUCOURT 106 VA 18
38 LIEUDIEU 151 TA 26
09 LIEURAC 219 EA 37
34 LIEURAN CABRIERES 213 LA 36
34 LIEURAN LES BEZIERS 214 LA 36
27 LIEUREY 37 Y 10
35 LIEURON 75 N 16
50 LIEUSAINT 33 Q 9
77 LIEUSAINT 62 HA 12
15 LIEUTADES 161 JA 29
60 LIEUVILLERS 26 HA 9
70 LIEVANS 88 YA 17
62 LIEVIN C 17 IA 4
02 LIEZ 28 LA 8
85 LIEZ 127 T 22
88 LIEZEY 89 AB 15
88 LIFFOL LE GRAND 67 VA 14
52 LIFFOL LE PETIT 67 VA 14
35 LIFFRE C 76 P 14
32 LIGARDES 186 Y 33
80 LIGESCOURT 16 EA 5
19 LIGINIAC 146 GA 27
86 LIGLET 114 BA 22
36 LIGNAC 114 BA 22
11 LIGNAIROLLES 221 FA 37
33 LIGNAN DE BAZAS 170 V 31
33 LIGNAN DE BORDEAUX 156 U 29
34 LIGNAN SUR ORB 213 KA 36
19 LIGNAREIX 146 GA 26
16 LIGNE 129 X 24
44 LIGNE C 94 Q 18
61 LIGNERES 37 X 12
62 LIGNEREUIL 17 HA 5
03 LIGNEROLLES 133 HA 23
21 LIGNEROLLES 86 SA 16
27 LIGNEROLLES 38 CA 11
36 LIGNEROLLES 116 GA 22
61 LIGNEROLLES 59 Z 13
88 LIGNEVILLE 67 XA 14
19 LIGNEYRAC 159 DA 28
10 LIGNIERES 84 OA 15
18 LIGNIERES C 116 GA 21
41 LIGNIERES 80 BA 16
80 LIGNIERES 27 IA 8
80 LIGNIERES CHATELAIN 25 EA 7
37 LIGNIERES DE TOURAINE 97 Y 18
80 LIGNIERES EN VIMEU 25 EA 7
72 LIGNIERES LA CARELLE 58 X 13
53 LIGNIERES ORGERES 58 V 13
16 LIGNIERES SONNEVILLE 142 V 26
55 LIGNIERES SUR AIRE 44 UA 12
56 LIGNOL 73 I 15
10 LIGNOL LE CHATEAU 66 RA 14
51 LIGNON 65 OA 13
89 LIGNORELLES 84 NA 16
61 LIGNOU 58 V 12
55 LIGNY EN BARROIS C 44 UA 12
71 LIGNY EN BRIONNAIS 135 PA 23
59 LIGNY HAUCOURT 18 LA 6
89 LIGNY LE CHATEL C 84 NA 16
45 LIGNY LE RIBAULT 81 EA 17
62 LIGNY LES AIRE 8 HA 4
62 LIGNY ST FLOCHEL 16 HA 5
62 LIGNY SUR CANCHE 16 GA 5
62 LIGNY THILLOY 17 JA 6
37 LIGRE 97 X 19
72 LIGRON 78 W 16
68 LIGSDORF 90 DB 18
37 LIGUEIL C 98 AA 19
24 LIGUEUX 144 AA 27
33 LIGUEUX 157 X 29
86 LIGUGE 113 Y 22
80 LIHONS 27 IA 7
60 LIHUS 26 FA 8
93 LILAS, LES C 40 HA 11
31 LILHAC 209 AA 36
59 LILLE P 9 KA 3
76 LILLEBONNE C 23 Z 8
35 LILLEMER 55 O 13
62 LILLERS C 8 HA 4
27 LILLY 25 DA 9
79 LIMALONGES 129 X 23
04 LIMANS 197 WA 33
58 LIMANTON 119 NA 20
69 LIMAS 136 RA 24
78 LIMAY C 39 EA 11
09 LIMBRASSAC 219 EA 37
02 LIME 28 MA 9
94 LIMEIL BREVANNES 40 HA 12
64 LIMENDOUS 207 V 36
37 LIMERAY 98 BA 18
67 LIMERSHEIM 70 EB 13
56 LIMERZEL 92 M 17
76 LIMESY 24 AA 8
78 LIMETZ VILLEZ 39 DA 10
24 LIMEUIL 158 AA 29
18 LIMEUX 100 GA 19
80 LIMEUX 16 EA 6
54 LIMEY REMENAUVILLE 45 WA 11
24 LIMEYRAT 158 AA 28
87 LIMOGES P 131 BA 25
77 LIMOGES FOURCHES 62 IA 12
46 LIMOGNE EN QUERCY C 174 EA 31
03 LIMOISE 118 KA 21
58 LIMON 118 LA 20
69 LIMONEST C 136 RA 25
63 LIMONS 133 LA 24
59 LIMONT FONTAINE 19 NA 5
07 LIMONY 150 RA 27
91 LIMOURS C 61 FA 12
11 LIMOUSIS 212 HA 36
11 LIMOUX S 221 GA 37
44 LIMOUZINIERE, LA 110 P 20
76 LIMPIVILLE 23 Y 8
46 LINAC 175 GA 30
23 LINARD 132 EA 22
87 LINARDS 145 DA 25
16 LINARS 143 W 26
91 LINAS 62 GA 12
08 LINAY 30 TA 8
86 LINAZAY 129 X 23
76 LINDEBEUF 24 AA 8
16 LINDOIS, LE 144 Z 25
57 LINDRE BASSE 47 AB 12
57 LINDRE HAUTE 47 AB 12
89 LINDRY 83 LA 16
70 LINEXERT 89 ZA 16
36 LINGE 114 BA 21
50 LINGEARD 57 S 12
14 LINGEVRES 35 T 10
62 LINGHEM 8 HA 4
67 LINGOLSHEIM 70 EB 13
50 LINGREVILLE 34 P 11
2B LINGUIZZETTA 228 MB 41
49 LINIERES BOUTON 97 W 18
86 LINIERS 113 Z 21
36 LINIEZ 115 EA 20
68 LINSDORF 90 DB 17
59 LINSELLES 9 KA 3
68 LINTHAL 90 CB 15
51 LINTHELLES 42 NA 12
51 LINTHES 42 NA 12
76 LINTOT 23 Z 8
76 LINTOT LES BOIS 24 BA 7
40 LINXE 183 R 33
55 LINY DEVANT DUN 30 TA 9
62 LINZEUX 16 GA 5
57 LIOCOURT 46 YA 11
80 LIOMER 25 EA 7
49 LION D'ANGERS, LE C 77 T 17
55 LION DEVANT DUN 30 TA 9
45 LION EN BEAUCE 61 FA 15
45 LION EN SULLIAS 82 HA 16
14 LION SUR MER 36 V 9
24 LIORAC SUR LOUYRE 158 Z 29
30 LIOUC 193 OA 33
19 LIOURDRES 159 EA 29
84 LIOUX 196 UA 33
23 LIOUX LES MONGES 133 HA 24
40 LIPOSTHEY 169 S 32
67 LIPSHEIM 70 EB 13
30 LIRAC 195 RA 33
49 LIRE 94 R 18
10 LIREY 64 OA 14
88 LIRONCOURT 88 WA 15
54 LIRONVILLE 45 WA 11
08 LIRY 30 RA 9
62 LISBOURG 8 GA 4
14 LISIEUX S 37 X 10
24 LISLE 143 Z 27
41 LISLE 80 BA 16
55 LISLE EN BARROIS 44 TA 11
55 LISLE EN RIGAULT 44 SA 12
81 LISLE SUR TARN C 189 EA 34
02 LISLET 29 OA 8
14 LISON 34 R 10
14 LISORES 36 X 11
27 LISORS 25 DA 9
09 LISSAC 210 DA 36
43 LISSAC 163 NA 28
46 LISSAC ET MOURET 174 FA 30
19 LISSAC SUR COUZE 159 DA 28
18 LISSAY LOCHY 116 HA 20
51 LISSE EN CHAMPAGNE 43 RA 12
91 LISSES 62 HA 13
63 LISSEUIL 133 JA 24
55 LISSEY 31 UA 9
69 LISSIEU 136 RA 25
77 LISSY 62 IA 12
33 LISTRAC DE DUREZE 157 W 30
33 LISTRAC MEDOC 155 T 28
40 LIT ET MIXE 183 Q 33
50 LITHAIRE 34 Q 9
14 LITTEAU 35 S 10
67 LITTENHEIM 49 DB 12
60 LITZ 26 GA 9
61 LIVAIE 58 W 13
14 LIVAROT C 36 X 11
54 LIVERDUN 46 XA 12
77 LIVERDY EN BRIE 40 JA 12
46 LIVERNON C 174 EA 30
81 LIVERS CAZELLES 189 FA 33
53 LIVET 77 U 15
72 LIVET EN SAOSNOIS 58 X 14
38 LIVET ET GAVET 167 WA 28
27 LIVET SUR AUTHOU 37 Z 10
95 LIVILLIERS 39 FA 10
12 LIVINHAC LE HAUT 175 GA 30
34 LIVINIERE, LA 212 IA 36
53 LIVRE 76 S 16
35 LIVRE SUR CHANGEON 76 Q 14
64 LIVRON 207 W 36
26 LIVRON SUR DROME 165 SA 30
14 LIVRY 35 T 10
58 LIVRY 118 KA 21
93 LIVRY GARGAN C 40 HA 11
51 LIVRY LOUVERCY 43 PA 10
77 LIVRY SUR SEINE 62 IA 13
67 LIXHAUSEN 49 EB 12
57 LIXHEIM 48 CB 12
57 LIXING LES ROUHLING 47 BB 10
57 LIXING LES ST AVOLD 47 AB 11
89 LIXY 63 KA 14
82 LIZAC 173 BA 32
86 LIZANT 129 X 24
36 LIZERAY 116 EA 20
23 LIZIERES 131 DA 23
25 LIZINE 107 XA 19
77 LIZINES 63 KA 13
56 LIZIO 74 L 16
65 LIZOS 208 X 36
02 LIZY 28 MA 8
77 LIZY SUR OURCQ C 41 JA 11
66 LLAGONNE, LA 222 GA 40
66 LLAURO 224 IA 39
66 LLO 222 FA 40
66 LLUPIA 224 IA 39
67 LOBSANN 49 FB 11
29 LOC BREVALAIRE 51 C 13
29 LOC EGUINER 52 E 13
29 LOC EGUINER ST THEGONNEC 52 F 13
22 LOC ENVEL 53 H 13
22 LOCARN 53 H 14
37 LOCHE SUR INDROIS 98 BA 19
37 LOCHES S 98 BA 19
10 LOCHES SUR OURCE 65 OA 15
14 LOCHEUR, LE 35 U 10
01 LOCHIEU 138 WA 24
67 LOCHWILLER 49 DB 12
56 LOCMALO 73 I 15
56 LOCMARIA 91 I 18
29 LOCMARIA BERRIEN 52 G 14
56 LOCMARIA GRAND CHAMP 74 K 16
29 LOCMARIA PLOUZANE 51 B 13
56 LOCMARIAQUER 91 J 17
29 LOCMELAR 52 E 13
56 LOCMINE C 73 J 16
56 LOCMIQUELIC 73 H 16
56 LOCOAL MENDON 73 I 16
62 LOCON 8 IA 4
60 LOCONVILLE 39 FA 10
56 LOCQUELTAS 74 K 16
29 LOCQUENOLE 52 F 12
59 LOCQUIGNOL 18 NA 5
29 LOCQUIREC 53 G 12
29 LOCRONAN 71 D 15
29 LOCTUDY 71 E 16
29 LOCUNOLE 73 H 15
03 LODDES 135 NA 23
31 LODES 217 Z 37
34 LODEVE S 191 LA 34
25 LODS 107 YA 19
70 LOEUILLEY 106 UA 18
80 LOEUILLY 26 GA 7
59 LOFFRE 18 KA 5
62 LOGE, LA 16 FA 4
10 LOGE AUX CHEVRES, LA 65 QA 14
85 LOGE FOUGEREUSE 111 T 21
10 LOGE POMBLIN, LA 84 OA 15
68 LOGELHEIM 90 DB 15
14 LOGES, LES 35 T 11
52 LOGES, LES 87 VA 16
76 LOGES, LES 23 X 8
78 LOGES EN JOSAS, LES 39 GA 12
50 LOGES MARCHIS, LES 56 R 13
10 LOGES MARGUERON, LES 64 OA 15
14 LOGES SAULCES, LES 36 V 11
50 LOGES SUR BRECEY, LES 56 R 12
77 LOGNES 40 IA 11
08 LOGNY BOGNY 29 OA 7
02 LOGNY LES AUBENTON 29 PA 7
29 LOGONNA DAOULAS 51 D 14
30 LOGRIAN FLORIAN 193 OA 33
28 LOGRON 60 CA 15
22 LOGUIVY PLOUGRAS 53 H 13
35 LOHEAC 75 O 16
64 LOHITZUN OYHERCQ 206 S 36
67 LOHR 48 CB 11
22 LOHUEC 53 G 13
53 LOIGNE SUR MAYENNE 77 T 16
28 LOIGNY LA BATAILLE 61 EA 15
49 LOIRE 94 S 17
17 LOIRE LES MARAIS 127 S 24
17 LOIRE SUR NIE 128 V 24
69 LOIRE SUR RHONE 150 RA 26
53 LOIRON C 76 S 15
61 LOISAIL 59 Z 13
55 LOISEY CULEY 44 UA 12
39 LOISIA 122 UA 22
73 LOISIEUX 152 WA 26
74 LOISIN 139 YA 23
55 LOISON 31 VA 9
62 LOISON SOUS LENS 17 JA 4
62 LOISON SUR CREQUOISE 16 FA 4
54 LOISY 46 XA 11
71 LOISY 121 SA 21
51 LOISY EN BRIE 42 NA 11
51 LOISY SUR MARNE 43 OA 12
51 LOIVRE 29 OA 9
17 LOIX 125 Q 23
50 LOLIF 56 Q 12
24 LOLME 158 AA 30
25 LOMBARD 106 WA 19
39 LOMBARD 122 VA 21
81 LOMBERS 189 GA 34
32 LOMBEZ C 209 AA 35
64 LOMBIA 207 W 36
65 LOMBRES 217 Y 37
45 LOMBREUIL 82 IA 15
72 LOMBRON 59 Y 15
59 LOMME C 9 JA 3
57 LOMMERANGE 32 XA 9
78 LOMMOYE 38 DA 11
65 LOMNE 216 X 37
70 LOMONT 89 AB 17
25 LOMONT SUR CRETE 107 ZA 18
01 LOMPNAS 138 VA 25
01 LOMPNIEU 138 VA 24
59 LOMPRET 9 JA 3
64 LONCON 207 U 35
76 LONDE, LA 24 AA 9
83 LONDE LES MAURES, LA 203 YA 37
16 LONDIGNY 129 X 24
76 LONDINIERES C 25 CA 7
80 LONG 16 FA 6
31 LONGAGES 210 CA 36
35 LONGAULNAY 75 O 14
80 LONGAVESNES 18 KA 6
21 LONGCHAMP 105 UA 18
52 LONGCHAMP 67 UA 15
88 LONGCHAMP 68 ZA 14
88 LONGCHAMP
SOUS CHATENOIS 67 WA 14
10 LONGCHAMP SUR AUJON 66 SA 15
27 LONGCHAMPS 25 DA 9
55 LONGCHAMPS SUR AIRE 44 UA 11
39 LONGCHAUMOIS 123 XA 22
39 LONGCOCHON 123 XA 21
52 LONGEAU PERCEY C 87 UA 16
21 LONGEAULT 105 TA 19
55 LONGEAUX 66 UA 12
25 LONGECHAUX 107 ZA 19
38 LONGECHENAL 152 UA 27
21 LONGECOURT EN PLAINE 105 TA 19
21 LONGECOURT LES CULETRE 104 QA 19
25 LONGEMAISON 107 ZA 19
71 LONGEPIERRE 121 TA 20
49 LONGERON, LE 110 R 20
69 LONGES 150 RA 26
69 LONGESSAIGNE 150 QA 25
70 LONGEVELLE 89 ZA 17
25 LONGEVELLE LES RUSSEY 108 AB 19
25 LONGEVELLE SUR DOUBS 108 AB 18
17 LONGEVES 127 S 23
85 LONGEVES 111 S 22
25 LONGEVILLE 107 YA 19
25 LONGEVILLE, LA 107 ZA 20
55 LONGEVILLE EN BARROIS 44 TA 12

57 LONGEVILLE LES METZ 46 XA 10
57 LONGEVILLE LES ST AVOLD 47 AB 10
52 LONGEVILLE SUR LA LAINES 65 RA 13
85 LONGEVILLE SUR MER 125 Q 22
10 LONGEVILLE SUR MOGNE 64 OA 14
25 LONGEVILLES MONT D'OR 123 YA 21
62 LONGFOSSE 7 EA 3
70 LONGINE, LA 89 ZA 16
91 LONGJUMEAU C 62 GA 12
54 LONGLAVILLE 31 WA 8
76 LONGMESNIL 25 DA 8
72 LONGNES 78 W 15
78 LONGNES 39 DA 11
61 LONGNY AU PERCHE C 59 AA 13
77 LONGPERRIER 40 IA 11
02 LONGPONT 41 KA 10
91 LONGPONT SUR ORGE 62 GA 12
10 LONGPRE LE SEC 65 QA 14
80 LONGPRE LES CORPS SAINTS 16 FA 6
14 LONGRAYE 35 T 10
16 LONGRE 129 W 24
76 LONGROY 15 DA 6
10 LONGSOLS 65 PA 13
49 LONGUE JUMELLES C 96 W 18
80 LONGUEAU 26 HA 7
53 LONGUEFUYE 77 T 16
76 LONGUEIL 24 AA 7
60 LONGUEIL ANNEL 27 JA 9
60 LONGUEIL STE MARIE 27 IA 9
62 LONGUENESSE 8 GA 3
61 LONGUENOE 58 W 13
76 LONGUERUE 24 CA 8
14 LONGUES SUR MER 35 T 9
95 LONGUESSE 39 FA 10
80 LONGUEVAL 17 JA 6
02 LONGUEVAL BARBONVAL 28 MA 9
14 LONGUEVILLE 35 S 9
47 LONGUEVILLE 171 X 31
50 LONGUEVILLE 56 P 11
62 LONGUEVILLE 7 EA 3
77 LONGUEVILLE 63 LA 13
59 LONGUEVILLE, LA 19 NA 5
10 LONGUEVILLE SUR AUBE 64 NA 13
76 LONGUEVILLE SUR SCIE C 24 BA 7
80 LONGUEVILLETTE 16 GA 6
54 LONGUYON C 31 VA 9
21 LONGVIC 105 TA 18
14 LONGVILLERS 35 T 10
62 LONGVILLERS 7 EA 4
78 LONGVILLERS 61 FA 13
08 LONGWE 30 RA 9
54 LONGWY C 31 WA 8
39 LONGWY SUR LE DOUBS 122 UA 20
61 LONLAY L'ABBAYE 57 T 12
61 LONLAY LE TESSON 58 V 12
16 LONNES 129 X 24
08 LONNY 29 RA 7
61 LONRAI 58 W 13
64 LONS 207 U 36
39 LONS LE SAUNIER P 122 VA 21
17 LONZAC 142 U 26
19 LONZAC, LE 145 DA 26
59 LOOBERGHE 8 GA 2
59 LOON PLAGE 8 GA 2
59 LOOS 9 KA 4
62 LOOS EN GOHELLE 17 IA 4
89 LOOZE 83 LA 15
29 LOPEREC 52 E 14
29 LOPERHET 52 D 14
2A LOPIGNA 227 JB 41
29 LOQUEFFRET 52 F 14
02 LOR 29 OA 9
25 LORAY 107 ZA 19
15 LORCIERES 162 LA 29
45 LORCY 82 HA 15
09 LORDAT 220 EA 38
61 LORE 57 U 13
67 LORENTZEN 48 CB 11
2B LORETO DI CASINCA 228 MB 40
2A LORETO DI TALLANO 229 KB 43
42 LORETTE 150 RA 26
50 LOREUR, LE 56 Q 11
41 LOREUX 99 EA 18
54 LOREY 68 YA 13
50 LOREY, LE 34 O 10
41 LORGES 80 DA 16
62 LORGIES 9 JA 4
83 LORGUES C 203 YA 35
56 LORIENT S 73 H 16
03 LORIGES 133 LA 23
17 LORIGNAC 141 T 26
79 LORIGNE 129 W 24
84 LORIOL DU COMTAT 195 SA 33
26 LORIOL SUR DROME C 165 SA 30
43 LORLANGES 148 LA 27
27 LORLEAU 25 DA 9
60 LORMAISON 39 FA 10
28 LORMAYE 60 DA 12
58 LORMES C 103 NA 18
33 LORMONT C 156 U 29
74 LORNAY 138 WA 24
54 LOROMONTZEY 68 ZA 13
35 LOROUX, LE 56 R 13
44 LOROUX BOTTEREAU, LE C 94 Q 19
09 LORP SENTARAILLE 218 BA 37
57 LORQUIN C 69 BB 12
77 LORREZ LE BOCAGE PREAUX C 63 JA 14
45 LORRIS C 82 HA 16
57 LORRY LES METZ 46 XA 10
57 LORRY MARDIGNY 46 XA 11
65 LORTET 216 Y 37
22 LOSCOUET SUR MEU 75 M 14
21 LOSNE 105 TA 19
40 LOSSE 171 W 32
19 LOSTANGES 159 EA 28
57 LOSTROFF 47 BB 11
29 LOTHEY 72 E 14
62 LOTTINGHEN 7 FA 3
35 LOU DU LAC, LE 75 N 14
72 LOUAILLES 78 V 16
77 LOUAN VILLEGRUIS FONTAINE 63 MA 12
22 LOUANNEC 53 H 12
37 LOUANS 98 Z 19
22 LOUARGAT 53 H 13
02 LOUATRE 41 LA 10
65 LOUBAJAC 215 W 37
07 LOUBARESSE 178 OA 30
15 LOUBARESSE 162 KA 29
09 LOUBAUT 218 CA 37
32 LOUBEDAT 185 W 34
24 LOUBEJAC 173 BA 30
09 LOUBENS 219 DA 37
33 LOUBENS 171 W 30
31 LOUBENS LAURAGAIS 211 EA 35
81 LOUBERS 189 FA 33
32 LOUBERSAN 209 Y 35
47 LOUBES BERNAC 157 X 30
63 LOUBEYRAT 133 JA 24
64 LOUBIENG 206 T 35
12 LOUBIERE, LA 175 IA 31
09 LOUBIERES 219 DA 37
79 LOUBIGNE 128 W 24
79 LOUBILLE 128 W 24
46 LOUBRESSAC 159 EA 29
61 LOUCE 58 W 12
14 LOUCELLES 35 U 10
33 LOUCHATS 170 U 31
62 LOUCHES 7 FA 3
03 LOUCHY MONTFAND 133 LA 23
65 LOUCRUP 216 W 37
22 LOUDEAC C 74 K 14
65 LOUDENVIELLE 216 Y 38
65 LOUDERVIELLE 217 Y 38
43 LOUDES C 163 NA 28
31 LOUDET 217 Z 37
57 LOUDREFING 47 BB 11
86 LOUDUN C 113 X 20
72 LOUE C 78 W 15
40 LOUER 184 S 34
49 LOUERRE 96 V 18
21 LOUESME 85 RA 16
37 LOUESTAULT 79 Z 17
60 LOUEUSE 25 EA 8
65 LOUEY 216 W 37
61 LOUGE SUR MAIRE 58 V 12
47 LOUGRATTE 172 Z 30
25 LOUGRES 108 AB 17
71 LOUHANS S 121 TA 21
64 LOUHOSSOA 205 O 36
19 LOUIGNAC 159 CA 27
79 LOUIN 112 V 20
44 LOUISFERT 94 Q 17
65 LOUIT 208 X 36
70 LOULANS VERCHAMP 107 YA 18
17 LOULAY C 128 U 24
39 LOULLE 122 WA 21
28 LOUPE, LA C 60 BA 13
02 LOUPEIGNE 42 MA 10
57 LOUPERSHOUSE 47 BB 10
33 LOUPES 156 U 29
53 LOUPFOUGERES 58 V 14
33 LOUPIA 221 FA 37
33 LOUPIAC 170 V 30
46 LOUPIAC 159 DA 29
81 LOUPIAC 189 EA 34
33 LOUPIAC DE LA REOLE 171 W 30
34 LOUPIAN 214 MA 35
30 LOUPLANDE 78 W 15
55 LOUPMONT 45 VA 11
55 LOUPPY LE CHATEAU 44 TA 11
55 LOUPPY SUR LOISON 31 UA 9
10 LOUPTIERE THENARD, LA 63 LA 13
59 LOURCHES 18 LA 5
31 LOURDE 217 Z 37
65 LOURDES C 216 W 37
64 LOURDIOS ICHERE 215 T 37
36 LOURDOUEIX ST MICHEL 132 EA 22
23 LOURDOUEIX ST PIERRE 131 EA 22
64 LOURENTIES 207 V 36
65 LOURES BAROUSSE 217 Z 37
49 LOURESSE ROCHEMENIER 96 V 19
35 LOURMAIS 55 O 13
84 LOURMARIN 196 UA 34
71 LOURNAND 120 RA 22
36 LOUROUER ST LAURENT 116 FA 21
37 LOUROUX, LE 98 AA 19
49 LOUROUX BECONNAIS, LE C 95 S 17
03 LOUROUX BOURBONNAIS 117 JA 22
03 LOUROUX DE BEAUNE 133 JA 23
03 LOUROUX DE BOUBLE 133 JA 23
03 LOUROUX HODEMENT 117 IA 22
40 LOURQUEN 184 T 34
32 LOURTIES MONBRUN 209 Z 35
45 LOURY 81 FA 15
32 LOUSLITGES 208 X 35
32 LOUSSOUS DEBAT 185 W 34
35 LOUTEHEL 75 N 15
57 LOUTZVILLER 48 DB 10
14 LOUVAGNY 36 W 11
49 LOUVAINES 77 T 17
39 LOUVATANGE 106 VA 19
78 LOUVECIENNES 39 GA 11
52 LOUVEMONT 66 SA 13
55 LOUVEMONT COTE DU POIVRE (VILLAGE RUINE) 44 UA 10
80 LOUVENCOURT 17 HA 6
39 LOUVENNE 122 UA 22
08 LOUVERGNY 30 RA 8
53 LOUVERNE 77 T 15
39 LOUVEROT, LE 122 VA 21
27 LOUVERSEY 38 AA 11
76 LOUVETOT 24 Z 8
64 LOUVIE JUZON 215 U 37
64 LOUVIE SOUBIRON 215 U 37
11 LOUVIERE LAURAGAIS, LA 211 EA 36
14 LOUVIERES 35 S 9
52 LOUVIERES 87 UA 15
61 LOUVIERES EN AUGE 36 W 11
27 LOUVIERS C 38 BA 10
53 LOUVIGNE 77 T 15
35 LOUVIGNE DE BAIS 76 Q 15
35 LOUVIGNE DU DESERT C 56 R 13
59 LOUVIGNIES QUESNOY 18 MA 5
14 LOUVIGNY 36 U 10
57 LOUVIGNY 46 YA 11
64 LOUVIGNY 207 U 35
72 LOUVIGNY 58 X 14
59 LOUVIL 9 KA 4
28 LOUVILLE LA CHENARD 61 EA 14
28 LOUVILLIERS EN DROUAIS 38 CA 12
28 LOUVILLIERS LES PERCHE 60 BA 12
51 LOUVOIS 42 OA 10
80 LOUVRECHY 26 HA 7
95 LOUVRES 40 HA 11
59 LOUVROIL 19 OA 5
27 LOUYE 38 CA 12
16 LOUZAC ST ANDRE 142 U 25
52 LOUZE 65 RA 13
72 LOUZES 59 X 13
17 LOUZIGNAC 128 V 25
45 LOUZOUER 82 JA 15
79 LOUZY 96 V 20
74 LOVAGNY 139 XA 24
56 LOYAT 74 L 15
39 LOYE, LA 106 VA 19
18 LOYE SUR ARNON 116 HA 21
71 LOYERE, LA 121 SA 20
01 LOYETTES 151 TA 25
69 LOZANNE 136 RA 25
17 LOZAY 128 U 24
82 LOZE 174 EA 32
62 LOZINGHEM 8 HA 4
50 LOZON 34 R 10
2B LOZZI 227 KB 40
36 LUANT 115 DA 21
72 LUART, LE 79 Z 15
40 LUBBON 171 W 32
57 LUBECOURT 47 ZA 11
19 LUBERSAC C 145 CA 27
54 LUBEY 45 WA 10
43 LUBILHAC 162 LA 27
88 LUBINE 69 CB 14
37 LUBLE 97 X 17
65 LUBRET ST LUC 208 X 36
65 LUBY BETMONT 208 X 36
12 LUC 175 HA 32
48 LUC 177 NA 30
65 LUC 216 X 37
83 LUC, LE C 203 YA 36
64 LUC ARMAU 208 W 36
26 LUC EN DIOIS C 180 UA 30
11 LUC SUR AUDE 221 GA 38
14 LUC SUR MER 36 V 9
11 LUC SUR ORBIEU 223 JA 37
64 LUCARRE 207 W 36
36 LUCAY LE LIBRE 100 FA 19
36 LUCAY LE MALE 99 CA 19
40 LUCBARDEZ ET BARGUES 184 U 33
2B LUCCIANA 226 MB 39
28 LUCE C 60 DA 13
61 LUCE 57 T 13
72 LUCE SOUS BALLON 78 X 14
72 LUCEAU 78 Y 16
64 LUCELLE 108 CB 18
69 LUCENAY 136 RA 24
71 LUCENAY L'EVEQUE C 104 PA 19
21 LUCENAY LE DUC 85 QA 17
58 LUCENAY LES AIX 118 MA 21
06 LUCERAM 199 DB 34
50 LUCERNE D'OUTREMER, LA 56 O 12
21 LUCEY 86 SA 16
54 LUCEY 45 WA 12
73 LUCEY 152 WA 25
64 LUCGARIER 207 V 36
86 LUCHAPT 130 AA 23
40 LUCHAT 141 T 25
72 LUCHE PRINGE 78 W 16
79 LUCHE SUR BRIOUX 128 V 23
79 LUCHE THOUARSAIS 112 V 20
80 LUCHEUX 17 HA 5
60 LUCHY 26 GA 8
74 LUCINGES 139 YA 23
33 LUCMAU 170 V 31
85 LUCON C 125 R 22
64 LUCQ DE BEARN 207 T 36
08 LUCQUY 29 OA 8
62 LUCS SUR BOULOGNE, LES 110 P 20
57 LUCY 47 ZA 11
76 LUCY 25 DA 7
02 LUCY LE BOCAGE 41 LA 10
89 LUCY LE BOIS 84 NA 17
89 LUCY SUR CURE 84 NA 17
89 LUCY SUR YONNE 84 MA 17
72 LUDE, LE C 78 X 17
51 LUDES 42 OA 10
33 LUDESSE 148 KA 26
09 LUDIES 219 EA 37
33 LUDON MEDOC 156 T 29
54 LUDRES 67 XA 12
40 LUE 169 S 32
49 LUE EN BAUGEOIS 96 V 17
68 LUEMSCHWILLER 90 DB 17
46 LUGAGNAC 174 EA 31
65 LUGAGNAN 216 W 37
33 LUGAIGNAC 156 V 29
12 LUGAN 175 GA 31
81 LUGAN 189 EA 34
15 LUGARDE 161 IA 27
33 LUGASSON 156 V 30
40 LUGLON 184 T 33
02 LUGNY 28 NA 7
71 LUGNY C 120 RA 22
18 LUGNY BOURBONNAIS 117 IA 20
18 LUGNY CHAMPAGNE 101 JA 19
71 LUGNY LES CHAROLLES 135 PA 22
2B LUGO DI NAZZA 228 LB 41
33 LUGON ET L'ILE DU CARNAY 156 U 29
33 LUGOS 169 S 31
74 LUGRIN 124 AB 22
62 LUGY 8 GA 4
25 LUHIER, LE 108 AB 19
49 LUIGNE 96 U 18
28 LUIGNY 60 BA 14
28 LUISANT 60 DA 13
77 LUISETAINES 63 KA 13
35 LUITRE 76 R 14
74 LULLIN 139 ZA 23
74 LULLY 139 ZA 23
38 LUMBIN 153 WA 27
62 LUMBRES C 8 GA 3
28 LUMEAU 61 EA 15
08 LUMES 29 RA 7
77 LUMIGNY NESLES ORMEAUX 41 JA 12
2B LUMIO 225 JB 39
12 LUNAC 175 FA 32
46 LUNAN 160 FA 30
24 LUNAS 157 Y 29
34 LUNAS C 191 KA 34
31 LUNAX 209 Z 36
41 LUNAY 79 AA 16
03 LUNEAU 135 OA 22
46 LUNEGARDE 174 EA 30
34 LUNEL C 193 OA 34
34 LUNEL VIEL 193 OA 34
76 LUNERAY 24 AA 7
18 LUNERY 116 GA 20
54 LUNEVILLE S 68 ZA 13
50 LUOT, LE 56 Q 12
54 LUPCOURT 68 YA 12
42 LUPE 150 RA 27
23 LUPERSAT 132 HA 24
32 LUPIAC 186 X 34
28 LUPLANTE 60 CA 14
32 LUPPE VIOLLES 185 V 34
57 LUPPY 46 YA 11
16 LUPSAULT 128 W 24
67 LUPSTEIN 49 DB 12
65 LUQUET 207 W 36
36 LURAIS 114 AA 21
28 LURAY 38 CA 12
64 LURBE ST CHRISTAU 215 T 37
01 LURCY 136 RA 24
58 LURCY LE BOURG 102 LA 19
03 LURCY LEVIS C 117 JA 21
42 LURE 135 OA 25
70 LURE S 89 ZA 17
36 LUREUIL 114 BA 21
2B LURI 226 MB 38
42 LURIECQ 149 OA 26
04 LURS 197 WA 33
18 LURY SUR ARNON C 100 FA 19
26 LUS LA CROIX HAUTE 166 WA 30
44 LUSANGER 94 P 17
31 LUSCAN 217 Z 37
24 LUSIGNAC 143 Y 27
86 LUSIGNAN C 113 X 22
47 LUSIGNAN PETIT 172 Y 32
03 LUSIGNY 118 MA 21
10 LUSIGNY SUR BARSE C 65 PA 14
21 LUSIGNY SUR OUCHE 104 RA 19
16 LUSSAC 129 Y 25
17 LUSSAC 142 U 26
33 LUSSAC C 156 W 29
86 LUSSAC LES CHATEAUX C 130 Z 22
87 LUSSAC LES EGLISES 131 BA 23
40 LUSSAGNET 185 V 34
64 LUSSAGNET LUSSON 207 V 35
30 LUSSAN C 178 PA 32
32 LUSSAN 209 Z 35
31 LUSSAN ADEILHAC 209 AA 36
17 LUSSANT 127 S 24
07 LUSSAS 178 QA 30
24 LUSSAS ET NONTRONNEAU 143 Z 26
23 LUSSAT 132 HA 23
63 LUSSAT 148 KA 25
37 LUSSAULT SUR LOIRE 98 AA 18
88 LUSSE 69 CB 14
79 LUSSERAY 128 V 23
65 LUSTAR 208 Y 36
58 LUTHENAY UXELOUP 118 LA 20
65 LUTILHOUS 216 Y 37
57 LUTTANGE 46 YA 10
68 LUTTENBACH PRES MUNSTER 90 CB 15
68 LUTTER 90 DB 18
68 LUTTERBACH 90 CB 16
28 LUTZ EN DUNOIS 80 CA 15
57 LUTZELBOURG 48 CB 12
67 LUTZELHOUSE 70 DB 13
88 LUVIGNY 69 CB 13
21 LUX 86 TA 17
31 LUX 211 EA 35
71 LUX 121 SA 21
16 LUXE 129 X 25
64 LUXE SUMBERRAUTE 206 R 36
51 LUXEMONT ET VILLOTTE 43 RA 12
70 LUXEUIL LES BAINS C 89 ZA 16
40 LUXEY 170 U 32
25 LUXIOL 107 YA 18
10 LUYERES 65 PA 13
37 LUYNES C 97 Z 18
65 LUZ ST SAUVEUR C 216 W 38
77 LUZANCY 41 KA 11
95 LUZARCHES C 40 HA 10
79 LUZAY 112 V 20
37 LUZE 113 Y 20
70 LUZE 89 AB 17
46 LUZECH C 173 CA 31
09 LUZENAC 220 EA 38
36 LUZERET 115 CA 22
50 LUZERNE, LA 35 S 10
63 LUZILLAT 133 LA 24
37 LUZILLE 98 BA 18
38 LUZINAY 151 SA 26
02 LUZOIR 19 OA 7
58 LUZY C 119 OA 21
55 LUZY ST MARTIN 30 TA 8
52 LUZY SUR MARNE 66 TA 15
02 LY FONTAINE 28 LA 7
07 LYAS 164 RA 30
74 LYAUD 139 ZA 23
36 LYE 99 DA 19
59 LYNDE 8 HA 3
70 LYOFFANS 89 ZA 17
69 LYON P 151 SA 25
27 LYONS LA FORET C 25 DA 9
58 LYS 103 MA 18
64 LYS 215 V 37
59 LYS LEZ LANNOY 9 KA 3
36 LYS ST GEORGES 115 EA 21

M

02 MAAST ET VIOLAINE 41 LA 9
52 MAATZ 87 UA 16
42 MABLY 135 OA 24
33 MACAU 156 T 28
64 MACAYE 205 Q 36
61 MACE 58 X 12
10 MACEY 64 NA 14
50 MACEY 56 Q 13
08 MACHAULT C 29 OA 9
77 MACHAULT 62 JA 13
85 MACHE 109 P 21
44 MACHECOUL C 109 O 20
02 MACHECOURT 28 NA 8
08 MACHEMONT 27 JA 9
57 MACHEREN 47 AB 10
42 MACHEZAL 136 PA 24
80 MACHIEL 16 EA 5
74 MACHILLY 139 YA 23
58 MACHINE, LA C 118 MA 20
36 MACHY 64 OA 15
80 MACHY 15 EA 5
67 MACKENHEIM 70 EB 14
67 MACKWILLER 48 CB 11
42 MACLAS 150 RA 27
02 MACOGNY 41 KA 10
71 MACON P 137 SA 23
88 MACONCOURT 67 XA 14
21 MACONGE 104 QA 19
39 MACORNAY 122 VA 21
73 MACOT LA PLAGNE 154 AB 26
17 MACQUEVILLE 142 V 25
02 MACQUIGNY 28 MA 7
47 MADAILLAN 172 Z 32
88 MADECOURT 68 XA 14
88 MADEGNEY 68 YA 14
62 MADELAINE SOUS MONTREUIL, LA 15 EA 4
59 MADELEINE, LA 9 KA 3
61 MADELEINE BOUVET, LA 59 AA 13
27 MADELEINE DE NONANCOURT, LA 38 CA 12
77 MADELEINE SUR LOING, LA 62 IA 14
41 MADELEINE VILLEFROUIN, LA 80 CA 16
15 MADIC 147 HA 27
09 MADIERE 219 DA 37
33 MADIRAC 156 U 30
65 MADIRAN 208 W 35
88 MADONNE ET LAMEREY 68 YA 14
19 MADRANGES 146 EA 26
53 MADRE 58 U 13
63 MADRIAT 148 KA 27
22 MAEL CARHAIX C 53 H 14
22 MAEL PESTIVIEN 53 H 13
67 MAENNOLSHEIM 49 DB 12
95 MAFFLIERS 40 GA 10
51 MAFFRECOURT 43 SA 10
34 MAGALAS 213 KA 35
16 MAGDELEINE, LA 129 W 24
31 MAGDELEINE SUR TARN, LA 188 DA 34
61 MAGE, LE 59 AA 13
51 MAGENTA 42 OA 11
30 MAGES, LES 178 PA 32
40 MAGESCQ 183 R 34
74 MAGLAND 140 AB 24
87 MAGNAC BOURG 145 DA 26
87 MAGNAC LAVAL C 130 BA 23
16 MAGNAC LAVALETTE VILLARS 143 X 26
16 MAGNAC SUR TOUVRE 143 X 26
32 MAGNAN 185 W 34
10 MAGNANT 65 QA 14
78 MAGNANVILLE 39 EA 11
32 MAGNAS 187 Z 33
23 MAGNAT L'ETRANGE 146 GA 25
79 MAGNE 128 U 23
86 MAGNE 129 Y 22
03 MAGNET 133 MA 23
51 MAGNEUX 28 NA 9
52 MAGNEUX 66 SA 13
42 MAGNEUX HAUTE RIVE 149 PA 26
50 MAGNEVILLE 33 P 9
10 MAGNICOURT 65 QA 13
62 MAGNICOURT EN COMTE 17 HA 5
62 MAGNICOURT SUR CANCHE 17 HA 5
21 MAGNIEN 104 QA 19
54 MAGNIERES 68 ZA 13
01 MAGNIEU 152 WA 25
95 MAGNILS REIGNIERS, LES 125 R 22
70 MAGNIVRAY 89 ZA 16
70 MAGNONCOURT 88 YA 16
70 MAGNORAY, LE 88 YA 17
28 MAGNY 60 CA 14
68 MAGNY 90 CB 17
89 MAGNY 84 OA 17
36 MAGNY, LE 116 FA 22
88 MAGNY, LE 68 YA 15
70 MAGNY, LES 89 ZA 17
25 MAGNY CHATELARD 107 YA 19
58 MAGNY COURS 118 KA 20
70 MAGNY DANIGON 89 ZA 17
14 MAGNY EN BESSIN 35 T 9
95 MAGNY EN VEXIN C 39 EA 10
10 MAGNY FOUCHARD 65 QA 14
70 MAGNY JOBERT 89 ZA 17
14 MAGNY LA CAMPAGNE 36 W 10
02 MAGNY LA FOSSE 18 LA 7
21 MAGNY LA VILLE 85 QA 17
21 MAGNY LAMBERT 85 QA 17
61 MAGNY LE DESERT 58 V 13
14 MAGNY LE FREULE 36 W 10
77 MAGNY LE HONGRE 40 JA 11
21 MAGNY LES AUBIGNY 105 TA 19
78 MAGNY LES HAMEAUX 39 FA 12
70 MAGNY LES JUSSEY 88 XA 16
21 MAGNY LES VILLERS 105 SA 19
58 MAGNY LORMES 103 NA 18
21 MAGNY MONTARLOT 105 UA 19
21 MAGNY ST MEDARD 105 TA 18
21 MAGNY SUR TILLE 105 TA 18
70 MAGNY VERNOIS 89 ZA 17
22 MAGOAR 53 I 13
11 MAGRIE 221 GA 37
81 MAGRIN 211 FA 35
68 MAGSTATT LE BAS 90 DB 17
68 MAGSTATT LE HAUT 90 DB 17
29 MAHALON 71 C 15
61 MAHERU 59 Y 12
25 MAICHE C 108 AB 19
54 MAIDIERES 45 XA 11
32 MAIGNAUT TAUZIA 186 Y 33
72 MAIGNE 78 W 15
60 MAIGNELAY MONTIGNY C 26 HA 8
11 MAILHAC 213 JA 36
87 MAILHAC SUR BENAIZE 131 CA 23
81 MAILHOC 189 FA 33
31 MAILHOLAS 210 CA 36
13 MAILLANE 195 RA 34
40 MAILLAS 170 V 32
01 MAILLAT 138 VA 23
37 MAILLE 97 Z 19
85 MAILLE 127 T 23
86 MAILLE 113 X 21
28 MAILLEBOIS 60 BA 12
76 MAILLERAYE SUR SEINE, LA 24 Z 9
40 MAILLERES 184 U 33
70 MAILLERONCOURT CHARETTE 88 YA 16
70 MAILLERONCOURT ST PANCRAS 88 XA 16
03 MAILLET 117 IA 22
36 MAILLET 115 EA 22
70 MAILLEY ET CHAZELOT 88 XA 17
85 MAILLEZAIS C 127 T 22
89 MAILLOT 63 LA 14
71 MAILLY 135 OA 23
51 MAILLY CHAMPAGNE 42 OA 10
89 MAILLY LA VILLE 84 NA 17
10 MAILLY LE CAMP 65 PA 12
89 MAILLY LE CHATEAU 84 MA 17
80 MAILLY MAILLET 17 IA 6
80 MAILLY RAINEVAL 26 HA 7
54 MAILLY SUR SEILLE 46 YA 11
21 MAILLYS, LES 106 UA 19
60 MAIMBEVILLE 26 HA 9
77 MAINCY 62 IA 13
16 MAINE DE BOIXE 129 X 25
16 MAINFONDS 143 W 26
59 MAING 18 MA 5
27 MAINNEVILLE 25 DA 9
23 MAINSAT 132 HA 24
62 MAINTENAY 16 EA 5
28 MAINTENON C 60 DA 13
57 MAINVILLERS 47 AB 11
28 MAINVILLIERS C 60 CA 13
45 MAINVILLIERS 62 GA 14
16 MAINXE 142 V 26
16 MAINZAC 143 Y 26
86 MAIRE 114 Z 20
79 MAIRE LEVESCAULT 129 W 23
59 MAIRIEUX 19 OA 5
08 MAIRY 30 TA 8
54 MAIRY MAINVILLE 31 WA 9
51 MAIRY SUR MARNE 43 QA 11
44 MAISDON SUR SEVRE 110 Q 19
21 MAISEY LE DUC 85 RA 16
80 MAISNIERES 15 DA 6
62 MAISNIL 16 HA 5
59 MAISNIL, LE 9 JA 4
62 MAISNIL LES RUITZ 17 IA 4
39 MAISOD 122 VA 22
10 MAISON DES CHAMPS 65 QA 14
58 MAISON DIEU, LA 103 MA 18
23 MAISON FEYNE 131 EA 23
61 MAISON MAUGIS 59 Z 13
80 MAISON PONTHIEU 16 FA 6
80 MAISON ROLAND 16 FA 5
77 MAISON ROUGE 63 KA 13
62 MAISONCELLE 16 GA 4
08 MAISONCELLE ET VILLERS 30 SA 9
60 MAISONCELLE ST PIERRE 26 GA 8

60 MAISONCELLE TUILERIE 26 GA 8
52 MAISONCELLES 67 VA 15
72 MAISONCELLES 79 Z 15
53 MAISONCELLES DU MAINE 77 T 15
77 MAISONCELLES EN BRIE 41 KA 11
77 MAISONCELLES EN GATINAIS 62 IA 14
14 MAISONCELLES LA JOURDAN 57 S 12
14 MAISONCELLES PELVEY 35 T 10
14 MAISONCELLES SUR AJON 35 U 10
18 MAISONNAIS 116 GA 21
87 MAISONNAIS SUR TARDOIRE 144 Z 25
79 MAISONNAY 128 W 23
86 MAISONNEUVE 112 W 21
23 MAISONNISSES 132 FA 24
11 MAISONS 223 IA 38
14 MAISONS 35 T 9
28 MAISONS 61 EA 13
94 MAISONS ALFORT C 40 HA 12
25 MAISONS DU BOIS
LIEVREMONT 107 YA 20
51 MAISONS EN CHAMPAGNE 43 QA 12
78 MAISONS LAFFITTE C 39 GA 11
10 MAISONS LES CHAOURCE 85 PA 15
10 MAISONS LES SOULAINES 65 RA 14
67 MAISONSGOUTTE 69 CB 14
79 MAISONTIERS 112 V 21
91 MAISSE 62 HA 13
02 MAISSEMY 27 KA 7
54 MAIXE 46 ZA 12
55 MAIZERAY 45 VA 10
57 MAIZEROY 47 ZA 10
57 MAIZERY 46 YA 10
14 MAIZET 35 U 10
55 MAIZEY 45 VA 11
80 MAIZICOURT 16 GA 5
14 MAIZIERES 36 V 11
52 MAIZIERES 66 TA 13
54 MAIZIERES 67 XA 13
62 MAIZIERES 17 HA 5
70 MAIZIERES 88 XA 17
10 MAIZIERES
LA GRANDE PAROISSE 64 NA 13
10 MAIZIERES LES BRIENNE 65 QA 13
57 MAIZIERES LES METZ C 46 YA 10
57 MAIZIERES LES VIC 69 AB 12
52 MAIZIERES SUR AMANCE 87 VA 16
42 MAIZILLY 135 PA 23
02 MAIZY 28 NA 9
04 MAJASTRES 198 YA 33
32 MALABAT 208 X 35
70 MALACHERE, LA 107 XA 18
01 MALAFRETAZ 137 TA 23
21 MALAIN 104 RA 18
88 MALAINCOURT 67 WA 14
52 MALAINCOURT SUR MEUSE 67 VA 14
92 MALAKOFF C 40 GA 11
55 MALANCOURT 44 TA 10
80 MALANDRY 30 TA 8
39 MALANGE 106 VA 19
25 MALANS 107 XA 19
70 MALANS 106 VA 18
56 MALANSAC 92 M 17
07 MALARCE SUR LA THINES 178 OA 31
26 MALATAVERNE 179 RA 31
84 MALAUCENE C 179 TA 32
57 MALAUCOURT SUR SEILLE 46 YA 11
76 MALAUNAY 24 BA 8
82 MALAUSE 187 AA 33
64 MALAUSSANNE 207 U 35
06 MALAUSSENE 199 CB 33
63 MALAUZAT 133 KA 25
54 MALAVILLERS 32 WA 9
71 MALAY 120 RA 22
89 MALAY LE GRAND 63 LA 14
89 MALAY LE PETIT 63 LA 14
15 MALBO 161 IA 29
07 MALBOSC 178 OA 31
70 MALBOUHANS 89 ZA 16
48 MALBOUZON 162 KA 30
25 MALBRANS 107 XA 19
25 MALBUISSON 123 YA 21
61 MALE 59 Z 14
09 MALEGOUDE 221 FA 37
84 MALEMORT DU COMTAT 196 TA 33
19 MALEMORT SUR CORREZE C 159 DA 28
26 MALENE, LA 177 LA 32
45 MALESHERBES C 62 HA 14
56 MALESTROIT C 74 L 16
61 MALETABLE 59 Z 13
12 MALEVILLE 175 FA 31
56 MALGUENAC 73 I 15
22 MALHOURE, LA 54 L 13
36 MALICORNAY 115 DA 21
03 MALICORNE 133 JA 23
89 MALICORNE 83 KA 16
72 MALICORNE SUR SARTHE C 78 W 16
21 MALIGNY 104 QA 19
89 MALIGNY 84 NA 16
04 MALIJAI 197 XA 33
59 MALINCOURT 18 LA 6
63 MALINTRAT 148 KA 25
26 MALISSARD 165 SA 29
16 MALAVILLE 143 W 26
04 MALLEFOUGASSE AUGES 197 WA 33
54 MALLELOY 46 YA 12
04 MALLEMOISSON 197 XA 33
13 MALLEMORT 196 TA 34
09 MALLEON 219 EA 37
23 MALLERET 146 GA 25
23 MALLERET BOUSSAC 132 GA 23
39 MALLEREY 122 UA 21
38 MALLEVAL 166 UA 28
42 MALLEVAL 150 RA 27
76 MALLEVILLE LES GRES 23 Z 7
27 MALLEVILLE SUR LE BEC 37 AA 10
85 MALLIEVRE 111 S 20
57 MALLING 32 YA 9
14 MALLOUE 35 S 11
02 MALMAISON, LA 29 OA 8
68 MALMERSPACH 90 BB 16
51 MALMY 43 SA 10
30 MALONS ET ELZE 178 OA 31
27 MALOUY 37 Z 10
80 MALPART 26 HA 8
25 MALPAS 123 YA 20
11 MALRAS 221 GA 37
43 MALREVERS 163 OA 28
57 MALROY 46 YA 10
71 MALTAT 119 NA 21
14 MALTOT 35 U 10
23 MALVAL 132 EA 23
43 MALVALETTE 149 PA 27
11 MALVES EN MINERVOIS 212 HA 36
31 MALVEZIE 217 Z 37
43 MALVIERES 149 NA 27
11 MALVIES 221 GA 37
44 MALVILLE 93 O 18
70 MALVILLERS 87 WA 16

54 MALZEVILLE 46 YA 12
48 MALZIEU FORAIN, LE 162 LA 29
48 MALZIEU VILLE, LE C 162 LA 29
02 MALZY 19 NA 7
72 MAMERS S 59 Y 14
62 MAMETZ 8 GA 3
80 MAMETZ 17 IA 6
54 MAMEY 45 XA 11
25 MAMIROLLE 107 YA 19
26 MANAS 179 SA 30
32 MANAS BASTANOUS 208 Y 36
24 MANAURIE 158 BA 29
54 MANCE 45 WA 10
28 MANCELIERE, LA 60 BA 12
50 MANCELLIERE SUR VIRE, LA 34 R 10
25 MANCENANS 107 ZA 18
25 MANCENANS LIZERNE 108 AB 18
71 MANCEY 121 SA 21
45 MANCHECOURT 62 HA 14
32 MANCIET 185 W 34
54 MANCIEULLES 31 WA 9
31 MANCIOUX 217 AA 37
51 MANCY 42 OA 11
30 MANDAGOUT 192 MA 33
15 MANDAILLES ST JULIEN 161 IA 28
06 MANDELIEU LA NAPOULE C 200 BB 35
57 MANDEREN 32 ZA 9
25 MANDEURE 108 AB 18
27 MANDEVILLE 38 BA 10
14 MANDEVILLE EN BESSIN 35 S 9
88 MANDRAY 69 BB 14
27 MANDRES 37 AA 12
54 MANDRES AUX QUATRE TOURS 45 WA 11
55 MANDRES EN BARROIS 66 UA 13
52 MANDRES LA COTE 66 UA 15
94 MANDRES LES ROSES 40 HA 12
88 MANDRES SUR VAIR 67 WA 14
70 MANDREVILLARS 89 AB 17
30 MANDUEL 193 QA 34
04 MANE 197 WA 33
31 MANE 217 AA 37
76 MANEGLISE 23 X 8
14 MANEHOUVILLE 24 BA 7
32 MANENT MONTANE 209 Z 36
14 MANERBE 36 X 10
55 MANGIENNES 31 VA 9
63 MANGLIEU 148 LA 26
54 MANGONVILLE 68 YA 13
12 MANHAC 175 HA 32
55 MANHEULLES 45 VA 10
57 MANHOUE 46 YA 11
02 MANICAMP 27 KA 8
21 MANIGOD 139 YA 25
62 MANIN 17 HA 5
62 MANINGHEM 7 FA 4
62 MANINGHEN HENNE 7 EA 3
76 MANIQUERVILLE 23 Y 8
21 MANLAY 104 PA 19
76 MANNEVILLE ES PLAINS 24 AA 7
76 MANNEVILLE LA GOUPIL 23 Y 8
14 MANNEVILLE LA PIPARD 37 X 10
27 MANNEVILLE LA RAOULT 23 Y 9
27 MANNEVILLE SUR RISLE 23 Z 9
76 MANNEVILLETTE 23 X 8
40 MANO 170 T 31
14 MANOIR, LE 35 T 9
27 MANOIR, LE 24 CA 9
52 MANOIS 66 UA 14
52 MANOM 32 YA 9
54 MANONCOURT EN VERMOIS 68 YA 12
54 MANONCOURT EN WOEVRE 45 XA 12
54 MANONVILLE 45 WA 11
54 MANONVILLER 68 AB 13
04 MANOSQUE C 197 WA 34
16 MANOT 130 Z 24
28 MANOU 60 BA 13
08 MANRE 43 RA 10
72 MANS, LE P 78 X 15
19 MANSAC 159 CA 28
65 MANSAN 208 X 36
23 MANSAT LA COURRIERE 187 AA 34
32 MANSEMPUY 187 AA 34
32 MANSENCOME 186 Y 34
09 MANSES 219 EA 37
72 MANSIGNE 78 X 16
16 MANSLE C 129 X 25
28 MANSO 227 JB 40
16 MANSONVILLE 187 AA 33
68 MANSPACH 90 CB 17
40 MANT 207 U 35
22 MANTALLOT 53 I 12
01 MANTENAY MONTLIN 121 TA 22
78 MANTES LA JOLIE S 39 EA 11
78 MANTES LA VILLE C 39 EA 11
66 MANTET 222 GA 40
05 MANTEYER 181 XA 31
37 MANTHELAN 98 AA 19
27 MANTHELON 38 BA 11
26 MANTHES 151 SA 27
61 MANTILLY 57 T 13
70 MANTOCHE 106 VA 18
39 MANTRY 122 VA 21
14 MANVIEUX 35 T 9
57 MANY 47 ZA 11
24 MANZAC SUR VERN 157 Z 28
63 MANZAT C 133 JA 24
01 MANZIAT 137 SA 22
52 MARAC 86 TA 15
88 MARAINVILLE SUR MADON 68 XA 13
54 MARAINVILLER 68 AB 13
60 MARAIS AUX 26 FA 9
91 MARAIS LA CHAPELLE, LE 36 W 11
27 MARAIS VERNIER 23 Y 9
32 MARAMBAT 186 Y 34
21 MARANDEUIL 105 UA 18
57 MARANGE SILVANGE C 46 XA 10
57 MARANGE ZONDRANGE 47 ZA 10
17 MARANS C 127 S 23
49 MARANS 77 S 17
33 MARANSIN 156 V 28
62 MARANT 16 EA 4
52 MARANVILLE 66 SA 15
08 MARANWEZ 29 PA 7
70 MARAST 88 YA 17
63 MARAT 148 MA 26
34 MARAUSSAN 213 KA 36
32 MARAVAT 187 Z 34
41 MARAY 100 EA 19
10 MARAYE EN OTHE 64 NA 14
50 MARBACHE 46 XA 12
59 MARBAIX 19 NA 6
27 MARBEUF 38 BA 10
52 MARBEVILLE 66 SA 14
28 MARBOUE 60 CA 15
01 MARBOZ 137 TA 23
08 MARBY 29 QA 7
19 MARC LA TOUR 160 EA 28
18 MARCAIS 116 HA 21

37 MARCAY 97 X 19
86 MARCAY 113 X 22
49 MARCE 96 V 17
37 MARCE SUR ESVES 98 Z 19
81 MARCEI 58 W 12
80 MARCELCAVE 26 HA 7
74 MARCELLAZ 139 YA 23
74 MARCELLAZ ALBANAIS 139 XA 25
21 MARCELLOIS 104 RA 18
47 MARCELLUS 171 W 31
33 MARCENAIS 156 V 28
03 MARCENAT 133 LA 23
15 MARCENAT 147 JA 27
21 MARCENAY 85 QA 16
42 MARCENOD 150 QA 26
50 MARCEY LES GREVES 56 O 12
61 MARCHAINVILLE 59 AA 13
02 MARCHAIS 28 NA 8
89 MARCHAIS BETON 83 KA 16
02 MARCHAIS EN BRIE 41 MA 11
01 MARCHAMP 152 VA 25
69 MARCHAMPT 136 QA 24
15 MARCHASTEL 161 IA 27
48 MARCHASTEL 176 KA 30
25 MARCHAUX C 107 XA 18
58 MARCHE, LA 102 KA 19
80 MARCHE ALLOUARDE 27 JA 7
80 MARCHELEPOT 27 JA 7
61 MARCHEMAISONS 59 X 13
77 MARCHEMORET 40 IA 10
41 MARCHENOIR C 80 CA 16
33 MARCHEPRIME 155 S 30
26 MARCHES 165 TA 29
73 MARCHES, LES 153 XA 26
21 MARCHESEUIL 104 PA 19
50 MARCHESIEUX 34 O 10
28 MARCHEVILLE 60 CA 14
55 MARCHEVILLE EN WOEVRE 45 VA 10
28 MARCHEZAIS 38 DA 12
59 MARCHIENNES C 18 LA 4
32 MARCIAC C 208 X 35
38 MARCIEU 166 VA 29
73 MARCIEUX 152 WA 26
71 MARCIGNY C 135 OA 23
21 MARCIGNY SOUS THIL 104 QA 18
46 MARCILHAC SUR CELE 174 EA 30
33 MARCILLAC 142 U 27
19 MARCILLAC LA CROISILLE 160 FA 27
19 MARCILLAC LA CROZE 159 EA 28
16 MARCILLAC LANVILLE 129 W 25
24 MARCILLAC ST QUENTIN 158 BA 29
12 MARCILLAC VALLON C 175 HA 31
63 MARCILLAT 133 KA 24
03 MARCILLAT EN COMBRAILLE C 133 IA 23
53 MARCILLE LA VILLE 57 U 14
35 MARCILLE RAOUL 56 P 13
35 MARCILLE ROBERT 76 Q 15
38 MARCILLOLES 151 TA 27
50 MARCILLY 56 R 12
77 MARCILLY 41 JA 11
69 MARCILLY D'AZERGUES 136 RA 25
52 MARCILLY EN BASSIGNY 87 VA 16
41 MARCILLY EN BEAUCE 79 AA 16
41 MARCILLY EN GAULT 99 EA 18
45 MARCILLY EN VILLETTE 81 FA 16
27 MARCILLY LA CAMPAGNE 38 BA 11
71 MARCILLY LA GUEURCE 135 PA 22
42 MARCILLY LE CHATEL 149 OA 25
10 MARCILLY LE HAYER C 64 MA 14
71 MARCILLY LES BUXY 120 RA 21
21 MARCILLY LES VITTEAUX 104 QA 18
21 MARCILLY OGNY 104 OA 18
27 MARCILLY SUR EURE 38 CA 12
37 MARCILLY SUR MAULNE 97 X 17
51 MARCILLY SUR SEINE 64 NA 13
21 MARCILLY SUR TILLE 86 TA 17
37 MARCILLY SUR VIENNE 97 Y 19
62 MARCK 7 FA 2
67 MARCKOLSHEIM C 70 EB 14
42 MARCLOPT 149 PA 26
59 MARCOING C 18 KA 6
15 MARCOLES 160 HA 29
38 MARCOLLIN 151 TA 27
07 MARCOLS LES EAUX 164 OA 29
72 MARCON 79 Y 16
62 MARCONNE 16 FA 5
62 MARCONNELLE 16 FA 5
11 MARCORIGNAN 213 JA 36
91 MARCOUSSIS 62 GA 12
04 MARCOUX 181 YA 32
42 MARCOUX 149 OA 25
08 MARCQ 30 SA 9
78 MARCQ 39 EA 11
59 MARCQ EN BAROEUL C 9 KA 3
59 MARCQ EN OSTREVENT 18 KA 5
02 MARCY 28 LA 7
58 MARCY 102 LA 18
69 MARCY 136 RA 24
69 MARCY L'ETOILE 150 RA 25
02 MARCY SOUS MARLE 28 NA 7
51 MARDEUIL 42 OA 10
45 MARDIE 81 FA 16
61 MARDILLY 37 X 11
52 MARDOR 86 TA 16
69 MARDORE 136 PA 24
45 MAREAU AUX BOIS 61 GA 15
45 MAREAU AUX PRES 81 EA 16
72 MAREIL EN CHAMPAGNE 78 V 15
95 MAREIL EN FRANCE 40 HA 10
78 MAREIL LE GUYON 39 EA 12
78 MAREIL MARLY 39 FA 11
72 MAREIL SUR LOIR 78 W 16
78 MAREIL SUR MAULDRE 39 EA 11
52 MAREILLES 66 UA 14
62 MARENLA 16 EA 4
17 MARENNES C 126 R 25
69 MARENNES 151 SA 26
72 MARESCHE 78 X 14
59 MARESCHES 18 MA 5
62 MARESQUEL ECOUEMICOURT 16 FA 4
62 MAREST 16 HA 4
02 MAREST DAMPCOURT 27 KA 8
60 MAREST SUR MATZ 27 JA 8
32 MARESTAING 209 BA 35
80 MARESTMONTIERS 26 HA 8
62 MARESVILLE 7 EA 4
77 MARETS, LES 63 LA 12
59 MARETZ 18 LA 6
63 MAREUGHEOL 148 KA 26
16 MAREUIL 142 W 25
24 MAREUIL C 143 Y 26
80 MAREUIL CAUBERT 16 EA 6
51 MAREUIL EN BRIE 42 NA 11
02 MAREUIL EN DOLE 42 MA 10
60 MAREUIL LA MOTTE 27 JA 8
51 MAREUIL LE PORT 42 NA 10
77 MAREUIL LES MEAUX 40 JA 11
18 MAREUIL SUR ARNON 116 GA 20

51 MAREUIL SUR AY 42 OA 10
41 MAREUIL SUR CHER 99 CA 18
85 MAREUIL SUR LAY DISSAIS C 125 R 22
60 MAREUIL SUR OURCQ 41 KA 10
88 MAREY 67 WA 15
21 MAREY LES FUSSEY 105 SA 19
21 MAREY SUR TILLE 86 TA 17
51 MARFAUX 42 NA 10
02 MARFONTAINE 28 NA 7
33 MARGAUX 155 T 28
74 MARGENCEL 139 ZA 23
95 MARGENCY 40 GA 11
19 MARGERIDES 146 HA 26
42 MARGERIE CHANTAGRET 149 OA 26
51 MARGERIE HANCOURT 65 QA 13
26 MARGES 165 SA 28
02 MARGIVAL 28 LA 9
81 MARGNES, LE 190 IA 34
08 MARGNY 31 UA 8
51 MARGNY 42 MA 11
60 MARGNY AUX CERISES 27 JA 8
60 MARGNY LES COMPIEGNE 27 JA 9
60 MARGNY SUR MATZ 27 JA 8
28 MARGON 59 AA 14
34 MARGON 214 LA 35
32 MARGOUET MEYMES 186 X 34
50 MARGUERAY 56 R 11
30 MARGUERITTES C 193 QA 34
33 MARGUERON 157 X 30
32 MARGUESTAU 185 W 33
08 MARGUT 31 UA 8
07 MARIAC 164 QA 29
80 MARICOURT 17 JA 6
06 MARIE 199 CB 33
57 MARIEULLES 46 XA 11
80 MARIEUX 17 HA 6
39 MARIGNA SUR VALOUSE 122 VA 22
17 MARIGNAC 142 U 26
31 MARIGNAC 217 Z 38
82 MARIGNAC 187 AA 34
26 MARIGNAC EN DIOIS 166 UA 29
31 MARIGNAC LASCLARES 210 BA 36
31 MARIGNAC LASPEYRES 209 AA 36
2A MARIGNANA 227 JB 41
13 MARIGNANE C 201 TA 36
49 MARIGNE 77 T 16
72 MARIGNE LAILLE 78 Y 16
53 MARIGNE PEUTON 77 S 16
74 MARIGNIER 139 ZA 24
01 MARIGNIEU 138 WA 25
03 MARIGNY 118 KA 21
39 MARIGNY 122 WA 21
50 MARIGNY C 34 R 10
51 MARIGNY 64 NA 12
71 MARIGNY 120 QA 21
79 MARIGNY 128 U 23
86 MARIGNY BRIZAY 113 Y 21
86 MARIGNY CHEMEREAU 113 X 22
02 MARIGNY EN ORXOIS 41 KA 10
58 MARIGNY L'EGLISE 103 OA 18
21 MARIGNY LE CAHOUET 104 QA 18
10 MARIGNY LE CHATEL 64 NA 13
21 MARIGNY LES REULLEE 121 SA 20
45 MARIGNY LES USAGES 81 FA 15
37 MARIGNY MARMANDE 113 Y 20
74 MARIGNY ST MARCEL 139 XA 25
58 MARIGNY SUR YONNE 103 MA 18
16 MARILLAC LE FRANC 143 Y 25
49 MARILLAIS, LE 94 R 18
85 MARILLET 111 T 22
33 MARIMBAULT 170 V 31
57 MARIMONT LES BENESTROFF 47 AB 11
74 MARIN 139 ZA 22
95 MARINES C 39 FA 10
42 MARINGES 150 PA 26
63 MARINGUES C 133 LA 24
03 MARIOL 133 MA 24
83 MARIONS 171 W 31
71 MARIZY 120 QA 22
02 MARIZY ST MARD 41 KA 10
02 MARIZY STE GENEVIEVE 41 KA 10
02 MARLE C 28 NA 7
08 MARLEMONT 29 QA 7
67 MARLENHEIM 49 DB 12
74 MARLENS 153 YA 25
80 MARLERS 25 EA 7
77 MARLES EN BRIE 41 JA 12
62 MARLES LES MINES 17 HA 4
62 MARLES SUR CANCHE 16 EA 4
42 MARLHES 150 OA 27
31 MARLIAC 210 DA 36
21 MARLIENS 105 TA 19
01 MARLIEUX 137 TA 24
74 MARLIOZ 139 XA 24
57 MARLY 46 YA 10
59 MARLY 18 MA 5
02 MARLY GOMONT 19 NA 7
95 MARLY LA VILLE 40 HA 10
78 MARLY LE ROI C 39 FA 11
71 MARLY SOUS ISSY 119 OA 21
71 MARLY SUR ARROUX 119 PA 21
18 MARMAGNE 100 GA 19
21 MARMAGNE 85 QA 17
71 MARMAGNE 120 QA 20
47 MARMANDE S 171 X 31
15 MARMANHAC 161 HA 28
89 MARMEAUX 84 OA 17
46 MARMINIAC 173 BA 30
47 MARMONT PACHAS 187 Z 33
61 MARMOUILLE 58 X 12
67 MARMOUTIER C 49 DB 12
24 MARNAC 158 BA 29
69 MARNAND 136 PA 24
38 MARNANS 151 TA 27
81 MARNAVES 174 FA 32
70 MARNAY C 106 WA 18
71 MARNAY 121 SA 21
86 MARNAY 129 Y 22
52 MARNAY SUR MARNE 86 TA 15
10 MARNAY SUR SEINE 64 MA 13
74 MARNAZ 139 ZA 24
44 MARNE, LA 109 O 20
61 MARNEFER 37 Z 11
79 MARNES 112 W 20
92 MARNES LA COQUETTE 39 GA 11
39 MARNEZIA 122 VA 21
12 MARNHAGUES ET LATOUR 191 KA 33
39 MARNOZ 122 WA 20
62 MAROEUIL 17 IA 5
59 MAROILLES 19 NA 6
41 MAROLLE EN SOLOGNE, LA 81 EA 17
14 MAROLLES 37 Y 10
41 MAROLLES 80 CA 17
51 MAROLLES 43 RA 12
60 MAROLLES 41 KA 10
91 MAROLLES EN BEAUCE 61 GA 13
77 MAROLLES EN BRIE 41 KA 12
94 MAROLLES EN BRIE 40 IA 12

91 MAROLLES EN HUREPOIX 62 GA 13
10 MAROLLES LES BAILLY 65 PA 14
72 MAROLLES LES BRAULTS C 59 Y 14
28 MAROLLES LES BUIS 60 AA 14
72 MAROLLES LES ST CALAIS 79 AA 15
10 MAROLLES SOUS LIGNIERES 84 OA 15
77 MAROLLES SUR SEINE 63 KA 13
72 MAROLLETTE 59 Y 13
42 MAROLS 149 OA 26
76 MAROMME C 24 BA 9
36 MARON 116 EA 20
54 MARON 67 XA 12
88 MARONCOURT 68 YA 14
40 MARPAPS 184 T 35
59 MARPENT 19 OA 5
35 MARPIRE 76 O 15
80 MARQUAIX 17 KA 7
24 MARQUAY 158 BA 29
62 MARQUAY 16 HA 5
31 MARQUEFAVE 210 CA 36
60 MARQUEGLISE 27 IA 8
11 MARQUEIN 211 EA 36
65 MARQUERIE 208 X 36
76 MARQUES 25 EA 7
59 MARQUETTE EN OSTREVANT 18 LA 5
59 MARQUETTE LEZ LILLE 9 KA 3
08 MARQUIGNY 30 RA 8
59 MARQUILLIES 9 JA 4
62 MARQUION C 18 KA 5
62 MARQUISE C 7 EA 3
80 MARQUIVILLERS 27 IA 8
66 MARQUIXANES 222 HA 39
37 MARRAY 79 Z 17
55 MARRE 44 UA 10
39 MARRE, LA 122 WA 21
07 MARS 164 PA 28
30 MARS 192 MA 33
42 MARS 135 PA 23
23 MARS, LES 133 HA 24
54 MARS LA TOUR 45 WA 10
08 MARS SOUS BOURCQ 30 RA 9
58 MARS SUR ALLIER 118 KA 20
11 MARSA 221 GA 38
16 MARSAC 143 W 25
23 MARSAC 131 DA 24
65 MARSAC 208 W 36
82 MARSAC 187 AA 33
63 MARSAC EN LIVRADOIS 149 NA 26
44 MARSAC SUR DON 93 P 17
24 MARSAC SUR L'ISLE 158 Z 28
45 MARSAINVILLIERS 62 GA 14
17 MARSAIS 128 T 23
85 MARSAIS STE RADEGONDE 111 S 22
57 MARSAL 47 AB 12
81 MARSAL 190 GA 33
24 MARSALES 173 AA 30
32 MARSAN 187 Z 34
24 MARSANEIX 158 AA 28
51 MARSANGIS 64 NA 12
89 MARSANGY 63 LA 15
21 MARSANNAY LA COTE 105 SA 18
21 MARSANNAY LE BOIS 105 TA 18
26 MARSANNE C 179 SA 30
33 MARSAS 156 U 28
65 MARSAS 216 X 37
63 MARSAT 134 KA 25
26 MARSAZ 165 SA 28
32 MARSEILLAN 208 Y 35
34 MARSEILLAN 214 MA 36
65 MARSEILLAN 208 X 36
13 MARSEILLE P 202 UA 36
60 MARSEILLE EN BEAUVAISIS C 25 FA 8
18 MARSEILLES LES AUBIGNY 101 JA 19
11 MARSEILLETTE 221 HA 37
34 MARSILLARGUES 193 PA 34
17 MARSILLY 125 R 23
57 MARSILLY 46 YA 10
32 MARSOLAN 187 Z 33
51 MARSON C 43 QA 11
55 MARSON SUR BARBOURE 66 UA 12
01 MARSONNAS 137 TA 23
31 MARSOULAS 218 BA 37
81 MARSSAC SUR TARN 189 FA 33
27 MARTAGNY 25 EA 9
71 MARTAILLY LES BRANCION 120 RA 22
80 MARTAINNEVILLE 15 EA 6
14 MARTAINVILLE 36 V 11
27 MARTAINVILLE 23 Y 9
76 MARTAINVILLE EPREVILLE 24 CA 9
86 MARTAIZE 112 W 20
46 MARTEL C 159 DA 29
54 MARTHEMONT 67 XA 13
57 MARTHILLE 47 ZA 11
73 MARTHOD 153 ZA 25
16 MARTHON 143 Y 26
12 MARTIEL 174 FA 31
39 MARTIGNA 138 VA 22
30 MARTIGNARGUES 193 PA 33
33 MARTIGNAS SUR JALLE 155 T 29
01 MARTIGNAT 138 VA 23
49 MARTIGNE BRIAND 96 U 19
35 MARTIGNE FERCHAUD 76 Q 16
53 MARTIGNE SUR MAYENNE 77 T 14
02 MARTIGNY 28 MA 9
50 MARTIGNY 56 R 12
76 MARTIGNY 24 BA 7
02 MARTIGNY COURPIERRE 28 NA 9
71 MARTIGNY LE COMTE 120 PA 22
88 MARTIGNY LES BAINS 67 WA 15
88 MARTIGNY LES GERBONVAUX 67 WA 13
14 MARTIGNY SUR L'ANTE 36 V 11
13 MARTIGUES C 201 TA 36
33 MARTILLAC 156 U 30
76 MARTIN EGLISE 24 BA 7
54 MARTINCOURT 45 XA 11
60 MARTINCOURT 25 FA 8
55 MARTINCOURT SUR MEUSE 30 TA 8
85 MARTINET 109 P 21
30 MARTINET, LE 178 OA 32
62 MARTINPUICH 17 IA 6
50 MARTINVAST 33 P 8
88 MARTINVELLE 88 XA 15
31 MARTISSERRE 209 AA 36
36 MARTIZAY 114 BA 20
27 MARTOT 38 BA 9
14 MARTRAGNY 35 T 10
83 MARTRE, LA 198 AB 34
33 MARTRES 156 V 30
63 MARTRES D'ARTIERE, LES 148 LA 25
31 MARTRES DE RIVIERE 217 Z 37
63 MARTRES DE VEYRE, LES 148 KA 25
63 MARTRES SUR MORGE 134 KA 24
31 MARTRES TOLOSANE 218 AA 37
12 MARTRIN 190 IA 33
21 MARTROIS 104 QA 18
29 MARTYRE, LA 52 E 13
11 MARTYS, LES 212 GA 36
30 MARUEJOLS LES GARDON 193 OA 33

87 MARVAL 144 AA 26
08 MARVAUX VIEUX 30 RA 9
48 MARVEJOLS C 176 LA 31
25 MARVELISE 89 ZA 17
55 MARVILLE 31 UA 9
28 MARVILLE MOUTIERS BRULE 60 CA 12
71 MARY 120 QA 21
77 MARY SUR MARNE 41 KA 11
56 MARZAN 92 M 17
81 MARZENS 189 EA 34
58 MARZY 118 KA 20
06 MAS, LE 198 BB 34
13 MAS BLANC DES ALPILLES 195 RA 34
11 MAS CABARDES C 212 HA 36
47 MAS D'AGENAIS, LE C 171 X 31
23 MAS D'ARTIGE, LE 146 GA 25
32 MAS D'AUVIGNON 186 Y 33
09 MAS D'AZIL, LE C 218 CA 37
48 MAS D'ORCIERES 177 NA 31
34 MAS DE LONDRES 192 NA 34
43 MAS DE TENCE, LE 164 QA 28
11 MAS DES COURS 221 HA 37
82 MAS GRENIER 188 BA 33
48 MAS ST CHELY 177 LA 31
11 MAS STES PUELLES 211 EA 36
23 MASBARAUD MERIGNAT 131 EA 24
64 MASCARAAS HARON 207 V 35
32 MASCARAS 208 X 35
65 MASCARAS 216 X 37
31 MASCARVILLE 211 EA 35
46 MASCLAT 159 CA 29
68 MASEVAUX C 90 BB 16
64 MASLACQ 206 T 35
87 MASLEON 145 DA 25
41 MASLIVES 80 DA 17
81 MASNAU MASSUGUIES, LE 190 HA 34
59 MASNIERES 18 KA 6
59 MASNY 18 KA 5
66 MASOS, LOS 222 HA 39
64 MASPARRAUTE 206 R 36
64 MASPIE LALONQUERE
JUILLACQ 207 W 36
47 MASQUIERES 173 BA 31
31 MASSABRAC 210 CA 36
11 MASSAC 223 IA 38
17 MASSAC 128 V 25
81 MASSAC SERAN 189 EA 34
81 MASSAGUEL 212 GA 35
79 MASSAIS 96 V 20
81 MASSALS 190 HA 34
30 MASSANES 193 OA 33
89 MASSANGIS 84 OA 17
09 MASSAT C 219 CA 38
18 MASSAY 100 FA 19
48 MASSEGROS, LE C 176 KA 32
33 MASSEILLES 171 W 31
47 MASSELS 172 AA 32
44 MASSERAC 93 O 17
19 MASSERET 145 DA 26
32 MASSEUBE C 209 Z 35
15 MASSIAC C 162 KA 27
38 MASSIEU 152 VA 27
01 MASSIEUX 137 SA 24
51 MASSIGES 43 RA 10
16 MASSIGNAC 144 Z 25
01 MASSIGNIEU DE RIVES 152 WA 25
30 MASSILARGUES ATTUECH 193 OA 33
71 MASSILLY 120 RA 22
21 MASSINGY 85 RA 16
74 MASSINGY 138 WA 25
21 MASSINGY LES SEMUR 85 OA 17
21 MASSINGY LES VITTEAUX 104 RA 18
86 MASSOGNES 112 W 21
06 MASSOINS 199 CB 33
74 MASSONGY 139 YA 23
47 MASSOULES 172 AA 31
33 MASSUGAS 157 X 30
71 MASSY 120 RA 22
76 MASSY 25 CA 8
91 MASSY C 40 GA 12
59 MASTAING 18 LA 5
01 MATAFELON GRANGES 138 VA 23
34 MATELLES, LES C 192 NA 34
66 MATEMALE 222 GA 39
17 MATHA C 128 V 25
10 MATHAUX 65 QA 14
25 MATHAY 108 AB 18
39 MATHENAY 122 VA 20
17 MATHES, LES 141 R 25
14 MATHIEU 36 V 10
52 MATHONS 66 TA 13
76 MATHONVILLE 25 CA 8
51 MATIGNICOURT GONCOURT 43 RA 12
22 MATIGNON C 55 M 13
80 MATIGNY 27 KA 7
51 MATOUGUES 43 PA 11
71 MATOUR C 136 QA 23
2B MATRA 228 MB 41
62 MATRINGHEM 8 GA 4
88 MATTAINCOURT 67 XA 14
54 MATTEXEY 68 ZA 13
08 MATTON ET CLEMENCY 30 TA 8
67 MATZENHEIM 70 EB 13
38 MAUBEC 151 TA 26
82 MAUBEC 187 AA 34
84 MAUBEC 196 TA 34
08 MAUBERT FONTAINE 29 OA 7
59 MAUBEUGE C 19 OA 5
65 MAUBOURGUET C 208 W 35
91 MAUCHAMPS 61 GA 13
76 MAUCOMBLE 24 CA 8
64 MAUCOR 207 V 36
80 MAUCOURT 27 KA 8
60 MAUCOURT 27 IA 7
55 MAUCOURT SUR ORNE 45 VA 10
95 MAUDETOUR EN VEXIN 39 EA 10
34 MAUGUIO C 194 OA 35
55 MAULAN 44 TA 12
86 MAULAY 113 X 20
59 MAULDE 18 LA 4
78 MAULE 39 EA 11
79 MAULEON C 111 T 20
65 MAULEON BAROUSSE C 217 Z 38
32 MAULEON D'ARMAGNAC 185 V 33
64 MAULEON LICHARRE C 206 S 36
60 MAULERS 26 GA 8
78 MAULETTE 39 DA 12
49 MAULEVRIER 95 T 20
76 MAULEVRIER STE GERTRUDE 24 Z 8
32 MAULICHERES 185 W 34
44 MAUMUSSON 94 R 17
82 MAUMUSSON 187 AA 33
32 MAUMUSSON LAGUIAN 207 W 35
76 MAUNY 24 AA 9
10 MAUPAS 64 OA 15
32 MAUPAS 185 V 34
77 MAUPERTHUIS 41 KA 12
50 MAUPERTUIS 34 R 11
50 MAUPERTUS SUR MER 33 O 8
86 MAUPREVOIR 129 Y 23
76 MAUQUENCHY 25 DA 8
31 MAURAN 218 BA 37
64 MAURE 208 W 36
35 MAURE DE BRETAGNE C 75 N 16
78 MAURECOURT 39 FA 11
77 MAUREGARD 40 IA 11
02 MAUREGNY EN HAYE 28 NA 8
34 MAUREILHAN 213 KA 36
66 MAUREILLAS LAS ILLAS 224 JA 40
31 MAUREMONT 211 EA 35
24 MAURENS 157 Y 29
31 MAURENS 211 EA 35
32 MAURENS 209 AA 35
81 MAURENS SCOPONT 211 EA 35
78 MAUREPAS C 39 FA 12
80 MAUREPAS 17 JA 6
31 MAURESSAC 210 CA 36
30 MAURESSARGUES 193 PA 33
31 MAUREVILLE 211 EA 35
15 MAURIAC S 160 GA 28
33 MAURIAC 157 W 30
40 MAURIES 207 V 35
15 MAURINES 162 KA 29
59 MAUROIS 18 MA 6
56 MAURON C 74 M 15
32 MAUROUX 187 AA 33
46 MAUROUX 173 BA 31
40 MAURRIN 184 U 34
15 MAURS C 160 GA 30
51 MAURUPT LE MONTOIS 44 SA 12
66 MAURY 223 IA 38
2B MAUSOLEO 225 KB 40
19 MAUSSAC 146 GA 26
13 MAUSSANE LES ALPILLES 195 SA 34
70 MAUSSANS 107 XA 18
23 MAUTES 132 HA 24
55 MAUVAGES 67 VA 13
31 MAUVAISIN 210 DA 36
07 MAUVES 165 SA 28
61 MAUVES SUR HUISNE 59 Z 13
44 MAUVES SUR LOIRE 94 Q 18
31 MAUVEZIN 209 AA 36
32 MAUVEZIN C 187 AA 34
65 MAUVEZIN 216 X 37
40 MAUVEZIN D'ARMAGNAC 185 W 33
09 MAUVEZIN DE PRAT 218 BA 37
09 MAUVEZIN DE STE CROIX 218 CA 37
36 MAUVIERES 114 BA 22
21 MAUVILLY 85 RA 16
58 MAUX 103 NA 19
31 MAUZAC 210 CA 36
24 MAUZAC
ET GRAND CASTANG 158 AA 29
79 MAUZE SUR LE MIGNON C 127 T 23
79 MAUZE THOUARSAIS 112 V 20
24 MAUZENS ET MIREMONT 158 AA 29
63 MAUZUN 148 LA 25
41 MAVES 80 CA 16
21 MAVILLY MANDELOT 104 RA 19
57 MAXE, LA 46 YA 10
35 MAXENT 75 N 15
54 MAXEVILLE 46 XA 12
88 MAXEY SUR MEUSE 67 VA 13
55 MAXEY SUR VAISE 67 VA 13
74 MAXILLY SUR LEMAN 124 AB 22
21 MAXILLY SUR SAONE 106 UA 18
46 MAXOU 173 CA 31
57 MAXSTADT 47 AB 11
77 MAY EN MULTIEN 41 KA 10
49 MAY SUR EVRE, LE 95 S 19
14 MAY SUR ORNE 36 V 10
24 MAYAC 144 AA 27
53 MAYENNE S 57 T 14
72 MAYET C 78 X 16
03 MAYET D'ECOLE, LE 133 LA 23
03 MAYET DE MONTAGNE, LE C 135 NA 24
40 MAYLIS 184 T 34
39 MAYNAL 122 UA 22
83 MAYONS, LES 203 YA 36
02 MAYOT 28 LA 8
46 MAYRAC 159 DA 29
12 MAYRAN 175 HA 31
31 MAYREGNE 217 Z 38
07 MAYRES 178 OA 30
63 MAYRES 149 NA 27
38 MAYRES SAVEL 166 WA 29
11 MAYREVILLE 211 EA 36
46 MAYRINHAC LENTOUR 160 EA 29
11 MAYRONNES 221 HA 37
60 MAYSEL 40 HA 10
81 MAZAMET C 212 HA 35
84 MAZAN 195 TA 33
07 MAZAN L'ABBAYE 163 OA 30
41 MAZANGE 79 AA 16
83 MAZAUGUES 203 WA 36
63 MAZAYE 147 JA 25
49 MAZE 96 V 18
85 MAZEAU, LE 127 T 23
23 MAZEIRAT 132 FA 23
88 MAZELEY 68 YA 14
17 MAZERAY 128 T 24
09 MAZERES 211 DA 36
33 MAZERES 170 V 31
65 MAZERES DE NESTE 217 Z 37
64 MAZERES LEZONS 207 U 36
31 MAZERES SUR SALAT 217 AA 37
03 MAZERIER 134 KA 24
08 MAZERNY 30 RA 8
16 MAZEROLLES 143 Y 25
17 MAZEROLLES 142 T 26
40 MAZEROLLES 184 U 34
64 MAZEROLLES 207 U 35
65 MAZEROLLES 208 X 36
86 MAZEROLLES 130 Z 22
11 MAZEROLLES DU RAZES 221 FA 37
25 MAZEROLLES LE SALIN 106 WA 19
54 MAZERULLES 46 YA 12
43 MAZET ST VOY 163 PA 28
86 MAZEUIL 112 W 21
43 MAZERAT AUROUZE 162 MA 28
43 MAZEYRAT D'ALLIER 162 MA 28
24 MAZEYROLLES 173 BA 30
23 MAZIERE
AUX BONS HOMMES, LA 133 HA 25
16 MAZIERES 143 Z 25
37 MAZIERES DE TOURAINE 97 Y 18
79 MAZIERES EN GATINE C 112 V 22
49 MAZIERES EN MAUGES 95 T 19
47 MAZIERES NARESSE 172 Z 30
79 MAZIERES SUR BERONNE 128 V 23
71 MAZILLE 136 RA 22
62 MAZINGARBE 17 IA 4
62 MAZINGHEM 8 HA 4
59 MAZINGHIEN 18 MA 6
33 MAZION 156 T 28
03 MAZIRAT 133 HA 23
88 MAZIROT 68 XA 14
80 MAZIS, LE 25 EA 7
63 MAZOIRES 148 KA 27
65 MAZOUAU 216 Y 37
11 MAZUBY 221 FA 38
08 MAZURES, LES 29 RA 7
2B MAZZOLA 228 MB 40
04 MEAILLES 198 AB 33
15 MEALLET 161 HA 27
23 MEASNES 131 EA 22
28 MEAUCE 60 BA 13
38 MEAUDRE 166 VA 28
50 MEAUFFE, LA 34 R 10
22 MEAUGON, LA 54 K 13
03 MEAULNE 117 IA 21
80 MEAULTE 17 IA 6
50 MEAUTIS 34 O 9
77 MEAUX S 41 JA 11
69 MEAUX LA MONTAGNE 136 QA 24
82 MEAUZAC 188 CA 33
35 MECE 76 O 14
46 MECHMONT 173 DA 30
57 MECLEUVES 46 YA 11
59 MECQUIGNIES 19 NA 5
55 MECRIN 45 VA 12
51 MECRINGES 41 MA 11
78 MEDAN 39 FA 11
61 MEDAVY 58 X 12
63 MEDEYROLLES 149 NA 27
25 MEDIERE 107 ZA 18
16 MEDILLAC 143 W 27
17 MEDIS 141 S 26
88 MEDONVILLE 67 VA 14
35 MEDREAC 75 N 14
53 MEE 77 S 16
28 MEE, LE 80 CA 15
77 MEE SUR SEINE, LE 62 IA 13
40 MEES 183 R 34
04 MEES, LES C 197 XA 33
72 MEES, LES 58 X 14
57 MEGANGE 47 ZA 10
74 MEGEVE 140 ZA 25
74 MEGEVETTE 139 ZA 23
22 MEGRIT 55 M 14
80 MEHARICOURT 27 IA 7
64 MEHARIN 206 R 36
41 MEHERS 99 DA 18
54 MEHONCOURT 68 ZA 13
61 MEHOUDIN 58 V 13
18 MEHUN SUR YEVRE C 100 GA 19
49 MEIGNANNE, LA 95 T 17
49 MEIGNE 96 V 19
49 MEIGNE LE VICOMTE 97 X 17
77 MEIGNEUX 63 KA 13
80 MEIGNEUX 26 FA 7
29 MEILARS 71 C 15
87 MEILHAC 144 BA 25
32 MEILHAN 209 Z 35
40 MEILHAN 184 T 34
47 MEILHAN SUR GARONNE C 171 W 31
19 MEILHARDS 145 DA 26
63 MEILHAUD 148 KA 26
35 MEILLAC 55 O 13
18 MEILLANT 117 HA 21
03 MEILLARD 134 LA 22
80 MEILLARD, LE 16 GA 6
85 MEILLERAIE TILLAY, LA 111 S 21
77 MEILLERAY 41 LA 12
44 MEILLERAYE DE BRETAGNE, LA 94 O 17
74 MEILLERIE 124 AB 22
03 MEILLERS 118 KA 22
64 MEILLON 207 V 36
01 MEILLONNAS 137 UA 23
21 MEILLY SUR ROUVRES 104 QA 19
57 MEISENTHAL 48 DB 11
67 MEISTRATZHEIM 70 EB 13
21 MEIX, LE 86 SA 17
51 MEIX ST EPOING, LE 42 MA 12
51 MEIX TIERCELIN, LE 65 QA 12
30 MEJANNES LE CLAP 178 PA 32
30 MEJANNES LES ALES 178 PA 32
2A MELA 230 LB 43
12 MELAGUES 191 KA 34
76 MELAMARE 23 Y 8
49 MELAY 95 T 19
52 MELAY 87 WA 16
71 MELAY 135 OA 23
61 MELE SUR SARTHE, LE C 59 Y 13
70 MELECEY 89 ZA 17
35 MELESSE 75 P 14
29 MELGVEN 72 F 16
60 MELICOCQ 27 JA 9
27 MELICOURT 37 Y 11
55 MELIGNY LE GRAND 45 VA 12
55 MELIGNY LE PETIT 44 UA 12
70 MELIN 87 WA 16
70 MELINCOURT 88 XA 16
70 MELISEY C 89 ZA 16
89 MELISEY 84 OA 16
12 MELJAC 175 HA 32
29 MELLAC 72 G 16
35 MELLE 56 R 13
79 MELLE C 128 V 23
71 MELLECEY 120 RA 20
79 MELLERAN 129 W 23
72 MELLERAY 59 AA 15
45 MELLEROY 83 JA 16
31 MELLES 217 AA 38
76 MELLEVILLE 15 DA 6
22 MELLIONNEC 73 I 14
60 MELLO 40 HA 10
21 MELOISEY 104 RA 19
56 MELRAND 73 I 15
67 MELSHEIM 49 DB 12
77 MELUN P 62 IA 13
04 MELVE 181 XA 31
77 MELZ SUR SEINE 63 LA 13
70 MEMBREY 87 WA 17
37 MEMBROLLE
SUR CHOISILLE, LA 98 Z 18
49 MEMBROLLE
SUR LONGUENEE, LE 95 T 17
41 MEMBROLLES 80 DA 15
88 MEMENIL 68 AB 14
67 MEMMELSHOFFEN 49 FB 11
25 MEMONT, LE 108 AB 19
89 MENADES 103 NA 18
88 MENARMONT 68 AB 13
41 MENARS 80 CA 17
63 MENAT C 133 JA 24
55 MENAUCOURT 44 UA 12
62 MENCAS 8 GA 4
67 MENCHHOFFEN 48 DB 11
48 MENDE P 177 MA 31
64 MENDIONDE 205 O 36
64 MENDITTE 206 S 37
64 MENDIVE 206 R 37
56 MENEAC 74 L 15
84 MENERBES 196 TA 34
76 MENERVAL 25 DA 8
78 MENERVILLE 39 DA 11
21 MENESBLE 86 SA 16
80 MENESLIES 15 DA 6
24 MENESPLET 157 W 28
27 MENESQUEVILLE 25 CA 9
21 MENESSAIRE 103 PA 19
58 MENESTREAU 102 LA 18
45 MENESTREAU EN VILLETTE 81 FA 16
15 MENET 147 IA 27
18 MENETOU COUTURE 101 JA 19
18 MENETOU RATEL 101 IA 18
18 MENETOU SALON 101 HA 19
36 MENETOU SUR NAHON 99 DA 19
18 MENETREOL
SOUS SANCERRE 101 JA 18
18 MENETREOL SUR SAULDRE 100 GA 18
36 MENETREOLS SOUS VATAN 115 EA 20
71 MENETREUIL 121 TA 21
21 MENETREUX LE PITOIS 85 QA 17
63 MENETROL 134 KA 25
39 MENETRU LE VIGNOBLE 122 VA 21
39 MENETRUX EN JOUX 122 WA 21
60 MENEVILLERS 26 IA 8
26 MENGLON 166 UA 30
79 MENIGOUTE C 112 W 22
53 MENIL 77 T 16
88 MENIL, LE 89 AB 16
08 MENIL ANNELLES 29 OA 9
55 MENIL AUX BOIS 44 UA 12
61 MENIL BERARD, LE 37 Y 12
61 MENIL BROUT, LE 58 X 13
61 MENIL CIBOULT, LE 57 T 12
61 MENIL DE BRIOUZE, LE 58 U 12
88 MENIL DE SENONES 69 BB 13
88 MENIL EN XAINTOIS 67 XA 14
61 MENIL ERREUX 58 X 13
61 MENIL FROGER 37 X 12
61 MENIL GONDOUIN 58 V 12
61 MENIL GUYON, LE 59 X 13
61 MENIL HERMEI 36 V 11
61 MENIL HUBERT EN EXMES 58 X 12
61 MENIL HUBERT SUR ORNE 35 U 11
61 MENIL JEAN 58 V 12
55 MENIL LA HORGNE 45 VA 12
54 MENIL LA TOUR 45 WA 12
08 MENIL LEPINOIS 28 LA 9
61 MENIL SCELLEUR, LE 58 W 12
88 MENIL SUR BELVITTE 68 AB 13
55 MENIL SUR SAULX 66 TA 12
61 MENIL VICOMTE, LE 37 Y 12
61 MENIL VIN 36 V 11
27 MENILLES 38 CA 11
49 MENITRE, LA 96 V 18
91 MENNECY C 62 HA 13
02 MENNESSIS 27 LA 7
41 MENNETOU SUR CHER C 100 EA 18
27 MENNEVAL 37 Z 10
02 MENNEVILLE 29 OA 9
62 MENNEVILLE 7 EA 3
02 MENNEVRET 18 MA 6
52 MENNOUVEAUX 66 UA 15
19 MENOIRE 159 EA 28
85 MENOMBLET 111 T 21
90 MENONCORT 90 BB 17
76 MENONVAL 25 DA 7
39 MENOTEY 106 VA 19
58 MENOU 102 LA 18
95 MENOUVILLE 39 FA 10
70 MENOUX 88 XA 16
36 MENOUX, LE 115 DA 22
38 MENS C 166 WA 29
24 MENSIGNAC 143 Y 27
57 MENSKIRCH 47 ZA 9
76 MENTHEVILLE 23 Y 8
74 MENTHON ST BERNARD 139 YA 25
74 MENTHONNEX EN BORNES 139 XA 24
74 MENTHONNEX
SOUS CLERMONT 139 XA 24
15 MENTIERES 162 KA 28
06 MENTON C 200 EB 34
62 MENTQUE NORTBECOURT 7 FA 3
95 MENUCOURT 39 FA 11
61 MENUS, LES 59 AA 13
31 MENVILLE 188 BA 34
36 MEOBECQ 115 CA 21
04 MEOLANS REVEL 182 ZA 31
49 MEON 97 X 17
83 MEOUNES LES MONTRIEUX 203 XA 36
41 MER C 80 DA 16
64 MERACQ 207 U 35
53 MERAL 76 S 15
09 MERAS 218 CA 37
62 MERCATEL 17 JA 5
09 MERCENAC 218 BA 37
21 MERCEUIL 121 SA 20
27 MERCEY 38 CA 10
25 MERCEY LE GRAND 106 WA 19
70 MERCEY SUR SAONE 87 WA 17
02 MERCIN ET VAUX 28 LA 9
62 MERCK ST LIEVIN 7 GA 3
59 MERCKEGHEM 8 GA 2
19 MERCOEUR C 160 FA 28
43 MERCOEUR 162 LA 28
07 MERCUER 178 PA 30
46 MERCUES 173 CA 31
71 MERCUREY 120 RA 20
26 MERCUROL 165 SA 28
73 MERCURY 153 YA 26
09 MERCUS GARRABET 219 DA 38
03 MERCY 118 MA 22
89 MERCY 84 MA 15
54 MERCY LE BAS 31 WA 9
54 MERCY LE HAUT 31 WA 9
22 MERDRIGNAC C 74 L 14
28 MERE 39 EA 12
89 MERE 84 NA 16
18 MEREAU 100 FA 19
80 MEREAUCOURT 26 FA 7
28 MEREGLISE 60 BA 14
80 MERELESSART 16 EA 6
32 MERENS 187 Z 34
09 MERENS LES VALS 220 EA 39
31 MERENVIELLE 210 BA 35
05 MEREUIL 180 VA 31
54 MEREVILLE 67 XA 13
91 MEREVILLE C 61 FA 14
27 MEREY 38 CA 11
25 MEREY SOUS MONTROND 107 XA 19
25 MEREY VIEILLEY 107 XA 18
51 MERFY 42 OA 9
10 MERGEY 64 OA 13
2B MERIA 226 MB 38
11 MERIAL 223 FA 38
62 MERICOURT 17 JA 5
78 MERICOURT 39 DA 11
80 MERICOURT EN VIMEU 26 FA 7
80 MERICOURT L'ABBE 17 IA 7
80 MERICOURT SUR SOMME 27 IA 7
95 MERIEL 39 GA 10
34 MERIFONS 213 LA 35
16 MERIGNAC 142 W 25
17 MERIGNAC 142 V 27
33 MERIGNAC C 155 T 29
33 MERIGNAS 156 W 29
01 MERIGNAT 138 UA 24
59 MERIGNIES 18 KA 4
36 MERIGNY 114 AA 21
09 MERIGON 218 BA 37
65 MERILHEU 216 X 37
22 MERILLAC 74 M 14
23 MERINCHAL 133 HA 24
84 MERINDOL 196 TA 34
26 MERINDOL LES OLIVIERS 180 TA 32
45 MERINVILLE 83 JA 15
10 MERIOT, LE 63 LA 14
64 MERITEIN 206 T 36
67 MERKWILLER PECHELBRONN 49 FB 11
38 MERLAS 152 VA 27
85 MERLATIERE, LA 110 Q 21
51 MERLAUT 43 RA 12
42 MERLE LEIGNECQ 149 OA 27
22 MERLEAC 73 J 14
61 MERLERAULT, LE C 37 Y 12
82 MERLES 187 AA 33
55 MERLES SUR LOISON 31 VA 9
56 MERLEVENEZ 73 I 16
02 MERLIEUX ET FOUQUEROLLES 28 MA 8
62 MERLIMONT 15 DA 4
19 MERLINES 147 HA 26
35 MERNEL 75 N 16
91 MEROBERT 61 FA 13
39 MERONA 122 VA 22
28 MEROUVILLE 61 FA 14
90 MEROUX MOVAL 89 BB 17
16 MERPINS 142 U 25
52 MERREY 67 VA 15
10 MERREY SUR ARCE 65 OA 15
61 MERRI 36 W 11
59 MERRIS 8 IA 3
89 MERRY LA VALLEE 83 LA 16
89 MERRY SEC 83 MA 17
89 MERRY SUR YONNE 84 MA 17
80 MERS LES BAINS 15 CA 6
36 MERS SUR INDRE 116 EA 21
57 MERSCHWEILLER 32 ZA 9
70 MERSUAY 88 XA 16
57 MERTEN 47 AB 10
52 MERTRUD 66 SA 13
68 MERTZEN 90 CB 17
67 MERTZWILLER 48 EB 11
60 MERU C 39 GA 10
02 MERVAL 28 NA 9
71 MERVANS 121 TA 21
85 MERVENT 111 T 22
31 MERVILLA 210 DA 35
31 MERVILLE 188 CA 34
59 MERVILLE C 8 IA 3
14 MERVILLE
FRANCEVILLE PLAGE 36 V 9
54 MERVILLER 69 AB 13
68 MERXHEIM 90 DB 16
73 MERY 153 XA 26
14 MERY CORBON 36 W 10
18 MERY ES BOIS 100 HA 18
60 MERY LA BATAILLE 27 IA 8
51 MERY PREMECY 42 NA 10
18 MERY SUR CHER 100 FA 19
77 MERY SUR MARNE 41 KA 11
95 MERY SUR OISE 39 GA 10
10 MERY SUR SEINE C 64 NA 13
22 MERZER, LE 53 J 13
25 MESANDANS 107 YA 18
44 MESANGER 94 R 18
76 MESANGUEVILLE 25 DA 8
02 MESBRECOURT RICHECOURT 28 MA 8
17 MESCHERS SUR GIRONDE 141 S 26
24 MESCOULES 157 Y 30
80 MESGE, LE 16 FA 7
10 MESGRIGNY 64 NA 13
74 MESIGNY 139 XA 24
56 MESLAN 73 H 15
41 MESLAND 80 BA 17
14 MESLAY 36 U 11
41 MESLAY 80 BA 16
53 MESLAY DU MAINE C 77 U 15
28 MESLAY LE GRENET 60 CA 14
28 MESLAY LE VIDAME 60 DA 14
25 MESLIERES 108 BB 18
22 MESLIN 54 L 13
25 MESMAY 106 WA 19
08 MESMONT 29 OA 8
21 MESMONT 104 RA 18
16 MESNAC 142 V 25
85 MESNARD LA BAROTIERE 110 R 20
39 MESNAY 122 WA 20
51 MESNEUX, LES 42 OA 10
61 MESNIERE, LA 59 Y 13
76 MESNIERES EN BRAY 25 CA 7
50 MESNIL, LE 33 P 9
50 MESNIL ADELEE, LE 56 R 12
50 MESNIL AMAND, LE 56 Q 11
77 MESNIL AMELOT, LE 40 IA 11
50 MESNIL AMEY, LE 34 R 10
50 MESNIL ANGOT, LE 34 R 10
14 MESNIL AU GRAIN, LE 35 T 10
50 MESNIL AU VAL, LE 33 P 8
50 MESNIL AUBERT, LE 34 Q 11
95 MESNIL AUBRY, LE 40 HA 10
14 MESNIL AUZOUF, LE 35 T 11
14 MESNIL BACLEY, LE 36 X 11
14 MESNIL BENOIST, LE 35 S 11
80 MESNIL BRUNTEL 27 JA 7
14 MESNIL CAUSSOIS, LE 35 S 11
14 MESNIL CLINCHAMPS 35 S 11
60 MESNIL CONTEVILLE, LE 26 FA 8
80 MESNIL DOMQUEUR 16 FA 6
14 MESNIL DURAND, LE 36 X 10
76 MESNIL DURDENT, LE 24 AA 7
80 MESNIL EN ARROUAISE 17 JA 6
60 MESNIL EN THELLE, LE 40 GA 10
49 MESNIL EN VALLEE, LE 95 S 18
76 MESNIL ESNARD, LE 24 BA 9
14 MESNIL EUDES, LE 36 X 10
50 MESNIL EURY, LE 34 R 10
76 MESNIL FOLLEMPRISE 24 CA 7
27 MESNIL FUGUET, LE 38 BA 10
50 MESNIL GARNIER, LE 56 Q 11
14 MESNIL GERMAIN, LE 36 X 11
50 MESNIL GILBERT, LE 56 R 12
14 MESNIL GUILLAUME, LE 37 X 10
27 MESNIL HARDRAY, LE 38 BA 11
50 MESNIL HERMAN, LE 34 R 11
27 MESNIL JOURDAIN, LE 38 BA 10
10 MESNIL LA COMTESSE 65 PA 13

Dép.	Commune		Page	Carré	
78	MESNIL LE ROI, LE		39	GA	11
10	MESNIL LETTRE		65	PA	13
76	MESNIL LIEUBRAY, LE		25	DA	8
80	MESNIL MARTINSART		17	IA	6
76	MESNIL MAUGER		25	DA	8
14	MESNIL MAUGER, LE		36	W	10
50	MESNIL OPAC, LE		34	R	11
50	MESNIL OZENNE, LE		56	R	12
76	MESNIL PANNEVILLE		24	AA	8
14	MESNIL PATRY, LE		35	U	10
50	MESNIL RAINFRAY, LE		56	R	12
76	MESNIL RAOUL		24	CA	9
50	MESNIL RAOULT, LE		34	R	11
76	MESNIL REAUME, LE		15	CA	6
14	MESNIL ROBERT, LE		35	S	11
50	MESNIL ROGUES, LE		56	O	11
27	MESNIL ROUSSET		37	Z	11
50	MESNIL ROUXELIN, LE		34	R	10
10	MESNIL SELLIERES		65	PA	14
14	MESNIL SIMON, LE		36	X	10
28	MESNIL SIMON, LE		38	DA	11
76	MESNIL SOUS JUMIEGES, LE		24	AA	9
27	MESNIL SOUS VIENNE		25	EA	9
78	MESNIL ST DENIS, LE		39	FA	12
60	MESNIL ST FIRMIN, LE		26	HA	8
80	MESNIL ST GEORGES		26	HA	8
02	MESNIL ST LAURENT		28	LA	7
10	MESNIL ST LOUP		64	NA	14
80	MESNIL ST NICAISE		27	JA	7
10	MESNIL ST PERE		65	PA	14
14	MESNIL SUR BLANGY, LE		37	X	10
60	MESNIL SUR BULLES, LE		26	HA	9
27	MESNIL SUR L'ESTREE		38	CA	12
51	MESNIL SUR OGER, LE		42	OA	11
60	MESNIL THERIBUS, LE		39	FA	9
28	MESNIL THOMAS, LE		60	BA	12
50	MESNIL TOVE, LE		57	S	12
50	MESNIL VENERON, LE		34	R	10
27	MESNIL VERCLIVES		25	DA	9
50	MESNIL VIGOT, LE		34	O	10
50	MESNIL VILLEMAN, LE		56	Q	11
14	MESNIL VILLEMENT, LE		36	V	11
50	MESNILBUS, LE		34	Q	10
50	MESNILLARD, LE		56	R	12
39	MESNOIS		122	VA	21
78	MESNULS, LES		39	EA	12
29	MESPAUL		52	E	12
64	MESPLEDE		207	T	35
03	MESPLES		132	HA	22
91	MESPUITS		62	GA	14
44	MESQUER		92	L	18
17	MESSAC		142	V	27
35	MESSAC		75	O	16
21	MESSANGES		105	SA	19
40	MESSANGES		183	Q	34
45	MESSAS		80	DA	16
79	MESSE		129	X	23
61	MESSEI	C	57	U	12
54	MESSEIN		67	XA	12
63	MESSEIX		147	HA	26
86	MESSEME		113	X	20
74	MESSERY		139	YA	23
71	MESSEY SUR GROSNE		120	RA	21
39	MESSIA SUR SORNE		122	VA	21
21	MESSIGNY ET VANTOUX		105	SA	18
69	MESSIMY		150	RA	25
01	MESSIMY SUR SAONE		136	RA	24
08	MESSINCOURT		30	TA	8
10	MESSON		64	OA	14
77	MESSY		40	IA	11
33	MESTERRIEUX		171	W	30
19	MESTES		146	GA	26
58	MESVES SUR LOIRE		102	KA	19
71	MESVRES	C	120	PA	20
25	METABIEF		123	YA	21
16	METAIRIES, LES		142	V	25
57	METAIRIES ST QUIRIN		69	BB	12
59	METEREN		8	IA	3
84	METHAMIS		196	TA	33
80	METIGNY		16	FA	7
57	METTING		48	CB	12
37	METTRAY		98	Z	18
57	METZ	P	46	YA	10
62	METZ EN COUTURE		18	KA	6
58	METZ LE COMTE		103	MA	18
10	METZ ROBERT		64	OA	15
74	METZ TESSY		139	XA	24
68	METZERAL		90	CB	15
57	METZERESCHE		32	YA	9
57	METZERVISSE	C	32	YA	9
57	METZING		47	BB	10
56	MEUCON		74	K	16
92	MEUDON	C	40	GA	12
21	MEUILLEY		105	SA	19
78	MEULAN	C	39	FA	11
76	MEULERS		24	CA	7
14	MEULLES		37	Y	11
21	MEULSON		85	RA	17
36	MEUNET PLANCHES		116	FA	20
36	MEUNET SUR VATAN		99	EA	19
45	MEUNG SUR LOIRE	C	81	EA	16
72	MEURCE		58	X	14
62	MEURCHIN		17	JA	4
70	MEURCOURT		88	YA	16
50	MEURDRAQUIERE, LA		56	Q	11
52	MEURES		66	TA	14
02	MEURIVAL		28	NA	9
17	MEURSAC		141	T	26
21	MEURSANGES		121	SA	20
21	MEURSAULT		120	RA	20
10	MEURVILLE		65	RA	14
41	MEUSNES		99	DA	19
39	MEUSSIA		122	WA	22
14	MEUVAINES		35	U	9
17	MEUX		142	V	27
60	MEUX, LE		27	IA	9
87	MEUZAC		145	DA	26
28	MEVOISINS		61	DA	13
26	MEVOUILLON		180	VA	32
01	MEXIMIEUX	C	137	TA	24
54	MEXY		31	WA	9
57	MEY		46	YA	10
68	MEYENHEIM		90	DB	16
38	MEYLAN	C	166	WA	28
19	MEYMAC	C	146	GA	26
30	MEYNES		193	QA	33
24	MEYRALS		158	BA	29
30	MEYRANNES		178	PA	32
13	MEYRARGUES		202	VA	35
07	MEYRAS		178	PA	30
13	MEYREUIL		202	VA	35
38	MEYRIE		151	UA	26
38	MEYRIEU LES ETANGS		151	TA	26
73	MEYRIEUX TROUET		152	WA	26
19	MEYRIGNAC L'EGLISE		146	EA	27
46	MEYRONNE		159	DA	29
04	MEYRONNES		182	AB	31
48	MEYRUEIS	C	177	LA	32
69	MEYS		150	QA	25
19	MEYSSAC	C	159	EA	28
07	MEYSSE		179	RA	30
38	MEYSSIES		151	TA	26
74	MEYTHET		139	XA	24
87	MEYZE, LA		144	BA	26
69	MEYZIEU	C	151	SA	25
53	MEZANGERS		77	U	14
34	MEZE	C	214	MA	36
04	MEZEL	C	197	YA	33
63	MEZEL		148	KA	25
81	MEZENS		188	DA	34
72	MEZERAY		78	W	16
43	MEZERES		163	OA	28
01	MEZERIAT		137	SA	23
80	MEZEROLLES		16	GA	5
11	MEZERVILLE		211	EA	36
14	MEZIDON CANON	C	36	W	10
35	MEZIERE, LA		75	O	14
28	MEZIERES AU PERCHE		60	CA	14
36	MEZIERES EN BRENNE	C	114	BA	20
28	MEZIERES EN DROUAIS		38	DA	12
45	MEZIERES EN GATINAIS		82	HA	15
80	MEZIERES EN SANTERRE		26	HA	7
27	MEZIERES EN VEXIN		38	DA	10
45	MEZIERES LEZ CLERY		81	EA	16
72	MEZIERES SOUS LAVARDIN		78	W	14
35	MEZIERES SUR COUESNON		76	Q	14
87	MEZIERES SUR ISSOIRE	C	130	AA	24
02	MEZIERES SUR OISE		28	LA	7
72	MEZIERES SUR PONTHOUIN		59	Y	14
78	MEZIERES SUR SEINE		39	EA	11
07	MEZILHAC		164	QA	29
89	MEZILLES		83	KA	16
47	MEZIN	C	186	X	33
90	MEZIRE		90	BB	17
40	MEZOS		183	R	33
02	MEZY MOULINS		41	MA	10
78	MEZY SUR SEINE		39	EA	11
58	MHERE		103	NA	19
24	MIALET		144	AA	26
30	MIALET		178	OA	32
64	MIALOS		207	U	35
80	MIANNAY		15	EA	6
58	MICHAUGUES		102	MA	18
68	MICHELBACH		90	CB	16
68	MICHELBACH LE BAS		90	DB	17
68	MICHELBACH LE HAUT		90	DB	17
89	MICHERY		63	KA	14
88	MIDREVAUX		67	VA	13
39	MIEGES		123	XA	21
32	MIELAN	C	208	Y	35
70	MIELLIN		89	AB	16
28	MIERMAIGNE		60	BA	14
46	MIERS		159	EA	29
39	MIERY		122	VA	20
67	MIETESHEIM		48	EB	11
74	MIEUSSY		139	ZA	23
61	MIEUXCE		58	W	13
89	MIGE		83	MA	17
89	MIGENNES	C	83	MA	15
09	MIGLOS		220	DA	38
86	MIGNALOUX BEAUVOIR		113	Y	22
70	MIGNAVILLERS		89	ZA	17
36	MIGNE		115	CA	21
86	MIGNE AUXANCES		113	X	21
45	MIGNERES		82	IA	15
45	MIGNERETTE		82	IA	15
54	MIGNEVILLE		69	AB	13
28	MIGNIERES		60	CA	14
39	MIGNOVILLARD		123	XA	21
36	MIGNY		116	FA	20
17	MIGRE		128	U	24
17	MIGRON		142	U	25
09	MIJANES		222	FA	39
01	MIJOUX		139	XA	22
72	MILESSE, LA		78	X	15
46	MILHAC		159	CA	29
24	MILHAC D'AUBEROCHE		158	AA	28
24	MILHAC DE NONTRON		144	BA	26
81	MILHARS		174	EA	32
31	MILHAS		217	AA	37
30	MILHAUD		193	PA	34
81	MILHAVET		189	FA	33
29	MILIZAC		51	C	13
86	MILLAC		130	Z	23
59	MILLAM		8	GA	2
41	MILLANCAY		99	EA	18
66	MILLAS	C	224	IA	39
12	MILLAU	S	191	KA	33
58	MILLAY		119	OA	20
76	MILLEBOSC		15	DA	6
78	MILLEMONT		39	EA	12
80	MILLENCOURT		17	IA	6
80	MILLENCOURT EN PONTHIEU		16	FA	6
21	MILLERY		85	PA	17
54	MILLERY		46	XA	12
69	MILLERY		150	RA	26
19	MILLEVACHES		146	FA	26
50	MILLIERES		34	Q	10
52	MILLIERES		66	UA	15
59	MILLONFOSSE		18	LA	4
50	MILLY		57	S	12
91	MILLY LA FORET	C	62	HA	13
71	MILLY LAMARTINE		136	RA	23
55	MILLY SUR BRADON		30	TA	9
60	MILLY SUR THERAIN		25	FA	8
78	MILON LA CHAPELLE		39	FA	12
40	MIMBASTE		183	S	35
13	MIMET		202	VA	36
21	MIMEURE		104	QA	19
40	MIMIZAN	C	169	R	32
51	MINAUCOURT LE MESNIL LES HURLUS		43	RA	10
34	MINERVE		213	IA	36
65	MINGOT		208	X	36
62	MINGOVAL		17	IA	5
35	MINIAC MORVAN		55	O	13
35	MINIAC SOUS BECHEREL		75	O	14
35	MINIHIC SUR RANCE, LE		55	N	13
22	MINIHY TREGUIER		53	I	12
54	MINORVILLE		45	WA	12
21	MINOT		86	SA	17
67	MINVERSHEIM		49	EB	12
24	MINZAC		157	W	29
74	MINZIER		139	XA	24
81	MIOLLES		190	HA	33
01	MIONNAY		137	SA	25
69	MIONS		151	SA	26
33	MIOS		169	S	30
64	MIOSSENS LANUSSE		207	V	35
04	MIRABEAU		197	XA	33
84	MIRABEAU		196	VA	34
07	MIRABEL		178	QA	30
82	MIRABEL		173	CA	32
26	MIRABEL AUX BARONNIES		179	TA	32
26	MIRABEL ET BLACONS		165	TA	30
32	MIRADOUX	C	187	Z	33
13	MIRAMAS		201	SA	35
17	MIRAMBEAU	C	142	U	27
31	MIRAMBEAU		209	AA	36
32	MIRAMONT D'ASTARAC		208	Y	35
31	MIRAMONT DE COMMINGES		217	Z	37
47	MIRAMONT DE GUYENNE		172	Y	30
82	MIRAMONT DE QUERCY		173	BA	32
32	MIRAMONT LATOUR		187	Z	34
40	MIRAMONT SENSACQ		207	V	35
32	MIRANDE	S	208	Y	35
81	MIRANDOL BOURGNOUNAC		175	GA	32
32	MIRANNES		208	Y	35
80	MIRAUMONT		17	IA	6
11	MIRAVAL CABARDES		212	HA	36
52	MIRBEL		66	TA	14
49	MIRE		77	U	16
86	MIREBEAU	C	113	X	21
21	MIREBEAU SUR BEZE	C	105	UA	18
39	MIREBEL		122	WA	21
88	MIRECOURT	C	67	XA	14
63	MIREFLEURS		148	KA	25
31	MIREMONT		210	CA	36
63	MIREMONT		133	IA	25
11	MIREPEISSET		213	JA	36
64	MIREPEIX		215	V	37
09	MIREPOIX	C	219	EA	37
32	MIREPOIX		187	Z	34
31	MIREPOIX SUR TARN		188	DA	34
34	MIREVAL		214	NA	35
11	MIREVAL LAURAGAIS		211	FA	36
01	MIRIBEL	C	137	SA	25
26	MIRIBEL		165	TA	28
38	MIRIBEL LANCHATRE		166	VA	29
38	MIRIBEL LES ECHELLES		152	VA	27
26	MIRMANDE		165	SA	30
71	MIROIR, LE		122	UA	22
80	MIRVAUX		16	HA	6
76	MIRVILLE		23	Y	8
26	MISCON		180	VA	30
27	MISEREY		38	CA	11
25	MISEREY SALINES		107	XA	18
01	MISERIEUX		137	SA	24
80	MISERY		27	JA	7
04	MISON		181	WA	32
79	MISSE		112	V	20
81	MISSECLE		189	FA	34
11	MISSEGRE		221	HA	37
21	MISSERY		104	QA	18
44	MISSILLAC		93	N	17
56	MISSIRIAC		74	M	16
40	MISSON		183	S	35
14	MISSY		35	U	10
02	MISSY AUX BOIS		27	LA	9
02	MISSY LES PIERREPONT		28	NA	8
02	MISSY SUR AISNE		28	LA	9
77	MISY SUR YONNE		63	KA	14
77	MITRY MORY	C	40	IA	11
78	MITTAINVILLE		61	DA	12
28	MITTAINVILLIERS		60	CA	13
67	MITTELBERGHEIM		70	DB	13
57	MITTELBRONN		48	CB	12
67	MITTELHAUSBERGEN		49	EB	12
67	MITTELHAUSEN		49	EB	12
67	MITTELSCHAEFFOLSHEIM		49	EB	12
68	MITTELWIHR		69	DB	14
57	MITTERSHEIM		47	BB	11
68	MITTLACH		90	BB	15
14	MITTOIS		36	W	11
68	MITZACH		90	BB	16
42	MIZERIEUX		149	PA	25
38	MIZOEN		167	XA	28
50	MOBECQ		34	P	10
2A	MOCA CROCE		229	KB	43
73	MODANE	C	168	AB	28
84	MODENE		179	TA	32
29	MOELAN SUR MER		72	G	16
59	MOERES, LES		8	IA	2
68	MOERNACH		90	CB	17
52	MOESLAINS		66	SA	12
51	MOEURS VERDEY		42	MA	12
59	MOEUVRES		17	KA	6
17	MOEZE		126	R	24
70	MOFFANS ET VACHERESSE		89	ZA	17
55	MOGEVILLE		45	VA	10
73	MOGNARD		153	XA	25
01	MOGNENEINS		137	SA	23
55	MOGNEVILLE		44	SA	12
60	MOGNEVILLE		26	HA	9
08	MOGUES		31	UA	8
56	MOHON		74	L	15
38	MOIDIEU DETOURBE		151	SA	26
91	MOIGNY SUR ECOLE		62	HA	13
70	MOIMAY		89	ZA	17
54	MOINEVILLE		45	WA	10
17	MOINGS		142	V	26
28	MOINVILLE LA JEULIN		61	EA	13
38	MOIRANS		152	VA	27
39	MOIRANS EN MONTAGNE	C	122	WA	22
47	MOIRAX		172	Z	32
69	MOIRE		136	RA	24
51	MOIREMONT		44	SA	10
55	MOIREY FLABAS CREPION		31	UA	9
39	MOIRON		122	VA	21
08	MOIRY		31	UA	8
44	MOISDON LA RIVIERE	C	94	O	17
77	MOISENAY		62	IA	13
80	MOISLAINS		17	JA	6
82	MOISSAC	C	173	BA	32
83	MOISSAC BELLEVUE		197	YA	34
48	MOISSAC VALLEE FRANCAISE		177	NA	32
87	MOISSANNES		131	DA	25
63	MOISSAT		148	LA	25
95	MOISSELLES		40	HA	10
39	MOISSEY		106	VA	19
38	MOISSIEU SUR DOLON		151	SA	27
78	MOISSON		39	EA	10
77	MOISSY CRAMAYEL		62	IA	12
58	MOISSY MOULINOT		103	NA	18
27	MOISVILLE		38	BA	11
41	MOISY		80	CA	16
2B	MOITA	C	228	MB	41
50	MOITIERS D'ALLONNE, LES		33	O	9
50	MOITIERS EN BAUPTOIS, LES		33	Q	9
21	MOITRON		86	SA	17
72	MOITRON SUR SARTHE		58	W	14
51	MOIVRE		43	RA	11
54	MOIVRONS		46	YA	11
56	MOLAC		74	L	16
76	MOLAGNIES		25	EA	8
02	MOLAIN		18	MA	6
39	MOLAIN		122	WA	20
39	MOLAMBOZ		122	VA	20
11	MOLANDIER		211	EA	36
31	MOLAS		209	AA	36
39	MOLAY		122	UA	20
70	MOLAY		87	WA	16
89	MOLAY		84	OA	16
14	MOLAY LITTRY, LE		35	S	10
83	MOLE, LA		204	ZA	36
28	MOLEANS		60	CA	15
15	MOLEDES		161	KA	27
65	MOLERE		216	X	37
21	MOLESMES		85	PA	15
89	MOLESMES		83	MA	17
48	MOLEZON		177	MA	32
60	MOLIENS		25	EA	8
24	MOLIERES		158	AA	29
46	MOLIERES		160	FA	29
82	MOLIERES	C	173	CA	32
91	MOLIERES, LES		61	FA	12
30	MOLIERES CAVAILLAC		192	MA	33
26	MOLIERES GLANDAZ		166	UA	30
30	MOLIERES SUR CEZE		178	PA	32
40	MOLIETS ET MAA		183	Q	34
02	MOLINCHART		28	MA	8
05	MOLINES EN QUEYRAS		168	BB	30
03	MOLINET		119	OA	22
41	MOLINEUF		80	BA	17
39	MOLINGES		138	WA	22
62	MOLINGHEM		8	HA	4
89	MOLINONS		64	MA	14
21	MOLINOT		120	RA	20
10	MOLINS SUR AUBE		65	QA	13
66	MOLITG LES BAINS		222	HA	39
70	MOLLANS		88	YA	17
26	MOLLANS SUR OUVEZE		180	TA	32
68	MOLLAU		90	BB	16
13	MOLLEGES		195	SA	34
03	MOLLES		133	MA	24
73	MOLLETTES, LES		153	XA	26
11	MOLLEVILLE		211	EA	36
80	MOLLIENS AU BOIS		16	HA	6
80	MOLLIENS DREUIL	C	26	FA	7
67	MOLLKIRCH		70	DB	13
15	MOLOMPIZE		162	KA	27
89	MOLOSMES		84	OA	16
21	MOLOY		86	SA	17
21	MOLPHEY		104	PA	18
39	MOLPRE		123	XA	21
57	MOLRING		47	AB	11
67	MOLSHEIM	S	70	EB	13
2B	MOLTIFAO		226	LB	40
39	MOLUNES, LES		138	WA	23
64	MOMAS		207	U	35
33	MOMBRIER		156	U	28
65	MOMERES		216	W	37
57	MOMERSTROFF		47	ZA	10
67	MOMMENHEIM		49	EB	12
40	MOMUY		184	T	35
64	MOMY		208	W	36
2A	MONACIA D'AULLENE		229	KB	44
2B	MONACIA D'OREZZA		228	MB	40
02	MONAMPTEUIL		28	MA	9
64	MONASSUT AUDIRACQ		207	V	36
12	MONASTERE, LE		175	IA	31
48	MONASTIER PIN MORIES, LE		176	LA	31
43	MONASTIER SUR GAZEILLE, LA	C	163	OA	29
39	MONAY		122	VA	20
47	MONBAHUS		172	Z	30
47	MONBALEN		172	Z	32
32	MONBARDON		209	Z	36
24	MONBAZILLAC		157	Y	29
82	MONBEQUI		188	CA	33
32	MONBLANC		209	BA	35
32	MONBRUN		187	BA	34
2B	MONCALE		225	JB	40
32	MONCASSIN		209	Y	35
31	MONCAUP		217	Z	37
64	MONCAUP		208	W	35
47	MONCAUT		172	Y	32
64	MONCAYOLLE LARRORY MENDIBIEU		206	S	36
72	MONCE EN BELIN		78	X	16
72	MONCE EN SAOSNOIS		59	Y	14
02	MONCEAU LE NEUF ET FAUCOUZY		28	MA	7
02	MONCEAU LE WAAST		28	NA	8
02	MONCEAU LES LEUPS		28	MA	8
59	MONCEAU ST WAAST		19	NA	6
02	MONCEAU SUR OISE		18	MA	7
60	MONCEAUX		26	IA	9
14	MONCEAUX, LES		36	X	10
61	MONCEAUX AU PERCHE		59	Z	13
14	MONCEAUX EN BESSIN		35	T	10
60	MONCEAUX L'ABBAYE		25	EA	8
58	MONCEAUX LE COMTE		103	MA	18
19	MONCEAUX SUR DORDOGNE		160	EA	28
54	MONCEL LES LUNEVILLE		68	ZA	13
54	MONCEL SUR SEILLE		46	ZA	12
88	MONCEL SUR VAIR		67	WA	13
08	MONCELLE, LA		30	SA	8
51	MONCETZ L'ABBAYE		65	RA	12
51	MONCETZ LONGEVAS		43	QA	11
25	MONCEY		107	XA	18
76	MONCHAUX SORENG		15	DA	7
59	MONCHAUX SUR ECAILLON		18	MA	5
59	MONCHEAUX		18	KA	4
62	MONCHEAUX LES FREVENT		16	HA	5
59	MONCHECOURT		18	KA	5
62	MONCHEL SUR CANCHE		16	GA	5
57	MONCHEUX		46	YA	11
62	MONCHIET		17	IA	5
62	MONCHY AU BOIS		17	IA	5
62	MONCHY BRETON		17	HA	4
62	MONCHY CAYEUX		16	GA	4
60	MONCHY HUMIERES		27	IA	9
80	MONCHY LAGACHE		27	KA	7
62	MONCHY LE PREUX		17	JA	5
60	MONCHY ST ELOI		40	HA	9
76	MONCHY SUR EU		15	DA	6
64	MONCLA		207	V	35
32	MONCLAR		185	W	33
47	MONCLAR	C	172	Y	31
82	MONCLAR DE QUERCY	C	188	DA	33
32	MONCLAR SUR LOSSE		208	Y	35
25	MONCLEY		106	WA	18
22	MONCONTOUR	C	54	K	14
86	MONCONTOUR	C	112	W	20
32	MONCORNEIL GRAZAN		209	Z	35
57	MONCOURT		68	AB	12
79	MONCOUTANT	C	111	U	21
47	MONCRABEAU		186	Y	33
61	MONCY		35	T	11
31	MONDAVEZAN		209	BA	36
57	MONDELANGE		46	YA	10
51	MONDEMENT MONTGIVROUX		42	NA	12
60	MONDESCOURT		27	KA	8
35	MONDEVERT		76	R	15
14	MONDEVILLE		36	V	10
91	MONDEVILLE		62	HA	13
62	MONDICOURT		17	HA	5
08	MONDIGNY		30	RA	8
31	MONDILHAN		209	Z	36
86	MONDION		113	Y	20
25	MONDON		107	YA	18
31	MONDONVILLE		188	CA	34
28	MONDONVILLE ST JEAN		61	EA	14
57	MONDORFF		32	YA	9
41	MONDOUBLEAU	C	79	AA	15
31	MONDOUZIL		210	DA	35
84	MONDRAGON		179	RA	32
14	MONDRAINVILLE		35	U	10
02	MONDREPUIS		19	OA	6
77	MONDREVILLE		62	IA	15
78	MONDREVILLE		39	DA	11
64	MONEIN	C	207	T	36
31	MONES		209	BA	36
09	MONESPLE		219	DA	37
03	MONESTIER		134	KA	23
07	MONESTIER		164	QA	28
24	MONESTIER		157	Y	29
63	MONESTIER, LE		148	MA	26
38	MONESTIER D'AMBEL		167	WA	30
38	MONESTIER DE CLERMONT	C	166	VA	29
38	MONESTIER DU PERCY, LE		166	VA	29
19	MONESTIER MERLINES		147	HA	26
19	MONESTIER PORT DIEU		147	HA	26
81	MONESTIES	C	189	FA	33
31	MONESTROL		211	EA	36
03	MONETAY SUR ALLIER		134	LA	22
03	MONETAY SUR LOIRE		135	NA	22
89	MONETEAU		83	MA	16
05	MONETIER ALLEMONT		181	XA	31
05	MONETIER LES BAINS, LE	C	167	ZA	29
24	MONFAUCON		157	X	29
65	MONFAUCON		208	X	35
32	MONFERRAN PLAVES		209	Z	35
32	MONFERRAN SAVES		209	BA	35
47	MONFLANQUIN	C	172	AA	31
32	MONFORT		187	AA	34
14	MONFREVILLE		35	S	9
47	MONGAILLARD		171	X	32
32	MONGAUSY		209	AA	35
33	MONGAUZY		171	W	30
40	MONGET		207	U	35
32	MONGUILHEM		185	V	34
47	MONHEURT		171	X	31
72	MONHOUDOU		59	Y	14
84	MONIEUX		196	UA	33
43	MONISTROL D'ALLIER		162	MA	29
43	MONISTROL SUR LOIRE	C	149	PA	27
32	MONLAUR BERNET		209	Y	36
65	MONLEON MAGNOAC		209	Y	36
43	MONLET		163	NA	28
32	MONLEZUN		208	X	35
32	MONLEZUN D'ARMAGNAC		185	V	34
65	MONLONG		208	Y	36
24	MONMADALES		158	Z	30
24	MONMARVES		158	Z	30
61	MONNAI		37	Y	11
37	MONNAIE		79	AA	17
57	MONNEREN		47	ZA	9
63	MONNERIE LE MONTEL, LA		134	MA	25
91	MONNERVILLE		61	FA	14
02	MONNES		41	KA	10
39	MONNET LA VILLE		122	WA	21
39	MONNETAY		122	VA	22
74	MONNETIER MORNEX		139	YA	23
60	MONNEVILLE		39	FA	10
39	MONNIERES		106	UA	19
44	MONNIERES		94	Q	19
30	MONOBLET		192	NA	33
32	MONPARDIAC		208	X	35
24	MONPAZIER	C	173	AA	30
64	MONPEZAT		208	W	35
24	MONPLAISANT		158	AA	29
33	MONPRIMBLANC		170	V	30
16	MONS		128	W	25
17	MONS		128	V	25
30	MONS		178	PA	32
31	MONS		210	DA	35
34	MONS		213	JA	35
63	MONS		133	LA	24
83	MONS		198	AB	34
80	MONS BOUBERT		15	EA	6
59	MONS EN BAROEUL		9	KA	3
02	MONS EN LAONNOIS		28	MA	8
77	MONS EN MONTOIS		63	KA	13
59	MONS EN PEVELE		18	KA	4
24	MONSAC		158	Z	29
24	MONSAGUEL		157	Z	30
24	MONSEC		143	Y	27
33	MONSEGUR	C	171	W	30
40	MONSEGUR		207	U	35
47	MONSEGUR		172	AA	31
64	MONSEGUR		208	W	35
15	MONSELIE, LA		147	HA	27
47	MONSEMPRON LIBOS		173	AA	31
85	MONSIREIGNE		111	S	21
69	MONSOLS	C	136	QA	23
38	MONSTEROUX MILIEU		151	SA	27
80	MONSURES		26	GA	8
67	MONSWILLER		49	DB	12
64	MONT		207	T	35
65	MONT		217	Y	38
71	MONT		119	NA	21
88	MONT, LE		69	BB	13
62	MONT BERNANCHON		8	IA	4
14	MONT BERTRAND		35	S	11
54	MONT BONVILLERS		31	WA	9
76	MONT CAUVAIRE		24	BA	8
32	MONT D'ASTARAC		209	Z	36
02	MONT D'ORIGNY		28	MA	7
05	MONT DAUPHIN		168	AB	30
31	MONT DE GALIE		217	Z	37
76	MONT DE L'IF		24	AA	8
38	MONT DE LANS		167	XA	28
25	MONT DE LAVAL		108	AB	19
32	MONT DE MARRAST		208	Y	36
40	MONT DE MARSAN	P	184	U	33
25	MONT DE VOUGNEY		108	AB	19
55	MONT DEVANT SASSEY		30	TA	9
08	MONT DIEU, LE		30	SA	8
64	MONT DISSE		207	V	35
35	MONT DOL		55	O	13
63	MONT DORE		147	JA	26
58	MONT ET MARRE		103	MA	19
54	MONT L'ETROIT		67	WA	13
60	MONT L'EVEQUE		40	IA	10
08	MONT LAURENT		29	QA	9
70	MONT LE VERNOIS		88	XA	17
54	MONT LE VIGNOBLE		67	WA	12
88	MONT LES LAMARCHE		87	WA	15
88	MONT LES NEUFCHATEAU		67	VA	14
71	MONT LES SEURRE		121	TA	20
66	MONT LOUIS	C	222	GA	40
02	MONT NOTRE DAME		42	MA	9
61	MONT ORMEL		36	X	11
41	MONT PRES CHAMBORD		80	DA	17
81	MONT ROC		190	HA	34
74	MONT SAXONNEX		139	ZA	24
39	MONT SOUS VAUDREY		122	VA	20
60	MONT ST ADRIEN, LE		26	FA	9
76	MONT ST AIGNAN	C	24	BA	9

62 MONT ST ELOI 17 IA 5
02 MONT ST JEAN 29 PA 7
21 MONT ST JEAN 104 QA 18
72 MONT ST JEAN 58 W 14
70 MONT ST LEGER 87 WA 17
02 MONT ST MARTIN 42 MA 9
08 MONT ST MARTIN 30 RA 9
38 MONT ST MARTIN 152 VA 27
54 MONT ST MARTIN C 31 WA 8
50 MONT ST MICHEL, LE 56 P 12
02 MONT ST PERE 41 LA 10
08 MONT ST REMY 29 QA 9
89 MONT ST SULPICE 84 MA 15
71 MONT ST VINCENT C 120 QA 21
51 MONT SUR COURVILLE 42 MA 10
54 MONT SUR MEURTHE 68 ZA 13
39 MONT SUR MONNET 122 WA 21
61 MONTABARD 58 W 12
72 MONTABON 79 Y 17
50 MONTABOT 56 R 11
89 MONTACHER VILLEGARDIN 63 KA 14
32 MONTADET 209 AA 35
34 MONTADY 213 KA 36
09 MONTAGAGNE 219 CA 38
39 MONTAGNA LE RECONDUIT 122 UA 22
39 MONTAGNA LE TEMPLIER 138 UA 22
30 MONTAGNAC 193 PA 33
34 MONTAGNAC C 214 MA 35
24 MONTAGNAC D'AUBEROCHE 158 AA 28
24 MONTAGNAC LA CREMPSE 157 Y 29
04 MONTAGNAC MONTPEZAT 197 XA 34
47 MONTAGNAC SUR AUVIGNON 172 Y 32
47 MONTAGNAC SUR LEDE 172 AA 31
01 MONTAGNAT 137 UA 23
33 MONTAGNE 156 V 29
38 MONTAGNE 165 TA 28
44 MONTAGNE, LA 93 P 19
70 MONTAGNE, LA 89 AB 16
80 MONTAGNE FAYEL 16 FA 7
70 MONTAGNEY 106 VA 18
25 MONTAGNEY SERVIGNEY 88 YA 17
01 MONTAGNIEU 152 UA 25
38 MONTAGNIEU 152 UA 26
12 MONTAGNOL 191 JA 34
73 MONTAGNOLE 152 WA 26
42 MONTAGNY 135 PA 24
69 MONTAGNY 150 RA 26
73 MONTAGNY 154 ZA 26
60 MONTAGNY EN VEXIN 39 EA 10
21 MONTAGNY LES BEAUNE 121 SA 20
71 MONTAGNY LES BUXY 120 RA 21
74 MONTAGNY LES LANCHES 139 XA 25
21 MONTAGNY LES SEURRE 121 TA 20
71 MONTAGNY PRES LOUHANS 121 UA 21
60 MONTAGNY STE FELICITE 40 IA 10
71 MONTAGNY SUR GROSNE 136 QA 23
33 MONTAGOUDIN 171 W 30
24 MONTAGRIER C 143 Y 27
82 MONTAGUDET 173 BA 32
64 MONTAGUT 207 U 35
19 MONTAIGNAC ST HIPPOLYTE 146 FA 27
02 MONTAIGU 28 NA 8
39 MONTAIGU 122 VA 21
85 MONTAIGU C 110 Q 20
82 MONTAIGU DE QUERCY C 173 BA 31
50 MONTAIGU LA BRISETTE 33 Q 8
03 MONTAIGU LE BLIN 133 MA 23
50 MONTAIGU LES BOIS 56 R 11
31 MONTAIGU SUR SAVE 188 CA 34
03 MONTAIGUET EN FOREZ 135 NA 23
63 MONTAIGUT C 133 IA 23
23 MONTAIGUT LE BLANC 131 EA 24
63 MONTAIGUT LE BLANC 148 KA 26
72 MONTAILLE 79 Z 15
73 MONTAILLEUR 153 YA 26
09 MONTAILLOU 223 FA 38
73 MONTAIMONT 153 YA 27
39 MONTAIN 122 VA 21
82 MONTAIN 188 BA 33
28 MONTAINVILLE 60 DA 14
78 MONTAINVILLE 39 EA 11
66 MONTALBA LE CHATEAU 224 IA 39
79 MONTALEMBERT 129 X 24
78 MONTALET LE BOIS 39 EA 10
38 MONTALIEU VERCIEU 138 UA 25
82 MONTALZAT 174 DA 32
32 MONTAMAT 209 AA 35
58 MONTAMBERT 119 NA 21
46 MONTAMEL 173 DA 30
86 MONTAMISE 113 Y 21
14 MONTAMY 35 T 11
69 MONTANAY 137 SA 25
25 MONTANCY 108 BB 18
25 MONTANDON 108 BB 18
50 MONTANEL 56 Q 13
64 MONTANER C 208 W 36
01 MONTANGES 138 WA 23
81 MONTANS 189 EA 34
58 MONTAPAS 103 MA 19
42 MONTARCHER 149 OA 26
09 MONTARDIT 218 BA 37
64 MONTARDON 207 V 36
30 MONTAREN ET ST MEDIERS 193 QA 33
45 MONTARGIS S 82 IA 15
77 MONTARLOT 63 JA 14
70 MONTARLOT LES RIOZ 107 XA 18
34 MONTARNAUD 214 NA 35
58 MONTARON 119 NA 20
47 MONTASTRUC 172 Y 31
65 MONTASTRUC 208 Y 36
82 MONTASTRUC 188 CA 33
31 MONTASTRUC DE SALIES 217 AA 37
31 MONTASTRUC
LA CONSEILLERE C 188 DA 34
31 MONTASTRUC SAVES 209 BA 36
46 MONTAT, LE 173 CA 31
60 MONTATAIRE C 40 HA 10
35 MONTAUBAN DE BRETAGNE C 75 N 14
82 MONTAUBAN P 188 CA 33
31 MONTAUBAN DE LUCHON 217 Z 38
80 MONTAUBAN DE PICARDIE 17 JA 6
26 MONTAUBAN SUR L'OUVEZE 180 VA 32
34 MONTAUD 193 OA 34
38 MONTAUD 152 VA 27
53 MONTAUDIN 57 S 13
26 MONTAULIEU 180 TA 31
10 MONTAULIN 65 PA 14
27 MONTAURE 38 BA 10
11 MONTAURIOL 211 EA 36
47 MONTAURIOL 172 Z 30
66 MONTAURIOL 224 IA 39
81 MONTAURIOL 190 HA 33
83 MONTAUROUX 198 AB 35
09 MONTAUT 219 DA 37
24 MONTAUT 158 Z 30
31 MONTAUT 210 CA 36
32 MONTAUT 208 Y 36
40 MONTAUT 184 T 34
47 MONTAUT 172 Z 30
64 MONTAUT 215 V 37
32 MONTAUT LES CRENEAUX 187 Z 34
35 MONTAUTOUR 76 R 14
54 MONTAUVILLE 45 XA 11
59 MONTAY 18 MA 6
47 MONTAYRAL 173 BA 31
24 MONTAZEAU 157 X 29
11 MONTAZELS 221 GA 38
21 MONTBARD S 85 QA 17
82 MONTBARLA 173 BA 32
39 MONTBARREY C 122 VA 20
45 MONTBARROIS 82 HA 15
82 MONTBARTIER 188 CA 33
02 MONTBAVIN 28 MA 8
12 MONTBAZENS C 175 GA 31
34 MONTBAZIN 214 MA 35
37 MONTBAZON C 98 Z 18
09 MONTBEL 221 FA 37
48 MONTBEL 177 NA 30
25 MONTBELIARD S 89 AB 17
25 MONTBELIARDOT 108 AB 19
71 MONTBELLET 121 SA 22
25 MONTBENOIT C 107 ZA 20
31 MONTBERAUD 218 BA 37
31 MONTBERNARD 209 AA 36
31 MONTBERON 188 DA 34
44 MONTBERT 110 O 19
21 MONTBERTHAULT 103 PA 18
82 MONTBETON 188 CA 33
03 MONTBEUGNY 118 MA 22
72 MONTBIZOT 78 X 15
55 MONTBLAINVILLE 44 SA 10
34 MONTBLANC 214 LA 36
70 MONTBOILLON 106 WA 18
28 MONTBOISSIER 60 CA 14
66 MONTBOLO 224 IA 40
38 MONTBONNOT ST MARTIN 152 WA 27
23 MONTBOUCHER 131 EA 24
26 MONTBOUCHER SUR JABRON 179 SA 30
15 MONTBOUDIF 147 IA 27
90 MONTBOUTON 108 BB 18
45 MONTBOUY 82 JA 16
16 MONTBOYER 143 W 27
70 MONTBOZON C 107 YA 18
05 MONTBRAND 180 VA 30
55 MONTBRAS 67 WA 13
50 MONTBRAY 56 R 11
51 MONTBRE 42 OA 10
02 MONTBREHAIN 18 LA 6
26 MONTBRISON 179 SA 31
42 MONTBRISON S 149 OA 26
16 MONTBRON C 143 Y 26
57 MONTBRONN 48 DB 11
46 MONTBRUN 174 FA 31
48 MONTBRUN 177 MA 31
31 MONTBRUN BOCAGE 218 CA 37
11 MONTBRUN DES CORBIERES 212 IA 36
31 MONTBRUN LAURAGAIS 210 DA 35
26 MONTBRUN LES BAINS 180 UA 32
46 MONTCABRIER 173 BA 31
81 MONTCABRIER 211 EA 35
24 MONTCARET 157 W 29
38 MONTCARRA 152 UA 26
62 MONTCAVREL 7 EA 4
21 MONTCEAU ET ECHARNANT 104 RA 19
71 MONTCEAU LES MINES C 120 PA 21
01 MONTCEAUX 136 RA 24
71 MONTCEAUX L'ETOILE 135 OA 23
77 MONTCEAUX LES MEAUX 41 JA 11
77 MONTCEAUX LES PROVINS 41 MA 12
10 MONTCEAUX LES VAUDES 65 PA 14
71 MONTCEAUX RAGNY 121 SA 21
63 MONTCEL 134 KA 24
73 MONTCEL 153 XA 25
71 MONTCENIS C 120 QA 21
01 MONTCET 137 TA 23
70 MONTCEY 88 YA 17
38 MONTCHABOUD 166 WA 28
42 MONTCHAL 150 PA 25
02 MONTCHALONS 28 NA 8
14 MONTCHAMP 35 T 11
15 MONTCHAMP 162 KA 28
71 MONTCHANIN C 120 OA 21
52 MONTCHARVOT 87 WA 16
50 MONTCHATON 34 P 11
16 MONTCHAUDE 142 V 27
14 MONTCHAUVET 35 T 11
78 MONTCHAUVET 39 DA 11
26 MONTCHENU 165 SA 28
08 MONTCHEUTIN 30 SA 9
61 MONTCHEVREL 59 Y 13
36 MONTCHEVRIER 115 EA 22
04 MONTCLAR 181 YA 31
11 MONTCLAR 221 GA 37
12 MONTCLAR 190 IA 33
31 MONTCLAR DE COMMINGES 218 BA 37
31 MONTCLAR LAURAGAIS 211 EA 36
26 MONTCLAR SUR GERVANNE 165 TA 30
43 MONTCLARD 162 MA 27
46 MONTCLERA 173 BA 30
05 MONTCLUS 180 VA 31
30 MONTCLUS 178 QA 32
03 MONTCOMBROUX LES MINES 135 NA 23
71 MONTCONY 121 UA 21
45 MONTCORBON 83 KA 15
02 MONTCORNET 29 OA 8
08 MONTCORNET 29 RA 7
70 MONTCOURT 88 XA 15
77 MONTCOURT FROMONVILLE 62 IA 14
71 MONTCOY 121 SA 21
45 MONTCRESSON 82 JA 16
50 MONTCUIT 34 Q 10
46 MONTCUQ C 173 CA 31
39 MONTCUSEL 138 VA 22
08 MONTCY NOTRE DAME 29 RA 7
30 MONTDARDIER 192 MA 33
77 MONTDAUPHIN 41 LA 11
57 MONTDIDIER 47 AB 11
80 MONTDIDIER S 26 IA 8
70 MONTDORE 88 XA 16
46 MONTDOUMERC 174 DA 32
81 MONTDRAGON 189 FA 34
81 MONTDURAUSSE 188 DA 33
2B MONTE 228 MB 40
41 MONTEAUX 80 BA 17
50 MONTEBOURG C 33 Q 9
82 MONTECH C 188 CA 33
25 MONTECHEROUX 108 AB 18
2B MONTEGROSSO 225 JB 39
32 MONTEGUT 209 Z 35
40 MONTEGUT 185 V 33
65 MONTEGUT 217 Y 37
32 MONTEGUT ARROS 208 X 36
31 MONTEGUT BOURJAC 209 AA 36
09 MONTEGUT EN COUSERANS 218 BA 37
31 MONTEGUT LAURAGAIS 211 FA 35
09 MONTEGUT PLANTAUREL 219 DA 37
32 MONTEGUT SAVES 209 AA 35
03 MONTEIGNET SUR L'ANDELOT 134 LA 23
15 MONTEIL, LE 147 HA 27
43 MONTEIL, LE 163 OA 28
23 MONTEIL AU VICOMTE, LE 132 FA 24
14 MONTEILLE 36 W 10
12 MONTEILS 174 FA 32
30 MONTEILS 193 PA 33
82 MONTEILS 174 DA 32
63 MONTEL DE GELAT 133 IA 24
26 MONTELEGER 165 SA 29
26 MONTELIER 165 TA 29
26 MONTELIMAR C 179 RA 30
01 MONTELLIER, LE 137 TA 24
09 MONTELS 219 DA 37
34 MONTELS 213 JA 36
81 MONTELS 189 EA 33
16 MONTEMBOEUF C 143 Z 25
57 MONTENACH 32 ZA 9
53 MONTENAY 57 S 14
17 MONTENDRE C 142 U 27
73 MONTENDRY 153 YA 26
62 MONTENESCOURT 17 IA 5
56 MONTENEUF 74 M 16
77 MONTENILS 41 MA 11
25 MONTENOIS 108 AB 17
58 MONTENOISON 102 LA 19
54 MONTENOY 46 YA 12
60 MONTEPILLOY 40 IA 10
39 MONTEPLAIN 106 VA 19
51 MONTEPREUX 42 OA 12
56 MONTERBLANC 74 K 16
45 MONTEREAU 82 HA 16
77 MONTEREAU FAULT YONNE C 63 JA 13
77 MONTEREAU SUR LE JARD 62 IA 13
35 MONTERFIL 75 N 15
76 MONTEROLIER 25 CA 8
56 MONTERREIN 74 M 16
56 MONTERTELOT 74 L 16
66 MONTESCOT 224 JA 39
02 MONTESCOURT LIZEROLLES 28 LA 7
31 MONTESPAN 217 AA 37
34 MONTESQUIEU 213 LA 35
47 MONTESQUIEU 172 Y 32
82 MONTESQUIEU 173 BA 32
09 MONTESQUIEU AVANTES 218 BA 37
66 MONTESQUIEU DES ALBERES 224 JA 40
31 MONTESQUIEU GUITTAUT 209 Z 36
31 MONTESQUIEU LAURAGAIS 210 DA 36
31 MONTESQUIEU VOLVESTRE C 210 CA 36
32 MONTESQUIOU C 208 Y 35
70 MONTESSAUX 89 ZA 16
78 MONTESSON 39 GA 11
32 MONTESTRUC SUR GERS 187 Z 34
03 MONTET, LE C 134 KA 22
46 MONTET ET BOUXAL 160 FA 30
47 MONTETON 171 X 30
84 MONTEUX 195 SA 33
77 MONTEVRAIN 40 IA 11
38 MONTEYNARD 166 WA 29
12 MONTEZIC 161 IA 30
09 MONTFA 218 CA 37
81 MONTFA 190 GA 34
38 MONTFALCON 151 TA 27
50 MONTFARVILLE 33 R 8
02 MONTFAUCON 41 LA 11
25 MONTFAUCON 107 XA 19
30 MONTFAUCON 195 RA 33
46 MONTFAUCON 174 DA 30
49 MONTFAUCON C 110 R 19
55 MONTFAUCON D'ARGONNE C 44 TA 10
43 MONTFAUCON EN VELAY C 164 PA 28
93 MONTFERMEIL C 40 IA 11
82 MONTFERMIER 173 CA 32
63 MONTFERMY 133 IA 25
11 MONTFERRAND 211 EA 36
24 MONTFERRAND DU PERIGORD 158 AA 30
26 MONTFERRAND LA FARE 180 UA 31
25 MONTFERRAND LE CHATEAU 107 XA 19
38 MONTFERRAT 152 VA 26
83 MONTFERRAT 198 ZA 35
66 MONTFERRER 222 HA 40
09 MONTFERRIER 219 EA 38
34 MONTFERRIER SUR LEZ 192 NA 34
10 MONTFEY 84 NA 15
14 MONTFIQUET 35 S 10
39 MONTFLEUR 138 UA 23
53 MONTFLOURS 77 T 14
25 MONTFLOVIN 107 ZA 20
04 MONTFORT 197 XA 33
25 MONTFORT 106 WA 19
49 MONTFORT 96 V 19
64 MONTFORT 206 S 36
40 MONTFORT EN CHALOSSE C 184 S 34
78 MONTFORT L'AMAURY C 39 EA 12
72 MONTFORT LE GESNOIS C 79 Y 15
83 MONTFORT SUR ARGENS 203 XA 35
11 MONTFORT SUR BOULZANE 222 GA 39
35 MONTFORT SUR MEU C 75 N 15
27 MONTFORT SUR RISLE C 23 Z 9
12 MONTFRANC 190 IA 34
30 MONTFRIN 195 RA 34
26 MONTFROC 180 VA 32
04 MONTFURON 196 VA 34
09 MONTGAILLARD C 219 DA 38
11 MONTGAILLARD 223 IA 38
40 MONTGAILLARD 184 U 34
65 MONTGAILLARD 216 X 37
81 MONTGAILLARD 188 DA 33
82 MONTGAILLARD 187 AA 33
31 MONTGAILLARD DE SALIES 217 AA 37
31 MONTGAILLARD LAURAGAIS 211 EA 35
31 MONTGAILLARD SUR SAVE 209 Z 36
05 MONTGARDIN 181 YA 31
50 MONTGARDON 34 P 9
61 MONTGAROULT 58 W 12
09 MONTGAUCH 218 BA 37
61 MONTGAUDRY 59 Y 13
31 MONTGAZIN 210 CA 36
77 MONTGE EN GOELE 40 IA 11
31 MONTGEARD 210 DA 36
73 MONTGELLAFREY 153 YA 27
05 MONTGENEVRE 168 AB 29
51 MONTGENOST 64 MA 12
60 MONTGERAIN 26 HA 8
35 MONTGERMONT 75 O 14
91 MONTGERON C 40 HA 12
95 MONTGEROULT 39 FA 10
25 MONTGESOYE 107 YA 19
46 MONTGESTY 173 CA 30
81 MONTGEY 211 FA 35
19 MONTGIBAUD 145 CA 26
73 MONTGILBERT 153 YA 26
73 MONTGIROD 154 ZA 26
31 MONTGISCARD C 210 DA 35
36 MONTGIVRAY 116 FA 21
02 MONTGOBERT 41 KA 9
08 MONTGON 30 RA 8
11 MONTGRADAIL 221 FA 37
31 MONTGRAS 209 BA 35
15 MONTGRELEIX 147 JA 27
02 MONTGRU ST HILAIRE 41 LA 10
26 MONTGUERS 180 UA 32
10 MONTGUEUX 64 OA 14
49 MONTGUILLON 77 T 16
17 MONTGUYON C 156 V 28
55 MONTHAIRONS, LES 44 UA 11
28 MONTHARVILLE 60 CA 14
35 MONTHAULT 56 R 13
11 MONTHAUT 221 FA 37
21 MONTHELIE 120 RA 20
51 MONTHELON 42 OA 11
71 MONTHELON 120 PA 20
02 MONTHENAULT 28 MA 9
52 MONTHERIES 66 SA 14
60 MONTHERLANT 39 FA 9
08 MONTHERME C 20 RA 7
02 MONTHIERS 41 LA 10
01 MONTHIEUX 137 SA 24
73 MONTHION 153 YA 26
37 MONTHODON 79 AA 17
86 MONTHOIRON 113 Z 21
08 MONTHOIS C 30 RA 9
39 MONTHOLIER 122 VA 20
41 MONTHOU SUR BIEVRE 80 CA 17
41 MONTHOU SUR CHER 99 CA 18
50 MONTHUCHON 34 Q 10
02 MONTHUREL 42 MA 11
88 MONTHUREUX LE SEC 67 XA 14
88 MONTHUREUX SUR SAONE C 88 XA 15
77 MONTHYON 40 JA 11
2B MONTICELLO 225 KB 39
52 MONTIER EN DER C 65 RA 13
10 MONTIER EN L'ISLE 65 RA 14
10 MONTIERAMEY 65 PA 14
36 MONTIERCHAUME 115 EA 20
60 MONTIERS 26 IA 8
55 MONTIERS SUR SAULX C 66 UA 13
32 MONTIES 209 Z 36
24 MONTIGNAC C 158 BA 28
33 MONTIGNAC 156 V 30
65 MONTIGNAC 216 X 37
16 MONTIGNAC CHARENTE 143 X 25
47 MONTIGNAC DE LAUZUN 172 Y 30
16 MONTIGNAC LE COQ 143 X 27
47 MONTIGNAC TOUPINERIE 172 Y 30
30 MONTIGNARGUES 193 PA 33
16 MONTIGNE 142 W 25
53 MONTIGNE LE BRILLANT 77 T 15
49 MONTIGNE LES RAIRIES 78 V 17
49 MONTIGNE SUR MOINE 110 R 19
14 MONTIGNY 35 U 11
18 MONTIGNY 101 IA 19
45 MONTIGNY 61 GA 15
54 MONTIGNY 69 AB 13
72 MONTIGNY 58 X 13
76 MONTIGNY 24 AA 9
58 MONTIGNY AUX AMOGNES 118 LA 20
55 MONTIGNY DEVANT SASSEY 30 TA 9
02 MONTIGNY EN ARROUAISE 28 MA 7
59 MONTIGNY EN CAMBRESIS 18 LA 6
62 MONTIGNY EN GOHELLE C 9 JA 4
58 MONTIGNY EN MORVAN 103 NA 19
59 MONTIGNY EN OSTREVENT 18 KA 5
02 MONTIGNY L'ALLIER 41 KA 10
89 MONTIGNY LA RESLE 84 NA 16
78 MONTIGNY LE BRETONNEUX 39 FA 12
28 MONTIGNY LE CHARTIF 60 BA 14
02 MONTIGNY LE FRANC 28 NA 8
28 MONTIGNY LE GANNELON 80 CA 15
77 MONTIGNY LE GUESDIER 63 LA 13
77 MONTIGNY LENCOUP 63 KA 13
02 MONTIGNY LENGRAIN 27 KA 9
39 MONTIGNY LES ARSURES 122 WA 20
70 MONTIGNY LES CHERLIEU 87 WA 16
02 MONTIGNY LES CONDE 42 MA 11
95 MONTIGNY LES CORMEILLES 39 GA 11
80 MONTIGNY LES JONGLEURS 16 FA 5
57 MONTIGNY LES METZ C 46 XA 10
10 MONTIGNY LES MONTS 64 OA 15
55 MONTIGNY
LES VAUCOULEURS 67 VA 13
70 MONTIGNY LES VESOUL 88 XA 17
21 MONTIGNY MONTFORT 85 PA 17
21 MONTIGNY MORNAY
VILLENEUVE SUR VINGEANNE 87 UA 17
02 MONTIGNY SOUS MARLE 28 NA 7
21 MONTIGNY ST BARTHELEMY 104 PA 18
21 MONTIGNY SUR ARMANCON 104 QA 18
21 MONTIGNY SUR AUBE C 85 RA 15
28 MONTIGNY SUR AVRE 38 BA 12
58 MONTIGNY SUR CANNE 119 MA 20
54 MONTIGNY SUR CHIERS 31 VA 9
02 MONTIGNY SUR CRECY 28 MA 8
39 MONTIGNY SUR L'AIN 122 WA 21
80 MONTIGNY SUR L'HALLUE 17 HA 6
77 MONTIGNY SUR LOING 62 IA 14
08 MONTIGNY SUR MEUSE 20 RA 6
08 MONTIGNY SUR VENCE 30 RA 8
51 MONTIGNY SUR VESLE 28 NA 9
49 MONTILLIERS 96 U 19
89 MONTILLOT 84 NA 17
03 MONTILLY 118 LA 21
61 MONTILLY SUR NOIREAU 57 U 12
17 MONTILS 142 U 26
41 MONTILS, LES 80 CA 17
36 MONTIPOURET 116 FA 21
11 MONTIRAT 221 HA 37
81 MONTIRAT 175 GA 32
28 MONTIREAU 60 BA 13
32 MONTIRON 209 AA 35
25 MONTIVERNAGE 107 ZA 18
76 MONTIVILLIERS C 23 X 8
11 MONTJARDIN 221 FA 37
12 MONTJAUX 176 JA 32
60 MONTJAVOULT 39 EA 10
05 MONTJAY 180 VA 31
71 MONTJAY 121 UA 20
16 MONTJEAN 129 X 24
53 MONTJEAN 76 S 15
49 MONTJEAN SUR LOIRE 95 S 18
11 MONTJOI 221 HA 37
82 MONTJOI 173 AA 32
09 MONTJOIE EN COUSERANS 218 BA 37
25 MONTJOIE LE CHATEAU 108 BB 18
50 MONTJOIE ST MARTIN 56 Q 13
31 MONTJOIRE 188 DA 34
26 MONTJOUX 179 TA 31
26 MONTJOYER 179 SA 31
04 MONTJUSTIN 196 VA 34
70 MONTJUSTIN ET VELOTTE 88 YA 17
28 MONTLANDON 60 BA 13
11 MONTLAUR 223 IA 37
12 MONTLAUR 191 JA 33
31 MONTLAUR 210 DA 35
26 MONTLAUR EN DIOIS 180 UA 30
04 MONTLAUX 197 WA 33
46 MONTLAUZUN 173 BA 32
21 MONTLAY EN AUXOIS 104 PA 18
25 MONTLEBON 108 AB 19
36 MONTLEVICQ 116 FA 22
02 MONTLEVON 41 MA 11
91 MONTLHERY C 62 GA 12
45 MONTLIARD 82 HA 15
17 MONTLIEU LA GARDE C 142 V 27
95 MONTLIGNON 40 GA 11
21 MONTLIOT ET COURCELLES 85 QA 16
41 MONTLIVAULT 80 DA 17
60 MONTLOGNON 40 IA 10
02 MONTLOUE 29 OA 8
18 MONTLOUIS 116 GA 20
37 MONTLOUIS SUR LOIRE C 98 AA 18
03 MONTLUCON S 133 IA 23
01 MONTLUEL C 137 SA 25
77 MONTMACHOUX 63 JA 14
60 MONTMACQ 27 JA 9
95 MONTMAGNY 40 GA 11
25 MONTMAHOUX 107 XA 20
21 MONTMAIN 105 TA 19
76 MONTMAIN 24 CA 9
21 MONTMANCON 106 UA 18
03 MONTMARAULT C 133 JA 23
39 MONTMARLON 123 XA 20
60 MONTMARTIN 27 IA 9
50 MONTMARTIN EN GRAIGNES 34 R 9
10 MONTMARTIN LE HAUT 65 QA 14
50 MONTMARTIN SUR MER C 34 P 11
05 MONTMAUR 181 WA 30
11 MONTMAUR 211 EA 36
26 MONTMAUR EN DIOIS 166 UA 30
31 MONTMAURIN 209 Z 36
55 MONTMEDY C 31 UA 8
08 MONTMEILLANT 29 PA 8
71 MONTMELARD 136 QA 23
69 MONTMELAS ST SORLIN 136 RA 24
73 MONTMELIAN C 153 XA 26
01 MONTMERLE SUR SAONE 136 RA 24
61 MONTMERREI 58 W 12
83 MONTMEYAN 203 XA 35
26 MONTMEYRAN 165 SA 29
74 MONTMIN 139 YA 25
51 MONTMIRAIL C 42 MA 11
72 MONTMIRAIL C 59 AA 15
26 MONTMIRAL 165 TA 28
30 MONTMIRAT 193 OA 33
39 MONTMIREY LA VILLE 106 VA 19
39 MONTMIREY LE CHATEAU C 106 VA 19
16 MONTMOREAU ST CYBARD C 143 X 27
95 MONTMORENCY S 40 HA 11
10 MONTMORENCY BEAUFORT 65 QA 13
86 MONTMORILLON S 114 AA 22
05 MONTMORIN 180 VA 31
63 MONTMORIN 148 LA 25
39 MONTMOROT 122 VA 21
71 MONTMORT 119 OA 21
51 MONTMORT LUCY C 42 NA 11
88 MONTMOTIER 88 YA 15
21 MONTMOYEN 86 RA 16
15 MONTMURAT 175 GA 30
66 MONTNER 224 IA 38
21 MONTOILLOT 104 RA 18
44 MONTOIR DE BRETAGNE C 93 N 18
41 MONTOIRE SUR LE LOIR C 79 AA 16
57 MONTOIS LA MONTAGNE 45 XA 10
26 MONTOISON 165 SA 29
03 MONTOLDRE 133 LA 23
11 MONTOLIEU 212 GA 36
77 MONTOLIVET 41 LA 11
80 MONTONVILLERS 16 GA 6
03 MONTORD 134 KA 23
64 MONTORY 206 S 37
21 MONTOT 105 UA 19
70 MONTOT 87 WA 17
52 MONTOT SUR ROGNON 66 UA 14
34 MONTOULIERS 213 JA 36
09 MONTOULIEU 219 DA 38
34 MONTOULIEU 192 NA 33
31 MONTOULIEU ST BERNARD 209 AA 36
85 MONTOURNAIS 111 T 21
35 MONTOURS 56 O 13
53 MONTOURTIER 77 U 14
65 MONTOUSSE 216 Y 37
31 MONTOUSSIN 209 BA 36
57 MONTOY FLANVILLE 46 YA 10
34 MONTPELLIER P 194 OA 35
17 MONTPELLIER DE MEDILLAN 141 T 26
63 MONTPENSIER 133 LA 24
25 MONTPERREUX 123 YA 20
12 MONTPEYROUX 176 JA 30
24 MONTPEYROUX 157 W 29
34 MONTPEYROUX 192 MA 34
63 MONTPEYROUX 148 KA 26
30 MONTPEZAT 193 PA 34
32 MONTPEZAT 209 AA 36
47 MONTPEZAT 172 Y 31
82 MONTPEZAT DE QUERCY C 173 DA 32
07 MONTPEZAT SOUS BAUZON C 163 PA 30
50 MONTPINCHON 34 Q 11
81 MONTPINIER 190 GA 34
31 MONTPITOL 189 EA 34
55 MONTPLONNE 44 TA 12
49 MONTPOLLIN 96 W 17
24 MONTPON MENESTEROL C 157 X 28
71 MONTPONT EN BRESSE C 121 TA 22
10 MONTPOTHIER 63 MA 13
47 MONTPOUILLAN 171 W 31
31 MONTRABE 210 DA 35
50 MONTRABOT 35 S 10
01 MONTRACOL 137 TA 23
79 MONTRAVERS 111 T 20
07 MONTREAL 178 PA 31
11 MONTREAL C 212 GA 36
32 MONTREAL C 186 X 33
89 MONTREAL 84 OA 17
01 MONTREAL LA CLUSE 138 VA 23
26 MONTREAL LES SOURCES 180 UA 31
59 MONTRECOURT 18 LA 5
46 MONTREDON 175 GA 30
11 MONTREDON DES CORBIERES 223 JA 37
81 MONTREDON LABESSONNIE C 190 GA 34
43 MONTREGARD 164 PA 28
31 MONTREJEAU C 217 Z 37
44 MONTRELAIS 95 S 18
24 MONTREM 157 Z 28
37 MONTRESOR C 98 BA 19
71 MONTRET C 121 TA 21
28 MONTREUIL 38 CA 12
62 MONTREUIL S 16 EA 4
85 MONTREUIL 111 S 22
93 MONTREUIL C 40 HA 11
61 MONTREUIL AU HOULME 58 V 12
02 MONTREUIL AUX LIONS 41 KA 11
49 MONTREUIL BELLAY C 96 W 19
86 MONTREUIL BONNIN 113 X 22

35 MONTREUIL DES LANDES 76 R 14
14 MONTREUIL EN AUGE 36 W 10
76 MONTREUIL EN CAUX 24 BA 8
37 MONTREUIL EN TOURAINE 79 AA 17
49 MONTREUIL JUIGNE 95 T 17
27 MONTREUIL L'ARGILLE 37 Y 11
61 MONTREUIL LA CAMBE 36 W 11
72 MONTREUIL LE CHETIF 58 W 14
35 MONTREUIL LE GAST 75 O 14
72 MONTREUIL LE HENRI 79 Z 16
53 MONTREUIL POULAY 57 U 13
35 MONTREUIL SOUS PEROUSE 76 R 14
10 MONTREUIL SUR BARSE 65 PA 14
52 MONTREUIL SUR BLAISE 66 SA 13
60 MONTREUIL SUR BRECHE 26 GA 8
95 MONTREUIL SUR EPTE 39 EA 10
35 MONTREUIL SUR ILLE 75 P 14
49 MONTREUIL SUR LOIR 77 U 17
50 MONTREUIL SUR LOZON 34 R 10
49 MONTREUIL SUR MAINE 77 T 17
60 MONTREUIL SUR THERAIN 26 GA 9
52 MONTREUIL SUR THONNANCE 66 TA 13
58 MONTREUILLON 103 NA 19
54 MONTREUX 69 BB 13
90 MONTREUX CHATEAU 90 BB 17
68 MONTREUX JEUNE 90 BB 17
68 MONTREUX VIEUX 90 BB 17
49 MONTREVAULT C 94 R 18
38 MONTREVEL 152 UA 26
39 MONTREVEL 122 VA 22
01 MONTREVEL EN BRESSE C 137 TA 22
41 MONTRICHARD C 98 BA 18
73 MONTRICHER ALBANNE 153 ZA 27
82 MONTRICOUX 188 DA 33
41 MONTRIEUX EN SOLOGNE 81 EA 17
26 MONTRIGAUD 165 TA 28
74 MONTRIOND 140 AB 23
48 MONTRODAT 177 LA 30
87 MONTROL SENARD 130 AA 24
16 MONTROLLET 130 AA 24
69 MONTROMANT 150 QA 25
05 MONTROND 181 WA 31
39 MONTROND 122 WA 21
25 MONTROND LE CHATEAU 107 XA 19
42 MONTROND LES BAINS 149 PA 26
81 MONTROSIER 174 EA 32
69 MONTROTTIER 150 QA 25
76 MONTROTY 25 EA 9
92 MONTROUGE C 40 GA 12
41 MONTROUVEAU 79 Z 16
17 MONTROY 127 S 23
12 MONTROZIER 176 IA 31
77 MONTRY 40 JA 11
37 MONTS 98 Z 18
60 MONTS 39 FA 10
14 MONTS EN BESSIN 35 T 10
62 MONTS EN TERNOIS 16 HA 5
86 MONTS SUR GUESNES C 113 X 20
48 MONTS VERTS, LES 162 KA 29
12 MONTSALES 174 FA 31
04 MONTSALIER 196 VA 33
15 MONTSALVY C 161 HA 30
73 MONTSAPEY 153 YA 26
58 MONTSAUCHE LES SETTONS C 103 OA 19
52 MONTSAUGEON 87 UA 17
31 MONTSAUNES 217 AA 37
55 MONTSEC 45 WA 11
61 MONTSECRET 57 T 12
09 MONTSEGUR 219 EA 38
26 MONTSEGUR SUR LAUZON 179 SA 31
07 MONTSELGUES 178 OA 31
11 MONTSERET 223 JA 37
65 MONTSERIE 217 Y 37
09 MONTSERON 218 CA 37
38 MONTSEVEROUX 151 SA 27
49 MONTSOREAU 97 W 19
40 MONTSOUE 184 U 34
95 MONTSOULT 40 GA 10
53 MONTSURS C 77 U 15
50 MONTSURVENT 34 P 10
10 MONTSUZAIN 65 PA 13
70 MONTUREUX ET PRANTIGNY 87 VA 17
70 MONTUREUX LES BAULAY 88 XA 16
43 MONTUSCLAT 163 OA 28
25 MONTUSSAINT 32 YA 8
33 MONTUSSAN 156 U 29
81 MONTVALEN 188 DA 34
46 MONTVALENT 159 DA 29
73 MONTVALEZAN 154 BB 26
26 MONTVENDRE 165 SA 29
42 MONTVERDUN 149 OA 25
73 MONTVERNIER 153 YA 27
15 MONTVERT 160 GA 28
03 MONTVICQ 133 JA 23
14 MONTVIETTE 36 W 11
76 MONTVILLE 24 BA 8
50 MONTVIRON 56 Q 12
55 MONTZEVILLE 44 TA 10
47 MONVIEL 172 Z 30
11 MONZE 221 HA 37
50 MOON SUR ELLE 34 R 10
68 MOOSCH 90 CB 16
68 MOOSLARGUE 90 CB 17
58 MORACHES 102 MA 18
17 MORAGNE 127 T 24
28 MORAINVILLE 61 EA 13
27 MORAINVILLE JOUVEAUX 37 Y 10
78 MORAINVILLIERS 39 FA 11
69 MORANCE 136 RA 24
28 MORANCEZ 60 DA 13
52 MORANCOURT 66 SA 13
37 MORAND 79 BA 17
51 MORANGIS 42 NA 11
91 MORANGIS 40 GA 12
60 MORANGLES 40 GA 10
49 MORANNES 77 U 16
55 MORANVILLE 45 VA 10
38 MORAS 151 TA 25
26 MORAS EN VALLOIRE 151 SA 27
59 MORBECQUE 8 HA 3
39 MORBIER 123 XA 22
40 MORCENX C 183 S 33
80 MORCHAIN 27 JA 7
62 MORCHIES 17 JA 6
02 MORCOURT 28 LA 7
80 MORCOURT 26 IA 7
35 MORDELLES C 75 O 15
56 MOREAC 74 K 16
41 MOREE C 80 CA 16
85 MOREILLES 125 R 22
88 MORELMAISON 67 WA 14
10 MOREMBERT 65 PA 13
38 MORESTEL C 152 UA 25
77 MORET SUR LOING C 62 JA 13
38 MORETEL DE MAILLES 153 XA 27
38 MORETTE 152 UA 27
80 MOREUIL C 26 HA 7
71 MOREY 120 RA 20
21 MOREY ST DENIS 105 SA 19
39 MOREZ C 123 XA 22
54 MORFONTAINE 31 WA 9
40 MORGANX 207 U 35
55 MORGEMOULIN 45 VA 10
27 MORGNY 25 DA 9
02 MORGNY EN THIERACHE 29 OA 7
76 MORGNY LA POMMERAYE 24 CA 8
57 MORHANGE 47 AB 11
63 MORIAT 148 LA 27
76 MORIENNE 25 EA 7
60 MORIENVAL 41 JA 9
84 MORIERES LES AVIGNON 195 SA 33
28 MORIERS 60 DA 14
22 MORIEUX 54 L 13
04 MORIEZ 198 ZA 33
50 MORIGNY 35 R 11
91 MORIGNY CHAMPIGNY 61 GA 13
74 MORILLON 140 AB 24
62 MORINGHEM 8 GA 3
52 MORIONVILLIERS 66 UA 14
80 MORISEL 26 HA 7
88 MORIVILLE 68 ZA 14
54 MORIVILLER 68 ZA 13
88 MORIZECOURT 67 WA 15
33 MORIZES 171 W 30
64 MORLAAS C 207 V 36
18 MORLAC 116 GA 21
29 MORLAIX S 52 F 13
80 MORLANCOURT 17 IA 6
64 MORLANNE 207 U 35
71 MORLET 120 OA 20
55 MORLEY 66 TA 13
12 MORLHON LE HAUT 174 FA 32
60 MORLINCOURT 27 KA 8
85 MORMAISON 110 O 20
77 MORMANT C 63 JA 12
45 MORMANT SUR VERNISSON 82 IA 15
32 MORMES 185 V 34
84 MORMOIRON C 196 TA 33
16 MORNAC 143 X 25
17 MORNAC SUR SEUDRE 141 S 25
42 MORNAND 149 OA 25
26 MORNANS 179 TA 30
69 MORNANT C 150 RA 26
84 MORNAS 179 RA 32
71 MORNAY 120 QA 22
18 MORNAY BERRY 101 JA 19
18 MORNAY SUR ALLIER 118 KA 20
71 MOROGES 120 RA 21
18 MOROGUES 101 IA 19
2B MOROSAGLIA C 226 LB 40
25 MORRE 107 XA 19
02 MORSAIN 27 KA 9
51 MORSAINS 42 MA 12
50 MORSALINES 33 O 8
27 MORSAN 37 Z 10
91 MORSANG SUR ORGE C 62 HA 12
91 MORSANG SUR SEINE 62 HA 13
57 MORSBACH 47 BB 10
67 MORSBRONN LES BAINS 49 FB 11
67 MORSCHWILLER 49 EB 12
68 MORSCHWILLER LE BAS 90 CB 16
2B MORSIGLIA 226 MB 38
88 MORTAGNE 69 AB 14
61 MORTAGNE AU PERCHE S 59 Z 13
59 MORTAGNE DU NORD 18 LA 4
17 MORTAGNE SUR GIRONDE 141 T 26
85 MORTAGNE SUR SEVRE C 95 S 20
50 MORTAIN C 57 S 12
77 MORTCERF 41 JA 12
38 MORTE, LA 166 WA 28
25 MORTEAU C 108 ZA 19
14 MORTEAUX COULIBOEUF C 36 W 11
02 MORTEFONTAINE 27 KA 9
60 MORTEFONTAINE 40 IA 10
60 MORTEFONTAINE EN THELLE 39 GA 10
87 MORTEMART 130 AA 24
60 MORTEMER 27 IA 8
76 MORTEMER 25 DA 7
77 MORTERY 63 LA 13
18 MORTHOMIERS 100 GA 19
02 MORTIERS 28 MA 8
17 MORTIERS 142 V 27
86 MORTON 96 W 19
61 MORTREE C 58 W 12
23 MORTROUX 132 FA 22
68 MORTZWILLER 90 BB 16
62 MORVAL 17 JA 6
90 MORVILLARS 90 BB 17
50 MORVILLE 33 P 9
88 MORVILLE 67 WA 14
45 MORVILLE EN BEAUCE 61 GA 14
57 MORVILLE LES VIC 46 ZA 12
76 MORVILLE SUR ANDELLE 25 DA 9
57 MORVILLE SUR NIED 47 ZA 11
54 MORVILLE SUR SEILLE 46 YA 11
60 MORVILLERS 25 EA 8
80 MORVILLERS ST SATURNIN 25 EA 7
10 MORVILLIERS 65 RA 13
28 MORVILLIERS 60 AA 12
62 MORY 17 JA 6
60 MORY MONTCRUX 26 HA 8
74 MORZINE 140 AB 23
14 MOSLES 35 T 9
51 MOSLINS 42 OA 11
16 MOSNAC 143 W 26
17 MOSNAC 142 U 26
36 MOSNAY 115 DA 21
37 MOSNE 98 BA 18
66 MOSSET 222 HA 39
21 MOSSON 85 RA 16
12 MOSTUEJOULS 176 KA 32
70 MOTEY BESUCHE 106 VA 18
70 MOTEY SUR SAONE 87 WA 17
85 MOTHE ACHARD, LA C 109 P 21
79 MOTHE ST HERAY, LA C 128 V 22
67 MOTHERN 50 GB 11
29 MOTREFF 72 G 14
22 MOTTE, LA 74 K 14
83 MOTTE, LA 204 ZA 35
26 MOTTE CHALANCON, LA C 180 UA 31
84 MOTTE D'AIGUES, LA 196 VA 34
38 MOTTE D'AVEILLANS, LA 166 WA 29
26 MOTTE DE GALAURE, LA 165 SA 28
04 MOTTE DU CAIRE, LA C 181 XA 31
73 MOTTE EN BAUGES, LA 153 XA 25
05 MOTTE EN CHAMPSAUR, LA 167 XA 30
26 MOTTE FANJAS, LA 165 UA 28
36 MOTTE FEUILLY, LA 116 FA 22
61 MOTTE FOUQUET, LA 58 V 13
73 MOTTE SERVOLEX, LA C 152 WA 26
71 MOTTE ST JEAN, LA 119 OA 22
38 MOTTE ST MARTIN, LA 166 WA 29
21 MOTTE TERNANT, LA 104 PA 18
10 MOTTE TILLY, LA 63 LA 13
28 MOTTEREAU 60 BA 14
76 MOTTEVILLE 24 AA 8
38 MOTTIER 151 UA 27
73 MOTZ 138 WA 24
54 MOUACOURT 68 AB 12
44 MOUAIS 93 P 17
06 MOUANS SARTOUX 200 BB 35
54 MOUAVILLE 45 WA 10
35 MOUAZE 76 P 14
85 MOUCHAMPS 110 R 21
32 MOUCHAN 186 X 33
39 MOUCHARD 122 WA 20
50 MOUCHE, LA 56 Q 12
32 MOUCHES 208 Y 35
59 MOUCHIN 9 LA 4
60 MOUCHY LE CHATEL 26 GA 9
43 MOUDEYRES 163 OA 29
14 MOUEN 35 U 10
27 MOUETTES 38 CA 11
89 MOUFFY 83 MA 17
27 MOUFLAINES 38 DA 10
80 MOUFLERS 16 FA 6
80 MOUFLIERES 15 EA 7
06 MOUGINS C 200 BB 35
79 MOUGON 128 V 23
64 MOUGUERRE 205 Q 35
36 MOUHERS 115 EA 22
36 MOUHET 131 CA 22
64 MOUHOUS 207 V 35
33 MOUILLAC 156 U 28
82 MOUILLAC 174 EA 32
39 MOUILLE, LA 123 XA 22
52 MOUILLERON 86 TA 17
85 MOUILLERON EN PAREDS 111 S 21
85 MOUILLERON LE CAPTIF 110 Q 21
55 MOUILLY 45 VA 10
55 MOULAINVILLE 45 VA 10
81 MOULARES 190 GA 33
53 MOULAY 57 T 14
81 MOULAYRES 189 FA 34
65 MOULEDOUS 208 X 36
34 MOULES ET BAUCELS 192 NA 33
24 MOULEYDIER 158 Z 29
30 MOULEZAN 193 OA 33
28 MOULHARD 60 BA 14
61 MOULICENT 59 AA 13
16 MOULIDARS 142 W 26
33 MOULIETS ET VILLEMARTIN 157 W 29
49 MOULIHERNE 97 W 18
81 MOULIN MAGE 191 JA 34
09 MOULIN NEUF 221 FA 37
24 MOULIN NEUF 157 W 28
60 MOULIN SOUS TOUVENT 27 KA 9
76 MOULINEAUX 24 AA 9
14 MOULINES 36 V 11
50 MOULINES 57 S 13
06 MOULINET 199 DB 33
47 MOULINET 172 Z 31
45 MOULINET SUR SOLIN, LE 82 IA 16
02 MOULINS 28 MA 9
03 MOULINS P 118 LA 22
35 MOULINS 76 Q 15
89 MOULINS EN TONNERROIS 84 OA 16
58 MOULINS ENGILBERT C 119 NA 20
61 MOULINS LA MARCHE C 59 Y 12
72 MOULINS LE CARBONNEL 58 W 14
57 MOULINS LES METZ 46 XA 10
55 MOULINS ST HUBERT 30 TA 8
36 MOULINS SUR CEPHONS 115 DA 20
61 MOULINS SUR ORNE 58 W 12
89 MOULINS SUR OUANNE 83 LA 16
18 MOULINS SUR YEVRE 101 HA 19
09 MOULIS 218 BA 38
33 MOULIS EN MEDOC 155 T 28
86 MOULISMES 130 AA 23
62 MOULLE 8 GA 3
33 MOULON 156 V 29
45 MOULON 82 IA 15
55 MOULOTTE 45 WA 10
14 MOULT 36 V 10
65 MOUMOULOUS 208 X 36
64 MOUMOUR 206 T 36
12 MOUNES PROHENCOUX 191 JA 34
32 MOUREDE 186 X 34
33 MOURENS 171 V 30
64 MOURENX 207 T 36
12 MOURET 175 HA 31
63 MOUREUILLE 133 JA 23
34 MOUREZE 214 LA 35
13 MOURIES 195 SA 34
62 MOURIEZ 16 FA 5
23 MOURIOUX VIEILLEVILLE 131 DA 24
15 MOURJOU 175 HA 30
51 MOURMELON LE GRAND 43 QA 10
51 MOURMELON LE PETIT 43 PA 10
39 MOURNANS CHARBONNY 123 XA 21
08 MOURON 30 RA 9
58 MOURON SUR YONNE 103 NA 19
77 MOUROUX 41 KA 11
95 MOURS 40 GA 10
26 MOURS ST EUSEBE 165 TA 28
31 MOURVILLES BASSES 211 EA 35
31 MOURVILLES HAUTES 211 EA 35
40 MOUSCARDES 184 S 35
30 MOUSSAC 193 PA 33
86 MOUSSAC 130 Z 23
15 MOUSSAGES 161 HA 27
11 MOUSSAN 213 JA 36
35 MOUSSE 76 Q 15
77 MOUSSEAUX LES BRAY 63 KA 13
27 MOUSSEAUX NEUVILLE 38 CA 11
78 MOUSSEAUX SUR SEINE 39 EA 11
10 MOUSSEY 64 OA 14
57 MOUSSEY 69 AB 12
88 MOUSSEY 69 BB 13
39 MOUSSIERES, LES 138 WA 23
54 MOUSSON 46 XA 11
61 MOUSSONVILLIERS 59 AA 12
11 MOUSSOULENS 212 GA 36
51 MOUSSY 42 OA 11
58 MOUSSY 102 LA 19
95 MOUSSY 39 FA 10
77 MOUSSY LE NEUF 40 IA 10
77 MOUSSY LE VIEUX 40 IA 11
02 MOUSSY VERNEUIL 28 MA 9
31 MOUSTAJON 217 Z 38
22 MOUSTERU 53 I 13
40 MOUSTEY 169 T 31
47 MOUSTIER 171 X 30
59 MOUSTIER EN FAGNE 19 PA 6
19 MOUSTIER VENTADOUR 146 FA 27
04 MOUSTIERS STE MARIE C 197 YA 34
22 MOUSTOIR 53 H 14
56 MOUSTOIR AC 74 K 16
56 MOUSTOIR REMUNGOL 73 J 15
63 MOUTADE, LA 134 KA 24
38 MOUTARET, LE 153 XA 27
57 MOUTERHOUSE 48 DB 11
86 MOUTERRE SILLY 112 W 20
86 MOUTERRE SUR BLOURDE 130 AA 23
25 MOUTHE C 123 YA 21
25 MOUTHEROT, LE 106 WA 19
71 MOUTHIER EN BRESSE 122 UA 20
25 MOUTHIER HAUTE PIERRE 106 UA 19
16 MOUTHIERS SUR BOEME 143 X 26
11 MOUTHOUMET C 221 HA 38
23 MOUTIER D'AHUN 132 FA 24
23 MOUTIER MALCARD 132 FA 22
23 MOUTIER ROZEILLE 132 GA 24
28 MOUTIERS 61 EA 14
35 MOUTIERS 76 R 15
54 MOUTIERS 45 XA 10
73 MOUTIERS C 154 ZA 26
61 MOUTIERS AU PERCHE 59 AA 13
14 MOUTIERS EN AUGE, LES 36 W 11
14 MOUTIERS EN CINGLAIS, LES 36 U 11
89 MOUTIERS EN PUISAYE 83 KA 17
44 MOUTIERS EN RETZ, LES 109 N 19
14 MOUTIERS HUBERT, LES 37 X 11
85 MOUTIERS LES MAUXFAITS C 125 O 22
79 MOUTIERS SOUS ARGENTON 112 U 20
79 MOUTIERS SOUS CHANTEMERLE 111 T 21
21 MOUTIERS ST JEAN 85 PA 17
85 MOUTIERS SUR LE LAY 125 R 22
16 MOUTON 129 X 25
39 MOUTONNE 122 VA 22
16 MOUTONNEAU 129 X 24
39 MOUTOUX 123 XA 21
54 MOUTROT 67 WA 12
59 MOUVAUX 9 KA 3
11 MOUX 223 IA 37
58 MOUX EN MORVAN 103 PA 19
73 MOUXY 153 XA 25
60 MOUY C 26 GA 9
77 MOUY SUR SEINE 63 KA 13
37 MOUZAY 98 AA 19
55 MOUZAY 30 TA 9
44 MOUZEIL 94 Q 18
24 MOUZENS 158 BA 29
81 MOUZENS 211 FA 35
85 MOUZEUIL ST MARTIN 111 S 22
81 MOUZIEYS PANENS 189 FA 33
81 MOUZIEYS TEULET 190 GA 34
44 MOUZILLON 94 O 19
08 MOUZON C 30 TA 8
16 MOUZON 144 Z 25
02 MOY DE L'AISNE C 28 LA 7
14 MOYAUX 37 Y 10
05 MOYDANS 180 VA 31
74 MOYE 138 WA 25
88 MOYEMONT 68 ZA 14
54 MOYEN 68 ZA 13
80 MOYENCOURT 27 JA 7
80 MOYENCOURT LES POIX 26 FA 7
88 MOYENMOUTIER 69 BB 13
60 MOYENNEVILLE 27 IA 9
62 MOYENNEVILLE 17 IA 5
80 MOYENNEVILLE C 15 EA 6
57 MOYENVIC 46 ZA 12
57 MOYEUVRE GRANDE C 45 XA 10
57 MOYEUVRE PETITE 32 XA 10
50 MOYON 34 R 11
12 MOYRAZES 175 HA 31
60 MOYVILLERS 27 IA 9
63 MOZAC 134 KA 25
49 MOZE SUR LOUET 96 U 18
76 MUCHEDENT 24 BA 7
34 MUDAISON 194 OA 35
35 MUEL 75 N 15
68 MUESPACH 90 DB 17
68 MUESPACH LE HAUT 90 DB 17
40 MUGRON C 184 T 34
67 MUHLBACH SUR BRUCHE 69 DB 13
68 MUHLBACH SUR MUNSTER 90 BB 15
41 MUIDES SUR LOIRE 80 DA 17
60 MUIDORGE 26 GA 8
27 MUIDS 38 CA 10
80 MUILLE VILLETTE 27 KA 8
60 MUIRANCOURT 27 JA 8
51 MUIZON 42 NA 10
06 MUJOULS, LES 198 BB 33
69 MULATIERE, LA 150 RA 25
78 MULCENT 39 EA 11
57 MULCEY 47 AB 12
67 MULHAUSEN 48 EB 11
68 MULHOUSE S 90 DB 16
72 MULSANNE 78 X 16
41 MULSANS 80 CA 17
65 MUN 208 X 36
67 MUNCHHAUSEN 50 GB 11
68 MUNCHHOUSE 90 DB 16
62 MUNCQ NIEURLET 8 GA 2
67 MUNDOLSHEIM C 49 EB 12
50 MUNEVILLE LE BINGARD 34 Q 10
50 MUNEVILLE SUR MER 56 Q 11
17 MUNG, LE 127 T 25
57 MUNSTER 47 BB 11
68 MUNSTER C 90 CB 15
68 MUNTZENHEIM 70 DB 15
68 MUNWILLER 90 DB 15
12 MUR DE BARREZ C 161 IA 29
22 MUR DE BRETAGNE C 73 J 14
41 MUR DE SOLOGNE 99 DA 18
2B MURACCIOLE 228 LB 41
12 MURASSON 191 IA 34
03 MURAT 133 JA 22
15 MURAT C 161 JA 28
63 MURAT LE QUAIRE 147 IA 26
81 MURAT SUR VEBRE C 191 JA 34
2B MURATO C 226 MB 39
74 MURAZ, LA 139 YA 24
68 MURBACH 90 CB 15
38 MURE, LA C 166 WA 29
04 MURE ARGENS, LA 198 ZA 33
60 MUREAUMONT 25 EA 8
78 MUREAUX, LES 39 FA 11
26 MUREILS 165 SA 28
74 MURES 139 XA 25
31 MURET S 210 CA 35
02 MURET ET CROUTTES 41 LA 9
12 MURET LE CHATEAU 175 IA 31
38 MURETTE, LA 152 VA 27
38 MURIANETTE 166 WA 28
38 MURINAIS 166 UA 28
34 MURLES 192 NA 34
58 MURLIN 102 KA 19
2B MURO 225 KB 39
63 MUROL 147 JA 26
12 MUROLS 161 IA 30
17 MURON 127 S 24
36 MURS 114 BA 20
84 MURS 196 TA 33
49 MURS ERIGNE 95 U 18
01 MURS ET GELIGNIEUX 152 VA 26
08 MURTIN ET BOGNY 29 QA 7
55 MURVAUX 30 TA 9
34 MURVIEL LES BEZIERS C 213 KA 35
34 MURVIEL LES MONTPELLIER 214 NA 35
54 MURVILLE 31 WA 9
2A MURZO 227 JB 41
30 MUS 193 PA 34
02 MUSCOURT 28 NA 9
64 MUSCULDY 206 S 37
74 MUSIEGES 139 XA 24
21 MUSIGNY 104 QA 19
52 MUSSEY SUR MARNE 66 TA 13
24 MUSSIDAN C 157 Y 28
67 MUSSIG 70 DB 14
21 MUSSY LA FOSSE 85 QA 17
71 MUSSY SOUS DUN 136 PA 23
10 MUSSY SUR SEINE C 85 QA 15
39 MUTIGNEY 106 VA 18
51 MUTIGNY 42 OA 10
14 MUTRECY 36 U 10
67 MUTTERSHOLTZ 70 EB 14
67 MUTZENHOUSE 49 EB 12
67 MUTZIG 70 DB 13
83 MUY, LE C 204 ZA 35
55 MUZERAY 31 VA 9
56 MUZILLAC C 92 L 17
27 MUZY 38 CA 12
73 MYANS 153 XA 26
58 MYENNES 101 JA 18
25 MYON 107 XA 20

N

64 NABAS 206 S 36
16 NABINAUD 143 X 27
24 NABIRAT 159 CA 30
62 NABRINGHEN 7 EA 3
17 NACHAMPS 127 T 24
24 NADAILLAC 159 CA 28
46 NADAILLAC DE ROUGE 159 CA 29
03 NADES 133 JA 23
46 NADILLAC 174 DA 30
27 NAGEL SEEZ MESNIL 38 AA 11
81 NAGES 191 IA 34
30 NAGES ET SOLORGUES 193 PA 34
66 NAHUJA 222 FA 40
24 NAILHAC 158 BA 28
23 NAILLAT 131 DA 23
31 NAILLOUX C 210 DA 36
89 NAILLY 63 KA 14
86 NAINTRE 113 Y 21
91 NAINVILLE LES ROCHES 62 HA 13
25 NAISEY LES GRANGES 107 YA 19
55 NAIVES EN BLOIS 45 VA 12
55 NAIVES ROSIERES 44 TA 12
55 NAIX AUX FORGES 66 UA 12
56 NAIZIN 74 K 15
12 NAJAC C 174 FA 32
85 NALLIERS 111 S 22
86 NALLIERS 114 AA 21
09 NALZEN 219 EA 38
68 NAMBSHEIM 90 EB 15
60 NAMPCEL 27 KA 9
02 NAMPCELLES LA COUR 29 OA 7
80 NAMPONT 15 EA 5
80 NAMPS MAISNIL 26 GA 7
02 NAMPTEUIL SOUS MURET 28 LA 9
80 NAMPTY 26 GA 7
21 NAN SOUS THIL 104 QA 18
39 NANC LES ST AMOUR 122 UA 22
18 NANCAY 100 GA 18
39 NANCE 122 UA 21
73 NANCES 152 WA 26
16 NANCLARS 129 X 25
55 NANCOIS LE GRAND 44 UA 12
55 NANCOIS SUR ORNAIN 44 UA 12
17 NANCRAS 141 S 25
25 NANCRAY 107 YA 19
45 NANCRAY SUR RIMARDE 82 GA 15
39 NANCUISE 122 VA 22
54 NANCY P 46 XA 12
74 NANCY SUR CLUSES 139 ZA 24
42 NANDAX 135 PA 24
77 NANDY 62 IA 13
45 NANGEVILLE 62 GA 14
77 NANGIS C 63 KA 13
74 NANGY 139 YA 23
58 NANNAY 102 KA 18
25 NANS 107 ZA 17
39 NANS, LES 123 XA 21
83 NANS LES PINS 202 WA 36
25 NANS SOUS STE ANNE 107 XA 20
12 NANT C 192 LA 33
55 NANT LE GRAND 44 TA 12
55 NANT LE PETIT 44 TA 12
77 NANTEAU SUR ESSONNE 62 HA 14
77 NANTEAU SUR LUNAIN 62 JA 14
92 NANTERRE P 39 GA 11
44 NANTES P 93 P 19
38 NANTES ENRATIER 166 WA 29
79 NANTEUIL 112 V 22
24 NANTEUIL AURIAC DE BOURZAC 143 X 27
16 NANTEUIL EN VALLEE 129 Y 24
51 NANTEUIL LA FORET 42 OA 10
02 NANTEUIL LA FOSSE 41 LA 9
60 NANTEUIL LE HAUDOUIN C 40 JA 10
77 NANTEUIL LES MEAUX 41 JA 11
02 NANTEUIL NOTRE DAME 41 LA 10
08 NANTEUIL SUR AISNE 29 PA 8
77 NANTEUIL SUR MARNE 41 KA 11
39 NANTEY 122 UA 22
24 NANTHEUIL 144 AA 27
24 NANTHIAT 144 BA 27
87 NANTIAT C 130 BA 24
17 NANTILLE 128 U 25
55 NANTILLOIS 30 TA 9
70 NANTILLY 106 VA 18
38 NANTOIN 151 TA 27
55 NANTOIS 66 UA 12
71 NANTON 120 RA 21
77 NANTOUILLET 40 IA 11
21 NANTOUX 120 RA 20
01 NANTUA S 138 VA 23
80 NAOURS 16 GA 6
57 NARBEFONTAINE 47 ZA 10
25 NARBIEF 108 AB 19
11 NARBONNE S 223 JA 37
64 NARCASTET 207 V 36
52 NARCY 66 TA 13
58 NARCY 102 KA 19
45 NARGIS 62 IA 15
15 NARNHAC 161 IA 29
64 NARP 206 S 36
40 NARROSSE 183 S 34
48 NASBINALS C 176 KA 30
27 NASSANDRES 37 Z 10
40 NASSIET 184 T 35

03 NASSIGNY 117 IA 22
24 NASTRINGUES 157 X 29
01 NATTAGES 152 WA 25
67 NATZWILLER 69 CB 13
12 NAUCELLE C 175 HA 32
15 NAUCELLES 161 HA 29
33 NAUJAC SUR MER 141 R 27
33 NAUJAN ET POSTIAC 156 V 29
02 NAUROY 18 LA 6
12 NAUSSAC 174 FA 31
48 NAUSSAC 163 NA 30
24 NAUSSANNES 158 Z 30
72 NAUVAY 59 Y 14
12 NAUVIALE 175 HA 31
30 NAVACELLES 178 PA 32
64 NAVAILLES ANGOS 207 V 36
64 NAVARRENX C 206 T 36
41 NAVEIL 80 BA 16
70 NAVENNE 88 YA 17
03 NAVES 134 KA 23
19 NAVES C 145 EA 27
59 NAVES 18 LA 5
81 NAVES 212 GA 35
74 NAVES PARMELAN 139 YA 24
71 NAVILLY 121 TA 20
50 NAY 34 Q 10
64 NAY C 215 V 37
88 NAYEMONT LES FOSSES 69 BB 14
12 NAYRAC, LE 175 IA 30
37 NAZELLES NEGRON 98 AA 18
33 NEAC 156 V 29
56 NEANT SUR YVEL 74 M 15
53 NEAU 77 U 14
27 NEAUFLES AUVERGNY 37 Z 11
27 NEAUFLES ST MARTIN 39 EA 9
61 NEAUPHE SOUS ESSAI 58 X 13
61 NEAUPHE SUR DIVE 36 X 11
78 NEAUPHLE LE CHATEAU 39 FA 12
78 NEAUPHLE LE VIEUX 39 EA 12
78 NEAUPHLETTE 38 DA 11
42 NEAUX 135 PA 24
34 NEBIAN 214 LA 35
11 NEBIAS 221 GA 38
57 NEBING 47 AB 11
63 NEBOUZAT 147 JA 25
61 NECY 36 W 11
87 NEDDE 146 EA 25
62 NEDON 8 HA 4
62 NEDONCHEL 8 HA 4
67 NEEWILLER
PRES LAUTERBOURG 50 GB 11
05 NEFFES 181 XA 31
34 NEFFIES 214 LA 35
66 NEFIACH 224 IA 39
82 NEGREPELISSE C 188 DA 33
50 NEGREVILLE 33 P 9
24 NEGRONDES 144 AA 27
50 NEHOU 33 P 9
57 NELLING 47 BB 11
77 NEMOURS C 62 IA 14
62 NEMPONT ST FIRMIN 15 EA 5
31 NENIGAN 209 Z 36
36 NEONS SUR CREUSE 114 AA 21
83 NEOULES 203 XA 36
23 NEOUX 132 GA 24
55 NEPVANT 30 TA 8
47 NERAC S 171 Y 32
40 NERBIS 184 T 34
16 NERCILLAC 142 V 25
17 NERE 128 V 24
36 NERET 116 GA 22
33 NERIGEAN 156 V 29
86 NERIGNAC 130 Z 23
03 NERIS LES BAINS 133 IA 23
74 NERNIER 139 YA 22
28 NERON 60 DA 13
42 NERONDE C 135 PA 25
63 NERONDE SUR DORE 148 MA 25
18 NERONDES C 117 JA 20
38 NERPOL ET SERRES 152 UA 27
30 NERS 193 PA 33
16 NERSAC 143 W 26
42 NERVIEUX 149 PA 25
95 NERVILLE LA FORET 40 GA 10
60 NERY 41 JA 9
63 NESCHERS 148 KA 26
09 NESCUS 218 CA 37
80 NESLE C 27 JA 7
21 NESLE ET MASSOULT 85 QA 16
76 NESLE HODENG 25 DA 8
80 NESLE L'HOPITAL 25 EA 7
51 NESLE LA REPOSTE 64 MA 12
51 NESLE LE REPONS 42 NA 10
76 NESLE NORMANDEUSE 15 DA 7
62 NESLES 7 EA 3
02 NESLES LA MONTAGNE 41 LA 11
95 NESLES LA VALLEE 39 GA 10
80 NESLETTE 15 EA 7
85 NESMY 110 Q 21
45 NESPLOY 82 HA 15
19 NESPOULS 159 DA 28
2B NESSA 225 KB 39
65 NESTIER 217 Y 37
55 NETTANCOURT 44 SA 11
39 NEUBLANS ABERGEMENT 121 UA 20
67 NEUBOIS 70 DB 14
27 NEUBOURG, LE C 38 AA 10
25 NEUCHATEL URTIERE 108 AB 18
59 NEUF BERQUIN 8 IA 3
68 NEUF BRISACH C 90 DB 15
63 NEUF EGLISE 133 JA 24
76 NEUF MARCHE 25 EA 9
59 NEUF MESNIL 19 NA 5
76 NEUFBOSC 25 CA 8
50 NEUFBOURG, LE 57 S 12
88 NEUFCHATEAU S 67 WA 14
76 NEUFCHATEL EN BRAY C 25 DA 7
72 NEUFCHATEL EN SAOSNOIS 58 X 14
62 NEUFCHATEL HARDELOT 7 DA 4
02 NEUFCHATEL SUR AISNE C 29 OA 9
57 NEUFCHEF 32 XA 9
60 NEUFCHELLES 41 KA 10
33 NEUFFONS 171 W 30
58 NEUFFONTAINES 103 NA 18
57 NEUFGRANGE 48 CB 10
02 NEUFLIEUX 27 KA 8
08 NEUFLIZE 29 PA 9
08 NEUFMAISON 29 QA 7
54 NEUFMAISONS 69 BB 13
08 NEUFMANIL 29 RA 7
50 NEUFMESNIL 34 P 9
80 NEUFMOULIN 16 FA 6
57 NEUFMOULINS 69 BB 12
77 NEUFMOUTIERS EN BRIE 40 JA 12
50 NEUFOUR, LE 44 SA 10
57 NEUFVILLAGE 47 AB 11
60 NEUFVY SUR ARONDE 27 IA 8
67 NEUGARTHEIM ITTLENHEIM 49 EB 12
67 NEUHAEUSEL 50 GB 12
37 NEUIL 97 Y 19
65 NEUILH 216 W 37
17 NEUILLAC 142 U 26
36 NEUILLAY LES BOIS 115 DA 21
49 NEUILLE 96 W 18
37 NEUILLE LE LIERRE 79 AA 17
37 NEUILLE PONT PIERRE C 97 Y 17
27 NEUILLY 38 CA 11
58 NEUILLY 102 MA 19
89 NEUILLY 83 LA 16
03 NEUILLY EN DONJON 135 NA 23
18 NEUILLY EN DUN 117 IA 21
18 NEUILLY EN SANCERRE 101 IA 18
60 NEUILLY EN THELLE C 40 GA 10
95 NEUILLY EN VEXIN 39 FA 10
52 NEUILLY L'HOPITAL 16 FA 6
14 NEUILLY LA FORET 34 R 10
61 NEUILLY LE BISSON 58 X 13
37 NEUILLY LE BRIGNON 114 AA 20
80 NEUILLY LE DIEN 16 FA 5
03 NEUILLY LE REAL C 118 LA 22
53 NEUILLY LE VENDIN 58 V 13
21 NEUILLY LES DIJON 105 TA 18
52 NEUILLY LEVEQUE C 87 UA 16
93 NEUILLY PLAISANCE C 40 HA 11
60 NEUILLY SOUS CLERMONT 26 HA 9
02 NEUILLY ST FRONT C 41 LA 10
61 NEUILLY SUR EURE 59 AA 13
93 NEUILLY SUR MARNE C 40 HA 11
92 NEUILLY SUR SEINE C 40 GA 11
52 NEUILLY SUR SUIZE 86 TA 15
62 NEULETTE 16 GA 5
42 NEULISE 135 PA 24
17 NEULLES 142 U 26
56 NEULLIAC 73 J 15
41 NEUNG SUR BEUVRON C 81 EA 17
57 NEUNKIRCHEN
LES BOUZONVILLE 47 ZA 9
03 NEURE 117 JA 21
70 NEUREY EN VAUX 88 YA 16
70 NEUREY LES LA DEMIE 88 YA 17
15 NEUSSARGUES MOISSAC 161 JA 28
62 NEUVE CHAPELLE 9 JA 4
67 NEUVE EGLISE 69 DB 14
27 NEUVE GRANGE, LA 25 DA 9
27 NEUVE LYRE, LA 37 AA 11
02 NEUVE MAISON 19 OA 7
74 NEUVECELLE 124 ZA 22
15 NEUVEGLISE 161 JA 29
70 NEUVELLE LES CROMARY 107 XA 18
70 NEUVELLE LES LA CHARITE 88 XA 17
70 NEUVELLE LES LURE, LA 89 ZA 16
70 NEUVELLE LES SCEY, LA 88 WA 17
52 NEUVELLE LES VOISEY 87 WA 16
54 NEUVES MAISONS C 67 XA 12
88 NEUVEVILLE
DEVANT LEPANGES, LA 68 AB 14
88 NEUVEVILLE SOUS CHATENOIS 67 WA 14
88 NEUVEVILLE
SOUS MONTFORT, LA 67 XA 14
19 NEUVIC C 146 GA 27
24 NEUVIC C 157 Y 28
87 NEUVIC ENTIER 145 DA 25
17 NEUVICQ 142 V 27
17 NEUVICQ LE CHATEAU 142 V 25
72 NEUVILLALAIS 78 W 14
19 NEUVILLE 160 EA 28
63 NEUVILLE 148 LA 25
59 NEUVILLE, LA 17 KA 4
08 NEUVILLE A MAIRE, LA 30 SA 8
80 NEUVILLE AU BOIS 16 EA 6
62 NEUVILLE AU CORNET 16 HA 5
50 NEUVILLE AU PLAIN 33 Q 9
51 NEUVILLE AU PONT, LA 44 SA 10
45 NEUVILLE AUX BOIS C 81 FA 15
51 NEUVILLE AUX BOIS, LA 44 SA 11
08 NEUVILLE AUX JOUTES, LA 19 PA 7
51 NEUVILLE AUX LARRIS 42 NA 10
60 NEUVILLE BOSC 39 FA 10
02 NEUVILLE BOSMONT, LA 28 NA 8
62 NEUVILLE BOURJONVAL 17 KA 6
76 NEUVILLE
CHANT D'OISEL, LA 24 CA 9
80 NEUVILLE COPPEGUEULE 25 EA 7
60 NEUVILLE D'AUMONT, LA 26 GA 9
08 NEUVILLE DAY 30 RA 9
86 NEUVILLE DE POITOU C 113 X 21
27 NEUVILLE DU BOSC, LA 37 AA 10
59 NEUVILLE EN AVESNOIS 18 MA 5
50 NEUVILLE EN BEAUMONT 34 P 9
02 NEUVILLE EN BEINE, LA 27 KA 8
59 NEUVILLE EN FERRAIN 9 KA 3
60 NEUVILLE EN HEZ, LA 26 GA 9
08 NEUVILLE
EN TOURNE A FUY, LA 29 QA 9
55 NEUVILLE EN VERDUNOIS 44 UA 11
76 NEUVILLE FERRIERES 25 DA 8
60 NEUVILLE GARNIER, LA 26 FA 9
02 NEUVILLE HOUSSET, LA 28 NA 7
80 NEUVILLE LES BRAY, LA 17 IA 7
01 NEUVILLE LES DAMES 137 SA 23
58 NEUVILLE LES DECIZE 118 LA 21
02 NEUVILLE LES DORENGT, LA 18 NA 6
80 NEUVILLE LES LOEUILLY 26 GA 7
08 NEUVILLE LES THIS 29 QA 7
55 NEUVILLE LES VAUCOULEURS 67 VA 13
08 NEUVILLE LES WASIGNY, LA 29 QA 8
08 NEUVILLE LEZ BEAULIEU 29 PA 7
61 NEUVILLE PRES SEES 58 X 12
80 NEUVILLE SIRE BERNARD, LA 26 HA 7
62 NEUVILLE SOUS MONTREUIL 16 EA 4
02 NEUVILLE ST AMAND 28 LA 7
60 NEUVILLE ST PIERRE, LA 26 GA 8
59 NEUVILLE ST REMY 18 KA 5
62 NEUVILLE ST VAAST 17 IA 5
02 NEUVILLE SUR AILETTE 28 NA 9
01 NEUVILLE SUR AIN 138 UA 24
27 NEUVILLE SUR AUTHOU 37 Z 10
37 NEUVILLE SUR BRENNE 79 AA 17
59 NEUVILLE SUR ESCAUT 18 LA 5
45 NEUVILLE SUR ESSONNE, LA 62 HA 14
02 NEUVILLE SUR MARGIVAL 28 LA 9
95 NEUVILLE SUR OISE 39 FA 11
55 NEUVILLE SUR ORNAIN 44 TA 12
60 NEUVILLE SUR OUDEUIL, LA 26 FA 8
60 NEUVILLE SUR RESSONS, LA 27 IA 8
69 NEUVILLE SUR SAONE C 137 SA 25
72 NEUVILLE SUR SARTHE 78 X 15
10 NEUVILLE SUR SEINE 85 QA 15
61 NEUVILLE SUR TOUQUES 37 X 11
10 NEUVILLE SUR VANNES 64 NA 14
60 NEUVILLE VAULT, LA 25 FA 9
62 NEUVILLE VITASSE 17 JA 5
67 NEUVILLER LA ROCHE 69 CB 13
54 NEUVILLER
LES BADONVILLER 69 BB 13
54 NEUVILLER SUR MOSELLE 68 YA 13
88 NEUVILLERS SUR FAVE 69 BB 14
02 NEUVILLETTE 28 MA 7
80 NEUVILLETTE 16 GA 5
72 NEUVILLETTE EN CHARNIE 78 V 15
39 NEUVILLEY 122 VA 20
59 NEUVILLY 18 MA 6
55 NEUVILLY EN ARGONNE 44 TA 10
62 NEUVIREUIL 17 JA 5
08 NEUVIZY 29 QA 8
03 NEUVY 118 LA 22
41 NEUVY 80 DA 17
51 NEUVY 42 MA 12
61 NEUVY AU HOULME 58 V 12
79 NEUVY BOUIN 112 U 21
18 NEUVY DEUX CLOCHERS 101 IA 18
28 NEUVY EN BEAUCE 61 FA 14
72 NEUVY EN CHAMPAGNE 78 W 15
28 NEUVY EN DUNOIS 60 DA 14
49 NEUVY EN MAUGES 95 S 18
45 NEUVY EN SULLIAS 81 GA 16
71 NEUVY GRANDCHAMP 119 OA 21
18 NEUVY LE BARROIS 118 KA 20
37 NEUVY LE ROI C 79 Z 17
36 NEUVY PAILLOUX 115 EA 20
89 NEUVY SAUTOUR 84 NA 15
36 NEUVY ST SEPULCHRE C 115 EA 21
18 NEUVY SUR BARANGEON 100 GA 18
58 NEUVY SUR LOIRE 82 JA 17
68 NEUWILLER 90 EB 17
67 NEUWILLER LES SAVERNE 48 DB 11
05 NEVACHE 168 ZA 28
58 NEVERS P 118 KA 20
29 NEVEZ 72 F 16
11 NEVIAN 213 JA 36
76 NEVILLE 24 Z 7
50 NEVILLE SUR MER 33 O 8
45 NEVOY 82 IA 16
39 NEVY LES DOLE 122 VA 20
39 NEVY SUR SEILLE 122 VA 21
87 NEXON C 144 BA 25
39 NEY 122 WA 21
74 NEYDENS 139 XA 24
01 NEYROLLES, LES 138 VA 23
01 NEYRON 137 SA 25
78 NEZEL 39 EA 11
34 NEZIGNAN L'EVEQUE 214 LA 35
53 NIAFLES 76 S 16
09 NIAUX 219 DA 38
80 NIBAS 15 DA 6
45 NIBELLE 82 HA 15
04 NIBLES 181 XA 32
06 NICE P 200 CB 34
21 NICEY 85 PA 16
55 NICEY SUR AIRE 44 UA 11
47 NICOLE 171 Y 31
50 NICORPS 34 O 11
57 NIDERHOFF 69 BB 12
57 NIDERVILLER 69 CB 12
67 NIEDERBRONN LES BAINS C 48 EB 11
68 NIEDERBRUCK 89 BB 16
68 NIEDERENTZEN 90 DB 15
67 NIEDERHASLACH 69 DB 13
67 NIEDERHAUSBERGEN 49 EB 12
68 NIEDERHERGHEIM 90 DB 15
67 NIEDERLAUTERBACH 50 GB 11
67 NIEDERMODERN 48 EB 11
68 NIEDERMORSCHWIHR 69 CB 15
67 NIEDERNAI 70 EB 13
67 NIEDERROEDERN 50 GB 11
67 NIEDERSCHAEFFOLSHEIM 49 FB 12
67 NIEDERSOULTZBACH 48 DB 11
67 NIEDERSTEINBACH 48 EB 11
57 NIEDERSTINZEL 48 BB 11
57 NIEDERVISSE 47 ZA 10
62 NIELLES LES ARDRES 7 FA 2
62 NIELLES LES BLEQUIN 7 FA 3
62 NIELLES LES CALAIS 7 EA 2
59 NIEPPE 9 JA 3
59 NIERGNIES 18 LA 6
15 NIEUDAN 160 GA 29
86 NIEUIL L'ESPOIR 113 Y 22
16 NIEUL 129 Y 25
87 NIEUL C 130 BA 24
85 NIEUL LE DOLENT 110 P 21
17 NIEUL LE VIROUIL 142 U 27
17 NIEUL LES SAINTES 141 T 25
85 NIEUL SUR L'AUTISE 111 T 22
17 NIEUL SUR MER 126 R 23
17 NIEULLE SUR SEUDRE 141 S 25
59 NIEURLET 8 GA 3
01 NIEVROZ 137 TA 25
68 NIFFER 90 DB 17
36 NIHERNE 115 DA 20
52 NIJON 67 VA 14
57 NILVANGE 32 XA 9
30 NIMES P 193 OA 34
52 NINVILLE 67 UA 15
79 NIORT P 128 U 23
11 NIORT DE SAULT 221 FA 38
04 NIOZELLES 197 WA 33
34 NISSAN LEZ ENSERUNE 213 KA 36
65 NISTOS 217 Y 37
89 NITRY 84 NA 17
57 NITTING 69 BB 12
59 NIVELLE 18 MA 4
56 NIVILLAC 92 M 17
60 NIVILLERS C 26 GA 9
38 NIVOLAS VERMELLE 152 UA 26
01 NIVOLLET MONTGRIFFON 138 UA 24
55 NIXEVILLE BLERCOURT 44 UA 10
33 NIZAN, LE 170 V 31
31 NIZAN GESSE 209 Z 36
32 NIZAS 209 BA 35
34 NIZAS 214 LA 35
03 NIZEROLLES 133 MA 24
02 NIZY LE COMTE 29 OA 8
12 NOAILHAC 175 HA 30
19 NOAILHAC 159 DA 28
81 NOAILHAC 212 HA 35
33 NOAILLAC 171 W 31
33 NOAILLAN 170 V 31
19 NOAILLES 159 DA 28
60 NOAILLES C 26 GA 9
81 NOAILLES 189 FA 33
42 NOAILLY 135 OA 23
48 NOALHAC 162 KA 29
63 NOALHAT 133 LA 24
27 NOARDS 37 Y 10
2B NOCARIO 228 MB 40
61 NOCE C 59 Z 13
2B NOCETA 228 LB 41
71 NOCHIZE 135 PA 22
58 NOCLE MAULAIX, LA 119 NA 21
21 NOD SUR SEINE 85 QA 16
25 NODS 107 YA 19
31 NOE 210 CA 36
89 NOE 63 LA 14
35 NOE BLANCHE, LA 75 O 16
10 NOE LES MALLETS 65 QA 15
27 NOE POULAIN, LA 37 Y 10
25 NOEL CERNEUX 108 AB 19
49 NOELLET 94 R 17
42 NOES, LES 135 NA 24
10 NOES PRES TROYES, LES 64 OA 14
62 NOEUX LES AUXI 16 GA 5
62 NOEUX LES MINES C 17 IA 4
31 NOGARET 211 FA 35
32 NOGARO C 185 W 34
52 NOGENT C 67 UA 15
10 NOGENT EN OTHE 64 NA 15
51 NOGENT L'ABBESSE 42 PA 10
02 NOGENT L'ARTAUD 41 LA 11
72 NOGENT LE BERNARD 59 Y 14
28 NOGENT LE PHAYE 61 DA 13
28 NOGENT LE ROI C 60 DA 12
28 NOGENT LE ROTROU S 59 AA 14
27 NOGENT LE SEC 38 BA 11
21 NOGENT LES MONTBARD 85 QA 17
10 NOGENT SUR AUBE 65 PA 13
28 NOGENT SUR EURE 60 CA 13
72 NOGENT SUR LOIR 78 Y 17
94 NOGENT SUR MARNE S 40 HA 11
60 NOGENT SUR OISE C 40 HA 9
10 NOGENT SUR SEINE S 63 LA 13
45 NOGENT SUR VERNISSON 82 IA 16
02 NOGENTEL 41 LA 11
39 NOGNA 122 VA 21
64 NOGUERES 207 T 36
63 NOHANENT 147 KA 25
18 NOHANT EN GOUT 101 IA 19
18 NOHANT EN GRACAY 100 FA 19
36 NOHANT VIC 116 FA 21
66 NOHEDES 222 GA 39
82 NOHIC 188 DA 33
21 NOIDAN 104 QA 18
70 NOIDANS LE FERROUX 88 WA 17
70 NOIDANS LES VESOUL 88 XA 17
52 NOIDANT CHATENOY 87 UA 16
52 NOIDANT LE ROCHEUX 87 UA 16
32 NOILHAN 209 AA 35
60 NOINTEL 26 HA 9
95 NOINTEL 40 GA 10
76 NOINTOT 23 Y 8
02 NOIRCOURT 29 OA 8
25 NOIREFONTAINE 108 AB 18
60 NOIREMONT 26 GA 8
42 NOIRETABLE C 149 NA 25
51 NOIRLIEU 43 SA 11
85 NOIRMOUTIER EN L'ILE C 109 M 20
70 NOIRON 106 VA 18
21 NOIRON SOUS GEVREY 105 TA 19
21 NOIRON SUR BEZE 105 UA 18
21 NOIRON SUR SEINE 85 QA 15
25 NOIRONTE 106 WA 18
08 NOIRVAL 30 RA 9
94 NOISEAU 40 HA 12
77 NOISIEL C 40 IA 11
57 NOISSEVILLE 46 YA 10
93 NOISY LE GRAND C 40 HA 11
78 NOISY LE ROI 39 FA 11
93 NOISY LE SEC C 40 HA 11
77 NOISY RUDIGNON 63 JA 14
77 NOISY SUR ECOLE 62 HA 14
95 NOISY SUR OISE 40 HA 10
37 NOIZAY 98 AA 18
24 NOJALS ET CLOTTE 158 AA 30
27 NOJEON EN VEXIN 25 DA 9
21 NOLAY C 120 RA 20
58 NOLAY 102 LA 19
76 NOLLEVAL 25 DA 9
42 NOLLIEUX 149 OA 25
59 NOMAIN 18 LA 4
47 NOMDIEU 186 Y 33
52 NOMECOURT 66 TA 13
54 NOMENY C 46 YA 11
88 NOMEXY 68 YA 14
25 NOMMAY 89 AB 17
88 NOMPATELIZE 69 AB 14
16 NONAC 143 W 27
27 NONANCOURT C 38 BA 12
14 NONANT 35 T 10
61 NONANT LE PIN 58 X 12
19 NONARDS 159 EA 28
16 NONAVILLE 142 W 26
52 NONCOURT SUR LE RONGEANT 66 TA 13
63 NONETTE 148 LA 26
74 NONGLARD 139 XA 24
54 NONHIGNY 69 BB 13
07 NONIERES 164 QA 29
55 NONSARD LAMARCHE 45 WA 11
24 NONTRON S 144 Z 26
77 NONVILLE 62 IA 14
88 NONVILLE 67 XA 15
28 NONVILLIERS GRANDHOUX 60 BA 14
2B NONZA 226 MB 38
88 NONZEVILLE 68 ZA 14
59 NOORDPEENE 8 HA 3
62 NORDAUSQUES 7 FA 3
67 NORDHEIM 49 DB 12
67 NORDHOUSE 70 EB 13
62 NOREUIL 17 JA 5
21 NORGES LA VILLE 105 TA 18
61 NORMANDEL 59 Z 12
27 NORMANVILLE 38 BA 10
76 NORMANVILLE 23 Z 8
21 NORMIER 104 QA 18
14 NOROLLES 37 X 10
14 NORON L'ABBAYE 36 V 11
14 NORON LA POTERIE 35 T 10
60 NOROY 26 HA 9
70 NOROY LE BOURG C 88 YA 17
02 NOROY SUR OURCQ 41 KA 10
62 NORRENT FONTES C 8 HA 4
14 NORREY EN AUGE 36 W 11
51 NORROIS 43 RA 12
88 NORROY 67 WA 14
54 NORROY LE SEC 31 WA 9
57 NORROY LE VENEUR 46 XA 10
54 NORROY LES PONT A MOUSSON 45 XA 11
62 NORT LEULINGHEM 7 FA 3
44 NORT SUR ERDRE C 94 P 18
62 NORTKERQUE 7 FA 2
76 NORVILLE 23 Z 9
91 NORVILLE, LA 62 GA 13
05 NOSSAGE ET BENEVENT 180 WA 32
88 NOSSONCOURT 68 AB 13
56 NOSTANG 73 I 16
23 NOTH 131 DA 23
67 NOTHALTEN 70 DB 14
76 NOTRE DAME D'ALIERMONT 24 CA 7
49 NOTRE DAME D'ALLENCON 96 U 18
50 NOTRE DAME D'ELLE 35 S 10
27 NOTRE DAME D'EPINE 37 Z 10
14 NOTRE DAME D'ESTREES 36 W 10
37 NOTRE DAME D'OE 98 Z 18
73 NOTRE DAME
DE BELLECOMBE 139 ZA 25
76 NOTRE DAME DE BLIQUETUIT 24 Z 9
42 NOTRE DAME DE BOISSET 135 PA 24
76 NOTRE DAME
DE BONDEVILLE C 24 BA 9
50 NOTRE DAME DE CENILLY 34 R 11
38 NOTRE DAME DE COMMIERS 166 WA 28
14 NOTRE DAME DE COURSON 37 X 11
76 NOTRE DAME DE GRAVENCHON 23 Z 8
27 NOTRE DAME DE L'ISLE 38 DA 10
38 NOTRE DAME DE L'OSIER 152 UA 27
30 NOTRE DAME DE LA ROUVIERE 192 NA 33
14 NOTRE DAME DE LIVAYE 36 W 10
50 NOTRE DAME DE LIVOYE 56 R 12
34 NOTRE DAME DE LONDRES 192 NA 34
38 NOTRE DAME DE MESAGE 166 WA 28
85 NOTRE DAME DE MONTS 109 N 20
85 NOTRE DAME DE RIEZ 109 O 21
24 NOTRE DAME DE SANILHAC 158 Z 28
38 NOTRE DAME DE VAUX 166 WA 29
44 NOTRE DAME DES LANDES 93 P 18
73 NOTRE DAME DES MILLIERES 153 YA 26
76 NOTRE DAME DU BEC 23 X 8
73 NOTRE DAME DU CRUET 153 YA 27
27 NOTRE DAME DU HAMEL 37 Y 11
76 NOTRE DAME DU PARC 24 BA 7
72 NOTRE DAME DU PE 78 V 16
73 NOTRE DAME DU PRE 154 ZA 26
61 NOTRE DAME DU ROCHER 58 U 12
50 NOTRE DAME DU TOUCHET 57 S 13
28 NOTTONVILLE 60 DA 15
23 NOUAILLE, LA 146 FA 25
86 NOUAILLE MAUPERTUIS 113 Y 22
50 NOUAINVILLE 33 P 8
41 NOUAN LE FUZELIER 81 FA 17
72 NOUANS 58 X 14
37 NOUANS LES FONTAINES 99 CA 19
08 NOUART 30 TA 9
37 NOUATRE 97 Z 19
35 NOUAYE, LA 75 N 14
51 NOUE, LA 42 MA 12
31 NOUEILLES 210 DA 36
32 NOUGAROULET 187 Z 34
23 NOUHANT 132 HA 23
87 NOUIC 130 AA 24
65 NOUILHAN 208 W 35
17 NOUILLERS, LES 127 T 24
55 NOUILLONPONT 31 VA 9
57 NOUILLY 46 YA 10
32 NOULENS 186 X 34
60 NOURARD LE FRANC 26 HA 9
41 NOURRAY 80 BA 16
40 NOUSSE 184 S 34
57 NOUSSEVILLER LES BITCHE 48 DB 10
57 NOUSSEVILLER ST NABOR 47 BB 10
64 NOUSTY 207 V 36
62 NOUVELLE EGLISE 7 FA 2
80 NOUVION C 16 EA 5
02 NOUVION EN THIERACHE, LE C 19 NA 6
02 NOUVION ET CATILLON 28 MA 8
02 NOUVION LE COMTE 28 LA 8
02 NOUVION LE VINEUX 28 MA 8
08 NOUVION SUR MEUSE 30 RA 8
35 NOUVOITOU 76 P 15
02 NOUVRON VINGRE 27 KA 9
23 NOUZERINES 132 GA 22
23 NOUZEROLLES 131 EA 22
23 NOUZIERS 132 FA 22
37 NOUZILLY 79 Z 17
08 NOUZONVILLE C 29 RA 7
63 NOVACELLES 148 MA 27
73 NOVALAISE 152 WA 26
2B NOVALE 228 MB 40
57 NOVEANT SUR MOSELLE 45 XA 11
74 NOVEL 124 AB 22
2B NOVELLA 226 LB 39
13 NOVES 195 SA 33
54 NOVIANT AUX PRES 45 WA 11
90 NOVILLARD 90 BB 17
25 NOVILLARS 107 XA 18
60 NOVILLERS 40 GA 10
08 NOVION PORCIEN C 29 OA 8
08 NOVY CHEVRIERES 29 QA 8
22 NOYAL 54 L 13
35 NOYAL CHATILLON
SUR SEICHE 75 P 15
56 NOYAL MUZILLAC 92 L 17
56 NOYAL PONTIVY 73 J 15
35 NOYAL SOUS BAZOUGES 56 P 13
44 NOYAL SUR BRUTZ 76 Q 16
35 NOYAL SUR VILAINE 76 P 15
02 NOYALES 28 MA 7
56 NOYALO 92 K 17
49 NOYANT C 97 X 17
03 NOYANT D'ALLIER 118 KA 22
37 NOYANT DE TOURAINE 97 Z 19
02 NOYANT ET ACONIN 28 LA 9
49 NOYANT LA GRAVOYERE 94 S 16
49 NOYANT LA PLAINE 96 U 18
38 NOYAREY 152 VA 27
62 NOYELLE VION 17 HA 5
80 NOYELLES EN CHAUSSEE 16 FA 5
62 NOYELLES GODAULT 17 JA 4
62 NOYELLES LES HUMIERES 16 GA 5
59 NOYELLES LES SECLIN 9 KA 4
62 NOYELLES LES VERMELLES 17 IA 4
62 NOYELLES SOUS BELLONNE 17 JA 5
62 NOYELLES SOUS LENS C 17 JA 4
59 NOYELLES SUR ESCAUT 18 KA 6
80 NOYELLES SUR MER 15 EA 5
59 NOYELLES SUR SAMBRE 19 NA 6
59 NOYELLES SUR SELLE 18 LA 5
62 NOYELLETTE 17 IA 5
72 NOYEN SUR SARTHE 78 W 16
77 NOYEN SUR SEINE 63 LA 13
05 NOYER, LE 167 XA 30
18 NOYER, LE 101 IA 18
73 NOYER, LE 153 XA 25
27 NOYER EN OUCHE, LE 37 AA 11
45 NOYERS 82 HA 16
52 NOYERS 67 VA 15
89 NOYERS C 84 OA 17
27 NOYERS, LES 39 EA 10
55 NOYERS AUZECOURT 44 SA 11
14 NOYERS BOCAGE 35 T 10
08 NOYERS PONT MAUGIS 30 SA 8
60 NOYERS ST MARTIN 26 GA 8
41 NOYERS SUR CHER 99 CA 18
04 NOYERS SUR JABRON C 181 WA 32
60 NOYON C 27 JA 8
10 NOZAY 64 OA 13
44 NOZAY C 93 P 17
91 NOZAY 62 GA 12
39 NOZEROY C 123 XA 21
07 NOZIERES 164 OA 28
18 NOZIERES 116 HA 21
49 NUAILLE 95 T 19
17 NUAILLE D'AUNIS 127 S 23

17 NUAILLE SUR BOUTONNE 128 U 24
58 NUARS 103 NA 18
55 NUBECOURT 44 TA 11
95 NUCOURT 39 EA 10
86 NUEIL SOUS FAYE 113 X 20
79 NUEIL SUR ARGENT 111 T 20
49 NUEIL SUR LAYON 96 U 19
69 NUELLES 136 RA 25
72 NUILLE LE JALAIS 79 Y 15
53 NUILLE SUR VICOIN 77 T 15
51 NUISEMENT SUR COOLE 43 PA 11
89 NUITS 85 PA 16
21 NUITS ST GEORGES C 105 SA 19
76 NULLEMONT 25 DA 7
57 NULLY TREMILLY 66 SA 14
62 NUNCQ HAUTECOTE 16 GA 5
36 NURET LE FERRON 115 CA 21
01 NURIEUX VOLOGNAT 138 VA 23
80 NURLU 17 JA 6
46 NUZEJOULS 173 CA 31
66 NYER 222 GA 39
49 NYOISEAU 77 S 16
26 NYONS S 180 TA 31

O

67 OBENHEIM 70 EB 14
67 OBERBRONN 48 EB 11
68 OBERBRUCK 90 BB 16
68 OBERDORF 90 DB 17
67 OBERDORF SPACHBACH 49 FB 11
57 OBERDORFF 47 ZA 10
68 OBERENTZEN 90 DB 15
57 OBERGAILBACH 48 CB 10
67 OBERHASLACH 70 DB 13
67 OBERHAUSBERGEN 49 EB 12
68 OBERHERGHEIM 90 DB 15
67 OBERHOFFEN
LES WISSEMBOURG 49 FB 11
67 OBERHOFFEN SUR MODER 49 FB 12
68 OBERLARG 108 CB 18
67 OBERLAUTERBACH 50 GB 11
67 OBERMODERN ZUTZENDORF 48 EB 11
68 OBERMORSCHWIHR 90 DB 15
68 OBERMORSCHWILLER 90 DB 17
67 OBERNAI C 70 DB 13
67 OBERROEDERN 50 GB 11
68 OBERSAASHEIM 90 EB 15
67 OBERSCHAEFFOLSHEIM 70 EB 13
67 OBERSOULTZBACH 48 DB 11
67 OBERSTEINBACH 48 EB 11
57 OBERSTINZEL 48 BB 12
57 OBERVISSE 47 ZA 10
59 OBIES 19 NA 5
19 OBJAT 159 CA 27
62 OBLINGHEM 8 IA 4
59 OBRECHIES 19 OA 5
57 OBRECK 47 ZA 11
77 OBSONVILLE 62 HA 14
36 OBTERRE 114 BA 20
21 OBTREE 85 QA 16
2A OCANA 227 KB 42
61 OCCAGNES 58 W 12
52 OCCEY 87 UA 17
2B OCCHIATANA 225 KB 39
80 OCCOCHES 16 GA 5
80 OCHANCOURT 15 DA 6
08 OCHES 30 SA 8
54 OCHEY 67 WA 13
59 OCHTEZEELE 8 HA 3
77 OCQUERRE 41 KA 11
76 OCQUEVILLE 23 Z 7
50 OCTEVILLE C 33 P 8
50 OCTEVILLE L'AVENEL 33 Q 8
76 OCTEVILLE SUR MER 23 X 8
34 OCTON 192 LA 34
31 ODARS 210 DA 35
69 ODENAS 136 RA 24
68 ODEREN 90 BB 16
59 ODOMEZ 10 MA 4
65 ODOS 216 W 37
67 ODRATZHEIM 70 DB 13
88 OELLEVILLE 67 XA 13
67 OERMINGEN 48 CB 11
57 OETING 47 BB 10
62 OEUF EN TERNOIS 16 GA 5
02 OEUILLY 28 NA 9
51 OEUILLY 42 NA 10
40 OEYREGAVE 206 R 35
40 OEYRELUY 183 R 34
62 OFFEKERQUE 7 FA 2
90 OFFEMONT C 89 BB 17
67 OFFENDORF 50 FB 12
80 OFFIGNIES 25 EA 7
62 OFFIN 16 FA 4
39 OFFLANGES 106 VA 19
60 OFFOY 26 FA 8
80 OFFOY 27 KA 7
76 OFFRANVILLE C 24 BA 7
62 OFFRETHUN 7 EA 3
88 OFFROICOURT 67 XA 14
67 OFFWILLER 48 EB 11
64 OGENNE CAMPTORT 206 T 36
51 OGER 42 OA 11
64 OGEU LES BAINS 215 U 37
54 OGEVILLER 68 AB 13
2B OGLIASTRO 226 MB 38
02 OGNES 27 KA 8
51 OGNES 42 OA 12
60 OGNES 40 JA 10
54 OGNEVILLE 67 XA 13
60 OGNOLLES 27 JA 8
60 OGNON 40 IA 10
57 OGY 46 YA 10
59 OHAIN 19 OA 6
76 OHERVILLE 23 Z 8
02 OHIS 19 OA 7
67 OHLUNGEN 49 EB 12
67 OHNENHEIM 70 DB 14
85 OIE, L' 110 R 20
70 OIGNEY 88 WA 16
62 OIGNIES 17 JA 4
21 OIGNY 85 RA 17
41 OIGNY 79 AA 15
02 OIGNY EN VALLOIS 41 KA 10
69 OINGT 136 RA 24
28 OINVILLE SOUS AUNEAU 61 EA 13
28 OINVILLE ST LIPHARD 61 FA 14
78 OINVILLE SUR MONTCIENT 39 EA 11
79 OIRON 112 W 20
51 OIRY 42 OA 11
70 OISELAY ET GRACHAUX 106 WA 18
80 OISEMONT C 15 EA 6
21 OISILLY 105 UA 18
41 OISLY 99 CA 18
45 OISON 61 FA 15
53 OISSEAU 57 T 14
72 OISSEAU LE PETIT 58 W 14
76 OISSEL 24 BA 9
77 OISSERY 40 JA 10
80 OISSY 26 FA 7
02 OISY 18 MA 6
58 OISY 83 LA 17
59 OISY 18 LA 5
62 OISY LE VERGER 18 KA 5
72 OIZE 78 X 16
18 OIZON 101 HA 18
34 OLARGUES C 213 JA 35
63 OLBY 147 JA 25
2B OLCANI 226 MB 38
65 OLEAC DEBAT 208 X 36
65 OLEAC DESSUS 216 X 37
12 OLEMPS 175 HA 31
14 OLENDON 36 V 11
2B OLETTA C 226 MB 39
66 OLETTE C 222 GA 39
2A OLIVESE 226 KB 42
45 OLIVET C 81 FA 16
53 OLIVET 77 S 15
51 OLIZY 42 NA 10
08 OLIZY PRIMAT 30 RA 9
55 OLIZY SUR CHIERS 30 TA 8
88 OLLAINVILLE 67 WA 14
91 OLLAINVILLE 62 GA 13
25 OLLANS 107 YA 18
28 OLLE 60 CA 13
54 OLLEY 45 WA 10
02 OLLEZY 27 KA 7
83 OLLIERES 202 WA 35
74 OLLIERES, LES 139 YA 24
07 OLLIERES SUR EYRIEUX, LES 164 RA 29
63 OLLIERGUES C 148 MA 25
83 OLLIOULES C 202 WA 37
63 OLLOIX 147 KA 26
69 OLMES, LES 136 QA 25
63 OLMET 148 MA 25
34 OLMET ET VILLECUN 191 LA 34
2B OLMETA DI CAPOCORSO 226 MB 38
2B OLMETA DI TUDA 226 MB 39
2A OLMETO C 229 KB 43
2B OLMI CAPPELLA 225 KB 40
2A OLMICCIA 229 KB 43
2B OLMO 228 MB 40
85 OLONNE SUR MER 125 O 22
34 OLONZAC C 213 IA 36
64 OLORON STE MARIE S 215 T 37
12 OLS ET RINHODES 174 FA 31
68 OLTINGUE 90 DB 17
67 OLWISHEIM 49 EB 12
26 OMBLEZE 165 TA 29
60 OMECOURT 25 EA 8
54 OMELMONT 67 XA 13
04 OMERGUES, LES 180 VA 32
95 OMERVILLE 39 EA 10
2B OMESSA 228 LB 40
33 OMET 170 V 30
65 OMEX 215 W 37
51 OMEY 43 QA 11
08 OMICOURT 30 SA 8
80 OMIECOURT 27 JA 7
02 OMISSY 28 LA 7
61 OMMEEL 58 X 12
57 OMMERAY 68 AB 12
61 OMMOY 36 W 11
08 OMONT C 30 RA 8
76 OMONVILLE 24 BA 7
50 OMONVILLE LA PETITE 33 O 8
50 OMONVILLE LA ROGUE 33 O 8
15 OMPS 160 GA 29
11 OMS 224 IA 39
25 ONANS 107 ZA 17
40 ONARD 184 S 34
70 ONAY 106 VA 18
01 ONCIEU 138 UA 24
88 ONCOURT 68 YA 14
91 ONCY SUR ECOLE 62 HA 13
14 ONDEFONTAINE 35 T 11
31 ONDES 188 CA 34
40 ONDRES 183 Q 35
45 ONDREVILLE SUR ESSONNE 62 HA 14
40 ONESSE ET LAHARIE 183 R 33
12 ONET LE CHATEAU 175 HA 31
80 ONEUX 16 FA 6
04 ONGLES 197 WA 33
39 ONGLIERES 123 XA 21
10 ONJON 65 PA 13
58 ONLAY 119 NA 20
59 ONNAING 18 MA 5
74 ONNION 139 ZA 23
39 ONOZ 122 VA 22
60 ONS EN BRAY 25 FA 9
73 ONTEX 152 WA 25
54 ONVILLE 45 XA 11
41 ONZAIN 80 BA 17
31 OO 217 Y 38
59 OOST CAPPEL 8 IA 2
06 OPIO 200 BB 34
66 OPOUL PERILLOS 223 JA 38
84 OPPEDE 196 TA 34
04 OPPEDETTE 196 VA 33
70 OPPENANS 89 ZA 17
62 OPPY 17 JA 5
38 OPTEVOZ 152 UA 25
64 ORAAS 206 S 35
15 ORADOUR 161 JA 29
16 ORADOUR 128 W 24
16 ORADOUR FANAIS 130 Z 24
87 ORADOUR ST GENEST 130 BA 23
87 ORADOUR SUR GLANE 130 BA 24
87 ORADOUR SUR VAYRES C 144 AA 25
21 ORAIN 87 UA 17
02 ORAINVILLE 29 OA 9
04 ORAISON 197 WA 33
84 ORANGE C 179 SA 32
39 ORBAGNA 122 UA 21
51 ORBAIS L'ABBAYE 42 NA 11
81 ORBAN 189 FA 34
14 ORBEC C 37 Y 11
63 ORBEIL 148 LA 26
32 ORBESSAN 209 Z 35
68 ORBEY 69 CB 15
37 ORBIGNY 99 CA 19
52 ORBIGNY AU MONT 87 UA 16
52 ORBIGNY AU VAL 87 UA 16
85 ORBRIE, L' 111 T 22
41 ORCAY 100 FA 18
78 ORCEMONT 61 EA 13
18 ORCENAIS 116 HA 21
63 ORCET 148 KA 25
52 ORCEVAUX 86 TA 16
41 ORCHAISE 80 BA 17
39 ORCHAMPS 106 VA 19
25 ORCHAMPS VENNES 107 ZA 19
86 ORCHES 113 Y 20
59 ORCHIES C 18 LA 4
74 ORCIER 139 ZA 23
05 ORCIERES C 167 YA 30
26 ORCINAS 179 TA 31
63 ORCINES 147 JA 25
63 ORCIVAL 147 JA 25
51 ORCONTE 43 RA 12
32 ORDAN LARROQUE 186 Y 34
64 ORDIARP 206 S 37
65 ORDIZAN 216 X 37
33 ORDONNAC 141 S 27
01 ORDONNAZ 138 VA 25
31 ORE 217 Z 37
64 OREGUE 206 R 36
66 OREILLA 222 GA 39
73 ORELLE 168 ZA 28
80 ORESMAUX 26 GA 7
65 ORGAN 209 Y 36
25 ORGEANS BLANCHEFONTAINE 108 AB 18
16 ORGEDEUIL 143 Y 25
09 ORGEIX 220 EA 39
39 ORGELET C 122 VA 22
35 ORGERES 75 P 15
61 ORGERES 37 Y 12
28 ORGERES EN BEAUCE C 61 EA 15
78 ORGERUS 39 EA 11
52 ORGES 66 SA 15
21 ORGEUX 105 TA 18
02 ORGEVAL 28 NA 8
78 ORGEVAL 39 FA 11
09 ORGIBET 217 AA 38
50 ORGLANDES 33 Q 9
07 ORGNAC L'AVEN 178 QA 32
19 ORGNAC SUR VEZERE 145 DA 27
13 ORGON C 195 SA 34
82 ORGUEIL 188 CA 33
70 ORICOURT 89 ZA 17
65 ORIEUX 208 X 36
65 ORIGNAC 216 X 37
33 ORIGNE 170 U 31
53 ORIGNE 77 T 15
17 ORIGNOLLES 142 V 27
21 ORIGNY 85 RA 16
02 ORIGNY EN THIERACHE 19 OA 7
61 ORIGNY LE BUTIN 59 Y 13
61 ORIGNY LE ROUX 59 Y 14
10 ORIGNY LE SEC 64 NA 13
02 ORIGNY STE BENOITE 28 MA 7
64 ORIN 206 T 36
65 ORINCLES 216 W 37
57 ORIOCOURT 47 ZA 11
26 ORIOL EN ROYANS 165 UA 28
16 ORIOLLES 142 W 27
64 ORION 206 S 36
38 ORIS EN RATTIER 167 WA 29
40 ORIST 183 R 35
16 ORIVAL 143 W 27
76 ORIVAL 24 AA 9
45 ORLEANS P 81 FA 16
31 ORLEAT 134 LA 25
65 ORLEIX 208 X 36
24 ORLIAC 158 BA 30
19 ORLIAC DE BAR 145 EA 27
24 ORLIAGUET 159 CA 29
69 ORLIENAS 150 RA 26
09 ORLU 222 FA 39
28 ORLU 61 FA 14
94 ORLY C 40 HA 12
77 ORLY SUR MORIN 41 LA 11
52 ORMANCEY 86 TA 16
70 ORMENANS 107 YA 18
57 ORMERSVILLER 48 DB 10
10 ORMES 64 OA 13
27 ORMES 38 AA 10
45 ORMES 81 EA 15
51 ORMES 42 OA 10
71 ORMES 123 XA 21
86 ORMES, LES 114 Z 20
89 ORMES, LES 83 LA 16
54 ORMES ET VILLE 68 YA 13
77 ORMES SUR VOULZIE, LES 63 KA 13
77 ORMESSON 62 IA 14
94 ORMESSON SUR MARNE C 40 HA 12
70 ORMOICHE 88 YA 16
28 ORMOY 60 DA 12
70 ORMOY 88 XA 16
89 ORMOY 83 MA 15
91 ORMOY 62 HA 13
91 ORMOY LA RIVIERE 61 GA 13
60 ORMOY LE DAVIEN 41 JA 10
52 ORMOY LES SEXFONTAINES 66 TA 14
60 ORMOY VILLERS 40 JA 10
38 ORNACIEUX 151 TA 27
11 ORNAISONS 223 JA 37
25 ORNANS C 107 XA 19
55 ORNES 44 UA 10
01 ORNEX 139 XA 23
32 ORNEZAN 209 Z 35
46 ORNIAC 174 DA 31
09 ORNOLAC USSAT LES BAINS 219 DA 38
38 ORNON 167 XA 28
57 ORNY 46 YA 11
60 OROER 26 GA 9
65 OROIX 208 W 36
57 ORON 47 ZA 11
79 OROUX 112 W 21
78 ORPHIN 61 EA 13
05 ORPIERRE C 180 VA 32
52 ORQUEVAUX 66 UA 14
05 ORRES, LES 182 ZA 31
21 ORRET 85 RA 17
64 ORRIULE 206 S 36
28 ORROUER 60 CA 13
60 ORROUY 41 JA 9
60 ORRY LA VILLE 40 HA 10
59 ORS 18 MA 6
30 ORSAN 179 RA 32
64 ORSANCO 206 R 36
11 ORSANS 221 FA 37
25 ORSANS 107 ZA 19
91 ORSAY C 39 GA 12
68 ORSCHWIHR 90 CB 15
67 ORSCHWILLER 70 DB 14
36 ORSENNES 115 EA 22
59 ORSINVAL 18 MA 5
63 ORSONNETTE 148 LA 26
78 ORSONVILLE 61 EA 13
66 ORTAFFA 224 JA 39
2B ORTALE 228 MB 40
40 ORTHEVIELLE 183 R 35
64 ORTHEZ C 206 T 35
30 ORTHOUX
SERIGNAC QUILHAN 193 OA 33
10 ORTILLON 65 PA 13
2B ORTIPORIO 228 MB 40
2A ORTO 227 KB 41
88 ORTONCOURT 68 ZA 14
09 ORUS 219 DA 38
18 ORVAL 116 HA 21
50 ORVAL 34 Q 11
44 ORVAULT C 93 P 18
27 ORVAUX 38 BA 11
25 ORVE 107 ZA 18
91 ORVEAU 62 GA 13
45 ORVEAU BELLESAUVE 62 HA 14
21 ORVILLE 86 TA 17
36 ORVILLE 99 EA 19
45 ORVILLE 62 HA 14
61 ORVILLE 37 X 11
62 ORVILLE 17 HA 6
60 ORVILLERS SOREL 27 IA 8
78 ORVILLIERS 39 DA 11
10 ORVILLIERS ST JULIEN 64 NA 13
40 ORX 183 Q 35
64 OS MARSILLON 207 T 36
2A OSANI 227 IB 40
55 OSCHES 44 UA 11
68 OSENBACH 90 CB 15
71 OSLON 121 SA 21
02 OSLY COURTIL 27 LA 9
14 OSMANVILLE 34 R 9
18 OSMERY 117 IA 20
65 OSMETS 208 X 36
18 OSMOY 101 HA 19
78 OSMOY 39 EA 11
76 OSMOY ST VALERY 25 CA 7
52 OSNE LE VAL 66 TA 13
08 OSNES 30 TA 8
95 OSNY 39 FA 10
40 OSSAGES 184 S 35
64 OSSAS SUHARE 206 S 37
25 OSSE 107 YA 18
35 OSSE 76 Q 15
64 OSSE EN ASPE 215 T 37
66 OSSEJA 222 FA 40
25 OSSELLE 106 WA 19
65 OSSEN 216 W 37
64 OSSENX 206 S 36
64 OSSERAIN RIVAREYTE 206 S 36
64 OSSES 205 Q 36
10 OSSEY LES TROIS MAISONS 64 NA 13
65 OSSUN C 216 W 37
65 OSSUN EZ ANGLES 216 W 37
64 OSTABAT ASME 206 R 36
02 OSTEL 28 MA 9
68 OSTHEIM 70 DB 14
67 OSTHOFFEN 70 EB 13
67 OSTHOUSE 70 EB 13
62 OSTREVILLE 16 HA 5
59 OSTRICOURT 17 KA 4
67 OSTWALD 70 EB 13
2A OTA 227 JB 41
54 OTHE 31 UA 9
77 OTHIS 40 IA 10
57 OTTANGE 32 XA 9
67 OTTERSTHAL 49 DB 12
67 OTTERSWILLER 49 DB 12
68 OTTMARSHEIM 90 DB 16
57 OTTONVILLE 47 ZA 10
67 OTTROTT 70 DB 13
67 OTTWILLER 48 CB 11
58 OUAGNE 102 MA 18
76 OUAINVILLE 23 Z 7
89 OUANNE 83 LA 17
28 OUARVILLE 61 EA 14
14 OUBEAUX, LES 34 R 9
41 OUCHAMPS 99 CA 18
42 OUCHES 135 OA 24
41 OUCQUES 80 CA 16
76 OUDALLE 23 X 8
58 OUDAN 102 LA 18
60 OUDEUIL 26 FA 8
59 OUDEZEELE 8 HA 3
52 OUDINCOURT 66 TA 14
44 OUDON 94 O 18
14 OUDON, L' 36 W 11
57 OUDRENNE 32 YA 9
71 OUDRY 119 PA 22
65 OUEILLOUX 216 X 37
28 OUERRE 38 DA 12
29 OUESSANT C 51 A 12
14 OUFFIERES 35 U 11
70 OUGE 87 WA 16
21 OUGES 105 TA 18
39 OUGNEY 106 VA 19
25 OUGNEY DOUVOT 107 YA 18
58 OUGNY 103 NA 19
25 OUHANS 107 YA 20
43 OUIDES 163 NA 29
64 OUILLON 207 V 36
14 OUILLY DU HOULEY 37 Y 10
14 OUILLY LE TESSON 36 V 11
14 OUILLY LE VICOMTE 36 X 10
14 OUISTREHAM C 36 V 9
36 OULCHES 115 CA 21
02 OULCHES LA VALLEE FOULON 28 NA 9
02 OULCHY LA VILLE 41 LA 10
02 OULCHY LE CHATEAU C 41 LA 10
28 OULINS 38 DA 11
38 OULLES 167 XA 28
69 OULLINS C 150 RA 25
85 OULMES 111 T 22
58 OULON 102 LA 19
39 OUNANS 122 VA 20
34 OUPIA 213 IA 36
39 OUR 106 VA 19
60 OURCEL MAISON 26 GA 8
26 OURCHES 165 TA 29
55 OURCHES SUR MEUSE 45 VA 12
65 OURDE 217 Z 38
65 OURDIS COTDOUSSAN 216 W 37
65 OURDON 216 W 37
58 OUROUER 102 LA 19
18 OUROUER LES BOURDELINS 117 IA 20
69 OUROUX 136 RA 23
58 OUROUX EN MORVAN 103 OA 19
71 OUROUX SOUS LE BOIS
STE MARIE 135 PA 22
71 OUROUX SUR SAONE 121 SA 21
65 OURSBELILLE 208 W 36
62 OURTON 17 HA 4
76 OURVILLE EN CAUX C 23 Z 8
40 OUSSE SUZAN 184 T 33
39 OUSSIERES 122 VA 20
45 OUSSON SUR LOIRE 82 IA 17
45 OUSSOY EN GATINAIS 82 IA 16
09 OUST C 219 CA 38
80 OUST MAREST 15 DA 6
65 OUSTE 216 W 37
45 OUTARVILLE C 61 FA 14
51 OUTINES 65 RA 13
62 OUTREAU C 7 DA 3
80 OUTREBOIS 16 GA 5
52 OUTREMECOURT 67 VA 14
51 OUTREPONT 43 RA 12
01 OUTRIAZ 138 VA 24
25 OUVANS 107 ZA 18
62 OUVE WIRQUIN 7 GA 3
11 OUVEILLAN 213 JA 36
50 OUVILLE 34 O 11
76 OUVILLE L'ABBAYE 24 AA 8
14 OUVILLE LA BIEN TOURNEE 36 W 10
76 OUVILLE LA RIVIERE 24 AA 7
45 OUVROUER LES CHAMPS 81 GA 16
86 OUZILLY 113 Y 21
45 OUZOUER DES CHAMPS 82 IA 16
41 OUZOUER LE DOYEN 80 CA 15
41 OUZOUER LE MARCHE C 80 DA 16
45 OUZOUER SOUS BELLEGARDE 82 HA 15
45 OUZOUER SUR LOIRE C 82 HA 16
45 OUZOUER SUR TREZEE 82 JA 17
65 OUZOUS 215 W 37
70 OVANCHES 88 XA 17
80 OVILLERS LA BOISSELLE 17 IA 6
59 OXELAERE 8 HA 3
71 OYE 135 PA 23
25 OYE ET PALLET 123 YA 20
62 OYE PLAGE 7 FA 2
51 OYES 42 NA 12
38 OYEU 152 UA 27
01 OYONNAX C 138 VA 23
86 OYRE 114 Z 20
70 OYRIERES 87 VA 17
28 OYSONVILLE 61 FA 13
38 OYTIER ST OBLAS 151 SA 26
38 OZ 167 XA 28
01 OZAN 137 SA 22
05 OZE 181 WA 31
71 OZENAY 121 SA 22
64 OZENX MONTESTRUCQ 206 T 35
54 OZERAILLES 45 WA 10
50 OZEVILLE 33 O 9
52 OZIERES 67 UA 14
17 OZILLAC 142 U 27
77 OZOIR LA FERRIERE 40 IA 12
28 OZOIR LE BREUIL 80 DA 15
71 OZOLLES 136 QA 22
07 OZON 164 RA 28
65 OZON 216 X 37
77 OZOUER LE VOULGIS 62 IA 12
40 OZOURT 184 S 34

P

02 PAARS 28 MA 9
22 PABU 53 I 13
42 PACAUDIERE, LA C 135 NA 23
35 PACE 75 O 14
61 PACE 58 W 13
38 PACT 151 SA 27
89 PACY SUR ARMANCON 84 OA 16
27 PACY SUR EURE C 38 CA 11
11 PADERN 223 IA 38
81 PADIES 190 HA 33
46 PADIRAC 159 EA 29
88 PADOUX 68 ZA 14
87 PAGEAS 144 AA 25
39 PAGNEY 106 WA 19
54 PAGNEY DERRIERE BARINE 45 WA 12
39 PAGNOZ 122 WA 20
55 PAGNY LA BLANCHE COTE 67 WA 13
21 PAGNY LA VILLE 105 TA 19
21 PAGNY LE CHATEAU 105 TA 19
57 PAGNY LES GOIN 46 YA 11
55 PAGNY SUR MEUSE 45 VA 12
54 PAGNY SUR MOSELLE 45 XA 11
64 PAGOLLE 206 S 36
65 PAILHAC 216 Y 38
07 PAILHARES 164 OA 28
15 PAILHEROLS 161 IA 29
09 PAILHES 218 CA 37
34 PAILHES 213 KA 35
60 PAILLART 26 GA 8
17 PAILLE 128 U 24
59 PAILLENCOURT 18 LA 5
33 PAILLET 170 V 30
47 PAILLOLES 172 Z 31
89 PAILLY 63 LA 14
52 PAILLY, LE 87 UA 16
44 PAIMBOEUF C 93 N 18
22 PAIMPOL C 53 J 12
35 PAIMPONT 75 N 15
21 PAINBLANC 104 RA 19
88 PAIR ET GRANDRUPT 69 BB 14
02 PAISSY 28 NA 9
10 PAISY COSDON 64 NA 14
79 PAIZAY LE CHAPT 128 V 24
86 PAIZAY LE SEC 114 AA 21
79 PAIZAY LE TORT 128 V 23
16 PAIZAY NADOUIN EMBOURIE 128 W 24
38 PAJAY 151 TA 27
38 PALADRU 152 VA 26
11 PALAIRAC 223 IA 38
56 PALAIS, LE C 91 I 18
87 PALAIS SUR VIENNE, LE 131 CA 25
91 PALAISEAU S 39 GA 12
52 PALAISEUL 87 UA 16
11 PALAJA 221 HA 37
31 PALAMINY 210 BA 36
70 PALANTE 89 ZA 17
25 PALANTINE 106 WA 19
2B PALASCA 226 KB 39
66 PALAU DE CERDAGNE 222 FA 40
66 PALAU DEL VIDRE 224 JA 39
34 PALAVAS LES FLOTS 194 OA 35
19 PALAZINGES 159 EA 28
77 PALEY 63 JA 14
48 PALHERS 176 LA 31
71 PALINGES C 120 PA 22
10 PALIS 64 NA 14
25 PALISE 107 XA 18
19 PALISSE 146 GA 27
63 PALLADUC 133 MA 24
32 PALLANNE 208 X 35
71 PALLEAU 121 TA 20
88 PALLEGNEY 68 ZA 14
44 PALLET, LE 94 O 19
81 PALLEVILLE 211 FA 35
53 PALLU, LA 58 V 13
85 PALLUAU C 110 P 20
36 PALLUAU SUR INDRE 115 CA 20
16 PALLUAUD 143 X 27
73 PALLUD 139 ZA 25
62 PALLUEL 18 KA 5
12 PALMAS 176 JA 31
11 [illegible] JA 37
2A PALNECA 228 LB 42
42 PALOGNEUX 149 OA 25
04 PALUD SUR VERDON, LA 198 YA 34
76 PALUEL 23 Z 7
77 PAMFOU 62 JA 13
09 PAMIERS S 219 DA 37
81 PAMPELONNE C 175 GA 32
79 PAMPLIE 112 U 22
79 PAMPROUX 112 W 22

32	PANASSAC		209	Z	36
87	PANAZOL		145	CA	25
35	PANCE		75	P	16
52	PANCEY		66	UA	13
2B	PANCHERACCIA		228	MB	41
02	PANCY COURTECON		28	MA	9
19	PANDRIGNES		160	EA	27
57	PANGE	C	46	YA	10
21	PANGES		105	SA	18
27	PANILLEUSE		38	DA	10
38	PANISSAGE		152	UA	26
42	PANISSIERES		150	PA	25
32	PANJAS		185	W	34
44	PANNECE		94	R	17
45	PANNECIERES		61	GA	14
45	PANNES		82	IA	15
54	PANNES		45	WA	11
39	PANNESSIERES		122	VA	21
72	PANON		59	X	14
38	PANOSSAS		151	TA	25
48	PANOUSE, LA		162	MA	30
93	PANTIN	C	40	HA	11
37	PANZOULT		97	Y	19
02	PAPLEUX		19	NA	6
13	PARADOU		195	RA	34
18	PARASSY		101	HA	19
2B	PARATA		228	MB	40
78	PARAY DOUAVILLE		61	EA	13
03	PARAY LE FRESIL		119	MA	21
71	PARAY LE MONIAL	C	119	OA	22
03	PARAY SOUS BRIAILLES		133	LA	23
91	PARAY VIEILLE POSTE		40	HA	12
11	PARAZA		213	JA	36
64	PARBAYSE		207	U	36
76	PARC D'ANXTOT		23	Y	8
49	PARCAY LES PINS		97	X	18
37	PARCAY MESLAY		98	Z	18
37	PARCAY SUR VIENNE		97	Y	19
35	PARCE		76	R	14
72	PARCE SUR SARTHE		78	V	16
39	PARCEY		122	UA	20
01	PARCIEUX		137	SA	24
24	PARCOUL		157	W	28
62	PARCQ, LE	C	16	FA	5
02	PARCY ET TIGNY		41	LA	10
34	PARDAILHAN		213	JA	35
47	PARDAILLAN		171	X	30
64	PARDIES		207	T	36
64	PARDIES PIETAT		207	V	36
63	PARDINES		148	KA	26
65	PAREAC		216	W	37
55	PAREID		45	WA	10
33	PAREMPUYRE		156	T	29
72	PARENNES		78	V	15
63	PARENT		148	KA	26
63	PARENTIGNAT		148	LA	26
40	PARENTIS EN BORN	C	169	R	31
62	PARENTY		7	EA	4
88	PAREY SOUS MONTFORT		67	XA	14
54	PAREY ST CESAIRE		67	XA	13
02	PARFONDEVAL		29	PA	7
61	PARFONDEVAL		59	Y	13
02	PARFONDRU		28	NA	8
55	PARFONDRUPT		45	VA	10
14	PARFOURU SUR ODON		35	T	10
02	PARGNAN		28	NA	9
80	PARGNY		27	JA	7
02	PARGNY FILAIN		28	MA	9
02	PARGNY LA DHUYS		42	MA	11
02	PARGNY LES BOIS		28	MA	8
51	PARGNY LES REIMS		42	NA	10
88	PARGNY SOUS MUREAU		67	VA	14
51	PARGNY SUR SAULX		44	SA	12
10	PARGUES		85	PA	15
30	PARIGNARGUES		193	PA	34
35	PARIGNE		56	R	13
72	PARIGNE L'EVEQUE		78	Y	15
72	PARIGNE LE POLIN		78	X	16
53	PARIGNE SUR BRAYE		57	T	14
42	PARIGNY		135	OA	24
50	PARIGNY		56	R	12
58	PARIGNY LA ROSE		102	LA	18
58	PARIGNY LES VAUX		102	KA	19
75	PARIS	P	40	GA	11
71	PARIS L'HOPITAL		120	RA	20
81	PARISOT		189	EA	34
82	PARISOT		174	EA	32
15	PARLAN		160	GA	29
40	PARLEBOSCQ		185	W	33
89	PARLY		83	LA	16
95	PARMAIN		39	GA	10
38	PARMILIEU		138	UA	25
36	PARNAC		115	CA	22
46	PARNAC		173	CA	31
26	PARNANS		165	TA	28
18	PARNAY		117	IA	20
49	PARNAY		96	W	19
53	PARNE SUR ROC		77	T	15
60	PARNES		39	EA	10
52	PARNOY EN BASSIGNY		87	VA	15
55	PAROCHES, LES		45	VA	11
89	PARON		63	LA	14
25	PAROY		106	WA	19
77	PAROY		63	KA	13
52	PAROY SUR SAULX		66	UA	13
89	PAROY SUR THOLON		83	LA	15
36	PARPECAY		99	DA	19
02	PARPEVILLE		28	MA	7
47	PARRANQUET		172	AA	30
54	PARROY		46	ZA	12
10	PARS LES CHAVANGES		65	OA	13
10	PARS LES ROMILLY		64	NA	13
23	PARSAC		132	GA	23
79	PARTHENAY	S	112	V	21
35	PARTHENAY DE BRETAGNE		75	O	14
2A	PARTINELLO		227	JB	40
54	PARUX		69	BB	13
01	PARVES		152	WA	25
27	PARVILLE		38	BA	11
80	PARVILLERS LE QUESNOY		27	IA	7
16	PARZAC		129	Y	24
53	PAS, LE		57	T	13
79	PAS DE JEU		112	W	20
62	PAS EN ARTOIS	C	17	HA	6
61	PAS ST L'HOMER, LE		59	AA	13
89	PASILLY		84	OA	17
63	PASLIERES		133	MA	24
02	PASLY		28	LA	9
21	PASQUES		105	SA	18
39	PASQUIER, LE		122	WA	21
66	PASSA		224	JA	39
38	PASSAGE, LE		152	VA	26
47	PASSAGE, LE		172	Z	32
61	PASSAIS	C	57	T	13
25	PASSAVANT		107	YA	18
51	PASSAVANT EN ARGONNE		44	SA	11
70	PASSAVANT LA ROCHERE		88	XA	15
49	PASSAVANT SUR LAYON		96	U	19

60	PASSEL		27	JA	8
39	PASSENANS		122	VA	21
38	PASSINS		152	UA	25
16	PASSIRAC		142	W	27
25	PASSONFONTAINE		107	ZA	19
71	PASSY		120	QA	22
74	PASSY		140	AB	24
89	PASSY		63	LA	15
02	PASSY EN VALOIS		41	KA	10
51	PASSY GRIGNY		42	MA	10
02	PASSY SUR MARNE		42	MA	10
77	PASSY SUR SEINE		63	LA	13
2A	PASTRICCIOLA		227	KB	41
45	PATAY	C	81	EA	15
39	PATORNAY		122	WA	21
2B	PATRIMONIO		226	MB	39
64	PAU	P	207	U	36
45	PAUCOURT		82	JA	15
36	PAUDY		100	FA	19
32	PAUILHAC		187	Z	33
33	PAUILLAC	C	155	T	28
22	PAULE		73	H	14
15	PAULHAC		161	JA	28
31	PAULHAC		188	DA	34
43	PAULHAC		148	LA	27
48	PAULHAC EN MARGERIDE		162	LA	29
43	PAULHAGUET	C	162	MA	28
34	PAULHAN		214	LA	35
12	PAULHE		176	KA	32
15	PAULHENC		161	JA	29
47	PAULHIAC		172	AA	30
11	PAULIGNE		221	GA	37
24	PAULIN		159	CA	28
81	PAULINET		190	HA	34
37	PAULMY		114	AA	20
36	PAULNAY		114	BA	20
44	PAULX		109	O	20
24	PAUNAT		158	AA	29
24	PAUSSAC ET ST VIVIEN		143	Z	27
52	PAUTAINES AUGEVILLE		66	UA	14
08	PAUVRES		29	OA	9
02	PAVANT		41	LA	11
42	PAVEZIN		150	RA	26
32	PAVIE		209	Z	35
10	PAVILLON STE JULIE, LE		64	NA	14
93	PAVILLONS SOUS BOIS, LES	C	40	HA	11
76	PAVILLY	C	24	AA	8
10	PAYNS		64	OA	13
11	PAYRA SUR L'HERS		211	EA	36
46	PAYRAC	C	159	DA	29
86	PAYRE		129	X	23
46	PAYRIGNAC		159	CA	30
81	PAYRIN AUGMONTEL		212	HA	35
40	PAYROS CAZAUTETS		207	U	35
86	PAYROUX		129	Y	23
31	PAYSSOUS		217	Z	37
07	PAYZAC		178	PA	31
24	PAYZAC		144	BA	27
24	PAZAYAC		159	CA	28
11	PAZIOLS		223	IA	38
58	PAZY		103	MA	19
38	PEAGE DE ROUSSILLON, LE		150	RA	27
51	PEAS		42	NA	12
07	PEAUGRES		150	RA	27
56	PEAULE		92	M	17
85	PEAULT		125	R	22
32	PEBEES		209	BA	35
43	PEBRAC		162	MA	28
09	PECH		220	EA	38
11	PECH LUNA		211	EA	36
31	PECHABOU		210	DA	35
31	PECHARIC ET LE PY		219	EA	37
81	PECHAUDIER		211	FA	35
31	PECHBONNIEU		188	DA	34
31	PECHBUSQUE		210	DA	35
36	PECHEREAU, LE		115	DA	22
40	PECORADE		184	U	34
78	PECQ, LE	C	39	FA	11
59	PECQUENCOURT		18	KA	5
91	PECQUEUSE		61	FA	12
77	PECY		63	KA	12
22	PEDERNEC		53	I	13
34	PEGAIROLLES DE BUEGES		192	MA	34
34	PEGAIROLLES DE L'ESCALETTE		192	LA	34
06	PEGOMAS		200	BB	35
26	PEGUE, LE		179	TA	31
31	PEGUILHAN		209	Z	36
52	PEIGNEY		87	UA	16
56	PEILLAC		74	M	16
06	PEILLE		200	DB	34
06	PEILLON		200	DB	34
74	PEILLONNEX		139	YA	23
39	PEINTRE		106	VA	19
33	PEINTURES, LES		156	W	28
04	PEIPIN		181	XA	32
73	PEISEY NANCROIX		154	AB	26
10	PEL ET DER		65	OA	13
13	PELISSANNE	C	201	TA	35
38	PELLAFOL		167	WA	29
05	PELLEAUTIER		181	XA	31
32	PELLEFIGUE		209	AA	35
33	PELLEGRUE	C	157	X	30
31	PELLEPORT		188	BA	34
21	PELLEREY		86	RA	17
44	PELLERIN, LE	C	93	O	19
49	PELLERINE, LA		97	X	18
53	PELLERINE, LA		57	S	14
36	PELLEVOISIN		115	CA	20
49	PELLOUAILLES LES VIGNES		96	U	17
26	PELONNE		180	UA	31
48	PELOUSE		177	MA	30
25	PELOUSEY		106	WA	18
57	PELTRE		46	YA	10
42	PELUSSIN	C	150	RA	27
62	PELVES		17	JA	5
05	PELVOUX		167	ZA	29
77	PENCHARD		40	JA	11
29	PENCRAN		52	D	13
80	PENDE		15	DA	6
56	PENESTIN		92	L	17
22	PENGUILY		54	L	13
62	PENIN		17	HA	5
76	PENLY		15	CA	6
29	PENMARCH		71	D	16
11	PENNAUTIER		212	GA	36
81	PENNE		189	EA	33
06	PENNE, LA		199	BB	33
47	PENNE D'AGENAIS	C	172	AA	31
13	PENNE SUR HUVEAUNE, LA		202	VA	36
26	PENNE SUR L'OUVEZE, LA		180	TA	32
14	PENNEDEPIE		23	X	9
26	PENNES LE SEC		180	UA	30
13	PENNES MIRABEAU, LES	C	202	UA	36
70	PENNESIERES		88	XA	17
38	PENOL		151	TA	27
87	PENSOL		144	AA	26
2B	PENTA ACQUATELLA		228	MB	40
2B	PENTA DI CASINCA		228	MB	40

22	PENVENAN		53	I	12
06	PEONE		182	BB	32
11	PEPIEUX		212	IA	36
36	PERASSAY		116	GA	22
72	PERAY		59	Y	14
89	PERCENEIGE		63	LA	14
89	PERCEY		84	NA	15
70	PERCEY LE GRAND		87	UA	17
95	PERCHAY, LE		39	FA	10
18	PERCHE, LA		117	IA	21
32	PERCHEDE		185	W	34
38	PERCY		166	VA	29
50	PERCY	C	56	R	11
14	PERCY EN AUGE		36	W	10
78	PERDREAUVILLE		39	DA	11
17	PERE		127	T	24
65	PERE		216	X	37
09	PEREILLE		219	EA	38
2B	PERELLI		228	MB	40
59	PERENCHIES		9	JA	3
34	PERET		214	LA	35
19	PERET BEL AIR		146	FA	26
16	PEREUIL		143	W	26
07	PEREYRES		164	PA	29
32	PERGAIN TAILLAC		187	Z	33
2A	PERI		227	KB	42
38	PERIER, LE		167	XA	29
50	PERIERS	C	34	Q	10
14	PERIERS EN AUGE		36	W	10
14	PERIERS SUR LE DAN		36	V	10
16	PERIGNAC		143	W	26
17	PERIGNAC		142	U	26
63	PERIGNAT LES SARLIEVE		148	KA	25
63	PERIGNAT SUR ALLIER		148	KA	25
79	PERIGNE		128	V	23
42	PERIGNEUX		149	PA	27
03	PERIGNY		133	MA	23
14	PERIGNY		35	U	11
17	PERIGNY		126	R	23
41	PERIGNY		80	BA	16
94	PERIGNY		62	HA	12
10	PERIGNY LA ROSE		64	MA	13
24	PERIGUEUX	P	158	Z	28
33	PERISSAC		156	V	28
02	PERLES		28	MA	9
09	PERLES ET CASTELET		220	EA	39
46	PERN		173	CA	31
21	PERNAND VERGELESSES		105	SA	19
02	PERNANT		27	LA	9
37	PERNAY		97	Y	18
50	PERNELLE, LA		33	O	8
62	PERNES		16	HA	4
62	PERNES LES BOULOGNE		7	EA	3
84	PERNES LES FONTAINES	C	195	TA	33
80	PERNOIS		16	GA	6
2B	PERO CASEVECCHIE		228	MB	40
34	PEROLS		194	OA	35
19	PEROLS SUR VEZERE		146	FA	26
01	PERON		138	WA	23
01	PERONNAS	C	137	TA	23
71	PERONNE		121	SA	22
80	PERONNE	S	17	JA	7
59	PERONNE EN MELANTOIS		9	KA	4
28	PERONVILLE		80	DA	15
01	PEROUGES		137	TA	24
36	PEROUILLE, LA		115	DA	21
90	PEROUSE		89	BB	17
60	PEROY LES GOMBRIES		40	JA	10
19	PERPEZAC LE BLANC		159	CA	28
19	PERPEZAC LE NOIR		145	DA	27
63	PERPEZAT		147	IA	25
66	PERPIGNAN	P	224	JA	39
50	PERQUES, LES		33	P	9
40	PERQUIE		185	V	33
52	PERRANCEY				
	LES VIEUX MOULINS		86	TA	16
78	PERRAY EN YVELINES, LE		39	EA	12
71	PERRECY LES FORGES		120	PA	21
69	PERREON, LE		136	RA	24
22	PERRET		73	I	14
71	PERREUIL		120	QA	20
42	PERREUX	C	135	OA	24
89	PERREUX		83	KA	16
94	PERREUX SUR MARNE, LE	C	40	HA	11
01	PERREX		137	SA	23
63	PERRIER		148	KA	26
85	PERRIER, LE		109	N	20
61	PERRIERE, LA		59	Y	13
73	PERRIERE, LA		154	ZA	27
14	PERRIERES		36	W	11
50	PERRIERS EN BEAUFICEL		57	S	12
27	PERRIERS LA CAMPAGNE		37	AA	10
27	PERRIERS SUR ANDELLE		25	CA	9
74	PERRIGNIER		139	ZA	23
39	PERRIGNY		122	UA	21
89	PERRIGNY		83	MA	16
21	PERRIGNY LES DIJON		105	SA	18
89	PERRIGNY SUR ARMANCON		85	PA	17
21	PERRIGNY SUR L'OGNON		106	UA	18
71	PERRIGNY SUR LOIRE		119	NA	22
52	PERROGNEY LES FONTAINES		86	TA	16
50	PERRON, LE		35	S	10
22	PERROS GUIREC	C	53	H	12
61	PERROU		57	U	13
70	PERROUSE		107	XA	18
58	PERROY		102	KA	18
27	PERRUEL		25	CA	9
52	PERRUSSE		67	UA	15
37	PERRUSSON		98	BA	19
15	PERS		160	GA	29
79	PERS		129	W	23
45	PERS EN GATINAIS		63	JA	15
74	PERS JUSSY		139	YA	24
86	PERSAC		130	Z	23
95	PERSAN		40	GA	10
56	PERSQUEN		73	I	15
80	PERTAIN		27	JA	7
08	PERTHES		29	PA	9
52	PERTHES		66	SA	12
77	PERTHES	C	62	IA	13
10	PERTHES LES BRIENNE		65	QA	13
14	PERTHEVILLE NERS		36	W	11
66	PERTHUS, LE		224	JA	40
35	PERTRE, LE		76	R	15
84	PERTUIS	C	196	VA	34
43	PERTUIS, LE		163	OA	28
16	PERUSE, LA		130	Z	25
61	PERVENCHERES	C	59	Y	13
82	PERVILLE		172	AA	32
46	PESCADOIRES		173	BA	31
63	PESCHADOIRES		148	MA	25
19	PESCHER, LE		159	EA	28
25	PESEUX		108	AB	18
39	PESEUX		122	UA	20
63	PESLIERES		148	LA	27
70	PESMES	C	106	VA	18
33	PESSAC	C	156	T	29
33	PESSAC SUR DORDOGNE		157	W	29

32	PESSAN		209	Z	35
25	PESSANS		106	WA	19
63	PESSAT VILLE NEUVE		134	KA	24
39	PESSE, LA		138	WA	23
17	PESSINES		141	T	25
32	PESSOULENS		187	AA	34
67	PETERSBACH		48	CB	11
01	PETIT ABERGEMENT, LE		138	VA	24
44	PETIT AUVERNE		94	Q	17
24	PETIT BERSAC		143	X	27
74	PETIT BORNAND				
	LES GLIERES, LE		139	ZA	24
50	PETIT CELLAND, LE		56	R	12
76	PETIT COURONNE		24	BA	9
90	PETIT CROIX		90	BB	17
54	PETIT FAILLY		31	VA	9
59	PETIT FAYT		19	NA	6
35	PETIT FOUGERAY, LE		75	P	15
68	PETIT LANDAU		90	EB	16
44	PETIT MARS		94	Q	18
39	PETIT MERCEY		106	WA	19
10	PETIT MESNIL		65	QA	14
39	PETIT NOIR		121	UA	20
33	PETIT PALAIS ET CORNEMPS		156	W	29
37	PETIT PRESSIGNY, LE		114	AA	20
76	PETIT QUEVILLY, LE	C	24	BA	9
57	PETIT REDERCHING		48	DB	10
57	PETIT TENQUIN		47	BB	11
02	PETIT VERLY		18	MA	6
79	PETITE BOISSIERE, LA		111	T	20
25	PETITE CHAUX		123	XA	21
59	PETITE FORET		18	MA	5
88	PETITE FOSSE, LA		69	CB	14
03	PETITE MARCHE, LA		133	IA	23
67	PETITE PIERRE, LA	C	48	DB	11
88	PETITE RAON, LA		69	BB	13
57	PETITE ROSSELLE		47	BB	10
71	PETITE VERRIERE, LA		103	PA	19
90	PETITEFONTAINE		90	BB	16
08	PETITES ARMOISES, LES		30	SA	8
51	PETITES LOGES, LES		43	PA	10
90	PETITMAGNY		89	BB	16
54	PETITMONT		69	BB	13
14	PETIVILLE		36	V	10
76	PETIVILLE		23	Z	9
85	PETOSSE		111	S	22
2A	PETRETO BICCHISANO	C	229	KB	43
57	PETTONCOURT		46	ZA	12
54	PETTONVILLE		69	AB	13
33	PEUJARD		156	U	28
29	PEUMERIT		71	D	15
22	PEUMERIT QUINTIN		53	I	14
62	PEUPLINGUES		7	EA	2
53	PEUTON		77	T	16
55	PEUVILLERS		31	UA	9
12	PEUX ET COUFFOULEUX		191	JA	34
57	PEVANGE		47	AB	11
51	PEVY		28	NA	9
11	PEXIORA		211	FA	36
54	PEXONNE		69	BB	13
40	PEY		183	R	35
06	PEYMEINADE		200	BB	35
13	PEYNIER		202	VA	35
13	PEYPIN		202	VA	36
84	PEYPIN D'AIGUES		196	VA	34
23	PEYRABOUT		132	FA	24
09	PEYRAT, LE		221	FA	38
87	PEYRAT DE BELLAC		130	BA	23
23	PEYRAT LA NONIERE		132	GA	24
87	PEYRAT LE CHATEAU		145	EA	25
79	PEYRATTE, LA		112	V	21
65	PEYRAUBE		208	X	36
07	PEYRAUD		150	RA	27
40	PEYRE		207	U	35
32	PEYRECAVE		187	AA	33
11	PEYREFITTE DU RAZES		221	FA	37
11	PEYREFITTE SUR L'HERS		211	EA	36
81	PEYREGOUX		190	GA	34
40	PEYREHORADE	C	183	R	35
12	PEYRELEAU	C	176	KA	32
19	PEYRELEVADE		146	FA	25
64	PEYRELONGUE ABOS		208	W	35
30	PEYREMALE		178	OA	32
11	PEYRENS		211	FA	36
66	PEYRESTORTES		224	JA	39
65	PEYRET ST ANDRE		209	Y	36
11	PEYRIAC DE MER		223	JA	37
11	PEYRIAC MINERVOIS	C	212	IA	36
01	PEYRIAT		138	VA	23
47	PEYRIERE		171	X	30
01	PEYRIEU		152	VA	25
24	PEYRIGNAC		158	BA	28
65	PEYRIGUERE		208	X	36
87	PEYRILHAC		130	BA	24
24	PEYRILLAC ET MILLAC		159	CA	29
46	PEYRILLES		173	CA	30
26	PEYRINS		165	TA	28
19	PEYRISSAC		145	EA	26
31	PEYRISSAS		209	AA	36
81	PEYROLE		189	FA	34
30	PEYROLES		177	NA	32
11	PEYROLLES		221	GA	38
13	PEYROLLES EN PROVENCE	C	202	VA	35
04	PEYROULES		198	AB	34
65	PEYROUSE		215	W	37
31	PEYROUZET		209	AA	36
04	PEYRUIS	C	197	WA	33
65	PEYRUN		208	X	36
26	PEYRUS		165	TA	29
15	PEYRUSSE		161	JA	28
32	PEYRUSSE GRANDE		208	X	35
12	PEYRUSSE LE ROC		175	GA	31
32	PEYRUSSE MASSAS		187	Z	34
32	PEYRUSSE VIEILLE		208	X	35
24	PEYSAC LE MOUSTIER		158	BA	29
31	PEYSSIES		210	BA	36
01	PEYZIEUX SUR SAONE		137	SA	23
77	PEZARCHES		41	JA	12
72	PEZE LE ROBERT		78	W	14
34	PEZENAS	C	214	LA	35
34	PEZENES LES MINES		213	KA	35
11	PEZENS		212	GA	36
66	PEZILLA DE CONFLENT		222	HA	39
66	PEZILLA LA RIVIERE		224	IA	39
41	PEZOU		80	BA	16
24	PEZULS		158	AA	29
28	PEZY		61	DA	14
68	PFAFFENHEIM		90	DB	15
67	PFAFFENHOFFEN		48	EB	11
67	PFALZWEYER		48	CB	12
68	PFASTATT		90	CB	16
68	PFETTERHOUSE		90	CB	17
67	PFETTISHEIM		49	EB	12
67	PFULGRIESHEIM		49	EB	12
90	PHAFFANS		90	BB	17
59	PHALEMPIN		9	KA	4
57	PHALSBOURG	C	48	CB	12
57	PHILIPPSBOURG		48	EB	11

40	PHILONDENX		207	U	35
54	PHLIN		46	YA	11
66	PIA		224	JA	39
72	PIACE		58	X	14
33	PIAN MEDOC, LE		155	T	29
33	PIAN SUR GARONNE, LE		170	V	30
2A	PIANA	C	227	JB	41
2B	PIANELLO		228	MB	41
2B	PIANO		228	MB	40
2A	PIANOTOLLI CALDARELLO		230	KB	44
39	PIARDS, LES		122	WA	22
05	PIARRE, LA		180	VA	31
2B	PIAZZALI		228	MB	40
2B	PIAZZOLE		228	MB	40
57	PIBLANGE		47	ZA	10
31	PIBRAC		210	CA	35
39	PICARREAU		122	WA	21
50	PICAUVILLE		33	Q	9
21	PICHANGES		105	TA	18
63	PICHERANDE		147	IA	26
80	PICQUIGNY	C	16	GA	7
2B	PIE D'OREZZA		228	MB	40
48	PIED DE BORNE		178	OA	31
2B	PIEDICORTE DI GAGGIO		228	MB	41
2B	PIEDICROCE	C	228	MB	40
2B	PIEDIGRIGGIO		226	LB	40
2B	PIEDIPARTINO		228	MB	40
26	PIEGON		179	TA	32
26	PIEGROS LA CLASTRE		165	TA	30
04	PIEGUT		181	XA	31
24	PIEGUT PLUVIERS		144	Z	26
27	PIENCOURT		37	Y	10
54	PIENNES		31	WA	9
80	PIENNES ONVILLERS		26	IA	8
06	PIERLAS		199	BB	33
38	PIERRE, LA		153	XA	27
69	PIERRE BENITE		151	SA	25
87	PIERRE BUFFIERE	C	145	CA	25
38	PIERRE CHATEL		166	WA	29
71	PIERRE DE BRESSE	C	121	TA	20
54	PIERRE LA TREICHE		67	WA	12
77	PIERRE LEVEE		41	KA	11
51	PIERRE MORAINS		42	OA	11
54	PIERRE PERCEE		69	BB	13
89	PIERRE PERTHUIS		103	NA	18
71	PIERRECLOS		136	RA	23
70	PIERRECOURT		87	VA	17
76	PIERRECOURT		25	DA	7
06	PIERREFEU		199	CB	34
83	PIERREFEU DU VAR		203	XA	36
12	PIERREFICHE		176	JA	31
48	PIERREFICHE		163	NA	30
76	PIERREFIQUES		23	X	8
19	PIERREFITTE		145	DA	27
23	PIERREFITTE		132	GA	23
79	PIERREFITTE		112	V	20
88	PIERREFITTE		68	YA	14
14	PIERREFITTE EN AUGE		36	X	10
60	PIERREFITTE EN BEAUVAISIS		26	FA	9
14	PIERREFITTE EN CINGLAIS		36	U	11
45	PIERREFITTE ES BOIS		82	IA	17
65	PIERREFITTE NESTALAS		215	W	38
55	PIERREFITTE SUR AIRE	C	44	UA	11
03	PIERREFITTE SUR LOIRE		119	NA	22
41	PIERREFITTE SUR SAULDRE		81	GA	17
93	PIERREFITTE SUR SEINE	C	40	HA	11
60	PIERREFONDS		27	JA	9
25	PIERREFONTAINE				
	LES BLAMONT		108	BB	18
25	PIERREFONTAINE				
	LES VARANS	C	107	ZA	19
15	PIERREFORT	C	161	JA	29
80	PIERREGOT		16	HA	6
26	PIERRELATTE	C	179	RA	31
95	PIERRELAYE		39	GA	11
26	PIERRELONGUE		180	TA	32
02	PIERREMANDE		27	LA	8
62	PIERREMONT		16	GA	5
52	PIERREMONT SUR AMANCE		87	VA	16
02	PIERREPONT		28	NA	8
14	PIERREPONT		36	V	11
54	PIERREPONT		31	WA	9
80	PIERREPONT SUR AVRE		26	HA	8
88	PIERREPONT SUR L'ARENTELE		68	AB	14
04	PIERRERUE		197	WA	33
34	PIERRERUE		213	JA	35
14	PIERRES		35	T	11
28	PIERRES		60	DA	13
76	PIERREVAL		24	CA	8
04	PIERREVERT		197	WA	34
50	PIERREVILLE		33	O	9
54	PIERREVILLE		67	XA	13
57	PIERREVILLERS		46	XA	10
44	PIERRIC		93	O	17
51	PIERRY		42	OA	11
2B	PIETRA DI VERDE		228	MB	41
2B	PIETRACORBARA		226	MB	38
2B	PIETRALBA		226	LB	39
2B	PIETRASERENA		228	MB	41
2B	PIETRICAGGIO		228	MB	40
2A	PIETROSELLA		229	JB	43
2B	PIETROSO		228	LB	41
64	PIETS PLASENCE MOUSTROU		207	U	35
11	PIEUSSE		221	GA	37
50	PIEUX, LES	C	33	O	8
2B	PIEVE		226	LB	39
89	PIFFONDS		83	KA	15
2B	PIGNA		225	KB	39
34	PIGNAN	C	214	NA	35
83	PIGNANS		203	YA	36
02	PIGNICOURT		29	OA	9
63	PIGNOLS		148	LA	26
18	PIGNY		100	HA	19
62	PIHEM		8	GA	3
62	PIHEN LES GUINES		7	EA	2
2A	PILA CANALE		229	KB	43
16	PILLAC		143	X	27
39	PILLEMOINE		122	WA	21
26	PILLES, LES		180	TA	31
55	PILLON		31	VA	9
40	PIMBO		207	U	35
89	PIMELLES		85	PA	16
39	PIMORIN		122	VA	22
60	PIMPREZ		27	JA	8
70	PIN		106	WA	18
03	PIN, LE		135	NA	22
14	PIN, LE		37	Y	10
17	PIN, LE		142	V	27
30	PIN, LE		193	QA	33
38	PIN, LE		152	VA	26
39	PIN, LE		122	VA	21
44	PIN, LE		94	R	17
77	PIN, LE		40	IA	11
79	PIN, LE		111	T	20
82	PIN, LE		187	AA	33
61	PIN AU HARAS, LE		58	X	12
31	PIN BALMA		210	DA	35
49	PIN EN MAUGES, LE		95	S	18

61 PIN LA GARENNE, LE 59 Z 13
31 PIN MURELET, LE 209 BA 36
65 PINAS 217 Y 37
42 PINAY 135 PA 25
72 PINCE 77 U 16
47 PINDERES 171 W 32
86 PINDRAY 114 AA 22
85 PINEAUX, LES 110 R 21
47 PINEL HAUTERIVE 172 Z 31
34 PINET 214 MA 36
33 PINEUILH 157 X 29
10 PINEY C 65 PA 14
2B PINO 226 MB 38
43 PINOLS C 162 LA 28
02 PINON 28 LA 9
16 PINS, LES 143 Y 25
31 PINS JUSTARET 210 CA 35
46 PINSAC 159 DA 29
31 PINSAGUEL 210 CA 35
38 PINSOT 153 XA 27
65 PINTAC 208 W 36
27 PINTERVILLE 38 BA 10
55 PINTHEVILLE 45 VA 10
28 PINTHIERES, LES 39 DA 12
2B PIOBETTA 228 MB 40
2B PIOGGIOLA 225 KB 39
84 PIOLENC 179 RA 32
23 PIONNAT 132 FA 23
63 PIONSAT C 133 IA 24
79 PIOUSSAY 129 W 24
35 PIPRIAC C 75 N 16
82 PIQUECOS 173 CA 32
01 PIRAJOUX 137 UA 22
35 PIRE SUR SEICHE 76 Q 15
25 PIREY 107 XA 18
44 PIRIAC SUR MER 92 L 18
72 PIRMIL 78 W 16
50 PIROU 34 P 10
32 PIS 187 Z 34
17 PISANY 141 T 25
95 PISCOP 40 GA 11
27 PISEUX 38 BA 12
38 PISIEU 151 TA 27
60 PISSELEU 26 FA 8
52 PISSELOUP 87 WA 16
70 PISSEURE, LA 88 YA 16
40 PISSOS C 170 T 32
85 PISSOTTE 111 T 22
80 PISSY 26 GA 7
76 PISSY POVILLE 24 BA 8
89 PISY 85 PA 17
59 PITGAM 8 HA 2
45 PITHIVIERS S 62 GA 14
45 PITHIVIERS LE VIEIL 61 GA 14
02 PITHON 27 KA 7
27 PITRES 24 CA 9
62 PITTEFAUX 7 EA 3
01 PIZAY 137 TA 25
72 PIZIEUX 59 Y 14
24 PIZOU, LE 157 W 28
09 PLA, LE 222 FA 39
29 PLABENNEC C 51 D 13
53 PLACE 57 T 14
27 PLACES, LES 37 Y 10
25 PLACEY 106 WA 19
80 PLACHY BUYON 26 GA 7
14 PLACY 36 U 11
50 PLACY MONTAIGU 35 S 11
07 PLAGNAL, LE 163 OA 30
01 PLAGNE 138 WA 23
31 PLAGNE 218 BA 37
31 PLAGNOLE 210 BA 36
11 PLAIGNE 219 EA 37
60 PLAILLY 40 IA 10
25 PLAIMBOIS DU MIROIR 108 AB 19
25 PLAIMBOIS VENNES 107 ZA 19
18 PLAIMPIED GIVAUDINS 117 HA 20
67 PLAINE 69 CB 13
49 PLAINE, LA 95 T 19
57 PLAINE DE WALSCH 69 CB 12
22 PLAINE HAUTE 54 J 13
44 PLAINE SUR MER, LA 93 M 19
70 PLAINEMONT 88 YA 16
10 PLAINES ST LANGE 85 QA 15
88 PLAINFAING 69 BB 14
39 PLAINOISEAU 122 VA 21
25 PLAINS
ET GRANDS ESSARTS, LES 108 BB 18
22 PLAINTEL 54 K 13
60 PLAINVAL 26 HA 8
27 PLAINVILLE 37 Y 10
60 PLAINVILLE 26 HA 8
12 PLAISANCE 190 HA 33
24 PLAISANCE 157 Z 30
32 PLAISANCE C 208 W 35
86 PLAISANCE 130 AA 23
31 PLAISANCE DU TOUCH 210 CA 35
39 PLAISIA 122 VA 22
26 PLAISIANS 180 UA 32
78 PLAISIR C 39 FA 12
34 PLAISSAN 214 MA 35
16 PLAIZAC 142 W 25
38 PLAN 152 UA 27
31 PLAN, LE 218 BA 37
83 PLAN D' AUPS STE BAUME 202 WA 36
13 PLAN D'ORGON 195 SA 34
26 PLAN DE BAIX 165 TA 29
13 PLAN DE CUQUES 202 UA 36
83 PLAN DE LA TOUR 204 ZA 36
73 PLANAISE 153 XA 26
21 PLANAY 85 QA 16
73 PLANAY 154 AB 27
44 PLANCHE, LA 110 Q 20
70 PLANCHER BAS 89 AB 16
70 PLANCHER LES MINES 89 AB 16
73 PLANCHERINE 153 YA 26
61 PLANCHES 37 Y 12
39 PLANCHES EN MONTAGNE, LES C 123 XA 21
39 PLANCHES PRES ARBOIS, LES 122 WA 20
58 PLANCHEZ 103 OA 19
22 PLANCOET C 55 M 13
10 PLANCY L'ABBAYE 64 OA 13
25 PLANEE, LA 123 YA 20
66 PLANES 222 GA 40
66 PLANEZES 224 IA 38
42 PLANFOY 150 OA 27
22 PLANGUENOUAL 54 L 13
46 PLANIOLES 174 FA 30
71 PLANOIS, LE 121 UA 21
27 PLANQUAY, LE 37 Y 10
14 PLANQUERY 35 S 10
62 PLANQUES 16 FA 4
52 PLANRUPT 65 RA 13
30 PLANS, LES 178 PA 32
34 PLANS, LES 191 LA 34
01 PLANTAY, LE 137 TA 24
30 PLANTIERS, LES 177 NA 32
61 PLANTIS, LE 59 Y 13
10 PLANTY 64 MA 14
07 PLANZOLLES 178 PA 31
57 PLAPPEVILLE 46 XA 10
39 PLASNE 122 VA 21
27 PLASNES 37 Z 10
17 PLASSAC 142 U 26
33 PLASSAC 155 T 28
16 PLASSAC ROUFFIAC 143 W 26
17 PLASSAY 127 T 25
07 PLATS 164 RA 28
56 PLAUDREN 74 K 16
63 PLAUZAT 148 KA 26
11 PLAVILLA 221 FA 37
24 PLAZAC 158 BA 28
15 PLEAUX C 160 GA 28
22 PLEBOULLE 54 M 12
35 PLECHATEL 75 O 16
22 PLEDELIAC 55 M 13
22 PLEDRAN 54 K 13
22 PLEGUIEN 54 J 12
22 PLEHEDEL 53 J 12
35 PLEINE FOUGERES C 56 P 13
02 PLEINE SELVE 28 MA 7
33 PLEINE SELVE 142 U 27
76 PLEINE SEVE 24 Z 7
35 PLELAN LE GRAND C 75 N 15
22 PLELAN LE PETIT C 55 M 13
22 PLELAUFF 73 I 14
22 PLELO 54 J 13
22 PLEMET 74 L 14
22 PLEMY 54 K 14
22 PLENEE JUGON 54 M 14
22 PLENEUF VAL ANDRE C 54 L 13
39 PLENISE 123 XA 20
39 PLENISETTE 123 XA 21
35 PLERGUER 55 O 13
22 PLERIN C 54 K 13
22 PLERNEUF 54 J 13
56 PLESCOP 74 K 17
35 PLESDER 55 O 13
22 PLESIDY 53 I 13
22 PLESLIN TRIGAVOU 55 N 13
57 PLESNOIS 46 XA 10
52 PLESNOY 87 UA 16
22 PLESSALA 74 L 14
44 PLESSE 93 O 17
02 PLESSIER HULEU, LE 41 LA 10
80 PLESSIER ROZAINVILLERS, LE 26 IA 7
60 PLESSIER SUR BULLES, LE 26 GA 9
60 PLESSIER SUR ST JUST, LE 26 HA 8
77 PLESSIS AUX BOIS, LE 40 IA 11
10 PLESSIS BARBUISE 64 MA 13
60 PLESSIS BELLEVILLE, LE 40 IA 10
95 PLESSIS BOUCHARD, LE 40 GA 11
60 PLESSIS BRION, LE 27 JA 9
60 PLESSIS DE ROYE 27 JA 8
41 PLESSIS DORIN, LE 59 AA 15
77 PLESSIS FEU AUSSOUX, LE 41 KA 12
95 PLESSIS GASSOT, LE 40 HA 11
49 PLESSIS GRAMMOIRE, LE 96 U 17
14 PLESSIS GRIMOULT, LE 35 T 11
27 PLESSIS GROHAN, LE 38 BA 11
27 PLESSIS HEBERT, LE 38 CA 11
41 PLESSIS L'ECHELLE, LE 80 DA 16
77 PLESSIS L'EVEQUE, LE 40 JA 11
50 PLESSIS LASTELLE, LE 34 Q 9
95 PLESSIS LUZARCHES, LE 40 HA 10
49 PLESSIS MACE, LE 95 T 17
91 PLESSIS PATE, LE 62 GA 12
60 PLESSIS PATTE D'OIE, LE 27 KA 8
77 PLESSIS PLACY, LE 41 JA 10
92 PLESSIS ROBINSON, LE C 40 GA 12
91 PLESSIS ST BENOIST, LE 61 FA 13
89 PLESSIS ST JEAN 63 LA 14
27 PLESSIS STE OPPORTUNE, LE 37 AA 10
94 PLESSIS TREVISE, LE 40 IA 12
22 PLESSIX BALISSON 55 N 13
22 PLESTAN 54 L 13
22 PLESTIN LES GREVES C 52 G 12
22 PLEUBIAN 53 I 11
56 PLEUCADEUC 74 M 16
22 PLEUDANIEL 53 I 12
22 PLEUDIHEN SUR RANCE 55 N 13
56 PLEUGRIFFET 74 K 15
35 PLEUGUENEUC 55 O 13
86 PLEUMARTIN C 114 Z 21
35 PLEUMELEUC 75 O 14
22 PLEUMEUR BODOU 53 G 12
22 PLEUMEUR GAUTIER 53 I 12
39 PLEURE 122 UA 20
51 PLEURS 42 NA 12
35 PLEURTUIT 55 N 13
29 PLEUVEN 72 E 16
88 PLEUVEZAIN 67 WA 13
16 PLEUVILLE 113 Y 21
22 PLEVEN 54 M 13
22 PLEVIN 73 H 14
29 PLEYBEN C 72 F 14
29 PLEYBER CHRIST 52 F 13
79 PLIBOUX 129 X 23
51 PLICHANCOURT 43 RA 12
32 PLIEUX 187 Z 33
51 PLIVOT 42 OA 11
29 PLOBANNALEC 71 D 16
67 PLOBSHEIM 70 EB 13
56 PLOEMEL 91 I 17
56 PLOEMEUR C 73 H 16
56 PLOERDUT 73 H 15
56 PLOEREN 91 J 17
56 PLOERMEL C 74 M 15
22 PLOEUC SUR LIE C 54 K 14
29 PLOEVEN 71 D 14
22 PLOEZAL 53 I 12
29 PLOGASTEL ST GERMAIN C 71 D 15
29 PLOGOFF 71 B 15
29 PLOGONNEC 71 E 15
02 PLOISY 28 LA 9
50 PLOMB 56 Q 12
88 PLOMBIERES LES BAINS C 89 ZA 15
21 PLOMBIERES LES DIJON 105 SA 18
29 PLOMELIN 72 E 15
29 PLOMEUR 71 D 16
02 PLOMION 29 OA 7
29 PLOMODIERN 71 D 14
29 PLONEIS 71 D 15
29 PLONEOUR LANVERN 71 D 16
29 PLONEVEZ DU FAOU 52 F 14
29 PLONEVEZ PORZAY 71 D 15
22 PLOREC SUR ARGUENON 55 M 13
18 PLOU 100 GA 19
22 PLOUAGAT C 53 J 13
22 PLOUARET C 53 H 12
29 PLOUARZEL 51 B 13
22 PLOUASNE 75 N 14
56 PLOUAY C 73 H 16
22 PLOUBALAY C 55 N 13
22 PLOUBAZLANEC 53 I 12
22 PLOUBEZRE 53 H 12
29 PLOUDALMEZEAU C 51 C 13
29 PLOUDANIEL 51 D 13
29 PLOUDIRY C 52 E 13
22 PLOUEC DU TRIEUX 53 I 12
29 PLOUEDERN 52 D 13
29 PLOUEGAT GUERAND 52 G 12
29 PLOUEGAT MOYSAN 52 G 13
29 PLOUENAN 52 E 12
22 PLOUER SUR RANCE 55 N 13
29 PLOUESCAT C 52 E 12
22 PLOUEZEC 53 J 12
29 PLOUEZOCH 52 F 12
22 PLOUFRAGAN C 54 K 13
29 PLOUGAR 52 E 13
29 PLOUGASNOU 52 F 12
29 PLOUGASTEL DAOULAS 51 D 14
29 PLOUGONVELIN 51 B 14
29 PLOUGONVEN 52 G 13
22 PLOUGONVER 53 H 13
29 PLOUGOULM 52 E 12
56 PLOUGOUMELEN 91 J 17
29 PLOUGOURVEST 52 E 13
22 PLOUGRAS 53 G 13
22 PLOUGRESCANT 53 I 11
22 PLOUGUENAST C 74 K 14
29 PLOUGUERNEAU 51 C 12
29 PLOUGUERNEVEL 73 I 14
22 PLOUGUIEL 53 I 12
29 PLOUGUIN 51 C 13
22 PLOUHA C 54 J 12
56 PLOUHARNEL 91 I 17
29 PLOUHINEC 71 C 15
56 PLOUHINEC 73 I 17
29 PLOUIDER 51 D 12
29 PLOUIGNEAU C 52 G 13
22 PLOUISY 53 I 13
22 PLOULEC'H 53 G 12
22 PLOUMAGOAR 53 I 13
22 PLOUMILLIAU 53 G 12
29 PLOUMOGUER 51 B 13
29 PLOUNEOUR MENEZ 52 F 13
29 PLOUNEOUR TREZ 51 D 12
22 PLOUNERIN 53 G 13
29 PLOUNEVENTER 52 D 13
29 PLOUNEVEZ LOCHRIST 52 D 12
22 PLOUNEVEZ MOEDEC 53 H 13
22 PLOUNEVEZ QUINTIN 53 I 14
29 PLOUNEVEZEL 52 G 14
22 PLOURAC'H 53 G 13
56 PLOURAY 73 H 15
22 PLOURHAN 54 J 12
29 PLOURIN 51 B 13
29 PLOURIN LES MORLAIX 52 F 13
22 PLOURIVO 53 J 12
62 PLOUVAIN 17 JA 5
22 PLOUVARA 54 J 13
29 PLOUVIEN 51 C 13
29 PLOUVORN 52 E 13
29 PLOUYE 52 G 14
29 PLOUZANE 51 C 13
22 PLOUZELAMBRE 53 G 12
29 PLOUZEVEDE C 52 E 13
29 PLOVAN 71 D 16
02 PLOYART ET VAURSEINE 28 NA 9
60 PLOYRON, LE 26 IA 8
29 PLOZEVET 71 D 15
22 PLUDUAL 54 J 12
22 PLUDUNO 55 M 13
22 PLUFUR 53 G 12
29 PLUGUFFAN 71 E 15
56 PLUHERLIN 74 M 17
22 PLUMAUDAN 55 N 14
22 PLUMAUGAT 75 M 14
56 PLUMELEC 74 K 16
56 PLUMELIAU 73 J 15
56 PLUMELIN 73 J 16
56 PLUMERGAT 73 J 16
14 PLUMETOT 36 V 9
22 PLUMIEUX 74 L 15
39 PLUMONT 106 WA 19
56 PLUNERET 73 J 17
22 PLURIEN 54 L 12
22 PLUSQUELLEC 53 H 13
22 PLUSSULIEN 53 I 14
21 PLUVAULT 105 TA 19
21 PLUVET 105 UA 19
56 PLUVIGNER C 73 J 16
22 PLUZUNET 53 H 12
51 POCANCY 42 PA 11
35 POCE LES BOIS 76 O 15
37 POCE SUR CISSE 98 BA 18
33 PODENSAC C 170 U 30
05 POET, LE 181 WA 32
26 POET CELARD, LE 179 TA 30
26 POET EN PERCIP, LE 180 UA 32
26 POET LAVAL, LE 179 SA 31
26 POET SIGILLAT, LE 180 UA 31
80 POEUILLY 27 KA 7
64 POEY D'OLORON 206 T 36
64 POEY DE LESCAR 207 U 36
03 POEZAT 134 KA 24
2B POGGIO D'OLETTA 226 MB 39
2B POGGIO DI NAZZA 228 LB 41
2B POGGIO DI VENACO 228 LB 41
2B POGGIO MARINACCIO 228 MB 40
2B POGGIO MEZZANA 228 MB 40
2B POGGIOLO 227 KB 41
51 POGNY 43 QA 11
39 POIDS DE FIOLE 122 VA 21
77 POIGNY 63 LA 13
78 POIGNY LA FORET 61 EA 12
58 POIL 119 OA 20
08 POILCOURT SYDNEY 29 OA 9
34 POILHES 213 KA 36
72 POILLE SUR VEGRE 77 V 16
35 POILLEY 56 R 13
50 POILLEY 56 Q 12
51 POILLY 42 NA 10
45 POILLY LEZ GIEN 83 IA 17
89 POILLY SUR SEREIN 84 NA 16
89 POILLY SUR THOLON 83 LA 16
21 POINCON LES LARREY 85 OA 16
36 POINCONNET, LE 115 EA 21
77 POINCY 41 JA 11
52 POINSENOT 86 SA 16
52 POINSON LES FAYL 87 VA 16
52 POINSON LES GRANCEY 86 SA 16
52 POINSON LES NOGENT 87 UA 15
61 POINTEL 58 V 12
31 POINTIS DE RIVIERE 217 Z 37
31 POINTIS INARD 217 AA 37
39 POINTRE 106 VA 19
25 POINTVILLERS 106 WA 19
28 POINVILLE 61 FA 14
85 POIRE SUR VELLUIRE, LE 111 S 22
85 POIRE SUR VIE, LE C 110 P 21
85 POIROUX 125 P 22
38 POISAT 166 WA 28
52 POISEUL 87 VA 15
21 POISEUL LA GRANGE 86 SA 17
21 POISEUL LA VILLE ET
LAPERRIERE 85 RA 17
21 POISEUL LES SAULX 86 SA 17
58 POISEUX 102 KA 19
18 POISIEUX 100 FA 19
41 POISLAY, LE 80 BA 15
71 POISSON 135 PA 22
52 POISSONS C 66 TA 13
78 POISSY C 39 FA 11
28 POISVILLIERS 60 DA 13
74 POISY 139 XA 24
49 POITEVINIERE, LA 95 S 19
86 POITIERS P 113 Y 21
10 POIVRES 43 PA 12
51 POIX 43 RA 11
80 POIX DE PICARDIE C 26 FA 7
59 POIX DU NORD 18 MA 5
08 POIX TERRON 30 RA 8
01 POIZAT, LE 138 VA 23
70 POLAINCOURT
ET CLAIREFONTAINE 88 XA 16
31 POLASTRON 209 AA 36
32 POLASTRON 209 AA 35
69 POLEYMIEUX AU MONT D'OR 136 RA 25
38 POLIENAS 152 UA 27
17 POLIGNAC 142 V 27
43 POLIGNAC 163 NA 28
35 POLIGNE 75 P 16
05 POLIGNY 167 XA 30
10 POLIGNY 65 PA 14
39 POLIGNY C 122 WA 20
77 POLIGNY 62 IA 14
62 POLINCOVE 7 FA 3
10 POLISOT 65 PA 15
10 POLISY 85 PA 15
66 POLLESTRES 224 JA 39
01 POLLIAT 137 TA 23
01 POLLIEU 138 WA 25
69 POLLIONNAY 150 RA 25
15 POLMINHAC 161 IA 29
2B POLVEROSO 228 MB 40
51 POMACLE 29 PA 9
46 POMAREDE 173 BA 30
11 POMAREDE, LA 211 FA 36
40 POMAREZ 184 S 35
11 POMAS 221 GA 37
12 POMAYROLS 176 KA 31
33 POMEROL 156 V 29
34 POMEROLS 214 MA 36
69 POMEYS 150 QA 26
21 POMMARD 120 RA 20
62 POMMERA 17 HA 5
85 POMMERAIE
SUR SEVRE, LA 111 T 20
14 POMMERAYE, LA 36 U 11
49 POMMERAYE, LA 95 S 18
22 POMMERET 54 L 13
59 POMMEREUIL 18 MA 6
76 POMMEREUX 25 DA 8
76 POMMEREVAL 25 CA 7
53 POMMERIEUX 77 S 16
57 POMMERIEUX 46 XA 11
22 POMMERIT JAUDY 53 I 12
22 POMMERIT LE VICOMTE 53 I 12
26 POMMEROL 180 UA 31
77 POMMEUSE 41 KA 12
82 POMMEVIC 173 AA 32
62 POMMIER 17 IA 5
38 POMMIER DE BEAUREPAIRE 151 TA 27
02 POMMIERS 27 LA 9
30 POMMIERS 192 MA 33
36 POMMIERS 115 DA 22
42 POMMIERS 149 OA 25
69 POMMIERS 136 RA 24
38 POMMIERS LA PLACETTE 152 VA 27
17 POMMIERS MOULONS 142 V 27
70 POMOY 88 YA 17
79 POMPAIRE 112 V 21
33 POMPEJAC 170 V 31
31 POMPERTUZAT 210 DA 35
54 POMPEY C 46 XA 12
32 POMPIAC 209 BA 35
48 POMPIDOU, LE 177 MA 32
88 POMPIERRE 67 VA 14
25 POMPIERRE SUR DOUBS 107 ZA 18
47 POMPIEY 171 X 32
33 POMPIGNAC 156 U 29
30 POMPIGNAN 192 NA 33
82 POMPIGNAN 188 CA 34
47 POMPOGNE 171 W 32
77 POMPONNE 40 IA 11
24 POMPORT 157 Y 30
64 POMPS 207 U 35
11 POMY 221 FA 37
72 PONCE SUR LE LOIR 79 Z 16
21 PONCEY LES ATHEE 106 UA 19
21 PONCEY SUR L'IGNON 86 RA 17
62 PONCHEL, LE 16 FA 5
80 PONCHES ESTRUVAL 16 FA 5
60 PONCHON 26 GA 9
01 PONCIN C 138 UA 24
42 PONCINS 149 PA 25
33 PONDAURAT 171 W 31
18 PONDY, LE 117 IA 21
26 PONET ET ST AUBAN 166 UA 29
31 PONLAT TAILLEBOURG 217 Z 37
17 PONS C 142 U 26
32 PONSAMPERE 108 Y 35
32 PONSAN SOUBIRAN 209 Y 36
26 PONSAS 165 SA 28
64 PONSON DEBAT POUTS 208 W 36
64 PONSON DESSUS 208 W 36
38 PONSONNAS 166 WA 29
21 PONT 105 UA 19
59 PONT A MARCQ C 9 KA 4
54 PONT A MOUSSON C 46 XA 11
62 PONT A VENDIN 17 JA 4
02 PONT ARCY 28 MA 9
27 PONT AUDEMER C 23 Z 9
27 PONT AUTHOU 37 Z 10
29 PONT AVEN C 72 G 16
14 PONT BELLANGER 35 S 11
36 PONT CHRETIEN
CHABENET, LE 115 DA 21
29 PONT CROIX C 71 C 15
01 PONT D'AIN C 138 UA 24
39 PONT D'HERY 122 WA 20
14 PONT D'OUILLY 36 U 11
26 PONT DE BARRET 179 SA 30
38 PONT DE BEAUVOISIN, LE C 152 VA 26
73 PONT DE BEAUVOISIN, LE C 152 VA 26
29 PONT DE BUIS LES QUIMERCH 52 E 14
38 PONT DE CHERUY C 151 TA 25
38 PONT DE CLAIX, LE 166 WA 28
27 PONT DE L'ARCHE C 38 BA 9
26 PONT DE L'ISERE 165 SA 28
07 PONT DE LABEAUME 178 PA 30
81 PONT DE LARN 212 HA 35
80 PONT DE METZ 26 GA 7
48 PONT DE MONTVERT, LE C 177 NA 31
70 PONT DE PLANCHES, LE 88 WA 17
39 PONT DE POITTE 122 VA 21
25 PONT DE ROIDE C 108 AB 18
37 PONT DE RUAN 98 Z 18
12 PONT DE SALARS C 176 IA 32
01 PONT DE VAUX C 121 SA 22
01 PONT DE VEYLE C 137 SA 23
70 PONT DU BOIS 88 XA 15
47 PONT DU CASSE 172 Z 32
63 PONT DU CHATEAU C 148 LA 25
39 PONT DU NAVOY 122 WA 21
38 PONT EN ROYANS C 166 UA 28
21 PONT ET MASSENE 104 PA 18
38 PONT EVEQUE 151 SA 26
14 PONT FARCY 56 R 11
50 PONT HEBERT 34 R 10
29 PONT L'ABBE C 71 D 16
17 PONT L'ABBE D'ARNOULT 127 S 25
14 PONT L'EVEQUE C 36 X 9
60 PONT L'EVEQUE 27 JA 8
52 PONT LA VILLE 66 SA 15
88 PONT LES BONFAYS 68 XA 14
25 PONT LES MOULINS 107 YA 18
22 PONT MELVEZ 53 H 13
80 PONT NOYELLES 17 HA 7
35 PONT PEAN 75 O 15
80 PONT REMY 16 FA 6
43 PONT SALOMON 149 PA 27
56 PONT SCORFF C 73 H 16
30 PONT ST ESPRIT C 179 RA 32
02 PONT ST MARD 27 LA 7
44 PONT ST MARTIN 93 P 19
27 PONT ST PIERRE 24 CA 9
54 PONT ST VINCENT 67 XA 12
10 PONT STE MARIE 64 OA 14
60 PONT STE MAXENCE C 40 IA 9
70 PONT SUR L'OGNON 89 ZA 17
88 PONT SUR MADON 68 YA 14
55 PONT SUR MEUSE 45 VA 12
59 PONT SUR SAMBRE 19 NA 5
10 PONT SUR SEINE 64 MA 13
89 PONT SUR VANNE 63 LA 14
89 PONT SUR YONNE C 63 KA 14
69 PONT TRAMBOUZE 135 PA 24
64 PONTACQ C 215 W 37
21 PONTAILLER SUR SAONE C 106 UA 18
26 PONTAIX 166 UA 30
73 PONTAMAFREY
MONTPASCAL 153 YA 27
23 PONTARION C 132 EA 24
25 PONTARLIER S 123 YA 20
60 PONTARME 40 HA 10
50 PONTAUBAULT 56 Q 12
89 PONTAUBERT 84 NA 17
77 PONTAULT COMBAULT C 40 IA 12
63 PONTAUMUR C 133 IA 25
02 PONTAVERT 28 NA 9
77 PONTCARRE 40 IA 12
70 PONTCEY 88 XA 17
61 PONTCHARDON 37 X 11
38 PONTCHARRA 153 XA 27
69 PONTCHARRA SUR TURDINE 136 QA 25
23 PONTCHARRAUD 132 GA 25
44 PONTCHATEAU C 93 N 18
46 PONTCIRQ 173 CA 30
14 PONTECOULANT 35 U 11
66 PONTEILLA 224 JA 39
30 PONTEILS ET BRESIS 178 OA 31
40 PONTENX LES FORGES 169 R 32
73 PONTET, LE 153 YA 26
84 PONTET, LE 195 SA 33
25 PONTETS, LES 123 YA 21
83 PONTEVES 203 XA 35
24 PONTEYRAUD 157 X 28
51 PONTFAVERGER
MORONVILLIERS 43 PA 9
63 PONTGIBAUD C 147 JA 25
28 PONTGOUIN 60 BA 13
78 PONTHEVRARD 61 FA 13
51 PONTHION 43 RA 12
80 PONTHOILE 15 EA 5
29 PONTHOU, LE 52 G 13
39 PONTHOUX 138 WA 22
64 PONTIACQ VIELLEPINTE 208 W 36
49 PONTIGNE 96 W 17
89 PONTIGNY 84 NA 16
04 PONTIS 182 YA 31
56 PONTIVY S 73 J 15
41 PONTLEVOY 99 CA 18
53 PONTMAIN 56 R 13
95 PONTOISE P 39 FA 11
60 PONTOISE LES NOYON 27 KA 8
40 PONTONX SUR L'ADOUR 183 S 34
50 PONTORSON C 56 Q 13
24 PONTOURS 158 AA 29
71 PONTOUX 121 TA 20
57 PONTOY 46 YA 11
57 PONTPIERRE 47 AB 11
60 PONTPOINT 40 IA 9
22 PONTRIEUX C 53 I 12
02 PONTRU 27 KA 7
02 PONTRUET 27 KA 7
50 PONTS 56 Q 12
49 PONTS DE CE, LES C 96 U 18
76 PONTS ET MARAIS 15 CA 6
72 PONTVALLAIN C 78 X 16
34 POPIAN 214 MA 35
2B POPOLASCA 228 LB 40
56 PORCARO 75 M 16
57 PORCELETTE 47 AB 10
33 PORCHERES 157 W 28
87 PORCHERIE, LA 145 DA 26
60 PORCHEUX 25 FA 9
78 PORCHEVILLE 39 EA 11
38 PORCIEU AMBLAGNIEU 138 UA 25
22 PORDIC 54 K 13
33 PORGE, LE 155 R 29
44 PORNIC C 93 N 19
44 PORNICHET 92 M 18
60 PORQUERICOURT 27 JA 8
2B PORRI 228 MB 40
29 PORSPODER 51 B 13
01 PORT 138 VA 23
09 PORT, LE 219 CA 38
53 PORT BRILLET 76 S 15
17 PORT D'ENVAUX 127 T 25
13 PORT DE BOUC 201 SA 36
40 PORT DE LANNE 183 R 35
86 PORT DE PILES 114 Z 20
17 PORT DES BARQUES 126 R 24
14 PORT EN BESSIN HUPPAIN 35 T 9
11 PORT LA NOUVELLE 223 KA 37
29 PORT LAUNAY 72 E 14
80 PORT LE GRAND 15 EA 6

39 PORT LESNEY 122 WA 20
56 PORT LOUIS C 73 H 16
78 PORT MARLY, LE 39 GA 11
27 PORT MORT 38 CA 10
13 PORT ST LOUIS DU RHONE C 201 RA 36
44 PORT ST PERE 93 O 19
32 PORT STE FOY ET PONCHAPT 157 X 29
47 PORT STE MARIE C 172 Y 32
70 PORT SUR SAONE C 88 XA 17
54 PORT SUR SEILLE 46 YA 11
66 PORT VENDRES C 224 KA 40
78 PORT VILLEZ 38 DA 10
66 PORTA 220 EA 39
2B PORTA, LA C 228 MB 40
50 PORTBAIL 34 P 9
27 PORTE JOIE 38 CA 10
66 PORTE PUYMORENS 220 EA 39
62 PORTEL, LE C 7 DA 3
11 PORTEL DES CORBIERES 223 JA 37
27 PORTES 38 AA 11
30 PORTES 178 OA 32
17 PORTES EN RE, LES 125 P 23
26 PORTES EN VALDAINE 179 SA 31
26 PORTES LES VALENCE C 165 SA 29
64 PORTET 207 V 35
31 PORTET D'ASPET 217 AA 38
31 PORTET DE LUCHON 217 Y 38
31 PORTET SUR GARONNE 210 CA 35
33 PORTETS 156 U 30
88 PORTIEUX 68 YA 14
34 PORTIRAGNES 214 LA 36
2A PORTO VECCHIO C 230 LB 44
37 PORTS 113 Z 20
21 POSANGES 104 OA 18
27 POSES 38 CA 9
51 POSSESSE 43 RA 11
49 POSSONNIERE, LA 95 T 18
89 POSTOLLE, LA 63 MA 14
57 POSTROFF 48 CB 11
51 POTANGIS 64 MA 13
30 POTELIERES 178 PA 32
59 POTELLE 18 MA 5
61 POTERIE AU PERCHE, LA 59 Z 12
76 POTERIE CAP D'ANTIFER, LA 23 X 8
27 POTERIE MATHIEU, LA 37 Y 10
21 POTHIERES 85 OA 16
14 POTIGNY 36 V 11
80 POTTE 27 JA 7
10 POUAN LES VALLEES 64 OA 13
86 POUANCAY 96 W 19
49 POUANCE C 76 R 16
86 POUANT 113 X 20
31 POUBEAU 217 Y 38
31 POUCHARRAMET 210 BA 36
47 POUDENAS 186 X 33
40 POUDENX 207 U 35
81 POUDIS 211 FA 35
65 POUEYFERRE 215 V 37
49 POUEZE, LA 95 T 17
79 POUFFONDS 128 V 23
23 POUGE, LA 132 FA 24
34 POUGET, LE 214 MA 35
30 POUGNADORESSE 193 QA 33
79 POUGNE HERRISSON 112 U 21
01 POUGNY 138 WA 23
58 POUGNY 102 KA 18
58 POUGUES LES EAUX C 102 KA 19
10 POUGY 65 PA 13
17 POUILLAC 142 V 27
01 POUILLAT 138 UA 23
41 POUILLE 99 CA 18
85 POUILLE 111 S 22
86 POUILLE 113 Z 22
44 POUILLE LES COTEAUX 94 R 18
21 POUILLENAY 85 QA 17
25 POUILLEY FRANCAIS 106 WA 19
25 POUILLEY LES VIGNES 107 XA 18
40 POUILLON C 183 S 35
51 POUILLON 29 OA 9
71 POUILLOUX 120 QA 21
57 POUILLY 46 YA 10
60 POUILLY 39 FA 10
21 POUILLY EN AUXOIS C 104 QA 18
69 POUILLY LE MONIAL 136 RA 24
42 POUILLY LES FEURS 149 PA 25
42 POUILLY LES NONAINS 135 OA 24
42 POUILLY SOUS CHARLIEU 135 OA 23
58 POUILLY SUR LOIRE C 101 JA 18
55 POUILLY SUR MEUSE 30 TA 8
21 POUILLY SUR SAONE 121 TA 20
02 POUILLY SUR SERRE 28 MA 8
21 POUILLY SUR VINGEANNE 87 UA 17
34 POUJOL SUR ORB, LE 213 KA 35
34 POUJOLS 191 LA 34
36 POULAINES 99 EA 19
80 POULAINVILLE 16 GA 7
81 POULAN POUZOLS 189 GA 34
52 POULANGY 86 TA 15
29 POULDERGAT 71 D 15
22 POULDOURAN 53 I 12
29 POULDREUZIC 71 D 15
69 POULE LES ECHARMEAUX 136 OA 23
64 POULIACQ 207 V 35
88 POULIERES, LES 69 AB 14
25 POULIGNEY LUSANS 107 YA 18
36 POULIGNY NOTRE DAME 116 FA 22
36 POULIGNY ST MARTIN 116 FA 22
36 POULIGNY ST PIERRE 114 BA 21
44 POULIGUEN, LE 92 L 18
29 POULLAN SUR MER 71 D 15
29 POULLAOUEN 52 G 14
16 POULLIGNAC 142 W 27
30 POULX 193 QA 33
65 POUMAROUS 216 X 37
82 POUPAS 187 AA 33
28 POUPRY 61 EA 15
58 POUQUES LORMES 103 NA 18
48 POURCHARESSES 177 NA 31
07 POURCHERES 164 QA 30
83 POURCIEUX 202 WA 35
51 POURCY 42 OA 10
71 POURLANS 121 TA 20
57 POURNOY LA CHETIVE 46 XA 11
57 POURNOY LA GRASSE 46 YA 11
89 POURRAIN 83 LA 16
83 POURRIERES 202 WA 35
16 POURSAC 129 X 24
17 POURSAY GARNAUD 128 U 24
64 POURSIUGUES BOUCOUE 207 U 35
08 POURU AUX BOIS 30 TA 8
08 POURU ST REMY 30 TA 8
34 POUSSAN 214 MA 35
23 POUSSANGES 146 GA 25
88 POUSSAY 67 XA 14
58 POUSSEAUX 83 MA 17
47 POUSSIGNAC 171 W 31
14 POUSSY LA CAMPAGNE 36 V 10
12 POUSTHOMY 190 IA 34
33 POUT, LE 156 U 29
61 POUVRAI 59 Y 14
88 POUXEUX 68 ZA 15
65 POUY 209 Z 36
31 POUY DE TOUGES 210 BA 36
32 POUY LOUBRIN 209 Z 35
32 POUY ROQUELAURE 186 Y 33
10 POUY SUR VANNES 64 MA 14
65 POUYASTRUC C 208 X 36
40 POUYDESSEAUX 185 V 33
32 POUYDRAGUIN 185 W 34
32 POUYLEBON 208 X 35
65 POUZAC 216 X 37
85 POUZAUGES C 111 S 21
37 POUZAY 97 Z 19
31 POUZE 210 DA 35
30 POUZILHAC 195 RA 33
07 POUZIN, LE 164 RA 30
63 POUZOL 133 JA 24
34 POUZOLLES 213 LA 35
34 POUZOLS 214 MA 35
11 POUZOLS MINERVOIS 213 JA 36
03 POUZY MESANGY 118 KA 21
40 POYANNE 184 S 34
70 POYANS 106 UA 18
40 POYARTIN 184 S 34
26 POYOLS 180 UA 30
80 POZIERES 17 IA 6
34 PRADAL, LE 213 KA 35
63 PRADEAUX, LES 148 LA 26
26 PRADELLE 180 UA 30
43 PRADELLES C 163 NA 30
59 PRADELLES 8 IA 3
11 PRADELLES CABARDES 212 HA 36
11 PRADELLES EN VAL 221 HA 37
31 PRADERE LES BOURGUETS 210 BA 35
07 PRADES 178 PA 30
09 PRADES 219 EA 38
43 PRADES 162 MA 28
66 PRADES S 222 HA 39
81 PRADES 211 FA 35
12 PRADES D'AUBRAC 176 JA 31
34 PRADES LE LEZ 192 NA 34
12 PRADES SALARS 176 IA 32
34 PRADES SUR VERNAZOBRE 213 JA 35
83 PRADET, LE 203 XA 37
09 PRADETTES 219 EA 37
09 PRADIERES 219 DA 38
15 PRADIERS 161 JA 27
12 PRADINAS 175 GA 32
19 PRADINES 146 FA 26
42 PRADINES 135 PA 24
46 PRADINES 173 CA 31
07 PRADONS 178 QA 31
04 PRADS HAUTE BLEONE 182 ZA 32
79 PRAHECQ C 128 V 23
79 PRAILLES 128 V 23
73 PRALOGNAN LA VANOISE 154 AB 27
21 PRALON 104 RA 18
42 PRALONG 149 OA 26
07 PRANLES 164 QA 30
16 PRANZAC 143 Y 26
52 PRASLAY 86 TA 16
10 PRASLIN 85 PA 15
28 PRASVILLE 61 EA 14
22 PRAT 53 H 12
09 PRAT BONREPAUX 218 BA 37
2B PRATO DI GIOVELLINA 228 LB 40
24 PRATS DE CARLUX 159 CA 29
66 PRATS DE MOLLO LA PRESTE C 222 HA 40
66 PRATS DE SOURNIA 222 HA 39
24 PRATS DU PERIGORD 173 BA 30
81 PRATVIEL 211 FA 35
39 PRATZ 138 WA 22
52 PRAUTHOY C 87 UA 17
41 PRAY 80 BA 17
54 PRAYE 67 XA 13
09 PRAYOLS 219 DA 38
46 PRAYSSAC 173 BA 31
47 PRAYSSAS C 172 Y 32
74 PRAZ SUR ARLY 140 ZA 25
14 PRE D'AUGE, LE 36 X 10
53 PRE EN PAIL C 58 V 13
28 PRE ST EVROULT 60 DA 14
93 PRE ST GERVAIS, LE 40 HA 11
28 PRE ST MARTIN 60 DA 14
07 PREAUX 164 RA 28
36 PREAUX 115 CA 20
53 PREAUX 77 U 15
76 PREAUX 24 BA 9
27 PREAUX, LES 23 Y 9
14 PREAUX BOCAGE 35 U 10
61 PREAUX DU PERCHE 59 Z 14
14 PREAUX ST SEBASTIEN 37 Y 11
38 PREBOIS 166 VA 29
50 PRECEY 56 O 12
32 PRECHAC 187 Z 34
33 PRECHAC 170 U 31
65 PRECHAC 216 W 37
32 PRECHAC SUR ADOUR 208 W 36
64 PRECHACQ JOSBAIG 206 T 36
40 PRECHACQ LES BAINS 183 S 34
64 PRECHACQ NAVARRENX 206 T 36
42 PRECIEUX 149 PA 26
72 PRECIGNE 77 V 16
64 PRECILHON 215 U 37
50 PRECORBIN 35 S 10
18 PRECY 101 JA 19
89 PRECY LE SEC 84 NA 17
10 PRECY NOTRE DAME 65 QA 13
21 PRECY SOUS THIL C 104 PA 18
10 PRECY ST MARTIN 65 OA 13
77 PRECY SUR MARNE 40 IA 11
60 PRECY SUR OISE 40 HA 10
89 PRECY SUR VRIN 83 LA 15
62 PREDEFIN 16 GA 4
44 PREFAILLES 92 M 19
45 PREFONTAINES 62 IA 15
89 PREGILBERT 84 MA 17
17 PREGUILLAC 142 T 26
33 PREIGNAC 170 V 30
32 PREIGNAN 187 Z 34
70 PREIGNEY 87 WA 16
11 PREIXAN 221 GA 37
39 PREMANON 123 XA 22
21 PREMEAUX PRISSEY 105 SA 19
58 PREMERY C 102 LA 19
59 PREMESQUES 9 JA 3
01 PREMEYZEL 152 VA 25
34 PREMIAN 213 JA 35
21 PREMIERES 105 UA 19
10 PREMIERFAIT 64 OA 13
03 PREMILHAT 133 HA 23
01 PREMILLIEU 138 VA 25
02 PREMONT 18 LA 6
02 PREMONTRE 28 LA 8
46 PRENDEIGNES 160 FA 30
32 PRENERON 186 X 34
22 PRENESSAYE, LA 74 K 14
21 PRENOIS 105 SA 18
41 PRENOUVELLON 80 DA 15
39 PRENOVEL 122 WA 22
54 PRENY 45 XA 11
58 PREPORCHE 119 NA 20
61 PREPOTIN 59 Z 12
26 PRES, LES 180 VA 31
43 PRESAILLES 163 OA 29
59 PRESEAU 18 MA 5
25 PRESENTEVILLERS 108 AB 17
31 PRESERVILLE 210 DA 35
39 PRESILLY 122 VA 22
74 PRESILLY 139 XA 24
73 PRESLE 153 XA 27
14 PRESLES 35 T 11
38 PRESLES 166 UA 28
95 PRESLES 40 GA 10
77 PRESLES EN BRIE 40 IA 12
02 PRESLES ET BOVES 28 MA 9
02 PRESLES ET THIERNY 28 MA 8
18 PRESLY 100 HA 18
45 PRESNOY 82 HA 15
86 PRESSAC 130 Z 24
27 PRESSAGNY L'ORGUEILLEUX 38 DA 10
01 PRESSIAT 138 UA 23
16 PRESSIGNAC 144 Z 25
24 PRESSIGNAC VICQ 158 Z 29
52 PRESSIGNY 87 VA 16
79 PRESSIGNY 112 W 21
45 PRESSIGNY LES PINS 82 IA 16
38 PRESSINS 152 VA 26
62 PRESSY 16 HA 4
71 PRESSY SOUS DONDIN 120 OA 22
25 PRETIERE, LA 108 AB 18
39 PRETIN 122 WA 20
50 PRETOT STE SUZANNE 34 Q 9
76 PRETOT VICQUEMARE 24 AA 7
14 PRETREVILLE 37 X 10
71 PRETY 121 SA 22
55 PRETZ EN ARGONNE 44 TA 11
18 PREUILLY 100 GA 19
36 PREUILLY LA VILLE 114 AA 21
37 PREUILLY SUR CLAISE C 114 AA 20
62 PREURES 7 FA 4
67 PREUSCHDORF 49 FB 11
76 PREUSEVILLE 25 DA 7
54 PREUTIN HIGNY 31 WA 9
59 PREUX AU BOIS 18 MA 6
59 PREUX AU SART 18 NA 5
72 PREVAL 59 Z 14
72 PREVELLES 59 Y 14
48 PREVENCHERES 178 OA 31
18 PREVERANGES 132 GA 22
01 PREVESSIN MOENS 139 XA 23
49 PREVIERE, LA 94 R 16
60 PREVILLERS 26 FA 8
12 PREVINQUIERES 175 GA 31
57 PREVOCOURT 47 ZA 11
27 PREY 38 CA 11
88 PREY 68 AB 14
24 PREYSSAC D'EXCIDEUIL 144 BA 27
08 PREZ 29 PA 7
52 PREZ SOUS LAFAUCHE 67 VA 14
79 PRIAIRES 127 T 23
01 PRIAY 137 UA 24
02 PRIEZ 41 LA 10
17 PRIGNAC 128 U 25
33 PRIGNAC EN MEDOC 141 S 27
33 PRIGNAC ET MARCAMPS 156 U 28
24 PRIGONRIEUX 157 Y 29
38 PRIMARETTE 151 TA 27
29 PRIMELIN 71 C 15
18 PRIMELLES 116 GA 20
79 PRIN DEYRANCON 127 T 23
86 PRINCAY 113 X 20
35 PRINCE 76 R 14
51 PRINGY 43 OA 12
74 PRINGY 139 XA 24
77 PRINGY 62 HA 13
44 PRINQUIAU 93 N 18
48 PRINSUEJOLS 176 KA 30
67 PRINTZHEIM 49 DB 12
02 PRISCES 28 NA 7
59 PRISCHES 19 NA 6
36 PRISSAC 115 CA 22
71 PRISSE 136 RA 23
79 PRISSE LA CHARRIERE 128 U 23
07 PRIVAS P 164 RA 30
12 PRIVEZAC 175 GA 31
08 PRIX LES MEZIERES 29 RA 7
56 PRIZIAC 73 H 15
71 PRIZY 135 PA 22
70 PROISELIERE ET LANGLE, LA 89 ZA 16
24 PROISSANS 159 CA 29
02 PROISY 28 NA 7
02 PROIX 28 MA 7
32 PROJAN 207 V 35
46 PROMILHANES 174 EA 31
63 PROMPSAT 134 KA 24
63 PRONDINES 147 IA 25
60 PRONLEROY 26 IA 9
62 PRONVILLE 17 JA 6
26 PROPIAC 180 TA 32
69 PROPIERES 136 QA 23
2A PROPRIANO 229 KB 43
51 PROSNES 43 PA 10
51 PROUILLY 28 NA 9
31 PROUPIARY 217 AA 37
14 PROUSSY 35 U 11
02 PROUVAIS 29 OA 9
80 PROUVILLE 16 GA 6
59 PROUVY 18 LA 5
80 PROUZEL 26 GA 7
25 PROVENCHERE 108 AB 18
70 PROVENCHERE 88 XA 16
88 PROVENCHERES
LES DARNEY 67 XA 15
88 PROVENCHERES SUR FAVE C 69 CB 14
89 PROVENCY 84 OA 17
10 PROVERVILLE 65 RA 14
38 PROVEYSIEUX 152 WA 27
59 PROVILLE 18 KA 6
59 PROVIN 9 JA 3
77 PROVINS S 63 LA 13
02 PROVISEUX ET PLESNOY 29 OA 9
80 PROYART 27 IA 7
28 PRUDEMANCHE 38 BA 12
46 PRUDHOMAT 159 EA 29
66 PRUGNANES 221 HA 38
10 PRUGNY 64 OA 14
49 PRUILLE 95 T 17
72 PRUILLE L'EGUILLE 79 Y 16
72 PRUILLE LE CHETIF 78 X 15
12 PRUINES 175 HA 31
51 PRUNAY 43 PA 10
10 PRUNAY BELLEVILLE 64 NA 14
41 PRUNAY CASSEREAU 79 AA 17
78 PRUNAY EN YVELINES 61 EA 13
28 PRUNAY LE GILLON 61 DA 14
78 PRUNAY LE TEMPLE 39 EA 11
91 PRUNAY SUR ESSONNE 62 HA 14
2B PRUNELLI DI CASACCONI 228 MB 40
2B PRUNELLI DI FIUMORBO C 228 MB 42
07 PRUNET 178 PA 30
15 PRUNET 161 HA 29
31 PRUNET 211 EA 35
66 PRUNET ET BELPUIG 224 IA 39
05 PRUNIERES 181 YA 31
38 PRUNIERES 166 WA 29
48 PRUNIERES 162 LA 29
36 PRUNIERS 116 FA 21
41 PRUNIERS EN SOLOGNE 99 DA 18
2B PRUNO 228 MB 40
89 PRUNOY 83 KA 16
21 PRUSLY SUR OURCE 85 RA 16
10 PRUSY 84 OA 15
71 PRUZILLY 136 RA 23
67 PUBERG 48 DB 11
74 PUBLIER 124 ZA 22
39 PUBLY 122 VA 21
44 PUCEUL 93 P 17
09 PUCH, LE 222 FA 39
47 PUCH D'AGENAIS 171 X 32
27 PUCHAY 25 DA 9
80 PUCHEVILLERS 17 HA 6
34 PUECH, LE 191 LA 34
34 PUECHABON 192 MA 34
81 PUECHOURSI 211 FA 35
30 PUECHREDON 193 OA 33
52 PUELLEMONTIER 65 RA 13
25 PUESSANS 107 YA 18
84 PUGET 196 UA 34
06 PUGET ROSTANG 199 BB 33
83 PUGET SUR ARGENS 204 AB 35
06 PUGET THENIERS C 199 BB 33
83 PUGET VILLE 203 XA 36
25 PUGEY 107 XA 19
01 PUGIEU 138 VA 25
11 PUGINIER 211 FA 36
33 PUGNAC 156 U 28
79 PUGNY 112 U 21
73 PUGNY CHATENOD 153 XA 25
11 PUICHERIC 212 IA 36
88 PUID, LE 69 BB 13
79 PUIHARDY 111 U 22
34 PUILACHER 214 MA 35
11 PUILAURENS 221 GA 38
17 PUILBOREAU 126 R 23
08 PUILLY ET CHARBEAUX 31 UA 8
04 PUIMICHEL 197 XA 33
34 PUIMISSON 213 KA 35
04 PUIMOISSON 197 XA 34
28 PUISAYE, LA 60 AA 12
45 PUISEAUX C 62 HA 14
91 PUISELET LE MARAIS 62 GA 13
76 PUISENVAL 25 DA 7
28 PUISET, LE 61 EA 14
49 PUISET DORE, LE 94 R 19
08 PUISEUX 29 QA 8
28 PUISEUX 60 CA 12
60 PUISEUX EN BRAY 25 EA 9
95 PUISEUX EN FRANCE 40 HA 10
02 PUISEUX EN RETZ 41 KA 9
60 PUISEUX LE HAUBERGER 40 GA 10
95 PUISEUX PONTOISE 39 FA 10
51 PUISIEULX 42 OA 10
62 PUISIEUX 17 IA 6
77 PUISIEUX 41 JA 10
02 PUISIEUX ET CLANLIEU 28 MA 7
34 PUISSALICON 213 LA 35
33 PUISSEGUIN 156 W 29
34 PUISSERGUIER 213 KA 36
21 PUITS 85 QA 16
10 PUITS ET NUISEMENT 65 OA 14
60 PUITS LA VALLEE 26 GA 8
11 PUIVERT 221 FA 38
32 PUJAUDRAN 210 BA 35
30 PUJAUT 195 RA 33
65 PUJO 208 W 36
40 PUJO LE PLAN 185 V 34
33 PUJOLS C 157 W 29
47 PUJOLS 172 Z 31
09 PUJOLS, LES 219 EA 37
33 PUJOLS SUR CIRON 170 U 30
71 PULEY, LE 120 QA 21
21 PULIGNY MONTRACHET 120 RA 20
27 PULLAY 37 AA 12
54 PULLIGNY 68 XA 13
54 PULNEY 67 XA 13
54 PULNOY 46 YA 12
63 PULVERIERES 133 JA 25
68 PULVERSHEIM 90 CB 16
80 PUNCHY 27 JA 7
88 PUNEROT 67 WA 13
65 PUNTOUS 209 Y 36
39 PUPILLIN 122 WA 20
08 PURE 30 TA 8
70 PURGEROT 88 XA 16
70 PUSEY 88 XA 17
69 PUSIGNAN 151 TA 25
91 PUSSAY 61 FA 14
37 PUSSIGNY 113 Z 20
70 PUSY ET EPENOUX 88 XA 17
61 PUTANGES PONT ECREPIN C 58 V 12
92 PUTEAUX C 40 GA 11
14 PUTOT EN AUGE 36 W 10
14 PUTOT EN BESSIN 35 U 10
57 PUTTELANGE AUX LACS 47 BB 10
57 PUTTELANGE LES THIONVILLE 32 YA 9
57 PUTTIGNY 47 ZA 11
54 PUXE 45 WA 10
54 PUXIEUX 45 WA 10
25 PUY, LE 107 YA 18
33 PUY, LE 171 W 30
19 PUY D'ARNAC 159 EA 28
85 PUY DE SERRE 111 T 22
17 PUY DU LAC 127 T 24
43 PUY EN VELAY, LE P 163 NA 28
63 PUY GUILLAUME 133 MA 24
46 PUY L'EVEQUE C 173 BA 31
23 PUY MALSIGNAT 132 GA 24
49 PUY NOTRE DAME, LE 96 V 19
05 PUY SANIERES 182 ZA 30
05 PUY ST ANDRE 168 ZA 29
05 PUY ST EUSEBE 182 ZA 30
63 PUY ST GULMIER 147 IA 25
26 PUY ST MARTIN 179 SA 30
05 PUY ST PIERRE 168 ZA 29
05 PUY ST VINCENT 167 ZA 29
13 PUY STE REPARADE, LE 196 UA 34
33 PUYBARBAN 171 W 30
81 PUYBEGON 189 FA 34
46 PUYBRUN 159 EA 29
81 PUYCALVEL 189 FA 34
32 PUYCASQUIER 187 Z 34
81 PUYCELCI 189 EA 33
82 PUYCORNET 173 CA 32
31 PUYDANIEL 210 CA 36
65 PUYDARRIEUX 208 Y 36
86 PUYE, LA 114 AA 21
82 PUYGAILLARD DE LOMAGNE 187 AA 33
82 PUYGAILLARD DE QUERCY 188 DA 33
26 PUYGIRON 179 SA 31
81 PUYGOUZON 190 GA 33
73 PUYGROS 153 XA 26
46 PUYJOURDES 174 EA 31
82 PUYLAGARDE 174 EA 32
82 PUYLAROQUE 174 DA 32
81 PUYLAURENS C 211 FA 35
32 PUYLAUSIC 209 AA 35
13 PUYLOUBIER 202 VA 35
24 PUYMANGOU 157 W 28
31 PUYMAURIN 209 AA 36
84 PUYMERAS 179 TA 32
47 PUYMICLAN 171 Y 31
47 PUYMIROL C 172 AA 32
16 PUYMOYEN 143 X 26
33 PUYNORMAND 157 W 29
40 PUYOL CAZALET 207 U 35
64 PUYOO 206 S 35
17 PUYRAVAULT 127 T 23
85 PUYRAVAULT 125 R 22
16 PUYREAUX 129 X 25
24 PUYRENIER 143 Y 26
17 PUYROLLAND 127 T 24
32 PUYSEGUR 187 Z 34
31 PUYSSEGUR 187 BA 34
47 PUYSSERAMPION 171 X 30
66 PUYVALADOR 222 GA 39
84 PUYVERT 196 UA 34
80 PUZEAUX 27 JA 7
57 PUZIEUX 46 YA 11
88 PUZIEUX 67 XA 14
66 PY 222 GA 40
27 PYLE, LA 37 AA 10
80 PYS 17 IA 6

Q

59 QUAEDYPRE 8 HA 2
38 QUAIX EN CHARTREUSE 152 WA 27
18 QUANTILLY 100 HA 19
34 QUARANTE 213 JA 36
59 QUAROUBLE 18 MA 5
89 QUARRE LES TOMBES C 103 OA 18
70 QUARTE, LA 87 WA 16
63 QUARTIER, LE 133 IA 24
2A QUASQUARA 227 KB 42
08 QUATRE CHAMPS 30 RA 9
46 QUATRE ROUTES DU LOT, LES 159 EA 29
27 QUATREMARE 38 BA 10
67 QUATZENHEIM 49 EB 12
62 QUEANT 17 JA 5
86 QUEAUX 130 Z 23
35 QUEBRIAC 55 O 14
35 QUEDILLAC 75 N 14
73 QUEIGE 153 ZA 25
53 QUELAINES ST GAULT 77 T 15
62 QUELMES 7 GA 3
56 QUELNEUC 75 N 16
29 QUEMENEVEN 72 E 15
21 QUEMIGNY POISOT 105 SA 19
21 QUEMIGNY SUR SEINE 85 RA 17
22 QUEMPER GUEZENNEC 53 I 12
22 QUEMPERVEN 53 H 12
80 QUEND 15 DA 5
89 QUENNE 84 MA 16
70 QUENOCHE 107 XA 18
2A QUENZA 230 LB 43
62 QUERCAMPS 7 FA 3
2B QUERCITELLO 228 MB 40
59 QUERENAING 18 MA 5
09 QUERIGUT C 222 FA 39
62 QUERNES 8 HA 4
50 QUERQUEVILLE 33 O 8
49 QUERRE 77 T 17
29 QUERRIEN 72 G 15
80 QUERRIEU 17 HA 7
70 QUERS 89 ZA 16
60 QUESMY 27 KA 8
80 QUESNE, LE 25 EA 7
80 QUESNEL, LE 26 IA 7
60 QUESNEL AUBRY, LE 26 GA 8
59 QUESNOY, LE C 18 MA 5
62 QUESNOY EN ARTOIS, LE 16 FA 5
80 QUESNOY LE MONTANT 15 EA 6
80 QUESNOY SUR AIRAINES 16 FA 6
59 QUESNOY SUR DEULE C 9 KA 3
62 QUESQUES 7 FA 3
27 QUESSIGNY 38 CA 11
22 QUESSOY 54 K 13
56 QUESTEMBERT C 92 L 17
62 QUESTRECQUES 7 EA 3
38 QUET EN BEAUMONT 167 WA 29
21 QUETIGNY 105 TA 18
50 QUETTEHOU C 33 O 8
50 QUETTETOT 33 P 9
14 QUETTEVILLE 23 Y 9
50 QUETTREVILLE SUR SIENNE 34 Q 11
51 QUEUDES 64 NA 12
94 QUEUE EN BRIE, LA 40 IA 12
78 QUEUE LES YVELINES, LA 39 EA 12
63 QUEUILLE 133 JA 24
80 QUEVAUVILLERS 26 FA 7
56 QUEVEN 73 H 16
22 QUEVERT 55 N 13
76 QUEVILLON 24 AA 9
54 QUEVILLONCOURT 67 XA 13
76 QUEVREVILLE LA POTERIE 24 BA 9
33 QUEYRAC 141 S 27
43 QUEYRIERES 163 OA 28
24 QUEYSSAC 157 Y 29
19 QUEYSSAC LES VIGNES 159 EA 29
15 QUEZAC 160 GA 30
48 QUEZAC 177 MA 31
56 QUIBERON C 91 I 17
76 QUIBERVILLE 24 AA 7
50 QUIBOU 34 R 10
09 QUIE 219 DA 38
77 QUIERS 63 JA 12
45 QUIERS SUR BEZONDE 82 HA 15
62 QUIERY LA MOTTE 17 JA 5
02 QUIERZY 27 KA 8
62 QUIESTEDE 8 GA 3
59 QUIEVELON 19 OA 5
59 QUIEVRECHAIN 18 MA 5
76 QUIEVRECOURT 25 CA 7
59 QUIEVY 18 LA 6
62 QUILEN 7 FA 4
11 QUILLAN C 221 GA 38
27 QUILLEBEUF SUR SEINE C 23 Y 9
22 QUILLIO, LE 74 J 14

08 QUILLY 30 RA 9
44 QUILLY 93 N 18
56 QUILY 74 L 16
29 QUIMPER P 71 E 15
29 QUIMPERLE C 72 G 16
76 QUINCAMPOIX 24 BA 8
60 QUINCAMPOIX FLEUZY 25 EA 7
86 QUINCAY 113 X 21
21 QUINCEROT 85 PA 17
89 QUINCEROT 85 PA 15
21 QUINCEY 105 SA 19
70 QUINCEY 88 YA 17
69 QUINCIE EN BEAUJOLAIS 136 RA 24
38 QUINCIEU 152 UA 27
69 QUINCIEUX 136 RA 24
18 QUINCY 100 GA 19
02 QUINCY BASSE 28 LA 8
55 QUINCY LANDZECOURT 31 UA 9
21 QUINCY LE VICOMTE 85 PA 17
02 QUINCY SOUS LE MONT 28 MA 9
91 QUINCY SOUS SENART 62 HA 12
77 QUINCY VOISINS 41 JA 11
50 QUINEVILLE 33 Q 8
25 QUINGEY C 106 WA 19
60 QUINQUEMPOIX 26 HA 8
12 QUINS 175 HA 32
24 QUINSAC 144 Z 27
33 QUINSAC 156 U 30
04 QUINSON 197 XA 34
03 QUINSSAINES 133 HA 23
31 QUINT FONSEGRIVES 210 DA 35
74 QUINTAL 139 XA 25
72 QUINTE, LA 78 W 15
07 QUINTENAS 164 RA 28
22 QUINTENIC 54 L 13
39 QUINTIGNY 122 VA 21
11 QUINTILLAN 223 IA 38
22 QUINTIN C 54 J 13
22 QUIOU, LE 55 N 14
11 QUIRBAJOU 221 GA 38
80 QUIRY LE SEC 26 HA 8
30 QUISSAC C 193 OA 33
46 QUISSAC 174 EA 30
56 QUISTINIC 73 I 16
27 QUITTEBEUF 38 BA 10
80 QUIVIERES 27 KA 7
62 QUOEUX HAUT MAINIL 16 FA 5

R

81 RABASTENS C 189 EA 34
65 RABASTENS DE BIGORRE C 208 X 36
09 RABAT LES TROIS SEIGNEURS 219 DA 38
85 RABATELIERE, LA 110 R 20
49 RABLAY SUR LAYON 96 U 18
61 RABODANGES 58 V 12
05 RABOU 181 XA 30
66 RABOUILLET 222 HA 39
88 RACECOURT 68 YA 14
52 RACHECOURT SUR MARNE 66 TA 13
52 RACHECOURT SUZEMONT 66 SA 13
59 RACHES 18 KA 4
10 RACINES 84 NA 15
71 RACINEUSE, LA 121 TA 20
62 RACQUINGHEM 8 HA 3
57 RACRANGE 47 AB 11
70 RADDON ET CHAPENDU 89 ZA 16
56 RADENAC 74 K 15
27 RADEPONT 24 CA 9
62 RADINGHEM 7 GA 4
59 RADINGHEM EN WEPPES 9 JA 4
61 RADON 58 X 13
10 RADONVILLIERS 65 QA 14
68 RAEDERSDORF 90 DB 17
68 RAEDERSHEIM 90 DB 16
76 RAFFETOT 23 Y 8
15 RAGEADE 162 LA 28
41 RAHART 80 BA 16
72 RAHAY 79 AA 15
57 RAHLING 48 CB 11
25 RAHON 108 ZA 18
39 RAHON 106 UA 20
61 RAI 37 Z 12
50 RAIDS 34 Q 10
59 RAILLENCOURT STE OLLE 18 KA 5
66 RAILLEU 222 GA 39
08 RAILLICOURT 29 OA 8
02 RAILLIMONT 29 PA 8
59 RAIMBEAUCOURT 18 KA 4
39 RAINANS 106 UA 19
80 RAINCHEVAL 17 HA 6
70 RAINCOURT 88 WA 16
93 RAINCY, LE S 40 HA 11
76 RAINFREVILLE 24 AA 7
80 RAINNEVILLE 16 HA 6
59 RAINSARS 19 OA 6
88 RAINVILLE 67 WA 14
60 RAINVILLERS 25 FA 9
49 RAIRIES, LES 78 V 17
59 RAISMES 18 LA 5
09 RAISSAC 219 EA 38
11 RAISSAC D'AUDE 213 JA 36
11 RAISSAC SUR LAMPY 212 GA 36
55 RAIVAL 44 TA 11
16 RAIX 129 X 24
78 RAIZEUX 61 EA 12
01 RAMASSE 138 UA 23
83 RAMATUELLE 204 AB 36
05 RAMBAUD 181 XA 31
88 RAMBERVILLERS C 68 ZA 14
55 RAMBLUZIN
ET BENOITE VAUX 44 UA 11
78 RAMBOUILLET S 61 EA 12
55 RAMBUCOURT 45 WA 11
80 RAMBURELLES 15 EA 6
80 RAMBURES 15 EA 7
62 RAMECOURT 16 GA 5
88 RAMECOURT 67 XA 14
10 RAMERUPT C 65 PA 13
02 RAMICOURT 18 LA 6
59 RAMILLIES 18 LA 5
68 RAMMERSMATT 90 CB 16
88 RAMONCHAMP 89 AB 16
31 RAMONVILLE ST AGNE 210 DA 35
45 RAMOULU 62 GA 14
64 RAMOUS 206 S 35
59 RAMOUSIES 19 OA 6
32 RAMOUZENS 186 X 34
50 RAMPAN 34 R 10
24 RAMPIEUX 158 AA 30
77 RAMPILLON 63 KA 13
46 RAMPOUX 173 CA 30
01 RANCE 137 SA 24
25 RANCENAY 107 XA 19
08 RANCENNES 20 SA 6
10 RANCES 65 OA 13
69 RANCHAL 136 QA 23
39 RANCHOT 106 VA 19
14 RANCHY 35 T 10
16 RANCOGNE 143 Y 25
87 RANCON 130 BA 23
52 RANCONNIERES 87 VA 15
80 RANCOURT 17 JA 6
88 RANCOURT 68 XA 14
55 RANCOURT SUR ORNAIN 44 SA 12
71 RANCY 121 TA 21
63 RANDAN C 134 LA 24
73 RANDENS 153 YA 26
25 RANDEVILLERS 107 ZA 18
61 RANDONNAI 59 Z 12
61 RANES 58 V 12
25 RANG 107 ZA 18
62 RANG DU FLIERS 15 DA 4
52 RANGECOURT 67 VA 15
57 RANGEN 49 DB 12
57 RANGUEVAUX 32 XA 9
35 RANNEE 76 R 16
67 RANRUPT 69 CB 14
39 RANS 106 WA 19
62 RANSART 17 IA 5
68 RANSPACH 90 BB 16
68 RANSPACH LE BAS 90 DB 17
68 RANSPACH LE HAUT 90 DB 17
25 RANTECHAUX 107 YA 19
60 RANTIGNY 26 HA 9
86 RANTON 112 W 20
68 RANTZWILLER 90 DB 17
14 RANVILLE 36 V 10
16 RANVILLE BREUILLAUD 128 W 25
70 RANZEVELLE 88 XA 16
55 RANZIERES 45 VA 11
88 RAON AUX BOIS 68 ZA 15
88 RAON L'ETAPE C 69 BB 13
54 RAON LES LEAU 69 CB 13
88 RAON SUR PLAINE 69 CB 13
2B RAPAGGIO 228 MB 40
2B RAPALE 226 LB 39
88 RAPEY 68 YA 14
14 RAPILLY 36 V 11
51 RAPSECOURT 43 RA 11
60 RARAY 40 IA 10
55 RARECOURT 44 TA 10
66 RASIGUERES 224 IA 38
86 RASLAY 97 W 19
84 RASTEAU 179 SA 32
71 RATENELLE 121 SA 22
26 RATIERES 165 SA 28
71 RATTE 121 UA 21
67 RATZWILLER 48 CB 11
43 RAUCOULES 163 PA 28
54 RAUCOURT 46 YA 11
59 RAUCOURT AU BOIS 18 MA 5
08 RAUCOURT ET FLABA C 30 SA 8
15 RAULHAC 161 IA 29
40 RAURET 163 NA 29
50 RAUVILLE LA BIGOT 33 P 8
50 RAUVILLE LA PLACE 33 P 9
67 RAUWILLER 48 CB 12
33 RAUZAN 156 V 29
58 RAVEAU 102 KA 19
63 RAVEL 148 LA 25
60 RAVENEL 26 HA 8
50 RAVENOVILLE 33 R 9
88 RAVES 69 BB 14
89 RAVIERES 85 PA 16
53 RAVIGNY 58 W 13
57 RAVILLE 47 ZA 10
54 RAVILLE SUR SANON 46 ZA 12
39 RAVILLOLES 122 WA 22
73 RAVOIRE, LA C 153 XA 26
70 RAY SUR SAONE 88 WA 17
62 RAYE SUR AUTHIE 16 FA 5
47 RAYET 172 AA 30
18 RAYMOND 117 IA 20
25 RAYNANS 89 AB 17
83 RAYOL CANADEL SUR MER 203 ZA 37
81 RAYSSAC 190 HA 34
24 RAZAC D'EYMET 172 Y 30
24 RAZAC DE SAUSSIGNAC 157 X 29
24 RAZAC SUR L'ISLE 158 Z 28
70 RAZE 88 XA 17
31 RAZECUEILLE 217 AA 38
32 RAZENGUES 209 AA 35
87 RAZES 131 CA 24
47 RAZIMET 171 X 31
37 RAZINES 113 Y 20
66 REAL 222 GA 39
76 REALCAMP 25 DA 7
05 REALLON 182 YA 30
81 REALMONT C 190 GA 34
82 REALVILLE 174 DA 32
32 REANS 185 W 34
77 REAU 62 IA 12
38 REAUMONT 152 VA 27
85 REAUMUR 111 T 21
47 REAUP LISSE 186 X 33
26 REAUVILLE 179 SA 31
17 REAUX 142 U 26
77 REBAIS C 41 LA 11
62 REBECQUES 8 GA 3
64 REBENACQ 215 U 37
62 REBERGUES 7 FA 3
76 REBETS 25 CA 8
88 REBEUVILLE 67 WA 14
31 REBIGUE 210 DA 35
12 REBOURGUIL 191 IA 33
36 REBOURSIN 99 EA 19
45 REBRECHIEN 81 FA 15
62 REBREUVE RANCHICOURT 17 IA 4
62 REBREUVE SUR CANCHE 16 HA 5
62 REBREUVIETTE 16 HA 5
39 RECANOZ 122 VA 20
21 RECEY SUR OURCE C 86 SA 16
90 RECHESY 90 CB 17
54 RECHICOURT LA PETITE 46 ZA 12
57 RECHICOURT LE CHATEAU C 69 BB 12
55 RECICOURT 44 TA 10
28 RECLAINVILLE 61 EA 14
71 RECLESNE 104 PA 19
62 RECLINGHEM 8 GA 4
54 RECLONVILLE 68 AB 13
77 RECLOSES 62 IA 14
25 RECOLOGNE 106 WA 18
70 RECOLOGNE 87 WA 17
70 RECOLOGNE LES RIOZ 88 XA 17
26 RECOUBEAU JANSAC 166 UA 30
48 RECOULES D'AUBRAC 176 JA 30
48 RECOULES DE FUMAS 177 LA 30
12 RECOULES PREVINQUIERES 176 JA 31
62 RECOURT 17 KA 5
55 RECOURT LE CREUX 44 UA 11
90 RECOUVRANCE 90 BB 17
48 RECOUX, LE 176 KA 31
62 RECQUES SUR COURSE 7 EA 4
62 RECQUES SUR HEM 7 FA 3
59 RECQUIGNIES 19 OA 5
14 RECULEY, LE 35 S 11
25 RECULFOZ 123 XA 21
65 RECURT 208 Y 36
51 RECY 43 PA 11
57 REDANGE 32 WA 9
29 REDENE 73 H 16
30 REDESSAN 193 QA 34
57 REDING 48 CB 12
35 REDON S 93 N 17
11 REDORTE, LA 212 IA 36
04 REDORTIERS 196 VA 33
60 REEZ FOSSE MARTIN 41 JA 10
79 REFFANNES 112 V 22
55 REFFROY 66 UA 12
50 REFFUVEILLE 56 R 12
31 REGADES 217 Z 37
09 REGAT 219 EA 37
62 REGNAUVILLE 16 FA 5
88 REGNEVELLE 88 XA 15
50 REGNEVILLE SUR MER 34 P 11
55 REGNEVILLE SUR MEUSE 44 UA 10
88 REGNEY 68 YA 14
69 REGNIE DURETTE 136 RA 23
80 REGNIERE ECLUSE 16 EA 5
80 REGNIOWEZ 20 QA 7
02 REGNY 28 LA 7
42 REGNY 135 PA 24
44 REGRIPPIERE, LA 94 R 19
56 REGUINY 74 K 15
68 REGUISHEIM 90 DB 16
83 REGUSSE 203 XA 35
88 REHAINCOURT 68 ZA 14
54 REHAINVILLER 68 ZA 13
88 REHAUPAL 69 AB 15
88 REHERREY 69 AB 13
54 REHON 31 WA 9
67 REICHSFELD 70 DB 14
67 REICHSHOFFEN 48 EB 11
67 REICHSTETT 49 FB 12
16 REIGNAC 142 V 27
33 REIGNAC 142 U 27
37 REIGNAC SUR INDRE 98 AA 19
63 REIGNAT 148 LA 25
50 REIGNEVILLE BOCAGE 33 O 9
74 REIGNIER C 139 YA 23
18 REIGNY 116 HA 22
15 REILHAC 161 HA 29
46 REILHAC 174 EA 30
46 REILHAGUET 159 DA 30
26 REILHANETTE 180 UA 32
04 REILLANNE C 196 VA 33
54 REILLON 69 AB 12
60 REILLY 39 EA 10
51 REIMS S 42 OA 10
51 REIMS LA BRULEE 43 RA 12
67 REINHARDSMUNSTER 49 DB 12
68 REININGUE 90 CB 16
67 REIPERTSWILLER 48 DB 11
39 REITHOUSE 122 VA 22
32 REJAUMONT 186 Y 34
65 REJAUMONT 217 Y 37
59 REJET DE BEAULIEU 18 MA 6
88 RELANGES 67 XA 15
39 RELANS 122 UA 21
29 RELECQ KERHUON, LE 51 C 13
01 RELEVANT 137 SA 24
62 RELY 8 HA 4
80 REMAISNIL 16 GA 5
61 REMALARD C 59 AA 13
02 REMAUCOURT 28 LA 7
08 REMAUCOURT 29 PA 8
44 REMAUDIERE, LA 94 R 19
80 REMAUGIES 27 IA 8
77 REMAUVILLE 62 JA 14
55 REMBERCOURT SOMMAISNE 44 TA 11
54 REMBERCOURT SUR MAD 45 WA 11
60 REMECOURT 26 HA 9
57 REMELFANG 47 ZA 10
57 REMELFING 48 CB 10
57 REMELING 32 ZA 9
55 REMENNECOURT 44 SA 12
54 REMENOVILLE 68 ZA 13
60 REMERANGLES 26 GA 9
54 REMEREVILLE 46 ZA 12
57 REMERING 47 AB 10
57 REMERING LES PUTTELANGE 47 BB 11
51 REMICOURT 44 SA 11
88 REMICOURT 67 XA 14
80 REMIENCOURT 26 HA 7
02 REMIES 28 MA 8
02 REMIGNY 28 LA 8
71 REMIGNY 120 RA 20
57 REMILLY 46 YA 11
58 REMILLY 119 NA 20
08 REMILLY AILLICOURT 30 SA 8
21 REMILLY EN MONTAGNE 104 RA 18
08 REMILLY LES POTHEES 29 QA 7
50 REMILLY SUR LOZON 34 R 10
21 REMILLY SUR TILLE 105 TA 18
62 REMILLY WIRQUIN 8 GA 3
56 REMINIAC 74 M 16
88 REMIREMONT C 89 ZA 15
55 REMOIVILLE 31 UA 9
05 REMOLLON 181 XA 31
88 REMOMEIX 69 BB 14
54 REMONCOURT 69 AB 12
88 REMONCOURT 67 XA 14
25 REMONDANS VAIVRE 108 AB 18
25 REMORAY BOUJEONS 123 YA 21
44 REMOUILLE 110 Q 19
30 REMOULINS C 193 QA 33
88 REMOVILLE 67 WA 14
87 REMPNAT 146 EA 25
76 REMUEE, LA 23 Y 8
56 REMUNGOL 73 J 15
26 REMUZAT C 180 UA 31
60 REMY 27 IA 9
62 REMY 17 JA 5
35 RENAC 75 N 16
38 RENAGE 152 UA 27
42 RENAISON 135 NA 24
02 RENANSART 28 MA 7
70 RENAUCOURT 87 WA 17
63 RENAUDIE, LA 149 NA 25
49 RENAUDIERE, LA 94 R 19
88 RENAUVOID 68 YA 15
41 RENAY 80 BA 16
53 RENAZE 76 S 16
38 RENCUREL 166 UA 28
72 RENE 58 X 14
25 RENEDALE 107 YA 20
59 RENESCURE 8 HA 3
21 RENEVE 106 UA 18
78 RENNEMOULIN 39 FA 11
52 RENNEPONT 66 SA 15
35 RENNES P 75 O 15
53 RENNES EN GRENOUILLES 57 U 13
11 RENNES LE CHATEAU 221 GA 38
11 RENNES LES BAINS 221 HA 38
25 RENNES SUR LOUE 122 WA 20
02 RENNEVAL 29 OA 7
08 RENNEVILLE 29 PA 8
27 RENNEVILLE 25 CA 9
31 RENNEVILLE 211 EA 36
2A RENNO 227 JB 41
61 RENOUARD, LE 36 X 11
63 RENTIERES 148 KA 27
62 RENTY 7 FA 4
40 RENUNG 185 V 34
08 RENWEZ C 29 RA 7
33 REOLE, LA C 171 W 30
85 REORTHE, LA 110 R 21
05 REOTIER 168 ZA 30
54 REPAIX 69 AB 12
26 REPARA AURIPLES, LA 165 SA 30
16 REPARSAC 142 V 25
88 REPEL 67 XA 14
14 REPENTIGNY 36 W 10
01 REPLONGES 137 SA 23
74 REPOSOIR, LE 139 ZA 24
39 REPOTS, LES 122 UA 21
90 REPPE 90 BB 17
72 REQUEIL 78 X 16
12 REQUISTA C 190 HA 33
61 RESENLIEU 37 X 12
70 RESIE ST MARTIN, LA 106 VA 18
02 RESIGNY 29 PA 7
55 RESSON 44 TA 12
60 RESSONS L'ABBAYE 39 FA 9
02 RESSONS LE LONG 27 KA 9
60 RESSONS SUR MATZ C 27 IA 8
28 RESSUINTES, LES 59 AA 13
37 RESTIGNE 97 X 18
34 RESTINCLIERES 193 OA 34
79 RETAIL, LE 112 U 22
17 RETAUD 141 T 25
23 RETERRE 133 HA 24
08 RETHEL S 29 QA 8
02 RETHEUIL 27 KA 9
60 RETHONDES 27 JA 9
80 RETHONVILLERS 27 JA 7
50 RETHOVILLE 33 Q 8
35 RETIERS C 76 Q 16
40 RETJONS 185 V 33
57 RETONFEY 46 YA 10
76 RETONVAL 25 DA 7
43 RETOURNAC C 163 OA 28
67 RETSCHWILLER 49 FB 11
57 RETTEL 32 YA 9
62 RETY 7 EA 3
68 RETZWILLER 90 CB 17
25 REUGNEY 107 YA 20
03 REUGNY 117 IA 22
37 REUGNY 79 AA 17
51 REUIL 42 NA 10
77 REUIL EN BRIE 41 KA 11
60 REUIL SUR BRECHE 26 GA 8
27 REUILLY 38 CA 10
36 REUILLY 100 FA 19
02 REUILLY SAUVIGNY 42 MA 10
21 REULLE VERGY 105 SA 19
59 REUMONT 18 MA 6
47 REUNION, LA 171 X 32
67 REUTENBOURG 49 DB 12
51 REUVES 42 NA 12
76 REUVILLE 24 AA 7
14 REUX 36 X 10
51 REVEILLON 41 MA 12
61 REVEILLON 59 Z 13
31 REVEL C 211 FA 35
38 REVEL 166 WA 28
38 REVEL TOURDAN 151 TA 27
80 REVELLES 26 GA 7
30 REVENS 191 LA 33
38 REVENTIN VAUGRIS 151 SA 26
28 REVERCOURT 38 BA 12
04 REVEST DES BROUSSES 196 VA 33
04 REVEST DU BION 196 VA 33
83 REVEST LES EAUX, LE 203 XA 37
06 REVEST LES ROCHES 199 CB 33
04 REVEST ST MARTIN 197 WA 33
14 REVIERS 35 U 9
39 REVIGNY 122 VA 21
55 REVIGNY SUR ORNAIN C 44 SA 11
50 REVILLE 33 R 8
55 REVILLE AUX BOIS 31 UA 9
02 REVILLON 28 NA 9
08 REVIN C 20 RA 7
01 REVONNAS 137 UA 23
67 REXINGEN 48 CB 11
59 REXPOEDE 8 HA 2
57 REYERSVILLER 48 DB 11
19 REYGADE 160 FA 28
52 REYNEL 66 UA 14
66 REYNES 224 IA 40
82 REYNIES 188 CA 33
46 REYREVIGNES 174 FA 30
01 REYRIEUX C 137 SA 24
01 REYSSOUZE 121 SA 22
74 REYVROZ 139 ZA 23
18 REZAY 116 GA 21
44 REZE C 93 P 19
15 REZENTIERES 162 KA 28
57 REZONVILLE 45 XA 10
2A REZZA 227 KB 41
10 RHEGES 64 OA 13
35 RHEU, LE 75 O 15
67 RHINAU 70 EB 14
57 RHODES 47 BB 12
41 RHODON 80 CA 16
60 RHUIS 40 IA 9
61 RI 58 W 12
66 RIA SIRACH 222 HA 39
44 RIAILLE C 94 Q 17
81 RIALET, LE 212 HA 35
18 RIANS 101 IA 19
83 RIANS C 202 WA 35
56 RIANTEC 73 H 16
52 RIAUCOURT 66 TA 14
55 RIAVILLE 45 VA 10
24 RIBAGNAC 157 Y 30
64 RIBARROUY 207 V 35
11 RIBAUTE 223 IA 37
30 RIBAUTE LES TAVERNES 193 OA 33
53 RIBAY, LE 57 U 13
55 RIBEAUCOURT 66 UA 13
80 RIBEAUCOURT 16 FA 6
02 RIBEAUVILLE 18 MA 6
68 RIBEAUVILLE S 69 DB 14
60 RIBECOURT DRESLINCOURT C 27 JA 8
59 RIBECOURT LA TOUR 18 KA 6
02 RIBEMONT C 28 MA 7
80 RIBEMONT SUR ANCRE 17 HA 6
48 RIBENNES 177 LA 30
24 RIBERAC C 143 Y 27
07 RIBES 178 PA 31
05 RIBEYRET 180 VA 31
05 RIBIERS C 181 WA 32
11 RIBOUISSE 221 FA 37
83 RIBOUX 202 WA 36
42 RICAMARIE, LA 150 QA 27
76 RICARVILLE 23 Z 8
76 RICARVILLE DU VAL 24 CA 7
11 RICAUD 211 FA 36
65 RICAUD 216 X 37
10 RICEYS, LES C 85 QA 15
35 RICHARDAIS, LA 55 N 12
54 RICHARDMENIL 68 YA 13
91 RICHARVILLE 61 FA 13
57 RICHE 47 AB 11
37 RICHE, LA 98 Z 18
52 RICHEBOURG 86 TA 15
62 RICHEBOURG 8 IA 4
78 RICHEBOURG 39 DA 12
55 RICHECOURT 45 WA 11
37 RICHELIEU C 113 Y 20
57 RICHELING 47 BB 11
57 RICHEMONT 32 XA 9
76 RICHEMONT 25 DA 7
84 RICHERENCHES 179 SA 31
57 RICHEVAL 69 BB 12
27 RICHEVILLE 38 DA 10
67 RICHTOLSHEIM 70 EB 14
68 RICHWILLER 90 CB 16
32 RICOURT 208 X 35
60 RICQUEBOURG 27 IA 8
29 RIEC SUR BELON 72 G 16
68 RIEDISHEIM 90 DB 16
67 RIEDSELTZ 50 FB 11
68 RIEDWIHR 70 DB 15
21 RIEL LES EAUX 85 RA 15
80 RIENCOURT 16 FA 7
62 RIENCOURT LES BAPAUME 17 JA 6
62 RIENCOURT LES CAGNICOURT 17 JA 5
90 RIERVESCEMONT 89 BB 16
68 RIESPACH 90 DB 17
31 RIEUCAZE 217 Z 37
09 RIEUCROS 219 EA 37
59 RIEULAY 18 LA 5
31 RIEUMAJOU 211 EA 36
31 RIEUMES C 210 BA 36
12 RIEUPEYROUX C 175 GA 32
34 RIEUSSEC 212 IA 36
48 RIEUTORT DE RANDON 177 MA 30
31 RIEUX C 210 CA 36
51 RIEUX 42 MA 11
56 RIEUX 93 N 17
60 RIEUX 40 HA 9
76 RIEUX 15 DA 7
09 RIEUX DE PELLEPORT 219 DA 37
59 RIEUX EN CAMBRESIS 18 LA 5
11 RIEUX EN VAL 221 HA 37
11 RIEUX MINERVOIS 212 IA 36
04 RIEZ C 197 XA 34
66 RIGARDA 222 HA 39
06 RIGAUD 199 BB 33
12 RIGNAC C 175 GA 31
46 RIGNAC 159 EA 29
25 RIGNEY 107 YA 18
01 RIGNIEUX LE FRANC 137 TA 24
25 RIGNOSOT 107 YA 18
70 RIGNOVELLE 89 ZA 16
70 RIGNY 106 VA 18
10 RIGNY LA NONNEUSE 64 MA 13
55 RIGNY LA SALLE 67 WA 12
10 RIGNY LE FERRON 64 MA 14
55 RIGNY ST MARTIN 67 WA 12
71 RIGNY SUR ARROUX 119 OA 22
37 RIGNY USSE 97 X 18
32 RIGUEPEU 208 Y 35
87 RILHAC LASTOURS 144 BA 25
87 RILHAC RANCON 131 CA 25
19 RILHAC TREIGNAC 145 EA 26
19 RILHAC XAINTRIE 160 GA 28
25 RILLANS 107 YA 18
37 RILLE 97 X 18
69 RILLIEUX LA PAPE C 137 SA 25
51 RILLY LA MONTAGNE 42 OA 10
10 RILLY STE SYRE 64 OA 13
08 RILLY SUR AISNE 30 RA 9
41 RILLY SUR LOIRE 98 BA 18
37 RILLY SUR VIENNE 97 Y 19
52 RIMAUCOURT 66 UA 14
68 RIMBACH PRES GUEBWILLER 90 CB 16
68 RIMBACH PRES MASEVAUX 89 BB 16
68 RIMBACHZELL 90 CB 16
40 RIMBEZ ET BAUDIETS 185 W 33
62 RIMBOVAL 7 FA 4
48 RIMEIZE 162 LA 30
57 RIMLING 48 CB 10
08 RIMOGNE 29 QA 7
26 RIMON ET SAVEL 166 UA 30
23 RIMONDEIX 132 FA 23
33 RIMONS 171 W 30
09 RIMONT 218 CA 37
35 RIMOU 56 P 13
06 RIMPLAS 199 CB 33
67 RIMSDORF 48 CB 11
67 RINGELDORF 48 EB 11
67 RINGENDORF 49 EB 12
62 RINXENT 7 EA 3
33 RIOCAUD 157 X 30
31 RIOLAS 209 AA 36
34 RIOLS 213 JA 35
81 RIOLS, LE 174 FA 32
63 RIOM S 134 KA 25
15 RIOM ES MONTAGNES C 161 IA 27
26 RIOMS 180 UA 32
40 RION DES LANDES 183 S 33
33 RIONS 170 U 30
42 RIORGES 135 OA 24
43 RIOTORD 150 OA 27
17 RIOUX 141 T 26
16 RIOUX MARTIN 143 W 27
70 RIOZ C 107 XA 18
68 RIQUEWIHR 69 CB 14
63 RIS 133 MA 24
65 RIS 216 Y 38
91 RIS ORANGIS C 62 HA 12
32 RISCLE C 185 W 34
05 RISOUL 168 AB 30
05 RISTOLAS 168 BB 30
67 RITTERSHOFFEN 50 FB 11
57 RITZING 32 ZA 9
64 RIUPEYROUS 207 V 36
36 RIVARENNES 115 CA 21
37 RIVARENNES 97 Y 18
42 RIVAS 149 PA 26
42 RIVE DE GIER C 150 RA 26
60 RIVECOURT 27 IA 9
17 RIVEDOUX PLAGE 126 Q 23
64 RIVEHAUTE 206 S 36
11 RIVEL 221 FA 38

2B RIVENTOSA 228 LB 41
09 RIVERENERT 219 CA 38
69 RIVERIE 150 RA 26
80 RIVERY 26 HA 7
38 RIVES C 152 VA 27
47 RIVES 172 Z 30
34 RIVES, LES 191 LA 34
66 RIVESALTES C 224 JA 38
37 RIVIERE 97 X 19
62 RIVIERE 17 IA 5
33 RIVIERE, LA 156 V 29
38 RIVIERE, LA 152 VA 27
10 RIVIERE DE CORPS, LA 64 OA 14
25 RIVIERE DRUGEON, LA 123 YA 20
74 RIVIERE ENVERSE, LA 140 AB 24
52 RIVIERE LES FOSSES 86 TA 17
88 RIVIERE SAAS ET GOURBY 183 R 34
14 RIVIERE ST SAUVEUR, LA 23 X 9
12 RIVIERE SUR TARN 176 KA 32
16 RIVIERES 143 Y 25
30 RIVIERES 178 PA 32
81 RIVIERES 189 FA 33
51 RIVIERES HENRUEL, LES 65 OA 12
52 RIVIERES LE BOIS 87 UA 16
76 RIVILLE 23 Z 7
69 RIVOLET 136 RA 24
39 RIX 123 XA 21
58 RIX 102 MA 18
68 RIXHEIM 90 DB 16
39 RIXOUSE, LA 122 WA 22
52 RIZAUCOURT BUCHEY 66 SA 14
33 ROAILLAN 170 V 31
84 ROAIX 179 SA 32
42 ROANNE S 135 OA 24
15 ROANNES ST MARY 160 HA 29
88 ROBECOURT 67 VA 15
62 ROBECQ 8 IA 4
59 ROBERSART 18 MA 6
55 ROBERT ESPAGNE 44 SA 12
52 ROBERT MAGNY
LANEUVILLE A REMY 66 SA 13
76 ROBERTOT 24 Z 7
60 ROBERVAL 40 IA 9
30 ROBIAC ROCHESSADOULE 178 OA 32
04 ROBINE SUR GALABRE, LA 181 YA 32
84 ROBION 196 TA 34
46 ROC, LE 159 DA 29
56 ROC ST ANDRE, LE 74 L 16
46 ROCAMADOUR 159 DA 29
83 ROCBARON 203 XA 36
41 ROCE 80 BA 16
38 ROCHE 151 TA 26
42 ROCHE 149 OA 26
56 ROCHE BERNARD, LA C 92 M 17
44 ROCHE BLANCHE, LA 94 R 18
63 ROCHE BLANCHE, LA 148 KA 25
19 ROCHE CANILLAC, LA C 160 FA 28
24 ROCHE CHALAIS, LA 157 W 28
63 ROCHE CHARLES
LA MAYRAND 147 JA 26
37 ROCHE CLERMAULT, LA 97 X 19
63 ROCHE D'AGOUX 133 IA 24
26 ROCHE DE GLUN, LA 165 SA 28
05 ROCHE DE RAME, LA 168 ZA 30
22 ROCHE DERRIEN, LA C 53 I 12
05 ROCHE DES ARNAUDS, LA 181 XA 30
21 ROCHE EN BRENIL, LA 103 PA 18
43 ROCHE EN REGNIER 163 OA 28
70 ROCHE ET RAUCOURT 87 WA 17
95 ROCHE GUYON, LA 39 DA 10
87 ROCHE L'ABEILLE 145 CA 26
42 ROCHE LA MOLIERE 150 PA 27
19 ROCHE LE PEYROUX 146 HA 27
25 ROCHE LES CLERVAL 107 ZA 18
25 ROCHE LEZ BEAUPRE 107 XA 18
61 ROCHE MABILE, LA 58 W 13
29 ROCHE MAURICE, LA 52 D 13
70 ROCHE MOREY, LA 87 WA 16
63 ROCHE NOIRE, LA 148 KA 25
86 ROCHE POSAY, LA 114 AA 21
86 ROCHE RIGAULT, LA 113 X 20
26 ROCHE ST SECRET BECONNE 179 TA 31
74 ROCHE SUR FORON, LA C 139 YA 24
26 ROCHE SUR GRANE, LA 179 SA 30
26 ROCHE SUR LE BUIS, LA 180 UA 32
70 ROCHE SUR LINOTTE
ET SORANS LES CORDIERS 107 YA 18
85 ROCHE SUR YON, LA P 110 Q 21
21 ROCHE VANNEAU, LA 104 QA 18
71 ROCHE VINEUSE, LA 136 RA 23
26 ROCHEBAUDIN 179 SA 30
24 ROCHEBEAUCOURT
ET ARGENTINE, LA 143 Y 26
05 ROCHEBRUNE 181 YA 31
26 ROCHEBRUNE 180 TA 31
26 ROCHECHINARD 165 TA 28
87 ROCHECHOUART S 144 AA 25
07 ROCHECOLOMBE 178 QA 31
37 ROCHECORBON 98 Z 18
17 ROCHEFORT S 126 R 24
21 ROCHEFORT 85 RA 16
73 ROCHEFORT 152 VA 26
30 ROCHEFORT DU GARD 195 RA 33
56 ROCHEFORT EN TERRE C 74 M 16
26 ROCHEFORT EN VALDAINE 179 SA 31
78 ROCHEFORT EN YVELINES 61 FA 13
63 ROCHEFORT MONTAGNE C 147 JA 25
26 ROCHEFORT SAMSON 165 TA 29
52 ROCHEFORT SUR LA COTE 66 TA 14
49 ROCHEFORT SUR LOIRE 95 T 18
39 ROCHEFORT SUR NENON C 106 VA 19
16 ROCHEFOUCAULD, LA C 143 Y 25
26 ROCHEFOURCHAT 180 TA 30
04 ROCHEGIRON, LA 196 VA 33
26 ROCHEGUDE 179 RA 32
30 ROCHEGUDE 178 PA 32
25 ROCHEJEAN 123 YA 21
17 ROCHELLE, LA P 126 R 23
70 ROCHELLE, LA 87 WA 16
50 ROCHELLE NORMANDE, LA 56 Q 12
07 ROCHEMAURE C 179 RA 30
79 ROCHENARD 128 U 23
07 ROCHEPAULE 164 OA 28
21 ROCHEPOT, LA 120 RA 20
07 ROCHER 178 PA 30
86 ROCHEREAU, LE 113 X 21
23 ROCHES 132 FA 23
41 ROCHES 80 DA 16
52 ROCHES BETTAINCOURT 66 TA 14
38 ROCHES DE CONDRIEU, LES 150 RA 26
41 ROCHES L'EVEQUE, LES 79 AA 16
25 ROCHES LES BLAMONT 108 BB 18
86 ROCHES PREMARIE ANDILLE 113 Y 22
52 ROCHES SUR MARNE 66 SA 12
85 ROCHESERVIERE C 110 P 20
07 ROCHESSAUVE 164 RA 30
88 ROCHESSON 89 AB 15
52 ROCHETAILLEE 86 TA 16
69 ROCHETAILLEE SUR SAONE 137 SA 25
38 ROCHETOIRIN 152 UA 26
85 ROCHETREJOUX 111 S 21
04 ROCHETTE, LA 199 BB 33
05 ROCHETTE, LA 181 YA 30
07 ROCHETTE, LA 163 PA 29
16 ROCHETTE, LA 143 X 25
73 ROCHETTE, LA C 153 XA 26
77 ROCHETTE, LA 62 IA 13
26 ROCHETTE DU BUIS, LA 180 UA 32
50 ROCHEVILLE 33 P 8
57 ROCHONVILLERS 32 XA 9
60 ROCHY CONDE 26 GA 9
03 ROCLES 133 KA 22
07 ROCLES 178 PA 30
48 ROCLES 163 NA 30
62 ROCLINCOURT 17 JA 5
88 ROCOURT 67 WA 15
02 ROCOURT ST MARTIN 41 LA 10
14 ROCQUANCOURT 36 V 10
14 ROCQUE, LA 35 T 11
76 ROCQUEFORT 24 Z 8
60 ROCQUEMONT 40 IA 10
76 ROCQUEMONT 24 CA 8
60 ROCQUENCOURT 26 HA 8
78 ROCQUENCOURT 39 FA 11
14 ROCQUES 37 X 10
02 ROCQUIGNY 19 OA 6
08 ROCQUIGNY 29 PA 8
62 ROCQUIGNY 17 JA 6
08 ROCROI C 20 QA 7
57 RODALBE 47 AB 11
62 RODELINGHEM 7 FA 3
12 RODELLE 175 IA 31
57 RODEMACK 32 YA 9
68 RODEREN 90 CB 16
68 RODERN 70 DB 14
66 RODES 224 IA 39
12 RODEZ P 175 IA 31
30 RODILHAN 193 QA 34
11 RODOME 221 FA 38
53 ROE, LA 76 R 16
62 ROELLECOURT 16 HA 5
67 ROESCHWOOG 50 GB 11
59 ROEULX 18 LA 5
62 ROEUX 17 JA 5
72 ROEZE SUR SARTHE 78 W 16
89 ROFFEY 84 OA 16
15 ROFFIAC 161 KA 28
02 ROGECOURT 28 LA 8
76 ROGERVILLE 23 X 8
54 ROGEVILLE 45 XA 12
68 ROGGENHOUSE 90 DB 16
2B ROGLIANO C 226 MB 38
39 ROGNA 138 WA 23
13 ROGNAC 201 TA 35
73 ROGNAIX 153 ZA 26
13 ROGNES 196 UA 34
25 ROGNON 107 YA 18
13 ROGNONAS 195 RA 33
02 ROGNY 28 NA 7
89 ROGNY LES SEPT ECLUSES 82 JA 16
30 ROGUES 192 MA 33
80 ROGY 26 GA 8
28 ROHAIRE 59 AA 12
56 ROHAN C 74 K 15
67 ROHR 49 EB 12
57 ROHRBACH LES BITCHE C 48 DB 11
67 ROHRWILLER 49 FB 12
86 ROIFFE 97 W 19
07 ROIFFIEUX 150 RA 27
80 ROIGLISE 27 JA 8
21 ROILLY 104 PA 18
28 ROINVILLE 61 EA 13
91 ROINVILLE 61 FA 13
91 ROINVILLIERS 61 GA 14
80 ROISEL C 18 KA 6
55 ROISES, LES 67 VA 13
42 ROISEY 150 RA 27
38 ROISSARD 166 VA 29
77 ROISSY EN BRIE C 40 IA 12
95 ROISSY EN FRANCE 40 HA 11
61 ROIVILLE 37 X 11
08 ROIZY 29 PA 9
52 ROLAMPONT 87 UA 15
57 ROLBING 48 DB 10
88 ROLLAINVILLE 67 WA 14
62 ROLLANCOURT 16 FA 4
78 ROLLEBOISE 39 DA 11
76 ROLLEVILLE 23 X 8
80 ROLLOT 27 IA 8
79 ROM 129 X 23
63 ROMAGNAT 148 KA 25
33 ROMAGNE 156 V 30
35 ROMAGNE 76 R 14
86 ROMAGNE 129 X 23
08 ROMAGNE, LA 29 PA 8
49 ROMAGNE, LA 95 S 19
55 ROMAGNE SOUS LES COTES 31 UA 9
55 ROMAGNE
SOUS MONTFAUCON 30 TA 9
38 ROMAGNIEU 152 VA 26
50 ROMAGNY 57 S 12
68 ROMAGNY 90 CB 17
90 ROMAGNY
SOUS ROUGEMONT 90 BB 16
25 ROMAIN 107 YA 18
39 ROMAIN 106 WA 19
51 ROMAIN 28 NA 9
54 ROMAIN 68 YA 13
88 ROMAIN AUX BOIS 67 WA 15
52 ROMAIN SUR MEUSE 67 VA 14
93 ROMAINVILLE C 40 HA 11
27 ROMAN 38 BA 11
71 ROMANECHE THORINS 136 RA 23
39 ROMANGE 106 VA 19
01 ROMANS 137 SA 23
79 ROMANS 128 V 22
26 ROMANS SUR ISERE C 165 TA 28
67 ROMANSWILLER 49 DB 12
17 ROMAZIERES 128 V 24
35 ROMAZY 56 Q 13
68 ROMBACH LE FRANC 69 CB 14
57 ROMBAS C 32 XA 10
59 ROMBIES ET MARCHIPONT 18 MA 5
62 ROMBLY 8 HA 4
17 ROMEGOUX 127 T 25
57 ROMELFING 47 BB 11
71 ROMENAY 121 TA 22
02 ROMENY SUR MARNE 41 LA 11
59 ROMERIES 18 MA 5
02 ROMERY 28 NA 7
51 ROMERY 42 OA 10
60 ROMESCAMPS 25 EA 8
47 ROMESTAING 171 W 31
26 ROMEYER 166 UA 29
32 ROMIEU, LA 186 Y 33
51 ROMIGNY 42 NA 10
34 ROMIGUIERES 191 LA 34
35 ROMILLE 75 O 14
41 ROMILLY 79 BA 15
27 ROMILLY LA PUTHENAYE 37 AA 11
28 ROMILLY SUR AIGRE 80 CA 15
27 ROMILLY SUR ANDELLE 24 CA 9
10 ROMILLY SUR SEINE C 64 NA 13
88 ROMONT 68 ZA 14
41 ROMORANTIN LANTHENAY S 99 EA 18
07 ROMPON 164 RA 29
61 RONAI 58 V 12
10 RONCENAY 64 OA 14
27 RONCENAY AUTHENAY, LE 38 BA 11
50 RONCEY 34 Q 11
70 RONCHAMP 89 AB 17
25 RONCHAUX 106 WA 19
02 RONCHERES 42 MA 10
76 RONCHEROLLES EN BRAY 25 DA 8
76 RONCHEROLLES
SUR LE VIVIER 24 BA 9
59 RONCHIN 9 KA 4
76 RONCHOIS 25 DA 8
57 RONCOURT 45 XA 10
59 RONCQ 9 KA 3
17 RONDE, LA 127 T 23
50 RONDE HAYE, LA 34 O 10
25 RONDEFONTAINE 123 YA 21
81 RONEL 190 GA 34
61 RONFEUGERAI 57 U 12
03 RONGERES 133 MA 23
03 RONNET 133 IA 23
69 RONNO 136 QA 24
95 RONQUEROLLES 39 GA 10
16 RONSENAC 143 X 26
80 RONSSOY 18 KA 6
69 RONTALON 150 RA 26
64 RONTIGNON 207 V 36
55 RONVAUX 45 VA 10
59 ROOST WARENDIN 18 KA 4
90 ROPPE 89 BB 17
67 ROPPENHEIM 50 GB 11
68 ROPPENTZWILLER 90 DB 17
57 ROPPEVILLER 48 DB 10
84 ROQUE ALRIC, LA 179 TA 32
14 ROQUE BAIGNARD, LA 36 X 10
13 ROQUE D'ANTHERON, LA 196 UA 34
83 ROQUE ESCLAPON, LA 198 AB 34
24 ROQUE GAGEAC, LA 158 BA 29
12 ROQUE STE MARGUERITE, LA 176 KA 32
30 ROQUE SUR CEZE, LA 178 OA 32
84 ROQUE SUR PERNES, LA 195 TA 33
06 ROQUEBILLIERE C 199 DB 33
34 ROQUEBRUN 213 KA 35
32 ROQUEBRUNE 186 X 34
33 ROQUEBRUNE 171 W 30
06 ROQUEBRUNE CAP MARTIN 200 DB 34
83 ROQUEBRUNE SUR ARGENS 204 AB 35
83 ROQUEBRUSSANNE, LA C 203 WA 36
82 ROQUECOR 172 AA 32
81 ROQUECOURBE C 190 GA 34
11 ROQUECOURBE MINERVOIS 212 IA 36
30 ROQUEDUR 192 MA 33
11 ROQUEFERE 212 HA 36
11 ROQUEFEUIL 221 FA 38
09 ROQUEFIXADE 219 EA 38
32 ROQUEFORT 187 Z 34
40 ROQUEFORT C 185 V 33
47 ROQUEFORT 172 Z 32
11 ROQUEFORT DE SAULT 222 GA 39
11 ROQUEFORT DES CORBIERES 223 JA 37
13 ROQUEFORT LA BEDOULE 202 VA 36
09 ROQUEFORT LES CASCADES 219 EA 38
06 ROQUEFORT LES PINS 200 CB 34
31 ROQUEFORT SUR GARONNE 218 BA 37
12 ROQUEFORT SUR SOULZON 191 JA 33
32 ROQUELAURE 187 Z 34
32 ROQUELAURE ST AUBIN 187 AA 34
30 ROQUEMAURE C 195 RA 33
81 ROQUEMAURE 188 DA 34
32 ROQUEPINE 186 Y 33
34 ROQUEREDONDE 191 KA 34
31 ROQUES 210 CA 35
32 ROQUES 186 X 34
31 ROQUESERIERE 188 DA 34
34 ROQUESSELS 213 KA 35
06 ROQUESTERON C 199 BB 33
06 ROQUESTERON GRASSE 200 BB 34
11 ROQUETAILLADE 221 GA 37
62 ROQUETOIRE 8 GA 3
27 ROQUETTE, LA 38 CA 10
06 ROQUETTE SUR SIAGNE, LA 200 BB 35
06 ROQUETTE SUR VAR, LA 199 CB 34
31 ROQUETTES 210 CA 35
13 ROQUEVAIRE C 202 VA 36
81 ROQUEVIDAL 211 EA 35
64 ROQUIAGUE 206 S 37
33 ROQUILLE, LA 157 X 29
57 RORBACH LES DIEUZE 47 BB 11
68 RORSCHWIHR 70 DB 14
05 ROSANS C 180 UA 31
39 ROSAY 122 UA 22
76 ROSAY 24 CA 8
78 ROSAY 39 EA 11
27 ROSAY SUR LIEURE 25 DA 9
2A ROSAZIA 227 KB 41
57 ROSBRUCK 47 BB 10
29 ROSCANVEL 51 C 14
29 ROSCOFF 52 E 12
14 ROSEL 35 U 10
68 ROSENAU 90 EB 17
67 ROSENWILLER 70 DB 13
25 ROSET FLUANS 106 WA 19
70 ROSEY 88 XA 17
71 ROSEY 120 RA 21
67 ROSHEIM C 70 DB 13
70 ROSIERE, LA 89 AB 16
07 ROSIERES 178 PA 31
43 ROSIERES 163 OA 28
60 ROSIERES 40 IA 10
81 ROSIERES 190 GA 33
54 ROSIERES AUX SALINES 68 YA 13
54 ROSIERES EN HAYE 45 XA 12
80 ROSIERES EN SANTERRE C 27 IA 7
10 ROSIERES PRES TROYES 64 OA 14
25 ROSIERES SUR BARBECHE 108 AB 18
70 ROSIERES SUR MANCE 87 WA 16
19 ROSIERS D'EGLETONS 146 FA 27
19 ROSIERS DE JUILLAC 145 CA 27
49 ROSIERS SUR LOIRE, LES 96 V 18
34 ROSIS 213 JA 35
36 ROSNAY 114 CA 21
51 ROSNAY 42 NA 10
85 ROSNAY 125 Q 22
10 ROSNAY L'HOPITAL 65 OA 13
29 ROSNOEN 52 E 14
93 ROSNY SOUS BOIS C 40 HA 11
78 ROSNY SUR SEINE 39 DA 11
60 ROSOY 26 HA 9
60 ROSOY EN MULTIEN 41 KA 10
45 ROSOY LE VIEIL 63 JA 15
22 ROSPEZ 53 H 12
2B ROSPIGLIANI 228 LB 41
29 ROSPORDEN C 72 F 15
57 ROSSELANGE 32 XA 10
67 ROSSFELD 70 EB 14
01 ROSSILLON 138 VA 25
67 ROSTEIG 48 DB 11
22 ROSTRENEN C 73 H 14
59 ROSULT 18 LA 4
25 ROSUREUX 108 AB 19
39 ROTALIER 122 VA 21
60 ROTANGY 26 FA 8
67 ROTHAU 69 CB 13
67 ROTHBACH 48 EB 11
73 ROTHERENS 153 XA 26
10 ROTHIERE, LA 65 QA 14
60 ROTHOIS 26 FA 8
39 ROTHONAY 122 VA 22
61 ROTOURS, LES 58 V 12
14 ROTS 35 U 10
67 ROTT 49 FB 11
67 ROTTELSHEIM 49 EB 12
26 ROTTIER 180 UA 31
49 ROU MARSON 96 V 19
81 ROUAIROUX 212 IA 35
44 ROUANS 93 O 19
85 ROUAUDIERE, LA 76 R 16
59 ROUBAIX C 9 KA 3
11 ROUBIA 213 JA 36
06 ROUBION 199 BB 33
14 ROUCAMPS 35 T 11
59 ROUCOURT 18 KA 5
02 ROUCY 28 NA 9
56 ROUDOUALLEC 72 G 15
52 ROUECOURT 66 TA 14
31 ROUEDE 217 AA 37
61 ROUELLE 57 T 12
52 ROUELLES 86 TA 16
76 ROUEN P 24 BA 9
72 ROUESSE FONTAINE 58 X 14
72 ROUESSE VASSE 78 V 14
34 ROUET 192 NA 34
72 ROUEZ 78 W 15
68 ROUFFACH C 90 DB 15
39 ROUFFANGE 106 WA 19
15 ROUFFIAC 160 GA 28
16 ROUFFIAC 143 X 27
17 ROUFFIAC 142 U 25
81 ROUFFIAC 189 FA 33
11 ROUFFIAC D'AUDE 221 GA 37
11 ROUFFIAC DES CORBIERES 223 IA 38
31 ROUFFIAC TOLOSAN 188 DA 34
17 ROUFFIGNAC 142 U 27
24 ROUFFIGNAC DE SIGOULES 157 Y 29
24 ROUFFIGNAC ST CERNIN
DE REILHAC 158 AA 28
50 ROUFFIGNY 56 R 12
46 ROUFFILHAC 159 CA 29
51 ROUFFY 42 OA 11
44 ROUGE C 76 Q 16
61 ROUGE, LA 59 Z 14
27 ROUGE PERRIERS 37 AA 10
02 ROUGEFAY 16 GA 5
90 ROUGEGOUTTE 89 BB 16
21 ROUGEMONT 85 PA 17
25 ROUGEMONT C 88 YA 17
90 ROUGEMONT LE CHATEAU C 90 BB 16
27 ROUGEMONTIERS 24 Z 9
25 ROUGEMONTOT 107 YA 18
41 ROUGEOU 99 DA 18
02 ROUGERIES 28 NA 7
88 ROUGES EAUX, LES 69 AB 14
15 ROUGET, LE 160 GA 29
52 ROUGEUX 87 VA 16
83 ROUGIERS 202 WA 36
16 ROUGNAC 143 Y 26
23 ROUGNAT 133 HA 24
04 ROUGON 198 ZA 34
25 ROUHE 107 XA 19
57 ROUHLING 47 BB 10
16 ROUILLAC C 142 W 25
22 ROUILLAC 53 M 14
86 ROUILLE 112 W 22
72 ROUILLON 78 X 15
77 ROUILLY 63 LA 13
10 ROUILLY SACEY 65 PA 14
34 ROUJAN C 214 LA 35
25 ROULANS C 107 YA 18
88 ROULIER, LE 68 AB 14
72 ROULLEE 59 Y 13
11 ROULLENS 221 GA 37
16 ROULLET ST ESTEPHE 143 W 26
14 ROULLOURS 35 S 11
47 ROUMAGNE 172 Y 30
76 ROUMARE 24 AA 8
16 ROUMAZIERES LOUBERT 144 Z 25
15 ROUMEGOUX 160 GA 29
81 ROUMEGOUX 190 GA 34
09 ROUMENGOUX 221 FA 37
31 ROUMENS 211 FA 35
04 ROUMOULES 197 XA 34
67 ROUNTZENHEIM 50 GB 12
57 ROUPELDANGE 47 ZA 10
61 ROUPERROUX 58 W 13
72 ROUPERROUX LE COQUET 59 Y 14
02 ROUPY 27 KA 7
12 ROUQUETTE, LA 174 FA 32
06 ROURE 199 CB 33
06 ROURET, LE 200 BB 34
59 ROUSIES 19 OA 5
87 ROUSSAC 131 BA 24
26 ROUSSAS 179 SA 31
49 ROUSSAY 110 R 19
81 ROUSSAYROLLES 174 EA 32
60 ROUSSELOY 40 HA 9
12 ROUSSENNAC 175 GA 31
62 ROUSSENT 16 EA 5
48 ROUSSES 177 MA 32
39 ROUSSES, LES 123 XA 22
05 ROUSSET 181 YA 31
13 ROUSSET 202 VA 35
71 ROUSSET, LE 120 QA 22
26 ROUSSET LES VIGNES 179 TA 31
27 ROUSSIERE, LA 37 Z 11
26 ROUSSIEUX 180 VA 31
38 ROUSSILLON C 151 SA 27
84 ROUSSILLON 196 UA 33
71 ROUSSILLON EN MORVAN 103 OA 19
16 ROUSSINES 144 Z 25
36 ROUSSINES 115 CA 22
30 ROUSSON 178 PA 32
89 ROUSSON 63 LA 15
57 ROUSSY LE VILLAGE 32 YA 9
25 ROUTELLE 106 WA 19
76 ROUTES 24 Z 7
11 ROUTIER 221 GA 37
27 ROUTOT C 24 Z 9
11 ROUVENAC 221 GA 38
54 ROUVES 46 YA 11
30 ROUVIERE, LA 193 PA 33
59 ROUVIGNIES 18 LA 5
60 ROUVILLE 41 JA 10
76 ROUVILLE 23 Y 8
60 ROUVILLERS 26 IA 9
21 ROUVRAY 103 OA 18
27 ROUVRAY 38 CA 10
89 ROUVRAY 84 MA 16
76 ROUVRAY CATILLON 25 DA 8
28 ROUVRAY ST DENIS 61 FA 14
28 ROUVRAY ST FLORENTIN 61 DA 14
45 ROUVRAY STE CROIX 81 EA 15
80 ROUVREL 26 HA 7
14 ROUVRES 36 V 11
28 ROUVRES 38 DA 11
77 ROUVRES 40 IA 10
60 ROUVRES EN MULTIEN 41 KA 10
21 ROUVRES EN PLAINE 105 TA 19
55 ROUVRES EN WOEVRE 45 VA 10
88 ROUVRES EN XAINTOIS 67 XA 14
88 ROUVRES LA CHETIVE 67 WA 14
36 ROUVRES LES BOIS 99 DA 19
10 ROUVRES LES VIGNES 66 RA 14
21 ROUVRES SOUS MEILLY 104 RA 19
45 ROUVRES ST JEAN 61 GA 14
52 ROUVRES SUR AUBE 86 SA 16
55 ROUVROIS SUR MEUSE 45 VA 11
55 ROUVROIS SUR OTHAIN 31 VA 9
02 ROUVROY 28 LA 7
62 ROUVROY C 17 JA 5
80 ROUVROY EN SANTERRE 27 IA 7
60 ROUVROY LES MERLES 26 HA 8
51 ROUVROY RIPONT 43 RA 10
08 ROUVROY SUR AUDRY 29 QA 7
52 ROUVROY SUR MARNE 66 TA 14
02 ROUVROY SUR SERRE 29 PA 7
07 ROUX, LE 163 OA 30
50 ROUXEVILLE 35 S 10
44 ROUXIERE, LA 94 R 18
76 ROUXMESNIL BOUTEILLES 24 BA 7
58 ROUY 102 MA 19
80 ROUY LE GRAND 27 JA 7
80 ROUY LE PETIT 27 JA 7
09 ROUZE 222 FA 39
16 ROUZEDE 143 Z 25
15 ROUZIERS 160 GA 29
37 ROUZIERS DE TOURAINE 79 Z 17
13 ROVE, LE 202 UA 36
88 ROVILLE AUX CHENES 68 AB 13
54 ROVILLE DEVANT BAYON 68 YA 13
38 ROVON 166 UA 28
60 ROY BOISSY 25 FA 8
17 ROYAN C 141 R 26
38 ROYAS 151 TA 26
63 ROYAT C 147 KA 25
60 ROYAUCOURT 26 HA 8
02 ROYAUCOURT ET CHAILVET 28 MA 8
54 ROYAUMEIX 45 WA 12
38 ROYBON C 151 TA 27
70 ROYE 89 ZA 17
80 ROYE C 27 JA 8
60 ROYE SUR MATZ 27 IA 8
71 ROYER 121 SA 22
23 ROYERE DE VASSIVIERE C 146 FA 25
87 ROYERES 131 CA 25
26 ROYNAC 179 SA 30
62 ROYON 16 FA 4
76 ROYVILLE 24 AA 7
35 ROZ LANDRIEUX 55 O 13
35 ROZ SUR COUESNON 56 P 13
77 ROZAY EN BRIE C 63 JA 12
50 ROZEL, LE 33 O 9
54 ROZELIEURES 68 ZA 13
57 ROZERIEULLES 45 XA 10
88 ROZEROTTE 67 XA 14
32 ROZES 186 Y 34
02 ROZET ST ALBIN 41 LA 10
48 ROZIER, LE 176 KA 32
42 ROZIER COTES D'AUREC 149 OA 27
42 ROZIER EN DONZY 149 PA 25
45 ROZIERES EN BEAUCE 81 EA 15
02 ROZIERES SUR CRISE 28 LA 9
88 ROZIERES SUR MOUZON 67 WA 15
87 ROZIERS ST GEORGES 145 DA 25
02 ROZOY BELLEVALLE 41 LA 11
02 ROZOY SUR SERRE C 29 OA 8
58 RUAGES 103 NA 18
45 RUAN 61 FA 15
41 RUAN SUR EGVONNE 80 BA 15
72 RUAUDIN 78 X 15
08 RUBECOURT ET LAMECOURT 30 SA 8
77 RUBELLES 62 IA 13
80 RUBEMPRE 16 HA 6
14 RUBERCY 35 S 9
80 RUBESCOURT 26 IA 8
08 RUBIGNY 29 PA 8
59 RUBROUCK 8 HA 3
22 RUCA 54 M 13
33 RUCH 156 W 29
14 RUCQUEVILLE 35 T 10
24 RUDEAU LADOSSE 143 Y 26
46 RUDELLE 160 EA 30
80 RUE C 15 DA 5
60 RUE ST PIERRE, LA 26 GA 9
76 RUE ST PIERRE, LA 24 CA 8
68 RUEDERBACH 90 CB 17
28 RUEIL LA GADELIERE 38 BA 12
92 RUEIL MALMAISON C 39 GA 11
68 RUELISHEIM 90 DB 16
16 RUELLE SUR TOUVRE C 143 X 25
59 RUES DES VIGNES, LES 18 KA 6
59 RUESNES 18 MA 5
46 RUEYRES 160 EA 30
16 RUFFEC C 129 X 24
36 RUFFEC 114 BA 21
25 RUFFEY LE CHATEAU 106 WA 18
21 RUFFEY LES BEAUNE 121 SA 20
21 RUFFEY LES ECHIREY 105 TA 18
39 RUFFEY SUR SEILLE 122 VA 21
56 RUFFIAC 74 M 16
01 RUFFIEU 138 VA 24
73 RUFFIEUX C 138 WA 25
44 RUFFIGNE 76 P 16
27 RUGLES C 37 Z 12
88 RUGNEY 68 YA 14
89 RUGNY 85 PA 16
70 RUHANS 107 XA 18
72 RUILLE EN CHAMPAGNE 78 W 15
53 RUILLE FROID FONDS 77 T 16
53 RUILLE LE GRAVELAIS 76 S 15
72 RUILLE SUR LOIR 79 Z 16
62 RUISSEAUVILLE 16 FA 4
62 RUITZ 17 IA 4
12 RULLAC ST CIRQ 175 HA 32
14 RULLY 57 T 12

60 RULLY 40 IA 10
71 RULLY 120 RA 20
62 RUMAUCOURT 18 KA 5
59 RUMEGIES 18 LA 4
68 RUMERSHEIM LE HAUT 90 EB 16
14 RUMESNIL 36 W 10
08 RUMIGNY C 29 PA 7
80 RUMIGNY 26 GA 7
62 RUMILLY 7 FA 4
74 RUMILLY C 138 WA 25
59 RUMILLY EN CAMBRESIS 18 KA 6
10 RUMILLY LES VAUDES 65 PA 15
62 RUMINGHEM 7 GA 2
55 RUMONT 44 UA 11
77 RUMONT 62 HA 14
22 RUNAN 53 I 12
94 RUNGIS 40 HA 12
07 RUOMS 178 PA 31
77 RUPEREUX 63 LA 12
88 RUPPES 67 WA 13
52 RUPT 66 TA 13
55 RUPT AUX NONAINS 44 TA 12
55 RUPT DEVANT ST MIHIEL 44 UA 11
55 RUPT EN WOEVRE 44 UA 10
88 RUPT SUR MOSELLE 89 AB 15
55 RUPT SUR OTHAIN 31 UA 9
70 RUPT SUR SAONE 88 WA 17
57 RURANGE LES THIONVILLE 46 YA 10
25 RUREY 107 XA 19
2B RUSIO 228 LB 40
67 RUSS 69 CB 13
57 RUSSANGE 32 WA 9
25 RUSSEY, LE C 108 AB 19
14 RUSSY 35 T 9
60 RUSSY BEMONT 41 JA 10
68 RUSTENHART 90 DB 15
11 RUSTIQUES 212 HA 36
84 RUSTREL 196 VA 33
57 RUSTROFF 32 ZA 9
2B RUTALI 226 MB 39
10 RUVIGNY 65 PA 14
38 RUY 152 UA 26
62 RUYAULCOURT 17 KA 6
15 RUYNES EN MARGERIDE C 162 KA 28
76 RY 25 CA 9
39 RYE 122 UA 20
14 RYES C 35 T 9

S

77 SAACY SUR MARNE 41 KA 11
67 SAALES C 69 CB 14
76 SAANE ST JUST 24 AA 7
67 SAASENHEIM 70 EB 14
46 SABADEL LATRONQUIERE 160 FA 30
46 SABADEL LAUZES 174 DA 30
32 SABAILLAN 209 AA 35
65 SABALOS 208 X 36
09 SABARAT 218 CA 37
65 SABARROS 208 Y 36
32 SABAZAN 185 W 34
72 SABLE SUR SARTHE C 77 V 16
85 SABLES D'OLONNE, LES S 125 O 22
85 SABLES D'OLONNE, LES S 125 O 22
84 SABLET 179 SA 32
07 SABLIERES 178 OA 31
17 SABLONCEAUX 141 S 25
77 SABLONNIERES 41 LA 11
33 SABLONS 156 V 28
38 SABLONS 150 RA 27
31 SABONNERES 209 BA 35
08 SABOTTERIE, LA 30 RA 8
30 SABRAN 179 QA 32
40 SABRES C 170 T 32
31 SACCOURVIELLE 217 Z 38
53 SACE 77 T 14
50 SACEY 56 Q 13
37 SACHE 97 Z 19
62 SACHIN 16 HA 4
08 SACHY 30 TA 8
36 SACIERGES ST MARTIN 115 CA 22
91 SACLAS 61 GA 14
91 SACLAY 64 GA 12
02 SACONIN ET BREUIL 27 LA 9
65 SACOUE 217 Z 37
27 SACQ, LE 38 BA 11
21 SACQUENAY 87 UA 17
27 SACQUENVILLE 38 BA 10
51 SACY 42 OA 10
89 SACY 84 NA 17
60 SACY LE GRAND 26 HA 9
60 SACY LE PETIT 26 IA 9
32 SADEILLAN 208 Y 36
24 SADILLAC 157 Y 30
33 SADIRAC 156 U 29
65 SADOURNIN 208 Y 36
19 SADROC 159 DA 27
67 SAESSOLSHEIM 49 EB 12
54 SAFFAIS 68 YA 13
39 SAFFLOZ 122 WA 21
44 SAFFRE 94 P 17
21 SAFFRES 104 RA 18
24 SAGELAT 158 BA 29
23 SAGNAT 131 DA 23
07 SAGNES ET GOUDOULET 163 PA 29
18 SAGONNE 117 JA 20
71 SAGY 121 UA 21
95 SAGY 39 FA 10
66 SAHORRE 222 HA 39
26 SAHUNE 180 TA 31
76 SAHURS 24 AA 9
61 SAI 58 W 12
15 SAIGNES C 147 HA 27
46 SAIGNES 159 EA 29
80 SAIGNEVILLE 15 EA 6
84 SAIGNON 196 UA 34
31 SAIGUEDE 210 BA 35
42 SAIL LES BAINS 135 NA 23
42 SAIL SOUS COUZAN 149 OA 25
65 SAILHAN 216 Y 38
19 SAILLAC 159 DA 28
46 SAILLAC 174 EA 31
66 SAILLAGOUSE C 222 FA 40
26 SAILLANS C 165 TA 30
33 SAILLANS 156 V 29
63 SAILLANT 149 OA 26
87 SAILLAT SUR VIENNE 130 AA 25
71 SAILLENARD 122 UA 21
08 SAILLY 30 TA 8
52 SAILLY 66 TA 13
71 SAILLY 120 OA 22
78 SAILLY 39 EA 11
57 SAILLY ACHATEL 46 YA 11
80 SAILLY AU BOIS 17 IA 6
62 SAILLY EN OSTREVENT 17 JA 5
80 SAILLY FLIBEAUCOURT 15 EA 5
62 SAILLY LABOURSE 17 IA 4
80 SAILLY LAURETTE 17 IA 7
80 SAILLY LE SEC 17 IA 7
59 SAILLY LEZ CAMBRAI 18 KA 5
59 SAILLY LEZ LANNOY 9 KA 3
80 SAILLY SAILLISEL 17 JA 6
62 SAILLY SUR LA LYS 8 IA 3
69 SAIN BEL 150 QA 25
58 SAINCAIZE MEAUCE 118 KA 20
59 SAINGHIN EN MELANTOIS 9 KA 4
59 SAINGHIN EN WEPPES 9 JA 4
76 SAINNEVILLE 23 X 8
89 SAINPUITS 83 LA 17
35 SAINS 56 P 13
59 SAINS DU NORD 19 OA 6
80 SAINS EN AMIENOIS 26 GA 7
62 SAINS EN GOHELLE C 17 IA 4
62 SAINS LES FRESSIN 16 FA 4
62 SAINS LES MARQUION 18 KA 5
62 SAINS LES PERNES 16 HA 4
60 SAINS MORAINVILLERS 26 HA 8
02 SAINS RICHAUMONT C 28 NA 7
56 SAINT, LE 72 G 15
64 SAINT ABIT 207 V 36
56 SAINT ABRAHAM 74 L 16
80 SAINT ACHEUL 16 GA 5
16 SAINT ADJUTORY 143 Y 25
22 SAINT ADRIEN 53 I 13
12 SAINT AFFRIQUE C 191 JA 33
81 SAINT AFFRIQUE LES MONTAGNES 212 GA 35
22 SAINT AGATHON 53 I 13
41 SAINT AGIL 79 AA 15
02 SAINT AGNAN 42 MA 11
58 SAINT AGNAN 103 OA 18
71 SAINT AGNAN 119 NA 22
81 SAINT AGNAN 189 EA 34
89 SAINT AGNAN 63 KA 14
27 SAINT AGNAN DE CERNIERES 37 Z 11
26 SAINT AGNAN EN VERCORS 166 UA 29
14 SAINT AGNAN LE MALHERBE 35 U 11
61 SAINT AGNAN SUR ERRE 59 Z 14
61 SAINT AGNAN SUR SARTHE 59 Y 12
17 SAINT AGNANT C 127 S 25
23 SAINT AGNANT DE VERSILLAT 131 DA 23
23 SAINT AGNANT PRES CROCQ 146 HA 25
24 SAINT AGNE 158 Z 29
40 SAINT AGNET 207 V 35
38 SAINT AGNIN SUR BION 151 TA 26
63 SAINT AGOULIN 134 KA 24
07 SAINT AGREVE C 164 QA 28
08 SAINT AIGNAN 30 SA 8
33 SAINT AIGNAN 156 V 29
41 SAINT AIGNAN C 99 CA 18
56 SAINT AIGNAN 73 J 14
72 SAINT AIGNAN 59 Y 14
82 SAINT AIGNAN 187 BA 33
53 SAINT AIGNAN DE COUPTRAIN 58 V 13
14 SAINT AIGNAN DE CRAMESNIL 36 V 10
45 SAINT AIGNAN DES GUES 82 HA 16
18 SAINT AIGNAN DES NOYERS 117 JA 21
44 SAINT AIGNAN GRANDLIEU 93 P 19
45 SAINT AIGNAN LE JAILLARD 82 HA 16
53 SAINT AIGNAN SUR ROE C 76 R 16
76 SAINT AIGNAN SUR RY 25 CA 8
36 SAINT AIGNY 114 BA 21
17 SAINT AIGULIN 157 W 28
54 SAINT AIL 45 XA 10
71 SAINT ALBAIN 137 SA 22
01 SAINT ALBAN 138 UA 24
22 SAINT ALBAN 54 L 13
31 SAINT ALBAN 188 CA 34
07 SAINT ALBAN AURIOLLES 178 PA 31
07 SAINT ALBAN D'AY 164 RA 28
73 SAINT ALBAN DE MONTBEL 152 WA 26
38 SAINT ALBAN DE ROCHE 151 TA 26
73 SAINT ALBAN DES HURTIERES 153 YA 26
73 SAINT ALBAN DES VILLARDS 153 YA 27
38 SAINT ALBAN DU RHONE 150 RA 27
07 SAINT ALBAN EN MONTAGNE 163 NA 30
42 SAINT ALBAN LES EAUX 135 OA 24
73 SAINT ALBAN LEYSSE C 153 XA 26
48 SAINT ALBAN SUR LIMAGNOLE C 162 LA 29
38 SAINT ALBIN DE VAULSERRE 152 VA 26
30 SAINT ALEXANDRE 179 RA 32
02 SAINT ALGIS 28 NA 7
56 SAINT ALLOUESTRE 74 K 16
23 SAINT ALPINIEN 132 GA 24
63 SAINT ALYRE D'ARLANC 148 MA 27
63 SAINT ALYRE ES MONTAGNE 147 JA 27
09 SAINT AMADOU 219 EA 37
81 SAINT AMANCET 211 GA 35
23 SAINT AMAND 132 GA 24
50 SAINT AMAND 35 S 11
62 SAINT AMAND 17 IA 6
24 SAINT AMAND DE BELVES 158 BA 30
24 SAINT AMAND DE COLY 159 CA 28
24 SAINT AMAND DE VERGT 158 Z 29
27 SAINT AMAND DES HAUTES TERRES 38 AA 10
58 SAINT AMAND EN PUISAYE C 83 KA 17
23 SAINT AMAND JARTOUDEIX 131 DA 24
87 SAINT AMAND LE PETIT 145 EA 25
59 SAINT AMAND LES EAUX C 18 LA 4
41 SAINT AMAND LONGPRE C 79 BA 17
87 SAINT AMAND MAGNAZEIX 131 CA 23
18 SAINT AMAND MONTROND S 117 HA 21
51 SAINT AMAND SUR FION 43 RA 12
55 SAINT AMAND SUR ORNAIN 66 UA 12
79 SAINT AMAND SUR SEVRE 111 T 20
15 SAINT AMANDIN 147 IA 27
09 SAINT AMANS 219 DA 37
11 SAINT AMANS 211 FA 36
48 SAINT AMANS C 177 LA 30
82 SAINT AMANS DE PELLAGAL 173 BA 32
12 SAINT AMANS DES COTS C 175 IA 30
82 SAINT AMANS DU PECH 172 AA 32
81 SAINT AMANS SOULT C 212 HA 35
81 SAINT AMANS VALTORET 212 HA 35
16 SAINT AMANT 143 X 27
16 SAINT AMANT DE BOIXE C 143 X 25
16 SAINT AMANT DE BONNIEURE 129 X 25
16 SAINT AMANT DE GRAVES 142 W 26
16 SAINT AMANT DE NOUERE 143 W 25
63 SAINT AMANT ROCHE SAVINE C 148 MA 26
63 SAINT AMANT TALLENDE C 148 KA 26
68 SAINT AMARIN C 90 BB 16
71 SAINT AMBREUIL 121 SA 21
18 SAINT AMBROIX 116 GA 20
30 SAINT AMBROIX C 178 PA 32
88 SAINT AME 89 AB 15
39 SAINT AMOUR C 122 UA 22
71 SAINT AMOUR BELLEVUE 136 RA 23
58 SAINT ANDELAIN 101 JA 18
26 SAINT ANDEOL 165 TA 29
38 SAINT ANDEOL 166 VA 29
07 SAINT ANDEOL DE BERG 179 OA 31
48 SAINT ANDEOL DE CLERGUEMORT 177 NA 32
07 SAINT ANDEOL DE FOURCHADES 164 PA 29
07 SAINT ANDEOL DE VALS 164 QA 30
69 SAINT ANDEOL LE CHATEAU 150 RA 26
21 SAINT ANDEUX 103 OA 18
13 SAINT ANDIOL 195 SA 34
06 SAINT ANDRE 200 DB 34
31 SAINT ANDRE 209 AA 36
32 SAINT ANDRE 209 AA 35
66 SAINT ANDRE 224 JA 39
73 SAINT ANDRE 168 AB 28
81 SAINT ANDRE 190 HA 33
48 SAINT ANDRE CAPCEZE 178 OA 31
24 SAINT ANDRE D'ALLAS 158 BA 29
42 SAINT ANDRE D'APCHON 135 OA 24
05 SAINT ANDRE D'EMBRUN 182 ZA 30
14 SAINT ANDRE D'HEBERTOT 23 X 9
01 SAINT ANDRE D'HUIRIAT 137 SA 23
30 SAINT ANDRE D'OLERARGUES 178 QA 32
01 SAINT ANDRE DE BAGE 137 SA 23
74 SAINT ANDRE DE BOEGE 139 ZA 23
50 SAINT ANDRE DE BOHON 34 R 10
61 SAINT ANDRE DE BRIOUZE 58 V 12
34 SAINT ANDRE DE BUEGES 192 MA 34
43 SAINT ANDRE DE CHALENCON 149 OA 27
01 SAINT ANDRE DE CORCY 137 SA 24
07 SAINT ANDRE DE CRUZIERES 178 PA 32
33 SAINT ANDRE DE CUBZAC C 156 U 29
24 SAINT ANDRE DE DOUBLE 157 Y 28
50 SAINT ANDRE DE L'EPINE 35 S 10
27 SAINT ANDRE DE L'EURE C 38 CA 11
49 SAINT ANDRE DE LA MARCHE 95 S 19
48 SAINT ANDRE DE LANCIZE 177 NA 32
17 SAINT ANDRE DE LIDON 141 T 26
30 SAINT ANDRE DE MAJENCOULES 192 MA 33
61 SAINT ANDRE DE MESSEI 57 U 12
12 SAINT ANDRE DE NAJAC 174 FA 32
11 SAINT ANDRE DE ROQUELONGUE 223 JA 37
30 SAINT ANDRE DE ROQUEPERTUIS 178 QA 32
05 SAINT ANDRE DE ROSANS 180 VA 31
34 SAINT ANDRE DE SANGONIS 214 MA 35
40 SAINT ANDRE DE SEIGNANX 183 Q 35
30 SAINT ANDRE DE VALBORGNE C 177 NA 32
12 SAINT ANDRE DE VEZINES 176 LA 32
22 SAINT ANDRE DES EAUX 55 N 13
44 SAINT ANDRE DES EAUX 92 M 18
33 SAINT ANDRE DU BOIS 171 V 30
55 SAINT ANDRE EN BARROIS 44 TA 11
71 SAINT ANDRE EN BRESSE 121 TA 21
58 SAINT ANDRE EN MORVAN 103 NA 18
38 SAINT ANDRE EN ROYANS 166 UA 28
89 SAINT ANDRE EN TERRE PLAINE 84 OA 17
07 SAINT ANDRE EN VIVARAIS 164 QA 28
33 SAINT ANDRE ET APPELLES 157 X 29
60 SAINT ANDRE FARIVILLIERS 26 GA 8
85 SAINT ANDRE GOULE D'OIE 110 R 20
69 SAINT ANDRE LA COTE 150 QA 26
07 SAINT ANDRE LACHAMP 178 PA 31
01 SAINT ANDRE LE BOUCHOUX 137 TA 23
63 SAINT ANDRE LE COQ 133 LA 24
71 SAINT ANDRE LE DESERT 120 QA 22
38 SAINT ANDRE LE GAZ 152 VA 26
42 SAINT ANDRE LE PUY 149 PA 26
04 SAINT ANDRE LES ALPES C 198 ZA 33
10 SAINT ANDRE LES VERGERS 64 OA 14
59 SAINT ANDRE LEZ LILLE 9 KA 3
76 SAINT ANDRE SUR CAILLY 24 CA 8
14 SAINT ANDRE SUR ORNE 36 U 10
79 SAINT ANDRE SUR SEVRE 111 T 21
01 SAINT ANDRE SUR VIEUX JONC 137 TA 23
85 SAINT ANDRE TREIZE VOIES 110 Q 20
33 SAINT ANDRONY 156 T 28
28 SAINT ANGE ET TORCAY 60 BA 12
77 SAINT ANGE LE VIEL 63 JA 14
16 SAINT ANGEAU 129 X 25
03 SAINT ANGEL 133 IA 22
19 SAINT ANGEL 146 GA 26
63 SAINT ANGEL 133 JA 24
63 SAINT ANTHEME C 149 NA 26
21 SAINT ANTHOT 104 RA 18
15 SAINT ANTOINE 160 HA 30
25 SAINT ANTOINE 123 YA 21
32 SAINT ANTOINE 187 AA 33
33 SAINT ANTOINE 156 U 28
24 SAINT ANTOINE CUMOND 143 X 27
24 SAINT ANTOINE D'AUBEROCHE 158 AA 28
24 SAINT ANTOINE DE BREUILH 157 X 29
47 SAINT ANTOINE DE FICALBA 172 Z 31
33 SAINT ANTOINE DU QUEYRET 157 W 30
37 SAINT ANTOINE DU ROCHER 79 Z 17
38 SAINT ANTOINE L'ABBAYE 165 TA 28
76 SAINT ANTOINE LA FORET 23 Y 8
33 SAINT ANTOINE SUR L'ISLE 157 W 28
06 SAINT ANTONIN 199 BB 33
32 SAINT ANTONIN 187 AA 34
81 SAINT ANTONIN DE LACALM 190 GA 34
27 SAINT ANTONIN DE SOMMAIRE 37 Z 11
83 SAINT ANTONIN DU VAR 203 YA 35
82 SAINT ANTONIN NOBLE VAL C 174 EA 32
13 SAINT ANTONIN SUR BAYON 202 VA 35
36 SAINT AOUSTRILLE 116 FA 20
36 SAINT AOUT 116 FA 21
05 SAINT APOLLINAIRE 182 YA 30
21 SAINT APOLLINAIRE 105 TA 18
07 SAINT APOLLINAIRE DE RIAS 164 RA 29
69 SAINT APPOLINAIRE 136 QA 24
38 SAINT APPOLINARD 165 UA 28
42 SAINT APPOLINARD 150 RA 27
24 SAINT AQUILIN 157 Y 28
61 SAINT AQUILIN DE CORBION 59 Y 12
27 SAINT AQUILIN DE PACY 38 CA 11
31 SAINT ARAILLE 209 BA 36
32 SAINT ARAILLES 208 Y 35
43 SAINT ARCONS D'ALLIER 162 MA 28
43 SAINT ARCONS DE BARGES 163 OA 29
38 SAINT AREY 166 WA 29
35 SAINT ARMEL 76 P 15
56 SAINT ARMEL 92 K 17
64 SAINT ARMOU 207 V 36
66 SAINT ARNAC 222 HA 38
14 SAINT ARNOULT 23 X 9
41 SAINT ARNOULT 79 AA 16
60 SAINT ARNOULT 25 EA 8
76 SAINT ARNOULT 23 Z 8
28 SAINT ARNOULT DES BOIS 60 CA 13
78 SAINT ARNOULT EN YVELINES C 61 FA 13
32 SAINT ARROMAN 209 Y 35
65 SAINT ARROMAN 216 Y 37
82 SAINT ARROUMEX 187 BA 33
24 SAINT ASTIER C 157 Y 28
47 SAINT ASTIER 157 X 30
06 SAINT AUBAN C 198 AB 34
05 SAINT AUBAN D'OZE 181 WA 31
26 SAINT AUBAN SUR L'OUVEZE 180 UA 32
59 SAINT AUBERT 18 LA 5
61 SAINT AUBERT SUR ORNE 58 V 12
02 SAINT AUBIN 27 KA 8
10 SAINT AUBIN 64 MA 13
21 SAINT AUBIN 120 RA 20
36 SAINT AUBIN 116 FA 20
39 SAINT AUBIN 106 UA 19
40 SAINT AUBIN 184 T 34
47 SAINT AUBIN 172 AA 31
59 SAINT AUBIN 19 OA 6
62 SAINT AUBIN 15 EA 4
91 SAINT AUBIN 39 GA 12
76 SAINT AUBIN CELLOVILLE 24 BA 9
89 SAINT AUBIN CHATEAU NEUF 83 LA 16
61 SAINT AUBIN D'APPENAI 59 Y 13
14 SAINT AUBIN D'ARQUENAY 36 V 10
35 SAINT AUBIN D'AUBIGNE C 75 P 14
27 SAINT AUBIN D'ECROSVILLE 38 BA 10
33 SAINT AUBIN DE BLAYE 142 U 27
61 SAINT AUBIN DE BONNEVAL 37 Y 11
33 SAINT AUBIN DE BRANNE 156 V 29
24 SAINT AUBIN DE CADELECH 172 Y 30
61 SAINT AUBIN DE COURTERAIE 59 Y 12
76 SAINT AUBIN DE CRETOT 23 Z 8
24 SAINT AUBIN DE LANQUAIS 158 Z 29
72 SAINT AUBIN DE LOCQUENAY 58 W 14
49 SAINT AUBIN DE LUIGNE 95 T 18
33 SAINT AUBIN DE MEDOC 155 T 29
24 SAINT AUBIN DE NABIRAT 159 CA 30
27 SAINT AUBIN DE SCELLON 37 Y 10
50 SAINT AUBIN DE TERREGATTE 56 Q 13
14 SAINT AUBIN DES BOIS 56 R 11
28 SAINT AUBIN DES BOIS 60 CA 13
44 SAINT AUBIN DES CHATEAUX 76 O 16
58 SAINT AUBIN DES CHAUMES 103 NA 18
72 SAINT AUBIN DES COUDRAIS 59 Z 14
61 SAINT AUBIN DES GROIS 59 Z 14
27 SAINT AUBIN DES HAYES 37 Z 11
35 SAINT AUBIN DES LANDES 76 Q 15
85 SAINT AUBIN DES ORMEAUX 99 S 20
50 SAINT AUBIN DES PREAUX 56 P 12
35 SAINT AUBIN DU CORMIER C 76 O 14
53 SAINT AUBIN DU DESERT 58 V 14
35 SAINT AUBIN DU PAVAIL 76 Q 15
50 SAINT AUBIN DU PERRON 34 Q 10
79 SAINT AUBIN DU PLAIN 112 U 20
27 SAINT AUBIN DU THENNEY 37 Y 11
60 SAINT AUBIN EN BRAY 25 FA 9
71 SAINT AUBIN EN CHAROLLAIS 120 PA 22
76 SAINT AUBIN EPINAY 24 BA 9
53 SAINT AUBIN FOSSE LOUVAIN 57 S 13
85 SAINT AUBIN LA PLAINE 125 R 22
76 SAINT AUBIN LE CAUF 24 BA 7
79 SAINT AUBIN LE CLOUD 112 V 21
37 SAINT AUBIN LE DEPEINT 79 Y 17
27 SAINT AUBIN LE GUICHARD 37 Z 11
03 SAINT AUBIN LE MONIAL 117 JA 22
27 SAINT AUBIN LE VERTUEUX 37 Z 10
76 SAINT AUBIN LES ELBEUF 24 BA 9
58 SAINT AUBIN LES FORGES 102 KA 19
80 SAINT AUBIN MONTENOY 26 FA 7
80 SAINT AUBIN RIVIERE 25 EA 7
76 SAINT AUBIN ROUTOT 23 Y 8
60 SAINT AUBIN SOUS ERQUERY 26 HA 9
55 SAINT AUBIN SUR AIRE 44 UA 12
27 SAINT AUBIN SUR GAILLON 38 CA 10
71 SAINT AUBIN SUR LOIRE 119 NA 22
14 SAINT AUBIN SUR MER 36 U 9
76 SAINT AUBIN SUR MER 24 AA 7
27 SAINT AUBIN SUR QUILLEBEUF 23 Z 9
76 SAINT AUBIN SUR SCIE 24 BA 7
89 SAINT AUBIN SUR YONNE 83 LA 15
17 SAINT AUGUSTIN 141 R 25
19 SAINT AUGUSTIN 146 EA 27
77 SAINT AUGUSTIN 41 KA 12
49 SAINT AUGUSTIN DES BOIS 95 T 18
19 SAINT AULAIRE 159 CA 27
16 SAINT AULAIS LA CHAPELLE 142 W 26
24 SAINT AULAYE C 157 X 28
34 SAINT AUNES 194 OA 35
32 SAINT AUNIX LENGROS 208 W 35
38 SAINT AUPRE 152 VA 27
43 SAINT AUSTREMOINE 162 LA 28
87 SAINT AUVENT 144 AA 25
85 SAINT AVAUGOURD DES LANDES 125 Q 22
56 SAINT AVE 74 K 17
31 SAINT AVENTIN 217 Z 38
37 SAINT AVERTIN C 98 Z 18
16 SAINT AVIT 143 W 27
26 SAINT AVIT 165 SA 28
40 SAINT AVIT 184 U 33
41 SAINT AVIT 59 AA 15
47 SAINT AVIT 171 X 30
63 SAINT AVIT 133 HA 25
81 SAINT AVIT 211 FA 35
33 SAINT AVIT DE SOULEGE 157 X 29
23 SAINT AVIT DE TARDES 132 GA 24
24 SAINT AVIT DE VIALARD 158 AA 29
32 SAINT AVIT FRANDAT 187 Z 33
23 SAINT AVIT LE PAUVRE 132 FA 24
28 SAINT AVIT LES GUESPIERES 60 CA 14
24 SAINT AVIT RIVIERE 158 AA 30
24 SAINT AVIT SENIEUR 158 AA 30
33 SAINT AVIT ST NAZAIRE 157 X 29
57 SAINT AVOLD C 47 AB 10
73 SAINT AVRE 153 YA 27
45 SAINT AY 81 EA 16
59 SAINT AYBERT 18 MA 4
63 SAINT BABEL 148 LA 26
73 SAINT BALDOPH 166 WA 28
02 SAINT BANDRY 27 KA 9
39 SAINT BARAING 122 UA 20
87 SAINT BARBANT 130 AA 23
23 SAINT BARD 132 HA 24
26 SAINT BARDOUX 165 SA 28
22 SAINT BARNABE 74 K 15
38 SAINT BARTHELEMY 151 TA 27
40 SAINT BARTHELEMY 205 O 35
50 SAINT BARTHELEMY 57 S 12
56 SAINT BARTHELEMY 73 J 16
70 SAINT BARTHELEMY 89 AB 16
77 SAINT BARTHELEMY 41 LA 12
47 SAINT BARTHELEMY D'AGENAIS 172 Y 31
49 SAINT BARTHELEMY D'ANJOU 96 U 18
24 SAINT BARTHELEMY DE BELLEGARDE 157 X 28
24 SAINT BARTHELEMY DE BUSSIERE 144 Z 26
38 SAINT BARTHELEMY DE SECHILIENNE 166 WA 28
26 SAINT BARTHELEMY DE VALS 165 SA 28
07 SAINT BARTHELEMY LE MEIL 164 QA 29
07 SAINT BARTHELEMY GROZON 164 RA 29
07 SAINT BARTHELEMY LE PLAIN 164 RA 28
42 SAINT BARTHELEMY LESTRA 150 PA 25
07 SAINT BASILE 164 QA 29
88 SAINT BASLEMONT 67 XA 15
18 SAINT BAUDEL 116 GA 20
53 SAINT BAUDELLE 57 T 14
38 SAINT BAUDILLE DE LA TOUR 152 UA 25
38 SAINT BAUDILLE ET PIPET 166 WA 29
37 SAINT BAULD 98 AA 19
54 SAINT BAUSSANT 45 WA 11
09 SAINT BAUZEIL 219 DA 37
30 SAINT BAUZELY 193 PA 33
07 SAINT BAUZILE 164 RA 30
48 SAINT BAUZILE 177 MA 31
34 SAINT BAUZILLE DE LA SYLVE 214 MA 35
34 SAINT BAUZILLE DE MONTMEL 193 OA 34
34 SAINT BAUZILLE DE PUTOIS 192 NA 33
87 SAINT BAZILE 144 AA 25
19 SAINT BAZILE DE LA ROCHE 159 EA 28
19 SAINT BAZILE DE MEYSSAC 159 EA 28
31 SAINT BEAT C 217 Z 38
12 SAINT BEAULIZE 191 KA 33
82 SAINT BEAUZEIL 173 AA 31
12 SAINT BEAUZELY C 176 JA 32
81 SAINT BEAUZILE 189 EA 33
43 SAINT BEAUZIRE 162 LA 27
63 SAINT BEAUZIRE 148 KA 25
30 SAINT BENEZET 193 PA 33
01 SAINT BENIGNE 121 SA 22
59 SAINT BENIN 18 MA 6
58 SAINT BENIN D'AZY C 118 LA 20
58 SAINT BENIN DES BOIS 102 LA 19
85 SAINT BENOIST SUR MER 125 Q 22
10 SAINT BENOIST SUR VANNE 64 MA 14
01 SAINT BENOIT 152 VA 25
04 SAINT BENOIT 198 AB 33
11 SAINT BENOIT 221 FA 37
86 SAINT BENOIT 113 Y 22
14 SAINT BENOIT D'HEBERTOT 23 X 9
81 SAINT BENOIT DE CARMAUX 189 FA 33
27 SAINT BENOIT DES OMBRES 37 Z 10
35 SAINT BENOIT DES ONDES 55 O 12
36 SAINT BENOIT DU SAULT C 131 CA 22
26 SAINT BENOIT EN DIOIS 165 UA 30
88 SAINT BENOIT LA CHIPOTTE 68 AB 14
37 SAINT BENOIT LA FORET 97 Y 19
45 SAINT BENOIT SUR LOIRE 82 GA 16
10 SAINT BENOIT SUR SEINE 64 OA 14
43 SAINT BERAIN 162 MA 28
71 SAINT BERAIN SOUS SANVIGNES 120 PA 21
71 SAINT BERAIN SUR DHEUNE 120 RA 20
01 SAINT BERNARD 136 RA 24
21 SAINT BERNARD 105 TA 19
38 SAINT BERNARD 152 WA 27
68 SAINT BERNARD 90 CB 17
73 SAINT BERON 152 WA 26
53 SAINT BERTHEVIN C 77 S 15
53 SAINT BERTHEVIN LA TANNIERE 57 S 13
31 SAINT BERTRAND DE COMMINGES 217 Z 37
72 SAINT BIEZ EN BELIN 78 X 16
22 SAINT BIHY 53 J 13
06 SAINT BLAISE 200 CB 34
74 SAINT BLAISE 139 XA 24
38 SAINT BLAISE DU BUIS 152 VA 27
67 SAINT BLAISE LA ROCHE 69 CB 13
32 SAINT BLANCARD 209 Z 36
80 SAINT BLIMONT 15 DA 6
52 SAINT BLIN C 66 UA 14
64 SAINT BOES 206 S 35
41 SAINT BOHAIRE 80 CA 17
71 SAINT BOIL 120 RA 21
54 SAINT BOINGT 68 ZA 13
01 SAINT BOIS 152 VA 25
28 SAINT BOMER 59 AA 14
61 SAINT BOMER LES FORGES 57 T 12
51 SAINT BON 63 MA 12
73 SAINT BON TARENTAISE 154 AB 27
16 SAINT BONNET 142 W 26
19 SAINT BONNET AVALOUZE 160 EA 27
87 SAINT BONNET BRIANCE 145 DA 25
87 SAINT BONNET DE BELLAC 130 AA 23
38 SAINT BONNET DE CHAVAGNE 165 TA 28
48 SAINT BONNET DE CHIRAC 176 LA 31
15 SAINT BONNET DE CONDAT 161 JA 27
71 SAINT BONNET DE CRAY 135 PA 23
03 SAINT BONNET DE FOUR 133 JA 23
71 SAINT BONNET DE JOUX C 120 QA 22
48 SAINT BONNET DE MONTAUROUX 163 NA 29
69 SAINT BONNET DE MURE 151 SA 25
03 SAINT BONNET DE ROCHEFORT 134 KA 23
30 SAINT BONNET DE SALENDRINQUE 192 NA 33
15 SAINT BONNET DE SALERS 161 HA 28
26 SAINT BONNET DE VALCLERIEUX 165 TA 28
71 SAINT BONNET DE VIEILLE VIGNE 120 PA 22
69 SAINT BONNET DES BRUYERES 136 QA 23
42 SAINT BONNET DES QUARTS 135 NA 23
30 SAINT BONNET DU GARD 193 QA 33
19 SAINT BONNET ELVERT 160 FA 28
71 SAINT BONNET EN BRESSE 121 TA 20
05 SAINT BONNET EN CHAMPSAUR C 167 XA 30
19 SAINT BONNET L'ENFANTIER 145 DA 27
19 SAINT BONNET LA RIVIERE 145 CA 27
63 SAINT BONNET LE BOURG 148 MA 27
63 SAINT BONNET LE CHASTEL 148 MA 26
42 SAINT BONNET LE CHATEAU C 149 OA 27
42 SAINT BONNET LE COURREAU 149 OA 26
43 SAINT BONNET LE FROID 164 QA 28
69 SAINT BONNET LE TRONCY 136 OA 24
63 SAINT BONNET LES ALLIER 148 LA 25
42 SAINT BONNET LES OULES 150 PA 26
19 SAINT BONNET LES TOURS DE MERLE 160 FA 28
19 SAINT BONNET PRES BORT 147 HA 26
63 SAINT BONNET PRES ORCIVAL 147 JA 25
63 SAINT BONNET PRES RIOM 134 KA 24
17 SAINT BONNET SUR GIRONDE 141 T 27
03 SAINT BONNET TRONCAIS 117 IA 21

58	SAINT BONNOT		102	LA	19
18	SAINT BOUIZE		101	JA	18
89	SAINT BRANCHER		103	OA	18
37	SAINT BRANCHS		98	AA	19
22	SAINT BRANDAN		54	J	13
30	SAINT BRES		178	PA	32
32	SAINT BRES		187	AA	34
34	SAINT BRES		193	OA	34
30	SAINT BRESSON		192	MA	33
70	SAINT BRESSON		89	ZA	16
46	SAINT BRESSOU		160	FA	30
44	SAINT BREVIN LES PINS		93	N	19
35	SAINT BRIAC SUR MER		55	M	12
16	SAINT BRICE		142	V	25
33	SAINT BRICE		156	V	30
50	SAINT BRICE		56	O	12
53	SAINT BRICE		77	U	16
61	SAINT BRICE		57	T	13
77	SAINT BRICE		63	LA	13
51	SAINT BRICE COURCELLES		42	OA	10
50	SAINT BRICE DE LANDELLES		56	R	13
35	SAINT BRICE EN COGLES	C	56	Q	13
95	SAINT BRICE SOUS FORET		40	HA	11
61	SAINT BRICE SOUS RANES		58	V	12
87	SAINT BRICE SUR VIENNE		130	AA	25
22	SAINT BRIEUC	P	54	K	13
56	SAINT BRIEUC DE MAURON		74	M	15
35	SAINT BRIEUC DES IFFS		75	O	14
17	SAINT BRIS DES BOIS		142	U	25
89	SAINT BRIS LE VINEUX		84	MA	16
58	SAINT BRISSON		103	OA	18
45	SAINT BRISSON SUR LOIRE		82	IA	17
70	SAINT BROING		106	VA	18
21	SAINT BROING LES MOINES		86	SA	17
52	SAINT BROINGT LE BOIS		87	UA	16
52	SAINT BROINGT LES FOSSES		86	TA	16
35	SAINT BROLADRE		55	P	13
38	SAINT BUEIL		152	VA	26
72	SAINT CALAIS	C	79	Z	16
53	SAINT CALAIS DU DESERT		58	V	13
72	SAINT CALEZ EN SAOSNOIS		59	Y	14
13	SAINT CANNAT		202	UA	35
03	SAINT CAPRAIS		117	IA	22
18	SAINT CAPRAIS		116	GA	20
32	SAINT CAPRAIS		209	AA	35
46	SAINT CAPRAIS		173	BA	30
33	SAINT CAPRAIS DE BLAYE		142	U	27
33	SAINT CAPRAIS DE BORDEAUX		156	U	30
47	SAINT CAPRAIS DE LERM		172	Z	32
24	SAINT CAPRAISE D'EYMET		157	Y	30
24	SAINT CAPRAISE DE LALINDE		158	Z	29
22	SAINT CARADEC		74	K	14
56	SAINT CARADEC TREGOMEL		73	H	15
22	SAINT CARNE		55	N	13
22	SAINT CARREUC		54	K	13
24	SAINT CASSIEN		172	AA	30
38	SAINT CASSIEN		152	VA	27
73	SAINT CASSIN		152	WA	26
22	SAINT CAST LE GUILDO		55	M	12
64	SAINT CASTIN		207	V	36
72	SAINT CELERIN		59	Y	15
53	SAINT CENERE		77	U	15
61	SAINT CENERI LE GEREI		58	W	13
18	SAINT CEOLS		101	IA	19
46	SAINT CERE	C	160	FA	29
74	SAINT CERGUES		139	YA	23
15	SAINT CERNIN	C	160	HA	28
46	SAINT CERNIN		174	DA	30
24	SAINT CERNIN DE L'HERM		173	BA	30
24	SAINT CERNIN DE LABARDE		157	Z	30
19	SAINT CERNIN DE LARCHE		159	CA	28
17	SAINT CESAIRE		142	U	25
30	SAINT CESAIRE DE GAUZIGNAN		193	PA	33
06	SAINT CEZAIRE SUR SIAGNE		198	AB	35
31	SAINT CEZERT		188	BA	34
23	SAINT CHABRAIS		132	GA	23
05	SAINT CHAFFREY		168	AB	29
15	SAINT CHAMANT		161	HA	28
19	SAINT CHAMANT		160	FA	28
46	SAINT CHAMARAND		173	DA	30
13	SAINT CHAMAS		201	SA	35
24	SAINT CHAMASSY		158	AA	29
42	SAINT CHAMOND	C	150	QA	26
01	SAINT CHAMP		152	WA	25
30	SAINT CHAPTES	C	193	PA	33
14	SAINT CHARLES DE PERCY		35	T	11
53	SAINT CHARLES LA FORET		77	U	16
36	SAINT CHARTIER		116	FA	21
38	SAINT CHEF		152	UA	26
46	SAINT CHELS		174	EA	31
48	SAINT CHELY D'APCHER	C	162	LA	29
12	SAINT CHELY D'AUBRAC	C	176	JA	30
51	SAINT CHERON		65	QA	12
91	SAINT CHERON	C	61	FA	13
34	SAINT CHINIAN	C	213	JA	35
80	SAINT CHRIST BRIOST		27	JA	7
31	SAINT CHRISTAUD		218	BA	37
32	SAINT CHRISTAUD		208	X	35
42	SAINT CHRISTO EN JAREZ		150	QA	26
07	SAINT CHRISTOL		164	OA	29
34	SAINT CHRISTOL		193	OA	34
84	SAINT CHRISTOL		196	VA	33
30	SAINT CHRISTOL DE RODIERES		178	QA	32
30	SAINT CHRISTOL LES ALES		193	OA	33
33	SAINT CHRISTOLY DE BLAYE		156	U	28
33	SAINT CHRISTOLY MEDOC		141	T	27
03	SAINT CHRISTOPHE		133	MA	23
16	SAINT CHRISTOPHE		130	AA	24
17	SAINT CHRISTOPHE		127	S	23
23	SAINT CHRISTOPHE		132	EA	24
28	SAINT CHRISTOPHE		60	CA	15
69	SAINT CHRISTOPHE		136	OA	23
73	SAINT CHRISTOPHE		152	WA	26
81	SAINT CHRISTOPHE		174	FA	32
86	SAINT CHRISTOPHE		113	Y	20
02	SAINT CHRISTOPHE A BERRY		27	KA	9
43	SAINT CHRISTOPHE D'ALLIER		163	NA	29
61	SAINT CHRISTOPHE DE CHAULIEU		57	T	12
33	SAINT CHRISTOPHE DE DOUBLE		157	W	28
35	SAINT CHRISTOPHE DE VALAINS		56	O	14
33	SAINT CHRISTOPHE DES BARDES		156	W	29
35	SAINT CHRISTOPHE DES BOIS		76	R	14
10	SAINT CHRISTOPHE DODINICOURT		65	QA	13
49	SAINT CHRISTOPHE DU BOIS		95	S	19
50	SAINT CHRISTOPHE DU FOC		33	O	8
72	SAINT CHRISTOPHE DU JAMBET		58	W	14
85	SAINT CHRISTOPHE DU LIGNERON		109	O	20
53	SAINT CHRISTOPHE DU LUAT		77	U	15
36	SAINT CHRISTOPHE EN BAZELLE	C	99	EA	19
36	SAINT CHRISTOPHE EN BOUCHERIE		116	GA	21
71	SAINT CHRISTOPHE EN BRESSE		121	SA	21
71	SAINT CHRISTOPHE EN BRIONNAIS		135	PA	23
72	SAINT CHRISTOPHE EN CHAMPAGNE		78	W	15
38	SAINT CHRISTOPHE EN OISANS		167	YA	29
26	SAINT CHRISTOPHE ET LE LARIS		165	TA	28
49	SAINT CHRISTOPHE LA COUPERIE		94	R	19
18	SAINT CHRISTOPHE LE CHAUDRY		116	HA	22
61	SAINT CHRISTOPHE LE JAJOLET		58	W	12
27	SAINT CHRISTOPHE SUR AVRE		37	AA	12
27	SAINT CHRISTOPHE SUR CONDE		37	Z	9
43	SAINT CHRISTOPHE SUR DOLAISON		163	NA	28
38	SAINT CHRISTOPHE SUR GUIERS		152	WA	27
37	SAINT CHRISTOPHE SUR LE NAIS		97	Y	17
79	SAINT CHRISTOPHE SUR ROC		112	V	22
12	SAINT CHRISTOPHE VALLON		175	HA	31
33	SAINT CIBARD		157	W	29
07	SAINT CIERGE LA SERRE		164	RA	29
07	SAINT CIERGE SOUS LE CHEYLARD		164	OA	29
52	SAINT CIERGUES		86	TA	16
17	SAINT CIERS CHAMPAGNE		142	V	27
33	SAINT CIERS D'ABZAC		156	V	28
33	SAINT CIERS DE CANESSE		156	T	28
17	SAINT CIERS DU TAILLON		142	T	27
16	SAINT CIERS SUR BONNIEURE		129	X	25
33	SAINT CIERS SUR GIRONDE	C	141	T	27
81	SAINT CIRGUE		190	HA	33
43	SAINT CIRGUES		162	LA	28
46	SAINT CIRGUES		160	GA	30
15	SAINT CIRGUES DE JORDANNE		161	IA	28
15	SAINT CIRGUES DE MALBERT		160	HA	28
07	SAINT CIRGUES DE PRADES		178	PA	30
07	SAINT CIRGUES EN MONTAGNE		163	OA	30
19	SAINT CIRGUES LA LOUTRE		160	FA	28
63	SAINT CIRGUES SUR COUZE		148	KA	26
82	SAINT CIRICE		187	AA	33
24	SAINT CIRQ		158	AA	29
82	SAINT CIRQ		174	DA	32
46	SAINT CIRQ LAPOPIE		174	EA	31
46	SAINT CIRQ MADELON		159	CA	29
46	SAINT CIRQ SOUILLAGUET		159	DA	30
36	SAINT CIVRAN		115	CA	22
07	SAINT CLAIR		150	RA	27
46	SAINT CLAIR		173	CA	30
82	SAINT CLAIR		173	AA	32
86	SAINT CLAIR		112	W	20
27	SAINT CLAIR D'ARCEY		37	Z	10
61	SAINT CLAIR DE HALOUZE		57	T	12
38	SAINT CLAIR DE LA TOUR		152	UA	26
38	SAINT CLAIR DU RHONE		150	RA	27
95	SAINT CLAIR SUR EPTE		39	EA	10
38	SAINT CLAIR SUR GALAURE		151	TA	27
50	SAINT CLAIR SUR L'ELLE	C	35	S	10
76	SAINT CLAIR SUR LES MONTS		24	AA	8
32	SAINT CLAR	C	187	AA	33
31	SAINT CLAR DE RIVIERE		210	BA	35
16	SAINT CLAUD	C	129	Y	25
39	SAINT CLAUDE	S	122	WA	22
41	SAINT CLAUDE DE DIRAY		115	CA	22
02	SAINT CLEMENT		29	OA	7
03	SAINT CLEMENT		135	NA	24
07	SAINT CLEMENT		164	PA	29
15	SAINT CLEMENT		161	IA	29
19	SAINT CLEMENT		145	EA	27
30	SAINT CLEMENT		193	OA	34
54	SAINT CLEMENT		68	ZA	13
89	SAINT CLEMENT		63	LA	14
08	SAINT CLEMENT A ARNES		29	QA	9
49	SAINT CLEMENT DE LA PLACE		95	T	17
63	SAINT CLEMENT DE REGNAT		133	LA	24
34	SAINT CLEMENT DE RIVIERE		192	NA	34
63	SAINT CLEMENT DE VALORGUE		149	OA	26
69	SAINT CLEMENT DE VERS		136	QA	23
17	SAINT CLEMENT DES BALEINES		125	P	23
49	SAINT CLEMENT DES LEVEES		96	V	18
69	SAINT CLEMENT LES PLACES		150	QA	25
50	SAINT CLEMENT RANCOUDRAY		57	S	12
05	SAINT CLEMENT SUR DURANCE		168	ZA	30
71	SAINT CLEMENT SUR GUYE		120	RA	21
69	SAINT CLEMENT SUR VALSONNE		136	QA	24
79	SAINT CLEMENTIN		111	U	20
22	SAINT CLET		53	I	12
92	SAINT CLOUD	C	40	GA	11
28	SAINT CLOUD EN DUNOIS		80	DA	15
47	SAINT COLOMB DE LAUZUN		172	Y	30
44	SAINT COLOMBAN		110	P	20
73	SAINT COLOMBAN DES VILLARDS		153	YA	27
33	SAINT COME		170	V	31
12	SAINT COME D'OLT		176	JA	31
14	SAINT COME DE FRESNE		35	T	9
50	SAINT COME DU MONT		34	R	9
30	SAINT COME ET MARUEJOLS		193	PA	34
56	SAINT CONGARD		74	M	16
22	SAINT CONNAN		53	J	13
22	SAINT CONNEC		73	J	14
15	SAINT CONSTANT		175	GA	30
14	SAINT CONTEST		36	U	10
72	SAINT CORNEILLE		78	Y	15
61	SAINT CORNIER DES LANDES		57	T	12
68	SAINT COSME		90	BB	17
72	SAINT COSME EN VAIRAIS		59	Y	14
11	SAINT COUAT D'AUDE		212	IA	36
11	SAINT COUAT DU RAZES		221	FA	37
29	SAINT COULITZ		72	E	14
35	SAINT COULOMB		55	O	12
16	SAINT COUTANT		129	Y	24
79	SAINT COUTANT		129	W	23
17	SAINT COUTANT LE GRAND		127	T	24
32	SAINT CREAC		187	AA	33
65	SAINT CREAC		216	W	37
05	SAINT CREPIN		168	AB	30
17	SAINT CREPIN		127	T	24
60	SAINT CREPIN AUX BOIS		27	JA	9
24	SAINT CREPIN D'AUBEROCHE		158	AA	28
24	SAINT CREPIN DE RICHEMONT		144	Z	27
24	SAINT CREPIN ET CARLUCET		159	CA	29
60	SAINT CREPIN IBOUVILLERS		39	FA	10
76	SAINT CRESPIN		24	BA	7
49	SAINT CRESPIN SUR MOINE		110	R	19
32	SAINT CRICQ		187	BA	34
40	SAINT CRICQ CHALOSSE		184	T	34
40	SAINT CRICQ DU GAVE		206	S	35
40	SAINT CRICQ VILLENEUVE		184	U	33
16	SAINT CYBARDEAUX		143	W	25
24	SAINT CYBRANET		158	BA	29
19	SAINT CYPRIEN		159	CA	27
24	SAINT CYPRIEN	C	158	BA	29
42	SAINT CYPRIEN		149	PA	26
46	SAINT CYPRIEN		173	CA	32
66	SAINT CYPRIEN		224	JA	39
12	SAINT CYPRIEN SUR DOURDOU		175	HA	30
07	SAINT CYR		150	RA	27
50	SAINT CYR		33	Q	9
71	SAINT CYR		121	SA	21
86	SAINT CYR		113	Y	21
87	SAINT CYR		144	AA	25
69	SAINT CYR AU MONT D'OR		151	SA	25
42	SAINT CYR DE FAVIERES		135	OA	24
27	SAINT CYR DE SALERNE		37	Z	10
42	SAINT CYR DE VALORGES		136	PA	25
85	SAINT CYR DES GATS		111	S	22
50	SAINT CYR DU BAILLEUL		57	S	13
17	SAINT CYR DU DORET		127	S	23
41	SAINT CYR DU GAULT		79	BA	17
14	SAINT CYR DU RONCERAY		37	Y	10
95	SAINT CYR EN ARTHIES		39	EA	10
49	SAINT CYR EN BOURG		96	W	19
53	SAINT CYR EN PAIL		58	V	13
85	SAINT CYR EN TALMONDAIS		125	Q	22
45	SAINT CYR EN VAL		81	FA	16
78	SAINT CYR L'ECOLE	C	39	FA	12
27	SAINT CYR LA CAMPAGNE		38	BA	10
79	SAINT CYR LA LANDE		96	W	19
91	SAINT CYR LA RIVIERE		61	GA	14
19	SAINT CYR LA ROCHE		159	CA	27
61	SAINT CYR LA ROSIERE		59	Z	14
69	SAINT CYR LE CHATOUX		136	QA	24
53	SAINT CYR LE GRAVELAIS		76	S	15
24	SAINT CYR LES CHAMPAGNES		145	CA	27
89	SAINT CYR LES COLONS		84	NA	16
42	SAINT CYR LES VIGNES		150	PA	26
39	SAINT CYR MONTMALIN		122	WA	20
91	SAINT CYR SOUS DOURDAN		61	FA	13
69	SAINT CYR SUR LE RHONE		151	SA	26
37	SAINT CYR SUR LOIRE	C	98	Z	18
01	SAINT CYR SUR MENTHON		137	SA	23
83	SAINT CYR SUR MER		202	WA	37
77	SAINT CYR SUR MORIN		41	KA	11
36	SAINT CYRAN DU JAMBOT		114	BA	20
06	SAINT DALMAS LE SELVAGE		182	BB	32
46	SAINT DAUNES		173	CA	31
11	SAINT DENIS		212	GA	36
30	SAINT DENIS		178	PA	32
89	SAINT DENIS		63	LA	14
93	SAINT DENIS	S	40	HA	11
46	SAINT DENIS CATUS		173	CA	30
63	SAINT DENIS COMBARNAZAT		133	LA	24
76	SAINT DENIS D'ACLON		24	AA	7
53	SAINT DENIS D'ANJOU		77	U	16
27	SAINT DENIS D'AUGERONS		37	Y	11
28	SAINT DENIS D'AUTHOU		60	BA	14
17	SAINT DENIS D'OLERON		126	Q	24
72	SAINT DENIS D'ORQUES		78	V	15
42	SAINT DENIS DE CABANNE		135	PA	23
53	SAINT DENIS DE GASTINES		57	S	14
36	SAINT DENIS DE JOUHET		116	EA	22
45	SAINT DENIS DE L'HOTEL		81	GA	16
14	SAINT DENIS DE MAILLOC		37	Y	10
14	SAINT DENIS DE MERE		35	U	11
18	SAINT DENIS DE PALIN		117	HA	20
33	SAINT DENIS DE PILE		156	V	29
71	SAINT DENIS DE VAUX		120	RA	21
61	SAINT DENIS DE VILLENETTE		57	U	13
72	SAINT DENIS DES COUDRAIS		59	Y	14
27	SAINT DENIS DES MONTS		37	AA	10
87	SAINT DENIS DES MURS		145	DA	25
28	SAINT DENIS DES PUITS		60	BA	13
27	SAINT DENIS DU BEHELAN		38	AA	11
53	SAINT DENIS DU MAINE		77	U	15
85	SAINT DENIS DU PAYRE		125	R	22
17	SAINT DENIS DU PIN		128	U	24
01	SAINT DENIS EN BUGEY		137	UA	24
48	SAINT DENIS EN MARGERIDE		162	MA	30
45	SAINT DENIS EN VAL		81	FA	16
85	SAINT DENIS LA CHEVASSE		110	Q	20
27	SAINT DENIS LE FERMENT		25	EA	9
50	SAINT DENIS LE GAST		56	O	11
76	SAINT DENIS LE THIBOULT		25	CA	9
50	SAINT DENIS LE VETU		34	Q	11
01	SAINT DENIS LES BOURG		137	TA	23
46	SAINT DENIS LES MARTEL		159	DA	29
28	SAINT DENIS LES PONTS		80	CA	15
77	SAINT DENIS LES REBAIS		41	KA	11
14	SAINT DENIS MAISONCELLES		35	S	11
42	SAINT DENIS SUR COISE		150	OA	26
61	SAINT DENIS SUR HUISNE		59	Y	13
41	SAINT DENIS SUR LOIRE		80	CA	17
89	SAINT DENIS SUR OUANNE		83	KA	16
61	SAINT DENIS SUR SARTHON		58	W	13
76	SAINT DENIS SUR SCIE		24	BA	8
60	SAINT DENISCOURT		25	EA	8
62	SAINT DENOEUX		16	FA	4
22	SAINT DENOUAL		55	M	13
29	SAINT DERRIEN		52	E	13
71	SAINT DESERT		120	RA	21
14	SAINT DESIR		36	X	10
07	SAINT DESIRAT		150	RA	27
03	SAINT DESIRE		116	HA	22
30	SAINT DEZERY		193	PA	33
21	SAINT DIDIER		103	PA	18
35	SAINT DIDIER		76	O	15
39	SAINT DIDIER		122	VA	21
58	SAINT DIDIER		103	MA	18
84	SAINT DIDIER		195	TA	33
69	SAINT DIDIER AU MONT D'OR		150	RA	25
43	SAINT DIDIER D'ALLIER		163	NA	29
01	SAINT DIDIER D'AUSSIAT		137	TA	23
38	SAINT DIDIER DE BIZONNES		152	UA	26
01	SAINT DIDIER DE FORMANS		136	RA	24
38	SAINT DIDIER DE LA TOUR		152	UA	26
27	SAINT DIDIER DES BOIS		38	BA	10
71	SAINT DIDIER EN BRESSE		121	TA	20
71	SAINT DIDIER EN BRIONNAIS		135	OA	23
03	SAINT DIDIER EN DONJON		135	NA	22
43	SAINT DIDIER EN VELAY	C	150	PA	27
03	SAINT DIDIER LA FORET		133	LA	23
07	SAINT DIDIER SOUS AUBENAS		178	OA	30
61	SAINT DIDIER SOUS ECOUVES		58	W	13
69	SAINT DIDIER SOUS RIVERIE		150	RA	26
71	SAINT DIDIER SUR ARROUX		119	OA	20
69	SAINT DIDIER SUR BEAUJEU		136	OA	23
01	SAINT DIDIER SUR CHALARONNE		137	SA	23
43	SAINT DIDIER SUR DOULON		148	MA	27
42	SAINT DIDIER SUR ROCHEFORT		149	NA	25
88	SAINT DIE	S	69	BB	14
63	SAINT DIER D'AUVERGNE	C	148	MA	26
63	SAINT DIERY		147	KA	26
30	SAINT DIONIZY		193	PA	34
05	SAINT DISDIER		167	WA	30
29	SAINT DIVY		51	D	13
17	SAINT DIZANT DU BOIS		142	U	27
17	SAINT DIZANT DU GUA		141	T	27
52	SAINT DIZIER	S	66	SA	12
26	SAINT DIZIER EN DIOIS		180	UA	31
90	SAINT DIZIER L'EVEQUE		90	BB	17
23	SAINT DIZIER LA TOUR		132	GA	23
23	SAINT DIZIER LES DOMAINES		132	FA	23
23	SAINT DIZIER LEYRENNE		131	EA	24
56	SAINT DOLAY		93	N	17
23	SAINT DOMET		132	GA	24
35	SAINT DOMINEUC		55	O	14
22	SAINT DONAN		54	J	13
63	SAINT DONAT		147	IA	26
26	SAINT DONAT SUR L'HERBASSE	C	165	SA	28
64	SAINT DOS		206	S	35
18	SAINT DOULCHARD	C	100	GA	19
34	SAINT DREZERY		193	OA	34
41	SAINT DYE SUR LOIRE		80	DA	17
50	SAINT EBREMOND DE BONFOSSE		34	R	10
71	SAINT EDMOND		135	PA	23
38	SAINT EGREVE	C	152	VA	27
27	SAINT ELIER		38	AA	11
28	SAINT ELIPH		60	BA	13
32	SAINT ELIX		209	AA	35
31	SAINT ELIX LE CHATEAU		210	BA	36
31	SAINT ELIX SEGLAN		217	AA	37
32	SAINT ELIX THEUX		208	Y	35
53	SAINT ELLIER DU MAINE		56	R	13
61	SAINT ELLIER LES BOIS		58	W	13
01	SAINT ELOI		137	TA	24
23	SAINT ELOI		132	EA	24
58	SAINT ELOI		118	KA	20
27	SAINT ELOI DE FOURQUES		37	AA	10
29	SAINT ELOY		52	E	14
03	SAINT ELOY D'ALLIER		116	HA	22
18	SAINT ELOY DE GY		100	GA	19
63	SAINT ELOY LA GLACIERE		148	MA	26
63	SAINT ELOY LES MINES		133	JA	23
19	SAINT ELOY LES TUILERIES		145	CA	27
28	SAINT EMAN		60	CA	14
71	SAINT EMILAND		120	QA	20
33	SAINT EMILION		156	V	29
03	SAINT ENNEMOND		118	LA	21
37	SAINT EPAIN		97	Z	19
57	SAINT EPVRE		47	ZA	11
35	SAINT ERBLON		75	P	15
53	SAINT ERBLON		76	R	16
02	SAINT ERME OUTRE ET RAMECOURT		28	NA	8
91	SAINT ESCOBILLE		61	FA	13
64	SAINT ESTEBEN		206	R	36
24	SAINT ESTEPHE		144	Z	26
33	SAINT ESTEPHE		141	T	27
66	SAINT ESTEVE	C	224	JA	39
13	SAINT ESTEVE JANSON		196	UA	34
42	SAINT ETIENNE	P	150	PA	27
08	SAINT ETIENNE A ARNES		29	QA	9
62	SAINT ETIENNE AU MONT		7	DA	3
51	SAINT ETIENNE AU TEMPLE		43	QA	11
19	SAINT ETIENNE AUX CLOS		146	HA	26
15	SAINT ETIENNE CANTALES		160	GA	29
34	SAINT ETIENNE D'ALBAGNAN		213	JA	35
40	SAINT ETIENNE D'ORTHE		183	R	35
64	SAINT ETIENNE DE BAIGORRY	C	205	O	37
07	SAINT ETIENNE DE BOULOGNE		164	QA	30
85	SAINT ETIENNE DE BRILLOUET		111	S	22
15	SAINT ETIENNE DE CARLAT		161	IA	29
37	SAINT ETIENNE DE CHIGNY		97	Y	18
15	SAINT ETIENNE DE CHOMEIL		147	IA	27
38	SAINT ETIENNE DE CROSSEY		152	VA	27
73	SAINT ETIENNE DE CUINES		153	YA	27
07	SAINT ETIENNE DE FONTBELLON		178	OA	30
47	SAINT ETIENNE DE FOURGERES		172	Z	31
23	SAINT ETIENNE DE FURSAC		131	DA	23
34	SAINT ETIENNE DE GOURGAS		192	LA	34
30	SAINT ETIENNE DE L'OLM		193	PA	33
33	SAINT ETIENNE DE LISSE		156	W	29
07	SAINT ETIENNE DE LUGDARES	C	178	OA	30
15	SAINT ETIENNE DE MAURS		160	GA	30
44	SAINT ETIENNE DE MER MORTE		109	O	20
44	SAINT ETIENNE DE MONTLUC	C	93	O	18
24	SAINT ETIENNE DE PUYCORBIER		157	Y	28
07	SAINT ETIENNE DE SERRE		164	QA	29
38	SAINT ETIENNE DE ST GEOIRS	C	152	UA	27
06	SAINT ETIENNE DE TINEE	C	182	BB	32
82	SAINT ETIENNE DE TULMONT		188	DA	33
07	SAINT ETIENNE DE VALOUX		150	RA	27
03	SAINT ETIENNE DE VICQ		133	MA	23
47	SAINT ETIENNE DE VILLEREAL		172	AA	30
63	SAINT ETIENNE DES CHAMPS		147	IA	25
41	SAINT ETIENNE DES GUERETS		80	BA	17
69	SAINT ETIENNE DES OULLIERES		136	RA	24
30	SAINT ETIENNE DES SORTS		179	RA	32
01	SAINT ETIENNE DU BOIS		137	UA	23
85	SAINT ETIENNE DU BOIS		110	P	20
13	SAINT ETIENNE DU GRES		195	RA	34
22	SAINT ETIENNE DU GUE DE L'ISLE		74	K	15
76	SAINT ETIENNE DU ROUVRAY	C	24	BA	9
48	SAINT ETIENNE DU VALDONNEZ		177	MA	31
27	SAINT ETIENNE DU VAUVRAY		38	CA	10
43	SAINT ETIENNE DU VIGAN		163	NA	30
71	SAINT ETIENNE EN BRESSE		121	TA	21
35	SAINT ETIENNE EN COGLES		56	Q	13
05	SAINT ETIENNE EN DEVOLUY	C	167	XA	30
34	SAINT ETIENNE ESTRECHOUX		191	KA	34
27	SAINT ETIENNE L'ALLIER		37	Z	10
79	SAINT ETIENNE LA CIGOGNE		128	U	24
19	SAINT ETIENNE LA GENESTE		146	GA	26
14	SAINT ETIENNE LA THILLAYE		36	X	9
69	SAINT ETIENNE LA VARENNE		136	RA	24
43	SAINT ETIENNE LARDEYROL		163	OA	28
05	SAINT ETIENNE LE LAUS		181	YA	31
42	SAINT ETIENNE LE MOLARD		149	OA	25
04	SAINT ETIENNE LES ORGUES	C	197	WA	33
88	SAINT ETIENNE LES REMIREMONT		89	AB	15
60	SAINT ETIENNE ROILAYE		27	KA	9
27	SAINT ETIENNE SOUS BAILLEUL		38	CA	10
10	SAINT ETIENNE SOUS BARBUISE		64	OA	13
43	SAINT ETIENNE SUR BLESLE		148	KA	27
01	SAINT ETIENNE SUR CHALARONNE		137	SA	23
01	SAINT ETIENNE SUR REYSSOUZE		137	SA	22
51	SAINT ETIENNE SUR SUIPPE		29	OA	9
63	SAINT ETIENNE SUR USSON		148	LA	26
48	SAINT ETIENNE VALLEE FRANCAISE		177	NA	32
02	SAINT EUGENE		41	MA	11
17	SAINT EUGENE		142	V	26
71	SAINT EUGENE		120	PA	21
51	SAINT EULIEN		44	SA	12
51	SAINT EUPHRAISE ET CLAIRIZET		42	NA	10
21	SAINT EUPHRONE		104	QA	18
71	SAINT EUSEBE		120	QA	21
74	SAINT EUSEBE		139	XA	24
05	SAINT EUSEBE EN CHAMPSAUR		167	XA	30
74	SAINT EUSTACHE		139	XA	25
76	SAINT EUSTACHE LA FORET		23	Y	8
16	SAINT EUTROPE		143	X	27
47	SAINT EUTROPE DE BORN		172	Z	30
29	SAINT EVARZEC		72	E	15
61	SAINT EVROULT DE MONTFORT		37	Y	12
61	SAINT EVROULT NOTRE DAME DU BOIS		37	Y	12
33	SAINT EXUPERY		171	W	30
19	SAINT EXUPERY LES ROCHES		146	HA	26
89	SAINT FARGEAU	C	83	KA	17
77	SAINT FARGEAU PONTHIERRY		62	HA	13
03	SAINT FARGEOL		133	IA	23
64	SAINT FAUST		207	U	36
07	SAINT FELICIEN	C	164	RA	28
66	SAINT FELIU D'AMONT		224	IA	39
66	SAINT FELIU D'AVALL		224	IA	39
03	SAINT FELIX		133	MA	23
16	SAINT FELIX		143	W	27
17	SAINT FELIX		127	T	24
46	SAINT FELIX		175	GA	30
60	SAINT FELIX		26	GA	9
74	SAINT FELIX		139	XA	25
24	SAINT FELIX DE BOURDEILLES		143	Z	27
33	SAINT FELIX DE FONCAUDE		171	W	30
34	SAINT FELIX DE L'HERAS		191	LA	34
34	SAINT FELIX DE LODEZ		192	MA	34
12	SAINT FELIX DE LUNEL		175	HA	30
30	SAINT FELIX DE PALLIERES		193	OA	33
24	SAINT FELIX DE REILLAC ET MORTEMART		158	AA	28
09	SAINT FELIX DE RIEUTORD		219	EA	37
12	SAINT FELIX DE SORGUES		191	JA	33
09	SAINT FELIX DE TOURNEGAT		219	EA	37
24	SAINT FELIX DE VILLADEIX		158	Z	29
31	SAINT FELIX LAURAGAIS		211	FA	35
08	SAINT FERGEUX		29	PA	8
70	SAINT FERJEUX		89	ZA	17
33	SAINT FERME		171	W	30
31	SAINT FERREOL		209	Z	36
74	SAINT FERREOL		153	YA	25
43	SAINT FERREOL D'AUROURE		149	PA	27
63	SAINT FERREOL DES COTES		149	NA	26
26	SAINT FERREOL TRENTE PAS		180	TA	31
11	SAINT FERRIOL		221	GA	38
22	SAINT FIACRE		53	I	13
77	SAINT FIACRE		41	JA	11
44	SAINT FIACRE SUR MAINE		94	Q	19
23	SAINT FIEL		132	FA	23
05	SAINT FIRMIN	C	167	XA	29
54	SAINT FIRMIN		68	XA	13
58	SAINT FIRMIN		102	LA	19
71	SAINT FIRMIN		120	OA	20
45	SAINT FIRMIN DES BOIS		82	JA	15
41	SAINT FIRMIN DES PRES		80	BA	16
45	SAINT FIRMIN SUR LOIRE		82	IA	17
10	SAINT FLAVY		64	NA	13
2B	SAINT FLORENT		226	MB	39
45	SAINT FLORENT		82	HA	17
85	SAINT FLORENT DES BOIS		110	Q	21
49	SAINT FLORENT LE VIEIL	C	95	S	18
30	SAINT FLORENT SUR AUZONNET		178	OA	32
18	SAINT FLORENT SUR CHER		116	GA	20
36	SAINT FLORENTIN		99	EA	19
89	SAINT FLORENTIN	C	84	NA	15
63	SAINT FLORET		148	KA	26
62	SAINT FLORIS		8	IA	3
15	SAINT FLOUR	S	162	KA	28
63	SAINT FLOUR		148	MA	25
48	SAINT FLOUR DE MERCOIRE		163	NA	30
37	SAINT FLOVIER		114	BA	20
50	SAINT FLOXEL		33	Q	9
62	SAINT FOLQUIN		7	FA	2
69	SAINT FONS	C	151	SA	25
71	SAINT FORGEOT		120	PA	20
78	SAINT FORGET		39	FA	12
69	SAINT FORGEUX		136	OA	25
42	SAINT FORGEUX LESPINASSE		135	OA	24
53	SAINT FORT		77	T	16
17	SAINT FORT SUR GIRONDE		141	T	26
16	SAINT FORT SUR LE NE		142	V	26
07	SAINT FORTUNAT SUR EYRIEUX		164	RA	29
16	SAINT FRAIGNE		128	W	24
61	SAINT FRAIMBAULT		57	T	13
53	SAINT FRAIMBAULT DE PRIERES		57	U	14
31	SAINT FRAJOU		209	AA	36
73	SAINT FRANC		152	WA	26
58	SAINT FRANCHY		102	MA	19
73	SAINT FRANCOIS DE SALES		153	XA	25
57	SAINT FRANCOIS LACROIX		47	ZA	9
73	SAINT FRANCOIS LONGCHAMP		153	YA	27
29	SAINT FREGANT		51	D	12
19	SAINT FREJOUX		146	HA	26
48	SAINT FREZAL D'ALBUGES		177	NA	30
48	SAINT FREZAL DE VENTALON		177	NA	32
11	SAINT FRICHOUX		212	IA	36
23	SAINT FRION		132	GA	25
50	SAINT FROMOND		34	R	10
16	SAINT FRONT		129	X	25
43	SAINT FRONT		163	OA	29
24	SAINT FRONT D'ALEMPS		144	AA	27
24	SAINT FRONT DE PRADOUX		157	Y	28
24	SAINT FRONT LA RIVIERE		144	Z	26
47	SAINT FRONT SUR LEMANCE		173	AA	30
24	SAINT FRONT SUR NIZONNE		144	Z	26
17	SAINT FROULT		126	R	24
85	SAINT FULGENT	C	110	R	20
61	SAINT FULGENT DES ORMES		59	Y	14
80	SAINT FUSCIEN		26	GA	7
14	SAINT GABRIEL BRECY		35	U	9
48	SAINT GAL		177	LA	30

63 SAINT GAL SUR SIOULE 133 JA 24
42 SAINT GALMIER C 150 PA 26
70 SAINT GAND 88 WA 17
35 SAINT GANTON 75 O 16
14 SAINT GATIEN DES BOIS 23 X 9
31 SAINT GAUDENS S 217 Z 37
86 SAINT GAUDENT 129 X 24
11 SAINT GAUDERIC 221 FA 37
36 SAINT GAULTIER C 115 CA 21
81 SAINT GAUZENS 189 EA 34
40 SAINT GEIN 185 V 34
79 SAINT GELAIS 128 U 22
22 SAINT GELVEN 73 I 14
34 SAINT GELY DU FESC 192 NA 34
79 SAINT GENARD 128 W 23
87 SAINT GENCE 130 BA 24
79 SAINT GENEROUX 112 W 20
63 SAINT GENES CHAMPANELLE 147 KA 25
63 SAINT GENES CHAMPESPE 147 IA 26
33 SAINT GENES DE BLAYE 156 T 28
33 SAINT GENES DE CASTILLON 156 W 29
33 SAINT GENES DE FRONSAC 156 V 28
33 SAINT GENES DE LOMBAUD 156 V 30
63 SAINT GENES DU RETZ 134 KA 24
63 SAINT GENES LA TOURETTE 148 MA 26
03 SAINT GENEST 133 IA 23
88 SAINT GENEST 68 ZA 14
86 SAINT GENEST D'AMBIERE 113 Y 20
07 SAINT GENEST DE BEAUZON 178 PA 31
81 SAINT GENEST DE CONTEST 190 GA 34
07 SAINT GENEST LACHAMP 164 QA 29
42 SAINT GENEST LERPT 150 PA 26
42 SAINT GENEST MALIFAUX C 150 QA 27
87 SAINT GENEST SUR ROSELLE 145 CA 25
43 SAINT GENEYS
PRES ST PAULIEN 163 NA 28
02 SAINT GENGOULPH 41 LA 10
71 SAINT GENGOUX DE SCISSE 120 RA 22
71 SAINT GENGOUX
LE NATIONAL C 120 RA 21
24 SAINT GENIES 159 CA 29
31 SAINT GENIES BELLEVUE 188 DA 34
30 SAINT GENIES DE COMOLAS 195 RA 33
34 SAINT GENIES DE FONTEDIT 213 KA 35
30 SAINT GENIES DE MALGOIRES 193 PA 33
34 SAINT GENIES DE VARENSAL 191 JA 34
34 SAINT GENIES
DES MOURGUES 193 OA 34
04 SAINT GENIEZ 181 XA 32
12 SAINT GENIEZ D'OLT C 176 JA 31
19 SAINT GENIEZ O MERLE 160 FA 28
05 SAINT GENIS 181 WA 31
16 SAINT GENIS D'HIERSAC 143 W 25
17 SAINT GENIS DE SAINTONGE C 142 U 26
66 SAINT GENIS DES FONTAINES 224 JA 39
33 SAINT GENIS DU BOIS 156 V 30
69 SAINT GENIS L'ARGENTIERE 150 OA 25
69 SAINT GENIS LAVAL C 150 RA 25
69 SAINT GENIS LES OLLIERES 150 RA 25
01 SAINT GENIS POUILLY 139 XA 23
01 SAINT GENIS SUR MENTHON 137 SA 23
73 SAINT GENIX SUR GUIERS C 152 VA 26
36 SAINT GENOU 115 CA 20
37 SAINT GENOUPH 97 Z 18
38 SAINT GEOIRE EN VALDAINE C 152 VA 27
38 SAINT GEOIRS 152 UA 27
15 SAINT GEORGES 162 KA 28
16 SAINT GEORGES 129 X 24
32 SAINT GEORGES 187 AA 34
47 SAINT GEORGES 173 AA 31
57 SAINT GEORGES 69 BB 12
62 SAINT GEORGES 16 FA 5
82 SAINT GEORGES 174 DA 32
17 SAINT GEORGES ANTIGNAC 142 U 26
25 SAINT GEORGES ARMONT 107 ZA 18
24 SAINT GEORGES BLANCANEIX 157 Y 29
53 SAINT GEORGES BUTTAVENT 57 T 14
61 SAINT GEORGES D'ANNEBECQ 58 V 12
14 SAINT GEORGES D'AUNAY 35 T 11
43 SAINT GEORGES D'AURAC 162 MA 28
50 SAINT GEORGES D'ELLE 35 S 10
38 SAINT GEORGES
D'ESPERANCHE 151 TA 26
17 SAINT GEORGES D'OLERON 126 Q 24
34 SAINT GEORGES D'ORQUES 214 NA 35
42 SAINT GEORGES DE BAROILLE 135 OA 25
50 SAINT GEORGES DE BOHON 34 R 10
35 SAINT GEORGES DE CHESNE 76 Q 14
38 SAINT GEORGES
DE COMMIERS 166 WA 28
17 SAINT GEORGES DE DIDONNE 141 R 26
35 SAINT GEORGES
DE GREHAIGNE 56 P 13
72 SAINT GEORGES DE LA COUEE 79 Z 16
14 SAINT GEORGES DE LA RIVIERE 33 O 9
48 SAINT GEORGES DE LEVEJAC 176 KA 32
50 SAINT GEORGES DE LIVOYE 56 R 12
17 SAINT GEORGES
DE LONGUEPIERRE 128 U 24
12 SAINT GEORGES DE LUZENCON 191 JA 33
63 SAINT GEORGES DE MONS 133 JA 24
85 SAINT GEORGES DE MONTAIGU 110 Q 20
24 SAINT GEORGES
DE MONTCLARD 158 Z 29
79 SAINT GEORGES DE NOISNE 112 V 22
85 SAINT GEORGES
DE POINTINDOUX 110 P 21
18 SAINT GEORGES DE POISIEUX 117 HA 21
35 SAINT GEORGES
DE REINTEMBAULT 56 R 13
69 SAINT GEORGES DE RENEINS 136 RA 24
79 SAINT GEORGES DE REX 127 T 23
50 SAINT GEORGES DE ROUELLEY 57 T 13
17 SAINT GEORGES DES AGOUTS 141 T 27
17 SAINT GEORGES DES COTEAUX 141 T 25
49 SAINT GEORGES DES GARDES 95 T 19
61 SAINT GEORGES
DES GROSEILLERS 57 U 12
73 SAINT GEORGES
DES HURTIERES 153 YA 26
49 SAINT GEORGES
DES SEPT VOIES 96 V 18
17 SAINT GEORGES DU BOIS 127 T 23
49 SAINT GEORGES DU BOIS 96 V 17
72 SAINT GEORGES DU BOIS 78 W 15
27 SAINT GEORGES DU MESNIL 37 Z 10
72 SAINT GEORGES DU ROSAY 59 Y 14
27 SAINT GEORGES DU VIEVRE C 37 Z 10
14 SAINT GEORGES EN AUGE 36 W 11
42 SAINT GEORGES EN COUZAN C 149 OA 25
42 SAINT GEORGES
HAUTE VILLE 149 OA 26
23 SAINT GEORGES LA POUGE 132 FA 24
43 SAINT GEORGES LAGRICOL 149 NA 27
53 SAINT GEORGES LE FLECHARD 77 U 15
72 SAINT GEORGES LE GAULTIER 58 W 14
86 SAINT GEORGES
LES BAILLARGEAUX C 113 Y 21
07 SAINT GEORGES LES BAINS 164 RA 29
87 SAINT GEORGES LES LANDES 131 CA 23
50 SAINT GEORGES MONTCOCQ 34 R 10
27 SAINT GEORGES MOTEL 38 CA 12
23 SAINT GEORGES NIGREMONT 146 GA 25
63 SAINT GEORGES SUR ALLIER 148 LA 25
36 SAINT GEORGES SUR ARNON 116 FA 20
89 SAINT GEORGES SUR BAULCHE 83 MA 16
41 SAINT GEORGES SUR CHER 98 BA 18
53 SAINT GEORGES SUR ERVE 78 V 14
28 SAINT GEORGES SUR EURE 60 CA 13
76 SAINT GEORGES SUR FONTAINE 24 BA 8
59 SAINT GEORGES SUR L'AA 8 GA 2
18 SAINT GEORGES SUR LA PREE 100 FA 19
49 SAINT GEORGES SUR LAYON 96 U 19
49 SAINT GEORGES SUR LOIRE C 95 T 18
18 SAINT GEORGES
SUR MOULON 100 HA 19
01 SAINT GEORGES SUR RENON 137 SA 24
40 SAINT GEOURS D'AURIBAT 184 S 34
40 SAINT GEOURS DE MAREMNE 183 R 34
56 SAINT GERAND 73 J 15
03 SAINT GERAND DE VAUX 134 LA 22
03 SAINT GERAND LE PUY 133 MA 23
47 SAINT GERAUD 171 X 30
24 SAINT GERAUD DE CORPS 157 X 29
44 SAINT GEREON 94 R 18
07 SAINT GERMAIN 178 OA 30
10 SAINT GERMAIN 64 OA 14
54 SAINT GERMAIN 68 YA 13
70 SAINT GERMAIN 89 ZA 17
86 SAINT GERMAIN 114 AA 22
69 SAINT GERMAIN AU MONT D'OR 136 RA 25
23 SAINT GERMAIN BEAUPRE 131 DA 23
58 SAINT GERMAIN CHASSENAY 118 LA 21
53 SAINT GERMAIN D'ANXURE 57 T 14
72 SAINT GERMAIN D'ARCE 78 X 17
61 SAINT GERMAIN D'AUNAY 37 Y 11
14 SAINT GERMAIN D'ECTOT 35 T 10
50 SAINT GERMAIN D'ELLE 35 S 10
33 SAINT GERMAIN D'ESTEUIL 141 S 27
76 SAINT GERMAIN D'ETABLES 24 BA 7
24 SAINT GERMAIN DE BELVES 158 BA 29
48 SAINT GERMAIN
DE CALBERTE C 177 NA 32
61 SAINT GERMAIN
DE CLAIREFEUILLE 37 X 12
16 SAINT GERMAIN
DE CONFOLENS 130 Z 24
53 SAINT GERMAIN DE COULAMER 58 V 14
27 SAINT GERMAIN DE FRESNEY 38 CA 11
33 SAINT GERMAIN DE GRAVE 170 V 30
01 SAINT GERMAIN DE JOUX 138 WA 23
61 SAINT GERMAIN DE LA COUDRE 59 Z 14
78 SAINT GERMAIN DE LA GRANGE 39 FA 11
33 SAINT GERMAIN DE LA RIVIERE 156 V 29
14 SAINT GERMAIN DE LIVET 36 X 10
79 SAINT GERMAIN
DE LONGUE CHAUME 112 V 21
17 SAINT GERMAIN DE LUSIGNAN 142 U 27
17 SAINT GERMAIN
DE MARENCENNES 127 S 24
61 SAINT GERMAIN DE MARTIGNY 59 Y 13
21 SAINT GERMAIN DE MODEON 103 PA 18
16 SAINT GERMAIN DE MONTBRON 143 Y 26
14 SAINT GERMAIN
DE MONTGOMMERY 36 X 11
27 SAINT GERMAIN DE PASQUIER 38 BA 10
85 SAINT GERMAIN DE PRINCAY 111 S 21
03 SAINT GERMAIN DE SALLES 134 KA 23
14 SAINT GERMAIN DE TALLEVENDE
LA LANDE VAUMONT 57 S 12
50 SAINT GERMAIN
DE TOURNEBUT 33 Q 8
50 SAINT GERMAIN
DE VARREVILLE 33 R 9
17 SAINT GERMAIN DE VIBRAC 142 V 27
27 SAINT GERMAIN DES ANGLES 38 BA 10
18 SAINT GERMAIN DES BOIS 117 HA 20
58 SAINT GERMAIN DES BOIS 102 MA 18
89 SAINT GERMAIN DES CHAMPS 103 OA 18
76 SAINT GERMAIN
DES ESSOURTS 24 CA 8
03 SAINT GERMAIN DES FOSSES 133 LA 23
61 SAINT GERMAIN DES GROIS 59 AA 13
24 SAINT GERMAIN DES PRES 144 AA 27
45 SAINT GERMAIN DES PRES 82 JA 15
49 SAINT GERMAIN DES PRES 95 S 18
81 SAINT GERMAIN DES PRES 211 FA 35
50 SAINT GERMAIN DES VAUX 33 O 8
46 SAINT GERMAIN DU BEL AIR C 173 DA 30
71 SAINT GERMAIN DU BOIS C 121 UA 21
61 SAINT GERMAIN DU CORBEIS 58 W 13
14 SAINT GERMAIN DU CRIOULT 35 T 11
14 SAINT GERMAIN DU PERT 34 R 9
35 SAINT GERMAIN DU PINEL 76 R 15
71 SAINT GERMAIN DU PLAIN C 121 SA 21
33 SAINT GERMAIN DU PUCH 156 V 29
18 SAINT GERMAIN DU PUY 101 HA 19
24 SAINT GERMAIN
DU SALEMBRE 157 Y 28
17 SAINT GERMAIN DU SEUDRE 141 T 26
48 SAINT GERMAIN DU TEIL C 176 KA 31
71 SAINT GERMAIN
EN BRIONNAIS 135 PA 23
35 SAINT GERMAIN EN COGLES 56 R 13
78 SAINT GERMAIN EN LAYE S 39 FA 11
39 SAINT GERMAIN
EN MONTAGNE 123 XA 21
24 SAINT GERMAIN ET MONS 157 Z 29
85 SAINT GERMAIN L'AIGUILLER 111 S 21
63 SAINT GERMAIN L'HERM C 148 MA 26
14 SAINT GERMAIN
LA BLANCHE HERBE 36 U 10
27 SAINT GERMAIN LA CAMPAGNE 37 Y 10
73 SAINT GERMAIN
LA CHAMBOTTE 152 WA 25
42 SAINT GERMAIN LA MONTAGNE 136 QA 23
60 SAINT GERMAIN LA POTERIE 25 FA 9
51 SAINT GERMAIN LA VILLE 43 QA 11
14 SAINT GERMAIN LANGOT 36 V 11
43 SAINT GERMAIN LAPRADE 163 OA 28
42 SAINT GERMAIN LAVAL C 135 OA 25
77 SAINT GERMAIN LAVAL 63 KA 13
19 SAINT GERMAIN LAVOLPS 146 GA 26
77 SAINT GERMAIN LAXIS 62 IA 13
90 SAINT GERMAIN LE CHATELET 90 BB 17
53 SAINT GERMAIN LE FOUILLOUX 77 T 15
28 SAINT GERMAIN LE GAILLARD 60 CA 13
50 SAINT GERMAIN LE GAILLARD 33 O 9
53 SAINT GERMAIN LE GUILLAUME 77 S 14
21 SAINT GERMAIN LE ROCHEUX 85 RA 16
14 SAINT GERMAIN LE VASSON 36 V 11
61 SAINT GERMAIN LE VIEUX 59 Y 12
63 SAINT GERMAIN LEMBRON C 148 LA 26
39 SAINT GERMAIN LES ARLAY 122 VA 21
91 SAINT GERMAIN LES ARPAJON 62 GA 12
87 SAINT GERMAIN LES BELLES C 145 DA 26
71 SAINT GERMAIN LES BUXY 120 RA 21
91 SAINT GERMAIN LES CORBEIL C 62 HA 12
01 SAINT GERMAIN
LES PAROISSES 152 VA 25
21 SAINT GERMAIN LES SENAILLY 85 PA 17
19 SAINT GERMAIN LES VERGNES 159 DA 27
42 SAINT GERMAIN LESPINASSE 135 OA 24
63 SAINT GERMAIN
PRES HERMENT 147 IA 25
21 SAINT GERMAIN SOURCE SEINE 85 RA 17
76 SAINT GERMAIN SOUS CAILLY 24 BA 8
77 SAINT GERMAIN SOUS DOUE 41 KA 11
27 SAINT GERMAIN SUR AVRE 38 CA 12
50 SAINT GERMAIN SUR AY 34 P 10
80 SAINT GERMAIN SUR BRESLE 25 EA 7
76 SAINT GERMAIN SUR EAULNE 25 DA 7
77 SAINT GERMAIN SUR ECOLE 62 HA 13
35 SAINT GERMAIN SUR ILLE 75 P 14
69 SAINT GERMAIN
SUR L'ARBRESLE 136 RA 25
55 SAINT GERMAIN SUR MEUSE 45 VA 12
49 SAINT GERMAIN SUR MOINE 94 R 19
77 SAINT GERMAIN SUR MORIN 40 JA 11
01 SAINT GERMAIN SUR RENON 137 TA 24
74 SAINT GERMAIN SUR RHONE 138 WA 24
72 SAINT GERMAIN SUR SARTHE 58 X 14
50 SAINT GERMAIN SUR SEVES 34 Q 10
37 SAINT GERMAIN SUR VIENNE 97 W 19
27 SAINT GERMAIN VILLAGE 23 Y 9
08 SAINT GERMAINMONT 29 PA 8
32 SAINT GERME 185 V 34
60 SAINT GERMER DE FLY 25 EA 9
31 SAINT GERMIER 211 EA 35
32 SAINT GERMIER 187 AA 34
79 SAINT GERMIER 112 W 22
81 SAINT GERMIER 190 GA 34
43 SAINT GERON 148 LA 27
15 SAINT GERONS 160 GA 29
30 SAINT GERVAIS 179 RA 32
33 SAINT GERVAIS 156 U 28
38 SAINT GERVAIS 166 VA 28
85 SAINT GERVAIS 109 N 20
95 SAINT GERVAIS 39 EA 10
63 SAINT GERVAIS D'AUVERGNE C 133 JA 24
72 SAINT GERVAIS DE VIC 79 AA 16
61 SAINT GERVAIS DES SABLONS 36 W 11
61 SAINT GERVAIS DU PERRON 58 X 13
72 SAINT GERVAIS EN BELIN 78 X 16
71 SAINT GERVAIS EN VALLIERE 121 SA 20
41 SAINT GERVAIS LA FORET 80 CA 17
74 SAINT GERVAIS LES BAINS C 140 AB 25
86 SAINT GERVAIS
LES TROIS CLOCHERS C 113 Y 20
63 SAINT GERVAIS
SOUS MEYMONT 148 MA 25
71 SAINT GERVAIS
SUR COUCHES 120 QA 20
34 SAINT GERVAIS SUR MARE C 191 KA 34
26 SAINT GERVAIS
SUR ROUBION 179 SA 30
30 SAINT GERVASY 193 QA 33
63 SAINT GERVAZY 148 KA 27
24 SAINT GERY 157 Y 29
46 SAINT GERY C 174 DA 31
24 SAINT GEYRAC 158 AA 28
51 SAINT GIBRIEN 43 PA 11
22 SAINT GILDAS 53 J 13
56 SAINT GILDAS DE RHUYS 92 J 17
44 SAINT GILDAS DES BOIS C 93 N 17
30 SAINT GILLES C 193 QA 34
35 SAINT GILLES 75 O 14
36 SAINT GILLES 115 DA 22
50 SAINT GILLES 34 R 10
51 SAINT GILLES 42 MA 9
71 SAINT GILLES 120 RA 20
22 SAINT GILLES
VIEUX MARCHE 73 J 14
85 SAINT GILLES CROIX DE VIE C 109 O 21
76 SAINT GILLES DE CRETOT 23 Z 8
76 SAINT GILLES DE LA NEUVILLE 23 Y 8
61 SAINT GILLES DES MARAIS 57 T 13
22 SAINT GILLES DU MENE 74 L 14
22 SAINT GILLES LES BOIS 53 I 12
87 SAINT GILLES LES FORETS 145 DA 26
22 SAINT GILLES PLIGEAUX 53 I 13
07 SAINT GINEIS EN COIRON 179 QA 30
74 SAINT GINGOLPH 124 AB 22
73 SAINT GIROD 139 XA 25
09 SAINT GIRONS S 218 BA 37
64 SAINT GIRONS 184 S 35
33 SAINT GIRONS D'AIGUEVIVES 156 U 28
64 SAINT GLADIE
ARRIVE MUNEIN 206 S 36
22 SAINT GLEN 54 L 14
29 SAINT GOAZEC 72 F 14
02 SAINT GOBAIN 28 LA 8
02 SAINT GOBERT 28 NA 7
64 SAINT GOIN 206 T 36
45 SAINT GONDON 82 HA 17
35 SAINT GONDRAN 75 O 14
35 SAINT GONLAY 75 N 15
56 SAINT GONNERY 74 K 15
40 SAINT GOR 185 V 33
56 SAINT GORGON 92 M 17
88 SAINT GORGON 68 AB 14
25 SAINT GORGON MAIN 107 YA 20
22 SAINT GOUENO 74 L 14
41 SAINT GOURGON 80 BA 17
16 SAINT GOURSON 129 X 24
23 SAINT GOUSSAUD 131 DA 24
80 SAINT GRATIEN 16 HA 6
95 SAINT GRATIEN C 40 GA 11
58 SAINT GRATIEN SAVIGNY 119 MA 20
56 SAINT GRAVE 74 M 16
35 SAINT GREGOIRE 75 P 14
81 SAINT GREGOIRE 190 GA 33
17 SAINT GREGOIRE D'ARDENNES 142 U 26
27 SAINT GREGOIRE DU VIEVRE 37 Z 10
32 SAINT GRIEDE 185 W 34
16 SAINT GROUX 129 X 25
22 SAINT GUEN 73 J 14
34 SAINT GUILHEM LE DESERT 192 MA 34
38 SAINT GUILLAUME 166 VA 29
35 SAINT GUINOUX 55 O 13
34 SAINT GUIRAUD 192 LA 34
56 SAINT GUYOMARD 74 L 16
43 SAINT HAON 163 NA 29
42 SAINT HAON LE CHATEL C 135 OA 24
42 SAINT HAON LE VIEUX 135 NA 24
42 SAINT HEAND C 150 PA 26
22 SAINT HELEN 55 N 13
21 SAINT HELIER 104 RA 18
76 SAINT HELLIER 24 BA 7
44 SAINT HERBLAIN C 93 P 19
44 SAINT HERBLON 94 R 18
63 SAINT HERENT 148 KA 26
29 SAINT HERNIN 72 G 14
22 SAINT HERVE 74 K 14
03 SAINT HILAIRE 118 KA 22
11 SAINT HILAIRE C 221 GA 37
25 SAINT HILAIRE 107 YA 18
31 SAINT HILAIRE 210 CA 36
43 SAINT HILAIRE 148 LA 27
46 SAINT HILAIRE 160 GA 29
63 SAINT HILAIRE 133 IA 24
91 SAINT HILAIRE 61 FA 13
38 SAINT HILAIRE (DU TOUVET) 152 WA 27
51 SAINT HILAIRE AU TEMPLE 43 QA 10
87 SAINT HILAIRE BONNEVAL 145 CA 25
62 SAINT HILAIRE COTTES 8 HA 4
42 SAINT HILAIRE CUSSON
LA VALMITTE 149 OA 27
24 SAINT HILAIRE D'ESTISSAC 157 Y 28
30 SAINT HILAIRE D'OZILHAN 195 RA 33
34 SAINT HILAIRE DE BEAUVOIR 193 OA 34
38 SAINT HILAIRE DE BRENS 151 UA 26
30 SAINT HILAIRE DE BRETHMAS 193 PA 33
61 SAINT HILAIRE DE BRIOUZE 58 V 12
44 SAINT HILAIRE DE CHALEONS 93 O 19
44 SAINT HILAIRE DE CLISSON 110 Q 19
18 SAINT HILAIRE DE COURT 100 FA 19
18 SAINT HILAIRE DE GONDILLY 101 JA 19
38 SAINT HILAIRE DE LA COTE 152 UA 27
33 SAINT HILAIRE DE LA NOAILLE 171 W 30
48 SAINT HILAIRE DE LAVIT 177 NA 32
85 SAINT HILAIRE DE LOULAY 110 Q 20
47 SAINT HILAIRE DE LUSIGNAN 172 Y 32
85 SAINT HILAIRE DE RIEZ 109 N 21
17 SAINT HILAIRE
DE VILLEFRANCHE C 128 U 25
85 SAINT HILAIRE DE VOUST 111 T 21
35 SAINT HILAIRE DES LANDES 76 O 14
85 SAINT HILAIRE DES LOGES C 111 T 22
17 SAINT HILAIRE DU BOIS 142 U 27
33 SAINT HILAIRE DU BOIS 171 W 30
50 SAINT HILAIRE DU HARCOUET C 56 R 13
53 SAINT HILAIRE DU MAINE 57 S 14
38 SAINT HILAIRE DU ROSIER 165 TA 28
18 SAINT HILAIRE EN LIGNIERES 116 GA 21
58 SAINT HILAIRE EN MORVAN 103 NA 19
55 SAINT HILAIRE EN WOEVRE 45 WA 10
19 SAINT HILAIRE FOISSAC 146 GA 27
58 SAINT HILAIRE FONTAINE 119 MA 21
63 SAINT HILAIRE LA CROIX 133 KA 24
85 SAINT HILAIRE LA FORET 125 P 22
61 SAINT HILAIRE LA GERARD 58 W 12
41 SAINT HILAIRE LA GRAVELLE 80 BA 15
79 SAINT HILAIRE LA PALUD 127 T 23
23 SAINT HILAIRE LA PLAINE 132 FA 24
87 SAINT HILAIRE LA TREILLE 131 CA 23
23 SAINT HILAIRE LE CHATEAU 132 EA 24
61 SAINT HILAIRE LE CHATEL 59 Z 13
51 SAINT HILAIRE LE GRAND 43 QA 10
72 SAINT HILAIRE LE LIERRU 59 Y 15
51 SAINT HILAIRE LE PETIT 43 QA 10
85 SAINT HILAIRE LE VOUHIS 110 R 21
45 SAINT HILAIRE LES ANDRESIS 83 KA 15
19 SAINT HILAIRE LES COURBES 145 EA 26
63 SAINT HILAIRE LES MONGES 147 IA 25
87 SAINT HILAIRE LES PLACES 144 BA 26
59 SAINT HILAIRE LEZ CAMBRAI 18 LA 5
19 SAINT HILAIRE LUC 146 GA 27
50 SAINT HILAIRE PETITVILLE 34 R 9
19 SAINT HILAIRE PEYROUX 159 DA 28
42 SAINT HILAIRE SOUS CHARLIEU 135 PA 24
10 SAINT HILAIRE SOUS ROMILLY 64 MA 13
45 SAINT HILAIRE ST MESMIN 81 EA 16
36 SAINT HILAIRE SUR BENAIZE 114 BA 22
61 SAINT HILAIRE SUR ERRE 59 Z 14
59 SAINT HILAIRE SUR HELPE 19 NA 6
45 SAINT HILAIRE SUR PUISEAUX 82 IA 16
61 SAINT HILAIRE SUR RISLE 37 Y 12
28 SAINT HILAIRE SUR YERRE 80 CA 15
19 SAINT HILAIRE TAURIEUX 160 EA 28
78 SAINT HILARION 61 EA 12
77 SAINT HILLIERS 63 LA 12
12 SAINT HIPPOLYTE 161 IA 30
15 SAINT HIPPOLYTE 161 IA 27
17 SAINT HIPPOLYTE 127 S 24
25 SAINT HIPPOLYTE C 89 AB 16
33 SAINT HIPPOLYTE 156 W 29
37 SAINT HIPPOLYTE 98 BA 19
66 SAINT HIPPOLYTE 224 JA 38
68 SAINT HIPPOLYTE 70 DB 14
30 SAINT HIPPOLYTE DE CATON 193 PA 33
30 SAINT HIPPOLYTE
DE MONTAIGU 193 QA 33
30 SAINT HIPPOLYTE DU FORT C 192 NA 33
84 SAINT HIPPOLYTE
LE GRAVEYRON 179 TA 32
38 SAINT HONORE 166 WA 29
76 SAINT HONORE 24 BA 7
58 SAINT HONORE LES BAINS 119 NA 20
43 SAINT HOSTIEN 163 OA 28
57 SAINT HUBERT 46 YA 10
71 SAINT HURUGE 120 QA 21
14 SAINT HYMER 36 X 10
39 SAINT HYMETIERE 138 VA 22
22 SAINT IGEAUX 73 I 14
12 SAINT IGEST 175 FA 31
31 SAINT IGNAN 217 Z 37
63 SAINT IGNAT 133 LA 24
71 SAINT IGNY DE ROCHE 136 PA 23
69 SAINT IGNY DE VERS 136 QA 23
15 SAINT ILLIDE 160 GA 28
78 SAINT ILLIERS LA VILLE 38 DA 11
78 SAINT ILLIERS LE BOIS 38 DA 11
43 SAINT ILPIZE 162 LA 28
51 SAINT IMOGES 42 OA 10
62 SAINT INGLEVERT 7 EA 2
38 SAINT ISMIER C 152 WA 27
12 SAINT IZAIRE 190 IA 33
04 SAINT JACQUES 198 YA 33
76 SAINT JACQUES D'ALIERMONT 24 CA 7
63 SAINT JACQUES D'AMBUR 133 IA 24
07 SAINT JACQUES D'ATTICIEUX 150 RA 27
35 SAINT JACQUES DE LA LANDE 75 P 15
50 SAINT JACQUES DE NEHOU 33 P 9
79 SAINT JACQUES DE THOUARS 112 V 20
69 SAINT JACQUES DES ARRETS 136 RA 23
15 SAINT JACQUES DES BLATS 161 IA 28
41 SAINT JACQUES DES GUERETS 79 AA 16
05 SAINT JACQUES
EN VALGODEMARD 167 XA 30
76 SAINT JACQUES SUR DARNETAL 24 CA 9
22 SAINT JACUT DE LA MER 55 M 13
22 SAINT JACUT DU MENE 74 L 14
56 SAINT JACUT LES PINS 92 M 17
19 SAINT JAL 145 DA 27
50 SAINT JAMES C 56 Q 13
64 SAINT JAMMES 207 V 36
59 SAINT JANS CAPPEL 8 IA 3
31 SAINT JEAN 188 DA 34
58 SAINT JEAN AUX AMOGNES 118 LA 20
08 SAINT JEAN AUX BOIS 29 PA 7
60 SAINT JEAN AUX BOIS 27 JA 9
42 SAINT JEAN BONNEFONDS 150 QA 26
56 SAINT JEAN BREVELAY C 74 K 16
06 SAINT JEAN CAP FERRAT 200 DB 34
07 SAINT JEAN CHAMBRE 164 QA 29
09 SAINT JEAN D'AIGUES VIVES 219 EA 38
12 SAINT JEAN D'ALCAPIES 191 JA 33
17 SAINT JEAN D'ANGELY S 128 U 24
17 SAINT JEAN D'ANGLE 127 S 25
69 SAINT JEAN D'ARDIERES 136 RA 23
73 SAINT JEAN D'ARVES 167 YA 28
73 SAINT JEAN D'ARVEY 153 XA 26
72 SAINT JEAN D'ASSE 78 X 14
24 SAINT JEAN D'ATAUX 157 Y 28
43 SAINT JEAN D'AUBRIGOUX 149 NA 27
74 SAINT JEAN D'AULPS 140 AB 23
38 SAINT JEAN D'AVELANNE 152 VA 26
24 SAINT JEAN D'ESTISSAC 157 Y 28
39 SAINT JEAN D'ETREUX 122 UA 22
24 SAINT JEAN D'EYRAUD 157 Y 29
38 SAINT JEAN D'HERANS 166 WA 29
63 SAINT JEAN D'HEURS 148 LA 25
33 SAINT JEAN D'ILLAC 155 T 29
88 SAINT JEAN D'ORMONT 69 BB 14
11 SAINT JEAN DE BARROU 223 JA 38
57 SAINT JEAN DE BASSEL 47 BB 12
91 SAINT JEAN DE BEAUREGARD 61 GA 12
73 SAINT JEAN DE BELLEVILLE 153 ZA 27
85 SAINT JEAN DE BEUGNE 125 R 22
33 SAINT JEAN DE BLAIGNAC 156 W 29
21 SAINT JEAN DE BOEUF 104 RA 19
44 SAINT JEAN DE BOISEAU 93 O 19
10 SAINT JEAN DE BONNEVAL 64 OA 14
38 SAINT JEAN DE BOURNAY C 151 TA 26
45 SAINT JEAN DE BRAYE C 81 FA 16
34 SAINT JEAN DE BUEGES 192 MA 34
30 SAINT JEAN DE CEYRARGUES 193 PA 33
73 SAINT JEAN DE CHEVELU 152 WA 25
24 SAINT JEAN DE COLE 144 AA 27
34 SAINT JEAN DE CORNIES 193 OA 34
73 SAINT JEAN DE COUZ 152 WA 26
30 SAINT JEAN DE CRIEULON 193 OA 33
34 SAINT JEAN DE CUCULLES 192 NA 34
50 SAINT JEAN DE DAYE C 34 R 10
47 SAINT JEAN DE DURAS 171 X 30
76 SAINT JEAN DE FOLLEVILLE 23 Y 8
34 SAINT JEAN DE FOS 192 MA 34
01 SAINT JEAN DE GONVILLE 139 XA 23
34 SAINT JEAN DE LA BLAQUIERE 192 LA 34
49 SAINT JEAN DE LA CROIX 95 T 18
61 SAINT JEAN DE LA FORET 59 Z 13
50 SAINT JEAN DE LA HAIZE 56 O 12
27 SAINT JEAN DE LA LEQUERAYE 37 Z 10
72 SAINT JEAN DE LA MOTTE 78 W 16
76 SAINT JEAN DE LA NEUVILLE 23 Y 8
73 SAINT JEAN DE LA PORTE 153 XA 26
50 SAINT JEAN DE LA RIVIERE 33 O 9
45 SAINT JEAN DE LA RUELLE C 81 EA 16
46 SAINT JEAN DE LAUR 174 EA 31
40 SAINT JEAN DE LIER 184 S 34
49 SAINT JEAN DE LINIERES 95 T 18
17 SAINT JEAN DE LIVERSAY 127 S 23
14 SAINT JEAN DE LIVET 37 X 10
21 SAINT JEAN DE LOSNE C 105 UA 19
64 SAINT JEAN DE LUZ C 205 P 36
81 SAINT JEAN DE MARCEL 190 GA 33
40 SAINT JEAN DE MARSACQ 183 Q 35
30 SAINT JEAN DE MARUEJOLS
ET AVEJAN 178 PA 32
73 SAINT JEAN DE MAURIENNE S 153 YA 27
34 SAINT JEAN DE MINERVOIS 213 JA 36
38 SAINT JEAN DE MOIRANS 152 VA 27
85 SAINT JEAN DE MONTS C 109 N 21
07 SAINT JEAN DE MUZOLS 164 RA 28
43 SAINT JEAN DE NAY 163 NA 28
01 SAINT JEAN DE NIOST 137 TA 25
11 SAINT JEAN DE PARACOL 221 GA 38
28 SAINT JEAN DE REBERVILLIERS 60 CA 12
81 SAINT JEAN DE RIVES 189 EA 34
86 SAINT JEAN DE SAUVES 113 X 20
50 SAINT JEAN DE SAVIGNY 35 S 10
30 SAINT JEAN DE SERRES 193 OA 33
74 SAINT JEAN DE SIXT 139 ZA 24
38 SAINT JEAN DE SOUDAIN 152 UA 26
74 SAINT JEAN DE THOLOME 139 ZA 24
79 SAINT JEAN DE THOUARS 112 V 20
47 SAINT JEAN DE THURAC 172 Z 32
01 SAINT JEAN DE THURIGNEUX 137 SA 24
69 SAINT JEAN DE TOUSLAS 150 RA 26
71 SAINT JEAN DE TREZY 120 QA 20
30 SAINT JEAN DE VALERISCLE 178 OA 32
81 SAINT JEAN DE VALS 190 GA 34
38 SAINT JEAN DE VAULX 166 WA 28
71 SAINT JEAN DE VAUX 120 RA 20
34 SAINT JEAN DE VEDAS 214 NA 35
09 SAINT JEAN DE VERGES 219 DA 37
12 SAINT JEAN DELNOUS 190 HA 33
50 SAINT JEAN DES BAISANTS 35 S 10
61 SAINT JEAN DES BOIS 57 T 12
50 SAINT JEAN DES CHAMPS 56 Q 12
72 SAINT JEAN DES ECHELLES 59 Z 15
14 SAINT JEAN DES ESSARTIERS 35 S 11
49 SAINT JEAN DES MAUVRETS 96 U 18
63 SAINT JEAN DES OLLIERES 148 LA 26
69 SAINT JEAN DES VIGNES 136 RA 25
51 SAINT JEAN DEVANT POSSESSE 43 RA 11
72 SAINT JEAN DU BOIS 78 W 16
82 SAINT JEAN DU BOUZET 187 AA 33
12 SAINT JEAN DU BRUEL 192 LA 33
76 SAINT JEAN DU CARDONNAY 24 BA 8
09 SAINT JEAN DU CASTILLONNAIS 217 AA 38
50 SAINT JEAN DU CORAIL 57 S 12
50 SAINT JEAN DU CORAIL
DES BOIS 56 R 12
29 SAINT JEAN DU DOIGT 52 F 12
09 SAINT JEAN DU FALGA 219 DA 37
30 SAINT JEAN DU GARD C 177 NA 32
30 SAINT JEAN DU PIN 178 OA 32
27 SAINT JEAN DU THENNEY 37 Y 11
26 SAINT JEAN EN ROYANS C 166 UA 28
63 SAINT JEAN EN VAL 148 LA 26
12 SAINT JEAN ET ST PAUL 191 JA 33
41 SAINT JEAN FROIDMENTEL 80 CA 15
22 SAINT JEAN KERDANIEL 53 J 13
57 SAINT JEAN KOURTZERODE 48 CB 12
69 SAINT JEAN LA BUSSIERE 136 PA 24
48 SAINT JEAN LA FOUILLOUSE 163 MA 30
56 SAINT JEAN LA POTERIE 93 N 17
42 SAINT JEAN LA VETRE 149 NA 25
43 SAINT JEAN LACHALM 163 NA 29
46 SAINT JEAN LAGINESTE 160 EA 29
66 SAINT JEAN LASSEILLE 224 JA 39
14 SAINT JEAN LE BLANC 35 T 11
45 SAINT JEAN LE BLANC C 81 FA 16
07 SAINT JEAN LE CENTENIER 179 QA 30
32 SAINT JEAN LE COMTAL 209 Y 35
50 SAINT JEAN LE THOMAS 56 P 12
01 SAINT JEAN LE VIEUX 138 UA 24
38 SAINT JEAN LE VIEUX 167 WA 28

Dép.	Commune		Page	Carreau	
64	SAINT JEAN LE VIEUX		206	R	37
55	SAINT JEAN LES BUZY		45	WA	10
77	SAINT JEAN LES DEUX JUMEAUX		41	KA	11
54	SAINT JEAN LES LONGUYON		31	UA	9
46	SAINT JEAN LESPINASSE		160	EA	29
31	SAINT JEAN LHERM		188	DA	34
87	SAINT JEAN LIGOURE		145	CA	25
46	SAINT JEAN MIRABEL		175	FA	30
64	SAINT JEAN PIED DE PORT	C	205	R	37
28	SAINT JEAN PIERRE FIXTE		59	AA	14
66	SAINT JEAN PLA DE CORTS		224	JA	40
64	SAINT JEAN POUDGE		207	V	35
32	SAINT JEAN POUTGE		186	Y	34
57	SAINT JEAN ROHRBACH		47	BB	11
07	SAINT JEAN ROURE		164	OA	29
67	SAINT JEAN SAVERNE		49	DB	12
42	SAINT JEAN SOLEYMIEUX	C	149	OA	26
37	SAINT JEAN ST GERMAIN		98	BA	19
63	SAINT JEAN ST GERVAIS		148	LA	27
42	SAINT JEAN ST MAURICE SUR LOIRE		135	OA	24
05	SAINT JEAN ST NICOLAS		167	YA	30
35	SAINT JEAN SUR COUESNON		76	Q	14
53	SAINT JEAN SUR ERVE		77	U	15
53	SAINT JEAN SUR MAYENNE		77	T	15
51	SAINT JEAN SUR MOIVRE		43	QA	11
01	SAINT JEAN SUR REYSSOUZE		137	TA	22
51	SAINT JEAN SUR TOURBE		43	RA	10
01	SAINT JEAN SUR VEYLE		137	SA	23
35	SAINT JEAN SUR VILAINE		76	Q	15
29	SAINT JEAN TROLIMON		71	D	16
04	SAINT JEANNET		197	XA	33
06	SAINT JEANNET		200	CB	34
18	SAINT JEANVRIN		116	GA	21
74	SAINT JEOIRE	C	139	ZA	23
73	SAINT JEOIRE PRIEURE		153	XA	26
07	SAINT JEURE D'ANDAURE		164	QA	28
07	SAINT JEURE D'AY		164	RA	28
43	SAINT JEURES		163	PA	28
44	SAINT JOACHIM		92	M	18
42	SAINT JODARD		135	PA	25
55	SAINT JOIRE		66	UA	13
50	SAINT JORES		34	Q	9
74	SAINT JORIOZ		139	YA	25
31	SAINT JORY		188	CA	34
24	SAINT JORY DE CHALAIS		144	AA	26
24	SAINT JORY LAS BLOUX		144	AA	27
42	SAINT JOSEPH		150	RA	26
50	SAINT JOSEPH		33	P	8
38	SAINT JOSEPH DE RIVIERE		152	WA	27
07	SAINT JOSEPH DES BANCS		164	QA	30
62	SAINT JOSSE		15	EA	4
22	SAINT JOUAN DE L'ISLE		75	M	14
35	SAINT JOUAN DES GUERETS		55	N	13
14	SAINT JOUIN		36	W	10
76	SAINT JOUIN BRUNEVAL		23	X	8
61	SAINT JOUIN DE BLAVOU		59	Y	13
79	SAINT JOUIN DE MARNES		112	W	20
79	SAINT JOUIN DE MILLY		111	T	21
87	SAINT JOUVENT		131	BA	24
25	SAINT JUAN		107	YA	18
22	SAINT JUDOCE		55	N	14
12	SAINT JUERY		190	IA	33
48	SAINT JUERY		162	KA	29
81	SAINT JUERY		190	GA	33
85	SAINT JUIRE CHAMPGILLON		111	S	21
31	SAINT JULIA		211	EA	35
11	SAINT JULIA DE BEC		221	GA	38
21	SAINT JULIEN		105	TA	18
22	SAINT JULIEN		54	K	13
31	SAINT JULIEN		210	BA	36
34	SAINT JULIEN		213	JA	35
39	SAINT JULIEN	C	138	UA	22
69	SAINT JULIEN		136	RA	24
83	SAINT JULIEN		197	WA	34
88	SAINT JULIEN		88	WA	15
19	SAINT JULIEN AUX BOIS		160	GA	28
33	SAINT JULIEN BEYCHEVELLE		155	T	28
07	SAINT JULIEN BOUTIERES		164	QA	29
43	SAINT JULIEN CHAPTEUIL	C	163	OA	28
43	SAINT JULIEN D'ANCE		149	OA	27
40	SAINT JULIEN D'ARMAGNAC		185	W	33
48	SAINT JULIEN D'ARPAON		177	MA	32
04	SAINT JULIEN D'ASSE		197	XA	33
24	SAINT JULIEN D'EYMET		157	Y	30
42	SAINT JULIEN D'ODDES		135	OA	25
24	SAINT JULIEN DE BOURDEILLES		143	Z	27
11	SAINT JULIEN DE BRIOLA		221	FA	37
30	SAINT JULIEN DE CASSAGNAS		178	PA	32
41	SAINT JULIEN DE CHEDON		99	CA	18
71	SAINT JULIEN DE CIVRY		135	PA	22
44	SAINT JULIEN DE CONCELLES		94	O	19
63	SAINT JULIEN DE COPPEL		148	LA	25
24	SAINT JULIEN DE CREMPSE		157	Y	29
09	SAINT JULIEN DE GRAS CAPOU		219	EA	37
71	SAINT JULIEN DE JONZY		135	PA	23
17	SAINT JULIEN DE L'ESCAP		128	U	24
38	SAINT JULIEN DE L'HERMS		151	TA	27
27	SAINT JULIEN DE LA LIEGUE		38	CA	10
30	SAINT JULIEN DE LA NEF		192	NA	33
24	SAINT JULIEN DE LAMPON		159	CA	29
14	SAINT JULIEN DE MAILLOC		37	Y	10
30	SAINT JULIEN DE PEYROLAS		179	QA	32
38	SAINT JULIEN DE RAZ		152	VA	27
15	SAINT JULIEN DE TOURSAC		160	GA	29
44	SAINT JULIEN DE VOUVANTES	C	94	R	17
43	SAINT JULIEN DES CHAZES		162	MA	28
85	SAINT JULIEN DES LANDES		109	P	21
85	SAINT JULIEN DES POINTS		178	OA	32
07	SAINT JULIEN DU GUA		164	QA	30
43	SAINT JULIEN DU PINET		163	OA	28
81	SAINT JULIEN DU PUY		189	FA	34
89	SAINT JULIEN DU SAULT	C	83	LA	15
07	SAINT JULIEN DU SERRE		178	QA	30
53	SAINT JULIEN DU TERROUX		57	U	13
48	SAINT JULIEN DU TOURNEL		177	MA	31
04	SAINT JULIEN DU VERDON		198	ZA	33
05	SAINT JULIEN EN BEAUCHENE		180	WA	30
40	SAINT JULIEN EN BORN		183	R	33
05	SAINT JULIEN EN CHAMPSAUR		167	XA	30
74	SAINT JULIEN EN GENEVOIS	S	139	XA	23
42	SAINT JULIEN EN QUINT		166	UA	29
07	SAINT JULIEN EN ST ALBAN		164	RA	30
26	SAINT JULIEN EN VERCORS		166	UA	28
81	SAINT JULIEN GAULENE		190	HA	33
86	SAINT JULIEN L'ARS	C	113	Y	22
07	SAINT JULIEN LA GENESTE		133	IA	24
23	SAINT JULIEN LA GENETE		133	HA	23
42	SAINT JULIEN LA VETRE		149	NA	25
07	SAINT JULIEN LABROUSSE		164	QA	29
23	SAINT JULIEN LE CHATEL		132	GA	24
14	SAINT JULIEN LE FAUCON		36	X	10
19	SAINT JULIEN LE PELERIN		160	FA	28
87	SAINT JULIEN LE PETIT		145	EA	25
07	SAINT JULIEN LE ROUX		164	RA	29
19	SAINT JULIEN LE VENDOMOIS		145	CA	26
54	SAINT JULIEN LES GORZE		45	WA	11
57	SAINT JULIEN LES METZ		46	YA	10
25	SAINT JULIEN LES MONTBELIARD		89	AB	17
30	SAINT JULIEN LES ROSIERS		178	OA	32
25	SAINT JULIEN LES RUSSEY		108	AB	19
10	SAINT JULIEN LES VILLAS		64	OA	14
19	SAINT JULIEN MAUMONT		159	EA	28
43	SAINT JULIEN MOLHESABATE		164	OA	28
42	SAINT JULIEN MOLIN MOLETTE		150	RA	27
73	SAINT JULIEN MONT DENIS		153	ZA	27
19	SAINT JULIEN PRES BORT		146	HA	27
63	SAINT JULIEN PUY LAVEZE		147	IA	26
55	SAINT JULIEN SOUS LES COTES		45	VA	12
69	SAINT JULIEN SUR BIBOST		150	QA	25
14	SAINT JULIEN SUR CALONNE		37	X	9
41	SAINT JULIEN SUR CHER		99	EA	18
71	SAINT JULIEN SUR DHEUNE		120	QA	21
01	SAINT JULIEN SUR REYSSOUZE		137	TA	22
61	SAINT JULIEN SUR SARTHE		59	Y	13
01	SAINT JULIEN SUR VEYLE		137	SA	23
07	SAINT JULIEN VOCANCE		164	QA	28
87	SAINT JUNIEN	C	130	AA	25
23	SAINT JUNIEN LA BREGERE		131	EA	25
87	SAINT JUNIEN LES COMBES		130	BA	24
57	SAINT JURE		46	YA	11
04	SAINT JURS		197	YA	33
01	SAINT JUST		137	UA	23
07	SAINT JUST		179	RA	32
15	SAINT JUST		162	KA	29
18	SAINT JUST		117	HA	20
24	SAINT JUST		143	Y	27
27	SAINT JUST		38	DA	10
34	SAINT JUST		193	OA	34
35	SAINT JUST		75	N	16
63	SAINT JUST		149	NA	26
38	SAINT JUST CHALEYSSIN		151	SA	26
69	SAINT JUST D'AVRAY		136	QA	24
38	SAINT JUST DE CLAIX		166	UA	28
42	SAINT JUST EN BAS		149	NA	25
77	SAINT JUST EN BRIE		63	KA	12
60	SAINT JUST EN CHAUSSEE	C	26	HA	8
42	SAINT JUST EN CHEVALET	C	135	NA	24
11	SAINT JUST ET LE BEZU		221	GA	38
30	SAINT JUST ET VACQUIERES		193	PA	33
64	SAINT JUST IBARRE		206	R	37
42	SAINT JUST LA PENDUE		135	PA	25
87	SAINT JUST LE MARTEL		131	CA	25
17	SAINT JUST LUZAC		127	S	25
43	SAINT JUST MALMONT		150	PA	27
43	SAINT JUST PRES BRIOUDE		162	LA	27
51	SAINT JUST SAUVAGE		64	NA	13
42	SAINT JUST ST RAMBERT	C	149	PA	26
49	SAINT JUST SUR DIVE		96	W	19
12	SAINT JUST SUR VIAUR		175	HA	32
32	SAINT JUSTIN		208	X	35
40	SAINT JUSTIN		185	V	33
22	SAINT JUVAT		55	N	14
08	SAINT JUVIN		30	SA	9
36	SAINT LACTENCIN		115	DA	20
69	SAINT LAGER		136	RA	24
07	SAINT LAGER BRESSAC		164	RA	30
39	SAINT LAMAIN		122	VA	21
14	SAINT LAMBERT		35	U	11
78	SAINT LAMBERT		39	FA	12
49	SAINT LAMBERT DU LATTAY		95	T	18
08	SAINT LAMBERT ET MONT DE JEUX		30	RA	8
49	SAINT LAMBERT LA POTHERIE		95	T	17
61	SAINT LAMBERT SUR DIVE		58	X	12
61	SAINT LANGIS LES MORTAGNE		59	Y	13
65	SAINT LANNE		208	W	35
65	SAINT LAON		112	W	20
09	SAINT LARY		217	AA	38
32	SAINT LARY		186	Y	34
31	SAINT LARY BOUJEAN		209	Z	36
65	SAINT LARY SOULAN		216	Y	38
38	SAINT LATTIER		165	TA	28
22	SAINT LAUNEUC		74	M	14
63	SAINT LAURE		133	LA	24
08	SAINT LAURENT		29	RA	7
18	SAINT LAURENT		100	GA	19
22	SAINT LAURENT		53	I	12
23	SAINT LAURENT		132	FA	23
31	SAINT LAURENT		209	AA	36
47	SAINT LAURENT		172	Y	32
56	SAINT LAURENT SUR OUST		74	M	16
58	SAINT LAURENT		101	JA	18
74	SAINT LAURENT		139	YA	24
62	SAINT LAURENT BLANGY		17	JA	5
64	SAINT LAURENT BRETAGNE		207	V	36
43	SAINT LAURENT CHABREUGES		162	LA	27
69	SAINT LAURENT D'AGNY		150	RA	26
30	SAINT LAURENT D'AIGOUZE		194	PA	35
71	SAINT LAURENT D'ANDENAY		120	QA	21
33	SAINT LAURENT D'ARCE		156	U	28
69	SAINT LAURENT D'OINGT		136	QA	24
12	SAINT LAURENT D'OLT		176	KA	31
26	SAINT LAURENT D'ONAY		165	TA	28
16	SAINT LAURENT DE BELZAGOT		142	X	27
76	SAINT LAURENT DE BREVEDENT		23	X	8
30	SAINT LAURENT DE CARNOLS		179	OA	32
66	SAINT LAURENT DE CERDANS		224	IA	40
16	SAINT LAURENT DE CERIS		129	Y	24
69	SAINT LAURENT DE CHAMOUSSET	C	150	QA	25
16	SAINT LAURENT DE COGNAC		142	U	25
14	SAINT LAURENT DE CONDEL		36	U	11
50	SAINT LAURENT DE CUVES		56	R	12
40	SAINT LAURENT DE GOSSE		206	R	35
86	SAINT LAURENT DE JOURDES		129	Y	22
17	SAINT LAURENT DE LA BARRIERE		127	T	24
11	SAINT LAURENT DE LA CABRERISSE		223	IA	37
49	SAINT LAURENT DE LA PLAINE		95	T	18
17	SAINT LAURENT DE LA PREE		127	S	24
66	SAINT LAURENT DE LA SALANQUE	C	224	JA	38
85	SAINT LAURENT DE LA SALLE		111	S	22
12	SAINT LAURENT DE LEVEZOU		176	JA	32
37	SAINT LAURENT DE LIN		97	X	17
69	SAINT LAURENT DE MURE		151	TA	25
48	SAINT LAURENT DE MURET		176	KA	30
65	SAINT LAURENT DE NESTE	C	217	Y	37
50	SAINT LAURENT DE TERREGATTE		56	R	13
48	SAINT LAURENT DE TREVES		177	MA	32
69	SAINT LAURENT DE VAUX		150	RA	25
48	SAINT LAURENT DE VEYRES		162	KA	30
30	SAINT LAURENT DES ARBRES		195	RA	33
49	SAINT LAURENT DES AUTELS		94	R	18
24	SAINT LAURENT DES BATONS		158	Z	29
27	SAINT LAURENT DES BOIS		38	CA	11
41	SAINT LAURENT DES BOIS		80	CA	16
16	SAINT LAURENT DES COMBES		143	W	27
33	SAINT LAURENT DES COMBES		156	W	29
24	SAINT LAURENT DES HOMMES		157	X	28
53	SAINT LAURENT DES MORTIERS		77	U	16
24	SAINT LAURENT DES VIGNES		157	Y	29
33	SAINT LAURENT DU BOIS		171	W	30
05	SAINT LAURENT DU CROS		181	XA	30
14	SAINT LAURENT DU MONT		36	W	10
49	SAINT LAURENT DU MOTTAY		95	S	18
07	SAINT LAURENT DU PAPE		164	RA	29
33	SAINT LAURENT DU PLAN		171	W	30
38	SAINT LAURENT DU PONT	C	152	WA	27
27	SAINT LAURENT DU TENCEMENT		37	Y	11
06	SAINT LAURENT DU VAR	C	200	CB	34
04	SAINT LAURENT DU VERDON		197	XA	34
38	SAINT LAURENT EN BEAUMONT		166	WA	29
71	SAINT LAURENT EN BRIONNAIS		135	PA	23
76	SAINT LAURENT EN CAUX		24	AA	7
37	SAINT LAURENT EN GATINES		79	AA	17
39	SAINT LAURENT EN GRANDVAUX	C	123	XA	21
26	SAINT LAURENT EN ROYANS		166	UA	28
42	SAINT LAURENT LA CONCHE		149	PA	25
28	SAINT LAURENT LA GATINE		38	DA	12
39	SAINT LAURENT LA ROCHE		122	VA	21
24	SAINT LAURENT LA VALLEE		158	BA	30
30	SAINT LAURENT LA VERNEDE		178	QA	32
30	SAINT LAURENT LE MINIER		192	MA	33
07	SAINT LAURENT LES BAINS		178	OA	30
87	SAINT LAURENT LES EGLISES		131	DA	24
46	SAINT LAURENT LES TOURS		160	FA	29
46	SAINT LAURENT LOLMIE		173	CA	32
33	SAINT LAURENT MEDOC	C	155	S	28
41	SAINT LAURENT NOUAN		80	DA	16
42	SAINT LAURENT ROCHEFORT		149	OA	25
07	SAINT LAURENT SOUS COIRON		178	QA	30
87	SAINT LAURENT SUR GORRE	C	144	AA	25
24	SAINT LAURENT SUR MANOIRE		158	AA	28
14	SAINT LAURENT SUR MER		35	S	9
55	SAINT LAURENT SUR OTHAIN		31	VA	9
01	SAINT LAURENT SUR SAONE		137	SA	23
85	SAINT LAURENT SUR SEVRE		111	S	20
79	SAINT LAURS		111	U	22
06	SAINT LEGER		198	AB	33
16	SAINT LEGER		143	W	26
17	SAINT LEGER		142	U	26
47	SAINT LEGER		171	Y	32
53	SAINT LEGER		77	U	15
62	SAINT LEGER		17	JA	5
73	SAINT LEGER		153	YA	27
77	SAINT LEGER		41	LA	11
60	SAINT LEGER AUX BOIS		27	JA	9
76	SAINT LEGER AUX BOIS		25	DA	7
23	SAINT LEGER BRIDEREIX		131	DA	23
33	SAINT LEGER DE BALSON		170	U	31
58	SAINT LEGER DE FOUGERET		119	NA	20
79	SAINT LEGER DE LA MARTINIERE		128	W	23
86	SAINT LEGER DE MONTBRILLAIS		96	W	19
79	SAINT LEGER DE MONTBRUN		96	W	20
48	SAINT LEGER DE PEYRE		177	LA	30
27	SAINT LEGER DE ROTES		37	Z	10
28	SAINT LEGER DES AUBEES		61	EA	13
49	SAINT LEGER DES BOIS		95	T	18
35	SAINT LEGER DES PRES		56	P	13
58	SAINT LEGER DES VIGNES		118	LA	20
71	SAINT LEGER DU BOIS		120	QA	20
76	SAINT LEGER DU BOURG DENIS		24	BA	9
27	SAINT LEGER DU GENNETEY		37	Z	9
48	SAINT LEGER DU MALZIEU		162	LA	29
84	SAINT LEGER DU VENTOUX		180	UA	32
14	SAINT LEGER DUBOSQ		36	W	10
60	SAINT LEGER EN BRAY		26	FA	9
78	SAINT LEGER EN YVELINES		39	EA	12
87	SAINT LEGER LA MONTAGNE		131	CA	24
23	SAINT LEGER LE GUERETOIS		131	EA	23
18	SAINT LEGER LE PETIT		102	KA	19
80	SAINT LEGER LES AUTHIE		17	HA	6
80	SAINT LEGER LES DOMART		16	GA	6
05	SAINT LEGER LES MELEZES		181	YA	30
71	SAINT LEGER LES PARAY		119	OA	22
44	SAINT LEGER LES VIGNES		93	O	19
87	SAINT LEGER MAGNAZEIX		131	CA	23
10	SAINT LEGER PRES TROYES		64	OA	14
71	SAINT LEGER SOUS BEUVRAY	C	119	OA	20
10	SAINT LEGER SOUS BRIENNE		65	OA	13
49	SAINT LEGER SOUS CHOLET		95	S	19
71	SAINT LEGER SOUS LA BUSSIERE		136	QA	23
10	SAINT LEGER SOUS MARGERIE		65	QA	13
80	SAINT LEGER SUR BRESLE		25	EA	7
71	SAINT LEGER SUR DHEUNE		120	RA	20
42	SAINT LEGER SUR ROANNE		135	OA	24
61	SAINT LEGER SUR SARTHE		59	Y	13
03	SAINT LEGER SUR VOUZANCE		135	OA	22
21	SAINT LEGER TRIEY		106	UA	18
89	SAINT LEGER VAUBAN		103	OA	18
86	SAINT LEOMER		114	BA	22
03	SAINT LEON		134	MA	22
31	SAINT LEON		210	DA	36
33	SAINT LEON		156	V	30
47	SAINT LEON		171	X	32
24	SAINT LEON D'ISSIGEAC		158	Z	30
24	SAINT LEON SUR L'ISLE		157	Y	28
24	SAINT LEON SUR VEZERE		158	BA	28
32	SAINT LEONARD		187	AA	34
51	SAINT LEONARD		42	OA	10
62	SAINT LEONARD		7	DA	3
76	SAINT LEONARD		23	Y	7
88	SAINT LEONARD		69	BB	14
87	SAINT LEONARD DE NOBLAT	C	145	DA	25
72	SAINT LEONARD DES BOIS		58	W	14
61	SAINT LEONARD DES PARCS		59	Y	12
41	SAINT LEONARD EN BEAUCE		80	CA	16
12	SAINT LEONS		176	JA	32
03	SAINT LEOPARDIN D'AUGY		118	KA	21
56	SAINT LERY		74	M	15
60	SAINT LEU D'ESSERENT		40	HA	10
95	SAINT LEU LA FORET	C	40	GA	11
65	SAINT LEZER		208	W	36
49	SAINT LEZIN		95	T	18
81	SAINT LIEUX LAFENASSE		190	GA	34
81	SAINT LIEUX LES LAVAUR		189	EA	34
79	SAINT LIN		112	V	22
04	SAINT LIONS		198	ZA	33
09	SAINT LIZIER	C	218	BA	37
32	SAINT LIZIER DU PLANTE		209	AA	36
50	SAINT LO	P	34	R	10
50	SAINT LO D'OURVILLE		34	P	9
40	SAINT LON LES MINES		183	R	35
72	SAINT LONGIS		59	Y	14
22	SAINT LORMEL		55	M	13
39	SAINT LOTHAIN		122	VA	20
32	SAINT LOUBE		209	AA	35
33	SAINT LOUBERT		170	V	30
33	SAINT LOUBES		156	U	29
40	SAINT LOUBOUER		184	U	34
14	SAINT LOUET SUR SEULLES		35	T	10
50	SAINT LOUET SUR VIRE		35	S	11
57	SAINT LOUIS		69	CB	12
68	SAINT LOUIS		90	EB	17
33	SAINT LOUIS DE MONTFERRAND		156	U	29
24	SAINT LOUIS EN L'ISLE		157	Y	28
11	SAINT LOUIS ET PARAHOU		221	GA	38
57	SAINT LOUIS LES BITCHE		48	DB	11
03	SAINT LOUP		133	LA	23
17	SAINT LOUP		127	T	24
23	SAINT LOUP		132	GA	23
39	SAINT LOUP		121	UA	20
41	SAINT LOUP		99	EA	18
50	SAINT LOUP		56	O	12
58	SAINT LOUP		42	NA	12
58	SAINT LOUP		101	JA	18
69	SAINT LOUP		136	QA	25
82	SAINT LOUP		187	AA	33
31	SAINT LOUP CAMMAS		188	DA	34
08	SAINT LOUP CHAMPAGNE		29	PA	9
89	SAINT LOUP D'ORDON		83	KA	15
10	SAINT LOUP DE BUFFIGNY		64	MA	13
14	SAINT LOUP DE FRIBOIS		36	W	10
49	SAINT LOUP DE GONOIS		82	JA	15
71	SAINT LOUP DE LA SALLE		121	SA	20
77	SAINT LOUP DE NAUD		63	KA	13
71	SAINT LOUP DE VARENNES		121	SA	21
18	SAINT LOUP DES CHAUMES		116	HA	20
45	SAINT LOUP DES VIGNES		82	HA	15
53	SAINT LOUP DU DORAT		77	U	16
53	SAINT LOUP DU GAST		57	U	13
31	SAINT LOUP EN COMMINGES		209	Z	36
14	SAINT LOUP HORS		35	T	10
79	SAINT LOUP LAMAIRE	C	112	V	21
70	SAINT LOUP NANTOUARD		106	WA	18
52	SAINT LOUP SUR AUJON		86	TA	16
70	SAINT LOUP SUR SEMOUSE	C	88	YA	16
08	SAINT LOUP TERRIER		30	RA	8
61	SAINT LOYER DES CHAMPS		58	W	12
28	SAINT LUBIN DE CRAVANT		38	BA	12
28	SAINT LUBIN DE LA HAYE		39	DA	12
28	SAINT LUBIN DES JONCHERETS		38	BA	12
41	SAINT LUBIN EN VERGONNOIS		80	CA	17
27	SAINT LUC		38	CA	11
28	SAINT LUCIEN		61	DA	12
51	SAINT LUMIER EN CHAMPAGNE		43	RA	12
51	SAINT LUMIER LA POPULEUSE		43	SA	12
44	SAINT LUMINE DE CLISSON		110	Q	19
44	SAINT LUMINE DE COUTAIS		109	O	19
35	SAINT LUNAIRE		55	N	12
28	SAINT LUPERCE		60	CA	13
39	SAINT LUPICIN		122	WA	22
10	SAINT LUPIEN		64	MA	14
10	SAINT LYE		64	OA	14
45	SAINT LYE LA FORET		81	FA	15
44	SAINT LYPHARD		92	M	18
31	SAINT LYS	C	210	BA	35
35	SAINT M'HERVE		76	R*	14
35	SAINT M'HERVON		75	N	14
33	SAINT MACAIRE	C	170	V	30
49	SAINT MACAIRE DU BOIS		96	V	19
49	SAINT MACAIRE EN MAUGES		95	S	19
27	SAINT MACLOU		23	Y	9
76	SAINT MACLOU DE FOLLEVILLE		24	BA	8
76	SAINT MACLOU LA BRIERE		23	Y	8
86	SAINT MACOUX		129	X	24
22	SAINT MADEN		55	N	14
33	SAINT MAGNE		170	T	31
33	SAINT MAGNE DE CASTILLON		156	W	29
63	SAINT MAIGNER		133	IA	24
17	SAINT MAIGRIN		142	V	27
04	SAINT MAIME		197	WA	33
24	SAINT MAIME DE PEREYROL		158	Z	28
23	SAINT MAIXANT		132	GA	24
33	SAINT MAIXANT		170	V	30
72	SAINT MAIXENT		59	Z	15
79	SAINT MAIXENT DE BEUGNE		111	T	22
79	SAINT MAIXENT L'ECOLE	C	112	V	22
85	SAINT MAIXENT SUR VIE		109	O	21
28	SAINT MAIXME HAUTERIVE		60	BA	13
35	SAINT MALO	S	55	N	12
56	SAINT MALO DE BEIGNON		75	N	15
44	SAINT MALO DE GUERSAC		93	N	18
50	SAINT MALO DE LA LANDE	C	34	P	10
35	SAINT MALO DE PHILY		75	O	16
56	SAINT MALO DES TROIS FONTAINES		74	L	15
85	SAINT MALO DU BOIS		111	S	20
58	SAINT MALO EN DONZIOIS		102	LA	18
35	SAINT MALON SUR MEL		75	N	15
69	SAINT MAMERT		136	OA	23
30	SAINT MAMERT DU GARD	C	193	PA	33
31	SAINT MAMET		217	Z	38
15	SAINT MAMET LA SALVETAT	C	160	GA	29
77	SAINT MAMMES		62	IA	13
94	SAINT MANDE	C	40	HA	11
17	SAINT MANDE SUR BREDOIRE		128	V	24
83	SAINT MANDRIER SUR MER	C	203	XA	37
14	SAINT MANVIEU BOCAGE		35	S	11
14	SAINT MANVIEU NORREY		35	U	10
15	SAINT MARC		162	KA	29
23	SAINT MARC A FRONGIER		132	GA	24
23	SAINT MARC A LOUBAUD		146	FA	25
41	SAINT MARC DU COR		79	AA	15
13	SAINT MARC JAUMEGARDE		202	VA	35
79	SAINT MARC LA LANDE		112	U	22
35	SAINT MARC LE BLANC		56	O	14
35	SAINT MARC SUR COUESNON		76	Q	14
21	SAINT MARC SUR SEINE		85	QA	16
35	SAINT MARCAN		56	P	13
08	SAINT MARCEAU		30	RA	8
72	SAINT MARCEAU		78	X	14
01	SAINT MARCEL		137	SA	24
08	SAINT MARCEL		29	QA	7
27	SAINT MARCEL		38	DA	10
36	SAINT MARCEL		115	DA	21
54	SAINT MARCEL		45	XA	10
56	SAINT MARCEL		74	L	16
70	SAINT MARCEL		87	WA	16
71	SAINT MARCEL		121	SA	21
73	SAINT MARCEL		154	ZA	26
38	SAINT MARCEL BEL ACCUEIL		151	TA	26
81	SAINT MARCEL CAMPES		189	FA	33
07	SAINT MARCEL D'ARDECHE		179	RA	31
42	SAINT MARCEL D'URFE		135	NA	25
30	SAINT MARCEL DE CAREIRET		178	QA	32
42	SAINT MARCEL DE FELINES		135	PA	25
24	SAINT MARCEL DU PERIGORD		158	Z	29
03	SAINT MARCEL EN MARCILLAT		133	IA	23
03	SAINT MARCEL EN MURAT		133	KA	23
69	SAINT MARCEL L'ECLAIRE		136	OA	25
07	SAINT MARCEL LES ANNONAY		150	RA	27
26	SAINT MARCEL LES SAUZET		179	SA	30
26	SAINT MARCEL LES VALENCE		165	SA	29
31	SAINT MARCEL PAULEL		188	DA	34
11	SAINT MARCEL SUR AUDE		213	JA	36
71	SAINT MARCELIN DE CRAY		120	QA	22
38	SAINT MARCELLIN	C	166	UA	28
42	SAINT MARCELLIN EN FOREZ		149	PA	26
84	SAINT MARCELLIN LES VAISON		179	TA	32
31	SAINT MARCET		217	Z	37
24	SAINT MARCORY		158	AA	30
14	SAINT MARCOUF		35	S	10
50	SAINT MARCOUF		33	Q	9
02	SAINT MARD		28	MA	9
17	SAINT MARD		127	T	24
54	SAINT MARD		68	YA	13
77	SAINT MARD		40	IA	11
80	SAINT MARD		27	IA	8
61	SAINT MARD DE RENO		59	Z	13
71	SAINT MARD DE VAUX		120	RA	20
51	SAINT MARD LES ROUFFY		42	OA	11
51	SAINT MARD SUR AUVE		43	RA	11
51	SAINT MARD SUR LE MONT		44	SA	11
76	SAINT MARDS		24	BA	7
27	SAINT MARDS DE BLACARVILLE		23	Z	9
27	SAINT MARDS DE FRESNE		37	Y	10
10	SAINT MARDS EN OTHE		64	NA	14
23	SAINT MARIEN		132	GA	22
33	SAINT MARIENS		156	U	28
61	SAINT MARS D'EGRENNE		57	T	13
72	SAINT MARS D'OUTILLE		78	Y	16
44	SAINT MARS DE COUTAIS		93	O	19
72	SAINT MARS DE LOCQUENAY		78	Y	16
44	SAINT MARS DU DESERT		94	Q	18
53	SAINT MARS DU DESERT		58	V	14
72	SAINT MARS LA BRIERE		79	Y	15
44	SAINT MARS LA JAILLE	C	94	R	17
85	SAINT MARS LA REORTHE		111	S	20
72	SAINT MARS SOUS BALLON		78	X	14
53	SAINT MARS SUR COLMONT		57	T	14
53	SAINT MARS SUR LA FUTAIE		57	S	13
77	SAINT MARS VIEUX MAISONS		41	LA	12
66	SAINT MARSAL		224	IA	39
07	SAINT MARTIAL		164	PA	29
15	SAINT MARTIAL		161	KA	29
16	SAINT MARTIAL		143	W	27
17	SAINT MARTIAL		128	U	24
30	SAINT MARTIAL		192	NA	33
33	SAINT MARTIAL		171	V	30
24	SAINT MARTIAL D'ALBAREDE		144	BA	27
24	SAINT MARTIAL D'ARTENSET		157	X	28
19	SAINT MARTIAL DE GIMEL		160	EA	27
17	SAINT MARTIAL DE MIRAMBEAU		142	U	27
24	SAINT MARTIAL DE NABIRAT		159	CA	30
24	SAINT MARTIAL DE VALETTE		144	Z	26
17	SAINT MARTIAL DE VITATERNE		142	U	26
19	SAINT MARTIAL ENTRAYGUES		160	FA	28
23	SAINT MARTIAL LE MONT		132	FA	24
23	SAINT MARTIAL LE VIEUX		146	GA	26
87	SAINT MARTIAL SUR ISOP		130	AA	23
17	SAINT MARTIAL SUR NE		142	U	26
24	SAINT MARTIAL VIVEYROL		143	Y	27
32	SAINT MARTIN		208	Y	35
54	SAINT MARTIN		69	AB	13
56	SAINT MARTIN		74	M	16
65	SAINT MARTIN		216	W	37
66	SAINT MARTIN		222	HA	38
67	SAINT MARTIN		69	DB	14
83	SAINT MARTIN		203	WA	35
76	SAINT MARTIN AU BOSC		25	EA	7
62	SAINT MARTIN AU LAERT		8	GA	3
76	SAINT MARTIN AUX ARBRES		24	AA	8
60	SAINT MARTIN AUX BOIS		26	HA	8
76	SAINT MARTIN AUX BUNEAUX		23	Y	7
51	SAINT MARTIN AUX CHAMPS		43	QA	12
14	SAINT MARTIN AUX CHARTRAINS		23	X	9
71	SAINT MARTIN BELLE ROCHE		137	SA	22
74	SAINT MARTIN BELLEVUE		139	XA	24
62	SAINT MARTIN BOULOGNE		7	DA	3
15	SAINT MARTIN CANTALES		160	GA	28
23	SAINT MARTIN CHATEAU		145	EA	25
62	SAINT MARTIN CHOQUEL		7	EA	3
47	SAINT MARTIN CURTON		171	W	31
45	SAINT MARTIN D'ABBAT		81	GA	16
51	SAINT MARTIN D'ABLOIS		42	NA	11
26	SAINT MARTIN D'AOUT		151	SA	27
64	SAINT MARTIN D'ARBEROUE		206	R	36
73	SAINT MARTIN D'ARC		167	ZA	28
49	SAINT MARTIN D'ARCE		96	W	17
07	SAINT MARTIN D'ARDECHE		179	QA	32
32	SAINT MARTIN D'ARMAGNAC		185	W	34
64	SAINT MARTIN D'ARROSSA		205	O	36
17	SAINT MARTIN D'ARY		156	V	28
50	SAINT MARTIN D'AUBIGNY		34	Q	10
50	SAINT MARTIN D'AUDOUVILLE		33	Q	8
18	SAINT MARTIN D'AUXIGNY	C	100	HA	19
71	SAINT MARTIN D'AUXY		120	QA	21
61	SAINT MARTIN D'ECUBLEI		37	Z	12
06	SAINT MARTIN D'ENTRAUNES		182	AB	32
42	SAINT MARTIN D'ESTREAUX		135	NA	23
62	SAINT MARTIN D'HARDINGHEM		7	FA	4
38	SAINT MARTIN D'HERES	C	166	WA	28
58	SAINT MARTIN D'HEUILLE		102	KA	19
63	SAINT MARTIN D'OLLIERES		148	MA	27
40	SAINT MARTIN D'ONEY		184	T	33
89	SAINT MARTIN D'ORDON		83	KA	15
09	SAINT MARTIN D'OYDES		219	DA	37
38	SAINT MARTIN D'URIAGE		166	WA	28
01	SAINT MARTIN DE BAVEL		138	VA	25
47	SAINT MARTIN DE BEAUVILLE		172	AA	32
73	SAINT MARTIN DE BELLEVILLE		154	ZA	27
79	SAINT MARTIN DE BERNEGOUE		128	V	23
14	SAINT MARTIN DE BIENFAITE LA CRESSONNIERE		37	Y	11
14	SAINT MARTIN DE BLAGNY		35	S	10
50	SAINT MARTIN DE BONFOSSE		34	R	10
76	SAINT MARTIN DE BOSCHERVILLE		24	AA	9
14	SAINT MARTIN DE BOSSENAY		64	MA	13
48	SAINT MARTIN DE BOUBAUX		177	NA	32
78	SAINT MARTIN DE BRETHENCOURT		61	FA	13
04	SAINT MARTIN DE BROMES		197	WA	34
09	SAINT MARTIN DE CARALP		219	DA	37
84	SAINT MARTIN DE CASTILLON		196	VA	34
50	SAINT MARTIN DE CENILLY		34	Q	11
38	SAINT MARTIN DE CLELLES		166	VA	29
71	SAINT MARTIN DE COMMUNE		120	QA	20
53	SAINT MARTIN DE CONNEE		78	V	14
17	SAINT MARTIN DE COUX		156	W	28
13	SAINT MARTIN DE CRAU		201	SA	35
14	SAINT MARTIN DE FONTENAY		36	V	10
85	SAINT MARTIN DE FRAIGNEAU		111	T	22
24	SAINT MARTIN DE FRESSENGEAS		144	AA	27
43	SAINT MARTIN DE FUGERES		163	OA	29

32	SAINT MARTIN DE GOYNE		187	Z	33
24	SAINT MARTIN DE GURSON		157	X	29
40	SAINT MARTIN DE HINX		183	R	35
17	SAINT MARTIN DE JUILLERS		128	U	24
87	SAINT MARTIN DE JUSSAC		130	AA	25
34	SAINT MARTIN DE L'ARCON		213	JA	35
84	SAINT MARTIN DE LA BRASQUE		196	VA	34
38	SAINT MARTIN DE LA CLUZE		166	VA	29
14	SAINT MARTIN DE LA LIEUE		37	X	10
21	SAINT MARTIN DE LA MER		104	PA	19
49	SAINT MARTIN DE LA PLACE		96	V	18
73	SAINT MARTIN DE LA PORTE		153	ZA	27
36	SAINT MARTIN DE LAMPS		115	DA	20
50	SAINT MARTIN DE LANDELLES		56	R	13
48	SAINT MARTIN DE LANSUSCLE		177	NA	32
33	SAINT MARTIN DE LAYE		156	V	28
12	SAINT MARTIN DE LENNE		176	JA	31
33	SAINT MARTIN DE LERM		171	W	30
71	SAINT MARTIN DE LIXY		135	PA	23
34	SAINT MARTIN DE LONDRES	C	192	NA	34
79	SAINT MARTIN DE MACON		96	W	20
14	SAINT MARTIN DE MAILLOC		37	X	10
14	SAINT MARTIN DE MIEUX		36	V	11
28	SAINT MARTIN DE NIGELLES		61	DA	12
05	SAINT MARTIN DE QUEYRIERES		168	ZA	29
17	SAINT MARTIN DE RE	C	126	Q	23
24	SAINT MARTIN DE RIBERAC		143	Y	27
71	SAINT MARTIN DE SALENCEY		120	OA	22
14	SAINT MARTIN DE SALLEN		35	U	11
79	SAINT MARTIN DE SANZAY		96	V	19
40	SAINT MARTIN DE SEIGNANX	C	183	Q	35
33	SAINT MARTIN DE SESCAS		171	V	30
79	SAINT MARTIN DE ST MAIXENT		128	V	22
07	SAINT MARTIN DE VALAMAS	C	164	QA	29
30	SAINT MARTIN DE VALGALGUES		178	OA	32
50	SAINT MARTIN DE VARREVILLE		33	R	9
38	SAINT MARTIN DE VAULSERRE		152	VA	26
46	SAINT MARTIN DE VERS		174	DA	30
47	SAINT MARTIN DE VILLEREAL		172	AA	30
11	SAINT MARTIN DE VILLEREGLAN		221	GA	37
14	SAINT MARTIN DES BESACES		35	S	11
41	SAINT MARTIN DES BOIS		79	AA	16
18	SAINT MARTIN DES CHAMPS		101	JA	19
29	SAINT MARTIN DES CHAMPS		52	F	13
50	SAINT MARTIN DES CHAMPS		56	Q	12
77	SAINT MARTIN DES CHAMPS		41	LA	12
78	SAINT MARTIN DES CHAMPS		39	EA	11
89	SAINT MARTIN DES CHAMPS		83	KA	17
24	SAINT MARTIN DES COMBES		158	Z	29
14	SAINT MARTIN DES ENTREES		35	T	10
85	SAINT MARTIN DES FONTAINES		111	S	22
03	SAINT MARTIN DES LAIS		119	MA	21
61	SAINT MARTIN DES LANDES		58	W	13
85	SAINT MARTIN DES MONTS		59	Z	15
72	SAINT MARTIN DES NOYERS		110	R	21
63	SAINT MARTIN DES OLMES		149	NA	26
61	SAINT MARTIN DES PEZERITS		59	Y	12
63	SAINT MARTIN DES PLAINS		148	LA	26
22	SAINT MARTIN DES PRES		53	J	14
11	SAINT MARTIN DES PUITS		223	IA	37
85	SAINT MARTIN DES TILLEULS		110	R	20
14	SAINT MARTIN DON		35	S	11
76	SAINT MARTIN DU BEC		23	X	8
33	SAINT MARTIN DU BOIS		156	V	28
49	SAINT MARTIN DU BOIS		77	T	16
77	SAINT MARTIN DU BOSCHET		41	LA	12
16	SAINT MARTIN DU CLOCHER		129	X	24
49	SAINT MARTIN DU FOUILLOUX		95	T	18
79	SAINT MARTIN DU FOUILLOUX		112	W	21
01	SAINT MARTIN DU FRENE		138	VA	23
71	SAINT MARTIN DU LAC		135	OA	23
53	SAINT MARTIN DU LIMET		76	R	16
76	SAINT MARTIN DU MANOIR		23	X	8
14	SAINT MARTIN DU MESNIL OURY		36	X	11
01	SAINT MARTIN DU MONT		138	UA	24
21	SAINT MARTIN DU MONT		104	RA	18
71	SAINT MARTIN DU MONT		121	UA	21
33	SAINT MARTIN DU PUY		171	W	30
58	SAINT MARTIN DU PUY		103	NA	18
71	SAINT MARTIN DU TARTRE		120	RA	21
89	SAINT MARTIN DU TERTRE		63	LA	14
95	SAINT MARTIN DU TERTRE		40	HA	10
27	SAINT MARTIN DU TILLEUL		37	Z	10
06	SAINT MARTIN DU VAR		200	CB	34
61	SAINT MARTIN DU VIEUX BELLEME		59	Y	13
76	SAINT MARTIN DU VIVIER		24	BA	9
77	SAINT MARTIN EN BIERE		62	HA	13
71	SAINT MARTIN EN BRESSE	C	121	TA	20
76	SAINT MARTIN EN CAMPAGNE		15	CA	6
71	SAINT MARTIN EN GATINOIS		121	SA	20
69	SAINT MARTIN EN HAUT		150	QA	26
26	SAINT MARTIN EN VERCORS		166	UA	28
32	SAINT MARTIN GIMOIS		209	AA	35
61	SAINT MARTIN L'AIGUILLON		58	V	12
86	SAINT MARTIN L'ARS		129	Y	23
24	SAINT MARTIN L'ASTIER		157	Y	28
51	SAINT MARTIN L'HEUREUX		43	QA	10
76	SAINT MARTIN L'HORTIER		25	CA	7
27	SAINT MARTIN LA CAMPAGNE		38	BA	10
78	SAINT MARTIN LA GARENNE		39	EA	11
19	SAINT MARTIN LA MEANNE		160	FA	28
71	SAINT MARTIN LA PATROUILLE		120	QA	21
42	SAINT MARTIN LA PLAINE		150	RA	26
42	SAINT MARTIN LA SAUVETE		135	OA	25
46	SAINT MARTIN LABOUVAL		174	EA	31
33	SAINT MARTIN LACAUSSADE		156	T	28
81	SAINT MARTIN LAGUEPIE		174	FA	32
11	SAINT MARTIN LALANDE		211	FA	36
85	SAINT MARTIN LARS EN STE HERMINE		111	S	21
37	SAINT MARTIN LE BEAU		98	AA	18
50	SAINT MARTIN LE BOUILLANT		56	R	12
01	SAINT MARTIN LE CHATEL		137	TA	23
26	SAINT MARTIN LE COLONEL		166	UA	29
76	SAINT MARTIN LE GAILLARD		15	CA	6
50	SAINT MARTIN LE GREARD		33	P	8
50	SAINT MARTIN LE HEBERT		33	P	8
87	SAINT MARTIN LE MAULT		131	BA	22
60	SAINT MARTIN LE NOEUD		26	FA	9
24	SAINT MARTIN LE PIN		144	Z	26
46	SAINT MARTIN LE REDON		173	BA	31
11	SAINT MARTIN LE VIEIL		212	GA	36
87	SAINT MARTIN LE VIEUX		144	BA	25
38	SAINT MARTIN LE VINOUX		166	WA	28
04	SAINT MARTIN LES EAUX		197	WA	33
52	SAINT MARTIN LES LANGRES		86	TA	16
79	SAINT MARTIN LES MELLE		128	V	23
04	SAINT MARTIN LES SEYNE		181	YA	31
42	SAINT MARTIN LESTRA		150	QA	25
60	SAINT MARTIN LONGUEAU		26	IA	9
11	SAINT MARTIN LYS		221	GA	38
76	SAINT MARTIN OSMONVILLE		24	CA	8
47	SAINT MARTIN PETIT		171	X	30
02	SAINT MARTIN RIVIERE		18	MA	6
19	SAINT MARTIN SEPERT		145	DA	27
71	SAINT MARTIN SOUS MONTAIGU		120	RA	20
15	SAINT MARTIN SOUS VIGOUROUX		161	JA	29
27	SAINT MARTIN ST FIRMIN		37	Z	9
23	SAINT MARTIN STE CATHERINE		131	DA	24
89	SAINT MARTIN SUR ARMANCON		84	OA	16
62	SAINT MARTIN SUR COJEUL		17	JA	5
59	SAINT MARTIN SUR ECAILLON		18	MA	5
73	SAINT MARTIN SUR LA CHAMBRE		153	YA	27
07	SAINT MARTIN SUR LAVEZON		179	RA	30
51	SAINT MARTIN SUR LE PRE		43	PA	11
58	SAINT MARTIN SUR NOHAIN		102	KA	18
59	SAINT MARTIN SUR OCRE		82	IA	17
89	SAINT MARTIN SUR OCRE		83	LA	16
89	SAINT MARTIN SUR OUANNE		83	KA	16
87	SAINT MARTIN TERRESSUS		131	DA	24
15	SAINT MARTIN VALMEROUX		160	HA	28
06	SAINT MARTIN VESUBIE	C	199	CB	33
03	SAINT MARTINIEN		133	HA	23
31	SAINT MARTORY	C	217	AA	37
16	SAINT MARY		129	Y	25
16	SAINT MARY LE PLAIN		162	KA	28
51	SAINT MASMES		29	PA	9
87	SAINT MATHIEU	C	144	Z	25
34	SAINT MATHIEU DE TREVIERS		192	NA	34
85	SAINT MATHURIN		125	P	22
49	SAINT MATHURIN SUR LOIRE		96	V	18
46	SAINT MATRE		173	BA	31
22	SAINT MAUDAN		74	K	15
22	SAINT MAUDEZ		55	N	13
35	SAINT MAUGAN		75	N	15
80	SAINT MAULVIS		25	EA	7
18	SAINT MAUR		116	GA	21
32	SAINT MAUR		208	Y	35
36	SAINT MAUR		115	DA	20
39	SAINT MAUR		122	VA	21
60	SAINT MAUR		25	FA	8
50	SAINT MAUR DES BOIS		56	R	12
94	SAINT MAUR DES FOSSES	C	40	HA	12
28	SAINT MAUR SUR LE LOIR		60	DA	14
52	SAINT MAURICE		87	UA	16
58	SAINT MAURICE		102	MA	19
63	SAINT MAURICE		148	KA	25
67	SAINT MAURICE		70	DB	14
94	SAINT MAURICE		40	HA	12
54	SAINT MAURICE AUX FORGES		69	BB	13
89	SAINT MAURICE AUX RICHES HOMMES		64	MA	14
25	SAINT MAURICE COLOMBIER		108	AB	18
39	SAINT MAURICE CRILLAT		122	WA	22
07	SAINT MAURICE D'ARDECHE		178	QA	31
76	SAINT MAURICE D'ETELAN		23	Z	9
07	SAINT MAURICE D'IBIE		178	QA	31
01	SAINT MAURICE DE BEYNOST		137	SA	25
30	SAINT MAURICE DE CAZEVIEILLE		193	PA	33
01	SAINT MAURICE DE GOURDANS		137	TA	25
47	SAINT MAURICE DE LESTAPEL		172	Z	30
43	SAINT MAURICE DE LIGNON		149	PA	27
01	SAINT MAURICE DE REMENS		137	UA	24
73	SAINT MAURICE DE ROTHERENS		152	WA	26
71	SAINT MAURICE DE SATONNAY		136	RA	22
17	SAINT MAURICE DE TAVERNOLE		142	U	26
48	SAINT MAURICE DE VENTALON		177	NA	32
71	SAINT MAURICE DES CHAMPS		120	RA	21
16	SAINT MAURICE DES LIONS		130	Z	24
85	SAINT MAURICE DES NOUES		111	T	21
61	SAINT MAURICE DU DESERT		58	U	12
07	SAINT MAURICE EN CHALENCON		164	RA	29
50	SAINT MAURICE EN COTENTIN		33	P	9
42	SAINT MAURICE EN GOURGOIS		149	PA	27
46	SAINT MAURICE EN QUERCY		160	FA	30
71	SAINT MAURICE EN RIVIERE		121	SA	20
38	SAINT MAURICE EN TRIEVES		166	VA	30
05	SAINT MAURICE EN VALGODEMARD		167	XA	29
38	SAINT MAURICE L'EXIL		150	RA	27
86	SAINT MAURICE LA CLOUERE		129	Y	22
79	SAINT MAURICE LA FOUGEREUSE		96	U	19
23	SAINT MAURICE LA SOUTERRAINE		131	DA	23
85	SAINT MAURICE LE GIRARD		111	T	21
89	SAINT MAURICE LE VIEIL		83	LA	16
87	SAINT MAURICE LES BROUSSES		145	CA	25
61	SAINT MAURICE LES CHARENCEY		59	AA	12
71	SAINT MAURICE LES CHATEAUNEUF		135	PA	23
71	SAINT MAURICE LES COUCHES		120	OA	20
91	SAINT MAURICE MONTCOURONNE		61	GA	13
34	SAINT MAURICE NAVACELLES		192	MA	34
23	SAINT MAURICE PRES CROCQ		132	GA	25
63	SAINT MAURICE PRES PIONSAT		133	IA	24
55	SAINT MAURICE SOUS LES COTES		45	VA	11
28	SAINT MAURICE ST GERMAIN		60	BA	13
40	SAINT MAURICE SUR ADOUR		184	U	34
45	SAINT MAURICE SUR AVEYRON		82	JA	16
69	SAINT MAURICE SUR DARGOIRE		150	RA	26
26	SAINT MAURICE SUR EYGUES		179	SA	32
45	SAINT MAURICE SUR FESSARD		82	IA	15
61	SAINT MAURICE SUR HUISNE		59	Z	13
88	SAINT MAURICE SUR MORTAGNE		68	ZA	13
88	SAINT MAURICE SUR MOSELLE		89	BB	16
21	SAINT MAURICE SUR VINGEANNE		87	UA	17
89	SAINT MAURICE THIZOUAILLE		83	LA	16
47	SAINT MAURIN		172	AA	32
54	SAINT MAX	C	46	YA	12
80	SAINT MAXENT		15	EA	6
30	SAINT MAXIMIN		193	OA	33
38	SAINT MAXIMIN		153	XA	27
60	SAINT MAXIMIN		40	HA	10
83	SAINT MAXIMIN LA STE BAUME	C	202	WA	35
79	SAINT MAXIRE		112	U	22
26	SAINT MAY		180	UA	31
22	SAINT MAYEUX		73	J	14
87	SAINT MEARD		145	DA	26
24	SAINT MEARD DE DRONE		143	Y	27
24	SAINT MEARD DE GURCON		157	X	29
16	SAINT MEDARD		142	V	26
17	SAINT MEDARD		142	V	27
31	SAINT MEDARD		217	AA	37
32	SAINT MEDARD		208	Y	35
36	SAINT MEDARD		115	CA	20
46	SAINT MEDARD		173	CA	31
57	SAINT MEDARD		47	AB	12
64	SAINT MEDARD		207	U	35
79	SAINT MEDARD		128	V	23
17	SAINT MEDARD D'AUNIS		127	S	23
24	SAINT MEDARD D'EXCIDEUIL		144	BA	27
33	SAINT MEDARD D'EYRANS		156	U	30
33	SAINT MEDARD DE GUIZIERES		156	W	28
24	SAINT MEDARD DE MUSSIDAN		157	Y	28
46	SAINT MEDARD DE PRESQUE		160	EA	29
42	SAINT MEDARD EN FOREZ		150	PA	26
33	SAINT MEDARD EN JALLES	C	155	T	29
23	SAINT MEDARD LA ROCHETTE		132	GA	24
46	SAINT MEDARD NICOURBY		160	FA	30
35	SAINT MEDARD SUR ILLE		75	P	14
29	SAINT MEEN		52	D	13
35	SAINT MEEN LE GRAND	C	75	M	14
49	SAINT MELAINE SUR AUBANCE		96	U	18
07	SAINT MELANY		178	OA	31
22	SAINT MELOIR		55	M	13
35	SAINT MELOIR DES ONDES		55	O	12
44	SAINT MEME LE TENU		109	O	20
16	SAINT MEME LES CARRIERES		142	V	26
16	SAINT MEME LES CARRIERES		128	U	25
51	SAINT MEMMIE		43	QA	11
88	SAINT MENGE		67	XA	14
08	SAINT MENGES		30	SA	7
03	SAINT MENOUX		118	KA	21
19	SAINT MERD DE LAPLEAU		160	FA	27
23	SAINT MERD LA BREUILLE		147	HA	25
19	SAINT MERD LES OUSSINES		146	FA	26
77	SAINT MERY		62	JA	13
27	SAINT MESLIN DU BOSC		37	AA	10
77	SAINT MESMES		40	IA	11
10	SAINT MESMIN		64	OA	13
21	SAINT MESMIN		104	RA	18
24	SAINT MESMIN		145	CA	27
85	SAINT MESMIN		111	T	21
19	SAINT MEXANT		145	DA	27
32	SAINT MEZARD		187	Z	33
71	SAINT MICAUD		120	QA	21
02	SAINT MICHEL		19	PA	7
09	SAINT MICHEL		219	DA	37
16	SAINT MICHEL		143	W	26
31	SAINT MICHEL		218	BA	37
32	SAINT MICHEL		208	Y	36
34	SAINT MICHEL		192	LA	34
45	SAINT MICHEL		82	HA	15
64	SAINT MICHEL		206	R	37
82	SAINT MICHEL		187	AA	33
44	SAINT MICHEL CHEF CHEF		93	N	19
07	SAINT MICHEL D'AURANCE		164	QA	29
30	SAINT MICHEL D'EUZET		179	QA	32
76	SAINT MICHEL D'HALESCOURT		25	DA	8
46	SAINT MICHEL DE BANNIERES		159	EA	29
07	SAINT MICHEL DE BOULOGNE		164	QA	30
33	SAINT MICHEL DE CASTELNAU		171	W	32
07	SAINT MICHEL DE CHABRILLANOUX		164	RA	29
05	SAINT MICHEL DE CHAILLOL		167	YA	30
72	SAINT MICHEL DE CHAVAIGNES		79	Z	15
48	SAINT MICHEL DE DEZE		177	NA	32
24	SAINT MICHEL DE DOUBLE		157	X	28
53	SAINT MICHEL DE FEINS		77	U	16
33	SAINT MICHEL DE FRONSAC		156	V	29
50	SAINT MICHEL DE LA PIERRE		34	Q	10
53	SAINT MICHEL DE LA ROE		76	R	16
11	SAINT MICHEL DE LANES		211	EA	36
33	SAINT MICHEL DE LAPUJADE		171	W	30
14	SAINT MICHEL DE LIVET		36	X	11
66	SAINT MICHEL DE LLOTES		224	IB	39
73	SAINT MICHEL DE MAURIENNE	C	167	ZA	28
24	SAINT MICHEL DE MONTAIGNE		157	W	29
50	SAINT MICHEL DE MONTJOIE		57	S	12
22	SAINT MICHEL DE PLELAN		55	M	13
33	SAINT MICHEL DE RIEUFRET		170	U	30
38	SAINT MICHEL DE ST GEOIRS		152	UA	27
81	SAINT MICHEL DE VAX		174	EA	32
23	SAINT MICHEL DE VEISSE		132	FA	24
24	SAINT MICHEL DE VILLADEIX		158	Z	29
18	SAINT MICHEL DE VOLANGIS		101	HA	19
61	SAINT MICHEL DES ANDAINES		57	U	13
38	SAINT MICHEL EN BEAUMONT		167	WA	29
36	SAINT MICHEL EN BRENNE		114	BA	20
22	SAINT MICHEL EN GREVE		53	G	12
85	SAINT MICHEL EN L'HERM		125	Q	22
40	SAINT MICHEL ESCALUS		183	R	33
49	SAINT MICHEL ET CHANVEAUX		94	R	17
04	SAINT MICHEL L'OBSERVATOIRE		196	VA	33
81	SAINT MICHEL LABADIE		190	HA	33
85	SAINT MICHEL LE CLOUCQ		111	T	22
38	SAINT MICHEL LES PORTES		166	VA	29
46	SAINT MICHEL LOUBEJOU		160	EA	29
85	SAINT MICHEL MONT MERCURE		111	S	20
62	SAINT MICHEL SOUS BOIS		7	FA	4
37	SAINT MICHEL SUR LOIRE		97	Y	18
88	SAINT MICHEL SUR MEURTHE		69	BB	14
91	SAINT MICHEL SUR ORGE	C	62	GA	12
42	SAINT MICHEL SUR RHONE		150	RA	27
26	SAINT MICHEL SUR SAVASSE		165	TA	28
62	SAINT MICHEL SUR TERNOISE		16	HA	5
61	SAINT MICHEL TUBOEUF		37	Z	12
55	SAINT MIHIEL	C	45	VA	11
13	SAINT MITRE LES REMPARTS		201	TA	35
44	SAINT MOLF		92	L	18
59	SAINT MOMELIN		8	GA	3
32	SAINT MONT		185	V	34
07	SAINT MONTANT		179	RA	31
89	SAINT MORE		84	NA	17
23	SAINT MOREIL		131	EA	25
08	SAINT MOREL		30	RA	9
33	SAINT MORILLON		170	U	30
38	SAINT MURY MONTEYMOND		167	XA	28
63	SAINT MYON		134	KA	24
67	SAINT NABOR		70	DB	13
88	SAINT NABORD		68	ZA	15
10	SAINT NABORD SUR AUBE		65	PA	13
82	SAINT NAUPHARY		188	DA	33
30	SAINT NAZAIRE		179	RA	32
44	SAINT NAZAIRE	S	92	M	18
66	SAINT NAZAIRE		224	JA	39
11	SAINT NAZAIRE D'AUDE		213	JA	36
34	SAINT NAZAIRE DE LADAREZ		213	KA	35
34	SAINT NAZAIRE DE PEZAN		194	OA	35
82	SAINT NAZAIRE DE VALENTANE		173	BA	32
30	SAINT NAZAIRE DES GARDIES		193	OA	33
26	SAINT NAZAIRE EN ROYANS		165	TA	28
26	SAINT NAZAIRE LE DESERT		180	UA	30
38	SAINT NAZAIRE LES EYMES		152	WA	27
17	SAINT NAZAIRE SUR CHARENTE		126	R	24
63	SAINT NECTAIRE		147	JA	26
24	SAINT NEXANS		157	Z	29
29	SAINT NIC		71	D	14
22	SAINT NICODEME		53	H	14
62	SAINT NICOLAS		17	IA	5
02	SAINT NICOLAS AUX BOIS		28	LA	8
76	SAINT NICOLAS D'ALIERMONT		24	CA	7
27	SAINT NICOLAS D'ATTEZ		37	AA	12
76	SAINT NICOLAS DE BLIQUETUIT		24	Z	8
37	SAINT NICOLAS DE BOURGUEIL		97	X	18
47	SAINT NICOLAS DE LA BALERME		172	Z	32
82	SAINT NICOLAS DE LA GRAVE	C	187	BA	33
76	SAINT NICOLAS DE LA HAIE		23	Z	8
76	SAINT NICOLAS DE LA TAILLE		23	Y	8
38	SAINT NICOLAS DE MACHERIN		152	VA	27
50	SAINT NICOLAS DE PIERREPONT		34	P	9
54	SAINT NICOLAS DE PORT	C	68	YA	12
44	SAINT NICOLAS DE REDON	C	93	N	17
61	SAINT NICOLAS DE SOMMAIRE		37	Z	12
03	SAINT NICOLAS DES BIEFS		135	NA	24
50	SAINT NICOLAS DES BOIS		56	R	12
61	SAINT NICOLAS DES BOIS		58	W	13
61	SAINT NICOLAS DES LAITIERS		37	Y	11
37	SAINT NICOLAS DES MOTETS		79	BA	17
27	SAINT NICOLAS DU BOSC		37	AA	10
22	SAINT NICOLAS DU PELEM	C	53	I	14
56	SAINT NICOLAS DU TERTRE		74	M	16
10	SAINT NICOLAS LA CHAPELLE		64	MA	13
73	SAINT NICOLAS LA CHAPELLE		139	ZA	25
21	SAINT NICOLAS LES CITEAUX		105	TA	19
69	SAINT NIZIER D'AZERGUES		136	QA	24
42	SAINT NIZIER DE FORNAS		149	OA	27
38	SAINT NIZIER DU MOUCHEROTTE		166	VA	28
01	SAINT NIZIER LE BOUCHOUX		121	TA	22
01	SAINT NIZIER LE DESERT		137	TA	24
42	SAINT NIZIER SOUS CHARLIEU		135	OA	23
71	SAINT NIZIER SUR ARROUX		119	PA	20
56	SAINT NOLFF		74	K	16
78	SAINT NOM LA BRETECHE	C	39	FA	11
73	SAINT OFFENGE DESSOUS		153	XA	25
73	SAINT OFFENGE DESSUS		153	XA	25
14	SAINT OMER		35	U	11
62	SAINT OMER	S	8	GA	3
62	SAINT OMER CAPELLE		7	GA	2
60	SAINT OMER EN CHAUSSEE		26	FA	8
38	SAINT ONDRAS		152	VA	26
35	SAINT ONEN LA CHAPELLE		75	M	14
23	SAINT ORADOUX DE CHIROUZE		146	GA	25
23	SAINT ORADOUX PRES CROCQ		132	HA	25
32	SAINT ORENS		187	AA	34
31	SAINT ORENS DE GAMEVILLE		210	DA	35
32	SAINT ORENS POUY PETIT		186	Y	33
32	SAINT OST		208	Y	36
17	SAINT OUEN		128	V	25
41	SAINT OUEN		80	BA	16
80	SAINT OUEN		16	GA	6
93	SAINT OUEN	C	40	GA	11
27	SAINT OUEN D'ATTEZ		37	AA	12
17	SAINT OUEN D'AUNIS		127	S	23
61	SAINT OUEN DE LA COUR		59	Z	13
72	SAINT OUEN DE MIMBRE		58	W	14
27	SAINT OUEN DE PONTCHEUIL		38	AA	10
61	SAINT OUEN DE SECHEROUVRE		59	Y	12
27	SAINT OUEN DE THOUBERVILLE		24	AA	9
35	SAINT OUEN DES ALLEUX		76	O	14
14	SAINT OUEN DES BESACES		35	S	11
27	SAINT OUEN DES CHAMPS		23	Z	9
53	SAINT OUEN DES TOITS		77	S	15
53	SAINT OUEN DES VALLONS		77	U	14
51	SAINT OUEN DOMPROT		65	QA	12
76	SAINT OUEN DU BREUIL		24	BA	8
14	SAINT OUEN DU MESNIL OGER		36	W	10
27	SAINT OUEN DU TILLEUL		38	AA	9
72	SAINT OUEN EN BELIN		78	X	16
77	SAINT OUEN EN BRIE		63	JA	13
72	SAINT OUEN EN CHAMPAGNE		78	V	15
95	SAINT OUEN L'AUMONE	C	39	GA	11
35	SAINT OUEN LA ROUERIE		56	Q	13
61	SAINT OUEN LE BRISOULT		58	V	13
14	SAINT OUEN LE HOUX		36	X	11
76	SAINT OUEN LE MAUGER		24	AA	7
14	SAINT OUEN LE PIN		36	X	10
88	SAINT OUEN LES PAREY		67	WA	14
37	SAINT OUEN LES VIGNES		98	BA	18
28	SAINT OUEN MARCHEFROY		38	DA	11
76	SAINT OUEN SOUS BAILLY		24	CA	7
87	SAINT OUEN SUR GARTEMPE		130	BA	23
61	SAINT OUEN SUR ITON		37	Z	12
58	SAINT OUEN SUR LOIRE		118	LA	20
61	SAINT OUEN SUR MAIRE		58	V	12
77	SAINT OUEN SUR MORIN		41	KA	11
10	SAINT OULPH		64	NA	13
63	SAINT OURS		147	JA	25
73	SAINT OURS		153	XA	25
18	SAINT OUTRILLE		99	EA	19
50	SAINT OVIN		56	Q	12
73	SAINT OYEN		153	ZA	26
29	SAINT PABU		51	C	13
76	SAINT PAER		24	AA	8
14	SAINT PAIR		36	V	10
50	SAINT PAIR SUR MER		56	P	12
43	SAINT PAL DE CHALENCON		149	OA	27
43	SAINT PAL DE MONS		150	PA	27
43	SAINT PAL DE SENOUIRE		162	MA	27
03	SAINT PALAIS		132	GA	22
18	SAINT PALAIS		100	HA	19
33	SAINT PALAIS		142	T	27
64	SAINT PALAIS	C	206	S	36
17	SAINT PALAIS DE NEGRIGNAC		142	V	27
17	SAINT PALAIS DE PHIOLIN		142	T	26
16	SAINT PALAIS DU NE		142	V	26
17	SAINT PALAIS SUR MER		141	R	26
24	SAINT PANCRACE		144	Z	27
73	SAINT PANCRACE		153	YA	27
38	SAINT PANCRASSE		152	WA	27
54	SAINT PANCRE		31	VA	8
40	SAINT PANDELON		183	R	34
46	SAINT PANTALEON		173	CA	31
84	SAINT PANTALEON		196	TA	33
19	SAINT PANTALEON DE LAPLEAU		146	GA	27
19	SAINT PANTALEON DE LARCHE		159	CA	28
26	SAINT PANTALEON LES VIGNES		179	SA	31
24	SAINT PANTALY D'ANS		144	AA	27
24	SAINT PANTALY D'EXCIDEUIL		144	BA	27
11	SAINT PAPOUL		211	FA	36
33	SAINT PARDON DE CONQUES		170	V	30
17	SAINT PARDOULT		128	U	24
63	SAINT PARDOUX		133	KA	24
79	SAINT PARDOUX		112	V	22
87	SAINT PARDOUX		131	CA	24
19	SAINT PARDOUX CORBIER		145	DA	27
23	SAINT PARDOUX D'ARNET		132	HA	25
24	SAINT PARDOUX DE DRONE		143	Y	27
47	SAINT PARDOUX DU BREUIL		171	X	31
24	SAINT PARDOUX ET VIELVIC		158	AA	30
47	SAINT PARDOUX ISAAC		172	Y	30
19	SAINT PARDOUX L'ORTIGIER		145	DA	27
19	SAINT PARDOUX LA CROISILLE		160	FA	27
24	SAINT PARDOUX LA RIVIERE	C	144	Z	26
19	SAINT PARDOUX LE NEUF		146	HA	26
23	SAINT PARDOUX LE NEUF		132	GA	24
19	SAINT PARDOUX LE VIEUX		146	GA	26
23	SAINT PARDOUX LES CARDS		132	GA	24
23	SAINT PARDOUX MORTEROLLES		132	EA	25
34	SAINT PARGOIRE		214	MA	35
58	SAINT PARIZE EN VIRY		118	LA	21
58	SAINT PARIZE LE CHATEL		118	KA	20
10	SAINT PARRES AUX TERTRES		64	OA	14
10	SAINT PARRES LES VAUDES		65	PA	14
12	SAINT PARTHEM		175	GA	30
47	SAINT PASTOUR		172	Z	31
65	SAINT PASTOUS		216	W	37
72	SAINT PATERNE	C	58	X	13
37	SAINT PATERNE RACAN		97	Y	17
77	SAINT PATHUS		40	JA	10
37	SAINT PATRICE		97	Y	18
50	SAINT PATRICE DE CLAIDS		34	O	10
61	SAINT PATRICE DU DESERT		58	V	13
06	SAINT PAUL		200	CB	34
19	SAINT PAUL		160	FA	28
33	SAINT PAUL		156	T	28
60	SAINT PAUL		26	FA	9
61	SAINT PAUL		57	T	12
65	SAINT PAUL		217	Y	37
73	SAINT PAUL		152	WA	25
87	SAINT PAUL		145	CA	25
88	SAINT PAUL		67	WA	14
04	SAINT PAUL (SUR UBAYE)		182	AB	31
02	SAINT PAUL AUX BOIS		27	KA	8
81	SAINT PAUL CAP DE JOUX	C	211	FA	35
82	SAINT PAUL D'ESPIS		173	AA	32
38	SAINT PAUL D'IZEAUX		152	UA	27
31	SAINT PAUL D'OUEIL		217	Z	38
42	SAINT PAUL D'UZORE		149	OA	25
32	SAINT PAUL DE BAISE		186	Y	34
66	SAINT PAUL DE FENOUILLET	C	221	HA	38
27	SAINT PAUL DE FOURQUES		37	AA	10
09	SAINT PAUL DE JARRAT		219	EA	38
46	SAINT PAUL DE LOUBRESSAC		173	DA	32
15	SAINT PAUL DE SALERS		161	HA	28
24	SAINT PAUL DE SERRE		158	Z	28
43	SAINT PAUL DE TARTAS		163	NA	29
01	SAINT PAUL DE VARAX		137	TA	24
38	SAINT PAUL DE VARCES		166	VA	28
46	SAINT PAUL DE VERN		160	FA	29
42	SAINT PAUL DE VEZELIN		135	OA	25
15	SAINT PAUL DES LANDES		160	GA	29
49	SAINT PAUL DU BOIS		95	U	19
14	SAINT PAUL DU VERNAY		35	T	10
40	SAINT PAUL EN BORN		169	R	32
74	SAINT PAUL EN CHABLAIS		124	AB	22
42	SAINT PAUL EN CORNILLON		149	PA	27
83	SAINT PAUL EN FORET		198	AB	35
79	SAINT PAUL EN GATINE		111	T	21
42	SAINT PAUL EN JAREZ		150	RA	26
85	SAINT PAUL EN PAREDS		111	S	20
34	SAINT PAUL ET VALMALLE		214	NA	35
30	SAINT PAUL LA COSTE		178	OA	32
24	SAINT PAUL LA ROCHE		144	BA	26
48	SAINT PAUL LE FROID		162	MA	29
72	SAINT PAUL LE GAULTIER		58	W	14
07	SAINT PAUL LE JEUNE		178	PA	31
40	SAINT PAUL LES DAX		183	R	34
13	SAINT PAUL LES DURANCE		196	VA	34
30	SAINT PAUL LES FONTS		195	RA	33
38	SAINT PAUL LES MONESTIER		166	VA	29
26	SAINT PAUL LES ROMANS		165	TA	28
24	SAINT PAUL LIZONNE		143	X	27
85	SAINT PAUL MONT PENIT		109	P	20
73	SAINT PAUL SUR ISERE		153	ZA	26
31	SAINT PAUL SUR SAVE		188	CA	34
26	SAINT PAUL TROIS CHATEAUX	C	179	RA	31
11	SAINT PAULET		211	EA	36
30	SAINT PAULET DE CAISSON		179	RA	32
43	SAINT PAULIEN	C	163	NA	28
72	SAINT PAVACE		78	X	15
31	SAINT PE D'ARDET		217	Z	37
65	SAINT PE DE BIGORRE	C	216	W	37
64	SAINT PE DE LEREN		206	R	35
31	SAINT PE DELBOSC		209	Z	36
47	SAINT PE ST SIMON		186	X	33
64	SAINT PEE SUR NIVELLE		205	P	36
28	SAINT PELLERIN		80	BA	15
50	SAINT PELLERIN		34	R	9
35	SAINT PERAN		75	N	15
45	SAINT PERAVY LA COLOMBE		81	EA	15
07	SAINT PERAY	C	165	SA	29
40	SAINT PERDON		184	U	34
24	SAINT PERDOUX		157	Z	30
46	SAINT PERDOUX		174	FA	30
35	SAINT PERE		55	O	13
58	SAINT PERE		101	JA	18
89	SAINT PERE		103	NA	18
44	SAINT PERE EN RETZ	C	93	N	19
45	SAINT PERE SUR LOIRE		82	HA	16
58	SAINT PEREUSE		103	NA	19
35	SAINT PERN		75	N	14
56	SAINT PERREUX		93	N	17
22	SAINT PEVER		53	I	13
33	SAINT PEY D'ARMENS		156	W	29
33	SAINT PEY DE CASTETS		156	W	29
10	SAINT PHAL		64	OA	15
85	SAINT PHILBERT DE BOUAINE		110	P	20
44	SAINT PHILBERT DE GRAND LIEU	C	109	P	19
14	SAINT PHILBERT DES CHAMPS		37	X	10
49	SAINT PHILBERT DU PEUPLE		96	W	18
49	SAINT PHILBERT EN MAUGES		95	S	19
27	SAINT PHILBERT SUR BOISSEY		37	AA	10
61	SAINT PHILBERT SUR ORNE		36	U	11
27	SAINT PHILBERT SUR RISLE		23	Z	9
21	SAINT PHILIBERT		105	SA	19
56	SAINT PHILIBERT		91	J	17
33	SAINT PHILIPPE D'AIGUILLE		156	W	29
33	SAINT PHILIPPE DU SEIGNAL		157	X	29
28	SAINT PIAT		60	DA	13
04	SAINT PIERRE		199	BB	33
15	SAINT PIERRE		146	HA	27

Dép.	Commune		Page	Carré	
31	SAINT PIERRE		211	EA	35
39	SAINT PIERRE		122	WA	21
51	SAINT PIERRE		43	PA	11
67	SAINT PIERRE		70	DB	13
08	SAINT PIERRE A ARNES		29	QA	9
02	SAINT PIERRE AIGLE		27	KA	9
05	SAINT PIERRE AVEZ		181	WA	32
14	SAINT PIERRE AZIF		36	W	9
23	SAINT PIERRE BELLEVUE		132	FA	24
76	SAINT PIERRE BENOUVILLE		24	AA	7
67	SAINT PIERRE BOIS		70	DB	14
59	SAINT PIERRE BROUCK		8	GA	2
14	SAINT PIERRE CANIVET		36	V	11
23	SAINT PIERRE CHERIGNAT		131	DA	24
63	SAINT PIERRE COLAMINE		147	JA	26
73	SAINT PIERRE D'ALBIGNY	C	153	XA	26
38	SAINT PIERRE D'ALLEVARD		153	XA	27
73	SAINT PIERRE D'ALVEY		152	WA	26
17	SAINT PIERRE D'AMILLY		127	T	23
05	SAINT PIERRE D'ARGENCON		180	VA	31
50	SAINT PIERRE D'ARTHEGLISE		33	P	9
32	SAINT PIERRE D'AUBEZIES		208	X	35
33	SAINT PIERRE D'AURILLAC		170	V	30
27	SAINT PIERRE D'AUTILS		38	CA	10
38	SAINT PIERRE D'ENTREMONT		152	WA	27
61	SAINT PIERRE D'ENTREMONT		57	T	12
73	SAINT PIERRE D'ENTREMONT		152	WA	27
86	SAINT PIERRE D'EXIDEUIL		129	X	23
24	SAINT PIERRE D'EYRAUD		157	Y	29
64	SAINT PIERRE D'IRUBE	C	205	Q	35
17	SAINT PIERRE D'OLERON	C	126	Q	24
27	SAINT PIERRE DE BAILLEUL		38	CA	10
33	SAINT PIERRE DE BAT		170	V	30
73	SAINT PIERRE DE BELLEVILLE		153	YA	26
42	SAINT PIERRE DE BOEUF		150	RA	27
38	SAINT PIERRE DE BRESSIEUX		151	UA	27
47	SAINT PIERRE DE BUZET		171	X	32
27	SAINT PIERRE DE CERNIERES		37	Z	11
69	SAINT PIERRE DE CHANDIEU		151	SA	26
38	SAINT PIERRE DE CHARTREUSE		152	WA	27
38	SAINT PIERRE DE CHERENNES		166	UA	28
72	SAINT PIERRE DE CHEVILLE		79	Y	17
24	SAINT PIERRE DE CHIGNAC	C	158	AA	28
47	SAINT PIERRE DE CLAIRAC		172	AA	32
24	SAINT PIERRE DE COLE		144	AA	27
07	SAINT PIERRE DE COLOMBIER		164	PA	30
27	SAINT PIERRE DE CORMEILLES		37	Y	10
50	SAINT PIERRE DE COUTANCES		34	O	11
73	SAINT PIERRE DE CURTILLE		152	WA	25
24	SAINT PIERRE DE FRUGIE		144	BA	26
23	SAINT PIERRE DE FURSAC		131	DA	23
73	SAINT PIERRE DE GENEBROZ		152	WA	26
36	SAINT PIERRE DE JARDS		100	FA	19
17	SAINT PIERRE DE JUILLERS		128	U	24
17	SAINT PIERRE DE L'ILE		128	U	24
34	SAINT PIERRE DE LA FAGE		192	LA	34
31	SAINT PIERRE DE LAGES		210	DA	35
36	SAINT PIERRE DE LAMPS		115	DA	20
86	SAINT PIERRE DE MAILLE		114	AA	21
14	SAINT PIERRE DE MAILLOC		37	X	10
76	SAINT PIERRE DE MANNEVILLE		24	AA	9
38	SAINT PIERRE DE MEAROZ		166	WA	29
38	SAINT PIERRE DE MESAGE		166	WA	28
13	SAINT PIERRE DE MEZOARGUES		195	RA	34
33	SAINT PIERRE DE MONS		170	V	31
48	SAINT PIERRE DE NOGARET		176	KA	31
35	SAINT PIERRE DE PLESGUEN		55	O	13
09	SAINT PIERRE DE RIVIERE		219	DA	38
27	SAINT PIERRE DE SALERNE		37	Z	10
50	SAINT PIERRE DE SEMILLY		35	S	10
73	SAINT PIERRE DE SOUCY		153	XA	26
81	SAINT PIERRE DE TRIVISY		190	HA	34
76	SAINT PIERRE DE VARENGEVILLE		24	AA	8
71	SAINT PIERRE DE VARENNES		120	QA	20
84	SAINT PIERRE DE VASSOLS		195	TA	33
66	SAINT PIERRE DELS FORCATS		222	GA	40
72	SAINT PIERRE DES BOIS		78	W	15
11	SAINT PIERRE DES CHAMPS		223	IA	37
37	SAINT PIERRE DES CORPS	C	98	Z	18
79	SAINT PIERRE DES ECHAUBROGNES		111	T	20
27	SAINT PIERRE DES FLEURS		38	AA	10
14	SAINT PIERRE DES IFS		36	X	10
27	SAINT PIERRE DES IFS		37	Z	9
76	SAINT PIERRE DES JONQUIERES		25	DA	7
53	SAINT PIERRE DES LANDES		76	R	14
61	SAINT PIERRE DES LOGES		37	Y	12
53	SAINT PIERRE DES NIDS		58	W	13
72	SAINT PIERRE DES ORMES		59	Y	14
48	SAINT PIERRE DES TRIPIERS		176	LA	32
27	SAINT PIERRE DU BOSGUERARD		37	AA	10
14	SAINT PIERRE DU BU		36	V	11
43	SAINT PIERRE DU CHAMP		149	NA	27
85	SAINT PIERRE DU CHEMIN		111	T	21
14	SAINT PIERRE DU FRESNE		35	T	11
14	SAINT PIERRE DU JONQUET		36	W	10
72	SAINT PIERRE DU LOROUER		79	Z	16
27	SAINT PIERRE DU MESNIL		37	Z	11
14	SAINT PIERRE DU MONT		35	S	9
40	SAINT PIERRE DU MONT		184	U	33
58	SAINT PIERRE DU MONT		102	LA	18
17	SAINT PIERRE DU PALAIS		156	V	28
91	SAINT PIERRE DU PERRAY		62	HA	12
61	SAINT PIERRE DU REGARD		35	U	11
27	SAINT PIERRE DU VAL		23	Y	9
27	SAINT PIERRE DU VAUVRAY		38	CA	10
50	SAINT PIERRE EGLISE	C	33	Q	8
74	SAINT PIERRE EN FAUCIGNY		139	ZA	24
76	SAINT PIERRE EN PORT		23	Y	7
76	SAINT PIERRE EN VAL		15	CA	6
21	SAINT PIERRE EN VAUX		104	QA	19
60	SAINT PIERRE ES CHAMPS		25	EA	9
43	SAINT PIERRE EYNAC		163	OA	28
63	SAINT PIERRE LA BOURLHONNE		149	NA	25
61	SAINT PIERRE LA BRUYERE		59	AA	14
53	SAINT PIERRE LA COUR		76	S	15
27	SAINT PIERRE LA GARENNE		38	CA	10
42	SAINT PIERRE LA NOAILLE		135	OA	23
69	SAINT PIERRE LA PALUD		150	RA	25
61	SAINT PIERRE LA RIVIERE		58	X	12
07	SAINT PIERRE LA ROCHE		179	RA	30
14	SAINT PIERRE LA VIEILLE		35	U	11
46	SAINT PIERRE LAFEUILLE		174	DA	31
50	SAINT PIERRE LANGERS		56	Q	12
03	SAINT PIERRE LAVAL		135	NA	23
76	SAINT PIERRE LAVIS		23	Z	8
23	SAINT PIERRE LE BOST		132	GA	22
63	SAINT PIERRE LE CHASTEL		147	JA	25
58	SAINT PIERRE LE MOUTIER	C	118	KA	21
48	SAINT PIERRE LE VIEUX		162	LA	29
71	SAINT PIERRE LE VIEUX		136	QA	23
76	SAINT PIERRE LE VIEUX		24	AA	7
85	SAINT PIERRE LE VIEUX		111	T	22
76	SAINT PIERRE LE VIGER		24	AA	7
60	SAINT PIERRE LES BITRY		27	KA	9
18	SAINT PIERRE LES BOIS		116	GA	21
76	SAINT PIERRE LES ELBEUF		38	BA	9
18	SAINT PIERRE LES ETIEUX		117	IA	21
02	SAINT PIERRE LES FRANQUEVILLE		28	NA	7
77	SAINT PIERRE LES NEMOURS		62	IA	14
49	SAINT PIERRE MONTLIMART		95	S	18
56	SAINT PIERRE QUIBERON		91	I	17
63	SAINT PIERRE ROCHE		147	JA	25
07	SAINT PIERRE ST JEAN		178	OA	31
14	SAINT PIERRE SUR DIVES	C	36	W	11
07	SAINT PIERRE SUR DOUX		164	QA	28
47	SAINT PIERRE SUR DROPT		171	X	30
53	SAINT PIERRE SUR ERVE		77	U	15
53	SAINT PIERRE SUR ORTHE		78	V	14
08	SAINT PIERRE SUR VENCE		30	RA	8
14	SAINT PIERRE TARENTAINE		35	T	11
46	SAINT PIERRE TOIRAC		174	FA	31
02	SAINT PIERREMONT		28	NA	8
08	SAINT PIERREMONT		30	SA	9
88	SAINT PIERREMONT		68	ZA	13
07	SAINT PIERREVILLE	C	164	QA	29
55	SAINT PIERREVILLERS		31	VA	9
03	SAINT PLAISIR		117	JA	21
31	SAINT PLANCARD		217	Z	37
50	SAINT PLANCHERS		56	P	12
36	SAINT PLANTAIRE		115	EA	22
71	SAINT POINT		136	RA	23
25	SAINT POINT LAC		123	YA	20
50	SAINT POIS	C	56	R	12
53	SAINT POIX		76	S	15
29	SAINT POL DE LEON	C	52	F	12
59	SAINT POL SUR MER		8	HA	2
62	SAINT POL SUR TERNOISE	C	16	HA	5
42	SAINT POLGUES		135	OA	24
11	SAINT POLYCARPE		221	GA	37
79	SAINT POMPAIN		111	T	22
24	SAINT POMPONT		158	BA	30
15	SAINT PONCY		162	KA	28
04	SAINT PONS		182	AB	31
07	SAINT PONS		179	RA	30
34	SAINT PONS DE MAUCHIENS		214	MA	35
34	SAINT PONS DE THOMIERES	C	213	IA	35
30	SAINT PONS LA CALM		178	QA	32
03	SAINT PONT		133	LA	23
17	SAINT PORCHAIRE	C	141	T	25
82	SAINT PORQUIER		188	BA	33
22	SAINT POTAN		55	M	13
10	SAINT POUANGE		64	OA	14
03	SAINT POURCAIN SUR BESBRE		119	MA	22
03	SAINT POURCAIN SUR SIOULE	C	133	LA	23
88	SAINT PRANCHER		67	XA	14
43	SAINT PREJET ARMANDON		162	MA	27
43	SAINT PREJET D'ALLIER		162	MA	29
28	SAINT PREST		60	DA	13
16	SAINT PREUIL		142	V	26
07	SAINT PRIEST		164	QA	30
23	SAINT PRIEST		132	HA	24
69	SAINT PRIEST	C	151	SA	25
63	SAINT PRIEST BRAMEFANT		133	LA	24
03	SAINT PRIEST D'ANDELOT		134	KA	24
19	SAINT PRIEST DE GIMEL		146	EA	27
63	SAINT PRIEST DES CHAMPS		133	IA	24
42	SAINT PRIEST EN JAREZ		150	QA	26
03	SAINT PRIEST EN MURAT		133	JA	23
23	SAINT PRIEST LA FEUILLE		131	DA	23
18	SAINT PRIEST LA MARCHE		116	GA	22
23	SAINT PRIEST LA PLAINE		131	DA	23
42	SAINT PRIEST LA PRUGNE		135	NA	24
42	SAINT PRIEST LA ROCHE		135	OA	24
42	SAINT PRIEST LA VETRE		149	NA	25
24	SAINT PRIEST LES FOUGERES		144	BA	26
87	SAINT PRIEST LIGOURE		145	CA	26
23	SAINT PRIEST PALUS		131	DA	25
87	SAINT PRIEST SOUS AIXE		144	BA	25
87	SAINT PRIEST TAURION		131	CA	25
38	SAINT PRIM		150	RA	27
07	SAINT PRIVAT		178	QA	30
19	SAINT PRIVAT	C	160	FA	28
34	SAINT PRIVAT		192	LA	34
43	SAINT PRIVAT D'ALLIER		163	MA	29
30	SAINT PRIVAT DE CHAMPCLOS		178	QA	32
48	SAINT PRIVAT DE VALLONGUE		177	NA	32
24	SAINT PRIVAT DES PRES		143	X	27
30	SAINT PRIVAT DES VIEUX		178	PA	32
43	SAINT PRIVAT DU DRAGON		162	LA	28
48	SAINT PRIVAT DU FAU		162	LA	29
57	SAINT PRIVAT LA MONTAGNE		45	XA	10
71	SAINT PRIVE		120	QA	21
89	SAINT PRIVE		83	JA	17
03	SAINT PRIX		133	MA	23
07	SAINT PRIX		164	QA	29
71	SAINT PRIX		119	OA	20
95	SAINT PRIX		40	GA	11
21	SAINT PRIX LES ARNAY		104	OA	19
46	SAINT PROJET		159	DA	30
82	SAINT PROJET		174	EA	32
15	SAINT PROJET DE SALERS		161	HA	28
16	SAINT PROJET ST CONSTANT		143	Y	25
85	SAINT PROUANT		111	S	21
45	SAINT PRYVE ST MESMIN		81	EA	16
32	SAINT PUY		186	Y	33
59	SAINT PYTHON		18	LA	5
17	SAINT QUANTIN DE RANCANNE		142	T	26
22	SAINT QUAY PERROS		53	H	12
22	SAINT QUAY PORTRIEUX		54	K	12
02	SAINT QUENTIN	S	28	LA	7
76	SAINT QUENTIN AU BOSC		15	CA	7
33	SAINT QUENTIN DE BARON		156	V	29
61	SAINT QUENTIN DE BLAVOU		59	Y	13
33	SAINT QUENTIN DE CAPLONG		157	X	29
16	SAINT QUENTIN DE CHALAIS		143	W	27
27	SAINT QUENTIN DES ISLES		37	Z	11
60	SAINT QUENTIN DES PRES		25	EA	8
47	SAINT QUENTIN DU DROPT		172	Z	30
49	SAINT QUENTIN EN MAUGES		95	S	18
80	SAINT QUENTIN EN TOURMONT		15	DA	5
38	SAINT QUENTIN FALLAVIER		151	TA	26
23	SAINT QUENTIN LA CHABANNE		132	GA	25
80	SAINT QUENTIN LA MOTTE CROIX AU BAILLY		15	DA	6
30	SAINT QUENTIN LA POTERIE		193	QA	33
09	SAINT QUENTIN LA TOUR		221	FA	37
08	SAINT QUENTIN LE PETIT		29	OA	8
51	SAINT QUENTIN LE VERGER		64	NA	12
53	SAINT QUENTIN LES ANGES		77	S	16
49	SAINT QUENTIN LES BEAUREPAIRE		78	W	17
61	SAINT QUENTIN LES CHARDONNETS		57	T	12
51	SAINT QUENTIN LES MARAIS		43	RA	12
16	SAINT QUENTIN SUR CHARENTE		130	Z	25
51	SAINT QUENTIN SUR COOLE		43	PA	11
37	SAINT QUENTIN SUR INDROIS		98	BA	19
38	SAINT QUENTIN SUR ISERE		152	VA	27
50	SAINT QUENTIN SUR LE HOMME		56	Q	12
58	SAINT QUENTIN SUR NOHAIN		102	KA	18
63	SAINT QUENTIN SUR SAUXILLANGES		148	LA	26
63	SAINT QUINTIN SUR SIOULE		134	KA	24
09	SAINT QUIRC		210	DA	36
57	SAINT QUIRIN		69	CB	12
24	SAINT RABIER		158	BA	28
71	SAINT RACHO		136	QA	23
26	SAINT RAMBERT D'ALBON		150	RA	27
01	SAINT RAMBERT EN BUGEY	C	138	UA	24
24	SAINT RAPHAEL		144	BA	27
83	SAINT RAPHAEL	C	204	AB	35
42	SAINT REGIS DU COIN		150	QA	27
37	SAINT REGLE		98	BA	18
07	SAINT REMEZE		178	OA	31
54	SAINT REMIMONT		68	YA	13
88	SAINT REMIMONT		67	WA	14
01	SAINT REMY		137	TA	23
12	SAINT REMY		174	FA	31
14	SAINT REMY		35	U	11
19	SAINT REMY		146	GA	26
21	SAINT REMY		85	PA	17
24	SAINT REMY		157	X	29
70	SAINT REMY		88	XA	16
71	SAINT REMY		121	SA	21
79	SAINT REMY		128	U	22
88	SAINT REMY		69	BB	14
62	SAINT REMY AU BOIS		16	FA	5
54	SAINT REMY AUX BOIS		68	ZA	13
02	SAINT REMY BLANZY		41	LA	10
76	SAINT REMY BOSCROCOURT		15	CA	6
59	SAINT REMY CHAUSSEE		19	NA	6
63	SAINT REMY DE BLOT		133	JA	24
63	SAINT REMY DE CHARGNAT		148	LA	26
15	SAINT REMY DE CHAUDES AIGUES		161	KA	29
73	SAINT REMY DE MAURIENNE		153	YA	27
13	SAINT REMY DE PROVENCE	C	195	SA	34
72	SAINT REMY DE SILLE		78	W	14
50	SAINT REMY DES LANDES		34	P	9
72	SAINT REMY DES MONTS		59	Y	14
59	SAINT REMY DU NORD		19	OA	5
35	SAINT REMY DU PLAIN		56	P	14
72	SAINT REMY DU VAL		58	X	14
51	SAINT REMY EN BOUZEMONT ST GENEST ET ISSON	C	65	RA	12
60	SAINT REMY EN L'EAU		26	HA	9
49	SAINT REMY EN MAUGES		94	R	18
03	SAINT REMY EN ROLLAT		133	LA	23
78	SAINT REMY L'HONORE		39	FA	12
55	SAINT REMY LA CALONNE		45	VA	10
77	SAINT REMY LA VANNE		41	LA	12
49	SAINT REMY LA VARENNE		96	V	18
08	SAINT REMY LE PETIT		29	PA	9
78	SAINT REMY LES CHEVREUSE		39	FA	12
10	SAINT REMY SOUS BARBUISE		64	OA	13
51	SAINT REMY SOUS BROYES		42	NA	12
28	SAINT REMY SUR AVRE		38	CA	12
51	SAINT REMY SUR BUSSY		43	QA	10
86	SAINT REMY SUR CREUSE		114	Z	20
63	SAINT REMY SUR DUROLLE	C	134	MA	25
29	SAINT RENAN	C	51	C	13
26	SAINT RESTITUT		179	RA	31
85	SAINT REVEREND		109	O	21
58	SAINT REVERIEN		102	MA	19
22	SAINT RIEUL		54	L	13
72	SAINT RIGOMER DES BOIS		58	X	13
41	SAINT RIMAY		79	AA	16
80	SAINT RIQUIER		16	FA	6
76	SAINT RIQUIER EN RIVIERE		25	DA	7
76	SAINT RIQUIER ES PLAINS		23	Z	7
42	SAINT RIRAND		135	NA	24
29	SAINT RIVOAL		52	E	14
19	SAINT ROBERT		159	CA	27
47	SAINT ROBERT		172	AA	32
37	SAINT ROCH		97	Z	18
61	SAINT ROCH SUR EGRENNE		57	T	13
17	SAINT ROGATIEN		126	R	23
16	SAINT ROMAIN		143	X	27
21	SAINT ROMAIN		120	RA	20
63	SAINT ROMAIN		149	NA	26
86	SAINT ROMAIN		129	Y	23
69	SAINT ROMAIN AU MONT D'OR		136	RA	25
07	SAINT ROMAIN D'AY		164	RA	28
42	SAINT ROMAIN D'URFE		135	NA	25
17	SAINT ROMAIN DE BENET		141	S	25
76	SAINT ROMAIN DE COLBOSC	C	23	Y	8
38	SAINT ROMAIN DE JALIONAS		151	TA	25
07	SAINT ROMAIN DE LERPS		165	SA	29
24	SAINT ROMAIN DE MONPAZIER		158	AA	30
69	SAINT ROMAIN DE POPEY		136	QA	25
38	SAINT ROMAIN DE SURIEU		151	SA	27
69	SAINT ROMAIN EN GAL		151	SA	26
69	SAINT ROMAIN EN GIER		150	RA	26
42	SAINT ROMAIN EN JAREZ		150	QA	26
84	SAINT ROMAIN EN VIENNOIS		179	TA	32
24	SAINT ROMAIN ET ST CLEMENT		144	AA	27
42	SAINT ROMAIN LA MOTTE		135	OA	24
33	SAINT ROMAIN LA VIRVEE		156	U	29
43	SAINT ROMAIN LACHALM		150	PA	27
47	SAINT ROMAIN LE NOBLE		172	AA	32
89	SAINT ROMAIN LE PREUX		83	LA	15
42	SAINT ROMAIN LE PUY		149	PA	26
42	SAINT ROMAIN LES ATHEUX		150	PA	27
71	SAINT ROMAIN SOUS GOURDON		120	OA	21
71	SAINT ROMAIN SOUS VERSIGNY		119	PA	21
41	SAINT ROMAIN SUR CHER		99	CA	18
17	SAINT ROMAIN SUR GIRONDE		141	T	27
26	SAINT ROMAN		166	UA	30
30	SAINT ROMAN DE CODIERES		192	NA	33
84	SAINT ROMAN DE MALEGARDE		179	SA	32
38	SAINT ROMANS		166	UA	28
79	SAINT ROMANS DES CHAMPS		128	V	23
79	SAINT ROMANS LES MELLE		128	V	23
31	SAINT ROME		211	EA	36
12	SAINT ROME DE CERNON		191	JA	33
48	SAINT ROME DE DOLAN		176	KA	32
12	SAINT ROME DE TARN	C	191	JA	33
50	SAINT ROMPHAIRE		34	R	11
31	SAINT RUSTICE		188	CA	34
76	SAINT SAENS	C	24	CA	8
76	SAINT SAIRE		25	DA	8
12	SAINT SALVADOU		174	FA	32
19	SAINT SALVADOUR		145	EA	27
81	SAINT SALVI DE CARCAVES		190	IA	34
47	SAINT SALVY		172	Y	32
81	SAINT SALVY DE LA BALME		212	HA	35
14	SAINT SAMSON		36	W	10
53	SAINT SAMSON		58	V	13
50	SAINT SAMSON DE BONFOSSE		34	R	11
27	SAINT SAMSON DE LA ROQUE		23	Y	9
60	SAINT SAMSON LA POTERIE		25	EA	8
22	SAINT SAMSON SUR RANCE		55	N	13
63	SAINT SANDOUX		148	KA	26
12	SAINT SANTIN		175	GA	30
15	SAINT SANTIN CANTALES		160	GA	28
15	SAINT SANTIN DE MAURS		175	GA	30
47	SAINT SARDOS		172	Y	31
82	SAINT SARDOS		188	BA	33
18	SAINT SATUR		101	JA	18
15	SAINT SATURNIN		161	IA	27
16	SAINT SATURNIN		143	W	26
18	SAINT SATURNIN		116	GA	22
48	SAINT SATURNIN		176	KA	31
51	SAINT SATURNIN		64	NA	12
63	SAINT SATURNIN		148	KA	26
72	SAINT SATURNIN		78	X	15
12	SAINT SATURNIN DE LENNE		176	KA	31
34	SAINT SATURNIN DE LUCIAN		192	LA	34
17	SAINT SATURNIN DU BOIS		127	T	23
53	SAINT SATURNIN DU LIMET		76	R	16
84	SAINT SATURNIN LES APT		196	UA	33
84	SAINT SATURNIN LES AVIGNON		195	SA	33
49	SAINT SATURNIN SUR LOIRE		96	U	18
24	SAINT SAUD LACOUSSIERE		144	AA	26
80	SAINT SAUFLIEU		26	GA	7
58	SAINT SAULGE	C	102	MA	19
59	SAINT SAULVE		18	MA	5
15	SAINT SAURY		160	GA	29
17	SAINT SAUVANT		142	U	25
86	SAINT SAUVANT		129	W	22
63	SAINT SAUVES D'AUVERGNE		147	IA	26
05	SAINT SAUVEUR		182	ZA	31
21	SAINT SAUVEUR		106	UA	18
24	SAINT SAUVEUR		158	Z	29
29	SAINT SAUVEUR		52	E	13
31	SAINT SAUVEUR		188	CA	34
33	SAINT SAUVEUR		155	S	28
38	SAINT SAUVEUR		166	UA	28
54	SAINT SAUVEUR		69	BB	13
60	SAINT SAUVEUR		27	JA	9
70	SAINT SAUVEUR	C	89	ZA	16
80	SAINT SAUVEUR		16	GA	7
86	SAINT SAUVEUR		114	Z	20
30	SAINT SAUVEUR CAMPRIEU		177	LA	32
17	SAINT SAUVEUR D'AUNIS		127	S	23
76	SAINT SAUVEUR D'EMALLEVILLE		23	Y	8
61	SAINT SAUVEUR DE CARROUGES		58	W	13
07	SAINT SAUVEUR DE CRUZIERES		178	PA	32
49	SAINT SAUVEUR DE FLEE		77	T	16
48	SAINT SAUVEUR DE GINESTOUX		162	MA	30
49	SAINT SAUVEUR DE LANDEMONT		94	R	18
47	SAINT SAUVEUR DE MEILHAN		171	W	31
07	SAINT SAUVEUR DE MONTAGUT		164	RA	29
48	SAINT SAUVEUR DE PEYRE		176	LA	30
50	SAINT SAUVEUR DE PIERREPONT		34	P	9
33	SAINT SAUVEUR DE PUYNORMAND		157	W	29
35	SAINT SAUVEUR DES LANDES		56	Q	14
26	SAINT SAUVEUR EN DIOIS		165	TA	30
89	SAINT SAUVEUR EN PUISAYE	C	83	KA	17
42	SAINT SAUVEUR EN RUE		150	QA	27
26	SAINT SAUVEUR GOUVERNET		180	UA	31
50	SAINT SAUVEUR LA POMMERAYE		56	O	11
63	SAINT SAUVEUR LA SAGNE		148	MA	27
46	SAINT SAUVEUR LA VALLEE		174	DA	30
24	SAINT SAUVEUR LALANDE		157	X	29
50	SAINT SAUVEUR LE VICOMTE	C	33	P	9
50	SAINT SAUVEUR LENDELIN	C	34	Q	10
77	SAINT SAUVEUR LES BRAY		63	KA	13
28	SAINT SAUVEUR MARVILLE		60	CA	13
77	SAINT SAUVEUR SUR ECOLE		62	IA	13
06	SAINT SAUVEUR SUR TINEE	C	199	CB	33
03	SAINT SAUVIER		132	GA	22
32	SAINT SAUVY		187	AA	34
33	SAINT SAVIN	C	156	U	28
38	SAINT SAVIN		152	UA	26
65	SAINT SAVIN		215	W	38
86	SAINT SAVIN	C	114	AA	22
17	SAINT SAVINIEN	C	127	T	25
86	SAINT SAVIOL		129	X	23
13	SAINT SAVOURNIN		202	VA	36
23	SAINT SEBASTIEN		131	DA	22
38	SAINT SEBASTIEN		166	WA	29
30	SAINT SEBASTIEN D'AIGREFEUILLE		178	OA	32
27	SAINT SEBASTIEN DE MORSENT		38	BA	11
50	SAINT SEBASTIEN DE RAIDS		34	Q	10
44	SAINT SEBASTIEN SUR LOIRE		93	P	19
86	SAINT SECONDIN		129	Y	23
29	SAINT SEGAL		52	E	14
35	SAINT SEGLIN		75	N	16
58	SAINT SEINE		119	NA	21
21	SAINT SEINE EN BACHE		106	UA	19
21	SAINT SEINE L'ABBAYE	C	104	RA	18
21	SAINT SEINE SUR VINGEANNE		87	UA	17
33	SAINT SELVE		170	U	30
50	SAINT SENIER DE BEUVRON		56	Q	13
50	SAINT SENIER SOUS AVRANCHES		56	Q	12
37	SAINT SENOCH		98	AA	19
35	SAINT SENOUX		75	O	16
34	SAINT SERIES		193	OA	34
07	SAINT SERNIN		178	QA	30
11	SAINT SERNIN		211	EA	36
47	SAINT SERNIN		157	X	30
71	SAINT SERNIN DU BOIS		120	QA	20
71	SAINT SERNIN DU PLAIN		120	RA	20
81	SAINT SERNIN LES LAVAUR		211	FA	35
12	SAINT SERNIN SUR RANCE	C	190	IA	33
89	SAINT SEROTIN		63	KA	14
22	SAINT SERVAIS		53	H	13
29	SAINT SERVAIS		52	E	13
56	SAINT SERVANT		74	L	16
19	SAINT SETIERS		146	GA	25
33	SAINT SEURIN DE BOURG		156	T	28
33	SAINT SEURIN DE CADOURNE		141	T	27
33	SAINT SEURIN DE CURSAC		156	T	28
17	SAINT SEURIN DE PALENNE		142	U	26
24	SAINT SEURIN DE PRATS		157	W	29
33	SAINT SEURIN SUR L'ISLE		157	W	28
33	SAINT SEVE		171	W	30
40	SAINT SEVER	C	184	U	34
14	SAINT SEVER CALVADOS	C	35	R	11
65	SAINT SEVER DE RUSTAN		208	X	36
17	SAINT SEVER DE SAINTONGE		142	U	25
12	SAINT SEVER DU MOUSTIER		190	IA	34
16	SAINT SEVERIN		143	X	27
24	SAINT SEVERIN D'ESTISSAC		157	Y	28
17	SAINT SEVERIN SUR BOUTONNE		128	U	24
30	SAINT SIFFRET		193	QA	33
45	SAINT SIGISMOND		81	EA	15
49	SAINT SIGISMOND		95	S	18
74	SAINT SIGISMOND		140	AB	24
85	SAINT SIGISMOND		127	T	23
17	SAINT SIGISMOND DE CLERMONT		142	U	26
23	SAINT SILVAIN BAS LE ROC		132	GA	23
23	SAINT SILVAIN BELLEGARDE		132	GA	24
23	SAINT SILVAIN MONTAIGUT		131	EA	23
23	SAINT SILVAIN SOUS TOULX		132	GA	23
27	SAINT SIMEON		37	Y	9
61	SAINT SIMEON		57	T	13
77	SAINT SIMEON		41	KA	12
38	SAINT SIMEON DE BRESSIEUX		151	TA	27
16	SAINT SIMEUX		142	W	26
02	SAINT SIMON	C	27	KA	7
15	SAINT SIMON		161	HA	29
16	SAINT SIMON		142	W	26
46	SAINT SIMON		174	EA	30
17	SAINT SIMON DE BORDES		142	U	27
17	SAINT SIMON DE PELLOUAILLE		141	T	26
74	SAINT SIXT		139	YA	24
42	SAINT SIXTE		149	OA	25
47	SAINT SIXTE		172	AA	32
19	SAINT SOLVE		145	CA	27
69	SAINT SORLIN		150	RA	26
73	SAINT SORLIN D'ARVES		167	YA	28
17	SAINT SORLIN DE CONAC		141	T	27
38	SAINT SORLIN DE MORESTEL		152	UA	26
38	SAINT SORLIN DE VIENNE		151	SA	26
01	SAINT SORLIN EN BUGEY		138	UA	25
26	SAINT SORLIN EN VALLOIRE		151	SA	27
03	SAINT SORNIN		133	JA	22
16	SAINT SORNIN		143	Y	25
17	SAINT SORNIN		141	S	25
87	SAINT SORNIN LA MARCHE		130	AA	23
19	SAINT SORNIN LAVOLPS		145	CA	27
87	SAINT SORNIN LEULAC		131	CA	23
32	SAINT SOULAN		209	AA	35
59	SAINT SOUPLET		18	MA	6
51	SAINT SOUPLET SUR PY		43	QA	10
77	SAINT SOUPPLETS		40	JA	11
46	SAINT SOZY		159	DA	29
88	SAINT STAIL		69	CB	14
35	SAINT SULIAC		55	N	13
01	SAINT SULPICE		137	TA	23
41	SAINT SULPICE		80	CA	17
46	SAINT SULPICE		174	EA	30
49	SAINT SULPICE		96	U	18
53	SAINT SULPICE		77	T	16
58	SAINT SULPICE		102	LA	19
60	SAINT SULPICE		26	GA	9
63	SAINT SULPICE		147	IA	26
70	SAINT SULPICE		89	ZA	17
73	SAINT SULPICE		152	WA	26
81	SAINT SULPICE		189	EA	34
17	SAINT SULPICE D'ARNOULT		141	S	25
24	SAINT SULPICE D'EXCIDEUIL		144	BA	27
16	SAINT SULPICE DE COGNAC		142	U	25
33	SAINT SULPICE DE FALEYRENS		156	V	29
91	SAINT SULPICE DE FAVIERES		61	GA	13
27	SAINT SULPICE DE GRIMBOUVILLE		23	Y	9
33	SAINT SULPICE DE GUILLERAGUES		171	W	30
24	SAINT SULPICE DE MAREUIL		143	Y	26
33	SAINT SULPICE DE POMMIERS		171	W	30
24	SAINT SULPICE DE ROUMAGNAC		157	Y	28
17	SAINT SULPICE DE ROYAN		141	S	25
16	SAINT SULPICE DE RUFFEC		129	Y	24
35	SAINT SULPICE DES LANDES		75	P	16
44	SAINT SULPICE DES LANDES		94	R	17
38	SAINT SULPICE DES RIVOIRES		152	VA	26
85	SAINT SULPICE EN PAREDS		111	S	21
33	SAINT SULPICE ET CAMEYRAC		156	U	29
35	SAINT SULPICE LA FORET		76	P	14
87	SAINT SULPICE LAURIERE		131	DA	24
23	SAINT SULPICE LE DUNOIS		131	EA	23
23	SAINT SULPICE LE GUERETOIS		132	EA	23
85	SAINT SULPICE LE VERDON		110	Q	20
19	SAINT SULPICE LES BOIS		146	GA	26
23	SAINT SULPICE LES CHAMPS	C	132	FA	24
87	SAINT SULPICE LES FEUILLES	C	131	CA	23
31	SAINT SULPICE SUR LEZE		210	CA	36
61	SAINT SULPICE SUR RISLE		37	Z	12
54	SAINT SUPPLET		31	WA	9
14	SAINT SYLVAIN		36	V	10
19	SAINT SYLVAIN		160	EA	28
76	SAINT SYLVAIN		23	Z	7
49	SAINT SYLVAIN D'ANJOU		96	U	17
07	SAINT SYLVESTRE		164	RA	29
74	SAINT SYLVESTRE		139	XA	25
87	SAINT SYLVESTRE		131	CA	24
59	SAINT SYLVESTRE CAPPEL		8	HA	3
27	SAINT SYLVESTRE DE CORMEILLES		37	Y	10
63	SAINT SYLVESTRE PRAGOULIN		133	LA	24
47	SAINT SYLVESTRE SUR LOT		172	AA	31
18	SAINT SYMPHORIEN		116	GA	20
27	SAINT SYMPHORIEN		23	Y	9
33	SAINT SYMPHORIEN	C	170	U	31
48	SAINT SYMPHORIEN		162	MA	29
72	SAINT SYMPHORIEN		78	W	15
79	SAINT SYMPHORIEN		128	U	23
71	SAINT SYMPHORIEN D'ANCELLES		136	RA	23
69	SAINT SYMPHORIEN D'OZON	C	151	SA	26
42	SAINT SYMPHORIEN DE LAY	C	135	PA	24
07	SAINT SYMPHORIEN DE MAHUN		164	QA	28
71	SAINT SYMPHORIEN DE MARMAGNE		120	PA	20
12	SAINT SYMPHORIEN DE THENIERES		161	IA	30
71	SAINT SYMPHORIEN DES BOIS		135	PA	23
61	SAINT SYMPHORIEN DES BRUYERES		37	Z	12
50	SAINT SYMPHORIEN DES MONTS		57	S	13
28	SAINT SYMPHORIEN LE CHATEAU		61	EA	13
50	SAINT SYMPHORIEN LE VALOIS		34	P	9
07	SAINT SYMPHORIEN SOUS CHOMERAC		164	RA	30

69 SAINT SYMPHORIEN SUR COISE C 150 QA 26
87 SAINT SYMPHORIEN , SUR COUZE 131 CA 24
21 SAINT SYMPHORIEN SUR SAONE 105 UA 19
29 SAINT THEGONNEC C 52 F 13
22 SAINT THELO 74 J 14
30 SAINT THEODORIT 193 OA 33
38 SAINT THEOFFREY 166 WA 29
73 SAINT THIBAUD DE COUZ 152 WA 26
10 SAINT THIBAULT 65 PA 14
21 SAINT THIBAULT 104 QA 18
60 SAINT THIBAULT 25 EA 8
77 SAINT THIBAULT DES VIGNES 40 IA 11
02 SAINT THIBAUT 28 MA 9
34 SAINT THIBERY 214 LA 36
39 SAINT THIEBAUD 122 WA 20
52 SAINT THIEBAULT 67 VA 14
51 SAINT THIERRY 29 OA 9
29 SAINT THOIS 72 F 14
02 SAINT THOMAS 28 NA 9
31 SAINT THOMAS 210 BA 35
17 SAINT THOMAS DE CONAC 141 T 27
53 SAINT THOMAS DE COURCERIERS 58 V 14
51 SAINT THOMAS EN ARGONNE 43 SA 10
26 SAINT THOMAS EN ROYANS 166 UA 28
42 SAINT THOMAS LA GARDE 149 OA 26
07 SAINT THOME 179 RA 31
29 SAINT THONAN 51 D 13
35 SAINT THUAL 55 O 14
35 SAINT THURIAL 75 O 15
56 SAINT THURIAU 73 J 15
27 SAINT THURIEN 23 Z 9
29 SAINT THURIEN 72 G 15
42 SAINT THURIN 149 NA 25
62 SAINT TRICAT 7 EA 2
22 SAINT TRIMOEL 54 L 13
84 SAINT TRINIT 196 UA 33
01 SAINT TRIVIER DE COURTES C 121 TA 22
01 SAINT TRIVIER SUR MOIGNANS C 137 SA 24
33 SAINT TROJAN 156 U 28
17 SAINT TROJAN LES BAINS 126 R 25
83 SAINT TROPEZ C 204 AB 36
56 SAINT TUGDUAL 73 H 15
72 SAINT ULPHACE 59 Z 14
68 SAINT ULRICH 90 CB 17
35 SAINT UNIAC 75 N 14
29 SAINT URBAIN 52 D 13
85 SAINT URBAIN 109 N 20
52 SAINT URBAIN MACONCOURT 66 TA 13
47 SAINT URCISSE 172 AA 32
81 SAINT URCISSE 188 DA 33
15 SAINT URCIZE 176 JA 30
10 SAINT USAGE 65 RA 15
21 SAINT USAGE 105 TA 19
71 SAINT USUGE 121 UA 21
51 SAINT UTIN 65 OA 13
26 SAINT UZE 165 SA 28
76 SAINT VAAST D'EQUIQUEVILLE 24 CA 7
60 SAINT VAAST DE LONGMONT 40 IA 9
76 SAINT VAAST DIEPPEDALLE 24 Z 7
76 SAINT VAAST DU VAL 24 BA 8
14 SAINT VAAST EN AUGE 36 W 9
59 SAINT VAAST EN CAMBRESIS 18 LA 5
80 SAINT VAAST EN CHAUSSEE 16 GA 6
50 SAINT VAAST LA HOUGUE 33 Q 8
60 SAINT VAAST LES MELLO 40 HA 10
14 SAINT VAAST SUR SEULLES 35 T 10
17 SAINT VAIZE 142 T 25
70 SAINT VALBERT 89 ZA 16
36 SAINT VALENTIN 116 EA 20
85 SAINT VALERIEN 111 S 22
89 SAINT VALERIEN 63 KA 14
60 SAINT VALERY 25 EA 7
76 SAINT VALERY EN CAUX C 24 Z 7
80 SAINT VALERY SUR SOMME C 15 DA 5
71 SAINT VALLERIN 120 RA 21
16 SAINT VALLIER 142 W 27
26 SAINT VALLIER C 164 RA 28
71 SAINT VALLIER 120 QA 21
88 SAINT VALLIER 68 YA 14
06 SAINT VALLIER DE THIEY C 198 BB 34
52 SAINT VALLIER SUR MARNE 87 UA 16
79 SAINT VARENT C 112 V 20
23 SAINT VAURY C 131 EA 23
62 SAINT VENANT 8 IA 4
43 SAINT VENERAND 163 MA 29
58 SAINT VERAIN 83 KA 17
05 SAINT VERAN 168 BB 30
38 SAINT VERAND 166 UA 28
69 SAINT VERAND 136 QA 24
71 SAINT VERAND 136 RA 23
43 SAINT VERT 148 MA 27
19 SAINT VIANCE 159 DA 28
41 SAINT VIATRE 81 FA 17
44 SAINT VIAUD 93 N 18
72 SAINT VICTEUR 58 W 14
03 SAINT VICTOR 133 IA 22
07 SAINT VICTOR 164 RA 28
15 SAINT VICTOR 160 GA 28
24 SAINT VICTOR 143 Y 27
27 SAINT VICTOR D'EPINE 37 Z 10
28 SAINT VICTOR DE BUTHON 60 BA 13
38 SAINT VICTOR DE CESSIEU 152 UA 26
27 SAINT VICTOR DE CHRETIENVILLE 37 Y 10
30 SAINT VICTOR DE MALCAP 178 PA 32
38 SAINT VICTOR DE MORESTEL 152 VA 25
61 SAINT VICTOR DE RENO 59 Z 13
30 SAINT VICTOR DES OULES 193 OA 33
23 SAINT VICTOR EN MARCHE 132 EA 24
12 SAINT VICTOR ET MELVIEU 191 JA 33
76 SAINT VICTOR L'ABBAYE 24 BA 8
30 SAINT VICTOR LA COSTE 195 RA 33
63 SAINT VICTOR LA RIVIERE 147 JA 26
43 SAINT VICTOR MALESCOURS 150 PA 27
63 SAINT VICTOR MONTVIANEIX 133 MA 24
09 SAINT VICTOR ROUZAUD 219 DA 37
43 SAINT VICTOR SUR ARLANC 149 NA 27
27 SAINT VICTOR SUR AVRE 37 AA 12
21 SAINT VICTOR SUR OUCHE 104 RA 19
42 SAINT VICTOR SUR RHINS 135 PA 24
13 SAINT VICTORET 202 TA 36
19 SAINT VICTOUR 146 HA 26
87 SAINT VICTURNIEN 130 BA 25
43 SAINT VIDAL 163 NA 28
27 SAINT VIGOR 38 CA 10
76 SAINT VIGOR D'YMONVILLE 23 Y 9
14 SAINT VIGOR DES MEZERETS 35 T 11
50 SAINT VIGOR DES MONTS 56 R 11
14 SAINT VIGOR LE GRAND 35 T 9
31 SAINT VINCENT 211 EA 35
43 SAINT VINCENT 163 OA 28
63 SAINT VINCENT 162 KA 28
64 SAINT VINCENT 215 V 37
82 SAINT VINCENT 174 DA 32
71 SAINT VINCENT BRAGNY 119 OA 22
76 SAINT VINCENT CRAMESNIL 23 Y 8
34 SAINT VINCENT D'OLARGUES 213 JA 35
34 SAINT VINCENT DE BARBEYRARGUES 192 NA 34
07 SAINT VINCENT DE BARRES 179 RA 30
42 SAINT VINCENT DE BOISSET 135 OA 24
24 SAINT VINCENT DE CONNEZAC 157 Y 28
24 SAINT VINCENT DE COSSE 158 BA 29
07 SAINT VINCENT DE DURFORT 164 RA 29
47 SAINT VINCENT DE LAMONTJOIE 186 Y 33
38 SAINT VINCENT DE MERCUZE 153 WA 27
33 SAINT VINCENT DE PAUL 156 U 29
40 SAINT VINCENT DE PAUL 183 S 34
33 SAINT VINCENT DE PERTIGNAS 156 W 29
69 SAINT VINCENT DE REINS 136 QA 24
15 SAINT VINCENT DE SALERS 161 HA 28
40 SAINT VINCENT DE TYROSSE C 183 Q 34
27 SAINT VINCENT DES BOIS 38 CA 10
44 SAINT VINCENT DES LANDES 94 Q 17
71 SAINT VINCENT DES PRES 120 QA 22
72 SAINT VINCENT DES PRES 59 Y 14
27 SAINT VINCENT DU BOULAY 37 Y 10
72 SAINT VINCENT DU LOROUER 79 Y 16
46 SAINT VINCENT DU PENDIT 160 FA 29
71 SAINT VINCENT EN BRESSE 121 TA 21
24 SAINT VINCENT JALMOUTIERS 157 X 28
79 SAINT VINCENT LA CHATRE 128 W 23
26 SAINT VINCENT LA COMMANDERIE 165 TA 29
24 SAINT VINCENT LE PALUEL 159 CA 29
04 SAINT VINCENT LES FORTS 182 ZA 31
82 SAINT VINCENT LESPINASSE 173 AA 32
46 SAINT VINCENT RIVE D'OLT 173 CA 31
85 SAINT VINCENT STERLANGES 110 R 21
85 SAINT VINCENT SUR GRAON 125 O 22
04 SAINT VINCENT SUR JABRON 181 WA 32
85 SAINT VINCENT SUR JARD 125 P 22
24 SAINT VINCENT SUR L'ISLE 144 AA 27
56 SAINT VINCENT SUR OUST 93 N 16
25 SAINT VIT 106 WA 19
73 SAINT VITAL 153 YA 26
47 SAINT VITE 173 AA 31
18 SAINT VITTE 117 HA 22
87 SAINT VITTE SUR BRIANCE 145 DA 26
17 SAINT VIVIEN 126 R 24
24 SAINT VIVIEN 157 X 29
33 SAINT VIVIEN DE BLAYE 156 U 28
33 SAINT VIVIEN DE MEDOC C 141 R 27
33 SAINT VIVIEN DE MONSEGUR 171 X 30
03 SAINT VOIR 134 MA 22
29 SAINT VOUGAY 52 E 13
51 SAINT VRAIN 43 RA 12
91 SAINT VRAIN 62 GA 13
22 SAINT VRAN 74 L 14
01 SAINT VULBAS 137 UA 25
59 SAINT WAAST 19 NA 5
76 SAINT WANDRILLE RANCON 24 AA 8
95 SAINT WITZ 40 IA 10
17 SAINT XANDRE 126 R 23
40 SAINT YAGUEN 184 T 33
71 SAINT YAN 135 OA 22
19 SAINT YBARD 145 DA 27
09 SAINT YBARS 210 CA 36
91 SAINT YON 61 GA 13
03 SAINT YORRE 133 MA 24
23 SAINT YRIEIX LA MONTAGNE 132 FA 25
87 SAINT YRIEIX LA PERCHE C 145 CA 26
19 SAINT YRIEIX LE DEJALAT 146 FA 26
23 SAINT YRIEIX LES BOIS 132 FA 24
87 SAINT YRIEIX SOUS AIXE 130 BA 25
16 SAINT YRIEIX SUR CHARENTE 143 X 25
71 SAINT YTHAIRE 120 RA 22
63 SAINT YVOINE 148 LA 26
29 SAINT YVY 72 F 15
33 SAINT YZAN DE SOUDIAC 156 U 28
33 SAINT YZANS DE MEDOC 141 T 27
83 SAINT ZACHARIE 202 WA 36
76 SAINTE ADRESSE 23 W 9
63 SAINTE AGATHE 148 MA 25
76 SAINTE AGATHE D'ALIERMONT 25 CA 7
42 SAINTE AGATHE EN DONZY 136 PA 25
42 SAINTE AGATHE LA BOUTERESSE 149 OA 25
06 SAINTE AGNES 200 DB 34
38 SAINTE AGNES 153 WA 27
39 SAINTE AGNES 122 UA 21
46 SAINTE ALAUZIE 173 CA 32
24 SAINTE ALVERE C 158 AA 29
15 SAINTE ANASTASIE 161 JA 28
30 SAINTE ANASTASIE 193 PA 33
83 SAINTE ANASTASIE SUR ISSOLE 203 XA 36
25 SAINTE ANNE 123 XA 20
32 SAINTE ANNE 187 AA 34
41 SAINTE ANNE 80 BA 16
56 SAINTE ANNE D'AURAY 73 J 17
87 SAINTE ANNE ST PRIEST 145 EA 25
44 SAINTE ANNE SUR BRIVET 93 N 18
38 SAINTE ANNE SUR GERVONDE 151 TA 26
35 SAINTE ANNE SUR VILAINE 75 O 16
77 SAINTE AULDE 41 KA 11
32 SAINTE AURENCE CAZAUX 208 Y 36
62 SAINTE AUSTREBERTHE 16 FA 5
76 SAINTE AUSTREBERTHE 24 BA 8
57 SAINTE BARBE 46 YA 10
88 SAINTE BARBE 69 AB 13
27 SAINTE BARBE SUR GAILLON 38 CA 10
47 SAINTE BAZEILLE 171 W 31
76 SAINTE BEUVE EN RIVIERE 25 DA 7
38 SAINTE BLANDINE 152 UA 26
79 SAINTE BLANDINE 128 V 23
56 SAINTE BRIGITTE 73 I 14
11 SAINTE CAMELLE 211 EA 36
62 SAINTE CATHERINE 17 IA 5
63 SAINTE CATHERINE 148 MA 26
69 SAINTE CATHERINE 150 QA 26
37 SAINTE CATHERINE DE FIERBOIS 98 Z 19
36 SAINTE CECILE 99 EA 19
50 SAINTE CECILE 56 R 11
71 SAINTE CECILE 136 RA 22
85 SAINTE CECILE 110 R 21
30 SAINTE CECILE D'ANDORGE 178 OA 32
81 SAINTE CECILE DU CAYROU 189 EA 33
84 SAINTE CECILE LES VIGNES 179 SA 32
61 SAINTE CERONNE LES MORTAGNE 59 Z 13
72 SAINTE CEROTTE 79 Z 16
32 SAINTE CHRISTIE 187 Z 34
32 SAINTE CHRISTIE D'ARMAGNAC 185 W 34
49 SAINTE CHRISTINE 95 S 18
63 SAINTE CHRISTINE 133 JA 24
05 SAINTE COLOMBE 180 VA 32
16 SAINTE COLOMBE 129 Y 25
17 SAINTE COLOMBE 142 V 27
21 SAINTE COLOMBE 104 QA 18
25 SAINTE COLOMBE 123 YA 20
33 SAINTE COLOMBE 156 W 29
35 SAINTE COLOMBE 76 O 16
40 SAINTE COLOMBE 184 U 34
46 SAINTE COLOMBE 160 FA 30
50 SAINTE COLOMBE 33 P 9
69 SAINTE COLOMBE 151 SA 26
76 SAINTE COLOMBE 24 AA 7
77 SAINTE COLOMBE 63 LA 13
89 SAINTE COLOMBE 84 OA 17
47 SAINTE COLOMBE DE DURAS 157 X 30
66 SAINTE COLOMBE DE LA COMMANDERIE 224 IA 39
48 SAINTE COLOMBE DE PEYRE 176 KA 30
47 SAINTE COLOMBE DE VILLENEUVE 172 Z 31
58 SAINTE COLOMBE DES BOIS 102 KA 18
47 SAINTE COLOMBE EN BRUILHOIS 172 Y 32
27 SAINTE COLOMBE LA COMMANDERIE 38 AA 10
27 SAINTE COLOMBE PRES VERNON 38 CA 10
42 SAINTE COLOMBE SUR GAND 135 PA 25
11 SAINTE COLOMBE SUR GUETTE 222 GA 38
11 SAINTE COLOMBE SUR L'HERS 221 FA 38
89 SAINTE COLOMBE SUR LOING 83 KA 17
21 SAINTE COLOMBE SUR SEINE 85 OA 16
64 SAINTE COLOME 215 U 37
69 SAINTE CONSORCE 150 RA 25
01 SAINTE CROIX 137 TA 25
02 SAINTE CROIX 28 NA 9
12 SAINTE CROIX 174 FA 31
24 SAINTE CROIX 158 AA 30
26 SAINTE CROIX 165 UA 30
46 SAINTE CROIX 173 BA 31
71 SAINTE CROIX 121 TA 22
81 SAINTE CROIX 189 FA 33
04 SAINTE CROIX A LAUZE 196 VA 33
68 SAINTE CROIX AUX MINES 69 CB 14
30 SAINTE CROIX DE CADERLE 192 NA 33
24 SAINTE CROIX DE MAREUIL 143 Y 26
34 SAINTE CROIX DE QUINTILLARGUES 193 OA 34
04 SAINTE CROIX DE VERDON 197 XA 34
33 SAINTE CROIX DU MONT 170 V 30
42 SAINTE CROIX EN JAREZ 150 RA 26
68 SAINTE CROIX EN PLAINE 90 DB 15
14 SAINTE CROIX GRAND TONNE 35 U 10
50 SAINTE CROIX HAGUE 33 O 8
27 SAINTE CROIX SUR AIZIER 23 Z 9
76 SAINTE CROIX SUR BUCHY 25 CA 8
14 SAINTE CROIX SUR MER 35 U 9
61 SAINTE CROIX SUR ORNE 58 V 12
48 SAINTE CROIX VALLEE FRANCAISE 177 NA 32
09 SAINTE CROIX VOLVESTRE C 218 BA 37
32 SAINTE DODE 208 Y 36
79 SAINTE EANNE 128 V 22
64 SAINTE ENGRACE 206 T 37
48 SAINTE ENIMIE C 177 LA 31
43 SAINTE EUGENIE DE VILLENEUVE 162 MA 28
07 SAINTE EULALIE 163 PA 29
11 SAINTE EULALIE 212 GA 36
15 SAINTE EULALIE 160 HA 28
33 SAINTE EULALIE 156 U 29
48 SAINTE EULALIE 162 MA 29
24 SAINTE EULALIE D'ANS 144 BA 27
24 SAINTE EULALIE D'EYMET 157 Y 30
12 SAINTE EULALIE D'OLT 176 JA 31
12 SAINTE EULALIE DE CERNON 191 KA 33
40 SAINTE EULALIE EN BORN 169 R 32
26 SAINTE EULALIE EN ROYANS 166 UA 28
01 SAINTE EUPHEMIE 136 RA 24
26 SAINTE EUPHEMIE SUR OUVEZE 180 UA 32
60 SAINTE EUSOYE 26 GA 8
36 SAINTE FAUSTE 115 EA 20
19 SAINTE FEREOLE 159 DA 27
23 SAINTE FEYRE 132 FA 23
23 SAINTE FEYRE LA MONTAGNE 132 GA 25
85 SAINTE FLAIVE DES LOUPS 110 P 21
33 SAINTE FLORENCE 156 W 29
85 SAINTE FLORENCE 110 R 21
43 SAINTE FLORINE 148 LA 27
09 SAINTE FOI 221 FA 37
19 SAINTE FORTUNADE 159 EA 28
40 SAINTE FOY 185 V 33
71 SAINTE FOY 135 OA 23
76 SAINTE FOY 24 BA 7
85 SAINTE FOY 125 P 22
31 SAINTE FOY D'AIGREFEUILLE 210 DA 35
24 SAINTE FOY DE BELVES 158 BA 30
24 SAINTE FOY DE LONGAS 158 Z 29
14 SAINTE FOY DE MONTGOMMERY 36 X 11
31 SAINTE FOY DE PEYROLIERES 210 BA 35
69 SAINTE FOY L'ARGENTIERE 150 QA 25
33 SAINTE FOY LA GRANDE C 157 X 29
33 SAINTE FOY LA LONGUE 171 W 30
69 SAINTE FOY LES LYON C 150 RA 25
42 SAINTE FOY ST SULPICE 149 PA 25
73 SAINTE FOY TARENTAISE 154 BB 26
61 SAINTE GAUBURGE STE COLOMBE 37 Y 12
17 SAINTE GEMME 141 S 25
32 SAINTE GEMME 187 AA 34
33 SAINTE GEMME 171 W 30
36 SAINTE GEMME 115 CA 20
51 SAINTE GEMME 42 MA 10
79 SAINTE GEMME 112 V 20
81 SAINTE GEMME 190 GA 33
18 SAINTE GEMME EN SANCERROIS 101 JA 18
85 SAINTE GEMME LA PLAINE 125 R 22
47 SAINTE GEMME MARTAILLAC 171 X 31
28 SAINTE GEMME MORONVAL 38 DA 12
41 SAINTE GEMMES 80 CA 16
49 SAINTE GEMMES D'ANDIGNE 77 S 17
53 SAINTE GEMMES LE ROBERT 77 V 14
49 SAINTE GEMMES SUR LOIRE 95 U 18
02 SAINTE GENEVIEVE 29 OA 8
50 SAINTE GENEVIEVE 33 Q 8
54 SAINTE GENEVIEVE 46 XA 11
60 SAINTE GENEVIEVE 40 GA 9
76 SAINTE GENEVIEVE 25 DA 8
45 SAINTE GENEVIEVE DES BOIS 82 JA 16
91 SAINTE GENEVIEVE DES BOIS C 62 HA 12
27 SAINTE GENEVIEVE LES GASNY 38 DA 10
12 SAINTE GENEVIEVE SUR ARGENCE C 161 IA 29
33 SAINTE HELENE 155 S 29
48 SAINTE HELENE 177 MA 31
56 SAINTE HELENE 73 I 16
71 SAINTE HELENE 120 RA 21
88 SAINTE HELENE 68 AB 14
76 SAINTE HELENE BONDEVILLE 23 Y 7
73 SAINTE HELENE DU LAC 153 XA 26
73 SAINTE HELENE SUR ISERE 153 YA 26
85 SAINTE HERMINE C 125 R 22
14 SAINTE HONORINE DE DUCY 35 T 10
14 SAINTE HONORINE DES PERTES 35 T 9
14 SAINTE HONORINE DU FAY 35 U 10
61 SAINTE HONORINE LA CHARDONNE 35 U 11
61 SAINTE HONORINE LA GUILLAUME 58 V 12
24 SAINTE INNOCENCE 157 Y 30
26 SAINTE JALLE 180 UA 31
72 SAINTE JAMME SUR SARTHE 78 X 15
01 SAINTE JULIE 137 UA 25
82 SAINTE JULIETTE 173 BA 32
12 SAINTE JULIETTE SUR VIAUR 175 HA 32
66 SAINTE LEOCADIE 222 FA 40
17 SAINTE LHEURINE 142 U 26
31 SAINTE LIVRADE 187 BA 34
47 SAINTE LIVRADE SUR LOT C 172 Z 31
36 SAINTE LIZAIGNE 116 FA 20
38 SAINTE LUCE 167 WA 29
44 SAINTE LUCE SUR LOIRE 94 Q 18
2A SAINTE LUCIE DE TALLANO 230 KB 43
18 SAINTE LUNAISE 116 HA 20
89 SAINTE MAGNANCE 103 OA 18
43 SAINTE MARGUERITE 162 MA 28
88 SAINTE MARGUERITE 69 BB 14
14 SAINTE MARGUERITE D'ELLE 35 S 10
61 SAINTE MARGUERITE DE CARROUGES 58 V 13
27 SAINTE MARGUERITE DE L'AUTEL 37 AA 11
14 SAINTE MARGUERITE DE VIETTE 36 X 11
14 SAINTE MARGUERITE DES LOGES 36 X 11
27 SAINTE MARGUERITE EN OUCHE 37 Z 11
07 SAINTE MARGUERITE LAFIGERE 178 OA 31
76 SAINTE MARGUERITE SUR DUCLAIR 24 AA 8
76 SAINTE MARGUERITE SUR FAUVILLE 23 Z 8
76 SAINTE MARGUERITE SUR MER 24 AA 7
05 SAINTE MARIE 180 UA 31
08 SAINTE MARIE 30 RA 9
15 SAINTE MARIE 161 JA 29
25 SAINTE MARIE 89 AB 17
32 SAINTE MARIE 187 AA 34
35 SAINTE MARIE 75 N 17
58 SAINTE MARIE 102 LA 19
65 SAINTE MARIE 217 Z 37
66 SAINTE MARIE 224 KA 39
51 SAINTE MARIE A PY 43 OA 10
76 SAINTE MARIE AU BOSC 23 X 8
57 SAINTE MARIE AUX CHENES 45 XA 10
68 SAINTE MARIE AUX MINES C 69 CB 14
59 SAINTE MARIE CAPPEL 8 HA 3
38 SAINTE MARIE D'ALLOIX 153 XA 27
73 SAINTE MARIE D'ALVEY 152 VA 26
24 SAINTE MARIE DE CHIGNAC 158 AA 28
73 SAINTE MARIE DE CUINES 153 YA 27
40 SAINTE MARIE DE GOSSE 183 R 35
17 SAINTE MARIE DE RE 126 Q 23
27 SAINTE MARIE DE VATIMESNIL 39 DA 10
87 SAINTE MARIE DE VAUX 130 BA 25
76 SAINTE MARIE DES CHAMPS 24 AA 8
50 SAINTE MARIE DU BOIS 57 S 13
53 SAINTE MARIE DU BOIS 57 U 13
51 SAINTE MARIE DU LAC NUISEMENT 65 RA 13
38 SAINTE MARIE DU MONT 153 WA 27
50 SAINTE MARIE DU MONT 33 R 9
70 SAINTE MARIE EN CHANOIS 89 ZA 16
70 SAINTE MARIE EN CHAUX 88 YA 16
62 SAINTE MARIE KERQUE 8 GA 2
21 SAINTE MARIE LA BLANCHE 121 SA 20
61 SAINTE MARIE LA ROBERT 58 V 12
19 SAINTE MARIE LAPANOUZE 147 HA 27
14 SAINTE MARIE LAUMONT 35 S 11
14 SAINTE MARIE OUTRE L'EAU 35 S 11
21 SAINTE MARIE SUR OUCHE 105 SA 18
27 SAINTE MARTHE 37 AA 11
47 SAINTE MARTHE 171 X 31
10 SAINTE MAURE 64 OA 14
47 SAINTE MAURE DE PEYRIAC 186 X 33
37 SAINTE MAURE DE TOURAINE C 98 Z 19
83 SAINTE MAXIME 204 AB 36
17 SAINTE MEME 128 U 25
51 SAINTE MENEHOULD S 44 SA 10
32 SAINTE MERE 187 Z 33
50 SAINTE MERE EGLISE C 33 Q 9
78 SAINTE MESME 61 FA 13
24 SAINTE MONDANE 159 CA 29
18 SAINTE MONTAINE 82 GA 17
24 SAINTE NATHALENE 159 CA 29
79 SAINTE NEOMAYE 128 V 22
01 SAINTE OLIVE 137 SA 24
61 SAINTE OPPORTUNE 57 U 12
27 SAINTE OPPORTUNE DU BOSC 37 AA 10
27 SAINTE OPPORTUNE LA MARE 23 Y 9
24 SAINTE ORSE 158 BA 28
72 SAINTE OSMANE 79 Z 16
79 SAINTE OUENNE 112 U 22
89 SAINTE PALLAYE 84 NA 17
69 SAINTE PAULE 136 QA 24
44 SAINTE PAZANNE 93 O 19
85 SAINTE PEXINE 125 R 22
50 SAINTE PIENCE 56 Q 12
54 SAINTE POLE 69 AB 13
02 SAINTE PREUVE 28 NA 8
12 SAINTE RADEGONDE 175 IA 31
17 SAINTE RADEGONDE 127 S 25
24 SAINTE RADEGONDE 172 Z 30
32 SAINTE RADEGONDE 187 Z 34
33 SAINTE RADEGONDE 157 W 29
71 SAINTE RADEGONDE 119 OA 21
79 SAINTE RADEGONDE 112 V 20
86 SAINTE RADEGONDE 114 Z 21
85 SAINTE RADEGONDE DES NOYERS 125 R 22
17 SAINTE RAMEE 141 T 27
70 SAINTE REINE 87 WA 17
73 SAINTE REINE 153 XA 26
44 SAINTE REINE DE BRETAGNE 93 M 18
57 SAINTE RUFFINE 46 XA 10
21 SAINTE SABINE 104 RA 19
24 SAINTE SABINE BORN 172 AA 30
72 SAINTE SABINE SUR LONGEVE 78 X 15
10 SAINTE SAVINE C 64 OA 14
61 SAINTE SCOLASSE SUR SARTHE 59 Y 13
80 SAINTE SEGREE 26 FA 7
29 SAINTE SEVE 52 F 13
16 SAINTE SEVERE 142 V 25
36 SAINTE SEVERE SUR INDRE C 116 FA 22
43 SAINTE SIGOLENE C 149 PA 27
18 SAINTE SOLANGE 101 IA 19
79 SAINTE SOLINE 129 W 23
16 SAINTE SOULINE 143 W 27
17 SAINTE SOULLE 127 S 23
09 SAINTE SUZANNE 210 CA 36
25 SAINTE SUZANNE 89 AB 17
53 SAINTE SUZANNE C 78 V 15
50 SAINTE SUZANNE SUR VIRE 34 R 10
33 SAINTE TERRE 156 W 29
03 SAINTE THERENCE 133 IA 23
18 SAINTE THORETTE 100 GA 19
22 SAINTE TREPHINE 73 I 14
24 SAINTE TRIE 144 BA 27
04 SAINTE TULLE 197 WA 34
11 SAINTE VALIERE 213 JA 36
08 SAINTE VAUBOURG 29 RA 9
79 SAINTE VERGE 96 V 20
89 SAINTE VERTU 84 NA 16
50 SAINTENY 34 Q 10
17 SAINTES S 142 T 25
13 SAINTES MARIES DE LA MER C 194 QA 35
60 SAINTINES 41 JA 9
91 SAINTRY SUR SEINE 62 HA 12
77 SAINTS 41 KA 12
89 SAINTS 83 LA 17
52 SAINTS GEOSMES 87 UA 16
28 SAINVILLE 61 FA 13
86 SAIRES 113 X 20
61 SAIRES LA VERRERIE 57 U 12
11 SAISSAC C 212 GA 36
80 SAISSEVAL 26 GA 7
71 SAISY 120 RA 20
79 SAIVRES 112 V 22
81 SAIX 212 GA 35
86 SAIX 97 W 19
05 SAIX, LE 181 WA 31
39 SAIZENAY 122 WA 20
54 SAIZERAIS 45 XA 12
58 SAIZY 103 NA 18
31 SAJAS 209 BA 36
24 SALAGNAC 144 BA 27
38 SALAGNON 152 UA 26
38 SALAISE SUR SANNE 151 SA 27
39 SALANS 106 WA 19
34 SALASC 213 LA 35
33 SALAUNES 155 S 29
07 SALAVAS 178 QA 31
01 SALAVRE 137 UA 22
30 SALAZAC 179 QA 32
41 SALBRIS C 100 FA 18
48 SALCES, LES 176 KA 31
65 SALECHAN 217 Z 38
31 SALEICH 217 AA 37
17 SALEIGNES 128 V 24
66 SALEILLES 224 JA 39
07 SALELLES, LES 178 OA 31
48 SALELLES, LES 176 LA 31
60 SALENCY 27 KA 8
67 SALENTHAL 49 DB 12
05 SALEON 181 WA 31
05 SALERANS 180 WA 32
31 SALERM 209 AA 36
83 SALERNES C 203 YA 35
15 SALERS C 161 HA 28
74 SALES 139 XA 25
59 SALESCHES 18 MA 5
38 SALETTE FALLAVAUX, LA 167 XA 29
26 SALETTES 179 SA 30
43 SALETTES 163 OA 29
80 SALEUX 26 GA 7
2A SALICE 227 KB 41
2B SALICETO 228 LB 40
81 SALIES 189 GA 33
64 SALIES DE BEARN C 206 S 35
31 SALIES DU SALAT C 217 AA 37
04 SALIGNAC 181 XA 32
33 SALIGNAC 156 U 28
17 SALIGNAC DE MIRAMBEAU 142 U 27
24 SALIGNAC EYVIGNES C 159 CA 29
17 SALIGNAC SUR CHARENTE 142 U 26
39 SALIGNEY 106 VA 19
85 SALIGNY 110 Q 20
89 SALIGNY 63 LA 14
18 SALIGNY LE VIF 101 IA 19
03 SALIGNY SUR ROUDON 119 NA 22
65 SALIGOS 216 W 38
30 SALINDRES 178 PA 32
30 SALINELLES 193 OA 34
15 SALINS 160 HA 28
77 SALINS 63 KA 13
39 SALINS LES BAINS C 122 WA 20
73 SALINS LES THERMES 153 ZA 26
21 SALIVES 86 SA 17
06 SALLAGRIFFON 199 BB 33
74 SALLANCHES C 140 ZA 24
62 SALLAUMINES 17 JA 4
71 SALLE, LA 137 SA 22
88 SALLE, LA 69 AB 14
49 SALLE DE VIHIERS, LA 95 T 19
38 SALLE EN BEAUMONT, LA 167 WA 29
49 SALLE ET CHAPELLE AUBRY, LA 95 S 18
05 SALLE LES ALPES, LA 168 ZA 29
48 SALLE PRUNET, LA 177 MA 32
33 SALLEBOEUF 156 U 29
63 SALLEDES 148 LA 26
11 SALLELES CABARDES 212 HA 36
11 SALLELES D'AUDE 213 JA 36
14 SALLEN 35 S 10
14 SALLENELLES 36 V 10
74 SALLENOVES 139 XA 24
85 SALLERTAINE 109 N 20
33 SALLES 169 S 30
47 SALLES 172 AA 31
65 SALLES 215 W 37
79 SALLES 128 W 22
81 SALLES 189 FA 33
33 SALLES, LES 157 W 29
42 SALLES, LES 135 NA 25
65 SALLES ADOUR 216 X 37
69 SALLES ARBUISSONNAS EN BEAUJOLAIS 136 RA 24
12 SALLES COURBATIES 174 FA 31
12 SALLES CURAN C 176 JA 32

16 SALLES D'ANGLES 142 V 26
32 SALLES D'ARMAGNAC 185 W 34
11 SALLES D'AUDE 213 KA 36
16 SALLES DE BARBEZIEUX 142 W 26
24 SALLES DE BELVES 173 BA 30
16 SALLES DE VILLEFAGNAN 129 X 24
30 SALLES DU GARDON, LES 178 OA 32
31 SALLES ET PRATVIEL 217 Z 38
12 SALLES LA SOURCE 175 HA 31
16 SALLES LAVALETTE 143 X 27
87 SALLES LAVAUGUYON, LES 144 Z 25
64 SALLES MONGISCARD 206 S 35
26 SALLES SOUS BOIS 179 SA 31
31 SALLES SUR GARONNE 210 BA 36
11 SALLES SUR L'HERS C 211 EA 36
17 SALLES SUR MER 126 R 24
83 SALLES SUR VERDON, LES 197 YA 34
64 SALLESPISSE 206 T 35
55 SALMAGNE 44 UA 12
21 SALMAISE 104 RA 18
67 SALMBACH 50 GB 11
12 SALMIECH 175 IA 32
59 SALOME 9 JA 4
10 SALON 64 OA 12
24 SALON 158 Z 28
13 SALON DE PROVENCE C 201 TA 35
19 SALON LA TOUR 145 DA 26
57 SALONNES 46 ZA 12
71 SALORNAY SUR GUYE 120 RA 22
80 SALOUEL 26 GA 7
62 SALPERWICK 8 GA 3
09 SALSEIN 218 BA 38
66 SALSES LE CHATEAU 223 JA 38
11 SALSIGNE 212 HA 36
42 SALT EN DONZY 150 PA 25
81 SALVAGNAC C 189 EA 33
12 SALVAGNAC CAJARC 174 EA 31
82 SALVETAT BELMONTET, LA 188 DA 33
31 SALVETAT LAURAGAIS, LA 211 EA 35
12 SALVETAT PEYRALES, LA C 175 GA 32
31 SALVETAT ST GILLES, LA 210 CA 35
34 SALVETAT SUR AGOUT, LA C 213 IA 35
11 SALVEZINES 222 GA 38
46 SALVIAC C 173 CA 30
42 SALVIZINET 149 PA 25
11 SALZA 221 HA 37
43 SALZUIT 162 MA 28
40 SAMADET 207 U 35
31 SAMAN 209 Z 36
32 SAMARAN 209 Y 36
32 SAMATAN C 209 AA 35
47 SAMAZAN 171 X 31
41 SAMBIN 99 CA 18
89 SAMBOURG 84 OA 16
59 SAMEON 18 LA 4
62 SAMER C 7 EA 3
21 SAMEREY 106 UA 19
64 SAMES 206 R 35
86 SAMMARCOLLES 97 X 19
77 SAMMERON 41 KA 11
74 SAMOENS C 140 AB 24
01 SAMOGNAT 138 VA 23
55 SAMOGNEUX 44 UA 10
77 SAMOIS SUR SEINE 62 IA 13
33 SAMONAC 156 U 28
77 SAMOREAU 62 IA 13
31 SAMOUILLAN 209 AA 36
02 SAMOUSSY 28 NA 8
39 SAMPANS 106 UA 19
55 SAMPIGNY 45 VA 12
71 SAMPIGNY LES MARANGES 120 RA 20
2A SAMPOLO 228 LB 42
07 SAMPZON 178 PA 31
25 SAMSON 106 WA 19
64 SAMSONS LION 207 W 35
65 SAMURAN 217 Z 37
2B SAN DAMIANO 228 MB 40
2B SAN GAVINO D'AMPUGNANI 228 MB 40
2A SAN GAVINO DI CARBINI 230 LB 43
2B SAN GAVINO DI FIUMORBO 228 LB 42
2B SAN GAVINO DI TENDA 226 LB 39
2B SAN GIOVANNI DI MORIANI 228 MB 40
2B SAN GIULIANO 228 MB 40
2B SAN LORENZO 228 LB 40
2B SAN MARTINO DI LOTA C 226 MB 39
2B SAN NICOLAO 228 MB 40
31 SANA 209 BA 36
83 SANARY SUR MER 202 WA 37
71 SANCE 137 SA 23
18 SANCERGUES C 101 JA 19
18 SANCERRE C 101 JA 18
25 SANCEY LE GRAND 107 ZA 18
25 SANCEY LE LONG 108 AB 18
28 SANCHEVILLE 61 DA 14
88 SANCHEY 68 YA 14
18 SANCOINS C 117 JA 20
27 SANCOURT 25 EA 9
59 SANCOURT 18 KA 5
80 SANCOURT 27 KA 7
54 SANCY 31 WA 9
77 SANCY 41 JA 11
02 SANCY LES CHEMINOTS 28 MA 9
77 SANCY LES PROVINS 41 LA 12
67 SAND 70 EB 13
28 SANDARVILLE 60 CA 14
88 SANDAUCOURT 67 WA 14
45 SANDILLON 81 FA 16
76 SANDOUVILLE 23 Y 8
01 SANDRANS 137 SA 24
62 SANGATTE 7 EA 2
62 SANGHEN 7 FA 3
40 SANGUINET 169 R 31
07 SANILHAC 178 PA 31
30 SANILHAC SAGRIES 193 OA 33
23 SANNAT 132 HA 24
14 SANNERVILLE 36 V 10
84 SANNES 196 UA 34
95 SANNOIS C 40 GA 11
65 SANOUS 208 W 36
57 SANRY LES VIGY 46 YA 10
57 SANRY SUR NIED 46 YA 10
88 SANS VALLOIS 67 XA 14
66 SANSA 222 GA 39
15 SANSAC DE MARMIESSE 160 GA 29
15 SANSAC VEINAZES 161 HA 30
79 SANSAIS 128 T 23
32 SANSAN 209 Z 35
43 SANSSAC L'EGLISE 163 NA 28
03 SANSSAT 133 MA 23
2A SANT'ANDREA D'ORCINO 227 JB 42
2B SANT'ANDREA DI BOZIO 228 LB 41
2B SANT'ANDREA DI COTONE 228 MB 40
2B SANT'ANTONINO 225 KB 39
2B SANTA LUCIA DI MERCURIO 228 LB 40
2B SANTA LUCIA DI MORIANI 228 MB 40
2B SANTA MARIA DI LOTA 226 MB 38
2A SANTA MARIA FIGANIELLA 229 KB 43
2B SANTA MARIA POGGIO 228 MB 40
2A SANTA MARIA SICHE C 227 KB 42
2B SANTA REPARATA DI BALAGNA 225 KB 39
2B SANTA REPARATA DI MORIANI 228 MB 40
39 SANTANS 122 VA 20
45 SANTEAU 81 GA 15
29 SANTEC 52 E 12
21 SANTENAY 120 RA 20
41 SANTENAY 80 BA 17
94 SANTENY 40 IA 12
59 SANTES 9 JA 4
28 SANTEUIL 61 EA 13
95 SANTEUIL 39 FA 10
89 SANTIGNY 84 OA 17
28 SANTILLY 61 EA 15
71 SANTILLY 120 RA 21
2B SANTO PIETRO DI TENDA 226 LB 39
2B SANTO PIETRO DI VENACO 228 LB 41
25 SANTOCHE 89 ZA 16
21 SANTOSSE 120 RA 20
18 SANTRANGES 82 IA 17
12 SANVENSA 174 FA 32
71 SANVIGNES LES MINES 120 PA 21
86 SANXAY 112 W 22
79 SANZAY 112 U 20
54 SANZEY 45 WA 12
14 SAON 35 S 9
25 SAONE 107 XA 19
14 SAONNET 35 S 9
06 SAORGE 199 EB 33
72 SAOSNES 59 X 14
26 SAOU 165 TA 30
61 SAP, LE 37 Y 11
61 SAP ANDRE, LE 37 Y 11
51 SAPIGNICOURT 65 RA 12
62 SAPIGNIES 17 JA 6
08 SAPOGNE ET FEUCHERES 30 RA 8
08 SAPOGNE SUR MARCHE 31 UA 8
39 SAPOIS 123 XA 21
88 SAPOIS 89 AB 15
02 SAPONAY 41 MA 10
70 SAPONCOURT 88 XA 16
74 SAPPEY, LE 139 XA 24
38 SAPPEY EN CHARTREUSE, LE 152 WA 27
32 SARAMON C 209 AA 35
45 SARAN 81 EA 15
25 SARAZ 107 XA 20
40 SARBAZAN 185 V 33
72 SARCE 78 X 16
61 SARCEAUX 58 W 12
95 SARCELLES C 40 HA 11
38 SARCENAS 152 WA 27
52 SARCEY 66 UA 15
69 SARCEY 136 QA 25
32 SARCOS 209 Z 36
60 SARCUS 25 EA 8
51 SARCY 42 NA 10
30 SARDAN 193 OA 33
23 SARDENT 132 EA 24
38 SARDIEU 151 TA 27
63 SARDON 134 KA 24
58 SARDY LES EPIRY 103 NA 19
64 SARE 205 P 36
72 SARGE LES LE MANS 78 X 15
41 SARGE SUR BRAYE 79 AA 15
2A SARI D'ORCINO C 227 JB 42
2A SARI SOLENZARA 230 MB 43
65 SARIAC MAGNOAC 209 Z 36
65 SARLABOUS 216 X 37
24 SARLANDE 144 BA 26
24 SARLAT LA CANEDA S 159 CA 29
24 SARLIAC SUR L'ISLE 144 AA 27
65 SARNIGUET 208 X 36
60 SARNOIS 25 FA 8
51 SARON SUR AUBE 64 NA 13
65 SARP 217 Z 37
64 SARPOURENX 206 T 35
32 SARRAGACHIES 185 W 34
25 SARRAGEOIS 123 YA 21
32 SARRAGUZAN 208 Y 36
57 SARRALBE C 47 BB 11
57 SARRALTROFF 48 BB 12
19 SARRAN 146 FA 27
64 SARRANCE 215 T 37
65 SARRANCOLIN 216 Y 38
32 SARRANT 187 AA 34
07 SARRAS 164 RA 28
24 SARRAZAC 144 BA 27
46 SARRAZAC 159 DA 28
40 SARRAZIET 184 U 34
67 SARRE UNION C 48 CB 11
57 SARREBOURG S 48 CB 12
31 SARRECAVE 209 Z 36
57 SARREGUEMINES S 48 CB 10
57 SARREINSMING 48 CB 10
31 SARREMEZAN 209 Z 36
67 SARREWERDEN 48 BB 11
52 SARREY 87 UA 15
65 SARRIAC BIGORRE 208 X 36
84 SARRIANS 195 SA 33
49 SARRIGNE 96 U 17
39 SARROGNA 122 VA 22
2A SARROLA CARCOPINO 227 JB 42
40 SARRON 207 V 35
65 SARROUILLES 208 X 36
19 SARROUX 147 HA 27
51 SARRY 43 QA 11
71 SARRY 135 OA 23
89 SARRY 84 OA 17
62 SARS, LE 17 IA 6
59 SARS ET ROSIERES 18 LA 4
62 SARS LE BOIS 17 HA 5
59 SARS POTERIES 19 OA 6
2A SARTENE S 229 KB 43
88 SARTES 67 VA 14
50 SARTILLY C 56 Q 12
62 SARTON 17 HA 6
78 SARTROUVILLE C 39 GA 11
36 SARZAY 116 EA 21
56 SARZEAU C 92 K 17
41 SASNIERES 79 AA 16
71 SASSANGY 120 RA 21
41 SASSAY 99 DA 18
59 SASSEGNIES 19 NA 5
38 SASSENAGE 166 VA 28
71 SASSENAY 121 SA 20
76 SASSETOT LE MALGARDE 24 AA 7
76 SASSETOT LE MAUCONDUIT 23 Y 7
76 SASSEVILLE 23 Z 7
27 SASSEY 38 CA 10
55 SASSEY SUR MEUSE 30 TA 9
36 SASSIERGES ST GERMAIN 116 FA 21
65 SASSIS 216 W 38
14 SASSY 36 W 11
69 SATHONAY CAMP 137 SA 25
69 SATHONAY VILLAGE 137 SA 25
07 SATILLIEU C 164 RA 28
38 SATOLAS ET BONCE 151 TA 25
34 SATURARGUES 193 OA 34
31 SAUBENS 210 CA 35
40 SAUBION 183 O 34
64 SAUBOLE 208 W 36
40 SAUBRIGUES 183 Q 35
40 SAUBUSSE 183 R 34
33 SAUCATS 170 T 30
64 SAUCEDE 206 T 36
28 SAUCELLE, LA 60 BA 12
76 SAUCHAY 15 CA 7
62 SAUCHY CAUCHY 18 KA 5
62 SAUCHY LESTREE 18 KA 5
12 SAUCLIERES 192 LA 33
10 SAUCLY 66 SA 14
62 SAUDEMONT 17 KA 5
51 SAUDOY 64 NA 12
52 SAUDRON 66 UA 13
55 SAUDRUPT 44 TA 12
39 SAUGEOT 122 WA 21
40 SAUGNAC ET CAMBRAN 183 S 34
40 SAUGNACQ ET MURET 169 T 31
33 SAUGON 156 U 28
43 SAUGUES C 162 MA 29
64 SAUGUIS ST ETIENNE 206 S 37
18 SAUGY 116 FA 20
12 SAUJAC 174 FA 31
17 SAUJON C 141 S 25
05 SAULCE, LA 181 XA 31
26 SAULCE SUR RHONE 165 SA 30
08 SAULCES CHAMPENOISES 29 QA 9
08 SAULCES MONCLIN 29 OA 8
03 SAULCET 133 LA 23
02 SAULCHERY 41 LA 11
62 SAULCHOY 16 EA 5
60 SAULCHOY, LE 26 GA 8
80 SAULCHOY SOUS POIX 26 FA 7
88 SAULCY, LE 69 BB 13
88 SAULCY SUR MEURTHE 69 BB 14
25 SAULES 107 YA 19
71 SAULES 120 RA 21
86 SAULGE 130 AA 22
49 SAULGE L'HOPITAL 96 U 18
53 SAULGES 77 U 15
16 SAULGOND 130 AA 24
46 SAULIAC SUR CELE 174 EA 31
21 SAULIEU C 104 PA 18
52 SAULLES 87 VA 16
55 SAULMORY ET VILLEFRANCHE 30 TA 9
36 SAULNAY 115 CA 20
54 SAULNES 31 WA 8
28 SAULNIERES 60 CA 12
35 SAULNIERES 75 P 16
70 SAULNOT 89 AB 17
57 SAULNY 46 XA 10
21 SAULON LA CHAPELLE 105 TA 19
21 SAULON LA RUE 105 TA 19
10 SAULSOTTE, LA 64 MA 13
84 SAULT C 196 UA 33
01 SAULT BRENAZ 138 UA 25
64 SAULT DE NAVAILLES 184 T 35
08 SAULT LES RETHEL 29 QA 9
08 SAULT ST REMY 29 PA 9
59 SAULTAIN 18 MA 5
62 SAULTY 17 HA 5
55 SAULVAUX 45 VA 12
70 SAULX C 88 YA 16
21 SAULX LE DUC 86 SA 17
55 SAULX LES CHAMPLON 45 VA 10
91 SAULX LES CHARTREUX 62 GA 12
78 SAULX MARCHAIS 39 EA 11
54 SAULXEROTTE 67 WA 13
67 SAULXURES 69 CB 13
88 SAULXURES LES BULGNEVILLE 67 WA 14
54 SAULXURES LES NANCY 46 YA 12
54 SAULXURES LES VANNES 67 WA 13
88 SAULXURES SUR MOSELOTTE C 89 AB 15
18 SAULZAIS LE POTIER C 117 HA 21
03 SAULZET 134 KA 23
63 SAULZET LE FROID 147 JA 26
59 SAULZOIR 18 LA 5
04 SAUMANE 196 VA 33
30 SAUMANE 177 NA 32
84 SAUMANE DE VAUCLUSE 195 TA 33
47 SAUMEJAN 171 W 32
28 SAUMERAY 60 CA 14
47 SAUMONT 172 Y 32
76 SAUMONT LA POTERIE 25 DA 8
33 SAUMOS 155 S 29
49 SAUMUR S 96 W 19
37 SAUNAY 79 AA 17
23 SAUNIERE, LA 132 FA 24
71 SAUNIERES 121 TA 20
76 SAUQUEVILLE 24 BA 7
79 SAURAIS 112 V 21
09 SAURAT 219 DA 38
63 SAURET BESSERVE 133 JA 24
63 SAURIER 148 KA 26
68 SAUSHEIM 90 DB 16
34 SAUSSAN 214 NA 35
28 SAUSSAY 38 CA 11
76 SAUSSAY 24 AA 8
27 SAUSSAY LA CAMPAGNE 25 DA 9
27 SAUSSAYE, LA 38 BA 10
50 SAUSSEMESNIL 33 Q 8
81 SAUSSENAC 190 GA 33
31 SAUSSENS 211 EA 35
04 SAUSSES 198 AB 33
13 SAUSSET LES PINS 201 TA 36
76 SAUSSEUZEMARE EN CAUX 23 X 8
21 SAUSSEY 104 RA 19
50 SAUSSEY 34 O 11
24 SAUSSIGNAC 157 Y 29
34 SAUSSINES 193 OA 34
21 SAUSSY 105 SA 18
09 SAUTEL 219 EA 37
33 SAUTERNES 170 U 31
34 SAUTEYRARGUES 193 OA 34
66 SAUTO 222 GA 40
44 SAUTRON 93 P 18
61 SAUVAGERE, LA 58 U 12
69 SAUVAGES, LES 136 PA 24
16 SAUVAGNAC 144 Z 25
47 SAUVAGNAS 172 Z 32
63 SAUVAGNAT 147 IA 25
63 SAUVAGNAT STE MARTHE 148 KA 26
25 SAUVAGNEY 106 WA 18
64 SAUVAGNON 207 U 36
03 SAUVAGNY 133 JA 22
42 SAUVAIN 149 NA 26
15 SAUVAT 147 HA 27
30 SAUVE C 193 OA 33
33 SAUVE, LA 156 V 30
64 SAUVELADE 206 T 36
01 SAUVERNY 139 XA 23
63 SAUVESSANGES 149 NA 27
32 SAUVETAT, LA 186 Y 34
63 SAUVETAT, LA 148 KA 26
47 SAUVETAT DE SAVERES, LA 172 AA 32
47 SAUVETAT DU DROPT, LA 172 Y 30
47 SAUVETAT SUR LEDE, LA 172 Z 31
30 SAUVETERRE 195 RA 33
32 SAUVETERRE 209 AA 35
65 SAUVETERRE 208 X 35
81 SAUVETERRE 212 HA 35
82 SAUVETERRE 173 CA 32
64 SAUVETERRE DE BEARN C 206 S 36
31 SAUVETERRE DE COMMINGES 217 Z 37
33 SAUVETERRE DE GUYENNE C 156 W 30
12 SAUVETERRE DE ROUERGUE 175 GA 32
47 SAUVETERRE LA LEMANCE 173 BA 30
47 SAUVETERRE ST DENIS 172 Z 32
32 SAUVIAC 208 Y 36
33 SAUVIAC 171 V 31
34 SAUVIAN 214 LA 36
63 SAUVIAT 148 MA 25
87 SAUVIAT SUR VIGE 131 DA 24
16 SAUVIGNAC 142 W 27
70 SAUVIGNEY LES GRAY 106 WA 18
70 SAUVIGNEY LES PESMES 106 VA 18
55 SAUVIGNY 67 WA 13
89 SAUVIGNY LE BEUREAL 84 OA 17
89 SAUVIGNY LE BOIS 84 OA 17
58 SAUVIGNY LES BOIS 118 LA 20
08 SAUVILLE 30 RA 8
88 SAUVILLE 67 WA 14
80 SAUVILLERS MONGIVAL 26 HA 7
32 SAUVIMONT 209 AA 35
55 SAUVOY 67 VA 12
46 SAUX 173 BA 31
31 SAUX ET POMAREDE 217 Z 37
63 SAUXILLANGES C 148 LA 26
06 SAUZE 198 AB 33
05 SAUZE DU LAC, LE 181 YA 31
79 SAUZE VAUSSAIS C 129 X 23
36 SAUZELLES 114 BA 21
26 SAUZET 179 SA 30
30 SAUZET 193 PA 33
46 SAUZET 173 CA 31
81 SAUZIERE ST JEAN, LA 189 EA 33
56 SAUZON 91 I 18
31 SAVARTHES 217 AA 37
07 SAVAS 150 RA 27
38 SAVAS MEPIN 151 TA 26
26 SAVASSE 179 RA 30
44 SAVENAY C 93 O 18
82 SAVENES 188 CA 34
23 SAVENNES 132 EA 24
63 SAVENNES 147 HA 26
49 SAVENNIERES 95 T 18
09 SAVERDUN C 210 DA 36
31 SAVERES 210 BA 36
67 SAVERNE S 49 DB 12
80 SAVEUSE 26 GA 7
71 SAVIANGES 120 RA 21
10 SAVIERES 64 OA 13
39 SAVIGNA 122 VA 22
12 SAVIGNAC 174 FA 31
33 SAVIGNAC 171 W 31
47 SAVIGNAC DE DURAS 157 X 30
33 SAVIGNAC DE L'ISLE 156 V 29
24 SAVIGNAC DE MIREMONT 158 AA 29
24 SAVIGNAC DE NONTRON 144 Z 26
24 SAVIGNAC LEDRIER 145 CA 27
24 SAVIGNAC LES EGLISES C 144 AA 27
09 SAVIGNAC LES ORMEAUX 220 EA 39
32 SAVIGNAC MONA 209 BA 35
47 SAVIGNAC SUR LEYZE 172 AA 31
30 SAVIGNARGUES 193 OA 33
86 SAVIGNE 129 Y 23
72 SAVIGNE L'EVEQUE 78 X 15
72 SAVIGNE SOUS LE LUDE 78 W 17
37 SAVIGNE SUR LATHAN 97 Y 18
01 SAVIGNEUX 137 SA 24
42 SAVIGNEUX 149 OA 26
60 SAVIGNIES 25 FA 9
50 SAVIGNY 34 Q 11
52 SAVIGNY 87 VA 16
69 SAVIGNY 150 QA 25
74 SAVIGNY 139 XA 24
88 SAVIGNY 68 YA 14
71 SAVIGNY EN REVERMONT 122 UA 21
18 SAVIGNY EN SANCERRE 101 JA 18
18 SAVIGNY EN SEPTAINE 101 HA 19
89 SAVIGNY EN TERRE PLAINE 84 OA 17
37 SAVIGNY EN VERON 97 X 19
21 SAVIGNY LE SEC 105 TA 18
77 SAVIGNY LE TEMPLE C 62 IA 13
50 SAVIGNY LE VIEUX 56 R 13
21 SAVIGNY LES BEAUNE 104 RA 19
86 SAVIGNY LEVESCAULT 113 Y 22
58 SAVIGNY POIL FOL 119 NA 21
86 SAVIGNY SOUS FAYE 113 X 20
21 SAVIGNY SOUS MALAIN 104 RA 18
08 SAVIGNY SUR AISNE 30 RA 9
51 SAVIGNY SUR ARDRES 42 NA 10
41 SAVIGNY SUR BRAYE C 79 AA 16
89 SAVIGNY SUR CLAIRIS 83 KA 15
71 SAVIGNY SUR GROSNE 120 RA 21
91 SAVIGNY SUR ORGE C 62 HA 12
71 SAVIGNY SUR SEILLE 121 TA 21
21 SAVILLY 104 PA 19
05 SAVINES LE LAC C 182 ZA 31
77 SAVINS 63 KA 13
84 SAVOILLAN 180 UA 32
21 SAVOISY 85 QA 16
21 SAVOLLES 105 UA 18
37 SAVONNIERES 97 Z 18
55 SAVONNIERES DEVANT BAR 44 TA 12
55 SAVONNIERES EN PERTHOIS 66 TA 12
21 SAVOUGES 105 TA 19
05 SAVOURNON 181 WA 31
70 SAVOYEUX 87 WA 17
02 SAVY 27 KA 7
62 SAVY BERLETTE 17 IA 5
74 SAXEL 139 ZA 23
58 SAXI BOURDON 102 MA 19
54 SAXON SION 67 XA 13
63 SAYAT 147 KA 25
30 SAZE 195 RA 33
36 SAZERAY 132 FA 22
03 SAZERET 133 JA 23
37 SAZILLY 97 Y 19
65 SAZOS 216 W 38
29 SCAER C 72 G 15
2B SCATA 228 MB 40
24 SCEAU ST ANGEL 144 Z 26
07 SCEAUTRES 179 RA 30
89 SCEAUX 84 OA 17
92 SCEAUX C 40 GA 12
49 SCEAUX D'ANJOU 77 T 17
45 SCEAUX DU GATINAIS 62 IA 15
72 SCEAUX SUR HUISNE 59 Z 15
25 SCEY MAISIERES 107 XA 19
70 SCEY SUR SAONE ET ST ALBIN C 88 WA 17
67 SCHAEFFERSHEIM 70 EB 13
67 SCHAFFHOUSE PRES SELTZ 50 GB 11
67 SCHAFFHOUSE SUR ZORN 49 EB 12
57 SCHALBACH 48 CB 12
67 SCHALKENDORF 48 EB 11
67 SCHARRACHBERGHEIM IRMSTETT 70 EB 13
67 SCHEIBENHARD 50 GB 11
67 SCHERLENHEIM 49 EB 12
67 SCHERWILLER 70 DB 14
67 SCHILLERSDORF 48 EB 11
67 SCHILTIGHEIM C 50 FB 12
67 SCHIRMECK C 69 CB 13
67 SCHIRRHEIN 49 FB 12
67 SCHIRRHOFFEN 49 FB 12
67 SCHLEITHAL 50 GB 11
68 SCHLIERBACH 90 DB 17
57 SCHMITTVILLER 48 CB 11
57 SCHNECKENBUSCH 48 CB 12
67 SCHNERSHEIM 49 EB 12
67 SCHOENAU 70 EB 14
67 SCHOENBOURG 48 CB 11
57 SCHOENECK 47 BB 10
67 SCHOENENBOURG 49 FB 11
67 SCHOPPERTEN 48 BB 11
57 SCHORBACH 48 DB 10
67 SCHWEIGHOUSE SUR MODER 48 EB 11
68 SCHWEIGHOUSE THANN 90 CB 16
67 SCHWENHEIM 49 DB 12
57 SCHWERDORFF 47 ZA 9
57 SCHWEYEN 48 DB 10
67 SCHWINDRATZHEIM 49 EB 12
68 SCHWOBEN 90 DB 17
67 SCHWOBSHEIM 70 EB 14
79 SCIECQ 128 U 22
74 SCIENTRIER 139 YA 24
32 SCIEURAC ET FLOURES 208 X 35
74 SCIEZ 139 YA 23
79 SCILLE 111 U 21
74 SCIONZIER C 139 ZA 24
2B SCOLCA 226 MB 39
86 SCORBE CLAIRVAUX 113 Y 20
29 SCRIGNAC 52 G 13
51 SCRUPT 43 RA 12
57 SCY CHAZELLES 46 XA 10
70 SCYE 88 XA 17
32 SEAILLES 186 X 34
43 SEAUVE SUR SEMENE, LA 149 PA 27
12 SEBAZAC CONCOURES 175 IA 31
27 SEBECOURT 37 AA 11
50 SEBEVILLE 33 Q 9
02 SEBONCOURT 18 MA 6
59 SEBOURG 18 MA 5
12 SEBRAZAC 175 IA 31
64 SEBY 207 U 35
70 SECENANS 89 ZA 17
08 SECHAULT 43 RA 10
07 SECHERAS 164 RA 28
08 SECHEVAL 29 RA 7
38 SECHILIENNE 166 WA 28
25 SECHIN 107 YA 18
59 SECLIN C 9 JA 4
79 SECONDIGNE SUR BELLE 128 V 23
79 SECONDIGNY C 112 U 21
57 SECOURT 46 YA 11
14 SECQUEVILLE EN BESSIN 35 U 10
08 SEDAN S 30 SA 8
31 SEDEILHAC 217 Z 37
26 SEDERON C 180 VA 32
64 SEDZE MAUBECQ 207 W 36
64 SEDZERE 207 V 36
67 SEEBACH 50 GB 11
61 SEES C 58 X 12
73 SEEZ 154 AB 26
47 SEGALAS 172 Z 30
65 SEGALAS 208 X 36
15 SEGALASSIERE, LA 160 GA 29
56 SEGLIEN 73 I 15
01 SEGNY 139 XA 23
16 SEGONZAC C 142 V 26
19 SEGONZAC 159 CA 27
24 SEGONZAC 157 Y 28
32 SEGOS 207 V 35
32 SEGOUFIELLE 210 BA 35
49 SEGRE S 77 S 17
31 SEGREVILLE 211 EA 35
72 SEGRIE 78 W 14
61 SEGRIE FONTAINE 35 U 11
21 SEGROIS 105 SA 19
36 SEGRY 116 FA 20
49 SEGUINIERE, LA 95 S 19
12 SEGUR 176 JA 32
81 SEGUR, LE 174 FA 32
19 SEGUR LE CHATEAU 145 CA 27
15 SEGUR LES VILLAS 161 JA 27
09 SEGURA 219 EA 37
84 SEGURET 179 TA 32
65 SEGUS 216 W 37
65 SEICH 217 Y 37
54 SEICHAMPS 46 YA 12
45 SEICHEBRIERES 81 GA 15
54 SEICHEPREY 45 WA 11
49 SEICHES SUR LE LOIR C 96 U 17
11 SEIGNALENS 221 FA 37
17 SEIGNE 128 V 24
89 SEIGNELAY C 83 MA 16
55 SEIGNEULLES 44 TA 11
40 SEIGNOSSE 183 Q 34
21 SEIGNY 85 QA 17
41 SEIGY 99 CA 19
31 SEILH 188 CA 34
19 SEILHAC C 145 EA 27
31 SEILHAN 217 Z 37
41 SEILLAC 80 BA 17
83 SEILLANS 198 AB 35
01 SEILLONNAZ 138 VA 25
83 SEILLONS SOURCE D'ARGENS 203 WA 35
77 SEINE PORT 62 IA 13
57 SEINGBOUSE 47 AB 10
32 SEISSAN 209 Z 35
09 SEIX 218 BA 38
35 SEL DE BRETAGNE, LE C 75 P 16
54 SELAINCOURT 67 XA 13
02 SELENS 27 KA 8
67 SELESTAT S 70 DB 14
79 SELIGNE 128 V 23
39 SELIGNEY 122 VA 20
53 SELLE CRAONNAISE, LA 76 R 16
35 SELLE EN COGLES, LA 56 Q 13
45 SELLE EN HERMOY, LA 82 JA 15
35 SELLE EN LUITRE, LA 76 R 14
35 SELLE GUERCHAISE, LA 76 R 15
61 SELLE LA FORGE, LA 57 U 12

45 SELLE SUR LE BIED, LA 82 JA 15
27 SELLES 23 Y 9
51 SELLES 43 PA 9
62 SELLES 7 FA 3
70 SELLES 88 XA 15
41 SELLES ST DENIS 100 FA 18
41 SELLES SUR CHER C 99 DA 18
36 SELLES SUR NAHON 115 DA 20
39 SELLIERES C 122 VA 20
41 SELOMMES C 80 CA 16
25 SELONCOURT 108 BB 18
21 SELONGEY C 86 TA 17
04 SELONNET 181 YA 31
67 SELTZ C 50 GB 11
02 SELVE, LA 29 OA 8
12 SELVE, LA 175 HA 32
09 SEM 220 DA 38
81 SEMALENS 211 FA 35
61 SEMALLE 58 X 13
21 SEMAREY 104 RA 18
43 SEMBADEL 163 MA 27
47 SEMBAS 172 Z 32
37 SEMBLANCAY 79 Z 17
36 SEMBLECAY 99 EA 19
32 SEMBOUES 208 X 35
65 SEMEAC C 208 X 36
64 SEMEACQ BLACHON 208 W 35
57 SEMECOURT 46 XA 10
58 SEMELAY 119 NA 20
33 SEMENS 170 V 30
89 SEMENTRON 83 LA 17
59 SEMERIES 19 OA 6
41 SEMERVILLE 80 CA 15
21 SEMEZANGES 105 SA 19
32 SEMEZIES CACHAN 209 Z 35
08 SEMIDE 29 RA 9
17 SEMILLAC 142 T 27
70 SEMMADON 88 WA 16
10 SEMOINE 42 OA 12
21 SEMOND 85 QA 16
25 SEMONDANS 89 AB 17
38 SEMONS 151 TA 27
59 SEMOUSIES 19 OA 6
17 SEMOUSSAC 142 T 27
52 SEMOUTIERS MONTSAON 66 TA 15
45 SEMOY 81 FA 15
32 SEMPESSERRE 187 Z 33
60 SEMPIGNY 27 JA 8
62 SEMPY 16 FA 4
21 SEMUR EN AUXOIS C 85 PA 17
71 SEMUR EN BRIONNAIS C 135 OA 23
72 SEMUR EN VALLON 79 Z 15
17 SEMUSSAC 141 S 26
08 SEMUY 30 RA 9
40 SEN, LE 170 U 32
65 SENAC 208 X 36
88 SENAIDE 87 WA 15
46 SENAILLAC LATRONQUIERE 160 FA 29
46 SENAILLAC LAUZES 174 EA 30
21 SENAILLY 85 PA 17
89 SENAN 83 LA 16
28 SENANTES 61 DA 12
60 SENANTES 25 EA 9
31 SENARENS 209 BA 36
70 SENARGENT MIGNAFANS 89 ZA 17
80 SENARPONT 25 EA 7
13 SENAS 195 TA 34
39 SENAUD 138 UA 22
81 SENAUX 190 IA 34
24 SENCENAC
PUY DE FOURCHES 144 Z 27
09 SENCONAC 219 EA 38
33 SENDETS 171 W 31
56 SENE 92 K 17
30 SENECHAS 178 OA 31
12 SENERGUES 175 HA 30
47 SENESTIS 171 X 31
43 SENEUJOLS 163 NA 29
04 SENEZ 198 ZA 33
15 SENEZERGUES 160 HA 30
31 SENGOUAGNET 217 AA 37
46 SENIERGUES 174 DA 30
86 SENILLE 113 Z 21
62 SENINGHEM 7 FA 3
62 SENLECQUES 7 FA 3
60 SENLIS S 40 IA 10
62 SENLIS 7 GA 4
80 SENLIS LE SEC 17 IA 6
78 SENLISSE 39 FA 12
18 SENNECAY 116 HA 20
71 SENNECEY LE GRAND C 121 SA 21
21 SENNECEY LES DIJON 105 TA 18
45 SENNELY 81 GA 17
37 SENNEVIERES 98 BA 19
76 SENNEVILLE SUR FECAMP 23 Y 7
89 SENNEVOY LE BAS 85 PA 16
89 SENNEVOY LE HAUT 85 PA 16
55 SENON 31 VA 9
28 SENONCHES C 60 BA 13
28 SENONCOURT 88 XA 16
55 SENONCOURT LES MAUJOUY 44 UA 10
88 SENONES C 69 BB 13
88 SENONGES 67 XA 15
53 SENONNES 76 R 16
60 SENOTS 39 FA 10
81 SENOUILLAC 189 FA 33
50 SENOVILLE 33 O 9
71 SENOZAN 137 SA 22
89 SENS S 63 LA 14
18 SENS BEAUJEU 101 IA 18
35 SENS DE BRETAGNE 76 P 14
71 SENS SUR SEILLE 121 UA 21
09 SENTEIN 217 AA 38
80 SENTELIE 26 FA 8
09 SENTENAC D'OUST 218 BA 38
09 SENTENAC DE SEROU 219 CA 38
68 SENTHEIM 90 BB 16
61 SENTILLY 58 W 12
59 SENTINELLE, LA 18 MA 5
65 SENTOUS 208 Y 36
08 SENUC 30 SA 9
22 SENVEN LEHART 53 J 13
89 SEPEAUX 83 KA 15
59 SEPMERIES 18 MA 5
37 SEPMES 98 Z 19
68 SEPPOIS LE BAS 90 CB 17
68 SEPPOIS LE HAUT 90 CB 17
61 SEPT FORGES 57 U 13
14 SEPT FRERES 35 S 11
76 SEPT MEULES 15 CA 6
51 SEPT SAULX 43 PA 10
77 SEPT SORTS 41 KA 11
14 SEPT VENTS 35 S 10
38 SEPTEME 151 SA 26
13 SEPTEMES LES VALLONS 202 UA 36
78 SEPTEUIL 39 EA 11
82 SEPTFONDS 174 DA 32
25 SEPTFONTAINES 107 YA 20

39 SEPTMONCEL 138 WA 22
02 SEPTMONTS 28 LA 9
55 SEPTSARGES 30 TA 9
02 SEPTVAUX 28 LA 8
55 SEPVIGNY 67 VA 13
79 SEPVRET 128 W 23
31 SEPX 217 AA 37
59 SEQUEDIN 9 JA 4
02 SEQUEHART 28 LA 7
61 SEQUESTRE, LE 189 FA 33
02 SERAIN 18 LA 6
08 SERAINCOURT 29 PA 8
95 SERAINCOURT 39 EA 11
19 SERANDON 146 GA 27
06 SERANON 198 AB 34
60 SERANS 39 EA 10
61 SERANS 55 V 12
54 SERANVILLE 68 ZA 13
59 SERANVILLERS FORENVILLE 18 LA 6
02 SERAUCOURT LE GRAND 27 KA 7
88 SERAUMONT 67 VA 13
28 SERAZEREUX 60 DA 13
03 SERBANNES 133 LA 24
89 SERBONNES 63 KA 14
02 SERCHES 28 LA 9
88 SERCOEUR 68 ZA 14
59 SERCUS 8 HA 3
71 SERCY 120 RA 21
66 SERDINYA 222 GA 39
32 SERE 209 Z 36
65 SERE EN LAVEDAN 215 W 37
65 SERE LANSO 216 W 37
65 SERE RUSTAING 208 X 36
88 SERECOURT 67 WA 15
87 SEREILHAC 144 BA 25
57 SEREMANGE ERZANGE 32 XA 9
32 SEREMPUY 187 AA 34
81 SERENAC 190 GA 33
56 SERENT 74 L 16
60 SEREVILLERS 26 HA 8
27 SEREZ 38 CA 11
38 SEREZIN DE LA TOUR 152 UA 26
69 SEREZIN DU RHONE 151 SA 26
24 SERGEAC 158 BA 28
39 SERGENAUX 122 UA 20
39 SERGENON 122 UA 20
89 SERGINES C 63 LA 14
01 SERGY 139 XA 23
02 SERGY 42 MA 10
62 SERICOURT 16 GA 5
15 SERIERS 162 KA 29
60 SERIFONTAINE 25 EA 9
46 SERIGNAC 173 BA 31
82 SERIGNAC 187 BA 33
47 SERIGNAC PEBOUDOU 172 Z 30
47 SERIGNAC SUR GARONNE 172 Y 32
34 SERIGNAN 213 LA 36
84 SERIGNAN DU COMTAT 179 SA 32
85 SERIGNE 111 S 22
61 SERIGNY 59 Z 14
86 SERIGNY 113 Y 20
19 SERILHAC 159 EA 28
02 SERINGES ET NESLES 42 MA 10
45 SERIS 80 DA 16
71 SERLEY 121 TA 21
58 SERMAGES 103 NA 19
49 SERMAISE 96 V 17
91 SERMAISE 61 FA 13
45 SERMAISES 62 GA 14
60 SERMAIZE 27 JA 8
51 SERMAIZE LES BAINS 44 SA 12
90 SERMAMAGNY 89 BB 17
39 SERMANGE 106 VA 19
2B SERMANO C 228 LB 40
63 SERMENTIZON 148 MA 25
38 SERMERIEU 152 UA 25
67 SERMERSHEIM 70 EB 14
71 SERMESSE 121 TA 20
51 SERMIERS 42 OA 10
89 SERMIZELLES 84 NA 17
02 SERMOISE 28 LA 9
58 SERMOISE SUR LOIRE 118 KA 20
01 SERMOYER 121 SA 22
23 SERMUR 132 HA 24
30 SERNHAC 193 QA 33
88 SEROCOURT 67 WA 14
65 SERON 208 W 36
38 SERPAIZE 151 SA 26
11 SERPENT, LA 221 GA 38
62 SERQUES 8 GA 3
52 SERQUEUX 87 WA 15
76 SERQUEUX 25 DA 8
27 SERQUIGNY 37 Z 10
2A SERRA DI FERRO 229 JB 43
2B SERRA DI FIUMORBO 228 MB 42
2A SERRA DI SCOPAMENE C 230 LB 43
66 SERRALONGUE 222 HA 40
74 SERRAVAL 139 YA 25
12 SERRE, LA 190 IA 33
23 SERRE BUSSIERE
VIEILLE, LA 132 GA 24
39 SERRE LES MOULIERES 106 WA 19
25 SERRE LES SAPINS 106 WA 19
05 SERRES C 180 WA 31
11 SERRES 221 GA 38
54 SERRES 46 ZA 12
64 SERRES CASTET 207 V 36
24 SERRES ET MONTGUYARD 172 Y 30
40 SERRES GASTON 207 U 35
64 SERRES MORLAAS 207 V 36
64 SERRES STE MARIE 207 U 36
09 SERRES SUR ARGET 219 DA 38
40 SERRESLOUS ET ARRIBANS 184 T 34
2A SERRIERA 227 JB 41
07 SERRIERES C 150 RA 27
71 SERRIERES 136 RA 23
01 SERRIERES DE BRIORD 138 UA 25
73 SERRIERES EN CHAUTAGNE 138 WA 25
01 SERRIERES SUR AIN 138 UA 23
89 SERRIGNY 84 OA 16
71 SERRIGNY EN BRESSE 121 TA 20
77 SERRIS 40 JA 11
54 SERROUVILLE 32 WA 9
30 SERRUELLES 116 HA 20
16 SERS 143 Y 26
65 SERS 216 W 38
02 SERVAIS 28 LA 8
02 SERVAL 28 MA 9
70 SERVANCE 89 AB 16
24 SERVANCHES 157 X 28
63 SERVANT 133 JA 23
01 SERVAS 137 TA 23
30 SERVAS 178 PA 32
76 SERVAVILLE SALMONVILLE 24 CA 9
48 SERVERETTE 162 LA 30
26 SERVES SUR RHONE 165 SA 28
34 SERVIAN C 214 LA 35
48 SERVIERES 177 LA 30

19 SERVIERES LE CHATEAU 160 FA 28
30 SERVIERS ET LABAUME 193 PA 33
81 SERVIES 189 FA 34
11 SERVIES EN VAL 221 HA 37
01 SERVIGNAT 121 TA 22
70 SERVIGNEY 88 YA 16
50 SERVIGNY 34 O 10
57 SERVIGNY LES RAVILLE 47 ZA 10
57 SERVIGNY LES STE BARBE 46 YA 10
28 SERVILLE 38 DA 12
03 SERVILLY 133 MA 23
25 SERVIN 107 ZA 18
62 SERVINS 17 IA 4
50 SERVON 56 Q 12
77 SERVON 40 IA 12
51 SERVON MELZICOURT 43 SA 10
35 SERVON SUR VILAINE 76 P 15
74 SERVOZ 140 AB 24
08 SERY 29 PA 8
89 SERY 84 NA 17
02 SERY LES MEZIERES 28 LA 7
60 SERY MAGNEVAL 40 JA 10
51 SERZY ET PRIN 42 NA 10
67 SESSENHEIM 50 GB 12
34 SETE C 214 NA 36
62 SETQUES 8 GA 3
95 SEUGY 40 HA 10
08 SEUIL 29 QA 9
55 SEUIL D'ARGONNE C 44 TA 11
03 SEUILLET 133 MA 23
37 SEUILLY 97 X 19
41 SEUR 80 CA 17
17 SEURE, LE 142 U 25
21 SEURRE C 121 TA 20
80 SEUX 26 GA 7
55 SEUZEY 45 VA 11
42 SEVELINGES 135 PA 24
90 SEVENANS 89 BB 17
44 SEVERAC 93 N 17
12 SEVERAC L'EGLISE 176 JA 31
12 SEVERAC LE CHATEAU C 176 KA 31
70 SEVEUX 87 WA 17
22 SEVIGNAC 54 M 14
64 SEVIGNACQ 207 V 35
64 SEVIGNACQ MEYRACQ 215 U 37
61 SEVIGNY 58 W 12
08 SEVIGNY LA FORET 29 OA 7
08 SEVIGNY WALEPPE 29 OA 8
76 SEVIS 24 BA 8
61 SEVRAI 58 W 12
93 SEVRAN C 40 HA 11
92 SEVRES C 39 GA 12
86 SEVRES ANXAUMONT 113 Y 22
71 SEVREY 121 SA 21
74 SEVRIER 139 XA 25
18 SEVRY 101 JA 19
68 SEWEN 89 BB 16
19 SEXCLES 160 FA 28
54 SEXEY AUX FORGES 67 XA 12
54 SEXEY LES BOIS 45 XA 12
52 SEXFONTAINES 66 TA 14
63 SEYCHALLES 148 LA 25
47 SEYCHES C 171 X 30
04 SEYNE C 182 YA 31
83 SEYNE SUR MER, LA C 203 WA 37
30 SEYNES 178 PA 32
74 SEYNOD C 139 XA 25
31 SEYRE 210 DA 36
40 SEYRESSE 183 R 34
01 SEYSSEL C 138 WA 24
74 SEYSSEL C 138 WA 24
31 SEYSSES 210 CA 35
32 SEYSSES SAVES 210 BA 35
38 SEYSSINET PARISET 166 VA 28
38 SEYSSINS 166 VA 28
38 SEYSSUEL 151 SA 26
74 SEYTHENEX 153 YA 25
74 SEYTROUX 140 ZA 23
51 SEZANNE C 42 NA 12
65 SIARROUY 208 W 36
43 SIAUGUES STE MARIE 162 MA 28
29 SIBIRIL 52 E 12
29 SIBIVILLE 16 GA 5
38 SICCIEU ST JULIEN
ET CARISIEU 152 UA 25
58 SICHAMPS 102 LA 19
68 SICKERT 90 BB 16
50 SIDEVILLE 33 P 8
18 SIDIAILLES 116 GA 22
17 SIECQ 128 V 25
67 SIEGEN 50 GB 11
89 SIEGES, LES 64 MA 14
57 SIERCK LES BAINS C 32 YA 9
68 SIERENTZ C 90 DB 17
57 SIERSTHAL 48 DB 11
76 SIERVILLE 24 BA 8
40 SIEST 183 R 35
31 SIEURAC 189 FA 34
09 SIEURAS 218 CA 37
38 SIEVOZ 166 WA 29
67 SIEWILLER 48 CB 11
06 SIGALE 200 BB 34
33 SIGALENS 171 W 31
11 SIGEAN C 223 JA 37
45 SIGLOY 81 GA 16
31 SIGNAC 217 Z 38
83 SIGNES 203 WA 36
52 SIGNEVILLE 66 TA 14
08 SIGNY L'ABBAYE C 29 QA 8
08 SIGNY LE PETIT C 19 PA 7
08 SIGNY MONTLIBERT 31 UA 8
77 SIGNY SIGNETS 41 KA 11
16 SIGOGNE 142 V 25
68 SIGOLSHEIM 70 DB 15
04 SIGONCE 197 WA 33
05 SIGOTTIER 180 VA 31
24 SIGOULES C 157 Y 30
85 SIGOURNAIS 111 S 21
04 SIGOYER 181 XA 32
05 SIGOYER 181 XA 31
09 SIGUER 220 DA 38
77 SIGY 63 KA 13
76 SIGY EN BRAY 25 DA 8
71 SIGY LE CHATEL 120 OA 22
56 SILFIAC 73 I 15
07 SILHAC 164 RA 29
38 SILLANS 152 UA 27
83 SILLANS LA CASCADE 203 YA 35
86 SILLARS 114 Z 22
33 SILLAS 171 W 31
72 SILLE LE GUILLAUME C 78 W 14
72 SILLE LE PHILIPPE 59 Y 15
57 SILLEGNY 46 XA 11
51 SILLERY 43 PA 10
25 SILLEY AMANCEY 107 XA 19
25 SILLEY BLEFOND 107 YA 18
74 SILLINGY 139 XA 24
61 SILLY EN GOUFFERN 58 W 12

57 SILLY EN SAULNOIS 46 YA 11
02 SILLY LA POTERIE 41 KA 10
60 SILLY LE LONG 40 JA 10
57 SILLY SUR NIED 46 YA 10
60 SILLY TILLARD 26 GA 9
55 SILMONT 44 TA 12
67 SILTZHEIM 48 CB 10
2B SILVARECCIO 228 MB 40
52 SILVAROUVRES 66 RA 15
64 SIMACOURBE 207 V 35
71 SIMANDRE 121 SA 21
01 SIMANDRE SUR SURAN 138 UA 23
69 SIMANDRES 151 SA 26
71 SIMARD 121 TA 21
62 SIMENCOURT 17 IA 5
24 SIMEYROLS 159 CA 29
13 SIMIANE COLLONGUE 202 UA 36
04 SIMIANE LA ROTONDE 196 VA 33
32 SIMORRE 209 Z 35
53 SIMPLE 77 S 16
59 SIN LE NOBLE 18 KA 5
38 SINARD 166 VA 29
02 SINCENY 27 LA 8
21 SINCEY LES ROUVRAY 103 PA 18
40 SINDERES 183 S 33
63 SINGLES 147 HA 26
24 SINGLEYRAC 157 Y 30
08 SINGLY 30 RA 8
67 SINGRIST 49 DB 12
09 SINSAT 219 DA 38
65 SINZOS 208 X 36
32 SION 185 W 34
44 SION LES MINES 75 P 16
19 SIONIAC 159 EA 29
88 SIONNE 67 VA 13
54 SIONVILLER 46 ZA 12
24 SIORAC DE RIBERAC 157 Y 28
24 SIORAC EN PERIGORD 158 BA 29
50 SIOUVILLE HAGUE 33 O 8
32 SIRAC 187 AA 34
62 SIRACOURT 16 GA 5
65 SIRADAN 217 Z 38
15 SIRAN 160 GA 29
34 SIRAN 212 IA 36
65 SIREIX 215 V 38
16 SIREUIL 143 W 26
39 SIROD 123 XA 21
64 SIROS 207 U 36
2B SISCO 226 MB 38
02 SISSONNE C 28 NA 8
02 SISSY 28 LA 7
82 SISTELS 187 AA 33
04 SISTERON C 181 WA 32
84 SIVERGUES 196 UA 34
71 SIVIGNON 136 QA 22
54 SIVRY 46 YA 11
51 SIVRY ANTE 44 SA 11
77 SIVRY COURTRY 62 IA 13
55 SIVRY LA PERCHE 44 UA 10
55 SIVRY SUR MEUSE 31 UA 9
83 SIX FOURS LES PLAGES C 202 WA 37
74 SIXT FER A CHEVAL 140 AB 24
35 SIXT SUR AFF 75 N 16
29 SIZUN C 52 E 13
86 SMARVES 113 Y 22
76 SMERMESNIL 25 DA 7
2A SOCCIA 227 KB 41
25 SOCHAUX C 89 BB 17
88 SOCOURT 68 YA 13
59 SOCX 8 HA 2
31 SODE 217 Z 38
49 SOEURDRES 77 U 16
77 SOGNOLLES EN MONTOIS 63 KA 13
51 SOGNY AUX MOULINS 43 OA 11
51 SOGNY EN L'ANGLE 43 SA 12
14 SOIGNOLLES 36 V 11
77 SOIGNOLLES EN BRIE 62 IA 12
78 SOINDRES 39 EA 11
70 SOING CUBRY
CHARENTENAY 88 WA 17
41 SOINGS EN SOLOGNE 99 DA 18
21 SOIRANS 105 UA 19
02 SOISSONS S 28 LA 9
21 SOISSONS SUR NACEY 106 UA 18
77 SOISY BOUY 63 LA 13
95 SOISY
SOUS MONTMORENCY C 40 GA 11
91 SOISY SUR ECOLE 62 HA 13
91 SOISY SUR SEINE 62 HA 12
02 SOIZE 29 OA 8
28 SOIZE 59 AA 14
51 SOIZY AUX BOIS 42 NA 12
69 SOLAIZE 151 SA 26
2B SOLARO 228 MB 42
67 SOLBACH 69 CB 13
04 SOLEILHAS 198 AB 34
25 SOLEMONT 108 AB 18
60 SOLENTE 27 JA 8
66 SOLER, LE 224 JA 39
26 SOLERIEUX 179 SA 31
77 SOLERS 62 IA 12
59 SOLESMES C 18 MA 5
72 SOLESMES 77 V 16
38 SOLEYMIEU 152 UA 25
42 SOLEYMIEUX 149 OA 26
40 SOLFERINO 169 S 32
57 SOLGNE 46 YA 11
14 SOLIERS 36 V 10
87 SOLIGNAC 145 CA 25
43 SOLIGNAC SOUS ROCHE 149 OA 27
43 SOLIGNAC SUR LOIRE C 163 NA 29
63 SOLIGNAT 148 KA 26
61 SOLIGNY LA TRAPPE 59 Z 12
10 SOLIGNY LES ETANGS 63 MA 13
2A SOLLACARO 229 KB 43
73 SOLLIERES SARDIERES 154 AB 27
83 SOLLIES PONT C 203 XA 37
83 SOLLIES TOUCAS 203 XA 36
83 SOLLIES VILLE 203 XA 37
71 SOLOGNY 136 RA 22
32 SOLOMIAC 187 AA 34
59 SOLRE LE CHATEAU C 19 OA 5
59 SOLRINNES 19 OA 5
45 SOLTERRE 82 IA 16
71 SOLUTRE POUILLY 136 RA 23
59 SOMAIN 18 LA 5
25 SOMBACOUR 123 YA 20
21 SOMBERNON C 104 RA 18
62 SOMBRIN 17 HA 5
65 SOMBRUN 208 W 35
49 SOMLOIRE 95 T 19
59 SOMMAING 18 MA 5
52 SOMMANCOURT 66 SA 13
71 SOMMANT 104 PA 19
08 SOMMAUTHE 30 SA 9
51 SOMME BIONNE 43 RA 10
51 SOMME SUIPPE 43 QA 10
51 SOMME TOURBE 43 RA 10

51 SOMME VESLE 43 RA 11
51 SOMME YEVRE 43 RA 11
89 SOMMECAISE 83 KA 16
55 SOMMEDIEUE 44 UA 10
55 SOMMEILLES 44 SA 11
02 SOMMELANS 41 LA 10
55 SOMMELONNE 44 TA 12
51 SOMMEPY TAHURE 43 QA 10
08 SOMMERANCE 30 SA 9
52 SOMMERECOURT 67 VA 14
60 SOMMEREUX 26 FA 8
02 SOMMERON 19 OA 6
14 SOMMERVIEU 35 T 9
54 SOMMERVILLER 46 ZA 12
76 SOMMERY 25 DA 8
76 SOMMESNIL 24 Z 8
51 SOMMESOUS 43 PA 12
25 SOMMETTE, LA 107 ZA 19
02 SOMMETTE EAUCOURT 27 KA 7
10 SOMMEVAL 64 OA 14
52 SOMMEVOIRE 66 SA 13
30 SOMMIERES C 193 OA 34
86 SOMMIERES DU CLAIN 129 Y 23
79 SOMPT 128 W 23
51 SOMPUIS C 43 QA 12
51 SOMSOIS 65 OA 12
08 SON 29 PA 8
46 SONAC 174 EA 30
78 SONCHAMP 61 EA 13
88 SONCOURT 67 WA 13
52 SONCOURT SUR MARNE 66 TA 14
68 SONDERNACH 90 CB 15
68 SONDERSDORF 90 DB 17
38 SONE, LA 166 UA 28
60 SONGEONS C 25 EA 8
39 SONGESON 122 WA 21
01 SONGIEU 138 VA 24
51 SONGY 43 QA 12
12 SONNAC 175 GA 30
17 SONNAC 128 V 25
11 SONNAC SUR L'HERS 221 FA 37
38 SONNAY 151 SA 27
73 SONNAZ 152 WA 26
16 SONNEVILLE 142 W 25
02 SONS ET RONCHERES 28 MA 7
01 SONTHONNAX LA MONTAGNE 138 VA 23
37 SONZAY 97 Y 17
40 SOORTS HOSSEGOR 183 Q 34
68 SOPPE LE BAS 90 CB 16
68 SOPPE LE HAUT 90 CB 16
09 SOR 218 BA 38
70 SORANS LES BREUREY 107 XA 18
02 SORBAIS 19 NA 7
32 SORBETS 185 W 34
40 SORBETS 207 V 35
55 SORBEY 31 VA 9
57 SORBEY 46 YA 10
03 SORBIER 134 MA 22
05 SORBIERS 180 VA 31
42 SORBIERS 150 QA 26
2B SORBO OCAGNANO 228 MB 40
2A SORBOLLANO 230 LB 43
08 SORBON 29 PA 8
34 SORBS 192 LA 33
08 SORCY BAUTHEMONT 29 QA 8
55 SORCY ST MARTIN 45 VA 12
40 SORDE L'ABBAYE 206 R 35
40 SORE C 170 U 32
65 SOREAC 208 X 36
66 SOREDE 224 JA 39
80 SOREL 17 KA 6
80 SOREL EN VIMEU 16 FA 6
28 SOREL MOUSSEL 38 CA 11
81 SOREZE 211 FA 35
09 SORGEAT 220 EA 39
24 SORGES 144 AA 27
84 SORGUES 195 SA 33
37 SORIGNY 98 Z 19
44 SORINIERES, LES 93 P 19
2B SORIO 226 LB 39
89 SORMERY 64 NA 15
08 SORMONNE 29 OA 7
19 SORNAC C 146 GA 26
70 SORNAY 106 VA 18
71 SORNAY, BOCCA DI 121 TA 21
54 SORNEVILLE 46 ZA 12
76 SORQUAINVILLE 23 Z 8
62 SORRUS 15 EA 4
40 SORT EN CHALOSSE 183 S 34
50 SORTOSVILLE 33 O 9
50 SORTOSVILLE EN BEAUMONT 33 O 9
47 SOS 186 X 33
06 SOSPEL C 199 DB 34
86 SOSSAIS 113 Y 20
65 SOST 217 Z 38
2A SOTTA 230 LB 44
50 SOTTEVAST 33 P 8
50 SOTTEVILLE 33 O 8
76 SOTTEVILLE LES ROUEN C 24 BA 9
76 SOTTEVILLE SOUS LE VAL 24 BA 9
76 SOTTEVILLE SUR MER 24 AA 7
46 SOTURAC 173 BA 31
57 SOTZELING 47 AB 11
51 SOUAIN PERTHES
LES HURLUS 43 QA 10
81 SOUAL 211 FA 35
28 SOUANCE AU PERCHE 59 AA 14
66 SOUANYAS 222 GA 39
62 SOUASTRE 17 IA 6
34 SOUBES 192 LA 34
17 SOUBISE 127 S 24
65 SOUBLECAUSE 208 W 35
17 SOUBRAN 142 U 27
23 SOUBREBOST 132 EA 24
53 SOUCE 57 T 13
49 SOUCELLES 96 U 17
07 SOUCHE, LA 178 PA 30
62 SOUCHEZ 17 IA 5
57 SOUCHT 48 DB 11
39 SOUCIA 122 WA 22
69 SOUCIEU EN JARREST 150 RA 25
46 SOUCIRAC 174 DA 30
01 SOUCLIN 138 UA 25
02 SOUCY 27 KA 9
89 SOUCY 63 LA 14
19 SOUDAINE LAVINADIERE 145 EA 26
44 SOUDAN 76 O 16
79 SOUDAN 112 W 22
24 SOUDAT 143 Z 26
41 SOUDAY 79 AA 15
51 SOUDE 43 PA 12
19 SOUDEILLES 146 FA 27
30 SOUDORGUES 192 NA 33
51 SOUDRON 43 PA 11
31 SOUEICH 217 AA 37
09 SOUEIX ROGALLE 218 BA 38
81 SOUEL 189 FA 33
65 SOUES 208 X 36

80 SOUES 16 FA 6
41 SOUESMES 100 GA 18
67 SOUFFELWEYERSHEIM 49 FB 12
67 SOUFFLENHEIM 50 GB 11
16 SOUFFRIGNAC 143 Y 26
36 SOUGE 115 DA 20
41 SOUGE 79 Z 16
72 SOUGE LE GANELON 58 W 14
35 SOUGEAL 56 P 13
89 SOUGERES EN PUISAYE 83 LA 17
11 SOUGRAIGNE 221 HA 38
45 SOUGY 81 EA 15
58 SOUGY SUR LOIRE 118 LA 20
55 SOUHESMES RAMPONT, LES 44 TA 10
21 SOUHEY 85 QA 17
62 SOUICH, LE 16 HA 5
11 SOUILHANELS 211 FA 36
11 SOUILHE 211 FA 36
46 SOUILLAC C 159 DA 29
72 SOUILLE 78 X 15
55 SOUILLY C 44 UA 11
09 SOULA 219 EA 38
33 SOULAC SUR MER 141 R 26
15 SOULAGES 162 LA 28
12 SOULAGES BONNEVAL 176 JA 30
10 SOULAINES DHUYS C 65 RA 13
49 SOULAINES SUR AUBANCE 96 U 18
49 SOULAIRE ET BOURG 96 U 17
28 SOULAIRES 61 DA 13
09 SOULAN 219 CA 38
51 SOULANGES 43 QA 12
18 SOULANGIS 101 HA 19
14 SOULANGY 36 V 11
11 SOULATGE 221 HA 38
52 SOULAUCOURT
SUR MOUZON 67 VA 14
24 SOULAURES 173 AA 30
25 SOULCE CERNAY 108 BB 18
53 SOULGE SUR OUETTE 77 U 15
34 SOULIE, LE 212 IA 35
51 SOULIERES 42 OA 11
33 SOULIGNAC 156 V 30
72 SOULIGNE FLACE 78 W 15
72 SOULIGNE SOUS BALLON 78 X 15
17 SOULIGNONNE 141 T 25
10 SOULIGNY 64 OA 14
72 SOULITRE 79 Y 15
85 SOULLANS 109 O 21
50 SOULLES 34 R 11
65 SOULOM 215 W 38
46 SOULOMES 174 DA 30
88 SOULOSSE
SOUS ST ELOPHE 67 VA 13
68 SOULTZ HAUT RHIN C 90 CB 16
67 SOULTZ LES BAINS 70 DB 13
67 SOULTZ SOUS FORETS C 49 FB 11
68 SOULTZBACH LES BAINS 90 CB 15
68 SOULTZEREN 90 CB 15
68 SOULTZMATT 90 CB 15
44 SOULVACHE 76 Q 16
89 SOUMAINTRAIN 84 NA 15
23 SOUMANS 132 GA 23
47 SOUMENSAC 172 Y 30
17 SOUMERAS 142 U 27
34 SOUMONT 192 LA 34
14 SOUMONT ST QUENTIN 36 V 11
64 SOUMOULOU 207 V 36
11 SOUPEX 211 FA 36
02 SOUPIR 28 MA 9
77 SOUPPES SUR LOING 62 IA 14
40 SOUPROSSE 184 T 34
64 SOURAIDE 205 Q 36
25 SOURANS 108 AB 18
69 SOURCIEUX LES MINES 150 RA 25
02 SOURD, LE 28 NA 7
50 SOURDEVAL C 57 S 12
50 SOURDEVAL LES BOIS 56 Q 11
80 SOURDON 26 HA 8
77 SOURDUN 63 LA 13
56 SOURN, LE 73 J 15
66 SOURNIA C 222 HA 39
15 SOURNIAC 160 GA 27
04 SOURRIBES 181 XA 32
28 SOURS 61 DA 13
19 SOURSAC 160 GA 27
24 SOURZAC 157 Y 28
23 SOUS PARSAT 132 FA 24
46 SOUSCEYRAC C 160 FA 29
17 SOUSMOULINS 142 V 27
26 SOUSPIERRE 179 SA 31
33 SOUSSAC 157 W 30
33 SOUSSANS 155 T 28
21 SOUSSEY SUR BRIONNE 104 QA 18
30 SOUSTELLE 178 OA 32
40 SOUSTONS C 183 O 34
38 SOUSVILLE 166 WA 29
42 SOUTERNON 135 OA 25
23 SOUTERRAINE, LA C 131 DA 23
79 SOUTIERS 112 V 22
39 SOUVANS 122 VA 20
30 SOUVIGNARGUES 193 OA 34
16 SOUVIGNE 129 W 24
37 SOUVIGNE 97 Y 17
79 SOUVIGNE 128 V 22
72 SOUVIGNE SUR MEME 59 Z 14
72 SOUVIGNE SUR SARTHE 77 U 16
03 SOUVIGNY C 118 KA 22
37 SOUVIGNY DE TOURAINE 98 BA 18
41 SOUVIGNY EN SOLOGNE 81 GA 17
65 SOUYEAUX 208 X 36
49 SOUZAY CHAMPIGNY 96 W 19
69 SOUZY 150 QA 25
91 SOUZY LA BRICHE 61 GA 13
28 SOVERIA 228 LB 40
26 SOYANS 179 SA 30
16 SOYAUX C 143 X 26
25 SOYE 107 ZA 18
18 SOYE EN SEPTAINE 117 HA 20
80 SOYECOURT 27 JA 7
52 SOYERS 87 VA 16
07 SOYONS 165 SA 29
67 SPARSBACH 48 DB 11
72 SPAY 78 X 15
68 SPECHBACH LE BAS 90 CB 17
68 SPECHBACH LE HAUT 90 CB 17
2B SPELONCATO 225 KB 39
06 SPERACEDES 198 AB 34
29 SPEZET 72 G 14
57 SPICHEREN 47 BB 10
55 SPINCOURT C 31 VA 9
59 SPONVILLE 45 WA 10
10 SPOY 65 RA 14
21 SPOY 105 TA 18
59 SPYCKER 8 GA 2
22 SQUIFFIEC 53 I 12
68 STAFFELFELDEN 90 CB 16
93 STAINS C 40 HA 11
55 STAINVILLE 66 TA 12
59 STAPLE 8 HA 3
67 STATTMATTEN 50 GB 12
2B STAZZONA 228 MB 40
59 STEENBECQUE 8 HA 3
59 STEENE 8 HA 2
59 STEENVOORDE C 8 IA 3
59 STEENWERCK 8 IA 3
67 STEIGE 69 CB 14
68 STEINBACH 90 CB 16
67 STEINBOURG 49 DB 12
68 STEINBRUNN LE BAS 90 DB 17
68 STEINBRUNN LE HAUT 90 DB 17
67 STEINSELTZ 49 FB 11
68 STEINSOULTZ 90 DB 17
55 STENAY C 30 TA 9
67 STERNENBERG 90 CB 17
68 STETTEN 90 DB 17
89 STIGNY 85 PA 16
67 STILL 70 DB 13
57 STIRING WENDEL C 47 BB 10
08 STONNE 30 SA 8
68 STORCKENSOHN 89 BB 16
68 STOSSWIHR 90 CB 15
67 STOTZHEIM 70 EB 14
67 STRASBOURG P 70 FB 13
59 STRAZEELE 8 IA 3
46 STRENQUELS 159 DA 29
68 STRUETH 90 CB 17
67 STRUTH 48 CB 11
57 STUCKANGE 32 YA 9
67 STUNDWILLER 50 GB 11
67 STURZELBRONN 48 EB 10
67 STUTZHEIM OFFENHEIM 49 EB 12
90 SUARCE 90 CB 17
16 SUAUX 129 Y 25
18 SUBDRAY, LE 116 GA 20
37 SUBLAINES 98 BA 18
14 SUBLES 35 T 10
18 SUBLIGNY 101 IA 18
50 SUBLIGNY 56 Q 12
89 SUBLIGNY 63 KA 14
09 SUC ET SENTENAC 220 DA 38
38 SUCCIEU 152 UA 26
44 SUCE SUR ERDRE 94 P 18
94 SUCY EN BRIE C 40 HA 12
41 SUEVRES 80 DA 17
63 SUGERES 148 LA 26
08 SUGNY 30 RA 9
64 SUHESCUN 206 R 36
71 SUIN 120 QA 22
51 SUIPPES C 43 QA 10
57 SUISSE 47 ZA 11
51 SUIZY LE FRANC 42 NA 11
01 SULIGNAT 137 SA 23
14 SULLY 35 T 9
60 SULLY 25 EA 8
71 SULLY 120 OA 20
45 SULLY LA CHAPELLE 81 GA 15
58 SULLY LA TOUR 102 KA 18
45 SULLY SUR LOIRE C 82 HA 16
56 SULNIAC 92 L 17
30 SUMENE C 192 NA 33
68 SUNDHOFFEN 90 DB 15
67 SUNDHOUSE 70 EB 14
39 SUPT 123 XA 20
63 SURAT 133 LA 24
09 SURBA 219 DA 38
67 SURBOURG 49 FB 11
80 SURCAMPS 16 FA 6
87 SURDOUX 145 DA 26
61 SURE 59 Y 13
92 SURESNES C 40 GA 11
72 SURFONDS 79 Y 15
02 SURFONTAINE 28 MA 7
17 SURGERES C 127 T 24
58 SURGY 83 MA 17
88 SURIAUVILLE 67 WA 14
79 SURIN 112 U 22
86 SURIN 129 Y 24
16 SURIS 130 Z 25
01 SURJOUX 138 WA 24
25 SURMONT 108 AB 18
62 SURQUES 7 FA 3
14 SURRAIN 35 S 9
50 SURTAINVILLE 33 O 9
27 SURTAUVILLE 38 BA 10
61 SURVIE 36 X 11
14 SURVILLE 23 X 9
27 SURVILLE 38 BA 10
50 SURVILLE 34 P 9
95 SURVILLIERS 40 HA 10
08 SURY 29 RA 7
45 SURY AUX BOIS 82 HA 15
18 SURY EN VAUX 101 JA 18
18 SURY ES BOIS 101 IA 18
42 SURY LE COMTAL 149 PA 26
18 SURY PRES LERE 82 JA 17
56 SURZUR 92 K 17
64 SUS 206 T 36
62 SUS ST LEGER 17 HA 5
64 SUSMIOU 206 T 36
87 SUSSAC 145 DA 26
34 SUSSARGUES 193 OA 34
03 SUSSAT 133 KA 23
21 SUSSEY 104 OA 19
38 SUSVILLE 166 WA 29
01 SUTRIEU 138 VA 24
09 SUZAN 219 DA 37
08 SUZANNE 30 RA 8
80 SUZANNE 17 IA 6
52 SUZANNECOURT 66 TA 13
27 SUZAY 38 DA 10
26 SUZE 165 TA 30
26 SUZE LA ROUSSE 179 SA 32
72 SUZE SUR SARTHE, LA C 78 W 16
84 SUZETTE 179 TA 32
60 SUZOY 27 JA 8
02 SUZY 28 MA 8
08 SY 30 SA 8
79 SYAM 123 XA 21
27 SYLVAINS LES MOULINS 38 BA 11
12 SYLVANES 191 JA 34
88 SYNDICAT, LE 89 AB 15

T

64 TABAILLE USQUAIN 206 S 36
33 TABANAC 156 U 30
73 TABLE, LA 153 YA 26
85 TABLIER, LE 110 Q 21
09 TABRE 219 EA 37
16 TACHE, LA 129 Y 25
32 TACHOIRES 209 Z 35
78 TACOIGNIERES 39 DA 11
58 TACONNAY 102 MA 18
22 TADEN 55 N 13
64 TADOUSSE USSAU 207 V 35
2B TAGLIO ISOLACCIO 228 MB 40
71 TAGNIERE, LA 120 PA 21
08 TAGNON 29 PA 9
68 TAGOLSHEIM 90 CB 17
68 TAGSDORF 90 DB 17
43 TAILHAC 162 LA 28
84 TAILLADES 195 TA 34
33 TAILLAN MEDOC, LE 155 T 29
55 TAILLANCOURT 67 VA 13
17 TAILLANT 127 T 25
61 TAILLEBOIS 57 U 12
17 TAILLEBOURG 127 T 25
47 TAILLEBOURG 171 X 31
33 TAILLECAVAT 171 X 30
25 TAILLECOURT 89 BB 17
85 TAILLEE, LA 127 S 22
02 TAILLEFONTAINE 27 KA 9
50 TAILLEPIED 33 P 9
66 TAILLET 224 IA 39
08 TAILLETTE 20 QA 7
35 TAILLIS 76 R 14
08 TAILLY 30 TA 9
21 TAILLY 121 SA 20
80 TAILLY 16 FA 7
26 TAIN L'HERMITAGE C 165 SA 28
89 TAINGY 83 LA 17
88 TAINTRUX 69 BB 14
59 TAISNIERES EN THIERACHE 19 NA 6
59 TAISNIERES SUR HON 19 NA 5
71 TAISSY 42 OA 10
81 TAIX 189 GA 33
71 TAIZE 120 RA 22
79 TAIZE 112 W 20
16 TAIZE AIZIE 129 X 24
08 TAIZY 29 PA 8
65 TAJAN 217 Y 37
11 TALAIRAN 223 IA 37
33 TALAIS 141 R 26
57 TALANGE 46 YA 10
21 TALANT 105 SA 18
2B TALASANI 228 MB 40
42 TALAUDIERE, LA 150 OA 26
65 TALAZAC 208 W 36
41 TALCY 80 DA 16
89 TALCY 84 OA 17
33 TALENCE C 156 T 29
07 TALENCIEUX 164 RA 28
35 TALENSAC 75 O 15
01 TALISSIEU 138 WA 25
15 TALIZAT 161 KA 28
25 TALLANS 107 YA 18
05 TALLARD C 181 XA 31
25 TALLENAY 107 XA 18
63 TALLENDE 148 KA 26
40 TALLER 183 R 33
74 TALLOIRES 139 YA 25
2B TALLONE 228 MB 41
79 TALLUD, LE 112 V 21
85 TALLUD STE GEMME 111 S 21
80 TALMAS 16 HA 6
21 TALMAY 106 UA 18
17 TALMONT SUR GIRONDE 141 S 26
85 TALMONT ST HILAIRE C 125 P 22
60 TALMONTIERS 25 EA 9
02 TALON 102 MA 18
58 TALUS ST PRIX 42 NA 11
51 TALUYERS 150 RA 26
69 TAMERVILLE 33 Q 8
50 TAMNAY EN BAZOIS 103 NA 19
58 TAMNIES 158 BA 29
24 TANAVELLE 161 JA 28
15 TANAY 105 UA 18
21 TANCARVILLE 23 Y 9
76 TANCOIGNE 96 U 19
49 TANCON 135 PA 23
71 TANCONVILLE 69 BB 13
54 TANCROU 41 KA 11
77 TANCUA 123 XA 22
39 TANGRY 16 HA 4
62 TANINGES C 140 ZA 24
74 TANIS 56 Q 13
50 TANLAY 84 OA 16
89 TANNAY 30 SA 8
08 TANNAY C 103 MA 18
58 TANNERON 200 BB 35
83 TANNERRE EN PUISAYE 83 KA 16
89 TANNIERES 42 MA 9
02 TANNOIS 44 TA 12
55 TANQUES 58 W 12
61 TANTONVILLE 67 XA 13
54 TANU, LE 56 Q 12
50 TANUS 175 GA 32
81 TANVILLE 58 W 13
61 TANZAC 141 T 26
17 TAPONAS 136 RA 23
69 TAPONNAT FLEURIGNAC 143 Y 25
16 TARABEL 211 EA 35
31 TARADEAU 203 ZA 35
83 TARARE C 136 QA 25
69 TARASCON C 195 RA 34
13 TARASCON SUR ARIEGE C 219 DA 38
09 TARASTEIX 208 W 36
65 TARBES P 208 W 36
65 TARCENAY 107 XA 19
25 TARDES 132 HA 23
23 TARDETS SORHOLUS C 206 S 37
64 TARDIERE, LA 111 T 21
85 TARDINGHEN 7 DA 2
62 TARENTAISE 150 QA 27
42 TARERACH 222 HA 39
66 TARGASSONNE 222 FA 40
66 TARGET 134 KA 23
03 TARGON C 156 V 30
33 TARNAC 146 FA 25
19 TARNES 156 V 29
33 TARNOS 183 Q 35
40 TARON SADIRAC VIELLENAVE 207 V 35
64 TARQUIMPOL 47 AB 12
57 TARRANO 228 MB 40
2B TARSAC 185 W 34
32 TARSACQ 207 U 36
64 TARSUL 86 SA 17
21 TART L'ABBAYE 105 TA 19
21 TART LE BAS 105 TA 19
21 TART LE HAUT 105 TA 19
21 TARTARAS 150 RA 26
42 TARTAS C 184 S 34
40 TARTECOURT 88 XA 16
70 TARTIERS 28 LA 9
02 TARTIGNY 26 HA 8
60 TARTONNE 198 YA 33
04 TARTRE, LE 122 UA 21
71 TARTRE GAUDRAN, LE 39 DA 12
78 TARZY 29 PA 7
08 TASQUE 208 W 35
32 TASSE 78 V 16
72 TASSENIERES 122 VA 20
39 TASSILLE 78 W 15
72 TASSIN LA DEMI LUNE C 151 SA 25
69 TASSO 228 LB 42
2A TATINGHEM 8 GA 3
62 TATRE, LE 142 V 27
16 TAUGON 127 S 23
17 TAULE C 52 F 12
29 TAULIGNAN 179 SA 31
26 TAULIS 224 IA 40
66 TAUPONT 74 L 15
56 TAURIAC 156 U 28
33 TAURIAC 159 EA 29
46 TAURIAC 188 DA 33
81 TAURIAC DE CAMARES 191 JA 34
12 TAURIAC DE NAUCELLE 175 GA 32
12 TAURIERS 178 PA 30
07 TAURIGNAN CASTET 218 BA 37
09 TAURIGNAN VIEUX 218 BA 37
09 TAURINYA 222 HA 39
66 TAURIZE 221 HA 37
11 TAUSSAC 161 IA 29
12 TAUSSAC LA BILLIERE 213 KA 35
34 TAUTAVEL 223 IA 38
66 TAUVES C 147 IA 26
63 TAUXIERES MUTRY 42 OA 10
51 TAUXIGNY 98 AA 19
37 TAVACO 227 KB 42
2A TAVANT 97 Y 19
37 TAVAUX 106 UA 19
39 TAVAUX ET PONTSERICOURT 28 OA 7
02 TAVEL 195 RA 33
30 TAVERA 227 KB 42
2A TAVERNAY 120 PA 20
71 TAVERNES C 203 XA 35
83 TAVERNY C 39 GA 11
95 TAVERS 80 DA 16
45 TAVEY 89 AB 17
70 TAXAT SENAT 134 KA 23
03 TAXENNE 106 VA 19
39 TAYAC 157 W 29
33 TAYBOSC 187 Z 34
32 TAYRAC 175 GA 32
12 TAYRAC 172 AA 32
47 TAZILLY 119 OA 21
58 TECH, LE 222 HA 40
66 TECHE 166 UA 28
38 TECOU 189 FA 34
81 TEICH, LE 169 S 30
33 TEIGNY 103 MA 18
58 TEIL, LE 179 RA 31
07 TEILHEDE 134 KA 24
63 TEILHET 219 EA 37
09 TEILHET 133 JA 24
63 TEILLAY 76 P 16
35 TEILLE 94 Q 18
44 TEILLE 78 X 14
72 TEILLET 190 HA 34
81 TEILLET ARGENTY 133 HA 23
03 TEILLOTS 159 CA 27
24 TEISSIERES DE CORNET 160 HA 29
15 TEISSIERES LES BOULIES 161 HA 29
15 TELGRUC SUR MER 51 D 14
29 TELLANCOURT 31 VA 8
54 TELLECEY 105 UA 18
21 TELLIERES LE PLESSIS 59 Y 12
61 TELOCHE 78 X 16
72 TEMPLE, LE 155 S 29
33 TEMPLE, LE 79 AA 15
41 TEMPLE DE BRETAGNE, LE 93 O 18
44 TEMPLE LAGUYON 144 BA 27
24 TEMPLE SUR LOT, LE 172 Y 31
47 TEMPLEMARS 9 KA 4
59 TEMPLEUVE 9 KA 4
59 TEMPLEUX LA FOSSE 17 JA 6
80 TEMPLEUX LE GUERARD 17 KA 6
80 TENAY 138 VA 24
01 TENCE C 164 PA 28
43 TENCIN 153 XA 27
38 TENDE C 199 EB 33
06 TENDON 68 AB 15
88 TENDRON 117 JA 20
18 TENDU 115 DA 21
36 TENEUR 16 GA 4
62 TENNIE 78 W 15
72 TENTELING 47 BB 10
57 TERCE 113 Z 22
86 TERCILLAT 132 FA 22
23 TERCIS LES BAINS 183 R 34
40 TERDEGHEM 8 HA 3
59 TERGNIER C 27 LA 8
02 TERJAT 133 IA 23
03 TERMES 30 SA 9
08 TERMES 223 IA 37
11 TERMES 162 KA 29
48 TERMES D'ARMAGNAC 185 W 34
32 TERMIGNON 154 AB 27
73 TERMINIERS 81 EA 15
28 TERNAND 136 QA 24
69 TERNANT 128 U 24
17 TERNANT 105 SA 19
21 TERNANT 119 NA 21
58 TERNANT LES EAUX 148 KA 26
63 TERNAS 16 HA 5
62 TERNAT 86 TA 16
52 TERNAY 79 AA 16
41 TERNAY 151 SA 26
69 TERNAY 96 W 19
86 TERNES, LES 161 KA 29
15 TERNUAY MELAY
ET ST HILAIRE 89 AB 16
70 TERNY SORNY 28 LA 9
02 TERRAMESNIL 16 HA 6
80 TERRASSE, LA 153 WA 27
38 TERRASSE SUR DORLAY, LA 150 QA 26
42 TERRASSON LA VILLEDIEU C 159 CA 28
24 TERRATS 224 IA 39
66 TERRAUBE 187 Z 33
32 TERRE CLAPIER 190 GA 34
81 TERRE NATALE C 87 VA 16
52 TERREBASSE 209 AA 36
31 TERREFONDREE 86 SA 16
21 TERREHAULT 59 Y 14
72 TERRES DE CHAUX, LES 108 AB 18
25 TERRISSE, LA 161 JA 30
12 TERROLES 221 GA 37
11 TERRON SUR AISNE 30 RA 9
08 TERROU 160 FA 29
46 TERSANNE 151 SA 27
26 TERSANNES 130 BA 23
87 TERSSAC 189 FA 33
81 TERTE ST DENIS, LE 39 DA 11
78 TERTRY 27 KA 7
80 TERVILLE 32 XA 9
57 TESSANCOURT SUR AUBETTE 39 FA 11
78 TESSE FROULAY 57 U 13
61 TESSE LA MADELEINE 57 U 13
61 TESSEL 35 U 10
14 TESSON 141 T 26
17 TESSONNIERE 112 V 20
79 TESSOUALE, LA 95 S 20
49 TESSY SUR VIRE C 34 R 11
50 TESTE DE BUCH, LA C 169 R 30
33 TETAIGNE 30 TA 8
08 TETEGHEM 8 HA 2
59 TETERCHEN 47 ZA 10
57 TETHIEU 183 S 34
40 TETING SUR NIED 47 AB 10
57 TEUILLAC 156 U 28
33 TEULAT 211 EA 35
81 TEURTHEVILLE BOCAGE 33 O 8
50 TEURTHEVILLE HAGUE 33 O 8
50 TEYJAT 143 Z 26
24 TEYRAN 193 OA 34
34 TEYSSIERES 179 TA 31
26 TEYSSIEU 160 FA 29
46 TEYSSODE 211 FA 35
81 THAAS 64 NA 12
51 THAIMS 141 T 26
17 THAIRE 127 S 24
17 THAIX 119 NA 20
58 THAL DRULINGEN 48 CB 11
67 THAL MARMOUTIER 49 DB 12
67 THALAMY 147 HA 26
19 THANN S 90 CB 16
68 THANNENKIRCH 69 CB 14
68 THANVILLE 70 DB 14
67 THAON 35 U 10
14 THAON LES VOSGES 68 ZA 14
88 THARAUX 178 PA 32
30 THAROISEAU 103 NA 18
89 THAROT 84 NA 17
89 THAUMIERS 117 IA 20
18 THAURON 131 EA 24
23 THAUVENAY 101 JA 18
18 THEBE 217 Z 38
65 THEDING 47 BB 10
57 THEDIRAC 173 CA 30
46 THEGRA 159 EA 29
46 THEHILLAC 93 N 17
56 THEIL, LE 134 KA 23
03 THEIL, LE 33 Q 8
50 THEIL, LE C 59 Z 14
61 THEIL BOCAGE, LE 35 T 11
14 THEIL DE BRETAGNE, LE 76 Q 15
35 THEIL EN AUGE, LE 23 X 9
14 THEIL NOLENT, LE 37 Z 10
27 THEIL RABIER 129 W 24
16 THEIL SUR VANNE 63 LA 14
89 THEILLAY 100 FA 18
41 THEILLEMENT 37 AA 9
27 THEIX 92 K 17
56 THEIZE 136 RA 24
69 THEL 136 QA 24
69 THELIGNY 59 AA 14
72 THELIS LA COMBE 150 QA 27
42 THELOD 67 XA 13
54 THELONNE 30 SA 8
08 THELUS 17 JA 5
62 THEMERICOURT 39 FA 10
95 THEMINES 159 EA 30
46 THEMINETTES 160 EA 30
46 THENAC 141 T 26
17 THENAC 157 Y 30
24 THENAILLES 29 OA 7
02 THENAY 115 CA 21
36 THENAY 99 CA 18
41 THENELLES 28 MA 7
02 THENESOL 153 ZA 25
73 THENEUIL 97 Y 19
37 THENEUILLE 117 JA 21
03 THENEZAY C 112 W 21
79 THENIOUX 100 FA 18
18 THENISSEY 85 RA 17
21 THENISY 63 KA 13
77 THENNELIERES 65 PA 14
10 THENNES 26 HA 7
80 THENON C 158 BA 28
24 THENORGUES 30 SA 9
08 THEOULE SUR MER 200 BB 35
06 THERDONNE 26 GA 9
60 THERINES 25 FA 8
60 THERMES MAGNOAC 209 Z 36
65 THERONDELS 161 IA 29
12 THEROUANNE 8 GA 3
62 THEROULDEVILLE 23 Y 7
76 THERVAY 106 VA 19
39 THESEE 99 CA 18
41 THESY 122 WA 20
39 THEULEY 87 WA 17
70 THEUS 181 YA 31
05 THEUVILLE 61 DA 14
28 THEUVILLE 39 FA 10
95 THEUVILLE AUX MAILLOTS 23 Y 7
76 THEVET ST JULIEN 116 FA 21
36 THEVILLE 33 Q 8
50 THEVRAY 37 Z 11
27 THEY SOUS MONTFORT 67 XA 14
88 THEY SOUS VAUDEMONT 67 XA 13
54 THEYS 153 XA 27
38 THEZA 224 JA 39
66 THEZAC 141 T 26
17 THEZAC 173 BA 31
47 THEZAN DES CORBIERES 223 IA 37
11 THEZAN LES BEZIERS 213 KA 36
34 THEZE 181 WA 32
04 THEZE C 207 V 35
64 THEZEY ST MARTIN 46 YA 11
54 THEZIERS 195 RA 33
30 THEZILLIEU 138 VA 25
01 THEZY GLIMONT 26 HA 7
80 THIAIS C 40 HA 12
94 THIANCOURT 90 BB 17
90 THIANGES 118 MA 20
58 THIANT 18 LA 5
59 THIAT 130 AA 23
87 THIAUCOURT REGNIEVILLE C 45 WA 11
54 THIAVILLE SUR MEURTHE 69 AB 13
54 THIBERVILLE C 37 Y 10
27 THIBIE 43 PA 11
51 THIBIVILLERS 39 FA 9
60 THIBOUVILLE 37 AA 10
27 THICOURT 47 ZA 11
57 THIEBAUMENIL 68 ZA 13
54 THIEBLEMONT FAREMONT C 43 RA 12
51 THIEBOUHANS 108 BB 18
25 THIEFFRAIN 65 QA 14
10 THIEFFRANS 88 YA 17
70 THIEFOSSE 89 AB 15
88 THIEL SUR ACOLIN 118 MA 22
03 THIEMBRONNE 7 FA 4
62 THIENANS 107 YA 18
70 THIENNES 8 HA 3
59 THIEPVAL 17 IA 6
80 THIERGEVILLE 23 Y 8
76 THIERNU 28 NA 7
02 THIERS S 134 MA 25
63

60 THIERS SUR THEVE 40 IA 10
27 THIERVILLE 37 Z 9
55 THIERVILLE SUR MEUSE 44 UA 10
06 THIERY 199 BB 33
60 THIESCOURT 27 JA 8
76 THIETREVILLE 23 Y 8
28 THIEULIN, LE 60 BA 13
80 THIEULLOY L'ABBAYE 26 FA 7
80 THIEULLOY LA VILLE 26 FA 7
60 THIEULOY ST ANTOINE 25 FA 8
62 THIEULOYE, LA 17 HA 4
60 THIEUX 26 GA 8
77 THIEUX 40 IA 11
14 THIEVILLE 36 W 11
62 THIEVRES 17 HA 6
62 THIEVRES 17 HA 6
80 THIEVRES 17 HA 6
15 THIEZAC 161 IA 28
45 THIGNONVILLE 61 GA 14
01 THIL 137 SA 25
10 THIL 65 RA 14
31 THIL 188 BA 34
51 THIL 29 OA 9
54 THIL 32 WA 9
27 THIL, LE 25 DA 9
76 THIL MANNEVILLE 24 BA 7
76 THIL RIBERPRE, LE 25 DA 8
71 THIL SUR ARROUX 119 OA 20
08 THILAY 29 RA 7
95 THILLAY, LE 40 HA 11
52 THILLEUX 65 RA 13
27 THILLIERS EN VEXIN, LES 39 DA 10
51 THILLOIS 42 OA 10
55 THILLOMBOIS 44 UA 11
55 THILLOT 45 VA 11
88 THILLOT, LE C 89 AB 16
37 THILOUZE 97 Z 19
28 THIMERT GATELLES 60 CA 13
57 THIMONVILLE 47 ZA 11
45 THIMORY 82 IA 16
08 THIN LE MOUTIER 29 OA 8
63 THIOLIERES 148 MA 26
03 THIONNE 134 MA 22
57 THIONVILLE S 32 YA 9
76 THIOUVILLE 23 Z 8
88 THIRAUCOURT 67 XA 14
85 THIRE 111 S 22
28 THIRON GARDAIS C 60 BA 14
08 THIS 29 RA 7
25 THISE 107 XA 18
28 THIVARS 60 DA 13
59 THIVENCELLE 18 MA 4
60 THIVERNY 40 HA 10
78 THIVERVAL GRIGNON 39 FA 11
52 THIVET 87 UA 15
24 THIVIERS C 144 AA 27
28 THIVILLE 80 CA 15
36 THIZAY 116 FA 20
37 THIZAY 97 X 19
69 THIZY C 136 PA 24
89 THIZY 84 OA 17
04 THOARD 181 XA 32
38 THODURE 151 TA 27
72 THOIGNE 58 X 14
30 THOIRAS 193 OA 33
72 THOIRE SOUS CONTENSOR 58 X 14
72 THOIRE SUR DINAN 79 Y 16
21 THOIRES 85 RA 15
39 THOIRETTE 138 VA 23
39 THOIRIA 122 WA 22
01 THOIRY 139 XA 23
73 THOIRY 153 XA 26
78 THOIRY 39 EA 11
01 THOISSEY C 136 RA 23
39 THOISSIA 122 UA 22
21 THOISY LA BERCHERE 104 QA 18
21 THOISY LE DESERT 104 OA 19
80 THOIX 26 FA 8
52 THOL LES MILLIERES 67 UA 15
86 THOLLET 130 BA 22
74 THOLLON 124 AB 22
13 THOLONET, LE 202 VA 35
88 THOLY, LE 89 AB 15
27 THOMER LA SOGNE 38 BA 11
77 THOMERY 62 IA 13
21 THOMIREY 104 RA 19
24 THONAC 158 BA 28
74 THONES C 139 YA 25
52 THONNANCE LES JOINVILLE 66 TA 13
52 THONNANCE LES MOULINS 66 UA 13
55 THONNE LA LONG 31 UA 8
55 THONNE LE THIL 31 UA 8
55 THONNE LES PRES 31 UA 8
55 THONNELLE 31 UA 8
74 THONON LES BAINS S 123 ZA 22
88 THONS, LES 88 WA 15
57 THONVILLE 47 ZA 11
84 THOR, LE 195 SA 33
45 THORAILLES 82 JA 15
25 THORAISE 106 WA 19
04 THORAME BASSE 198 ZA 33
04 THORAME HAUTE 182 ZA 32
43 THORAS 162 MA 29
41 THORE LA ROCHETTE 79 AA 16
72 THOREE LES PINS 78 W 17
74 THORENS GLIERES C 139 YA 24
89 THOREY 84 OA 16
21 THOREY EN PLAINE 105 TA 19
54 THOREY LYAUTEY 67 XA 13
21 THOREY SOUS CHARNY 104 QA 18
21 THOREY SUR OUCHE 104 RA 19
79 THORIGNE 128 V 23
49 THORIGNE D'ANJOU 77 T 17
53 THORIGNE EN CHARNIE 77 V 15
35 THORIGNE FOUILLARD 76 P 14
72 THORIGNE SUR DUE 79 Y 15
79 THORIGNY 128 U 23
85 THORIGNY 110 R 21
77 THORIGNY SUR MARNE C 40 IA 11
89 THORIGNY SUR OREUSE 63 LA 14
83 THORONET, LE 203 YA 35
07 THORRENC 150 RA 27
10 THORS 66 RA 14
17 THORS 128 V 25
80 THORY 26 HA 8
89 THORY 84 NA 17
21 THOSTE 104 PA 18
18 THOU 101 IA 18
45 THOU 82 JA 17
17 THOU, LE 127 S 24
49 THOUARCE C 96 U 18
44 THOUARE SUR LOIRE 94 Q 18
79 THOUARS C 112 V 20
09 THOUARS SUR ARIZE 218 CA 37
47 THOUARS SUR GARONNE 171 Y 32
85 THOUARSAIS BOUILDROUX 111 S 21
51 THOULT TROSNAY, LE 42 NA 11
08 THOUR, LE 29 OA 8
49 THOUREIL, LE 96 V 18
35 THOURIE 76 Q 16
87 THOURON 131 CA 24
60 THOUROTTE 27 JA 9
41 THOURY 80 DA 17
77 THOURY FEROTTES 63 JA 14
32 THOUX 187 BA 34
53 THUBOEUF 57 U 13
02 THUEL, LE 29 OA 8
66 THUES ENTRE VALLS 222 GA 39
07 THUEYTS C 178 PA 30
08 THUGNY TRUGNY 29 QA 9
73 THUILE, LA 153 XA 26
04 THUILES, LES 182 ZA 31
54 THUILLEY AUX GROSEILLES 67 XA 13
88 THUILLIERES 67 XA 14
66 THUIR C 224 IA 39
27 THUIT, LE 38 CA 10
27 THUIT ANGER, LE 38 BA 9
27 THUIT HEBERT 24 AA 9
27 THUIT SIGNOL, LE 38 AA 10
27 THUIT SIMER, LE 38 AA 10
25 THULAY 108 BB 18
54 THUMEREVILLE 45 WA 10
59 THUMERIES 17 KA 4
59 THUN L'EVEQUE 18 LA 5
59 THUN ST AMAND 18 LA 4
59 THUN ST MARTIN 18 LA 5
86 THURAGEAU 113 X 21
86 THURE 113 Y 20
63 THURET 133 LA 24
71 THUREY 121 TA 21
25 THUREY LE MONT 107 XA 18
69 THURINS 150 RA 25
21 THURY 120 OA 20
89 THURY 83 LA 17
60 THURY EN VALOIS 41 KA 10
14 THURY HARCOURT C 35 U 11
60 THURY SOUS CLERMONT 26 GA 9
74 THUSY 139 XA 24
65 THUY 208 X 36
74 THYEZ 139 ZA 24
65 TIBIRAN JAUNAC 217 Y 37
61 TICHEVILLE 37 X 11
21 TICHEY 121 UA 20
67 TIEFFENBACH 48 CB 11
49 TIERCE C 77 U 17
54 TIERCELET 32 WA 9
35 TIERCENT, LE 56 Q 14
14 TIERCEVILLE 35 U 9
32 TIESTE URAGNOUX 208 W 35
48 TIEULE, LE 176 KA 31
85 TIFFAUGES 110 R 20
77 TIGEAUX 41 JA 12
91 TIGERY 62 HA 12
09 TIGNAC 220 EA 38
49 TIGNE 96 U 19
88 TIGNECOURT 67 WA 15
73 TIGNES 154 BB 26
06 TIGNET, LE 198 BB 35
38 TIGNIEU JAMEYZIEU 151 TA 25
62 TIGNY NOYELLE 15 EA 5
45 TIGY 81 GA 16
21 TIL CHATEL 86 TA 17
40 TILH 184 S 35
65 TILHOUSE 216 Y 37
32 TILLAC 208 X 35
28 TILLAY LE PENEUX 61 EA 14
60 TILLE 26 GA 9
21 TILLENAY 106 UA 19
76 TILLEUL, LE 23 X 8
27 TILLEUL DAME AGNES 37 AA 11
27 TILLEUL LAMBERT, LE 38 AA 10
27 TILLEUL OTHON, LE 37 AA 10
88 TILLEUX 67 WA 14
49 TILLIERES 94 R 19
27 TILLIERES SUR AVRE 38 BA 12
80 TILLOLOY 27 IA 8
79 TILLOU 128 W 23
51 TILLOY ET BELLAY 43 RA 11
80 TILLOY FLORIVILLE 15 DA 6
80 TILLOY LES CONTY 26 GA 7
62 TILLOY LES HERMAVILLE 17 HA 5
62 TILLOY LES MOFFLAINES 17 JA 5
59 TILLOY LEZ CAMBRAI 18 KA 5
59 TILLOY LEZ MARCHIENNES 18 LA 4
27 TILLY 38 DA 10
36 TILLY 131 BA 22
78 TILLY 39 DA 11
62 TILLY CAPELLE 16 GA 4
14 TILLY LA CAMPAGNE 36 V 10
55 TILLY SUR MEUSE 44 UA 11
14 TILLY SUR SEULLES C 35 T 10
62 TILQUES 8 GA 3
70 TINCEY ET PONTREBEAU 87 WA 17
61 TINCHEBRAY C 57 T 12
80 TINCOURT BOUCLY 17 KA 7
62 TINCQUES 17 HA 5
57 TINCRY 47 ZA 11
62 TINGRY 7 EA 4
51 TINQUEUX 42 OA 10
35 TINTENIAC C 75 O 14
71 TINTRY 120 OA 20
58 TINTURY 119 MA 20
43 TIRANGES 149 OA 27
32 TIRENT PONTEJAC 209 AA 35
50 TIREPIED 56 O 12
89 TISSEY 84 NA 16
80 TITRE, LE 16 EA 5
45 TIVERNON 61 FA 15
15 TIVIERS 162 KA 28
33 TIZAC DE CURTON 156 V 29
33 TIZAC DE LAPOUYADE 156 V 28
24 TOCANE ST APRE 143 Y 27
27 TOCQUEVILLE 23 Z 9
50 TOCQUEVILLE 33 Q 8
76 TOCQUEVILLE EN CAUX 24 AA 7
76 TOCQUEVILLE LES MURS 23 Y 8
76 TOCQUEVILLE SUR EU 15 CA 6
76 TOEUFLES 15 EA 6
08 TOGES 30 RA 9
51 TOGNY AUX BOEUFS 43 QA 11
2A TOLLA 227 KB 42
88 TOLLAINCOURT 67 WA 15
62 TOLLENT 16 FA 5
50 TOLLEVAST 33 P 8
77 TOMBE, LA 63 KA 13
47 TOMBEBOEUF 172 Y 31
54 TOMBLAINE C 46 YA 12
2B TOMINO 226 MB 38
26 TONILS, LES 180 TA 30
81 TONNAC 189 EA 33
17 TONNAY BOUTONNE C 127 T 24
17 TONNAY CHARENTE C 127 S 24
47 TONNEINS C 171 Y 31
89 TONNERRE C 84 OA 16
50 TONNEVILLE 33 0 8
54 TONNOY 68 YA 13
22 TONQUEDEC 53 H 12
35 TORCE 76 R 15
72 TORCE EN VALLEE 59 Y 15
53 TORCE VIVIERS EN CHARNIE 77 V 15
52 TORCENAY 87 UA 16
61 TORCHAMP 57 T 13
38 TORCHEFELON 152 UA 26
01 TORCIEU 138 UA 24
62 TORCY 16 FA 4
71 TORCY 120 QA 21
77 TORCY S 40 IA 11
02 TORCY EN VALOIS 41 LA 10
21 TORCY ET POULIGNY 85 PA 17
10 TORCY LE GRAND 65 PA 13
76 TORCY LE GRAND 24 BA 7
10 TORCY LE PETIT 65 PA 13
76 TORCY LE PETIT 24 BA 7
66 TORDERES 224 IA 39
14 TORDOUET 37 Y 11
49 TORFOU 110 R 19
91 TORFOU 62 GA 13
50 TORIGNI SUR VIRE C 35 S 11
30 TORNAC 193 OA 33
52 TORNAY 87 VA 17
76 TORP MESNIL, LE 24 AA 8
25 TORPES 106 WA 19
71 TORPES 122 UA 20
27 TORPT, LE 23 Y 9
14 TORQUESNE, LE 36 X 10
66 TORREILLES 224 JA 38
16 TORSAC 143 X 26
43 TORSIAC 148 KA 27
63 TORTEBESSE 147 IA 25
62 TORTEFONTAINE 16 FA 5
62 TORTEQUESNE 17 KA 5
18 TORTERON 117 JA 20
14 TORTEVAL QUESNAY 35 T 10
03 TORTEZAIS 117 JA 22
14 TORTISAMBERT 36 X 11
10 TORVILLIERS 64 OA 14
17 TORXE 127 T 24
27 TOSNY 38 CA 10
40 TOSSE 183 Q 34
01 TOSSIAT 137 UA 23
65 TOSTAT 208 X 36
27 TOSTES 38 BA 10
88 TOTAINVILLE 67 WA 14
76 TOTES C 24 BA 8
18 TOUCHAY 116 GA 21
26 TOUCHE, LA 179 SA 31
44 TOUCHES, LES 94 Q 18
17 TOUCHES DE PERIGNY, LES 128 V 24
89 TOUCY C 83 LA 16
06 TOUDON 199 CB 33
06 TOUET DE L'ESCARENE 199 DB 34
06 TOUET SUR VAR 199 BB 33
82 TOUFFAILLES 173 BA 32
59 TOUFFLERS 9 LA 3
14 TOUFFREVILLE 36 V 10
27 TOUFFREVILLE 25 DA 9
76 TOUFFREVILLE LA CABLE 23 Z 8
76 TOUFFREVILLE LA CORBELINE 24 AA 8
76 TOUFFREVILLE SUR EU 15 CA 6
32 TOUGET 187 AA 34
31 TOUILLE 218 BA 37
21 TOUILLON 85 QA 17
25 TOUILLON ET LOUTELET 123 YA 21
32 TOUJOUSE 185 V 34
54 TOUL S 45 WA 12
07 TOULAUD 164 RA 29
33 TOULENNE 170 V 30
08 TOULIGNY 29 RA 8
02 TOULIS ET ATTENCOURT 28 NA 8
83 TOULON P 203 WA 37
03 TOULON SUR ALLIER 118 LA 22
71 TOULON SUR ARROUX C 119 PA 21
12 TOULONJAC 174 FA 31
66 TOULOUGES C 224 JA 39
31 TOULOUSE P 210 CA 35
39 TOULOUSE LE CHATEAU 122 VA 20
40 TOULOUZETTE 184 T 34
23 TOULX STE CROIX 132 GA 23
14 TOUQUES 23 X 9
62 TOUQUET PARIS PLAGE, LE 7 DA 4
61 TOUQUETTES 37 Y 12
77 TOUQUIN 41 KA 12
06 TOUR, LA 199 CB 33
74 TOUR, LA 139 ZA 23
24 TOUR BLANCHE, LA 143 Y 27
84 TOUR D'AIGUES, LA 196 VA 34
63 TOUR D'AUVERGNE, LA C 147 IA 26
46 TOUR DE FAURE 174 EA 31
69 TOUR DE SALVAGNY, LA 150 RA 25
25 TOUR DE SCAY, LA 106 VA 18
09 TOUR DU CRIEU, LA 219 EA 37
39 TOUR DU MEIX, LA 122 VA 22
56 TOUR DU PARC, LE 92 K 17
38 TOUR DU PIN, LA S 152 UA 26
14 TOUR EN BESSIN 35 T 9
42 TOUR EN JAREZ, LA 150 QA 26
41 TOUR EN SOLOGNE 80 DA 17
37 TOUR ST GELIN, LA 97 Y 19
34 TOUR SUR ORB, LA 191 KA 34
41 TOURAILLES 80 BA 17
61 TOURAILLES, LES 57 U 12
34 TOURBES 214 LA 35
08 TOURCELLES CHAUMONT 30 RA 9
29 TOURCH 72 F 15
59 TOURCOING C 9 KA 3
32 TOURDUN 208 X 35
42 TOURETTE, LA 149 OA 27
11 TOURETTE CABARDES, LA 212 GA 36
06 TOURETTE DU CHATEAU 199 CB 33
14 TOURGEVILLE 36 W 9
49 TOURLANDRY, LA 95 T 19
50 TOURLAVILLE C 33 P 8
47 TOURLIAC 172 AA 30
60 TOURLY 39 FA 10
59 TOURMIGNIES 9 KA 4
39 TOURMONT 122 VA 20
61 TOURNAI SUR DIVE 58 W 12
32 TOURNAN 209 AA 35
77 TOURNAN EN BRIE C 40 JA 12
25 TOURNANS 107 YA 18
08 TOURNAVAUX 29 RA 7
65 TOURNAY C 216 X 37
14 TOURNAY SUR ODON 35 T 10
33 TOURNE, LE 156 U 30
14 TOURNEBU 36 V 11
32 TOURNECOUPE 187 AA 34
27 TOURNEDOS BOIS HUBERT 38 BA 10
27 TOURNEDOS SUR SEINE 38 CA 9
31 TOURNEFEUILLE 210 CA 35
06 TOURNEFORT 199 CB 33
62 TOURNEHEM SUR LA HEM 7 FA 3
12 TOURNEMIRE 191 KA 33
15 TOURNEMIRE 161 HA 28
08 TOURNES 29 RA 7
14 TOURNEUR, LE 35 S 11
27 TOURNEVILLE 38 BA 10
14 TOURNIERES 35 S 10
11 TOURNISSAN 223 IA 37
45 TOURNOISIS 80 DA 15
73 TOURNON 153 YA 26
47 TOURNON D'AGENAIS C 173 BA 31
36 TOURNON ST MARTIN C 114 AA 21
37 TOURNON ST PIERRE 98 AA 19
07 TOURNON SUR RHONE S 164 RA 28
65 TOURNOUS DARRE 208 Y 36
65 TOURNOUS DEVANT 208 Y 36
71 TOURNUS C 121 SA 22
27 TOURNY 38 DA 10
61 TOUROUVRE C 59 Z 13
11 TOUROUZELLE 213 IA 36
11 TOURREILLES 221 GA 37
31 TOURREILLES, LES 217 Z 37
32 TOURRENQUETS 187 Z 34
06 TOURRETTE LEVENS 200 DB 34
83 TOURRETTES 198 AB 35
26 TOURRETTES, LES 179 SA 30
06 TOURRETTES SUR LOUP 200 CB 34
16 TOURRIERS 143 X 25
37 TOURS 98 Z 18
73 TOURS EN SAVOIE 153 ZA 26
80 TOURS EN VIMEU 15 EA 6
51 TOURS SUR MARNE 42 OA 10
63 TOURS SUR MEYMONT 148 MA 25
79 TOURTENAY 96 W 19
08 TOURTERON C 30 RA 8
24 TOURTOIRAC 144 BA 27
83 TOURTOUR 203 YA 35
09 TOURTOUSE 218 BA 37
47 TOURTRES 172 Y 31
09 TOURTROL 219 EA 37
83 TOURVES 203 WA 36
14 TOURVILLE EN AUGE 23 X 9
27 TOURVILLE LA CAMPAGNE 38 AA 10
76 TOURVILLE LA CHAPELLE 25 CA 7
76 TOURVILLE LA RIVIERE 24 BA 9
76 TOURVILLE LES IFS 23 Y 8
76 TOURVILLE SUR ARQUES 24 BA 7
14 TOURVILLE SUR ODON 35 U 10
27 TOURVILLE
SUR PONT AUDEMER 23 Y 9
50 TOURVILLE SUR SIENNE 34 P 11
28 TOURY 61 FA 14
58 TOURY LURCY 118 LA 21
58 TOURY SUR JOUR 118 LA 21
63 TOURZEL RONZIERES 148 KA 26
76 TOUSSAINT 23 Y 7
69 TOUSSIEU 151 SA 26
01 TOUSSIEUX 137 SA 24
77 TOUSSON 62 HA 14
78 TOUSSUS LE NOBLE 39 GA 12
27 TOUTAINVILLE 23 Y 9
71 TOUTENANT 30 TA 9
80 TOUTENCOURT 17 HA 6
31 TOUTENS 211 EA 35
49 TOUTLEMONDE 95 T 19
16 TOUVERAC 142 V 27
38 TOUVET, LE C 153 WA 27
27 TOUVILLE 24 Z 9
44 TOUVOIS 109 P 20
16 TOUVRE 143 X 26
16 TOUZAC 142 V 26
46 TOUZAC 173 BA 31
2B TOX 228 MB 41
19 TOY VIAM 146 FA 26
14 TRACY BOCAGE 35 T 10
60 TRACY LE MONT 27 KA 9
60 TRACY LE VAL 27 KA 9
58 TRACY SUR LOIRE 101 JA 18
14 TRACY SUR MER 35 T 9
69 TRADES 136 OA 23
67 TRAENHEIM 70 DB 13
57 TRAGNY 46 YA 11
10 TRAINEL 63 LA 13
45 TRAINOU 81 FA 15
76 TRAIT, LE 24 AA 9
70 TRAITIEFONTAINE 107 XA 18
73 TRAIZE 152 WA 26
63 TRALAIGUES 133 IA 24
2B TRALONCA 228 LB 40
22 TRAMAIN 54 M 13
71 TRAMAYES C 136 RA 23
71 TRAMBLY 136 OA 23
62 TRAMECOURT 16 GA 4
51 TRAMERY 42 NA 10
65 TRAMEZAIGUES 216 X 38
38 TRAMOLE 151 TA 26
54 TRAMONT EMY 67 XA 13
54 TRAMONT LASSUS 67 XA 13
54 TRAMONT ST ANDRE 67 WA 13
01 TRAMOYES 137 SA 25
88 TRAMPOT 66 UA 14
85 TRANCHE SUR MER, LA 125 Q 23
01 TRANCLIERE, LA 137 TA 24
28 TRANCRAINVILLE 61 EA 14
72 TRANGE 78 X 15
36 TRANGER, LE 115 CA 20
10 TRANNES 65 RA 14
88 TRANQUEVILLE GRAUX 67 WA 13
35 TRANS 56 P 13
53 TRANS 58 V 14
83 TRANS EN PROVENCE 204 ZA 35
44 TRANS SUR ERDRE 94 O 17
80 TRANSLAY, LE 15 EA 6
62 TRANSLOY, LE 17 JA 6
36 TRANZAULT 115 EA 21
78 TRAPPES C 39 FA 12
11 TRASSANEL 212 HA 36
68 TRAUBACH LE BAS 90 CB 17
68 TRAUBACH LE HAUT 90 CB 17
11 TRAUSSE 212 IA 36
84 TRAVAILLAN 179 SA 32
02 TRAVECY 28 LA 8
32 TRAVERSERES 209 Z 35
70 TRAVES 88 XA 17
81 TRAVET, LE 190 GA 34
79 TRAYES 112 U 21
56 TREAL 74 M 16
50 TREAUVILLE 33 O 8
29 TREBABU 51 B 14
03 TREBAN 134 KA 22
81 TREBAN 190 HA 33
81 TREBAS 190 HA 33
22 TREBEDAN 55 N 13
11 TREBES 212 HA 36
22 TREBEURDEN 53 G 12
65 TREBONS 216 X 37
31 TREBONS DE LUCHON 217 Z 38
31 TREBONS SUR LA GRASSE 211 EA 35
22 TREBRIVAN 53 H 14
22 TREBRY 54 L 14
21 TRECLUN 105 UA 19
51 TRECON 42 OA 11
22 TREDANIEL 54 L 14
22 TREDARZEC 53 I 12
22 TREDIAS 55 M 14
56 TREDION 74 L 16
22 TREDREZ 53 G 12
22 TREDUDER 53 G 12
02 TREFCON 27 KA 7
35 TREFFENDEL 75 N 15
29 TREFFIAGAT 71 D 16
44 TREFFIEUX 94 P 17
56 TREFFLEAN 92 K 17
38 TREFFORT 166 VA 29
01 TREFFORT CUISIAT C 138 UA 23
22 TREFFRIN 53 G 14
29 TREFLAOUENAN 52 E 12
29 TREFLEVENEZ 52 E 13
29 TREFLEZ 52 D 12
51 TREFOLS 41 MA 12
22 TREFUMEL 55 N 14
29 TREGARANTEC 51 D 13
29 TREGARVAN 51 D 14
22 TREGASTEL 53 H 12
22 TREGLAMUS 53 H 13
29 TREGLONOU 51 C 13
22 TREGOMEUR 54 J 13
22 TREGON 55 M 13
22 TREGONNEAU 53 I 12
29 TREGOUREZ 72 F 15
22 TREGROM 53 H 13
29 TREGUENNEC 71 D 16
22 TREGUEUX 54 K 13
22 TREGUIDEL 54 J 12
22 TREGUIER C 53 I 12
29 TREGUNC 72 F 16
41 TREHET 79 Z 16
56 TREHORENTEUC 74 M 15
29 TREHOU, LE 52 E 13
19 TREIGNAC C 145 EA 26
03 TREIGNAT 132 GA 23
89 TREIGNY 83 KA 17
11 TREILLES 223 JA 38
45 TREILLES EN GATINAIS 82 IA 15
44 TREILLIERES 93 P 18
52 TREIX 66 TA 14
85 TREIZE SEPTIERS 110 R 20
85 TREIZE VENTS 111 S 20
82 TREJOULS 173 CA 32
48 TRELANS 176 KA 31
49 TRELAZE 96 U 18
22 TRELEVERN 53 H 12
42 TRELINS 149 OA 25
24 TRELISSAC 158 AA 28
22 TRELIVAN 55 N 13
50 TRELLY 34 O 11
59 TRELON C 19 OA 6
02 TRELOU SUR MARNE 42 MA 10
29 TREMAOUEZAN 51 D 13
22 TREMARGAT 53 I 14
76 TREMAUVILLE 23 Z 8
17 TREMBLADE, LA C 141 R 25
35 TREMBLAY 56 P 13
49 TREMBLAY, LE 94 S 17
93 TREMBLAY EN FRANCE C 40 HA 11
28 TREMBLAY LES VILLAGES 60 CA 12
27 TREMBLAY OMONVILLE, LE 37 AA 10
78 TREMBLAY
SUR MAULDRE, LE 39 FA 12
54 TREMBLECOURT 45 WA 12
70 TREMBLOIS, LE 106 VA 18
08 TREMBLOIS LES CARIGNAN 31 UA 8
08 TREMBLOIS LES ROCROI 29 OA 7
35 TREMEHEUC 55 P 13
22 TREMEL 53 G 12
22 TREMELOIR 54 J 13
49 TREMENTINES 95 T 19
29 TREMEOC 71 D 16
22 TREMEREUC 55 N 13
57 TREMERY 46 YA 10
22 TREMEUR 55 M 14
22 TREMEVEN 53 J 12
29 TREMEVEN 72 G 16
38 TREMINIS 166 WA 30
70 TREMOINS 89 AB 17
24 TREMOLAT 158 AA 29
47 TREMONS 173 AA 31
49 TREMONT 96 U 19
61 TREMONT 59 X 12
55 TREMONT SUR SAULX 44 TA 12
88 TREMONZEY 88 YA 15
22 TREMOREL 74 M 14
15 TREMOUILLE 147 IA 27
63 TREMOUILLE ST LOUP 147 HA 26
12 TREMOUILLES 175 IA 32
09 TREMOULET 219 EA 37
22 TREMUSON 54 J 13
39 TRENAL 122 UA 21
40 TRENSACQ 170 T 32
47 TRENTELS 172 AA 31
22 TREOGAN 73 H 14
29 TREOGAT 71 D 16
28 TREON 60 CA 12
29 TREOUERGAT 51 C 13
51 TREPAIL 42 PA 10
76 TREPORT, LE 15 CA 6
25 TREPOT 107 XA 19
14 TREPREL 36 V 11
38 TREPT 151 UA 25
55 TRESAUVAUX 45 VA 10
35 TRESBOEUF 76 P 16
62 TRESCAULT 18 KA 6
26 TRESCHENU CREYERS 166 VA 30
05 TRESCLEOUX 180 VA 31
70 TRESILLEY 88 XA 18
51 TRESLON 42 NA 10
58 TRESNAY 118 KA 21
46 TRESPOUX RASSIELS 173 CA 31
30 TRESQUES 179 QA 32
34 TRESSAN 214 MA 35
25 TRESSANDANS 88 YA 17
57 TRESSANGE 32 XA 9
35 TRESSE 55 O 13
66 TRESSERRE 224 JA 39
73 TRESSERVE 152 WA 26
33 TRESSES 156 U 29
22 TRESSIGNAUX 54 J 12
59 TRESSIN 9 KA 4
72 TRESSON 79 Z 16
03 TRETEAU 134 MA 22
77 TRETOIRE, LA 41 LA 11
13 TRETS C 202 VA 35
80 TREUX 17 IA 6
77 TREUZY LEVELAY 62 JA 14
22 TREVE 74 K 14
90 TREVENANS 89 BB 17
22 TREVENEUC 54 J 12
55 TREVERAY 66 UA 12
22 TREVEREC 53 I 12
35 TREVERIEN 55 O 14

30 TREVES C 192 LA 33
69 TREVES 150 RA 26
81 TREVIEN 189 GA 33
14 TREVIERES C 35 S 9
73 TREVIGNIN 153 XA 25
66 TREVILLACH 222 HA 39
11 TREVILLE 211 FA 36
25 TREVILLERS 108 BB 18
89 TREVILLY 84 OA 17
03 TREVOL 118 LA 21
22 TREVOU TREGUIGNEC 53 H 12
01 TREVOUX C 136 RA 24
29 TREVOUX, LE 72 G 16
22 TREVRON 55 N 13
03 TREZELLES 133 MA 23
22 TREZENY 53 H 12
11 TREZIERS 221 FA 37
29 TREZILIDE 52 E 12
63 TREZIOUX 148 MA 25
16 TRIAC LAUTRAIT 142 W 25
34 TRIADOU, LE 192 NA 34
85 TRIAIZE 125 R 22
50 TRIBEHOU 34 R 10
89 TRICHEY 85 PA 15
60 TRICOT 26 IA 8
60 TRIE CHATEAU 39 EA 9
60 TRIE LA VILLE 39 EA 9
65 TRIE SUR BAISE C 208 Y 36
78 TRIEL SUR SEINE C 39 FA 11
67 TRIEMBACH AU VAL 70 DB 14
54 TRIEUX 32 WA 9
83 TRIGANCE 198 ZA 34
44 TRIGNAC 93 M 18
51 TRIGNY 28 NA 9
45 TRIGUERES 83 JA 15
77 TRILBARDOU 40 JA 11
66 TRILLA 222 HA 39
77 TRILPORT 41 JA 11
67 TRIMBACH 50 GB 11
35 TRIMER 55 O 14
86 TRIMOUILLE, LA C 114 BA 22
45 TRINAY 81 FA 15
15 TRINITAT, LA 161 JA 30
06 TRINITE, LA 200 DB 34
27 TRINITE, LA 38 CA 11
50 TRINITE, LA 56 R 12
73 TRINITE, LA 153 XA 26
27 TRINITE DE REVILLE, LA 37 Z 11
27 TRINITE
DE THOUBERVILLE, LA 24 AA 9
61 TRINITE DES LAITIERS, LA 37 Y 12
76 TRINITE DU MONT, LA 23 Z 8
56 TRINITE PORHOET, LA C 74 L 15
56 TRINITE SUR MER, LA 91 J 17
56 TRINITE SURZUR, LA 92 L 17
26 TRIORS 165 TA 28
15 TRIOULOU, LE 175 GA 30
41 TRIPLEVILLE 80 DA 15
76 TRIQUERVILLE 23 Z 8
27 TRIQUEVILLE 23 Y 9
59 TRITH ST LEGER 18 MA 5
57 TRITTELING 47 AB 10
71 TRIVY 136 QA 22
15 TRIZAC 161 HA 27
17 TRIZAY 127 S 25
28 TRIZAY COUTRETOT
ST SERGE 59 AA 14
28 TRIZAY LES BONNEVAL 60 CA 14
14 TROARN C 36 V 10
19 TROCHE 145 DA 27
21 TROCHERES 105 UA 18
77 TROCY EN MULTIEN 41 JA 10
02 TROESNES 41 KA 10
22 TROGUERY 53 I 12
37 TROGUES 97 Y 19
55 TROIS DOMAINES, LES 44 UA 11
23 TROIS FONDS 132 GA 23
51 TROIS FONTAINES L'ABBAYE 44 SA 12
14 TROIS MONTS 35 U 10
86 TROIS MOUTIERS, LES C 97 W 19
15 TROIS PALIS 143 W 26
16 TROIS PIERRES, LES 23 Y 8
51 TROIS PUITS 42 OA 10
58 TROIS VEVRES 118 LA 20
64 TROIS VILLES 206 S 37
57 TROISFONTAINES 69 CB 12
52 TROISFONTAINES LA VILLE 66 SA 13
50 TROISGOTS 34 R 11
60 TROISSEREUX 26 FA 9
51 TROISSY 42 NA 10
62 TROISVAUX 16 HA 4
59 TROISVILLES 18 MA 6
70 TROMAREY 106 WA 18
57 TROMBORN 47 ZA 10
32 TRONCENS 208 X 35
38 TRONCHE, LA 166 WA 28
35 TRONCHET, LE 55 O 13
72 TRONCHET, LE 78 W 14
89 TRONCHOY 84 OA 16
71 TRONCHY 121 TA 21
27 TRONCQ, LE 38 AA 10
54 TRONDES 45 WA 12
03 TRONGET 133 KA 22
14 TRONQUAY, LE 35 T 10
27 TRONQUAY, LE 25 DA 9
58 TRONSANGES 102 KA 19
54 TRONVILLE 45 WA 10
55 TRONVILLE EN BARROIS 44 TA 12
41 TROO 79 AA 16
60 TROSLY BREUIL 27 JA 9
02 TROSLY LOIRE 27 LA 8
10 TROUANS 65 PA 12
65 TROUBAT 217 Z 38
21 TROUHANS 105 UA 19
21 TROUHAUT 105 TA 18
66 TROUILLAS 224 JA 39
65 TROULEY LABARTHE 208 X 36
60 TROUSSENCOURT 26 GA 8
55 TROUSSEY 45 VA 12
60 TROUSSURES 26 FA 9
25 TROUVANS 107 YA 18
76 TROUVILLE 23 Z 8
27 TROUVILLE LA HAULE 23 Z 9
14 TROUVILLE SUR MER C 36 W 9
18 TROUY 116 HA 20
09 TROYE D'ARIEGE 219 EA 37
10 TROYES P 64 OA 14
55 TROYON 44 UA 11
71 TRUCHERE, LA 121 SA 22
67 TRUCHTERSHEIM C 49 EB 12
02 TRUCY 28 MA 9
58 TRUCY L'ORGUEILLEUX 102 LA 18
89 TRUCY SUR YONNE 84 MA 17
12 TRUEL, LE 191 IA 33
21 TRUGNY 121 TA 20
26 TRUINAS 179 TA 30
60 TRUMILLY 40 JA 10
61 TRUN C 36 W 11
14 TRUNGY 35 T 10
14 TRUTTEMER LE GRAND 57 T 12
14 TRUTTEMER LE PETIT 57 T 12
37 TRUYES 98 AA 18
62 TUBERSENT 7 EA 4
11 TUCHAN C 223 IA 38
54 TUCQUEGNIEUX 31 WA 9
19 TUDEILS 159 EA 28
32 TUDELLE 186 X 34
72 TUFFE C 59 Y 15
17 TUGERAS ST MAURICE 142 U 27
02 TUGNY ET PONT 27 KA 7
42 TUILIERE, LA 135 NA 24
26 TULETTE 179 SA 32
19 TULLE P 159 EA 27
38 TULLINS C 152 VA 27
80 TULLY 15 DA 6
02 TUPIGNY 18 MA 6
69 TUPIN ET SEMONS 150 RA 26
44 TURBALLE, LA 92 L 18
06 TURBIE, LA 200 DB 34
21 TURCEY 104 RA 18
68 TURCKHEIM 69 CB 15
19 TURENNE 159 DA 28
16 TURGON 129 Y 24
10 TURGY 84 OA 15
89 TURNY 84 NA 15
49 TURQUANT 96 W 19
57 TURQUESTEIN BLANCRUPT 69 CB 13
50 TURQUEVILLE 33 Q 9
76 TURRETOT 23 X 8
04 TURRIERS C 181 XA 31
24 TURSAC 158 BA 29
16 TUSSON 129 W 24
65 TUZAGUET 217 Y 37
33 TUZAN, LE 170 T 31
16 TUZIE 129 X 24

U

67 UBERACH 48 EB 11
88 UBEXY 68 YA 14
04 UBRAYE 198 AB 33
2A UCCIANI 227 KB 42
07 UCEL 178 OA 30
40 UCHACQ ET PARENTIS 184 U 33
30 UCHAUD 193 PA 34
84 UCHAUX 179 RA 32
09 UCHENTEIN 218 BA 38
71 UCHIZY 121 SA 22
71 UCHON 120 PA 20
57 UCKANGE 32 XA 9
68 UEBERSTRASS 90 CB 17
68 UFFHEIM 90 DB 17
68 UFFHOLTZ 90 CB 16
73 UGINE C 153 ZA 25
65 UGLAS 217 Y 37
65 UGNOUAS 208 W 36
54 UGNY 31 VA 9
80 UGNY L'EQUIPEE 27 KA 7
02 UGNY LE GAY 27 KA 8
55 UGNY SUR MEUSE 67 VA 12
64 UHART CIZE 205 Q 37
64 UHART MIXE 206 S 36
67 UHLWILLER 49 EB 12
67 UHRWILLER 48 EB 11
79 ULCOT 96 U 19
91 ULIS, LES C 61 GA 12
60 ULLY ST GEORGES 40 GA 9
49 ULMES, LES 96 V 19
28 UMPEAU 61 EA 13
09 UNAC 220 EA 38
21 UNCEY LE FRANC 104 OA 18
51 UNCHAIR 42 NA 9
68 UNGERSHEIM 90 DB 16
42 UNIAS 149 PA 26
10 UNIENVILLE 65 OA 14
42 UNIEUX 149 PA 27
31 UNION, L' 188 DA 34
28 UNVERRE 60 BA 14
09 UNZENT 219 DA 37
05 UPAIX 181 WA 32
26 UPIE 165 SA 29
66 UR 222 FA 40
31 URAU 217 AA 37
2A URBALACONE 229 KB 43
66 URBANYA 222 GA 39
67 URBEIS 69 CB 14
68 URBES 89 BB 16
42 URBISE 135 NA 23
03 URCAY 117 IA 21
02 URCEL 28 MA 9
90 URCEREY 89 AB 17
36 URCIERS 116 GA 22
64 URCUIT 205 Q 35
21 URCY 105 SA 18
32 URDENS 187 Z 34
64 URDES 207 U 35
64 URDOS 215 U 38
64 UREPEL 205 Q 37
40 URGONS 207 U 35
32 URGOSSE 185 W 34
88 URIMENIL 68 ZA 15
67 URMATT 69 DB 13
64 UROST 207 V 36
61 UROU ET CRENNES 58 W 12
64 URRUGNE 205 P 36
09 URS 220 EA 38
68 URSCHENHEIM 90 DB 15
64 URT 205 Q 35
2B URTACA 226 LB 39
25 URTIERE 108 BB 19
54 URUFFE 67 WA 13
24 URVAL 158 AA 29
10 URVILLE 65 RA 14
14 URVILLE 36 V 11
50 URVILLE 33 O 9
88 URVILLE 67 WA 14
50 URVILLE NACQUEVILLE 33 O 8
02 URVILLERS 28 LA 7
77 URY 62 IA 14
58 URZY 102 KA 19
95 US 39 FA 10
07 USCLADES ET RIEUTORD 163 PA 30
34 USCLAS D'HERAULT 214 MA 35
34 USCLAS DU BOSC 192 LA 34
74 USINENS 138 WA 24
19 USSAC 159 DA 28
09 USSAT 219 DA 38
79 USSEAU 128 T 23
86 USSEAU 113 Y 20
15 USSEL 161 JA 28
19 USSEL S 146 HA 26
46 USSEL 174 DA 30
03 USSEL D'ALLIER 134 KA 23
63 USSON 148 LA 26
86 USSON DU POITOU 129 Z 23
42 USSON EN FOREZ 149 OA 27
14 USSY 36 V 11
77 USSY SUR MARNE 41 KA 11
64 USTARITZ C 205 O 36
09 USTOU 219 CA 38
06 UTELLE 199 CB 33
67 UTTENHEIM 70 EB 13
67 UTTENHOFFEN 48 EB 11
67 UTTWILLER 48 DB 11
04 UVERNET FOURS 182 AB 31
71 UXEAU 119 OA 21
88 UXEGNEY 68 YA 14
39 UXELLES 119 OA 21
59 UXEM 8 HA 2
65 UZ 215 W 38
40 UZA 183 R 33
64 UZAN 207 U 35
18 UZAY LE VENON 117 HA 20
46 UZECH 173 CA 30
64 UZEIN 207 U 36
22 UZEL C 74 J 14
25 UZELLE 107 ZA 18
88 UZEMAIN 68 YA 15
07 UZER 178 PA 31
65 UZER 216 X 37
19 UZERCHE C 145 DA 27
30 UZES C 193 QA 33
33 UZESTE 170 V 31
64 UZOS 207 V 36

V

72 VAAS 78 X 17
81 VABRE C 190 HA 34
12 VABRE TIZAC 175 GA 32
15 VABRES 162 KA 28
30 VABRES 192 NA 33
12 VABRES L'ABBAYE 191 JA 33
55 VACHERAUVILLE 44 UA 10
04 VACHERES 196 VA 33
26 VACHERES EN QUINT 165 TA 29
74 VACHERESSE 140 AB 23
88 VACHERESSE
ET LA ROUILLIE, LA 67 WA 15
27 VACHERIE, LA 38 BA 10
14 VACOGNES NEUILLY 35 U 10
14 VACQUERIE, LA 35 S 10
34 VACQUERIE ET ST MARTIN
DE CASTRIES, LA 192 MA 34
62 VACQUERIE LE BOUCQ 16 GA 5
62 VACQUERIETTE ERQUIERES 16 FA 5
54 VACQUEVILLE 69 AB 13
84 VACQUEYRAS 179 SA 32
34 VACQUIERES 193 OA 34
31 VACQUIERS 188 DA 34
39 VADANS 122 VA 20
70 VADANS 106 VA 18
55 VADELAINCOURT 44 TA 10
51 VADENAY 43 OA 10
02 VADENCOURT 18 MA 7
80 VADENCOURT 17 HA 6
55 VADONVILLE 45 VA 12
07 VAGNAS 178 PA 31
88 VAGNEY 89 AB 15
57 VAHL EBERSING 47 AB 11
57 VAHL LES BENESTROFF 47 AB 11
57 VAHL LES FAULQUEMONT 47 AB 11
53 VAIGES 77 U 15
34 VAILHAN 214 LA 35
34 VAILHAUQUES 192 NA 34
12 VAILHOURLES 174 FA 32
46 VAILLAC 174 DA 30
52 VAILLANT 86 TA 16
10 VAILLY 64 OA 14
74 VAILLY 139 ZA 23
02 VAILLY SUR AISNE C 28 MA 9
18 VAILLY SUR SAULDRE C 101 IA 18
50 VAINS 56 Q 12
85 VAIRE 109 O 21
25 VAIRE ARCIER 107 YA 18
25 VAIRE LE PETIT 107 XA 18
80 VAIRE SOUS CORBIE 17 HA 7
77 VAIRES SUR MARNE C 40 IA 11
84 VAISON LA ROMAINE C 179 TA 32
82 VAISSAC 188 DA 33
70 VAITE 87 WA 17
70 VAIVRE, LA 88 YA 16
70 VAIVRE ET MONTOILLE 88 XA 17
83 VAL, LE 203 XA 35
88 VAL D'AJOL, LE 89 ZA 16
10 VAL D'AUZON 65 PA 13
39 VAL D'EPY 138 UA 22
52 VAL D'ESNOMS, LE 86 TA 17
73 VAL D'ISERE 154 BB 26
35 VAL D'IZE 76 O 14
55 VAL D'ORNAIN 44 TA 12
10 VAL D'ORVIN 64 MA 14
27 VAL DAVID, LE 38 CA 11
57 VAL DE BRIDE 47 AB 11
04 VAL DE CHALVAGNE 198 AB 33
74 VAL DE FIER 138 WA 24
70 VAL DE GOUHENANS, LE 89 ZA 17
57 VAL DE GUEBLANGE, LE 47 BB 11
76 VAL DE LA HAYE 24 BA 9
89 VAL DE MERCY 84 MA 17
52 VAL DE MEUSE C 87 VA 15
27 VAL DE REUIL C 38 BA 10
25 VAL DE ROULANS 107 YA 18
76 VAL DE SAANE 24 AA 8
51 VAL DE VESLE 43 PA 10
51 VAL DE VIERE 43 RA 12
51 VAL DES MARAIS 42 OA 11
05 VAL DES PRES 168 AB 29
54 VAL ET CHATILLON 69 BB 13
26 VAL MARAVEL 180 VA 30
70 VAL ST ELOI, LE 88 YA 16
91 VAL ST GERMAIN, LE 61 FA 13
50 VAL ST PERE, LE 56 Q 12
21 VAL SUZON 105 SA 18
12 VALADY 175 HA 31
27 VALAILLES 37 Z 10
41 VALAIRE 99 CA 18
49 VALANJOU 95 U 19
26 VALAURIE 179 SA 31
04 VALAVOIRE 181 XA 32
70 VALAY 106 VA 18
63 VALBELEIX 147 JA 26
04 VALBELLE 181 WA 32
55 VALBOIS 45 VA 11
38 VALBONNAIS C 167 WA 29
06 VALBONNE 200 BB 35
31 VALCABRERE 217 Z 37
50 VALCANVILLE 33 Q 8
66 VALCEBOLLERE 222 FA 40
63 VALCIVIERES 149 NA 26
52 VALCOURT 66 SA 12
25 VALDAHON 107 YA 19
60 VALDAMPIERRE 39 FA 9
06 VALDEBLORE 199 CB 33
50 VALDECIE, LE 33 P 9
81 VALDERIES C 190 GA 33
06 VALDEROURE 198 AB 34
68 VALDIEU LUTRAN 90 BB 17
86 VALDIVIENNE 114 Z 22
90 VALDOIE C 89 BB 17
26 VALDROME 180 VA 31
81 VALDURENQUE 212 GA 35
42 VALEILLE 150 PA 25
82 VALEILLES 173 AA 31
01 VALEINS 137 SA 24
39 VALEMPOULIERES 122 WA 20
36 VALENCAY C 99 DA 19
16 VALENCE 129 Y 25
26 VALENCE P 165 SA 29
82 VALENCE C 173 AA 32
82 VALENCE D'ALBIGEOIS C 190 HA 33
77 VALENCE EN BRIE 63 JA 13
32 VALENCE SUR BAISE C 186 Y 33
59 VALENCIENNES S 18 MA 5
38 VALENCIN 151 SA 26
38 VALENCOGNE 152 VA 26
72 VALENNES 79 AA 15
04 VALENSOLE C 197 XA 34
25 VALENTIGNEY C 108 AB 18
31 VALENTINE 217 Z 37
94 VALENTON C 40 HA 12
34 VALERGUES 193 OA 34
04 VALERNES 181 XA 32
60 VALESCOURT 26 HA 9
15 VALETTE 161 IA 27
38 VALETTE, LA 166 WA 29
83 VALETTE DU VAR, LA C 203 XA 37
24 VALEUIL 144 Z 27
33 VALEYRAC 141 S 27
73 VALEZAN 154 AB 26
67 VALFF 70 EB 13
39 VALFIN SUR VALOUSE 138 VA 22
34 VALFLAUNES 192 NA 34
42 VALFLEURY 150 OA 26
61 VALFRAMBERT 58 X 13
88 VALFROICOURT 68 XA 14
07 VALGORGE C 178 OA 30
54 VALHEY 46 ZA 12
62 VALHUON 16 HA 4
19 VALIERGUES 146 GA 26
03 VALIGNAT 134 KA 23
03 VALIGNY 117 JA 21
80 VALINES 15 DA 6
38 VALJOUFFREY 167 XA 29
15 VALJOUZE 162 KA 28
42 VALLA, LA 149 NA 25
42 VALLA EN GIER, LA 150 QA 27
30 VALLABREGUES 195 RA 34
30 VALLABRIX 193 QA 33
89 VALLAN 83 MA 16
95 VALLANGOUJARD 39 FA 10
79 VALLANS 128 U 23
10 VALLANT ST GEORGES 64 OA 13
06 VALLAURIS C 200 CB 35
2B VALLE D'ALESANI 228 MB 40
2B VALLE D'OREZZA 228 MB 40
2B VALLE DI CAMPOLORO 227 JB 42
2A VALLE DI MEZZANA 227 JB 42
2B VALLE DI ROSTINO 226 LB 40
2B VALLECALLE 226 MB 39
17 VALLEE, LA 127 S 25
02 VALLEE AU BLE, LA 28 NA 7
02 VALLEE MULATRE, LA 18 MA 6
31 VALLEGUE 211 EA 35
74 VALLEIRY 139 XA 24
18 VALLENAY 116 HA 21
10 VALLENTIGNY 65 RA 13
57 VALLERANGE 47 AB 11
30 VALLERARGUES 178 PA 32
30 VALLERAUGUE C 192 MA 33
37 VALLERES 97 Y 18
52 VALLERET 66 SA 13
24 VALLEREUIL 157 Y 28
70 VALLEROIS LE BOIS 88 YA 17
70 VALLEROIS LORIOZ 88 XA 17
25 VALLEROY 107 XA 18
52 VALLEROY 87 VA 16
54 VALLEROY 45 WA 10
88 VALLEROY AUX SAULES 68 XA 14
88 VALLEROY LE SEC 67 XA 14
89 VALLERY 63 KA 14
31 VALLESVILLES 210 DA 35
44 VALLET C 94 R 19
27 VALLETOT 23 Z 9
2B VALLICA 226 KB 40
10 VALLIERES 84 OA 15
23 VALLIERES 132 FA 24
74 VALLIERES 139 XA 25
41 VALLIERES LES GRANDES 98 BA 18
30 VALLIGUIERES 193 OA 33
76 VALLIQUERVILLE 24 Z 8
73 VALLOIRE 167 ZA 28
54 VALLOIS 68 ZA 13
88 VALLOIS, LES 68 XA 14
03 VALLON EN SULLY 117 IA 22
07 VALLON PONT D'ARC C 178 QA 31
72 VALLON SUR GEE 78 W 15
74 VALLORCINE 140 BB 24
05 VALLOUISE 168 ZA 29
66 VALMANYA 222 HA 39
34 VALMASCLE 213 LA 35
73 VALMEINIER 167 ZA 28
57 VALMESTROFF 32 YA 9
11 VALMIGERE 221 HA 37
95 VALMONDOIS 39 GA 10
57 VALMONT 47 AB 10
76 VALMONT C 23 Y 7
57 VALMUNSTER 47 ZA 10
51 VALMY 43 RA 10
50 VALOGNES C 33 O 8
24 VALOJOULX 158 BA 28
25 VALONNE 108 AB 18
25 VALOREILLE 108 AB 18
26 VALOUSE 180 TA 31
46 VALPRIONDE 173 BA 31
43 VALPRIVAS 149 OA 27
91 VALPUISEAUX 62 GA 13
34 VALRAS PLAGE 214 LA 36
84 VALREAS C 179 SA 31
34 VALROS 214 LA 36
46 VALROUFIE 174 DA 31
09 VALS 219 EA 37
52 VALS DES TILLES 86 TA 16
43 VALS LE CHASTEL 162 MA 27
07 VALS LES BAINS C 178 QA 30
43 VALS PRES LE PUY 163 NA 28
14 VALSEME 36 X 10
05 VALSERRES 181 XA 31
69 VALSONNE 136 QA 24
88 VALTIN, LE 90 BB 15
15 VALUEJOLS 161 JA 28
07 VALVIGNERES 179 QA 31
63 VALZ SOUS CHATEAUNEUF 148 LA 27
12 VALZERGUES 175 GA 31
51 VANAULT LE CHATEL 43 RA 11
51 VANAULT LES DAMES 43 RA 11
79 VANCAIS 129 W 23
72 VANCE 79 Z 16
67 VANCELLE, LA 70 DB 14
25 VANCLANS 107 YA 19
01 VANDEINS 137 TA 23
54 VANDELAINVILLE 45 XA 11
70 VANDELANS 107 YA 18
54 VANDELEVILLE 67 XA 13
60 VANDELICOURT 27 IA 8
58 VANDENESSE 119 NA 20
21 VANDENESSE EN AUXOIS 104 RA 19
51 VANDEUIL 42 NA 9
51 VANDIERES 42 NA 10
54 VANDIERES 45 XA 11
54 VANDOEUVRE LES NANCY C 46 XA 12
25 VANDONCOURT 89 BB 16
17 VANDRE 127 T 24
27 VANDRIMARE 25 CA 9
08 VANDY 30 RA 9
10 VANLAY 84 OA 15
21 VANNAIRE 85 QA 16
70 VANNE 88 WA 17
79 VANNEAU, LE 127 T 23
57 VANNECOURT 47 ZA 11
27 VANNECROCQ 23 Y 9
56 VANNES P 92 K 17
54 VANNES LE CHATEL 67 WA 13
45 VANNES SUR COSSON 81 GA 16
39 VANNOZ 122 WA 21
07 VANOSC 164 OA 28
07 VANS, LES C 178 PA 31
57 VANTOUX 46 YA 10
70 VANTOUX ET LONGEVELLE 106 WA 18
92 VANVES C 40 GA 12
21 VANVEY 85 RA 16
77 VANVILLE 63 KA 13
24 VANXAINS 157 X 28
57 VANY 46 YA 10
17 VANZAC 142 V 27
79 VANZAY 129 X 23
74 VANZY 138 WA 24
81 VAOUR C 189 EA 33
38 VARACIEUX 152 UA 27
44 VARADES C 95 S 18
83 VARAGES 203 XA 35
24 VARAIGNES 143 Z 26
46 VARAIRE 174 EA 31
17 VARAIZE 128 U 24
01 VARAMBON 137 UA 24
21 VARANGES 105 TA 19
54 VARANGEVILLE 46 YA 12
14 VARAVILLE 36 V 10
38 VARCES ALLIERES ET RISSET 166 VA 28
23 VAREILLES 131 DA 23
71 VAREILLES 135 PA 23
89 VAREILLES 63 MA 14
82 VAREN 174 EA 32
76 VARENGEVILLE SUR MER 24 BA 7
50 VARENGUEBEC 34 Q 9
49 VARENNE, LA 94 Q 18
71 VARENNE L'ARCONCE 135 PA 23
71 VARENNE ST GERMAIN 135 OA 22
71 VARENNE SUR LE DOUBS 121 TA 20
24 VARENNES 158 Z 29
31 VARENNES 211 EA 35
37 VARENNES 98 AA 19
80 VARENNES 17 HA 6
82 VARENNES 188 DA 33
86 VARENNES 113 X 21
89 VARENNES 84 NA 16
45 VARENNES CHANGY 82 IA 16
55 VARENNES EN ARGONNE C 44 SA 10
91 VARENNES JARCY 62 IA 12
71 VARENNES LE GRAND 121 SA 21
71 VARENNES LES MACON 137 SA 23
58 VARENNES LES NARCY 102 KA 19
71 VARENNES SOUS DUN 136 PA 23
43 VARENNES ST HONORAT 162 MA 28
71 VARENNES ST SAUVEUR 121 TA 22
03 VARENNES SUR ALLIER C 133 LA 23
36 VARENNES SUR FOUZON 99 DA 19
49 VARENNES SUR LOIRE 97 W 19
63 VARENNES SUR MORGE 134 KA 24
77 VARENNES SUR SEINE 63 JA 14
03 VARENNES SUR TECHE 133 MA 23
63 VARENNES SUR USSON 148 LA 26
58 VARENNES VAUZELLES 102 KA 19
47 VARES 172 Y 31
60 VARESNES 27 KA 8
39 VARESSIA 122 VA 22
19 VARETZ 159 DA 28
09 VARILHES C 219 DA 37
60 VARINFROY 41 KA 10
02 VARISCOURT 29 OA 9
28 VARIZE 60 DA 15
57 VARIZE 47 ZA 10
88 VARMONZEY 68 YA 14
55 VARNEVILLE 45 VA 11
76 VARNEVILLE BRETTEVILLE 24 BA 8
70 VAROGNE 88 YA 16
21 VAROIS ET CHAIGNOT 105 TA 18
50 VAROUVILLE 33 O 8
49 VARRAINS 96 W 19
77 VARREDDES 41 JA 11
05 VARS 182 AB 30
16 VARS 143 X 25
70 VARS 87 VA 17
19 VARS SUR ROSEIX 159 CA 27
57 VARSBERG 47 AB 10
17 VARZAY 141 T 25
58 VARZY C 102 LA 18
27 VASCOEUIL 25 CA 9
79 VASLES 112 W 21
57 VASPERVILLER 69 CB 12
63 VASSEL 148 LA 25
18 VASSELAY 100 HA 19
38 VASSELIN 152 UA 26
02 VASSENS 27 KA 9
02 VASSENY 28 MA 9
26 VASSIEUX EN VERCORS 166 UA 29
51 VASSIMONT ET CHAPELAINE 43 PA 12
55 VASSINCOURT 44 SA 12
02 VASSOGNE 28 NA 9
76 VASSONVILLE 24 BA 8
14 VASSY C 35 T 11
89 VASSY 85 PA 17
50 VAST, LE 33 Q 8
50 VASTEVILLE 33 O 8
43 VASTRES, LES 164 PA 29
36 VATAN C 99 EA 19
54 VATHIMENIL 68 ZA 13
76 VATIERVILLE 25 DA 7
38 VATILIEU 152 UA 27

57 VATIMONT 47 ZA 11
51 VATRY 43 PA 12
76 VATTETOT SOUS BEAUMONT 23 Y 8
76 VATTETOT SUR MER 23 X 7
27 VATTEVILLE 38 CA 10
76 VATTEVILLE LA RUE 24 Z 9
14 VAUBADON 35 S 10
71 VAUBAN 135 PA 23
55 VAUBECOURT C 44 TA 11
88 VAUBEXY 68 YA 14
14 VAUCELLES 35 T 9
02 VAUCELLES ET BEFFECOURT 28 MA 8
25 VAUCHAMPS 107 YA 18
51 VAUCHAMPS 42 MA 11
10 VAUCHASSIS 64 OA 14
60 VAUCHELLES 27 JA 8
80 VAUCHELLES LES AUTHIE 17 HA 6
80 VAUCHELLES LES DOMART 16 FA 6
80 VAUCHELLES LES QUESNOY 16 FA 6
21 VAUCHIGNON 120 RA 20
10 VAUCHONVILLIERS 65 OA 14
70 VAUCHOUX 88 XA 17
49 VAUCHRETIEN 96 U 18
51 VAUCIENNES . 42 NA 10
60 VAUCIENNES 41 KA 10
58 VAUCLAIX 103 NA 19
51 VAUCLERC 43 RA 12
25 VAUCLUSE 108 AB 19
25 VAUCLUSOTTE 108 AB 18
10 VAUCOGNE 65 PA 13
70 VAUCONCOURT NERVEZAIN 88 WA 17
55 VAUCOULEURS C 67 VA 12
54 VAUCOURT 69 AB 12
77 VAUCOURTOIS 41 JA 11
92 VAUCRESSON 39 GA 11
60 VAUDANCOURT 39 EA 10
71 VAUDEBARRIER 135 PA 22
49 VAUDELNAY 96 V 19
14 VAUDELOGES 36 W 11
51 VAUDEMANGES 43 PA 10
54 VAUDEMONT 67 XA 13
10 VAUDES 65 PA 14
51 VAUDESINCOURT 43 QA 10
02 VAUDESSON 28 MA 9
89 VAUDEURS 64 MA 15
07 VAUDEVANT 164 RA 28
54 VAUDEVILLE 68 YA 13
88 VAUDEVILLE 68 ZA 14
55 VAUDEVILLE LE HAUT 67 VA 13
95 VAUDHERLAND 40 HA 11
54 VAUDIGNY 68 YA 13
39 VAUDIOUX, LE 122 WA 21
55 VAUDONCOURT 31 VA 9
88 VAUDONCOURT 67 WA 14
77 VAUDOUE, LE 62 HA 14
77 VAUDOY EN BRIE 63 KA 12
57 VAUDRECHING 47 ZA 9
52 VAUDRECOURT 67 VA 14
52 VAUDREMONT 66 SA 15
27 VAUDREUIL, LE 38 BA 10
31 VAUDREUILLE 211 FA 36
50 VAUDREVILLE 33 Q 8
39 VAUDREY 122 VA 20
62 VAUDRICOURT 17 IA 4
80 VAUDRICOURT 15 DA 6
50 VAUDRIMESNIL 34 Q 10
62 VAUDRINGHEM 7 FA 3
25 VAUDRIVILLERS 107 ZA 18
14 VAUDRY 35 S 11
25 VAUFREY 108 BB 18
84 VAUGINES 196 UA 34
69 VAUGNERAY C 150 RA 25
91 VAUGRIGNEUSE 61 GA 12
91 VAUHALLAN 40 GA 12
38 VAUJANY 167 XA 28
93 VAUJOURS 40 IA 11
49 VAULANDRY 96 W 17
15 VAULMIER, LE 161 IA 28
38 VAULNAVEYS LE BAS 166 WA 28
38 VAULNAVEYS LE HAUT 166 WA 28
87 VAULRY 130 BA 24
89 VAULT DE LUGNY 84 NA 17
62 VAULX 16 FA 5
74 VAULX 139 XA 24
69 VAULX EN VELIN C 151 SA 25
38 VAULX MILIEU 151 TA 26
62 VAULX VRAUCOURT 17 JA 6
60 VAUMAIN, LE 25 EA 9
03 VAUMAS 119 MA 22
04 VAUMEILH 181 XA 32
60 VAUMOISE 41 JA 10
89 VAUMORT 63 LA 14
24 VAUNAC 144 AA 27
26 VAUNAVEYS LA ROCHETTE 165 TA 30
61 VAUNOISE 59 Y 14
76 VAUPALIERE, LA 24 BA 9
28 VAUPILLON 60 BA 13
10 VAUPOISSON 65 PA 13
55 VAUQUOIS 44 TA 10
95 VAUREAL 39 FA 11
12 VAUREILLES 175 GA 31
02 VAUREZIS 28 LA 9
60 VAUROUX, LE 25 FA 9
79 VAUSSEROUX 112 V 22
79 VAUTEBIS 112 V 22
90 VAUTHIERMONT 90 BB 17
53 VAUTORTE 57 S 14
13 VAUVENARGUES 202 VA 35
30 VAUVERT C 193 PA 34
14 VAUVILLE 36 W 9
50 VAUVILLE 33 O 8
70 VAUVILLERS C 88 XA 15
80 VAUVILLERS 27 IA 7
03 VAUX 133 IA 22
31 VAUX 211 EA 35
57 VAUX 46 XA 10
86 VAUX 129 X 23
02 VAUX ANDIGNY 18 MA 6
08 VAUX CHAMPAGNE 29 QA 9
55 VAUX DEVANT DAMLOUP 44 UA 10
80 VAUX EN AMIENOIS 16 GA 6
69 VAUX EN BEAUJOLAIS 136 QA 24
01 VAUX EN BUGEY 138 UA 24
08 VAUX EN DIEULET 30 SA 9
71 VAUX EN PRE 120 RA 21
02 VAUX EN VERMANDOIS 27 KA 7
25 VAUX ET CHANTEGRUE 123 YA 20
16 VAUX LAVALETTE 143 X 27
70 VAUX LE MONCELOT 106 WA 18
77 VAUX LE PENIL 62 IA 13
08 VAUX LES MOURON 30 RA 9
08 VAUX LES MOUZON 30 TA 8
55 VAUX LES PALAMEIX 45 VA 11
25 VAUX LES PRES 106 WA 19
08 VAUX LES RUBIGNY 29 PA 8
39 VAUX LES ST CLAUDE 138 WA 22
80 VAUX MARQUENNEVILLE 16 EA 6
08 VAUX MONTREUIL 29 QA 8

16 VAUX ROUILLAC 142 W 25
21 VAUX SAULES 105 SA 18
52 VAUX SOUS AUBIGNY 87 UA 17
14 VAUX SUR AURE 35 T 9
52 VAUX SUR BLAISE 66 SA 13
27 VAUX SUR EURE 38 CA 11
77 VAUX SUR LUNAIN 63 JA 14
17 VAUX SUR MER 141 R 26
39 VAUX SUR POLIGNY 122 VA 20
78 VAUX SUR SEINE 39 FA 11
14 VAUX SUR SEULLES 35 T 10
80 VAUX SUR SOMME 17 HA 7
52 VAUX SUR ST URBAIN 66 TA 13
86 VAUX SUR VIENNE 113 Z 20
08 VAUX VILLAINE 29 OA 7
02 VAUXAILLON 28 LA 9
52 VAUXBONS 86 TA 16
02 VAUXBUIN 27 LA 9
02 VAUXCERE 28 MA 9
69 VAUXRENARD 136 RA 23
02 VAUXTIN 28 MA 9
55 VAVINCOURT C 44 TA 11
51 VAVRAY LE GRAND 43 RA 12
51 VAVRAY LE PETIT 43 RA 12
54 VAXAINVILLE 69 AB 13
88 VAXONCOURT 68 ZA 14
57 VAXY 47 ZA 11
44 VAY 93 P 17
09 VAYCHIS 220 EA 39
46 VAYLATS 174 DA 31
46 VAYRAC C 159 EA 29
33 VAYRES 156 V 29
87 VAYRES 144 AA 25
91 VAYRES SUR ESSONNE 62 HA 13
43 VAZEILLES LIMANDRE 163 NA 28
43 VAZEILLES PRES SAUGUES 162 MA 29
82 VAZERAC 173 CA 32
03 VEAUCE 134 KA 23
42 VEAUCHE 149 PA 26
42 VEAUCHETTE 149 PA 26
18 VEAUGUES 101 IA 18
26 VEAUNES 165 SA 28
76 VEAUVILLE LES BAONS 24 AA 8
76 VEAUVILLE LES QUELLES 24 Z 7
09 VEBRE 220 EA 38
15 VEBRET 147 HA 27
48 VEBRON 177 MA 32
57 VECKERSVILLER 48 CB 11
57 VECKRING 47 ZA 9
88 VECOUX 89 AB 15
80 VECQUEMONT 26 HA 7
52 VECQUEVILLE 66 TA 13
84 VEDENE 195 SA 33
15 VEDRINES ST LOUP 162 LA 28
19 VEGENNES 159 EA 29
54 VEHO 68 AB 13
37 VEIGNE 98 Z 18
74 VEIGY FONCENEX 139 YA 23
81 VEILHES 211 EA 35
41 VEILLEINS 99 EA 18
21 VEILLY 104 RA 19
19 VEIX 146 EA 26
54 VELAINE EN HAYE 46 XA 12
54 VELAINE SOUS AMANCE 46 YA 12
55 VELAINES 44 UA 12
38 VELANNE 152 VA 26
21 VELARS SUR OUCHE 104 RA 18
13 VELAUX 202 UA 35
60 VELENNES 26 GA 9
80 VELENNES 26 FA 7
70 VELESMES ECHEVANNE 106 WA 18
25 VELESMES ESSARTS 106 WA 19
70 VELET 106 VA 18
34 VELIEUX 213 IA 36
24 VELINES C 157 W 29
78 VELIZY VILLACOUBLAY C 39 GA 12
70 VELLE LE CHATEL 88 XA 17
54 VELLE SUR MOSELLE 68 YA 13
86 VELLECHES 113 Y 20
70 VELLECHEVREUX ET COURBENANS 89 ZA 17
70 VELLECLAIRE 106 WA 18
70 VELLEFAUX 88 XA 17
70 VELLEFREY ET VELLEFRANGE 106 WA 18
70 VELLEFRIE 88 YA 16
70 VELLEGUINDRY ET LEVRECEY 88 XA 17
70 VELLEMINFROY 88 YA 17
70 VELLEMOZ 106 WA 18
84 VELLERON 195 TA 33
25 VELLEROT LES BELVOIR 108 ZA 18
25 VELLEROT LES VERCEL 107 ZA 19
36 VELLES 115 DA 21
52 VELLES 87 WA 16
90 VELLESCOT 90 BB 17
25 VELLEVANS 107 ZA 18
70 VELLEXON QUEUTREY ET VAUDEY 87 WA 17
70 VELLOREILLE LES CHOYE 106 WA 18
85 VELLUIRE 127 S 22
21 VELOGNY 104 QA 18
2B VELONE ORNETO 228 MB 40
70 VELORCEY 88 YA 16
55 VELOSNES 31 UA 8
88 VELOTTE ET TATIGNECOURT 68 YA 14
62 VELU 17 JA 6
57 VELVING 47 ZA 10
51 VELYE 42 OA 11
15 VELZIC 161 HA 28
95 VEMARS 40 IA 10
27 VENABLES 38 CA 10
2B VENACO C 228 LB 41
85 VENANSAULT 110 P 21
06 VENANSON 199 CB 33
21 VENAREY LES LAUMES C 85 QA 17
19 VENARSAL 159 DA 28
03 VENAS 117 IA 22
84 VENASQUE 196 TA 33
06 VENCE C 200 CB 34
34 VENDARGUES 193 OA 34
03 VENDAT 133 LA 23
33 VENDAYS MONTALIVET 141 R 27
59 VENDEGIES AU BOIS 18 MA 5
59 VENDEGIES SUR ECAILLON 18 MA 5
35 VENDEL 76 Q 14
50 VENDELEE, LA 34 O 10
02 VENDELLES 27 KA 7
34 VENDEMIAN 214 MA 35
71 VENDENESSE LES CHAROLLES 120 PA 22
71 VENDENESSE SUR ARROUX 119 OA 21
67 VENDENHEIM 49 EB 12
14 VENDES 35 T 10
02 VENDEUIL 28 LA 8
60 VENDEUIL CAPLY 26 GA 8
14 VENDEUVRE 36 W 11
86 VENDEUVRE DU POITOU 113 X 21
10 VENDEUVRE SUR BARSE C 65 QA 14
59 VENDEVILLE 9 KA 4

02 VENDHUILE 18 KA 6
02 VENDIERES 41 LA 11
62 VENDIN LE VIEIL 17 JA 4
62 VENDIN LES BETHUNE 8 IA 4
31 VENDINE 211 EA 35
36 VENDOEUVRES 115 CA 21
24 VENDOIRE 143 X 27
41 VENDOME S 80 BA 16
42 VENDRANGES 135 PA 24
85 VENDRENNES 110 R 20
34 VENDRES 213 KA 36
08 VENDRESSE 30 RA 8
02 VENDRESSE BEAULNE 28 MA 9
77 VENDREST 41 KA 11
10 VENDUE MIGNOT, LA 64 OA 14
30 VENEJAN 179 RA 32
13 VENELLES 202 UA 35
17 VENERAND 127 T 25
70 VENERE 106 VA 18
38 VENERIEU 151 TA 26
02 VENEROLLES 18 MA 6
31 VENERQUE 210 DA 35
81 VENES 190 GA 34
18 VENESMES 116 GA 20
76 VENESTANVILLE 24 AA 7
60 VENETTE 27 IA 9
77 VENEUX LES SABLONS 62 IA 14
54 VENEY 69 AB 13
50 VENGEONS 57 S 12
25 VENISE 107 XA 18
70 VENISEY 88 XA 16
69 VENISSIEUX C 151 SA 25
02 VENIZEL 28 LA 9
89 VENIZY 84 NA 15
25 VENNANS 107 YA 18
45 VENNECY 81 FA 15
25 VENNES 107 ZA 19
54 VENNEZEY 68 ZA 13
27 VENON 38 BA 10
38 VENON 166 WA 28
38 VENOSC 167 XA 29
89 VENOUSE 84 NA 16
89 VENOY 84 MA 16
33 VENSAC 141 R 27
63 VENSAT 134 KA 24
13 VENTABREN 202 UA 35
05 VENTAVON 181 WA 31
51 VENTELAY 28 NA 9
09 VENTENAC 219 EA 37
11 VENTENAC CABARDES 212 GA 36
11 VENTENAC EN MINERVOIS 213 JA 36
04 VENTEROL 181 XA 31
26 VENTEROL 179 TA 31
27 VENTES, LES 38 BA 11
61 VENTES DE BOURSE, LES 59 X 13
76 VENTES ST REMY 24 CA 8
43 VENTEUGES 162 MA 29
51 VENTEUIL 42 NA 10
73 VENTHON 153 ZA 25
2B VENTISERI 228 MB 42
16 VENTOUSE 129 Y 24
88 VENTRON 89 BB 15
61 VENTROUZE, LA 59 Z 12
2B VENZOLASCA 228 MB 40
50 VER 56 Q 11
28 VER LES CHARTRES 60 DA 13
60 VER SUR LAUNETTE 40 IA 10
14 VER SUR MER 35 U 9
33 VERAC 156 V 29
42 VERANNE 150 RA 27
34 VERARGUES 193 OA 34
11 VERAZA 221 GA 37
60 VERBERIE 27 IA 9
52 VERBIESLES 66 TA 15
25 VERCEL VILLEDIEU LE CAMP C 107 ZA 19
59 VERCHAIN MAUGRE 18 MA 5
74 VERCHAIX 140 AB 24
26 VERCHENY 165 TA 30
49 VERCHERS SUR LAYON, LES 96 V 19
62 VERCHIN 16 GA 4
62 VERCHOCQ 7 FA 4
39 VERCIA 122 UA 21
26 VERCLAUSE 180 UA 31
26 VERCOIRAN 180 UA 32
80 VERCOURT 15 EA 5
04 VERDACHES 181 YA 32
81 VERDALLE 212 GA 35
33 VERDELAIS 170 V 30
77 VERDELOT 41 LA 11
54 VERDENAL 69 AB 13
60 VERDEREL LES SAUQUEUSE 26 FA 8
60 VERDERONNE 26 HA 9
41 VERDES 80 CA 15
2B VERDESE 228 MB 40
64 VERDETS 207 T 36
81 VERDIER, LE 189 EA 33
83 VERDIERE, LA 203 XA 35
18 VERDIGNY 101 JA 18
16 VERDILLE 128 W 25
02 VERDILLY 41 LA 10
24 VERDON 158 Z 29
51 VERDON 42 MA 11
33 VERDON SUR MER, LE 141 R 26
21 VERDONNET 85 PA 16
09 VERDUN 219 EA 38
55 VERDUN S 44 UA 10
11 VERDUN EN LAURAGAIS 211 FA 36
82 VERDUN SUR GARONNE C 188 CA 34
71 VERDUN SUR LE DOUBS C 121 SA 20
18 VEREAUX 117 JA 20
73 VEREL DE MONTBEL 152 WA 26
73 VEREL PRAGONDRAN 153 XA 26
37 VERETZ 98 AA 18
70 VEREUX 87 VA 17
31 VERFEIL C 189 EA 34
82 VERFEIL 174 EA 32
30 VERFEUIL 178 QA 32
57 VERGAVILLE 47 AB 11
35 VERGEAL 76 R 15
70 VERGENNE, LA 89 ZA 17
35 VERGER, LE 75 O 15
17 VERGEROUX 127 S 24
39 VERGES 122 VA 21
76 VERGETOT 23 X 8
43 VERGEZAC 163 NA 28
30 VERGEZE 193 PA 34
63 VERGHEAS 133 IA 24
80 VERGIES 15 EA 7
89 VERGIGNY 84 NA 15
71 VERGISSON 136 RA 23
17 VERGNE 128 U 24
17 VERGNE, LA 128 U 24
32 VERGOIGNAN 185 V 34
50 VERGONCEY 56 Q 13
43 VERGONGHEON 148 LA 27
49 VERGONNES 94 R 16
04 VERGONS 198 ZA 33
25 VERGRANNE 107 ZA 18

24 VERGT C 158 Z 28
24 VERGT DE BIRON 172 AA 30
02 VERGUIER, LE 18 KA 7
39 VERIA 122 UA 22
83 VERIGNON 198 YA 34
28 VERIGNY 60 CA 13
42 VERIN 150 RA 26
17 VERINES 127 S 23
71 VERISSEY 121 TA 21
01 VERJON 138 UA 22
71 VERJUX 121 SA 20
70 VERLANS 89 AB 17
82 VERLHAC TESCOU 188 DA 33
89 VERLIN 83 LA 15
62 VERLINCTHUN 7 EA 3
59 VERLINGHEM 9 JA 3
32 VERLUS 207 V 35
02 VERMAND C 27 KA 7
80 VERMANDOVILLERS 27 IA 7
62 VERMELLES 17 IA 4
89 VERMENTON C 84 NA 17
88 VERMONT, LE 69 CB 13
49 VERN D'ANJOU 77 S 17
35 VERN SUR SEICHE 75 P 15
18 VERNAIS 117 IA 21
69 VERNAISON 150 RA 26
09 VERNAJOUL 219 DA 37
51 VERNANCOURT 44 SA 11
49 VERNANTES 97 W 18
39 VERNANTOIS 122 VA 21
30 VERNAREDE, LA 178 OA 32
38 VERNAS 151 UA 25
43 VERNASSAL 163 NA 28
09 VERNAUX 220 EA 38
69 VERNAY 136 QA 23
74 VERNAZ, LA 140 ZA 23
25 VERNE 107 YA 18
13 VERNEGUES 196 TA 34
23 VERNEIGES 132 GA 23
73 VERNEIL, LE 153 YA 26
72 VERNEIL LE CHETIF 78 X 16
03 VERNEIX 133 IA 22
36 VERNELLE, LA 99 DA 19
31 VERNET 210 CA 35
03 VERNET, LE 133 MA 24
04 VERNET, LE 182 ZA 32
09 VERNET, LE 219 DA 37
43 VERNET, LE 163 MA 28
63 VERNET LA VARENNE 148 MA 26
66 VERNET LES BAINS 222 HA 39
63 VERNET STE MARGUERITE, LE 147 JA 26
63 VERNEUGHEOL 147 HA 25
16 VERNEUIL 144 Z 25
18 VERNEUIL 117 IA 20
51 VERNEUIL 42 NA 10
58 VERNEUIL 118 MA 20
03 VERNEUIL EN BOURBONNAIS 134 KA 23
60 VERNEUIL EN HALATTE 40 HA 9
55 VERNEUIL GRAND 31 UA 8
77 VERNEUIL L'ETANG 62 JA 12
37 VERNEUIL LE CHATEAU 97 Y 19
87 VERNEUIL MOUSTIERS 130 BA 23
55 VERNEUIL PETIT 31 UA 8
02 VERNEUIL SOUS COUCY 28 LA 8
27 VERNEUIL SUR AVRE C 37 AA 12
36 VERNEUIL SUR IGNERAIE 116 FA 21
37 VERNEUIL SUR INDRE 98 BA 19
78 VERNEUIL SUR SEINE 39 FA 11
02 VERNEUIL SUR SERRE 28 MA 8
87 VERNEUIL SUR VIENNE 130 BA 25
27 VERNEUSSES 37 Y 11
57 VERNEVILLE 45 XA 10
72 VERNIE 78 W 14
25 VERNIERFONTAINE 107 YA 19
63 VERNINES 147 JA 26
09 VERNIOLLE 219 DA 37
38 VERNIOZ 151 SA 27
50 VERNIX 56 R 12
49 VERNOIL 96 W 18
39 VERNOIS, LE 122 VA 21
25 VERNOIS LES BELVOIR 108 AB 18
21 VERNOIS LES VESVRES 86 TA 17
70 VERNOIS SUR MANCE 87 WA 16
15 VERNOLS 161 JA 27
07 VERNON 178 PA 31
27 VERNON C 38 DA 10
86 VERNON 113 Y 22
10 VERNONVILLIERS 65 RA 14
07 VERNOSC LES ANNONAY 164 RA 28
21 VERNOT 86 SA 17
70 VERNOTTE, LA 88 WA 17
41 VERNOU EN SOLOGNE 81 EA 17
77 VERNOU LA CELLE SUR SEINE 62 JA 13
37 VERNOU SUR BRENNE 98 AA 18
28 VERNOUILLET 38 CA 12
78 VERNOUILLET 39 FA 11
01 VERNOUX 121 TA 22
79 VERNOUX EN GATINE 112 U 21
07 VERNOUX EN VIVARAIS C 164 RA 29
79 VERNOUX SUR BOUTONNE 128 V 23
89 VERNOY 63 KA 15
25 VERNOY, LE 89 AB 17
03 VERNUSSE 133 JA 23
57 VERNY C 46 YA 11
2A VERO 227 KB 42
89 VERON 63 LA 15
26 VERONNE 165 TA 30
21 VERONNES 86 TA 17
71 VEROSVRES 136 QA 22
08 VERPEL 30 SA 9
38 VERPILLIERE, LA C 151 TA 26
80 VERPILLIERES 27 JA 8
10 VERPILLIERES SUR OURCE 85 QA 15
13 VERQUIERES 195 SA 34
62 VERQUIN 8 IA 4
73 VERRENS ARVEY 153 YA 26
34 VERRERIES DE MOUSSANS 212 IA 35
21 VERREY SOUS DREE 104 RA 18
21 VERREY SOUS SALMAISE 104 RA 18
10 VERRICOURT 65 PA 13
49 VERRIE 96 V 18
85 VERRIE, LA 111 S 20
78 VERRIERE, LA 39 FA 12
08 VERRIERES 30 SA 9
10 VERRIERES 65 PA 14
12 VERRIERES 176 KA 32
16 VERRIERES 142 V 26
51 VERRIERES 44 SA 10
61 VERRIERES 59 AA 13
63 VERRIERES 147 KA 26
86 VERRIERES 130 Z 22
25 VERRIERES DE JOUX 124 ZA 20
25 VERRIERES DU GROSBOIS 107 YA 19
42 VERRIERES EN FOREZ 149 OA 26
91 VERRIERES LE BUISSON 40 GA 12
86 VERRUE 113 X 20

79 VERRUYES 112 V 22
46 VERS 174 DA 31
71 VERS 121 SA 21
74 VERS 139 XA 24
39 VERS EN MONTAGNE 122 WA 20
30 VERS PONT DU GARD 193 OA 33
39 VERS SOUS SELLIERES 122 VA 20
26 VERS SUR MEOUGE 180 VA 32
80 VERS SUR SELLES 26 GA 7
78 VERSAILLES P 39 GA 12
01 VERSAILLEUX 137 TA 24
14 VERSAINVILLE 36 V 11
42 VERSANNE, LA 150 QA 27
71 VERSAUGUES 135 OA 22
52 VERSEILLES LE BAS 87 UA 16
52 VERSEILLES LE HAUT 87 UA 16
02 VERSIGNY 28 LA 8
60 VERSIGNY 40 IA 10
12 VERSOLS ET LAPEYRE 191 JA 33
14 VERSON 35 U 10
01 VERSONNEX 139 XA 23
74 VERSONNEX 138 WA 24
38 VERSOUD, LE 166 WA 28
40 VERT 184 U 33
78 VERT 39 EA 11
79 VERT, LE 128 U 24
28 VERT EN DROUAIS 38 CA 12
91 VERT LE GRAND 62 HA 13
91 VERT LE PETIT 62 HA 13
77 VERT ST DENIS 62 IA 13
51 VERT TOULON 42 NA 11
59 VERTAIN 18 MA 5
63 VERTAIZON C 148 LA 25
39 VERTAMBOZ 122 WA 21
21 VERTAULT 85 PA 16
24 VERTEILLAC C 143 Y 27
47 VERTEUIL D'AGENAIS 172 Y 31
16 VERTEUIL SUR CHARENTE 129 X 24
73 VERTHEMEX 152 WA 26
33 VERTHEUIL 141 S 27
63 VERTOLAYE 149 NA 26
62 VERTON 15 EA 4
44 VERTOU C 94 Q 19
38 VERTRIEU 138 UA 25
51 VERTUS C 42 OA 11
16 VERVANT 129 X 25
17 VERVANT 128 U 24
88 VERVEZELLE 69 AB 14
02 VERVINS S 28 NA 7
55 VERY 44 TA 10
71 VERZE 136 RA 22
11 VERZEILLE 221 GA 37
51 VERZENAY 42 PA 10
51 VERZY C 43 PA 10
52 VESAIGNES SOUS LAFAUCHE 67 UA 14
52 VESAIGNES SUR MARNE 87 UA 15
01 VESANCY 139 XA 22
26 VESC 180 TA 31
90 VESCEMONT 89 BB 16
57 VESCHEIM 48 CB 12
39 VESCLES 138 VA 22
01 VESCOURS 121 SA 22
2B VESCOVATO C 228 MB 40
18 VESDUN 116 HA 22
51 VESIGNEUL SUR MARNE 43 QA 11
01 VESINES 137 SA 22
78 VESINET, LE C 39 GA 11
02 VESLES ET CAUMONT 28 NA 8
02 VESLUD 28 NA 8
27 VESLY 39 DA 10
50 VESLY 34 P 10
70 VESOUL P 88 YA 17
14 VESPIERE, LA 37 Y 11
07 VESSEAUX 178 OA 30
50 VESSEY 56 Q 13
30 VESTRIC ET CANDIAC 193 PA 34
21 VESVRES 104 QA 18
52 VESVRES SOUS CHALANCEY 86 TA 17
95 VETHEUIL 39 EA 10
74 VETRAZ MONTHOUX 139 YA 23
90 VETRIGNE 89 BB 17
36 VEUIL 99 DA 19
02 VEUILLY LA POTERIE 41 KA 10
76 VEULES LES ROSES 24 AA 7
76 VEULETTES SUR MER 23 Z 7
03 VEURDRE, LE 118 KA 21
38 VEUREY VOROIZE 152 VA 27
51 VEUVE, LA 43 PA 11
41 VEUVES 98 BA 18
21 VEUVEY SUR OUCHE 104 RA 19
21 VEUXHAULLES SUR AUBE 85 RA 15
39 VEVY 122 VA 21
88 VEXAINCOURT 69 BB 13
14 VEY, LE 35 U 11
05 VEYNES C 181 WA 31
87 VEYRAC 130 BA 25
07 VEYRAS 164 QA 30
63 VEYRE MONTON C 148 KA 26
12 VEYREAU 177 LA 32
74 VEYRIER DU LAC 139 XA 25
15 VEYRIERES 146 HA 27
19 VEYRIERES 146 HA 26
24 VEYRIGNAC 159 CA 29
24 VEYRINES DE DOMME 158 BA 29
24 VEYRINES DE VERGT 158 AA 28
38 VEYRINS THUELLIN 152 VA 26
50 VEYS, LES 34 R 9
38 VEYSSILIEU 151 TA 26
60 VEZ 41 KA 10
15 VEZAC 161 HA 29
24 VEZAC 158 BA 29
89 VEZANNES 84 NA 16
02 VEZAPONIN 27 KA 9
15 VEZE 161 JA 27
25 VEZE, LA 107 XA 19
89 VEZELAY C 103 NA 18
54 VEZELISE C 67 XA 13
90 VEZELOIS 89 BB 17
15 VEZELS ROUSSY 161 IA 29
30 VEZENOBRES C 193 PA 33
38 VEZERONCE CURTIN 152 UA 26
70 VEZET 88 WA 17
43 VEZEZOUX 148 LA 27
51 VEZIER, LE 41 MA 12
86 VEZIERES 97 X 19
27 VEZILLON 38 CA 10
02 VEZILLY 42 MA 10
35 VEZIN LE COQUET 75 O 15
89 VEZINNES 84 OA 16
49 VEZINS 95 T 19
12 VEZINS DE LEVEZOU C 176 JA 32
72 VEZOT 59 X 14
2B VEZZANI C 228 LB 41
28 VIABON 61 EA 14
12 VIALA DU PAS DE JAUX 191 KA 33
12 VIALA DU TARN 191 JA 33
48 VIALAS 177 NA 31

Dép.	Commune		Page	Carré	
64	VIALER		207	V	35
19	VIAM		146	EA	26
81	VIANE		190	IA	34
21	VIANGES		104	PA	19
47	VIANNE		171	X	32
10	VIAPRES LE PETIT		64	OA	13
95	VIARMES	C	40	HA	10
34	VIAS		214	LA	36
46	VIAZAC		174	FA	30
12	VIBAL, LE		175	IA	32
57	VIBERSVILLER		47	BB	11
76	VIBEUF		24	AA	8
16	VIBRAC		142	W	26
17	VIBRAC		142	V	27
72	VIBRAYE	C	79	Z	15
21	VIC DE CHASSENAY		104	PA	18
21	VIC DES PRES		104	RA	19
65	VIC EN BIGORRE	C	208	W	36
34	VIC LA GARDIOLE		214	NA	35
32	VIC FEZENSAC	C	186	Y	34
63	VIC LE COMTE	C	148	LA	26
30	VIC LE FESQ		193	OA	34
21	VIC SOUS THIL		104	PA	18
02	VIC SUR AISNE	C	27	KA	9
15	VIC SUR CERE	C	161	IA	29
57	VIC SUR SEILLE	C	46	ZA	12
09	VICDESSOS	C	220	DA	38
50	VICEL, LE		33	Q	8
63	VICHEL		148	KA	27
02	VICHEL NANTEUIL		41	LA	10
28	VICHERES		59	AA	14
88	VICHEREY		67	XA	13
03	VICHY	S	133	LA	23
2A	VICO	C	227	JB	41
80	VICOGNE, LA		16	HA	6
22	VICOMTE SUR RANCE, LA		55	N	13
03	VICQ		134	KA	23
52	VICQ		87	VA	15
59	VICQ		18	MA	4
78	VICQ		39	EA	12
40	VICQ D'AURIBAT		184	S	34
36	VICQ EXEMPLET		116	GA	21
87	VICQ SUR BREUILH		145	CA	26
86	VICQ SUR GARTEMPE		114	AA	21
36	VICQ SUR NAHON		99	DA	19
14	VICQUES		36	W	11
14	VICTOT PONTFOL		36	W	10
61	VIDAI		59	Y	13
46	VIDAILLAC		174	EA	31
23	VIDAILLAT		132	FA	24
83	VIDAUBAN		203	ZA	35
50	VIDECOSVILLE		33	Q	8
87	VIDEIX		144	Z	25
91	VIDELLES		62	HA	13
65	VIDOU		208	Y	36
50	VIDOUVILLE		35	S	10
65	VIDOUZE		208	W	35
60	VIEFVILLERS		26	FA	8
49	VIEIL BAUGE, LE		96	W	17
51	VIEIL DAMPIERRE, LE		44	SA	11
27	VIEIL EVREUX, LE		38	CA	11
62	VIEIL HESDIN		16	GA	5
62	VIEIL MOUTIER		7	FA	3
43	VIEILLE BRIOUDE		162	LA	27
62	VIEILLE CHAPELLE		8	IA	4
62	VIEILLE EGLISE		7	FA	2
78	VIEILLE EGLISE EN YVELINES		61	FA	12
39	VIEILLE LOYE, LA		106	VA	19
27	VIEILLE LYRE, LA		37	Z	11
31	VIEILLE TOULOUSE		210	DA	35
45	VIEILLES MAISONS SUR JOUDRY		82	HA	16
15	VIEILLESPESSE		162	KA	28
15	VIEILLEVIE		175	HA	30
31	VIEILLEVIGNE		210	DA	36
44	VIEILLEVIGNE		110	Q	20
25	VIEILLEY		107	XA	18
21	VIEILMOULIN		104	RA	18
02	VIEL ARCY		28	MA	9
08	VIEL ST REMY		29	QA	8
32	VIELLA		207	W	35
65	VIELLA		216	W	38
65	VIELLE ADOUR		216	X	37
65	VIELLE AURE	C	216	Y	38
65	VIELLE LOURON		216	Y	38
40	VIELLE SOUBIRAN		185	V	33
40	VIELLE ST GIRONS		183	Q	33
40	VIELLE TURSAN		184	U	34
64	VIELLENAVE D'ARTHEZ		207	U	36
64	VIELLENAVE DE NAVARRENX		206	T	36
64	VIELLESEGURE		206	T	36
58	VIELMANAY		102	KA	18
81	VIELMUR SUR AGOUT	C	211	FA	35
43	VIELPRAT		163	OA	29
02	VIELS MAISONS		41	LA	11
21	VIELVERGE		106	UA	18
79	VIENNAY		112	V	21
38	VIENNE	S	151	SA	26
95	VIENNE EN ARTHIES		39	EA	10
14	VIENNE EN BESSIN		35	T	9
45	VIENNE EN VAL		81	GA	16
51	VIENNE LA VILLE		44	SA	10
51	VIENNE LE CHATEAU		44	SA	10
84	VIENS		196	VA	33
88	VIENVILLE		69	BB	14
65	VIER BORDES		216	W	37
23	VIERSAT		132	HA	23
28	VIERVILLE		61	FA	13
50	VIERVILLE		34	R	9
14	VIERVILLE SUR MER		35	S	9
18	VIERZON	S	100	FA	19
02	VIERZY		41	LA	9
59	VIESLY		18	MA	6
14	VIESSOIX		35	T	11
25	VIETHOREY		107	ZA	18
01	VIEU		138	VA	25
01	VIEU D'IZENAVE		138	VA	24
03	VIEURE		117	JA	22
34	VIEUSSAN		213	JA	35
28	VIEUVICQ		60	CA	14
53	VIEUVY		57	S	13
14	VIEUX		35	U	10
81	VIEUX		189	EA	33
59	VIEUX BERQUIN		8	IA	3
40	VIEUX BOUCAU LES BAINS		183	Q	34
14	VIEUX BOURG		23	X	9
22	VIEUX BOURG, LE		53	J	13
16	VIEUX CERIER, LE		129	Y	24
77	VIEUX CHAMPAGNE		63	KA	13
25	VIEUX CHARMONT		89	BB	17
21	VIEUX CHATEAU		103	OA	18
59	VIEUX CONDE		18	MA	4
68	VIEUX FERRETTE		90	CB	17
14	VIEUX FUME		36	W	10
08	VIEUX LES ASFELD		29	OA	9
57	VIEUX LIXHEIM		48	CB	12
76	VIEUX MANOIR		24	CA	8
22	VIEUX MARCHE, LE		53	H	12
24	VIEUX MAREUIL		143	Y	27
59	VIEUX MESNIL		19	NA	5
60	VIEUX MOULIN		27	JA	9
88	VIEUX MOULIN		69	BB	13
14	VIEUX PONT		36	W	11
61	VIEUX PONT		58	W	12
27	VIEUX PORT		23	Z	9
59	VIEUX RENG		19	OA	5
76	VIEUX ROUEN SUR BRESLE		25	EA	7
76	VIEUX RUE, LA		24	CA	9
16	VIEUX RUFFEC		129	Y	24
68	VIEUX THANN		90	CB	16
35	VIEUX VIEL		56	P	13
27	VIEUX VILLEZ		38	CA	10
35	VIEUX VY SUR COUESNON		76	Q	14
65	VIEUZOS		209	Y	36
21	VIEVIGNE		105	TA	18
52	VIEVILLE		66	TA	14
54	VIEVILLE EN HAYE		45	WA	11
21	VIEVY		104	OA	19
41	VIEVY LE RAYE		80	CA	16
65	VIEY		216	W	38
38	VIF	C	166	VA	28
02	VIFFORT		41	MA	11
30	VIGAN, LE	S	192	MA	33
46	VIGAN, LE		159	CA	30
15	VIGEAN, LE		160	HA	28
86	VIGEANT, LE		130	Z	23
87	VIGEN, LE		145	CA	25
19	VIGEOIS	C	145	DA	27
65	VIGER		216	W	37
23	VIGEVILLE		132	FA	23
2A	VIGGIANELLO		229	KB	43
45	VIGLAIN		82	GA	16
80	VIGNACOURT		16	GA	6
2B	VIGNALE		226	MB	39
14	VIGNATS		36	W	11
40	VIGNAU, LE		185	V	34
31	VIGNAUX		187	BA	34
05	VIGNEAUX, LES		168	ZA	29
65	VIGNEC		216	X	38
77	VIGNELY		40	JA	11
60	VIGNEMONT		27	JA	9
64	VIGNES		207	U	35
89	VIGNES		103	OA	17
48	VIGNES, LES		176	LA	32
52	VIGNES LA COTE		66	UA	14
55	VIGNEUL SOUS MONTMEDY		31	UA	8
54	VIGNEULLES		68	YA	13
55	VIGNEULLES LES HATTONCHATEL	C	45	WA	11
44	VIGNEUX DE BRETAGNE		93	O	18
02	VIGNEUX HOCQUET		29	OA	7
91	VIGNEUX SUR SEINE	C	40	HA	12
11	VIGNEVIEILLE		221	HA	37
38	VIGNIEU		152	UA	26
35	VIGNOC		75	O	14
58	VIGNOL		103	MA	18
21	VIGNOLES		105	SA	19
16	VIGNOLLES		142	W	26
19	VIGNOLS		145	CA	27
33	VIGNONET		156	V	29
52	VIGNORY	C	66	TA	14
55	VIGNOT		45	VA	12
18	VIGNOUX SOUS LES AIX		101	HA	19
18	VIGNOUX SUR BARANGEON		100	GA	19
57	VIGNY		46	YA	11
95	VIGNY	C	39	FA	10
36	VIGOULANT		132	FA	22
31	VIGOULET AUZIL		210	DA	35
36	VIGOUX		115	DA	22
86	VIGUERON		187	BA	33
57	VIGY	C	46	YA	10
49	VIHIERS	C	95	U	19
36	VIJON		132	GA	22
54	VILCEY SUR TREY		45	XA	11
22	VILDE GUINGALAN		55	N	13
03	VILHAIN, LE		117	JA	22
16	VILHONNEUR		143	Y	25
91	VILLABE		62	HA	13
18	VILLABON		101	IA	19
24	VILLAC		159	CA	28
10	VILLACERF		64	OA	13
54	VILLACOURT		68	YA	13
10	VILLADIN		64	MA	14
70	VILLAFANS		89	ZA	17
68	VILLAGE NEUF		90	EB	17
21	VILLAINES EN DUESMOIS		85	QA	17
72	VILLAINES LA CARELLE		59	X	13
72	VILLAINES LA GONAIS		59	Z	15
53	VILLAINES LA JUHEL	C	58	V	14
21	VILLAINES LES PREVOTES		85	PA	17
37	VILLAINES LES ROCHERS		97	Y	19
95	VILLAINES SOUS BOIS		40	HA	10
72	VILLAINES SOUS LUCE		79	Y	16
72	VILLAINES SOUS MALICORNE		78	W	16
76	VILLAINVILLE		23	X	8
27	VILLALET		38	BA	11
11	VILLALIER		212	HA	36
45	VILLAMBLAIN		80	DA	15
24	VILLAMBLARD	C	157	Z	28
35	VILLAMEE		56	R	13
28	VILLAMPUY		80	DA	15
33	VILLANDRAUT	C	170	U	31
37	VILLANDRY		97	Y	18
11	VILLANIERE		212	HA	36
2A	VILLANOVA		227	KB	41
58	VILLAPOURCON		119	OA	20
05	VILLAR D'ARENE		167	YA	28
11	VILLAR EN VAL		221	HA	37
05	VILLAR LOUBIERE		167	XA	29
11	VILLAR ST ANSELME		221	GA	37
05	VILLAR ST PANCRACE		168	AB	29
23	VILLARD		131	EA	23
74	VILLARD		139	ZA	23
38	VILLARD BONNOT		153	WA	27
73	VILLARD D'HERY		153	XA	26
38	VILLARD DE LANS	C	166	VA	28
73	VILLARD LEGER		153	YA	26
38	VILLARD NOTRE DAME		167	XA	28
38	VILLARD RECULAS		167	XA	28
38	VILLARD REYMOND		166	WA	29
73	VILLARD SALLET		153	XA	26
38	VILLARD ST CHRISTOPHE		166	WA	29
39	VILLARD ST SAUVEUR		138	WA	22
39	VILLARD SUR BIENNE		122	WA	22
73	VILLARD SUR DORON		153	ZA	25
11	VILLARDEBELLE		221	HA	37
11	VILLARDONNEL		212	GA	36
39	VILLARDS D'HERIA		122	WA	22
74	VILLARDS SUR THONES		139	YA	24
73	VILLAREMBERT		153	YA	27
70	VILLARGENT		89	ZA	17
21	VILLARGOIX		104	PA	18
73	VILLARGONDRAN		153	YA	27
31	VILLARIES		188	DA	34
73	VILLARLURIN		154	ZA	26
73	VILLARODIN BOURGET		168	AB	28
73	VILLAROGER		154	BB	26
73	VILLAROUX		153	XA	26
24	VILLARS		79	Z	17
28	VILLARS		60	DA	14
42	VILLARS		150	PA	26
84	VILLARS		196	UA	33
71	VILLARS, LE		121	SA	21
04	VILLARS COLMARS		182	ZA	32
52	VILLARS EN AZOIS		65	RA	15
17	VILLARS EN PONS		141	T	26
21	VILLARS ET VILLENOTTE		85	OA	17
21	VILLARS FONTAINE		105	SA	19
70	VILLARS LE PAUTEL		88	WA	16
90	VILLARS LE SEC		108	BB	18
25	VILLARS LES BLAMONT		108	BB	18
17	VILLARS LES BOIS		142	U	25
01	VILLARS LES DOMBES	C	137	TA	24
52	VILLARS SANTENOGE		86	SA	16
25	VILLARS SOUS DAMPJOUX		108	AB	18
25	VILLARS SOUS ECOT		108	AB	18
25	VILLARS ST GEORGES		106	WA	19
06	VILLARS SUR VAR	C	199	CB	33
11	VILLARZEL CABARDES		212	HA	36
11	VILLARZEL DU RAZES		221	GA	37
11	VILLASAVARY		211	FA	36
31	VILLATE		210	CA	35
31	VILLAUDRIC		188	DA	34
11	VILLAUTOU		219	EA	37
41	VILLAVARD		79	AA	16
74	VILLAZ		139	YA	24
60	VILLE		27	JA	8
67	VILLE	C	69	CB	14
54	VILLE AU MONTOIS		31	WA	9
54	VILLE AU VAL		46	XA	11
10	VILLE AUX BOIS, LA		65	RA	13
02	VILLE AUX BOIS LES DIZY, LA		29	OA	8
02	VILLE AUX BOIS LES PONTAVERT, LA		28	NA	9
41	VILLE AUX CLERCS, LA		80	BA	15
37	VILLE AUX DAMES, LA		98	Z	18
92	VILLE D'AVRAY		39	GA	11
55	VILLE DEVANT BELRAIN		44	UA	11
55	VILLE DEVANT CHAUMONT		31	UA	9
2B	VILLE DI PARASO		225	KB	39
2B	VILLE DI PIETRABUGNO		226	MB	39
82	VILLE DIEU DU TEMPLE, LA		188	BA	33
51	VILLE DOMMANGE		42	OA	10
91	VILLE DU BOIS, LA		62	GA	12
25	VILLE DU PONT		107	ZA	20
52	VILLE EN BLAISOIS		66	SA	13
74	VILLE EN SALLAZ		139	ZA	23
51	VILLE EN SELVE		42	OA	10
51	VILLE EN TARDENOIS	C	42	NA	10
54	VILLE EN VERMOIS		68	YA	12
55	VILLE EN WOEVRE		45	VA	10
35	VILLE ES NONAIS, LA		55	N	13
54	VILLE HOUDLEMONT		31	VA	8
74	VILLE LA GRAND		139	YA	23
58	VILLE LANGY		118	MA	20
80	VILLE LE MARCLET		16	FA	6
02	VILLE SAVOYE		42	MA	9
38	VILLE SOUS ANJOU		151	SA	27
10	VILLE SOUS LA FERTE		65	RA	15
51	VILLE SOUS ORBAIS, LA		42	MA	11
77	VILLE ST JACQUES		63	JA	14
80	VILLE SUR ANCRE		17	IA	6
10	VILLE SUR ARCE		65	QA	15
55	VILLE SUR COUSANCES		44	TA	10
88	VILLE SUR ILLON		68	YA	14
69	VILLE SUR JARNIOUX		136	RA	24
08	VILLE SUR LUMES		29	RA	7
08	VILLE SUR RETOURNE		29	OA	9
55	VILLE SUR SAULX		44	TA	12
10	VILLE SUR TERRE		65	RA	14
51	VILLE SUR TOURBE	C	43	RA	10
54	VILLE SUR YRON		45	WA	10
28	VILLEAU		61	DA	14
61	VILLEBADIN		58	X	12
41	VILLEBAROU		80	CA	17
50	VILLEBAUDON		34	R	11
11	VILLEBAZY		221	HA	37
77	VILLEBEON		63	JA	14
49	VILLEBERNIER		96	W	18
21	VILLEBERNY		104	OA	18
21	VILLEBICHOT		105	TA	19
89	VILLEBLEVIN		63	KA	14
01	VILLEBOIS		138	UA	25
16	VILLEBOIS LAVALETTE	C	143	X	26
26	VILLEBOIS LES PINS		180	VA	31
28	VILLEBON		60	BA	13
91	VILLEBON SUR YVETTE	C	40	GA	12
89	VILLEBOUGIS		63	KA	14
37	VILLEBOURG		79	Y	17
41	VILLEBOUT		80	BA	15
47	VILLEBRAMAR		172	Y	31
03	VILLEBRET		133	IA	23
82	VILLEBRUMIER	C	188	DA	33
18	VILLECELIN		116	GA	20
77	VILLECERF		62	JA	14
54	VILLECEY SUR MAD		45	XA	11
39	VILLECHANTRIA		138	UA	22
41	VILLECHAUVE		79	AA	17
69	VILLECHENEVE		150	QA	25
10	VILLECHETIF		65	PA	14
89	VILLECHETIVE		64	MA	15
50	VILLECHIEN		57	S	13
89	VILLECIEN		83	LA	15
55	VILLECLOYE		31	UA	8
12	VILLECOMTAL		175	IA	31
32	VILLECOMTAL SUR ARROS		208	X	36
21	VILLECOMTE		86	TA	17
91	VILLECONIN		61	GA	13
80	VILLECOURT		27	JA	7
94	VILLECRESNES	C	40	HA	12
83	VILLECROZE		203	YA	35
11	VILLEDAIGNE		213	JA	36
15	VILLEDIEU		161	KA	28
21	VILLEDIEU		85	QA	16
84	VILLEDIEU		179	TA	32
17	VILLEDIEU, LA		128	V	24
23	VILLEDIEU, LA		146	FA	25
48	VILLEDIEU, LA		162	MA	30
25	VILLEDIEU, LES		123	YA	21
86	VILLEDIEU DU CLAIN, LA	C	113	Y	22
70	VILLEDIEU EN FONTENETTE, LA		88	YA	16
49	VILLEDIEU LA BLOUERE		94	R	19
41	VILLEDIEU LE CHATEAU		79	Z	16
61	VILLEDIEU LES BAILLEUL		58	W	12
50	VILLEDIEU LES POELES	C	56	R	11
36	VILLEDIEU SUR INDRE		115	DA	20
37	VILLEDOMAIN		99	CA	19
37	VILLEDOMER		79	AA	17
17	VILLEDOUX		125	R	23
11	VILLEDUBERT		212	HA	36
16	VILLEFAGNAN	C	129	W	24
89	VILLEFARGEAU		83	MA	16
87	VILLEFAVARD		131	BA	23
21	VILLEFERRY		104	QA	18
11	VILLEFLOURE		221	HA	37
79	VILLEFOLLET		128	V	23
38	VILLEFONTAINE	C	151	TA	26
11	VILLEFORT		221	FA	38
48	VILLEFORT	C	178	OA	31
32	VILLEFRANCHE		209	Z	35
89	VILLEFRANCHE		83	KA	15
81	VILLEFRANCHE D'ALBIGEOIS	C	190	HA	33
03	VILLEFRANCHE D'ALLIER		133	JA	22
66	VILLEFRANCHE DE CONFLENT		222	HA	39
31	VILLEFRANCHE DE LAURAGAIS	C	211	EA	36
24	VILLEFRANCHE DE LONCHAT	C	157	W	29
12	VILLEFRANCHE DE PANAT		190	IA	33
12	VILLEFRANCHE DE ROUERGUE	S	174	FA	31
24	VILLEFRANCHE DU PERIGORD	C	173	BA	30
47	VILLEFRANCHE DU QUEYRAN		171	X	32
26	VILLEFRANCHE LE CHATEAU		180	VA	32
41	VILLEFRANCHE SUR CHER		99	EA	18
06	VILLEFRANCHE SUR MER	C	200	DB	34
69	VILLEFRANCHE SUR SAONE	S	136	RA	24
41	VILLEFRANCOEUR		80	CA	17
70	VILLEFRANCON		106	WA	18
64	VILLEFRANQUE		205	Q	35
65	VILLEFRANQUE		208	W	35
11	VILLEGAILHENC		212	GA	36
16	VILLEGATS		129	X	24
27	VILLEGATS		38	DA	11
71	VILLEGAUDIN		121	TA	21
18	VILLEGENON		101	IA	18
11	VILLEGLY		212	HA	36
36	VILLEGONGIS		115	DA	20
33	VILLEGOUGE		156	V	29
36	VILLEGOUIN		115	CA	20
52	VILLEGUSIEN LE LAC		87	UA	16
41	VILLEHERVIERS		99	EA	18
16	VILLEJESUS		129	W	25
16	VILLEJOUBERT		143	X	25
94	VILLEJUIF	C	40	HA	12
91	VILLEJUST		62	GA	12
84	VILLELAURE		196	UA	34
37	VILLELOIN COULANGE		99	CA	19
65	VILLELONGUE		216	W	38
11	VILLELONGUE D'AUDE		221	FA	37
66	VILLELONGUE DE LA SALANQUE		224	JA	39
66	VILLELONGUE DELS MONTS		224	JA	40
10	VILLELOUP		64	NA	14
82	VILLEMADE		188	CA	33
11	VILLEMAGNE		211	FA	36
34	VILLEMAGNE L'ARGENTIERE		213	KA	35
79	VILLEMAIN		128	W	24
45	VILLEMANDEUR		82	IA	15
89	VILLEMANOCHE		63	KA	14
41	VILLEMARDY		80	BA	16
77	VILLEMARECHAL		63	JA	14
77	VILLEMAREUIL		41	JA	11
31	VILLEMATIER		188	DA	34
10	VILLEMAUR SUR VANNE		64	NA	14
65	VILLEMBITS		208	Y	36
60	VILLEMBRAY		25	EA	9
77	VILLEMER		62	JA	14
89	VILLEMER		83	MA	16
10	VILLEMEREUIL		64	OA	14
28	VILLEMEUX SUR EURE		60	DA	12
38	VILLEMOIRIEU		151	TA	25
10	VILLEMOIRON EN OTHE		64	NA	14
49	VILLEMOISAN		95	S	18
91	VILLEMOISSON SUR ORGE		62	GA	12
66	VILLEMOLAQUE		224	JA	39
93	VILLEMOMBLE	C	40	HA	11
42	VILLEMONTAIS		135	OA	24
02	VILLEMONTOIRE		41	LA	9
10	VILLEMORIEN		65	PA	15
17	VILLEMORIN		128	V	24
86	VILLEMORT		114	AA	22
01	VILLEMOTIER		137	UA	22
11	VILLEMOUSTAUSSOU		212	HA	36
45	VILLEMOUTIERS		82	HA	15
10	VILLEMOYENNE		65	PA	14
65	VILLEMUR		209	Z	36
31	VILLEMUR SUR TARN	C	188	DA	34
45	VILLEMURLIN		82	HA	17
04	VILLEMUS		197	WA	34
10	VILLENAUXE LA GRANDE	C	64	MA	13
77	VILLENAUXE LA PETITE		63	LA	13
40	VILLENAVE		184	S	33
33	VILLENAVE D'ORNON	C	156	U	29
33	VILLENAVE DE RIONS		156	V	30
65	VILLENAVE PRES BEARN		208	W	36
65	VILLENAVE PRES MARSAC		208	W	36
89	VILLENAVOTTE		63	KA	14
01	VILLENEUVE		137	SA	24
04	VILLENEUVE		197	WA	33
09	VILLENEUVE		218	AA	38
12	VILLENEUVE	C	174	FA	31
33	VILLENEUVE		156	T	28
63	VILLENEUVE		148	KA	26
23	VILLENEUVE, LA		132	HA	24
71	VILLENEUVE, LA		121	TA	20
10	VILLENEUVE AU CHATELOT, LA		64	MA	13
10	VILLENEUVE AU CHEMIN		64	NA	15
10	VILLENEUVE AU CHENE, LA		65	QA	14
70	VILLENEUVE BELLENOYE ET LA MAIZE, LA		88	YA	16
43	VILLENEUVE D'ALLIER		162	LA	28
25	VILLENEUVE D'AMONT		123	XA	20
59	VILLENEUVE D'ASCQ	C	9	KA	3
59	VILLENEUVE D'ASCQ	C	9	KA	3
59	VILLENEUVE D'ASCQ	C	9	KA	3
39	VILLENEUVE D'AVAL		122	WA	20
06	VILLENEUVE D'ENTRAUNES		182	AB	32
09	VILLENEUVE D'OLMES		219	EA	38
07	VILLENEUVE DE BERG	C	178	QA	30
47	VILLENEUVE DE DURAS		157	X	30
66	VILLENEUVE DE LA RAHO		224	JA	39
38	VILLENEUVE DE MARC		151	TA	26
40	VILLENEUVE DE MARSAN	C	185	V	33
31	VILLENEUVE DE RIVIERE		217	Z	37
09	VILLENEUVE DU LATOU		218	CA	37
09	VILLENEUVE DU PAREAGE		219	DA	37
78	VILLENEUVE EN CHEVRIE, LA		38	DA	11
71	VILLENEUVE EN MONTAGNE		120	RA	21
41	VILLENEUVE FROUVILLE		80	CA	16
89	VILLENEUVE L'ARCHEVEQUE	C	64	MA	14
11	VILLENEUVE LA COMPTAL		211	FA	36
17	VILLENEUVE LA COMTESSE		128	U	23
89	VILLENEUVE LA DONDAGRE		63	LA	15
92	VILLENEUVE LA GARENNE	C	40	GA	11
89	VILLENEUVE LA GUYARD		63	KA	14
51	VILLENEUVE LA LIONNE		41	MA	12
66	VILLENEUVE LA RIVIERE		224	JA	39
77	VILLENEUVE LE COMTE		40	JA	12
94	VILLENEUVE LE ROI	C	40	HA	12
31	VILLENEUVE LECUSSAN		217	Y	37
30	VILLENEUVE LES AVIGNON	C	195	RA	33
34	VILLENEUVE LES BEZIERS		213	LA	36
77	VILLENEUVE LES BORDES		63	KA	13
31	VILLENEUVE LES BOULOC		188	DA	34
63	VILLENEUVE LES CERFS		133	LA	24
51	VILLENEUVE LES CHARLEVILLE, LA		42	NA	12
39	VILLENEUVE LES CHARNOD		138	UA	23
21	VILLENEUVE LES CONVERS, LA		85	RA	17
11	VILLENEUVE LES CORBIERES		223	JA	38
89	VILLENEUVE LES GENETS		83	KA	16
81	VILLENEUVE LES LAVAUR		211	EA	35
34	VILLENEUVE LES MAGUELONE		214	NA	35
11	VILLENEUVE LES MONTREAL		221	GA	37
60	VILLENEUVE LES SABLONS		39	FA	10
06	VILLENEUVE LOUBET		200	CB	34
11	VILLENEUVE MINERVOIS		212	HA	36
51	VILLENEUVE RENNEVILLE CHEVIGNY		42	OA	11
21	VILLENEUVE SOUS CHARIGNY		104	OA	18
77	VILLENEUVE SOUS DAMMARTIN		40	IA	11
39	VILLENEUVE SOUS PYMONT		122	VA	21
60	VILLENEUVE SOUS THURY		41	KA	10
77	VILLENEUVE ST DENIS		40	IA	12
94	VILLENEUVE ST GEORGES	C	40	HA	12
02	VILLENEUVE ST GERMAIN		28	LA	9
28	VILLENEUVE ST NICOLAS		61	DA	14
89	VILLENEUVE ST SALVES		84	MA	16
51	VILLENEUVE ST VISTRE ET VILLEVOTTE		64	NA	12
03	VILLENEUVE SUR ALLIER		118	LA	21
91	VILLENEUVE SUR AUVERS		62	GA	13
77	VILLENEUVE SUR BELLOT		41	LA	11
18	VILLENEUVE SUR CHER		116	GA	20
45	VILLENEUVE SUR CONIE		80	DA	15
02	VILLENEUVE SUR FERE		42	MA	10
47	VILLENEUVE SUR LOT	S	172	Z	31
60	VILLENEUVE SUR VERBERIE		40	IA	9
81	VILLENEUVE SUR VERE		189	FA	33
89	VILLENEUVE SUR YONNE	C	83	LA	15
31	VILLENEUVE TOLOSANE		210	CA	35
34	VILLENEUVETTE		214	LA	35
78	VILLENNES SUR SEINE		39	FA	11
31	VILLENOUVELLE		211	EA	35
77	VILLENOY		40	JA	11
36	VILLENTROIS		99	DA	19
41	VILLENY		81	EA	17
53	VILLEPAIL		58	V	13
77	VILLEPARISIS		40	IA	11
70	VILLEPAROIS		88	YA	17
26	VILLEPERDRIX		180	TA	31
37	VILLEPERDUE		98	Z	19
89	VILLEPERROT		63	KA	14
11	VILLEPINTE		211	FA	36
93	VILLEPINTE	C	40	HA	11
41	VILLEPORCHER		79	AA	17
44	VILLEPOT		76	R	16
78	VILLEPREUX		39	FA	11
76	VILLEQUIER		23	Z	8
02	VILLEQUIER AUMONT		27	KA	8
18	VILLEQUIERS		101	JA	19
57	VILLER		47	AB	11
41	VILLERABLE		79	BA	16
41	VILLERBON		80	CA	17
47	VILLEREAL	C	172	Z	30
45	VILLEREAU		81	FA	15
59	VILLEREAU		18	MA	5
42	VILLEREST		135	OA	24
02	VILLERET		18	KA	7
10	VILLERET		65	RA	14
01	VILLEREVERSURE		138	UA	23
41	VILLERMAIN		80	DA	16
41	VILLEROMAIN		80	BA	16
95	VILLERON		40	HA	10
11	VILLEROUGE TERMENES		223	IA	37
77	VILLEROY		40	JA	11
80	VILLEROY		15	EA	7
89	VILLEROY		63	KA	14
55	VILLEROY SUR MEHOLLE		67	VA	12
42	VILLERS		135	PA	23
88	VILLERS		68	YA	14
02	VILLERS AGRON AIGUIZY		42	NA	10
51	VILLERS ALLERAND		42	OA	10
62	VILLERS AU BOIS		17	IA	5
62	VILLERS AU FLOS		17	JA	6
59	VILLERS AU TERTRE		18	KA	5
51	VILLERS AUX BOIS		42	OA	11
80	VILLERS AUX ERABLES		26	HA	7
51	VILLERS AUX NOEUDS		42	OA	10
55	VILLERS AUX VENTS		44	SA	11
14	VILLERS BOCAGE	C	35	T	10
80	VILLERS BOCAGE	C	16	GA	6
70	VILLERS BOUTON		107	XA	18
80	VILLERS BRETONNEUX		26	HA	7
62	VILLERS BRULIN		17	HA	5
25	VILLERS BUZON		106	WA	19
80	VILLERS CAMPSART		25	EA	7
14	VILLERS CANIVET		36	V	11
80	VILLERS CARBONNEL		27	JA	7
08	VILLERS CERNAY		30	TA	8
62	VILLERS CHATEL		17	IA	5
70	VILLERS CHEMIN ET MONT LES ETRELLES		106	WA	18
25	VILLERS CHIEF		107	ZA	19
02	VILLERS COTTERETS	C	41	KA	10
55	VILLERS DEVANT DUN		30	TA	9
08	VILLERS DEVANT LE THOUR		29	OA	8
08	VILLERS DEVANT MOUZON		30	SA	8
76	VILLERS ECALLES		24	AA	8
51	VILLERS EN ARGONNE		44	SA	11
95	VILLERS EN ARTHIES		39	EA	10
59	VILLERS EN CAUCHIES		18	LA	5
54	VILLERS EN HAYE		45	XA	12
61	VILLERS EN OUCHE		37	Y	11
02	VILLERS EN PRAYERES		28	MA	9
27	VILLERS EN VEXIN		39	DA	10
39	VILLERS FARLAY	C	122	WA	20
80	VILLERS FAUCON		18	KA	6
51	VILLERS FRANQUEUX		29	OA	9
25	VILLERS GRELOT		107	YA	18
59	VILLERS GUISLAIN		18	KA	6
02	VILLERS HELON		41	LA	10
62	VILLERS L'HOPITAL		16	GA	5
54	VILLERS LA CHEVRE		31	VA	8
25	VILLERS LA COMBE		107	ZA	19
21	VILLERS LA FAYE		105	SA	19
54	VILLERS LA MONTAGNE		31	WA	9
70	VILLERS LA VILLE		89	ZA	17
51	VILLERS LE CHATEAU		43	PA	11
25	VILLERS LE LAC		108	AB	19

Dép.	Commune		Page	Carré	
54	VILLERS LE ROND		31	VA	9
02	VILLERS LE SEC		28	MA	7
51	VILLERS LE SEC		44	SA	12
55	VILLERS LE SEC		66	UA	12
70	VILLERS LE SEC		88	YA	17
08	VILLERS LE TILLEUL		30	RA	8
08	VILLERS LE TOURNEUR		29	QA	8
39	VILLERS LES BOIS		122	VA	20
62	VILLERS LES CAGNICOURT		17	JA	5
02	VILLERS LES GUISE		18	MA	7
70	VILLERS LES LUXEUIL		88	YA	16
55	VILLERS LES MANGIENNES		31	VA	9
54	VILLERS LES MOIVRONS		46	YA	12
54	VILLERS LES NANCY		46	XA	12
36	VILLERS LES ORMES		115	DA	20
21	VILLERS LES POTS		106	UA	19
80	VILLERS LES ROYE		27	IA	8
51	VILLERS MARMERY		43	PA	10
59	VILLERS OUTREAUX		18	LA	6
70	VILLERS PATER		107	YA	18
21	VILLERS PATRAS		85	QA	15
59	VILLERS PLOUICH		18	KA	6
59	VILLERS POL		18	MA	5
39	VILLERS ROBERT		122	VA	20
21	VILLERS ROTIN		106	UA	19
08	VILLERS SEMEUSE	C	29	RA	7
62	VILLERS SIR SIMON		17	HA	5
59	VILLERS SIRE NICOLE		19	OA	5
80	VILLERS SOUS AILLY		16	FA	6
25	VILLERS SOUS CHALAMONT		123	XA	20
51	VILLERS SOUS CHATILLON		42	NA	10
76	VILLERS SOUS FOUCARMONT		25	DA	7
25	VILLERS SOUS MONTROND		107	XA	19
55	VILLERS SOUS PAREID		45	WA	10
54	VILLERS SOUS PRENY		45	XA	11
60	VILLERS SOUS ST LEU		40	HA	10
60	VILLERS ST BARTHELEMY		25	FA	9
02	VILLERS ST CHRISTOPHE		27	KA	7
60	VILLERS ST FRAMBOURG		40	IA	10
60	VILLERS ST GENEST		41	JA	10
25	VILLERS ST MARTIN		107	ZA	18
60	VILLERS ST PAUL		40	HA	9
60	VILLERS ST SEPULCRE		26	GA	9
57	VILLERS STONCOURT		47	ZA	10
60	VILLERS SUR AUCHY		25	EA	9
80	VILLERS SUR AUTHIE		15	EA	5
08	VILLERS SUR BAR		30	SA	8
60	VILLERS SUR BONNIERES		25	FA	8
60	VILLERS SUR COUDUN		27	JA	9
02	VILLERS SUR FERE		42	MA	10
08	VILLERS SUR LE MONT		30	RA	8
27	VILLERS SUR LE ROULE		38	CA	10
14	VILLERS SUR MER		36	W	9
55	VILLERS SUR MEUSE		44	UA	11
57	VILLERS SUR NIED		47	ZA	11
70	VILLERS SUR PORT		88	XA	16
70	VILLERS SUR SAULNOT		89	AB	17
60	VILLERS SUR TRIE		39	EA	9
80	VILLERS TOURNELLE		26	HA	8
70	VILLERS VAUDEY		87	WA	17
60	VILLERS VERMONT		25	EA	8
60	VILLERS VICOMTE		26	GA	8
39	VILLERSERINE		122	VA	20
70	VILLERSEXEL	C	89	ZA	17
54	VILLERUPT	C	32	WA	9
14	VILLERVILLE		23	X	9
10	VILLERY		64	OA	14
01	VILLES		138	WA	24
84	VILLES SUR AUZON		196	TA	33
60	VILLESELVE		27	KA	8
51	VILLESENEUX		42	OA	11
46	VILLESEQUE		173	CA	31
11	VILLESEQUE DES CORBIERES		223	JA	37
11	VILLESEQUELANDE		212	GA	36
11	VILLESISCLE		211	FA	36
34	VILLESPASSANS		213	JA	36
11	VILLESPY		211	FA	36
93	VILLETANEUSE		40	HA	11
34	VILLETELLE		193	PA	34
23	VILLETELLE, LA		132	HA	24
89	VILLETHIERRY		63	KA	14
47	VILLETON		171	X	31
24	VILLETOUREIX		143	Y	27
11	VILLETRITOULS		221	HA	37
41	VILLETRUN		80	BA	16
54	VILLETTE		31	VA	9
78	VILLETTE		39	EA	11
14	VILLETTE, LA		35	U	11
38	VILLETTE D'ANTHON		151	TA	25
38	VILLETTE DE VIENNE		151	SA	26
39	VILLETTE LES ARBOIS		122	WA	20
39	VILLETTE LES DOLE		106	VA	19
01	VILLETTE SUR AIN		137	UA	24
10	VILLETTE SUR AUBE		64	OA	13
27	VILLETTES		38	BA	10
43	VILLETTES, LES		149	PA	27
69	VILLEURBANNE	C	151	SA	25
89	VILLEVALLIER		83	LA	15
77	VILLEVAUDE		40	IA	11
51	VILLEVENARD		42	NA	11
49	VILLEVEQUE		96	U	17
34	VILLEVEYRAC		214	MA	35
30	VILLEVIEILLE		193	OA	34
39	VILLEVIEUX		122	UA	21
07	VILLEVOCANCE		164	RA	28
45	VILLEVOQUES		82	IA	15
41	VILLEXANTON		80	CA	16
17	VILLEXAVIER		142	U	27
39	VILLEY, LE		122	VA	20
54	VILLEY LE SEC		45	XA	12
54	VILLEY ST ETIENNE		45	XA	12
21	VILLEY SUR TILLE		86	TA	17
27	VILLEZ SOUS BAILLEUL		38	CA	10
27	VILLEZ SUR LE NEUBOURG		37	AA	10
69	VILLIE MORGON		136	RA	23
36	VILLIERS		114	BA	20
86	VILLIERS		113	X	21
95	VILLIERS ADAM		40	GA	10
37	VILLIERS AU BOUIN		97	X	17
51	VILLIERS AUX CORNEILLES		64	MA	13
53	VILLIERS CHARLEMAGNE		77	T	16
17	VILLIERS COUTURE		128	V	24
77	VILLIERS EN BIERE		62	IA	13
79	VILLIERS EN BOIS		128	U	23
27	VILLIERS EN DESOEUVRE		38	DA	11
52	VILLIERS EN LIEU		44	SA	12
21	VILLIERS EN MORVAN		104	PA	19
79	VILLIERS EN PLAINE		111	U	22
50	VILLIERS FOSSARD		34	R	10
10	VILLIERS HERBISSE		64	OA	12
91	VILLIERS LE BACLE		39	GA	12
95	VILLIERS LE BEL	C	40	HA	11
10	VILLIERS LE BOIS		85	PA	15
21	VILLIERS LE DUC		85	RA	16
78	VILLIERS LE MAHIEU		39	EA	11
28	VILLIERS LE MORHIER		61	DA	12
50	VILLIERS LE PRE		56	Q	13
16	VILLIERS LE ROUX		129	X	24
14	VILLIERS LE SEC		35	U	9
52	VILLIERS LE SEC		66	TA	15
58	VILLIERS LE SEC		102	LA	18
95	VILLIERS LE SEC		40	HA	10
52	VILLIERS LES APREY		86	TA	16
89	VILLIERS LES HAUTS		85	PA	16
89	VILLIERS LOUIS		63	LA	14
77	VILLIERS SOUS GREZ		62	IA	14
61	VILLIERS SOUS MORTAGNE		59	Z	13
10	VILLIERS SOUS PRASLIN		65	PA	15
89	VILLIERS ST BENOIT		83	KA	16
02	VILLIERS ST DENIS		41	LA	11
78	VILLIERS ST FREDERIC		39	FA	12
77	VILLIERS ST GEORGES	C	63	LA	12
28	VILLIERS ST ORIEN		60	DA	15
79	VILLIERS SUR CHIZE		128	V	24
41	VILLIERS SUR LOIR		79	BA	16
94	VILLIERS SUR MARNE	C	40	HA	12
77	VILLIERS SUR MORIN		41	JA	11
91	VILLIERS SUR ORGE		62	GA	12
77	VILLIERS SUR SEINE		63	LA	13
52	VILLIERS SUR SUIZE		86	TA	15
89	VILLIERS SUR THOLON		83	LA	16
58	VILLIERS SUR YONNE		102	MA	18
89	VILLIERS VINEUX		84	NA	15
41	VILLIERSFAUX		79	BA	16
01	VILLIEU LOYES MOLLON		137	TA	24
57	VILLING		47	AB	9
16	VILLOGNON		129	X	25
89	VILLON		85	PA	16
88	VILLONCOURT		68	ZA	14
14	VILLONS LES BUISSONS		36	U	10
45	VILLORCEAU		80	DA	16
63	VILLOSANGES		133	IA	24
60	VILLOTRAN		26	FA	9
88	VILLOTTE		67	WA	15
55	VILLOTTE DEVANT LOUPPY		44	TA	11
21	VILLOTTE ST SEINE		104	RA	18
55	VILLOTTE SUR AIRE		44	UA	11
21	VILLOTTE SUR OURCE		85	RA	16
88	VILLOUXEL		67	VA	14
77	VILLUIS		63	LA	13
08	VILLY		30	TA	8
89	VILLY		84	NA	16
14	VILLY BOCAGE		35	T	10
21	VILLY EN AUXOIS		104	RA	18
10	VILLY EN TRODES		65	QA	14
76	VILLY LE BAS		15	DA	7
10	VILLY LE BOIS		64	OA	14
74	VILLY LE BOUVERET		139	XA	24
10	VILLY LE MARECHAL		64	OA	14
21	VILLY LE MOUTIER		105	SA	19
74	VILLY LE PELLOUX		139	XA	24
14	VILLY LEZ FALAISE		36	V	11
70	VILORY		88	YA	16
55	VILOSNES HARAUMONT		30	TA	9
57	VILSBERG		48	CB	12
53	VIMARCE		78	V	14
12	VIMENET		176	JA	31
88	VIMENIL		68	AB	14
73	VIMINES		152	WA	26
14	VIMONT		36	V	10
45	VIMORY		82	IA	15
61	VIMOUTIERS	C	36	X	11
77	VIMPELLES		63	KA	13
62	VIMY	C	17	JA	5
77	VINANTES		40	IA	11
11	VINASSAN		223	KA	37
17	VINAX		128	V	24
38	VINAY	C	166	UA	28
51	VINAY		42	NA	11
66	VINCA	C	222	HA	39
39	VINCELLES		122	UA	21
51	VINCELLES		42	MA	10
71	VINCELLES		121	TA	21
89	VINCELLES		84	MA	17
89	VINCELOTTES		84	MA	16
94	VINCENNES	C	40	HA	11
39	VINCENT		122	UA	21
88	VINCEY		68	YA	14
62	VINCLY		8	GA	4
77	VINCY MANOEUVRE		41	JA	10
02	VINCY REUIL ET MAGNY		29	OA	8
71	VINDECY		135	OA	23
50	VINDEFONTAINE		34	Q	9
16	VINDELLE		143	X	25
51	VINDEY		42	NA	12
81	VINDRAC ALAYRAC		189	FA	33
10	VINETS		65	PA	13
36	VINEUIL		115	DA	20
41	VINEUIL	C	80	CA	17
60	VINEUIL ST FIRMIN		40	HA	10
71	VINEUSE, LA		120	RA	22
07	VINEZAC		178	PA	31
66	VINGRAU		223	JA	38
61	VINGT HANAPS		58	X	13
76	VINNEMERVILLE		23	Z	7
89	VINNEUF		63	KA	14
18	VINON		101	JA	18
83	VINON SUR VERDON		197	WA	34
83	VINS SUR CARAMY		203	XA	35
26	VINSOBRES		179	SA	31
81	VINTROU, LE		212	HA	35
63	VINZELLES		133	LA	24
71	VINZELLES		136	RA	23
74	VINZIER		140	ZA	22
07	VINZIEUX		150	RA	27
88	VIOCOURT		67	WA	14
64	VIODOS ABENSE DE BAS		206	S	36
62	VIOLAINES		9	JA	4
42	VIOLAY		136	PA	25
84	VIOLES		179	SA	32
52	VIOLOT		87	UA	16
34	VIOLS EN LAVAL		192	NA	34
34	VIOLS LE FORT		192	NA	34
88	VIOMENIL		68	YA	15
07	VION		164	RA	28
72	VION		78	V	16
73	VIONS		138	WA	25
57	VIONVILLE		45	XA	10
32	VIOZAN		209	Y	36
03	VIPLAIX		116	HA	22
09	VIRA		219	EA	37
66	VIRA		222	HA	38
81	VIRAC		189	FA	33
50	VIRANDEVILLE		33	O	8
15	VIRARGUES		161	JA	28
47	VIRAZEIL		171	X	31
14	VIRE	S	35	S	11
71	VIRE		121	SA	22
72	VIRE EN CHAMPAGNE		77	V	15
46	VIRE SUR LOT		173	BA	31
89	VIREAUX		84	OA	16
54	VIRECOURT		68	YA	13
33	VIRELADE		170	U	30
08	VIREUX MOLHAIN		20	RA	6
08	VIREUX WALLERAND		20	RA	6
50	VIREY		56	R	13
71	VIREY LE GRAND		121	SA	20
10	VIREY SOUS BAR		65	PA	15
51	VIRGINY		43	RA	10
01	VIRIAT	C	137	TA	23
42	VIRICELLES		150	QA	26
38	VIRIEU	C	152	VA	26
01	VIRIEU LE GRAND	C	138	VA	25
01	VIRIEU LE PETIT		138	WA	24
42	VIRIGNEUX		150	QA	25
01	VIRIGNIN		152	WA	25
38	VIRIVILLE		151	TA	27
63	VIRLET		133	IA	23
57	VIRMING		47	AB	11
78	VIROFLAY	C	39	GA	12
17	VIROLLET		141	T	26
80	VIRONCHAUX		16	EA	5
27	VIRONVAY		38	CA	10
33	VIRSAC		156	U	28
17	VIRSON		127	S	23
76	VIRVILLE		23	Y	8
39	VIRY		138	WA	23
71	VIRY		120	PA	22
74	VIRY		139	XA	24
91	VIRY CHATILLON	C	62	HA	12
02	VIRY NOUREUIL		27	KA	8
62	VIS EN ARTOIS		17	JA	5
84	VISAN		179	SA	32
63	VISCOMTAT		148	MA	25
65	VISCOS		216	W	38
21	VISERNY		85	PA	17
65	VISKER		216	W	37
80	VISMES		15	EA	6
70	VISONCOURT		88	YA	16
43	VISSAC AUTEYRAC		162	MA	28
30	VISSEC		192	MA	33
35	VISSEICHE		76	O	15
81	VITERBE		189	FA	34
54	VITERNE		67	XA	13
27	VITOT		38	AA	10
15	VITRAC		160	GA	29
24	VITRAC		159	CA	29
63	VITRAC		133	JA	24
12	VITRAC EN VIADENE		161	JA	29
16	VITRAC ST VINCENT		143	Y	25
19	VITRAC SUR MONTANE		146	FA	27
61	VITRAI SOUS LAIGLE		37	Z	12
03	VITRAY		117	IA	21
28	VITRAY EN BEAUCE		60	CA	14
35	VITRE	C	76	R	15
79	VITRE		128	V	23
39	VITREUX		106	VA	19
54	VITREY		67	XA	13
70	VITREY SUR MANCE	C	87	WA	16
54	VITRIMONT		68	ZA	13
05	VITROLLES		181	XA	31
13	VITROLLES	C	202	UA	35
84	VITROLLES EN LUBERON		196	VA	34
45	VITRY AUX LOGES		81	GA	15
62	VITRY EN ARTOIS	C	17	JA	5
71	VITRY EN CHAROLLAIS		119	OA	22
52	VITRY EN MONTAGNE		86	TA	16
51	VITRY EN PERTHOIS		43	RA	12
51	VITRY LA VILLE		43	QA	11
58	VITRY LACHE		102	MA	19
10	VITRY LE CROISE		65	QA	15
51	VITRY LE FRANCOIS	S	43	RA	12
71	VITRY LES CLUNY		120	RA	22
52	VITRY LES NOGENT		87	UA	15
71	VITRY SUR LOIRE		119	NA	21
57	VITRY SUR ORNE		32	XA	10
94	VITRY SUR SEINE	C	40	HA	12
55	VITTARVILLE		31	UA	9
21	VITTEAUX	C	104	QA	18
76	VITTEFLEUR		23	Z	7
88	VITTEL	C	67	XA	14
57	VITTERSBOURG		47	BB	11
57	VITTONCOURT		47	ZA	11
54	VITTONVILLE		46	XA	11
80	VITZ SUR AUTHIE		16	FA	5
74	VIUZ EN SALLAZ		139	ZA	23
74	VIUZ LA CHIESAZ		139	XA	25
02	VIVAISE		28	MA	8
42	VIVANS		135	OA	23
2B	VIVARIO		228	LB	41
64	VIVEN		207	U	35
63	VIVEROLS	C	149	NA	27
66	VIVES		224	IA	39
52	VIVEY		86	TA	16
66	VIVIER, LE		222	HA	38
08	VIVIER AU COURT		30	SA	7
35	VIVIER SUR MER, LE		55	O	12
02	VIVIERES		41	KA	9
07	VIVIERS	C	179	RA	31
57	VIVIERS		47	ZA	11
89	VIVIERS		84	NA	16
73	VIVIERS DU LAC		152	WA	26
88	VIVIERS LE GRAS		67	WA	15
81	VIVIERS LES LAVAUR		211	EA	35
81	VIVIERS LES MONTAGNES		212	GA	35
88	VIVIERS LES OFFROICOURT		67	XA	14
10	VIVIERS SUR ARTAUT		65	QA	15
54	VIVIERS SUR CHIERS		31	VA	9
09	VIVIES		219	EA	37
12	VIVIEZ		175	GA	30
16	VIVILLE		142	W	26
72	VIVOIN		58	X	14
86	VIVONNE	C	113	X	22
49	VIVY		96	W	18
21	VIX		85	QA	16
85	VIX		127	S	22
38	VIZILLE	C	166	WA	28
65	VIZOS		216	W	38
07	VOCANCE		164	QA	28
63	VODABLE		148	KA	26
68	VOEGTLINSHOFFEN		90	CB	15
57	VOELFLING LES BOUZONVILLE		47	AB	9
67	VOELLERDINGEN		48	CB	11
16	VOEUIL ET GIGET		143	X	26
68	VOGELGRUN		90	EB	15
73	VOGLANS		152	WA	26
07	VOGUE		178	QA	30
02	VOHARIES		28	NA	7
55	VOID VACON	C	45	VA	12
10	VOIGNY		65	RA	14
51	VOILEMONT		43	SA	10
25	VOILLANS		107	ZA	18
52	VOILLECOMTE		66	SA	13
57	VOIMHAUT		47	ZA	11
54	VOINEMONT		68	YA	13
63	VOINGT		147	HA	25
77	VOINSLES		41	JA	12
51	VOIPREUX		42	OA	11
25	VOIRES		107	YA	19
38	VOIRON	C	152	VA	27
27	VOISCREVILLE		37	AA	9
28	VOISE		61	EA	13
77	VOISENON		62	IA	13
52	VOISEY		87	WA	16
52	VOISINES		86	TA	16
89	VOISINES		63	LA	14
78	VOISINS LE BRETONNEUX		39	FA	12
38	VOISSANT		152	VA	26
17	VOISSAY		127	T	24
39	VOITEUR	C	122	VA	21
70	VOIVRE, LA		89	ZA	16
88	VOIVRE, LA		69	BB	14
88	VOIVRES, LES		68	YA	15
72	VOIVRES LES LE MANS		78	W	15
59	VOLCKERINCKHOVE		8	GA	3
71	VOLESVRES		119	PA	22
68	VOLGELSHEIM		90	EB	15
89	VOLGRE		83	LA	16
67	VOLKSBERG		48	CB	11
63	VOLLORE MONTAGNE		148	MA	25
63	VOLLORE VILLE		148	MA	25
57	VOLMERANGE LES BOULAY		47	ZA	10
57	VOLMERANGE LES MINES		32	XA	9
57	VOLMUNSTER	C	48	DB	10
21	VOLNAY		120	RA	20
72	VOLNAY		79	Y	15
70	VOLON		87	WA	17
04	VOLONNE	C	181	XA	32
2B	VOLPAJOLA		228	MB	40
57	VOLSTROFF		32	YA	9
26	VOLVENT		180	UA	30
63	VOLVIC		133	KA	25
04	VOLX		197	WA	33
88	VOMECOURT		68	ZA	14
88	VOMECOURT SUR MADON		68	XA	14
52	VONCOURT		87	VA	16
08	VONCQ		30	RA	9
21	VONGES		106	UA	18
01	VONGNES		138	WA	25
01	VONNAS		137	SA	23
70	VORAY SUR L'OGNON		107	XA	18
38	VOREPPE		152	VA	27
43	VOREY	C	163	OA	28
02	VORGES		28	MA	8
25	VORGES LES PINS		107	XA	19
18	VORLY		117	HA	20
18	VORNAY		117	IA	20
39	VOSBLES		138	VA	23
21	VOSNE ROMANEE		105	SA	19
10	VOSNON		64	NA	15
37	VOU		98	AA	19
51	VOUARCES		64	NA	13
21	VOUDENAY		104	QA	19
10	VOUE		65	PA	13
52	VOUECOURT		66	TA	14
70	VOUGECOURT		88	XA	15
21	VOUGEOT		105	SA	19
10	VOUGREY		65	PA	15
42	VOUGY		135	OA	24
74	VOUGY		139	ZA	24
16	VOUHARTE		143	W	25
17	VOUHE		127	T	23
79	VOUHE		112	V	22
70	VOUHENANS		89	ZA	17
79	VOUILLE		128	V	23
86	VOUILLE	C	113	X	21
85	VOUILLE LES MARAIS		127	S	22
51	VOUILLERS		44	SA	12
36	VOUILLON		116	FA	20
14	VOUILLY		35	S	9
25	VOUJEAUCOURT		108	AB	18
21	VOULAINES LES TEMPLIERS		85	RA	16
77	VOULANGIS		41	JA	11
86	VOULEME		129	X	24
16	VOULGEZAC		143	X	26
86	VOULON		129	X	22
02	VOULPAIX		28	NA	7
07	VOULTE SUR RHONE, LA	C	164	RA	29
79	VOULTEGON		111	U	20
77	VOULTON		63	LA	12
77	VOULX		63	JA	14
86	VOUNEUIL SOUS BIARD		113	X	21
86	VOUNEUIL SUR VIENNE	C	113	Y	21
38	VOUREY		152	VA	27
69	VOURLES		150	RA	26
03	VOUSSAC		133	KA	23
89	VOUTENAY SUR CURE		84	NA	17
19	VOUTEZAC		145	DA	27
16	VOUTHON		143	Y	26
55	VOUTHON BAS		67	VA	13
55	VOUTHON HAUT		67	VA	13
53	VOUTRE		78	V	15
85	VOUVANT		111	T	22
37	VOUVRAY	C	98	AA	18
72	VOUVRAY SUR HUISNE		59	Z	15
72	VOUVRAY SUR LOIR		79	Y	17
88	VOUXEY		67	WA	14
86	VOUZAILLES		112	W	21
16	VOUZAN		143	Y	26
18	VOUZERON		100	GA	18
08	VOUZIERS	S	30	RA	9
41	VOUZON		81	FA	17
51	VOUZY		42	OA	11
28	VOVES	C	61	DA	14
74	VOVRAY EN BORNES		139	XA	24
02	VOYENNE		28	NA	8
80	VOYENNES		27	JA	7
57	VOYER		69	CB	12
56	VRAIE CROIX, LA		74	L	17
80	VRAIGNES EN VERMANDOIS		27	KA	7
80	VRAIGNES LES HORNOY		26	FA	7
52	VRAINCOURT		66	TA	14
27	VRAIVILLE		38	BA	10
51	VRAUX		43	PA	11
88	VRECOURT		67	VA	14
59	VRED		18	LA	5
70	VREGILLE		106	WA	18
02	VREGNY		28	LA	9
80	VRELY		27	IA	7
50	VRETOT, LE		33	P	9
39	VRIANGE		106	VA	19
08	VRIGNE AUX BOIS		30	SA	7
08	VRIGNE MEUSE		30	SA	8
45	VRIGNY		81	GA	15
51	VRIGNY		42	OA	10
61	VRIGNY		58	W	12
44	VRITZ		94	R	17
08	VRIZY		30	RA	9
60	VROCOURT		25	FA	8
51	VROIL		44	SA	11
80	VRON		15	EA	5
57	VRONCOURT		67	XA	13
52	VRONCOURT LA COTE		67	VA	14
88	VROVILLE		68	YA	14
57	VRY		46	YA	10
24	VUE		93	O	19
25	VUILLAFANS		107	YA	19
25	VUILLECIN		123	YA	20
02	VUILLERY		28	LA	9
10	VULAINES		64	MA	14
77	VULAINES LES PROVINS		63	KA	13
77	VULAINES SUR SEINE		62	IA	13
74	VULBENS		138	WA	24
57	VULMONT		46	YA	11
39	VULVOZ		138	WA	23
70	VY LE FERROUX		88	XA	17
70	VY LES FILAIN		88	YA	17
70	VY LES LURE		89	ZA	17
70	VY LES RUPT		88	WA	17
70	VYANS LE VAL		89	AB	17
25	VYT LES BELVOIR		108	AB	18

W

Dép.	Commune		Page	Carré	
62	WABEN		15	EA	5
60	WACQUEMOULIN		26	IA	9
62	WACQUINGHEN		7	EA	3
08	WADELINCOURT		30	SA	8
08	WAGNON		29	OA	8
59	WAHAGNIES		17	KA	4
68	WAHLBACH		90	DB	17
67	WAHLENHEIM		49	EB	12
62	WAIL		16	GA	5
62	WAILLY		17	IA	5
62	WAILLY BEAUCAMP		15	EA	4
68	WALBACH		90	CB	15
67	WALBOURG		49	FB	11
67	WALCK, LA		48	EB	11
67	WALDERSBACH		69	CB	13
67	WALDHAMBACH		48	CB	11
57	WALDHOUSE		48	DB	10
68	WALDIGHOFEN		90	DB	17
67	WALDOLWISHEIM		49	DB	12
57	WALDWEISTROFF		47	ZA	9
57	WALDWISSE		32	ZA	9
68	WALHEIM		90	CB	17
59	WALINCOURT SELVIGNY		18	LA	6
59	WALLERS		18	LA	5
59	WALLERS TRELON		19	PA	6
59	WALLON CAPPEL		8	HA	3
57	WALSCHBRONN		48	DB	10
57	WALSCHEID		69	CB	12
57	WALTEMBOURG		48	CB	12
68	WALTENHEIM		90	DB	17
67	WALTENHEIM SUR ZORN		49	EB	12
55	WALY		44	TA	11
59	WAMBAIX		18	LA	6
62	WAMBERCOURT		16	FA	4
60	WAMBEZ		25	EA	8
59	WAMBRECHIES		9	KA	3
62	WAMIN		16	FA	4
76	WANCHY CAPVAL		24	CA	7
62	WANCOURT		17	JA	5
59	WANDIGNIES HAMAGE		18	LA	5
67	WANGEN		49	DB	12
67	WANGENBOURG ENGENTHAL		48	CB	12
59	WANNEHAIN		9	LA	4
62	WANQUETIN		17	IA	5
67	WANTZENAU, LA		49	FB	12
08	WARCQ		29	RA	7
55	WARCQ		45	VA	10
62	WARDRECQUES		8	GA	3
51	WARGEMOULIN HURLUS		43	RA	10
80	WARGNIES		16	GA	6
59	WARGNIES LE GRAND		18	MA	5
59	WARGNIES LE PETIT		18	MA	5
59	WARHEM		8	HA	2
59	WARLAING		18	LA	4
62	WARLENCOURT EAUCOURT		17	JA	6
62	WARLINCOURT LES PAS		17	HA	5
80	WARLOY BAILLON		17	HA	6
60	WARLUIS		26	GA	9
62	WARLUS		17	IA	5
80	WARLUS		26	FA	7
62	WARLUZEL		17	HA	5
51	WARMERIVILLE		29	PA	9
08	WARNECOURT		29	RA	7
59	WARNETON		9	JA	3
80	WARSY		27	IA	8
80	WARVILLERS		27	IA	7
08	WASIGNY		29	QA	8
59	WASNES AU BAC		18	LA	5
59	WASQUEHAL		9	KA	3
67	WASSELONNE	C	49	DB	12
68	WASSERBOURG		90	CB	15
02	WASSIGNY	C	18	MA	6
52	WASSY	C	66	SA	13
62	WAST, LE		7	EA	3
02	WATIGNY		19	PA	7
55	WATRONVILLE		45	VA	10
59	WATTEN		8	GA	3
59	WATTIGNIES		9	KA	4
59	WATTIGNIES LA VICTOIRE		19	OA	5
59	WATTRELOS		9	KA	3
68	WATTWILLER		90	CB	16
60	WAVIGNIES		26	HA	8
54	WAVILLE		45	XA	11
62	WAVRANS SUR L'AA		8	GA	3
62	WAVRANS SUR TERNOISE		16	GA	4
59	WAVRECHAIN SOUS DENAIN		18	LA	5
59	WAVRECHAIN SOUS FAULX		18	LA	5
55	WAVRILLE		31	UA	9
59	WAVRIN		9	JA	4
59	WAZIERS		18	KA	5
68	WECKOLSHEIM		90	DB	15
68	WEGSCHEID		90	BB	16
67	WEINBOURG		48	DB	11
67	WEISLINGEN		48	CB	11
67	WEITBRUCH		49	FB	12
67	WEITERSWILLER		48	DB	11
60	WELLES PERENNES		26	HA	8
59	WEMAERS CAPPEL		8	HA	3
68	WENTZWILLER		90	DB	17
68	WERENTZHOUSE		90	DB	17
59	WERVICQ SUD		9	KA	3
59	WEST CAPPEL		8	HA	2
68	WESTHALTEN		90	CB	15
67	WESTHOFFEN		49	DB	12
67	WESTHOUSE		70	EB	13
67	WESTHOUSE MARMOUTIER		49	DB	12
62	WESTREHEM		8	HA	4
68	WETTOLSHEIM		90	CB	15
67	WEYER		48	CB	11
67	WEYERSHEIM		49	FB	12
68	WICKERSCHWIHR		70	DB	15
67	WICKERSHEIM WILSHAUSEN		49	EB	12
62	WICQUINGHEM		7	FA	4
59	WICRES		9	JA	4
62	WIDEHEM		7	EA	4
68	WIDENSOHEN		90	DB	15
02	WIEGE FATY		28	NA	7
80	WIENCOURT L'EQUIPEE		26	IA	7
62	WIERRE AU BOIS		7	EA	3
62	WIERRE EFFROY		7	EA	3
57	WIESVILLER		48	CB	10
59	WIGNEHIES		19	OA	6
08	WIGNICOURT		29	QA	8

68	WIHR AU VAL		90	CB	15
68	WILDENSTEIN		89	BB	15
67	WILDERSBACH		69	CB	13
62	WILLEMAN		16	GA	5
59	WILLEMS		9	KA	3
62	WILLENCOURT		16	FA	5
68	WILLER		90	DB	17
68	WILLER SUR THUR		90	CB	16
55	WILLERONCOURT		44	UA	12
62	WILLERVAL		17	JA	5
57	WILLERWALD		48	BB	11
67	WILLGOTTHEIM		49	EB	12
08	WILLIERS		31	UA	8
59	WILLIES		19	OA	6
67	WILWISHEIM		49	DB	12
62	WIMEREUX		7	DA	3
62	WIMILLE		7	DA	3
67	WIMMENAU		48	DB	11
02	WIMY		19	OA	7
67	WINDSTEIN		48	EB	11
67	WINGEN		49	FB	11
67	WINGEN SUR MODER		48	DB	11
67	WINGERSHEIM		49	EB	12
62	WINGLES	C	9	JA	4
68	WINKEL		90	CB	18
59	WINNEZEELE		8	HA	3
57	WINTERSBOURG		48	CB	12
67	WINTERSHOUSE		49	EB	12
67	WINTZENBACH		50	GB	11
68	WINTZENHEIM	C	90	DB	15
67	WINTZENHEIM KOCHERSBERG		49	DB	12
62	WIRWIGNES		7	EA	3
80	WIRY AU MONT		16	EA	6
67	WISCHES		69	CB	13
88	WISEMBACH		69	CB	14
55	WISEPPE		30	TA	9
62	WISMES		7	FA	3
62	WISQUES		8	GA	3
62	WISSANT		7	DA	2
67	WISSEMBOURG	S	49	FB	11
02	WISSIGNICOURT		28	LA	8
91	WISSOUS		40	HA	12
51	WITRY LES REIMS		29	PA	9
68	WITTELSHEIM		90	CB	16
68	WITTENHEIM	C	90	DB	16
62	WITTERNESSE		8	GA	4
67	WITTERNHEIM		70	EB	14
68	WITTERSDORF		90	CB	17
67	WITTERSHEIM		49	EB	12
62	WITTES		8	HA	3
67	WITTISHEIM		70	EB	14
57	WITTRING		48	CB	10
67	WIWERSHEIM		49	EB	12
62	WIZERNES		8	GA	3
55	WOEL		45	WA	11
57	WOELFLING LES SARREGUEMINES		48	CB	10
67	WOERTH	C	49	FB	11
80	WOIGNARUE		15	DA	6
55	WOIMBEY		44	UA	11
80	WOINCOURT		15	DA	6
57	WOIPPY	C	46	XA	10
80	WOIREL		16	EA	6
68	WOLFERSDORF		90	CB	17
68	WOLFGANTZEN		90	EB	15
67	WOLFISHEIM		70	EB	13
67	WOLFSKIRCHEN		48	CB	11
67	WOLSCHHEIM		49	DB	12
68	WOLSCHWILLER		90	DB	18
67	WOLXHEIM		70	DB	13
59	WORMHOUT	C	8	HA	2
57	WOUSTVILLER		47	BB	10
68	WUENHEIM		90	CB	16
57	WUISSE		47	AB	11
59	WULVERDINGHE		8	GA	3
95	WY DIT JOLI VILLAGE		39	EA	10
59	WYLDER		8	HA	2

X

88	XAFFEVILLERS		68	AB	13
47	XAINTRAILLES		171	X	32
79	XAINTRAY		112	U	22
16	XAMBES		143	X	25
54	XAMMES		45	WA	11
88	XAMONTARUPT		68	AB	15
57	XANREY		46	ZA	12
85	XANTON CHASSENON		111	T	22
88	XARONVAL		68	YA	13
54	XERMAMENIL		68	ZA	13
88	XERTIGNY	C	68	ZA	15
54	XEUILLEY		67	XA	13
54	XIROCOURT		68	XA	13
55	XIVRAY ET MARVOISIN		45	WA	11
54	XIVRY CIRCOURT		31	WA	9
57	XOCOURT		47	ZA	11
88	XONRUPT LONGEMER		89	BB	15
54	XONVILLE		45	WA	10
57	XOUAXANGE		69	BB	12
54	XOUSSE		69	AB	12
54	XURES		68	AB	12

Y

80	Y		27	JA	7
76	YAINVILLE		24	AA	9
80	YAUCOURT BUSSUS		16	FA	6
40	YCHOUX		169	S	32
15	YDES		147	HA	27
76	YEBLERON		23	Y	8
77	YEBLES		62	IA	12
73	YENNE	C	152	WA	25
28	YERMENONVILLE		61	DA	13
91	YERRES	C	40	HA	12
76	YERVILLE	C	24	AA	8
45	YEVRE LA VILLE		62	GA	14
28	YEVRES		60	BA	14
10	YEVRES LE PETIT		65	QA	13
22	YFFINIAC		54	K	13
40	YGOS ST SATURNIN		184	T	33
03	YGRANDE		117	JA	22
76	YMARE		24	BA	9
28	YMERAY		61	EA	13
28	YMONVILLE		61	EA	14
15	YOLET		161	HA	29
08	YONCQ		30	SA	8
80	YONVAL		15	EA	6
63	YOUX		133	IA	23
76	YPORT		23	X	7
76	YPREVILLE BIVILLE		23	Z	8
76	YQUEBEUF		24	CA	8
50	YQUELON		56	P	11
63	YRONDE ET BURON		148	LA	26
89	YROUERRE		84	OA	16
63	YSSAC LA TOURETTE		134	KA	24
19	YSSANDON		159	CA	28
43	YSSINGEAUX	S	163	PA	28
15	YTRAC		160	HA	29
62	YTRES		17	JA	6
57	YUTZ	C	32	YA	9
76	YVECRIQUE		24	AA	8
08	YVERNAUMONT		30	RA	8
86	YVERSAY		113	X	21
17	YVES		126	R	24
61	YVETEAUX, LES		58	V	12
76	YVETOT	C	24	Z	8
50	YVETOT BOCAGE		33	P	9
22	YVIAS		53	I	12
16	YVIERS		142	W	27
22	YVIGNAC		55	M	14
76	YVILLE SUR SEINE		24	AA	9
74	YVOIRE		139	YA	22
41	YVOY LE MARRON		81	EA	17
33	YVRAC		156	U	29
16	YVRAC ET MALLEYRAND		143	Y	25
61	YVRANDES		57	T	12
72	YVRE L'EVEQUE		78	X	15
72	YVRE LE POLIN		78	X	16
80	YVRENCH		16	FA	5
80	YVRENCHEUX		16	FA	5
80	YZENGREMER		15	DA	6
49	YZERNAY		95	T	20
69	YZERON		150	QA	25
03	YZEURE	C	118	LA	22
37	YZEURES SUR CREUSE		114	AA	21
80	YZEUX		16	FA	6
40	YZOSSE		183	S	34

Z

68	ZAESSINGUE		90	DB	17
2B	ZALANA		228	MB	41
57	ZARBELING		47	AB	11
59	ZEGERSCAPPEL		8	HA	2
67	ZEHNACKER		49	DB	12
67	ZEINHEIM		49	DB	12
68	ZELLENBERG		70	DB	14
67	ZELLWILLER		70	EB	13
59	ZERMEZEELE		8	HA	3
2A	ZERUBIA		230	KB	43
57	ZETTING		48	CB	10
2A	ZEVACO		226	KB	42
2A	ZICAVO	C	228	LB	42
2A	ZIGLIARA		227	KB	43
2B	ZILIA		225	KB	39
57	ZILLING		48	CB	12
68	ZILLISHEIM		90	DB	17
68	ZIMMERBACH		90	CB	15
68	ZIMMERSHEIM		90	DB	16
57	ZIMMING		47	ZA	10
88	ZINCOURT		68	ZA	14
67	ZINSWILLER		48	EB	11
67	ZITTERSHEIM		48	DB	11
67	ZOEBERSDORF		49	DB	12
57	ZOMMANGE		47	AB	12
2A	ZONZA		230	LB	43
62	ZOTEUX		7	FA	4
62	ZOUAFQUES		7	FA	3
57	ZOUFFTGEN		32	XA	9
2A	ZOZA		230	KB	43
2B	ZUANI		228	MB	41
62	ZUDAUSQUES		8	GA	3
62	ZUTKERQUE		7	FA	2
59	ZUYDCOOTE		8	HA	2
59	ZUYTPEENE		8	HA	3

BELGIQUE

AALST	**S** Chef-lieu d'arrondissement	10	**OA 2**
Nom	**P** Chef-lieu de province	Page	Coordonnées

AALST (ALOST)	S	10	OA	2
AALTER		2	LA	1
AARLEN/ARLON	P	31	WA	8
AARSCHOTT		12	SA	2
AARTSELAAR		3	OA	1
AAT/ATH	S	10	NA	3
AISEAU PRESLES		20	RA	4
ALKEN		13	UA	2
ALOST/AALST	S	10	OA	2
ALVERINGEM		8	IA	2
AMBLEVE/AMEL		22	XA	5
AMEL (AMBLEVE)		22	XA	5
AMMAY		13	UA	4
ANDENNE		12	TA	4
ANDERLECHT		11	PA	3
ANDERLUES		19	PA	4
ANHEE		20	SA	5
ANS		13	VA	3
ANTHISNES		13	VA	4
ANTOING		9	LA	4
ANTWERPEN (ANVERS)	P	3	PA	1
ANVERS/ANTWERPEN	P	3	PA	1
ANZEGEM		10	LA	3
ARDOOIE		9	KA	2
ARENDONK		4	TA	0
ARLON (AARLEN)	P	31	WA	8
AS		13	VA	2
ASSE		11	PA	2
ASSENEDE		2	NA	1
ASSESSE		20	SA	5
ATH (AAT)	S	10	NA	3
ATTERT		31	WA	7
AUBANGE		31	WA	8
AUBEL		14	WA	3
AUDENARDE/OUDENAARDE	S	10	MA	2
AUDERGHEM (OUDERGEM)		11	QA	3
AVELGEM		9	LA	3
AWANS		13	UA	3
AYWAILLE		13	VA	4
BAARLE HERTOG (BAERLE DUC)		4	SA	0
BAELEN		14	XA	3
BAERLE DUC/BAARLE HERTOG		4	SA	0
BALEN		4	TA	1
BASSE SAMBRE		12	RA	4
BASSENGE(BITSINGEN)		13	VA	3
BASTENAKEN/BASTOGNE	S	21	VA	6
BASTOGNE (BASTENAKEN)	S	21	VA	6
BEAUMONT		19	PA	5
BEAURAING		20	SA	6
BEAUVECHAIN (BEVEKOM)		12	RA	3
BEERNEM		2	LA	1
BEERSE		4	SA	0
BEERSEL		11	PA	3
BEGIJNENDIJK		12	RA	2
BEKKEVOORT		12	SA	2
BELOEIL		10	NA	4
BERCHEM		3	OA	1
BERCHEM STE AGATHE/ SINT AGATHA BERCHEM		11	PA	2
BERGEN (MONS)	P	19	OA	4
BERINGEN		12	TA	2
BERLAAR		4	RA	1
BERLARE		10	OA	2
BERLOZ		12	TA	3
BERNISSART		18	MA	4
BERTEM		11	RA	2
BERTOGNE		21	VA	6
BERTRIX		30	TA	7
BEVEKOM/BEAUVECHAIN		12	RA	3
BEVER (BIEVENE)		10	OA	3
BEVEREN (Waas)		3	PA	1
BEYNE HEUSAY		13	VA	4
BIERBEEK		12	RA	3
BIEVENE/BEVER		10	OA	3
BIEVRE		20	SA	7
BILZEN		13	VA	2
BINCHE		19	PA	4
BITSINGEN/BASSENGE		13	VA	3
BLANKENBERGE		1	KA	0
BLEGNY		13	WA	3
BOCHOLT		5	VA	1
BOECHOUT		3	OA	1
BONHEIDEN		11	QA	2
BOOM		3	QA	1
BOORTMEERBEEK		11	QA	2
BORGERHOUT		3	OA	1
BORGLOON		13	UA	3
BORGWORM/WAREMME	S	12	TA	3
BORNEM		3	PA	1
BORSBEEK		3	OA	1
BOUILLON		30	TA	7
BOURG LEOPOLD/ LEOPOLDSBURG		4	TA	1
BOUSSU		19	NA	4
BOUTERSEM		12	RA	3
BRAINE L'ALLEUD (EIGENBRAKEL)		11	PA	3
BRAINE LE CHATEAU (KASTEELBRAKEL)		11	PA	3
BRAINE LE COMTE ('S GRAVENBRAKEL)		11	PA	4
BRAIVES		12	TA	3
BRAKEL		10	NA	3
BRASSHAAT		3	QA	1
BRECHT		4	RA	0
BREDENE		1	JA	1
BREE		5	VA	1
BRUGELETTE		10	NA	4
BRUGES (BRUGGE)	P	2	LA	1
BRUGGE/BRUGES	P	2	LA	1
BRUNEHAUT		9	LA	4
BRUSSEL/BRUXELLES	P	11	PA	2
BRUXELLES/BRUSSEL	P	11	PA	3
BUGGENHOUT		11	PA	2
BULLANGE/BUTGENBACH (BULLINGEN)		22	YA	4
BULLINGEN (BUTGENBACH/BULLANGE)		22	YA	4
BURDINNE		12	TA	4
BURG REULAND		22	XA	5
BUTGENBACH (BULLINGEN/BULLANGE)		22	YA	4
CELLES (Les Tournai)		10	MA	3
CERFONTAINE		19	QA	6
CHAPELE LEZ HERLAIMONT		19	PA	4
CHARLEROI	S	19	QA	4
CHASTRE		12	RA	4
CHATELET		20	QA	5
CHAUDFONTAINE		13	VA	4
CHAUMONT GISTOUX		12	RA	3
CHIEVRES		10	NA	4
CHIMAY		19	PA	6
CHINY		31	UA	7
CINEY		21	TA	5
CLAVIER		21	UA	4
COLFONTAINE		18	NA	4
COMINES/KOMEN		9	JA	3
COURCELLES		19	PA	4
COURT ST ETIENNE		11	QA	3
COURTRAI (KORTRIJK)	S	9	LA	3
COUVIN		20	OA	6
CRISNEE		13	UA	3
DALHEM		13	WA	3
DAMME		2	LA	1
DAVERDISSE		21	TA	6
DE HAAN		1	KA	1
DE PANNE/LA PANNE		1	IA	1
DE PINTE		10	MA	2
DEERIJK		9	LA	2
DEINZE		10	MA	2
DENDERLEEUW		10	OA	2
DENDERMONDE/TERMONDE	S	10	OA	2
DENTERGEM		9	LA	2
DESSEL		4	TA	1
DESTELBERGEN		10	NA	2
DEURNE (Antwerpen)		3	QA	1
DIEPENBEEK		13	UA	2
DIEST		12	TA	2
DIKSMUIDE/DIXMUDE	S	9	JA	2
DILBEEK		11	PA	3
DILSEN		13	VA	2
DINANT	S	20	SA	5
DISON		14	WA	4
DIXMUDE (DISKMUIDE)	S	9	JA	2
DOISCHE		20	RA	6
DONCEEL		13	UA	3
DOORNIK (TOURNAI)	S	9	LA	4
DOUR		19	NA	5
DROGENBOS		11	PA	3
DUFFEL		3	QA	1
DURBUY		21	UA	5
ECAUSSINNES		11	PA	4
EDEGEM		3	OA	1
EDINGEN (ENGHIEN)		10	OA	3
EEKLO	S	2	MA	1
EGHEZEE		12	SA	4
EIGENBRAKEL/ BRAINE L'ALLEUD		11	PA	3
EKERREN		3	QA	1
ELLEZELLES/ELZELE		10	MA	3
ELSENE/IXELLES		11	QA	3
ELZELE (ELLEZELLES)		10	MA	3
ENGHIEN (EDINGEN)		10	OA	3
ENGIS		13	UA	4
EREZEE		21	VA	5
ERPE MERE		10	OA	2
ERQUELINNES		19	OA	5
ESNEUX		13	VA	4
ESPIERRES HELCHIN/ SPIERE HELKIJN		9	LA	3
ESSEN		3	OA	0
ESTAIMPUIS		9	LA	3
ESTINNES		19	OA	5
ETALLE		31	VA	8
ETTERBEEK		11	OA	3
EUPEN		14	XA	3
EVERE		11	QA	2
EVERGEM		2	MA	1
FAIMES		13	UA	3
FARCIENNES		20	QA	4
FAUVILLERS		31	VA	7
FERNELMONT		12	SA	4
FERRIERES		21	VA	5
FEXHE LE HAUT CLOCHER		13	UA	3
FEXHE SLINS		13	VA	3
FLEMALLE		13	UA	4
FLERON		13	VA	3
FLEURUS		11	QA	4
FLOBECQ/VLOESBERG		10	NA	3
FLOREFFE		20	RA	4
FLORENNES		20	RA	5
FLORENVILLE		31	UA	8
FONTAINE L'EVEQUE		19	PA	4
FOREST/VORST		11	PA	3
FOSSES LA VILLE		20	RA	5
FOURONS (VOEREN)		14	WA	3
FRAISNES LEZ ANVAING		10	MA	3
FRAMERIES		18	NA	4
FROIDCHAPELLE		19	PA	6
FURNES (VEURNE)	S	8	IA	2
GALMAARDEN/GAMMERAGES		10	OA	3
GAMMERAGES (GALMAARDEN)		10	OA	3
GAND (GENT)	P	10	MA	2
GANSHOREN		11	PA	2
GAVERE		10	MA	2
GEDINNE		20	SA	6
GEEL		4	SA	1
GEER		12	TA	3
GEETBETS		12	TA	2
GELDENAKEN (JODOIGNE)		12	SA	3
GEMBLOUX SUR ORNEAU		12	RA	4
GENAPPE/GENEPIEN		11	QA	4
GENEPIEN (GENAPPE)		11	QA	4
GENK		13	VA	2
GENT/GAND	P	10	MA	2
GERAARDSBERGEN/GRAMMONT		10	NA	3
GERPINNES		20	QA	5
GESVES		21	TA	4
GINGELOM		12	TA	3
GISTEL		1	JA	1
GLAAIEN (GLONS)		13	VA	3
GLABBEEK ZUURBEMDE		12	SA	2
GLONS/GLAAIEN		13	VA	3
GOETSENHOVEN/GOSSONCOURT		12	SA	3
GOOIK		10	OA	3
GOSSONCOURT (GOETSENHOVEN)		12	SA	3
GOUVY		22	WA	5
GRACE HOLLOGNE		13	VA	3
GRAMMONT (GERAARSBERGEN)		10	NA	3
GRAVEN (GREZ DOICEAU)		12	RA	3
GREZ DOICEAU/GRAVEN		12	RA	3
GRIMBERGEN		11	PA	2
GROBBENDONK		4	RA	1
HAACHT		12	RA	2
HAALTERT		10	OA	2
HABAY		31	VA	8
HAL (HALLE)	S	11	PA	3
HALEN		12	TA	2
HALLE/HAL	S	11	PA	3
HAM		4	TA	1
HAM SUR HEURE NALINNES		19	QA	5
HAMME (Durme)		3	OA	1
HAMOIR		21	VA	4
HAMOIS		21	TA	5
HAMONT ACHEL		5	VA	1
HANNUIT (HANNUT)		12	TA	3
HANNUT/HANNUIT		12	TA	3
HARELBEKE		9	LA	3
HASSELT	P	13	UA	2
HASTIERE		20	RA	5
HAVELANGE		21	TA	5
HECHTEL EKSEL		5	UA	1
HEERS		13	UA	3
HEIST OP DEN BERG		12	RA	2
HEKELGEM		10	OA	2
HELECINE		12	SA	3
HEMIKSEM		3	PA	1
HENSIES		18	MA	4
HERBEUMONT		30	TA	7
HERENT		12	RA	2
HERENTALS		4	RA	1
HERENTHOUT		4	RA	1
HERK DE STAD/HERK LA VILLE		12	TA	2
HERK LA VILLE (HERK DE STAD)		12	TA	2
HERNE		10	OA	3
HERON		12	TA	4
HERSELT		12	SA	2
HERSTAL		13	VA	3
HERSTAPPE		13	UA	3
HERVE		13	WA	3
HERZELE		10	NA	2
HEUSDEN ZOLDER		13	UA	2
HEUVELLAND		9	JA	3
HOBOKEN		3	PA	1
HOEGAARDEN		12	SA	3
HOEI (HUY)	S	13	UA	4
HOEILAART		11	QA	3
HOELSELT		13	UA	2
HOLSBEEK		12	RA	2
HONNELLES		18	NA	5
HOOGLEDE		9	KA	2
HOOGSTATEN		4	RA	0
HOREBEKE		10	NA	3
HOTTON		21	UA	5
HOUFFALIZE		22	WA	6
HOUTALEN HELCHTEREN		13	UA	2
HOUTHULST		9	JA	2
HOUYET		20	SA	5
HOVE		3	QA	1
HULDENBERG		11	QA	3
HULSHOUT		12	RA	2
HUY (HOEI)	S	13	UA	4
ICHTEGEM		1	JA	1
IEPER/YPRES	S	9	JA	2
INCOURT		12	RA	3
INGELMUNSTER		9	LA	2
ITTER (ITTRE)		11	PA	3
ITTRE/ITTER		11	PA	3
IXELLES (ELSENE)		11	OA	3
IZEGEM		9	KA	2
JABBEKE		1	KA	1
JALHAY		14	XA	4
JEMEPPE SUR SAMBRE		12	RA	4
JETTE		11	PA	2
JEUK/GOYER		12	TA	3
JODOIGNE/GELDENAKEN		12	SA	3
JUPRELLE		13	VA	3
JURBEKE/JURBISE		10	OA	4
KALMTHOUT		3	QA	0
KAMPENHOUT		11	QA	2
KAPELLE OP DEN BOS		11	OA	2
KAPELLEN (Antwerpen)		3	QA	0
KAPRIJKE		2	MA	1
KASTEELBRAKEL/ BRAINE LE CHATEAU		11	PA	3
KASTERLEE		4	SA	1
KEERBERGEN		12	RA	2
KELMIS/LA CALAMINE		14	XA	3
KINROOI		5	WA	1
KLUISBERGEN		10	MA	3
KNESSELARE		2	LA	1
KNOKKE HEIST		2	LA	0
KOEKELARE		1	JA	1
KOEKELBERG		11	PA	2
KOKSIJDE		1	IA	1
KOMEN (COMINES)		9	JA	3
KONTICH		3	QA	1
KORTEMARK		9	KA	2
KORTENAKEN		12	TA	2
KORTENBERG		11	QA	2
KORTESSEM		13	UA	2
KORTRIJK/COURTRAI	S	9	LA	3
KRAINEM		11	QA	2
KRUIBEKE		3	PA	1
KRUISHOUTEM		10	MA	2
KUURNE		9	LA	2
LA BRUYERE		12	SA	4
LA CALAMINE (KELMIS)		14	XA	3
LA HULPE/TERHULPEN		11	QA	3
LA PANNE (DE PANNE)		1	IA	1
LA ROCHE EN ARDENNE		21	VA	5
LAAKDAL		12	SA	2
LAARNE		10	NA	2
LANAKEN		13	VA	2
LANDEN		12	TA	3
LANGEMARK POELKAPELLE		9	JA	2
LE ROEULX		11	OA	4
LEAU (ZOUTLEEUW)		12	TA	3
LEBBEKE		11	PA	2
LEDE		10	OA	2
LEDEGEM		9	KA	3
LEGLISE		31	VA	7
LENDELEDE		9	KA	2
LENNIK		11	PA	3
LENS		10	NA	4
LEOPOLDSBURG/ BOURG LEOPOLD		4	TA	1
LES BONS VILLERS		11	QA	4
LESSEN (LESSINES)		10	NA	3
LESSINES/LESSEN		10	NA	3
LEUVEN/LOUVAIN	P	11	RA	2
LEUZE EN HAINAUT		10	MA	4
LIBIN		21	UA	6
LIBRAMONT CHEVIGNY		21	UA	7
LICHTERVELDE		9	KA	2

LIEDEKERKE		10	OA	2
LIEGE/LUIK	P	13	VA	3
LIER/LIERRE		4	RA	1
LIERDE		10	NA	3
LIERNEUX		22	WA	5
LIERRE (LIER)		4	RA	1
LIJSEM (LINCENT)		12	TA	3
LILLE		4	SA	1
LIMBOURG/LIMBURG		14	XA	4
LINCENT/LIJSEM		12	TA	3
LINKEBEEK		11	PA	3
LINT		3	OA	1
LINTER		12	SA	3
LO RENINGE		8	IA	2
LOBBES		19	PA	5
LOCHRISTI		2	NA	1
LOKEREN		3	OA	1
LOMMEL		5	UA	1
LONDERZEEL		11	PA	2
LONTZEN		14	XA	3
LOUVAIN (LEUVEN)	P	11	RA	2
LOUVIERE, LA		19	PA	4
LOVENDEGEM		2	MA	1
LUBBEEK		12	SA	2
LUIK (LIEGE)	P	13	VA	3
LUMMMEN		12	TA	2
MAARKEDAL		10	MA	3
MAASEIK	S	5	WA	1
MAASMECHELEM		13	VA	2
MACHELEN (Brussel)		11	QA	2
MALDEGEM		2	LA	1
MALINES (MECHELEN)	S	11	OA	2
MALMEDY		22	XA	4
MANAGE		11	PA	4
MANHAY		21	VA	5
MARCHE EN FAMENNE		21	UA	5
MARCHIN		12	TA	4
MARTELANGE		31	VA	7
MECHELEN/MALINES	S	11	QA	2
MEERHOUT		4	TA	1
MEEUWEN GRUITRODE		5	VA	1
MEISE		11	PA	2
MEIX DEVANT VIRTON		31	VA	8
MELLE		10	NA	2
MENEN/MENIN		9	KA	3
MERBES LE CHATEAU		19	PA	5
MERCHTEM		11	PA	2
MERELBEKE		10	NA	2
MERKSEM		3	QA	1
MERKSPLAS		4	SA	0
MESANCY		31	WA	8
MESEN/MESSINES		9	JA	3
MESSINES (MESEN)		9	JA	3
METTET		20	RA	5
MEULEBEKE		9	LA	2
MIDDELKERKE		1	JA	1
MODAVE		21	UA	4
MOERBEKE (Waas)		3	OA	1
MOESKROEN (MOUSCRON)	S	9	KA	3
MOL		4	TA	1
MOLENBEEK ST JEAN / SINT JANS MOLENBEEK		11	PA	2
MOMIGNIES		19	PA	6
MONS/BERGEN	P	19	OA	4
MONT DE L'ENCLUS		10	MA	3
MONT ST GUIBERT		11	QA	3
MONTIGNY LE TILLEUL		19	QA	5
MOORSLEDE		9	KA	2
MORLANWELZ		19	PA	4
MORTSEL		3	QA	1
MOUSCRON/MOESKROEN	S	9	KA	3
MUSSON		31	VA	8
NAMUR/NAMEN	P	12	SA	4
NANDRIN		13	UA	4
NASSOGNE		21	UA	6
NAZARETH		10	MA	2
NEERPELT		5	UA	1
NEUFCHATEAU	S	31	UA	7
NEUPRE		13	UA	4
NEVELE		10	MA	2
NIEL		3	PA	1
NIEUPORT (NIEUWPOORT)		1	IA	1
NIEUWERKERKEN (Saint Truiden)		12	TA	2
NIEUWPOORT/NIEUPORT		1	IA	1
NIJEN		4	RA	1
NIJVEL (NIVELLES)	S	11	PA	4
NINOVE		10	OA	3
NIVELLES/NIJVEL	S	11	PA	4
OERLE (OREYE)		13	UA	3
OHEY		21	TA	4
OLEN		4	SA	1
OLNE		13	WA	4
ONHAYE		20	SA	5
OOSTENDE/OSTENDE	S	1	JA	1
OOSTERZELE		10	NA	2
OOSTKAMP		2	LA	1
OOSTROZEBEKE		9	LA	2
OPGLABBEEK		13	VA	2
OPWIJK		11	PA	2
OPZULLIK (SILLY)		10	OA	3
OREYE/OERLE		13	UA	3
ORP JAUCHE		12	SA	3
OSTENDE (OOSTENDE)	S	1	JA	1
OTTIGNIES LOUVAIN LA NEUVE		11	QA	3
OUD HEVERLEE		12	RA	3
OUD TURNHOUT		4	SA	0
OUDENAARDE/AUDENARDE	S	10	MA	2
OUDENBURG		1	KA	1
OUDERGEM (AUDERGHEM)		11	OA	3
OUFFET		21	UA	4
OUPEYE		13	VA	3
OVERIJSE		11	QA	3
OVERPELT		5	UA	1
PALISEUL		21	TA	7
PECQ		9	LA	3
PEER		5	UA	1
PEPINGEN		11	PA	3
PEPINSTER		14	WA	4
PERUWELZ		10	MA	4
PERWEZ/PERWIJS		12	SA	4
PHILIPPEVILLE	S	20	OA	5
PITTEM		9	LA	2
PLOMBIERES		14	XA	3
PONT A CELLES		11	PA	4
POPERINGE		8	IA	2
PROFONDEVILLE		20	SA	5
PUTTE		11	RA	2
QUAREGNON		19	NA	4
QUEVY		19	OA	5
QUIEVRAIN		18	NA	4
RAEREN		14	XA	3
RAMILLIES		12	SA	3
RANST		4	OA	1
RAVELS		4	SA	0
REBECQ		11	PA	3
REMICOURT		13	UA	3
RENAIX (RONSE)		10	MA	3
RENDEUX		21	VA	5
RETIE		4	TA	1
RHODE ST GENESE/ SINT GENESIUS RODE		11	PA	3
RIEMST		13	VA	3
RIJKEVORSEL		4	RA	0
RIXENSART		11	QA	3
ROCHEFORT		21	TA	6
ROESELARE/ROULERS	S	9	KA	2
RONSE/RENAIX		10	MA	3
ROOSDAAL		10	OA	3
ROTSELAAR		12	RA	2
ROULERS (ROESELARE)	S	9	KA	2
ROUVROY		31	VA	8
RUISELEDE		9	LA	2
RUMES		9	LA	4
RUMST		11	OA	2
S GRAVENBRAKEL/ BRAINE LE COMTE		11	PA	4
SAINT GEORGES SUR MEUSE		13	UA	4
SAINT GHISLAIN		19	NA	4
SAINT GILLES/SINT GILLIS		11	PA	3
SAINT HUBERT		21	UA	6
SAINT JOSSE TEN NOODE/ SINT JOOST TEN NODE		11	QA	2
SAINT LEGER (en Gaume)		31	VA	8
SAINT NICOLAS		13	VA	3
SAINT NICOLAS (SINT NIKLAAS)	S	3	PA	1
SAINT TROND (SINT TRUIDEN)		12	TA	3
SAINT VITH (SANKT VITH)		22	XA	5
SAINTE ODE		21	VA	6
SAMBREVILLE		20	QA	4
SANKT VITH/SAINT VITH		22	XA	5
SCHAARBEEK/SCHAERBEEK		11	QA	2
SCHERPENHEUVEL ZICHEM		12	SA	2
SCHILDE		4	RA	1
SCHOTEN		3	QA	1
SENEFFE		11	PA	4
SERAING		13	VA	4
SILLY/OPZULLIK		10	OA	3
SINT AGATHA BERCHEM/ BERCHEM STE AGATHE		11	PA	2
SINT AMANDS		11	PA	2
SINT GENESIUS RODE/ RHODE ST GENESE		11	PA	3
SINT GILLIS (SAINT GILLES)		11	PA	3
SINT GILLIS WAAS		3	PA	1
SINT JANS MOLENBEEK/ MOLENBEEK ST JEAN		11	PA	2
SINT JOOST TEN NODE/ SAINT JOSSE TEN NOODE		11	OA	2
SINT KATELIJNE WAVER		11	QA	2
SINT LAMBRECHTS WOLUWE/ WOLUWE ST LAMBERT		11	QA	3
SINT LAUREINS		2	MA	1
SINT LIEVENS HOUTEM		10	NA	2
SINT MARTENS LATEM		10	MA	2
SINT NIKLAAS/SAINT NICOLAS	S	3	PA	1
SINT PIETERS LEEUW		11	PA	3
SINT PIETERS WOLUWE/ WOLUWE ST PIERRE		11	OA	3
SINT RENELDE (SAINTES)		11	PA	3
SINT TRUIDEN/SAINT TROND		12	TA	3
SIVRY RANCE		19	PA	5
SOIGNIES/ZINNIK	S	11	OA	4
SOMBREFFE		11	RA	4
SOMME LEUZE		21	UA	5
SOUMAGNE		13	WA	4
SPA		14	WA	4
SPIERE HELKIJN/ ESPIERRES HELCHIN		9	LA	3
SPRIMONT		13	VA	4
STABROEK		3	QA	0
STADEN		9	KA	2
STAVELOT		22	WA	4
STEENOKKERZEEL		11	QA	2
STEKENE		3	OA	1
STOUMONT		22	WA	4
TAMISE (TEMSE)		3	PA	1
TELLIN		21	TA	6
TEMSE/TAMISE		3	PA	1
TENNEVILLE		21	VA	6
TERHULPEN (LA HULPE)		11	QA	3
TERMONDE (DENDERMONDE)	S	10	OA	2
TERNAT		11	PA	2
TERVUREN		11	OA	3
TESSENDERLO		12	TA	2
THEUX		14	WA	4
THIMISTER CLERMONT		14	WA	3
THUIN	S	19	PA	5
TIELT	S	9	LA	2
TIELT WINGE		12	SA	2
TIENEN/TIRLEMONT		12	SA	3
TINLOT		13	UA	4
TINTIGNY		31	VA	8
TIRLEMONT (TIENEN)		12	SA	3
TONGEREN/TONGRES	S	13	VA	3
TONGRES (TONGEREN)	S	13	VA	3
TORHOUT		9	KA	2
TOURNAI/DOORNIK	S	9	LA	4
TREMELO		12	RA	2
TROIS POINTS		22	WA	5
TROOZ		13	WA	4
TUBIZE/TUBEZE		11	PA	3
UCCLE/UKKEL		11	PA	3
UKKEL/UCCLE		11	PA	3
VAUX SUR SURE		21	VA	7
VERLAINE		13	UA	4
VERVIERS	S	14	WA	4
VEURNE/FURNES	S	8	IA	2
VIELSALM		22	WA	5
VILLERS LA VILLE		11	QA	4
VILLERS LE BOUILLET		13	UA	4
VILVOORDE/VILVORDE	S	11	OA	2
VIROINVAL		20	QA	6
VIRTON	S	31	VA	8
VISE/WEZET		13	VA	3
VLETEREN		8	IA	2
VLOESBERG (FLOBECQ)		10	NA	3
VOEREN/FOURONS		14	WA	3
VORSELAAR		4	RA	1
VORST/FOREST		11	PA	3
VOSSELAAR		4	SA	0
VRESSE SUR SEMOIS		30	SA	7
WAARSCHOOT		2	MA	1
WAASMUNSTER		3	OA	1
WACHTEBEKE		2	NA	1
WAIMES/ WEISMES		22	XA	4
WALCOURT		19	QA	5
WALHAIN		12	RA	4
WANZE		12	TA	4
WAREGEM		9	LA	2
WAREMME/BORGWORM	S	12	TA	3
WASSEIGES		12	SA	4
WATERLOO		11	QA	3
WATERMAAL BOSVOORDE/ WATERMAEL BOITSFORT		11	QA	3
WATERMAEL BOITSFORT/ WATERMAAL BOSVOORDE		11	QA	3
WAVRE/WAVER	P	11	RA	3
WEISMES (WAIMES)		22	XA	4
WELKENRAEDT		14	XA	3
WELLEN		13	UA	3
WELLIN		21	TA	6
WEMMEL		11	PA	2
WERVIK		9	KA	3
WESTERLO		4	SA	1
WESTMALLE		4	RA	1
WETTEREN		10	NA	2
WEVELGEM		9	KA	3
WEZEMBEEK OPPEM		11	QA	2
WEZET (VISE)		13	VA	3
WICHELEN		10	OA	2
WIELSBEKE		9	LA	2
WIJNEGEM		3	QA	1
WILLEBROEK		11	OA	2
WILRIJK		3	QA	1
WINGENE		9	LA	2
WOLUWE ST LAMBERT/ SINT LAMBRECHTS WOLUWE		11	QA	3
WOLUWE ST PIERRE/ SINT PIETERS WOLUWE		11	OA	3
WOMMELGEM		3	QA	1
WORTEGEM PETEGEM		10	MA	3
WUUSTWEZEL		4	RA	0
YPRES (IEPER)	S	9	JA	2
YVOIR		20	SA	5
ZANDHOVEN		4	RA	1
ZAVENTEM		11	QA	2
ZEDELGEM		1	KA	1
ZELE		3	OA	1
ZELZATE		2	NA	1
ZEMST		11	QA	2
ZINGEM		10	MA	2
ZINNIK (SOIGNIES)	S	10	OA	4
ZOERSEL		4	RA	1
ZOMERGEM		2	MA	1
ZONHOVEN		13	UA	2
ZONNEBEKE		9	JA	2
ZOTTEGEM		10	NA	2
ZOUTLEEUW/LEAU		12	TA	3
ZUIENKERKE		1	KA	1
ZULTE		10	LA	2
ZUTENDAAL		13	VA	2
ZWALM		10	NA	2
ZWEVEGEM		9	LA	3
ZWIJNDRECHT		3	PA	1

LUXEMBOURG

ARSDORF		31	WA	7
ASSELBORN		22	XA	6
BASCHARAGE		32	WA	8
BASTENDORF		32	XA	7
BEAUFORT		32	YA	7
BECH		32	YA	7
BECKERICH		31	WA	7
BERDORF		32	YA	7
BERG		32	XA	7
BERTRANGE		32	XA	8
BETTBORN		32	WA	7
BETTEMBOURG		32	XA	8
BETTENDORF		22	YA	7
BETZDORF		32	YA	8
BIGONVILLE		31	WA	7
BISSEN		32	XA	7
BOEVANGE (Clervaux)		22	XA	6
BOEVANGE SUR ATTERT		32	XA	7
BOULAIDE		22	WA	7
BOURSCHEID		22	XA	7
BOUS		32	YA	8
BURMERANGE		32	YA	9
CAPELLEN	C	32	XA	8
CLEMENCY		31	WA	8
CLERVAUX	C	22	XA	6
CONSDORF		32	YA	7
CONSTHUM		22	XA	6
CONTERN		32	YA	8
DALHEIM		32	YA	8
DIEKIRCH	S	22	XA	7
DIFFERDANGE		31	WA	8
DIPPACH		32	XA	8
DUDELANGE		32	XA	9
ECHTERNACH	C	32	ZA	7
ELL		31	WA	7
ERMSDORF		32	YA	7
ERPELDANGE (sur Sure)		22	XA	7
ESCH SUR ALZETTE	C	32	XA	9
ESCH SUR SURE		22	WA	7
ESCHWEILER		22	WA	6
ETTELBRUCK		32	XA	7
FEULEN		22	XA	7
FISCHBACH		32	YA	7
FLAXWEILER		32	YA	8
FOLSCHETTE		31	WA	7
FOUHREN		22	YA	7
FRISANGE		32	YA	8
GARNICH		32	XA	8
GOESDORF		22	XA	7
GREVENMACHER	S	32	YA	8
GROSBOUS		32	XA	7
HACHIVILLE		22	WA	6
HARLANGE		22	WA	7
HEFFINGEN		32	YA	7
HEIDERSCHEID		22	XA	7
HEINERSCHEID		22	XA	6
HESPERANGE		32	YA	8
HOBSCHEID		32	WA	8
HOSCHEID		22	XA	7
HOSINGEN		22	XA	6
JUNGLINSTER		32	YA	8
KAUTENBACH		22	XA	6
KAYL		32	XA	9
KEHLEN		32	XA	8
KOERICH		32	XA	8
KOPSTAL		32	XA	8
LAROCHETTE		32	YA	7
LENNINGEN		32	YA	8
LEUDELANGE		32	XA	8
LINTGEN		32	XA	8
LORENTZWEILER		32	XA	8
LUXEMBOURG	P	32	YA	8
MAMER		32	XA	8
MANTERNACH		32	ZA	8
MECHER		31	WA	7
MEDERNACH		32	YA	7
MERSCH		32	XA	7
MERTERT		32	ZA	8
MERTZIG		32	XA	7
MOMPACH		32	ZA	7
MONDERCANGE		32	XA	8
MONDORF LES BAINS		32	YA	8
MUNSHAUSEN		22	XA	6
NEUNHAUSEN		22	WA	7
NIEDERANVEN		32	YA	8
NOMMERN		32	YA	7
OBERWAMPACH		22	WA	6
PERLE		31	WA	7
PETANGE		31	WA	8
PUTSCHEID		22	XA	6
RECKANGE SUR MESS		32	XA	8
REDANGE	C	31	WA	7
REISDORF		22	YA	7
REMERSCHEN		32	YA	9
REMICH	C	32	YA	8
RODENBOURG		32	YA	8
ROESER		32	XA	8
ROSPORT		32	ZA	7
RUMELANGE		32	XA	9
SAEUL		32	XA	7
SANDWEILER		32	YA	8
SANEM		32	WA	8
SCHIEREN		32	XA	7
SCHIFFLANGE		32	XA	8
SCHUTTRANGE		32	YA	8
SEPTFONTAINES		32	WA	8
STADTBREDIMUS		32	YA	8
STEINFORT		32	WA	8
STEINSEL		32	XA	8
STRASSEN		32	XA	8
TROISVIERGE		22	XA	6
TUNTANGE		32	XA	8
USELDANGE		32	XA	7
VIANDEN	C	22	YA	7
VICHTEN		32	XA	7
WAHL		32	WA	7
WALDBILLIG		32	YA	7
WALDBREDIMUS		32	YA	8
WALFERDANGE		32	XA	8
WEILER LA TOUR		32	YA	8
WEIMERSKRICH		32	XA	8
WEISWANPACH		22	XA	6
WELLENSTEIN		32	YA	8
WILTZ	C	22	XA	6
WILWERWILTZ		22	XA	6
WINSELER		22	WA	6
WORMELDANGE		32	YA	8

MONACO

CONDAMINE, LA	200	DB	34
MONACO	200	DB	34
MONTE CARLO	200	DB	34